2022

## GAAS GUIDE

A Comprehensive Restatement of Standards for Auditing, Attestation, Compilation, and Review

MARK S. BEASLEY, Ph.D., CPA

## Editorial Staff

Editor .................................................... Mary P. Taylor
Production ................... Jennifer Schencker, Manjula Mahalingam, and Anbarasu Anbumani

This publication is designed to provide accurate and authoritative information in regard to the subject matter covered. It is sold with the understanding that the publisher is not engaged in rendering legal, accounting or other professional service. If legal advice or other expert assistance is required, the services of a competent professional person should be sought. All views expressed in this publication are those of the author and not necessarily those of the publisher or any other person.

ISBN: 978-0-8080-5640-9

© 2021 CCH Incorporated and its affiliates. All rights reserved.
2700 Lake Cook Road
Riverwoods, IL 60015
800 344 3734
CCHCPELink.com

No claim is made to original government works; however, within this publication, the following are subject to CCH Incorporated's copyright: (1) the gathering, compilation, and arrangement of such government materials; (2) the magnetic translation and digital conversion of data, if applicable; (3) the historical, statutory and other notes and references; and (4) the commentary and other materials.

Do not send returns to the above address. If for any reason you are not satisfied with your book purchase, it can easily be returned within 30 days of shipment. Please go to *support.cch.com/returns* to initiate your return. If you require further assistance with your return, please call: (800) 344-3734 M-F, 8 a.m. – 6 p.m. CT.

Printed in Canada

# GAAS Guide
by Mark S. Beasley

## Highlights

CCH's *GAAS Guide* highlights key aspects of professional standards, including recent pronouncements, for CPAs involved in audit, attestation, preparation, compilation, and review services engagements. The 2022 *GAAS Guide* includes detailed analyses of critical components of the complete listing of Statements on Auditing Standards (SASs), Statements on Standards for Attestation Engagements (SSAEs), and Statements on Standards for Accounting and Review Services (SSARS), along with numerous practitioner aids that can easily be incorporated into any CPA firm's practice.

## 2022 Edition

The 2022 Edition of CCH's *GAAS Guide* has been updated to reflect the latest available professional standards. This edition now reflects all the changes resulting from the efforts of the American Institute of Certified Public Accountants (AICPA) to revise auditing standards to incorporate revisions and amendments contained in new standards up through SAS No. 142, *Audit Evidence*, that will become effective for audits of financial statement periods ending on or after December 15, 2022. Additionally, this edition of the *GAAS Guide* briefly highlights how the following new SASs will impact auditing standards once they become effective for audits of financial statement periods ending on or after December 15, 2023:

- SAS No. 143, *Auditing Accounting Estimates and Related Disclosures*
- SAS No. 144, *Amendments to AU-C Sections 501, 540, and 620 Related to the Use of Specialists and the Use of Pricing Information Obtained from External Information Sources*

This 2022 Edition also highlights key provisions included in the exposure draft of a proposed new SAS, *Understanding the Entity and its Environment and Assessing the Risks of Material Misstatement*, issued in August 2020.

The 2022 Edition of the *GAAS Guide* also includes coverage of recently issued SSAEs and SSARSs including the following:

- Statement on Standards for Attestation Engagements (SSAE) No. 21, *Direct Examination Engagements*, which becomes effective for examination reports dated on or after June 15, 2022.
- Statement on Standards for Attestation Engagements (SSAE) No. 22, *Review Engagements*, which becomes effective for practitioner's review reports dated on or after June 15, 2022.
- SSARS No. 25, *Materiality in a Review of Financial Statements and Adverse Conclusions*, which becomes effective for engagements performed in accordance with SSARS for periods ending on or after December 15, 2021.

## Highlights

The 2022 *GAAS Guide* also highlights recently issued audit, attestation, and SSARS interpretations, and it summarizes current exposure drafts of proposed new standards.

The extensive coverage of these AICPA standards is particularly relevant to CPAs who serve nonpublic entity clients. The guidance contained in this edition is also relevant to CPAs who serve public company clients. Although the Public Company Accounting Oversight Board (PCAOB) is responsible for establishing professional standards applicable to audits of public companies, this edition includes summaries of issues having implications for audits of public companies. These summaries, labeled "Public Company Implication," are incorporated throughout the coverage of the AICPA's AU-Cs. CPAs who audit public companies will find that these summaries help them identify key differences between audits of public and nonpublic companies. Our summaries of PCAOB Auditing Standards reflect the most recently issued standards including PCAOB AS-3101 (*The Auditor's Report on an Audit of Financial Statements When the Auditor Expresses an Unqualified Opinion and Related Amendments to PCAOB Standards*) issued in June 2017, as well as AS-2501 (*Auditing Accounting Estimates, Including Fair Value Measurements*) and AS-1210 (*Using the Work of an Auditor-Engaged Specialist*) issued by the PCAOB in December 2018 and approved by the Securities and Exchange Commission (SEC) in July 2019.

Owing to the attention focused on corporate scandals involving allegations of fraudulent financial reporting, the need for auditors to detect material misstatements due to fraud is critical. To help sensitize CPAs to issues affecting auditor responsibility for fraud, this edition contains "Fraud Pointers," which integrate fraud issues related to a particular professional standard's requirement. This should aid CPAs in considering fraud risks throughout the entire audit engagement.

To keep CPAs abreast of potential changes affecting the AICPA Professional Standards and other developments affecting auditing practice, this edition contains overviews of outstanding exposure drafts. Throughout the book, highlights labeled "Important Notice for 2022" explain key elements of potential changes, including proposed redrafts of existing professional standards and other regulatory changes, alerting CPAs to issues that may affect their engagements.

This 2022 Edition continues to provide what has always been the most important feature of the *GAAS Guide*—readability. While practitioners are responsible for ensuring that their engagements comply with the applicable authoritative guidance in the professional standards (SASs, SSAEs, SSARS, PCAOB), this *Guide* provides a useful resource to better understand key elements of those standards. The utmost care has been exercised to avoid the difficult language and to follow the organization of the original pronouncements. Essential material is placed at your fingertips for quick integration into your practice. There is no more need to wonder exactly what a standard means or how it is to be used in a real engagement.

## Automate your CCH Engagement Guides with ProSystem *fx* Engagement

By integrating your CCH *Engagement Guides* with ProSystem *fx* Engagement, you can achieve a fully paperless audit workflow. ProSystem *fx* Engagement, a member of the CCH ProSystem *fx* Office suite, enables firms to increase convenience and efficiency by automating workpaper preparation, management, and workflow within a state-of-the-art paperless engagement system. ProSystem *fx* and CCH are pleased to offer this high-quality combination of software and content to the accounting community. To sample ProSystem *fx* Engagement, please call 1-800-PFX-9998, or visit the ProSystem *fx* web site at CCHGroup.com/ProSystem.

## CCH® CPELink

Wolters Kluwer's goal is to provide you with the clearest, most concise, and up-to-date accounting and auditing information to help further your professional development, as well as a convenient method to help you satisfy your continuing professional education requirements. CCH® CPELink* offers a complete line of webinars and self-study courses covering complex and constantly evolving accounting and auditing issues. We are continually adding new programs to help you stay current on all the latest developments. The CCH® CPELink self-study courses are available 24 hours a day, seven days a week. You'll get immediate exam results and certification. To view our complete accounting and auditing course catalog, go to: *cchcpelink.com*.

## Accounting Research Manager®

**Accounting Research Manager®** is the most comprehensive, up-to-date, and objective online database of financial reporting literature. It includes all authoritative and proposed accounting, auditing, and SEC literature, plus independent, expert-written interpretive guidance. And, in addition to our standard accounting and SEC libraries, you can enjoy the full spectrum of financial reporting with our Audit library.

The Audit library covers auditing standards, attestation engagement standards, accounting and review services standards, audit risk alerts, and other vital auditing-related guidance. You'll also have online access to our best-selling *GAAS Practice Manual*, *Knowledge-Based Audits*™ *of Commercial Entities*, *Knowledge-Based Audits*™ *of Employee Benefit Plans*, *Knowledge-Based Audits*™ *of Financial Institutions*, *Knowledge-Based Preparation, Compilation, and Review Engagements*, *CPA's Guide to Effective Engagement Letters*, and *CPA's Guide to Management Letter Comments*, and be kept up-to-date on the latest authoritative literature via the *GAAS Update Service*.

---

*Wolters Kluwer is registered with the National Association of State Boards of Accountancy (NASBA) as a sponsor of continuing professional education on the National Registry of CPE Sponsors. State Boards of Accountancy have the final authority on the acceptance of individual course for CPE credit. Complaints regarding registered sponsors may be submitted to the National Registry of CPE Sponsors through its website: www.nasbaregistry.org.

With **Accounting Research Manager**®, you maximize the efficiency of your research time, while enhancing your results. Learn more about our content and our experts by visiting us at **accountingresearchmanager.com**.

**10/21**

© 2021 CCH Incorporated and its affiliates. All rights reserved.

# Contents

| | |
|---|---|
| Table of Exhibits | xi |
| Preface | xxiii |
| About the Author | xxvii |

**AU-C Preface: Preface to the Codification of Statements on Auditing Standards: Principles Underlying an Audit Conducted in Accordance with Generally Accepted Auditing Standards**

| | |
|---|---|
| AU-C Preface: Codification of Statements on Auditing Standards | 1002 |

**AU-C 200: General Principles and Responsibilities**

| | |
|---|---|
| Section 200: Overall Objectives of the Independent Auditor and the Conduct of an Audit in Accordance with Generally Accepted Auditing Standards | 2002 |
| Section 210: Terms of Engagement | 2024 |
| Section 220: Quality Control for an Engagement Conducted in Accordance with Generally Accepted Auditing Standards | 2039 |
| Section 230: Audit Documentation | 2049 |
| Section 240: Consideration of Fraud in a Financial Statement Audit | 2065 |
| Section 250: Consideration of Laws and Regulations in an Audit of Financial Statements | 2093 |
| Section 260: The Auditor's Communication with Those Charged with Governance | 2102 |
| Section 265: Communicating Internal Control Related Matters Identified in an Audit | 2118 |

**AU-C 300 & 400: Risk Assessment and Response to Assessed Risks**

| | |
|---|---|
| Section 300: Planning an Audit | 3002 |
| Section 315: Understanding the Entity and Its Environment and Assessing the Risks of Material Misstatements | 3017 |
| Section 320: Materiality in Planning and Performing an Audit | 3060 |
| Section 330: Performing Audit Procedures in Response to Assessed Risks and Evaluating the Audit Evidence Obtained | 3067 |
| Section 402: Audit Considerations Relating to an Entity Using a Service Organization | 4001 |
| Section 450: Evaluation of Misstatements Identified During the Audit | 4012 |

**AU-C 500: Audit Evidence**

| | |
|---|---|
| Section 500: Audit Evidence | 5002 |
| Section 501: Audit Evidence—Specific Considerations for Selected Items | 5013 |
| Section 505: External Confirmations | 5039 |

Section 510: Opening Balances—Initial Audit Engagements, Including Reaudit Engagements .......................... 5054
Section 520: Analytical Procedures ........................ 5062
Section 530: Audit Sampling .............................. 5080
Section 540: Auditing Accounting Estimates, Including Fair Value Accounting Estimates and Related Disclosures .............. 5117
Section 550: Related Parties .............................. 5146
Section 560: Subsequent Events and Subsequently Discovered Facts ................................................. 5160
Section 570: The Auditor's Consideration of an Entity's Ability to Continue as a Going Concern ........................... 5174
Section 580: Written Representations ...................... 5188
Section 585: Consideration of Omitted Procedures after the Report Release Date .......................................... 5201

**AU-C 600: Using the Work of Others**

Section 600: Special Considerations—Audits of Group Financial Statements (Including the Work of Component Auditors) .... 6002
Section 610: Using the Work of Internal Auditors ............ 6027
Section 620: Using the Work of an Auditor's Specialist ........ 6038

**AU-C 700: Audit Conclusions and Reporting**

Section 700: Forming an Opinion and Reporting on Financial Statements ............................................ 7002
Section 701: Communicating Key Audit Matters in the Independent Auditor's Report ......................... 7022
Section 703: Forming an Opinion and Reporting on Financial Statements of Employee Benefit Plans Subject to ERISA ...... 7028
Section 705: Modifications to the Opinion in the Independent Auditor's Report ..................................... 7047
Section 706: Emphasis-of-Matter Paragraphs and Other-Matter Paragraphs in the Independent Auditor's Report ........... 7067
Section 708: Consistency of Financial Statements ............. 7076
Section 720: Other Information in Documents Containing Audited Financial Statements .................................. 7081
Section 725: Supplementary Information in Relation to the Financial Statements as a Whole ....................... 7089
Section 730: Required Supplementary Information ............ 7097

**AU-C 800: Special Considerations**

Section 800: Special Considerations—Audits of Financial Statements Prepared in Accordance with Special Purpose Frameworks ........................................... 8002
Section 805: Special Considerations—Audits of Single Financial Statements and Specific Elements, Accounts or Items of a Financial Statement .................................. 8014

Section 806: Reporting on Compliance with Aspects of Contractual Agreements or Regulatory Requirements in Connection with Audited Financial Statements.................................. 8024
Section 810: Engagements to Report on Summary Financial Statements............................................................. 8029

## AU-C 900: Special Considerations in the United States

Section 905: Alert That Restricts the Use of the Auditor's Written Communication ........................................ 9002
Section 910: Financial Statements Prepared in Accordance with a Financial Reporting Framework Generally Accepted in Another Country............................................................. 9006
Section 915: Reports on Application of Requirements of an Applicable Financial Reporting Framework................ 9015
Section 920: Letters for Underwriters and Certain Other Requesting Parties ..................................... 9021
Section 925: Filings with the U.S. Securities and Exchange Commission under the Securities Act of 1933 .............. 9044
Section 930: Interim Financial Information .................. 9051
Section 935: Compliance Audits............................. 9075
Section 940: An Audit of Internal Control over Financial Reporting That Is Integrated with an Audit of Financial Statements ..... 9087
Section 945: Auditor Involvement with Exempt Offering Documents ................................................ 9120

## AT-C Section: Statements on Standards for Attestation Engagements

Preface: Codification of Statements on Standards for Attestation Engagements............................................... 10,002
Section 100: Common Concepts .............................. 10,005
Section 105: Concepts Common to All Attestation Engagements . 10,005
Section 200: Level of Service .............................. 10,024
Section 205: Assertion-Based Examination Engagements ....... 10,024
Section 206: Direct Examination Engagements ................ 10,057
Section 210: Review Engagements ........................... 10,065
Section 215: Agreed-Upon Procedures Engagements ........... 10,091
Section 300: Subject Matter ................................ 10,104
Section 305: Prospective Financial Information ............... 10,104
Section 310: Reporting on Pro Forma Financial Information ..... 10,122
Section 315: Compliance Attestation ........................ 10,135
Section 320: Reporting on an Examination of Controls at a Service Organization Relevant to User Entities' Internal Control over Financial Reporting....................................... 10,150
Section 395: Management's Discussion and Analysis .......... 10,172

**AR-C Section: Statements on Standards for Accounting and Review Services**
    Section 60: General Principles for Engagements Performed in Accordance with Statements on Standards for Accounting and Review Services ....................................... 11,002
    Section 70: Preparation of Financial Statements .............. 11,016
    Section 80: Compilation Engagements ..................... 11,025
    Section 90: Review of Financial Statements ................. 11,041
    Section 100: Special Considerations—International Reporting Issues........................................... 11,109
    Section 120: Compilation of Pro Forma Financial Information ... 11,116
*Accounting Resources on the Web*     12,001
*Cross-Reference*     13,001
*Index*     14,001

# Table of Exhibits

The following Exhibits, are located in Wolters Kluwer's *2022 GAAS Guide*.

| Exhibit | GAAS Guide Reference |
|---|---|
| Exhibit AU-C 200-1—Professional Skepticism | AU-C 200: General Principles and Responsibilities |
| Exhibit AU-C 210-1—Audit Engagement Letter | AU-C 200: General Principles and Responsibilities |
| Exhibit AU-C 210-2—Prospective Client Evaluation Form | AU-C 200: General Principles and Responsibilities |
| Exhibit AU-C 230-1—AU-Cs That Identify Specific Audit Documentation Requirements | AU-C 200: General Principles and Responsibilities |
| Exhibit AU-C 230-2—Letter for Regulatory Agency That Requests Access to Audit Documentation | AU-C 200: General Principles and Responsibilities |
| Exhibit AU-C 240-1—Guidance for Auditing Revenue in Certain Industries | AU-C 200: General Principles and Responsibilities |
| Exhibit AU-C 260-1—Topic and Nature of Communications about Significant Findings | AU-C 200: General Principles and Responsibilities |
| Exhibit AU-C 265-1—Examples of Possible Deficiencies | AU-C 200: General Principles and Responsibilities |
| Exhibit AU-C 265-2—Example of a Written Communication about Significant Deficiencies and Material Weaknesses | AU-C 200: General Principles and Responsibilities |
| Exhibit AU-C 265-3—Examples of Possible Material Weaknesses: Small Business Enterprise | AU-C 200: General Principles and Responsibilities |
| Exhibit AU-C 300-1—Audit Engagement Planning Checklist | 400: Risk Assessment and Response to Assessed Risks |
| Exhibit AU-C 315-1—Examples of Industry, Regulatory, and Other External Factors | 400: Risk Assessment and Response to Assessed Risks |
| Exhibit AU-C 315-2—Nature of the Entity and Relevant Standards of Financial Reporting | 400: Risk Assessment and Response to Assessed Risks |
| Exhibit AU-C 315-3—Examples of Elements of the Control Environment | 400: Risk Assessment and Response to Assessed Risks |

| Exhibit | GAAS Guide Reference |
|---|---|
| Exhibit AU-C 315-4—Examples of Factors Affecting Entity Risks | 400: Risk Assessment and Response to Assessed Risks |
| Exhibit AU-C 315-5—Objectives of Information Systems | 400: Risk Assessment and Response to Assessed Risks |
| Exhibit AU-C 315-6—Examples of Control Activities Germane to Internal Control over Financial Reporting | 400: Risk Assessment and Response to Assessed Risks |
| Exhibit AU-C 315-7—Application of Internal Control Concepts to Small and Midsized Entities | 400: Risk Assessment and Response to Assessed Risks |
| Exhibit AU-C 315-8—Factors That Might Indicate a Heightened Risk of Material Misstatement | 400: Risk Assessment and Response to Assessed Risks |
| Exhibit AU-C 330-1—Relationship of Assessed Risks of Material Misstatement and Auditor's Responses | 400: Risk Assessment and Response to Assessed Risks |
| Exhibit AU-C 330-2—Decision Tree for Designing and Performing Current Year Tests of Controls | 400: Risk Assessment and Response to Assessed Risks |
| Exhibit AU-C 330-3—Examples of Substantive Procedures Relevant to Inventory Assertions | 400: Risk Assessment and Response to Assessed Risks |
| Exhibit AU-C 330-4—Examples of Roll Forward of Substantive Procedures from Interim to Period End | 400: Risk Assessment and Response to Assessed Risks |
| Exhibit AU-C 450-1—Checklist of Qualitative Factors in Determining Materiality | 400: Risk Assessment and Response to Assessed Risks |
| Exhibit AU-C 450-2—SEC Staff Accounting Bulletin (SAB-99): "Materiality" | 400: Risk Assessment and Response to Assessed Risks |
| Exhibit AU-C 501-1—Audit Program: Inventory Observation Procedures Discovered after the Report Release Date | AU-C 500: Audit Evidence |
| Exhibit AU-C 501-2—Confirmation Request for Inventory Held by Another Party | AU-C 500: Audit Evidence |
| Exhibit AU-C 501-3—Illustrative Audit Inquiry Letter to Legal Counsel | AU-C 500: Audit Evidence |

| Exhibit | GAAS Guide Reference |
|---|---|
| Exhibit AU-C 501-4—Illustrative Audit Inquiry Letter to Legal Counsel Whereby Management Has Requested That the Lawyer Prepare the List of Pending or Threatened Litigation, Claims, and Assessments | AU-C 500: Audit Evidence |
| Exhibit AU-C 505-1—Positive Confirmation | AU-C 500: Audit Evidence |
| Exhibit AU-C 505-2—Negative Confirmation | AU-C 500: Audit Evidence |
| Exhibit AU-C 505-3—Obligation under Long-Term Leases | AU-C 500: Audit Evidence |
| Exhibit AU-C 505-4—Mortgage Obligation | AU-C 500: Audit Evidence |
| Exhibit AU-C 505-5—Audit Program—Confirmation of Accounts Receivable | AU-C 500: Audit Evidence |
| Exhibit AU-C 505-6—Summary of Accounts Receivable Confirmation Statistics | AU-C 500: Audit Evidence |
| Exhibit AU-C 510-1—Letter of Understanding from Predecessor to Successor Auditor | AU-C 500: Audit Evidence |
| Exhibit AU-C 510-2—Client Consent and Acknowledgment Letter | AU-C 500: Audit Evidence |
| Exhibit AU-C 520-1—Documentation of the Effect of Analytical Procedures on the Planning of Substantive Audit Procedures | AU-C 500: Audit Evidence |
| Exhibit AU-C 520-2—Performance of Analytical Procedures | AU-C 500: Audit Evidence |
| Exhibit AU-C 520-3—Example of Final Analytical Review | AU-C 500: Audit Evidence |
| Exhibit AU-C 530-1—Audit Judgment Factors Used in Non-Statistical and Statistical Sampling to Determine Sample Size for Tests of Controls | AU-C 500: Audit Evidence |
| Exhibit AU-C 530-2—Audit Judgment Factors Used to Determine Sample Size for Substantive Procedures | AU-C 500: Audit Evidence |
| Exhibit AU-C 530-3—Illustrative Sample Sizes | AU-C 500: Audit Evidence |

| Exhibit | GAAS Guide Reference |
|---|---|
| Exhibit AU-C 530-4—Selecting the Sample | AU-C 500: Audit Evidence |
| Exhibit AU-C 530-5—Misstatements and Professional Judgment | AU-C 500: Audit Evidence |
| Exhibit AU-C 530-6—Required Sample Size for Non-Statistical Tests of Details | AU-C 500: Audit Evidence |
| Exhibit AU-C 540-1—Nonauthoritative Guidance for Auditing Soft Accounting Information | AU-C 500: Audit Evidence |
| Exhibit AU-C 540-2—Common Financial Statement Estimates Requiring Auditor Evaluation | AU-C 500: Audit Evidence |
| Exhibit AU-C 560-1—Subsequent Events Audit Program | AU-C 500: Audit Evidence |
| Exhibit AU-C 560-2—Discovery of Facts after the Date of the Report | AU-C 500: Audit Evidence |
| Exhibit AU-C 570-1—Conditions and Events That May Raise a Substantial-Doubt Question | AU-C 500: Audit Evidence |
| Exhibit AU-C 570-2—Plans and Factors Relevant to the Evaluation of Management's Plans | AU-C 500: Audit Evidence |
| Exhibit AU-C 570-3—Going-Concern Section When Management's Statement is Required | AU-C 500: Audit Evidence |
| Exhibit AU-C 570-4—Evaluating an Entity's Ability to Continue as a Going Concern | AU-C 500: Audit Evidence |
| Exhibit AU-C 580-1—Management Representation Letter | AU-C 500: Audit Evidence |
| Exhibit AU-C 580-2—Additional Requirements for Written Representations | AU-C 500: Audit Evidence |
| Exhibit AU-C 585-1—Omission of Engagement Procedures Discovered after the Report Release Date | AU-C 500: Audit Evidence |
| Exhibit AU-C 600-1—Reference to the Work of Another Auditor in the Audit Report | AU-C 600: Using the Work of Others |

| Exhibit | GAAS Guide Reference |
|---|---|
| Exhibit AU-C 620-1—Considerations for Inclusion in an Agreement between the Auditor and an Auditor's External Specialist | AU-C 600: Using the Work of Others |
| Exhibit AU-C 700-1—Standard Unmodified Auditor's Report | AU-C 700: Audit Conclusions and Reporting |
| Exhibit AU-C 703-1—Auditor's Report on Financial Statements for a Defined Contribution Retirement Plan Subject to ERISA | AU-C 700: Audit Conclusions and Reporting |
| Exhibit AU-C 703-2—Auditor's Report on Financial Statements for a Defined Contribution Retirement Plan Subject to ERISA When Management Elects an ERISA Section 103(a)(3)(C) Audit | AU-C 700: Audit Conclusions and Reporting |
| Exhibit AU-C 705-1—Qualified Auditor's Report Due to Material Misstatement | AU-C 700: Audit Conclusions and Reporting |
| Exhibit AU-C 705-2—Qualified Auditor's Report Due to Inadequate Disclosure | AU-C 700: Audit Conclusions and Reporting |
| Exhibit AU-C 705-3—Adverse Auditor's Report | AU-C 700: Audit Conclusions and Reporting |
| Exhibit AU-C 705-4—Qualified Auditor's Report Because of a Scope Limitation | AU-C 700: Audit Conclusions and Reporting |
| Exhibit AU-C 705-5—Disclaimer Report | AU-C 700: Audit Conclusions and Reporting |
| Exhibit AU-C 705-6—Auditor's Report on Comparative Financial Statements with Unmodified Prior-Year Opinion and Modified Current-Year Opinion | AU-C 700: Audit Conclusions and Reporting |
| Exhibit AU-C 706-1—Auditing Standards Requiring Emphasis-of-Matter Paragraphs and Other-Matter Paragraphs | AU-C 700: Audit Conclusions and Reporting |
| Exhibit AU-C 706-2—Auditor's Report with Emphasis-of-Matter Paragraph | AU-C 700: Audit Conclusions and Reporting |
| Exhibit AU-C 706-3—Auditor's Report with Other-Matter Paragraph | AU-C 700: Audit Conclusions and Reporting |

| Exhibit | GAAS Guide Reference |
|---|---|
| Exhibit AU-C 720-1—Other Information Section to be Included in the Auditor's Report Related to Other Information Included in the Annual Report and Auditor Has Not Identified an Uncorrected Material Misstatement | AU-C 700: Audit Conclusions and Reporting |
| Exhibit AU-C 720-2—Other Information Section to be Included in the Auditor's Report Related to Other Information Included in the Annual Report and Auditor Has Concluded That an Uncorrected Material Misstatement Exists | AU-C 700: Audit Conclusions and Reporting |
| Exhibit AU-C 725-1—Supplementary Information Section in Auditor's Report Used When Reporting on Supplementary Information | AU-C 700: Audit Conclusions and Reporting |
| Exhibit AU-C 725-2—Reporting on Supplementary Information Separately from the Financial Statements as a Whole | AU-C 700: Audit Conclusions and Reporting |
| Exhibit AU-C 730-1—Required Supplementary Information Section in Auditor's Report When Reporting on Supplementary Information | AU-C 700: Audit Conclusions and Reporting |
| Exhibit AU-C 800-1—Special Purpose Frameworks and Reporting Requirements | AU-C 800: Special Considerations |
| Exhibit AU-C 800-2—Independent Auditor's Report on Cash-Based Financial Statements | AU-C 800: Special Considerations |
| Exhibit AU-C 800-3—Independent Auditor's Report on Financial Statements Prepared in Accordance with a Regulatory Basis of Accounting and Intended for General Use | AU-C 800: Special Considerations |
| Exhibit AU-C 805-1—Auditor's Report on a Single Financial Statement | AU-C 800: Special Considerations |
| Exhibit AU-C 805-2—Auditor's Report on a Specific Element, Account, or Item of a Financial Statement | AU-C 800: Special Considerations |

## Table of Exhibits

| Exhibit | GAAS Guide Reference |
|---|---|
| Exhibit AU-C 806-1—Separate Auditor's Report on Compliance with Aspects of Contractual Agreements | AU-C 800: Special Considerations |
| Exhibit AU-C 810-1—Report on Summary Financial Statements with an Unmodified Opinion Dated after the Date of the Auditor's Report on the Audited Financial Statements | AU-C 800: Special Considerations |
| Exhibit AU-C 905-1—List of Statements on Auditing Standards Containing Requirements for an Alert as to the Intended Use of an Auditor's Written Communication | AU-C 900: Special Considerations in the United States |
| Exhibit AU-C 910-1—U.S. Form of Auditor's Report on Financial Statements That Are Also Intended for Use in the U.S. | AU-C 900: Special Considerations in the United States |
| Exhibit AU-C 910-2—U.S. Form of Auditor's Report on Financial Statements Intended for Use Only Outside the U.S. | AU-C 900: Special Considerations in the United States |
| Exhibit AU-C 915-1—Accountant's Report on the Application of Accounting Principles | AU-C 900: Special Considerations in the United States |
| Exhibit AU-C 920-1—Representation Letter from Requesting Parties | AU-C 900: Special Considerations in the United States |
| Exhibit AU-C 920-2—Sample Comfort Letter for a 1933 Act Offering | AU-C 900: Special Considerations in the United States |
| Exhibit AU-C 925-1—Disclosure in "Experts" Section of a Registration Statement Filed under the Securities Act of 1933 | AU-C 900: Special Considerations in the United States |
| Exhibit AU-C 925-2—Disclosure That Includes the Auditor's Review Report on Unaudited Interim Financial Information | AU-C 900: Special Considerations in the United States |
| Exhibit AU-C 930-1—Management Representation Letter for a Review of Interim Financial Information | AU-C 900: Special Considerations in the United States |
| Exhibit AU-C 930-2—Standard Review Report on Interim Financial Information | AU-C 900: Special Considerations in the United States |

| Exhibit | GAAS Guide Reference |
|---|---|
| Exhibit AU-C 930-3—Modification of Review Report on Interim Financial Information Due to a Departure from the Applicable Financial Reporting Framework | AU-C 900: Special Considerations in the United States |
| Exhibit AU-C 930-4—Modification of Review Report on Interim Financial Statements Due to Inadequate Disclosure | AU-C 900: Special Considerations in the United States |
| Exhibit AU-C 930-5—Separate Section Related to a Going Concern Issue Referred to in the Previous Audit Report | AU-C 900: Special Considerations in the United States |
| Exhibit AU-C 930-6—Separate Section Related to a Going Concern Issue Not Referred to in the Previous Audit Report | AU-C 900: Special Considerations in the United States |
| Exhibit AU-C 940-1—Combined Report Expressing an Unmodified Opinion on ICFR and on the Financial Statements | AU-C 900: Special Considerations in the United States |
| Exhibit AU-C 940-2—Written Communication of Significant Deficiencies and Material Weaknesses | AU-C 900: Special Considerations in the United States |
| Exhibit AU-C 945-1—Examples of Exempt Securities and Exempt Transactions | AU-C 900: Special Considerations in the United States |
| Exhibit AU-C 945-2—Example Terms for Inclusion in Engagement Letters | AU-C 900: Special Considerations in the United States |
| Exhibit AU-C 945-3—Example of an Inclusion Letter | AU-C 900: Special Considerations in the United States |
| Exhibit AT-C 105-1—Acceptable Level of Detection Risk | AT-C Section: Statements on Standards for Attestation Engagements |
| Exhibit AT-C 205-1—Types of Modified Opinions | AT-C Section: Statements on Standards for Attestation Engagements |
| Exhibit AT-C 205-2—Examination Report—Subject Matter | AT-C Section: Statements on Standards for Attestation Engagements |
| Exhibit AT-C 205-3—Assertion-Based Examination Report—Assertion | AT-C Section: Statements on Standards for Attestation Engagements |
| Exhibit AT-C 206-1—Direct Examination Report—Measurement | AT-C Section: Statements on Standards for Attestation Engagements |

| Exhibit | GAAS Guide Reference |
|---|---|
| Exhibit AT-C 206-2—Direct Examination Report—Evaluation | AT-C Section: Statements on Standards for Attestation Engagements |
| Exhibit AT-C 210-1—Review Report—Subject Matter | AT-C Section: Statements on Standards for Attestation Engagements |
| Exhibit AT-C 210-2—Review Report—Assertion | AT-C Section: Statements on Standards for Attestation Engagements |
| Exhibit AT-C 215-1—AUP Engagement Report | AT-C Section: Statements on Standards for Attestation Engagements |
| Exhibit AT-C 305-1—Report on an Examination of a Forecast | AT-C Section: Statements on Standards for Attestation Engagements |
| Exhibit AT-C 305-2—Report on an Examination of a Projection | AT-C Section: Statements on Standards for Attestation Engagements |
| Exhibit AT-C 305-3—AUP Engagement Report for a Financial Forecast | AT-C Section: Statements on Standards for Attestation Engagements |
| Exhibit AT-C 310-1—Examination Report on Pro Forma Financial Information | AT-C Section: Statements on Standards for Attestation Engagements |
| Exhibit AT-C 310-2—Review Report on Pro Forma Financial Information | AT-C Section: Statements on Standards for Attestation Engagements |
| Exhibit AT-C 315-1—Examination on Compliance with Specified Requirements | AT-C Section: Statements on Standards for Attestation Engagements |
| Exhibit AT-C 315-2—Examination on Management's Assertion Concerning Compliance with Specified Requirements | AT-C Section: Statements on Standards for Attestation Engagements |
| Exhibit AT-C 315-3—AUP Report on Compliance with Specified Requirements | AT-C Section: Statements on Standards for Attestation Engagements |
| Exhibit AT-C 315-4—AUP Report on Internal Control over Compliance with Specified Requirements | AT-C Section: Statements on Standards for Attestation Engagements |
| Exhibit AT-C 320-1—Type 1 Report | AT-C Section: Statements on Standards for Attestation Engagements |
| Exhibit AT-C 320-2—Type 2 Report | AT-C Section: Statements on Standards for Attestation Engagements |
| Exhibit AT-C 395-1—Examination Report on an Entity's MD&A Presentation | AT-C Section: Statements on Standards for Attestation Engagements |
| Exhibit AT-C 395-2—Review Report on an Entity's MD&A Presentation | AT-C Section: Statements on Standards for Attestation Engagements |

| Exhibit | GAAS Guide Reference |
|---|---|
| Exhibit AR-C 60-1—Other Preparation, Compilation, and Review Publications | AR-C Section: Statements on Standards for Accounting and Review Services |
| Exhibit AR-C 70-1—Preparation of Financial Statements versus Assistance in Preparing Financial Statements | AR-C Section: Statements on Standards for Accounting and Review Services |
| Exhibit AR-C 70-2—Preparation of Financial Statements Engagement Letter | AR-C Section: Statements on Standards for Accounting and Review Services |
| Exhibit AR-C 80-1—Compilation Engagement Letter | AR-C Section: Statements on Standards for Accounting and Review Services |
| Exhibit AR-C 80-2—Standard Accountant's Compilation Report | AR-C Section: Statements on Standards for Accounting and Review Services |
| Exhibit AR-C 80-3—Compilation Report When Independence Is Impaired | AR-C Section: Statements on Standards for Accounting and Review Services |
| Exhibit AR-C 80-4—Compilation Report Disclosing a GAAP Departure | AR-C Section: Statements on Standards for Accounting and Review Services |
| Exhibit AR-C 90-1—Review Engagement Letter | AR-C Section: Statements on Standards for Accounting and Review Services |
| Exhibit AR-C 90-2—Management Representation Letter | AR-C Section: Statements on Standards for Accounting and Review Services |
| Exhibit AR-C 90-3—Standard Accountant's Review Report | AR-C Section: Statements on Standards for Accounting and Review Services |
| Exhibit AR-C 90-4—Review Program | AR-C Section: Statements on Standards for Accounting and Review Services |
| Exhibit AR-C 90-5—Review Questionnaire Checklist | AR-C Section: Statements on Standards for Accounting and Review Services |
| Exhibit AR-C 90-6—Inquiry Checklist for a Review Engagement | AR-C Section: Statements on Standards for Accounting and Review Services |
| Exhibit AR-C 90-7—Analytical Procedures for a Review Engagement | AR-C Section: Statements on Standards for Accounting and Review Services |
| Exhibit AR-C 90-8—Documenting Expectations When Performing Analytical Procedures in a Review Engagement | AR-C Section: Statements on Standards for Accounting and Review Services |
| Exhibit AR-C 90-9—Considering Going Concern | AR-C Section: Statements on Standards for Accounting and Review Services |

| Exhibit | GAAS Guide Reference |
|---|---|
| Exhibit AR-C 100-1—Accountant's Compilation Report on Financial Statements Prepared in Accordance With a Financial Reporting Framework Generally Accepted in Another Country Performed in Accordance With SSARS and Another Set of Compilation Standards and the Financial Statements Are Intended for Use Only Outside the United States | AR-C Section: Statements on Standards for Accounting and Review Services |
| Exhibit AR-C 100-2—Accountant's Compilation Report on Financial Statements Prepared in Accordance With a Financial Reporting Framework Generally Accepted in Another Country Performed in Accordance With SSARS and Another Set of Compilation Standards and the Financial Statements Are Also Intended for Use in the United States | AR-C Section: Statements on Standards for Accounting and Review Services |
| Exhibit AR-C 100-3—Accountant's Review Report on Financial Statements Prepared in Accordance With a Financial Reporting Framework Generally Accepted in Another Country Performed in Accordance With SSARS and Another Set of Compilation Standards and the Financial Statements Are Intended for Use Only Outside the United States | AR-C Section: Statements on Standards for Accounting and Review Services |
| Exhibit AR-C 100-4—Accountant's Review Report on Financial Statements Prepared in Accordance With a Financial Reporting Framework Generally Accepted in Another Country Performed in Accordance With SSARS and Another Set of Review Standards and the Financial Statements Are Also Intended for Use in the United States | AR-C Section: Statements on Standards for Accounting and Review Services |

| Exhibit | GAAS Guide Reference |
|---|---|
| Exhibit AR-C 120-1—Accountant's Compilation Report on Pro Forma Financial Information | AR-C Section: Statements on Standards for Accounting and Review Services |

# Preface

CCH's 2022 *GAAS Guide* describes the engagement standards, practices, and procedures in use today, including Statements on Auditing Standards (SASs) and their Interpretations, Statements on Standards for Attestation Engagements (SSAEs) and their Interpretations, and Statements on Standards on Accounting and Review Services (SSARS) and their Interpretations.

The 2022 Edition of the *GAAS Guide* has been updated to reflect the latest available professional standards and includes coverage of the following recently issued auditing standards:

- SAS No. 134, *Auditor Reporting and Amendments, Including Amendments Addressing Disclosures in the Audit of Financial Statements*
- SAS No. 135, *Omnibus Statement on Auditing Standards—2019*
- SAS No. 136, *Forming an Opinion and Reporting on Financial Statements of Employee Benefit Plans Subject to ERISA*
- SAS No. 137, *The Auditor's Responsibilities Relating to Other Information Included in Annual Reports*
- SAS No. 138, *Amendments to the Description of the Concept of Materiality*
- SAS No. 139, *Amendments to AU-C Sections 800, 805, and 810 to Incorporate Auditor Reporting Changes from SAS No. 134*
- SAS No. 140, *Amendments to AU-C Sections 725, 730, 930, 935, and 940 to Incorporate Auditor Reporting Changes from SAS Nos. 134 and 137*
- SAS No. 141, *Amendment to the Effective Dates of SAS Nos. 134-140*
- SAS No. 142, *Audit Evidence*

All of these new SASs, except for SAS No. 142, become effective for audits of financial statement periods ending on or after December 15, 2021. SAS No. 142 becomes effective for audits of financial statement periods ending on or after December 15, 2022.

In July 2020, the AICPA Auditing Standards Board (ASB) issued SAS No. 143, *Auditing Accounting Estimates and Related Disclosures*, and in June 2021, the ASB issued SAS No. 144, *Amendments to AU-C Sections 501, 540, and 620 Related to the Use of Specialists and the Use of Pricing Information Obtained from External Information Sources*. Because SAS No. 143 and SAS No. 144 do not become effective until audits of financial statement periods ending on or after December 15, 2023, this edition of the *GAAS Guide* briefly highlights where they will impact auditing standards given they will not directly impact 2022 audits.

The 2022 *GAAS Guide* also briefly highlights how the August 2020 exposure draft of a proposed new SAS, *Understanding the Entity and its Environment and Assessing the Risks of Material Misstatement*, will impact auditing standards.

This edition also includes coverage of these recently issued SSAEs and SSARS:

- Statement on Standards for Attestation Engagements (SSAE) No. 21, *Direct Examination Engagements*, which becomes effective for examination reports dated on or after June 15, 2022.
- Statement on Standards for Attestation Engagements (SSAE) No. 22, *Review Engagements*, which becomes effective for practitioner's review reports dated on or after June 15, 2022.
- Statement on Standards for Accounting and Review Services (SSARS) No. 25, *Materiality in a Review of Financial Statements and Adverse Conclusions*, which becomes effective for engagements performed in accordance with SSARS for periods ending on or after December 15, 2021.

The 2022 *GAAS Guide* also highlights recently issued audit and SSARS interpretations, and it summarizes current exposure drafts of proposed new standards.

Each section is organized using a consistent structure that is simple and insightful. The opening of each section begins with a list of "Authoritative Pronouncements" that identifies the specific professional standards pertinent to that section. That list is followed by an "Overview" that highlights key provisions of the relevant section, followed by "Definitions," then by "Requirements" that identify the essential professional responsibilities that must be satisfied in each part of your engagement, which are presented in a numbered fashion to highlight their key provisions. Next, under the label "Analysis and Application of Procedures," you will find a concise discussion of how each specific requirement should be applied. Finally, many of the sections contain "Practitioner Aids" to help you apply the promulgated standards to your specific engagements.

A continuing feature of the 2022 Edition is the inclusion throughout most sections of additional insights to help you identify unique issues related to your implementation of the professional standards requirements, including suggestions to help you better plan and execute your engagements. This highlighted guidance is summarized as one of the following:

- Engagement Strategy
- Fraud Pointer
- Important Notice for 2022
- Observation
- Planning Aid Reminder
- Public Company Implication

These highlights are easy to find and can help you understand many of the important subtleties contained in the professional standards guidance.

The AICPA's Auditing Standards Board issues auditing standards applicable to the audits of nonpublic companies, whereas the Public Company Accounting Oversight Board (PCAOB) establishes auditing and other professional standards for registered public accounting firms. While the 2022 Edition of the *GAAS Guide* focuses on those auditing standards applicable to nonpublic company audits, it also contains Public Company Implications that highlight issues that are unique for audits of public companies.

These Public Company Implications reflect the recently completed PCAOB project to re-codify PCAOB Auditing Standards into a new organizational format and they provide an overview of the PCAOB's most recently issued auditing standards including PCAOB AS-3101 (*The Auditor's Report on an Audit of Financial Statements When the Auditor Expresses an Unqualified Opinion and Related Amendments to PCAOB Standards*) issued in June 2017, as well as AS-2501 (*Auditing Accounting Estimates, Including Fair Value Measurements*) and AS-1210 (*Using the Work of an Auditor-Engaged Specialist*) issued by the PCAOB in December 2018 and approved by the SEC in July 2019. The 2022 Edition of the *GAAS Guide* also includes summaries of a number of PCAOB exposure drafts and recently issued Staff Alerts and other notices.

This 2022 Edition continues to provide what has always been the most important feature of the *GAAS Guide*—readability. While practitioners are responsible for ensuring that their engagements comply with the applicable authoritative guidance in the professional standards (SASs, SSAEs, SSARS, PCAOB), this *Guide* provides a useful resource to better understand key elements of those standards. The utmost care has been exercised to avoid the difficult language and to follow the organization of the original pronouncements. Essential material is placed at your fingertips for quick integration into your practice. There is no more need to wonder exactly what a standard means or how it is to be used in a real engagement.

## Acknowledgments

Thanks are due to James L. Ulvog, CPA, of Alta Loma, CA, for his thoughtful, thorough review of the 2022 Edition.

*Mark S. Beasley*
Raleigh, North Carolina

# About the Author

**Mark S. Beasley** is the KPMG Professor of Accounting in the Department of Accounting at North Carolina State University, in Raleigh, N.C., where he teaches auditing and risk management courses in the undergraduate and masters programs. He served as a member of the COSO Board for over seven years and has participated in a number of other national-level risk management initiatives. He served on the Advisory Council that helped develop COSO's initial *Enterprise Risk Management—Integrated Framework* issued in 2004, and he also worked with COSO on its 2017 revision of that framework. He recently served on the United Nations' Internal Control Advisory Group that advised the UN Controller on COSO-based best practices related to internal controls. Dr. Beasley received a BS in accounting from Auburn University and a Ph.D. from Michigan State University. He is a Certified Public Accountant (CPA) in North Carolina and has worked in public accounting, where he was an Audit Manager with EY. Dr. Beasley also worked as a Technical Manager with the American Institute of Certified Public Accountants's (AICPA's) Auditing Standards Division in New York City. He is a member of the AICPA and the American Accounting Association. Dr. Beasley also serves as Director of North Carolina State University's Enterprise Risk Management Initiative, which provides thought leadership on enterprise risk management and its integration with strategy planning and governance.

Dr. Beasley actively conducts research related to financial statement fraud, corporate governance, enterprise risk management, and auditor quality. His work has been published in journals such as *Journal of Accounting Research, Contemporary Accounting Research, Auditing: A Journal of Practice & Theory, Accounting Horizons, Journal of the American Taxation Association, Journal of Accountancy, Strategic Finance, Financial Management,* and *The CPA Journal,* among numerous others. He served on the AICPA's Antifraud Programs and Controls Task Force, in addition to serving on Auditing Standards Board task forces, including the SAS No. 99 Fraud Task Force. He has also been extensively involved in conducting staff training for two of the Big Four accounting firms. Dr. Beasley is a co-author of several continuing education courses, an auditing textbook, and an auditing casebook.

# AU-C Preface
# Preface to the Codification of Statements on Auditing Standards: Principles Underlying an Audit Conducted in Accordance with Generally Accepted Auditing Standards

## AU-C Preface

# CODIFICATION OF STATEMENTS ON AUDITING STANDARDS

## Preface

The preface contains the principles underlying an audit conducted in accordance with generally accepted auditing standards. The principles provide a framework to help explain an audit and understand it; however, these principles are not requirements and do not carry any authority.

## Purpose of an Audit

An audit's purpose is to increase the degree of confidence users can place in an entity's financial statements. The auditor achieves this purpose by expressing an opinion on "whether the financial statements are prepared, in all material respects, in accordance with the applicable financial reporting framework."

## Responsibilities

The auditor is responsible for:
- Having appropriate competence and capabilities to perform the audit.
- Complying with relevant ethical requirements, including independence and due care requirements.
- Maintaining professional skepticism and exercising professional judgment throughout the planning and performance of the audit.

## Performance

The auditor obtains reasonable assurance about whether the financial statements as a whole are free from material misstatement, whether due to fraud or error, in order to express an opinion.

Reasonable assurance is a high, but not absolute, level of assurance that is attained by:
- Adequately planning the work and properly supervising any assistants.
- Determining the appropriate materiality level(s).
- Obtaining a sufficient understanding of the entity and its environment, including its internal control, to identify and assess the risks of material misstatement whether due to error or fraud.
- Obtaining sufficient appropriate audit evidence supporting the conclusion relating to the absence or existence of material misstatements by designing and implementing appropriate responses to assessed risks.

Absolute assurance is unable to be obtained due to inherent limitations arising from the nature of financial reporting, the nature of audit procedures, and the need for audits to be conducted within a reasonable period of time at a reasonable cost.

## Reporting

The auditor must either express in his or her written report an opinion regarding the financial statements taken as a whole or state that an opinion cannot be expressed.

# AU-C 200
# General Principles and Responsibilities

| | | |
|---|---|---|
| Section 200: | Overall Objectives of the Independent Auditor and the Conduct of an Audit in Accordance with Generally Accepted Auditing Standards .................................. | 2002 |
| Section 210: | Terms of Engagement .............................. | 2024 |
| Section 220: | Quality Control for an Engagement Conducted in Accordance with Generally Accepted Auditing Standards ........... | 2039 |
| Section 230: | Audit Documentation .............................. | 2047 |
| Section 240: | Consideration of Fraud in a Financial Statement Audit ...... | 2065 |
| Section 250: | Consideration of Laws and Regulations in an Audit of Financial Statements ...................................... | 2093 |
| Section 260: | The Auditor's Communication with Those Charged with Governance ................................... | 2102 |
| Section 265: | Communicating Internal Control Related Matters Identified in an Audit .......................................... | 2118 |

# SECTION 200

# OVERALL OBJECTIVES OF THE INDEPENDENT AUDITOR AND THE CONDUCT OF AN AUDIT IN ACCORDANCE WITH GENERALLY ACCEPTED AUDITING STANDARDS

## Authoritative Pronouncements

SAS-122—Statements on Auditing Standards: Clarification and Recodification

SAS-123—Omnibus Statement on Auditing Standards—2011

SAS-134—Auditor Reporting and Amendments, Including Amendments Addressing Disclosures in the Audit of Financial Statements

SAS-136—Forming an Opinion and Reporting on Financial Statements of Employee Benefit Plans Subject to ERISA

SAS-138—Amendments to the Description of the Concept of Materiality

SAS-141—Amendment to the Effective Dates of SAS Nos. 134-140

SAS-142—Audit Evidence

SAS-143—Auditing Accounting Estimates and Related Disclosures

## Overview

This section describes the auditor's overall objectives; the nature and scope of an audit designed to enable the auditor to meet those objectives; the scope, authority, and structure of GAAS; and requirements establishing the auditor's general responsibilities in all engagements conducted in accordance with GAAS, including the obligation to comply with GAAS.

One overall objective of the auditor is to obtain reasonable assurance about whether the financial statements as a whole are free from material misstatement, whether due to fraud or error. This enables the auditor to express an opinion on whether the financial statements are presented fairly in all material respects in accordance with an applicable financial reporting framework. Reasonable assurance is obtained when sufficient appropriate audit evidence has been obtained to reduce the audit risk to an acceptably low level. The auditor cannot provide absolute assurance, because of inherent limitations resulting in most audit evidence being persuasive rather than conclusive.

> **PLANNING AID REMINDER:** If reasonable assurance cannot be obtained and a qualified audit opinion is insufficient, GAAS requires the auditor disclaim an opinion or withdraw from the engagement if doing so is not prohibited by law or regulation.

The auditor is to express an opinion, or disclaim an opinion, when he or she is associated with financial information. An auditor is associated with financial information when he or she has performed sufficient audit procedures to be able to report in compliance with GAAS.

Another overall objective of the auditor is to report on the financial statements and communicate as required by GAAS in accordance with his or her findings. An audit conducted in accordance with GAAS and the relevant ethical requirements allows the auditor to form an audit opinion. The form of opinion expressed depends on the applicable financial reporting framework, laws, and regulations. In some circumstances the auditor may provide an opinion on specific matters other than the financial statements, such as on the effectiveness of internal control, in which case, additional work would be required to provide such an opinion. The audit opinion does not provide assurance about the entity's future viability or management's efficiency or effectiveness in conducting the entity's affairs.

An audit is conducted to provide users with additional confidence in the financial statements. In planning and performing an audit, the auditor is required to identify and assess risks of material misstatement, whether due to fraud or error, based on an understanding of the entity and its environment, including its internal control; obtain sufficient appropriate audit evidence about whether material misstatements exist by designing and implementing appropriate responses to the assessed risks; and form an opinion on the financial statements, or conclude that an opinion cannot be formed, based on an evaluation of the audit evidence obtained.

Materiality is applied in planning and performing an audit and in evaluating the effects of identified misstatements on the audit and uncorrected misstatements on the financial statements. Misstatements are generally considered material if they could reasonably be expected to influence the economic decisions of users relying on the financial statements. The auditor's judgment of materiality may be affected by his or her perception of users' financial information needs and the size and nature of a misstatement. Auditors are responsible for detecting misstatements that are material at the opinion level, which is generally the financial statements as a whole or, for governmental entities, each reporting unit.

**IMPORTANT NOTICE FOR 2022:** In December 2019, the AICPA's Auditing Standards Board (ASB) issued SAS No. 138 titled *Amendments to the Description of the Concept of Materiality* to align the materiality concepts discussed in auditing standards, including AU-C 200, with the definition of materiality used by the U.S. judicial system, the PCAOB auditing standards, and the Financial Accounting Standards Board (FASB). The FASB aligned its definition of materiality in August 2018 to be consistent with the U.S. judicial system and other U.S. standards setters and regulators. The ASB believes it is in the public interest to eliminate existing inconsistencies in definitions of materiality used. The U.S. judicial system defines misstatement as material if there is "**substantial likelihood** that a reasonable shareholder **would** consider it important" whereas existing auditing standards define a misstatement as material if it "**could reasonably be expected to** influence the judgment of a reasonable person." The effective date of the amendment is for audits of financial statements for periods ending on or after December 15, 2021.

An entity's financial statements are prepared and presented by management with oversight from those charged with governance. While GAAS does not impose responsibilities on management or those charged with governance, an audit conducted in accordance with GAAS presumes that both parties have fundamental responsibilities that are not relieved by the conduct of an audit.

**IMPORTANT NOTICE FOR 2022:** In May 2019, the AICPA's Auditing Standards Board (ASB) issued SAS No. 134 titled *Auditor Reporting and Amendments, Including Amendments Addressing Disclosures in the Audit of Financial Statements*, to revise the auditor's report and to amend various AU-C sections to heighten the auditor's focus on disclosures throughout the process of auditing financial statements. Originally, the effective date of SAS No. 134 was for audits of financial statements periods ending on or after December 15, 2020, with early implementation **not** permitted. However, the ASB's issuance of SAS No. 141, *Amendment to the Effective Dates of SAS Nos. 134-140*, extended the effective date to December 15, 2021, in order to provide more time for firms to implement SAS No. 134 in light of the effect of the coronavirus pandemic. While SAS No. 141 allows for early implementation of SAS No. 134, the ASB recommends that SAS Nos. 134-140 be implemented concurrently. When SAS No. 134 becomes effective at the end of 2021, it will amend the definition of "financial statements" to also note that "Disclosures comprise explanatory or descriptive information, set out as required, expressly or permitted or otherwise allowed by the applicable financial reporting framework, on the face of a financial statement or in the notes, or incorporated therein by reference when expressly permitted."

## Definitions

| | |
|---|---|
| Applicable financial reporting framework | The financial reporting framework adopted by management and those charged with governance (as applicable) for preparing and presenting financial statements that is acceptable given the nature of the entity and the objective of the financial statements, or that is required by law or regulation. Applicable financial reporting frameworks include U.S. GAAP, GAAP for private companies developed by the FASB's Private Company Council, IFRS, and IFRS for small and medium-sized entities (SMEs). |
| Audit risk | Risk that the auditor expresses an inappropriate audit opinion when the financial statements are materially misstated, which is a function of the risks of material misstatement and detection risk. |
| Auditor | The person or persons conducting the audit, typically the engagement partner, other engagement team members, the firm, or their governmental equivalents. |
| Detection risk | Risk that the procedures performed by the auditor to reduce audit risk to an acceptably low level will not detect an existing misstatement that could be material, either individually or when aggregated with other misstatements. |

§ 200 • Overall Objectives  **2005**

| | |
|---|---|
| Financial reporting framework | A set of criteria used to determine measurement, recognition, presentation, and disclosure of all material items appearing in the financial statements. Examples include accounting principles generally accepted in the United States (U.S. GAAP), International Financial Reporting Standards (IFRS) issued by the International Accounting Standards Board, and special-purpose frameworks. |
| | A fair presentation framework requires compliance with framework requirements and acknowledges that to achieve fair presentation of the financial statements, management may need to provide disclosures beyond those specifically required in the framework, or, in rare circumstances, to depart from a framework requirement. If a financial reporting framework requires compliance with framework requirements but does not make either of the preceding acknowledgments, it is not a fair presentation framework. |
| Financial statements | A structured representation of historical financial information intended to communicate an entity's economic resources or obligations at a point in time or changes therein for a period of time in accordance with a financial reporting framework. Related disclosures are included, which typically summarize significant accounting policies and other explanatory information. The term "financial statements" may refer to a single financial statement or a complete set. |
| Historical financial information | Information expressed in financial terms in relation to a particular entity, derived primarily from that entity's accounting system, about past economic events, conditions, or circumstances. |
| Interpretive publications | GAAS auditing interpretations and exhibits, auditing guidance in AICPA Audit and Accounting Guides, and AICPA Auditing Statements of Position. |
| Management | The person(s) with executive responsibility for the conduct of the entity's operations, which may include some or all of those charged with governance. |
| Misstatement | A difference between the amount, classification, presentation, or disclosure of a reported financial statement item and that which is required for the item to be in accordance with the applicable financial reporting framework. If expressing an opinion regarding the fair presentation of the financial statements in all material respects, misstatements include adjustments of items that the auditor judges necessary for such fair presentation. Misstatements may be due to fraud or error. |
| Other auditing publications | Publications other than interpretive publications, including auditing articles in professional journals and the AICPA's *CPA Letter*, continuing professional education programs and other instruction materials, textbooks, guidebooks, audit programs, and checklists; and other auditing publications from the AICPA, state CPA societies, other organizations, and individuals. |

| | |
|---|---|
| Premise, relating to the responsibilities of management and those charged with governance (as appropriate) on which an audit is conducted *or* premise | Management and those charged with governance (as appropriate) have the following responsibilities that are fundamental to conducting an audit in accordance with GAAS:<br><br>(1) To prepare and present (fairly present in the case of a fair presentation framework such as GAAS) the financial statements in accordance with the applicable financial reporting framework, including designing, implementing, and maintaining internal control relevant to the preparation and presentation of financial statements free from material misstatement; and<br><br>(2) To provide the auditor with access to all information relevant to financial statement preparation and fair presentation of which management and those charged with governance (as appropriate) are aware, additional information the auditor may request from management and those charged with governance for the purpose of the audit, and unrestricted access to persons within the entity from whom the auditor needs to obtain audit evidence. |
| Professional judgment | The application of relevant training, knowledge, and experience, within the context provided by auditing, accounting, and ethical standards, in making informed decisions about the appropriate courses of action in the circumstances of the audit engagement. |
| Professional skepticism | An attitude that includes a questioning mind, being alert to conditions that may indicate possible misstatement due to fraud or error, and a critical assessment of audit evidence. |
| Reasonable assurance | In the context of financial statement audits, a high, but not absolute, level of assurance. |
| Risk of material misstatement | Risk that the financial statements are materially misstated prior to the audit, which at the assertion level is the risk that a misstatement could occur in an assertion about a class of transaction, account balance, or disclosure that could be material, either individually or when aggregated with other misstatements.<br><br>There are two components of the risk of material misstatement. Inherent risk is the risk before considering any related controls. Control risk is the risk that a material misstatement will not be prevented, or detected and corrected, on a timely basis by the entity's internal control. |
| Those charged with governance | The person(s) or organization(s) responsible for overseeing the strategic direction of the entity and the obligations related to the accountability of the entity, which includes overseeing the financial reporting process. Those charged with governance may include management personnel. |

**PUBLIC COMPANY IMPLICATION:** The PCAOB uses a topical system for integrating the Board's standards and those interim auditing standards that are still in effect. The topics selected generally follow the flow of the audit process. Moreover, the PCAOB uses a single, integrated numbering system that is different from the numbering systems used by other standard setters (an AS prefix is used, and a 4-digit number). PCAOB auditing standards are organized using the following topics: (1) general auditing standards, (2) audit procedures,

(3) auditor reporting, (4) matters related to filings under federal securities laws, and (5) other matters associated with audits. In addition, the PCAOB rescinded the interim auditing standards in Section 150 (*Generally Accepted Auditing Standards*), Section 201 (*Nature of the General Standards*), Section 410 (*Adherence to Generally Accepted Accounting Principles*), Section 532 (*Restricting the Use of an Auditor's Report*), and Section 901 (*Public Warehouses—Controls and Auditing Procedures for Goods Held*).

## Requirements

The auditor is presumptively required to adhere to the following guidance when conducting an audit in accordance with GAAS:

1. Comply with relevant ethical requirements relating to financial statement audit engagements.
2. Plan and perform an audit with professional skepticism.
3. Exercise professional judgment in planning and performing an audit.
4. To obtain reasonable assurance, obtain sufficient appropriate audit evidence to reduce audit risk to an acceptably low level, allowing reasonable conclusions to be drawn on which to base an audit opinion.

> **IMPORTANT NOTICE FOR 2022:** In July 2020, the AICPA Auditing Standards Board (ASB) issued SAS No. 142, *Audit Evidence*, which supersedes AU-C 500 (*Audit Evidence*) and amends various other sections, including AU-C 200, in the professional standards. This new SAS addresses the evolving nature of business and audit services and issues that include the use of emerging technologies by both preparers and auditors, audit data analytics (ADA), the application of professional skepticism, the expanding use of external information sources as audit evidence, and more broadly, the accuracy, completeness, and reliability of audit evidence. SAS No. 142 is effective for audits of financial statements for periods ending on or after December 15, 2022.

5. Comply with all AU-C sections relevant to the audit. AU-C sections are relevant when the section is in effect and the circumstances addressed by the AU-C exist.
6. Have an understanding of the entire text of an AU-C section, including its application and explanatory material, in order to understand its objectives and properly apply its requirements.
7. Do not represent compliance with GAAS in the audit report unless the requirements of AU-C 200 and all other AU-C sections relevant to the audit have been complied with.
8. To achieve the auditor's overall objectives, when planning and performing the audit use the objectives stated in relevant AU-C sections and consider the interrelationships among GAAS to (1) determine whether any audit procedures additional to those required by individual AU-C sections are necessary to pursue the objectives stated in each AU-C

section and (2) to evaluate whether sufficient appropriate audit evidence has been obtained.

9. Comply with each requirement of an AU-C section unless the entire AU-C section is not relevant to the audit, the requirement is not relevant because it is conditional and the condition does not exist, or, in rare circumstances, it is necessary to depart from a presumptively mandatory requirement.

10. The degree of responsibility imposed on auditors by professional requirements depends on the type of requirement.
    a. For an unconditional requirement, indicated by the word *must* in GAAS, the auditor must comply with the requirement in all cases where it is relevant.
    b. For a presumptively mandatory requirement, indicated by the word *should* in GAAS, the auditor must comply with the requirement in all cases where it is relevant except in rare circumstances when the auditor judges it necessary to depart from such requirement.

11. The need to depart from a presumptively mandatory requirement is expected to occur only when the requirement is for a specific procedure to be performed that would be ineffective in achieving the requirement's intent in the circumstances. In these situations, alternative audit procedures should be performed to achieve the intent of that requirement.

12. Consider interpretive publications applicable to the audit.

13. If auditing guidance from another auditing publication is applied, use professional judgment to assess the relevance and appropriateness of that guidance to the circumstances of the audit.

14. If an objective in a relevant AU-C section cannot be achieved, evaluate whether that prevents the auditor from achieving his or her overall objectives, thereby requiring the auditor to modify the audit opinion or withdraw from the engagement in accordance with GAAS. Failure to achieve an objective represents a significant finding or issue requiring documentation.

---

**IMPORTANT NOTICE FOR 2022:** In July 2020, the AICPA Auditing Standards Board (ASB) issued SAS No. 143, *Auditing Accounting Estimates and Related Disclosures*, which supersedes AU-C 540 (*Auditing Accounting Estimates, Including Fair Value Accounting Estimates, and Related Disclosures*) and amends various other sections, including AU-C 200, in the professional standards. The new SAS begins with an explanation of the nature of accounting estimates and how they can vary widely in nature and are required to be made by management when monetary amounts cannot be directly observed. The measurement of amounts is subject to estimation uncertainty, which reflects inherent limitations in the knowledge or data. These limitations give rise to inherent subjectivity and variation in measurement outcomes. Although the guidance in SAS No. 143 applies to all accounting estimates, the degree to which an accounting estimate is subject to estimation uncertainty will vary substantially. Therefore, SAS No. 143 recognizes that the nature, timing, and extent of the risk assessment and further audit procedures required will vary in relation to the estimation uncertainty and the assessment of the related risks of material misstatement. The ASB is coordinating the effective date of SAS No. 143 with the effective date of a proposed new SAS, *Understanding the Entity and Its Environment and Assessing the Risks of Material Misstatement*, which is under consideration by the ASB at the time this edition of the *GAAS Guide* was prepared. SAS No. 143 does not become effective until audits of financial statements for periods ending on or after December 15, 2023, which is consistent with the date in the proposed new standard. As a result, this AU-C reflects existing auditing standards requirements. Updates to reflect SAS No. 143 will occur in the next edition of the *GAAS Guide*.

*Financial Statement Preparation*

Although the auditor expresses an opinion on the client's financial statements, the responsibility for the financial statements rests with management. Nonetheless, the auditor can make suggestions to the client about the form and content of the financial statements or may draft the financial statements based on information the client provides.

**PUBLIC COMPANY IMPLICATION:** Section 302 of the Sarbanes-Oxley Act of 2002 (SOX) requires the CEO and CFO of public companies to prepare a written statement that certifies the appropriateness of the annual and quarterly financial statements and disclosures, including certification that based on their knowledge those financial statements and disclosures fairly present, in all material respects, the operations and financial condition of the issuer. Thus, in an audit of a public company's financial statements, the auditor would not be responsible for drafting the financial statements based on information provided by the client. Rather, management is responsible for preparing the financial statements. Although similar public certifications by the senior officers of private companies are not required, representations similar to those required by Section 302 are often included in the management representation letter signed by the senior officers of private companies.

Management is responsible for identifying the applicable financial reporting framework for the entity's financial statements and making judgments regarding reasonable accounting estimates and appropriate accounting policies in the context of that framework when preparing the financial statements. The applicable financial reporting framework may encompass financial accounting standards established by an authorized or recognized standards-setting organization and legislative or regulatory requirements. Other sources that may encompass or provide direction on the application of financial reporting frameworks include the legal and ethical environment, published accounting interpretations and views on emerging accounting issues, widely recognized general and industry practices, and accounting literature. If a conflict exists between information from different sources, the source with the highest authority prevails.

> **PLANNING AID REMINDER:** The responsibilities of management and those charged with governance are very important to the conduct of an audit, so the auditor is required to obtain the agreement of the client regarding those responsibilities prior to accepting an audit engagement.

The form and content of the financial statements are determined by the financial reporting framework used. There are general purpose and special purpose financial statements, prepared to meet the financial information needs of a wide range of users or those of specific users, respectively. There are fair presentation frameworks, such as U.S. GAAP or IFRS, including versions of each for smaller companies, and regulatory or contractual-based frameworks. The financial reporting framework also determines what constitutes a complete set of financial statements. Many frameworks are intended to provide information about an entity's financial position, financial performance, and cash flows. For these frameworks, a complete set of financial statements might include a balance sheet, income statement, statement of changes in equity, cash flow statement, and related notes. For other frameworks, a single financial statement and its related notes may constitute a complete set of financial statements.

*Ethical Requirements*

The auditor is subject to the ethical requirements prescribed by the AICPA Code of Professional Conduct, to more restrictive rules of state boards of accountancy and applicable regulatory agencies, and, in the case of audits of governmental entities, to *Government Auditing Standards*. The AICPA Code of Professional Conduct establishes the fundamental principles of professional ethics, which include responsibilities, the public interest, integrity, the scope and nature of services, objectivity and independence, and due care.

> **PRACTICE POINTER:** Many state boards of accountancy require CPAs licensed in their state to comply with the AICPA Code of Professional Conduct and other AICPA authoritative standards even if those CPAs are not members of the AICPA. The AICPA's Code of Professional Conduct (Code) is structured in several parts, including guidance applicable to all members in addition to separate guidance for members in public practice and guidance for members in business. The Code includes a *conceptual framework approach* (also known as the "threats and safeguard approach") to help members evaluate compliance with the Code.

> **OBSERVATION:** Statement on Quality Control Standards No. 8 (*A Firm's System of Quality Control*) details firm responsibilities for establishing policies and procedures to obtain reasonable assurance that the firm and its personnel comply with relevant ethical requirements, including those pertaining to independence. AU-C 220 allows that the engagement team can rely on the firm's quality control system in meeting quality control responsibilities for an audit engagement unless the engagement partner determines it is inappropriate to do so.

> **IMPORTANT NOTICE FOR 2022:** In February 2021, the AICPA's Auditing Standards Board (ASB) issued an exposure draft of two proposed new Statements on Quality Management Standards-Quality Management, *A Firm's System of Quality Management* and *Engagement Quality Reviews*, and a proposed new SAS *Quality Management for an Engagement Conducted in Accordance with Generally Accepted Auditing Standards*. The proposals are intended to update those standards in light of how the environment in which audit firms have evolved, including the use of technology and evolving regulation, and to address concerns noted by peer reviews. The comment period was extended to August 2021.

The auditor must be independent of the entity in order to perform a GAAS audit unless (1) GAAS provides differently or (2) the auditor is required by law or regulation to accept the engagement and report on the financial statements. Unless one of these exceptions applies, the auditor is precluded from issuing a report under GAAS if he or she lacks independence.

The need for independence in both fact and appearance is a result of the auditor's responsibility to users of the financial statements. Because the users of financial statements have no way of verifying the fairness of the financial statements, they must rely on the work of an independent auditor. If it is suspected that the auditor is not independent, then the integrity and fairness of the financial statements are questionable and the auditor's assurance is of little value to the reader. The auditor is also required to use due care, meaning he or she should have the appropriate competence and capabilities to perform the audit and issue an appropriate auditor's report. The AICPA Code of Professional Conduct is applicable to professional services provided by a CPA that require independence.

> **PUBLIC COMPANY IMPLICATIONS:** If the client is a public entity, regulations established by the Securities and Exchange Commission and the Public Company Accounting Oversight Board (PCAOB) must be considered. SOX authorizes the PCAOB to issue independence and ethics standards applicable to audits of public company financial statements. Additionally, SOX explicitly includes provisions related to the performance of nonaudit services, audit partner rotation, and auditor acceptance of employment at the client. In April 2003, the PCAOB adopted the provisions of the AICPA's Code of Professional Conduct on integrity and objectivity as its "Interim Ethics Standards." The PCAOB also designated the previous Rule 101 of the Code of Professional Conduct and the related interpretations and ethical rulings plus Standards Nos. 1, 2, and 3, and Interpretations 99-1, 00-1, and 00-2 of the Independence Standards Board (ISB) as its "Interim Independence Standards." ISB Standard No. 1 and Interpretations 00-1 and 00-2 have been superseded by PCAOB Rule 3526. Other than these changes, aspects of the prior AICPA Code of Professional Conduct are still in force for public company audits.
>
> PCAOB Rule 3526 requires the registered public accounting firm to make certain disclosures to the client's audit committee regarding independence both before it accepts an initial engagement and no less frequently than yearly

thereafter. Before accepting an initial engagement, the registered firm must (1) communicate in writing to the audit committee all relationships between the firm and the potential client and individuals in financial reporting oversight roles at the potential client that may potentially affect the firm's independence and (2) discuss with the audit committee the potential independence effects of these relationships. These communications must be updated at least annually. And, at least annually, the registered firm must communicate to the audit committee in writing that the firm is independent. The registered firm must document these communications.

PCAOB Rule 3520 requires registered public accounting firms to be independent of their clients. Under Rule 3521, a registered public accounting firm is not independent if it performs any service for a client during the audit or professional engagement period for a contingent fee or commission. Under Rule 3522, a registered public accounting firm is not independent if it performs tax services during the audit or professional engagement period that involve the marketing, planning, or opining in favor of the tax treatment of a transaction if the transaction is confidential (i.e., the taxpayer cannot disclose the transaction) or involves an aggressive tax position as defined by the PCAOB. The audit period is the period covered by the financial statements being audited or reviewed. The professional engagement period begins on the earlier of when the initial engagement letter is signed or the audit, review, or attest procedures begin, and it ends when the registered firm or the client notifies the SEC that there is no longer a client relationship. In addition, under Rule 3523 a registered public accounting firm is generally not independent if it provides tax services to a client person in a financial reporting oversight role or a family member of such a person during the professional engagement period. A person in a financial reporting oversight role has the ability to influence the contents of the financial statements or those who prepare the financial statements (e.g., board members, CEO, president, CFO, COO, general counsel, chief accounting officer, controller, director of internal audit, director of financial reporting, treasurer). However, if a board member is in a financial reporting oversight role solely because he or she is a member of the board, the registered firm is not prohibited from providing tax services to the board member. Finally, if a registered public accounting firm seeks to perform allowable tax services or allowable nonaudit services related to internal control over financial reporting for a client, the registered firm, as required by the Sarbanes-Oxley Act, must obtain pre-approval from the audit committee to perform the service. In either instance, the registered firm must (1) describe in writing to the audit committee the scope of the service and the potential effect of the service on the firm's independence and (2) document the substance of its discussion with the audit committee (Rule 3524 and Rule 3525). Additionally, in the case of allowable tax services, the registered firm must disclose (1) the fee structure for the arrangement, (2) the existence of any side letter or other amendment or agreement related to the service, and (3) whether the registered firm has any referral agreement, referral fee, or fee-sharing arrangement with a third party related to the service (Rule 3524).

PCAOB Rule 3502 prohibits an individual at a registered public accounting firm from knowingly or recklessly taking an action, or failing to take a required action, where the individual's behavior is likely to lead to the registered firm's violation of the Sarbanes-Oxley Act, PCAOB rules and standards, SEC rules, or provisions of the securities laws.

**PUBLIC COMPANY IMPLICATION:** The PCAOB's Staff Audit Practice Alert No. 10 (*Maintaining and Applying Professional Skepticism in Audits*) states that professional skepticism is essential to effective performance of an audit. The auditor cannot exercise due professional care unless he or she is professionally skeptical. To be professionally skeptical, the auditor should maintain a questioning mind and critically assess audit evidence. Although professional skepticism is required throughout the audit, skepticism is particularly important when auditing areas involving significant management judgments, transactions outside the normal course of business, and with a higher risk of fraud. Practice Alert 10 identifies a number of threats to maintaining an appropriate level of professional skepticism, including (1) incentives or pressures to build or maintain a long-term audit engagement, (2) an inappropriate level of trust or confidence in management, and (3) excessive workload demands. In addition, skepticism can be impaired by the auditor's desire to (1) avoid significant conflicts with management, (2) provide an unqualified audit opinion before the company's filing deadline, (3) achieve high client satisfaction ratings, (4) keep audit costs low, and (5) cross-sell other services. Professional skepticism can be enhanced by (1) consistent communication by senior firm leadership as to the importance of professional skepticism in performing high quality audits; (2) a performance appraisal, promotion, and compensation process that emphasizes audit quality; (3) assigning personnel to engagements who have the needed knowledge, skill, and ability; (4) maintaining appropriate documentation, recognizing that more extensive documentation is needed for those areas that require greater judgment; and (5) monitoring the effective application of the firm's quality control system. Although the firm can facilitate individual auditors maintaining an appropriate level of professional skepticism, it is ultimately up to the individual auditor to be professionally skeptical. Skepticism is needed throughout the engagement—first, in identifying and assessing risks of material misstatement; second, in performing tests of controls and substantive procedures; and third, in evaluating audit results to form an opinion. In their efforts to be professionally skeptical, auditors and audit firms must remember that their overriding duty is to put the interests of investors first.

## *Professional Skepticism*

Every task performed by a professional person is approached with a mental attitude. In an audit engagement, that mental attitude is described as professional skepticism. The auditor's use of professional skepticism is important for reducing the risks of overlooking unusual circumstances, over-generalizing audit conclusions, or using inappropriate assumptions to determine the nature, timing, and extent and evaluate the results of audit procedures. Professional skepticism involves being alert to contradictory audit evidence, information that causes the reliability of documents or responses to inquiries to be questioned, conditions that may indicate fraud, and circumstances suggesting the need for additional audit procedures beyond those required by GAAS.

**FRAUD POINTER:** In enforcement actions against auditors the SEC frequently cites lack of due professional care and lack of appropriate professional skepticism. Auditors need to avoid simply accepting management assertions at face value or ignoring known management integrity issues.

Auditors can be affected by unconscious or conscious biases that can impact their professional judgment, including the design of further audit procedures and evaluation of evidence obtained. Maintaining an awareness of biases, such as the tendency to place more weight on events or experiences that immediately come to mind or are readily available than those that are not (availability bias) or a tendency to place more weight on information that corroborates an existing belief than information that contradicts that belief (confirmation bias), is important for the auditor to continually monitor as they made those judgments.

Professional skepticism does not suggest that the auditor assumes the client's management is dishonest or that everything management says is incorrect.

---

**FRAUD POINTER:** AU-C 240 emphasizes the importance of exercising professional skepticism when assessing the risk of material misstatements in the financial statements due to fraud. First, the auditor should approach the engagement with a questioning mind-set that recognizes that fraud is possible in any entity, regardless of the auditor's prior experience with the entity and the auditor's views about management integrity. Second, the auditor should critically evaluate evidence obtained throughout the performance of audit procedures by always questioning whether the evidence obtained suggests that fraud might be present. The auditor should not let his or her beliefs about management's integrity allow him or her to accept less than persuasive evidence.

---

While the auditor is required to consider the reliability of information to be used as audit evidence, he or she may assume records and documents are genuine unless there is reason to believe otherwise. If there is doubt about a record or document's authenticity, the auditor must investigate further and determine what additional audit procedures are needed to resolve the matter.

*Professional Judgment*

Exercising professional judgment throughout the audit is important, especially regarding matters such as:

- Materiality and audit risk;
- The nature, timing, and extent of audit procedures used to meet GAAS requirements and gather audit evidence;
- Evaluating if sufficient appropriate audit evidence has been obtained and GAAS and overall objectives have been achieved;
- Evaluating management's judgments in applying the applicable financial reporting framework; and
- Drawing conclusions based on the audit evidence obtained.

Professional judgment does not provide justification for decisions not otherwise supported by the facts and circumstances of the engagement or by sufficient appropriate audit evidence. When matters are particularly difficult or contentious, the auditor may consult with engagement team members or others to assist in making informed and reasonable judgments. Significant professional judgments made in reaching conclusions on significant audit matters should be documented such that an experienced auditor with no previous connection to the audit is able to understand those judgments. Documenting the auditor's thought process in the form of a memo may be helpful if the engagement is subject to peer review or is later subject to a dispute. Professional judgments can be evaluated based on whether a judgment reflects competent and appropriate application of auditing standards and accounting principles given the facts and circumstances known to the auditor up to the date of his or her report.

## Sufficient Appropriate Audit Evidence

Obtaining and evaluating audit evidence comprises most of the auditor's work in forming an audit opinion. Audit evidence is cumulative in nature and is primarily obtained from audit procedures performed during the audit, but it may also be obtained from previous audits if the auditor has evaluated the effect any changes since that audit or from a firm's quality control procedures for client acceptance and continuance. Audit evidence may be information that supports or contradicts management assertions and, in some cases, the absence of information may constitute audit evidence such as when management refuses to provide a requested representation.

The auditor uses professional judgment in determining whether sufficient appropriate audit evidence has been obtained. Sufficiency and appropriateness of audit evidence are interrelated. Sufficiency is a measure of the quantity of audit evidence and the quantity needed generally increases as the auditor's assessment of the risks of material misstatement increases and as the quality of audit evidence decreases. However, increased quantity may not be able to compensate for poor-quality audit evidence. Appropriateness is a measure of the quality, or relevance and reliability, of audit evidence. The reliability of audit evidence is affected by its source, its nature, and the circumstances under which it is obtained.

## Audit Risk

The assessment of audit risk is a matter of professional judgment based on audit procedures to obtain information about that risk and other evidence obtained throughout the audit. Audit risk is a function of the risks of material misstatement and detection risk.

### Risks of material misstatement

Risks of material misstatement exist at two levels:

1. *Overall financial statement level* Risks relating pervasively to the financial statements as a whole that may affect several assertions.
2. *Assertion level* Risks relating to particular classes of transactions, account balances, and disclosures that are assessed to determine the nature, timing, and extent of further audit procedures necessary to obtain sufficient appropriate audit evidence.

There are two components of risks of material misstatement, inherent risk and control risk, which exist independently of the audit. Inherent risks may vary among assertions due to factors such as complex calculations, estimates subject to significant uncertainty, or circumstances of the entity and its environment. Control risk is a function of the effectiveness of management's design, implementation, and maintenance of internal control relevant to financial reporting. Control risk may be reduced by effective internal controls but can never be eliminated due to inherent limitations such as the potential for human error, collusion, or management override of controls. The auditor may assess inherent and control risk either separately or on a combined basis, and may make this assessment using either quantitative or qualitative measures of risk.

*Detection risk*

Detection risk is the other component affecting audit risk and it relates to the nature, timing, and extent of audit procedures. For a given level of audit risk, there is an inverse relationship between the acceptable level of detection risk and the assessed risks of material misstatement at the assertion level. For example, the greater the risk level, the lower the detection risk that the auditor can accept. Lower detection risk means that the audit evidence needs to be more persuasive. Detection risk is a function of an audit procedure's effectiveness and its application by the auditor. Adequate planning, proper assignment of engagement team personnel, use of professional skepticism, and supervision and review of audit work performed increase the effectiveness of an audit procedure and its application and decrease the chance that an auditor might select an inappropriate audit procedure, misapply an appropriate audit procedure, or misinterpret audit results. Due to the inherent limitations of an audit, detection risk can be reduced but not eliminated.

*Inherent limitations of an audit*

The inherent limitations of an audit prevent the auditor from obtaining absolute assurance that the financial statements are free from material misstatement; therefore, there is a risk that some material misstatements of the financial statements may not be detected. Discovery of such a material misstatement does not necessarily indicate a failure to conduct an audit in accordance with GAAS. Whether the auditor has performed an audit in accordance with GAAS is determined by the audit procedures performed in the circumstances, the sufficiency and appropriateness of the audit evidence obtained, and the suitability of the auditor's report based on an evaluation of the evidence given the auditor's overall objectives.

---

**PLANNING AID REMINDER:** Inherent limitations and matters of difficulty, time, or cost do not provide a valid basis for the auditor to omit an audit procedure for which there is no alternative or to be satisfied with evidence that is less than persuasive.

---

The principal inherent limitations of an audit arise from:
- The nature of financial reporting.
- The nature of audit procedures.
- The need for the audit to be conducted in a reasonable period of time at a reasonable cost.

The nature of financial reporting is such that for many financial statement items there is a degree of uncertainty and management must make judgments, which results in financial statements having an inherent level of variability. This is often the case with accounting estimates and, while the variability cannot be eliminated, the auditor should consider the reasonableness of estimates as well as the qualitative aspects of the entity's accounting practices including indicators of bias in management's judgments.

The nature of audit procedures is such that there are practical and legal limitations on the auditor's ability to obtain audit evidence. When performing audit procedures, the auditor cannot be certain that information is complete, because management or others may not provide all the relevant information intentionally or unintentionally or fraud may exist, causing the auditor to believe invalid audit evidence is valid. Also, since an audit is not an official investigation of wrongdoing, the auditor does not have specific legal powers such as the power of search that would be necessary for such an investigation.

The need for the audit to be conducted in a reasonable period of time at a reasonable cost means that it may be impracticable to address all information that may exist or pursue every matter exhaustively, because there is a balance that needs to be struck between the reliability of information and its cost. The auditor should plan the audit so it will be performed effectively, undertake greater audit effort in areas most expected to contain risks of material misstatement, and use testing and other means to examine populations for misstatements. The auditor is required to have a basis for the identification and assessment of risks of material misstatement at the financial statement and assertion levels by performing risk assessment procedures and related activities and to use testing and other means of examining populations to provide a reasonable basis for drawing conclusions about the population.

> **OBSERVATION:** Other AU-C sections identify specific audit procedures to use to reduce the effect of inherent limitations due to certain assertions or subject matters such as fraud (AU-C 240), related-party relationships and transactions (AU-C 550), noncompliance with laws and regulations (AU-C 250), and events or conditions that may affect an entity's ability to continue as a going concern (AU-C 570).

## *Nature and Content of GAAS*

The AICPA Code of Professional Conduct requires an auditor comply with Statements on Auditing Standards (SASs) issued by the Auditing Standards Board. GAAS provides the auditor with guidance regarding his or her overall objectives and general responsibilities. For some engagements, the auditor may be required to comply with auditing requirements in addition to GAAS, such as *Government Auditing Standards*. In these circumstances, GAAS does not override laws or regulations that govern an audit, but an audit conducted to adhere to those laws and regulations may not comply with GAAS. The auditor may also conduct an audit in accordance with GAAS and PCAOB standards, International Standards on Auditing (ISAs), *Government Auditing Standards*, or the auditing standards of a specific country or jurisdiction, in which case the auditor may need to perform additional audit procedures to comply with those standards as well.

AU-C sections clearly state the scope, effective date, and any specific limitation on that AU-C's applicability and, unless otherwise stated, may be applied before the effective date specified. An AU-C contains both professional requirements and related guidance in applying it. In fulfilling professional responsibilities, the auditor should consider the entire text of an AU-C.

---

**PUBLIC COMPANY IMPLICATION:** An auditor's professional requirements as specified in AU-C 200 are quite similar to an auditor's professional requirements in the audit of a public company, as specified by the PCAOB in Rule 3101 (Certain Terms Used in Auditing and Related Professional Practice Standards).

---

The related guidance in an AU-C is also referred to as application or explanatory material and is intended to be descriptive rather than imperative (i.e., it does not impose a performance obligation upon the auditor). For example, explanatory material may (1) further explain the meaning of a requirement or what it is intended to cover, (2) include particular audit procedures that may be appropriate, and (3) provide additional information that the auditor may find helpful in applying his or her professional judgment. The procedures or actions suggested by the explanatory material are denoted by the words *may*, *might*, or *could*.

The application and other explanatory material may include introductory material, definitions, appendixes, and additional considerations specific to audits of governmental and smaller, less complex entities. Introductory material may explain the AU-C section's purpose and scope, relationship to other AU-C sections, subject matter, context, and responsibilities of the auditor and others in relation to the AU-C's subject matter. Definitions provide the meanings attributed to certain terms for purposes of GAAS that will carry the same meaning throughout GAAS unless otherwise indicated but are not intended to override definitions established for other purposes. When an AU-C provides considerations specific to smaller, less complex entities, they typically refer to an entity with ownership and management concentrated in one or a small number of individuals that has simple transactions or recordkeeping, or few products, lines of business, internal controls, levels of management, or personnel.

### *Objectives in AU-C Sections*

AU-C sections contain objectives that link the requirements of that AU-C section to the auditor's overall objectives, assisting the auditor in understanding what needs to be accomplished and how to accomplish it and in deciding whether more needs to be done to achieve the objectives given the circumstances of the audit. Objectives in AU-C sections are subject to inherent limitations and should be understood in the context of the auditor's overall objectives and as they relate to the objectives and requirements of other relevant AU-C sections.

While proper application of the requirements of relevant AU-Cs is expected to provide the auditor with sufficient basis for achieving his or her objectives, the auditor must determine the audit procedures that are necessary to fulfill GAAS requirements and achieve GAAS objectives. In some cases, this may mean the auditor needs to perform audit procedures in addition to those required by GAAS in order to meet the objectives specified in GAAS.

If the auditor concludes that sufficient appropriate audit evidence has not been obtained to achieve his or her overall objectives, the auditor may:

- Evaluate whether further relevant audit evidence has or will be obtained by complying with other AU-C sections,
- Extend the work performed in applying one or more requirements, and
- Perform other procedures the auditor judges necessary in the circumstances.

**PLANNING AID REMINDER:** If none of these procedures is practical or possible, sufficient appropriate audit evidence will not be obtained and the auditor will need to determine the effect on his or her report or on his or her ability to complete the engagement.

*Complying with Relevant Requirements*

An AU-C may specify that an auditor "should consider" a procedure. In this instance, there is a presumptive requirement that the auditor will consider the procedure. However, although an auditor essentially has to consider the procedure, he or she does not necessarily have to perform the procedure.

An auditor may, in rare circumstances, depart from a presumptively mandatory requirement. In these situations, the auditor must document why he or she departed from the requirement and how he or she accomplished the objective of the presumptively mandatory requirement through other procedures.

**ENGAGEMENT STRATEGY:** An engagement planning strategy is to start with the assumption that all AU-Cs apply, given that most are relevant in every audit. As planning proceeds, the auditor might identify exceptions that exist for unique situations. For example, the use of specialists, audits of service organizations, or the audit of fair values might not be applicable. Auditors may wish to identify a list of the most frequent exceptions, which could be used when planning all audit engagements, and assume that all other AU-Cs are applicable.

**PUBLIC COMPANY IMPLICATION:** PCAOB standards are very similar to AU-C 200 as it relates to the auditor's performance responsibility. The PCAOB's Rule 3101 (Certain Terms Used in Auditing and Related Professional Practice Standards) states that PCAOB standards create unconditional responsibilities, presumptively mandatory responsibilities, and responsibilities to consider. Unconditional responsibilities are denoted by the words *must*, *shall*, and *is required*. Presumptively mandatory responsibilities are denoted by the word *should*. Responsibilities to consider are denoted by the words *may*, *might*, *could*, and similar language.

## Interpretive Publications

Interpretative publications are issued under the authority of the Auditing Standards Board. Guidelines established in interpretative publications are not auditing standards but, rather, provide specific direction on how auditing standards are to be observed in particular situations, especially for clients who operate in specialized industries.

Auditing Interpretations are discussed throughout this text. AICPA Audit and Accounting Guides, which are listed below, and AICPA Statements of Position (Auditing and Attestation) may be purchased from the AICPA:

- Airlines
- Analytical Procedures
- Assessing and Responding to Audit Risk in a Financial Statement Audit
- Audit Sampling
- Auditing Derivative Instruments, Hedging Activities, and Investments in Securities
- Auditing Revenue in Certain Industries
- Brokers and Dealers in Securities
- Casinos
- Compilation and Review Engagements
- Construction Contractors
- Depository and Lending Institutions: Banks and Savings Institutions, Credit Unions, Finance Companies, and Mortgage Companies
- Employee Benefit Plans
- Entities with Oil and Gas Producing Activities
- Government Auditing Standards and Circular A-133 Audits
- Health Care Entities
- Investment Companies
- Life and Health Insurance Entities
- Not-for-Profit Entities
- Property and Liability Insurance Entities
- Prospective Financial Information
- Service Organizations: Applying SSAE No. 16, Reporting on Controls at Service Organizations (SOC 1)
- State and Local Governments

## Other Auditing Publications

An auditor is not "expected to be aware of the full body of other auditing publications," and such publications have no authoritative status. In determining whether another auditing publication is relevant and appropriate, the auditor may presume publications published by the AICPA and reviewed by the AICPA Audit and Attest Standards Staff are appropriate. For other publications, the auditor may consider the degree to which the publication is recognized as being helpful in understanding and applying GAAS and the issuer or author is recognized as an authority in auditing matters.

---

**PLANNING AID REMINDER:** The auditor's responsibilities to follow professional requirements do not apply to Auditing Interpretations issued by the Auditing Standards Board or to any other interpretive guidance or other auditing publications. Therefore, the words *must* or *should* in an interpretive document do *not* represent unconditional or presumptively mandatory requirements, respectively. However, if the auditor does not follow the guidance in the ASB's Auditing Interpretations, he or she will need to be prepared to defend his or her work.

---

## Failure to Achieve an Objective

The auditor uses judgment to determine whether objectives have been achieved. Circumstances that may cause failure to achieve an objective include those preventing the auditor from complying with the relevant requirements of an AU-C section or that result in it not being practical or possible for the auditor to obtain the necessary audit evidence to achieve the objective. The auditor documents a failure to achieve an objective to provide evidence of the basis for his or her conclusions about achievement of his or her overall objectives and to assist in making that evaluation.

# Practitioner's Aid

Professional skepticism is a key element to exercising due professional care in the conduct of an audit. The practitioner's aid presented in Exhibit AU-C 200-1 is based on the guidance provided in the AICPA's Practice Alert 98-2 (*Professional Skepticism and Related Topics*). Practice Alerts are based on existing auditing standards and are issued by the AICPA to help practitioners improve the efficiency and effectiveness of their audits.

## EXHIBIT AU-C 200-1—PROFESSIONAL SKEPTICISM

| Key Questions on Skepticism | Suggested Guidance Provided by Practice Alert 98-2 |
| --- | --- |
| • What is professional skepticism? | Professional skepticism is an attitude that includes a questioning mind and working practices that encompass a critical assessment of audit evidence. |
| • Should professional skepticism be exercised throughout the audit? | Because audit evidence is gathered and evaluated throughout an engagement, professional skepticism must be exercised throughout the entire engagement. |
| • Does professional skepticism mean that statements made by management should never be accepted? | The auditor should strike a balance between disbelief and unquestioning acceptance. Generally, there is a need to corroborate management's responses. |
| • What level of evidence should the auditor obtain in exercising professional skepticism? | Evidence should be persuasive rather than convincing. |
| • Do representations by management provide persuasive evidence? | Representations by management, without further corroboration, rarely provide persuasive evidence. |
| • What are some audit areas that may demand particular scrutiny? | Management responses to questions resulting from the application of analytical procedures. |
| | Representations regarding recoverability of assets or deferred charges. |
| | Accruals (or lack thereof), particularly for unusual events or transactions. |
| | Substance of large and unusual (particularly period-end) transactions. |
| | Vague contract terms or conditions. |
| | Existence of nonstandard journal entries. |
| | Lack of copies of original documents. |
| | Presence of fraud or illegal acts. |
| • Which conditions related to nonstandard journal entries may suggest heightened skepticism with respect to a particular account balance? | Journal entries processed outside the normal course of business. |
| | Transactions that are complex or unusual in nature. |
| | Estimates and period-end adjustments. |
| | Journal entries indicative of potential problems with the accounting systems. |
| | Item has been prone to client error in the past. |
| | Item has not been reconciled on a timely basis or contains old reconciling items. |
| | Represents a particular risk specific to the client's industry. |

| Key Questions on Skepticism | Suggested Guidance Provided by Practice Alert 98-2 |
|---|---|
| | Represents account balances affecting the company's book value and liquidity (e.g., account balances that are used in determining loan covenant ratios). |
| • Does the use of photocopies or draft copies (rather than originals) have an effect on audit skepticism? | Yes; it may be more difficult to identify alterations on photocopied material, and draft copies might not include all relevant information. With the use of scanners, original documents can be altered in a way that makes detection especially difficult. |
| • When presented with photocopied documents, what alternative procedures are available to the auditor? | The auditor should consider whether the originals should be obtained and inspected. |
| • Should the auditor accept fax or e-mail confirmation responses? | The auditor should consider whether (1) to confirm the information over the telephone and/or (2) to request that the original confirmation be returned directly to the auditor. |

# SECTION 210

# TERMS OF ENGAGEMENT

## Authoritative Pronouncements

SAS-122—Statements on Auditing Standards: Clarification and Recodification

SAS-134—Auditor Reporting and Amendments, Including Amendments Addressing Disclosures in the Audit of Financial Statements

SAS-135—Omnibus Statement on Auditing Standards—2019

SAS-137—The Auditor's Responsibilities Relating to Other Information Included in Annual Reports

SAS-141—Amendment to Effective Dates of SAS Nos. 134-140

## Overview

AU-C 210 provides the auditor with guidance regarding his or her responsibilities in agreeing on the terms of the audit engagement with management and those charged with governance (as appropriate). The auditor should only accept or continue an audit engagement when the basis upon which the audit is to be performed has been agreed upon by establishing the presence of the preconditions for an audit and confirming that the auditor and management and those charged with governance (as appropriate) share a common understanding of the terms of the audit engagement.

**IMPORTANT NOTICE FOR 2022:** In February 2022, The AICPA's Auditing Standards Board (ASB) issued an exposure draft of a proposed new SAS, *Inquiries of the Predecessor Auditor Regarding Fraud and Noncompliance with Laws and Regulations*, that includes proposed amendments to AU-C 210. The proposed revisions would require the auditor, once management authorizes the predecessor auditor to respond to inquiries from the auditor, to inquire of the predecessor auditor regarding identified or suspected fraud or noncompliance with laws or regulations (NOCLAR). The exposure draft also emphasizes that the absence of authorization by management to make inquiries of the predecessor auditor should alert the auditor to carefully consider engagement acceptance. The ASB believes this approach is similar to auditor responsibilities under PCAOB Auditing Standards. The comment period on the exposure draft ended June 30, 2021.

**PLANNING AID REMINDER:** AU-C 210 addresses audit preconditions that are within the entity's control, whereas AU-C 220 deals with the auditor's responsibilities that are within his or her control regarding the acceptance of an audit engagement.

## Definitions

| | |
|---|---|
| Preconditions for an audit | The use by management of an acceptable financial reporting framework in the preparation of the financial statements and the agreement of management and, when appropriate, those charged with governance to the premise on which an audit is conducted. |
| Recurring audit | An audit engagement for an existing audit client for whom the auditor performed the preceding audit. |
| Management | In AU-C 210, the term "management" should be read as "management and, when appropriate, those charged with governance" unless the context suggests otherwise. |

## Requirements

The auditor is presumptively required to perform the following procedures when agreeing to the terms of an audit engagement with management:

1. To determine whether the preconditions for an audit are present:
   a. Determine whether the financial reporting framework to be applied in the financial statement preparation is acceptable.
   b. Obtain management's agreement that it acknowledges and understands its responsibility (1) for preparing and fairly presenting the financial statements in accordance with the applicable financial reporting framework; (2) for designing, implementing, and maintaining internal control relevant to preparing and fairly presenting financial statements free from material misstatement due to fraud or error; and (3) to provide the auditor with access to all information management is aware of that is relevant to the financial statements' preparation and fair presentation, additional information the auditor may request from management for purposes of the audit, and unrestricted access to persons within the entity from whom the auditor needs to obtain audit evidence. A discussion of these issues between the auditor, management, and those charged with governance is good client relations and establishes a record of understanding.
2. Do not accept an engagement if management or those charged with governance impose a scope limitation that the auditor believes will result in a disclaimer of opinion on the financial statements as a whole unless the audit is required by law or regulation, in which case, the auditor is permitted but not required to accept the engagement.
3. If the preconditions for an audit are not present, discuss the matter with management. Do not accept the engagement unless required by law or regulation if the financial reporting framework to be applied in preparing the financial statements is unacceptable or management's agreement of its acknowledgment and understanding of its responsibilities has not been obtained.
4. Agree upon the audit engagement terms with management.
5. Record agreed-upon terms of the audit engagement in an engagement letter or other suitable form of written agreement that includes:

a. The financial statement audit's objective and scope;

b. The auditor's responsibilities;

c. Management's responsibilities;

d. A statement that because of the inherent limitations of an audit and those of internal control, there is some risk that some material misstatements may not be detected even though the audit is planned and performed properly in accordance with GAAS;

e. Identification of the applicable financial reporting framework for the financial statement presentation; and

f. Reference to the expected form and content of any reports the auditor will issue and a statement that in some circumstances a report may differ from its expected form and content.

6. Before accepting an initial audit or reaudit engagement, request the entity's permission to inquire of any predecessor auditor about matters that will assist in determining whether to accept the engagement and request the entity's authorization of the predecessor auditor to fully respond to the auditor's inquiries. If an entity refuses to authorize the predecessor auditor to respond in full or in part, inquire about the reasons and consider the implications in deciding whether to accept the engagement.

7. If the predecessor auditor provides no response or a limited response, consider the implications in deciding whether to accept the engagement. Evaluate a predecessor auditor's response before accepting the engagement.

8. On recurring audits, evaluate whether the terms of the audit engagement need to be revised. If the terms do not need revision, remind the entity of the engagement terms and document that reminder.

9. Do not agree to a change in the audit engagement terms when there is no reasonable justification for the change.

10. If prior to completing the audit engagement the auditor is requested to change the audit engagement to an engagement that provides a lower level of assurance, determine whether there is reasonable justification for the change.

11. If the audit engagement terms are changed, the auditor and management should agree on and record the new engagement terms in an engagement letter or other suitable written agreement.

12. If the auditor concludes there is no reasonable justification for the change in audit engagement terms and is not permitted by management to continue the original audit engagement, he or she should withdraw from the engagement when possible under law and regulation; communicate the circumstances to those charged with governance; and determine if any legal, contractual, or other obligation exists to report the circumstances to other parties, such as owners or regulators.

13. If law or regulation prescribes a specific layout, form, or wording of the auditor's report that differs significantly from GAAS requirements, evaluate whether users might misunderstand the auditor's report and, if so, whether the auditor would be permitted to reword the prescribed form to be in accordance with GAAS requirements or attach a separate report. Do not accept the engagement unless required by law or regulation if rewording the form or attaching a separate report would not be permitted or would not mitigate the risk of users misunderstanding the auditor's report. An audit conducted in accordance with such law or regulation does not comply with GAAS; so, the auditor should not make reference in his or her report to the audit having been conducted in accordance with GAAS.

---

**PLANNING AID REMINDER:** Practitioners who perform audits of employee benefit plans to comply with U.S. Department of Labor (DOL) audit requirements should be aware that those requirements extend beyond requirements in generally accepted auditing standards. Recently, the DOL has studied a number of audits of employee benefit plans and found that 39% of those audits contained major deficiencies. The DOL found that the smaller the number of firm engagements to conduct audits of employee benefit plans, the larger the rate of deficiencies. In response to this finding, the DOL has called for federal legislation that would allow the U.S. Secretary of Labor to establish standards for employee benefit plans audits as well as additional education for practitioners who perform those audits. Practitioners should obtain a sufficient understanding of DOL audit requirements before accepting an engagement to audit an employee benefit plan.

---

## Analysis and Application of Procedures

### Preconditions for an Audit

The auditor should determine whether the financial reporting framework to be applied to the financial statements is acceptable in determining whether the preconditions for an audit exist. An acceptable financial reporting framework provides the auditor with suitable criteria or benchmarks for auditing the financial statements by allowing reasonably consistent evaluation or measurement of a subject matter using professional judgment. The framework also provides the criteria for management to fairly present the entity's financial statements. Factors that may impact the auditor's determination of the acceptability of a financial reporting framework include the nature of the entity, the purpose and nature of the financial statements, and whether the financial reporting framework is prescribed by law or regulation.

Financial statements may be prepared in accordance with a financial reporting framework designed to meet the common financial information needs of a wide range of users. These general purpose financial reporting frameworks are established by bodies designated by the AICPA Council in Part 1.320 of the AICPA Code of Professional Conduct to establish such principles and include the following:

- The Financial Accounting Standards Board's (FASB) *Accounting Standards Codification,* promulgated by the FASB;
- International Financial Reporting Standards, promulgated by the International Accounting Standards Board;
- Statements of the Governmental Accounting Standards Board (GASB), promulgated by the GASB; and
- Statements of Federal Financial Accounting Standards, promulgated by the Federal Accounting Standards Advisory Board.

Financial statements may also be prepared in accordance with a special purpose framework, such as one prescribed by law or regulation, and the acceptability of special purpose financial statements is addressed in AU-C 800.

**PLANNING AID REMINDER:** If after accepting an audit engagement the applicable financial reporting framework is found to be unacceptable and use of the framework is not prescribed by law or regulation, management may decide to use another acceptable framework. If this occurs, the previously agreed-upon engagement terms will no longer be accurate and new terms should be agreed upon and recorded to reflect the framework change.

The auditor also needs to obtain management's agreement that it acknowledges and understands its responsibilities in establishing whether the preconditions for an audit exist. This agreement helps prevent misunderstandings about the respective responsibilities of management and the auditor. The auditor may want to make management aware that written representations of its fulfillment of certain responsibilities will be required by AU-C 580, other AU-C sections, and possibly in support of other audit evidence. If management will not acknowledge its responsibilities or agree with the expectation to provide written representations, the auditor will not be able to obtain sufficient appropriate audit evidence and the engagement should not be accepted unless required to do so by law or regulation. If required to accept the engagement, the auditor may need to explain to management the importance of these matters and their implications for the auditor's report.

**ENGAGEMENT STRATEGY:** As a precondition of the audit of special purpose financial statements, AU-C 800 requires the auditor to obtain management's agreement that it acknowledges and understands its responsibility to include all informative disclosures that are appropriate for the special purpose framework used.

Management is responsible for maintaining the internal control necessary for the preparation and fair presentation of the financial statements. Management determines what internal control is necessary by considering management's needs, the complexity of the business, the nature of the entity's risks, and relevant laws or regulations. Internal control only provides reasonable assurance about achieving the entity's financial reporting objectives due to its inherent limitations, and an audit does not act as a substitute for management's maintenance of the necessary internal control. Management's agreement about its responsibility for internal control does not imply that the auditor will find that the entity's internal control has achieved its purpose or is free of deficiencies.

The auditor should consider whether to accept an audit engagement when there is a scope limitation imposed by management. Some scope limitations do not preclude the auditor from accepting the engagement, such as restrictions imposed by management that the auditor believes will result in a qualified opinion or restrictions imposed by circumstances beyond management's control. If an entity is required by law or regulation to have an audit and management imposes a scope limitation the auditor expects will result in disclaiming an opinion on the financial statements as a whole, the auditor is neither precluded from nor required to accept the engagement.

*Agreement on Audit Engagement Terms*

The auditor reaches an agreement on the terms of the audit engagement with management or those charged with governance of the entity. If the agreement on engagement terms is only with those charged with governance, the auditor is still required to obtain management's agreement that it acknowledges and understands its responsibilities. Agreeing on audit engagement terms before the audit begins helps to avoid misunderstandings, reducing the risk that the entity may rely inappropriately on the auditor to protect the entity against certain risks or to perform certain functions that are the entity's responsibility. The form and content of the audit engagement letter varies; information on the auditor's responsibilities may be based on the summary of those responsibilities contained in AU-C 200 (*Overall Objectives of the Independent Auditor and the Conduct of an Audit in Accordance with Generally Accepted Auditing Standards*) and the description of management's responsibilities is addressed in the requirements of AU-C 210.

The understanding between the auditor and the client may also include the following:

- Elaboration of the audit scope, including reference to the guidance the auditor adheres to;
- Coordination regarding the planning of the engagement and performance of the audit, including information about the engagement team;
- Communication of key audit matters (KAMs);
- The form of any other communication of the audit engagement results;
- Arrangements regarding audit planning and performance, including the audit team composition;
- That, at the conclusion of the engagement, management will provide the auditor with a letter that confirms certain representations made during the audit;
- Clarification that the auditor will have access to all information that management used to prepare the financial statements and related disclosures;

- Management's agreement to provide the auditor with draft financial statements and accompanying information, including that relevant to their preparation and fair presentation, in time to allow the auditor to complete the audit in the proposed timetable;
- Management's agreement regarding matters related to other information to be included in the annual report and related auditor reporting on other information;
- Management's agreement to inform the auditor of subsequent events it becomes aware of that may affect the financial statements;
- The basis on which fees are computed and any billing arrangements; and
- A request for management to agree to the terms of the engagement and acknowledge receipt of the engagement letter.

---

**IMPORTANT NOTICE FOR 2022:** In May 2019, the AICPA's Auditing Standards Board (ASB) issued SAS No. 134 titled *Auditor Reporting and Amendments, Including Amendments Addressing Disclosures in the Audit of Financial Statements* that makes significant changes to the auditor's report, including the ability to communicate key audit matters (KAMs) in the auditor's report. SAS No. 134 also includes conforming amendments to other AU-C sections, including AU-C 210. SAS No. 134 amends AU-C 210 to note that when the auditor is engaged to report on KAMs the auditor may include in the engagement letter an acknowledgment that management has requested that the auditor communicate KAMs in the auditor's report. Originally, these changes were not to become effective until late 2020, given the effective date of SAS No. 134 was for audits of financial statements periods ending on or after December 15, 2020. However, the ASB's issuance of SAS No. 141, *Amendment to the Effective Dates of SAS Nos. 134-140*, extended the effective date of SAS No. 134 to December 15, 2021, in order to provide more time for firms to implement SAS No. 134 in light of the effect of the coronavirus pandemic. While SAS No. 141 allows for early implementation of SAS No. 134, the ASB recommends that SAS Nos. 134-140 be implemented concurrently.

---

**OBSERVATION:** AU-C 265 requires the auditor of financial statements to communicate in writing to management and those charged with governance significant deficiencies and material weaknesses that were identified. Although an audit of financial statements is not designed to perform procedures to detect control deficiencies, AU-C 265 requires communication when the auditor identifies significant deficiencies and material weaknesses in internal control over financial reporting.

---

**PUBLIC COMPANY IMPLICATION:** The Sarbanes-Oxley Act of 2002 (SOX) requires all public companies to issue an internal control report that includes management's assessment of the effectiveness of internal controls. Furthermore, the auditor must attest to and issue a report on management's assessment of internal control for the large accelerated filer public companies. Thus, in the audit of accelerated filer public companies, the auditor must issue an opinion on the financial statements and an opinion on internal controls. The audit of financial statements and the audit of internal controls are meant to be integrated. For this reason, when obtaining an understanding with the client in the audit of a public company, the auditor must modify the discussion to reflect the unique responsibility for internal controls that is applicable to public companies.

Some other matters, such as the following, may also be included as part of the understanding with the client when relevant:

- An acknowledgment if management has engaged the auditor to communicate KAMs;
- Arrangements concerning involvement of specialists or internal auditors, if applicable;
- Arrangements involving a predecessor auditor;
- Any limitation or other arrangements regarding the liability of the auditor or the client, such as indemnification to the auditor for liability arising from known misrepresentations to the auditor by management (regulators may restrict or prohibit such liability limitation arrangements);
- Conditions under which access to the auditor's documentation may be granted to others;
- Additional services to be provided relating to regulatory requirements; and
- Arrangements regarding other services to be provided in connection with the engagement.

Exhibit AU-C 210-1 provides an example of an audit engagement letter demonstrating the incorporation of many of these matters.

## Communications with the Predecessor Auditor

A successor auditor is required to communicate with the predecessor auditor before accepting an engagement; however, an auditor may make a proposal on an engagement before the communication has been made. More than one auditor may make a proposal on the same engagement. Under this circumstance, the predecessor auditor is not expected to respond to inquiries made by the auditor until (1) the client has selected a successor auditor and (2) the successor auditor has accepted the engagement subject to the consideration of the responses received from the predecessor auditor. The responsibility to initiate the communication, which can be either oral or written, rests with the successor auditor.

**ENGAGEMENT STRATEGY:** Rule 1.700 of the AICPA's Code of Professional Conduct prohibits an auditor from disclosing confidential information except when the client agrees to the disclosure. To reconcile the requirements of AU-C 210 with Rule 1.700, the successor auditor should ask the prospective client to grant permission to discuss the impending engagement with the predecessor auditor. The client should not place any restrictions on the exchange of information between the successor and predecessor auditors. If the successor auditor cannot obtain required information from the predecessor auditor because of client restrictions, the successor auditor should consider the reasons for the restrictions and take the circumstances into consideration when deciding whether to accept the client. Likewise, the auditor is required by Rule 1.700 to keep information obtained from the predecessor auditor confidential regardless of whether the engagement is accepted.

The predecessor auditor is expected to respond promptly and fully to the successor auditor's inquiries in accordance with the Code of Professional Conduct unless there are unusual circumstances such as pending, threatened, or potential ligation or disciplinary proceedings. Under these circumstances, the predecessor auditor may decide to not respond fully to the inquiries but should clearly state that the response is limited.

Inquiries directed by the successor auditor to the predecessor auditor may include matters such as the following:

- Information related to the integrity of management;
- Disagreements between the predecessor auditor and the client concerning accounting principles, audit procedures, or other "similarly significant matters";
- The predecessor auditor's understanding of the nature of the entity's relationships with related parties and significant unusual transactions;
- Predecessor auditor's communications with management and those charged with governance concerning fraud, illegal acts by the client, and matters related to the client's internal control; and
- The predecessor auditor's understanding of the reason for the change in auditors.

**IMPORTANT NOTICE FOR 2022:** In May 2019, the AICPA's Auditing Standards Board (ASB) issued SAS No. 135 titled *Omnibus Statement on Auditing Standards—2019* that includes amendments to various AU-C sections. SAS No. 135 notes that the auditor may want to also inquire about the predecessor auditor's understanding of the nature of the entity's relationships and transactions with related parties and significant unusual transactions. The original effective date of SAS No. 135 was for audits of financial statements periods ending on or after December 15, 2020, with early implementation **not** permitted. However, the ASB's issuance of SAS No. 141, *Amendment to the Effective Dates of SAS Nos. 134-140*, extended the effective date of SAS No. 135 to December 15, 2021, in order to provide more time for firms to implement SAS No. 135 in light of the effect of the coronavirus pandemic. While SAS No. 141 allows for early implementation of SAS No. 135, the ASB recommends that SAS Nos. 134-140 be implemented concurrently.

**FRAUD POINTER:** AU-C 240 notes that the auditor should consider other information obtained in an audit, such as procedures related to the acceptance and continuance of clients, when assessing the risks of material misstatements due to fraud. Information obtained from the predecessor auditor about management's integrity, disagreements between management and the predecessor auditor, and the reasons for the change in auditors can provide relevant insights to the successor auditor, particularly when combined with other information gathered by the successor auditor to assess fraud risks.

---

**PLANNING AID REMINDER:** When the most recent financial statements have been compiled or reviewed, a successor-predecessor auditor relationship does not exist; however, the auditor is not prohibited from following the guidance established by AU-C 510.

---

*Recurring Audits*

When deciding if the terms of a recurring audit engagement need to be revised, the auditor may consider the following factors:

- Indications that the entity misunderstands the nature and scope of the audit;
- Any revised or special terms of the audit engagement;
- A change of senior management;
- Significant changes in ownership or the nature or size of the entity's business; and
- Changes in the legal or regulatory requirements, the financial reporting framework adopted in preparing the financial statements, or other reporting requirements.

If the terms of a recurring audit engagement do not need to be revised, the auditor reminds the entity of those terms via a written or oral reminder. If the reminder is oral, the auditor may document the reminder by including with whom the discussion took place, when, and the significant points discussed.

*Accepting a Change in the Audit Engagement Terms*

The auditor considers whether to agree to a change in audit engagement terms based on whether there is a reasonable justification for the change. Reasonable bases for requesting a change in terms include changing circumstances affecting the entity's requirements or misunderstandings about the nature of the service originally requested. Change requests may be unreasonable if the change relates to information that is incorrect, incomplete, or otherwise unsatisfactory; for example, if the auditor is requested to change an audit to a review engagement to avoid a qualified opinion or a disclaimer of opinion.

If the auditor concludes that there is a reasonable justification for changing an audit engagement to a review or other service, the report on the other service will not reference the original audit engagement or any procedures performed in the original audit engagement unless the revised engagement is an agreed-upon procedures engagement and reference to those procedures is a normal part of the report.

In circumstances where the auditor is conducting an audit in accordance with a law or regulation that prescribes an audit report that is not in compliance with GAAS, conducting the audit in accordance with GAAS may not be mentioned in the report. Regardless, the auditor is encouraged to apply GAAS to the extent practicable in the audit, including the AU-C sections addressing the auditor's report.

## Practitioner's Aids

*EXHIBIT AU-C 210-1—AUDIT ENGAGEMENT LETTER*

To the [appropriate representative of those charged with governance] of Averroes Company:

[*The objective and scope of the audit*]

You have requested that we audit the financial statements of Averroes Company, which comprise the balance sheet as of December 31, 20X5, and the related statements of income, changes in stockholders' equity, and cash flows for the year then ended. We are pleased to confirm our acceptance and our understanding of this audit engagement by means of this letter. Our audit will be conducted with the objective of our expressing an opinion on the financial statements.

The objectives of our audit are to obtain reasonable assurance about whether the financial statements as a whole are free from material misstatement, whether due to fraud or error, and to issue an auditor's report that includes our opinion. Reasonable assurance is a high level of assurance but is not absolute assurance and therefore is not a guarantee that an audit conducted in accordance with auditing standards generally accepted in the United States of America (GAAS) will always detect a material misstatement when it exists. Misstatements can arise from fraud or error and are considered material if, individually or in the aggregate, they could reasonably be expected to influence the economic decisions of users made on the basis of these financial statements.

[*Auditor's responsibilities*]

We will conduct our audit in accordance with GAAS. As part of an audit in accordance with GAAS, we exercise professional judgment and maintain professional scepticism throughout the audit. We also, identify and assess the risks of material misstatement of the financial statements, whether due to fraud or error, design and perform audit procedures responsive to those risks, and obtain audit evidence that is sufficient and appropriate to provide a basis for our opinion. The risk of not detecting a material misstatement resulting from fraud is higher than for one resulting from error, as fraud may involve collusion, forgery, intentional omissions, misrepresentations, or the override of internal control. Also, we obtain and understanding of internal control relevant to the audit in order to design audit procedures that are appropriate in the circumstances, but not for the purpose of expressing an opinion on the effectiveness of the entity's internal control. However, we will communicate to you in writing concerning any significant deficiencies or material weaknesses in internal control relevant to the audit of the financial statements that we have identified during the audit. In addition, we evaluate the appropriateness of accounting policies used and the reasonableness of accounting estimates made by management, as well as evaluate the overall presentation of the financial statements, including the disclosures, and whether the financial statements represent the underlying transactions and events in a manner that achieves fair presentation. Furthermore, we conclude, based on the audit evidence obtained, whether there are conditions or events, considered in the aggregate, that raise substantial doubt about Averroes Company's ability to continue as a going concern for a reasonable period of time.

Because of the inherent limitations of an audit, together with the inherent limitations of internal control, an unavoidable risk that some material misstatements may not be detected exists, even though the audit is properly planned and performed in accordance with GAAS.

[*Management's responsibilities and identification of the applicable financial reporting framework*]

Our audit will be conducted on the basis that management and, where appropriate, those charged with governance acknowledge and understand that they have responsibility:

a. For the preparation and fair presentation of the financial statements in accordance with accounting principles generally accepted in the United States;

b. For the design, implementation, and maintenance of internal control relevant to the preparation and fair presentation of financial statements that are free from material misstatement, whether due to fraud or error; and

c. To provide us with:

   i. Access to all information of which management is aware that is relevant to the preparation and fair presentation of the financial statements such as records, documentation, and other matters;

   ii. Additional information that we may request from management for the purpose of the audit; and

   iii. Unrestricted access to persons within the entity from whom we determine it necessary to obtain audit evidence.

As part of our audit process, we will request from management and, where appropriate, those charged with governance, written confirmation concerning representations made to us in connection with the audit.

[*Other relevant information*]

[*Insert other information, such as fee arrangements, billings and other specific terms, as appropriate.*]

**[Reporting]**

[*Insert appropriate reference to the expected form and content of the auditor's report. Example follows:*]

We will issue a written report upon completion of our audit of Averroes Company's financial statements. Our report will be addressed to the board of directors of Averroes Company. Circumstances may arise in which our report may differ from its expected form and content based on the results of our audit. Depending on the nature of these circumstances, it may be necessary for us to modify our opinion, add an emphasis-of-matter paragraph or other-matter paragraph to our auditor's report, or if necessary, withdraw from the engagement.

We will also issue a written report on [*Insert appropriate reference to other auditor's reports expected to be issued*] upon completion of our audit.

Please sign and return the attached copy of this letter to indicate your acknowledgment of, and agreement with, the arrangements for our audit of the financial statements including our respective responsibilities.

Averroes Company

Acknowledged and agreed on behalf of Averroes Company by

(signed)

Name and Title:

Date:

---

Exhibit AU-C 210-2 is a prospective client evaluation form that can be helpful in determining whether a client should be accepted. Once a client is accepted, the form can be used as an integral part of the planning of the accepted engagement.

## EXHIBIT AU-C 210-2—PROSPECTIVE CLIENT EVALUATION FORM

Use this form to document the evaluation of a prospective client who has requested audited financial statements. The memo format is only a guide. The auditor should exercise professional judgment to determine how the form should by modified by adding, deleting, or revising captions to the memo format.

The evaluation process does not imply that our firm is vouching for the integrity or reliability of the prospective client.

Name of Prospective Client: _____

Date of Financial Statements: _____

1. Describe how contact was established with the prospective client.

_____

_____

_____

2. Provide a background of the principals that represent the client.

_____

_____

_____

3. Describe the nature of the products and/or services provided by the prospective client.

_____

_____

_____

4. Describe the services and dates of services provided by the predecessor CPA.

_____

_____

_____

5. Explain the reason(s) why the prospective client has decided to seek the services of another CPA.

_____
_____
_____

6. Summarize the explanation for the change of accountants as understood by the predecessor CPA. (If the predecessor CPA firm has not been contacted, provide the reason that contact was not made.)

_____
_____
_____

7. Summarize the history of the prospective client and other CPA firms (other than the predecessor CPA firm) that have provided service for the past 10 years.

_____
_____
_____

8. Explain why the client desires audited financial statements, and identify external parties who may rely on the statements (however, identifying parties that may rely on the financial statements may create privity issues if there is litigation).

_____
_____
_____

9. Describe any litigation that the client and its principals have been involved in during the past 5 years.

_____
_____
_____

10. Summarize information obtained from credit bureaus, etc., concerning the credit rating of the client and its principals.

_____
_____
_____

11. Other information: _____

_____

_____

Prepared By: _____
Date: _____
Client Accepted (Yes or No): _____
Acceptance Date: _____
Signature of CPA: _____

# SECTION 220

# QUALITY CONTROL FOR AN ENGAGEMENT CONDUCTED IN ACCORDANCE WITH GENERALLY ACCEPTED AUDITING STANDARDS

## Authoritative Pronouncements

SAS-122—Statements on Auditing Standards: Clarification and Recodification

SAS-134—Auditor Reporting and Amendments, Including Amendments Addressing Disclosures in the Audit of Financial Statements

SAS-136—Forming an Opinion and Reporting on Financial Statements of Employee Benefit Plans Subject to ERISA

SAS-141—Amendment to Effective Dates of SAS Nos. 134-140

SQCS-8—A Firm's System of Quality Control (Redrafted)

## Overview

AU-C 220 provides auditors with guidance regarding their responsibilities for quality control procedures in audits of financial statements, engagement quality control reviews, and other engagements conducted in accordance with generally accepted auditing standards (GAAS).

**OBSERVATION:** AU-C 220 is applicable to auditors in government audit organizations who perform financial audits in accordance with GAAS.

According to Statement on Quality Control Standards (SQCS) No. 8 (*A Firm's System of Quality Control*), an accounting firm should adopt a system of quality controls to provide reasonable assurance that the firm and its personnel comply with professional standards and applicable legal and regulatory requirements and the reports issued by the firm or engagement partners are appropriate in the circumstances. Quality control standards relate to the conduct of a firm's audit practice, and those quality control standards should be implemented for each audit to provide the auditor with reasonable assurance at the engagement level as well. The engagement team may rely on the firm's quality control system unless the engagement partner determines it is inappropriate to do so based on available information.

SQCS-8 notes that the firm's system of quality control should include policies and procedures addressing each of the following elements:

- Leadership responsibilities for quality within the firm (the "tone at the top"),
- Relevant ethical requirements,

- Acceptance and continuance of client relationships and specific engagements,
- Human resources,
- Engagement performance, and
- Monitoring.

---

**PUBLIC COMPANY IMPLICATION:** PCAOB AS-1220 (*Engagement Quality Review*) establishes quality review standards for audits of public companies. Unlike the concurring review requirement adopted by the PCAOB as part of its interim standards, which only pertained to firms that were members of the AICPA's SECPS, AS-1220 applies to all firms registered with the PCAOB. In addition to applying to audits performed under PCAOB standards, AS-1220 also applies to reviews. However, the procedures required to be performed by the engagement quality reviewer for a review of interim financial information is more limited. For all such engagements, an engagement review is conducted before the report is issued. The engagement reviewer is required to be a partner of the firm performing the engagement, another person in an equivalent position in the firm, or an individual outside the firm who is associated with a registered public accounting firm. The engagement reviewer is required to have competence, independence, integrity, and objectivity. He or she is required to have the level of competence needed to have an overall responsibility for a comparable engagement. To maintain objectivity, the engagement reviewer would not be permitted to make decisions for the engagement team, supervise the team, or assume responsibilities of the team. Certain review procedures are required on every audit engagement, and review procedures generally involve discussions with engagement personnel and review of documents. Review procedures must be performed with due professional care and professional skepticism. Required engagement quality review procedures are more limited when the service being reviewed is an interim review. In addition, the engagement quality reviewer would be required to review documentation in the areas that he or she reviewed. The engagement quality reviewer would be required to assess whether this documentation indicates that the engagement team responded appropriately to significant risks and whether the documentation supports conclusions reached by the engagement team. The engagement quality reviewer must adequately document his or her review procedures. Finally, the firm is not permitted to issue its report (or communicate its conclusion to the client if no report was to be issued) until the engagement quality reviewer granted his or her concurring approval.

---

The AICPA Professional Issues Task Force published Practice Alert No. 01-1 (*Common Peer Review Recommendations*), which identifies common peer review findings that are helpful to professionals as they consider critical and significant issues in planning and performing audits. The issues are grouped in the following categories: (1) implementation of new professional standards or pronouncements, (2) application of U.S. GAAP pertaining to equity transactions, (3) application of U.S. GAAP pertaining to revenue recognition considerations, (4) documentation of audit procedures and audit findings, and (5) miscellaneous findings. Practice Alerts can be downloaded from the AICPA website (http://www.aicpa.org).

## Definitions

| | |
|---|---|
| Engagement partner | The partner or other person in the firm who is responsible for the audit engagement, its performance, and the auditor's report issued by the firm and who has the appropriate authority from any required professional, legal, or regulatory bodies. |
| Engagement quality control review | A process designed to provide an objective evaluation before the report release date of the significant judgments made and conclusions reached by the engagement team in formulating the auditor's report. This process is only for those audit engagements for which the firm has determined an engagement quality control review is required. |
| Engagement quality control reviewer | A partner, staff member, suitably qualified external person, or a team of such people, none of whom are part of the engagement team, with sufficient and appropriate experience and authority to objectively evaluate the significant judgments made and the conclusions reached by the engagement team in formulating the auditor's report. |
| Engagement team | All partners or staff performing the engagement and any individuals, except for external specialists, engaged by the firm or a network firm who perform audit procedures on the engagement. |
| Firm | A form of organization permitted by law or regulation whose characteristics conform to resolutions of the Council of the AICPA and that practices public accounting. |
| Monitoring | An ongoing process of considering and evaluating the firm's system of quality control, including inspection or a periodic review of engagement documentation, reports, and clients' financial statements for a selection of completed engagements, designed to provide the firm with reasonable assurance that its system of quality control is designed appropriately and operating effectively. |
| Network firm | A firm or other entity that belongs to a network as defined below. |
| Network | An association of entities that includes at least one firm that cooperate for the purpose of enhancing the firms' ability to provide professional services and that share at least one of the following characteristics: (1) use of a common brand name; (2) common control among the firms through ownership, management, or some other means; (3) profits or costs, excluding the costs of operating the network; (4) costs of developing audit methodologies, manuals, and training; (5) common business strategy, including accountability for performance related to the strategy; (6) significant professional resources; and (7) required common quality control procedures. |
| Partner | Any individual with authority to bind the firm in the performance of a professional services engagement. This may include an employee who has not assumed the benefits and risks of ownership. |
| Personnel | Partners and staff. |
| Professional standards | Standards established by bodies that set auditing and attest standards applicable to the engagement being performed and relevant ethical requirements. |

| | |
|---|---|
| Relevant ethical requirements | Ethical requirements the engagement team and engagement quality control reviewer are subject to, consisting of the AICPA Code of Professional Conduct and the more restrictive rules of applicable state boards of accountancy and applicable regulatory agencies. |
| Staff | Professionals other than partners, including any specialists employed by the firm. |
| Suitably qualified external person | An individual outside the firm with the competence and capabilities to act as an engagement partner (e.g., a partner of another firm). |

## Requirements

The auditor is presumptively required to perform the following procedures regarding quality control procedures for financial statement audits:

### *Engagement Partner Responsibilities*

1. Take responsibility for the overall quality on each assigned audit engagement. Certain procedures may be delegated to engagement team members, their work may be used, and the firm's quality control system may be relied upon.

2. Observe and inquire as necessary throughout the audit for evidence of noncompliance with relevant ethical requirements by engagement team members.

3. If the engagement partner becomes aware that engagement team members have not complied with relevant ethical requirements, consult with others in the firm to determine the appropriate action.

4. Form a conclusion on compliance with independence requirements relevant to the audit engagement and, in doing so:

   a. Obtain relevant information from the firm and network firms (as applicable) to identify and evaluate circumstances and relationships that threaten independence.

   b. Evaluate information on any identified breaches of the firm's independence policies and procedures to determine whether they threaten independence.

   c. Take appropriate action to eliminate or reduce threats to independence to an acceptable level by applying safeguards or withdrawing from the engagement if appropriate and possible under law or regulation. Promptly report any inability to resolve the matter to the firm so the firm may take appropriate action.

5. Determine that appropriate procedures regarding client and audit engagement acceptance and continuance have been followed and that the conclusions reached are appropriate.

6. If the engagement partner obtains information that would have caused the firm to decline the audit engagement had the information been available, promptly communicate that information to the firm so the firm and engagement partner can take the necessary action.

7. Determine that the engagement team and any auditor's specialists have the appropriate competence and capabilities to (1) perform the audit engagement in accordance with professional standards and applicable legal and regulatory requirements and (2) enable an auditor's report to be issued that is appropriate in the circumstances.

8. Take responsibility for (1) the direction, supervision, and performance of the audit engagement in compliance with professional standards, applicable legal and regulatory requirements, and the firm's policies and procedures and (2) the auditor's report being appropriate in the circumstances.

9. Take responsibility for reviews being performed in accordance with the firm's review policies and procedures.

10. On or before the date of the auditor's report, review the audit documentation and talk with the engagement team to determine that sufficient appropriate audit evidence has been obtained to support the conclusions reached and for the auditor's report to be issued.

11. With regards to consultations:
    a. Take responsibility for the engagement team consulting as appropriate on difficult or contentious matters.
    b. Determine that the engagement team consulted appropriately during the engagement, both within the team and between the team and others inside or outside the firm.
    c. Determine that the party consulted agreed with the nature and scope of consultations and understood the conclusions resulting from the consultations.
    d. Determine that the conclusions resulting from consultations have been implemented.

12. For any audit engagements requiring an engagement quality control review:
    a. Determine that an engagement quality control reviewer has been appointed.
    b. Discuss significant findings or issues arising during the audit engagement or the engagement quality control review with the engagement quality control reviewer.
    c. Do not release the auditor's report until the completion of the engagement quality control review.

## *Engagement Quality Control Reviewer Responsibilities*

13. Objectively evaluate the significant judgments made and conclusions reached by the engagement team in formulating the auditor's report. This evaluation should involve:
    a. Discussion of significant findings or issues with the engagement partner,
    b. Review of the financial statements and the proposed auditor's report,
    c. Review of selected audit documentation relating to the significant judgments made and conclusions reached by the engagement team, and
    d. Evaluation of the conclusions reached in formulating the auditor's report and consideration of whether the proposed auditor's report is appropriate.

## *Differences of Opinion*

14. If differences of opinion arise within the engagement team with those consulted or between the engagement partner and the engagement quality control reviewer where applicable, the firm's policies and procedures for resolving differences of opinion should be followed by the engagement team.

## Monitoring

15. With regards to the monitoring process, the engagement partner should consider:

    a. The results of the firm's monitoring process based on the latest information the engagement partner received from the firm and other network firms (as applicable).

    b. Whether noted deficiencies in that information may affect the audit engagement.

## Documentation

16. The following audit documentation should be included:

    a. Issues identified regarding compliance with relevant ethical requirements and their resolution;

    b. Conclusions on compliance with independence requirements relevant to the audit engagement and any relevant discussions with the firm supporting these conclusions;

    c. Conclusions regarding client and audit engagement acceptance and continuance; and

    d. The nature, scope, and conclusions of consultations during the audit engagement.

17. For an engagement quality control review, the engagement quality control reviewer should document:

    a. The performance of procedures required by the firm's policies on engagement quality control review,

    b. The date that the engagement quality control review was completed, and

    c. That the reviewer is unaware of any unresolved matters that would cause the reviewer to believe that the significant judgments made and conclusions reached by the engagement team were inappropriate.

---

**PLANNING AID REMINDER:** Practitioners who perform audits of employee benefit plans to comply with U.S. Department of Labor (DOL) audit requirements should be aware that those requirements extend beyond requirements in generally accepted auditing standards. Recently, the DOL has studied a number of audits of employee benefit plans and found that 39% of those audits contained major deficiencies. The DOL found that the smaller the number of firm engagements to conduct audits of employee benefit plans, the larger the rate of deficiencies. In response to this finding, the DOL has called for federal legislation that would allow the U.S. Secretary of Labor to establish standards for employee benefit plans audits as well as additional education for practitioners who perform those audits. Practitioners should obtain a sufficient understanding of DOL audit requirements before accepting an engagement to audit an employee benefit plan.

## Analysis and Application of Procedures

*Engagement Partner Responsibilities*

*Audit quality responsibilities*

By taking responsibility for the overall quality on an audit engagement, the engagement partner emphasizes that quality is essential to performing audit engagements and, more specifically, to:

- Performing work that complies with professional standards and legal and regulatory requirements,
- Complying with applicable firm quality control policies and procedures,
- Issuing auditor's reports appropriate to the circumstances, and
- The engagement team's ability to raise concerns without fear of reprisal.

*Relevant ethical requirements*

In considering relevant ethical requirements, the engagement partner may look to the fundamental principles of professional ethics established by the AICPA Code of Professional Conduct: responsibilities, the public interest, integrity, objectivity and independence, and due care.

The engagement partner must form a conclusion regarding compliance with independence requirements relevant to the audit engagement. If threats to independence are identified that cannot be reduced to an acceptable level, appropriate action may involve eliminating the activity or interest that creates the threat or withdrawing from the engagement if possible under law or regulation.

*Client and audit engagement acceptance and continuance*

Information such as the following can assist the engagement partner in determining whether conclusions regarding client and audit engagement acceptance and continuance are appropriate:

- The integrity of the entity's principal owners, key management, and those charged with governance.
- Whether the engagement team is competent and has the necessary capabilities, time, and resources to perform the audit engagement.
- Whether the firm and engagement team can comply with relevant ethical requirements.
- The implications of significant findings or issues arising during the current or previous audit engagement on relationship continuance.

*Engagement team assignment*

The engagement partner may determine the capabilities and competence of the engagement team as a whole, by considering factors such as the team's:

- Understanding and practical experience with similar audit engagements;
- Understanding of professional standards, legal and regulatory requirements, and the firm's quality control policies and procedures;
- Technical expertise, including IT and other specialized areas of accounting and auditing;

- Knowledge of the client's industry; and
- Ability to apply professional judgment.

*Engagement performance*

The engagement partner takes responsibility for the direction, supervision, performance, and review of the audit engagement. To direct the engagement team, that engagement partner may inform the team of matters such as the following:

- Team member responsibilities, including the need to comply with relevant ethical requirements and to plan and perform the audit with professional skepticism;
- Responsibilities of each partner involved in the audit engagement;
- Objectives of the work to be performed;
- Nature of the entity's business;
- Risk-related issues;
- Problems that may arise; and
- The detailed approach to performance of the engagement.

Supervision of the engagement team may involve tracking audit engagement progress; considering the competence and capabilities of individual team members; identifying matters for consultation or consideration by qualified engagement team members; and addressing significant findings or issues arising during the audit engagement, considering their significance, and appropriately modifying the planned approach.

Review responsibilities and procedures are determined based on the guidance in SQCS-8 that suitably experienced team members review the work of other team members and involve consideration of whether:

- Work was performed according to professional, legal, and regulatory requirements;
- Significant findings or issues for further consideration were raised;
- Appropriate consultations occurred and their conclusions were documented and implemented;
- The nature, timing, and extent of work performed was appropriate, does not need to be revised, supports the conclusions reached, and was appropriately documented;
- Evidence obtained is sufficient and appropriate to support the auditor's report; and
- Objectives of the engagement procedures were achieved.

The engagement partner may review items relating to critical areas of judgment, significant risks, or other areas the partner considers important to ensure significant findings and issues are resolved on or before the date of the auditor's report. If an engagement partner takes over during an audit, in order to assume the necessary responsibilities, he or she may apply these review procedures to the work performed up to the date of change.

> **PLANNING AID REMINDER:** The engagement partner may, but is not required to, review all audit documentation. The partner is required to document the extent and timing of the reviews.

Direction, supervision, and review of an engagement team member with specialized expertise may include agreeing to the nature, scope, and objectives of that member's work; the respective roles of that member and the rest of the team; the nature, timing, and extent of communication between that member and the rest of the team; and evaluating the adequacy, relevance, reasonableness, and consistency of that member's work and findings with other audit evidence.

*Consultations*

Engagement team members have a professional responsibility to bring difficult or contentious matters that may require consultation to the attention of the appropriate personnel. Consultations will be most effective when those consulted have the appropriate knowledge, authority, and experience and are given the relevant facts to enable them to provide informed advice. The engagement team may consult with those outside the firm if the firm lacks appropriate internal resources.

*Engagement Quality Control Review*

The engagement quality control review should be completed before the auditor's report is released; however, review documentation may be completed after the report release date as part of final audit file assembly. If the review is completed after the date of the auditor's report and identifies the need for additional procedures or evidence, the report date is changed to the date when those additional procedures are completed or the additional evidence is obtained.

The engagement partner, by remaining alert to changes in circumstances, can identify situations where an engagement quality control review becomes necessary during the course of the engagement. For some firms, none of the firm's audit engagements may meet the criteria that would require an engagement quality control review.

> **OBSERVATION:** The engagement partner's responsibilities for the audit engagement and its performance are not reduced by the performance of an engagement quality control review.

An engagement quality control review's extent may vary depending on audit complexity and the risk of an inappropriate auditor's report and may include consideration of matters such as:

- Significant risks identified during the audit and responses to those risks, including fraud risk;
- Judgments made, especially regarding materiality and significant risks;
- The significance and handling of misstatements identified during the audit;

- Matters to be communicated to management, those charged with governance, and regulatory bodies where applicable;
- The engagement team's evaluation of the firm's independence for purposes of the audit;
- Whether appropriate consultations took place on matters involving differences of opinion or other difficult or contentious matters and the conclusions of these consultations; and
- Whether audit documentation reviewed reflects the work performed related to significant judgments and supports the conclusions reached.

When management has engaged the auditor to communicate key audit matters (KAMs), the engagement quality review would also consider the conclusions reached by the engagement team in formulating the auditor's report, including the determination of KAMs to be communicated and not communicated, or the determination that there are no KAMs to communicate.

---

**IMPORTANT NOTICE FOR 2022:** In May 2019, the AICPA's Auditing Standards Board (ASB) issued SAS No. 134 titled *Auditor Reporting and Amendments, Including Amendments Addressing Disclosures in the Audit of Financial Statements* that makes significant changes to the auditor's report, including the ability to communicate key audit matters (KAMs) in the auditor's report. SAS No. 134 also includes conforming amendments to other AU-C sections, including AU-C 220. SAS No. 134 amends AU-C 220 to note that when the auditor is engaged to report on KAMs the engagement quality reviewer would also include considerations reached by the engagement team related to the KAMs communicated. Originally, these changes were not to become effective until late 2020, given the effective date of SAS No. 134 was for audits of financial statements periods ending on or after December 15, 2020, with early implementation **not** permitted. However, the ASB's issuance of SAS No. 141, *Amendment to the Effective Dates of SAS Nos. 134-140*, extended the effective date of SAS No. 134 to December 15, 2021, in order to provide more time for firms to implement SAS No. 134 in light of the effect of the coronavirus pandemic. While SAS No. 141 allows for early implementation of SAS No. 134, the ASB recommends that SAS Nos. 134-140 be implemented concurrently.

---

## Monitoring

When considering whether deficiencies in monitoring affect the audit engagement, the engagement partner may determine that measures the firm took to resolve the deficiency are sufficient in the context of the audit.

---

**OBSERVATION:** AU-C 220 points out that if a firm is found to have deficiencies in its system of quality control or violates specific policies or controls, it does not mean that a particular audit engagement was not performed in accordance with generally accepted auditing standards or that the auditor's report was not appropriate.

# SECTION 230

# AUDIT DOCUMENTATION

## Authoritative Pronouncements

SAS-122—Statements on Auditing Standards: Clarification and Recodification

SAS-134—Auditor Reporting and Amendments, Including Amendments Addressing Disclosures in the Audit of Financial Statements

SAS-137—The Auditor's Responsibilities Relating to Other Information Included in Annual Reports

SAS-141—Amendment to Effective Dates of SAS Nos. 134-140

SAS-142—Audit Evidence

SAS-143—Auditing Accounting Estimates and Related Disclosures

SAS Interpretation 1—Providing Access to or Copies of Audit Documentation to a Regulator

## Overview

Audit documentation (working papers) should (1) support the auditor's representation that the engagement has been planned and performed in accordance with GAAS and applicable legal and regulatory requirements and (2) substantiate the type of audit report (such as an unqualified or qualified opinion) issued. However, the specific type, content, and extent of documentation is to some degree dependent upon the characteristics of the particular engagement and the audit methodology employed. The specific nature of the audit documentation is a matter of the auditor's professional judgment, recognizing that such professional judgment needs to be reasonable and in accordance with professional norms.

The auditor must prepare audit documentation for each engagement in sufficient detail for an experienced auditor with no previous involvement with the engagement to understand the following:

- The nature, timing, and extent of audit procedures performed;

- The results of the audit tests performed and the evidence collected; and

- Conclusions drawn on significant matters and significant professional judgments made in reaching these conclusions.

## Definitions

| | |
|---|---|
| Audit documentation | Record of audit procedure performed, audit evidence obtained, and conclusions the auditor reached. Also called working papers or workpapers. |
| Audit file | One or more folders or other storage media, in physical or electronic form, containing the records that constitute the audit documentation for a specific engagement. |
| Documentation completion date | Date, no later than 60 days following the report release date, on which the auditor has assembled for retention a complete and final set of documentation in the audit file. |
| Experienced auditor | An individual (whether internal or external to the firm) who has practical audit experience and a reasonable understanding of audit processes, GAAS and applicable legal and regulatory requirements, the business environment in which the entity operates, and auditing and financial reporting issues relevant to the entity's industry. (Practical audit experience does not mean the auditor is required to have performed comparable audits.) |
| Report release date | Date the auditor grants the entity permission to use the auditor's report in connection with the financial statements. |

## Requirements

The auditor is required to perform the following procedures related to audit documentation:

### Timely Preparation of Audit Documentation

1. Prepare audit documentation on a timely basis.

### Documentation of Audit Procedures Performed and Audit Evidence Obtained

2. Prepare audit documentation sufficient to enable an experienced auditor with no previous connection to the audit to understand (*a*) the nature, timing, and extent of the audit procedures performed to comply with GAAS and applicable legal and regulatory requirements; (*b*) the results of audit procedures performed and the audit evidence obtained; and (*c*) conclusions reached on significant audit findings and significant professional judgments made in reaching those conclusions.

3. To document the nature, timing, and extent of audit procedures performed, record (*a*) the identifying characteristics of the specific items or matters tested, (*b*) who performed the audit work and the date work was completed, and (*c*) who reviewed the audit work and the date and extent of the review.

4. Include in the audit documentation abstracts or copies of significant contracts or agreements that were inspected during the audit.

5. Document discussions of significant findings with management, those charged with governance, and others. Include the nature of the findings discussed, and when and with whom the discussions occurred.

6. If information was identified that is inconsistent with the auditor's final conclusion regarding a significant finding, document how the inconsistency was addressed.

7. Document the justification for any departure from a relevant presumptively mandatory requirement. Also document how the alternative audit procedures performed were sufficient to achieve the intent of that requirement.

8. Additional documentation is required for matters arising after the date of the auditor's report. Document (*a*) the circumstances encountered; (*b*) new or additional audit procedures performed, audit evidence obtained, conclusions reached, and their effect on the audit report; and (*c*) when and by who changes to the audit documentation were made and reviewed.

## Assembly and Retention of the Final Audit File

9. Document the report release date in the audit documentation.

10. Complete the administrative process of assembling the final audit file on a timely basis, no later than the documentation completion date (i.e., no later than 60 days following the report release date).

11. Do not discard any audit documentation after the documentation completion date before the end of the specified retention period, a minimum of five years from the report release date.

12. If audit documentation needs to be modified or added to after the documentation completion date, document the specific reasons for making the changes and when and by whom the changes were made and reviewed.

---

**IMPORTANT NOTICE FOR 2022:** In July 2020, the AICPA Auditing Standards Board (ASB) issued SAS No. 143, *Auditing Accounting Estimates and Related Disclosures*, which supersedes AU-C 540 (*Auditing Accounting Estimates, Including Fair Value Accounting Estimates, and Related Disclosures*) and amends various other sections, including AU-C 230, in the professional standards. The new SAS begins with an explanation of the nature of accounting estimates and how they can vary widely in nature and are required to be made by management when monetary amounts cannot be directly observed. The measurement of amounts is subject to estimation uncertainty, which reflects inherent limitations in the knowledge or data. These limitations give rise to inherent subjectivity and variation in measurement outcomes. Although the guidance in SAS No. 143 applies to all accounting estimates, the degree to which an accounting estimate is subject to estimation uncertainty will vary substantially. Therefore, SAS No. 143 recognizes that the nature, timing, and extent of the risk assessment and further audit procedures required will vary in relation to the estimation uncertainty and the assessment of the related risks of material misstatement. The ASB is coordinating the effective date of SAS No. 143 with the effective date of a proposed new SAS, *Understanding the Entity and Its Environment and Assessing the Risks of Material Misstatement*, which was under consideration by the ASB at the time this edition of the *GAAS Guide* was being prepared. SAS No. 143 does not become effective until audits of financial statements for periods ending on or after December 15, 2023, which is consistent with the date in the proposed new standard. As a result, this AU-C reflects existing auditing standards requirements. Updates to reflect SAS No. 143 will occur in the next edition of the *GAAS Guide*.

---

**PUBLIC COMPANY IMPLICATION:** PCAOB Staff Audit Practice Alert No. 14 (*Improper Alteration of Audit Documentation*) reminds auditors of the potentially severe sanctions associated with improperly altering audit documentation. Improper alteration, especially in connection with an inspection or investigation, violates the Board's rules. The Staff Audit Practice Alert emphasizes that AS

1215 (originally issued as AS 3) requires the completion of a complete and final set of audit documentation within 45 days of the report release date. After this date, audit documentation may not be deleted or discarded. Additional documentation may be added, if the additional documentation is dated, identified as to individual and reason for the addition. Registered firms have an obligation to ensure that work papers are properly archived, that no improper alterations occur after archival, and that PCAOB inspectors are provided originally-archived documentation, supplemented, if appropriate, with additions that meet the above criteria.

## Analysis and Application of Procedures

### Timely Preparation of Audit Documentation

Timely preparation of audit documentation enhances audit quality and facilitates the effective review and evaluation of audit evidence obtained and conclusions reached before the auditor's report is finalized.

> **PLANNING AID REMINDER:** The report release date is often the date the auditor delivers the audit report to the entity. However, when there are delays in releasing the report, the auditor may become aware of a fact that might have affected the audit report if it was known. AU-C 561 addresses the auditor's responsibilities in such circumstances.

### Documentation of Audit Procedures Performed and Audit Evidence Obtained

*Sufficiency of audit documentation for an experienced auditor*

The form, content, and extent of audit documentation will vary, and the following factors should be considered:

- Size and complexity of the entity,
- Identified risks of material misstatement,
- Degree of professional judgment required to perform the procedures and evaluate the results,
- Nature of audit procedures used,
- Significance of the audit evidence obtained,
- Nature and extent of identified exceptions,
- Need to document a conclusion (or the basis for a conclusion) that is not evident from reviewing the documentation of the work performed, and
- Audit methodology and tools used.

Audit documentation (which may be in hard-copy form, electronic form, or other medium) developed for an engagement should demonstrate that the three standards of fieldwork were satisfied. The documentation generally includes the following:

- Audit plans,
- Analyses,

- Issues memoranda,
- Confirmation letters,
- A representation letter,
- Checklists,
- Correspondence concerning and summaries of significant findings or issues, and
- Abstracts/copies of entity documents (including significant contracts or agreements that support the accounting for specific transactions).

The auditor is not required to include items such as superseded, incomplete, corrected, or duplicate documents in the audit documentation. The auditor also cannot rely on oral explanations to support the work performed or the conclusions reached, although oral explanations can supplement the audit documentation.

Compliance with AU-C 230 will generally result in sufficient, appropriate audit documentation; however, other AU-C sections contain specific documentation requirements applicable to particular circumstances (see Exhibit AU-C 230-1). Audit documentation serves to provide evidence that the audit complies with GAAS. However, the auditor is not required to document every matter considered during the audit. Furthermore, the auditor is not required to separately document compliance for matters for which the existing audit documentation demonstrates compliance; for example:

- An audit plan demonstrates the auditor has planned the audit.
- A signed engagement letter demonstrates the auditor's agreement to the terms of the audit engagement with management or those charged with governance.
- A qualified auditor's report demonstrates compliance with GAAS requirements to express a qualified opinion.

There are various ways compliance with general audit requirements can be demonstrated. For example, professional skepticism may be documented by evidence of specific procedures performed to corroborate management's responses to the auditor's inquiries. Engagement partner responsibility for the direction, supervision, and performance of the audit in compliance with GAAS may be documented by the partner's involvement in team discussions about the susceptibility of the entity's financial statements to material misstatements.

Significant audit findings or issues encountered during an engagement should be documented. The following are examples of significant findings or issues:

- Significant matters related to the selection, application, and consistency of significant accounting practices, particularly related to accounting for complex or unusual transactions and the accounting for items dependent on estimates, uncertainties, and management assumptions.
- Matters leading to significant risks.

- The results of audit procedures suggesting that the financial statements could be materially misstated.
- The results of audit procedures suggesting a need to revise the auditor's assessment of and response to the risks of material misstatement.
- The application of required audit procedures was difficult.
- Findings that could lead to a modification of the standard auditor's report.

The form, content, and extent of audit documentation regarding significant findings will vary depending on the extent of professional judgment exercised. It is appropriate for the auditor to document professional judgments when the findings, issues, and judgments are significant, as in the following circumstances:

- When considering information or factors that should be considered and the consideration is significant.
- When concluding as to the reasonableness of areas of subjective judgments.
- When concluding as to a document's authenticity when conditions caused the auditor to believe the document may not be authentic.

**ENGAGEMENT STRATEGY:** The auditor may find it helpful to prepare a completion memorandum, or summary of the significant issues or findings identified during the audit and how they were addressed. This summary can facilitate effective and efficient reviews and inspections of the audit documentation as well as help the auditor identify any AU-C section objectives not being achieved that could prevent him or her from achieving the overall objectives of the auditor.

In auditing smaller, less complex entities, audit documentation will generally be less extensive. However, documentation should still be sufficient for an experienced auditor to determine if a GAAS audit was performed, because the audit may be subject to external review.

*Identification of items tested and of the preparer and reviewer*

Documenting the identifying characteristics of items tested improves the auditor's ability to review and supervise work performed and to investigate exceptions and inconsistencies. For example, if 50 payroll transactions are tested as part of the tests of controls, the audit documentation must specifically identify which 50 items were tested possibly by listing the payroll check numbers. Likewise, if accounts are confirmed as part of the audit of receivables, the specific accounts confirmed must be documented.

**PLANNING AID REMINDER:** In some instances, it is not necessary to specifically list each item tested. For example, if systematic sampling is used it is sufficient to identify the starting point and the sampling interval. However, the method of documentation must enable an experienced auditor to reconstruct which specific sample items were tested as part of the engagement.

The requirement for documenting who reviewed audit work and the date and extent of the review does not require each individual working paper to contain evidence of its review. What must be documented is what audit work was reviewed, who reviewed the work, and when it was reviewed.

*Documentation of discussions of significant findings*

Documentation of discussions of significant findings with management, those charged with governance, or other personnel within or external to the entity such as those providing professional advice, is not limited to auditor-prepared documentation. Documentation may include documents such as entity-prepared minutes of meetings if they provide an appropriate record of the discussion.

---

**IMPORTANT NOTICE FOR 2022:** In May 2019, the AICPA's Auditing Standards Board (ASB) issued SAS No. 134 titled *Auditor Reporting and Amendments, Including Amendments Addressing Disclosures in the Audit of Financial Statements* that makes significant changes to the auditor's report, including the ability to communicate key audit matters (KAMs) in the auditor's report. SAS No. 134 also includes conforming amendments to other AU-C sections, including AU-C 230. SAS No. 134 amends AU-C 230 to note that when the auditor may want to prepare audit documentation in those circumstances where the auditor is engaged to report on KAMs but the auditor determines that there are no KAMs to be communicated. Originally, these changes were not to become effective until late 2020, given the effective date of SAS No. 134 was for audits of financial statements periods ending on or after December 15, 2020, with early implementation **not** permitted. However, the ASB's issuance of SAS No. 141, *Amendment to the Effective Dates of SAS Nos. 134-140*, extended the effective date of SAS No. 134 to December 15, 2021, in order to provide more time for firms to implement SAS No. 134 in light of the effect of the coronavirus pandemic. While SAS No. 141 allows for early implementation of SAS No. 134, the ASB recommends that SAS Nos. 134-140 be implemented concurrently.

---

*Documentation of inconsistencies*

Documentation of information identified that is inconsistent with the auditor's final conclusion may include procedures performed and documentation of consultations or resolutions of differences in professional judgment among the engagement team or between the engagement team and others consulted.

---

**ENGAGEMENT STRATEGY:** Documentation as discussed in AU-C 230 is essential in supporting an auditor against claims of malpractice. Auditors should ensure that their audit procedures, results, and conclusions are well documented and carefully reviewed. Such steps are an important part of minimizing liability risk.

---

*Documentation of departure from a relevant requirement*

GAAS requires the auditor to comply with requirements that are relevant to the audit. Accordingly, the auditor is only required to document departure from relevant requirements. Requirements are not relevant in cases where (1) the AU-

C section is not relevant or (2) the requirement is conditional and the condition does not exist.

*Matters arising after the date of the auditor's report*

Circumstances in which the auditor performs audit procedures or draws new conclusions after the date of his or her report are rare, but they do occur. Such circumstances include when the auditor becomes aware of facts that existed at the date of his or her report that might have caused the opinion in the report to be modified or the financial statements to be amended or when the auditor concludes necessary audit procedures were omitted.

## Assembly and Retention of the Final Audit File

*Assembly of the audit file on a timely basis*

While 60 days is the normal period of time auditors have to complete assembling the audit file, auditors may have fewer than 60 days to complete this process due to statutes, regulations, or the firm's quality control policies. Prior to the documentation completion date, the auditor may change the audit documentation to:

- Complete the documentation and assembly of the audit evidence that was gathered prior to the date of the auditor's report,
- Assemble the audit file (e.g., delete or discard superseded documentation and cross-reference working papers),
- Sign off on file completion checklists, and
- Add information to the file received after the date of the auditor's report (e.g., an original of a confirmation that was previously faxed).

**ENGAGEMENT STRATEGY:** The auditor is required to document auditor independence and staff training. The most efficient means of documenting these items may be centrally within the firm, although the firm can choose to include the documentation at the engagement level.

*Retention of the audit file*

Audit documentation should be retained for a period of time that is sufficient to meet the quality control policies of the CPA firm, and any applicable legal or regulatory requirements, which may in some instances specify retention periods longer than five years.

**PUBLIC COMPANY IMPLICATIONS:** The Sarbanes-Oxley Act of 2002 (SOX) required the PCAOB to adopt an auditing standard that requires auditors to prepare and maintain audit documentation for a period of at least seven years. The nature and extent of documentation retained must be in sufficient detail to support the auditor's conclusions. SOX makes the knowing and willful destruction of audit documentation within the seven-year period a criminal offense. The PCAOB's AS-1215 (*Audit Documentation*) contains the audit documentation requirements applicable to audits of public companies. The PCAOB states that a failure to prepare adequate audit documentation is serious, and inadequate audit documentation in a high-risk area is a *very serious* (authors' emphasis) violation of PCAOB standards. The PCAOB also states that an oral explanation of audit procedures without written documentary evidence is insufficient. In addition, audit documentation should be prepared at the time the audit procedure is performed. Failure to maintain sufficient documentation leads to the presumption that the procedures were not applied, the evidence was not obtained, and the conclusions reached lacked adequate support. AU-C 230 bears many similarities to AS-1215. The PCAOB's Staff Audit Practice Alert No. 14 (*Improper Alteration of Audit Documentation*) clarifies that audit documentation cannot be deleted or discarded after the documentation completion date, which is to be no later than 45 days after the report release date. Any additions to the audit documentation must indicate the date the information was added, the name of the person who prepared the additional documentation, and the reason for adding it.

---

Audit documentation is the property of the auditor. The auditor may at his or her option make available to the client copies of the audit documentation as long as the effectiveness and integrity of the audit process is not compromised. In addition, governmental regulators may have a right to the audit documentation based on law, regulation, or the audit contract. When regulators request access to audit documentation, the auditor should consider the following guidance:

- Consider notifying the client that regulators have requested access to the audit documentation, and state that the auditor intends to comply with the request.
- Make arrangements (time, date, place, etc.) with the regulators concerning access to the audit documentation.
- Establish procedures that allow the auditor to maintain control over the audit documentation.

In addition to the above procedures, the auditor should consider sending a letter to the regulatory agency (probably requesting a signed acknowledgment of receipt of the letter) that explains the role of the auditor and the nature of the audit documentation. (Exhibit AU-C 230-2 is an example of such a letter.) The auditor should not agree to transfer the ownership of the audit documentation to the regulatory agency.

---

**PLANNING AID REMINDER:** Interpretation 1 of AU-C 230 notes that a regulator may request access to the audit documentation before the audit has been completed and the report has been released. The interpretation notes that because the audit documentation may change prior to completion of the audit, it is preferable that access be delayed until all the audit procedures have been completed and all internal reviews have been performed.

---

When a regulatory agency requests the auditor's audit documentation but there is no legal basis for the request (no applicable law, regulation, or audit contract requirement), the auditor should evaluate the purpose for the request. That evaluation should include consultation with legal counsel. If the auditor agrees with the request, the auditor should obtain permission for access to the audit documentation from the client (preferably in writing). In some instances, the client may request an inspection of the audit documentation before granting the regulatory agency access to it. If the auditor agrees to the client's request, the auditor should maintain control over the audit documentation.

Some regulatory agencies may hire a third party to inspect audit documentation. Under this circumstance, the auditor should follow the same procedures that would apply if the regulatory agency itself were inspecting the audit documentation. In addition, the auditor should obtain from the regulatory agency a statement (preferably in writing) that the third party is "acting on behalf of the regulator and agreement from the third party that he or she is subject to the same restriction on disclosure and use of audit documentation and the information contained therein as the regulator."

**OBSERVATION:** The guidance in this section does not apply to requests from (1) the Internal Revenue Service, (2) peer review programs (and similar programs) established by the AICPA or state societies of CPAs, (3) proceedings arising from alleged violations of ethical standards, or (4) subpoenas.

*Modification of addition of audit documentation after the document completion date*

The auditor may find it necessary to modify or add audit documentation after the documentation completion date to clarify existing audit documentation in response to comments received during monitoring inspections. All new documentation created, including notes made on preexisting documents, should be dated and initialled.

## Practitioner's Aids

Exhibit AU-C 230-1 is a checklist for audit documentation required by various AU-C sections.

**EXHIBIT AU-C 230-1—AU-Cs THAT IDENTIFY SPECIFIC AUDIT DOCUMENTATION REQUIREMENTS**

| Reference | Nature of Documentation |
|---|---|
| AU-C 210, *Terms of Engagement* (paragraphs .10, .13, and .16) | The agreed-upon terms of the engagement should be documented in the engagement letter or other suitable written agreement. |
| | For recurring engagements when the auditor concludes the terms of the preceding engagement do not need to be revised, the auditor should remind management and the terms and the reminder should be documented. |
| | When there are changes to the terms of the engagement, the new terms should be documented in an engagement letter or other suitable form of written agreement. |
| AU-C 220, *Quality Control for an Engagement Conducted in Accordance with Generally Accepted Auditing Standards* (paragraphs .25 and .26) | Issues and conclusions reached related to compliance with ethical and independence requirements and acceptance and continuance of client relationships. |

| Reference | Nature of Documentation |
|---|---|
| | The engagement quality reviewer should document that procedures required for the quality review have been performed, the date the review was completed, and that the reviewer is not aware of any unresolved matters that would cause him or her to believe that the significant judgments that the engagement team made and the conclusions it reached were not appropriate. |
| AU-C 240, *Consideration of Fraud in a Financial Statement Audit* (paragraphs .43-.46) | Document the audit team brainstorming discussion on fraud (when it occurred, who participated, what was discussed, conclusions reached). |
| | Procedures performed to identify and assess the risks of material misstatement due to fraud. |
| | Risks identified and the auditor's response (both the overall responses and responses at the assertion level). |
| | If revenue recognition is not identified as a risk factor, the reasons why. |
| | Results of procedures related to management override of controls. |
| | Other conditions or analytical procedures that led the auditor to perform additional auditing procedures. |
| | Fraud-related communications to management, the audit committee, and others. |
| AU-C 250, *Consideration of Laws and Regulations in an Audit of Financial Statements* (paragraph .28) | Description of the identified or suspected noncompliance with laws and regulations and the results of discussion with management, and those charged with governance. |
| AU-C 260, *The Auditor's Communication with Those Charged with Governance* (paragraph .20) | Required communications to those charged with governance about matters involving the auditor's responsibilities, the planned scope and timing of the audit, and significant audit findings. |
| AU-C 265, *Communicating Internal Control Related Matters Identified in an Audit* (paragraphs .11-.16) | Communication of significant deficiencies and material weaknesses in internal control made to management and those charged with governance. |
| AU-C 300, *Planning an Audit* (paragraph .14) | Document the overall audit strategy, the audit plan, and any significant changes made during the audit engagement to the overall audit strategy or to the audit plan. |
| AU-C 315, *Understanding the Entity and Its Environment and Assessing the Risks of Material Misstatement* (paragraph .33) | Audit team discussion of the susceptibility of the client's financial statements to error or fraud (when the discussion occurred, who participated, subjects discussed, and planned audit responses). |
| | The auditor's understanding of the entity's environment and its internal control (including sources of information and risk assessment procedures). |

| Reference | Nature of Documentation |
|---|---|
| | The auditor's assessment of the risk of material misstatement at the financial statement level and the assertion level and the auditor's basis for these assessments. |
| | Risks identified and evaluation of related controls. |
| AU-C 320, *Materiality in Planning and Performing an Audit* (paragraph .14) | Materiality for financial statements as a whole. |
| | Materiality level(s) for particular classes of transactions, account balances, or disclosures. |
| | Performance materiality. |
| AU-C 330, *Performing Audit Procedures in Response to Assessed Risks and Evaluating the Audit Evidence Obtained* (paragraphs .30-.33) | Overall audit response to the assessed risk of misstatement at the financial statement level. |
| | Nature, timing, and extent of further audit procedures performed. |
| | Linkage of procedures to risks at the assertion level. |
| | Results of audit procedures. |
| | Decision regarding the operating effectiveness of controls obtained in a prior audit and their use in the current audit. |
| | Determination not to use external confirmation procedures for accounts receivable when the account balance is material. |
| | Demonstrate that the financial statements agree or reconcile with the underlying accounting records. |
| AU-C 450, *Evaluation of Misstatements Identified during the Audit* (paragraph .12) | Amount below which misstatements would be regarded as clearly trivial. |
| | All misstatements accumulated during the audit and whether they have been corrected. |
| | The auditor's conclusion about whether uncorrected misstatements are material, individually or in the aggregate, and the basis for that conclusion. |
| AU-C 501, *Audit Evidence—Specific Considerations for Selected Items* (paragraph .20) | Basis for determination to not seek direct communication with the entity's legal counsel. |
| AU-C 520, *Analytical Procedures* (paragraph .08) | When substantive analytical procedures are performed, document (1) expectations where not evident from work performed, (2) results of comparing expectations to recorded amounts or ratios computed, and (3) additional procedures (and their results) arising from identifying unexpected results. |

| Reference | Nature of Documentation |
|---|---|
| AU-C 540, *Auditing Accounting Estimates, Including Fair Value Accounting Estimates, and Related Disclosures* (paragraph .22) | For those accounting estimates leading to significant risks, the basis for the auditor's conclusions about the reasonableness of accounting estimates and their disclosure. Indicators of possible management bias, if any. |
| AU-C 550, *Related Parties* (paragraph .28) | Names of identified related parties and the nature of the related-party relationships. |
| AU-C 570, *Going Concern* (paragraph .18) | Document (1) circumstances that raised substantial doubt about the entity's ability to continue as a going concern, (2) elements of management's plans the auditor considered significant in overcoming adverse conditions, (3) procedures performed to evaluate management's plans, (4) audit conclusions, and (5) the effect of the matter on the financial statements and the audit report. |
| AU-C 600, *Special Considerations—Audits of Group Financial Statements (Including the Work of Component Auditors)* (paragraphs .49-.64) | Document (1) an analysis of the components and the type of work to be performed on the information of the components, (2) those components for which reference in the auditor's report to the component auditors will be made, (3) written communications between the group engagement team and component auditors, (4) the financial statements of the component and the component auditor's report, and the nature, timing, and extent of the group engagement team's involvement in the work performed by the component auditor. |
| AU-C 610, *Using the Work of Internal Auditors* (paragraphs .33-.35) | If the external auditor uses the work of the internal auditor, document (1) the evaluation of the objectivity, competence, and quality control of the internal audit function; (2) the nature and extent of the work used; and (3) the procedures, including reperformance, performed to evaluate the adequacy of the internal audit work. If the external auditor uses internal auditors to provide direct assistance, document (1) threats to internal audit's objectivity, including safeguards to reduce or eliminate the threats, (2) internal audit's competence, (3) the basis for deciding on the nature and extent of work performed by internal audit, (4) the nature and extent of the external auditor's testing of internal audit's work, and (5) the workpapers prepared by internal audit. If the external auditor relies on either the work of internal audit or internal audit to provide direct assistance, the evaluation of whether the external auditor is still sufficiently involved in the audit to express an opinion. |

| Reference | Nature of Documentation |
|---|---|
| AU-C 701, *Communicating Key Audit Matters in the Independent Auditor's Report* | The matters that required significant auditor attention and the rationale for determining whether or not each matter is a key audit matter. When there are no key audit matters, the rationale for that determination. Also, the auditor must document the rationale for not communicating a key audit matter in the auditor's report. |
| AU-C 720, *The Auditor's Responsibilities Related to Other Information Included in Annual Reports* | The procedures performed on other information in the annual report and the final version of the other information on which the auditor performed the work. |
| AU-C 915, *Reports on Application of Requirements of an Applicable Financial Reporting Framework* (paragraph .13) | The reporting accountant's rationale for not consulting with the continuing accountant. |
| AU-C 930, *Interim Financial Information* (paragraphs .42-.43) | Documentation in support of the review of interim financial information, including:<br>• Nature, timing, and extent of procedures performed and results.<br>• Results of review procedures performed and evidence obtained.<br>• Findings or issues that may indicate that the interim financial information is materially misstated, the auditor's actions to address these findings, and the basis for the final conclusions reached. |
| AU-C 935, *Compliance Audits* (paragraphs .39-.42) | Document certain oral communications to management and the audit committee or its equivalent. |

Exhibit AU-C 230-2 is an example of a letter that may be sent to a regulatory agency in response to its request for access to the auditor's documentation.

## EXHIBIT AU-C 230-2—LETTER FOR REGULATORY AGENCY THAT REQUESTS ACCESS TO AUDIT DOCUMENTATION

Your representatives have requested access to our audit documentation in connection with our audit of the December 31, 20X8 financial statements of [*name of client*]. It is our understanding that the purpose of your request is [*state purpose: for example*, "to facilitate your regulatory examination"].

Our audit of [*name of client*]'s December 31, 20X8 financial statements was conducted in accordance with auditing standards generally accepted in the United States of America, the objective of which is to form an opinion as to whether the financial statements, which are the responsibility and representations of management, present fairly, in all material respects, the financial position, results of operations, and cash flows in conformity with generally accepted accounting principles. Under generally accepted auditing standards, we have the responsibility, within the inherent limitations of the auditing process, to design our audit to provide reasonable assurance that errors and fraud that have a material effect on the financial statements will be detected, and to exercise due care in the conduct of our audit. The concept of selective testing of the data being audited, which involved judgment both as to the number of transactions to be audited and as to the areas to be tested, has been generally accepted as a valid and sufficient basis for an audit to express an opinion on financial statements. Thus, our audit, based on the concept of selective testing, is subject to the inherent risk that material errors or fraud, if they exist, would not be detected. In addition, an audit does not address the possibility that material errors or fraud may occur in the future. Also, our use of professional judgment and the assessment of materiality for the purpose of our audit means that matters may have existed that would have been assessed differently by you.

The audit documentation was prepared for the purpose of providing the principal support for our report on [*name of client*]'s December 31, 20X8, financial statements and to aid in the conduct and supervision of our audit. The audit documentation is the principal record of auditing procedures performed, evidence obtained, and conclusions reached in the engagement. The auditing procedures that were performed were limited to those we considered necessary under generally accepted auditing standards to enable us to formulate and express an opinion on the financial statements taken as a whole. Accordingly, we make no representation as to the sufficiency or appropriateness, for your purposes, of either the information contained in our audit documentation or our auditing procedures. In addition, any notations, comments, and individual conclusions appearing on any of the audit documents do not stand alone, and should not be read as an opinion on any individual amounts, accounts, balances, or transactions.

Our audit of [*name of client*]'s December 31, 20X8, financial statement was performed for the purpose stated above and has not been planned or conducted in contemplation of your [*state purpose: for example*, "regulatory examination"] or for the purpose of assessing [*name of client*]'s compliance with laws and regulations. Therefore, items of possible interest to you may not have been specifically addressed. Accordingly, our audit and the audit documentation prepared in connection therewith, should not supplant other inquiries and procedures that should be undertaken by the [*name of regulatory agency*] for the purpose of monitoring and regulating the financial affairs of the [*name of client*]. In addition, we have not audited any financial statements of [*name of client*] since [*date of audited balance sheet referred to in the first paragraph above*] nor have we performed any auditing procedures since [*date*], the date of our auditor's report, and significant events or circumstances may have occurred since that date.

The audit documentation constitutes and reflects work performed or evidence obtained by [*name of auditor*] in its capacity as independent auditor for [*name of client*]. The documents contain trade secrets and confidential commercial and financial information of our firm and [*name of client*] that is privileged and confidential, and we expressly reserve all rights with respect to disclosures to third parties. Accordingly, we request confidential treatment under the Freedom of Information Act or similar laws and regulations when requests are made for the audit documentation or information contained therein or any derived therefrom. We further request that written notice be given to our firm before distribution of the information in the audit documentation [*or copies thereof*] to others, including other governmental agencies, except when such distribution is required by law or regulations. [*If it is expected that copies will be requested, add the following:* Any copies of our audit documentation that we agree to provide you will be identified as "Confidential Treatment Requested by [*name of auditor, address, and telephone number*]."]

The above illustrative letter should be appropriately modified to reflect the circumstances of the engagement. Some of the modifications that may be needed include the following:

- When the audit has been conducted in accordance with GAAS and other established auditing procedures (such as generally accepted governmental auditing standards), the letter should be appropriately modified.
- When the audit was conducted in accordance with the Single Audit Act of 1984, and other federal audit requirements, the letter should be modified to explain the object of the audit.
- When the letter is sent to the regulatory agency at the request of management (rather than by law, regulation, or audit contract), the letter should state that "the management of X Company has authorized us to provide you access to our audit documentation in order to facilitate your regulatory examination."
- When the financial statements are based on regulatory accounting principles, the letter should be appropriately modified.
- When the regulatory agency has asked for photocopies of the audit documentation, the letter should state that "any photocopies of our audit documentation we agree to provide you will be identified as 'Confidential Treatment Request by [*name of auditor, address, telephone number*].'"
- When the audit engagement has not been completed, the letter should be modified to describe that fact and to put the regulatory agency on guard that the workpapers may change based on the performance of additional audit procedures (generally, the auditor should not agree to supply the regulatory agency with incomplete audit documentation).

# SECTION 240

# CONSIDERATION OF FRAUD IN A FINANCIAL STATEMENT AUDIT

## Authoritative Pronouncements

SAS-122—Statements on Auditing Standards: Clarification and Recodification

SAS-134—Auditor Reporting and Amendments, Including Amendments Addressing Disclosures in the Audit of Financial Statements

SAS-135—Omnibus Statement on Auditing Standards—2019

SAS-136—Forming an Opinion and Reporting on Financial Statements of Employee Benefit Plans Subject to ERISA

SAS-141—Amendment to Effective Dates of SAS Nos. 134-140

SAS-143—Auditing Accounting Estimates and Related Disclosures

## Overview

AU-C 240 states that an auditor "is responsible for obtaining reasonable assurance that the financial statements as a whole are free from material misstatement, whether caused by fraud or error." Auditing standards note that the presence of intent distinguishes errors and fraud. Unintentional misstatements are errors, whereas intentional misstatements are due to fraud. AU-C 240 states that the auditor "is concerned with fraud that causes a material misstatement in the financial statements" and identifies the two relevant types of fraud, namely (1) misstatements arising from fraudulent financial reporting and (2) misstatements arising from misappropriations of assets.

The risk of the auditor not detecting a material misstatement due to fraud is higher than the risk of not detecting a material misstatement due to error. This is because there are often attempts to conceal fraud and there may be collusion, making detection even more difficult. Management fraud is also more difficult to detect than employee fraud because of management's ability to manipulate procedures or override controls. Therefore, while obtaining reasonable assurance throughout the audit, the auditor is responsible for maintaining an attitude of professional skepticism.

The auditor has three main objectives when considering fraud in a financial statement audit: (1) to identify and assess the risk of material misstatement of the financial statement due to fraud, (2) to obtain sufficient appropriate audit evidence about the assessed risks of material misstatement due to fraud, through designing and implementing appropriate responses, and (3) to respond appropriately to identified or suspected fraud. Due to the inherent limitations of an audit, an unavoidable risk exists that some material misstatements of the financial statements may not be detected, even though the audit is properly planned and performed in accordance with GAAS.

**PUBLIC COMPANY IMPLICATION:** PCAOB auditing standards emphasize the importance of considering fraud risk in a financial statement audit, and they require the auditor to integrate his or her assessment of fraud risk into his or her general risk-assessment procedures. In particular, a discussion of fraud risk is contained in AS-1101, AS-2101, AS-2110, AS-2301, and AS-2810. AS-2110 and AS-2301 provide the most detailed discussion of the auditor's responsibility in assessing and responding to fraud risk. Although there are a number of differences between the PCAOB's and ASB's risk standards, the risk-assessment concepts contained in the PCAOB standards should be familiar to most auditors. As is currently the case, audit risk is the risk that the auditor will issue an inappropriate opinion on financial statements that are materially misstated. The auditor is to reduce audit risk to a low level through the application of audit procedures. As a result, the amount of audit effort devoted to particular accounts, classes of transactions, and disclosures should vary based on their respective risk.

While AU-C 240 outlines the auditor's responsibilities to detect material misstatements due to fraud, it is important to remember that the primary responsibility for the prevention and detection of fraud rests with those charged with governance of the entity and management. Those charged with governance should consider the potential for override of internal controls or other inappropriate influence over the financial reporting process. Management should place a strong emphasis on fraud prevention and exhibit a strong commitment to creating a culture of honesty and ethical behavior.

**IMPORTANT NOTICE FOR 2022:** In May 2019, the AICPA's Auditing Standards Board (ASB) issued SAS No. 134 titled *Auditor Reporting and Amendments, Including Amendments Addressing Disclosures in the Audit of Financial Statements* that amends various AU-C sections to focus the auditor's attention on disclosures earlier in the process of auditing financial statements. SAS No. 134 amends AU-C 240 to emphasize the need for auditors, when assessing the risks of material misstatement arising from fraud, to consider whether management may have omitted, obscured, or misstated disclosures required by the applicable financial reporting framework. Originally, the effective date of SAS No. 134 was for audits of financial statements periods ending on or after December 15, 2020, with early application **not** permitted. However, the ASB's issuance of SAS No. 141, *Amendment to the Effective Dates of SAS Nos. 134-140*, extended the effective date of SAS No. 134 to December 15, 2021, in order to provide more time for firms to implement SAS No. 134 in light of the effect of the coronavirus pandemic. While SAS No. 141 allows for early implementation of SAS No. 134, the ASB recommends that SAS Nos. 134-140 be implemented concurrently.

**IMPORTANT NOTICE FOR 2022:** In May 2019, the AICPA's Auditing Standards Board (ASB) issued SAS No. 135 titled *Omnibus Statement on Auditing Standards—2019* that includes amendments to various AU-C sections. SAS No. 135 incorporates some of the guidance in PCAOB Auditing Standards related to communications with audit committees by adding requirements to AU-C 260 for the auditor to communicate to those charged with governance the auditor's views relating to an entity's significant unusual transactions and the potential effects of uncorrected misstatements on future-period financial statements. SAS No. 135 also amends AU-C 240 to define significant unusual transactions as *"significant transactions that are outside the normal course of business for the entity or that otherwise appear to be unusual due to their timing, size, or nature."* The amendment to AU-C 240 also requires the auditor to inquire of management whether the entity has entered into any significant unusual transactions, and, if so, the nature, terms, and business purpose (or lack thereof) of those transactions and whether such transactions involved related parties. Originally, the effective date of SAS No. 135 was for audits of financial statements periods ending on or after December 15, 2020, with early application **not** permitted. However, the ASB's issuance of SAS No. 141, *Amendment to the Effective Dates of SAS Nos. 134-140*, extended the effective date of SAS No. 135 to December 15, 2021, in order to provide more time for firms to implement SAS No. 135 in light of the effect of the coronavirus pandemic. While SAS No. 141 allows for early implementation of SAS No. 135, the ASB recommends that SAS Nos. 134-140 be implemented concurrently.

## Definitions

| | |
|---|---|
| Fraud | An intentional act by one or more individuals among management, those charged with governance, employees, or third parties involving the use of deception that results in a misstatement in financial statements that are the subject of an audit. |
| Fraud risk factors | Events or conditions that indicate an incentive or pressure to perpetrate fraud, provide an opportunity to commit fraud, or indicate attitudes or rationalizations to justify a fraudulent action. |
| Significant unusual transactions | Significant transactions that are outside the normal course of business for the entity or that otherwise appear to be unusual due to their timing, size, or nature. |

**PUBLIC COMPANY IMPLICATION:** The PCAOB has issued AS-2410 (*Related Parties: Amendments to Certain PCAOB Auditing Standards Regarding Significant Unusual Transactions and Other Amendments to PCAOB Auditing Standards*), which changes the audit guidance in the areas of related-party transactions (RPTs), significant unusual transactions, and financial relationships and transactions with executive officers. The PCAOB has combined these three areas into a single standard because of the potential relationships between RPTs, significant unusual transactions, and financial relationships and transactions with executive officers. In auditing RPTs, the standard requires the auditor to (1) perform procedures to understand the company's relationships and transactions with related parties, including transactions with related parties that were modified during the period under audit; (2) evaluate whether the company has properly identified its related parties and transactions with them; (3) perform additional procedures if undisclosed (by management) related parties or related-party transactions are discovered by the auditor; (4) perform specific procedures for those RPTs required to be disclosed in the financial statements or that are identified as a significant risk; and (5) communicate to the audit committee the auditor's evaluation of the company's identification of, accounting for, and disclosure of RPTs.

AS-2410 also amends the PCAOB's existing requirements on the consideration of fraud in an audit. The PCAOB describes a "significant unusual transaction" as one that is outside the normal course of business for the company or that otherwise appears unusual because of the transaction's timing, size, or nature. In auditing significant unusual transactions, the standard requires the auditor to (1) perform procedures to identify significant unusual transactions; (2) perform procedures to determine whether the significant unusual transaction has a business purpose and, if so, to understand that purpose; and (3) consider whether the transaction may have been entered into to commit financial reporting fraud or conceal a misappropriation of assets. The PCAOB's standard amends the Board's risk assessment standards to require the auditor to obtain an understanding of the company's financial relationships and transactions with executive officers, including executive compensation arrangements. Specifically, AS-2410 requires the auditor to consider whether executive compensation arrangements may create an incentive or pressure for the company to achieve certain operating results or financial position.

## Requirements

The auditor is presumptively required to perform the following procedures in considering the possibility that fraud related to financial statements exists in an audit engagement:

### Professional Skepticism

1. Maintain an attitude of professional skepticism throughout the audit. Recognize the possibility that a material misstatement due to fraud could exist regardless of past experience of the honesty and integrity of management and those charged with governance.

2. Records and documents may be accepted as genuine unless there are conditions leading the auditor to believe a document may not be authentic or may have undisclosed modified terms, in which case the auditor should investigate further.

3. Investigate further inconsistent or otherwise unsatisfactory responses to inquiries of management, those charged with governance, or others.

### Discussion among the Engagement Team

4. Key engagement team members, including the engagement partner, should exchange ideas and discuss how and where the entity's financial statements, including statements and disclosures, may be susceptible to material misstatement due to fraud, how management could perpetrate and conceal fraudulent financial reporting, and how entity assets could be misappropriated. Emphasis should be placed on known external and internal fraud risk factors affecting the entity, the risk of management override of controls, circumstances that might be indicative of earnings management or manipulation of other financial measures, the importance of maintaining professional skepticism throughout the audit, and how the auditor might respond to the susceptibility of the entity's financial statements to material misstatement due to fraud.

5. Communication about the risks of material misstatement due to fraud should continue among team members throughout the audit.

## Risk Assessment Procedures and Related Activities

6. Inquire of management regarding its assessment of the risk that the financial statements may be materially misstated due to fraud; its process for identifying, responding to, and monitoring risks of fraud in the entity as well as any communication with those charged with governance regarding this process; communication to employees regarding its views on business practices and ethical behaviour; and whether the entity has entered into any significant unusual transactions, and, if so, the nature, terms, and business purposes of those transactions.

7. Inquire of management and others within the entity as appropriate, including internal audit if it exists, to determine whether they have knowledge of any actual, suspected, or alleged fraud affecting the entity.

8. If there is an internal audit function, inquire whether it has performed any procedures to identify or detect fraud during the year, if management has responded satisfactorily to any findings of these procedures, obtain its views about the risks of fraud, and inquire about their awareness of any significant unusual transactions.

9. Obtain an understanding of how those charged with governance exercise oversight of management's processes for identifying and responding to fraud risks and the internal control established to mitigate those risks (unless all of those charged with governance are involved with managing the entity).

10. Inquire of those charged with governance regarding their views about the risks of fraud and whether they have knowledge of any actual, suspected, or alleged fraud affecting the entity. These inquiries are made in part to corroborate management responses.

11. Evaluate analytical procedures performed as part of risk assessment procedures, including procedures relating to revenue accounts, to identify any unusual or unexpected relationships that indicate risks of material misstatement due to fraud.

12. Consider whether other information obtained indicates risks of material misstatement due to fraud.

13. Evaluate whether information obtained from the risk assessment procedures, including analytical procedures performed, and related activities performed indicate the presence of one or more fraud risk factors, because these may indicate risks of material misstatement due to fraud.

## Identification and Assessment of Risks of Material Misstatement Due to Fraud

14. Identify and assess the risks of material misstatement due to fraud throughout the audit at the financial statement level, and at the assertion level for classes of transactions, account balances, and disclosures.

15. Presume that risks of fraud in revenue recognition exist and evaluate which revenue types, transactions, or assertions create these risks.

16. Treat assessed risks of material misstatement due to fraud as significant risks. Obtain an understanding of the entity's controls relevant to these risks and evaluate if the design and implementation of these controls mitigate fraud risks.

## Responses to Assessed Risks of Material Misstatement Due to Fraud

17. Determine overall responses to address the assessed risks of material misstatement due to fraud at the financial statement level. In determining these responses, assign and supervise personnel considering their knowledge, skill, and abilities and the assessment of the risks of material misstatement due to fraud for the engagement; evaluate whether the entity's selection and application of accounting policies is indicative of fraudulent financial reporting; and incorporate an element of unpredictability in selecting the nature, timing, and extent of audit procedures.

18. Design and perform further audit procedures whose nature, timing, and extent are responsive to the assessed risks of material misstatement due to fraud at the assertion level.

19. Design and perform audit procedures responsive to the risks of management override of controls.

   a. Test the appropriateness of journal entries and adjustments by (1) obtaining an understanding of the entity's financial reporting process and controls as well as of control design and implementation; (2) inquiring about inappropriate or unusual activity of those involved in the financial reporting process; (3) considering fraud risk indicators, controls, the nature and complexity of accounts, and entries processed outside the normal course of business; (4) selecting entries and adjustments made at the end of a reporting period; and (5) considering the need to test entries and adjustments throughout the period.

   b. Review accounting estimates by evaluating whether management judgments in making estimates indicate a possible bias that may represent a risk of material misstatement due to fraud. If there is a possible bias, reevaluate accounting estimates taken as a whole and perform a retrospective review of management judgments related to significant and highly sensitive accounting estimates in the prior year's financial statements.

   c. Evaluate whether the business rationale of significant transactions outside the normal course of business or otherwise unusual transactions suggests the transactions may have been entered into to engage in fraud.

   d. Determine whether audit procedures other than those already identified need to be performed in order to respond to the identified risks of management override of controls.

---

**IMPORTANT NOTICE FOR 2022:** In July 2020, the AICPA Auditing Standards Board (ASB) issued SAS No. 143, *Auditing Accounting Estimates and Related Disclosures*, which supersedes AU-C 540 (*Auditing Accounting Estimates, Including Fair Value Accounting Estimates, and Related Disclosures*) and amends various other sections including AU-C 240 in the professional standards. The new SAS begins with an explanation of the nature of accounting estimates and how they can vary widely in nature and are required to be made by management when monetary amounts cannot be directly observed. The measurement of amounts is subject to estimation uncertainty, which reflects inherent limitations in the knowledge or data. These limitations give rise to inherent subjectivity and variation in measurement outcomes. Although the guidance in SAS No. 143 applies to all accounting estimates, the degree to which an accounting estimate is subject to estimation uncertainty will vary substantially. Therefore, SAS No.

143 recognizes that the nature, timing, and extent of the risk assessment and further audit procedures required will vary in relation to the estimation uncertainty and the assessment of the related risks of material misstatement. The ASB is coordinating the effective date of SAS No. 143 with the effective date of a proposed new SAS, *Understanding the Entity and Its Environment and Assessing the Risks of Material Misstatement*, which is under consideration by the ASB at the time this edition of the *GAAS Guide* was prepared. SAS No. 143 does not become effective until audits of financial statements for periods ending on or after December 15, 2023, which is consistent with the date in the proposed new standard. As a result, this AU-C reflects existing auditing standards requirements. Updates to reflect SAS No. 143 will occur in the next edition of the *GAAS Guide*.

## *Evaluation of Audit Evidence*

20. Evaluate whether the results of audit procedures, including analytical procedures, indicate a previously unrecognized risk of material misstatement due to fraud. If not already performed, perform analytical procedures relating to revenue through the end of the reporting period to identify any unusual or unexpected relationships that indicate risks of material misstatement due to fraud at this time. When significant unusual transactions are identified, evaluate whether the business purpose surrounding the transaction might suggest that it might have been entered into to engage in fraudulent financial reporting or to conceal misappropriation of assets.

21. Evaluate whether identified misstatements are indicative of fraud. If misstatements do indicate fraud, evaluate the implications for other aspects of the audit, including the evaluation of materiality, management and employee integrity, and reliability of management representations.

22. If an identified misstatement may be the result of fraud and management is believed to be involved, reevaluate the assessment of the risks of material misstatement due to fraud and the impact on procedures that respond to these risks. Consider whether the circumstances indicate possible collusion involving management, employees, or third parties.

23. Evaluate the audit implications when the auditor concludes or is unable to conclude whether the financial statements are materially misstated as a result of fraud.

## *Auditor Unable to Continue the Engagement*

24. If the ability to continue performing the audit due to a misstatement resulting from fraud or suspected fraud is questioned, determine the professional and legal responsibilities applicable, including any requirement to report to those who made the audit appointment or to regulatory authorities and consider whether withdrawal from the engagement is appropriate or legally permitted. If the auditor withdraws, discuss the withdrawal and its reasons with the appropriate level of management and those charged with governance and determine if a professional or legal requirement exists to report the withdrawal and its reasons to those who made the audit appointment or to regulatory authorities.

## *Communications to Management and Those Charged with Governance*

25. Inform the appropriate level of management on a timely basis of any fraud identified and of information indicating fraud may exist.

26. Communicate with those charged with governance (unless all of those charged with governance are involved in managing the entity) on a timely basis regarding identified or suspected fraud involving management, employees with significant internal control roles, or others where the fraud results in a material misstatement in the financial statements.

27. Communicate with those charged with governance any other fraud-related matters that are relevant to their responsibilities in the auditor's judgment.

## Communications to Regulatory and Enforcement Authorities

28. Determine whether the auditor has a responsibility to report the occurrence of or suspicion of fraud to a party outside the entity. There are some circumstances in which the auditor's legal responsibilities may override the duty of confidentiality to the client.

## Documentation

29. Documentation of the understanding of the entity and its environment and the assessment of the risk of material misstatement should include significant decisions reached during the engagement team discussion regarding the susceptibility of the entity's financial statements to material misstatement due to fraud; how the discussion occurred, when it occurred, and who participated; and the identified and assessed risks of material misstatement due to fraud at the financial statement and assertion level.

30. Documentation of the responses to the assessed risks of material misstatement should include overall responses to the assessed risks of material misstatement due to fraud at the financial statement level, the nature, timing, and extent of audit procedures, and the linkage of those procedures with the assessed risks of material misstatement due to fraud at the assertion level. This documentation should also include the results of audit procedures, including those addressing the risk of management override of controls.

31. Document communication about fraud made to management, those charged with governance, regulators, and others.

32. Document the reasons for a conclusion that the presumption of the existence of a risk of material misstatement due to fraud related to revenue recognition is not applicable to an engagement.

# Analysis and Application of Procedures

## Characteristics of Fraud

### Fraudulent financial reporting

The intentional misstatement of information (through either commission or omission) in financial statements is referred to as "fraudulent financial reporting." Intent is often difficult to determine and the audit is not designed to determine intent, but to obtain reasonable assurance about whether the financial statements as a whole are free from material misstatement, whether due to fraud or error. Fraudulent financial reporting may be caused in an effort to manage earnings and often involves management override of controls. AU-C 240 lists the following as examples of fraudulent financial reporting:

- Intentional misapplications of accounting principles relating to amounts, classification, manner of presentation, or disclosure (e.g., disclosing a loss contingency based on the standards established by generally accepted accounting principles when, in fact, the contingency should be accrued).

- Manipulation, falsification, or alteration of the accounting records or supporting documents that financial statements are prepared from (e.g., the inclusion of false amounts in the accounts receivable subsidiary ledger).
- Misrepresentation in or intentional omission from the financial statements and disclosures of events, transactions, or other significant information.

*Misappropriation of assets*

Theft of assets that results in the misstatement of financial statements is referred to as "misappropriation of assets" (theft or defalcation). Misappropriation can result from a variety of deliberate actions, such as the unauthorized removal of inventory and the payment for assets that have never been received by the client. The auditor is required to plan and perform the audit to detect material misstatements due to misappropriation of assets.

---

**OBSERVATION:** In 2010, the Committee of Sponsoring Organizations of the Treadway Commission (COSO) issued a study titled "Fraudulent Financial Reporting 1998-2007: An Analysis of U.S. Public Companies" that examined about 350 cases of SEC enforcement actions against public companies alleging financial statement fraud. Of those cases, the majority involved fraudulent financial reporting. Only 14% of the cases involved misappropriations of assets. However, auditors of nonpublic entities might conclude that the risk of material misstatements due to misappropriations of assets is likely to be higher in nonpublic companies than in public companies.

---

*Consideration of Fraud in Governmental and Not-for-Profit Audits*

The auditor's responsibilities relating to fraud in an audit of a governmental or not-for-profit entity may be a result of additional legislation, regulation, and requirements. Thus, an auditor may have a responsibility to consider risks of fraud beyond considering risks of material misstatement of the financial statements for these entities.

*Professional Skepticism*

An important element in identifying fraudulent financial statements is the mindset of professional skepticism that the auditor brings to an engagement. An auditor should guard against becoming complacent in the collection and evaluation of audit evidence even when past experience with the client has provided no indication of dishonesty or deception on the part of management. Although fraud is not a purely random event, the auditor should always consider that fraud could occur in any audit engagement no matter what the circumstances.

---

**PLANNING AID REMINDER:** Common characteristics of litigation against auditors related to fraudulent financial statements include (1) accepting management's representations without obtaining corroborative evidence, (2) allowing management to influence the scope of audit procedures, and (3) ignoring conditions that suggest that there is an unreasonable degree of risk related to the engagement.

The auditor is not expected to be an authentication expert, but when conditions lead the auditor to believe a document may not be authentic or may have undisclosed modified terms, he or she should investigate further, possibly by confirming directly with a third party or using the work of a specialist to assess the document's authenticity.

*Discussion among the Engagement Team*

The extent of the discussion among the engagement team and how it occurs will vary across engagements and may depend on factors such as whether there should be multiple discussions in audits involving multiple locations, whether to include specialists assigned to the audit team in discussions, and whether to consult with others internal or external to the firm to acquire additional information, if appropriate.

The discussion may include a consideration of matters such as management's involvement in overseeing employees with access to cash or assets susceptible to misappropriation, unusual or unexplained changes in behavior or lifestyle of management or employees the audit team is aware of, types of circumstances that might indicate the possibility of fraud, the risk that management may attempt to present disclosures in an obscure manner, how unpredictability will be incorporated into audit procedures, which audit procedures might be selected to respond to fraud risks, and any allegations of fraud the auditor is aware of.

**ENGAGEMENT STRATEGY:** The discussion or process may be performed prior to the execution of the other procedures listed in AU-C 240 (and discussed in the remainder of this Section) or as part of those procedures. In practice, the discussion for the potential for material misstatement of the financial statements due to fraud will generally be fluid and take a course dictated to some degree by the developments during the engagement. It is not particularly important when this procedure is performed but rather it is the professional attitude maintained by the auditor with respect to the procedure that is important. If the procedure is merely part of a checklist along with other audit procedures, it is unlikely that an effective audit will be performed. On the other hand, if the auditor believes that fraud could arise in any engagement and he or she remains sensitive to this possibility throughout the engagement, the chance of identifying material fraudulent financial statements will be enhanced.

**FRAUD POINTER:** If conducted with the appropriate mind-set, the brainstorming among audit team members about how and where they believe material misstatements due to fraud might occur and how management could perpetrate and conceal fraud can provide important insights to all audit team members about the presence of fraud risks. By setting aside prior beliefs about management's integrity, the brainstorming session can be an effective tool in reminding audit team members about the importance of maintaining an appropriate questioning mind-set that recognizes that fraud is possible in any engagement. The brainstorming session is meant to be a dialogue of information exchanged between all audit team members, not a one-way communication from the audit partner or manager to all other audit team members. Even though a sole practitioner has no team members, he or she should document his or her thoughts on these matters.

## Risk Assessment Procedures and Related Activities

To assess the risk of material misstatement due to fraud, AU-C 240 requires, as part of an auditor's development of an understanding of the client's business and industry, that the following procedures be performed as the basis for identifying risks of material misstatement due to fraud:

- Make inquiries of appropriate personnel in order to identify their views on the risks of fraud and how those risks have been addressed.
- Consider unusual or unexpected relationships that have been identified during the performance of analytical procedures as part of the planning the engagement.
- Consider whether other information provides insight into the possible existence of fraud risk factors.
- Consider whether fraud risk factors exist.

**FRAUD POINTER:** AU-C 240 notes that the set of information to be gathered by the auditor to assess fraud risks should be comprehensive and should not be solely based on a completed fraud risk factor checklist. Auditors assess fraud risk factors and combine that information with information obtained through inquiries of others within the entity, from the performance of planning phase analytical procedures, and through the performance of other procedures. More complete sets of information from multiple sources are expected to increase the auditor's ability to identify circumstances where fraud risk is heightened.

### Information gathered through inquiries

The auditor's inquiry of management regarding the nature, extent, and frequency of management's assessment of the risk of fraud and prevention and detection controls in place are relevant to the auditor's understanding of the entity's control environment. Management's failure to perform such an assessment may, in some circumstances, indicate management does not place much importance on internal control. In smaller, less complex entities management's assessment may focus on the risks of employee fraud or misappropriation of assets.

**ENGAGEMENT STRATEGY:** AU-C 580 requires that the client make certain written representations concerning fraud that relate to management's knowledge of fraud or suspected fraud affecting the entity that involve management, employees who have significant roles in internal control, or others where fraud could materially misstate financial statements. The representations also relate to management's knowledge of fraud or suspected fraud received from communications by others, such as employees, former employees, analysts, regulators, and short sellers, among others. As auditors make the required AU-C 240 inquiries, an effective engagement strategy is to consider making specific inquiries of the items to be explicitly addressed in the management representation letter. The auditor might find it helpful to state at the time of inquiry that he or she will be requesting written representations of management's responses at the end of fieldwork. That might lead to less confusion at the end of fieldwork, because the representation letter is signed by management.

The auditor may direct inquiries about the existence or suspicion of fraud to others within the entity to corroborate management responses or to provide information regarding possible management override of controls. Inquiries may be directed to operating personnel not directly involved in the financial reporting process, employees with different authority levels, employees involved in initiating, processing, or recording complex or unusual transactions or their supervisors, in-house legal counsel, the chief ethics officer or equivalent person, or those charged with dealing with fraud allegations. These inquiries are one way in which the auditor exercises professional skepticism of management responses.

**FRAUD POINTER:** Forensic experts note that the use of inquiry can be an effective tool in fraud investigation. People who might be reluctant to voluntarily share information about actual or possible fraud are often more likely to reveal that information if directly asked. As a result, auditors should take seriously the inquiries they make of those within an entity—the information obtained could be invaluable.

The auditor is also responsible for obtaining an understanding of the oversight exercised by those charged with governance over management's processes for identifying and responding to fraud risks and the internal control established to mitigate those risks. To obtain this understanding, the auditor may attend meetings where these discussions occur, read minutes from these meetings, or make inquiries of those charged with governance.

**FRAUD POINTER:** In January 2005, the AICPA's Antifraud Programs and Controls Task Force issued a document entitled "Management Override of Internal Controls: The Achilles' Heel of Fraud Prevention," which provides guidance to audit committees to help them address the ever-present fraud risk resulting from management override of internal control. The document notes that the audit committee, or the board when there is no audit committee, plays a vital role in overseeing the actions of management. For many organizations, the audit committee is in the best position to most likely prevent, deter, and detect fraud resulting from management override of controls. The document identifies specific actions an audit committee can take to address the risk of management override of internal controls. Auditors may find the document helpful in their discussions with audit committees about how the audit committee is addressing this ever-present risk of fraud. This document was updated in 2016.

*Information gathered through analytical procedures*

Analytical procedures performed during planning may help identify the risks of material misstatements due to fraud. The degree of reliance that can be placed on analytical procedures is dependent on the source, completeness, and reliability of the data; the level of the disaggregation; and the nature of the analysis. For example, analytical procedures performed during planning that indicate risks of material misstatement due to fraud may be performed at a high level and need to be combined with further audit evidence to identify risks of material misstatement due to fraud.

---

**ENGAGEMENT STRATEGY:** Analytical procedures relating to revenue that may identify unusual or unexpected relationships indicating risks of material misstatement due to fraud may include a comparison of sales volume based on recorded revenue with production capacity as an excess of sales volume over production capacity could indicate recording fictitious sales. Another analytical procedure that may be performed is a trend analysis of revenues and sales returns by month during and shortly after the reporting period to identify the existence of undisclosed side agreements allowing customers to return goods that would preclude revenue recognition. A trend analysis of sales by month compared with units shipped could identify a material misstatement of recorded revenues.

---

*Information gathered through other procedures*

Other information obtained through the performance of other procedures might provide insight into the possible existence of fraud risk. Specific information about risks of material misstatement due to fraud should be combined with other information, such as the following, that has come to the auditor's attention:

- Discussions among engagement personnel (as discussed earlier),
- Information considered when the engagement was accepted (if a new engagement) or continued, and
- Results from the review of interim financial statements.

*Information gathered through considering fraud risk factors*

AU-C 240 describes fraud risk factors as "events or conditions that indicate an incentive or pressure to commit fraud or provide an opportunity to commit fraud." For example, a fraud risk factor exists if key management personnel's compensation is significantly dependent on operating results. The circumstance does not mean that fraud exists but rather that the likelihood of fraud is influenced by the circumstance and as the number of fraud risk factors increases the audit approach must reflect that environment.

---

**FRAUD POINTER:** Three conditions are present when fraud exists: (1) an incentive or pressure that motivates management or others to engage in fraud, (2) an opportunity for the individual to carry out the fraud, (3) the perpetrator has an attitude or set of ethical beliefs that allow him or her to justify committing an unethical or dishonest act. AU-C 240 organizes the examples of fraud risk factors along these three conditions of fraud. When auditors identify fraud risk factors across the three conditions, fraud risk is likely to be high. Likewise, the absence of one or all three of the conditions listed above does not suggest that the auditor should conclude that the possibility of fraudulent acts is nonexistent or very low. In fact, it is often difficult for an auditor to observe management's attitude or ability to rationalize a fraudulent act, because it involves management's state of mind.

In smaller, less complex entities some of these considerations may be less relevant. For example, there may not be a written code of conduct, but there may be a culture emphasizing integrity and ethical behavior. Failure to have certain controls can often be compensated by other conditions in the entity. However, management dominated by one individual can be a weakness because of the potential for management override of controls.

Indicators may suggest that significant unusual transactions may have been entered into to engage in fraudulent financial reporting or to conceal misappropriation of assets. Examples of factors might include transactions whose form is overly complex, transactions where management is emphasizing the accounting treatment than the economic substance of the transaction, transactions with related parties previously undisclosed to the auditor, or transactions that lack commercial or economic substance.

## *Identification and Assessment of Risks of Material Misstatement Due to Fraud*

Material misstatement due to fraudulent financial reporting of revenue recognition is ordinarily a presumed risk that varies across entities according to their particular circumstances, pressures, and incentives. However, this presumption of risk may be rebutted if the auditor concludes no risk of material misstatement due to fraud related to revenue recognition exists for a particular audit.

> **FRAUD POINTER:** Fraudulent financial reporting enforcement actions issued by the SEC often highlight cases that involve revenue recognition. AU-C 240 states that "the auditor should ordinarily presume that there is a risk of material misstatement due to fraud relating to revenue recognition."

In obtaining an understanding of the design, implementation, and monitoring of the entity's controls relevant to fraud risks, the auditor may learn that management has chosen to accept certain risks rather than establish controls. This understanding can be useful to the auditor in identifying fraud risk factors that could affect the assessment of the risks that the financial statements may contain material misstatements due to fraud.

## *Responses to Assessed Risks of Material Misstatement Due to Fraud*

After completion of the procedures described so far, the auditor is in a position to determine how to respond to identified risks of material misstatements due to fraud through the performance of audit procedures. AU-C 240 states that the auditor may respond by modifying:

1. The overall approach to the audit at the financial statement level;
2. The nature, timing, and extent of procedures at the assertion level;

3. The procedures related to possible management override of controls; and
4. Other audit procedures.

*Overall approach to the audit at the financial statement level*

AU-C 240 states that the auditor's overall responses to address the assessment of risks of material misstatement generally reflect an increased level of professional skepticism.

Assignment and supervision of personnel is one overall response and, in some instances, it is appropriate for the auditor to assign personnel with special skills, such as information technology or even forensic experience, or for more experienced auditors to participate in the engagement. The intensity of the supervision of the engagement should reflect the assessed level of risk.

Unpredictability of audit procedures is another overall response that is important to help prevent individuals in the entity who are familiar with the normal audit procedures from being able to conceal fraudulent financial reporting. As the assessment of the risks of material misstatement due to fraud increases, the auditor should likewise increase the unpredictability of the audit approach. This strategy may range from changing the timing of audit procedures to varying the locations of procedures.

As the risk of fraud increases at the financial statement level, the auditor's concern with the appropriateness and quality of accounting principles selected and applied should increase. For example, the auditor should consider if management appears to be selecting and applying accounting principles that consistently have the same overall impact on the financial statements (e.g., consistently increase earnings before taxes).

*Nature, timing, and extent of procedures at the assertion level*

The specific nature (i.e., use procedures that generate more reliable evidence), timing (i.e., perform procedures at or near year-end), and extent (i.e., the size of the audit sample) of audit procedures are affected by the assessed of risks of material misstatement due to fraud at the assertion level.

*Procedures related to possible management override of controls*

AU-C 240 recognizes that management is in a unique position to engage in fraud by bypassing existing controls. Therefore, an auditor must always consider the risk of management override of controls.

Fraudulent financial reporting often involves recording inappropriate or unauthorized journal entries throughout the year or at period end or making adjustments to amounts reported in the financial statement that are not reflected in formal journal entries. Thus, the auditor should review journal entries and other adjustments to assess their appropriateness. When the auditor is selecting specific journal entries and other adjustments for testing (as well as the nature and timing of how those entries will be tested), there are several relevant factors:

- Fraud risk factors or other conditions that relate to specific classes of entries.
- The quality of controls that relate to entries, including whether entries are processed manually or automated.
- The financial reporting process and the client's evidential support (including electronic support) for entries.
- Entries with unusual characteristics such as unique authorization sources, posting dates, dollar amounts, and accounts involved.
- Entries that affect accounts that are characterized by their complexity, high degree of subjectivity because of estimates, past history of errors, or identification with risk factors suggesting possible material misstatement due to fraud.
- Entries that are not considered part of the routine (sales, purchases, payroll, etc.) journal entries made during the period.

**PLANNING AID REMINDER:** AU-C 240 points out that in planning which entries should be tested, the auditor should take into consideration that fraudulent entries are often made at the end of an accounting period.

The preparation of financial statements requires the inclusion of significant accounting estimates that are based on the judgment of management. Fraudulent financial reporting is often executed through the manipulation of accounting estimates. AU-C 540 (*Auditing Accounting Estimates, Including Fair Value Accounting Estimates, and Related Disclosures*) requires the auditor to perform a retrospective review as a risk assessment procedure, and the auditor may include any review of management's judgments and assumptions to look for biases that could represent a risk of material misstatement due to fraud as part of this review. The purpose of the review is to indicate the existence of any possible management bias, not to question the auditor's professional judgments made in the prior year based on available information.

**ENGAGEMENT STRATEGY:** Challenging estimates made by a client and supporting those challenges can be difficult; however, AU-C 240 requires that the auditor perform a retrospective review of estimates made in previous years by the client. If the client has exhibited consistent bias in the past, that history should be considered in assessing material misstatement due to fraud. As part of the engagement strategy, the auditor should have access to information obtained in prior years about significant estimates in order to evaluate the consistency of management's assumptions and judgments in the current year relative to prior years.

In considering management override of controls, the auditor also analyzes the business basis for significant unusual transactions. Business transactions should make sense given the fundamental characteristics of a client. Transactions that appear unusual to the auditor should be investigated in order to determine their rationale. This process should include the following procedures:

- Consider whether the transaction is overly complex.
- Determine whether the transaction has been discussed with the audit committee or board of directors.
- Consider whether the transaction is driven by its accounting implication rather than sound business strategy.
- Determine whether a transaction that involves unconsolidated related parties has been properly reviewed and approved by the audit committee or board of directors.
- Determine whether a transaction involves a (1) previously unidentified related party or (2) party that cannot fulfill its obligation without support from the client.

---

**ENGAGEMENT STRATEGY:** AU-C 240 points out that because management can override controls, it is unlikely that audit risk can be reduced to an appropriately low level by performing only tests of controls. As a result, substantive testing is likely to be part of the engagement strategy.

---

*Evaluation of Audit Evidence*

AU-C 240 emphasizes the critical evaluation of audit evidence related to the occurrence of possible fraud that is primarily qualitative, based on the auditor's judgment. This evaluation can provide additional insight into risks of material misstatement due to fraud and whether there is a need to perform additional audit procedures.

*Evaluating the results of analytical procedures performed as part of substantive tests or in the overall review stage of the engagement*

As required by AU-C 520 (*Analytical Procedures*), analytical procedures should be performed as part of the overall review of financial information and considered for possible performance as part of substantive procedures. The performance of these latter (non-planning stage) analytical procedures might identify fraud risks that had not previously come to the auditor's attention.

---

**PLANNING AID REMINDER:** AU-C 240 requires (as part of the overall review stage of the engagement) the auditor to apply substantive analytical procedures to revenue through the end of the period.

---

Professional judgment must be exercised to identify trends and relationships that appear to be unusual and therefore subject to further investigation; however, AU-C 240 points out that unusual relationships might come to the auditor's attention "because management or employees generally are unable to manipulate certain information to create seemingly normal or expected relationships." For example, the following unexpected relationships might be based on fraudulent activities:

- There are material differences between sales according to the accounting records and sales according to production reports because fictitious sales

have been recorded by the management personnel who had access to the accounting records but not to production statistics.
- There are unusual relationships between the current year's inventory, accounts payable, sales, or costs of goods sold and those of the previous year because of inventory theft and the perpetrator was unable to adjust the affected accounts.
- There is an unusual relationship between net income and cash flows from operations because fictitious revenue was recorded through receivables and not cash.

**FRAUD POINTER:** AU-C 240 states that unusual and unexpected relationships involving year-end revenue and income should be particularly relevant to the auditor's concern with the possible existence of fraudulent financial statements. For example, the recognition of unusually large amounts of revenue from unusual transactions needs to be considered by the auditor.

**FRAUD POINTER:** The auditor should evaluate management's responses to inquiries (particularly inquiries related to substantive analytical procedures and analytical procedures performed as part of the overall review stage of the audit) to determine whether the responses are vague, implausible, or inconsistent with other evidence obtained. Management representations on significant issues should be supported by corroborating audit evidence.

*Responding to misstatements that might relate to fraud*

When a fraudulent act or possible fraudulent act is discovered and that act does not appear to have a material impact on the financial statements, the auditor should nonetheless consider the implications of the fraud, especially the person(s) involved in the act. For example, if the fraudulent act that has financial statement implications was conducted by a high-level management individual, the auditor should consider whether the circumstance calls into question the integrity of management and the reliability of previously obtained evidence. Also, if there are numerous misstatements, even if their cumulative effect is not material, this may be indicative of fraud risk because fraud is rarely an isolated occurrence.

**PLANNING AID REMINDER:** The identification of fraudulent acts has an effect on the auditor's determination of materiality because the level of materiality is a function of both quantitative and qualitative factors. That is, if fraudulent misstatements are identified during the engagement, the level of materiality for the engagement decreases.

*Auditor Unable to Continue the Engagement*

The auditor may question the ability to continue performing the audit under circumstances such as the following:

- The entity does not take action the auditor considers appropriate regarding fraud, even if the fraud is not material to the financial statements.
- The auditor's work indicates the financial statements have a significant risk of material and pervasive fraud.
- The auditor has significant concern about the competence or integrity of management or those charged with governance.

The auditor may find it appropriate to seek legal advice in considering whether to withdraw from an engagement and determining an appropriate course of action. Factors that could impact the auditor's decision to withdraw include the involvement of management or those charged with governance and the effects on the auditor from continuing to have an association with the entity. For example, concerns about management's integrity may arise on the day the auditor plans to sign the auditor report. Even at that point, the auditor may need to perform additional procedures or consider withdrawal. It is important to note that withdrawal may not be an option to auditors on some governmental and not-for-profit audits due to mandates, public interest considerations, contractual requirements, or law or regulation.

*Communications to Management and Those Charged with Governance*

When the auditor believes fraud might have occurred (whether consequential or inconsequential), the matter should be communicated to the appropriate level of management. In communications with those charged with governance, the auditor may communicate orally or in writing. AU-C 260 identifies factors to consider in making this determination, but the auditor may consider documenting all of these communications in writing given their sensitive nature.

---

**ENGAGEMENT STRATEGY:** The auditor and the audit committee should come to an understanding about the need for communication with the audit committee when lower-level employees are involved in fraudulent acts.

---

There are several examples of other fraud-related matters the auditor may wish to discuss with those charged with governance, including the auditor's evaluation of the entity's control environment, management actions that may be indicative of fraudulent financial reporting, and significant deficiencies or material weaknesses in controls to address risks of material misstatement due to fraud.

*Communications to Regulatory and Enforcement Authorities*

Generally, the auditor is not required to communicate the possible or actual existence of fraud to other parties due to the confidential relationship with the client; however, AU-C 316 points out that it might be necessary to communicate such information under the following circumstances:

- Communication might be required by statute, regulation, courts of law, or waived by agreement.
- There may be a statutory duty to report the occurrence of fraud to supervisory authorities.
- There may be a duty to report misstatements to authorities if management and those charged with governance fail to take corrective action.

**RISK ASSESSMENT STRATEGY:** The auditor should consider seeking legal counsel when determining whether a third party should be informed of possible fraud related to a client's financial statements.

## Practitioner's Aid

Exhibit AU-C 240-1 discusses authoritative guidance that is helpful in the audit of revenue reported in a client's financial statements. Exhibit AU-C 240-1 summarizes an approach described in the AICPA's Audit Guide *Auditing Revenue in Certain Industries*. The Audit Guide (which is available for purchase from the AICPA) notes that based on SEC Accounting and Auditing Enforcement Releases from between January 1987 and 1997, "more than half of the frauds involved overstating revenues by recording them either fictitiously or prematurely." The FASB's new revenue recognition standard, *Revenue from Contracts with Customers (Topic 606)* (ASU 2014-09), requires the application of greater judgment, thereby increasing the opportunity for preparer error and fraud.

### EXHIBIT AU-C 240-1—GUIDANCE FOR AUDITING REVENUE IN CERTAIN INDUSTRIES

Revenue should be recognized when it has been earned or substantially earned. Generally this means that revenue is recorded when goods are delivered or services are performed. Management has the primary responsibility for the fair presentation of revenue and related accounts such as allowances for uncollectible accounts, sales returns, and provisions for customer rebates and refunds. The AICPA's Audit Guide *Auditing Revenue in Certain Industries* points out that factors such as the (1) tone at the top, (2) role of the audit committee, (3) effectiveness of the internal audit function, and (4) adoption of effective internal control have an impact on the proper reporting of revenue in the financial statements based on U.S. GAAP.

The recognition of revenue consistent with U.S. GAAP can involve the application of a variety of pronouncements, including the following:

- ASC 360-20 (Real Estate Sales)
- ASC 470-40 (Product Financing Arrangements)
- ASC 605 (Revenue Recognition)
- ASC 952 (Franchisors)
- ASC 985 (Software)

The Audit Guide identifies the following specific factors that might indicate that a client is not reporting revenues in accordance with U.S. GAAP:

- Side agreements
- Channel stuffing
- Related-party transactions and significant unusual transactions
- Nature of business and accounting for revenue
- Integrity of evidence

*Side agreements*

Arrangements whereby the normal terms of a sale are modified in order to encourage a particular customer to accept shipment of goods that it would generally not accept (or record as a purchase) constitute a side agreement. These arrangements are generally characterized as relieving "the customer of some of the risk and rewards of ownership." Side agreements often result in revenue being recorded when the recognition is not in accordance with U.S. GAAP. Since side agreements are an exception to the normal sales conditions and are known only to a few key management personnel, this circumstance presents a challenge to the auditor; however, the Audit Guide points out that being aware that such an agreement could exist is a starting point for discovering their actual existence.

> **FRAUD POINTER:** The existence of side agreements undisclosed by management to the auditor is a significant fraud risk factor and potentially calls into question the integrity of top management. Side agreements can be either written or oral. The auditor should usually inquire about the existence of side agreements during the confirmation process.

*Channel stuffing*

The Audit Guide defines the channel stuffing strategy as a "marketing practice that suppliers sometimes use to boost sales by inducing distributors to buy substantially more inventory than they can promptly resell." The client's objective is to record more sales in the current period than would typically be recorded if sales were simply driven by market conditions. The auditor should be alert to identifying irregular sales patterns and consider their effect on the current financial statements. For example, there may be a need to create or increase provisions for returned goods or special discounts related to side agreements.

*Related-party transactions and significant unusual transactions*

Related-party transactions can be the basis for the recording of fraudulent transactions. For example, a client might sell inventory or capital assets to a related-party at an inflated price. The Audit Guide points out that individual related-party transactions that are kept relatively small but executed frequently could nonetheless have a material impact on the financial statements.

Another transaction type that can result in the reporting of fraudulent information in the financial statements involves highly complex transactions whether or not they involve related parties.

*Nature of business and accounting for revenue*

Revenue is generally recognized when earned; however, the nature of the client's industry can increase the risk that fraudulent revenue recognition schemes are present. The Audit Guide reminds auditors to consider factors such as the following as they relate to the probability that a client could inappropriately recognize revenue:

- The manner by which the client recognizes revenue based on the nature of its industry
- A recent change in the manner by which a client recognizes revenue
- The existence of client sales and payment terms that differ from industry norms or the client's normal internal policies
- Shipment policies that provide a basis for the inappropriate recognition of revenue

**PUBLIC COMPANY IMPLICATION:** The SEC staff has issued guidance specific to revenue recognition that is relevant to auditors of public companies. SAB-101 and SAB-104 summarize the SEC staff's views of the appropriate accounting for revenue recognition in financial statements. The guidance includes an analysis of the criteria that must be satisfied in order to recognize revenue. Auditors of public companies should consider the guidance in SAB-101 and SAB-104.

*Integrity of evidence*

The integrity of the evidence that supports the recognition of revenue is another risk factor that should be considered by the auditor. The Audit Guide lists the following as some of the conditions related to evidence that can suggest the improper recording of revenue:

- Responses from management with respect to revenue recognition are "inconsistent, vague, or implausible."
- Audit evidence to support revenue transactions is missing.
- Company personnel have signed bills of lading (rather than the common carrier).
- Shipping documents have been altered.

---

## Indicators of Improper Revenue Recognition

There is no comprehensive checklist to determine when conditions suggest that a client might be inappropriately recording revenue; however, the Audit Guide presents the following (categorized as (1) absence of an agreement, (2) lack of delivery, and (3) incomplete earnings process) as indicators that should raise the auditor's suspicions about fraudulent revenue transactions.

*Absence of an agreement*

- Sales are based on letters of intent rather than signed contracts or agreements.
- Goods are shipped before they are authorized by a customer.
- Sales are recorded at the date of shipment to a new customer even though the customer can return the goods with no obligation.
- Sales are recorded even though the customer has the right to cancel the sale.
- Sales are recorded even though certain terms of the agreement, such as a consignment sales arrangement, have not been satisfied.

*Lack of delivery*
- Sales are recorded before delivery occurs.
- Sales are based on transactions that were executed after the end of the accounting period.
- Sales are based on shipments to warehouses or other locations that have not been authorized by the customer.
- Sales are recorded but a critical component of the order has not been shipped.
- Sales are recorded based on the receipt of purchase orders.

*Incomplete earnings process*
- Sales are recorded but receipt of payment from the customer is based on other material conditions that must be satisfied by the client.
- Sales are recorded but goods are unassembled.
- Sales are recorded based on shipments to freight forwarders but the goods will be returned to the client for modifications as dictated by the customer.
- Sales are recorded even though the client is obliged to perform additional work (such as debugging a client application).

**Audit Procedures**

The Audit Guide lists the following as authoritative and nonauthoritative procedures that the auditor should consider in obtaining "reasonable assurance about whether the financial statements are free of material misstatement, whether caused by error or fraud":

- Determine an appropriate audit risk level.
- Develop knowledge of the business.
- Consider internal control over revenue recognition.
- Consider fraud in the financial statements.
- Consider related-party transactions.
- Perform analytical procedures.
- Perform cutoff tests, vouch transactions, and perform other tests.
- Send appropriate confirmations.
- Evaluate accounting estimates related to revenue transactions.
- Observe inventory.
- Obtain appropriate management representations.
- Consider the adequacy of financial statement disclosures.
- Evaluate audit evidence.

*Determine an appropriate audit risk level*

The auditor's awareness of fraud risk factors, related-party transactions, and other questionable revenue recognition characteristics of a client can occur as part of accepting or continuing an engagement, as part of planning the engagement, and as part of developing an understanding of a client's business and environment, including its internal control, or during the performance of tests of controls and substantive procedures. For this reason, during the entire engagement the auditor may need to reevaluate the levels of inherent risk and control risk related to revenue recognition to determine the nature, timing, and extent of audit procedures appropriate for the audit of revenue and related accounts.

*Develop knowledge of the business*

The Audit Guide notes that an auditor should be aware of a variety of characteristics of a client's revenue recognition process, including the following:

- Products and services sold;
- The effect of seasonal or cyclical trends on revenue;
- Marketing and sales policies, both internal and industry-wide;
- Policies with respect to pricing, returns, discount credit granting, and payment terms;
- Personnel (particularly in the marketing and sales activities) who record sales, extend credit, and authorize shipments;
- Compensation benefits that are related to sales volume;
- Classes and categories of customers;
- The client's role in "placing products with end users, and how the company manages, tracks and controls its inventory that is held by distributors"; and
- Accounting principles that are appropriate for the client's sales activities.

The Audit Guide points out that making inquiries of appropriate management personnel can help to better understand high-audit-risk conditions such as unusual or complex revenue transactions and sales contracts with unusual or complex terms.

**FRAUD POINTER:** Making appropriate inquiries is only a starting point in determining whether the client has recognized revenue inappropriately. The auditor should attempt to corroborate representations obtained through inquiry using other audit procedures, such as obtaining written confirmation from an independent source.

The auditor should read sales contracts in order to understand the responsibilities accepted by the client and their implications for revenue recognition. The Audit Guide notes that reading sales contracts and sales correspondence might alert the auditor to the existence of side agreements.

When a client executes complex sales agreements or is involved in related-party transactions, care must be taken in the assignment of personnel to ensure that the training and experience of an auditor is sufficient for the demands of this phase of the engagement. In some instances, it is appropriate to seek expert assistance from members of the firm who are not part of the engagement, and in some instances it is necessary to use the work of an outside specialist.

*Consider internal control over revenue recognition*

As with other significant components of a client's internal control, the auditor should develop an understanding of internal control over revenue transactions that satisfies the requirements established by AU-C 315 (*Understanding the Entity and Its Environment and Assessing the Risks of Material Misstatement*). Internal control related to revenue recognition should, among other things, include an understanding of (1) how nonstandard revenue contracts are approved, (2) the accounting implications for changing standard contracts, (3) the development of estimates related to revenue transactions, and (4) related-party transactions. Based on the auditor's understanding of internal control related to revenue recognition, an appropriate level of control risk should be assessed and in turn tests of controls should be performed. If the results from performing tests of controls suggest that internal control over revenue recognition is ineffective, the nature, timing, or extent of substantive procedures must be modified in order to provide more persuasive audit evidence.

*Consider fraud in the financial statements*

AU-C 240 requires that an auditor specifically assess the risk of material misstatement of the financial statements due to fraud and consider that assessment in designing the audit procedures to be performed. The Audit Guide points out that the auditor's assessment relative to financial statement fraud is dependent upon factors such as (1) professional skepticism and its effect on the nature, timing, and extent of audit procedures, (2) management's selection and application of accounting principles for revenue recognition, and (3) management's ability to circumvent internal control related to revenue recognition.

*Consider related-party transactions*

AU-C 550 (*Related Parties*) provides guidance for the planning and application of procedures for related-party transactions. The Audit Guide identifies the following as procedures that may be appropriate for substantive procedures for revenue recognition that involves a related party:

- Understand the purpose of the transaction.
- Examine documentation that supports the transaction.
- Determine whether the board of directors (or other appropriate personnel) has approved the transaction.
- Confirm the details of the transaction with external parties.
- When the transaction raises questions about its substance, refer to various sources of information to determine whether the transaction appears to be reasonable.
- When the transaction creates material uncollected balances or obligations, obtain information about the financial viability of the related party.

*Perform analytical procedures*

AU-C 520 (*Analytical Procedures*) provides guidance for the performance of analytical procedures in an audit engagement. The Audit Guide notes that the following analytical procedures "are particularly useful in identifying unusual fluctuations in the revenue cycle that warrant additional consideration":

- Compare monthly and quarterly sales to comparable periods for the current year and previous years and evaluate the amounts in the context of current industry conditions and current client strategies.
- Review sales recorded a few days before and a few days after the end of the year.
- Compare gross profit ratios to those for previous years and to budgeted amounts, and evaluate the amounts in the context of current industry conditions and current client strategies.
- Compare the amount of inventory in the distribution channel with the amounts for prior periods to consider whether there may be channel stuffing.
- Compare the trends of sales in the distributor channel and evaluate the amounts in the context of current industry conditions and current client strategies.
- Compare revenue deductions, such as discounts, to those of the previous year and budgeted amounts, and evaluate the amounts in the context of current industry conditions and current client strategies.
- Evaluate sales credits and returns after the end of the year with regard to the figures for similar periods of the previous year to determine whether there may have been contingent sales or other unusual sales arrangements.
- Evaluate the ratio of returns and allowances to sales.
- Compare the aged trial balance of receivables with those of previous years.
- Evaluate the amount of cash receipts collected after the end of the year to cash receipts activities during the year to determine whether receipts are unusually slow to materialize.

*Perform cutoff tests, vouch transactions, and perform other tests*

The auditor should perform appropriate cutoff tests, vouch transactions, and perform other audit procedures to determine whether sales and related transactions are recorded in the appropriate accounting period.

*Send appropriate confirmations*

AU-C 505 (*External Confirmations*) provides guidance for the use of confirmations in an audit engagement. The Audit Guide notes that the auditor should consider confirming the details of complicated or unusual sales transactions, including possible unfilled obligations on the part of the client.

---

**PLANNING AID REMINDER:** AU-C 240 states that there is generally a heightened risk of fraud involving revenue recognition. Therefore, the auditor should consider confirming the terms of material revenue transactions, including inquiring about the existence of side agreements. The auditor should be more likely to confirm the terms of revenue transactions if they are unusual or complex. In addition, AICPA Practice Alert 03-1 (*Audit Confirmations*) states that the auditor should be more likely to confirm transaction terms and the existence of side agreements if any of the following conditions exist: (1) significant sales or sales volume at or near the end of the reporting period, (2) use of nonstandard contracts or contract clauses, (3) use of letters of authorization instead of signed contracts or agreements, (4) altered dates on contracts or shipping documents, (5) contracts or agreements that are linked with each other or that happen concurrently (e.g., sales to and purchases from the same party), (6) lack of evidence that the customer has accepted the product, (7) presence of bill-and-hold transactions, (8) sales with extended payment terms or nonstandard installment receivables, (9) sales without involvement from the accounting/finance department or where the accounting/finance department does not monitor relationships with distributors/retailers, (10) unusual sales volume to distributors/retailers, (11) sales involving a commitment for future upgrades, especially if not involving software, (12) sales involving significant uncertainties or obligations for the seller, (13) sales to value-added resellers or distributors whose financial viability is questionable, (14) an abnormally large increase in a receivable from a customer, and (15) aggressive accounting policies and practices by the client.

*Evaluate accounting estimates related to revenue transactions*

AU-C 540 (*Auditing Accounting Estimates, Including Fair Value Accounting Estimates, and Related Disclosures*) describes the auditor's responsibilities and the audit procedures with respect to estimates that are part of the client's financial statements. The Audit Guide notes that this general guidance should be applied to material accounts such as sales, sales returns, the allowance for doubtful accounts, and revenue recognized under the percentage-of-completion method used to account for long-term construction contracts.

*Observe inventory*

The Audit Guide reminds auditors that appropriate cutoff procedures for the observation of inventories at the end of the year have implications for the recognition of revenues in the proper accounting period. In addition, the Guide notes that if a client has numerous shipping facilities the auditor should (1) observe inventory counts at all locations on the same date or (2) observe only some of the locations on an unannounced basis. Also, if the client is in an industry where inventory obsolescence is an issue, the auditor should determine whether client personnel used to count the inventory have the expertise to identify obsolete inventory.

*Obtain appropriate management representations*

AU-C 580 (*Written Representations*) provides guidance in obtaining written representations from a client. The Audit Guide states that some of the items that should be considered for representation by the client are as follows:

- There has been no fraud that could have a material effect on the financial statements.
- Related-party transactions, including sales and amounts receivable from related parties, have been properly recorded and disclosed.
- All financial records and related data have been made available.
- Significant estimates and material concentrations that are required to be disclosed.

- The effects of any uncorrected financial statement misstatements aggregated by the auditor during the current engagement and pertaining to the latest period presented are immaterial, both individually and in the aggregate, to the financial statements taken as a whole. (A summary of such items should be included in or attached to the letter.)

If the client has been involved in unusual revenue transactions, the auditor should consider whether it is appropriate to ask for representation concerning the details of these transactions.

*Consider the adequacy of financial statement disclosures*

The financial statements should reflect disclosures "with regard to revenue recognition policies, information about major customers or significant concentrations of credit risk, related-party transactions, and the effect of significant revisions to estimates in percentage-of-completion contracts."

*Evaluate audit evidence*

The Audit Guide points out that "to the extent the auditor remains in substantial doubt about any assertion of material significance, he or she must refrain from forming an opinion until he or she has obtained sufficient appropriate audit evidence to remove such substantial doubt, or the auditor must express a qualified or disclaimer of opinion."

---

**OBSERVATION:** In addition to providing general guidance for the audit of revenue and related accounts, the Audit Guide provides specific guidance for the high-technology manufacturing industry.

---

## SECTION 250

## CONSIDERATION OF LAWS AND REGULATIONS IN AN AUDIT OF FINANCIAL STATEMENTS

### Authoritative Pronouncements

SAS-122—Statements on Auditing Standards: Clarification and Recodification

### Overview

The laws and regulations an entity is subject to constitute its legal and regulatory framework. The effect of laws and regulations on the financial statements of entities varies widely. Some laws and regulations have a direct effect on the determination of material amounts and disclosures in the financial statements, and for these laws and regulations the auditor must obtain sufficient appropriate audit evidence. Other laws and regulations do not have a direct effect on the entity's financial statements, but compliance may be fundamental to operating aspects of the business such that noncompliance may have a material effect on the financial statements. For these laws and regulations, the auditor is required to perform specified audit procedures that may identify instances of noncompliance with these laws and regulations. The auditor may also become aware of acts of noncompliance through other audit procedures during the audit, so it is important to maintain an attitude of professional skepticism throughout the audit.

> **PLANNING AID REMINDER:** AU-C 250 establishes professional standards relating to the auditor's responsibility for considering laws and regulations in the course of the audit of the entity's financial statements. An auditor might accept other engagements that impose a different responsibility for detecting illegal acts. Such engagements include professional services subject to governmental auditing standards or special engagements designed to determine compliance with specific laws or regulations.

In general, the auditor lacks the expertise and is not responsible for identifying and evaluating all acts of noncompliance with laws and regulations. The auditor is responsible for "obtaining reasonable assurance that the financial statements, as a whole, are free from material misstatement, whether caused by fraud or error." Even if an audit is properly performed and planned in accordance with GAAS, there is a risk that material misstatements may not be detected. There are several inherent limitations that may prevent the auditor from detecting material misstatements resulting from noncompliance with laws and regulations: (1) many laws and regulations primarily relate to the operating aspects of an entity and may not affect the financial statements or be captured by the entity's financial reporting information systems; (2) noncompliance may involve acts of concealment such as collusion, management override of controls, or intentional misrepresentation to the auditor; and (3) whether an act constitutes noncompliance is ultimately a matter for a court of law and legal determination.

The more removed an act of noncompliance becomes from events and transactions reflected in the financial statements, the less likely the auditor is to become aware of the noncompliant act. However, if the auditor does detect noncompliance, regardless of its materiality level, other aspects of the audit may be impacted, such as the auditor's consideration of management or employee integrity. AU-C 250 provides the auditor with the guidance to respond to identified or suspected noncompliance with laws or regulations appropriately.

**PLANNING AID REMINDER:** There are some specific statutory requirements that require the auditor to report on the entity's compliance with certain provisions of laws or regulations as part of the financial statement audit. AU-C 705 addresses the auditor's reporting responsibilities in these circumstances.

## Definition

Noncompliance — Acts of intentional or unintentional omission or commission by the entity which are contrary to prevailing laws or regulations. Acts of noncompliance include transactions entered into by the entity, in the name of the entity, or on its behalf by those charged with governance, management, or employees. Noncompliance does not include personal misconduct by those charged with governance, management, or employees of the entity that is unrelated to the entity's business activities.

## Requirements

The auditor is presumptively required to perform the following procedures in considering laws and regulations in a financial statement audit:

### Consideration of Compliance with Laws and Regulations

1. As part of obtaining an understanding of the entity and its environment, obtain a general understanding of the legal and regulatory framework applicable to the entity and its industry and how the entity is complying with that framework.

2. Obtain sufficient appropriate audit evidence regarding material amounts and disclosures in the financial statements for which the provisions of laws and regulations are generally recognized to have a direct effect on their determination.

3. Perform the following audit procedures that may identify instances of noncompliance with other laws and regulations that may have a material effect on the financial statements:

    a. Inquire of management (and those charged with governance as appropriate) as to whether the entity is in compliance with such laws and regulations, and

    b. Inspect any correspondence with relevant licensing or regulatory authorities.

4. Remain alert during the audit to the possibility that instances of noncompliance or suspected noncompliance may be brought to the auditor's attention through other audit procedures.

5. If noncompliance is not identified or suspected, the auditor is not required to perform additional audit procedures regarding the entity's compliance with laws and regulations.

## Audit Procedures When Noncompliance Is Identified or Suspected

6. If noncompliance with laws and regulations is identified or suspected, obtain an understanding of the nature and circumstances of occurrence of the act and further information to evaluate the possible effect on the financial statements.

7. If noncompliance is suspected, discuss the matter with management (and those charged with governance as appropriate). Consider the need to obtain legal advice if management or those charged with governance do not provide sufficient information supporting the entity's compliance with laws and regulations and the auditor judges the effect of the suspected noncompliance may be material to the financial statements.

8. If sufficient information about suspected noncompliance cannot be obtained, evaluate the effect of the lack of sufficient appropriate audit evidence on the auditor's opinion.

9. Evaluate the implications of noncompliance on other aspects of the audit, including the auditor's risk assessment and the reliability of written representations, and take appropriate action.

## Reporting Identified or Suspected Noncompliance

10. Communicate matters involving identified or suspected noncompliance with laws and regulations that are not clearly inconsequential with those charged with governance unless all of those individuals are involved in the entity's management and already aware of these matters.

11. If the auditor judges identified or suspected noncompliance to be intentional and material, communicate the matter to those charged with governance as soon as practicable.

12. If the auditor suspects management or those charged with governance of being involved in noncompliance, communicate the matter to the entity's next higher existing level of authority. Consider the need to obtain legal advice if no such higher authority exists or the auditor believes the communication may not be acted upon or is unsure of whom to report the matter to.

13. If the auditor concludes that the noncompliance has a material effect on the financial statements that is not adequately reflected in the financial statements, the auditor should express a qualified or adverse opinion on the financial statements.

14. If management or those charged with governance prevent the auditor from obtaining sufficient appropriate audit evidence to evaluate whether potentially material noncompliance has or is likely to have occurred, that is a limitation on the scope of the audit and the auditor should express a qualified opinion or disclaim an opinion on the financial statements.

15. If the auditor is unable to determine whether noncompliance has occurred due to circumstances other than limitations imposed by management or those charged with governance, evaluate the effect on his or her opinion.

16. If noncompliance with laws and regulation is identified or suspected, determine whether the auditor has a responsibility to report this noncompliance to parties outside the entity.

**OBSERVATION:** AU-C 250 specifically requires the auditor to inspect correspondence, if any, with the relevant licensing or regulatory authorities. Auditing standards previously noted that an audit performed in accordance with GAAS provided no assurance that noncompliance with laws and regulations would be detected or that contingent liabilities that might result would be disclosed. However, the Clarified SASs now state that because of the inherent limitations in an audit, some material misstatements in the financial statements may not be detected, even though the audit is properly planned and performed with in accordance with GAAS. The concept of "no assurance" is different from the concept described as "inherent limitations of an audit."

*Documentation*

Document identified or suspected noncompliance with laws and regulations and the results of discussion with management, those charged with governance where applicable, and other parties inside and outside the entity.

## Analysis and Application of Procedures

*Management Responsibilities*

Management, with oversight from those charged with governance, is responsible for ensuring the entity's operations are conducted in accordance with laws and regulations. To prevent and detect noncompliance with laws and regulations, an entity may employ policies and procedures such as monitoring legal requirements; using appropriate internal control systems; and developing, training employees on, and monitoring compliance with a code of conduct. Large entities may support these activities by assigning responsibilities to an audit committee or the internal audit, legal, or compliance function.

**PLANNING AID REMINDER:** The auditor should request a written representation from the entity stating that no violations or possible violations of laws or regulations have occurred that may require accrual or disclosure in the financial statements. Management should also represent that it has informed the auditor of all possible illegal acts that it is aware of. Written representations provided by management provide audit evidence about management's knowledge of identified or suspected noncompliance with laws and regulations. However, these representations do not provide sufficient appropriate audit evidence on their own and do not affect the nature and extent of other audit evidence the auditor must obtain.

## Consideration of Compliance with Laws and Regulations

*Obtaining an understanding of the legal and regulatory framework*

Procedures the auditor may use to obtain a general understanding of the legal and regulatory framework and the entity's compliance with that framework include the following:

- Using the auditor's existing understanding of the entity's industry, regulatory, and other external factors;
- Updating the understanding of laws and regulations that directly determine reported amounts and disclosures in the financial statements;
- Inquiring of management as to other laws and regulations that may have a fundamental effect on the entity's operations;
- Inquiring of management as to the entity's policies and procedures regarding compliance with laws and regulations and those adopted to identify, evaluate, and account for litigation claims;
- Inquiring of management as to the use of management representations and entity-issued directives concerning compliance with laws and regulations; and
- Considering the auditor's knowledge of the entity's history of noncompliance with laws and regulations.

*Laws and regulations with direct effects on financial statements*

Generally, the auditor takes into consideration laws and regulations that directly apply to the determination of financial statement amounts or disclosures when planning his or her audit procedures. These laws and regulations may include those relating to the form and content of financial statements, industry-specific financial reporting issues, accounting for transactions under government contracts, and the accrual or recognition of expenses for income tax or pension costs. For example, the auditor would likely evaluate compliance with Internal Revenue Code and related regulations when determining whether the provision for income taxes is fairly presented in the financial statements. The auditor's responsibility for detecting illegal acts relating to laws and regulations having a direct and material effect on the financial statements is the same as the responsibility relating to the detection of errors and fraud. The auditor must design the audit to provide reasonable assurance of detecting such acts.

*Laws and regulations with indirect effects on financial statements*

Most laws and regulations have only an indirect effect on financial statements; that is, when noncompliance related to this type of law or regulation has occurred, the effects are often indirect in that they only require disclosure in the financial statements based on their classification as a contingent liability. Laws and regulations of this type may include those related to securities trading, occupational safety and health, food and drug administration, environmental protection, equal employment, and antitrust violations.

Noncompliant acts of this type are generally related to the operations of the organization rather than to the financial and accounting aspects of the entity and could have a fundamental effect on the entity's operations by causing it to cease operations or creating a going concern. Furthermore, under many circumstances, the auditor lacks sufficient basis for determining whether this type of law or regulation has been violated.

## Audit Procedures When Noncompliance Is Identified or Suspected

*Indicators of noncompliance*

AU-C 250 lists the following as examples of specific information that raises questions about the existence of noncompliance with laws and regulations:

- Unauthorized or improperly recorded transactions.
- Investigation by a governmental or regulatory agency, or payment of fines or penalties.
- Noncompliance with laws or regulations cited in reports of examinations by regulatory agencies made available to the auditor.
- Payments for unspecified services or loans to consultants, affiliates, employees, or government officials or employees.
- Sales commissions or agents' fees that appear excessive in relation to those normally paid by the client or to the services actually received.
- Unusual payments in cash, purchases of bank cashiers' checks in amounts payable to bearer, or transfers to numbered bank accounts.
- Purchases made at prices significantly above or below market price.
- Unusual transactions with companies registered in tax havens.
- Payments for goods or services made to countries other than those from which the goods or services originated.
- Existence of an information system that fails, by design or by accident, to provide an adequate audit trail or sufficient audit evidence.
- Unfavorable media comment.
- Failure to file tax returns or pay government duties or similar fees common to the entity's industry or the nature of its business.

*Perform appropriate audit procedures*

If it is necessary to obtain a further understanding of the identified or suspected noncompliant act, perform additional procedures such as the following:

- Inspect supporting documentation and compare it with the accounting records;
- Confirm information with other parties and intermediaries;
- Determine if the transaction has been properly authorized; and
- Consider whether other, similar transactions have occurred, and attempt to identify them.

Further information to consider in evaluating the possible effect of noncompliant acts on the financial statements includes:

- The quantitative and qualitative materiality of the effect of noncompliance on the financial statements.
- If the potential financial consequences require accrual or disclosure under the applicable financial reporting framework.
- If the potential financial consequences are so serious that the financial statements may not be fairly presented or may be otherwise misleading.

When management cannot provide sufficient information to demonstrate that a noncompliant act did not take place, the auditor may consult with the entity's legal counsel or external legal counsel. If it is not appropriate for the auditor to consult with the entity's legal counsel or the auditor is not satisfied with the counsel's opinion, it may be appropriate for the auditor to consult his or her own legal counsel regarding the existence of a noncompliant act, the possible legal consequences including the possibility of fraud, and any further action the auditor should take.

> **FRAUD POINTER:** The client is normally expected to perform an investigation if an illegal act might have occurred. (These investigations are typically performed by an outside law firm with the assistance of forensic accountants under the supervision of the audit committee.) The auditor should request that he or she be allowed to attend the presentation of the investigation team's report at the completion of the engagement and discuss the results of the investigation with senior management and the audit committee.

*Evaluate the implications of noncompliance*

The implications of noncompliant acts on other aspects of the audit are particularly applicable to the evaluation of the reliability of management representations. Such facts as the perpetrators involved, the methods of concealment, and the nature of internal control procedures overridden should be considered in the evaluation. In circumstances where management or those charged with governance do not take remedial actions the auditor considers appropriate, the auditor may question his or her ability to rely on management representations and the potential effects of continuing association with the entity. These circumstances may cause the auditor to seek legal advice in considering withdrawal from the engagement. If withdrawal is prohibited by law or regulation, the auditor may consider alternative actions such as describing the noncompliance in an Other Matter(s) paragraph in the auditor's report.

> **OBSERVATION:** The possible loss arising from the illegal act should be evaluated to determine whether the amount is material. All costs related to the loss, such as penalties and fines, should be considered. The need for accrual and/or disclosure in the financial statements should be evaluated in the context of guidelines codified in ASC 450 (Contingencies). The auditor must consider both quantitative and qualitative factors in evaluating the materiality of the illegal act. Qualitative factors are often more important than the immediate quantitative effect in evaluating the materiality of an illegal act. For example, penalties and fines can sometimes exceed the amount of the illegal act itself.

The illegal act should also be evaluated to determine whether other aspects of the engagement are affected. This is particularly applicable to the evaluation of the reliability of management representations. Such facts as the perpetrators involved, the methods of concealment, and the nature of internal control procedures overridden should be considered in the evaluation.

**FRAUD POINTER:** An AICPA Practice Alert on illegal acts states that the auditor is to evaluate management's conclusions after receiving the investigation report. After the auditor considers the results of the special investigation and discusses the investigation report with senior management and the audit committee, he or she must determine (1) whether additional audit procedures need to be performed, (2) the nature of any needed disclosures in the financial statements and notes, (3) whether internal control deficiencies exist and need to be communicated, and (4) whether the audit report needs to be modified. The auditor should also consider whether it is appropriate to withdraw from the engagement.

## *Reporting Identified or Suspected Noncompliance*

The auditor's communication of identified or suspected noncompliance to those charged with governance may include the following:

- Description of the noncompliant act,
- Circumstances surrounding the noncompliant act, and
- Auditor's evaluation of the effects of the noncompliant act on the financial statements.

**FRAUD POINTER:** If members of senior management are involved in the illegal act, the auditor should communicate directly with the audit committee (or equivalent individuals). The communication can be written or oral, and in either case it should be adequately documented in the audit files.

The auditor may reach an agreement with those charged with governance in advance regarding the nature of matters to be communicated in order to avoid communicating clearly inconsequential matters.

**ENGAGEMENT STRATEGY:** If the auditor finds it necessary to issue a qualified or adverse opinion or a disclaimer of opinion on the financial statements and management or those charged with governance refuse to accept this modified opinion, the auditor may withdraw from the engagement and indicate the reasons for withdrawal in writing to those charged with governance.

Notifying parties external to the entity about the occurrence of a noncompliant act is generally not required; however, AU-C 250 notes that, under the following circumstances, the auditor may be called on to inform another party of a noncompliant act:

- Inquiries received from a successor auditor.
- Subpoena issued by a court.
- Governmental audit requirements applicable to entities that have received financial aid.

**ENGAGEMENT STRATEGY:** Because of the confidential relationship between the entity and the auditor, the auditor may find it advisable to contact legal counsel before noncompliant acts are disclosed to outside parties.

Audits of governmental agencies may have additional reporting requirements relating to compliance with laws, regulations, and provision of contracts or grant agreements and may require communicating instances of noncompliance to appropriate oversight bodies and funding agencies.

# SECTION 260

# THE AUDITOR'S COMMUNICATION WITH THOSE CHARGED WITH GOVERNANCE

## Authoritative Pronouncements

SAS-122—Statements on Auditing Standards: Clarification and Recodification

SAS-123—Omnibus Statement on Auditing Standards—2011

SAS-134—Auditor Reporting and Amendments, Including Amendments Addressing Disclosures in the Audit of Financial Statements

SAS-135—Omnibus Statement on Auditing Standards—2019

SAS-137—The Auditor's Responsibilities Relating to Other Information Included in Annual Reports

SAS-141—Amendment to Effective Dates of SAS Nos. 134-140

SAS-143—Auditing Accounting Estimates and Related Disclosures

## Overview

Effective governance over the entity's processes, including those related to financial reporting, is a critical element of an entity's internal controls. Persons should be in place who have responsibility for overseeing the strategic direction of the entity and obligations related to the accountability of the entity to its key stakeholders, including oversight of the financial reporting process. Governance structures vary by entity, often depending on the entity's size and organizational structure.

AU-C 260 establishes standards and provides guidance on the auditor's communication with those charged with governance in relation to the audit of financial statements. The intent of AU-C 260 is to provide a framework for an effective two-way communication between the auditor and those charged with governance, and it identifies specific matters to be communicated. Auditors are additionally required to communicate matters that in their judgment are significant and relevant to the responsibilities of those charged with governance for overseeing the financial reporting process. AU-C 260 does not preclude the auditor from communicating other matters in addition to those required.

The principal purposes of the auditor's communications with those charged with governance include the following:

- Communicate clearly the responsibilities of the auditor in relation to the financial statement audit, including an overview of the scope and timing of the audit.

- Obtain information relevant to the audit from those charged with governance.

- Provide those charged with governance with timely information about observations arising from the audit that are relevant to their governance responsibilities in the oversight of the financial reporting processes.
- Promote effective two-way communication between the auditor and those charged with governance.

The intended recipient of the auditor's communication is *those charged with governance*, which may vary across entities. For many, those charged with governance include the board of directors or its audit committee. For others, those charged with governance may reside outside the entity, such as a government agency, or those charged with governance may include those who have management responsibilities. Determination of who those charged with governance are is based on the auditor's judgment.

---

**IMPORTANT NOTICE FOR 2022:** In May 2019, the AICPA's Auditing Standards Board (ASB) issued SAS No. 134 titled *Auditor Reporting and Amendments, Including Amendments Addressing Disclosures in the Audit of Financial Statements*, to revise the auditor's report and to amend various AU-C sections to heighten the auditor's focus on disclosures throughout the process of auditing financial statements. Those changes also resulted in conforming amendments to other AU-C sections, including AU-C 260. The most significant change to AU-C 260 is the requirement for the auditor to communicate with those charged with governance about (1) the terms of the engagement, (2) significant risks identified by the auditor and how the auditor plans to address areas of higher risks, (3) unexpected modifications to the overall audit strategy, and (4) circumstances that affect the form and content of the auditor's report, such as a modified opinion, inclusion of an emphasis-of-matter or other-matter paragraph, or the communication of key audit matters (KAMs) in the auditor's report. Originally, the effective date of SAS No. 134 was for audits of financial statements periods ending on or after December 15, 2020, with early implementation **not** permitted. However, the ASB's issuance of SAS No. 141, *Amendment to the Effective Dates of SAS Nos. 134-140*, extended the effective date of SAS No. 134 to December 15, 2021, in order to provide more time for firms to implement SAS No. 134 in light of the effect of the coronavirus pandemic. While SAS No. 141 allows for early implementation of SAS No. 134, the ASB recommends that SAS Nos. 134-140 be implemented concurrently.

---

**IMPORTANT NOTICE FOR 2022:** In May 2019, the AICPA's Auditing Standards Board (ASB) issued SAS No. 135 titled *Omnibus Statement on Auditing Standards—2019* that includes amendments to various AU-C sections. SAS No. 135 incorporates some of the guidance in PCAOB Auditing Standards related to communications with audit committees to add requirements to AU-C 260 for the auditor to communicate to those charged with governance the auditor's views relating to an entity's significant unusual transactions and matters that are difficult or contentious for which the auditor consulted outside the engagement team and that are relevant to those charged with governance. The communication of significant unusual transactions may include (1) the auditor's views on the policies and practices management used to account for significant transactions and (2) the auditor's understanding of the business purpose of significant unusual transactions. SAS No. 135 also amends AU-C 260 to require the auditor to communicate the potential effects of uncorrected misstatements on future-period financial statements. Originally, the effective date of SAS No. 135 was for audits of financial statements periods ending on or after December 15, 2020, with early application **not** permitted. However, the ASB's issuance of SAS No. 141, *Amendment to the Effective Dates of SAS Nos. 134-140*, extended the effective date of SAS No. 135 to December 15, 2021, in order to provide more time for firms to implement SAS No. 135 in light of the effect of the coronavirus pandemic. While SAS No. 141 allows for early implementation of SAS No. 135, the ASB recommends that SAS Nos. 134-140 be implemented concurrently.

## Definitions

| | |
|---|---|
| Those charged with governance | The person(s) or organization(s) with responsibility for overseeing the strategic direction of the entity, the obligations related to the accountability of the entity, and the financial reporting process. May include management personnel; for example, executive members or a governance board or an owner-manager. |
| Management | The person(s) with executive responsibility for the conduct of the entity's operations. May include some or all of those charged with governance. |

**PUBLIC COMPANY IMPLICATION:** The PCAOB's issuance of AS-3101 (*The Auditor's Report on an Audit of Financial Statements When the Auditor Expresses an Unqualified Opinion and Related Amendments to PCAOB Standards*) in 2017 requires the auditor (1) to describe critical audit matters in the audit report and (2) to disclose the tenure of the audit firm as auditor. The PCAOB's AS 3101 describes critical audit matters as those audit matters that are communicated, or are required to be communicated, to the audit committee that (1) relate to accounts or disclosures that are material to the financial statements and (2) involve especially challenging, subjective, or complex auditor judgment. The auditor's report includes (1) identification of the critical audit matter, (2) description of why the auditor concluded that the item was a critical audit matter, (3) description of how the critical audit matter was addressed in the audit, and (4) reference to the relevant financial statement accounts and disclosures affected by the critical audit matter.

**PUBLIC COMPANY IMPLICATION:** PCAOB Auditing Standard AS-2410 (*Related Parties: Amendments to Certain PCAOB Auditing Standards Regarding Significant Unusual Transactions and Other Amendments to PCAOB Auditing Standards*) contains audit guidance in the areas of related-party transactions (RPTs), significant unusual transactions, and financial relationships and transactions with executive officers. The PCAOB combined these three areas into a single standard because of the potential relationships between RPTs, significant unusual transactions, and financial relationships and transactions with executive officers. In auditing RPTs, the standard requires the auditor to (1) perform procedures to understand the company's relationships and transactions with related parties, including transactions with related parties that were modified during the period under audit; (2) evaluate whether the company has properly identified its related parties and transactions with them; (3) perform additional procedures if undisclosed (by management) related parties or related-party transactions are discovered by the auditor; (4) perform specific procedures for those RPTs required to be disclosed in the financial statements or that are identified as a significant risk; and (5) communicate to the audit committee the auditor's evaluation of the company's identification of, accounting for, and disclosure of RPTs.

AS-2410 also includes the PCAOB's requirements on the consideration of fraud in an audit. The PCAOB describes a "significant unusual transaction" as one that is outside the normal course of business for the company or that otherwise appears unusual because of the transaction's timing, size, or nature. In auditing significant unusual transactions, the standard requires the auditor to (1) perform procedures to identify significant unusual transactions; (2) perform procedures to determine whether the significant unusual transaction has a business purpose and, if so, to understand that purpose; and (3) consider whether the transaction may have been entered into to commit financial reporting fraud or conceal a misappropriation of assets. AS-2410 requires the auditor to consider whether executive compensation arrangements may create an incentive or pressure for the company to achieve certain operating results or financial position.

## Requirements

The auditor is required to perform the following procedures related to communications with those charged with governance:

### Those Charged with Governance

1. Determine the appropriate people to communicate with in the entity's governance structure.

2. When communicating with a subgroup of those charged with governance, determine if there is an additional need to communicate with the governing body.

3. If matters have been communicated to those involved in managing the entity who also have governance responsibilities, those matters do not need to be communicated again to the same individual in their governance role. This does not preclude the need for all those who would be communicated with in their governance capacity to be adequately informed.

### Matters to Be Communicated

4. The auditor's responsibilities in relation to the financial statements should be communicated. This includes the auditor's responsibility for forming and expressing an opinion on whether the financial statements are prepared, in all material respects, in conformity with the applicable financial reporting framework. This also includes communicating that the financial statement audit does not relieve management or those charged with governance of their responsibilities.

5. Communicate an overview of the planned scope and timing of the audit, including communication about significant risks identified by the auditor.

6. Communicate any significant findings or issues, including the auditor's views about qualitative aspects of the entity's significant accounting practices, significant unusual transactions, significant difficulties encountered during the audit, disagreements with management, or difficult or contentious matters that the auditor consulted outside the engagement team that are significant and relevant to those charged with governance. Also communicate significant findings that in the auditor's judgment are relevant to the responsibilities of those charged with governance for overseeing the financial reporting process, and communicate circumstances that affect the auditor's report.

---

**IMPORTANT NOTICE FOR 2022:** In July 2020, the AICPA Auditing Standards Board (ASB) issued SAS No. 143, *Auditing Accounting Estimates and Related Disclosures*, which supersedes AU-C 540 (*Auditing Accounting Estimates, Including Fair Value Accounting Estimates, and Related Disclosures*) and amends various other sections, including AU-C 501, in the professional standards. The new SAS begins with an explanation of the nature of accounting estimates and how they can vary widely in nature and are required to be made by management when monetary amounts cannot be directly observed. The measurement of amounts is subject to estimation uncertainty, which reflects inherent limitations in the knowledge or data. These limitations give rise to inherent subjectivity and variation in measurement outcomes. Although the guidance in SAS No. 143 applies to all accounting estimates, the degree to which an accounting estimate is subject to estimation uncertainty will vary substantially. Therefore, SAS No. 143 recognizes that the nature, timing, and extent of the risk assessment and further audit procedures required will vary in relation to the estimation uncertainty and the assessment of the related risks of material misstatement. The ASB is coordinating the effective date of SAS No. 143 with the effective date of a proposed new SAS, *Understanding the Entity and Its Environment and Assessing the Risks of Material Misstatement*, which was under consideration by the ASB at the time this edition of the *GAAS Guide* was being prepared. SAS No. 143 does not become effective until audits of financial statements for periods ending on or after December 15, 2023, which is consistent with the date in the proposed new standard. As a result, this AU-C reflects existing auditing standards requirements. Updates to reflect SAS No. 143 will occur in the next edition of the *GAAS Guide*.

---

7. Communicate nontrivial uncorrected misstatements and any effect they may have on the auditor's opinion. Identify any material uncorrected misstatements individually and request they be corrected. Also communicate the effect of any uncorrected misstatements related to prior periods or uncorrected misstatements or matters that could potentially cause future-period financial statements to be materially misstated, even though those matters are immaterial to the current year financial statements under audit.

8. If there are members of those charged with governance that are not involved in managing the entity, additional information needs to be communicated. These communications should include material, corrected misstatements and significant findings or issues that have been shared with management; the auditor's views on significant matters management discussed with other accountants; and written representations the auditor is requesting.

## The Communication Process

9. Communicate the form, timing, and expected general content of communications.

10. Communicate significant findings or issues in writing when, using professional judgment, oral communication is not adequate. This communication does not need to include matters that have been communicated by management with those charged with governance and satisfactorily resolved, unless any matters were omitted or not sufficiently communicated by management. The auditor does not need to communicate the information at the same level of detail as management as long as the auditor participated with management in the discussions and adequately confirmed that the communications were adequate.

11. Any written communication related to this standard is a by-product report and should include an indication that its use should be restricted to those charged with governance and, if appropriate, management.

12. Communicate with those charged with governance on a timely basis.

13. Evaluate the adequacy of the two-way communication for the purpose of the audit. If there has been inadequate communication, evaluate any effect on the assessment of risks of material misstatement and ability to obtain sufficient appropriate audit evidence.

## Documentation

14. Document any oral communications related to AU-C 260, including when and to whom the communications occurred. Retain a copy of any written communications related to AU-C 260 as part of the audit documentation. Also include documentation of matters required to be communicated to those charged with governance that were communicated by management, not the auditor.

---

**PUBLIC COMPANY IMPLICATION:** AS-1301 (*Communications with Audit Committees*) requires that an engagement letter document the terms of the audit engagement with the audit committee. The engagement letter documents the objectives of the audit and the respective responsibilities of the auditor and management

The auditor is to provide an overview of the overall audit strategy to the audit committee. Aspects of the overall audit strategy that are to be communicated are (1) the timing of the audit; (2) significant risks identified by the auditor; (3) the external auditor's planned use of internal audit; (4) names, locations, and planned responsibilities of other audit firms or other personnel who are not employed by the auditor, and the basis for the auditor's determination that he or she can serve as the principal auditor; and (5) significant changes to the audit strategy and the reasons for those changes.

The auditor must communicate to the audit committee information about the results of the audit, including information on the company's accounting policies and practices and the auditor's evaluation of the quality of the company's financial reporting. With respect to accounting policies and practices, the auditor is to communicate (1) management's initial selection of, or changes to, accounting policies and practices, including the effects of these policies and practices on the financial statements and disclosures; (2) the company's critical accounting policies and practices, and the reason the policies and practices are considered the most critical; (3) the company's critical accounting estimates, including a description of the process used by management to develop these estimates, any significant changes to the process, and significant assumptions used in developing the estimates; and (4) significant unusual transactions, which are defined as transactions outside the normal course of business or that are unusual due to their size, timing, or nature. With respect to the auditor's evaluation of the quality of the company's financial reporting, he or she is to communicate (1) qualitative aspects of significant accounting policies and practices, including cases where the auditor has identified management bias in its judgments; (2) the auditor's assessment of management's disclosures related to critical accounting policies and practice; (3) the auditor's conclusions as to the reasonableness of the company's critical accounting estimates; (4) significant unusual transactions, including the auditor's understanding of the business rationale for these transactions; (5) the auditor's conclusion as to whether the presentation of the financial statements and notes is in conformity with U.S. GAAP or another accepted financial reporting framework; and (6) alternative treatments allowed under U.S. GAAP (or another acceptable framework) and the auditor's preferred treatment.

In addition to the above, the auditor is to communicate to the audit committee (1) the auditor's responsibility for any other information in a document containing audited financial statements; (2) difficult or contentious matters where the auditor consulted outside the engagement team; (3) when management consults with another accountant to the extent the auditor is aware of this fact, and the auditor's view on the issue; (4) if the auditor has substantial doubt about the company's ability to continue as a going concern and, if the auditor's doubt is alleviated by management plans, the nature of those plans; (5) a schedule of uncorrected misstatements; (6) disagreements with management; and (7) difficulties encountered in performing the audit. These communications are to occur before the issuance of the audit report. With the exception of the engagement letter, the other required communications can be written or oral but, if they are oral, the nature of the communications must be documented.

## Analysis and Application of Procedures

### Those Charged with Governance

*Determine the appropriate recipients of the auditor's communication*

The intended recipients of the auditor's communication are those charged with governance, which varies from one entity to another. The auditor's understanding of the entity's governance structure and processes obtained in connection with the requirements in AU-C 315 provides relevant input to his or her determination of the appropriate recipients of his or her communication.

Those charged with governance might include one or more of the following:

- Board of directors or supervisory board.
- Subgroup of the board, such as the audit committee.
- Partners or proprietors.
- Committee of management or trustees.
- Owner-manager or sole trustee.

AU-C 260 does not establish communication requirements with an entity's management or owners unless they also are charged with a governance role.

In many instances, communication with the audit committee (or another equivalent subgroup of those charged with governance) adequately fulfills the auditor's responsibility to communicate with those charged with governance. Audit committees exist in many entities and are often responsible for oversight of the financial reporting process.

**PUBLIC COMPANY IMPLICATION:** Both the New York Stock Exchange and the NASDAQ require registrants to have audit committees. The Sarbanes-Oxley Act of 2002 (SOX) specifically mandates that the audit committee of a public company be directly responsible for the appointment, compensation, and oversight of the work of the auditor. In effect, the audit committee, and not the management, of a public company is to be viewed as "the client."

The auditor's determination of whether communication with the audit committee (or equivalent subgroup) fulfills the requirements to communicate with those charged with governance should include consideration of the following:

- The respective responsibilities of the governing body and the subgroup,
- The nature of the matter to be communicated,
- Relevant legal or regulatory requirements,
- The authority of the subgroup to take action in relation to the information communicated,
- The ability of the subgroup to provide further information and explanations needed by the auditor, and
- Whether there are potential conflicts of interest between the subgroup and the other members of the governing body.

In making this determination, the auditor should assess how effectively the subgroup communicates relevant information with the governing body. To protect communication channels, the auditor may include an explicit statement in the engagement terms retaining the right to communicate directly with the governing body. For many entities, the auditor will determine that the audit committee constitutes the appropriate communication recipients.

**OBSERVATION:** In evaluating audit committees or other subgroups of those charged with governance, the auditor should assess whether the audit committee or subgroup exercises good governance principles. Effective audit committee processes include facilitating access between the auditor and the audit committee, including regular meetings with the auditor and the audit committee chair and others on the audit committee, with at least one of those meetings each year occurring without management present.

## Matters to Be Communicated

*Auditor's responsibilities related to the financial statement audit*

The auditor should communicate to those charged with governance the auditor's responsibilities under auditing standards. These communications may include the following responsibilities:

- Performing the audit in accordance with GAAS and designing the audit for purposes of expressing an opinion on the financial statements. GAAS require matters to be communicated, including matters arising during the audit that are relevant to those charged with governance.
- Considering internal control over financial reporting for purposes of designing audit procedures, but not for purposes of expressing an opinion on the effectiveness of the entity's internal control over financial reporting.
- Communicating only those matters related to the financial statement audit that in the auditor's professional judgment are relevant to the financial reporting oversight responsibilities of those charged with governance.
- Communicating other matters required by laws or regulations, by agreement with the entity, or by additional engagement requirements.
- If engaged to communicate key audit matters, the auditor will be communicating those matters to those charged with governance.
- Communicating matters related to other information in the annual report.

**ENGAGEMENT STRATEGY:** The auditor may communicate these required matters regarding the auditor's GAAS responsibilities through an engagement letter or other form of written agreement, as long as that agreement is provided to those charged with governance.

While the auditor's report affirms the auditor's independence, it may be appropriate to communicate with those charged with governance circumstances or relationships such as financial interests, business or family relationships, or nonaudit services that the auditor considered in concluding that independence was not impaired.

**OBSERVATION:** It may be particularly appropriate to communicate matters that could bear on independence with those charged with governance in audits of public interest entities. Public interest entities include those subject to Securities and Exchange Commission reporting requirements as well as other entities with audited financial statements directly relied upon by significant numbers of stakeholders or indirectly relied upon through regulatory oversight such that an audit failure involving the entity could cause significant harm to the public.

*Overview of the planned scope and timing of the audit*

The auditor should communicate with those charged with governance an overview of the planned scope and timing of the audit. Communication of these matters may assist the auditor in better understanding the entity and its environment. These communications also assist those charged with governance in understanding better the consequences of the auditor's work for their oversight activities and help those charged with governance better understand the auditor's consideration of risks and materiality.

The auditor should exercise caution when communicating matters related to the planned scope and timing of the audit. It is important that the auditor's communication of these matters not compromise the effectiveness of the audit. This caution is especially relevant when those charged with governance are involved in managing the entity, such as an owner-manager. The auditor should avoid disclosing information that makes his or her audit procedures predictable. The auditor may broadly describe broad factors related to materiality, but avoid describing specific thresholds or amounts.

Typical matters related to the planned scope and timing that the auditor may communicate include the following:

- How the auditor plans to address significant risks of material misstatements;
- The auditor's approach to internal control;
- The application of materiality in the context of an audit; and
- The extent to which the auditor will use internal audit, if applicable.

Discussions with those charged with governance about the planned scope and timing of the audit may provide the auditor with useful insights about their attitude and actions. For example, the communications may reveal information about the attitudes, awareness, and actions of those charged with governance regarding their responsibilities for the oversight of the financial reporting process, including responsibility for internal control and assessing fraud risk.

Communications may provide the views of those charged with governance regarding issues such as the allocation of responsibilities between management and those charged with governance; the entity's strategies and related risks that could result in material misstatements, including how the auditor plans to address higher areas of risk concerns and communicate about significant risks; matters warranting particular attention during the audit; and significant communications with regulators. Discussions may also cover the actions of those charged with governance in response to previous communications with the auditor and in response to developments in laws, accounting standards, and corporate governance practices. If the auditor is engaged to communicate key audit matters, the auditor may communicate the auditor's views about areas that may be key audit matters.

If unexpected events, changes in conditions, or audit evidence obtained from the performance of procedures changes the overall audit strategy and audit plan, the auditor may communicate with those charged with governance about such matters and update initial discussions. The auditor may also communicate matters discussed with the engagement quality control reviewer.

*Significant findings from the audit*

A primary component of the required auditor communications is to inform those charged with governance about significant findings from the audit. Communications about significant findings from the audit include matters that directly relate to the financial reporting oversight of those charged with governance. Exhibit AU-C 260-1 summarizes the topics that AU-C 260 states should be communicated with those charged with governance and describes what the nature of those communications may include.

---

**ENGAGEMENT STRATEGY:** Audit evidence may include additional information requested from those charged with governance as part of the communication of significant findings. For example, the auditor may want to confirm that he or she has the same understanding of significant issues as those charged with governance.

---

**PLANNING AID REMINDER:** If the auditor encounters significant difficulties in the audit, such difficulties may constitute a scope limitation that leads to a modification of his or her opinion.

---

## The Communication Process

*Establishing the communication process*

Clear communications about the auditor's GAAS responsibilities, the planned audit scope and timing, and the nature of expected communications strengthen the communications between the auditor and those charged with governance. Thus, AU-C 260 requires the auditor to establish a mutual understanding of these matters with those charged with governance. If the terms of engagement are agreed upon with those charged with governance, the auditor may provide those charged with governance a copy of the engagement letter to communicate about matters relevant to the audit.

Clarification of the purpose, form, and process of the required communications with those charged with governance in advance of making the required communications contributes to effective two-way communication. Explicit understanding about the auditor's expectation that the communication is designed to be a two-way communication reinforces to those charged with governance the importance of their providing relevant information to the auditor that might affect the audit of financial statements, including any modifications to the audit report. AU-C 260 does not preclude the auditor from discussing matters with management or the internal auditor before communicating with those charged with governance when appropriate.

*Form of communication*

For a matter not required to be communicated in writing, whether to communicate orally or in writing is determined by the auditor's judgment. In making those determinations, the auditor should consider the following matters:

- Significance of the particular matter;
- Whether the matter has been satisfactorily resolved and whether it will be included in the auditor's report;
- Whether management previously communicated the matter to those charged with governance;
- The size, operating structure, control environment, and legal structure of the entity;
- Legal or regulatory requirements to communicate certain audit findings in writing;
- Amount of ongoing contact and dialogue the auditor has with those charged with governance and the expectations of those charged with governance; and
- Whether there have been significant changes in the composition and membership of the governing body.

**ENGAGEMENT STRATEGY:** If a matter is discussed with an individual member of those charged with governance, the auditor may summarize the matter in later communications to ensure that all of those charged with governance have full and balanced information.

**ENGAGEMENT STRATEGY:** Documentation of oral communication may include entity-prepared copies of minutes if they are an appropriate record of the communication.

**IMPORTANT NOTICE FOR 2022:** In May 2019, the AICPA's Auditing Standards Board (ASB) issued SAS No. 135 titled *Omnibus Statement on Auditing Standards—2019* that includes amendments to various AU-C sections. SAS No. 135 incorporates some of the guidance in PCAOB Auditing Standards related to communications with audit committees. SAS No. 135 notes that if management communicated some or all of the matters the auditor is required to communicate and, as a result, the auditor did not communicate these matters at the same level of detail as management, the auditor should include a copy or summary of management's communications provided to those charged with governance in the audit documentation. Originally, the effective date of SAS No. 135 was for audits of financial statements periods ending on or after December 15, 2020, with early application **not** permitted. However, the ASB's issuance of SAS No. 141, *Amendment to the Effective Dates of SAS Nos. 134-140*, extended the effective date of SAS No. 135 to December 15, 2021, in order to provide more time for firms to implement SAS No. 135 in light of the effect of the coronavirus pandemic. While SAS No. 141 allows for early implementation of SAS No. 135, the ASB recommends that SAS Nos. 134-140 be implemented concurrently.

*Timing of communication*

The appropriate timing of communications will vary with the circumstances, depending on the significance and nature of the matter and the action expected to be taken by those charged with governance. Matters related to audit planning, such as the overview of the auditor's responsibilities and the planned scope and timing of the audit, are likely to be discussed early in the engagement as part of clarifying the terms of the engagement. Significant findings from the audit may be communicated as they are encountered (e.g., significant difficulties, uncorrected misstatements, matters requiring significant auditor attention, significant findings, etc.) so that they can be overcome in a timely fashion. The auditor may also communicate preliminary views on key audit matters, if engaged to report on key audit matters.

*Adequacy of communication*

The evaluation of the two-way communication between the auditor and those charged with governance can be supported based on observations from audit procedures performed for other purposes. Such observations of those charged with governance may include:

- Appropriateness and timeliness of actions taken in response to matters communicated by the auditor;
- Apparent openness in communications with the auditor;
- Willingness and capacity to meet with the auditor without management present;
- Apparent ability to understand matters raised by the auditor, often exhibited by extent of probing and questioning recommendations;
- Difficulty in establishing a mutual understanding of the form, timing, and expected general content of communications; and
- For those charged with governance also involved in managing the entity, awareness of how matters discussed with the auditor affect their governance and management responsibilities.

Inadequate communication may signal an ineffective control environment, which should impact the auditor's assessment of risk of material misstatements, and it may signal an increased risk that the auditor may not have obtained all the audit evidence required to form an opinion on the financial statements. To address concerns about the adequacy of the communications, the auditor may discuss concerns with those charged with governance. If the situation remains unresolved, the auditor may consider modifying the opinion on the financial statements due to a scope limitation, obtaining legal advice, communicating with those outside the entity (e.g., regulators, shareholders, responsible government agencies), or withdrawing from the engagement.

AU-C 260 does not change requirements in other standards to communicate certain matters to those charged with governance. The following communications required by other standards remain in effect:

- Communications with the audit committee or others with equivalent authority and responsibility pertaining to illegal acts that come to the auditor's attention (see AU-C 250).
- Communications to management and the audit committee or others with equivalent authority and responsibility when the auditor becomes aware during the audit that the entity is subject to an audit requirement that may not be encompassed in the terms of the engagement, and that an audit in accordance with generally accepted auditing standards may not satisfy the relevant legal, regulatory, or contractual requirements (see AU-C 935).
- Required direct inquiry of the audit committee (or at least its chair) regarding the audit committee's views about the risk of fraud and whether the audit committee has knowledge of any fraud or suspected fraud affecting the entity (see AU-C 240).
- Communications to those charged with governance about fraud caused by senior management and fraud (whether caused by senior management or others) that causes a material misstatement in the financial statements (see AU-C 240).
- Communications in writing to management and those charged with governance regarding control deficiencies identified during an audit that upon evaluation are considered to be significant deficiencies or material weaknesses (see AU-C 265).
- Consideration of communication of the nature of significant assumptions used in fair value measurements, the degree of subjectivity involved in the development of the assumption, and the relative materiality of the items being measured at fair value to the financial statements as a whole (see AU-C 540).
- Communications with those charged with governance regarding the auditor's responsibility with respect to other information, any procedures performed relating to the other information, and the results (see AU-C 720).

## Practitioner's Aid

Exhibit AU-C 260-1 presents examples of significant findings from the audit that generally are communicated by the auditor to those charged with governance.

# EXHIBIT AU-C 260-1 TOPIC AND NATURE OF COMMUNICATIONS ABOUT SIGNIFICANT FINDINGS

| Topic of Communication | Nature of Communication |
|---|---|
| Qualitative aspects of entity's significant accounting practices | • Appropriateness and acceptability of accounting policies to the circumstances |
| | • Initial selection of and changes to accounting policies, including application of new pronouncements |
| | • Effect of significant accounting policies in controversial or emerging areas |
| | • Effect of the timing of transactions in relation to the period they are recorded |
| | • Identification of and process used to make accounting estimates |
| | • Indicators of possible management bias |
| | • Risks of material misstatement due to significant accounting estimates |
| | • Financial statement disclosure of estimation uncertainty |
| | • Issues involved and judgments made in preparing sensitive financial statement disclosures |
| | • Overall neutrality, consistency, and clarity of disclosures in financial statements |
| | • Extent to which financial statements are potentially impacted by significant disclosed uncertainties, unusual transactions, and selective correction of misstatements |
| | • Factors affecting asset and liability carrying values |
| Significant difficulties encountered during the audit | • Significant delays in management providing required information |
| | • Unnecessarily short time frame to complete the audit |
| | • Extensive unexpected effort required to obtain sufficient, appropriate evidence |
| | • Restrictions imposed by management on the auditors |
| | • Unavailability of expected information |
| | • Management unwilling to provide information about plans to deal with conditions that led the auditor to believe there is substantial doubt about the entity's ability to continue as a going concern |
| Significant unusual transactions | • Auditor views on the policies and practices management used to account for significant unusual transactions |
| | • Auditor's understanding of the business purpose for significant unusual transactions |
| Disagreements with management | • Disagreements with management are required to be communicated (whether or not satisfactorily resolved) about matters that individually or in the aggregate could be significant to the financial statements |

| Topic of Communication | Nature of Communication |
|---|---|
| | • Significant disagreements with management concerning applicability of accounting principles, scope of the engagement, or wording of the audit report |
| Uncorrected misstatements | • Information about overall number and monetary effect of individually immaterial uncorrected misstatements |
| | • Discussion of the implications of failure to correct known and likely misstatements |
| Corrected misstatements | • Any corrected immaterial misstatements that could indicate a particular bias in financial statement preparation |
| Significant issues discussed or subject to correspondence with management | • Issues may include business conditions affecting the entity that increase the risk of material misstatement and discussions in connection with the retention of the auditor or discussions about the application of accounting principles and auditing standards |
| Written representations | • Provision of a copy of management's written representations to those charged with governance |

# SECTION 265

## COMMUNICATING INTERNAL CONTROL RELATED MATTERS IDENTIFIED IN AN AUDIT

### Authoritative Pronouncements

SAS-122—Statements on Auditing Standards: Clarification and Recodification

SAS-130—An Audit of Internal Control over Financial Reporting That Is Integrated with an Audit of Financial Statements

SAS-135—Omnibus Statement on Auditing Standards—2019

SAS Interpretation 1—Communication of Significant Deficiencies and Material Weaknesses Prior to Completion of the Compliance Audit for Participants in Office of Management and Budget Single Audit Act Pilot Project

SAS Interpretation 2—Communication of Significant Deficiencies and Material Weaknesses Prior to Completion of the Compliance Audit for Auditors That Are Not Participants in Office of Management and Budget Single Audit Act Pilot Project

SAS Interpretation 3—Appropriateness of Identifying No Significant Deficiencies or No Material Weaknesses in an Interim Communication

### Overview

AU-C 265 provides the auditor with guidance on appropriately communicating internal control deficiencies identified during the audit to those charged with governance and management. The auditor may identify internal control deficiencies while identifying and assessing the risks of material misstatement as well as during other phases of the audit. AU-C 265 specifies which identified deficiencies are required to be communicated to those charged with governance and management. However, the auditor is not precluded from communicating other identified internal control matters that are not required to be communicated.

> **PLANNING AID REMINDER:** AU-C 265 is not applicable if the auditor is engaged to perform an audit of internal control over financial reporting that is integrated with a financial statement audit. AU-C 940 (*An Audit of Internal Control Over Financial Reporting That Is Integrated With an Audit of Financial Statements*) applies in these circumstances.

> **PUBLIC COMPANY IMPLICATIONS:** The Sarbanes-Oxley Act of 2002 (SOX) requires the auditor of an accelerated filer public company to issue a report on the operating effectiveness of its internal control over financial reporting. The audit of internal controls and the audit of the financial statements of a public company are to be integrated. In order to provide reasonable assurance about

the operating effectiveness of internal controls, the auditor is to perform tests of controls over financial reporting. Information about significant deficiencies and material weaknesses obtained through work performed as part of the financial statement audit should be considered when reporting on internal controls (and vice versa).

## Definitions

| | |
|---|---|
| Deficiency in internal control over financial reporting | Exists when the design or operation of a control does not allow management or employees, in the normal course of performing their assigned functions, to prevent or detect and correct misstatements on a timely basis. |
| | A *design* deficiency exists when a control needed to meet the control objective is missing or an existing control is not properly designed such that the control objective would not be met even if the control operated as designed. |
| | A deficiency in *operation* exists when a properly designed control does not operate as designed or when the person performing the control does not have the necessary authority or competence to effectively perform the control. |
| Material weakness | A deficiency or combination of deficiencies in internal control over financial reporting such that there is a reasonable possibility that a material misstatement of the entity's financial statements will not be prevented or detected and corrected on a timely basis. A reasonable possibility exists when the likelihood of an event is either reasonably possible, where the likelihood of occurrence is more than remote but less than likely, or probable, where the event is likely to occur. |
| Reasonably possible | The chance of the future event or events occurring is more than remote but less than likely. |
| Probable | The future event or events are likely to occur. |
| Significant deficiency | A deficiency or combination of deficiencies in internal control over financial reporting that is less severe than a material weakness yet important enough to merit attention by those charged with governance. |

**PUBLIC COMPANY IMPLICATIONS:** PCAOB Staff Audit Practice Alert No. 11 (*Considerations for Audits of Internal Control over Financial Reporting*) identifies common deficiencies in audits of internal control over financial reporting (ICFR), and highlights factors for auditors to consider when performing audits of ICFR. Common inspection deficiencies related to ICFR audits include the auditor's failure to (1) identify and sufficiently test controls relevant to the risk of material misstatement, (2) sufficiently test the design and operating effectiveness of management review controls, (3) sufficiently update the results from testing controls at an interim date to year-end, (4) sufficiently test controls over system-generated data, (5) adequately test the work of others, and (6) adequately evaluate identified control deficiencies. The Audit Practice Alert provides guidance to auditors in risk assessment, selecting controls to test, testing management review controls, testing information technology controls (including controls over systems-generated data and reports), roll-forward testing of controls, using the work of others, and evaluating identified control deficiencies.

## Requirements

The auditor is presumptively required to perform the following procedures with respect to the communication of internal control related matters to management and those charged with governance:

1. Determine whether internal control deficiencies have been identified based on the audit work performed.
2. If internal control deficiencies have been identified, determine whether they constitute significant deficiencies or material weaknesses individually or in combination based on audit work performed.
3. If an internal control deficiency or combination of deficiencies is initially determined to not be a material weakness, consider whether prudent officials using the same facts and circumstances would likely reach the same conclusion.
4. Communicate significant deficiencies and material weaknesses identified during the audit, including those that were remediated during the audit, in writing to those charged with governance on a timely basis.
5. Communicate to management at an appropriate level of responsibility on a timely basis:
    a. In writing, unless doing so is inappropriate, significant deficiencies and material weaknesses communicated or intended to be communicated with those charged with governance.
    b. In writing or orally, other internal control deficiencies identified during the audit not otherwise communicated to management that the auditor judges to be sufficiently important to merit management's attention. If these deficiencies are communicated orally, document the communication.
6. Communications to those charged with governance and management should be made no later than 60 days following the report release date.
7. Written communication of significant deficiencies and material weaknesses should include:
    a. The definitions of the terms "material weakness" and, when relevant, "significant deficiency."
    b. A description of the material weaknesses and significant deficiencies and an explanation of their potential effects.
    c. Sufficient information for those charged with governance and management to understand the context of the communication, including explanations that (1) the audit's purpose was to express an opinion on the financial statements; (2) the audit included consideration of internal control over financial reporting to design appropriate audit procedures, but not to express an opinion on the effectiveness of

internal control; (3) the auditor is not expressing an opinion on internal control effectiveness; and (4) the auditor's consideration of internal control was not designed to identify all deficiencies that might be significant deficiencies or material weaknesses, so unidentified deficiencies, significant deficiencies, or material weaknesses may exist.

   d. A restriction on the use of the communication to those charged with governance, management, others within the organization, and any specified governmental authority to which the auditor is required to report.

8. A written communication issued stating that no material weaknesses were identified during the audit should include the matters described in paragraph 7(a), (c), and (d).

9. A written communication should *not* be issued that states that no significant deficiencies were identified in an audit.

## Analysis and Application of Procedures

*Identifying Deficiencies in Internal Control and Evaluating Their Severity*

The auditor is required to obtain an understanding of internal control relevant to the audit when identifying and assessing the risks of material misstatement. In making those risk assessments and when performing further audit procedures in response to those risks, the auditor may identify deficiencies in internal control. While the purpose of the audit is not to express an opinion on internal controls, the auditor may identify deficiencies that would be appropriate to communicate to those charged with governance. AU-C 265 provides guidance regarding those communications.

The auditor may communicate his or her findings with management when determining whether internal control deficiencies have been identified. It is appropriate to discuss these issues with a level of management familiar with the internal control area in question and with the authority to take remedial actions on any control deficiencies identified. The auditor may obtain other relevant information to consider from these discussions such as:

- Management's understanding of the actual or suspected causes of deficiencies,
- Exceptions management may have noted that arose from deficiencies, and
- Preliminary indications from management of its response to the findings.

**OBSERVATION:** Smaller, less complex entities may have less segregation of duties or more informal controls than larger organizations. However, this may not indicate that control deficiencies exist, because management authority and oversight may act effectively as controls, reducing the need for more detailed control activities.

> **PLANNING AID REMINDER:** An auditor may decide not to test controls and instead perform all substantive audit procedures. AICPA Technical Practice Aid 8200.15 notes that the decision to not test controls does not automatically mean there is a control deficiency that must be evaluated. If the auditor decides not to test a control because it is nonexistent or is not properly designed, then that would represent a control deficiency that needs to be assessed in order to determine whether it is a significant deficiency or material weakness. If the design of the control is appropriate but the auditor decides not to test it for other reasons, then he or she has not identified a control deficiency.

AU-C 265 requires the auditor to determine whether identified control deficiencies, individually or in combination, are significant deficiencies or material weaknesses. The determination of whether a control deficiency constitutes a significant deficiency or material weakness is a matter of professional judgment. When making this determination, the auditor considers the likelihood and magnitude of misstatement.

> **PLANNING AID REMINDER:** The auditor is not obtaining an understanding of internal control for the purpose of expressing an opinion on internal control. Thus, significant deficiencies and material weaknesses may exist even if the auditor has not identified misstatements during the audit.

> **PLANNING AID REMINDER:** Internal control deficiencies might be discovered during various phases of the engagement. Deficiencies can be related to any of the five components of internal control. In addition, deficiencies can arise because of poor design or poor operation of the control. For example, a deficiency could be related to lack of proper segregation of duties and responsibilities (design within internal control) or lack of timely preparation of bank reconciliations (execution within internal control).

Several factors can affect the likelihood that a deficiency might fail to prevent or detect and correct a misstatement. Examples of such factors include the nature of the account balance or transaction, the susceptibility of assets or liabilities to loss, the subjectivity, complexity, and judgment required to determine the amount involved, the cause and frequency of exceptions due to the control deficiency, the interactions of the control with other controls and other control deficiencies, and the importance of the controls to the financial reporting process.

The magnitude of the misstatement caused by a control deficiency may be affected by size of the financial statement amounts or disclosures impacted by the deficiency and by the volume of activity in an account balance or class of transactions. The magnitude of a potential misstatement is generally limited to overstating an account balance or transaction total by the recorded amount, while understatements could be larger. Some control deficiencies may be individually insignificant; however, when combined with other deficiencies that affect the same account balance or disclosure, the combination of deficiencies can increase the risks of misstatement to the extent that a significant deficiency or material weakness exists.

AU-C 265 identifies specific indicators of material weaknesses in internal control:

- Ineffective oversight of the entity's financial reporting and internal control by those charged with governance.
- Restatement of previously issued financial statements to reflect the correction of a misstatement.
- Identification by the auditor of a material misstatement in the financial statements not initially identified by the entity's internal control.
- Identification of fraud of any magnitude on the part of senior management.

Exhibit AU-C 265-1 provides guidance regarding what items may be considered deficiencies in internal control over financial reporting.

*Communicating internal control deficiencies*

AU-C 265 requires the auditor's communication of significant deficiencies and material weaknesses to be in writing. This communication requirement applies to all significant deficiencies or material weaknesses identified during the current audit in addition to significant deficiencies and material weaknesses communicated in previous audits that have not yet been remediated. If the entity has chosen not to act on a previously identified significant deficiency or material weakness with no rational explanation, that decision could constitute a significant deficiency or material weakness.

The timing of required written communications is best if made by the report release date, although AU-C 265's requirement is that the written communication be made no later than 60 days after the report release date. Some matters may be communicated to management or those charged with governance at an earlier date to allow management the opportunity to remediate the deficiency on a timely basis. The early communication does not have to be in writing, however, the auditor must ultimately communicate all significant deficiencies and material weaknesses in writing.

**OBSERVATION:** For some significant deficiencies or material weaknesses, management or those charged with governance may make a conscious decision to accept the risk of the deficiency leading to a material misstatement due to the cost or other considerations associated with remediating the deficiency. Despite management's decision, the auditor is still required to communicate all significant deficiencies and material weaknesses.

**PUBLIC COMPANY IMPLICATIONS:** In the audit of internal control over financial reporting required by SOX for public companies, the presence of one or more material weaknesses prohibits the auditor from concluding that internal control over financial reporting is operating effectively.

The level of detail the auditor communicates regarding identified significant deficiencies and material weaknesses is subject to the auditor's professional judgment. Factors that may impact the level of detail communicated include the nature, size, and complexity of the entity; the nature of the significant deficiencies and material weaknesses identified; the entity's governance composition; and any legal or regulatory requirements about the communication of internal control deficiencies.

**PLANNING AID REMINDER:** In some circumstances, it may not be appropriate for the auditor to communicate significant deficiencies and material weaknesses to management because identified deficiencies may cause the auditor to question management's integrity or competence. In these situations, the auditor should, as appropriate, follow the guidance in either AU-C 250 on reporting identified or suspected noncompliance with laws and regulations when those charged with governance are involved in the noncompliance or AU-C 240 on communicating to those charged with governance when fraud or suspected fraud involving management has been identified.

If deficiencies other than significant deficiencies or material weaknesses have been reported to management in a prior period and management has chosen not to remedy the deficiencies, the auditor does not need to communicate the deficiencies again during the current audit. However, if there has been a change in management or new information has arisen affecting the auditor's understanding of the deficiencies, the auditor may find it appropriate to recommunicate these deficiencies. The failure of management to remedy previously communicated internal control deficiencies may constitute a significant deficiency that requires communication with those charged with governance. When reporting on other internal control deficiencies identified in the audit, those charged with governance may wish to be informed of any such deficiencies communicated to management.

**OBSERVATION:** The appropriate level of management is the one that has responsibility and authority to evaluate the deficiencies in internal control and to take necessary remedial action. For significant deficiencies and material weaknesses, the appropriate level is likely to be the CEO or CFO. Other deficiencies might be appropriately communicated to operational management.

While the auditor should explain the potential effects of the deficiencies in his or her written communication of significant deficiencies and material weaknesses, the effects do not need to be quantified. Other items the auditor may include in the written communication include the following:

- Inherent limitations of internal control, including the potential for management override of controls;
- The specific nature and extent of the auditor's consideration of internal control during the audit;
- Suggestions for remedial action on identified deficiencies; and
- Management's actual or proposed responses and a statement about whether the auditor has taken any steps to verify if management's responses have been implemented.

Management may prepare a written response to the auditor's communication regarding significant deficiencies and material weaknesses. This response may include information such as a description of corrective actions taken by the entity, the entity's plans to implement new controls, or a statement indicating that management believes the costs of correcting a deficiency outweigh the benefits. If such a response is included in a document containing the auditor's written communication of significant deficiencies and material weaknesses, the auditor may add a paragraph such as the following to his or her written communication disclaiming an opinion on management's response:

> X Corporation's written response to the significant deficiencies [*and material weaknesses*] identified in our audit was not subjected to the auditing procedures applied in the audit of the financial statements and, accordingly, we express no opinion on it.

A written communication stating that no material weaknesses were identified in the audit does not provide any assurance about the effectiveness of an entity's internal control over financial reporting. However, management or those charged with governance may request that this communication be made or it may be required by some governmental entities and the auditor is not precluded from issuing such a communication. The auditor is precluded from issuing a written communication indicating that no significant deficiencies were identified during the audit due to its potential to be misunderstood or misused.

## Practitioner's Aids

Exhibit AU-C 265-1 includes examples from AU-C 265 of circumstances that indicate possible control deficiencies, significant deficiencies, or material weaknesses. Exhibit AU-C 265-2 is an example of a written communication encompassing AU-C 265's requirements. Exhibit AU-C 265-3 contains examples of possible material weaknesses for a small business enterprise.

### *EXHIBIT AU-C 265-1—EXAMPLES OF POSSIBLE DEFICIENCIES*

- Deficiencies in internal control design
    - —Inadequate overall internal control design over financial statement preparation
    - —Inadequate design over a significant account or process
    - —Inadequate documentation of internal control
    - —Insufficient control consciousness across the organization

—Evidence of ineffective aspects of the control environment

—Evidence of an ineffective entity risk assessment process

—Evidence of an ineffective response to identified significant risks

—Inadequate segregation of duties

—Absent or inadequate controls over safeguarding of assets

—Inadequate design of information technology general and application controls

—Unqualified or inadequately trained employees or management

—Inadequate design of monitoring controls

—Absence of an internal process to report deficiencies in internal control to management on a timely basis

—Absence of a risk assessment process in an entity where one would ordinarily be established

- Failures in the operation of internal control

—Evidence of failure in the operation of an effectively designed control over a significant account or process

—Evidence of failure of the information and communication component of internal control to provide complete and accurate output because of deficiencies in timeliness, completeness, or accuracy

—Evidence of failure of controls designed to safeguard assets from loss, damage, or misappropriation

—Lack of performance of reconciliations of significant accounts

—Presence of undue bias or lack of objectivity by those responsible for accounting decisions

—Misrepresentation by client personnel to the auditor

—Management override of controls

—Failure of an application control caused by a deficiency in the design or operation of an IT general control

—An observed deviation rate exceeding the auditor's expected deviation rate in a test of the operating effectiveness of a control

---

## EXHIBIT AU-C 265-2—EXAMPLE OF A WRITTEN COMMUNICATION ABOUT SIGNIFICANT DEFICIENCIES AND MATERIAL WEAKNESSES

To Management and [*identify the body or individuals charged with governance, such as the entity's Board of Directors*] of X Corporation

In planning and performing our audit of the financial statements of X Corporation as of and for the year ended December 31, 20X5, in accordance with auditing standards generally accepted in the United States of America, we considered X Corporation's internal control over financial reporting (internal control) as a basis for designing audit procedures that are appropriate in the circumstances for the purpose of expressing our opinion on the financial statements, but not for the purpose of expressing an opinion on the effectiveness of X

Corporation's internal control. Accordingly, we do not express an opinion on the effectiveness of the company's internal control.

Our consideration of internal control was for the limited purpose described in the preceding paragraph and was not designed to identify all deficiencies in internal control that might be [*material weaknesses or significant deficiencies or material weaknesses*] and therefore, [*material weaknesses or significant deficiencies or material weaknesses*] may exist that were not identified. However, as discussed below, we identified certain deficiencies in internal control that we consider to be [*material weaknesses* or *significant deficiencies* or *material weaknesses and significant deficiencies*].

A deficiency in internal control exists when the design or operation of a control does not allow management or employees, in the normal course of performing their assigned functions, to prevent, or detect and correct, misstatements on a timely basis. A material weakness is a deficiency, or combination of deficiencies, in internal control, such that there is a reasonable possibility that a material misstatement of the entity's financial statements will not be prevented, or detected and corrected, on a timely basis. [*We consider the following deficiencies in X Corporation's internal control to be material weaknesses:*]

[*Describe the material weaknesses that were identified and explain their potential effects.*]

[*A significant deficiency is a deficiency, or combination of deficiencies, in internal control that is less severe than a material weakness, yet important enough to merit attention by those charged with governance. We consider the following deficiencies in X Corporation's internal control to be significant deficiencies:*]

[*Describe the significant deficiencies that were identified and explain their potential effects.*]

[*If the auditor is communicating significant deficiencies and did not identify any material weaknesses, the auditor may state that none of the identified significant deficiencies are considered to be material weaknesses.*]

This communication is intended solely for the information and use of management, [*identify those charged with governance*], others within the organization, and [*identify any governmental authorities to which the auditor is required to report*] and is not intended to be and should not be used by anyone other than these specified parties.

[*Auditor's Signature*]

[*Date*]

---

## EXHIBIT AU-C 265-3—EXAMPLES OF POSSIBLE MATERIAL WEAKNESSES: SMALL BUSINESS ENTERPRISE

Determining whether a specific condition is a material weakness is based on exercising professional judgment in the context of the existing characteristics of a particular client. The following list includes examples of conditions that the auditor may identify as a material weakness for a small business enterprise. The list is illustrative only and is not intended to be comprehensive. Also, because the assumption is that the client is a small business enterprise, there is an emphasis on cash and related cash transactions, inventory, and property, plant, and equipment.

- *Cash and credit sales*

    —Credit sales are approved by the bookkeeper, who is responsible for the write-off of bad debts.

    —A bookkeeper maintains cash receipts records, opens the mail, and prepares the bank deposit.

    —Cash payments for expenditures using cash receipts for the day.

    —Cash receipts are deposited at the end of the week, net of expenditures paid during the week.

    —Several sales clerks have access to the single cash drawer used during the day to record cash sales.

    —Cash registers used during the day are not read and reconciled after the end of each shift.

    —A bookkeeper is responsible for the purchase of goods and services.

    —There is no formal documentation that shows that goods purchased were received.

    —Documentation to support cash disbursements is maintained on a haphazard basis.

    —The office manager authorizes the payment of invoices, prepares checks, and reconciles the bank statements.

- *Cash and purchases of goods and services*

    —Purchase orders are not used to authorize the acquisition of goods and services.

    —Invoices and other supporting documentation are not marked as "cancelled" or "paid."

    —The hiring and firing of employees is not centralized.

    —Paychecks are given to an immediate supervisor for distribution.

    —The number of hours or days worked is not controlled through the use of time clocks or otherwise approved by supervisory personnel.

    —An unusually large amount of petty cash is maintained, and support for expenditures is lacking.

    —Numerous checking accounts are used, and prenumbered checks are not accounted for.

    —Numerous employees are authorized to sign checks.

    —Checks are often written to "cash."

    —Bank reconciliations are seldom prepared.

- *Inventory controls*

    —The periodic inventory count is not under the control of the owner or manager.

    —The inventory is not subject to reasonable limited access (for both employees and customers) based on the characteristics of the business.

—Inventory shipments to customers are not based on appropriate shipping authorization.

—Inventory receipts are not properly counted and inspected.

—The year-end inventory summarization is not analyzed and evaluated by the owner or manager for unusual variations in gross profit percentages, obsolete inventory lines, unreasonable inventory counts, missing items, inappropriate cost data, etc.

- *Property, plant, and equipment*

    —A plant ledger is not maintained.

    —The owner or manager does not periodically verify the existence and condition of property items.

    —The sale of used property items is not approved by the owner or manager.

# AU-C 300 & 400
# Risk Assessment and Response to Assessed Risks

| Section 300: | Planning an Audit ............................... | 3002 |
| Section 315: | Understanding the Entity and Its Environment and Assessing the Risks of Material Misstatements ................ | 3017 |
| Section 320: | Materiality in Planning and Performing an Audit .......... | 3060 |
| Section 330: | Performing Audit Procedures in Response to Assessed Risks and Evaluating the Audit Evidence Obtained ........... | 3067 |
| Section 402: | Audit Considerations Relating to an Entity Using a Service Organization ................................. | 4001 |
| Section 450: | Evaluation of Misstatements Identified During the Audit ..... | 4012 |

# SECTION 300

# PLANNING AN AUDIT

## Authoritative Pronouncements

SAS-122—Statements on Auditing Standards: Clarification and Recodification

SAS-134—Auditor Reporting and Amendments, Including Amendments Addressing Disclosures in the Audit of Financial Statements

SAS-141—Amendment to Effective Dates of SAS Nos. 134-140

## Overview

AU-C 300 recognizes that the successful completion of an audit engagement is a difficult task and, like most difficult tasks, requires proper planning. The auditor's objective is to plan the audit so that it is performed effectively. AU-C 300 primarily considers the auditor's responsibility to plan an audit in the context of a recurring audit. Additional considerations relevant to initial audit engagements are addressed in AU-C 600 (*Special Considerations—Audits of Group Financial Statements (Including the Work of Component Auditors)*).

Adequate planning of an audit benefits the financial statement audit in many ways, including:

- Helping to identify important areas of the audit and potential problems in a timely manner;
- Determining personnel requirements;
- Determining how to use a firm's resources in an effective and efficient manner;
- Helping in the direction, supervision, and review of the work of engagement team members; and
- Helping with any necessary coordination of work done by auditors of components and specialists.

The nature, timing, and extent of planning depend on (1) the size and complexity of the entity, (2) the auditor's previous experience serving the entity, and (3) changes in circumstances that occur during the audit engagement.

The audit plan must be responsive to the auditor's identification of the risk of material misstatement. Although planning begins before the auditor begins fieldwork, planning is not a discrete process but, rather, is an iterative process that continues until the current audit engagement is completed. As the auditor performs planned audit procedures, he or she considers the need to revise the nature, timing, and extent of audit procedures that were selected during the initial phase of planning the audit.

§ 300 • Planning an Audit    3003

**IMPORTANT NOTICE FOR 2022:** In May 2019, the AICPA's Auditing Standards Board (ASB) issued SAS No. 134 titled *Auditor Reporting and Amendments, Including Amendments Addressing Disclosures in the Audit of Financial Statements* to revise the auditor's report and to amend various AU-C sections to heighten the auditor's focus on disclosures throughout the process of auditing financial statements. SAS No. 134 focuses the auditor's attention on disclosures earlier in the process of auditing financial statements by amending AU-C 300 to emphasize the importance of giving appropriate attention to, and planning adequate time for addressing disclosures in the same way as classes of transactions, events, and account balances, and early consideration of matters such as significant new or revised disclosures. This consideration would include the processes management uses to identify and prepare the disclosures required by the applicable financial reporting framework, including disclosures containing information that is obtained from outside the general and subsidiary ledgers. Originally, the effective date of SAS No. 134 was for audits of financial statements periods ending on or after December 15, 2020, with early implementation **not** permitted. However, the ASB's issuance of SAS No. 141, *Amendment to the Effective Dates of SAS Nos. 134-140*, extended the effective date of SAS No. 134 to December 15, 2021, in order to provide more time for firms to implement SAS No. 134 in light of the effect of the coronavirus pandemic. While SAS No. 141 allows for early implementation of SAS No. 134, the ASB recommends that SAS Nos. 134-140 be implemented concurrently.

---

**PUBLIC COMPANY IMPLICATION:** PCAOB Auditing Standards AS-2101 (*Audit Planning*) and AS-1201 (*Supervision of the Audit Engagement*) contain guidance related to audit planning and supervision. AS-2101 establishes requirements related to planning the audit, including requirements related to developing an appropriate audit strategy and audit plan. AS-1201 describes the auditor's responsibilities for supervising the engagement, and it applies to the engagement partner and other audit team members who assist the partner in supervising others. Although there are a number of differences between the PCAOB's and the ASB's standards, the risk-assessment concepts contained in the PCAOB standards should be familiar to most auditors. As is currently the case, audit risk is the risk that the auditor will issue an inappropriate opinion on financial statements that are materially misstated. The auditor is to reduce audit risk to a low level through the application of audit procedures. As a result, the amount of audit effort devoted to particular accounts, classes of transactions, and disclosures should vary based on their respective risk.

---

## Requirements

The auditor is presumptively required to perform the following procedures related to planning an audit:

1. The engagement partner and other key engagement team members should be involved in planning the audit. This includes planning and participating in the engagement team member discussion.

2. At the beginning of the current audit engagement, perform the following activities:
    a. Perform procedures regarding continuing the client relationship and the specific audit engagement as required by AU-C 220 (*Quality Control for an Engagement Conducted in Accordance with Generally Accepted Auditing Standards*).
    b. Evaluate compliance with ethical requirements, including independence, as required by AU-C 220.
    c. Establish an understanding of the engagement terms as required by AU-C 210 (*Terms of Engagement*).
3. Establish an overall audit strategy setting the scope, timing, and direction of the audit and that guides development of the audit plan. In establishing the audit strategy, the auditor should:
    a. Identify the engagement's characteristics defining its scope;
    b. Determine the engagement's reporting objectives in order to plan the audit's timing and the nature of the required communications;
    c. Consider significant factors, determined using professional judgment, directing the engagement team's efforts;
    d. Consider the results of preliminary engagement activities and whether any knowledge the engagement partner gained on other engagements performed for the entity is relevant; and
    e. Determine the nature, extent, and timing of resources necessary to perform the engagement.
4. Develop an audit plan, including descriptions of:
    a. The nature and extent of planned risk assessment procedures as determined by AU-C 315;
    b. The nature, timing, and extent of planned further audit procedures at the relevant assertion level as determined by AU-C 330; and
    c. Other planned audit procedures that are required for the engagement to comply with GAAS.
5. Update and revise the overall audit strategy and plan as necessary during the course of the audit.
6. Plan the nature, timing, and extent of direction and supervision of engagement team members and review of their work.
7. Consider whether specialized skills are needed to perform the audit and, if they are, seek the assistance of an audit staff professional or an outside professional. The auditor should have sufficient knowledge to communicate the objectives of the other professional's work; evaluate whether the specified audit procedures will meet the auditor's objectives; and evaluate the results of the audit procedures applied as they relate to the nature, timing, and extent of further planned audit procedures.

8. Document (1) the overall audit strategy, (2) the audit plan, and (3) any significant changes made during the audit engagement to the overall audit strategy or plan and the reasons for those changes.
9. Perform the following activities prior to starting an initial audit:
   a. Perform procedures regarding the acceptance of the client relationship and specific audit engagement as required by AU-C 220.
   b. Communicate with the predecessor auditor when there is a change of auditors in accordance with AU-C 210.

## Analysis and Application of Procedures

*Discussion among Key Engagement Team Members*

Key engagement team members are required to discuss the risks of material misstatement of the financial statements due to error or fraud. This discussion improves the effectiveness and efficiency of the planning process by drawing on the experience of the engagement partner and other team members and by helping team members understand how the results of audit procedures they perform may affect other aspects of the audit, such as the nature, timing, and extent of further audit procedures.

*Preliminary Engagement Activities*

The required preliminary engagement activities allow the auditor to assess certain conditions relating to the audit. One important aspect evaluated with these procedures is management integrity. The auditor also needs to ascertain that he or she is independent and that there is no misunderstanding with the client regarding engagement terms before commencing the audit engagement.

For a continuing engagement, these preliminary procedures often occur shortly after the completion of the previous audit engagement.

---

**PLANNING AID REMINDER:** Although the auditor evaluates client continuance, ethical requirements, and independence before commencing the engagement, he or she needs to monitor these aspects throughout the period of the professional engagement.

---

*Develop an Overall Strategy for the Audit Engagement*

The specific audit strategy for an engagement is based on the characteristics of the client. Specific factors that the auditor should consider include the following:

- Characteristics of the client's business and the related industry implications (e.g., the financial reporting framework that provide the client's basis of reporting, locations, etc.);
- The nature of reports expected to be rendered, including deadlines and key dates for expected communications and the involvement of other auditors, including internal auditors;

- Preliminary judgment of materiality levels, and material locations and account balances (including setting materiality levels for auditors of other locations);
- Conditions where there may be a higher risk of material misstatement;
- Whether to test the operating effectiveness of internal control; and
- Identification of recent events affecting the entity or its industry, including recent financial reporting developments.

**PLANNING AID REMINDER:** The auditor should also consider his or her knowledge gained from performing other engagements for the entity.

In developing an overall audit strategy, the auditor should consider (1) the scope of the audit engagement and (2) the engagement's reporting objectives, timing, and required communications. In determining the scope of the audit engagement, the auditor may consider the following:

- Industry-specific reporting requirements;
- Expected audit coverage (e.g., number of client locations where audit procedures are going to be performed);
- Nature of control relationships between a parent and a subsidiary;
- Use of other auditors;
- The entity's reporting currency;
- Any statutory or regulatory audit requirements;
- The use of client personnel (e.g., internal audit) in performing the audit engagement;
- The client's use of service organizations, and how the auditor will test the design and operating effectiveness of controls at the service organization;
- The auditor's planned use of audit evidence obtained in prior periods;
- The effect of information technology on audit procedures, including the availability of electronic data and the use of computer-assisted audit techniques;
- The availability of client personnel and data;
- Engagement budgeting, including allocating sufficient time to audit areas with greater risk;
- Audit areas with a higher risk of material misstatement;
- The entity's volume of transactions (which may affect whether the auditor decides to test the operating effectiveness of internal control);
- Management's commitment to internal control and the results of previous evaluations of the operating effectiveness of internal control, including management's efforts to remedy significant deficiencies or material weaknesses; and
- Significant recent developments affecting the entity (e.g., business, industry, legal, regulatory).

**PLANNING AID REMINDER:** When practitioners are engaged to perform audits that involve reporting to government entities (e.g., an employee benefit plan audit conducted in accordance with the U.S. Department of Labor requirements), the auditor should understand those requirements to ensure he or she understands the nature and extent of requirements imposed by government regulations that extend beyond GAAS.

In determining the engagement's reporting objectives, timing, and required communications, the auditor may consider:

- Due dates of financial reports, including interim reports;
- Planned meeting dates with management and those charged with governance;
- The expected type and timing of reports to be issued (e.g., audit report, management letter, etc.);
- Periodic updates to management on the progress of the audit throughout the engagement;
- The type and timing of reports from other auditors involved in performing the engagement;
- The schedule of audit team meetings during the audit and the planned schedule for reviewing audit work; and
- Whether there are any required communications with third parties.

**PUBLIC COMPANY IMPLICATIONS:** SOX and revised SEC rules prohibit the auditor of a public company from performing certain nonaudit services for that company. Many of these services were prohibited under existing SEC rules on independence adopted in November 2000. SOX requires that any allowed nonaudit service be preapproved by the audit committee of the public company. There are a number of differences between SEC/PCAOB independence rules and the independence rules that apply to auditors of private (non-SEC registrants) companies.

An outcome of preparing the audit strategy is that it helps the auditor determine the allocation of audit resources; for example:

- The nature of audit staff to assign to specific audit areas (e.g., assign experienced staff to high-risk areas).
- The number of staff to assign to specific audit areas.
- The timing of when audit staff are to be assigned.
- The supervision, management, and direction of audit staff.

> **ENGAGEMENT STRATEGY:** The audit strategy helps in developing the audit plan, but preparing the strategy and developing the plan are not unrelated or sequential processes. The audit strategy and plan are highly interrelated, and changes to one will likely result in changes to the other.

Because the nature, timing, and extent of audit planning depends in part on the size and complexity of the client, the planning for a small entity does not have to be complex or time-consuming. A brief memorandum that outlines issues from the previous audit, updated based on conversations with the owner-manager, can serve as the basis for planning the current audit.

## Communications with Management and Those Charged with Governance

The auditor is required to communicate an overview of the audit's planned scope and timing with those charged with governance of the entity. These discussions are intended to facilitate the effective administration of the engagement. Those communication responsibilities are addressed in AU-C 260 (*The Auditor's Communication with Those Charged with Governance*).

> **ENGAGEMENT STRATEGY:** The auditor may discuss aspects of the audit plan with the entity's management; however, the overall audit strategy and plan are the auditor's responsibility. Furthermore, care should be taken in discussions with entity management to maintain the effectiveness of the audit. For example, discussing the details of audit procedures with management could compromise audit effectiveness by making the audit procedures too predictable.

## Develop an Audit Plan

The auditor should prepare a detailed audit plan that reflects the overall strategy for performing the audit engagement. The audit plan will include the nature, timing, and extent of further audit procedures to be performed by the engagement team. Planning for these procedures occurs throughout the audit, and may be adjusted as the auditor conducts risk assessment procedures and further audit procedures, such as tests of the operating effectiveness of controls, and substantive procedures.

> **ENGAGEMENT STRATEGY:** The auditor may need to revise the original audit strategy and plan as a result of a change in circumstances or the results of audit procedures that were performed. For example, audit evidence obtained through substantive procedures that contradicts earlier evidence gathered through tests of controls may cause the auditor to revise the assessment of risk and amend the audit strategy and plan.

Planning the nature, timing, and extent of the direction and supervision of engagement team members and the review of their work depends on many factors, such as:

- Entity complexity and size,
- Area of the audit,
- Assessed risks of material misstatement (i.e., higher assessed risks of material misstatement typically correspond to increased extent and timeliness of supervision and increased review of team member work), and
- Competence of team members performing the audit work.

In audits carried out by a sole practitioner, there is no direction, supervision, or review of others' work. In these circumstances, the auditor may want to consult with other suitably experienced auditors if complex or unusual issues are involved.

The determination of the nature, timing, and extent of planned risk assessment procedures and further audit procedures also includes procedures related to disclosures in the financial statements. Consideration of disclosures in the planning process helps the auditor give attention to and plan time for addressing disclosures, including consideration of new or revised disclosures.

## Consider Whether Specialized Skills Are Needed to Perform the Audit Engagement

Specialized skills are often needed in performing an audit (e.g., information technology, valuation, forensic, etc.). The audit engagement team often needs an individual possessing information technology (IT) skills to (1) determine the effect of IT on the audit, (2) understand IT controls, and (3) design and perform tests of IT controls and substantive procedures. An IT professional is more likely to be needed on the engagement if:

- The entity's systems and IT controls are complex,
- The entity has made significant changes to existing systems or has implemented new systems,
- The entity has significant involvement with electronic commerce,
- The entity uses emerging technologies,
- Significant audit evidence is available only in electronic form, or
- Significant data sharing exists among systems.

An IT specialist may perform the following audit procedures: (1) analyze how the entity initiates, authorizes, records, processes, and reports transactions; (2) analyze the design of the entity's internal controls; (3) inspect the entity's system documentation; (4) observe the operation of IT controls; and (5) plan and perform tests of IT controls.

## Documentation

The auditor's documentation of the overall audit strategy should communicate significant matters to the engagement team and include key decisions made to properly plan the audit, such as the overall scope, timing, and conduct of the audit. This documentation may be in the form of a memorandum.

Documentation of the audit plan records the planned nature, timing, and extent of risk assessment procedures and further audit procedures at the relevant assertion level that respond to the assessed risks. For this, the auditor may use standard audit programs or audit completion checklists tailored to the specific audit engagement.

Recording significant changes made to the audit strategy or plan during the audit and the reasons for those changes helps to explain why changes were made, that appropriate responses were taken to changes that occurred, and also describes the final audit strategy and plan adopted.

*Considerations Relevant to Initial Audit Engagements*

In a first-year audit, the auditor should also consider the following factors in developing the audit strategy and plan:

- The need to make arrangements with the previous auditor to review their documentation; see AU-C 510 (*Opening Balances—Initial Audit Engagements, Including Reaudit Engagements*).
- Any major issues discussed with management before being retained, the need to communicate these issues to those charged with governance, and the effect of these issues on the audit strategy and audit plan.
- The need to obtain appropriate audit evidence for account balances as of the beginning of the year.
- Other steps required by the firm's system of quality control (e.g., the involvement of a second partner to review the audit plan before work begins).

---

**PLANNING AID REMINDER:** The process of planning the audit is typically more extensive in the first year of an engagement than in later years.

---

AU-C 510 requires the auditor to communicate with the predecessor auditor before accepting an engagement. Inquiry of the predecessor auditor might provide useful information relevant to the successor auditor's decision about whether to accept the engagement.

## Practitioner's Aid

*Use a Planning Checklist*

The auditor may use an engagement planning checklist to control the planning phase of the audit engagement. Exhibit AU-C 300-1 is an example of such a checklist.

### EXHIBIT AU-C 300-1—AUDIT ENGAGEMENT PLANNING CHECKLIST

Use the following checklist as a guide for planning audit procedures in a continuing engagement. The checklist is only a guide, and professional judgment should be exercised to determine how the checklist should be modified by revising the questions listed or adding questions to it where appropriate.

Check the appropriate response. If the question is not relevant to this particular audit engagement, place "N/A" (not applicable) in the space provided for the audit documentation reference. If additional explanation is needed with respect to a question, provide a proper cross-reference to another audit schedule.

Client Name: _____

Date of Financial Statements: _____

| | Yes | No | Audit Documentation Reference |
|---|---|---|---|
| 1. Is the scope of the audit engagement limited to a single financial statement? | _____ | _____ | _____ |
| • If yes, have we identified the notes and other disclosures that are appropriate for a single financial statement presentation? | _____ | _____ | _____ |
| • If yes, are the other financial statements going to be available for our perusal in order to identify events, transactions, and balances that may have implications for the audited financial statements? | _____ | _____ | _____ |
| 2. Are comparative financial statements presented? | _____ | _____ | _____ |
| • If yes, are we responsible for reporting on the previous year's financial statements? | _____ | _____ | _____ |
| 3. If a predecessor CPA is reporting on the previous year's financial statements, have we: | | | |
| • Discussed relevant matters with the predecessor CPA before accepting the engagement? | _____ | _____ | _____ |
| • Considered what matters to discuss with the predecessor CPA? | _____ | _____ | _____ |
| • Arranged to communicate matters discovered in the current engagement to the predecessor CPA? | _____ | _____ | _____ |

|  | Yes | No | Audit Documentation Reference |
|---|---|---|---|
| • Arranged to provide the predecessor with a preliminary draft of the current and previous year's financial statements and our audit report? | _____ | _____ | _____ |
| • Considered the format and content of the representation letter to be issued to the predecessor CPA? | _____ | _____ | _____ |
| 4. Have we considered the effect on audit procedures if the client has decided not to present a statement of cash flows? | _____ | _____ | _____ |
| 5. If the client has decided to present supplementary information, which is not part of the basic financial statements, are we engaged to review the supplementary information? | _____ | _____ | _____ |
| 6. If a portion of the financial statements is audited by another CPA, have we determined whether we can serve as the principal CPA? | _____ | _____ | _____ |
| 7. If we can serve as the principal CPA, have we considered whether to refer in our audit report to the work done by the other CPA? | _____ | _____ | _____ |
| 8. Have we identified the bases (operating income, total assets, etc.) and percentages of those amounts that should be used by subordinates to identify material misstatement? | _____ | _____ | _____ |
| 9. In designing the specific inquiries to be made, have we considered: | | | |
| • The nature and materiality of items? | _____ | _____ | _____ |
| • The likelihood of misstatement? | _____ | _____ | _____ |
| • Knowledge obtained during current and previous engagements? | _____ | _____ | _____ |

§ 300 • *Planning an Audit* **3013**

|  | Yes | No | Audit Documentation Reference |
|---|---|---|---|
| • The stated qualifications of the entity's accounting personnel? | _____ | _____ | _____ |
| • The extent to which a particular item is affected by management's judgment? | _____ | _____ | _____ |
| • The inadequacies in the entity's underlying financial data? | _____ | _____ | _____ |
| • The potential for related-party transactions? | _____ | _____ | _____ |

10. Have we acquired an adequate understanding of specialized accounting principles and practices of the client's industry by:

| | Yes | No | Audit Documentation Reference |
|---|---|---|---|
| • Reviewing relevant AICPA Accounting/Audit Guides? | _____ | _____ | _____ |
| • Reviewing financial statements of other entities in the same industry? | _____ | _____ | _____ |
| • Consulting with other individuals familiar with accounting practices in the specialized industry? | _____ | _____ | _____ |
| • Evaluating impact of any changes in accounting principles? | _____ | _____ | _____ |
| • Reading periodicals, textbooks, and other publications? | _____ | _____ | _____ |
| • Performing other procedures? (Describe.) | _____ | _____ | _____ |

11. Have we developed an understanding of the client's organization, including:

| | Yes | No | Audit Documentation Reference |
|---|---|---|---|
| • The form of business organization? | _____ | _____ | _____ |
| • The history of the client? | _____ | _____ | _____ |
| • The principals involved in the organization by review of the organizational chart or similar analysis? | _____ | _____ | _____ |
| • Changes in capital structure? | _____ | _____ | _____ |
| • Other relevant matters? (Describe.) | _____ | _____ | _____ |

|  | Yes | No | Audit Documentation Reference |
|---|---|---|---|
| 12. Have we developed an understanding of the client's operating characteristics, including: | | | |
| • An understanding of the client's products and services? | _____ | _____ | _____ |
| • Identification of operating locations? | _____ | _____ | _____ |
| • An understanding of production methods? | _____ | _____ | _____ |
| • Degree of reliance on information technology, including the use of outside service centers? | _____ | _____ | _____ |
| • Other operating characteristics? (Describe.) | _____ | _____ | _____ |
| 13. Have we developed an understanding of the nature of the client's assets, liabilities, revenues, and expenses by: | | | |
| • Reviewing the client's chart of accounts? | _____ | _____ | _____ |
| • Reviewing the previous year's financial statements? | _____ | _____ | _____ |
| • Considering the relationships between specific accounts and the nature of the client's business? | _____ | _____ | _____ |
| • Performing other procedures? (Describe.) | _____ | _____ | _____ |
| 14. Have we made inquiries concerning accounting principles, practices, and methods, including processes used to identify and prepare disclosures? | _____ | _____ | _____ |
| 15. Have we made inquiries concerning the accounting procedures and processes used by the client, including: | | | |
| • Recording transactions? | _____ | _____ | _____ |
| • Classifying transactions? | _____ | _____ | _____ |
| • Summarizing transactions? | _____ | _____ | _____ |

|  | Yes | No | Audit Documentation Reference |
|---|---|---|---|

- Accumulating information for making disclosures in the financial statements? _____ _____ _____
- Other accounting procedures? (Describe.) _____ _____ _____

16. Have we obtained an adequate understanding of internal control over financial reporting, including whether to test the operating effectiveness of controls? _____ _____ _____

17. Have we made inquiries concerning the effect on the financial statements due to actions taken at meetings of:
    - Stockholders? _____ _____ _____
    - The board of directors? _____ _____ _____
    - Other committees? (Describe.) _____ _____ _____

18. If there were changes in the application of accounting principles:
    - Did the change in accounting principle include the adoption of another acceptable accounting principle? _____ _____ _____
    - Was the change properly justified? _____ _____ _____
    - Were the effects of the change presented in the financial statements, including adequate disclosure, in a manner consistent with U.S. GAAP? _____ _____ _____
    - Were there other matters that we took into consideration? _____ _____ _____

19. Have we made inquiries concerning changes in the client's business activities or industry that may require the adoption of different accounting principles, and have we considered the implication of this change for the financial statements? _____ _____ _____

|  | Yes | No | Audit Documentation Reference |
|---|---|---|---|
| 20. Have we made inquiries concerning the occurrence of events subsequent to the date of the financial statements that may require: | | | |
| • Adjustments to the financial statements? | _____ | _____ | _____ |
| • Disclosures in the financial statements? | _____ | _____ | _____ |
| 21. Have we considered whether other professional services are needed in order to complete the audit engagement, including: | | | |
| • Preparing a working trial balance? | _____ | _____ | _____ |
| • Preparing adjusting journal entries? | _____ | _____ | _____ |
| • Consulting matters fundamental to the preparation of acceptable financial statements? | _____ | _____ | _____ |
| • Preparing tax returns? | _____ | _____ | _____ |
| • Providing bookkeeping or data-processing services that do not include the generation of financial statements? | _____ | _____ | _____ |
| • Other services considered necessary before an audit can be performed? (Describe.) | _____ | _____ | _____ |
| 22. Have we performed preliminary analytical procedures as required by AU-C 520? | _____ | _____ | _____ |
| 23. Have we obtained reports from other CPA(s) who reported on the financial statements of components of the client-reporting entity if we have decided to rely on their reports? | _____ | _____ | _____ |

Prepared By: _____

Date: _____

# SECTION 315

## UNDERSTANDING THE ENTITY AND ITS ENVIRONMENT AND ASSESSING THE RISKS OF MATERIAL MISSTATEMENTS

### Authoritative Pronouncements

SAS-122—Statements on Auditing Standards: Clarification and Recodification

SAS-134—Auditor Reporting and Amendments, Including Amendments Addressing Disclosures in the Audit of Financial Statements

SAS-135—Omnibus Statement on Auditing Standards—2019

SAS-141—Amendment to Effective Dates of SAS Nos. 134-140

SAS-142—Audit Evidence

### Overview

The Preface to the Codification of Statements on Auditing Standards notes that the auditor is to obtain a sufficient understanding of the entity and its environment, including its internal control, to identify and assess the risk of material misstatement of the financial statements whether caused by error or fraud. This understanding is also used by the auditor to plan the nature, timing, and extent of further audit procedures (i.e., tests of operating effectiveness of controls and substantive procedures) to respond to the assessed risks of material misstatement.

---

**IMPORTANT NOTICE FOR 2022:** In August 2020, the AICPA Auditing Standards Board (ASB) issued an exposure draft of a proposed new Statement on Auditing Standard, *Understanding the Entity and its Environment and Assessing the Risks of Material Misstatement*, that would supersede AU-C 315 (same title) and amend various other sections of auditing standards. The goal of this proposed new standard is to modernize the risk assessment standard by enhancing the requirements and guidance with respect to identifying and assessing the risks of material misstatement. In particular, the guidance is intended to address the work effort related to gaining an understanding of the entity's system of internal control and assessing control risk, in part because deficiencies in the process of obtaining the required understanding of internal control is a common audit issue identified by practice monitoring programs worldwide. While the proposed SAS does not change key concepts associated with audit risk, it provides expanded guidance to emphasize the importance of an effective risk assessment for entities of all sizes. If approved, the proposed SAS would become effective for audits of financial statements for periods ending on or after December 15, 2023, which is consistent with the effective date of SAS No. 143, *Auditing Accounting Estimates and Related Disclosures*.

## Definitions

| | |
|---|---|
| Assertions | Management representations embodied in the financial statements and used by the auditor to consider the different types of potential misstatements that may occur. |
| Relevant assertion | A financial statement assertion that has a reasonable possibility of containing one or more misstatements that would cause the financial statements to be materially misstated. The determination of relevance is made without regard to the effect of internal controls. |
| Business risk | A risk resulting from the setting of inappropriate objectives and strategies or from significant conditions, events, circumstances, actions, or inactions that could adversely affect an entity's ability to achieve its objectives and execute its strategies. |
| Internal control | A process—effected by those charged with governance, management, and other personnel—designed to provide the entity with reasonable assurance about the achievement of the entity's objectives with regard to (1) reliability of financial reporting, (2) effectiveness and efficiency of operations, and (3) compliance with applicable laws and regulations. Internal control over safeguarding of assets against unauthorized acquisition, use, or disposition may include controls relating to financial reporting and operations objectives. |
| Risk assessment procedures | Audit procedures performed to obtain an understanding of the entity and its environment, including the entity's internal control, to identify and assess the risks of material misstatement, whether due to fraud or error, at the financial statement and assertion levels. |
| Significant risk | An identified and assessed risk of material misstatement that, in the auditor's judgment, requires special audit consideration. |

---

**PUBLIC COMPANY IMPLICATION:** The PCAOB's AS-2410 (*Related Parties: Amendments to Certain PCAOB Auditing Standards Regarding Significant Unusual Transactions and Other Amendments to PCAOB Auditing Standards*) contains the audit guidance in the areas of related-party transactions (RPTs), significant unusual transactions, and financial relationships and transactions with executive officers. The PCAOB combined these three areas into a single standard because of the potential relationships between RPTs, significant unusual transactions, and financial relationships and transactions with executive officers. In auditing RPTs, the standard requires the auditor to (1) perform procedures to understand the company's relationships and transactions with related parties, including transactions with related parties that were modified during the period under audit; (2) evaluate whether the company has properly identified its related parties and transactions with them; (3) perform additional procedures if undisclosed (by management) related parties or related-party transactions are discovered by the auditor; (4) perform specific procedures for those RPTs required to be disclosed in the financial statements or that are identified as a significant risk; and (5) communicate to the audit committee the auditor's evaluation of the company's identification of, accounting for, and disclosure of RPTs.

AS-2410 also includes requirements for the consideration of fraud in an audit. The PCAOB describes a "significant unusual transaction" as one that is outside the normal course of business for the company or that otherwise appears unusual because of the transaction's timing, size, or nature. In auditing significant unusual transactions, the standard requires the auditor to (1) perform procedures to identify significant unusual transactions; (2) perform procedures to determine whether the significant unusual transaction has a business purpose and, if so, to understand that purpose; and (3) consider whether the transaction may have been entered into to commit financial reporting fraud or conceal a misappropriation of assets. The PCAOB's standard requires the auditor to obtain an understanding of the company's financial relationships and transactions with executive officers, including executive compensation arrangements. Specifically, AS-2410 requires the auditor to consider whether executive compensation arrangements may create an incentive or pressure for the company to achieve certain operating results or financial position.

---

**PUBLIC COMPANY IMPLICATION:** PCAOB Staff Audit Practice Alert No. 11 identifies common deficiencies in audits of internal control over financial reporting (ICFR), and highlights factors for auditors to consider when performing audits of ICFR. Common inspection deficiencies related to ICFR audits include the auditor's failure to: (1) identify and sufficiently test controls relevant to the risk of material misstatement, (2) sufficiently test the design and operating effectiveness of management review controls, (3) sufficiently update the results from testing controls at an interim date to year-end, (4) sufficiently test controls over system-generated data, (5) adequately test the work of others, and (6) adequately evaluate identified control deficiencies. The Audit Practice Alert provides guidance to auditors in risk assessment, selecting controls to test, testing management review controls, testing information technology controls (including controls over systems-generated data and reports), roll-forward testing of controls, using the work of others, and evaluating identified control deficiencies.

---

## Requirements

The auditor is presumptively required to perform the following procedures in developing an understanding of the entity and its environment and assessing the risks of material misstatements:

### Risk Assessment Procedures

1. Perform the following risk assessment procedures to provide a basis for identifying and assessing risks of material misstatements at the financial statement and assertion levels:

    a. Inquiries of management and others within the entity who may have information that could assist in identifying risks of material misstatement,

    b. Analytical procedures, and

    c. Observation and inspection.

    These procedures alone do not provide sufficient appropriate audit evidence on which to base the audit opinion.

2. Consider whether information obtained from the client acceptance or continuance process is relevant to identifying risks of material misstatement.

3. If the engagement partner has performed other engagements for the entity, that partner should consider any information relevant to identifying risks of material misstatement.

4. If the auditor intends to use information from previous experience with the entity or from procedures performed in previous audits, perform audit procedures to establish the continued relevance of that information to the current audit.

5. During planning, consider the results of the assessed risk of material misstatement due to fraud along with other information gathered in the process of identifying risks of material misstatement.

6. The engagement partner and other key engagement team members should discuss the susceptibility of the entity's financial statements to material misstatement and application of the applicable financial reporting framework to the entity. The engagement partner should determine which matters are communicated to engagement team members who are not involved in the discussion.

**IMPORTANT NOTICE FOR 2022:** In July 2020, the AICPA Auditing Standards Board (ASB) issued SAS No. 142, *Audit Evidence*, which supersedes AU-C 500 (*Audit Evidence*) and amends various other sections, including AU-C 315, in the professional standards. This new SAS addresses the evolving nature of business and audit services and issues that include the use of emerging technologies by both preparers and auditors, audit data analytics (ADA), the application of professional skepticism, the expanding use of external information sources as audit evidence, and, more broadly, the accuracy, completeness, and reliability of audit evidence. This SAS is effective for audits of financial statements for periods ending on or after December 15, 2022.

## Understanding the Entity and Its Environment

7. Obtain an understanding of:

   a. Relevant industry, regulatory, and other external factors, including the applicable financial reporting framework.

   b. The entity's nature, including its operations, ownership and governance structures, types of investments being made and planned, including investments in entities formed to accomplish specific objectives, their structure, and how they are financed.

   c. The entity's selection and application of accounting policies, including the reasons for any changes. Evaluate whether policies are appropriate for its business and consistent with the applicable financial reporting framework and accounting policies used in its industry.

   d. The entity's objectives and strategies and related business risks that may result in risks of material misstatement.

   e. The measurement and review of the entity's financial performance.

## Understanding the Entity's Internal Control

8. Obtain an understanding of internal control relevant to the audit. Whether a control is relevant to the audit is a matter of professional judgment. Most relevant controls are likely to relate to financial reporting, but not all controls related to financial reporting will be relevant.

### § 315 • *Understanding the Entity and Its Environment*  3021

> **IMPORTANT NOTICE FOR 2022:** The exposure draft of a proposed new Statement on Auditing Standard, *Understanding the Entity and its Environment and Assessing the Risks of Material Misstatement,* issued in August 2020 makes it clear that the required understanding of internal control includes understanding each of the five components of the system of internal control: (1) control environment; (2) risk assessment; (3) information and communication; (4) control activities; and (5) monitoring.

9. Evaluate the design of controls relevant to the audit and determine whether they have been implemented by performing procedures in addition to inquiry of the entity's personnel.

10. Obtain an understanding of the control environment. Evaluate whether (1) management, with the oversight of those charged with governance, has created and maintained a culture of honesty and ethical behavior and (2) strengths in the control environment provide an appropriate foundation for the other internal control components, or if deficiencies in the control environment undermine other components.

11. Obtain an understanding of whether the entity has a process for identifying business risks relevant to financial reporting objectives, estimating their significance, assessing their likelihood of occurrence, and deciding about actions to address those risks.

12. If the entity has established a risk assessment process, obtain an understanding of it and its results. If the auditor identifies risks of material misstatement that management failed to identify, evaluate whether an underlying risk exists that would be expected to be identified by the entity's risk assessment process. If such a risk exists, obtain an understanding of why the process failed to identify it and evaluate whether the process is appropriate to its circumstances or if a significant deficiency or material weakness exists in the process.

13. If the entity has not established a risk assessment process or has an ad-hoc process, discuss with management whether business risks relevant to financial reporting objectives have been identified and how they have been addressed. Evaluate whether the absence of a documented risk assessment process is appropriate in the circumstances or represents a significant deficiency or material weakness in the entity's internal control.

14. Obtain an understanding of the information system, including the related business processes relevant to financial reporting including relevant aspects of the system that impact disclosures in the financial statements, including the following areas:

    a. Classes of transactions in the entity's operations significant to the financial statements.

    b. Procedures within manual and IT systems by which those transactions are initiated, authorized, recorded, processed, corrected as necessary, transferred to the general ledger, and reported in the financial statements.

    c. Related accounting records, in manual or electronic form, supporting information and specific accounts in the financial statements that are used to initiate, authorize, record, process, correct as necessary, transfer to the general ledger, and report transactions.

    d. How the information system captures events and conditions significant to the financial statements other than transactions.

e. The financial reporting process used to prepare the entity's financial statements, including significant accounting estimates and disclosures.

f. Controls surrounding journal entries, including nonstandard journal entries used to record nonrecurring, unusual transactions or adjustments.

---

**IMPORTANT NOTICE FOR 2022:** The exposure draft of a proposed new Statement on Auditing Standard, *Understanding the Entity and its Environment and Assessing the Risks of Material Misstatement*, issued in August 2020 would require the auditor to understand the related IT environment in order to gain a high-level understanding of the nature and complexity of the IT environment and its supporting processes to determine which applications and aspects of the IT environment are subject to risks. This helps the auditor identify risks that might affect the design, implementation, and operating effectiveness of automated controls. The proposed revision would require the auditor to identify general IT controls relevant to the audit, including evaluation of their design and implementation. This would include identification of IT general controls that address risks related to the design, implementation, and operating effectiveness of automated controls important to addressing the risks of material misstatement.

---

15. Obtain an understanding of how the entity communicates financial reporting roles and responsibilities and significant matters relating to financial reporting, including (1) communications between management and those charged with governance and (2) external communications, such as those with regulatory authorities.

16. Obtain an understanding of control activities relevant to the audit. Relevant activities are those the auditor judges necessary to understand in order to assess the risks of material misstatement at the assertion level and design further audit procedures responsive to assessed risks. Obtain an understanding of the entity's process of reconciling detailed records to the general ledger for material account balances and of how the entity has responded to risks arising from IT.

17. Obtain an understanding of the major activities the entity uses to monitor internal control over financial reporting, including those related to control activities relevant to the audit and how the entity initiates corrective actions to its controls.

18. If the entity has an internal audit function, obtain an understanding of the nature of its responsibilities, how it fits in the entity's organizational structure, and the activities it performs or will perform in order to determine the internal audit function's relevance to the audit.

19. Obtain an understanding of the sources of information used in the entity's monitoring activities and the reasons management considers the information to be sufficiently reliable for monitoring.

## *Identifying and Assessing the Risks of Material Misstatement*

20. Identify and assess the risks of material misstatement at (1) the financial statement level and (2) the relevant assertion level related to each material class of transactions, account balance, and disclosure to provide a basis for designing and performing further audit procedures. To do this:

a. Identify risks throughout the process of obtaining an understanding of the entity and its environment, including relevant controls that relate to the risks, and considering the classes of transactions, account balances, and disclosures in the financial statements.

b. Assess identified risks and evaluate whether they relate pervasively to the financial statements as a whole and may affect many assertions.

c. Relate identified risks to what can go wrong at the assertion level, taking into account relevant controls the auditor intends to test.

d. Consider the likelihood of one or more misstatements and whether the potential misstatement is of a magnitude that could result in a material misstatement.

---

**IMPORTANT NOTICE FOR 2022:** Risks at the financial statement level relate pervasively to the financial statements as a whole and potentially affect many assertions, while risks of material misstatement at the assertion level consists of two components: inherent risk and control risk. The exposure draft of a proposed new Statement on Auditing Standard, *Understanding the Entity and its Environment and Assessing the Risks of Material Misstatement*, issued in August 2020 would require the auditor to conduct a separate assessment of inherent risk and control risk. To assess inherent risk, the auditor should assess the likelihood and magnitude of misstatement. If the auditor plans to test the operating effectiveness of controls, the auditor should assess control risks. The proposed SAS makes it clear that, if the auditor does not plan to test the operating effectiveness of controls, control risk is assessed at maximum and the resulting assessment of the risk of material misstatement is the same as the assessment of inherent risk.

---

21. Determine whether any risks identified in the risk assessment process are significant risks in the auditor's judgment, excluding the effects of identified controls related to the risk. Consider the following in determining significant risks:

    a. Whether the risk is a risk of fraud.

    b. Whether the risk requires special attention because it is related to significant economic, accounting, or other developments.

    c. The complexity of transactions.

    d. Whether the risk involves significant transactions with related parties.

    e. The degree of subjectivity in the measurement of financial information related to the risk, especially those measurements involving a wide range of measurement uncertainty.

    f. Whether the risk involves significant unusual transactions.

22. If it is determined that a significant risk exists, obtain an understanding of the entity's controls, including control activities, relevant to that risk and evaluate whether such controls have been suitably designed and implemented to mitigate such risks.

---

**IMPORTANT NOTICE FOR 2022:** The exposure draft of a proposed new Statement on Auditing Standard, *Understanding the Entity and its Environment and Assessing the Risks of Material Misstatement*, issued in August 2020 emphasizes that significant risks are based on inherent risks alone, excluding the effects of identified controls related to the risks.

23. It may not be possible or practicable to obtain sufficient appropriate audit evidence from substantive procedures alone for some risks, such as those relating to the inaccurate or incomplete recording of routine and significant classes of transactions or account balances that often permit highly automated processing with little manual intervention. For such risks, obtain an understanding of the entity's controls over those risks.

24. If new information or audit evidence from performing further audit procedures is obtained that is inconsistent with the audit evidence on which the auditor originally based his or her assessment of risks of material misstatement at the assertion level, revise the assessment and modify the further planned audit procedures accordingly.

## Documentation

25. Document:
    a. The required discussion among the engagement team, significant decisions reached, how and when the discussion occurred, and the participating audit team members.
    b. Key elements of the understanding obtained regarding each specified aspect of the entity and its environment and each internal control component, the sources of information from which the understanding was obtained, and the risk assessment procedures performed.
    c. Identified and assessed risks of material misstatement at the financial statement and assertion levels.
    d. Identified significant risks and risks for which substantive procedures alone do not provide sufficient appropriate audit evidence, and related controls about which the auditor has obtained an understanding.

## Analysis and Application of Procedures

### Risk Assessment Procedures

Although much of the auditor's effort in identifying and assessing risks occurs in planning the audit, the auditor should continue to assess risk throughout the audit and, if necessary, modify his or her overall risk evaluation and the nature, timing, and extent of audit procedures to reflect any modification to his or her initial risk assessments. The extent of the understanding of the entity required is determined by the auditor's professional judgment and should be sufficient to identify and assess the risks of material misstatement, whether due to error or fraud, related to amounts or disclosures in the financial statements. The auditor's required depth of understanding is less than that of the entity's management.

**PLANNING AID REMINDER:** In assessing the entity's risks, the auditor should also be mindful of the specific fraud-risk-assessment requirements contained in AU-C 240 (*Consideration of Fraud in a Financial Statement Audit*). For example, AU-C 240 requires the auditor to assess the risk of material misstatement due to fraud and to modify audit procedures in response to this risk. A heightened risk of material misstatement due to fraud might call for an overall response (e.g., more supervision, more experienced staff, greater skepticism); a response tailored to classes of transactions, account balances, or disclosures (e.g., modify the nature, timing, and extent of audit procedures to be performed); or both.

---

The auditor should (1) perform analytical procedures, (2) make inquiries of management and others within the entity, and (3) observe activities and inspect documents and records in performing risk assessment procedures. Although the auditor should perform all three of these risk assessment procedures, he or she is not required to perform all three of these procedures for every area of risk being assessed.

The auditor may perform other risk assessment procedures in addition to the three types of procedures that are required. For example, the auditor may make inquiries of individuals outside the entity (e.g., the entity's outside counsel, bankers, and valuation experts). The auditor also may examine information developed by outside sources (e.g., analyst reports, reports by credit rating agencies, trade journals, etc.).

---

**ENGAGEMENT STRATEGY:** In performing risk assessment procedures the auditor may also gather evidence about the operating effectiveness of controls even though the risk assessment procedures were not specifically designed to accomplish this purpose. Also, due to efficiency concerns, the auditor may choose to perform tests of controls or substantive procedures at the same time that he or she performs risk assessment procedures.

---

*Inquiries of management and others*

Auditors direct many of their inquiries to management and to those responsible for the entity's financial reporting process. In addition, an auditor may want to extend his or her inquiries to other parties within the entity. These other parties can often provide a valuable (different) perspective that may be useful in identifying risks of material misstatement. In deciding on other parties to talk with and on what to ask, an auditor should focus on obtaining information that will help him or her identify risks of material misstatement. Other parties that may be uniquely helpful to the auditor, and the types of information they might provide, are as follows:

| Internal Party | Type of Risk Information Provided |
|---|---|
| Those charged with governance | An understanding of the entity's control environment |
| Internal audit | Results of audits performed during the year, including control deficiencies that were identified and management's responses to these findings |
| Those involved with initiating, authorizing, processing, or recording complex or unusual transactions | An understanding of the business purpose of the transaction, the accounting policy that was selected, and how it was applied |

| Internal Party | Type of Risk Information Provided |
|---|---|
| In-house legal counsel | Pending or threatened litigation, compliance with laws or regulations, any known or suspected fraud, and an understanding of contract terms and provisions with financial reporting implications |
| Marketing or sales personnel | Changes in marketing strategies, sales trends, or agreements with customers |

*Analytical procedures*

AU-C 520 (*Analytical Procedures*) requires the auditor to perform analytical procedures in planning the audit. These procedures are useful in obtaining an understanding of the entity and its environment and in identifying financial statement risk areas. Analytical procedures may also help the auditor identify unusual transactions and events. In performing analytical procedures, the auditor should develop his or her own independent expectation as to the recorded account balance or ratio. A difference between the auditor's expectation and the entity's recorded account balance (or a ratio computed using recorded account balances) may indicate a higher risk of material misstatement.

> **FRAUD POINTER:** Auditors sometimes perform analytical procedures at a highly aggregated level. For example, an auditor might compare the entity's recorded total revenue amount to his or her expectation of total revenue. Analytical procedures performed at such an aggregated level may not be effective in identifying risks of material misstatement. The auditor should consider performing analytical procedures on a more disaggregated basis (e.g., analyze revenue amounts by quarter or month, by operating unit, by product line, etc.).

*Observation and inspection*

Auditors typically observe procedures and inspect documents and records in assessing client risks. Examples of these activities include the following:

- Tour some of the entity's locations and plants;
- Observe the operations of the entity, including selected control procedures;
- Inspect documents, records, and control manuals; and
- Read reports prepared by management, internal audit, and those charged with governance.

*Prior-period information*

Based on prior experience with the entity, the auditor may have knowledge of the nature of the entity and its environment, its internal control, past misstatements, management's efforts to correct past misstatements, and significant changes the entity has undergone since the prior period. This knowledge is useful in assessing risks in the current year's audit, including risks related to disclosures required by the applicable financial reporting framework. When performing audit procedures to assess the continued relevance of prior period information, the auditor may make inquiries and perform walk-throughs of relevant systems.

## Required discussion among the audit team

The audit team should discuss the risks of material misstatement in the client's financial statements, whether caused by error or fraud. This discussion may occur at the same time as the audit team brainstorming session required by AU-C 240.

> **PLANNING AID REMINDER:** AU-C 240 requires the audit team to brainstorm on where and how an entity's financial statements might be susceptible to material misstatement due to fraud. AU-C 315 extends this requirement—requiring a discussion of where and how the entity's financial statements are susceptible to material misstatement, whether caused by fraud or by error.

All audit members need not take part in the discussion, nor is it necessary for them to be informed of all decisions reached in the discussion. The engagement partner or a delegate may communicate appropriate portions of the discussion to other engagement team members and a communication plan may be useful for this purpose.

> **ENGAGEMENT STRATEGY:** A sole practitioner may be performing the audit. In this case, he or she is responsible for considering the risks of material misstatement in the client's financial statements.

The required audit team discussion provides more experienced engagement team members with an opportunity to share their knowledge, allows an exchange of information among engagement team members, helps team members to identify those aspects of the entity's financial statements that are susceptible to material misstatement that are being assigned to each audit team member, and provides a way for team members to share new information obtained throughout the audit regarding the risk assessment.

## Understanding the Entity and Its Environment

> **PUBLIC COMPANY IMPLICATION:** The PCAOB's Staff Audit Practice Alert No. 3 (*Audit Considerations in the Current Economic Environment*) states that events in the financial markets and the economy may have implications for the valuation, impairment, or recoverability of assets and for the completeness and valuation of liabilities. Staff Audit Practice Alert No. 3 is designed to help auditors identify matters that may affect audit risk and thereby require additional audit effort. Practice Alert 3 provides guidance on (1) overall audit considerations, (2) auditing fair value measurements, (3) auditing accounting estimates, (4) auditing the adequacy of disclosures, (5) the auditor's consideration of an entity's ability to continue as a going concern, and (6) additional audit considerations in other areas. As it relates to overall audit considerations, Practice Alert 3 provides guidance on planning, fraud, internal controls, substantive procedures, and audit committee communications. For example, relating to internal controls, controls over the identification and review of assets for recoverability and impairment and controls over the use of specialists may require additional audit attention Staff

Audit Practice Alert No. 3 emphasizes that Practice Alert No. 2 (*Matters Related to Auditing Fair Value Measurements of Financial Instruments and the Use of Specialists*) remains applicable in the current environment. The Practice Alert 3 reminds auditors of the sensitivity of various accounting estimates, the approaches that the auditor should consider in auditing estimates, and that the auditor should perform a retrospective review of significant accounting estimates from the prior year. Such a retrospective review may identify deficiencies in the client's estimation process, including possible management bias. With respect to disclosures, the Practice Alert 3 reminds auditors of the client's disclosure obligations related to significant risks and uncertainties. Practice Alert 3 reminds auditors that in a case of the omission of a required disclosure, the auditor should issue a qualified or adverse report. Practice Alert 3 emphasizes the requirements in AU-C 570 (*Going Concern*). In addition to the factors listed in AU-C 570 that relate to management's plans to mitigate the conditions or events that give rise to the going-concern doubt, the auditor may also consider the client's participation in a program of federal assistance. Finally, Practice Alert 3 suggests that audit risk may be elevated in the following areas as a result of the current economic environment: (1) consolidation, (2) contingencies and guarantees, (3) derivatives, especially credit derivatives, (4) debt obligations, (5) deferred tax assets, (6) goodwill, intangibles, and other long-lived assets, (7) inventory, (8) other-than-temporary impairment of investment securities, (9) pension and other postretirement benefits, (10) receivables, (11) restructuring, (12) revenue recognition, and (13) share-based payments.

*Industry, regulatory, and other external factors*

The auditor should understand the industry and regulatory factors that affect the client. These factors include industry conditions, regulations affecting the client, the legal and political environment, environmental requirements affecting the client including requirements related to disclosures, and other factors. Some industries pose unique risks of material misstatements (e.g., financial institutions, high-technology companies), and the auditor should consider whether the engagement is staffed with individuals who possess an appropriate degree of industry expertise. Exhibit AU-C 315-1 provides examples of industry, regulatory, and other external factors.

The regulatory environment in which the entity operates may have an impact on accounting principles and industry-specific factors, laws and regulations, government policies, tax implications, and other regulatory issues that may impact financial reporting and the risk of material misstatement.

*Nature of the entity*

The auditor should understand the nature of the entity in order to be informed about the classes of transactions, account balances, and disclosures that are likely to appear in the entity's financial statements. For example, an entity with a complex structure (e.g., numerous subsidiaries, a number of which are located in foreign locations) may present issues related to preparing consolidated financial statements, the allocation of goodwill across different operating units, asset impairment testing, and foreign currency translation. Also, understanding the relationships between management, owners, and those charged with governance is useful in identifying related-party transactions. Significant changes the entity has undergone from prior periods may change or increase the risks of material misstatement. Exhibit AU-C 315-2 provides examples of entity-specific factors to consider and their link to relevant standards of financial reporting (U.S. GAAP).

---

**OBSERVATION:** Entities may be formed by entities to accomplish a specific purpose, such as variable interest entities, and financial reporting frameworks often specify conditions that amount to control or circumstances under which an entity should be considered for consolidation for which a detailed understanding of the agreements involving the entity formed for a specific purpose is involved.

---

**IMPORTANT NOTICE FOR 2022:** The exposure draft of a proposed new Statement on Auditing Standard, *Understanding the Entity and its Environment and Assessing the Risks of Material Misstatement*, issued in August 2020 emphasizes that while size of the entity matters, it is the level of complexity in the nature of the entity and its financial reporting that is the primary driver of scalability. Even smaller entities have complex business models and financial reporting processes, which require the performance of detailed risk assessments.

---

*Entity's selection and application of accounting policies*

The auditor's understanding of the entity's selection and application of accounting policies may include the following matters:

- Entity's method of accounting for significant and unusual transactions;
- Effect of significant accounting policies in areas lacking authoritative guidance or consensus;
- Significant changes in the entity's accounting policies and disclosures and the reasons for these changes;
- Financial reporting standards, laws, and regulations that are new to the entity and the entity's adoption plans; and
- Financial reporting competencies of personnel involved in selecting and applying significant new or complex accounting standards.

*Objectives and strategies of the entity and the resulting business risks*

The auditor should obtain an understanding of the entity's objectives and strategies as well as the business risks that result from them. Objectives are management's overall plans for the entity. For governmental entity audits, management objectives may be influenced by legislation, regulation, and public accountability concerns. Strategies are management's detailed approach for accomplishing its objectives. Business risks are those factors that might prevent the entity from achieving its objectives or implementing its strategies, as well as the risk that the entity has designed flawed objectives or strategies. Entity objectives and strategies are dynamic, changing, and evolve over time.

> **OBSERVATION:** The entity's business risks encompass the risk of material misstatement in the financial statements and include risks that may extend beyond risks related to financial reporting.

> **IMPORTANT NOTICE FOR 2022:** In May 2019, the AICPA's Auditing Standards Board (ASB) issued SAS No. 135 titled *Omnibus Statement on Auditing Standards—2019* that includes amendments to various AU-C sections. SAS No. 135 amends AU-C 240 to add a definition for significant unusual transactions. SAS No. 135 also amends AU-C 315 to note that in exercising professional judgment about what risks are significant risks, the auditor should consider whether the risk involved significant unusual transactions. Originally, the effective date of SAS No. 135 was for audits of financial statements periods ending on or after December 15, 2020, with early application **not** permitted. However, the ASB's issuance of SAS No. 141, *Amendment to the Effective Dates of SAS Nos. 134-140*, extended the effective date of SAS No. 135 to December 15, 2021, in order to provide more time for firms to implement SAS No. 135 in light of the effect of the coronavirus pandemic. While SAS No. 141 allows for early implementation of SAS No. 135, the ASB recommends that SAS Nos. 134-140 be implemented concurrently.

The successful identification of client business risks helps the auditor assess the risks of material misstatement in the financial statements; however, the auditor is not expected to identify all business risks. Rather, the auditor focuses on business risks that have financial statement implications. Examples of client strategies and factors affecting the client's business and the related business risks include the following:

| Client Strategy or Factor Affecting the Client's Business | Business Risk |
| --- | --- |
| Expansion into new markets | The client lacks the expertise and personnel needed to effectively compete in the new markets; failure to accurately forecast demand |
| Introduction of new products | Lack of customer acceptance; cost overruns in producing the product; lack of historical data on customer returns and warranty claims; increased liability exposure |
| Issuance of new accounting pronouncements | The client implements the new pronouncement incorrectly or fails to apply it |
| Changes in industry-specific regulations | Loss of key licenses; increased compliance costs; increased liability exposure |
| Issuance of new equity or debt securities | Failure to complete the offering in the amount expected; additional restrictions imposed on the entity's operations |
| Introduction of a new information processing system | Existing systems and processes are not compatible; failure to effectively manage the conversion from the old system to the new system |

*Financial performance of the entity*

The measurement of the entity's financial performance—whether via internal or external measures—creates performance pressure on management. This performance pressure can appropriately cause management to take steps to improve the entity's operating performance but in some instances performance pressure can lead to inappropriate managerial actions that result in material misstatements in the financial statements.

Management may use the following internally generated performance measures in evaluating the entity's financial performance:

- Key performance indicators and operating ratios;
- Measures of employee performance;
- Actual-to-budget comparisons;
- Comparative financial statements;
- Department, division, or subsidiary performance reports; and
- Comparison of the entity's performance with that of competitors.

In smaller entities, management inquiry may reveal a lack of processes in place to internally measure and review financial performance, which could indicate an increased risk that misstatements may not be detected and corrected. The auditor's use of performance measures may help him or her identify risks of material misstatement. For example, client growth that significantly outpaces that of the rest of the industry may be a risk factor. Unexplained client growth may be of particular concern when coupled with very aggressive employee compensation plans (a high ratio of variable-based compensation to fixed compensation).

**OBSERVATION:** Management's measurement, review, and investigation of (unexpected) financial performance are not part of the monitoring element of internal control; rather, such activity is a type of manual detective control activity.

*Internal Control Components*

The auditor should obtain an understanding of the following five components of internal control:

1. *Control environment* The control environment sets the tone of an organization, which influences the control consciousness of its employees. The control environment is the foundation for all other components of internal control, because it provides discipline and structure.
2. *Risk assessment by the entity* Risk assessment is the process that an entity must conduct in order to identify and assess any relevant risks to its objectives. Once this assessment is performed, management must determine how the risks should be managed.
3. *Information and communication systems* Information and communication systems are used to identify, capture, and exchange the information needed for employees to carry out their responsibilities.

4. *Control activities* Control activities are the policies and procedures that help ensure that management directives are carried out.
5. *Monitoring* Monitoring is a process that an entity uses to assess the quality of its internal control performance over time.

---

**OBSERVATION:** The above five components of internal control and the guidance in AU-C 315 are based on COSO's *Internal Control—Integrated Framework*, originally issued by it in 1992, but revised in 2013. The updated *Framework* retains the core definition of internal control and the five components of internal control. And, the requirement to consider the five components to assess the effectiveness of internal control remains fundamentally unchanged.

---

**PUBLIC COMPANY IMPLICATION:** The Sarbanes-Oxley Act of 2002 (SOX) requires all public companies to issue an "internal control report" that includes the following: (1) a statement that management is responsible for establishing and maintaining adequate internal control over financial reporting and (2) an assessment of the effectiveness of internal control over financial reporting as of the end of the company's fiscal year. Auditors are also required to perform a separate evaluation of the effectiveness of internal control for large, accelerated filers. Related SEC rules require management to explicitly state their responsibility for internal control and to identify material weaknesses in internal control. The framework that management uses as a basis for its evaluation of internal control must be one that has been established by a body or group that followed a due-process procedure that allowed for public comment. Most public companies use COSO's *Internal Control—Integrated Framework*. The concepts in AU-C 315 are based on that framework.

---

**FRAUD POINTER:** Gaining an understanding of internal control provides useful information about the presence of one of the three fraud conditions: opportunity. Nonexistent or deficient internal controls can provide management or employees with opportunities or circumstances that allow them to carry out material misstatements in the financial statements. For this reason, auditors should consider the information they obtain through understanding internal control as they evaluate the presence of other risk factors related to conditions of fraud. The more fraud risk factors the auditor observes, the greater the likelihood of a material misstatement due to the occurrence of fraud.

---

**IMPORTANT NOTICE FOR 2022:** The exposure draft of a proposed new Statement on Auditing Standard, *Understanding the Entity and its Environment and Assessing the Risks of Material Misstatement*, issued in August 2020 differentiates indirect controls from direct controls. **Indirect controls** are controls that are typically more "indirect" in nature given they generally do not directly address the risks of material misstatement at the assertion level. Rather, they are more indicative of risks at the financial statement level. The three components of internal control that are "indirect controls" include the control environment, risk assessment, and monitoring. **Direct controls** are controls that typically directly address the risks of material misstatement at the assertion level. The two components of internal control that are "direct controls" include information system and communication and control activities.

*Control environment*

The success or failure of internal control depends on the environment in which the internal control process takes place (i.e., the control environment). The control environment is also referred to as "the tone at the top," and it is the foundation for all the other elements of internal control. AU-C 315 identifies the following as elements that affect an entity's control environment:

- Integrity and ethical values,
- Commitment to competence,
- Participation of those charged with governance,
- Management's philosophy and operating style,
- Organizational structure,
- Assignment of authority and responsibility, and
- Human resource policies and practices.

Exhibit AU-C 315-3 provides examples of elements of the control environment.

The effectiveness of an entity's controls cannot exceed the integrity and ethical values of those who design, administer, and monitor controls. Given this fact, an entity's control consciousness is heavily influenced by those charged with governance.

**FRAUD POINTER:** The AICPA's thought paper entitled *Management Override of Internal Controls: The Achilles' Heel of Fraud Prevention*, updated in 2016, provides guidance to audit committees to help them address the ever-present risk of fraud resulting from management override of internal control. The document notes that the audit committee (or the board where there is no audit committee) plays a vital role in overseeing the actions of management. For many organizations, the audit committee is in the best position to prevent, deter, and detect fraud resulting from management override of controls. The document identifies specific actions an audit committee can take to address the risk of management override of internal controls. Auditors may find the document helpful as they assess the "participation of those charged with governance" element of the control environment.

*Risk assessment by the entity*

The design of internal control related to financial reporting should include management's identification, analysis, and management of risk factors that may prevent financial statements from being prepared in accordance with U.S. GAAP. When designing internal controls, management should consider "external and internal events, and circumstances that may occur and adversely affect an entity's ability to initiate, authorize, record, process, and report financial data consistent with the assertions of management in the financial statements." Risk assessment is an ongoing process, and Exhibit AU-C 315-4 provides examples of factors affecting entity risks.

**OBSERVATION:** In 2004, the Committee of Sponsoring Organizations of the Treadway Commission (COSO) issued an enterprise risk management framework, *Enterprise Risk Management—Integrated Framework*, to assist boards of directors, management, and others within entities to effectively manage risks across the enterprise. Many organizations have implemented enterprise risk management processes that helps the board and senior management identify, assess, and manage the entity's most significant risk exposures. Practitioners should discuss with boards and senior management the nature of processes an entity's leadership uses to monitor the organizations' most significant risks, including information about the most significant business risk exposures.

**PUBLIC COMPANY IMPLICATION:** COSO's 2017 *Enterprise Risk Management: Integrating with Strategy and Performance* is likely to be particularly useful to auditors of public companies who are assessing an entity's risk assessment process as part of auditing the effectiveness of internal control over financial reporting.

*Information and communication systems*

The auditor needs to obtain an understanding of the entity's financial reporting system. A financial reporting system generally consists of computer hardware, software, people, automated and manual procedures, and data used by the entity to initiate, authorize, record, process, and report its transactions and events and maintain accountability for assets, liabilities, and equity. The information system may be heavily automated, but it often includes some manual or human-performed processes. Additionally, the information system includes the use of standard and nonstandard journal entries. All these, and other, aspects of the information system should be considered as part of the assessment of risks related to financial reporting.

Sometimes the financial statements contain information that is generated outside the general and subsidiary ledgers, such as information from lease agreements, information from the entity's risk management system, and information from financial models. The auditor should use professional judgment to determine what aspects of those systems should be part of the auditor's understanding.

Exhibit AU-C 315-5 provides a description of information systems' objectives. The quality of information generated by the system affects management's ability to make appropriate decisions and reliably report financial information.

The auditor also needs to understand how the entity communicates to individuals their roles and responsibilities related to the financial reporting process. Communication occurs in written form (e.g., manuals), orally, electronically, and through management actions.

**IMPORTANT NOTICE FOR 2022:** As computing technologies continue to rapidly evolve, a number of organizations are turning to cloud computing to expand their computing resources while avoiding significant investments in IT infrastructure, training, personnel, and software. Despite a number of benefits that cloud computing options provide, a number of risks accompany those benefits. To help organizations manage risks associated with cloud computing, COSO has a thought paper, *Enterprise Risk Management for Cloud Computing*, which establishes a common language and foundation for assessing and overseeing risks from a holistic perspective. The document can be downloaded from COSO for free at www.coso.org.

---

**IMPORTANT NOTICE FOR 2022:** In May 2019, the AICPA's Auditing Standards Board (ASB) issued SAS No. 134 titled *Auditor Reporting and Amendments, Including Amendments Addressing Disclosures in the Audit of Financial Statements* to revise the auditor's report and to amend various AU-C sections to heighten the auditor's focus on disclosures throughout the process of auditing financial statements. SAS No. 134 focuses the auditor's attention on disclosures earlier in the process of auditing financial statements by amending AU-C 315 to acknowledge, and give prominence to, disclosures where the information is not derived from the accounting system. SAS No. 134 also amends AU-C 315 to remind the auditor to consider whether changes in financial reporting requirements or the entity's environment, financial condition, or activities may result in significant new or revised disclosures. Originally, the effective date of SAS No. 134 was for audits of financial statements periods ending on or after December 15, 2020, with early implementation **not** permitted. However, the ASB's issuance of SAS No. 141, *Amendment to the Effective Dates of SAS Nos. 134-140*, extended the effective date of SAS No. 134 to December 15, 2021, in order to provide more time for firms to implement SAS No. 134 in light of the effect of the coronavirus pandemic. While SAS No. 141 allows for early implementation of SAS No. 134, the ASB recommends that SAS Nos. 134-140 be implemented concurrently.

---

*Control activities*

Control activities are those policies and procedures that help ensure that management's objectives and strategies are carried out. Within the domain of financial reporting controls, control activities should be designed to address risks of material misstatement to the financial statements, including disclosures. Examples of control activities are authorizations, performance reviews, information processing, physical controls, and segregation of duties. Control activities may be within IT or manual systems. Exhibit AU-C 315-6 provides other examples of control activities germane to internal control over financial reporting. The auditor typically does not obtain an understanding of the control activities related to every relevant assertion or each transaction class, account balance, and disclosure in the financial statements.

**ENGAGEMENT STRATEGY:** The requirement that the auditor obtain an understanding of all five components of internal control does not suggest that this gathering of information is accomplished as five distinct tasks. The auditor might, for example, develop an understanding of some control activities as part of his or her consideration of the information and communication component of internal control.

## Monitoring

Once internal controls are implemented, management must assess the controls (both from a design perspective and an operational perspective) on a timely basis and make modifications when appropriate. Monitoring of controls involves assessing the quality of internal control performance over time, and is accomplished through ongoing activities, separate evaluations, or both.

Ongoing monitoring should be part of the routine activities of effective internal control, and include supervisory and management activities. The entity's internal audit function may be relevant to the audit if its responsibilities and activities are related to the entity's financial reporting, including monitoring of internal controls, and the auditor expects to use some of the internal auditors' work. In these circumstances, the guidance in AU-C 610 applies. In addition, external parties can have an important role in monitoring internal controls. For example, as part of its role, a regulatory agency might evaluate internal control or the client's customers might complain about billing errors or incorrect shipment of materials. All of these factors make up the monitoring component of internal control.

## Auditor objectives related to internal control

The auditor's primary objective in understanding internal control is to understand whether and how a control prevents, or detects and corrects, material misstatements in relevant assertions related to classes of transactions, account balances, or disclosures. The primary objective is not necessarily to evaluate each of the five internal control components. Therefore, an auditor may define internal control using different terminology or a different framework as long as the internal control objectives underlying the five internal control components are met.

The auditor should obtain an understanding of internal control over financial reporting sufficient to understand the design of controls and whether the controls have been implemented. The auditor uses this knowledge to (1) identify the types of possible misstatements, (2) identify the factors that affect the risk of material misstatement, and (3) design further audit procedures (tests of the operating effectiveness of controls and substantive procedures).

**PLANNING AID REMINDER:** AICPA Technical Practice Aid TIS 8200.05 clarifies that the auditor is required to obtain an understanding of internal control in every audit, even if he or she believes that internal control is not effective. This requirement applies even if the auditor intends to design a substantive audit approach and not rely on controls. Additionally, AICPA Technical Practice Aid

TIS 8200.11 notes that the auditor cannot skip the evaluation and documentation of controls when he or she believes the controls over financial reporting are nonexistent or ineffective. The auditor is required to obtain a sufficient understanding of internal controls to assess their design and implementation. The purpose of obtaining such an understanding in every audit is to evaluate the design of controls to provide the auditor with information to assess the risk of material misstatements. When the auditor believes, based on his or her understanding of internal controls, that controls do not exist to prevent or detect material misstatements in financial statements, he or she would plan and perform substantive procedures to respond to the assessed risks. The auditor needs to be satisfied that only performing substantive procedures provides sufficient appropriate evidence to support his or her opinion. Additionally, the auditor must evaluate identified control deficiencies to determine whether any are deemed to be significant deficiencies or material weaknesses for communication in writing to management and those charged with governance.

*Relevant assertions*

The auditor obtains an understanding of the entity and its environment, including internal controls, to assess the risk of material misstatements in the financial statements. Misstatements arise when assertions made by management in the preparation and presentation of financial statements are violated. The assertions are made by management implicitly and explicitly when they prepare and present financial information in accordance with the applicable financial reporting framework. These assertions relate to the recognition, measurement, presentation, and disclosure of the various elements of the financial statements. These assertions encompass the following two categories:

1. Assertions related to classes of transactions and
2. Assertions related to account balances at the end of the period.

**IMPORTANT NOTICE FOR 2022:** In May 2019, the AICPA's Auditing Standards Board (ASB) issued SAS No. 134 titled *Auditor Reporting and Amendments, Including Amendments Addressing Disclosures in the Audit of Financial Statements* to revise the auditor's report and to amend various AU-C sections to heighten the auditor's focus on disclosures throughout the process of auditing financial statements. SAS No. 134 amends AU-C 315 to revise the assertions for presentation and disclosure to promote their more consistent and effective use by integrating the relevant assertions relating to disclosures within the other categories of assertions rather than keeping them as separate assertions. As a result, the assertions related to classes of transactions now include a new presentation assertion and the assertions related to account balances also now include a new classification and presentation assertion. The assertions related to presentation and disclosure will no longer be as a separate category from the other categories of assertions once SAS No. 134 becomes effective. Originally, the effective date of SAS No. 134 was for audits of financial statements periods ending on or after December 15, 2020, with early implementation **not** permitted. However, the ASB's issuance of SAS No. 141, *Amendment to the Effective Dates of SAS Nos. 134-140*, extended the effective date of SAS No. 134 to December 15, 2021, in order to provide more time for firms to implement SAS No. 134 in light of the effect of the coronavirus pandemic. While SAS No. 141

allows for early implementation of SAS No. 134, the ASB recommends that SAS Nos. 134-140 be implemented concurrently.

There are six assertions that relate to classes of transactions and events, and related disclosures, for the period under audit:

1. *Occurrence* The entity has entered into the transactions and events that are recorded.
2. *Completeness* All transactions and events that affected the entity during the period have been recorded.
3. *Accuracy* Transactions and events are recorded at the right amount.
4. *Cutoff* Transactions and events are recorded in the right period.
5. *Classification* Transactions and events are recorded in the right account.
6. *Presentation* Transactions and events are appropriately summarized and clearly described, and disclosures are relevant and understandable.

There are six assertions that relate to account balances and related disclosures at the end of the period under audit:

1. *Existence* Assets, liabilities, and owners' interests exist.
2. *Rights and obligations* The entity holds or controls the rights to recorded assets, and recorded liabilities are obligations of the entity.
3. *Completeness* All of the entity's assets, liabilities, and owners' interests have been recorded, and all related disclosures that should be included have been included.
4. *Accuracy, valuation, and allocation* Assets, liabilities, and owners' interests have been properly recorded and disclosed at appropriate amounts.
5. *Classification* Assets, liabilities, and owner's interests have been recorded in the proper accounts.
6. *Presentation* Assets, liabilities, and owner's interests are summarized and clearly described and related disclosures are understandable and relevant.

**OBSERVATION:** The auditor may use the list of assertions or develop his or her own list of assertions (as long as the objectives underlying the foregoing assertions are met).

The auditor uses the assertions to form the basis for the assessment of risks of material misstatement and to design and perform further audit procedures. The risk of material misstatement may relate directly to a particular assertion for classes of transactions, account balances, or disclosures or it may pertain to the financial statements taken as a whole. If the risk of material misstatement pertains to the overall financial statements, many assertions will be affected.

## Understanding the Entity's Internal Control

The auditor is required to obtain an understanding of internal control in every engagement in order to assess the risks of material misstatement and to have an adequate basis to plan the nature, timing, and extent of audit procedures that are responsive to these risks.

> **PLANNING AND REMINDER:** AU-C 315 requires the auditor to obtain an understanding of internal control. Auditors may perform walk-throughs of transactions to confirm their understanding of internal control relevant to transaction processing. Walk-throughs are considered to be a good practice, and an auditor might (although is not required to) perform a walk-through of significant accounting cycles every year. AICPA Technical Practice Aid TIS 8200.12 notes that a walk-through performed every year might be an effective technique that the auditor performs to update his or her understanding of the control in order to allow him or her to rely on certain audit evidence obtained in prior years that is based on the continued performance of that control in the current fiscal period. In that instance, the walk-through may be an efficient and effective technique to obtain an understanding of the continued relevance of the audit evidence obtained in prior years. Furthermore, when performing a walk-through of controls, the auditor might identify improvements to the controls that the client should consider implementing. A by-product of obtaining an understanding of controls is that suggestions for improvements can be made to the client, which adds value to the audit process.

> **PUBLIC COMPANY IMPLICATION:** SOX requires all public companies to issue an "internal control report" by management. Furthermore, SOX requires that auditors of the larger, accelerated filer public companies issue a separate opinion based on their evaluation of the effectiveness of internal control over financial reporting. Auditors of all entities, including auditors of public companies, must obtain an understanding of internal control over financial reporting. Auditors of accelerated filer public companies must also perform tests of controls in every audit that are sufficient to provide separate assurance about the design and operating effectiveness of internal control over financial reporting.

*Limitations and general characteristics of internal control*

Internal control is subject to limitations through unintentional means such as faulty decision-making and human error or through intentional means, including collusion to circumvent controls and management override of controls. Because of this, internal control can only provide reasonable assurance, not absolute assurance, that the entity is achieving its financial reporting objectives. In smaller entities, sufficient segregation of duties may not be practicable but this internal control deficiency can be compensated for through more effective oversight than in a larger entity. Finally, a basic concept in the design of internal control is the expectation that controls must be cost-effective. That is, the benefits derived from an internal control procedure should exceed the cost of adopting the procedure. When designing an internal control, an entity cannot measure the cost-benefit relation precisely, but a reasonable analysis combined with appropriate judgment and estimates is useful.

---

**FRAUD POINTER:** One of the limitations of internal control is that management is in a unique position to commit fraud because it can override established controls. The risk of management override when the entity is run by an owner-manager depends heavily on the entity's control environment and on the owner-manager's attitude toward internal control. Since the risk of management override of internal control is present in virtually all audits, AU-C 240 mandates that certain audit procedures be performed in every audit to respond to the ever-present risk of management override. Auditors must (1) examine journal entries and other adjustments, (2) review accounting estimates for bias, and (3) evaluate the business reason for significant unusual transactions.

---

Entities' internal control systems often combine manual and automated elements with characteristics relevant to the auditor's risk assessment and further audit procedures. Manual controls (1) may be independent of IT, (2) may use information generated by the IT system, (3) may be used to monitor IT functioning and automated controls, and (4) may be used to handle exceptions from normal transaction processing. An entity's use of IT may affect internal control components related to financial reporting, operations, or compliance objectives as well as the way in which transactions are initiated, authorized, recorded, processed, and reported. The nature and characteristics of the entity's information system will cause the extent and nature of the risks to internal control to vary among entities.

The use of IT-based controls can benefit internal control because of the following IT system characteristics:
- Predefined business rules and complicated calculations can be consistently applied by IT to a large number of similar transactions;
- Information can be processed accurately by IT and be available to internal users in a timely fashion;
- A variety of analytical tools can be applied by IT to the processed information;
- An entity's IT-based activities and its policies and procedures can be better monitored;
- The risk that IT controls can be circumvented can be reduced; and
- Security controls for applications, databases, and operating systems can be implemented to enhance the effective segregation of duties.

On the other hand, the use of IT controls introduces a variety of specific risks related to the internal control environment. Risks that are related to IT-based controls can arise through the following situations:
- A reliance on automated procedures that are incorrectly processing data or that are processing incorrect data;
- Changing, destroying, or introducing new data into the system without proper authorization;

- IT personnel gaining excess access privileges thereby breaking down segregation of duties;
- An unauthorized change of data in a master file;
- An unauthorized change to a system or a program;
- The failure to make necessary changes to a system or a program;
- Inappropriate manual intervention (i.e., override of IT-based processing); or
- The potential loss of data.

Although IT controls offer many advantages and are increasingly common in today's business environment, manual controls may be more appropriate where judgment and discretion are needed. For example, manual controls are particularly germane in the case of (1) transactions that are large, unusual, or nonrecurring; (2) transactions or events where defining or predicting misstatements is difficult; (3) rapidly changing circumstances where a unique or custom control response may be needed; and (4) monitoring the performance of automated controls. However, manual controls have a number of limitations, and therefore their use may be less suitable for high-volume or recurring transactions. It is easier to bypass, override, or ignore manual controls than IT controls, and manual controls are more prone to error or mistake. The auditor cannot assume that manual controls have been applied on a consistent basis. As a result, the auditor should test a sample of transactions where the manual control is expected to operate to evaluate the operating effectiveness of any manual control that the auditor plans to rely on.

---

**PLANNING AID REMINDER:** If the auditor decides to use an outside professional with specialized IT skills to evaluate and test IT systems and controls, the guidance in AU-C 620 (*Using the Work of an Auditor's Specialist*) should be followed.

---

*Controls relevant to the audit*

AU-C 315 notes that management develops internal control related to a broad spectrum of objectives ranging from financial reporting matters to the efficient execution of operational activities. However, the auditor's consideration of internal controls in an audit of financial statements is specific. The auditor is concerned with internal control and its components as they relate to the reliability of financial reporting. More specifically, the auditor is concerned with relevant assertions over classes of transactions, account balances, and presentation and disclosure.

The auditor is not required to assess all controls that are designed to reduce the risk of a material misstatement in the financial statements. The determination of which controls to be assessed is a function of the auditor's professional judgment. However, in exercising his or her professional judgment, the auditor should consider the following:

- Materiality of the assertion related to the class of transaction, account balance, or disclosure that the control pertained to;
- The entity's size (see Exhibit AU-C 315-7 for examples of the application of internal control concepts to small and midsize entities);
- The nature of the entity's business (e.g., organizational and ownership characteristics) and information systems;
- The diversity and complexity of the entity's operations;
- Legal and regulatory requirements; and
- Whether and how a control, alone or in combination with others, prevents or detects and corrects material misstatement.

**PLANNING AID REMINDER:** During the planning stage of the audit engagement, the auditor's responsibility to gain an understanding of internal control is limited to understanding the design of the system of controls and determining whether internal controls are in place; it does not include determining whether those controls are operating effectively. (Determining whether controls are operating effectively is part of further audit procedures, which are discussed in AU-C 330.)

The auditor is not primarily concerned with controls related to the efficiency and effectiveness of operations or compliance with laws and regulations; however, these controls may be relevant if they relate to the generation of information or data that the auditor will use in performing other audit procedures. For example, quality control data may be useful for testing the assertion in the financial statements that the allowance for returned goods is properly valued. Likewise, controls related to compliance with laws and regulations are likely to be relevant if noncompliance could have a material and direct effect on financial statement amounts and disclosures (e.g., compliance with income tax laws and regulations).

*Determine the extent of internal control understanding needed*

The auditor needs to test whether controls have been designed and implemented (i.e., the control exists and is being used). The focus is on determining whether the control is likely to prevent (or detect and correct) material misstatements in the financial statements. A control that is improperly designed may represent a material weakness, and the auditor will have to make this evaluation.

An auditor evaluates the design and implementation of controls by performing a combination of procedures—inquiry, observation, inspection of documents and reports, and tracing transactions through the accounting system. Reliance on inquiry alone is not sufficient. In most cases, obtaining an understanding of the design of a control is not sufficient to conclude that the control is operating effectively. However, if the control is automated, and the entity has strong general computer controls (particularly over computer security and program changes), the auditor's testing of the design and implementation of an automated control may provide evidence of the operating effectiveness of the control.

> **FRAUD POINTER:** AU-C 240 reminds the auditor that as part of gaining an understanding of an entity's internal control, he or she should evaluate whether the internal controls that address identified risks of material misstatement due to fraud have been suitably designed and placed in operation. These controls may be specific controls designed to mitigate specific fraud risks, or they may be broad programs and controls designed to prevent, deter, and detect fraud.

*Understanding the internal control component: control environment*

The auditor should obtain an understanding of the attitudes, awareness, and actions of management and those charged with governance toward internal control and its importance in the entity. In other words, the auditor attempts to assess the entity's "tone at the top"—that is, how important are strong internal controls and reliable financial reporting to those ultimately responsible for the entity's operations and performance? It is this control environment that sets the tone of the organization and provides a foundation for the other internal control components.

> **PLANNING AID REMINDER:** The control environment may be less formal in smaller entities than larger entities. AICPA Technical Practice Aid TIS 8200.08 reminds auditors that auditing standards require the auditor to understand all components of internal control, including the control environment, sufficiently to evaluate the design of the controls and to determine whether they have been placed in operation. Even in smaller entities, auditors may rely on the control environment to determine the nature, timing, and extent of further audit procedures. Thus, auditors are required to understand the control environment even when it is less formal. When auditors rely on aspects of the control environment, they are required to test those controls. Because of the potential impact on audit strategy, auditors are encouraged to evaluate the control environment early in the audit process.

The auditor should evaluate whether control environment elements have been implemented. For example, an entity may claim to have a hotline process, but the auditor should determine whether the hotline has been established, whether employees know about it, and whether it is being used. Also, an entity may state that employees must sign an acknowledgment on a yearly basis that they are in compliance with the entity's code of conduct, but is there any evidence that these employee certifications are taking place and does the entity follow up with employees who fail to provide the certification? The auditor should obtain sufficient, appropriate audit evidence through inquiries, supplemented with observation and inspection, to determine whether control environment elements have been implemented.

Some elements of an entity's control environment have a pervasive effect on assessing the risks of material misstatement, one of which is the role of those charged with governance. The auditor should consider the independence from management of those charged with governance (e.g., the board of directors, audit committee). For example, if management's compensation is highly variable and that variability is tied (directly or indirectly) to reported financial results (e.g., bonuses, stock options, grants, and other awards) there is a tension between management's desire to increase their compensation and the requirement to produce accurate financial statements. Those charged with governance are one of the few checks on management's behavior in this situation; however, the effectiveness of these individuals in acting as a check on management is often dependent on their independence from management.

Other factors that may impact the effectiveness of the control environment include whether those charged with governance understand the entity's business transactions and the extent to which they evaluate whether the financial statements are prepared in accordance with the applicable financial reporting framework. Although nonpublic companies are not required to have financial experts among those charged with governance, the entity's control environment is likely to be stronger if individuals with financial expertise are involved in overseeing the affairs of the entity.

In making an overall evaluation of the control environment component, the auditor should consider the strengths and weaknesses in the various control environment elements. A strong control environment reduces the risk of material misstatement, particularly the risk of material misstatement due to fraud. Because the control environment is the foundation for all the other elements of internal control, this component has a pervasive effect on the risks of material misstatement and therefore the auditor's evaluation of the nature, timing, and extent of further audit procedures. However, the operation of the control environment is not specific enough to provide substantial audit comfort that material misstatements in individual classes of transactions, account balances, or disclosures will be prevented or detected.

*Understanding the internal control component: risk assessment by the entity*

When the auditor is obtaining an understanding of the entity's risk assessment process, the determination of whether that risk assessment process is appropriate to the entity's circumstances is a matter of judgment.

---

**IMPORTANT NOTICE FOR 2022:** To help organizations strengthen their risk assessment processes, COSO has a thought paper, *Risk Assessment in Practice*, which contains guidance about techniques that can be used by management and boards to assess the likelihood, impact, and other dimensions of potential risk events. The paper, which can be downloaded from COSO for free at www.coso.org, provides application examples and best practice guidance about the process of assessing the significance of risk events for the entity.

---

*Understanding the internal control component: information and communication system*

Auditors should obtain an understanding of related business processes of the entity to further the understanding of the entity's information system relevant to financial reporting. Related business processes include developing, purchasing, producing, selling, and distributing an entity's products and services, ensuring compliance with laws and regulations, and recording information including financial reporting and accounting information.

**ENGAGEMENT STRATEGY:** When transaction totals are entered into the general ledger automatically and when financial statements are prepared using IT, there may be little in the way of an audit trail. In these situations, it is important that the auditor be able to rely on the client's IT controls. Also, the auditor may want to consider having a computer audit specialist on the engagement and/or using computer-assisted audit techniques.

---

**FRAUD POINTER:** To address the risk of management override of internal controls, AU-C 240 requires the auditor in every audit to examine journal entries and other adjustments for evidence of possible misstatements. The required understanding of both automated and manual procedures related to the process for recording journal entries and adjustments helps the auditor in examining journal entries and other adjustments for evidence of possible misstatements. The auditor's understanding of the entity's financial reporting process can help in identifying the type, number, and monetary value of journal entries and other adjustments that are typically made in preparing the financial statements.

---

The auditor should understand how the entity communicates financial reporting roles and responsibilities to affected employees and how it communicates matters related to financial reporting to affected parties. Communication often occurs through policy manuals and financial reporting manuals, which the auditor may consider examining. Employees should understand how their roles and responsibilities relate to the work of others, and they should understand the entity's processes for reporting financial reporting exceptions to their supervisors and other levels of management within the entity.

*Understanding the internal control component: control activities*

In reviewing control activities, the auditor's primary consideration is understanding how a control activity alone or in combination with other control activities either prevents or detects and corrects material misstatements in the financial statements. The focus is on identifying and understanding relevant control activities, which are those related to significant risks and risks for which substantive procedures alone do not provide sufficient appropriate audit evidence as well as those that are relevant in the auditor's judgment, such as those in financial statement areas where a material misstatement is most likely to occur.

To understand how IT affects control activities, the auditor should obtain an understanding of both application controls and general computer controls. Application controls apply to processing transactions by individual applications and help to ensure transactions occurred, are authorized, and are completely and accurately recorded and processed. For example, the review and follow-up of items on a system-generated exception report depends on the accuracy of the underlying system-generated information.

The entity's control activities should be designed to respond to IT-related risks. For example, effective general computer controls reduce the risks associated with relying on application controls. The auditor's focus is on those controls that maintain the integrity and security of system-generated information (i.e., that prevent or detect unauthorized additions, modifications, or deletions to this information).

*Understanding the internal control component: monitoring*

Management often relies on internally generated information in performing monitoring activities. Management may assume that the information is accurate, but this assumption should not be made unless the controls over the generation of the information are designed and operating effectively or the accuracy of the information has been directly tested. The auditor should understand the information sources used by management in performing monitoring activities, and management's basis for relying on this information.

## Identifying and Assessing the Risks of Material Misstatement

*Assessment of risks of material misstatement at the financial statement and assertion levels*

The auditor uses the assertions described earlier to form the basis for the assessment of risks of material misstatement and to design and perform further audit procedures. The risk of material misstatement may relate directly to a particular assertion for classes of transactions, account balances, or disclosures or it may pertain to the financial statements taken as a whole. If the risk of material misstatement pertains to the overall financial statements, many assertions will be affected. Financial statement risks are often especially relevant to the auditor's assessment of the risks of material misstatement due to fraud. Risks related to the financial statements taken as a whole often may relate to a deficient control environment. Weaknesses in the control environment often have a pervasive effect on the audit and may call for an overall response by the auditor (e.g., assign more experienced personnel to the engagement, devote more partner and manager time to supervising the engagement, increase the overall skepticism that the engagement is performed with).

Risks of material misstatement at the assertion level should also be considered because they help to determine the nature, timing, and extent of further audit procedures necessary in the audit. Management implicitly or explicitly makes assertions about the classes of transaction and events for the period under audit, account balances at the end of the period, and presentation and disclosure. The auditor is then responsible for considering the types of potential misstatements that could occur regarding relevant assertions. Relevant assertions are those that have a reasonable possibility of containing misstatements that would cause the financial statements to be materially misstated.

The auditor's consideration of disclosures in the financial statements includes qualitative and quantitative disclosures. Qualitative aspects might include liquidity and debt covenants, circumstances triggering impairment losses, changes in accounting policies, related-party transactions, among other matters. Disclosures may be less detailed or less complex for smaller entities.

In gaining an understanding of an entity's internal control, the auditor may develop concerns regarding the integrity of the entity's management or the condition and reliability of an entity's records such that the auditor's opinion may need to be modified or the auditor may need to withdraw from the engagement where doing so is legally allowed.

---

**IMPORTANT NOTICE FOR 2022:** In May 2019, the AICPA's Auditing Standards Board (ASB) issued SAS No. 134 titled *Auditor Reporting and Amendments, Including Amendments Addressing Disclosures in the Audit of Financial Statements* to revise the auditor's report and to amend various AU-C sections to heighten the auditor's focus on disclosures throughout the process of auditing financial statements. SAS No. 134 amends AU-C 315 to remind the auditor that when assessing risks of material misstatements in the financial statements, the auditor should consider the risks of misstatement in not only quantitative aspects of disclosure but also qualitative aspects of disclosures. Originally, the effective date of SAS No. 134 was for audits of financial statements periods ending on or after December 15, 2020, with early implementation **not** permitted. However, the ASB's issuance of SAS No. 141, *Amendment to the Effective Dates of SAS Nos. 134-140*, extended the effective date of SAS No. 134 to December 15, 2021, in order to provide more time for firms to implement SAS No. 134 in light of the effect of the coronavirus pandemic. While SAS No. 141 allows for early implementation of SAS No. 134, the ASB recommends that SAS Nos. 134-140 be implemented concurrently.

---

*Auditor's evaluation of controls*

In evaluating controls, the auditor primarily focuses on those controls that are likely to prevent or detect and correct material misstatements in relevant assertions. The relevance of an assertion depends on its nature, the volume of transactions or data related to the assertion, and the nature and complexity of the systems the entity uses to process and control information supporting the assertion. In some cases, multiple controls must operate effectively to reduce the risk of material misstatement for a particular assertion to an appropriately low level. In other cases, a single control activity may be sufficient to achieve a control objective for a relevant assertion. For example, the entity's controls related to completing the count of physical inventory are designed to address the existence and completeness assertions for the inventory account balance.

Some controls are directly related to an assertion, while other controls are indirectly related to an assertion. For example, preventive controls, especially those that are control activities, tend to be directly related to an assertion. Detective controls (e.g., management reviews of business performance) are more likely to be indirectly related to an assertion. In general, more direct controls are more effective in reducing the risk of material misstatement.

> **OBSERVATION:** The auditor may identify deficiencies in internal control as part of the risk assessment process. If these deficiencies rise to the level of significant deficiencies or material weaknesses, they must be communicated in writing to those charged with governance.

*Significant risks requiring special audit attention*

Significant risks often relate to significant unusual transactions and judgmental matters, whereas less complex, routine transactions that are subject to systematic processing are less likely to produce significant risks. Exhibit AU-C 315-8 presents factors that may indicate a heightened risk of material misstatement. Issues requiring the auditor's attention are (1) risks related to unusual transactions, (2) risks related to judgmental matters, and (3) management controls over nonroutine transactions and judgmental matters.

> **IMPORTANT NOTICE FOR 2022:** The exposure draft of a proposed new Statement on Auditing Standard, *Understanding the Entity and its Environment and Assessing the Risks of Material Misstatement*, issued in August 2020 acknowledges that the determination of whether a risk is a significant risk requires application of professional judgment. A significant risk is not limited to those risks with both a higher likelihood of occurrence and higher magnitude of potential misstatement, should the risk occur. A significant risk could also include risks potentially lower in likelihood but for which the magnitude could be very high if it occurred.

Unusual transactions are more likely to represent a significant risk when (1) management is involved in specifying the accounting treatment, especially operating management, (2) the transaction involves complex accounting principles or computations, (3) the transaction is with related parties, (4) the transaction is not subject to the entity's normal internal control processes, and (5) there is extensive manual involvement in collecting and processing the data underlying the transaction.

Financial statement amounts and disclosures whose determination involves significant judgment, especially accounting estimates, are more likely to represent a significant risk. In particular, estimates that are dependent on the occurrence or nonoccurrence of future events are more prone to misstatement. In addition, judgments involving revenue recognition for certain types of transactions can be subject to differing interpretations, increasing the likelihood of a misstatement.

Although unusual transactions and judgmental matters are less likely to be subject to routine controls, management still needs to develop controls over these issues. The auditor should consider *whether* and *how* management responds to unusual transactions and judgmental matters. For example, when assumptions are involved in determining recorded amounts, the assumptions should be reviewed by senior management or experts. In addition, management should have implemented formal processes for developing significant accounting estimates, including review by senior management and, in some instances, those charged with governance.

> **OBSERVATION:** If the entity does not have effective controls over significant risks and the auditor evaluates this deficiency as either a significant deficiency or a material weakness, he or she should communicate this matter to those charged with governance.

*Risks for which substantive procedures alone are not sufficient*

The auditor may not be able to reduce detection risk to an acceptably low level using only substantive procedures when an entity processes significant classes of business transactions (e.g., revenues, purchases, cash receipts, and cash disbursements) entirely using automated processing. In these instances, audit evidence might exist only in electronic form and the reliability of such electronic evidence depends on the design and operating effectiveness of the controls over the generation of the evidence. There is also a heightened risk that information can be improperly initiated or altered if the initiation, authorization, recording, processing, or reporting of transactions occurs only in electronic form. In these circumstances, the auditor will have to rely on the effectiveness of internal controls, at least to some extent, to reduce detection risk to an appropriately low level.

*Assessment of risk throughout the engagement*

The auditor assesses the risk of material misstatement in the planning stage of the audit based on his or her understanding of the entity and its environment, including internal control. As the auditor performs further audit procedures, his or her initial assessment may change. For example, the auditor might find that controls that he or she planned to rely on are not operating effectively. The auditor might also find errors in performing substantive tests that are larger and more frequent than he or she expected based on his or her initial risk assessment. In these situations, the auditor should revise his or her risk assessments and modify the nature, timing, and extent of audit procedures as appropriate.

*Documentation*

The auditor uses his or her professional judgment in determining the nature and extent of documentation. The nature and extent of the auditor's documentation depends on (1) the nature, size, and complexity of the entity and its environment, including its internal control; (2) how much information is available from the entity; (3) the extent of the auditor's procedures; and (4) the auditor's specific audit methodology. Generally, the larger and more complex the entity and the greater the extent of the auditor's procedures, the more extensive the auditor's documentation will be. The extent of documentation sufficient for the auditors to obtain an appropriate understanding of the entity may also be greater if the engagement team is less experienced. Documentation may be carried forward and updated to reflect any changes in a recurring audit.

> **PLANNING AID REMINDER:** Although it is recommended that an entity document its controls so that the auditor can efficiently understand them, assess the risk of material misstatement, and test them for operating effectiveness, controls

do not have to be documented by the client for them to be tested. If the entity does not document a control and it is an important control, AU-C 315 requires the auditor to document the control as part of his or her risk assessment procedures to identify and assess the risks of material misstatements.

## Practitioner's Aids

The following exhibits may be used as practitioner's aids.

§ 315 • Understanding the Entity and Its Environment    **3051**

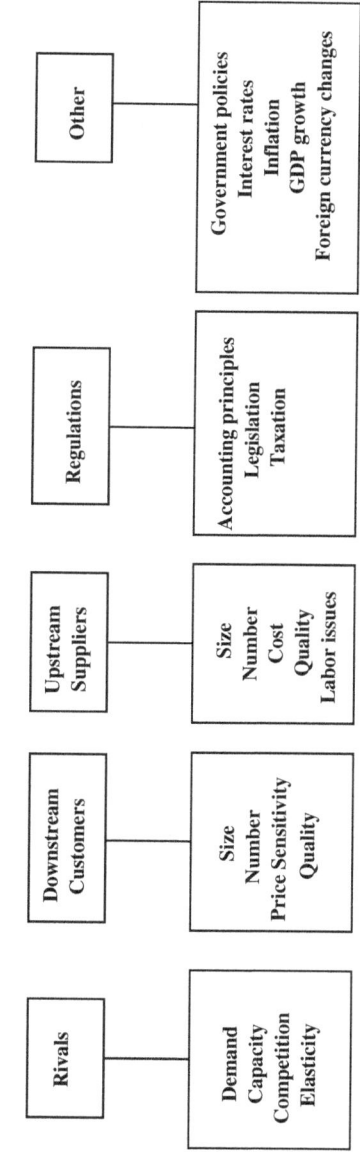

EXHIBIT AU-C 315-1—EXAMPLES OF INDUSTRY, REGULATORY, AND OTHER EXTERNAL FACTORS

# EXHIBIT AU-C 315-2—NATURE OF THE ENTITY AND RELEVANT STANDARDS OF FINANCIAL REPORTING

| Nature of the Entity | Examples | Relevant Standards of Financial Reporting[a] |
|---|---|---|
| Business operations | Geographic segments | ASC 280 |
| | Joint ventures | ASC 323 |
| | Key customers | ASC 280 |
| | Long-term supply contracts | ASC 440, ASC 470 |
| | Major customers | ASC 280 |
| | Pension, other postretirement benefits, and other postemployment benefits | ASC 715, ASC 712, ASC 958 |
| | Related-party transactions | ASC 850 |
| | Research and development activities | ASC 730, ASC 985 |
| | Sources of revenue | ASC 605 |
| | Stock option plans | ASC 718, ASC 505 |
| | Subsidiaries or divisions | ASC 810, ASC 840 |
| | Warranties | ASC 450 |
| Investments | Acquisitions, mergers, and disposals | ASC 350, ASC 805 |
| | Investments in securities | ASC 320, ASC 323 |
| | Derivatives | ASC 815 |
| | Capital expenditures | ASC 835 |
| Financing | Off-balance-sheet financing | ASC 460 |
| | Leasing | ASC 840 |
| Financial reporting | Revenue recognition | ASC 605 |
| | Fair-value accounting | ASC 820, ASC 825 |
| | Foreign currency transactions and translation | ASC 830 |

[a] Not a complete list. Readers desiring a more complete list or a detailed discussion of these pronouncements might refer to CCH's *GAAP Guide,* by Williams et al.

§ 315 • Understanding the Entity and Its Environment    3053

## EXHIBIT AU-C 315-3—EXAMPLES OF ELEMENTS OF THE CONTROL ENVIRONMENT

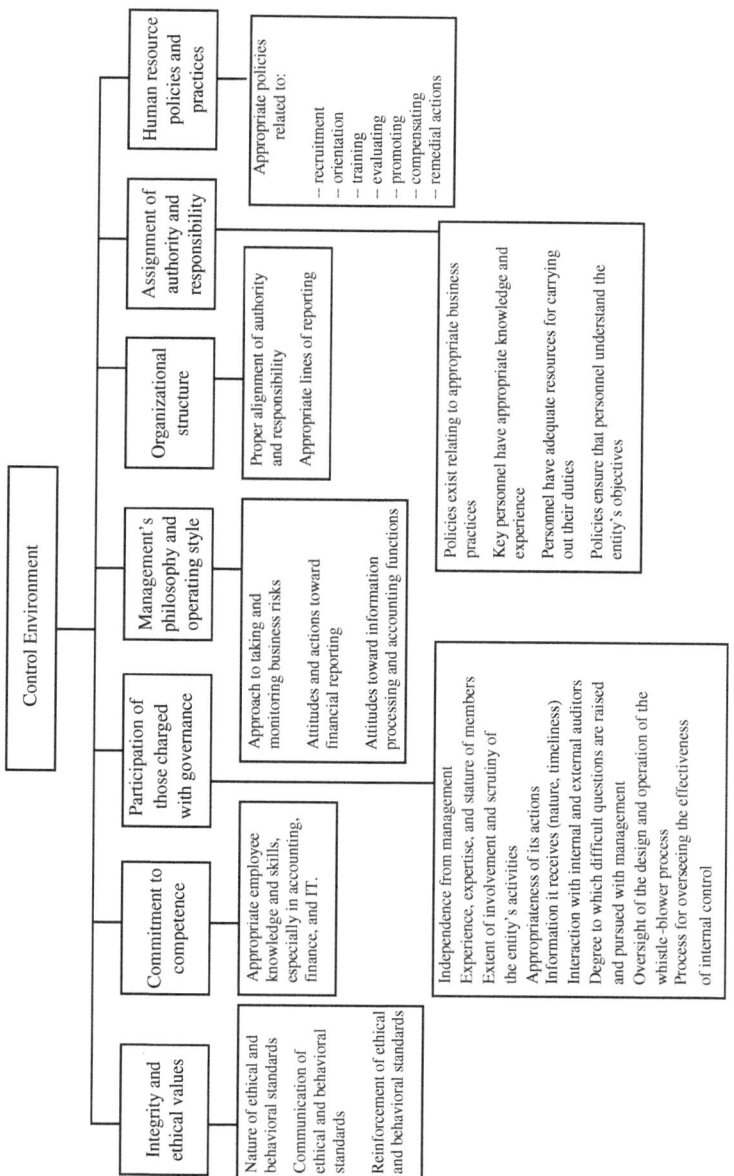

EXHIBIT AU-C 315-4—EXAMPLES OF FACTORS AFFECTING ENTITY RISKS

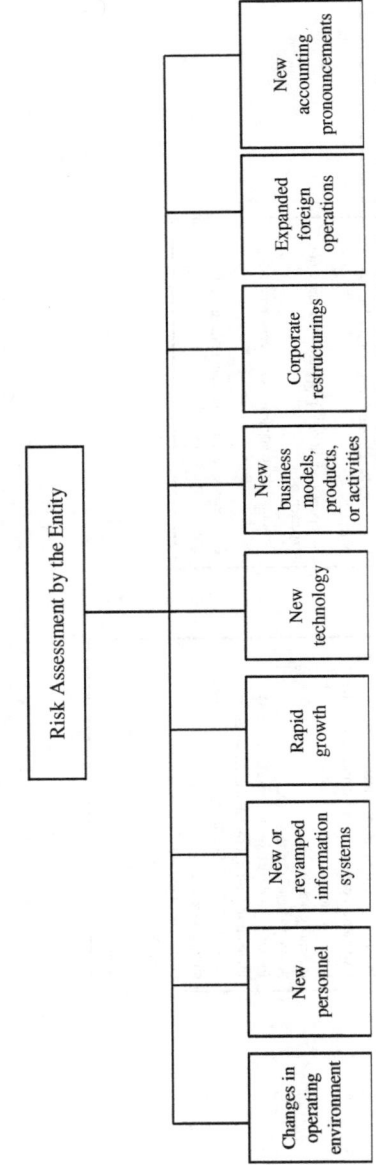

§ 315 • Understanding the Entity and Its Environment    **3055**

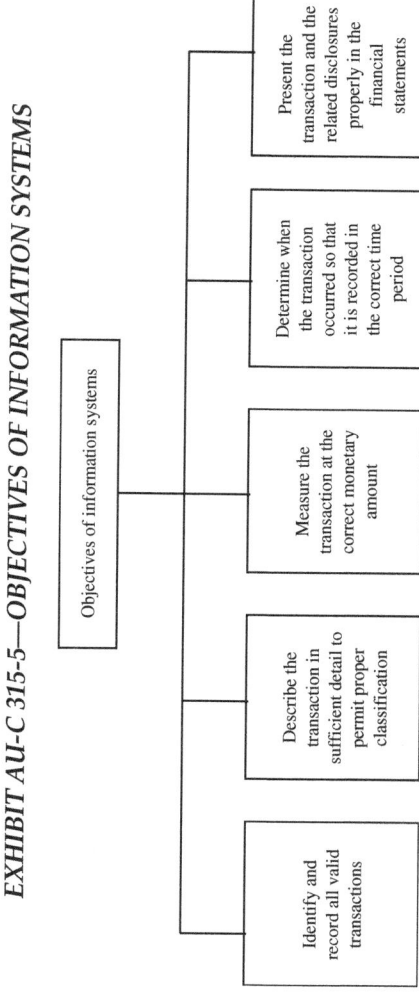

EXHIBIT AU-C 315-5—OBJECTIVES OF INFORMATION SYSTEMS

# EXHIBIT AU-C 315-6—EXAMPLES OF CONTROL ACTIVITIES GERMANE TO INTERNAL CONTROL OVER FINANCIAL REPORTING

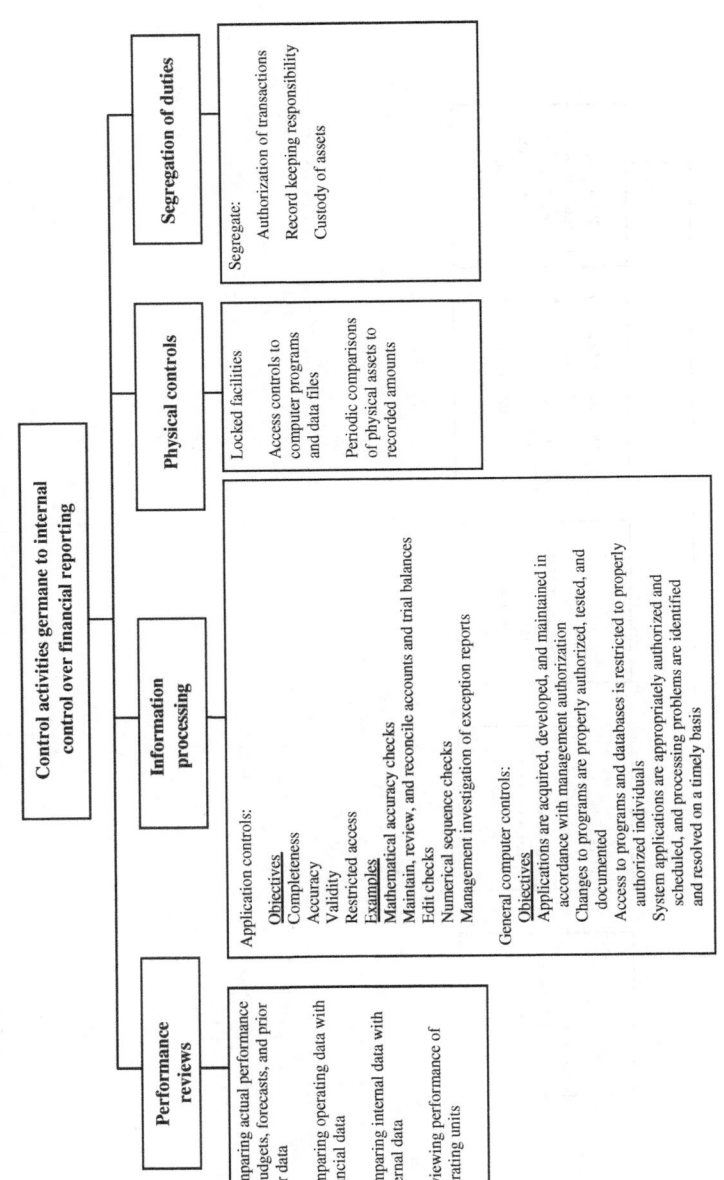

## EXHIBIT AU-C 315-7—APPLICATION OF INTERNAL CONTROL CONCEPTS TO SMALL AND MIDSIZED ENTITIES

Internal control is a critical element in helping the client to prepare financial statements that reflect U.S. generally accepted accounting principles (U.S. GAAP). However, AU-C 315 recognizes that internal control will often be designed and implemented differently for a large company than for a small or even a midsized company. For example, the five components of internal control may not be clearly distinguishable in a smaller entity; rather, the owner-manager in a smaller entity may perform functions that cut across the five components of internal control. Although the internal control objectives underlying the internal control components should be met in every entity regardless of size, how the control objectives are achieved can vary from client to client. For example, the following features of a small or midsized entity's internal control may be as effective as the features adopted by a larger entity:

- *Control environment* Controls related to the control environment might not be as extensively documented in a formal manner but, rather, may be communicated orally and by management example to affected personnel. For example, although a formal code of conduct might not be reduced to written form, the essence of such a code might be part of the culture of the entity. In addition, smaller companies might not have independent or outside members among the group charged with governance of the entity. In fact, in some very small entities, it is often the owner-manager him- or herself who is charged with governance.

- *Risk assessment by entity* Risk assessment related to the preparation of financial statements might be less formal in a small company. However, all entities regardless of size, should have established financial reporting objectives. They may just be implicit rather than explicit in smaller entities. It is often the case that because of their involvement in the day-to-day operations of the entity, key managerial personnel (including owner-managers), are fully aware of the relationship between various operational activities and financial reporting objectives. The auditor should discuss with management how risks are identified and how they are managed.

- *Information and communication systems* Documentation of the information and communication system and related controls might not be as extensive or formal in a small company. The active involvement by a relatively small number of managerial personnel might not require formal accounting manuals or sophisticated accounting records. Also, communication in a smaller entity is often easier to achieve.

- *Control activities* Management involvement might substitute for certain types of control activities in smaller entities (e.g., management may specifically authorize the entity to enter into transactions through its direct involvement). Segregation of duties can often be a challenge in a smaller entity. However, reasonable segregation of duties can often be achieved even in an entity with only a few employees through (1) appropriate assignment of responsibilities to these few individuals, (2) management oversight of incompatible activities, or (3) utilization of embedded controls in packaged software programs.

- *Monitoring* Ongoing monitoring activities in smaller entities are likely to be informal. However, management's day-to-day involvement in operational activities may provide an adequate separate evaluation of the effectiveness of the design and operation of internal control.

The auditor's process of obtaining an understanding of the entity and its environment is also typically different for a small entity than for a midsize or large entity. For example, smaller entities often don't reduce their objectives and strategies to written form. These entities also may not have formal processes for managing business risks. The auditor obtains an understanding of the entity and its environment through discussions with management, and through his or her observation of how the business is run (i.e., what the implicit objectives and strategies are) and risks are managed.

Smaller entities may not have a formal process for measuring and reviewing their financial performance. Management of these entities may nonetheless rely on key indicators that they know from experience are accurate barometers of business performance. The auditor should discuss how management measures and reviews the entity's financial performance and document this discussion in the workpapers.

## EXHIBIT AU-C 315-8—FACTORS THAT MIGHT INDICATE A HEIGHTENED RISK OF MATERIAL MISSTATEMENT

**Operating Factors**
- The entity operates in a region that is economically unstable (e.g., highly inflationary economies, countries with political and economic instability).
- The entity has operations in volatile markets (e.g., derivatives trading).
- The entity is struggling to meet objectives it has set, especially if the entity has publicly committed to meeting the objectives.
- The entity has begun offering new products or services.
- The entity has changed its sales, distribution, and production methods.
- There has been turnover among key personnel, especially among senior executives and individuals with financial reporting oversight responsibilities.
- The entity is subject to complex regulations.
- The entity's industry is subject to rapid changes.

**Financing Factors**
- The entity's ability to access capital and credit is constrained.
- The entity has completed a large acquisition or divestiture during the period under audit.
- The entity enters into complex alliances, joint venture agreements, special-purpose entities, and other types of off-balance-sheet financing.

**Financial Reporting Factors**

- There are questions about the ability of the entity to continue as a going concern.
- There are incentives for management and other personnel to engage in fraud.
- The entity lacks an adequate number of personnel with accounting and financial reporting skills.
- The entity has implemented a new information system or made significant modification to existing information systems.
- New accounting pronouncements apply to the entity.
- The entity has changed the accounting policies it uses or the methods used to apply an existing accounting policy.
- The entity's financial reports depend on complex measurements and/or highly subjective judgments (e.g., fair-value accounting).
- The entity enters into material related-party transactions.
- There are weaknesses in the entity's internal control over financial reporting.
- The entity has a history of past misstatements and/or significant material audit adjustments.
- Regulators or others are investigating or have alleged financial reporting improprieties.
- The entity faces pending litigation and other types of contingent liabilities.
- The entity has entered into large revenue transactions at the end of the period.
- The entity has entered into nonroutine and nonsystematic transactions that are material.
- The accounting for material transactions depends on management intent.

# SECTION 320

# MATERIALITY IN PLANNING AND PERFORMING AN AUDIT

## Authoritative Pronouncements

SAS-122—Statements on Auditing Standards: Clarification and Recodification

SAS-134—Auditor Reporting and Amendments, Including Amendments Addressing Disclosures in the Audit of Financial Statements

SAS-138—Amendments to the Description of the Concept of Materiality

SAS-141—Amendment to Effective Dates of SAS Nos. 134-140

## Overview

In determining the nature, timing, and extent of audit procedures, the auditor must consider, among other factors, materiality and audit risk. Considering materiality and audit risk helps the auditor in planning and performing the audit. AU-C 450 (*Evaluation of Misstatement Identified during the Audit*) provides the auditor with guidance in evaluating the effect of any identified misstatements on the audit and of any uncorrected misstatements on the financial statements, and in forming the opinion in the auditor's report.

"Materiality" is generally defined by financial reporting frameworks (such as the FASB's Statement of Financial Accounting Concepts No. 2 (CON-2) (Qualitative Characteristics of Accounting Information)) as omissions or misstatements of accounting information that have a substantial likelihood of influencing the judgment made by a reasonable person relying on the financial statements. Judgments about materiality are affected by the circumstances, including the size and nature of the misstatements, as well as by the common needs of the financial statement users, and those judgments may involve both quantitative and qualitative considerations.

"Audit risk" is the risk that the auditor may unknowingly fail to appropriately modify his or her opinion on financial statements that are materially misstated and is a function of the risks of material misstatement and detection risk. The concept of audit risk is based on the reality that the audit process can result in only reasonable assurance (not absolute assurance) that the auditor will detect material misstatements in financial statements, whether caused by error or fraud.

**OBSERVATION:** Materiality in an audit engagement relates to the assertions that are explicitly stated or implied in the financial statements. AU-C 315 outlines three classes of assertions: (1) assertions related to classes of transactions, (2) assertions related to account balances, and (3) assertions related to presentation and disclosure.

§ 320 • *Materiality in Planning* 3061

**IMPORTANT NOTICE FOR 2022:** In May 2019, the AICPA's Auditing Standards Board (ASB) issued SAS No. 134 titled *Auditor Reporting and Amendments, Including Amendments Addressing Disclosures in the Audit of Financial Statements* to revise the auditor's report and to amend various AU-C sections to heighten the auditor's focus on disclosures throughout the process of auditing financial statements. SAS No. 134 amends AU-C 320 to clarify the importance of considering whether misstatements in qualitative disclosures could be material. SAS No. 134 emphasizes that assessing whether misstatements in qualitative disclosures are material involves the use of professional judgment to determine whether there is a substantial likelihood that misstatements would influence the judgments made by a reasonable user of the financial statements. Originally, the effective date of SAS No. 134 was for audits of financial statements periods ending on or after December 15, 2020, with early implementation **not** permitted. However, the ASB's issuance of SAS No. 141, *Amendment to the Effective Dates of SAS Nos. 134-140*, extended the effective date of SAS No. 134 to December 15, 2021, in order to provide more time for firms to implement SAS No. 134 in light of the effect of the coronavirus pandemic. While SAS No. 141 allows for early implementation of SAS No. 134, the ASB recommends that SAS Nos. 134-140 be implemented concurrently.

---

**IMPORTANT NOTICE FOR 2022:** In December 2019, the AICPA's Auditing Standards Board (ASB) issued SAS No. 138 titled *Amendments to the Description of the Concept of Materiality* to align the materiality concepts discussed in auditing standards, including AU-C 320, with the definition of materiality used by the U.S. judicial system, the PCAOB auditing standards, and the Financial Accounting Standards Board (FASB). The FASB aligned its definition of materiality in August 2018 to be consistent with the U.S. judicial system and other U.S. standards setters and regulators. The ASB believes it is in the public interest to eliminate existing inconsistencies in definitions of materiality used. The U.S. judicial system defines a misstatement as material if there is "**substantial likelihood** that a reasonable shareholder **would** consider it important," whereas existing auditing standards define a misstatement as material if it "**could reasonably be expected to** influence the judgment of a reasonable person." The original effective date of the amendment was for audits of financial statements for periods ending on or after December 15, 2020. However, the ASB's issuance of SAS No. 141, *Amendment to the Effective Dates of SAS Nos. 134-140*, extended the effective date of SAS No. 138 to December 15, 2021, in order to provide more time for firms to implement SAS No. 134 in light of the effect of the coronavirus pandemic. While SAS No. 141 allows for early implementation of SAS No. 134, the ASB recommends that SAS Nos. 134-140 be implemented concurrently.

---

An auditor's opinion refers to materiality of the financial statements in the context of the financial statements taken as a whole. AU-C 320 notes that in performing the audit the auditor is concerned with matters that either individually or in the aggregate could be material to the financial statements. The auditor's responsibility is to plan and perform the audit to obtain reasonable assurance that material misstatements, whether caused by error or fraud, are detected. Reasonable assurance is achieved by obtaining sufficient appropriate audit evidence to reduce audit risk to the desired level. Judgments about materiality help the auditor determine the nature and extent of risk assessment procedures, identify and assess the risks of material misstatement, and determine further audit procedures.

**ENGAGEMENT STRATEGY:** The auditor is concerned with materiality levels during both the planning and evaluation phases of an engagement. Although conceptually it is possible, usually, the assessment of materiality levels will not be the same at the planning stage as at the evaluation stage. Because the auditor will have more complete information to better assess materiality for a particular engagement, the materiality level at the end of the audit can differ from the materiality used in the planning stage. In fact, if the level of materiality is significantly less at the evaluation stage than at the planning stage, the auditor will generally need to reevaluate the sufficiency of the audit procedures he or she has performed. See AU-C 450 for more specific guidance about materiality considerations when evaluating misstatements identified during the audit.

**PUBLIC COMPANY IMPLICATION:** PCAOB Auditing Standards AS-2101 (*Audit Planning*) and AS-1201 (*Supervision of the Audit Engagement*) affect audit planning and supervision. AS-2101 establishes requirements related to planning the audit, including requirements related to developing an appropriate audit strategy and audit plan. AS-1201 describes the auditor's responsibilities for supervising the engagement, and it applies to the engagement partner and other audit team members who assist the partner in supervising others. Although there are a number of differences between the PCAOB's and ASB's risk standards, the risk-assessment concepts contained in the PCAOB standards should be familiar to most auditors. Audit risk is the risk that the auditor will issue an inappropriate opinion on financial statements that are materially misstated. The auditor is to reduce audit risk to a low level through the application of audit procedures. As a result, the amount of audit effort devoted to particular accounts, classes of transactions, and disclosures should vary based on their respective risk.

## Definitions

| | |
|---|---|
| Performance materiality | Amount(s) set by the auditor at less than materiality to reduce the probability of the aggregate of uncorrected and undetected misstatements exceeding materiality to an appropriately low level. Performance materiality amount(s) can apply to the financial statements as a whole or to particular classes of transactions, account balances, or disclosures. Performance materiality is different from tolerable misstatement. |

## Requirements

The auditor is presumptively required to perform the following procedures in considering materiality when planning and performing the audit:

1. Determine materiality for the financial statements as a whole when establishing the overall audit strategy. Also determine materiality for

particular classes of transactions, account balances, or disclosures for which there is a substantial likelihood that misstatements in amounts smaller than materiality for the financial statements as a whole would influence judgments made by a reasonable financial statement user.

2. Determine performance materiality in order to assess the risks of material misstatement and determine the nature, timing, and extent of further audit procedures.

3. If the auditor becomes aware of information during the audit that would have caused different initial determinations of materiality, revise impacted materiality levels as appropriate.

4. If the auditor concludes a lower materiality level than that initially determined is appropriate for the financial statements as a whole or for particular classes of transactions, account balances, or disclosures, determine if it is necessary to revise performance materiality, and if the nature, timing, and extent of further audit procedures remain appropriate.

5. Documentation should include the following amounts and the factors considered in their determination:

    a. Materiality for the financial statements as a whole;

    b. Any applicable materiality levels for particular classes of transactions, account balances, or disclosures;

    c. Performance materiality; and

    d. Any revision of these materiality levels as the audit progressed.

## Analysis and Application of Procedures

*Determine Materiality during the Planning Phase of the Engagement*

The determination of materiality is a matter of professional judgment. Often the auditor applies a percentage to a chosen benchmark as a step in determining materiality for the financial statements as a whole. In identifying an appropriate benchmark, auditors often consider common financial statement elements (e.g., assets, liabilities, pre-tax income, etc.); specific financial statement accounts or elements, including disclosures, that will be the focus of financial statement users' attention; the nature of the entity, its industry, and the economic environment; the entity's ownership structure and financing methods; and the relative volatility of the benchmark. Appropriate benchmarks for a profit-oriented entity may be profit before tax, total revenues, or gross profit, while appropriate benchmarks for not-for-profit or governmental entities may be total cost, net cost, or asset value. The percentage to be applied to the chosen benchmark is subject to professional judgment and may vary depending on the benchmark chosen and the type of entity being audited. For example, assume that the auditor has established the following analysis as a preliminary step in establishing materiality levels in an engagement:

| Financial Statement Element | Financial Statements Amount (unaudited) | Percentage Misstatement Considered Material | Amount Misstatement Considered Material |
|---|---|---|---|
| Gross profit | $4,000,000 | 6% | $240,000 |
| Income before taxes from continuing items | 3,000,000 | 7% | 210,000 |
| Total assets | 4,000,000 | 10% | 400,000 |
| Current assets | 3,000,000 | 8% | 240,000 |

Although the auditor may be concerned with the misstatement of several financial statement elements, generally the smallest materiality level is used in the planning phase of the engagement. This approach is justified because of the interrelationship of the financial statements and the need for audit efficiency. In the current example, the overall materiality level for the financial statements would be $210,000.

---

**ENGAGEMENT STRATEGY:** When the auditor uses a single materiality threshold for all of the financial statements, the planned audit risk is lower for those items that have a materiality threshold level higher than the single materiality level selected for planning purposes. In the current example, the planned audit risk is lower for the balance sheet (total assets) because the materiality level is $210,000 rather than $400,000. However, AU-C 320 does allow the auditor to use two different levels of materiality for the income statement and balance sheet as part of the engagement strategy. In this example, the auditor may conclude that misstatements aggregating $210,000 are material to the income statement but that misstatements to the balance sheet would have to aggregate to $400,000, as long as balance sheet misstatements have no impact on the income statement.

---

Relevant financial data used in calculating the benchmark and materiality level generally include prior-period and period-to-date financial information, current period budgets or forecasts, and changes in the economy or the entity's industry. Determination of materiality levels is also based on the auditor's understanding of user needs and expectations and may be influenced by factors such as financial statement elements with a high degree of estimation uncertainty, or, for audits of governmental entities, by legislative and regulatory requirements. Once the materiality level is established, however, misstatements should be evaluated regardless of any inherent uncertainties. Furthermore, materiality levels relate to the financial reporting period being audited regardless of its length.

The auditor is required to consider whether there are circumstances where misstatements of particular classes of transactions, account balances, or disclosure of lesser amounts than the materiality level determined for the financial statements as a whole might affect economic decisions of users of the financial statements. For example, accounting standards, regulations, or laws may affect user expectations regarding the measurement or disclosure of certain items. Additionally, the industry or environment the entity operates in may place importance on key disclosures. Focus on a particular aspect of an entity's business that is disclosed separately in the financial statements may also affect user expectations. In considering whether establishing materiality levels for transaction classes, account balances, or disclosures is necessary, it may be useful to the auditor to obtain an understanding of the views and expectations of management and those charged with governance.

Misstatements are considered material if they could reasonably influence the economic decisions of users. Misstatements in qualitative disclosures could be material given the nature of the entity. For example, liquidity risk disclosures may be important to users of the financial statements for a financial institution.

**OBSERVATION:** In assessing the significance of a misstatement, the auditor should consider the pervasiveness of the misstatement (such as whether the amounts and presentation of numerous financial statement items are affected), and the effect of the misstatement on the financial statements taken as a whole.

**PUBLIC COMPANY IMPLICATION:** The SEC Staff has issued guidance about materiality considerations relevant to financial statements for public companies. SEC Staff Accounting Bulletin No. 99 (SAB-99) (Materiality) contains the SEC staff's views that the auditor's exclusive reliance on certain quantitative benchmarks to assess materiality in preparing financial statements and performing audits of those financial statements is inappropriate; misstatements are not immaterial simply because they fall beneath a numerical threshold. SAB-99 emphasizes the importance of evaluating qualitative aspects of materiality and provides guidance to auditors of useful qualitative characteristics to consider. Auditors of public companies should examine SAB-99's guidance.

**PLANNING AID REMINDER:** There is an inverse relationship between audit risk and materiality, which can be expressed in the following generalizations: (1) the risk that an item could be misstated by an extremely large amount is generally low and (2) the risk that an item could be misstated by an extremely small amount is generally high. Thus, as the planned level of materiality is reduced, the scope of the audit approach must be increased.

*Performance Materiality Considerations*

The auditor plans the audit to detect material misstatements, which could arise from an individual misstatement that is material or from the aggregation of individually immaterial misstatements. AU-C 320 requires the auditor to set performance materiality to reduce to an appropriately low level the probability that an aggregate of uncorrected and undetected misstatements exceeds materiality for the financial statements as a whole.

Performance materiality levels are determined using professional judgment. These levels are affected by the auditor's understanding of the entity, which includes information gathered during risk assessment procedures, the nature and extent of misstatements identified in prior audits, and the auditor's expectations regarding misstatements in the current audit. Tolerable misstatement is the application of performance materiality to a particular sampling procedure.

## Revision of Materiality Levels

The auditor should revise materiality levels if it appears that actual financial results will be significantly different from the anticipated results used to initially determine materiality of the financial statements, relevant transactions, account balances, or disclosures. Circumstances that could create a need to revise materiality levels include a change in the entity's circumstances, new information, or a change in the auditor's understanding of the entity and its operations as a result of performing further audit procedures.

---

**PLANNING AID REMINDER:** Materiality levels may be determined for planning purposes before financial statements are prepared. In these situations, the auditor may base materiality judgments on annualized interim financial statements or prior-period financial statements, adjusting for any relevant changes in the entity, industry, or economy.

---

# SECTION 330

## PERFORMING AUDIT PROCEDURES IN RESPONSE TO ASSESSED RISKS AND EVALUATING THE AUDIT EVIDENCE OBTAINED

### Authoritative Pronouncements

SAS-122—Statements on Auditing Standards: Clarification and Recodification

SAS-134—Auditor Reporting and Amendments, Including Amendments Addressing Disclosures in Financial Statements

SAS-135—Omnibus Statement on Auditing Standards—2019

SAS-136—Forming an Opinion and Reporting on Financial Statements of Employee Benefit Plans Subject to ERISA

SAS-142—Audit Evidence

### Overview

Auditing standards require the auditor to obtain sufficient appropriate audit evidence by performing audit procedures in response to the risks of material misstatements identified and assessed by the auditor. That audit evidence is obtained to afford a reasonable basis for an opinion regarding the financial statements as a whole. AU-C 330 establishes the standards and procedures to assist the auditor in fulfilling these requirements and provides guidance to assist the auditor with the following:

- Determining the overall response to the risk of material misstatement at the financial statement level.
- Designing and performing further audit procedures in response to risks of material misstatement at the relevant financial statement assertion level.
- Evaluating the sufficiency and appropriateness of audit evidence obtained.
- Satisfying the related documentation requirements.

The auditor's performance of risk assessment procedures should lead to the identification of those account balances, classes of transactions, or disclosures where material misstatements are most likely to occur. The risk assessment procedures should provide the basis for designing and performing further audit procedures. To reduce audit risk to an acceptably low level, the auditor performs further audit procedures, whose nature, timing, and extent are responsive to the assessed risks of material misstatement. AU-C 330 provides guidance to assist auditors in the design and performance of these further audit procedures to address the risks of material misstatement identified. Exhibit AU-C 330-1 provides an overview of the linkage between the assessed level of risk of material misstatements and the auditor's responses to the risks that are identified (described elsewhere in this section).

> **PUBLIC COMPANY IMPLICATION:** PCAOB Auditing Standards AS-2301 (*The Auditor's Responses to the Risks of Material Misstatement*) and AS-2810 (*Evaluating Audit Results*) provide guidance to the auditor in performing audit procedures. AS-2301 establishes requirements for responding to audit risk, both at the overall level and at the level of significant accounts and disclosures. AS-2810 describes the auditor's responsibilities for evaluating audit results. The auditor must evaluate whether he or she has obtained sufficient appropriate audit evidence, and he or she is required to consider (1) uncorrected misstatements and control deficiencies, (2) overall financial statement presentation, including disclosures, and (3) potential management bias in preparing the financial statements. Although there are a number of differences between the PCAOB's and ASB's risk standards, the risk-assessment concepts contained in the PCAOB standards should be familiar to most auditors. As is currently the case, audit risk is the risk that the auditor will issue an inappropriate opinion on financial statements that are materially misstated. The auditor is to reduce audit risk to a low level through the application of audit procedures. As a result, the amount of audit effort devoted to particular accounts, classes of transactions, and disclosures should vary based on their respective risk.

## Definitions

| | |
|---|---|
| Substantive procedure | An audit procedure, including tests of details and substantive analytical procedures, designed to detect material misstatements at the assertion level. |
| Test of controls | An audit procedure designed to evaluate the operating effectiveness of controls in preventing, or detecting and correcting, material misstatements at the assertion level. |

## Requirements

The auditor is presumptively required to perform the following procedures regarding audit procedures in response to assessed risks and evaluating the audit evidence obtained:

### Overall Responses

1. Design and implement overall responses to address the assessed risks of material misstatement at the financial statement level that are not biased toward evidence that is corroborative and against evidence that is contradictory. The auditor maintains professional skepticism, including when evaluating audit evidence.

### Assertion Level Responses

2. Design and perform further audit procedures with the nature, timing, and extent to respond to the assessed risks of material misstatement at the relevant assertion level.

3. When designing further audit procedures to perform:

a. Consider the reasons for the assessed risk of material misstatement at the relevant assertion level for each material class of transactions, account balance, and disclosure, including the inherent risk of material misstatement for each item and whether the risk assessment incorporates control risk thereby requiring the auditor to obtain evidence about the operating effectiveness of controls.

b. Obtain more persuasive audit evidence the higher the assessment of risk.

---

**IMPORTANT NOTICE FOR 2022:** In July 2020, the AICPA Auditing Standards Board (ASB) issued SAS No. 142, *Audit Evidence*, which supersedes AU-C 500 (*Audit Evidence*) and amends various other sections, including AU-C 330, in the professional standards. This new SAS addresses the evolving nature of business and audit services and issues that include the use of emerging technologies by both preparers and auditors, audit data analytics (ADA), the application of professional skepticism, the expanding use of external information sources as audit evidence, and, more broadly, the accuracy, completeness, and reliability of audit evidence. This SAS is effective for audits of financial statements for periods ending on or after December 15, 2022.

---

## *Tests of Controls*

4. Design and perform tests of controls to obtain sufficient appropriate audit evidence about the operating effectiveness of relevant controls at the assertion level when (1) the assessment of risks of material misstatement includes an expectation that controls are operating effectively or (2) substantive procedures cannot provide sufficient appropriate audit evidence alone.

5. Obtain more persuasive audit evidence through the performance of test of controls the greater the reliance on the effectiveness of a control.

6. When designing and performing tests of controls:

    a. Perform inquiry and other procedures to obtain audit evidence about controls' operating effectiveness, including how controls were applied at relevant times during the period under audit, the consistency of application, and by whom or what means they were applied, including whether the person performing the control has the authority and competence necessary to perform the control effectively.

    b. Determine whether the tested controls depend on other indirect controls and, if so, whether it is necessary to obtain audit evidence supporting the indirect controls' operating effectiveness.

7. Test controls for the particular time or throughout the period for which the auditor intends to rely on those controls.

8. When obtaining evidence about the operating effectiveness of controls during an interim period, (*a*) obtain audit evidence about significant changes to those controls subsequent to the interim period and (*b*) determine the additional audit evidence to be obtained for the remaining period.

9. Determine if it is appropriate to use audit evidence about the operating effectiveness of controls obtained in previous audits and, if so, the length of time that may elapse before retesting a control, by considering:

    a. The effectiveness of other elements of internal control,

    b. Risks arising from the characteristics of the control (e.g., characteristics of manual or automated controls),

c. The effectiveness of general IT controls,

d. The effectiveness of the control and its application including the nature and extent of deviations previously noted and if there have been personnel changes significantly affecting control application,

e. If the lack of change in a control poses a risk due to changing circumstances, and

f. The risks of material misstatement and the extent of reliance on the control.

10. If planning to use audit evidence about the operating effectiveness of controls from previous audits, perform audit procedures such as inquiry combined with observation or inspection to establish that information's continuing relevance to the current audit. If changes have occurred affecting the audit evidence's continuing relevance to the current audit, test the controls in the current audit. If such changes have not occurred, test the controls at least once every third audit, rotating testing so some controls are tested during each audit.

11. If planning to rely on controls over a significant risk, test the operating effectiveness of those controls in the current period.

12. When evaluating the operating effectiveness of relevant controls, evaluate whether misstatements detected by substantive procedures indicate the controls are not operating effectively. The absence of detected misstatements does not provide audit evidence that the controls are effective.

13. When deviations from controls the auditor intends to rely on are detected, make specific inquiries to understand the matter and its potential consequences. Determine whether (1) the tests of controls performed provide an appropriate basis for reliance on the controls, (2) additional tests of controls are necessary, or (3) the potential risks of misstatement need to be addressed using substantive procedures.

## *Substantive Procedures*

14. Design and perform substantive procedures for all relevant assertions related to each material class of transactions, account balance, and disclosure regardless of the assessed risks of material misstatement.

15. Consider whether external confirmation procedures should be performed as substantive audit procedures. External confirmations of accounts receivable are often necessary to reduce audit risk to an acceptably low level for the relevant assertion and should be used unless (1) the overall account balance is immaterial, (2) those confirmations would be ineffective, or (3) the assessed level of risk of material misstatement is low and sufficient appropriate audit evidence will be obtained by performing substantive procedures. If the auditor concludes external confirmation procedures for accounts receivable are not necessary, document the basis for that determination.

16. Perform audit procedures related to the financial statement closing process, such as agreeing or reconciling the financial statements with the underlying accounting records, including agreeing or reconciling information in disclosures, and examining material journal entries and other adjustments made during financial statement preparation. Accounting records alone do not constitute sufficient appropriate evidence.

17. If the assessed risk of material misstatement at the relevant assertion level is considered a significant risk, perform substantive procedures specifically responsive to that risk. When the response to a significant risk consists only of substantive procedures, those procedures should include tests of details.

18. When substantive procedures are performed at an interim date, cover the remaining period by performing (1) substantive procedures combined with tests of controls for the intervening period or (2) substantive procedures only if those procedures are sufficient to extend the audit conclusions from the interim date to period end.

19. If unexpected misstatements are detected at an interim date, evaluate whether the related assessment of risks and the planned nature, timing, and extent of substantive procedures covering the remaining period need to be modified.

## Selecting Items for Testing

20. Determine a means of selecting items for testing that is effective for the audit procedure when designing tests of controls and tests of details.

## Presentation and Disclosure

21. Perform audit procedures to evaluate whether the overall financial statement presentation and related disclosures are in accordance with the applicable financial reporting framework. The auditor should consider whether the financial statements are presented in a manner that reflects the appropriate classification and description of financial information and the underlying transactions, events, and conditions, and whether the financial statements reflect the appropriate presentation, structure, and content.

---

**IMPORTANT NOTICE FOR 2022:** In May 2019, the AICPA's Auditing Standards Board (ASB) issued SAS No. 134 titled *Auditor Reporting and Amendments, Including Amendments Addressing Disclosures in the Audit of Financial Statements* to revise the auditor's report and to amend various AU-C sections to heighten the auditor's focus on disclosures throughout the process of auditing financial statements. SAS No. 134 amends AU-C 330 to require auditors to evaluate whether the overall presentation of the financial statements including disclosures is in accordance with the applicable financial reporting framework. That would include substantive procedures related to the financial reporting closing process that agree or reconcile information in disclosures with the underlying accounting records. Originally, the effective date of SAS No. 134 was for audits of financial statements periods ending on or after December 15, 2020, with early implementation **not** permitted. However, the ASB's issuance of SAS No. 141, *Amendment to the Effective Dates of SAS Nos. 134-140*, extended the effective date of SAS No. 134 to December 15, 2021, in order to provide more time for firms to implement SAS No. 134 in light of the effect of the coronavirus pandemic. While SAS No. 141 allows for early implementation of SAS No. 134, the ASB recommends that SAS Nos. 134-140 be implemented concurrently.

---

## Sufficiency and Appropriateness of Audit Evidence

22. Before the audit's conclusion, based on audit procedures performed and audit evidence obtained, evaluate whether the assessments of the risks of material misstatement at the relevant assertion level remain appropriate.

23. Conclude whether sufficient appropriate audit evidence has been obtained at both the assertion level and the overall financial statement level. Consider all relevant audit evidence, whether it corroborates or contradicts financial statement assertions.

24. If sufficient appropriate audit evidence about a relevant assertion has not been obtained, attempt to obtain further audit evidence. If unable to obtain such evidence, express a qualified opinion or a disclaimer of opinion.

## Documentation

25. Document (*a*) the overall responses to address the assessed risks of material misstatement at the financial statement level and the nature, timing, and extent of further audit procedures performed; (*b*) the linkage of those procedures with the assessed risks at the relevant assertion level; and (*c*) the result of the audit procedures and the conclusions where they are not otherwise clear.

26. If planning to use audit evidence about the operating effectiveness of controls obtained in previous audits, document the conclusions reached about relying on those controls.

27. Documentation should demonstrate that the financial statements agree or reconcile with the underlying accounting records, including agreeing and reconciling disclosures.

## Analysis and Application of Procedures

### Overall Responses

The auditor's risk assessment procedures may identify risks pervasive to the financial statements. In particular, the auditor's understanding of the control environment obtained as part of the auditor's risk assessment procedures may affect the assessment of the risk of material misstatement at the overall financial statement level. When deficiencies in the control environment exist, the auditor's confidence in internal control and the reliability of evidence generated internally by the client's internal control system may lead the auditor to perform audit procedures closer to period end than at interim and seek more audit evidence from the performance of substantive procedures. Thus, consideration of matters affecting the control environment or other factors that affect the overall risks of material misstatements at the financial statement level has a significant effect on the general approach to the audit.

To respond to assessed risks of material misstatement at the financial statement level, the auditor's response may include the following:

- Emphasizing to the audit engagement team the importance of maintaining professional skepticism in gathering and evaluating audit evidence;
- Assigning more experienced staff or those with specialized skills or using specialists;
- Providing more supervision;
- Incorporating additional elements of unpredictability in the selection of further audit procedures to be performed; and
- Making general changes to the nature, timing, and extent of audit procedures.

## Assertion Level Responses

Based on his or her performance of risk assessment procedures, the auditor may identify risks of material misstatements at the relevant assertion level for account balances, classes of transactions, or disclosures. AU-C 330 requires the auditor to design and perform further audit procedures to respond to the assessed risks of material misstatements at the relevant assertion level. This ensures a direct linkage between the risk assessment and the nature, timing, and extent of further audit procedures. Further audit procedures may emphasize the performance of substantive procedures (a substantive approach) or use both tests of controls and substantive procedures (a combined approach).

---

**PLANNING AID REMINDER:** Although audit procedures performed in prior audits and example audit procedures in illustrative audit programs may be useful to the auditor, the assessment of the risk of material misstatement in the current period forms the primary basis for designing further audit procedures.

---

To determine the appropriateness of further audit procedures, the auditor considers several factors:

- The significance of the risk.
- The likelihood that a material misstatement will occur.
- The characteristics of the class of transactions, account balance, or disclosure involved.
- The nature of specific controls used by the entity, in particular, whether they are manual or automated.
- Whether the auditor expects to obtain audit evidence from tests of controls (to determine whether the controls are operating effectively to prevent or detect and correct material misstatements).

In some cases, the auditor may respond by only performing substantive procedures and exclude the effect of controls. However, in doing so, he or she must be satisfied that only performing substantive procedures for the relevant assertions is appropriate for effectively reducing detection risk to an acceptable level. Often, however, auditors determine that a combined approach of performing both tests of controls and substantive procedures is most effective.

---

**PLANNING AID REMINDER:** Because there are limitations in any system of internal control in preventing or detecting material misstatements, tests of controls do not eliminate the need for the performance of substantive procedures.

---

### Considering the nature of further audit procedures

The nature of the audit procedures is of most importance when designing and performing further audit procedures to respond to risks of material misstatement. The nature of further audit procedures refers to the purpose and type of further audit procedures. The purpose relates to whether the procedures are designed to be tests of controls or to provide substantive evidence about an account balance, class of transaction, or disclosure. The type of further audit procedure relates to whether the procedures involve inspection, observation, inquiry, confirmation, recalculation, reperformance, or analytical procedure.

As the risks of material misstatement for a relevant assertion increase, the auditor may modify the nature of the further audit procedure by changing the purpose from a test of control to a substantive procedure, because evidence from substantive procedures is often more reliable and relevant. The auditor may also modify the type of procedure in order to obtain evidence that is more reliable.

The reasons for the assessment of risk of material misstatement for the relevant assertion should affect the nature of the further audit procedures. Information affecting the auditor's assessment of inherent risk and his or her understanding of internal control will directly affect his or her determination of the appropriate nature of further audit procedures. For example, if the auditor believes internal controls are effectively designed and in operation, he or she may plan to perform tests of controls and modify the nature of substantive procedures accordingly. In other situations, when the auditor's assessment of risk of material misstatement is low, the auditor may conclude that the performance of substantive analytical procedures provides sufficient appropriate audit evidence.

*Considering the timing of further audit procedures*

Timing refers to when the auditor performs further audit procedures or the period or date that the audit evidence applies to. The auditor's decision about the timing of further audit procedures is affected by his or her assessment of the risks of material misstatement at the relevant assertion level. As the risks of material misstatement increase, the auditor may decide to perform substantive procedures closer to the period end, unannounced, or at unpredictable times.

When the auditor performs procedures before period end, he or she should consider the additional evidence that might be necessary for the remaining untested period. In some cases, audit procedures performed at interim periods help the auditor identify important matters at an early stage of the audit. Having determined that further audit tests are to be performed at earlier interim periods, the auditor should consider whether additional testing is required between the interim and period-end time frame.

The timing of the performance of audit procedures may be affected by when the relevant information is available. In some cases, electronic evidence may be overwritten and thus must be examined on a timely basis before that occurs. In other cases, the nature of risks may affect the timing of procedures. For example, if there is a risk of material misstatement related to the cutoff of revenue transactions, the auditor may wait to inspect transactions near period end. Certain audit procedures can only be performed at or after period end, such as reconciling accounting records to the financial statements. And, certain procedures can only be performed at or after period-end such as agreeing or reconciling information in the financial statements, including disclosures, with the underlying accounting records.

## Considering the extent of further audit procedures

The extent of further audit procedures encompasses the sufficiency or quantity of a specific audit procedure to be performed. Several factors affect the auditor's considerations of the extent of further audit procedures:

- Materiality level: Extent increases as materiality decreases.
- The assessed risk of material misstatement: As the risk increases, the extent may need to increase.
- The degree of assurance the auditor plans to obtain from the further audit procedures: The greater the assurance needs, the greater the extent of testing needed.

The increase in the extent of further audit procedures is effective as long as the nature of the test is relevant to the risks identified.

## Tests of Controls

Further audit procedures consist of tests of controls and substantive procedures. Tests of controls are only performed on controls that the auditor has determined to be suitably designed to prevent or detect and correct a material misstatement in a relevant assertion. Some controls are directly related to specific assertions, and other controls are related only indirectly to specific assertions. The more direct the relationship between controls and an assertion, the more likely the control can provide a basis for reducing the overall risk of material misstatement. If tests of controls show them to be operating effectively at the relevant assertion level and level of planned reliance, the extent of substantive procedures in the audit may be able to be reduced.

---

**PLANNING AID REMINDER:** The auditor performs tests of controls when he or she expects the operating effectiveness of controls to reduce his or her assessment of the risks of material misstatements or when substantive procedures alone will not provide sufficient appropriate evidence. According to AICPA Technical Practice Aid TIS 8200.06, the phrase "expectation of the operating effectiveness of controls" means that the auditor's understanding of all five components of internal control enable him or her to initially assess control risk at less than the maximum. In that case, the auditor's strategy is to perform a combination of tests of controls and substantive procedures. The auditor's initial assessment of control risk is preliminary and subject to satisfactory results from the tests of the operating effectiveness of those controls. An audit is usually more efficient when the auditor can rely to some degree on the client's internal control.

---

Although the objective of tests of controls differs from the auditor's risk assessment procedures, he or she may determine that testing the operating effectiveness of controls can be efficiently and effectively performed as part of procedures performed to assess their design and implementation. The auditor may also perform dual-purpose tests, performing a test of controls concurrently with a test of details on the same transaction. Dual-purpose tests are designed and evaluated by considering each purpose of the test separately.

*Nature and extent of tests of controls*

The nature of tests of controls ordinarily includes the following procedures:
- Inquiries of appropriate entity personnel;
- Inspection of documents, reports, or electronic files for indication of the performance of the control;
- Observation of the application of the control; and
- Reperformance by the auditor of the application of the control.

The nature of the test of controls is affected by the desired assurance to be obtained about the operating effectiveness of the controls. Evidence obtained from inspection or reperformance generally provides more assurance than evidence obtained from inquiry or observation. Furthermore, inquiry alone is not sufficient to obtain evidence about the operating effectiveness of controls. As the desired level of assurance from controls increases, auditors usually change the nature of tests of controls from a combination of inquiry and observation to inspection and reperformance.

The nature of tests of controls is directly affected by the nature of the underlying control. For some controls, operating effectiveness is best evidenced by documentation. In those situations, the auditor's tests of controls most likely involve inspection of documentation. For other controls, such as those related to the control environment, the most reliable and relevant evidence may be obtained through inquiry and observation.

The extent of tests of controls relates to the sufficiency of the tests. Several factors affect the extent of tests of controls:
- The frequency of the performance of the control by the entity during the period.
- The length of time during the audit period that the auditor is relying on the control.
- The relevance and reliability of the audit evidence to be obtained in supporting that the control prevents or detects and corrects material misstatements at the relevant financial statement level.
- The extent to which audit evidence is obtained from tests of other controls related to the relevant assertion.
- The extent to which the auditor plans to rely on the operating effectiveness of the control in the assessment of risk.
- The expected deviation from the control.

Because of the inherent consistency of IT processing, the nature and extent of the auditor's tests of an automated control may be affected by his or her testing of the operating effectiveness of IT general controls, particularly those related to security and program change controls. That is, the automated control might require limited testing because once the control is implemented it functions the same way each time unless the program or underlying data is changed. The auditor may test the automated control once it is implemented and then test the overall effectiveness of general IT controls to ensure that the automated control has not changed since it was implemented and that it continues to function effectively. This evaluation may require the skills of an IT specialist.

**IMPORTANT NOTICE FOR 2022:** In August 2020, the AICPA Auditing Standards Board (ASB) issued an exposure draft of a proposed new Statement on Auditing Standard, *Understanding the Entity and its Environment and Assessing the Risks of Material Misstatement*, that would supersede AU-C 315 (same title) and amend various other sections of auditing standards, including amendments to AU-C 330. The proposed changes to AU-C 330 include expanded guidance about the importance for the auditor to consider performing tests of controls that address risks related to the integrity of the entity's data or the accuracy and completeness of the entity's system-generated reports. That may include tests of IT general controls, particularly those that support the operating effectiveness of automated controls or the integrity of system-generated reports. If approved, the proposed SAS would become effective for audits of financial statements for periods ending on or after December 15, 2023, which is consistent with the effective date of SAS No. 143, *Auditing Accounting Estimates and Related Disclosures*.

*Timing of tests of controls*

The timing of the auditor's tests of controls depends on the period of time he or she intends to rely on those controls. If the auditor only intends to rely on the performance of controls as of a point in time (e.g., relying on controls related to the physical inventory taken as of the balance sheet date), tests of the controls may be conducted as of that particular time. If the auditor intends to rely on the performance of controls throughout the period under audit, the tests of controls should be performed to determine that they operated effectively during that period.

For many controls, the auditor's tests may be performed during an interim period and several factors affect the need for additional evidence about those controls during the remaining untested period:

- The significance of the assessed risks of material misstatements.
- The specific controls that were tested during the interim period, the results of those tests, and significant changes to those controls since testing.
- The degree to which audit evidence about the operating effectiveness of those controls was obtained.
- The length of the remaining period.
- The extent to which the auditor intends to reduce further substantive procedures based on the reliance of controls.
- The effectiveness of the control environment.

Additional evidence may be obtained by extending testing of the operating effectiveness of controls over the remaining period or testing the entity's monitoring of controls.

The auditor may be able to rely on tests of controls performed in prior-year audits. To rely on tests of controls performed in prior audits, the auditor must obtain evidence about whether changes in those specific controls have occurred subsequent to the prior-year audit. If changes have been made since the prior-year testing, the auditor may obtain evidence to determine whether the changes have affected the control's continued effective functioning. The evidence gathered about these changes may support increasing or decreasing the expected audit evidence to be obtained about the operating effectiveness of those controls in the current-year audit.

The auditor uses professional judgment in determining the reliance to be placed on prior-year audit evidence for controls that have not changed since they were last tested and do not mitigate significant risks. More frequent retesting of a control generally occurs when the control environment is weak, there is weak monitoring of controls, there is a significant manual element to the control, personnel changes have occurred that affect the application of the control, there are weak general IT controls, and there are other circumstances that indicate a need for changes in the control. By testing some controls each audit, the auditor obtains information about the continuing effectiveness of the control environment that can affect the decision to rely on evidence obtained in previous audits. Exhibit AU-C 330-2 provides a summary of decisions auditors make about the timing of the testing of controls for current-year audits.

## Operating Effectiveness of Controls

Deviations from controls the auditor intends to rely on may be detected and can be caused by factors such as personnel changes, seasonal fluctuations in transaction volume, and human error. The detected deviation rate may be significant enough to indicate that the control cannot be relied on to reduce risk at the relevant assertion level to the level assessed by the auditor. Furthermore, a material misstatement detected by the auditor's procedures that indicates the misstatement would not have been detected by the entity is an indicator of a material weakness in internal control.

## Substantive Procedures

Substantive procedures consist of two types: (1) substantive analytical procedures and (2) tests of details of classes of transactions, account balances, and disclosures.

Generally, the nature, timing, and extent of substantive procedures are affected by the assessed level of risk of material misstatement. However, AU-C 330 notes that the auditor should design and perform substantive procedures for all relevant assertions pertaining to each account balance, disclosure, and material class of transactions. As a result, substantive procedures are required in every audit because (1) the auditor's assessment of risks of material misstatements is judgmental and may not be sufficiently precise to identify all risks of material misstatements and (2) there are inherent limitations in any system of internal control.

**IMPORTANT NOTICE FOR 2022:** In May 2019, the AICPA's Auditing Standards Board (ASB) issued SAS No. 135 titled *Omnibus Statement on Auditing Standards—2019* that includes amendments to various AU-C sections. SAS No. 135

amends AU-C 240 to add a definition for significant unusual transactions. SAS No. 135 also amends AU-C 330 to note that because significant unusual transactions can affect the risks of material misstatements due to error or fraud, substantive procedures that take into account the types of potential misstatements that could result from significant unusual transactions may be necessary. Originally, the effective date of SAS No. 135 was for audits of financial statements periods ending on or after December 15, 2020, with early application **not** permitted. However, the ASB's issuance of SAS No. 141, *Amendment to the Effective Dates of SAS Nos. 134-140*, extended the effective date of SAS No. 135 to December 15, 2021, in order to provide more time for firms to implement SAS No. 135 in light of the effect of the coronavirus pandemic. While SAS No. 141 allows for early implementation of SAS No. 135, the ASB recommends that SAS Nos. 134-140 be implemented concurrently.

*Nature and extent of substantive procedures*

The nature of substantive procedures is directly affected by whether the procedure is a substantive analytical procedure or a test of details. Substantive analytical procedures are generally more applicable to larger volumes of transactions that tend to be predictable over time, such as income statement accounts. Tests of details are generally more appropriate for obtaining audit evidence about account balances, particularly existence and valuation.

The nature of substantive procedures should be responsive to the level of planned detection risk. In many instances the auditor's planned level of detection risk is affected by his or her tests of controls. Thus, the nature of substantive testing is affected by the audit evidence obtained through tests of controls. For example, substantive analytical procedures may be sufficiently responsive to the planned level of detection risk for some accounts, particularly when the tests of operating effectiveness have reduced the auditor's assessed level of the risk of material misstatements. In other situations, only a test of details or a combination of tests of details and substantive analytical procedures is appropriate to respond to the planned level of detection risk.

The nature of substantive procedures is directly affected by the nature of the relevant assertion. For example, to test the existence assertion, the nature of the auditor's substantive procedures should include the selection of items for testing from those recorded in the accounting records. To test the completeness assertion, the nature of the auditor's substantive procedures should include the selection of items for testing from audit evidence that indicates that an item has occurred and should be recorded in the accounting records. Exhibit AU-C 330-3 provides an example of illustrative substantive procedures linked to the inventory account balance assertions and the inventory presentation and disclosure assertions.

The extent of substantive testing may need to increase to achieve a reduced level of planned detection risk when results from tests of controls are unsatisfactory. The extent of substantive procedures is often addressed through the sample size examined in the substantive procedure. Other matters may also affect the extent of substantive procedures, including whether it is more effective to use other selective means of testing.

In considering whether to perform external confirmation procedures to provide audit evidence, the auditor should consider that confirmations may be relevant when addressing assertions related to many different items, including account balances, agreement terms, contracts, transactions with other parties, and the absence of certain conditions, such as "side agreements." Factors the auditor may consider in determining whether to perform external confirmation procedures include:

- The confirming party's knowledge of the subject matter;
- The willingness or ability of the confirming party to respond, which may affect whether the party responds, responds in a casual manner, or attempts to restrict reliance on the response;
- The confirming party's objectivity; and
- The ability of a confirmation performed for one purpose to provide audit evidence about other matters.

Confirmation of accounts receivable is a generally accepted auditing procedure, where accounts receivable refers to the entity's claims against customers from the sale of goods or services in the normal course of business and a financial institution's loans. Confirmations can also be effective in auditing many other areas: cash, notes receivable, inventory, consigned merchandise, construction and production contracts, investment securities, market values, accounts payable, notes payable, lines of credit, and actual and contingent liabilities. It is important to recognize that external confirmations provide more relevant audit evidence related to certain assertions such as existence than they do regarding other assertions such as recoverability of accounts receivable. The auditor may determine external confirmations would be ineffective if the auditor has reason to believe response rates would be inadequate or otherwise unreliable.

**PLANNING AID REMINDER:** The auditor's procedures examining adjustments made during the course of preparing the financial statements refers to journal entries and adjustments prepared by the entity during the process of preparing its financial statements, such as consolidating entries or elimination entries between subsidiaries. It does not refer to journal entries recorded by the entity in the general ledger during the year. However, AU-C 240 reminds auditors that they are required to design audit procedures to test the appropriateness of journal entries recorded by the entity in the general ledger during the year.

**FRAUD POINTER:** AU-C 240 requires the auditor to respond to the risk of management override of internal controls in every audit by examining journal entries. Thus, the auditor's examination of journal entries and other adjustments as part of his or her substantive procedures should be coordinated with the examination of journal entries required by AU-C 240 to address the ever-present risk of management override of internal control.

In addition to the foregoing required substantive procedures at the financial statement reporting level, AU-C 330 requires the auditor to perform substantive procedures for all significant risks. For example, if the auditor determines that the risk of material misstatement in accounts receivable is highly related to the existence assertion, the auditor may not only confirm outstanding account balances of related customer balances but also other details related to transactions affecting customers' account balances.

---

**PLANNING AID REMINDER:** In certain instances, the auditor may plan an all-substantive approach even if his or her understanding of internal control causes him or her to believe that controls are designed effectively. After the auditor obtains an understanding of the entity and its environment, including internal controls, and assesses the risk of material misstatement, he or she may consider the cost-benefit to determine the most effective set of further audit procedures. If the auditor believes that the benefit of testing the operating effectiveness of internal controls is less than the costs of testing them, he or she may acopt an audit strategy that consists solely of substantive procedures to respond to the risk of material misstatement.

---

*Timing of substantive procedures*

Similar to tests of controls, the auditor may decide to perform substantive procedures at an interim date or at periods close to or as of period end. When substantive procedures are performed at interim dates, there is a risk that material misstatement that exists at the period end will not be detected by the auditor. As the length of the period between interim testing and period end increases, this risk increases. As a result, when the auditor decides to perform substantive tests at an interim date, he or she should perform further substantive procedures, sometimes in combination with tests of controls, to cover the remaining period to provide a basis for extending the audit conclusions from interim substantive procedures to period end. Exhibit AU-C 330-4 provides an illustrative example of how interim substantive procedures can be rolled forward to period end.

Several factors affect the auditor's decision to perform substantive procedures at an interim date:

- The strength of the control environment and other relevant controls.
- The availability of information at a later date that is necessary for the auditor's procedures.
- The objective of the substantive procedure.
- The assessed risk of material misstatement.
- The nature of the account balance or class of transactions and relevant assertions.
- The ability of the auditor to reduce the risk that misstatements that exist at the period end are not detected by performing appropriate substantive procedures, including those combined with tests of controls.

**FRAUD POINTER:** When the auditor identifies risks of material misstatements due to fraud, one of his or her responses might include a change in the timing of substantive procedures to perform tests at or closer to the end of the reporting period.

Unlike the auditor's tests of controls, he or she is in most cases unable to rely on substantive procedures performed in prior audits to reduce detection risk in the current audit. Audit evidence obtained from prior audits typically provides little or no evidence to reduce detection risk in the current audit. As a result, substantive procedures should generally be performed during the current audit. However, in some cases the auditor may use audit evidence from a previous audit's substantive procedures if the evidence and subject matter have not fundamentally changed and audit procedures have been performed during the current period to establish its continuing relevance.

### Selecting Items for Testing

For a test to be effective, the auditor must obtain audit evidence to the extent that sufficient appropriate audit evidence will be obtained when combined with other audit evidence. Therefore, the items selected to be tested should be relevant, reliable, and sufficient for the auditor to draw valid conclusions, with an acceptable level of risk that the conclusion based on a selected sample may be different from the conclusion reached if the entire population was tested.

There are three methods the auditor can use to select items for testing, and any method may be appropriate given particular circumstances.

1. Select all items in a population: This may occur for tests of details and may be appropriate when the population is a small number of large-value items, there is a significant risk of material misstatement, or a complete examination is cost effective due to its repetitive nature.
2. Select specific items: This method is subject to nonsampling risk and items selected may include high value or key items, all items over a certain amount, or items to obtain information about certain matters. This method does not constitute audit sampling, so the results cannot be projected to the entire population, although they may provide some evidence about the remainder of the population.
3. Audit sampling: This method is designed to enable the auditor to draw conclusions about an entire population based on testing a sample of the population (discussed in AU-C 530).

### Sufficiency and Appropriateness of Audit Evidence

Auditing standards require the auditor to obtain sufficient appropriate audit evidence in order to obtain a reasonable basis for his or her opinion about the financial statements. The sufficiency and appropriateness of audit evidence to support the auditor's conclusions made throughout the audit are a matter of professional judgment. Several factors affect the sufficiency and appropriateness of audit evidence:

- Significance of the potential misstatement in the relevant assertion and the likelihood of it having a material effect on the financial statements.
- Effectiveness of management's responses and controls to address the risks.
- Experience gained during previous audits with respect to similar potential misstatements.
- Results of audit procedures performed, including whether such audit procedures identified specific instances of fraud or error.
- Source and reliability of audit evidence.
- Persuasiveness of audit evidence.
- Understanding of the entity and its environment, including its internal control.

The auditor's accumulation of audit evidence in an audit is cumulative and iterative. As the auditor performs the audit procedures and obtains related audit evidence, he or she should evaluate whether assessments of the risks of material misstatement at the relevant assertion level remain appropriate.

Evidence obtained from risk assessment procedures or further audit procedures, including tests of controls and substantive procedures, may have an impact on the nature, timing, and extent of audit procedures. For example, information may come to the auditor's attention that differs from the information he or she used to assess the risk of material misstatement or information obtained from tests of controls may identify deviations in those controls. That information may require the auditor to modify the assessed level of risk of material misstatement, in turn requiring changes in the nature, timing, or extent of other planned audit procedures that should be performed.

**FRAUD POINTER:** A deficiency commonly cited in SEC enforcement actions against auditors is their overreliance on internal controls, particularly their failure to expand testing in light of known control deficiencies. In some cases, auditors actually identified and documented significant control problems in specific areas and then failed to alter the audit testing in response to the heightened risk. In other cases, auditors assumed the presence of a baseline level of internal control despite documenting that the client essentially had no controls in place.

**FRAUD POINTER:** When the auditor identifies a material misstatement due to fraud, he or she should not assume that the fraud instance is an isolated occurrence. The auditor should consider the implications for the overall financial statement audit and may need to modify his or her overall response to the risk of material misstatements or his or her response at the relevant assertion level.

> **PUBLIC COMPANY IMPLICATION:** In December 2018, the PCAOB issued AS-1210, *Using the Work of an Auditor-Engaged Specialist*. The goal of this new standard is to amend existing PCAOB Auditing Standards to expand guidance related to the use of the work performed by specialists. AS-1210 provides specific guidance related to the use of company-employed specialists, auditor-employed specialists, and auditor-engaged specialists. In developing this new standard, the PCAOB noted that its inspections process has observed substantial variation in practice as to how auditors use the work of specialists and how they evaluate the work performed by specialists. For example, it has noted that auditors have failed to adequately evaluate the assumptions used by company specialists to develop fair value measurements and auditors have failed to consider contradictory evidence or issues raised by an auditor's specialist. The SEC approved AS-1210 in July 2019. The effective date is for audits of fiscal years ending on or after December 15, 2020.

*Documentation*

The form and extent of documentation is a matter of professional judgment influenced by the entity's nature, size, complexity, and internal control; availability of information from the entity; and the audit methodology and technology used in the audit.

## Practitioner's Aids

The following exhibits may be used as practitioner's aids.

## EXHIBIT AU-C 330-1—RELATIONSHIP OF ASSESSED RISKS OF MATERIAL MISSTATEMENT AND AUDITOR'S RESPONSES

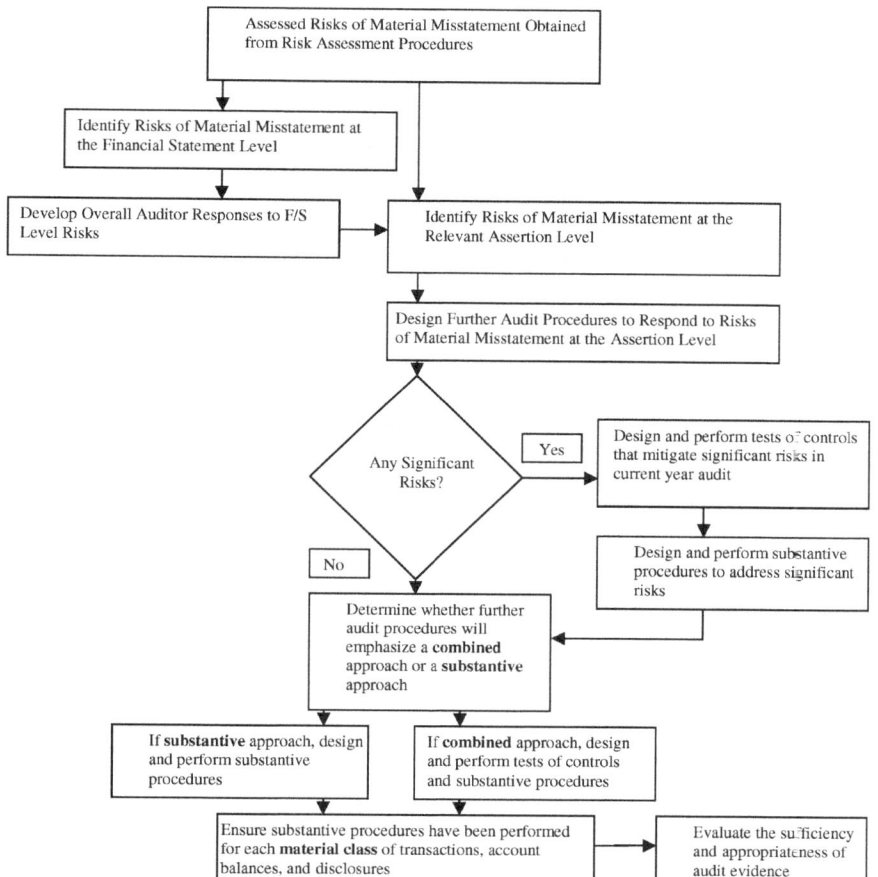

# EXHIBIT AU-C 330-2—DECISION TREE FOR DESIGNING AND PERFORMING CURRENT YEAR TESTS OF CONTROLS

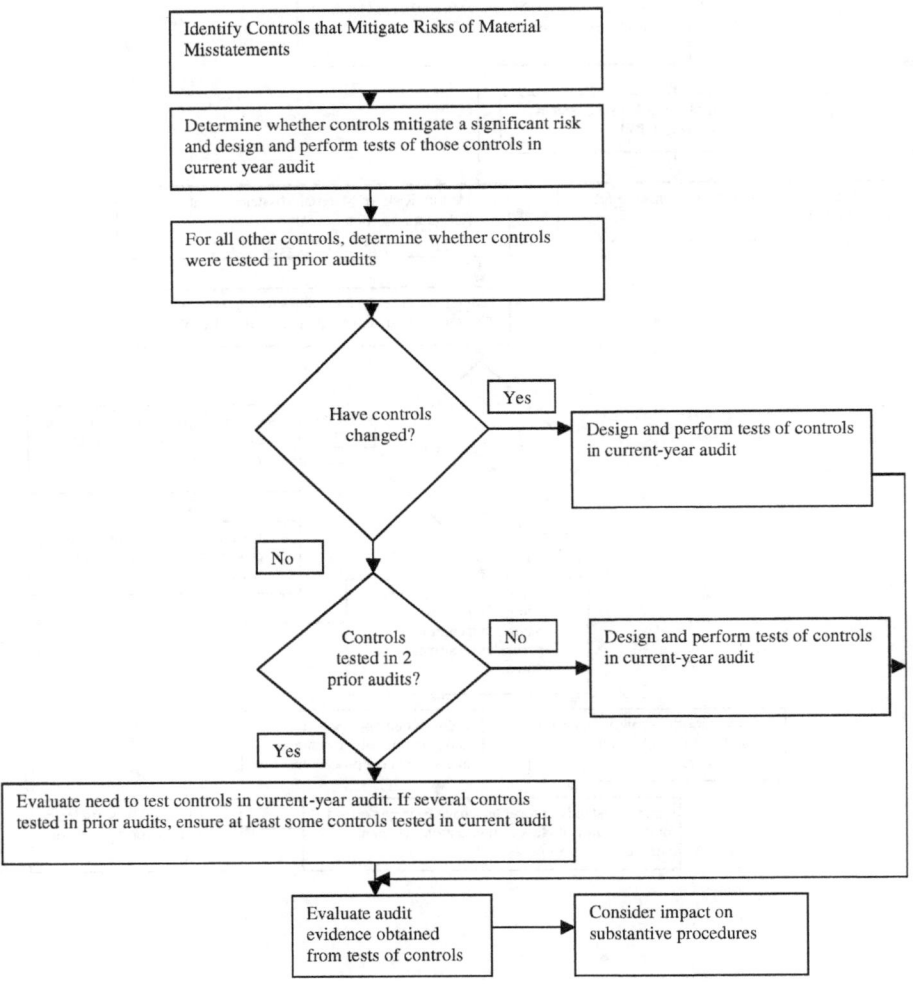

# EXHIBIT AU-C 330-3—EXAMPLES OF SUBSTANTIVE PROCEDURES RELEVANT TO INVENTORY ASSERTIONS

| Inventory Account Balance Assertions | Examples of Substantive Procedures |
|---|---|
| *Existence* Inventories included in the balance sheet physically exist | Conduct a physical examination of inventory items |
| | Obtain confirmation of inventory items held at outside locations |
| | Inspect documentation related to the purchase and sale of inventory between the physical inventory date and the balance sheet date |
| *Completeness* Inventory items on hand at the balance sheet date are included in the balance sheet. | Conduct a physical examination of inventory items and determine that the items are recorded in the inventory listing |
| | Inspect shipping and receiving transactions near year-end for recording in the proper period |
| *Valuation* Inventories are stated at cost (except when market is lower). | Examine invoices paid to vendors for inventory purchases and compare product unit prices to those appropriate given the underlying selected accounting policy (e.g. LIFO versus FIFO) |
| | Inspect inventory publications and other market data for current market prices and determine whether unit prices used to value inventory are at lower of cost or market |
| | Recalculate unit price times quantity for selected items included in the inventory listing |
| | Watch for evidence of slow-moving items while present for the physical examination of inventory |

| Inventory Account Balance Assertions | Examples of Substantive Procedures |
|---|---|
| *Rights and obligations* The entity has legal title or similar rights of ownership to the inventories. | Obtain confirmation of inventory held at other locations to confirm title of goods held |
| | Examine vendor invoices for evidence of consignment arrangements |
| | Examine sales invoices and related shipping documents to ensure inventories exclude items billed to customers or owned by others |

| Inventory Presentation and Disclosure Assertions | Examples of Substantive Procedures |
|---|---|
| *Rights and obligations* Any pledge or assignment of inventories is appropriately disclosed | Obtain confirmation of inventories pledged under loan agreements |
| *Completeness* The financial statements include all disclosures related to inventories specified by U.S. GAAP | Use a disclosure checklist to determine whether required U.S. GAAP disclosures are included in the footnotes |

| Inventory Account Balance Assertions | Examples of Substantive Procedures |
|---|---|
| *Understandability* Inventories are properly classified in the balance sheet as current assets and all related disclosures are understandable | Examine drafts of the financial statements for appropriate balance sheet classification<br><br>Read the inventory footnote disclosures for clarity |
| *Accuracy and valuation* The major categories of inventories and their bases of valuation are accurately disclosed in the financial statements. | Examine the drafts of the financial statements for appropriate disclosure |

## EXHIBIT AU-C 330-4—EXAMPLES OF ROLL FORWARD OF SUBSTANTIVE PROCEDURES FROM INTERIM TO PERIOD END

Professional judgment must be used to determine which balance sheet accounts can be subjected to substantive tests prior to the balance sheet date. To illustrate how this approach may be applied, assume that an auditor has decided to confirm accounts receivable at an interim date. The confirmation procedures normally applied at year-end would be applied to the trial balance of accounts receivable as of the interim date. Returned confirmations would be evaluated, and the auditor would develop various confirmation statistics. For transactions occurring after the interim date, the auditor would rely upon the client's internal control to process data in an acceptable manner. Summary data in the sales journal and cash receipts journal would be reviewed for unusual items. In addition, the client could be requested to prepare an aged trial balance at the end of the year, and the auditor could perform the analysis. During the review, the auditor would look for significant amounts from customers that were not listed on the interim trial balance. Other items that are unusual or that otherwise come to the attention of the auditor could be subject to confirmation as of the year-end date.

The following illustrates an audit schedule format that an auditor could use to document the approach of performing substantive tests on data processed by the client after the interim date:

*Averroes Company*
Analysis of Accounts Receivable from Interim to Year-End Date 12/31/X6

| | | |
|---|---:|---:|
| Accounts Receivable Balance @ 9/30/X6 | | $450,000 |
| | | See audit schedule @ AR110 |
| Sales — October[a] | 80,000 | |
| November[a] | 85,000 | |
| December[a] | 82,000 | |
| | | 247,000 |
| Cash receipts — October[b] | 78,000 | |
| November[b] | 81,000 | |
| December[b] | 79,000 | |
| | | 238,000 |

| | | |
|---|---|---|
| Write-offs — October[c] | 450 | |
| November[c] | 230 | |
| December[c] | 1,850 | |
| | | -2,530 |
| Accounts Receivable Balance @ 12/31/X6 | | $456,470 |

See audit schedule @ AR100

[a] Traced to Sales Journal—Footed November and December journals
[b] Traced to Cash Receipts Journal—Footed October
[c] Traced to approvals and reviewed with credit manager

Prepared By: JB

Date: 1/29/X7

AR101

# SECTION 402

## AUDIT CONSIDERATIONS RELATING TO AN ENTITY USING A SERVICE ORGANIZATION

### Authoritative Pronouncements

SAS-122—Statements on Auditing Standards: Clarification and Recodification

### Overview

The guidance established by AU-C 402 applies to the audit of a client that uses the services of another entity (service organization), whereby those services are considered to be part of the client's information system used to process transactions because they affect one or more of the following:

- Classes of transactions significant to the entity's financial statements.
- Procedures used to initiate, record, process, and report transactions in the financial statements.
- The client's accounting records, supporting information, and specific accounts in the financial statements.
- The procedures, both manual and automated, used to process accounting transactions (from the initiation of a transaction to the impact of the transaction on the financial statements).
- The process used to prepare the client's financial statements (including significant accounting estimates and disclosures).
- Procedures used to capture events and conditions, other than transactions, that are significant to the financial statements.
- Controls surrounding journal entries, including nonstandard journal entries used to record nonrecurring, unusual transactions, or adjustments.

The activities performed by the service organization may be considered part of the client's internal control and therefore may require that the auditor develop a sufficient understanding of the controls in place at the service organization's facilities. However, it may be costly to have the client's auditor visit the other organization to obtain such an understanding. Also, it could be disruptive to the other organization to have several of its customers' auditors review and test its internal control.

To provide a reasonable solution to this problem, the AICPA issued AU-C 402, which the auditor of a user entity should use in obtaining a sufficient understanding of the services provided by a service organization as well as effects on the user entity's internal control relevant to the audit in order to identify, assess, and respond to the risks of material misstatement. The nature and extent of the user auditor's work regarding the service organization's services depends on the nature and significance of the services to the entity and their relevance to the audit.

**OBSERVATION:** AU-C 402 provides guidance for the user auditor when a client uses a service organization. AT-C 320 contains the guidance for service auditors.

**PLANNING AID REMINDER:** The standards established by AU-C 402 are not applicable to the audit of a client's transactions that arise from financial interests in partnerships, corporations, and joint ventures, when the entity's proprietary interest is accounted for and reported. In addition, AU-C 402 would not apply when the service organization executes transactions based on specific authorization granted by the user organization. In that case, the client retains responsibility for authorizing the transactions and maintaining the related accountability. For example, the user auditor would not consider the control procedures of a broker that simply executes security transactions for the user organization.

## ROLE OF THE USER AUDITOR

When a user organization employs a service organization, the user organization's ability to institute effective internal controls over the activities performed by the service organization can vary.

In many instances, internal controls of the service organization are an extension of the user organization's accounting system. Generally, transactions authorized by the user organization are transferred to the service organization for additional processing, and internal controls are maintained by both the user and the service organization. In other instances, the service organization may execute transactions and maintain related accountability, and the user organization might not have effective internal controls over such transactions.

## Definitions

| | |
|---|---|
| Complementary user entity controls | Controls the service organization assumes will be implemented by user entities. If these controls are necessary to achieve the control objectives stated in management's description of the service organization's system, they should be identified as such in the description. |
| Report on management's description of a service organization's system and the suitability of the design of controls (type 1 report) | A report comprising (1) management's description of the service organization's system; (2) a written assertion by the service organization's management about whether in all material respects, based on suitable criteria and as of a specified date, management's description of the service organization's system fairly presents such system's design and implementation, and the controls related to the description's control objectives were suitably designed to achieve those objectives; and (3) a service auditor's report expressing an opinion on these written assertions. |
| Report on management's description of a service organization's system and the suitability of the design and operating effectiveness of controls (type 2 report) | A report comprising (1) management's description of the service organization's system; (2) a written assertion by the service organization's management about whether in all material respects, based on suitable criteria and throughout the specified period, the description of the service organization's system fairly presents such system's design and implementation, the controls related to the description's control objectives were suitably designed and operated effectively to achieve those objectives; and (3) a service auditor's report expressing an opinion on these written assertions and including a description of the service auditor's tests of controls and their results. |
| Service auditor | A practitioner who reports on controls at a service organization. |
| Service organization | An organization or segment of an organization providing services to user entities that are part of those user entities' information and communication systems relevant to financial reporting. |
| Service organization's system | Policies and procedures designed, implemented, and documented by management of the service organization to provide user entities with the services covered by the service auditor's report. Management's description of the service organization's system identifies the services covered; the period or date to which the description relates; the control objectives specified by management or an outside party, including specification of the outside party; and the related controls. |
| Subservice organization | A service organization used by another service organization to perform some of the services provided to user entities that are relevant to those user entities' internal control over financial reporting. |

| | |
|---|---|
| User auditor | An auditor who audits and reports on the financial statements of a user entity. |
| User entity | An entity that uses a service organization and whose financial statements are being audited. |

## Requirements

The user auditor is presumptively required to perform the following procedures in the financial statement audit of an entity that uses one or more service organizations:

### *Obtain an Understanding of the Services Provided by a Service Organization*

1. Obtain an understanding of how the user entity uses a service organization in its operations, including the nature and significance of services the service organization provides, including the user entity's internal control; the nature and materiality of transactions processed and accounts or financial reporting processes affected by the service organization; the degree of interaction between the service organization's and user entity's activities; and the nature of the relationship, including the contractual terms, between the organizations.

2. Obtain an understanding of internal control relevant to the audit by evaluating the design and implementation of relevant controls at the user entity, including controls applied to transactions processed by the service organization, relating to services performed by the service organization.

3. Determine whether a sufficient understanding of the user entity's internal control relevant to the audit has been obtained to provide a basis for the identification and assessment of risks of material misstatement. This evidence can be obtained from one or more of the following sources: information about the service organization available at the user entity, a type 1 or type 2 report, specific information obtained by contacting the service organization through the user entity, using another auditor to perform procedures providing the necessary information, or by visiting the service organization and performing these procedures.

### *Using a Service Auditor's Report*

4. The service auditor's professional reputation, competence, and independence from the service organization as well as the adequacy of the standards under which report was issued should be considered in determining the sufficiency and appropriateness of the audit evidence provided by a type 1 or type 2 report.

5. To use a type 1 or type 2 report as audit evidence about the design and implementation of controls at the service organization, evaluate whether the description of the service organization's system is as of or for an appropriate time period; evaluate the sufficiency and appropriateness of the evidence provided for the understanding of internal control relevant to the audit; and determine whether identified complementary user entity controls are relevant, and, if so, obtain an understanding of whether the user entity has designed and implemented such controls.

### *Responding to the Assessed Risks of Material Misstatement*

6. In responding to assessed risks, determine whether sufficient appropriate audit evidence concerning relevant financial statement assertions is available from records held at the user entity and, if not, perform further audit proce-

dures to obtain that evidence or ask the service auditor through the user entity to perform those procedures on the user auditor's behalf.

7. If the risk assessment includes an expectation that controls applied only at the service organization are operating effectively, the user auditor should obtain evidence about this operating effectiveness via one or more of the following procedures: obtaining and reading a type 2 report, performing appropriate tests of controls at the service organization, or using another auditor to perform tests of controls at the service organization on the user auditor's behalf.

8. To use a type 2 report as audit evidence about the operating effectiveness of controls at the service organization, perform the following procedures to determine whether the service auditor's report provides sufficient appropriate audit evidence to support the risk assessment: evaluate whether the report is for an appropriate time period; determine whether identified complementary user entity controls are relevant, and, if so, obtain an understanding of whether the user entity has designed, implemented, and tested the operating effectiveness of such controls; evaluate the adequacy of the period covered by the tests of controls and the time elapsed since the performance of the tests of controls; and evaluate whether the tests of controls and results described in the type 2 report are relevant to assertions in the user entity's financial statements.

9. If the user auditor plans to use a type 1 or type 2 report that excludes the services provided by a subservice organization and those services are relevant to the audit of the user entity's financial statements, apply the requirements of AU-C 402 with respect to the services provided by the subservice organization.

## *Fraud, Noncompliance, and Uncorrected Misstatements in Relation to Service Organization Activities*

10. Inquire of the user entity's management about whether the service organization has reported any fraud, noncompliance with laws and regulations, or uncorrected misstatements. If so, evaluate how such matters affect the nature, timing, and extent of further audit procedures.

### *Reporting by the User Auditor*

11. Modify the user auditor's report opinion in accordance with AU-C 705 (*Modifications to The Opinion in The Independent Auditor's Report*) if unable to obtain sufficient appropriate audit evidence regarding the services provided by the service organization relevant to the audit of the user entity's financial statements.

12. Do not refer to the work of a service auditor in a report containing an unmodified opinion.

13. Reference can be made to the work of a service auditor if the opinion is modified and reference to the work is relevant to an understanding of the modification. This reference should indicate that the user auditor's responsibility for the audit opinion is not diminished.

## Analysis and Application of Procedures

### *Obtain an Understanding of the Services Provided by a Service Organization*

Information about relevant controls instituted by a service organization can be identified from a number of sources, including the following:

- User manuals;
- System overviews;
- Technical manuals;
- The contract between the two parties; and
- Reports by other parties including the service auditor, internal auditors, and regulatory authorities.

When the activities performed by the service organization are routine and highly standardized, a review of information obtained by the user auditor in previous experience with the service center might be useful in planning the current engagement. Services provided by services organizations that are relevant to the audit include maintaining accounting records, managing assets, and initiating, recording, or processing transactions for user entities.

---

**OBSERVATION:** Smaller entities may use external bookkeeping services to process transactions, maintain accounting records, or prepare their financial statements. Use of such a service organization does not relieve management and those charged with governance of their responsibilities for the financial statements.

---

An understanding of service organization controls that affect a user entity's internal control may be necessary if the nature of the transactions processed is significant, even if the transactions processed and accounts affected do not appear material to the user entity's financial statements. The degree of interaction between the organizations is also important to consider, because the higher the degree of interaction between the organizations, the more likely the user entity will be able to implement effective controls over transactions performed by the service organization. For audits of governmental entities, additional audit procedures may be required such as obtaining and understanding of internal control over compliance, and performing tests of compliance and compliance controls.

Contractual terms or service level agreements between the organizations may provide for matters such as the information to be provided to the user entity, the form of records maintained and access to them, any indemnification to be provided to the user entity in the event of a performance failure, whether a type 1 or type 2 report will be provided, whether the user auditor has rights of access to the user entity's accounting records at the service organization, and whether the agreement allows for direct communication between the user auditor and the service auditor.

---

**PLANNING AID REMINDER:** While there are direct relationships between the service organization and user entity and between the service organization and service auditor, there is not a direct relationship between the user auditor and service auditor. Communication between the user auditor and service auditor are typically conducted through the user entity and service organization.

If it is not possible or practicable to obtain sufficient appropriate audit evidence about certain risks from substantive procedures alone, the controls over such risks are relevant to the audit and the user auditor is required to obtain an understanding about those controls. This situation can occur when highly automated processing gives rise to risks of inaccurate or incomplete recording of transactions and balances, a situation often present when a using a service organization.

The procedures the auditor determines are needed to provide a basis for the identification and assessment of the risks of material misstatement related to the user entity's use of the service organization may be influenced by factors such as the size of the organizations, the complexity of transactions and services involved, the service organization's location, whether the procedure will provide the user auditor with sufficient appropriate audit evidence, and the nature of the relationship between the user entity and service organization. In situations where a user entity outsources significant business units or functions and a type 1 or type 2 report is not available, visiting the service organization may be the most effective procedure for the user auditor to gain an understanding of controls at the service organization. In situations where a type 1 or type 2 report has been issued, the user auditor may also choose to use the service auditor to perform procedures to provide the necessary information about relevant controls at the service organization, following the guidance in AU-C 600 about using the work of another auditor.

## Using a Service Auditor's Report

The user auditor may make inquiries about the service auditor to the auditor's professional organization and other practitioners and inquire as to whether the service auditor is subject to regulatory oversight. If the service auditor practices in a jurisdiction with different standards, the user auditor may obtain information about those standards from the standard-setting organization in that jurisdiction.

**OBSERVATION:** A service auditor's report implies that the service auditor is independent of the service organization. However, the service auditor does not need to be independent of user entities.

**PLANNING AID REMINDER:** Standards put forth by a body designated by the Council of the AICPA pursuant to the "Compliance with Standards Rule" of the AICPA Code of Professional Conduct are presumed to be adequate. The IAASB is not one of these bodies, so the auditor may wish to use AT-C 320 (*Reporting on an Examination of Controls at a Service Organization Relevant to User Entities' Internal Control Over Financial Reporting*) as guidance if the service auditor's report is issued in accordance with International Standard on Assurance Engagements 3402 (*Assurance Reports on Controls at a Service Organization*) promulgated by the IAASB.

*Type 1 report*

A type 1 report can be useful to user auditors, particularly in providing an understanding of:

- Controls at the service organization affecting the user entity's transaction processing.
- The flow of transactions through the service organization's system to identify points where material misstatements in the user entity's financial statements could occur.
- Service organization control objectives relevant to the user entity's financial statement assertions.
- Whether service organization controls are suitably designed and implemented for detecting and correcting processing errors that could result in material misstatements in user entity financial statements.

---

**PLANNING AID REMINDER:** A type 1 report does not provide any evidence of the operating effectiveness of relevant controls.

---

A type 1 report is "as of" a date, and if that date is outside the user entity's reporting period, the report may still be used to provide the user auditor with a preliminary understanding of service organization controls if it is supplemented by additional current information. Procedures the user auditor may perform to update the information in a type 1 report include discussing changes at the service organization with user entity or service organization personnel or reviewing current documentation and correspondence issued by the service organization.

*Type 2 report*

The more overlap there is between the period covered by the type 2 report and the user entity's financial statement period, the more evidence a type 2 report typically provides. If there is little overlap between the two periods, additional audit evidence may be provided by an additional type 2 report covering the preceding or subsequent period, by obtaining additional evidence about significant changes in service organization controls outside the period covered by the report, or by performing additional audit procedures. Factors influencing the additional audit evidence obtained for the period not covered by the type 2 report include the following:

- Significance of the assessed risks of material misstatement at the assertion level,
- Significant changes to controls since they were tested,
- Degree to which audit evidence was obtained about the operating effectiveness of controls,
- Length of the remaining period,
- Extent to which the user auditor plans to reduce substantive testing based on reliance on controls, and
- Effectiveness of the user entity's control environment and monitoring controls.

If there is no overlap between the period of the type 2 report and the user entity's financial statement period, the user auditor cannot rely on the type 2 report to determine the operating effectiveness of the user entity's controls, because it provides no current period evidence.

If the user auditor believes the type 2 report does not provide sufficient audit evidence, the auditor may contact the service organization through the user entity to discuss the scope and result of the service auditor's work or to request that the service auditor perform additional procedures, or the user auditor may perform additional procedures.

A service auditor's report noting deviations or containing a modified opinion can still be used by the user auditor, and any deviation or modification should be considered in assessing the tests of controls performed by the service auditor.

**PUBLIC COMPANY IMPLICATION:** The Sarbanes-Oxley Act of 2002 (SOX) requires all public companies to issue an "internal control report" by management. Furthermore, SOX requires the auditor to issue a separate opinion based on his or her evaluation of the effectiveness of internal control over financial reporting. That responsibility includes a requirement for the auditor to arrive at his or her own assessment of the operating effectiveness of the internal controls. When auditing a public company that uses a service organization to process transactions relevant to financial statements, the auditor should consider the guidance contained in AU-C 402. In many cases the auditor is required to obtain a service auditor's report on a description of a service organization's system and the suitability of the design and operating effectiveness of controls.

*Communication of significant deficiencies and material weaknesses*

If a significant deficiency or material weakness in internal control is identified, the user auditor should communicate these deficiencies in writing on a timely basis to management and those charged with governance, following the guidance in AU-C 265. Control deficiencies that may be identified in an audit of a user entity related to use of a service organization include monitoring controls that are needed but have not been implemented by the user entity, complementary user entity controls identified in a type 1 or type 2 report that have not been implemented by the user entity, and controls needed at the service organization that were not implemented or are not operating effectively. The auditor may also communicate other control-related matters, such as deficiencies that are not significant deficiencies or material weaknesses.

*Type 1 and Type 2 reports that exclude the services of a subservice organization*

If a service organization uses a subservice organization, the service auditor's report may include or exclude the subservice organization's relevant control objectives and controls. These reporting methods are known as the inclusive method and carve-out method, respectively. If the service auditor's report (type 1 or 2) excludes the controls at the subservice organization and the services provided by the subservice organization are relevant to the audit of the entity's financial statement, the user auditor is required to apply the requirements of AU-C 402.

## Responding to the Assessed Risks of Material Misstatement

If a service organization maintains material elements of the user entity's accounting records, the user auditor may need direct access to those records to obtain sufficient appropriate audit evidence regarding the operation of controls over those records and to substantiate recorded transactions and balances. The user auditor may perform the following procedures in obtaining audit evidence for financial statement assertions about transactions and balances maintained by the service organization for a user entity:

- Inspect records and documents held by the user entity or service organization,
- Obtain confirmations of balances and transactions from the service organization if the user entity maintains independent records, and
- Perform analytical procedures on records maintained by the user entity or on reports received from the service organization.

The user auditor is required to design and perform tests of controls to obtain sufficient appropriate audit evidence concerning the operating effectiveness of relevant controls in a service organization when (1) the user auditor's assessment of risks of material misstatement includes an expectation that the controls at the service organization are operating effectively or (2) substantive procedures alone or in combination with tests of operating effectiveness of controls at the user entity cannot provide sufficient appropriate audit evidence at the assertion level. Risk assessments will be based on combined evidence from the user auditor's procedures and the service auditor's report. Procedures the user auditor may perform to test a user entity's controls over service organization activities include reperformance of items processed by the service organization and tests of the user entity's reconciliation of output reports with source documents.

In some circumstances, the user auditor may require additional information to evaluate how any reported matters affect the nature, timing, and extent of further audit procedures. When this occurs, the user auditor may consider contacting the service organization or service auditor to obtain that information.

## Fraud, Noncompliance, and Uncorrected Misstatements in Relation to Service Organization Activities

Some contracts between service organizations and user entities require the service organization to disclose to affected user entities any fraud, noncompliance with laws and regulations, or uncorrected misstatements attributable to the service organization. User auditors are required to make inquiries of the user entity management regarding any such matters that have been disclosed to the user entity by the service organization and the user auditor should evaluate the impact of such disclosures on the nature, timing, and extent of the auditor's further audit procedures.

## Reporting by the User Auditor

The user auditor may be unable to obtain sufficient appropriate audit evidence regarding the relevant services provided by the service organization, causing a scope limitation on the audit. The auditor may express a qualified opinion or disclaim an opinion depending on whether he or she considers the potential effects on the financial statements to be material, pervasive, or both. The user auditor may be unable to obtain sufficient appropriate audit evidence when:

- He or she is unable to obtain a sufficient understanding of services provided by the service organization and does not have a basis for identifying and assessing risks of material misstatement.
- His or her risk assessment includes an expectation that service organization controls are operating effectively but sufficient appropriate audit evidence to support this cannot be obtained.
- Sufficient appropriate audit evidence is only available from service organization records and he or she is unable to obtain direct access to these records.

The user auditor's report does not reference the service auditor's report as a basis for the user auditor's opinion on the user entity's financial statements. However, if the user auditor expresses a modified opinion because of a modified opinion in the service auditor's report, he or she is not precluded from referencing the service auditor's report. In these situations, the user auditor may need the consent of the service auditor to make such reference and the service auditor does not need to be referred to by name.

## SECTION 450

## EVALUATION OF MISSTATEMENTS IDENTIFIED DURING THE AUDIT

### Authoritative Pronouncements

SAS-122—Statements on Auditing Standards: Clarification and Recodification

SAS-134—Auditor Reporting and Amendments, Including Amendments Addressing Disclosures in the Audit of Financial Statements

SAS-136—Forming an Opinion and Reporting on Financial Statements of Employee Benefit Plans Subject to ERISA

SAS-137—The Auditor's Responsibilities Relating to Other Information Included in Annual Reports

SAS-138—Amendments to the Description of the Concept of Materiality

SAS-141—Amendment to the Effective Dates of SAS Nos. 134-140

### Overview

AU-C 450 guides the auditor in evaluating the effect of any misstatements to the financial statements identified during the audit and the effect of any uncorrected misstatements on the financial statements. AU-C 320 (*Materiality in Planning and Performing an Audit*) addresses the auditor's responsibilities in applying the concept of materiality in planning and performing an audit.

> **ENGAGEMENT STRATEGY:** The auditor is concerned with materiality levels during both the planning phase and the evaluation phase of an engagement. Although conceptually possible, generally, the assessment of materiality levels will not be the same at the planning stage as at the evaluation stage. Because the auditor will have more complete information to better assess materiality for a particular engagement, the materiality level at the end of the audit can differ from the materiality used in the planning stage. In fact, if the level of materiality is significantly less at the evaluation stage than at the planning stage, the auditor will generally need to reevaluate the sufficiency of the audit procedures he or she has performed.

> **IMPORTANT NOTICE FOR 2022:** In December 2019, the AICPA's Auditing Standards Board (ASB) issued SAS No. 138 titled *Amendments to the Description of the Concept of Materiality* to align the materiality concepts discussed in auditing standards, including AU-C 200, with the definition of materiality used by the U.S. judicial system, the PCAOB auditing standards, and the Financial Accounting Standards Board (FASB). The FASB aligned its definition of materiality in August 2018 to be consistent with the U.S. judicial system and other U.S. standards setters and regulators. The ASB believes it is in the public interest to

eliminate existing inconsistencies in definitions of materiality used. The U.S. judicial system defines a misstatement as material if there is **"substantial likelihood** that a reasonable shareholder **would** consider it important" whereas existing auditing standards define a misstatement as material if it **"could reasonably be expected to** influence the judgment of a reasonable person." The effective date of the amendment is for audits of financial statements for periods ending on or after December 15, 2021.

---

**IMPORTANT NOTICE FOR 2022:** In May 2019, the AICPA's Auditing Standards Board (ASB) issued SAS No. 134 titled *Auditor Reporting and Amendments, Including Amendments Addressing Disclosures in the Audit of Financial Statements* to revise the auditor's report and to amend various AU-C sections to heighten the auditor's focus on disclosures throughout the process of auditing financial statements. SAS No. 134 amends AU-C 450 to clarify that misstatements in financial statements can include inadequate or incomplete disclosures or omissions of disclosures required by the applicable financial reporting framework. SAS No. 134 notes that the requirement to accumulate misstatements (unless clearly trivial) includes the accumulation of misstatements in disclosures to determine the effect of such misstatements on the relevant disclosures and the financial statements as a whole. Because the misstatements in qualitative disclosures cannot be added together as is possible in the case of misstatements involving amounts, the determination of whether a misstatement in qualitative disclosure is material is a matter that involves the exercise of professional judgment. Originally, the effective date of SAS No. 134 was for audits of financial statements periods ending on or after December 15, 2020, with early implementation **not** permitted. However, the ASB's issuance of SAS No. 141, *Amendment to the Effective Dates of SAS Nos. 134-140*, extended the effective date to December 15, 2021, in order to provide more time for firms to implement SAS No. 134 in light of the effect of the coronavirus pandemic. While SAS No. 141 allows for early implementation of SAS No. 134, the ASB recommends that SAS Nos. 134-140 be implemented concurrently.

---

## Definitions

| | |
|---|---|
| Misstatement | Difference between a reported financial statement item's amount, classification, presentation, or disclosure and what is required for it to be in accordance with the applicable financial reporting framework. Misstatements can arise from error or fraud. In the context of the auditor's expressing an opinion on the financial statements, misstatements include adjustments of amounts, classifications, presentations, or disclosures that the auditor judges are necessary for the financial statements to be presented fairly in all material respects. |
| Uncorrected misstatements | Misstatements the auditor has accumulated during the audit that have not been corrected. |

## Requirements

The auditor is presumptively required to perform the following procedures in considering materiality when planning and performing the audit:

1. Accumulate misstatements identified during the audit, other than those that are clearly trivial.

2. Determine whether the overall audit strategy and audit plan need to be revised if:

    a. The nature and circumstances of occurrence of identified misstatements indicate that other misstatements may exist that could be material when aggregated with accumulated misstatements, or

    b. The aggregate of accumulated misstatements approaches materiality levels determined for the financial statements as a whole, classes of transactions, account balances, or disclosures.

3. Communicate all accumulated misstatements with the appropriate level of management on a timely basis. Request that management correct the misstatements.

4. If management, at the auditor's request, has examined and corrected the detected misstatements, perform the necessary additional audit procedures to determine if any misstatements remain.

5. If management refuses to correct some or all of the misstatements communicated by the auditor, obtain an understanding of management's reasons for not making the corrections and consider those reasons when evaluating whether the financial statements as a whole are free from material misstatement.

6. Prior to evaluating the effect of uncorrected misstatements, reassess the determination of materiality levels for the financial statements as a whole and any classes of transactions, account balances, or disclosures considered to determine whether those levels are still appropriate given the entity's actual financial results.

7. Determine whether uncorrected misstatements are material, individually or in the aggregate. Make this determination by considering the size, nature, and circumstances of the misstatements' occurrence and the effect of uncorrected misstatements related to prior periods in relation to the financial statements as a whole, relevant transaction classes, account balances, and disclosures.

8. Documentation should include:

    a. The amount below which misstatements are clearly regarded as trivial;

    b. All misstatements accumulated during the audit and whether they have been corrected; and

    c. The auditor's conclusion about whether uncorrected misstatements are material, individually or in aggregate, and the basis for that conclusion.

## Analysis and Application of Procedures

*Accumulating Identified Misstatements*

Misstatements arise due to error or fraud. They may exist as the result of various means, including inaccurate data gathering or processing, omission of amounts or disclosures, or use or accounting estimates that are clearly incorrect or that the auditor considers unreasonable, an inappropriate classification, aggregation or disaggregation of information, and the omission of disclosures necessary for fair presentation. There are three types of misstatements the auditor may encounter:

1. *Factual misstatements* Misstatements about which there is no doubt.
2. *Judgmental misstatements* Differences in judgment between management and the auditor concerning appropriate selection and application of accounting estimates and policies.
3. *Projected misstatements* The auditor's best estimate of misstatements in populations obtained by extrapolating misstatements identified in audit samples to the entire population.

When accumulating identified misstatements, the term "clearly trivial" does not have the same meaning as the term "not material." Clearly trivial misstatements will be of a lower order of magnitude than materiality levels or of a wholly different nature than those considered material, and will be of inconsequential amounts whether considered individually or in the aggregate. If there is any uncertainty about the triviality of a misstatement, it is not to be considered clearly trivial.

The auditor may designate an amount below which misstatements of amounts in the individual statements would be clearly trivial and not accumulate those misstatements because the auditor expects that the accumulation of such amounts clearly would not have a material effect on the financial statements. However, misstatements that are above the designated amount would be accumulated.

Misstatements in disclosures may also be clearly trivial whether taken individually or in the aggregate and whether judged based on size, nature, or circumstances. Misstatements in disclosures that are not clearly trivial would be accumulated to assist the auditor in evaluating their effect on the financial statements as a whole.

---

**OBSERVATION:** If the auditor has concluded, based on audit procedures employed, that a particular balance likely falls within a range, then the likely misstatement is the difference between the balance recorded in the financial statement and the upper or lower boundary of the range. For example, if the range is likely to be between $200,000 and $300,000 and the recorded balance is $315,000, the misstatement to be aggregated is $15,000 ($315,000 − $300,000). However, if the auditor's assessment of the balance is based on a point estimate (say, $290,000) rather than a range, the misstatement to be aggregated is the difference between the point estimate and the financial statement balance [in this case $25,000 ($315,000 − $290,000)].

### Considering Identified Misstatements during the Audit

The nature and circumstances of occurrence of a misstatement may indicate the misstatement is not the only instance of misstatement. This could be the case if the misstatement occurred due to a breakdown in internal control or from inappropriate assumptions or valuation methods commonly used by the entity.

If the auditor identifies misstatements during the audit that approach materiality levels, the risk that undetected misstatements may exceed materiality levels when combined with identified misstatements may be greater than is acceptable.

**OBSERVATION:** The current year's financial statements may be affected by misstatements from the prior year's engagement financial statements because such misstatements were not considered material and therefore no adjustment was made in the prior year. If the auditor believes that "there is an unacceptably high risk" that the current year's financial statements are materially misstated when the prior year's misstatements are taken into consideration, the auditor should include the likely misstatement amount due to the prior year's misstatement with the current year's likely misstatement amount to determine whether the current year's financial statements appear to be materially misstated.

### Communicating and Correcting Misstatements

The auditor should communicate all identified misstatements to an appropriate level of management. This communication should be made timely to allow management an opportunity to evaluate whether the items are misstatements and to take any necessary action. The appropriate level of management to receive the communication from the auditor is typically the level of management with the authority to take the appropriate action. In some cases, laws or regulations may prevent the auditor from communicating certain misstatements to management or others within the entity. In these circumstances, the auditor may consider seeking legal advice to understand his or her responsibilities.

Management's correction of all identified misstatements is preferable because it helps to maintain the accuracy of books and records and to prevent the risk of material misstatements in future financial statements due to the accumulation of effects of prior uncorrected misstatements. The auditor should request management to record adjustments needed to correct all factual misstatements, unless they are considered to be trivial, including the effect of prior-period misstatements. For projected material misstatements based on a sample, the auditor should request management to examine the class of transactions, account balance, or disclosure in order to identify and correct misstatements. For judgmental misstatements based on differences in estimates, the auditor should request management to review the assumptions and methods used in developing management's estimate.

If management decides not to correct some or all of the misstatements communicated by the auditor, he or she should consider the qualitative aspects of the entity's accounting practices and indicators of possible bias in management's judgments when determining the implications related to his or her report.

## Evaluating the Effect of Uncorrected Misstatements

If the auditor reassesses materiality during the audit and determines lower materiality levels are appropriate, then performance materiality levels as well as the nature, timing, and extent of further audit procedures will need to be reconsidered to ensure that sufficient appropriate audit evidence is obtained for the auditor to formulate an opinion.

There are several factors the auditor should consider in determining whether uncorrected misstatements are material, whether considered individually or in the aggregate. Uncorrected misstatements from different entity locations or found by other auditors performing portions of the audit should be included in evaluating the effects of uncorrected misstatements. Furthermore, the materiality of a misstatement in the audit of a governmental entity may be affected by legislation, regulation, or additional reporting responsibilities. While individual misstatements may be offset by other misstatements, this generally does not offset the misstatements' materiality. However, it may be appropriate to offset misstatements within the same class of transactions or account balance if the auditor determines the risk that further undetected misstatements may exist is acceptable.

The materiality of classification misstatements depends on several qualitative factors, including the effects of the misstatement on debt and contractual covenants, on individual line items or subtotals, and on key ratios. In some circumstances, the auditor may conclude that a classification misstatement is not material even if it exceeds materiality levels. This conclusion may be drawn if, for example, the misclassification amount is small in relation to the size of related balance sheet items and the misstatement does not impact the income statement or key ratios.

The objective of the auditor is to perform the audit to obtain reasonable assurance that misstatements that could be quantitatively material to the financial statements are detected. However, qualitative factors also contribute to the determination of materiality and may cause the auditor to determine a misstatement is material even if the amount of the misstatement is lower than the prescribed materiality levels. Exhibit AU-C 450-1 lists several qualitative factors the auditor may consider in determining a misstatement's materiality. It is important for the auditor to remember that existence of any of these qualitative factors does not necessarily mean a misstatement is material.

Each individual misstatement of a qualitative disclosure is considered to evaluate its effect on relevant disclosures, as well as its effect on the financial statements as a whole. The determination of whether a misstatement in a qualitative disclosure is material, is a matter of professional judgment.

The auditor considers uncorrected misstatements in amounts and disclosures to determine whether uncorrected misstatements by nature are material. Uncorrected misstatements may be considered material either individually or in combination with other misstatements. For example, identified errors may be recurring or pervasive or several misstatements may link to the same matter and when aggregated might affect the user's judgment of that matter.

> **FRAUD POINTER:** If a misstatement may be the result of fraud, AU-C 240 (*Consideration of Fraud in a Financial Statement Audit*) requires the auditor to consider the implications of the misstatement in relation to other aspects of the audit, even if the misstatement is not material to the financial statements as a whole.

*Document Audit Results Relating to Misstatements*

The auditor's documentation of uncorrected misstatements may consider the following:

- The aggregate effect of misstatements on the financial statements;
- Whether any materiality levels for particular classes of transactions, account balances, or disclosures have been exceeded; and
- The effect of uncorrected misstatements on key ratios or trends and compliance with legal, regulatory, and contractual requirements.

## Practitioner's Aids

*EXHIBIT AU-C 450-1—CHECKLIST OF QUALITATIVE FACTORS IN DETERMINING MATERIALITY*

The following qualitative factors may be relevant in determining the materiality of an item:

- Items that have an effect on ratios used to evaluate the entity's financial position, results of operations, or cash flows;
- Items that change losses to income or vice versa;
- Items that are relevant in determining whether loan covenants and similar items have been violated;
- Items that have an effect on materiality thresholds that are established by statute or regulation;
- Items that mask a change in earnings or other trends;
- Items that increase management's compensation;
- Items that are significant given the auditor's understanding of known previous communications to users;
- Items involving particular parties (such as related parties);
- Items that affect other information that will be communicated in documents containing the audited financial statements that are substantially likely to influence the judgment made by a reasonable user of the financial statements;
- Items that affect the sensitivity of the financial statements to possible fraud, illegal acts, or other similar situations;

- Items that are misclassified (such as misclassification of an item that should be considered operating but is classified as nonoperating);
- The omission of information that is not required by the applicable financial reporting framework but that the auditor judges to be important to the users' understanding of the entity's financial position, financial performance, or cash flows;
- The significance of the item in relationship to known user needs;
- The character of the misstatement (e.g., the degree to which an account balance is based on an estimate);
- The possible motivation of management for the misstatement;
- The existence of offsetting effects of individually significant items;
- The possibility that an item or incorrect selection or application of an accounting policy that is currently immaterial could have a material impact on subsequent financial statements;
- The cost of making a correction; and
- The risk that other undetected misstatements would affect the auditor's opinion.

### EXHIBIT AU-C 450-2—SEC STAFF ACCOUNTING BULLETIN (SAB-99): "MATERIALITY"

The Financial Accounting Standards Board (FASB) and the American Institute of Certified Public Accountants (AICPA) have provided little guidance for determining what constitutes a material item in financial statements. The Securities and Exchange Commission (SEC) has addressed this issue in a Staff Acccunting Bulletin (SAB) titled "Materiality" (SAB-99). Although the SEC addresses only publicly traded companies, SAB-99, discussed here, provides valuable guidance in the performance of audits in general. This Practitioner's Aid summarizes the guidance in the SAB.

SAB-99 discusses how the auditor of a public company should do the following:

- Assess materiality,
- Aggregate and net misstatements, and
- Consider immaterial misstatements that are intentional.

### Assessing Materiality

FASB Concepts Statement No. 2 (CON-2) (*Qualitative Characteristics of Accounting Information*) characterizes "materiality" as follows:

> The omission or misstatement of an item in a financial report is material if, in the light of surrounding circumstances, the magnitude of the item is such that it is probable that the judgment of a reasonable person relying upon the report would have been changed or influenced by the inclusion or correction of the item.

While everyone agrees with this description of materiality, applying the concept in practice requires a considerable amount of professional judgment. In many engagements, an auditor establishes a material threshold or a rule of thumb, such as 5% or 10%, and a misstatement(s) that is less than the specific threshold is not considered material. SAB-99 points out that the creation of a specific materiality percentage or dollar value for determining whether a particular item is material "has no basis in the accounting literature or the law."

An auditor deals with two broad types of materiality during an engagement. First, in order to help plan an engagement, the auditor must identify a materiality factor. That is, the auditor must make some determination of what may be material in determining the nature, timing, and extent of audit procedures. Generally, as the materiality threshold falls from, say, 10% to 5%, the extent of audit procedures that are necessary to achieve the auditor's objective is increased. The SEC has no problem with an auditor using preliminary definitions of "materiality" in determining the audit approach in a particular engagement.

The second type of materiality the auditor must address in an engagement involves determining whether specific misstatements are in the aggregate large enough for the auditor to conclude that the financial statements may be materially misstated. The SEC points out that in this phase of the audit engagement, using hard and fast materiality thresholds is not appropriate. That is, concluding whether or not an item is material is not a procedural process (asking whether an item exceeds a specific threshold) but rather an analytical process (asking whether it could affect one's assessment of a particular company). To support the argument that acceptance of the analytical process is the appropriate approach, the SEC refers to the following legal conclusion: "Magnitude by itself, without regard to the nature of the item and the circumstances in which the judgment has to be made, will not generally be a sufficient basis for a materiality judgment." That is, the SEC reminds auditors that both quantitative and qualitative factors must be considered in determining whether an item is material to the financial statements taken as a whole.

SAB-99 points out that the qualitative factors used to evaluate a matter that is below the quantitative threshold should include the following:

- Whether the misstatement arises from an item capable of precise measurement or from an estimate and, if from an estimate, the degree of imprecision inherent in the estimate;
- Whether the misstatement masks a change in earnings or other trends;
- Whether the misstatement hides a failure to meet analysts' consensus expectations for the enterprise;
- Whether the misstatement changes a loss into income or vice versa;
- Whether the misstatement concerns a segment or other portion of the registrant's business that has been identified as playing a significant role in the registrant's operations or profitability;
- Whether the misstatement affects the registrant's compliance with regulatory requirements;
- Whether the misstatement affects the registration's compliance with loan covenants or other contractual requirements;

- Whether the misstatement has the effect of increasing management's compensation—for example, by satisfying requirements for the award of bonuses or other forms of incentive compensation; and
- Whether the misstatement involves concealment of an unlawful transaction.

The SEC also notes that an auditor must be particularly careful when audit results suggest that management has intentionally made misstatements in the preparation of its financial statements that appear to have the objective of "managing earnings." In this regard, SAB-99 makes the following observation:

> The staff believes that investors generally would regard as significant a management practice to over- or under-state earnings up to an amount just short of a percentage threshold in order to "manage" earnings. Investors presumably also would regard as significant an accounting practice that, in essence, rendered all earnings figures subject to a management-directed margin of misstatement.

Based on the SEC's reasoning and plain common sense, an auditor should not establish a materiality threshold and then blindly apply it in an engagement. That is not exercising judgment; it is reducing the audit process to a mechanical process that can be more efficiently performed by a computer.

## Aggregating and Netting Misstatements

In determining whether financial statements are materially misstated, the misstatement should be evaluated both individually and in the aggregate. This determination should be made on the basis of both quantitative thresholds and qualitative factors (such as those discussed in the previous section), and the analysis should be directed to "individual line item amounts, subtotals, or totals in the financial statements."

When an individual item by itself is material, it is incorrect to offset its significance with another item that has the opposite impact on the financial statements. For example, if sales are materially overstated and cost of goods sold is materially overstated by more or less the same amount, it would not be proper to suggest that the income statement is not materially misstated because net income is not materially affected by the offsetting misstatements.

SAB-99 warns auditors that they must be careful when aggregating the effects of two or more misstatements that net to a smaller effect on a particular total or subtotal. This is especially true when two misstatements are offset and one is based on an estimate and the other on a precise measurement.

---

**ENGAGEMENT STRATEGY:** The auditor must take into consideration in the current engagement misstatements that were made in previous years but were considered immaterial. Those previous years' misstatements could have a material impact on the current year's financial statements, since the quantitative and qualitative factors that are relevant to identifying material items in the current engagement may have changed.

---

*Consider immaterial misstatements that are intentional*

SAB-99 raises the question of whether a client can make deliberate adjustments to its financial statements that are inconsistent with U.S. generally accepted accounting principles (U.S. GAAP) even though the effect is immaterial. The SEC takes the position that such action by a client is inappropriate and may in fact be in violation of securities laws that require that the books and records be accurate in "reasonable detail," a more stringent constraint than the materiality threshold. In determining what reasonable detail is, the auditor should consider the materiality factors (quantitative and qualitative factors discussed earlier) as well as additional factors such as the following:

- *The significance of the misstatement* Though registrants do not need to make finely calibrated determinations of significance with respect to immaterial items, it is "reasonable" to treat misstatements with clearly inconsequential effects differently than more significant ones.
- *How the misstatement arose* It is unlikely that it is ever "reasonable" for registrants to record misstatements or fail to correct known misstatements—even immaterial ones—if these actions are directed by or known to senior management and are for the purposes of "managing" earnings. On the other hand, insignificant misstatements that arise from the operation of systems or recurring processes in the normal course of business generally will not cause a registrant's books to be inaccurate "in reasonable detail."
- *The cost of correcting the misstatement* The books and records provisions of the Exchange Act do not require registrants to make major expenditures to correct small misstatements. However, if there is little cost or delay involved in correcting a misstatement, failing to do so is unlikely to be "reasonable."
- *The clarity of authoritative accounting guidance with respect to the misstatement* If reasonable minds may differ about the appropriate accounting treatment of a financial statement item, a failure to correct it may not cause the registrant's financial statements to be inaccurate "in reasonable detail." However, if there is little ground for reasonable disagreement, it becomes less reasonable to leave a misstatement uncorrected.

*The auditor's response to intentional misstatements*

Securities laws and auditing standards (AU-C 240 and AU-C 250 (*Consideration of Laws and Regulations in an Audit of Financial Statements*)) both require that an auditor report fraudulent acts to the appropriate level of management. If the auditor believes that a misstatement is, or may be, the result of fraud, he or she should consider the implications of the misstatement in relation to other aspects of the audit, even if the misstatement is not material to the financial statements.

> **ENGAGEMENT STRATEGY:** In addition to reporting fraudulent acts to the appropriate level of management, the auditor must also consider how the discovery of such facts affects the nature, timing, and extent of audit procedures. In some instances, it may be appropriate, after seeking competent legal advice, for the auditor to resign from an engagement.

*U.S. GAAP precedent over industry practice*

When there is a conflict between U.S. GAAP and industry accounting practice, clearly U.S. GAAP must be observed. Thus, if a client prepares a portion of its financial statements to conform to industry accounting practices that are inconsistent with U.S. GAAP, these departures must be evaluated to determine whether the financial statements are materially misstated.

*General comments*

The SEC recognizes that determining when financial statements are materially misstated can be a complex process. This is especially true when the application of U.S. GAAP to a particular transaction or balance is not clear. Under these conditions, a client may account for an item "based on analogies to similar situations or other factors." When these conditions arise, an auditor is encouraged to discuss ambiguous accounting and reporting issues with the SEC staff on a timely basis.

> **ENGAGEMENT STRATEGY:** When the client is not a public company, the auditor should have in place procedures that encourage staff accountants to discuss difficult reporting issues with appropriate personnel within the firm.

## AU-C 500
## Audit Evidence

| Section 500: | Audit Evidence | 5002 |
|---|---|---|
| Section 501: | Audit Evidence—Specific Considerations for Selected Items | 5013 |
| Section 505: | External Confirmations | 5039 |
| Section 510: | Opening Balances—Initial Audit Engagements, Including Reaudit Engagements | 5054 |
| Section 520: | Analytical Procedures | 5062 |
| Section 530: | Audit Sampling | 5080 |
| Section 540: | Auditing Accounting Estimates, Including Fair Value Accounting Estimates, and Related Disclosures | 5117 |
| Section 550: | Related Parties | 5146 |
| Section 560: | Subsequent Events and Subsequently Discovered Facts | 5160 |
| Section 570: | The Auditor's Consideration of an Entity's Ability to Continue as a Going Concern | 5174 |
| Section 580: | Written Representations | 5188 |
| Section 585: | Consideration of Omitted Procedures after the Report Release Date | 5201 |

# SECTION 500

# AUDIT EVIDENCE

## Authoritative Pronouncements

SAS-135—Omnibus Statement on Auditing Standards—2019

SAS-142—Audit Evidence

SAS Interpretation 1—The Effect of an Inability to Obtain Audit Evidence Relating to Income Tax Accruals (October 2011)

SAS Interpretation 2—Auditor of Participating Employer in a Governmental Cost-Sharing Multiple-Employer Pension Plan (April 2014)

SAS Interpretation 3—Auditor of Participating Employer in a Governmental Agent Multiple-Employer Pension Plan (June 2014)

## Overview

The "Preface to the Codification of Statements on Auditing Standards" notes that to obtain reasonable assurance, the auditor:

> Obtains sufficient appropriate audit evidence about whether material misstatements exist through designing and implementing appropriate responses to assessed risks.

AU-C 500 explains what constitutes audit evidence in a financial statement audit and addresses the auditor's responsibilities to design and perform audit procedures to inform the auditor's conclusion about whether sufficient appropriate audit evidence has been obtained to be able to draw reasonable conclusions on which to base the auditor's opinion.

AU-C 500 applies to all audit evidence obtained during the course of the audit. Other AU-C sections supplement this guidance by addressing additional details of audit evidence such as specific aspects of the audit, audit evidence to be obtained in relation to a particular topic, specific procedures to obtain audit evidence, and the evaluation of whether sufficient appropriate audit evidence has been obtained. Thus, both this section and other AU-C sections need to be considered to fulfil the auditor's responsibilities.

**IMPORTANT NOTICE FOR 2022:** In July 2020, the AICPA Auditing Standards Board (ASB) issued SAS No. 142, *Audit Evidence*, which supersedes AU-C 500 (*Audit Evidence*) and amends various other sections in the professional standards. This new SAS addresses the evolving nature of business and audit services and issues that include the use of emerging technologies by both preparers and auditors, audit data analytics (ADA), the application of professional skepticism, the expanding use of external information sources as audit evidence, and, more broadly, the accuracy, completeness, and reliability of audit evidence. This SAS is effective for audits of financial statements for periods ending on or after December 15, 2022.

## Definitions

| | |
|---|---|
| Appropriateness (of audit evidence) | Measure of the quality of audit evidence and its relevance and reliability in providing support for conclusions on which the auditor's opinion is based. |
| Audit evidence | Information used by the auditor in arriving at the conclusion on which the auditor's opinion is based. Audit evidence is information to which audit procedures have been applied and consists of information that corroborates or contradicts assertions in the financial statements. |
| External information source | An external individual or organization that provides information that is used by the entity in preparing the financial statements or that has been obtained by the auditor as audit evidence, when such information is suitable for use by a broad range of users. When financial information has been provided by an individual or organization acting in the capacity of management's specialist, service organization, or auditor's specialist, the individual or organization is not considered an external information source with respect to that particular information. |
| Sufficiency (of audit evidence) | Measure of the quantity of audit evidence. The quantity of audit evidence needed is affected by the auditor's assessment of the risks of material misstatement and by the quality of the audit evidence (e.g., its appropriateness). |

## Requirements

The auditor is presumptively required to perform the following procedures in collecting and evaluating audit evidence to support his or her opinion on the client's financial statements:

1. Consider the relevance and reliability of information, including its source, to be used as audit evidence when designing and performing audit procedures.

2. Evaluate whether such information is sufficiently reliable for the purposes of the audit by (1) obtaining audit evidence about the accuracy and completeness of the information and (2) evaluating whether the information is sufficiently precise and detailed.

3. Evaluate whether the information corroborates or contradicts assertions in the financial statements. If audit evidence obtained is inconsistent or contradicts assertions in the financial statements, or the auditor has doubts about the reliability of information to be used as audit evidence, the auditor should determine what modifications to audit procedures are necessary to resolve the matter and any effect of the matter on other aspects of the audit.

4. Consider whether the information used as audit evidence and the results of the auditor's procedures provide a basis for concluding on the sufficiency and appropriateness of audit evidence obtained.

5. When inconsistencies in information obtained are identified or doubts exist about the reliability of audit evidence, determine whether modifications or additions to audit procedures are necessary.

---

**PUBLIC COMPANY IMPLICATION:** Obtaining sufficient appropriate audit evidence as to whether the recognition, measurement, presentation, and disclosures related to revenue are in accordance with U.S. GAAP is a significant focus in most audit engagements. According to PCAOB Staff Audit Practice Alert No. 12 (*Matters Related to Auditing Revenue in an Audit of Financial Statements*), the Board's inspections over the years have found numerous deficiencies relating to auditing revenue. Among the areas where the PCAOB has found the most problems are (1) testing revenue recognition involving contracts, (2) evaluating revenue presentation (gross vs. net), (3) testing proper revenue cutoff, (4) evaluating whether required revenue-related disclosures are present, (5) responding to fraud risks related to revenue, (6) testing and evaluating revenue-related controls, (7) using sampling to test revenue, (8) using analytical procedures to test revenue, and (9) testing revenue when multiple locations are involved. Audit firms are encouraged to revisit their auditing methodologies and implementation of those methodologies related to revenue, as well as considering the need for additional employee training. Finally, the PCAOB indicates that greater partner and senior manager attention may be needed in ensuring that auditing standards are followed with respect to auditing revenue.

---

## Analysis and Application of Procedures

### Sufficient Appropriate Audit Evidence

Audit evidence is cumulative in nature, and includes evidence from (1) procedures performed during the audit, (2) results from prior-year audits, and (3) the firm's quality control process for client acceptance and continuance. Audit evidence includes both information that supports and information that contradicts management's assertions and in some cases may include the absence of information, such as when management refuses to provide a requested representation. Many types of audit procedures are performed to obtain audit evidence. Those include inspection, observation, confirmation, recalculation, reperformance, analytical procedures, and inquiry. Inquiry is one of these audit procedures that may provide important audit evidence, but that alone is not sufficient to test the operating effectiveness of controls and generally does not provide sufficient audit evidence of the absence of a material misstatement at the assertion level. Additionally, these procedures may be performed manually or using automated tools and techniques.

The auditor obtains reasonable assurance regarding his or her audit conclusions when sufficient appropriate audit evidence has been obtained to reduce audit risk to an acceptably low level. The sufficiency and appropriateness of audit evidence are interrelated and together they affect the persuasiveness of audit evidence. The conclusion about whether sufficient appropriate evidence has been obtained is made at both the financial statement and assertion levels. As the relevance and reliability of evidence increases, the quantity of evidence required may decrease. However, increased quantities of audit evidence may not compensate for poor-quality evidence. The reliability of audit evidence depends on its source, its nature, and the circumstances under which it is obtained. Audit judgment is used to determine when the audit evidence obtained is sufficient and appropriate to draw reasonable conclusions on which to base the audit opinion.

> **PUBLIC COMPANY IMPLICATION:** The PCAOB's AS-1105 (*Audit Evidence*) defines what constitutes audit evidence, and it provides guidance to the auditor of a public company in evaluating the sufficiency and appropriateness of audit evidence. Although there are a number of differences between the PCAOB's and ASB's risk standards, the risk-assessment concepts contained in the PCAOB standards should be familiar to most auditors. Audit risk is the risk that the auditor will issue an inappropriate opinion on financial statements that are materially misstated. The auditor is to reduce audit risk to a low level through the application of audit procedures. The guidance in AU-C 500 is largely consistent with AS-1105.

> **FRAUD POINTER:** A very common deficiency in enforcement actions against auditors is the auditor's failure to gather adequate audit evidence. In some cases, the SEC has highlighted specific areas where evidence was inadequate, such as auditors' examinations of draft contracts rather than final contracts and auditors' failure to obtain evidence related to all the steps in written audit programs. In these instances, the SEC believed the failure to gather adequate evidence prevented the auditors from detecting material misstatement due to fraud.

Audit evidence is obtained from a variety of sources and may reflect different forms of evidence, such as oral information, visual information, paper documents, electronic information, documents, and electronically stored data. Some audit evidence is obtained from audit procedures testing the accounting records to determine that the records are internally consistent and agree to the financial statements. Accounting records alone, however, do not provide sufficient appropriate audit evidence for the auditor's opinion. Additional assurance is typically obtained from consistent or corroborating audit evidence from other sources, such as those independent of the entity. Sources of information independent of the entity that the auditor may use as audit evidence may include third-party confirmations, analysts' reports, and benchmarking data about competitors. Sources also include management and information developed by the auditor.

*Audit Procedures*

The auditor obtains audit evidence by performing three types of procedures: (1) risk assessment procedures, (2) tests of controls, and (3) substantive procedures, which include tests of details and substantive analytical procedures. Tests of controls should be performed when required by auditing standards or when the auditor chooses to perform these tests.

The auditor may perform audit procedures manually or by using automated tools and techniques. Automated tools may be used to gather and organize data for analysis to perform both risk assessment and further audit procedures. Some information may only be available in automated form or at certain points in time, thereby, impacting the nature and timing of audit procedures performed.

Audit evidence gathering procedures used by the auditor include (1) inspection, (2) observation, (3) external confirmation, (4) recalculation, (5) reperformance, (6) analytical procedures, and (7) inquiry. In some cases, audit evidence gathered in previous years' audits may continue to provide sufficient appropriate audit evidence, but the auditor should perform audit procedures to ascertain the continuing relevance of this evidence from prior years.

**PLANNING AID REMINDER:** Often the accounting data and corroborating evidence only exist in electronic form, and that evidence may only exist at a certain point in time. As a result, some of that evidence may not be visible in written form and it might not be retrievable after certain points in time. As part of planning the audit, the auditor should identify the time that evidence might exist or is available and consider that timing when planning the audit. In some cases, the auditor might determine that the use of IT specialists is appropriate in performing the audit.

*Inspection*

Inspection involves examining documents or records or physically examining an asset (or using remote observation techniques). The reliability of the audit evidence obtained from inspecting documents or records varies depending on the nature and source of the documents and records, and on the strength of internal control for internally generated documents and records. Inspection of tangible assets can provide useful audit evidence regarding the existence of the asset. It is a less effective procedure for providing evidence related to valuation of an asset and the entity's right to use it. Inspection is sometimes paired with observation as an evidence-gathering technique—for example, auditors often inspect individual assets during a physical inventory observation. Automated tools may assist with inspection procedures, such as text-recognition software techniques.

*Observation*

Observation involves looking at a client-performed process or procedure (e.g., observation of the entity's process for counting inventory, observation of the performance of a control procedure). Automated tools, such as drone or video transmission, may be used to observe processes. Observation is limited to providing evidence about the state of a process or procedure at the time its performance is observed. Also, the very act of observing a process or procedure may change its performance—that is, client personnel may perform a process or procedure differently than normal when they know the auditor is watching.

*External confirmation*

A confirmation is a specific type of inquiry. It involves asking a third party to make a representation through a direct written response (in paper or electronic form) to the auditor about certain information or of an existing condition (e.g., confirmation of an accounts receivable balance). Often confirmations are used to provide audit evidence related to account balances, but they can also be used to confirm the existence of any agreements that may affect an account balance (e.g., a side agreement allowing a customer to return goods if the customer is not able to resell them).

*Recalculation*

Recalculation is a procedure that involves checking the mathematical accuracy of documents or records. In some situations, automated tools may allow for recalculation of 100% of a population.

*Reperformance*

The auditor may reperform a procedure or control that is part of the entity's internal control. For example, an entity may have a control that involves the assistant controller reviewing the account coding for cash disbursements. The auditor could reperform this procedure.

*Analytical procedures*

Analytical procedures involve analyzing the reasonableness of financial information by comparing it with other financial and nonfinancial data. For example, the auditor might evaluate the reasonableness of the allowance for doubtful accounts by relating the allowance to the ratio of days' sales in receivables. In performing analytical procedures, the auditor should develop his or her own independent expectation of the account balance (or ratio etc.) *before* performing the analytical procedure. The effectiveness of an analytical procedure largely depends on the auditor's subsequent investigation of fluctuations or relationships that are inconsistent with other data or that deviate significantly from the auditor's expectations.

---

**FRAUD POINTER:** In some cases, the auditor uses the prior year's audited balance as the implicit expectation and then focuses on differences between the recorded amount and the prior year's balance in performing the analytical procedure. In some cases, the *lack of a difference* between the recorded amount and the prior year's balance is just as problematic as the existence of a difference.

---

Scanning is a type of an analytical procedure. Scanning involves reviewing accounting records (e.g., transaction listings, subsidiary ledgers, general ledger control accounts, adjusting entries, suspense accounts, reconciliations) for large or unusual items and then testing them. The effectiveness of scanning depends on the auditor's ability to define unusual items. Scanning is implemented most effectively through the use of electronic auditing procedures. For example, audit data analytics may allow auditors to identify areas that might represent risks of material misstatement. Those procedures may include visualization of transaction details. Audit data analytic tools may also allow the auditor to scan 100% of a population for unusual characteristics.

*Inquiry*

Inquiry involves asking questions to obtain information from knowledgeable sources. The auditor should consider making inquiries of both financial and nonfinancial personnel and of personnel both inside and external to the entity. Inquiry involves both formal written inquiries and informal oral questions. While used extensively, inquiry is typically a complementary procedure to another audit evidence-gathering technique, and its effectiveness depends on the auditor's ability to evaluate the responses received.

Responses to inquiries may provide the auditor with new information, corroborative audit evidence, or contradictory audit evidence. The auditor may choose to modify or perform additional audit procedures based on his or her evaluation of these inquiry responses.

Inquiry may be used in assessing management intent where such intent is determinative of the accounting under U.S. GAAP (e.g., the classification of securities held as investments). Management may state that it has the positive intent and ability to hold a debt security to maturity, but finding evidence to corroborate this management representation may be difficult. In such cases, management's past history of doing what it says may provide evidence either to support or refute its representations.

---

**FRAUD POINTER:** Inquiry of senior management is likely to be particularly ineffective in cases of fraud where top management is involved. Note also that AU-C 240 (*Consideration of Fraud in a Financial Statement Audit*) requires the auditor to make certain inquiries related to the risk of fraud.

---

**ENGAGEMENT STRATEGY:** Some responses to inquiries are of sufficient importance that the auditor may wish to obtain written representations from management or those charged with governance.

---

*Relevance and Reliability*

The relevance and reliability of information impacts the quality of the audit evidence.

*Relevance*

Relevant audit evidence relates to the specific assertion being tested by the auditor. For example, observation of the client's physical inventory count provides relevant audit evidence related to the existence assertion for the inventory account balance. The direction of testing is a factor that affects the relevance of audit evidence.

The audit procedures used also affect the relevance of audit evidence. Certain audit procedures may provide audit evidence relevant to particular assertions but not others. The auditor should bear in mind that audit evidence provided about one assertion is not a substitute for audit evidence about another assertion. It is also important to remember that audit evidence from different procedures or sources may be relevant to the same assertion.

The relevance of information may be affected by the classes of transactions, account balances, disclosures or assertions to which the information relates, and by the time period related to the information. Information may be relevant to some assertions, but not others. Certain types of audit evidence may be relevant to one assertion, but not another. For example, evidence obtained from inspection of a physical asset is relevant to the existence assertion, but not rights and obligations.

*Reliability*

The reliability of audit evidence is determined by referring to its source, its nature, and the circumstances under which it is obtained. Attributes that impact the reliability of audit evidence include its accuracy, completeness, authenticity, and susceptibility to bias. Although there are exceptions to these general principles, audit evidence is more reliable when it:

- Is obtained from a knowledgeable, independent source external to the entity.
- Is produced by a system with effective internal control.
- Is obtained directly by the auditor (e.g., observation, reperformance) rather than indirectly (e.g., inquiry).
- Exists in documentary form.
- Exists in original form (rather than as a copy, fax, or document that has been transformed into electronic form).

---

**FRAUD POINTER:** Although the auditor is expected to evaluate the reliability of audit evidence, he or she is not expected to authenticate the validity of written documents. The auditor is not trained in authenticating documents and auditing standards do not expect auditors to have this expertise. Nonetheless, many frauds are perpetrated through the creation of bogus documentation or the alteration of legitimate documentation. The auditor should be cognizant of this risk, and may want to involve forensic specialists in high risk engagements, particularly where questions about the authenticity of documentation arise. If the auditor believes a document may not be authentic or unauthorized modifications to it have been made, the auditor may determine that additional audit procedures need to be performed.

---

Information that is more susceptible to bias is less reliable than information that is less susceptible to bias. Bias may exist when management prepares the information or when management interprets information as part of its decision making. AU-C 200 requires the auditor to exercise professional judgment, which includes determining the impact of management bias on information from both internal and external sources.

## Entity-Produced Information

The auditor often uses information produced by the entity as the source for other audit procedures. When the auditor uses client-generated information, he or she needs to test whether the information is accurate and complete. The auditor may test the completeness and accuracy of client-generated information at the same time that he or she is performing another audit procedure using that data. Rather than directly testing the accuracy and completeness of client-generated information, the auditor may, alternatively, test the controls over the production and maintenance of the information. The sources of information may be a combination of management and external parties.

---

**PLANNING AID REMINDER:** Due to concerns about IRS access to tax accrual papers, a client may fail to adequately document its income tax accrual or may deny the auditor access to this information. In accordance with Interpretation 1 of AU 500, limitations on access to information needed to audit the tax accrual will necessitate the auditor issuing either a qualified opinion or a disclaimer of opinion. Moreover, client requests for the auditor not to retain documentation of the client's support for its income tax accrual, or the auditor's evaluation thereof, cannot be honored if this request would preclude the auditor from adequately documenting the audit procedures performed, findings obtained, and conclusions reached. Finally, the auditor cannot rely on an opinion from in-house legal counsel, outside counsel, or third-party tax advisers as to the adequacy of the client's income tax accrual in lieu of the auditor's own procedures.

---

Sometimes the entity transforms information from its original form into an electronic or digitized form. The reliability of that information may depend on controls over the information's transformation and how the entity maintains it in that form. The auditor may test controls over the transformation and maintenance of that data.

Other times, information is electronically initiated, recorded, processed, or reported, making it only available in electronic form. In those instances, internal controls over the initiation and alteration of that information are especially important for the auditor to consider and perhaps test.

The entity may use a management's specialist to provide expertise in an area other than accounting or auditing that is used to assist in preparing its financial statements. In these situations, the auditor performs audit procedures to evaluate the specialist's work and the nature, timing, and extent of the audit procedures performed. Further guidance about the consideration of work performed by management specialists is addressed in AU-C 501 (*Audit Evidence—Specific Considerations for Selected Items*).

**PUBLIC COMPANY IMPLICATION:** In December 2018, the PCAOB issued AS-1210 (*Using the Work of an Auditor-Engaged Specialist*). The goal of this standard is to amend existing PCAOB Auditing Standards to expand guidance related to the use of the work performed by specialists. AS-1210 provides specific guidance related to the use of company-employed specialists, auditor-employed specialists, and auditor-engaged specialists. In developing this new standard, the PCAOB noted that its inspections process has observed substantial variation in practice as to how auditors use the work of specialists and how they evaluate the work performed by specialists. For example, it has noted that auditors have failed to adequately evaluate the assumptions used by company specialists to develop fair value measurements and auditors have failed to consider contradictory evidence or issues raised by an auditor's specialist. AS-1210 was approved by the SEC in July 2019. The effective date for AS-1210 is for audits of fiscal years ending on or after December 15, 2020.

## *Evidence That Is Inconsistent or of Doubtful Reliability*

AU-C 230 addresses specific documentation requirements for the auditor when the auditor identifies information that is inconsistent with the auditor's final conclusion regarding a significant finding or issue.

**PLANNING AID REMINDER:** A governmental entity may participate in a governmental cost-sharing multiple-employer pension plan. For example, employees of a city, county, or other municipality may participate in a pension plan offered by the state. The local governmental entity is required to report certain pension amounts in its own financial statements. Some of these amounts are calculated by the plan (e.g., the state pension plan) or the plan's actuary, and the underlying records may be maintained only by the plan. In accordance with Interpretation 2 of AU-C 500, the audited financial statements of the plan and additional unaudited information provided by the plan do not constitute sufficient appropriate audit evidence for the audit of the local governmental entity's own financial statements. Additional audit procedures need to be performed on the schedule of employer allocations, and certain key elements in a schedule of pension amounts including the net pension liability, total deferred inflows and outflows of resources, and total pension expense in order for the auditor of the local governmental entity to accumulate sufficient appropriate audit evidence. In auditing the local governmental entity's pension amounts, the audit report issued by the auditor of the plan can be considered as evidence by the local governmental entity's auditor. However, the local auditor should consider whether the plan's auditor's report and the accompanying schedules are adequate and appropriate, and whether the plan auditor has the necessary competence and independence. Interpretation 3 of AU-C 500 provides essentially the same guidance for governmental entities that participate in a governmental agent multiple-employer pension plan.

AU-C 330 (*Performing Audit Procedures in Response to Assessed Risks and Evaluating the Audit Evidence Obtained*) states that the auditor should consider all relevant audit evidence whether it corroborates or contradicts the assertions being tested. Information that is contradictory may be relevant even when the source is less reliable than corroborating information from more reliable sources. Contradictory information is not considered in isolation. In those instances, the auditor should consider the persuasiveness of the audit evidence as a whole, using professional skepticism and judgment.

Information obtained through inquiry is sometimes difficult to support management's intent. In those situations where corroborating information is mostly from inquiry, maintaining professional skepticism is particularly important.

# SECTION 501

## AUDIT EVIDENCE—SPECIFIC CONSIDERATIONS FOR SELECTED ITEMS

### Authoritative Pronouncements

SAS-122—Statements on Auditing Standards: Clarification and Recodification

SAS-136—Forming an Opinion and Reporting on Financial Statements of Employee Benefit Plans Subject to ERISA

SAS-142—Audit Evidence

SAS-143—Auditing Accounting Estimates and Related Disclosures

SAS-144—Amendments to AU-C Sections 501, 540, and 620 Related to the Use of Specialists and the Use of Pricing Information Obtained from External Information Sources

### Overview

AU-C 501 provides guidance for the auditor in obtaining sufficient appropriate audit evidence in accordance with relevant AU-Cs regarding the:

- Valuation of investments in securities and derivative instruments;
- Existence and condition of inventory;
- Completeness of litigation, claims, and assessments involving the entity;
- Presentation and disclosure of segment information in accordance with the applicable financial reporting framework; and
- Use of management's specialists.

---

**IMPORTANT NOTICE FOR 2022:** In July 2020, the AICPA Auditing Standards Board (ASB) issued SAS No. 142, *Audit Evidence*, which supersedes AU-C 500 (*Audit Evidence*) and amends various other sections, including AU-C 501 in the professional standards. This new SAS addresses the evolving nature of business and audit services and issues that include the use of emerging technologies by both preparers and auditors, audit data analytics (ADA), the application of professional skepticism, the expanding use of external information sources as audit evidence, and, more broadly, the accuracy, completeness, and reliability of audit evidence. This SAS is effective for audits of financial statements for periods ending on or after December 15, 2022.

---

**IMPORTANT NOTICE FOR 2022:** In July 2020, the AICPA Auditing Standards Board (ASB) issued SAS No. 143, *Auditing Accounting Estimates and Related Disclosures*, which supersedes AU-C 540 (*Auditing Accounting Estimates, Including Fair Value Accounting Estimates, and Related Disclosures*) and amends various other sections including AU-C 501 in the professional standards. The new SAS begins with an explanation of the nature of accounting estimates and how they can vary widely in nature and are required to be made by management when monetary amounts cannot be directly observed. The measurement of amounts is subject to estimation uncertainty, which reflects inherent limitations in the knowledge or data. These limitations give rise to inherent subjectivity and variation in measurement outcomes. Although the guidance in SAS No. 143 applies to all accounting estimates, the degree to which an accounting estimate is subject to estimation uncertainty will vary substantially. Therefore, SAS No. 143 recognizes that the nature, timing, and extent of the risk assessment and further audit procedures required will vary in relation to the estimation uncertainty and the assessment of the related risks of material misstatement. The ASB is coordinating the effective date of SAS No. 143 with the effective date of a proposed new SAS, *Understanding the Entity and Its Environment and Assessing the Risks of Material Misstatement*, which was under consideration by the ASB at the time this edition of the *GAAS Guide* was being prepared. SAS No. 143 does not become effective until audits of financial statements for periods ending on or after December 15, 2023, which is consistent with the date in the proposed new standard. As a result, this AU-C reflects existing auditing standards requirements. Updates to reflect SAS No. 143 will occur in the next edition of the *GAAS Guide*.

---

**IMPORTANT NOTICE FOR 2022:** In June 2021, the AICPA Auditing Standards Board (ASB) issued SAS No. 144, *Amendments to AU-C Sections 501, 540, and 620 Related to the Use of Specialists and the Use of Pricing Information Obtained from External Information Sources*, that amends AU-C 501 to provide guidance on applying SAS No. 143 when management has used the work of a specialist in making accounting estimates and to provide additional guidance about evaluating the work of management's specialist. For example, it highlights how the extent of the auditor's work on a model used to develop an estimate may depend on whether the model is commercially available or internally developed. SAS No. 144 does not become effective until audits of financial statements for periods ending on or after December 15, 2023, which is consistent with the effective date of SAS No. 143. As a result, this AU-C reflects existing auditing standards requirements. Updates to reflect SAS No. 144 will occur in the next edition of the *GAAS Guide*.

---

## Definitions

| | |
|---|---|
| Management's specialist | An individual or organization possessing expertise in a field other than accounting or auditing, whose work in that field is used by the entity to assist the entity in preparing the financial statements. |

## Requirements

The auditor is presumptively required to perform the following procedures in obtaining sufficient appropriate audit evidence for the following selected items:

## Investments in Securities Valued Based on Investee's Financial Results Excluding Investments Accounted for Using Equity Method of Accounting

1. When investments in securities are valued based on an investee's financial results (excluding investments accounted for using the equity method of accounting), obtain sufficient appropriate audit evidence supporting the investee's financial results by:

   a. Obtaining and reading the available financial statements of the investee and any accompanying audit report and determining if the audit report is satisfactory for this purpose.

   b. If the investee's financial statements are not audited or the audit report is not satisfactory, apply (or request the investor arrange with the investee to have another auditor apply) appropriate auditing procedures to the financial statements, considering the materiality of the investment to the investor entity's financial statements.

   c. Obtaining sufficient appropriate audit evidence if the carrying amount of the investment reflects factors not recognized in the investee's financial statements or fair values of assets that are materially different from the investee's carrying amounts.

   d. If there is a time lag between the date of the entity's and the investee's financial statements that could have a material effect on the entity's financial statements, determine if the entity's management has considered the lack of comparability and determine any effect this has on the auditor's report.

   If sufficient appropriate audit evidence cannot be obtained because the auditor is unable to perform one or more of these procedures, determine the effect on the auditor's opinion in accordance with AU-C 705 (*Modifications to the Opinion in the Independent Auditor's Report*).

2. To address subsequent events and transactions of the investee occurring after the date of the investee's financial statements but before the auditor's report date, obtain and read available interim financial statements of the investee and make appropriate inquiries of the investor's management to identify events and transactions that may be material to the investor's financial statements that need to be recognized or disclosed in the financial statements.

## Investments in Derivative Instruments and Securities Measured or Disclosed at Fair Value

3. Determine whether the applicable financial reporting framework specifies the method to be used to determine the fair value of the entity's derivative investments and investments in securities and evaluate whether the determination of fair value is consistent with the specific valuation method.

4. If fair value estimates of derivative instruments or securities are obtained from broker-dealer or other third-party sources based on proprietary valuation models, understand the method used in developing the estimate and consider the applicability of AU-C 500 (*Audit Evidence*).

5. If fair value estimates of derivative instruments or securities are developed by the entity using a valuation model, obtain evidence supporting management's assertions about fair value determined using the model.

## Impairment Losses

6. When considering impairment losses, evaluate management's conclusion about the need to recognize an impairment loss for a decline in a security's

fair value below its cost or carrying amount and obtain sufficient appropriate audit evidence supporting the amount of any impairment adjustment recorded, including evaluating whether the entity complied with the requirements of the applicable financial reporting framework.

7. Obtain sufficient appropriate audit evidence about the amount of unrealized appreciation or depreciation in the fair value of a derivative that is recognized or disclosed because of the ineffectiveness of a hedge, including evaluating whether the entity complied with the requirements of the applicable financial reporting framework.

---

**FRAUD POINTER:** Fraudulent financial reporting enforcement actions issued by the SEC often highlight cases that involve asset overstatements. Assets related to fair value measurement and disclosure might involve heightened fraud risk because of the significant opportunities for management to perpetrate fraud related to those accounts. The significant dependence on management assumptions and the related complexities associated with measuring and disclosing fair value instruments can create significant opportunities for management to engage in fraud. Conversely, in a private company the risk may be an understatement of assets (i.e., an overstatement of expenses) so as to reduce income taxes.

---

*Inventory*

8. If inventory is material to the financial statements, obtain sufficient appropriate audit evidence regarding its existence and condition by:

   a. Attending physical inventory counting, unless doing so is impracticable, to evaluate management's instructions and procedures for recording and controlling the results of the entity's physical inventory counting; observe the performance of management's count procedures; inspect the inventory; and perform test counts.

   b. Performing audit procedures over the entity's final inventory records to determine whether they accurately reflect actual inventory count results.

9. If physical inventory counting is conducted at a date other than the date of the financial statements, also perform audit procedures to obtain audit evidence about whether changes in inventory between the count date and the date of the financial statements are recorded properly.

10. If unable to attend physical inventory counting due to unforeseen circumstances, make or observe some physical counts on an alternative date and perform audit procedures on intervening transactions.

11. If attending physical inventory counting is impracticable, perform alternative audit procedures to obtain sufficient appropriate audit evidence regarding the existence and condition of inventory. If this is not possible, modify the opinion in the auditor's report in accordance with AU-C 705.

12. If there is inventory under custody and control of a third party that is material to the financial statements, obtain sufficient appropriate audit evidence about its existence and condition by requesting confirmation from the third party regarding the quantities and condition of inventory held on the entity's behalf and/or performing inspection or other audit procedures appropriate in the circumstances.

## Litigation, Claims, and Assessments

13. Design and perform audit procedures to identify litigation, claims, and assessments involving the entity that may give rise to a risk of material misstatement, including:
    a. Inquiring of management and, where applicable, others within the entity including in-house legal counsel;
    b. Obtaining from management a description and evaluation of litigation, claims, and assessments that existed at the date of the financial statements being reported on and during the period between the financial statements' date and the date the information is furnished, including an identification of matters referred to legal counsel;
    c. Reviewing minutes of meetings of those charged with governance; documents from management concerning litigation, claims, and assessments; and correspondence between the entity and its external legal counsel; and
    d. Reviewing legal expense accounts and invoices from external legal counsel.

14. For actual or potential litigation, claims, and assessments identified based on the above audit procedures, obtain audit evidence relevant to:
    a. The period in which the underlying cause for legal action occurred,
    b. The degree of probability of an unfavorable outcome, and
    c. The amount or range of potential loss.

15. If a risk of material misstatement regarding litigation or claims is identified or audit procedures indicate other material litigation or claims may exist, seek direct communication with the entity's external legal counsel. Communicate through a letter of inquiry, prepared by management and sent by the auditor, requesting the entity's external legal counsel communicate directly with the auditor.

16. In cases when the entity's in-house legal counsel has the responsibility for the entity's litigation, claims, and assessments, the auditor should also seek direct communication with the in-house legal counsel through a letter of inquiry. This communication is not a substitute for seeking direct communication with external legal counsel.

17. Document the basis for any determination not to seek direct communication with the entity's external legal counsel.

18. Request that management authorize the external legal counsel to discuss applicable matters with the auditor.

19. Letters of inquiry should include, but are not limited to, the following matters:
    a. Identification of the entity and its subsidiaries and the date of the audit.
    b. A list prepared by management or a request for legal counsel to prepare a list describing and evaluating pending or threatened litigation, claims, and assessments with respect to which the legal counsel has been engaged and has devoted substantive legal consultation or representation on behalf of the entity.
    c. A list prepared by management describing and evaluating unasserted claims and assessments management considers to be probable or assertion and that, if asserted, would have at least a reasonable possibility of an unfavorable outcome with respect to which the legal

counsel has been engaged and has devoted substantive legal consultation or representation on behalf of the entity.

   d. For each pending or threatened litigation, claim, and assessment listed, a request that legal counsel either provide the following information or comment on those matters on which legal counsel's views may differ from management's stated views:

     i. A description of the nature of the matter, the progress of the case to date, and the action the entity intends to take;
     ii. An evaluation of the likelihood of an unfavorable outcome and an estimate, if possible, of the amount or range of potential loss; and
     iii. An identification of the omission of any pending or threatened litigation, claims, and assessments from the list or a statement that the list of such matters is complete.

   e. For each unasserted claim and assessment listed, a request that legal counsel comment on those matters on which legal counsel's views may differ from management's stated views.

   f. A statement that management understands that legal counsel will advise and consult with the entity concerning disclosure and the requirements of the applicable financial reporting framework if legal counsel forms a professional conclusion that the entity should disclose or consider disclosing an unasserted possible claim or assessment.

   g. A request that the legal counsel confirm whether the understanding described in item (f) is correct.

   h. A request that the legal counsel specifically identify the nature of and the reasons for any limitation on the response.

   i. A request that the legal counsel specify the effective date of the response.

20. If the auditor is aware that an entity has changed legal counsel or the entity's legal counsel has resigned, he or she should consider inquiring of management or others about the reasons such legal counsel is no longer associated with the entity.

21. Modify the opinion in the auditor's report in accordance with AU-C 705 if (1) the entity's external legal counsel refuses to respond appropriately to the letter of inquiry and the auditor is unable to obtain sufficient appropriate audit evidence by performing alternative audit procedures or (2) management refuses to give the auditor permission to communicate or meet with the entity's external legal counsel.

## Segment Information

22. Obtain sufficient appropriate audit evidence regarding the presentation and disclosure of segment information in accordance with the applicable financial reporting framework by:

   a. Obtaining an understanding of management's methods in determining segment information, evaluating whether such methods are likely to result in disclosure in accordance with the applicable financial reporting framework, and testing the methods' application where appropriate.

   b. Performing analytical procedures or other audit procedures appropriate in the circumstances.

## Management Specialists

23. When management's specialists have prepared information that is to be used as audit evidence, the auditor should evaluate the capabilities, objectivity, and competence of the specialist, understand the work of the specialist, and evaluate whether that work is appropriate as audit evidence for the assertion examined.

# Analysis and Application of Procedures

## Investments in Securities and Derivative Instruments

Professional judgment may be involved in evaluating audit evidence regarding assertions about investments in securities and derivative instruments, especially valuation. AU-C 540 (*Auditing Accounting Estimates, Including Fair Value Accounting Estimates, and Related Disclosures*) addresses the auditor's responsibilities related to accounting estimates, including fair value accounting estimates, and related disclosures in a financial statement audit and the AICPA's Audit Guide *Auditing Derivative Instruments, Hedging Activities, and Investments in Securities* provides additional and more detailed guidance related to planning and performing procedures for assertions about derivative instruments, hedging activities, and investments in securities.

To obtain evidence about the cost of securities valued at cost, the auditor may inspect documentation of the purchase price, confirm with the issuer or holder, and test discount or premium amortization using recomputation or analytical procedures.

**FRAUD POINTER:** The auditor should consider the guidance established in AU-C 240 (*Consideration of Fraud in a Financial Statement Audit*) for the possibility of management override of controls related to fair value information presented in financial statements.

**ENGAGEMENT STRATEGY:** Although this may be obvious, the Auditing Standards Board recognizes that accounting standards, especially those related to fair value, are becoming sophisticated and that auditors must stay current with financial accounting theory. For example, the valuation and disclosures related to derivatives as codified in ASC 815 (*Derivatives and Hedging*) and the application of the standards related to goodwill as codified in ASC 350 (*Intangibles—Goodwill and Other*) can be challenging even to the most seasoned auditor. It is more important than ever that the auditor devote a part of his or her professional life to professional development in order to deliver an audit product that satisfies professional standards. In some instances, an effective engagement strategy includes the use of a specialist who is knowledgeable about fair value instruments, measurements, and disclosures.

**PLANNING AID REMINDER:** Although U.S. GAAP requires the investments to be recorded at fair value, a readily determinable fair value may not exist. For example, investments in a hedge fund may be reported at fair value even though fair value is not readily determinable. The hedge fund management might not provide details on how the fair value of its investments is determined, and it might only confirm the aggregate amount of a company's investment in the hedge fund. The receipt by an auditor of a confirmation where investments are confirmed on an aggregate basis is not sufficient. However, the existence assertion is supported if the auditor receives confirmation from the hedge fund as to the individual investments held by the fund. The valuation assertion is not supported even if the fund manager confirms the investments held by the hedge fund on an individual basis. Management, not the hedge fund manager, is responsible for determining the fair values of investments held by the fund. Management needs to develop a process for determining the fair value of investments held in the hedge fund. The auditor needs to (1) understand management's process, (2) evaluate whether the fair value measurements are in conformity with U.S. GAAP, and (3) test management's fair value determinations. If the auditor is unable to gather sufficient appropriate audit evidence related to either the existence or valuation assertions, a scope limitation may exist, requiring either a qualified audit opinion or a disclaimer of opinion.

### Investments in Securities Valued Based on Investee's Financial Results Excluding Investments Accounted for Using Equity Method of Accounting

To determine whether the auditor's report on an investee's financial statements is satisfactory, the auditor may make inquiries about the professional standing and reputation of the other auditor, visit the other auditor, discuss the audit procedures followed and their results, and review the other auditor's audit plan and documentation.

> **PLANNING AID REMINDER:** If investments are accounted for using the equity method of accounting, the auditor should follow the guidance in AU-C 600 (*Special Considerations—Audits of Group Financial Statements (Including the Work of Component Auditors)*).

The auditor may conclude after reading his or her report on an investee's financial statements that additional audit procedures are necessary to obtain sufficient appropriate audit evidence. Additional evidence could be needed because of significant differences in fiscal year-ends, significant differences in accounting principles, changes in ownership, or the significance of the investment to the investor's financial statements. Procedures the auditor may perform to obtain additional evidence include reviewing the investor's information about the investee such as investee minutes, budgets, and cash flow information, and inquiring of the investor's management about the investee's financial results. The auditor may need to obtain evidence related to transactions between the entity and the investee to evaluate that any unrealized profits and losses on transactions between the entity and investee were properly eliminated and that disclosures about material related-party transactions are adequate.

> **PLANNING AID REMINDER:** The client may have more than one valuation method and identified a range of significantly different estimates of fair value. In

that instance, the auditor evaluates how the client has investigated these differences in establishing a particular valuation.

A time lag in reporting between the date of the investor's and investee's financial statements could have a material effect on the investor's financial statements if the time lag is not consistent with the prior period in comparative statements or because a significant transactions occurred during the time lag. If a change in time lag occurs that has a material effect on the investor's financial statements, the auditor may be required to add an emphasis-of-matter paragraph to the auditor's report because the comparability of financial statements between periods has been materially affected by a change in reporting period.

**PLANNING AID REMINDER:** An entity may hold an interest in a trust that is managed by a third-party trustee. U.S. GAAP may require the assets in the trust to be reported at fair value (see ASC 958, *Not-for-Profit Entities*). The receipt of a confirmation from the trustee, where the investments held are confirmed on an aggregate basis, is not sufficient. However, the existence assertion is supported if the auditor receives confirmation from the trustee as to the individual investments held by the trustee. The valuation assertion is not supported even if the trustee confirms the investments held by the trust on an individual basis. Management, not the third-party trustee, is responsible for determining the fair values of investments held in the trust. Management needs to develop a process for determining the fair value of investments held in a trust. The auditor needs to (1) understand management's process, (2) evaluate whether the fair value measurements are in conformity with U.S. GAAP, and (3) test management's fair value determinations. If the auditor is unable to gather sufficient appropriate audit evidence related to either the existence or valuation assertions, a scope limitation may exist, requiring either a qualified audit opinion or a disclaimer of opinion.

*Investments in Derivative Instruments and Securities Measured or Disclosed at Fair Value*

The fair value of derivative instruments and securities may be available from quoted market prices for instruments and securities listed on national exchanges or over-the-counter markets. Quoted market prices from these sources generally provide sufficient evidence of fair value. Quoted market prices may also come from other sources such as broker-dealers who are market makers in the derivative or security or the National Quotation Bureau; the auditor may need special knowledge to understand the circumstances in which a quote was developed from one of these sources in order to use the quote to test valuation assertions.

**PUBLIC COMPANY IMPLICATION:** The PCAOB's Staff Audit Practice Alert No. 2 (*Matters Related to Auditing Fair Value Measurements of Financial Instruments and the Use of Specialists*) is designed to provide guidance related to auditing fair values, particularly in light of the FASB's guidance in ASC 820 (*Fair Value Measurements and Disclosures*). The auditor needs to understand the company's process for determining fair value measurements and disclosures, including related internal controls. The auditor should also evaluate whether (1) management's assumptions in determining fair value are reasonable and are not inconsistent with market information, (2) management's reliance on historical financial information continues to be justified (e.g., use of historical default rates may not be appropriate when credit markets are deteriorating), and (3) the company's determination of fair value is applied consistently and whether this is appropriate. For example, a company may apply a model consistently in determining fair value, but because of changes in the environment it may be more appropriate for the company to change the relative weights of model inputs. In addition, the auditor should recognize that model inputs based on the company's own data are generally more susceptible to bias and take appropriate audit steps to respond to this increased risk. Finally, U.S. GAAP provides many required disclosures relating to fair value measurements. The auditor needs to recognize that material disclosures that depart from U.S. GAAP represent a misstatement of the financial statements.

**PUBLIC COMPANY IMPLICATION:** The PCAOB's Staff Audit Practice Alert No. 4 (*Auditor Considerations Regarding Fair Value Measurements, Disclosures, and Other-than-Temporary Impairments*) is designed to inform auditors about the potential implications on annual audits and interim reviews of three former FASB Staff Positions (FSPs): (1) FSP FAS 157-4 (*Determining Fair Value When the Volume and Level of Activity for the Asset or Liability Have Significantly Decreased and Identifying Transactions That Are Not Orderly*), (2) FSP FAS 115-2 and FAS 124-2 (*Recognition and Presentation of Other-than-Temporary-Impairment*), and (3) FSP FAS 107-1 and APB 28-1 (*Interim Disclosures about Fair Value of Financial Instruments*). The guidance in these now superseded FSPs is incorporated in ASC 820 (*Fair Value Measurements and Disclosures*), ASC 320 (*Investments—Debt and Equity Securities*), and ASC 825 (*Financial Instruments*), respectively. Staff Audit Practice Alert No. 4 states that the auditor should include inquiries about the application of these FSPs in a review of interim financial information. For audits of financial statements, Practice Alert 4 emphasizes the need for auditors to obtain sufficient appropriate evidence to support accounting estimates, including their measurement and disclosure. For example, in certain cases the guidance in ASC 320 (*Investments—Debt and Equity Securities*) requires losses from other-than-temporary impairments to be separated between credit losses and other factors. Such a determination involves significant judgment. Practice Alert 4 also reminds auditors of their responsibility to read other information in documents containing interim and annual financial statements. If this other information is inconsistent with the financial statements, either the audit report, the financial statements, or the other information needs to be changed. The application of these FSPs may require communication to the audit committee because their application might involve a change in (1) accounting policy, (2) accounting estimates, (3) the process by which management develops sensitive estimates, and (4) the auditor's judgment about the quality, not just the acceptability, of the client's accounting policies. These required disclosures to the audit committee pertain to both annual audits and interim reviews.

If quoted market values are not available for a derivative instrument or security, fair value estimates may often be obtained from broker-dealers or other third-party sources based on proprietary valuation models or from the entity based on internally or externally developed valuation models. Obtaining an understanding of the valuation method used may include understanding whether a pricing model or cash flow projection was used. The auditor may also find it necessary to obtain estimates from more than one pricing source if, for example, the pricing source has a relationship with the entity that might impair its objectivity or the valuation is based on assumptions that are highly subjective or particularly sensitive to changes in the underlying circumstances.

---

**ENGAGEMENT STRATEGY:** Fair value information may be based on sensitive assumptions. That is, a change in an assumption can have a significant impact on the dollar value of fair value information. The auditor may consider encouraging management to use techniques such as sensitivity analysis to help identify particularly sensitive assumptions. If management has not used sensitivity analysis in this manner, the auditor should consider whether to use the approach as part of the engagement strategy to identify such assumptions.

---

**OBSERVATION:** When the client uses a valuation model to quantify measurements and disclosures, the auditor neither serves as an appraiser nor substitutes his or her judgment for that of the client. The auditor's role is to review the model and determine whether the client has used reasonable assumptions based on the relevant circumstances.

---

*Impairment Losses*

The auditor determines whether an impairment loss has been incurred by making judgments based on knowledge and experience about past and current events and assumptions about future events. These judgments are based on subjective and objective factors, the relevance of which may depend on whether they tend to corroborate or conflict with management's conclusions. Examples of such factors include:

- Fair value is significantly below cost or carrying value and the decline is attributable to adverse conditions specifically related to the security, industry, or geographic area; the decline has existed for an extended period of time; and management has the intent to sell the security or it is more likely than not that it will be required to sell the security before recovery for an equity security or before the security's anticipated recovery of its amortized cost basis for a debt security.
- The security has been downgraded by a rating agency.
- The financial condition of the issuer has deteriorated.
- Dividends have been reduced or eliminated or scheduled interest payments have not been made.
- The entity recorded losses from the security subsequent to the end of the reporting period.

Obtaining sufficient appropriate audit evidence about the unrealized appreciation or depreciation in the fair value of a derivative that is recognized or disclosed because of the ineffectiveness of a hedge may include understanding the methods used to determine whether the hedge is highly effective and to determine the ineffective portion of the hedge.

*Inventory*

Attendance at physical inventory counting may serve as a test of control, substantive procedure, or both, depending on the auditor's risk assessment, planned approach, and the specific procedures carried out. The following are examples of relevant matters for the auditor in planning attendance at physical inventory counting or in designing and performing audit procedures related to the existence and condition of inventory:

- The risks of material misstatement and the control risk related to inventory.
- Whether adequate procedures are expected to be established and proper instructions issued for physical inventory counting.
- The timing of physical inventory counting.
- Whether the entity maintains a perpetual inventory system.
- To determine at which locations attendance is appropriate, the locations at which inventory is held and the materiality and risks of material misstatement at different locations. AU-C 600 may be relevant if component auditors are involved in attending physical inventory counting at a remote location.
- Whether the assistance of an auditor's specialist is needed.

**FRAUD POINTER:** AU-C 240 notes that when the auditor believes there is a risk of material misstatement due to fraud, he or she may consider observing inventory on unexpected dates or at unexpected locations on a surprise basis. For situations in which the risk of material misstatement in inventory due to fraud is perceived to be high, AU-C 240 notes that the auditor's examination of the entity's inventory records might help identify locations or items that require specific attention during or after the physical count. For example, the auditor may decide to count inventory at multiple locations on the same date.

The auditor evaluates management's instructions and procedures for recording and controlling the results of the entity's physical inventory counting by examining whether they address, for example:

- The application of appropriate control activities such as count and recount procedures;
- The accurate identification of the stage of completion of work in progress; of slow-moving, obsolete, or damaged items; and of inventory owned by a third party, for example, on consignment;
- The procedures used to estimate physical quantities where applicable; and
- Control over inventory's movement between areas and its shipping and receipt before and after the cutoff date.

Observing the performance of management's count procedures assists the auditor in obtaining audit evidence that management's instructions and count procedures are designed and implemented adequately. Inspecting the inventory assists the auditor in verifying the existence of inventory and in identifying obsolete, damaged, or aging inventory. Performing test counts provides the auditor with audit evidence about the completeness and accuracy of management's count records. Exhibit AU-C 501-1 provides an example audit program for an inventory observation.

Entities may use an external firm that specializes in taking physical inventories to perform their inventory count. The auditor may be able to adjust the extent of work on the physical count of inventory because of the work of an outside inventory firm but the use of such a firm does not by itself provide the auditor with sufficient appropriate audit evidence regarding inventory. AU-C 500 requires the auditor to perform certain procedures if information to be used as audit evidence has been prepared using the work of a management's specialist. Procedures the auditor may perform to obtain sufficient appropriate audit evidence regarding inventory in these circumstances include examining the outside firm's program, observing its procedures and controls, evaluating the effectiveness of its procedures, recomputing calculations of the submitted inventory on a test basis, and applying appropriate tests to the intervening transactions. If there is any restriction on the auditor's judgment concerning the extent of the auditor's contact with the inventory, there may be a scope restriction, in which case AU-C 705 requires the auditor to modify the audit opinion due to the scope limitation.

---

**PLANNING AID REMINDER:** Some companies are in the business of counting, recording, and pricing inventories. The auditor's responsibility for the count and other tasks performed by an inventory-taking company is similar to the responsibility for tasks normally performed directly by the client. Therefore, the auditor should (1) review the client's inventory-counting program, (2) make or observe a test of physical counts, (3) make appropriate mathematical checks, and (4) test the valuation of the inventory.

---

If physical inventory counting is performed at a date other than the date of the financial statements, the auditor considers whether this is appropriate by evaluating the effectiveness of the design, implementation, and maintenance of controls over changes in inventory. If the entity has a perpetual inventory system, differences in the perpetual inventory records and actual physical inventory quantities on hand may indicate that the controls over changes in inventory are not operating effectively. Factors to consider when designing audit procedures to obtain audit evidence about whether changes in inventory amounts between the count date and final inventory records are recorded properly include whether the perpetual inventory records are properly adjusted; the reliability of the entity's perpetual inventory system; and the reasons for significant differences between the information obtained during the physical count and the perpetual inventory records.

> **ENGAGEMENT STRATEGY:** If an auditor has not substantiated the existence of inventory based on one of the approaches described above, testing solely the client's inventory records will not be sufficient to satisfy professional standards. Under this circumstance the auditor should observe the client's count or actually make inventory counts of the inventory and test intervening transactions between the count date and the balance sheet date. These procedures should be performed in concert with documentation created and procedures performed by the client.

> **FRAUD POINTER:** AU-C 240 notes that the auditor may request that the client count inventory at year-end or on a date closer to year-end to minimize the risk of inventory balances being manipulated between the count date and the balance sheet date.

Attendance at physical inventory counting may be impracticable due to the nature and location of the inventory. For example, the location may pose a safety threat to the auditor or the auditor may be auditing financial statements covering periods for which he or she has not observed or made some physical counts of prior inventories. However, matters of inconvenience, difficulty, time, or cost are not by themselves valid bases for the auditor to not attend physical inventory counting. If attendance at physical inventory counting is impracticable, the auditor may be able to obtain sufficient appropriate audit evidence about the existence and condition of inventory by performing alternative audit procedures such as inspecting documentation of subsequent sales of specific inventory items owned at the time of the physical inventory count, testing prior transactions, reviewing the records of prior counts, or applying gross profit tests or other analytical procedures. However, if the auditor is unable to obtain sufficient appropriate evidence about the existence of inventory, he or she may need to modify the auditor's report.

When inventory is held by a third party that is material to the financial statements, circumstances such as when there is doubt as to the third party's integrity and objectivity may make it appropriate for the auditor to perform audit procedures in place of or in addition to confirmation with the third party. An example confirmation is shown in Exhibit AU-C 501-2. Other audit procedures may include:

- Attending or arranging for another auditor to attend the third party's physical inventory count,
- Obtaining another auditor's report or service auditor's report on the adequacy of the third party's internal control for ensuring that the inventory is properly counted and adequately safeguarded,
- Inspecting documentation regarding inventory held by third parties, and
- Requesting confirmation from other parties when inventory has been pledged as collateral.

## Litigation, Claims, and Assessments

Litigation, claims, and assessments involving the entity may have a material effect on the financial statements and therefore be required to be disclosed or accounted for in the financial statements. Some legal matters involving the entity may not have a material effect on the financial statements such as matters unrelated to actual or potential litigation, claims, or assessments; matters that management or legal counsel have not devoted substantive attention to; matters for which the entity's insurance exceeds the amount sought from the entity; or matters that are clearly trivial to the financial statements.

Management is responsible for adopting policies and procedures to identify, evaluate, and account for litigation, claims, and assessments in order to prepare the financial statements in conformity with the applicable financial reporting framework. Because management is the primary source of information about events or conditions considered in the financial accounting for and reporting of litigation, claims, and assessments, the auditor's procedures regarding litigation, claims, and assessments may include:

- Discussing with management the policies and procedures adopted for identifying, evaluating, and accounting for litigation, claims, and assessments involving the entity that may give rise to a risk of material misstatement; and
- Obtaining a written representation from management that they have disclosed and accounted for all known actual or possible litigation and claims whose effects should be considered when preparing the financial statements in accordance with the applicable financial reporting framework.

Risk assessment procedures performed while obtaining an understanding of the entity and its environment may assist the auditor in becoming aware of litigation, claims, and assessments involving the entity. Examples of such procedures include reading minutes from meetings of directors and other bodies held during and subsequent to the audit period; reading documents such as contracts, loan agreements, leases, and correspondence from taxing or other governmental agencies; obtaining information concerning guarantees from bank confirmations; and inspecting other documents for possible guarantees by the entity. AU-C 250 details the auditor's responsibilities to obtain an understanding of the entity's legal and regulatory framework applicable to the entity and its industry or sector and how the entity is complying with that framework.

---

**ENGAGEMENT STRATEGY:** Audit evidence obtained for the purpose of identifying litigation, claims, and assessments that may give rise to a material misstatement may also provide audit evidence about other relevant considerations, such as valuation or measurement of litigation, claims, or assessments.

---

The auditor ordinarily lacks the expertise to evaluate litigation, claims, and assessments and therefore must rely a great deal on the client's lawyer regarding these matters. Direct communication with the entity's external legal counsel is the auditor's primary means of obtaining sufficient appropriate audit evidence about whether potentially material litigation, claims, and assessments are known, and management's estimates of the costs and financial implications are reasonable. An entity's inside counsel may provide the auditor with corroborating evidence.

**OBSERVATION:** The American Bar Association (ABA) has approved *Statement of Policy Regarding Lawyers' Responses to Auditor's Requests for Information* (the ABA Statement), which explains the concerns of the legal counsel and the nature of limitations that an auditor is likely to encounter in connection with seeking direct communication with the entity's legal counsel about litigation, claims, assessments, and unasserted claims. The ABA Statement is provided as an exhibit in AU-C 501.

**ENGAGEMENT STRATEGY:** Audit inquiry letters should be sent to those lawyers, which may be either inside counsel or outside lawyers, who have the primary responsibility for, and knowledge about, particular litigation, claims and assessments.

**PLANNING AID REMINDER:** AU-C 501 states that an external legal counsel's response to a letter of inquiry provide the auditor with sufficient appropriate evidence concerning the accounting for and reporting of pending and threatened litigation, claims, and assessments.

**FRAUD POINTER:** AU-C 240 requires the auditor to consider making inquiries of others separate from management about the risks of fraud. As part of these inquiries, auditors may make inquiries of in-house legal counsel about the risks of fraud.

In some situations, the auditor may find it necessary to meet with the entity's external legal counsel to discuss the likely outcome of litigation or claims or to seek clarification of matters noted by the legal counsel in the response to the auditor. This may occur when the auditor determines a matter is a significant risk, the matter is complex, or a disagreement exists between management and the entity's external legal counsel. These meetings typically require management's permission and are held with a member of management in attendance. Clarifications of matters should be adequately documented in the working papers.

The auditor is responsible for obtaining audit evidence about the status of litigation, claims, and assessments up to the date of the auditor's report. This evidence may be obtained by inquiry of management, including in-house legal counsel, or by obtaining updated information from the entity's external legal counsel.

> **ENGAGEMENT STRATEGY:** The lawyer's response to the auditor's letter of audit inquiry should be addressed to the auditor, should apply to circumstances that existed from the date of the balance sheet through the auditor's report date, and should have an effective date within two or three weeks of the report date. Clearly specifying the earliest acceptable effective date of legal counsel's response to the letter of inquiry to approximate the expected date of the audit report can help alleviate the need to obtain updated information from the entity's legal counsel.

If legal counsel limits the response to the letter of inquiry to matters counsel has given substantive attention to or to matters that are individually or collectively material to the financial statements using materiality limits agreed upon by the entity and auditor, these are not limitations on the scope of the audit. If legal counsel cannot respond about the likelihood of an unfavorable outcome of litigation, claims, and assessments or the amount or range of potential loss because of inherent uncertainties, the auditor may conclude that the financial statements are affected by an uncertainty concerning the outcome of a future event that is not able to be reasonable estimated. In these situations, AU-C 705 addresses any effect of legal counsel's response on the auditor's report.

> **PLANNING AID REMINDER:** If management imposes a scope limitation and the auditor cannot obtain sufficient appropriate audit evidence through alternative audit procedures, AU-C 705 requires the auditor to disclaim an opinion or to withdraw from the audit when practicable.

While the auditor would typically consider the inability to review information that could be significant to the audit as a scope limitation, this is not intended to apply to documents subject to the attorney-client privilege. To emphasize this, the letter of inquiry may contain language such as the following:

> We do not intend that either our request to you to provide information to our auditor or your response to our auditor should be construed in any way to constitute a waiver of the attorney-client privilege or the attorney work-product privilege.

This type of language does not constitute a scope limitation of legal counsel's response.

If the auditor believes there may be actual or potential litigation, claims, or assessments and the entity has not engaged legal counsel on these matters, he or she may discuss the possible need to consult legal counsel to assist in determining the appropriate measurement, recognition, or disclosure of related liabilities or loss contingencies in the financial statements. Refusal by management to consult legal counsel in this situation may result in a scope limitation that precludes an unqualified opinion.

> **OBSERVATION:** In some situations, legal counsel may be required by relevant ethical requirements to resign if the entity disregards legal counsel's advice concerning financial accounting and reporting for litigation, claims, and assessments.

Exhibit AU-C 501-3, which is taken from Appendix A of AU-C 501, illustrates an audit inquiry letter to legal counsel.

Exhibit AU-C 501-4 illustrates an audit inquiry letter whereby management has requested that the lawyer prepare the list of pending or threatened litigation, claims, and assessments.

## Segment Information

The auditor is responsible for the presentation and disclosure of segment information as it relates to the financial statements as a whole and so is not required to perform audit procedures necessary to express an opinion on the segment information by itself. When obtaining an understanding of management's methods in determining segment information and evaluating whether those methods are likely to result in disclosure in accordance with the applicable financial reporting framework, the following matters may be relevant:

- Sales, transfers, and charges between segments and elimination of intersegment amounts;
- Comparisons with budgets and other expected results;
- The allocation of assets and costs among segments;
- Consistency with prior periods and the adequacy of the disclosures with respect to inconsistencies; and
- Management's process for identifying segments requiring disclosure in accordance with the entity's financial reporting framework.

## Use of Management's Specialists

When information to be used as audit evidence is prepared by management's specialists, the auditor takes into account the significance of that specialist's work for the auditor's purposes. The auditor's procedures may be affected by factors such as the nature and complexity of the underlying issue that is the focus of the specialist, availability of other evidence, the risk of material misstatement that may be linked to the underlying issue, whether the specialist is employed by the entity or engaged as an external party by the entity, and the extent to which management can influence the work of the specialist, among other matters.

The auditor's consideration of the capabilities, competencies, and objectivity of the specialists include matters related to the level and nature of expertise of the specialist, their ability to exercise competency in the circumstances (such as geographic location, availability of time and resources), and the existence of possible bias, conflicts of interests, or influences of others. Information to be considered can come from a variety of sources, such as personal experience and discussions with the specialist, knowledge of their professional recognitions, published materials developed by the specialist, and whether their work is subject to technical standards compliance.

Threats to the specialist's objectivity can be reduced by safeguards, such as quality control procedures. Generally, threats to objectivity are less significant to specialists engaged by the entity than specialist employed by the entity. Ordinarily, specialists employed by the entity are not considered as more objective than other employees of the entity.

An understanding of the work of the specialist also includes an understanding of the field of expertise. That might include understanding about whether the specialist's field has areas of specialty within it that are specific to the audit and whether any professional standards and regulatory and legal requirements apply to the work of the specialist. When the management specialist is engaged by the entity, there is likely to be an engagement letter or other written form of agreement that might help the auditor consider the appropriateness of the specialist's work.

Evaluating the appropriateness of the specialist's work for audit evidence might include consideration of the relevance and reliability of the specialist's findings and conclusions, including consistency with other evidence, key assumptions made by the specialist, and evaluation of the source data used as the basis for that work.

## Practitioner's Aids

*EXHIBIT AU-C 501-1—AUDIT PROGRAM: INVENTORY OBSERVATION PROCEDURES DISCOVERED AFTER THE REPORT RELEASE DATE*

Use the following procedures as a guide for the observation of inventories. The audit program is only a guide, and professional judgment should be exercsed to determine how the procedures should be modified by revising procedures listed or adding procedures to the audit program.

Initial and date each procedure as it is completed. If the procedure is not relevant to this particular audit engagement, place "N/A" (not applicable) in the space provided for an initial.

Client Name: _____

Date of Financial Statements: _____

Audit Report Date: _____

| | | Yes | No | Audit Documentation Reference |
|---|---|---|---|---|
| **Planning Phase** | | | | |
| 1. | Review with appropriate personnel the inventory count procedures to be used by the client. | _____ | _____ | _____ |
| 2. | Attend meetings in which the client instructs personnel concerning the inventory count. | | | |

|   | Yes | No | Audit Documentation Reference |
|---|---|---|---|
| 3. Identify inventory count issues that need special attention (such as the use of a specialist, inventory held by consignees, inventory held for other parties). | _____ | _____ | _____ |
| 4. Determine the number of staff personnel and level of experience needed to cover the client's inventory count. | _____ | _____ | _____ |

**Inventory Count Phase**

|   | Yes | No | Audit Documentation Reference |
|---|---|---|---|
| 5. Meet with client personnel to identify any new issues that need to be addressed before the count begins. | _____ | _____ | _____ |
| 6. Determine whether inventory that should not be counted (such as consigned goods, inventory to be shipped during the day) has been appropriately segregated or otherwise identified. | _____ | _____ | _____ |
| 7. Obtain inventory control count information (such as range of ticket numbers or count sheet numbers to be used during the count). | _____ | _____ | _____ |
| 8. Obtain inventory cutoff information from the shipping department (such as bill of lading numbers) and the receiving department (such as receiving report numbers). | _____ | _____ | _____ |
| 9. Test inventory counts on a sample basis, and determine whether items are being counted and described correctly and identified as obsolete or damaged if appropriate. | _____ | _____ | _____ |
| 10. Record some test counts that can be used later to test the client's summarization of inventory counts. | _____ | _____ | _____ |
| 11. Determine whether all inventory items are counted and clearly marked as "counted." | _____ | _____ | _____ |

|  | Yes | No | Audit Documentation Reference |
|---|---|---|---|
| 12. Determine whether inventory that is moved from one location to another is appropriately identified to avoid double counting or omission from the count. | _____ | _____ | _____ |
| 13. Once the inventory count is completed, obtain inventory control information (such as last ticket or counting sheet number used). | _____ | _____ | _____ |

**Inventory Count Summary Phase**

|  | Yes | No | Audit Documentation Reference |
|---|---|---|---|
| 14. Trace inventory test counts made during the inventory count to client inventory summarization sheets. | _____ | _____ | _____ |
| 15. Determine whether inventory numbers used in the client's summarization sheets are consistent with inventory control information obtained at the conclusion of the physical inventory count. | _____ | _____ | _____ |
| 16. Select inventory amount in the inventory summarization, and trace to either (1) inventory test count information or (2) consistency of ticket control information. | _____ | _____ | _____ |
| 17. Determine whether inventory items identified as damaged or obsolete during the inventory count were appropriately identified in the client's inventory summarization. | _____ | _____ | _____ |
| 18. Determine whether inventory cutoff information obtained during the inventory count is consistent with sales information and purchases information shortly before and after the year-end date. | _____ | _____ | _____ |

Reviewed by: _____

Date: _____

## EXHIBIT AU-C 501-2—CONFIRMATION REQUEST FOR INVENTORY HELD BY ANOTHER PARTY

[*Client's Letterhead*]

[*Custodian's Name and Address*]

Dear:_____

In accordance with the request of our auditors, please confirm the correctness of the inventory items owned by us but held by your company as of December 31, 20X5. For your convenience we have included with this correspondence a list of these items based on our records.

Also, please answer the following questions:

1. How did you determine the number of inventory items held by you as of December 31, 20X5?

_____
_____
_____

2. Are any of the items held by you for us damaged?

_____
_____
_____

3. Are there any negotiable or nonnegotiable warehouse receipts issued, and if so, to your knowledge have any of the receipts been assigned or pledged?

_____
_____
_____

4. Are there any liens against the inventory?

_____
_____
_____

5. Do we owe you any amount of money as of December 31, 20X5?

_____
_____
_____

If the amounts and descriptions included in the attachment are correct, please sign the space provided and return this letter to our auditor in the enclosed self-addressed envelope.

If the amounts are incorrect or there is other relevant information that you want to communicate to our auditors, sign in the space provided, explain the difference in a separate letter, and return this letter and any other relevant information to our auditor in the enclosed self-addressed envelope.

Thank you for your prompt attention to this matter.

Very truly yours,

_____

[*Client's Signature*]

The above balance at the confirmation date is correct, except as noted on the back of this letter.

_____

[*Custodian's Signature*]
[*Title*]

## EXHIBIT AU-C 501-3—ILLUSTRATIVE AUDIT INQUIRY LETTER TO LEGAL COUNSEL

In connection with an audit of our financial statements at [*balance sheet date*] and for the [*period*] then ended, management of the Company has prepared, and furnished to our auditors [*name and address of auditors*], a description and evaluation of certain contingencies, including those set forth below involving matters with respect to which you have been engaged and to which you have devoted substantive attention on behalf of the Company in the form of legal consultation or representation. These contingencies are regarded by management of the Company as material for this purpose [*management may indicate a materiality limit if an understanding has been reached with the auditor*]. Your response should include matters that existed at [*balance sheet date*] and during the period from that date to the date of your response.

[*Alternative wording when management requests the lawyer to prepare the list that describes and evaluates pending or threatened litigation, claims, and assessments is as follows:*]

> In connection with an audit of our financial statements as of [*balance sheet date*] and for the [*period*] then ended, please furnish our auditors [*name and address of auditors*], with the information requested below concerning contingencies involving matters with respect to which you have devoted substantive attention on behalf of the Company in the form of legal consultation or representation. [*When a materiality limit has been established based on an understanding between management and the auditor, the following sentence should be added:* This request is limited to contingencies amounting to [*amount*] individually or items involving lesser amounts that exceed [*amount*] in the aggregate.]

Pending or Threatened Litigation [*excluding unasserted claims*]

> [*Ordinarily the information would include the following: (1) the nature of the litigation, (2) the progress of the case to date, (3) how management is responding or intends to respond to the litigation (for example, to contest the case vigorously or to seek an out-of-court settlement), and (4) an evaluation of the likelihood of an unfavorable outcome and an estimate, if one can be made, of the amount or range of potential loss.*] This letter will serve as our consent for you to

furnish to our auditor all the information requested herein. Accordingly, please furnish to our auditors such explanation, if any, that you consider necessary to supplement the foregoing information, including an explanation of those matters as to which your views may differ from those stated and an identification of the omission of any pending or threatened litigation, claims, and assessments or a statement that the list of such matters is complete.

[Alternative wording when management requests the lawyer to prepare the list that describes and evaluates pending or threatened litigation, claims, and assessments is as follows:

> Regarding pending or threatened litigation, claims, and assessments, please include in your response (1) the nature of the litigation, (2) the progress of the case to date, (3) how the Company is responding or intends to respond (for example, to contest the case vigorously or to seek an out-of-court settlement), and (4) an evaluation of the likelihood of an unfavorable outcome and an estimate, if one can be made, of the amount or range of potential loss.]

Unasserted Claims and Assessments [considered by management to be probable of assertion and that, if asserted, would have at least a reasonable possibility of an unfavorable outcome]

> [Ordinarily, management's information would include the following: (1) the nature of the matter, (2) how management intends to respond if the claim is asserted, and (3) an evaluation of the likelihood of an unfavorable outcome and an estimate, if one can be made, of the amount or range of potential loss.] Please furnish to our auditors such explanation, if any, that you consider necessary to supplement the foregoing information, including an explanation of those matters as to which your views may differ from those stated.

We understand that whenever, in the course of performing legal services for us with respect to a matter recognized to involve an unasserted possible claim or assessment that may call for financial statement disclosure, if you have formed a professional conclusion that we should disclose or consider disclosure concerning such possible claim or assessment, as a matter of professional responsibility to us, you will so advise us and will consult with us concerning the question of such disclosure and the applicable requirements of Financial Accounting Standards Board (FASB) *Accounting Standards Codification* (ASC) 450, *Contingencies*. Please specifically confirm to our auditors that our understanding is correct.

[Alternative wording when management requests the lawyer to prepare the list that describes and evaluates pending or threatened litigation, claims, and assessments is as follows:

> We have represented to our auditors that there are no unasserted possible claims or assessments that you have advised us are probable of assertion and must be disclosed in accordance with FASB ASC 450. We understand that whenever, in the course of performing legal services for us with respect to a matter recognized to involve an unasserted possible claim or assessment that may call for financial statement disclosure, you have formed a professional conclusion that we should disclose or consider disclosure concerning such possible claim or assessment, as a matter of professional responsibility to us, you will so advise us and will consult with us concerning the question of such disclosure and the applicable requirements of FASB ASC 450. Please specifically confirm to our auditors that our understanding is correct.]

Please specifically identify the nature of and reasons for any limitation on your response.

[*The auditor may request the client to inquire about additional matters—for example, unpaid or unbilled charges—or specified information on certain contractually assumed obligations of the company, such as guarantees or indebtedness of others.*]

[*Alternative wording when management requests the lawyer to prepare the list that describes and evaluates pending or threatened litigation, claims, and assessments is as follows:*]

> Your response should include matters that existed as of [*balance sheet date*] and during the period from that date to the effective date of your response. Please specifically identify the nature of and reasons for any limitations on your response. Our auditors expect to have the audit complete about [*expected completion date*]. They would appreciate receiving your reply by that date with a specified effective date no earlier than [*ordinarily two weeks before expected completion date*].]

[*Wording that could be used in an audit inquiry letter, instead of the heading and first paragraph, when the client believes that there are no unasserted claims or assessments (to be specified to the lawyer for comment) that are probable of assertion and that, if asserted, would have a reasonable possibility of an unfavorable outcome as specified by FASB ASC 450, is as follows:*]

> Unasserted claims and assessments—We have represented to our auditors that there are no unasserted possible claims that you have advised us are probable of assertion and must be disclosed, in accordance with FASB ASC 450, *Contingencies*. [*The second paragraph in the section relating to unasserted claims and assessments would not be altered.*]]

---

## EXHIBIT AU-C 501-4—ILLUSTRATIVE AUDIT INQUIRY LETTER TO LEGAL COUNSEL WHEREBY MANAGEMENT HAS REQUESTED THAT THE LAWYER PREPARE THE LIST OF PENDING OR THREATENED LITIGATION, CLAIMS, AND ASSESSMENTS

---

In connection with an audit of our financial statements as of [*balance sheet date*] and for the [*period*] then ended, please furnish our auditors, [*name and address of auditors*], with the information requested below concerning certain contingencies involving matters with respect to which you have devoted substantive attention on behalf of the Company in the form of legal consultation or representation. [*When a materiality limit has been established based on an understanding between management and the auditor, the following sentence should be added:* This request is limited to contingencies that amount to [*amount*] individually or items involving lesser amounts that exceed [*amount*] in the aggregate.]

*Pending or Threatened Litigation, Claims, and Assessments*

Regarding pending or threatened litigation, claims, and assessments, please include in your response (1) the nature of each matter; (2) the progress of each matter to date; (3) how the Company is responding or intends to respond (for example, to contest the case vigorously or seek an out-of-court settlement); and

(4) an evaluation of the likelihood of an unfavorable outcome and an estimate, if one can be made, of the amount or range or potential loss.

*Unasserted Claims and Assessments*

We have represented to our auditors that there are no unasserted possible claims or assessments that you have advised us are probable of assertion and must be disclosed in accordance with FASB Statement No. 5 (ASC 450). We understand that whenever, in the course of performing legal services for us with respect to a matter recognized to involve an unasserted possible claim or assessment that may call for financial statement disclosure, you have formed a professional conclusion that we should disclose or consider disclosure concerning such possible claim or assessment, as a matter of professional responsibility to us, you will so advise us and will consult with us concerning the question of such disclosure and the applicable requirements of ASC 450 (Contingencies). Please specifically confirm to our auditors that our understanding is correct.

*Other Matters*

Your response should include matters that existed as of [*balance-sheet date*] and during the period from that date to the effective date of your response.

Please specifically identify the nature of and reasons for any limitations on your response.

Our auditors expect to have the audit completed about [*expected completion date*]. They would appreciate receiving your reply by that date with a specified effective date no earlier than [*ordinarily two weeks before expected completion date*].

# SECTION 505

# EXTERNAL CONFIRMATIONS

## Authoritative Pronouncements

SAS-122—Statements on Auditing Standards: Clarification and Recodification

## Overview

The auditor can obtain audit evidence by confirming with, or acquiring information from, third parties. The confirmation process can be used as part of the audit of a number of account balances, transactions, and other information. For example, accounts receivable and payable may be confirmed with customers and vendors, respectively; a complex transaction may be confirmed with the counterparty; and the relationship between two (related) parties may be explained by the other party. The objective of the auditor in using external confirmation procedures is to design and perform the procedures to obtain relevant and reliable audit evidence.

In general, audit evidence obtained through the external confirmation process is often considered to be appropriate evidence. AU-C 500 reinforces this position, indicating that audit evidence is more reliable when it obtained from sources outside the entity, obtained directly by the auditor, and exists in documentary form, all of which are characteristics of external confirmations.

---

**PLANNING AID REMINDER:** AU-C 330 (*Performing Audit Procedures in Response to Assessed Risks and Evaluating the Audit Evidence Obtained*) requires the auditor to use external confirmation procedures for accounts receivable. While confirmation of accounts receivable is a generally accepted auditing procedure, confirmations can be effective in auditing many other areas: cash, notes receivable, inventory, consigned merchandise, construction and production contracts, investment securities, market values, accounts payable, notes payable, lines of credit, and actual and contingent liabilities. Confirmations can also be used to confirm the terms of unusual transactions and transactions with related parties.

## Definitions

| | |
|---|---|
| External confirmation | Audit evidence obtained as a direct written response to the auditor from a third party (the confirming party), in paper form, by electronic or other medium, or through the auditor's direct access to information held by a third party when the auditor is provided the information necessary to access the confirming party's data by the third party. If management provides the information necessary to access the confirming party's data, this does not meet the definition of an external confirmation. |
| Positive confirmation request | A request that the confirming party respond directly to the auditor providing the requested information or indicating whether the confirming party agrees with the information in the request. |
| Negative confirmation request | A request that the confirming party respond directly to the auditor only if the confirming party disagrees with the information provided in the request. |
| Nonresponse | A positive confirmation request the confirming party fails to respond or fully respond to, or a confirmation request returned undelivered. |
| Exception | A response indicating a difference between the information that is requested to be confirmed or that is contained in the entity's records and information provided by the confirming party. |

## Requirements

The auditor is presumptively required to perform the following procedures when using external confirmations:

1. Maintain control over confirmation requests by:
    a. Determining the information to be confirmed or requested,
    b. Selecting the appropriate confirming party,
    c. Designing the confirmation requests and determining that requests are directed to the appropriate confirming party and responses are coming directly to the auditor, and
    d. Sending the requests including any follow-up requests to the confirming party.
2. If management refuses to allow the auditor to send a confirmation request:
    a. Inquire about management's reasons for the refusal and seek audit evidence about the validity and reasonableness of those reasons.
    b. Evaluate the implications of management's refusal on the auditor's assessment of the relevant risks of material misstatement, including the risk of fraud, and on the nature, timing, and extent of other audit procedures.
    c. Perform alternative audit procedures designed to obtain relevant and reliable audit evidence.

3. If the auditor concludes management's refusal to allow the auditor to send a confirmation request is unreasonable or the auditor is unable to obtain reliable audit evidence from alternative audit procedures, communicate with those charged with governance and determine the implications for the audit and the auditor's opinion.
4. If factors are identified causing the auditor to doubt the reliability of a response to a confirmation request, obtain further audit evidences to resolve those doubts.
5. If the auditor determines that a response to a confirmation request is not reliable, evaluate the implications on the assessment of the relevant risks of material misstatement, including the risk of fraud, and on the nature, timing, and extent of other audit procedures.
6. For each nonresponse, perform alternative audit procedures to obtain relevant and reliable audit evidence.
7. If a written response to a positive confirmation request is necessary to obtain sufficient appropriate audit evidence, alternative audit procedures will not provide the required evidence. If confirmation is not obtained, determine the implications for the audit and the auditor's opinion.
8. Investigate exceptions to determine whether they indicate the presence of misstatements.
9. Negative confirmations provide less persuasive audit evidence than positive confirmations and should not be used as the sole substantive audit procedure to address an assessed risk of material misstatement at the assertion level unless the following four factors exist:
   a. The assessed risk of material misstatement is low and sufficient appropriate audit evidence has been obtained regarding the operating effectiveness of controls relevant to the assertion.
   b. The population of items subject to negative confirmation procedures consists of a large number of small, homogeneous account balances, transactions, or conditions.
   c. The expected exception rate is very low.
   d. The auditor is unaware of any circumstances that would cause recipients to disregard the confirmation requests.
10. Evaluate whether the results of the external confirmation procedures provide relevant and reliable audit evidence or if further audit evidence is necessary.

## Analysis and Application of Procedures

### External Confirmation Procedures

While external confirmation procedures are often used to confirm account balances or disclosures, they may also be used to confirm terms of agreements, contracts, or transactions between parties or to confirm the absence of other conditions, such as "side agreements."

> **PLANNING AID REMINDER:** AU-C 330 (*Performing Audit Procedures in Response to Assessed Risks and Evaluating the Audit Evidence Obtained*) requires the auditor to use external confirmation procedures for accounts receivable. Accounts receivable also encompass notes receivable and other receivables that use descriptive terms, assuming the account balance arose from the sale of goods or services in the normal course of business.

Confirmation requests should be addressed to respondents who, when they respond to the requests, will generate meaningful and appropriate audit evidence. When selecting the appropriate confirming party, the auditor should select a party believed to be knowledgeable about the information to be confirmed.

> **FRAUD POINTER:** The auditor should be aware that under some circumstances the level of professional skepticism should be increased, resulting in a closer scrutiny of the respondent's competence, knowledge, and objectivity. For example, increased skepticism is appropriate when there has been an unusual transaction or a significant balance or transaction. For these as well as other circumstances, the auditor may decide to investigate the characteristics of the respondents more closely or to employ other audit procedures to reduce the risk of material misstatements in the financial statements.

> **PLANNING AID REMINDER:** Auditors must be cautious when confirming the fair value of assets with parties that were originally involved in the acquisition of the assets being investigated. Because the respondent party might not provide objective evidence, the auditor should consider whether it is necessary to communicate with a party that is not involved in the transaction in order to collect appropriate audit evidence concerning the fair value of an asset.

The auditor should determine that external confirmation requests are properly addressed before they are sent out by testing the validity of some or all of the addresses, whether physical or electronic. The nature and extent of the procedures necessary to test addresses' validity depends on the risk associated with the type of confirmation or address.

> **ENGAGEMENT STRATEGY:** Confirmation requests (either positive or negative) may be returned as undeliverable. In this case, it is important for the auditor to corroborate that the intended recipient actually exists. AICPA Practice Alert 03-1 (*Audit Confirmations*) states that the auditor may want to discuss confirmations returned as undeliverable with a client official not related to the area being audited.

The reliability of the audit evidence obtained and the confirmation response rate may be directly affected by the design of the confirmation request. In designing the confirmation request, factors such as the following should be considered:

- Assertions being addressed;
- Identified risks of material misstatements, including fraud risks;
- Confirmation request layout and presentation;
- Prior auditor experience;
- Method of communication;
- Management authorization or encouragement to the confirming parties to respond to the auditor; some confirming parties may require management authorization before responding; and
- The respondent's ability to confirm or provide the requested information.

**ENGAGEMENT STRATEGY:** Although confirming accounts payable is not a generally accepted auditing procedure, accounts payable confirmations can be useful in providing audit evidence related to the existence and completeness assertions. In particular, it may be appropriate to send accounts payable confirmations to major suppliers, including those with small or zero balances. In addition, confirming accounts payable can be useful in detecting round-trip or linked transactions (an entity simultaneously sells to and buys from another party). AICPA Practice Alert 03-1 (*Audit Confirmations*) states that the following circumstances suggest that confirming accounts payable is appropriate: (1) the client has weak controls over payables and cash disbursements, (2) the client's industry poses a higher risk of unrecorded liabilities or inappropriate accounting, and (3) the complexity of the client's environment increases the risk of unrecorded liabilities. In confirming accounts payable, a blank confirmation request form is generally used. An important aspect of confirming accounts payable is the generation of a reliable and complete vendor list. The auditor should (1) review the accounts payable subsidiary ledger, (2) review invoice files by supplier, (3) review disbursement records by supplier, and (4) ask client personnel for the names of major suppliers. If an accounts payable confirmation is not returned, the auditor should perform alternative procedures, including examining subsequent cash disbursements. Subsequent cash disbursements might indicate amounts that should have been recorded as a liability at the balance sheet date.

One form of confirmation request is the positive external confirmation request and a response to such a request is generally expected to provide reliable evidence. A positive confirmation form may be designed in two ways. The information to be confirmed may be indicated in the confirmation request or the request may be blank, requiring the respondent to fill in the missing information. In either circumstance, audit evidence is dependent on the receipt of responses from the recipients of confirmation requests.

**ENGAGEMENT STRATEGY:** There is a trade-off between selecting the complete format and selecting the incomplete format as part of the engagement strategy. A risk exists when using the complete format that the confirming party may reply without verifying that the information is correct. When a respondent completes and returns an incomplete form, more appropriate evidence is created than when the respondent is simply asked to sign a complete confirmation form. However, when the incomplete form is used, the response rate will usually be lower and less accurate (sufficiency of evidence matter), and it may be necessary to perform alternative audit procedures to supplement the confirmation process. When a positive confirmation is used and the request is not returned, no evidence is created.

### Management Refuses to Allow the Auditor to Send a Confirmation Request

When evaluating the implications of management's refusal to allow the auditor to send a confirmation request, the auditor may find it necessary to revise the assessment of risks of material misstatement at the assertion level and modify planned audit procedures.

> **FRAUD POINTER:** If management's refusal is unreasonable, this may indicate the presence of a fraud risk factor that the auditor should evaluate.

In order to obtain sufficient evidence, the auditor should also perform alternative audit procedures, such as those used by the auditor in the event of nonresponses to confirmation requests.

> **OBSERVATION:** Clients sometimes ask the auditor not to send a confirmation request to a particular party. Often the stated reason is that there is a dispute between the client and the party as to the account balance. Audit Practice Alert 03-1 (*Audit Confirmations*) states that a dispute is not by itself a sufficient reason not to send a confirmation. Although there may be valid reasons for honoring a management request not to send a confirmation request to a particular party, the auditor should corroborate the reasons management is making this request. Simple reliance on management representations as corroboration is not sufficient. If the auditor concludes that management's request not to send a confirmation is not reasonable, and the restriction significantly limits the audit scope, he or she should normally either disclaim an opinion or withdraw from the engagement.

### Reliability of Confirmation Responses

The confirmation process should be executed so that the client does not have an opportunity to intercept requests when they are mailed or when they are returned from respondents. The confirmation process ideally involves the auditor mailing a confirmation request directly to a respondent and receiving the returned confirmation directly from the respondent. However, there is always some risk that confirmation responses may be intercepted, altered, or subject to fraud. Factors that may cause the auditor to doubt the reliability of the confirmation response include the response being received by the auditor indirectly or the response appearing to come from someone other than the intended confirming party. Risks the auditor should consider when determining the reliability of confirmation responses include:

- The information obtained may not be from an authentic source.
- A respondent may not be knowledgeable about the information to be confirmed.
- The integrity of the information may have been compromised.

Electronic responses such as fax or e-mail responses involve reliability risks that can be mitigated by using a secure confirmation environment. Tools such as encryption, electronic digital signatures, and procedures to verify website authenticity may help the auditor to improve the security of the electronic confirmation process. If relying on an electronic confirmation process, the auditor may use an assurance trust services report such as SysTrust to help assess the design and operating effectiveness of the controls related to the process and address reliability risks and concerns.

When the auditor has doubts about the reliability of a confirmation response to be used as audit evidence, he or she may determine additional or modified procedures are needed to resolve those doubts. Under these circumstances, the auditor may employ procedures such as the following:

- Verify the source and content of electronic response through a telephone call to the respondent.
- Request the respondent mail the original confirmation directly to the auditor if the response has been received indirectly.

A response to a confirmation request may contain restrictive language regarding its use. These restrictions may not create doubt about the reliability of the response if the restrictive language does not relate to the assertions being tested by the confirmation or if the restriction appears to be a boilerplate disclaimer of liability. However, if the restrictive language causes the auditor to have doubts about the completeness, accuracy, or reliability of the response, further audit evidence will need to be obtained to resolve those doubts. If the auditor concludes that a response is unreliable, he or she may find it necessary to revise the assessment of risks of material misstatement at the assertion level and modify planned audit procedures.

> **FRAUD POINTER:** If a response is unreliable, this may indicate the presence of a fraud risk factor that the auditor should evaluate.

*Oral Responses*

An oral response to a confirmation does not meet the definition of a confirmation request, because it is not written. Therefore, if external confirmation is required to provide sufficient appropriate audit evidence and an oral response is all the auditor receives, the auditor has not obtained the evidence needed.

> **ENGAGEMENT STRATEGY:** If an auditor has concluded that a direct written response to a positive confirmation is necessary to obtain sufficient appropriate evidence, the auditor may take the oral response to a confirmation request in consideration when determining the nature, timing, and extent of alternative

procedures. An appropriately documented oral response combined with the evidence the original confirmation request was based on may provide sufficient appropriate audit evidence for the auditor in certain circumstances. Appropriate documentation includes details such as the time and date of the conversation, the identity of the person providing the response, and the response provided. The auditor may also wish to perform additional procedures to establish the reliability of the oral confirmation.

*Nonresponses*

In the case of each nonresponse to a confirmation request, alternative audit procedures must be used. The specific nature of alternative procedures depends on the account balance or transaction and the adequacy of the client's internal control. For example, when a customer will not confirm an account receivable, the existence of the account could be substantiated through the review of a subsequent cash collection(s) or the inspection of documentation for the transaction(s) that created the year-end balance. A nonresponse to a confirmation request may cause the auditor to revise the assessed risk of material misstatement at the assertion level, to modify planned audit procedures, and to evaluate a newly indicated fraud risk factor.

It may be acceptable to omit the use of alternative procedures if both of the following two circumstances exist:

1. Unconfirmed balances do not appear to be unique.
2. Unconfirmed balances are immaterial when projected as 100% misstatements.

*Unconfirmed balances do not appear to be unique*

The auditor should review those accounts that respondents will not confirm to determine whether they are unusual. Although it is difficult to define "unusual," transactions that are complex and not routine, and balances that do not follow a dollar-value pattern, would increase the level of audit risk and generally preclude the auditor from omitting alternative procedures. For example, most auditors would be skeptical if most of the unconfirmed accounts receivable were from customers who also had other relationships with the client.

*Unconfirmed balances are immaterial*

The auditor may treat all accounts that respondents do not confirm as misstatements if collectively those misstatements could not have a material effect on the financial statements. In determining the misstatements, the auditor must project the assumed misstatements from the unconfirmed balances to the total population.

---

**PLANNING AID REMINDER:** AICPA Practice Alert 03-1 (*Audit Confirmations*) states that the auditor can increase confirmation response rates by (1) using clear wording, (2) sending the confirmation to a specific person, (3) naming the company being audited, (4) having the client manually sign the confirmation request, (5) providing deadlines for receiving a response, (6) sending second and third requests, and (7) calling the respondent for an oral confirmation and requesting that the written request be subsequently mailed. In addition, accounts receivable confirmation requests may receive greater attention if they are included with the monthly statement sent to the customer.

## When a Positive Confirmation Response Is Necessary to Obtain Sufficient Appropriate Audit Evidence

Circumstances that could cause a positive confirmation response to be necessary in order to obtain sufficient appropriate audit evidence include:

- Information to corroborate management's assertions is only available outside of the entity, and
- Specific fraud risk factors prevent the auditor from relying on evidence from the entity. These factors may include the risk of collusion or management override of controls.

## Exceptions

Exceptions may be used by the auditor to gauge the quality of confirmation responses from similar parties or accounts or the presence of deficiencies in the entity's internal control over financial reporting. Exceptions in confirmation responses may not indicate misstatements, but may be due to timing, measurement, or clerical errors in the external confirmation process. However, in some instances, exceptions may indicate misstatements or potential misstatements in the financial statements.

**FRAUD POINTER:** If the auditor identifies a misstatement, he or she is required to evaluate whether that misstatement indicates the presence of fraud.

## Negative Confirmations

A negative confirmation form requires the respondent to return the confirmation only if there is disagreement. When negative confirmations are not returned, the evidence generated is different from that generated when positive confirmations are used. That is, the lack of returned negative confirmations provides only implicit evidence that the information is correct.

**ENGAGEMENT STRATEGY:** Unreturned negative confirmations do not provide explicit evidence that the intended third parties received the confirmation requests and verified that the information contained on them is correct. Auditors should factor this limitation into their engagement strategy.

It is also important for the auditor to consider that confirming parties who disagree with the information on the negative confirmation request may be more likely to respond to the request if the perceived error is not in their favor and less likely to respond if the perceived error is in their favor. For example, negative confirmation requests may be useful in providing evidence about whether balances in account holders' bank deposit accounts are understated, but may be ineffective in providing evidence about whether those accounts are overstated.

*Evaluate the Audit Evidence Obtained*

---

**FRAUD POINTER:** Enforcement actions against auditors often result from deficiencies in the accounts receivable confirmation process. Some cases involved the failure to confirm accounts receivable; other cases involved auditors' failure to control the confirmation process (e.g., allowed the client to handle mailing and receipt of confirmations and the related responses). Finally, a number of auditors were cited for failing to perform alternative procedures when confirmations were not returned or were returned with material exceptions.

---

## Practitioner's Aids

In the confirmation of accounts receivable, the auditor may use a positive confirmation or a negative confirmation or a combination of both. An example of a positive confirmation is presented in Exhibit AU-C 505-1. An example of a negative confirmation is presented in Exhibit AU-C 505-2. Positive and negative confirmations may take a variety of forms. For example, the negative confirmation may be a stamp or a sticker placed directly on the monthly statements sent to the client's customers; for a positive confirmation it may be a letter in a format similar to the one used in Exhibit AU-C 505-1.

The standards related to the confirmation process apply to all confirmations, not just those that involve the confirmation of receivables. Exhibits AU-C 505-3 and AU-C 505-4 illustrate other types of confirmations, namely, the confirmation of a lease obligation and a mortgage obligation.

Exhibit AU-C 505-5 illustrates an audit program for the confirmation of accounts receivable.

Exhibit AU-C 505-6 provides an example of an audit schedule that summarizes the results of the accounts receivable confirmation process.

### EXHIBIT AU-C 505-1—POSITIVE CONFIRMATION

[*Client's Letterhead*]

---

[*Customer's Name and Address*]

Dear _____:

In accordance with the request of our auditors, please confirm the correctness of your account as listed below.

Account # _____

Date of Account Balance _____

(Confirmation Date)

Account Balance $ _____

If the amount is correct, sign in the space provided and return this letter to our auditor in the enclosed self-addressed envelope.

If the amount is incorrect, sign in the space provided, explain the difference on the back of this letter, and return this letter to our auditor in the enclosed self-addressed envelope.

This is not a request for payment.

Thank you for your prompt attention to this matter.

Very truly yours,

[*Client's Signature*]

The above balance at the confirmation date is correct, except as noted on the back of this letter.

[*Customer's Signature*]

[*Title*]

## EXHIBIT AU-C 505-2—NEGATIVE CONFIRMATION

CONFIRMATION REQUEST

Please examine this statement carefully. If it is not correct, please notify our auditors of any differences. For your convenience a stamped, self-addressed envelope is enclosed.

If you do not reply to this request, it will be assumed that the balance is correct.

This is not a request for payment.

## EXHIBIT AU-C 505-3—OBLIGATION UNDER LONG-TERM LEASES

[*Client's Letterhead*]

[*Lessor's Name and Address*]

Dear _____:

In accordance with the request of our auditors, please confirm the correctness of terms of our lease (and related matters) with your company.

Initial date of lease: _____

Monthly payments: $ _____

Number of months covered by the lease: _____

Renewal date (if applicable): _____

Monthly renewal payments $ _____

Period covered by renewal options: From: _____ To: _____

Purchase option (if applicable)

Purchase option price: $ _____

Dates covered by purchase option: From: _____ To: _____

Date of last lease payment received: _____

Other information:

_____
_____
_____

If the above information is correct, sign in the space provided and return this letter to our auditor in the enclosed self-addressed envelope.

If the above information is incorrect, sign in the space provided, explain the difference on the back of this letter, and return this letter to our auditor in the enclosed self-addressed envelope.

Thank you for your prompt attention to this matter.

Very truly yours,

_____

[*Client's Signature*]

The above information is correct, except as noted on the back of this letter.

_____

[*Lessor's Signature*] [*Title*]

## EXHIBIT AU-C 505-4—MORTGAGE OBLIGATION

[*Client's Letterhead*]

[*Mortgagor's Name and Address*]

Dear _____:

In accordance with the request of our auditors, please confirm the correctness of terms of our mortgage (and related matters) with your company.

    Initial date of mortgage: _____

    Monthly payments: $ _____

    Number of months covered by the mortgage: _____

    Interest rate: _____%;

    Unpaid balance as of (Date): $ _____

    Date of last mortgage payment received: _____

    Purpose of mortgage:

    _____

    _____

    Description of mortgaged property:

    _____

    _____

    Escrow amount held by you: $ _____

Amount of property taxes paid during (Date): $ _____

Amount of insurance paid during (Date): $ _____

Other information:

_____

_____

If the above information is correct, sign in the space provided and return this letter to our auditor in the enclosed self-addressed envelope.

If the above information is incorrect, sign in the space provided, explain the difference on the back of this letter, and return this letter to our auditor in the enclosed self-addressed envelope.

Thank you for your prompt attention to this matter.

Very truly yours,

_____

[*Client's Signature*]

The above information is correct, except as noted on the back of this letter.

_____

[*Mortgagor's Signature*] [*Title*]

_____

## *EXHIBIT AU-C 505-5—AUDIT PROGRAM—CONFIRMATION OF ACCOUNTS RECEIVABLE*

Use the following procedures as a guide for confirming accounts receivable. The audit program is only a guide, and professional judgment should be exercised to determine how the procedures should be modified by revising procedures listed or adding procedures to the audit program.

Initial and date each procedure as it is completed. If the procedure is not relevant to this particular audit engagement, place "N/A" (not applicable) in the space provided for an initial.

Client Name: _____

Date of Financial Statements: _____

Audit Report Date: _____

| | | *Yes* | *No* | *Audit Documentation Reference* |
|---|---|---|---|---|
| 1. | Obtain or prepare an aged trial balance of accounts receivable. | _____ | _____ | _____ |
| 2. | Foot and crossfoot the aged trial balance and trace the total to the general ledger. | _____ | _____ | _____ |

|  | Yes | No | Audit Documentation Reference |
|---|---|---|---|
| 3. Trace a sample of accounts listed on the aged trial balance to the account in the accounts receivable subsidiary ledger. | _____ | _____ | _____ |
| 4. Trace a sample of accounts in the accounts receivable subsidiary ledger to the aged trial balance. | _____ | _____ | _____ |
| 5. From the aged trial balance select a sample of account balances for confirmation. | _____ | _____ | _____ |
| 6. If confirmations are prepared by the client, substantiate the information on the confirmation with information contained in the subsidiary ledger. | _____ | _____ | _____ |
| 7. Mail confirmations directly with the U.S. Postal Service and include in the mailings a self-addressed return envelope. | _____ | _____ | _____ |
| 8. Trace returned confirmation to information contained in the list of confirmations mailed. | _____ | _____ | _____ |
| 9. Investigate exceptions noted in returned confirmation. | _____ | _____ | _____ |
| 10. Send second requests for confirmations not returned. | _____ | _____ | _____ |
| 11. Apply alternative procedures (such as review of subsequent cash collection and inspection of documentation that substantiate the original balance) to confirmations not returned. | _____ | _____ | _____ |
| 12. Prepare summary statistics based on confirmations mailed and results of confirmation process. | _____ | _____ | _____ |

Reviewed by: _____

Date: _____

# EXHIBIT AU-C 505-6—SUMMARY OF ACCOUNTS RECEIVABLE CONFIRMATION STATISTICS

Averroes Company Accounts Receivable Confirmation Statistics 12/31/X5

| | Dollar Value | Number of Accounts | Relative to Total Accounts Receivable | | Relative to Total Confirmations Sent | |
|---|---|---|---|---|---|---|
| | | | Dollar Value | Number of Accounts | Dollar Value | Number of Accounts |
| Total Accounts Receivable | $351,574.31 | 426 | | | | |
| Total Confirmations Mailed | 223,876.12 | 235 | 63.70% | 55.20% | | |
| Accounts Confirmed (including exceptions cleared) | 184,392.13 | 177 | 52.50% | 41.60% | 82.40% | 75.30% |
| Unconfirmed Accounts Verified through Alternative Procedures | 36,726.75 | 43 | 10.40% | 10.10% | 16.40% | 18.30% |
| Exceptions not cleared[a] | 2,757.24 | 15 | 0.80% | 3.50% | 1.20% | 6.40% |
| Totals | $223,876.12 | 235 | 63.70% | 55.20% | 100.00% | 100.00% |

[a] See analysis of exceptions not cleared at AR201.

Prepared By: *JB*

Date: *2/18/X6*

AR200

## SECTION 510

## OPENING BALANCES—INITIAL AUDIT ENGAGEMENTS, INCLUDING REAUDIT ENGAGEMENTS

### Authoritative Pronouncements

SAS-122—Statements on Auditing Standards: Clarification and Recodification

SAS-134—Auditor Reporting and Amendments, Including Amendments Addressing Disclosures in the Audit of Financial Statements

SAS-135—Omnibus Statement on Auditing Standards—2019

SAS-136—Forming an Opinion and Reporting on Financial Statements of Employee Benefit Plans Subject to ERISA

SAS-141—Amendment to Effective Dates of SAS Nos. 134-140

### Overview

AU-C 510 addresses the auditor's responsibilities in an initial audit engagement, including a reaudit engagement, with regards to opening balances. In these audit engagements, the auditor's objective is to obtain sufficient appropriate audit evidence about whether:

- Opening balances contain misstatements materially affecting the current period's financial statements.

- Appropriate accounting policies reflected in the opening balances are consistently applied in the current period's financial statements and any changes in these policies are properly accounted for, presented, and disclosed in accordance with the applicable financial reporting framework.

**PLANNING AID REMINDER:** The standards established by AU-C 510 do not apply to an engagement if the most recently audited financial statements are dated more than one year prior to the earliest period being audited.

Requirements to communicate with the predecessor auditor are addressed in AU-C 210 (*Terms of Engagement*).

## Definitions

| | |
|---|---|
| Initial audit engagement | An engagement in which the prior-period financial statements were either (1) not audited or (2) audited by a predecessor auditor. |
| Opening balances | Account balances existing at the beginning of the period that are based on prior-period closing balances and reflect prior-period events, transactions, and accounting policies. Opening balances include matters requiring disclosure that exist at the beginning of the period such as contingencies and commitments. |
| Predecessor auditor(s) | The auditor from a different audit firm who reported on the most recent audited financial statements and/or the auditor who was engaged to perform but did not complete an audit of the financial statements. |
| Reaudit | An initial audit engagement to audit financial statements that have been previously audited by a predecessor auditor. |

## Requirements

The auditor is presumptively required to perform the following procedures in an initial audit engagement:

*Audit Procedures*

1. Read the most recent financial statements, if any, and any predecessor auditor's report on those statements for information relevant to opening balances, including disclosures and consistency in the application of accounting policies.

2. If prior-period financial statements were audited by a predecessor auditor, request that the client authorize the predecessor auditor to share his or her audit documentation and to respond fully to inquiries by the current auditor to assist in engagement planning.

3. Obtain sufficient appropriate audit evidence about whether the opening balances contain misstatements materially affecting the current period's financial statements by:

    a. Determining if the prior-period closing balances were correctly brought forward to the current period or restated, if appropriate.
    b. Determining whether opening balances reflect application of appropriate accounting policies.
    c. Evaluating if audit procedures performed in the current period provide evidence relevant to the opening balances and reviewing the predecessor auditor's documentation when the prior-year financial statements were audited and/or performing specific audit procedures to obtain evidence regarding the opening balances.

4. If the auditor obtains evidence that the opening balances contain misstatements that could materially affect the current-period financial statements, perform appropriate additional audit procedures to determine the effect on the current-period financial statements. If the auditor concludes such misstatements exist in the current-period financial statements, communicate the misstatements to the appropriate level of management and those charged with governance.

5. Obtain sufficient appropriate audit evidence about whether accounting policies reflected in the opening balances are consistently applied in the

current period's financial statements and any changes in these policies are properly accounted for, presented, and disclosed in accordance with the applicable financial reporting framework.

6. If prior-period financial statements were audited by a predecessor auditor and the audit opinion was modified by the predecessor auditor, evaluate the effect of the matter causing the modification in assessing the risks of material misstatement in the current-period financial statements.

## Possible Misstatements in Financial Statements Reported on by a Predecessor Auditor

7. If the auditor becomes aware of information during the audit leading him or her to believe the financial statements reported on by the predecessor auditor may require revision, request that the client inform the predecessor auditor of the situation and arrange for the three parties to discuss the information and attempt to resolve the matter.

8. Communicate information regarding subsequent discovery of facts that may have affected audited financial statements previously reported on to the predecessor auditor.

9. If the client refuses to inform the predecessor auditor or the auditor is not satisfied with the matter's resolution, evaluate the implications on the current engagement and whether to resign from the engagement or, if law or regulation prevents the auditor from withdrawing, disclaim an opinion on the financial statements.

## Audit Conclusions and Reporting

10. Do not make reference in the audit report to the report or work of the predecessor auditor as part of the basis for the opinion.

11. If unable to obtain sufficient appropriate audit evidence regarding opening balances, express a qualified opinion or a disclaimer of opinion as appropriate.

12. If the auditor concludes the opening balances contain a misstatement materially affecting the current-period financial statements and the misstatement's effect is not properly accounted for, presented, or disclosed, express an opinion as appropriate.

13. If the auditor concludes that, in accordance with the applicable financial reporting framework, the current period's accounting policies are not consistently applied in relation to opening balances or a change in accounting policies is not properly accounted for, presented, or disclosed, express a qualified or adverse opinion as appropriate.

14. If the predecessor auditor's opinion regarding the prior-period financial statements was modified and that modification remains relevant and material to the current period financial statements, modify the opinion on the current-period financial statements.

# Analysis and Application of Procedures

## Audit Procedures

### Considerations when there is a predecessor auditor

Communications between the predecessor auditor and the successor auditor may be helpful in planning the audit engagement, but they do not have to be made before the auditor accepts the client. The auditor's communications with the predecessor auditor are guided by relevant ethical and professional requirements.

---

**PLANNING AID REMINDER:** When the most recent financial statements have been compiled or reviewed, a predecessor auditor does not exist; however, the current auditor is not prohibited from following the guidance established by AU-C 510.

---

Before allowing access to audit documentation, the predecessor auditor should reach an understanding with the successor auditor regarding the use of the audit documentation. This understanding may be documented in a letter prepared by the predecessor auditor and acknowledged by the successor. Exhibit AU-C 510-1 is an example of such a letter. In order to further document the process related to the review of the predecessor's audit documentation, the predecessor auditor may request a consent and acknowledgment letter from the client. Exhibit AU-C 510-2 is an example of such a letter.

---

**PLANNING AID REMINDER:** If the predecessor auditor denies or limits access to documentation or does not respond fully to inquiries, it may affect the successor auditor's assessment of risk or the nature, timing, and extent of the his or her procedures regarding opening balances.

---

Although the predecessor auditor must use professional judgment in determining which audit documentation should be made available to the auditor, AU-C 510 points out that generally the predecessor auditor grants access to audit files, such as those documenting (1) the planning of the engagement, (2) risk assessment procedures, (3) further audit procedures, (4) audit results, and (5) matters related to continuing accounting and auditing significance, such as analyses of balances and contingencies. In audits of governmental entities, there may be legal or regulatory restrictions limiting the auditor's access to information from the predecessor auditor. In these situations, audit evidence may need to be obtained through other means, or, if sufficient appropriate audit evidence cannot be obtained, the effect on the auditor's opinion should be considered.

---

**FRAUD POINTER:** When assessing the risks of material misstatements due to fraud, the auditor should consider other information obtained in an audit, such as procedures related to the acceptance and continuance of clients. Information obtained from the predecessor auditor about management's integrity, disagreements between management and the predecessor auditor, and the reasons for the change in auditors can provide relevant insights to the successor auditor, particularly when combined with other information gathered by the successor auditor to assess fraud risks.

> **IMPORTANT NOTICE FOR 2022:** In May 2019, the AICPA's Auditing Standards Board (ASB) issued SAS No. 135 titled *Omnibus Statement on Auditing Standards—2019* that includes amendments to various AU-C sections. SAS No. 135 amends AU-C 510 to note that the auditor's review of the predecessor auditor's documentation may include review of working papers related to related parties and significant unusual transactions. Originally, the effective date of SAS No. 135 was for audits of financial statements periods ending on or after December 15, 2020, with early application **not** permitted. However, the ASB's issuance of SAS No. 141, *Amendment to the Effective Dates of SAS Nos. 134-140*, extended the effective date to December 15, 2021, in order to provide more time for firms to implement SAS No. 135 in light of the effect of the coronavirus pandemic. While SAS No. 141 allows for early implementation of SAS No. 135, the ASB recommends that SAS Nos. 134-140 be implemented concurrently.

In addition to review of the predecessor auditor's audit documentation, the auditor may also assess the competence and independence of the predecessor auditor. The nature, timing, and extent of the auditor's audit procedures relating to opening balances and consistency of accounting principles may be affected by review of the predecessor auditor's working papers, but they, as well as the conclusions reached from these procedures, remain the sole responsibility of the current auditor.

> **OBSERVATION:** If the predecessor auditor is owed fees for prior work, he or she does not need to comply with a request until those fees are paid.

*Obtain audit evidence to support beginning account balances*

The nature and extent of audit procedures the auditor uses to obtain sufficient appropriate audit evidence about opening balances depends on many factors, including:

- The entity's accounting policies;
- The nature of the account balances, classes of transactions, and disclosures and the risks of material misstatement in the current-period financial statements;
- The significance of the opening balances relative to the current-period financial statements; and
- Whether the prior-period financial statements were audited and any modification to that audit opinion.

Current-period audit procedures may be useful in obtaining evidence about opening balances of some current assets and liabilities; for example, collection or payment during the current period provides some evidence about the opening balances of accounts receivable and accounts payable, respectively. The auditor may also obtain some evidence about the opening balances of noncurrent assets and liabilities through current-period audit procedures; for example, third-party confirmations may provide some evidence about the opening balances of long-term debts and investments. However, for many current and noncurrent asset and liability accounts additional audit procedures may be necessary.

---

**IMPORTANT NOTICE FOR 2022:** In May 2019, the AICPA's Auditing Standards Board (ASB) issued SAS No. 134 titled *Auditor Reporting and Amendments, Including Amendments Addressing Disclosures in the Audit of Financial Statements* that makes significant changes to the auditor's report, including the ability to communicate key audit matters (KAMs) in the auditor's report. SAS No. 134 also includes conforming amendments to other AU-C sections, including amendments to AU-C 510 to acknowledge that if the auditor encounters significant difficulty in obtaining sufficient appropriate audit evidence about whether the opening balances contain material misstatements that materially affect the current period's financial statements, the auditor may determine this to be a KAM. Originally, the effective date of SAS No. 134 was for audits of financial statements periods ending on or after December 15, 2020, with early implementation **not** permitted. However, the ASB's issuance of SAS No. 141, *Amendment to the Effective Dates of SAS Nos. 134-140*, extended the effective date to December 15, 2021, in order to provide more time for firms to implement SAS No. 134 in light of the effect of the coronavirus pandemic. While SAS No. 141 allows for early implementation of SAS No. 134, the ASB recommends that SAS Nos. 134-140 be implemented concurrently.

---

## *Audit Conclusions and Reporting*

When the auditor is unable to obtain sufficient appropriate audit evidence regarding the opening balances, the audit report may need to be modified in one of the following ways as appropriate:

- The auditor may issue a qualified opinion or a disclaimer of opinion, or
- The auditor may issue an opinion that is qualified or disclaimed regarding the results of operations and cash flows and unmodified regarding financial position.

## Practitioner's Aids

Exhibit AU-C 510-1 is an example of a letter of understanding between the predecessor and successor auditors. This letter is reproduced, with minor modifications, from Exhibit C of AU-C 315.

*EXHIBIT AU-C 510-1—LETTER OF UNDERSTANDING FROM PREDECESSOR TO SUCCESSOR AUDITOR*

---

We have previously audited, in accordance with auditing standards generally accepted in the United States of America, the December 31, 20X7, financial statements of Averroes Company. We rendered a report on those financial statements and have not performed any audit procedures subsequent to the audit report date. In connection with your audit of Averroes Company's 20X8 financial statements, you have requested access to our audit documentation prepared in connection with that audit. Averroes Company has authorized our firm to allow you to review the audit documentation.

Our audit, and the audit documentation prepared in connection therewith, of Averroes Company's financial statements was not planned or conducted in contemplation of your review. Therefore, items of possible interest to you may not have been specifically addressed. Our use of professional judgment and the assessment of audit risk and materiality for the purpose of our audit mean that matters may have existed that would have been assessed differently by you. We make no representation as to the sufficiency or appropriateness of the information in our audit documentation for your purposes.

We understand that the purpose of your review is to obtain information about Averroes Company and our 20X7 audit results to assist you in planning and performing your 20X8 audit of Averroes Company. For that purpose only, we will provide you access to our audit documentation that relates to that objective.

Upon request, we will provide copies of audit documentation that provides factual information about Averroes Company. You agree to subject any such copies or information otherwise derived from our audit documentation to your normal policy for retention of audit documentation and protection of confidential client information. Furthermore, in the event of a third-party request for access to your audit documentation prepared in connection with your audits of Averroes Company, you agree to obtain our permission before voluntarily allowing any such access to our audit documentation or information otherwise derived from our audit documentation, and to obtain on our behalf any releases that you obtain from such third party. You agree to advise us promptly and provide us with a copy of any subpoena, summons, or other court order for access to your audit documentation that include copies of our audit documentation or information otherwise derived therefrom.

Please confirm your agreement with the foregoing by signing and dating a copy of this letter and returning it to us.

Very truly yours,

[*Predecessor Auditor*]

By:

Accepted: [*Successor Auditor*]

By:

Date:

---

An additional paragraph may be added to the letter to provide the predecessor auditor with additional assurance concerning the use of audit documentation in order for the successor auditor to gain broader access to that documentation. An example of such a paragraph is reproduced from AU-C 510:

> Because your review of our audit documentation is undertaken solely for the purpose described previously and may not entail a review of all our audit documentation, you agree that (1) the information obtained from the review will not be used by you for any other purpose, (2) you will not comment, orally or in writing, to anyone as a result of that review about whether our audit was performed in accordance with generally accepted auditing standards, (3) you will not provide expert testimony or litigation support services or otherwise accept an engagement to comment on issues relating to the quality of our audit, and (4) you accept sole responsibility for the nature, timing, and extent of audit work performed and the conclusions reached in rendering your opinion on the 20X8 financial statements of Averroes Company.

Exhibit AU-C 510-2 is an example of a consent and acknowledgment letter the predecessor auditor may send to the client (reproduced from AU-C 510).

> **ENGAGEMENT STRATEGY:** Rule 1.700 of the Code of Professional Conduct prohibits an auditor from disclosing confidential information except when the client agrees to the disclosure. To reconcile the requirements of AU-C 510 with Rule 1.700, the successor auditor should ask the prospective client to grant permission to discuss the impending engagement with the predecessor auditor. The client should not place any restrictions on the exchange of information between the successor and predecessor auditors. If the successor auditor cannot obtain required information from the predecessor auditor because of client restrictions, the successor auditor should consider the reasons for the restrictions and take the circumstances into consideration when deciding whether to accept the client.

### EXHIBIT AU-C 510-2—CLIENT CONSENT AND ACKNOWLEDGMENT LETTER

You have given your consent to allow [*name of successor CPA firm*], as independent auditors for Averroes Company, access to our audit documentation for our audit of the December 31, 20X7, financial statement of Averroes Company. You also have given your consent to us to respond fully to [*name of successor CPA firm*] inquiries. You understand and agree that the review of our audit documentation is undertaken solely for the purpose of obtaining an understanding of Averroes and certain information about our audit to assist [*name of successor CPA firm*] in planning and performing the audit of the December 31, 20X8, financial statement of Averroes Company.

Please confirm your agreement with the foregoing by signing and dating a copy of this letter and returning it to us.

Attached is the form of the letter we will furnish [*name of successor CPA firm*] regarding the use of the audit documentation.

Very truly yours,

[*Predecessor Auditor*]
By:

Accepted:
[*Averroes Company*]
By:
Date:

# SECTION 520

# ANALYTICAL PROCEDURES

## Authoritative Pronouncements

SAS-122—Statements on Auditing Standards: Clarification and Recodification

## Overview

Analytical procedures are used to determine whether relationships between information presented in financial statements are consistent with the auditor's expectations. For example, if an auditor is aware that a client has invested heavily in new machinery, depreciation expense would be expected to be significantly greater in the current period than in the prior period. To successfully employ analytical procedures, an auditor must have a thorough knowledge of the client and the industry in which it operates.

AU-C 520 provides guidance to the auditor in using analytical procedures as substantive procedures and in performing analytical procedures near the end of an audit in order to help form an overall conclusion on the financial statements. AU-C 315 addresses the use of analytical procedures as risk assessment procedures and AU-C 330 addresses the nature, timing, and extent of audit procedures, including substantive analytical procedures, in response to assessed risks.

> **ENGAGEMENT STRATEGY:** The auditor must use professional judgment to determine whether analytical procedures should be used as a substantive procedure to collect audit evidence related to account balances or classes of transactions. Although AU-C 520 does not require that analytical procedures be used as part of substantive testing, it does imply that it may be difficult to achieve certain audit objectives efficiently without applying substantive analytical procedures.

## Definition

| | |
|---|---|
| Analytical procedures | Evaluations of financial information through analysis of plausible relationships among both financial and nonfinancial data, including any necessary investigation of identified fluctuations or relationships that are inconsistent with other relevant information or that differ significantly from expected values. |

## Requirements

The following are presumptively required of the auditor when performing substantive analytical procedures or analytical procedures used near the end of the audit to assist in forming an overall conclusion:

1. When designing and performing substantive analytical procedures, alone or in combination with tests of details:

a. Determine the suitability of the analytical procedures for the assertions being tested, considering the assessed risks of material misstatement and any tests of details used;
   b. Evaluate the reliability of the data the auditor's expectations are developed from, considering factors such as the source, comparability, nature and relevance of available information, and controls over preparation of the data;
   c. Develop an expectation of recorded amounts or ratios and evaluate whether the expectation combined with other audit evidence obtained is precise enough to identify a misstatement that, whether alone or with other misstatements, may cause material misstatement of the financial statements; and
   d. Determine the level of difference of recorded amounts from expected values that is acceptable and does not require any further investigation and compare the recorded amounts or ratios based on recorded amounts with the expectations.
2. Design and perform analytical procedures near the end of an audit to assist in drawing reasonable conclusions about whether the financial statements are consistent with the auditor's understanding of the entity.
3. If analytical procedures performed in accordance with AU-C 520 identify fluctuations or relationships that are inconsistent with other relevant information or that differ from expected values by a significant amount, investigate those differences by inquiring of management and obtaining appropriate audit evidence relevant to management's responses and performing any other necessary audit procedures.
4. When using substantive analytical procedures, document:
   a. The expectation of recorded amounts or ratios when the expectation is not otherwise readily determinable from existing documentation.
   b. Results of the comparison of the expectation to the recorded amounts or ratios.
   c. Any additional auditing procedures performed relating to fluctuations or relationships that are inconsistent with other relevant information or that differ from expected values by a significant amount and the results of such procedures.

## Analysis and Application of Procedures

### Analytical Procedures

Analytical procedures operate under the basic premise that plausible relationships among data may be reasonably expected to exist. The reasons for the plausibility of these relationships are important because apparently related data may not be related, which can lead to erroneous conclusions or an unexpected relationship may be able to provide important evidence.

Analytical procedures include considering comparisons of the entity's financial information with comparable prior-period information, anticipated entity results, and similar industry information. Analytical procedures also involve considering relationships among financial information elements expected to conform to a predictable pattern or between financial and nonfinancial information. Scanning is an analytical procedure used to identify significant or unusual items where the auditor uses professional judgment to review accounting data. Analytical procedures may be performed using many methods, from simple comparisons to complex analyses using statistical techniques, and may be applied at many different levels of aggregation.

---

**PUBLIC COMPANY IMPLICATION:** Guidance related to analytical procedures is contained in AS-2110, AS-2301, AS-2810, and AS-1105. Audit risk is the risk that the auditor will issue an inappropriate opinion on financial statements that are materially misstated. The auditor is to reduce audit risk to a low level through the application of audit procedures. As a result, the amount of audit effort, such as the performance of analytical procedures, devoted to particular accounts, classes of transactions, and disclosures should vary based on their respective risk.

---

The AICPA Audit Guide *Analytical Procedures* states that the process of using analytical procedures consists of four phases:

1. Formation of auditor expectations,
2. Identification of differences between account balances and auditor expectations,
3. Investigation of differences, and
4. Evaluation of results.

## *Formation of Auditor Expectations*

The auditor incorporates all of his or her experiences, both general and client-specific, to develop expectations of relationships between financial and nonfinancial data. Thus, at this stage the auditor must formulate an expectation about a relationship involving an amount that appears in the client's accounting system. Because of the varying nature of information processed and otherwise developed by a client, the Audit Guide notes that the effectiveness of developing an expectation depends on the following factors:

- Nature of account or assertion,
- Reliability and other characteristics of data, and
- Inherent precision of an analytical procedure.

*Nature of account or assertion*

Auditor expectations must be based on plausible relationships between financial and nonfinancial data. The more predictable a relationship, the more plausible the auditor's expectation. For example, there is a relationship between the amount of interest-bearing debt on the balance sheet (as reported throughout the year) and the interest expense reported on the operating statement. Developing an expected relationship between two amounts such as these is relatively easy to do; however, expectations about other relationships can be more difficult to identify with an acceptable degree of precision. For example, the relationship between accounts receivable and the allowance for uncollectible accounts can be difficult to predict if the client has changed its credit policies or the economics of the client's industry have significantly changed. The Audit Guide lists the following as examples of factors that an auditor may consider in establishing a relationship between accounts (assertions) on the financial statements:

- The degree of subjectivity exercised to develop the account balance (e.g., an account may simply be an aggregation of transactions (low degree of subjectivity) or be based on estimates (high degree of subjectivity));
- The product mix;
- The client's profile (e.g., the manner in which it distributes its products);
- Management's discretion;
- Various measurements of the client's environment (e.g., changes in economic, technological, or regulatory conditions); and
- The type of account (balance sheet or operating account).

*Reliability and other characteristics of data*

The precision of the auditor's expectation (how close the expectation is to the correct amount, not the reported amount) depends on the quality of the data used to form the expectation. If the reliability of the data is poor, the quality of the audit evidence created by performing an analytical procedure will be poor and perhaps irrelevant. The Audit Guide identifies the following as factors that are useful in determining the usefulness of data used to develop auditor expectations:

- The client's internal control (the stronger the internal control, the more reliable the data);
- The source of data (data based on outside parties are more reliable than internally generated data);
- Audited data (data that have been subjected to audit procedures (generally financial data) are more reliable than data that have not been audited (generally nonfinancial data)); and
- The degree of aggregation (the more aggregated data, the more difficult it is to develop a precise expectation).

**PLANNING AID REMINDER:** In addition to financial information, nonfinancial data may be taken into consideration as part of the performance of analytical procedures. For example, quality control reports prepared near year-end may identify production problems, which may suggest that significant amounts of inventory sold during the latter part of the year may be returned or may significantly increase future warranty claims.

*Inherent precision of an analytical procedure*

The Audit Guide broadly classifies analytical procedures as (1) trend analysis, (2) ratio analysis, (3) reasonableness test, and (4) regression analysis. These broad analytical procedures are not substitutes for one another. The auditor, using professional judgment, selects the appropriate analytical procedure based on the desired level of assurance that the account (assertion) is not materially misstated.

Trend analysis is based on the analysis of changes in a balance over a period of time that can vary from two years (the current year compared with the previous year) to several years. Generally, trend analysis is most effective when the client is in a stable environment. For example, the reasonableness of current year sales may be appropriately tested by comparing that amount to sales in the previous year if there is an absence of increased competition in the area serviced by the client, changing local economic conditions, changing consumer preferences, and an absence of change in a host of other environmental conditions.

The advantage of using trend analysis is its simplicity; however, its effectiveness is limited by the fact that it does not take into consideration changes in the client's environment. In addition, the use of this approach is based on an implicit rather than an explicit expectation. That is, in trend analysis the auditor does not explicitly establish an expected dollar amount but, rather, compares two numbers that because of changed conditions might not be comparable. Trend analysis is also limited to a single predictor and cannot take into consideration operating data or external data.

Ratio analysis can be used to compare the relationship between (1) accounts over time (inventory turnover), (2) an account and nonfinancial information (e.g., sales per square foot of space), (3) accounts of the client and data from the client's industry (e.g., the percentage of uncollectible accounts), and (4) a combination of the foregoing three items.

Like trend analysis, ratio analysis is most effective when the environmental characteristics of the client are stable; however, the Audit Guide points out that ratio analysis can be more effective than trend analysis "because comparisons between the balance sheet and operating statement can often reveal unusual fluctuations that an analysis of the individual accounts would not." Furthermore, using ratio analysis that is based in part on industry data can only be effective if the client's operating and financing activities do not deviate significantly from industry norms.

Reasonableness tests utilize financial and nonfinancial data to determine the acceptability of an account balance or a change in an account balance. For example, the current year's payroll expense expectation may take into consideration last year's account balance and other factors such as the average pay rate change, the timing of pay rate adjustments, and the expansion or contraction of the labor force. The advantage of a reasonableness test over trend analysis and ratio analysis is that in a reasonableness test the auditor takes into consideration a client's changed environment and, using professional judgment, assesses whether the current-year balance appears to be appropriate. In applying a reasonableness test the auditor must be careful to identify all the significant factors that could have an impact on the account balance being investigated.

Regression analysis is the most sophisticated analytical procedure in that it is based on a statistical model to predict the relationship between the account balance and various other factors. Generally, the difference between a reasonableness test and regression analysis is that regression analysis produces a quantitative prediction (expressed as a range) of what the current year's balance should be.

The most difficult analytical procedure to employ is regression analysis, but it has all of the advantages of reasonableness tests and, additionally, it provides a measure of statistical precision. That is, the auditor does not attempt to predict a single amount but, rather, estimates a projected amount plus or minus a dollar value.

---

**PLANNING AID REMINDER:** The effectiveness of analytical procedures is increased if the data sets are disaggregated. For example, applying a trend analysis approach to divisional information rather than consolidated financial information will generally result in more precise expectations. Be aware that when conducting regression analyses, one needs a sufficient number of data points to obtain a statistically valid result. Usually 18 to 20 data points are sufficient. Quarterly results can be used if the data are accurate. Microsoft Excel and other spreadsheet programs contain easy-to-use statistical analysis programs.

---

*Identification of differences between account balance and auditor expectations*

The second phase of the analytical procedure process is the identification of differences, which simply means that the auditor computes the difference between the expectation and the recorded account balance. The computed difference is then compared with the auditor's measure of materiality. When the analytical procedure is part of substantive testing, the auditor will accept the recorded amount balance when the difference is less than the materiality threshold for the account (e.g., the tolerable misstatement). If the difference is greater than the materiality threshold, the difference must be investigated.

*Investigation of differences*

The Audit Guide points out that differences between the expected amount and the recorded account balance can arise for one or more of the following reasons:

- The recorded account balance is misstated.
- The recorded account balance is affected by inherent factors related to the nature of the account to a degree not anticipated by the auditor.
- The expected amount is affected by the reliability of databases used to establish the expected amount to a degree not anticipated by the auditor.

Initially the auditor should evaluate the expectation results by determining whether there is an apparent problem with the precision of the estimate (the second and third items listed above). If it is concluded that the analytical procedure created a too imprecise expectation, then the auditor must decide whether the cost related to employing a more precise analytical procedure can be justified. For example, the auditor might have used trend analysis to develop an implicit expectation about a client's current sales figure, but if the difference between the expected amount and the recorded sales amount is too great, it may be concluded that regression analysis should be used to test the acceptability of the sales figure.

If the auditor concludes that the level of precision does not appear to be the reason for the unacceptable difference between the expected amount and the recorded amount, the investigation should consider whether there is a plausible explanation for the difference. Generally a plausible explanation is related to unexpected events, changes in the business environment, or accounting changes. The Audit Guide states that a plausible explanation should be evaluated in the context of such factors as the following:

- The development of audit evidence in other parts of the engagement, especially evidence obtained that relates to the database used to formulate the original expectation.
- Reports by management or the board of directors that identify and explain significant variances between budgeted and actual results.
- Relevant information identified in the minutes of the board of directors.
- Information about unusual events that occurred in previous years that may have reoccurred in the current period.

When an analytical procedure is performed as part of substantive testing, reasons that support a plausible explanation must be investigated and corroborated. The specific form of corroboration will depend on the nature of the account and the plausible explanation, but the Audit Guide notes that one or more of the following procedures may be useful to an auditor:

- Confirm related factors with outside parties.
- Make inquiries of internal personnel who did not provide the plausible explanation to the auditor.
- Perform other auditing procedures (perhaps on the data that were used to establish the expectation).
- Inspect documents that support the plausible explanation.

If the auditor cannot corroborate the plausible explanation, the difference must be evaluated as unexplained.

*Evaluation of results*

The final step in the analytical procedures process is the evaluation of results arising from the application of the procedure. Professional judgment must be exercised to determine how the results of applying an analytical procedure affect the audit engagement. The Audit Guide points out that "the auditor should attempt to quantify that portion of the difference for which plausible explanations can be obtained and, where appropriate, corroborate and determine that the amount that cannot be explained is sufficiently small to enable him or her to conclude on the absence of material misstatement." More specifically when a plausible explanation cannot be supported, the auditor should aggregate misstatements that the entity has not corrected in a way that enables him or her to consider whether, in relation to individual amounts, subtotals, or totals in the financial statements, they materially misstate the financial statements taken as a whole. Qualitative considerations also influence the auditor in reaching a conclusion as to whether misstatements are material.

## Substantive Analytical Procedures

In determining whether and to what extent analytical procedures should be used, an auditor should consider the relative effectiveness and efficiency of analytical procedures as compared to tests of details in reducing the risk of material misstatement and identifying potential misstatements. The effectiveness and efficiency of substantive analytical procedures depend on the following factors:

- Nature of the assertion being tested,
- Plausibility and predictability of the relationship,
- Reliability and availability of the data used to develop the expectation, and
- Precision of the expectation.

> **ENGAGEMENT STRATEGY:** Analytical data prepared by management may be effective if the auditor is satisfied that the data are properly prepared.

The applicability of analytical procedures for given assertions depends on the nature of the assertion and the risk of material misstatement. Because the auditor desires more persuasive audit evidence, a more predictable relationship is generally required. The following generalizations may be useful in identifying predictable relationships:

- Relationships in a relatively stable environment tend to be more predictable than those in an unstable environment. (For example, bad debts expense and credit sales tend to be closely related to a stable economic environment.)
- Relationships among data on the income statement tend to be more predictable than relationships among data on the balance sheet. (For example, sales and sales commission expense tend to be more closely related than trade accounts payable and inventories.)
- Relationships that are subject to management discretion are more difficult to evaluate. (For example, loss contingency accruals associated with the number of pending lawsuits tend not to be predictable.)

Substantive analytical procedures may be used in conjunction with tests of details to provide sufficient audit evidence on a particular assertion. In these circumstances, less persuasive analytical procedures may still be useful in providing corroborating evidence. Widely recognized trade ratios can also often be used effectively in substantive analytical procedures to support the reasonableness of recorded amounts.

> **PLANNING AID REMINDER:** Many relationships between financial statement items that may be used in the audit of business entities may not be relevant for

audits of governmental entities. For example, governmental entities may have little direct relationship between revenue and expenditure.

For the auditor to be able to draw an inference about an account balance or a class of transactions based on applying analytical procedures, the data from which the inference is made must be reliable and available. In evaluating the reliability of data, the following generalizations are useful:

- Audited data (current or prior years) are more reliable than unaudited data.
- Internal data tend to be more reliable when developed under an effective system of internal control.
- Data from an external source tend to be more reliable than data from an internal source.
- Data tend to be more reliable when they are comparable to other available information.
- Data tend to be more reliable when the auditor is satisfied as to their nature and relevance.

The auditor may consider testing the operating effectiveness of controls over the entity's preparation of information used in substantive analytical procedures. When these controls are effective, the auditor may have greater confidence in the reliability of the data and, therefore, in the results of the analytical procedures.

Because analytical procedures generally lead to fairly broad conclusions about assertions in the financial statements, an auditor should consider the precision of the established expectation. In some instances, an auditor may be satisfied with a fairly imprecise expectation. For example, expectations concerning the relationship between warranty expense and sales subject to warranty may be imprecise (say, from 1% to 8% of sales) if significant changes in warranty expenses are unlikely to have a material effect on the financial statements. On the other hand, a more precise expectation may be demanded for sales returns when the client is in an industry that experiences significant returns and a change of a percentage point or two could have a material effect on the financial statements.

A less precise expectation may be appropriate when the evidence from the substantive analytical procedure will be combined with audit evidence from tests of details. However, a more precise expectation is needed if the substantive analytical procedure is the only procedure planned to address a risk of misstatement for a relevant assertion.

The precision of an expectation is also affected by the level of aggregation of the information. Expectations developed at a disaggregated level increase the auditor's change of detecting material misstatements by decreasing the risk that offsetting factors may obscure material misstatements. The appropriate level of aggregation to use for analytical procedures is influenced by the entity's nature, size, and complexity.

When planning analytical procedures, the auditor should set the materiality thresholds for acceptable deviations from expected amounts. The amount of an acceptable deviation from the expected amount should be less than what is considered material when those deviations are combined with other errors in other account balances and classes of transactions. As the auditor's assessment of the risk of material misstatement increases, the persuasiveness of the audit evidence obtained should also increase. Therefore, as the assessed risk increases, the auditor's level of acceptable deviation from the expected amount will decrease.

## Analytical Procedures Performed to Assist in forming an Overall Conclusion

Analytical procedures performed near the end of the audit to assist the auditor in forming an overall conclusion may be similar to those used as risk assessment procedures. These procedures may include reading the financial statements, considering the adequacy of evidence obtained related to unusual or unexpected balances identified during the audit, and considering unusual or unexpected balances or relationships that were not previously identified. If the results of these analytical procedures reveal a previously unidentified risk of material misstatement, the auditor is required to revise his or her assessment of the risks of material misstatement and modify further planned audit procedures as appropriate.

## Investigating Results of Analytical Procedures

When the auditor is investigating differences between identified relationships and their expected values, he or she may obtain audit evidence relevant to management's responses by evaluating those responses in the context of the understanding of the entity and its environment and other audit evidence obtained during the course of the audit. Circumstances in which the auditor may find it necessary to perform other audit procedures may occur when management is unable to provide an explanation or when management's explanation combined with the evidence obtained relevant to management's response is not sufficient.

## Practitioner's Aids

Exhibit AU-C 520-1 and Exhibit AU-C 520-2 are examples of audit documentation that could be used to document the performance and results of analytical procedures. Exhibit AU-C 520-3 illustrates an approach to the performance of final analytical review.

*EXHIBIT AU-C 520-1—DOCUMENTATION OF THE EFFECT OF ANALYTICAL PROCEDURES ON THE PLANNING OF SUBSTANTIVE AUDIT PROCEDURES*

> Use this audit schedule to document the effect of analytical procedures on planned substantive audit procedures. The evaluation of the preliminary condition's effect on planned substantive audit procedures is preliminary, and the nature, extent, and timing of audit procedures may be revised based on additional information obtained during the engagement.

Client _____   Name: _____

Date of Financial Statements: _____

| Preliminary Condition | Implication of Preliminary Condition on Planning Substantive Audit Procedures | Substantive Audit Documentation Reference |
|---|---|---|
| • **Account Balance/Transaction:** <br> Description of preliminary condition: | Nature of Procedure: <br><br> Timing of Procedure: <br> Extent of Procedure: | |
| • **Account Balance/Transaction:** <br> Description of preliminary condition: | Nature of Procedure: <br><br> Timing of Procedure: <br> Extent of Procedure: | |
| • **Account Balance/Transaction:** <br> Description of preliminary condition: | Nature of Procedure: <br><br> Timing of Procedure: <br> Extent of Procedure: | |
| • **Account Balance/Transaction:** <br> Description of preliminary condition: | Nature of Procedure: <br><br> Timing of Procedure: <br> Extent of Procedure: | |
| • **Account Balance/Transaction:** <br> Description of preliminary condition: | Nature of Procedure: <br><br> Timing of Procedure: <br> Extent of Procedure: | |

Analysis Performed by: _____
Date: _____
Reviewed by: _____
Date: _____

## EXHIBIT AU-C 520-2—PERFORMANCE OF ANALYTICAL PROCEDURES

Use this form to document the performance of analytical procedures. The form is only a guide, and professional judgment should be exercised to determine how the form should be modified by omitting or adding analytical procedures.

Client Name: _____

Date of Financial Statements: _____

### COMPARISON OF CURRENT FINANCIAL STATEMENTS WITH COMPARABLE PRIOR-PERIOD FINANCIAL STATEMENTS

The following ratios were computed:

_____ Using financial data that reflect adjustments proposed to date.

_____ Using financial data that do not reflect adjustments.

## § 520 • Analytical Procedures

|   | Formula |
|---|---|
| **LIQUIDITY RATIOS** | |
| 1. Current ratio | $\dfrac{\text{Current Assets}}{\text{Current Liabilities}}$ |
| 2. Acid-test ratio | $\dfrac{\text{Quick Assets}}{\text{Current Liabilities}}$ |
| 3. Days' sales in accounts receivable | $\dfrac{\text{Average Accounts Receivable} \times 365 \text{ Days}}{\text{Net Credit Sales}}$ |
| 4. Current liabilities to total assets | $\dfrac{\text{Current Liabilities}}{\text{Total Assets}}$ |
| **ACTIVITY RATIOS** | |
| 1. Inventory turnover | $\dfrac{\text{Cost of Goods Sold}}{\text{Average Inventory}}$ |
| 2. Receivable turnover | $\dfrac{\text{Net Credit Sales}}{\text{Average Accounts Receivable}}$ |
| **OTHER RATIOS** | |
| 1. Asset turnover | $\dfrac{\text{Net Sales}}{\text{Average Total Assets}}$ |
| 2. Gross profit percentage | $\dfrac{\text{Gross Profit}}{\text{Net Sales}}$ |
| **PROFITABILITY RATIOS** | |
| 1. Bad debt to sales | $\dfrac{\text{Bad Debt Expense}}{\text{Net Sales}}$ |
| 2. Return on assets | $\dfrac{\text{Net Income}}{\text{Average Total Assets}}$ |
| 3. Return on equity | $\dfrac{\text{Net Income}}{\text{Average Total Equity}}$ |
| 4. Net margin | $\dfrac{\text{Net Income}}{\text{Net Sales}}$ |
| **COVERAGE RATIOS** | |
| 1. Debt to total assets | $\dfrac{\text{Total Debt}}{\text{Total Assets}}$ |
| 2. Interest expense to sales | $\dfrac{\text{Interest Expense}}{\text{Net Sales}}$ |
| 3. Number of times interest earned | $\dfrac{\text{Income before Interest and Taxes}}{\text{Interest Expenses}}$ |

## OTHER RATIOS

|   | | Formula |
|---|---|---|
| 1. | Effective tax rate | $\dfrac{\text{Income Taxes}}{\text{Income Before Taxes}}$ |
| 2. | Bad debt rate | $\dfrac{\text{Allowance for Bad Debts}}{\text{Accounts Receivable}}$ |
| 3. | Depreciation rate | $\dfrac{\text{Depreciation Expense}}{\text{Average Depreciable Property}}$ |
| 4. | Accounts payable to purchases | $\dfrac{\text{Accounts Payable}}{\text{Purchases}}$ |
| 5. | Dividend rate | $\dfrac{\text{Dividends}}{\text{Common Stock (Market Value)}}$ |
| 6. | Interest rate | $\dfrac{\text{Interest Expense}}{\text{Average Interest - Bearing Debt}}$ |
| 7. | Payroll rate | $\dfrac{\text{Payroll Expense}}{\text{Net Sales}}$ |
| 8. | Dividend return | $\dfrac{\text{Dividend Income}}{\text{Average Equity Investments}}$ |
| 9. | Interest income return | $\dfrac{\text{Interest Income}}{\text{Average Debt Investments}}$ |

## OTHER

### COMPARISON OF CURRENT FINANCIAL STATEMENTS WITH ANTICIPATED RESULTS

|   |   |   | 20XX |   |
|---|---|---|---|---|
| *Acct #* | *Account Name* | *Actual* | *Budgeted* | *Difference* |
| | Cash in bank—name | | | |
| | Petty cash | | | |
| | Cash in bank—payroll | | | |
| | Investment—marketable equity securities (current) | | | |
| | Allowance for decline in market value—marketable equity securities (current) | | | |
| | Accounts receivable | | | |
| | Allowance for doubtful accounts | | | |
| | Other receivables (current) | | | |
| | Accrued interest receivable | | | |
| | Notes receivable (current) | | | |
| | Discount on notes receivable | | | |
| | Dividends receivable | | | |
| | Inventory (year-end balance) | | | |
| | Prepaid insurance | | | |

| Acct # | Account Name | Actual | 20XX Budgeted | Difference |
|---|---|---|---|---|
| | Prepaid rent | | | |
| | Prepaid advertising | | | |
| | Land | | | |
| | Buildings | | | |
| | Accumulated depreciation—buildings | | | |
| | Delivery equipment | | | |
| | Accumulated depreciation—delivery equipment | | | |
| | Fixtures | | | |
| | Accumulated depreciation—fixtures | | | |
| | Office equipment | | | |
| | Accumulated depreciation—Office equipment | | | |
| | Property—capital leases | | | |
| | Investment—marketable equity securities (noncurrent) | | | |
| | Allowance for decline in market value—marketable equity securities (noncurrent) | | | |
| | Deferred bond issuance costs | | | |
| | Other receivables (noncurrent) | | | |
| | Investment—convertible bonds | | | |
| | Land held for investment | | | |
| | Accounts payable | | | |
| | Accrued liabilities | | | |
| | Payroll taxes and other withholdings | | | |
| | Interest payable | | | |
| | Notes payable | | | |
| | Discounts/premiums—notes payable | | | |
| | Obligations—capital leases (current) | | | |
| | Dividends payable | | | |
| | Income taxes payable | | | |
| | Notes payable (noncurrent) | | | |
| | Bonds payable | | | |
| | Discounts/premiums—bonds payable | | | |
| | Obligations—capital leases (noncurrent) | | | |
| | Common stock | | | |
| | Paid-in capital in excess of par | | | |
| | Unappropriated retained earnings | | | |

| Acct # | Account Name | Actual | 20XX Budgeted | Difference |
|---|---|---|---|---|
| | Appropriated retained earnings | | | |
| | Unrealized loss—marketable equity securities (noncurrent) | | | |
| | Sales | | | |
| | Sales returns and allowances | | | |
| | Sales discounts | | | |
| | Cost of goods sold | | | |
| | Purchases | | | |
| | Freight-in | | | |
| | Bad debt expense | | | |
| | Utilities expense | | | |
| | Travel expense | | | |
| | Advertising expense | | | |
| | Delivery expense | | | |
| | Miscellaneous expense | | | |
| | Insurance expense | | | |
| | Rent expense | | | |
| | Professional fees expense | | | |
| | Salaries and wages expense | | | |
| | Payroll taxes expense | | | |
| | Depreciation expense—buildings | | | |
| | Depreciation expense—delivery equipment | | | |
| | Depreciation expense—fixtures | | | |
| | Depreciation expense—office equipment | | | |
| | Depreciation expense—capital leases | | | |
| | Repairs and maintenance expense | | | |
| | Miscellaneous income | | | |
| | Extraordinary items | | | |
| | Dividend income | | | |
| | Interest income | | | |
| | Interest expense | | | |
| | Loss/gain on sale of assets | | | |
| | Unrealized loss—marketable equity securities | | | |
| | Recovery of market reduction of marketable equity securities (current) recorded in prior years | | | |
| | Loss on exchange of assets | | | |

| Acct # | Account Name | Actual | **20XX** Budgeted | Difference |
|---|---|---|---|---|
| | Loss due to permanent decline in value of security investments | | | |
| | Loss/gain on sale of investments | | | |
| | Income tax expense | | | |
| | Totals | | | |

Prepared By: _____

Reviewed By: _____

### STUDY OF FINANCIAL STATEMENT ELEMENTS AND UNEXPECTED RELATIONSHIPS

| Unexpected Relationships | Summary of Analysis |
|---|---|
| _____ | _____ |
| _____ | _____ |
| _____ | _____ |
| _____ | _____ |
| _____ | _____ |
| _____ | _____ |
| _____ | _____ |

### OTHER ANALYTICAL PROCEDURES

Summary of findings: _____

_____

_____

_____

Prepared By: _____

Date: _____

Reviewed By: _____

Date: _____

---

## EXHIBIT AU-C 520-3—EXAMPLE OF FINAL ANALYTICAL REVIEW

**Client:** _____

**Name:** _____

At this stage of the engagement it is important to consider the financial statements as a whole in light of the audit evidence that has been accumulated and in light of known and likely user expectations. The objective of this phase of the audit is to answer one very important question about the statement as they are presented:

Do these financial statement make sense?      Yes _____    No _____

Consider the following broad significant financial statement categories (please check):

Cash _____
Accounts receivable _____
Inventory _____
Fixed assets _____
Investments _____
Accounts payable & accrued expenses _____
Notes payable _____
Equity _____
Revenues _____
Cost of goods sold _____
Payroll _____
Other expenses _____

|  |  | Yes | No | N/A |
|---|---|---|---|---|
| 1. | Do they appear reasonable compared to | | | |
|  | a. Prior years? | _____ | _____ | _____ |
|  | b. Industry norms? | _____ | _____ | _____ |
|  | c. Current budget? | _____ | _____ | _____ |
| 2. | Do related data within the statement appear to be congruent? For example | _____ | _____ | _____ |
|  | a. Cost of sales compared to sales? | _____ | _____ | _____ |
|  | b. Cost of sales compared to inventory? | _____ | _____ | _____ |
|  | c. Payroll taxes, benefits, workers' compensation, compared to payroll? | _____ | _____ | _____ |
|  | d. Current assets compared to current liabilities? | _____ | _____ | _____ |
|  | e. Percent relations of income statement amounts to gross income? | _____ | _____ | _____ |
|  | f. Percent relations of significant expenses to total expenses? | _____ | _____ | _____ |
|  | g. Percent relation of significant assets/liabilities to total assets? | _____ | _____ | _____ |

|  | Yes | No | N/A |
|---|---|---|---|
| 3. Is there known nonfinancial information that corroborates financial data in the statements? | _____ | _____ | _____ |

Explain:

_____
_____
_____

4. Attach a draft copy of statements to this workpaper and make notations on them as appropriate.

# SECTION 530

# AUDIT SAMPLING

## Authoritative Pronouncements

SAS-122—Statements on Auditing Standards: Clarification and Recodification

SAS-142—Audit Evidence

## Overview

Auditors obtain appropriate audit evidence by performing audit procedures sufficient to afford a reasonable basis for an opinion on the financial statements. "Audit evidence" represents all the information used by an auditor in arriving at the conclusions that support his or her audit opinion.

Examining the documentation for every transaction of a business is costly and time-consuming. Because most audit objectives do not require that amount of evidence, auditors frequently use sampling techniques and procedures. AU-C 530 provides guidance regarding the auditor's use of statistical and non-statistical sampling when designing and selecting the audit sample, performing test of controls and tests of details, and evaluating sample results. The auditor's objective in using audit sampling is to provide a reasonable basis for drawing conclusions about the population from which the sample is selected.

> **PLANNING AID REMINDER:** AU-C 530 notes that there may be reasons other than performing sampling why an auditor would examine fewer than all of the items in a given population and that under these circumstances, the guidelines established in AU-C 530 are not applicable. One example is the auditor's performance of risk-assessment procedures to obtain an understanding of the entity and its environment, including its internal controls. Another example is an auditor deciding to confirm all receivables that have a balance of $1,000 or more. Previous AICPA Audit Risk Alerts point out that in this case the results of the confirmed items cannot be projected to the total balance of accounts receivable, because the auditor has not drawn a sample from all of the receivables. Sampling results cannot be projected to the population as a whole unless all of the items in the total population have had some chance for selection.

AU-C 530 endorses both a non-statistical approach and a statistical approach to sampling by concluding that either approach can provide sufficient audit evidence, as required by the third standard of fieldwork. Both non-statistical and statistical sampling are based on judgment, and the same factors are used in both approaches in order to determine the appropriate sample size and to evaluate the sample results.

§ 530 • *Audit Sampling*    **5081**

---

**PLANNING AID REMINDER:** For additional guidance, auditors may wish to reference the AICPA Audit Guide *Audit Sampling*, which provides practical guidance for auditors on the use of non-statistical and statistical sampling in auditing.

---

**IMPORTANT NOTICE FOR 2022:** In July 2020, the AICPA Auditing Standards Board (ASB) issued SAS No. 142, *Audit Evidence*, which supersedes AU-C 500 (*Audit Evidence*) and amends various other sections, including AU-C 530, in the professional standards. This SAS addresses the evolving nature of business and audit services and issues that include the use of emerging technologies by both preparers and auditors, audit data analytics (ADA), the application of professional skepticism, the expanding use of external information sources as audit evidence, and, more broadly, the accuracy, completeness, and reliability of audit evidence. This SAS is effective for audits of financial statements for periods ending on or after December 15, 2022.

---

## Definitions

| | |
|---|---|
| Audit sampling (sampling) | Selection and evaluation of a sample of items from a population of relevance to the audit (i.e., less than 100 percent of the population) such that the auditor expects the sample to be representative of the population and likely to provide a reasonable basis for conclusions about the population. A representative sample will result in conclusions that, subject to sampling risk limitations, are similar to those that would be drawn if the same procedures were applied to the population. |
| Population | The entire set of data from which a sample is selected and about which the auditor wishes to draw conclusions |
| Sampling risk | The risk that the auditor's conclusion based on a sample may be different from the conclusion if the entire population was subjected to the same audit procedure. Sampling risk can lead to two types of erroneous conclusions: <br> 1. The conclusion that controls are more effective than they actually are in a test of controls or that a material misstatement does not exist when it actually does in a test of details. This is the type of erroneous conclusion of primary concern to the auditor because it affects audit effectiveness and is more likely to lead to an inappropriate audit opinion. <br> 2. The conclusion that controls are less effective than they actually are in a test of controls or that a material misstatement exists when it actually does not in a test of details. This type of erroneous conclusion affects audit efficiency as it usually leads to additional work to establish that initial audit conclusions were incorrect, but audit effectiveness is not impacted. |
| Nonsampling risk | The risk that the auditor reaches an erroneous conclusion for any reason not related to sampling risk. |
| Sampling unit | Individual items constituting a population (may be physical items or monetary units). |

| | |
|---|---|
| Statistical sampling | An approach to sampling characterized by random selection of the sample items and the use of an appropriate statistical technique to evaluate sample results, including measurement of sampling risk. A sampling approach without these characteristics is considered non-statistical sampling. |
| Stratification | The process of dividing a population into subpopulations, each of which is a group of sampling units intended to have similar characteristics (often monetary value). |
| Tolerable misstatement | A monetary amount set by the auditor for which the auditor seeks to obtain an appropriate level of assurance that the set amount is not exceeded by the population's actual misstatement. |
| Tolerable rate of deviation | A rate of deviation set by the auditor for which the auditor seeks to obtain an appropriate level of assurance that the set deviation rate is not exceeded by the population's actual deviation rate. |

## Requirements

The auditor is presumptively required to use the following procedures when using audit sampling:

1. Consider the purpose of the audit procedure and the characteristics of the population from which the sample will be drawn when designing an audit sample.

2. Determine a sample size that will reduce sampling risk to an acceptably low level.

3. Select items for the sample such that there is a reasonable expectation that the sample is representative of the relevant population and likely to provide a reasonable basis for conclusions about the population.

4. Perform appropriate audit procedures on each item selected.

5. If an audit procedure is not applicable to a selected item, perform the procedure on a replacement item.

6. If unable to apply designed or suitable alternative audit procedures to a selected item, treat that item as a deviation from the prescribed control in a test of controls or a misstatement in a test of details.

7. Investigate the nature and cause of any identified deviations or misstatements and evaluate their possible effect on the purpose of the audit procedure and on other areas of the audit.

8. Project audit sampling results to the population.

9. Evaluate sample results, sampling risk, and whether the use of audit sampling provided a reasonable basis for conclusions about the population tested.

## Analysis and Application of Procedures

*Sample Design*

The auditor considers the purpose to be achieved and the combination of audit procedures likely to achieve that purpose when designing an audit sample. Considering this information helps the auditor to determine what population to sample and what conditions constitute a deviation or misstatement. The auditor is required to perform audit procedures to obtain evidence that the population from which the sample is drawn is complete. By considering the conditions constituting a deviation or misstatement, the auditor helps ensure that his or her evaluation of deviations or projection of misstatements contains all the deviations and misstatements and only conditions representing deviations or misstatements.

> **ENGAGEMENT STRATEGY:** Even if the auditor finds a condition during an audit procedure that does not constitute a deviation or misstatement, that condition may have an important effect on other areas of the audit.

When considering the characteristics of the population from which the sample will be drawn, the auditor may determine that the expected rate of deviation for a test of controls or the expected misstatement in a test of details is high. If the expected rate of deviation is unacceptably high, the auditor normally chooses not to perform the test of controls. If the expected misstatement is high, the auditor may use a larger sample size or examine the entire population in a test of details.

Nonsampling risk is a factor to be considered in the audit that cannot be measured, but it can be reduced to an acceptable level if an effective quality control system is implemented and the audit is adequately planned and supervised. Examples of nonsampling risk are (1) the selection of inappropriate auditing procedures and (2) the failure to identify an error on a document that the auditor is examining.

*Sample Size*

The auditor is responsible for obtaining sufficient appropriate audit evidence to reduce audit risk to an acceptably low level, allowing the auditor to draw reasonable conclusions on which to base the audit opinion. Sampling risk occurs because fewer than 100% of the sample units in a population are reviewed. For this reason, the auditor can reduce sampling risk by increasing the size of the sample. As detection risk for a specific audit objective decreases, the auditor's allowable risk of incorrect acceptance for the test of details decreases and the required sample size for the test increases.

> **FRAUD POINTER:** AU-C 240 notes that one of the auditor's overall responses to the risk of material misstatement due to fraud is to change the extent of audit procedures applied. When the risk of material misstatement due to fraud is considered high, auditors may decide to increase sample sizes or test the entire population instead of using a sample.

Sample size determination is influenced by many factors, such as the following.

For test of controls:

- Tolerable rate of deviation.
- Expected rate of deviation for the population to be tested.
- The desired level of assurance that the population's actual deviation rate does not exceed the tolerable deviation rate, which may be determined based on the extent to which the auditor's risk assessment takes relevant controls into account.
- The number of sampling units in a very small population (e.g., fewer than 500 sampling units).

For substantive tests of details:

- The desired level of assurance that the actual population misstatement does not exceed the tolerable misstatement, which may be determined based on the auditor's assessment of the risk of material misstatement and assurance obtained from other substantive procedures relating to the same assertion.
- To determine the desired level of assurance, the auditor would consider:
  — Tolerable misstatement,
  — Expected misstatement for the population,
  — Stratification of the population when performed, and
  — Number of sampling units in each stratum (for some sampling methods).

The auditor should not decide between using statistical or non-statistical sampling approaches based on sample size. Both approaches generally result in a similar sample size and the auditor using a non-statistical approach need not compute the corresponding sample size using statistical techniques. If the auditor uses a statistical approach, sample size will be determined from formulas or tables based on the factors described above. If a non-statistical approach is used, the auditor uses professional judgment to apply the above factors in determining sample size.

## Selecting Items for Testing

When selecting items for testing, the auditor may first examine items that have a higher risk of material misstatement and then use sampling to estimate some characteristic for the rest of the population. Statistical sampling selects items using random selection methods, including simple random, systematic random, monetary unit, and probability weighted selection. Non-statistical sampling uses haphazard or random-based selection to select sample items. The methods of selecting samples most frequently used are random, systematic, and haphazard selection.

## Performing Audit Procedures

When the auditor is unable to perform an audit procedure on a selected item, a replacement item may be used if the inability to perform the procedure does not represent a deviation from appropriate procedures by the entity. However, if the auditor's inability to perform an audit procedure on a selected item occurs because of a lack of evidence the entity should have, the auditor will need to evaluate the effect on the audit. The auditor should consider the items unable to be examined as deviations or misstatements and evaluate the effect on the sample results. If sample results do not change, examination of the items may not be necessary; if sample results do change such that the auditor would conclude there is a material misstatement or rate of deviation, the auditor is required to perform alternative audit procedures that would provide sufficient appropriate audit evidence to form a conclusion.

> **FRAUD POINTER:** In these circumstances, the auditor should also consider whether the reasons for his or her inability to examine the selected items have implications on the assessment of risks of material misstatement due to fraud, the assessed level of control risk the auditor expects to be supported, or the degree of reliance on management representations.

## Nature and Cause of Deviations and Misstatements

In examining the nature and causes of identified deviations and misstatements, the auditor should consider the qualitative aspects of the misstatements, including whether they were caused by fraud or error. Deviations and misstatements caused by fraud require a broader consideration of potential implications than those caused by error. The auditor may also notice a common feature in identified deviations or misstatements that may cause the auditor to extend his or her audit procedures to all the items in the population with that common feature.

> **ENGAGEMENT STRATEGY:** The auditor may also request that management examine a class of transactions, account balance, or disclosure to understand the cause of an identified misstatement, determine the actual misstatement amount, and adjust the financial statements appropriately.

## Projecting Misstatements

The auditor projects misstatements found in the sample in a test of details to the population, which provides an impression of the scale of the misstatement but may not be sufficient to determine an amount to be recorded. For tests of controls, the sample deviation rate represents the projected deviation rate for the population so no projection is necessary.

## Evaluating Audit Sample Results

If, in a test of controls, there is an unexpectedly high sample deviation rate, the assessed risks of material misstatement may be increased unless additional audit evidence is obtained supporting the initial assessment. If, in a test of details, there is an unexpectedly high misstatement amount in the sample, the auditor may conclude that a class of transactions or account balance is materially misstated unless further audit evidence is obtained that no material misstatement exists.

The tolerable misstatement amount set by the auditor is related to performance materiality. Performance materiality levels are determined to address the risk that when immaterial misstatements are aggregated, they may cause a material misstatement of the financial misstatements if a margin for potential undetected misstatements is not provided. Tolerable misstatement is the auditor's application of performance materiality to a particular sampling procedure and it may be the same or lower than the performance materiality level.

The projected misstatement is the auditor's best estimate of misstatement in a population in a test of details. As the projected misstatement amount approaches or exceeds the tolerable misstatement, the likelihood that the population's actual misstatement exceeds the tolerable misstatement increases. Also, if the projected misstatement is higher than the auditor's expectations, this could mean there is an unacceptable sampling risk that the actual population misstatement exceeds the tolerable misstatement. Under these circumstances, the auditor may consider the results of other audit procedures to assess the risks that the actual population misstatement exceeds the tolerable misstatement, and additional audit evidence may be obtained to reduce that risk.

If the auditor concludes that audit sampling has not provided a reasonable basis for conclusions about the tested population, the auditor may:

- Request management investigate identified misstatements and the potential for further misstatements and make any necessary adjustments; or
- Tailor the nature, timing, and extent of further audit procedures to best achieve the required assurance.

*Sampling Tests of Controls (Non-Statistical and Statistical Sampling Approaches)*

As stated earlier, attribute sampling measures the frequency of a specific occurrence in a particular population. This sampling technique is used to discover how often exceptions occur in the population under examination. Thus, attribute sampling is concerned with the qualitative characteristics of a sample—with tests of controls, which the auditor must perform in order to assess control risk at less than the maximum level.

## Promulgated Procedures Checklist

1. Determine the objectives of the test.
2. Define the deviation conditions.
3. Define the population:
    a. Define the period covered by the test.
    b. Define the sampling unit.
    c. Consider the completeness of the population.

4. Determine the method of selecting the sample:
    a. Random-number sampling.
    b. Systematic sampling.
    c. Other sampling.
5. Determine the sample size:
    a. Consider the allowable risk of assessing control risk too low.
    b. Consider the maximum rate of deviations from prescribed internal controls that would support the auditor's planned assessed level of control risk (tolerable rate).
    c. Consider the expected population deviation rate.
    d. Consider the effect of the population size.
    e. Consider statistical or non-statistical sampling methods.
6. Perform the sampling plan.
7. Evaluate the sample results:
    a. Calculate the deviation rate.
    b. Consider the sampling risk.
    c. Consider the qualitative aspects of the deviations.
    d. Reach an overall conclusion.
8. Document the sampling procedures.

## Analysis and Application of Procedures

### Step 1—Determine the objectives of the test

Generally, the use of sampling techniques in tests of controls applies only to those internal controls that generate documentary evidence. Thus, sampling techniques generally cannot be used in tests of controls for segregation of duties or the competency of personnel.

Tests of controls are concerned with determining whether a client's internal control operates in accordance with prescribed policies. Each internal control procedure has an objective and prescribed rules to obtain that objective. For example, in the credit department of a business, a control might state that orders must be appropriately approved for acceptance of credit risk before being processed. The objective of this control is to ensure that credit is approved before an order is accepted. This control must also include the prescribed rules for attaining the objective. One of the rules for attaining this particular objective for the credit department might be that no additional credit may be extended to any customer who has an outstanding balance more than sixty days old. The head of the credit department is responsible for ensuring that this control and its prescribed rules are consistently followed.

Every control objective must have one or more stated control techniques, which are designed to achieve the control objective.

Controls may be classified as preventive or detective. Preventive controls are established to prevent errors from occurring. Detective controls are established to detect errors that have occurred.

When performing tests of controls, the auditor must determine whether a specific internal control operates as designed and whether the control objective is being achieved. In this respect the auditor might be concerned with (1) who performed the control, (2) where the control was performed, and (3) whether the control was performed in accordance with prescribed policy.

The audit objective must be defined in terms of specific compliance characteristics that can be tested.

---

**FRAUD POINTER:** To address the ever-present risk of management override of internal control, AU-C 240 requires the auditor to examine journal entries and other adjustments for evidence of possible material misstatement due to fraud. One objective of the auditor's examination of journal entries is to determine the effectiveness of internal controls over journal entries and other adjustments. In light of the volume of journal entries to be examined as part of testing controls related to the journal entry process, auditors are likely to base their testing on samples of journal entries. Thus, the auditor's objective in this sample application is to obtain evidence that the internal controls over the journal entry process operate effectively.

---

**PUBLIC COMPANY IMPLICATIONS:** The Sarbanes-Oxley Act of 2002 (SOX) requires all accelerated filer public companies to issue a report by the auditor on the effectiveness of the entity's internal control over financial reporting. To provide the basis for the auditor's report on internal control, he or she performs tests of controls over financial reporting. In many circumstances, the auditor performs tests of controls of samples selected from the population of transactions subject to the internal controls being examined. Thus, the guidance in this section is especially relevant to public company auditors.

---

*Step 2—Define the deviation conditions*

A *deviation* is a departure from the prescribed internal control. The auditor must identify any significant deviation conditions that exist in a control. A significant deviation condition exists when a necessary step to achieve a particular internal control objective is not performed as prescribed. The auditor might consider that some internal controls, such as multiple approvals, are unimportant and need not be tested.

*Step 3—Define the population*

The population selected for examination must be complete and must provide the auditor with the opportunity to satisfy the established audit objective. A sample should be selected in a manner that is representative of the population from which it is selected. If the population is not complete in all respects, the selected sample will not be representative of the complete population. For example, the audit objective may be to determine whether all goods that are shipped are properly billed. For this audit objective, the auditor should define the population as bills of lading or other shipping records prepared during the audit period—rather than sales invoices, which may or may not represent goods that have been shipped.

### Step 3a—Define the period covered by the test

A conclusion can be drawn about a population only if all items in the population have a chance of being selected for examination. The population from which the sample is selected should include all transactions for the accounting period under examination. However, professional standards recognize that it may be appropriate to perform tests of controls at interim dates and review subsequent transactions when the auditor performs year-end audit procedures.

### Step 3b—Define the sampling unit

A population consists of a number of sampling units, such as cancelled checks or sales invoices. For example, if the audit objective is to determine whether vouchers have been properly approved, the sampling items may be the line items in the voucher register rather than the checks used to pay the vouchers. Once the auditor adequately defines the population, the sample unit should not be difficult to define.

### Step 3c—Consider the completeness of the population

The physical representation of the population must be consistent with the definition of the population. For example, the auditor might be concerned with all cash disbursements made during the period and define the population as all cancelled checks during the period. The auditor must determine that the defined population is complete; otherwise, a representative sample cannot be drawn from the population.

### Step 4—Determine the method of selecting the sample

Sampling units must be selected from the defined population so that each sampling unit has a chance of being selected. AU-C 530 requires that a representative sample be selected for both non-statistical sampling and statistical sampling. When statistical sampling is used, the sample must be selected on an unbiased basis (usually a random selection).

**ENGAGEMENT STRATEGY:** AU-C 530 notes that auditors should select sample items so that the sample is representative of the population. A representative sample is one in which all items in a population have an equal opportunity of being included in the sample. A randomly selected sample meets that definition, and random selection is often the technique used to select samples for statistical sampling applications. However, auditors also often use random selection techniques for non-statistical sampling plans to increase the likelihood that those samples are representative of the population. The use of a representative sample reduces sampling risk.

## Step 4a—Random-number sampling

A sample may be selected from the population on a random basis using random numbers generated by a computer or numbers chosen from a random-number table.

## Step 4b—Systematic sampling

The auditor may select a random sample using the systematic-selection method, whereby every $n$th item is selected. Systematic selection is also referred to as sequential sampling. The following steps should be followed when systematic selection is used:

1. Determine the population ($N$).
2. Determine the sample size ($n$).
3. Compute the interval size by dividing $N$ by $n$.
4. Select a random start (a random-number table can be used to determine the starting point).
5. Determine the sample items selected by successively adding the interval to the random starting point.

To illustrate the systematic-selection method, assume that the auditor has defined the population as 3,000 sales invoices listed in the sales journal ($N$) and would like to select 100 sales invoices for testing ($n$). Thus, the interval is every thirtieth sales invoice (3,000/100). If it is assumed that the auditor selects the number 12 as a random starting point, the first sales invoice selected would be the twelfth invoice, the second would be the forty-second invoice (12 + 30), and so on, until the sample of 100 items is selected.

A client might summarize or group a population in a specific order, and thus such a population would not be random. A sample selected from a non-random population using the systematic-selection method might not be appropriate for drawing statistical conclusions about a population, unless the auditor takes steps to solve the randomness problem. The auditor should examine the population to determine whether it has been grouped or summarized in a particular order. Inquiries of client personnel may also be made to ascertain how individual transactions are accumulated or individual balances listed. If the population is in a specific order, it should be stratified and proportional samples should be drawn from each stratum. In this event, the auditor might want to test one or more of the strata more extensively.

Even if the population is not in a specific order, it usually is advisable for the auditor to have two or more random starts.

## Step 4c—Other sampling

Block sampling refers to selecting contiguous sampling units, such as all checks numbered from 420 to 440. Block sampling cannot be used when the auditor uses a statistical sampling approach. When the auditor uses only a few blocks to select the sample, block sampling also would be inappropriate for a non-statistical sampling approach.

Haphazard sampling consists of selecting sampling units without any conscious bias. For example, the selection would be biased if the auditor had a tendency to select vendor folders that had the most vendor invoices in them. If properly applied, haphazard sampling can be used for non-statistical sampling but not for a statistical sampling approach.

*Step 5—Determine the sample size*

A considerable amount of professional judgment is necessary to determine the proper sample size. The method for reaching a decision for determining the sample size is the same for non-statistical sampling as it is for statistical sampling. In statistical sampling, the auditor will quantify the factors that are used to determine the sample size; in non-statistical sampling, the factors will be described in subjective terms. For example, in statistical sampling, the auditor may conclude that a 10% factor should be assigned to the risk of assessing control risk too low. In non-statistical sampling, the auditor may conclude that the client's internal controls appear to be well-designed. Both conclusions are highly subjective and are based on the same fundamental analysis, although the conclusion associated with statistical sampling is more precise.

**EXHIBIT AU-C 530-1—AUDIT JUDGMENT FACTORS USED IN NON-STATISTICAL AND STATISTICAL SAMPLING TO DETERMINE SAMPLE SIZE FOR TESTS OF CONTROLS**

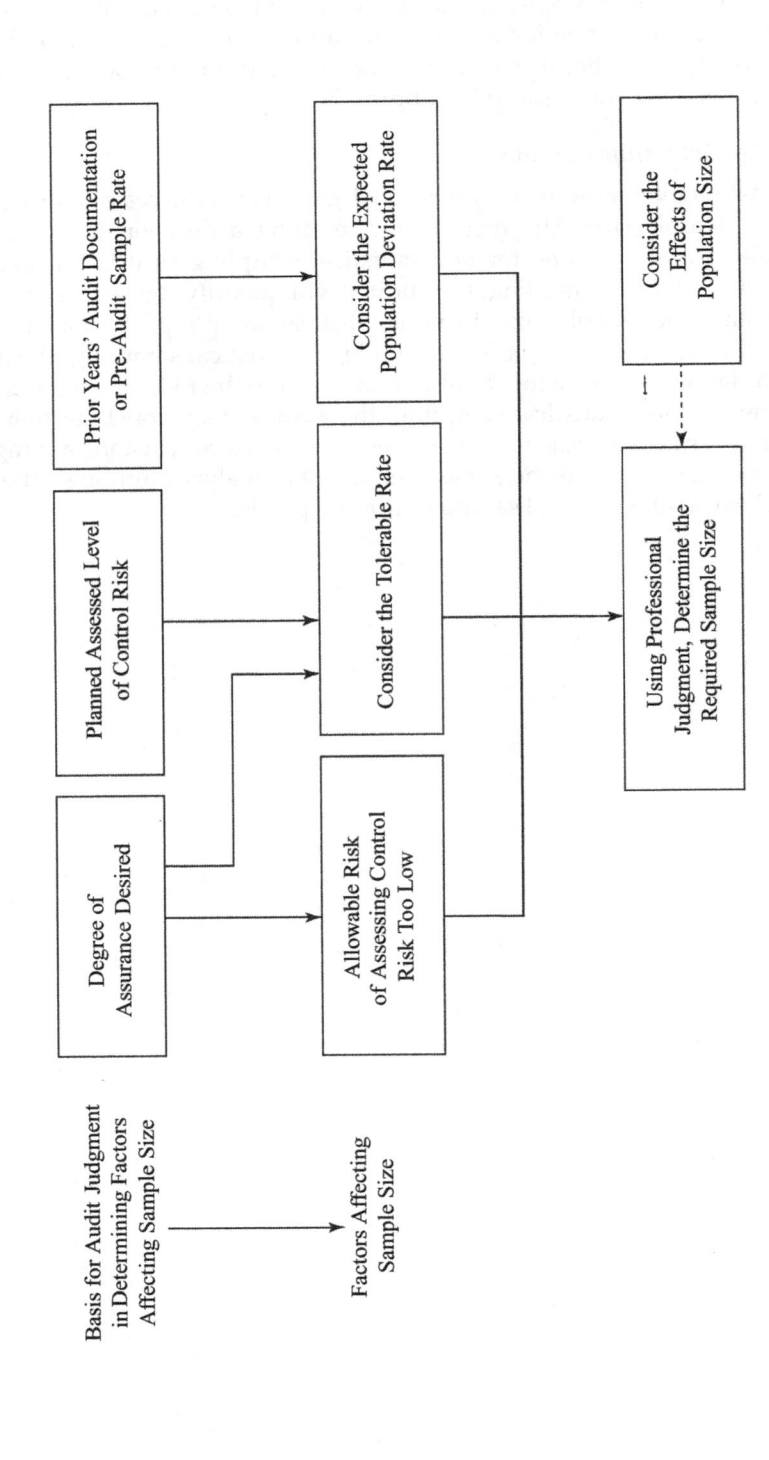

The audit decision process is summarized in Exhibit AU-C 530-1.

*Step 5a—Consider the allowable risk of assessing control risk too low*

The level of sampling risk is influenced by the size of the sample. There is always a risk that the auditor will not draw a representative sample. The larger the sample, the more audit hours it takes to test the sample. Achieving an acceptable level of sampling risk is the result of a trade-off between trying to avoid overauditing on the one hand and underauditing on the other.

Establishing an allowable risk of assessing control risk too low is a function of the degree of assurance indicated by the audit evidence selected as part of the sample process. If the auditor desires a high degree of assurance, it is necessary to establish a relatively small risk of assessing control risk too low. Establishing a small risk of assessing control risk too low will require that (assuming all other factors remain constant) the auditor increase the size of the sample. The larger the sample size, the higher the degree of assurance the auditor can offer about the effectiveness of internal control. For example, if using a non-statistical sample, the auditor must select a larger sample in order to establish a low risk of underestimating control risk rather than establishing a moderate risk of assessing control risk too low. When using statistical sampling, the auditor must select a larger sample size in order to make a statement about the maximum error rate at a 99% confidence level (or a 1% allowable risk of assessing control risk too low) rather than at a 90% confidence level.

*Step 5b—Consider the tolerable rate*

The "tolerable rate" is the maximum percentage of deviations (errors) in a population that an auditor will tolerate without changing the planned assessed level of control risk. The establishment of a tolerable rate in an engagement is based on (1) the planned assessed level of control risk and (2) the degree of assurance indicated by the audit evidence in the sample.

The planned assessed level of control risk results from obtaining an understanding of the client's internal control. Having gained an understanding of the client's internal control, the auditor then establishes the planned level of control risk, which in turn is a factor in determining the sample size for tests of control. For example, if an internal control is considered highly relevant to a critical financial statement assertion, the auditor would initially plan to rely relatively heavily on the control procedure and there would be a tendency to establish a small tolerable rate.

*Step 5c—Consider the expected population deviation rate*

The purpose of attribute sampling for non-statistical as well as statistical sampling is to provide some insight into the deviation rate of a particular characteristic in a population. For example, the auditor may be interested in the rate of pricing errors the client made in preparing customer invoices. However, before sampling can begin, the auditor must make a preliminary estimate of the deviation rate. The expected population deviation rate is the anticipated deviation rate in the entire population. Ideally, the estimate should be based on the results of audits of prior years, taking into consideration any subsequent modifications of the client's internal control. The auditor may review audit documentation for the last few years to obtain an idea of the expected population deviation rate. In a new engagement, the auditor can estimate the expected population deviation rate by selecting and auditing a preliminary sample of about 25 items. The results of the test should be properly documented, because the preliminary sample becomes part of the final sample.

As the expected population deviation rate approaches the tolerable rate that the auditor established, the required sample size increases because the auditor must make an allowance for sampling risk. That is, if the auditor establishes a tolerable rate of 5% but the preliminary estimate of the deviation rate is 4%, in most situations the risk is too great that the actual deviation rate is more than 5%. In non-statistical and statistical sampling, it is misleading to think of estimating a single error rate. It is more useful to think of estimating an error range. In the current example, if the auditor is using non-statistical sampling, it is better to think of the preliminary estimate of the deviation rate of being somewhere around 4%. If statistical sampling is used, the auditor may state that the estimated deviation rate is 4% plus or minus 2% (a range between 2% and 6%). Clearly, when the expected population deviation rate for a particular internal control is equal to or greater than the tolerable rate, the auditor should establish the control risk at its maximum level and generally not complete the test of controls, at least for the particular control(s) under investigation.

### Step 5d—Consider the effect of the population size

In most circumstances, the size of the population has little and sometimes no effect on the determination of the required sample size in attribute sampling.

### Step 5e—Consider a statistical or non-statistical sampling method

The auditor may use either a non-statistical sampling method or a statistical sampling method.

***Sample size and non-statistical sampling*** When using non-statistical sampling, the auditor takes into consideration the risk of assessing control risk too low, the tolerable rate, and the expected population deviation rate, and determines the sample size by professional judgment. The auditor should observe the following generalizations in determining the sample size when non-statistical sampling is employed:

- As the risk of assessing control risk too low increases, the required sample size decreases.
- As the risk of assessing control risk too low decreases, the required sample size increases.
- As the tolerable rate increases, the required sample size decreases.
- As the tolerable rate decreases, the required sample size increases.
- As the expected population deviation rate increases, the required sample size increases.
- As the expected population deviation rate decreases, the required sample size decreases.

*Sample size and statistical sampling* For statistical sampling, the auditor can use tables or computer applications to determine the appropriate sample size. To use either tables or computer applications, the following must be established by the auditor:

- The risk of assessing control risk too low,
- The tolerable error rate, and
- The expected population deviation rate.

For example, if an auditor established (1) the risk of assessing control risk too low at 5%, (2) a tolerable error rate of 9%, and (3) an expected population deviation rate of 4%, the required sample size would be about 100.

## Step 6—Perform the sampling plan

After the sample has been selected, the auditor should apply audit procedures to each sampling unit to determine whether there has been a deviation from the established internal control procedure. Usually, a deviation occurs if the auditor is unable to perform an audit procedure or apply alternative audit procedures to a sampling unit. As a general rule, sampling units that are selected but not examined, such as voided transactions or unused documents, should be replaced with new sampling units. Voided transactions or unused documents are not considered deviations if the established procedure of accounting for these items has been properly followed.

## Step 7—Evaluate the sample results

After the audit procedures have been applied to each sampling unit, and the deviations, if any, from the prescribed internal controls have been summarized, the auditor must evaluate the results of the sampling.

## Step 7a—Calculate the deviation rate

The deviation rate is computed by dividing the number of deviations by the number of units in the sample. The sample deviation rate is the auditor's best estimate of the population deviation rate.

## Step 7b—Consider the sampling risk

The auditor must consider the degree of sampling risk involved in the sample results. Sampling risk arises because the auditor does not examine all of the sampling units in a population. An auditor can reach an entirely different conclusion on the basis of sample results than if the entire population is examined. When the auditor's estimate of the population deviation is less than the tolerable rate for the population, there is still a possibility that the true deviation rate in the population (maximum population deviation) is greater than the tolerable rate. The auditor can determine the degree of sampling risk in the sample results by computing the maximum population deviation rate.

*Sampling risk and non-statistical sampling* When the auditor employs non-statistical sampling, the sampling risk cannot be quantified; the auditor should nonetheless take that risk into consideration in determining whether the potential error rate in the population is unacceptable. The auditor should observe the following generalizations when evaluating the results of non-statistical sampling:

- The auditor may rely on the planned assessed level of control risk when the auditor's best estimate of the population deviation rate (based on the sample results) is equal to or less than the expected population deviation rate.
- The auditor cannot rely on the planned assessed level of control risk when the auditor's best estimate of the population deviation rate is greater than the expected population deviation rate.

When the deviation rate is greater than the tolerable rate, the planned assessed level of control risk is not justified. Thus, the auditor may, for example, decide not to rely on the client's internal control (assess control risk at the maximum) in the performance of substantive procedures.

*Sampling risk and statistical sampling* When using statistical sampling, the auditor can use tables or computer applications to measure the allowance for sampling risk. To use either tables or computer applications, the following must be established by the auditor:

- The risk of assessing control risk too low,
- The number of actual deviations found in the sample,
- The sample size, and
- The expected deviation rate.

To illustrate the above procedures, assume that the risk the auditor has established for assessing control risk too low is 5%, the sample size established by the auditor is 100, the tolerable rate established by the auditor is 9%, and the expected population deviation rate established by the auditor is 4%. If the auditor examines the 100 sample units and discovers two errors, the maximum population deviation rate (obtained from tables in Appendix A of the AICPA's *Audit Sampling* Guide) is 6.2%. The maximum population deviation rate is also referred to as the upper limits or the upper precision limits.

In the above illustration, the auditor can be 95% certain that the maximum population deviation rate is 6.2%. The 95% certainty percentage is the complement of the 5% risk factor (100% minus 5%). Since the maximum deviation rate of 6.2% is less than the tolerable rate of 9% established by the auditor, the planned assessed level of control risk is not changed. However, when the maximum population deviation rate is greater than the tolerable rate established by the auditor, the planned assessed level of control risk is not justified.

*Step 7c—Consider the qualitative aspects of the deviations*

The auditor should consider the qualitative aspects of each deviation. The nature and cause of each deviation should be analyzed and deviations should be classified into unintentional deviations (errors) or intentional deviations (acts of fraud). The auditor should make a determination about whether the deviation resulted from a misunderstanding of instructions or from carelessness. The discovery of an act of fraud would require more attention from the auditor than the discovery of an error.

*Step 7d—Reach an overall conclusion*

The auditor must determine whether the overall audit approach supports the planned assessed level of control risk. To make this overall evaluation, the auditor should consider the following factors:

- Sample results of tests of controls,
- Results of inquiries about controls that do not leave an audit trail, and
- Results of observations concerning control procedures that are based on the segregation of responsibilities.

Professional judgment is required in reaching a conclusion on how the results of the tests of controls will affect the nature, timing, and extent of the subsequent substantive procedures.

*Step 8—Document the sampling procedures*

The auditor should consider the following matters for documentation in the audit files:

- Description of internal controls tested,
- Objective of the tests of controls,
- Definition of population and sampling unit,
- Definition of deviation conditions,
- Method of determining sample size,
- Method of sample selection,
- Description of audit procedures employed and list of deviations discovered by the auditor [deviations should be classified as unintentional and (suspected) intentional acts], and
- Evaluation of sample results and overall conclusions.

## Sampling in Tests of Details (Non-Statistical and Statistical Sampling Approaches)

Variable sampling (which is used in the performance of substantive tests of transactions and balances) is used to estimate the dollar value of a population and determine the reasonableness of financial statement balances. The purpose of substantive procedures is to obtain evidence of the validity and propriety of accounting balances and classes of transactions.

## Promulgated Procedures Checklist

The auditor may use the following steps to apply variable sampling to substantive procedures:

1. Determine the audit objective of the test.
2. Define the population:
   a. Define the sampling unit.
   b. Consider the completeness of the population.
   c. Identify individually significant items.
3. Choose an audit sampling technique.
4. Determine the sample size:
   a. Consider variations within the population.
   b. Consider the acceptable level of risk.
   c. Consider the tolerable misstatement.
   d. Consider the expected amount of misstatement.
   e. Consider the population size.
5. Determine the method of selecting the sample.
6. Perform the sampling plan.
7. Evaluate the sample results:
   a. Project the misstatement to the population and consider sampling risk.
   b. Consider the qualitative aspects of misstatements and reach an overall conclusion.
8. Document the sampling procedures.

## Analysis and Application of Procedures

*Step 1—Determine the audit objective of the test*

The audit objective of performing substantive procedures is to determine whether the dollar value assigned by management to an account balance or group of transactions is reasonable.

*Step 2—Define the population*

The population the auditor defines must include all items that are related to the audit objective of the procedures. If items relevant to the audit objective are omitted from the population, the audit objective of the procedure will not be achieved. For example, the audit objective may be to determine whether the repairs and maintenance expense account is reasonably stated. The definition of the population could be all line items that make up the detail of the account, but such a definition would probably be deficient because other accounts—especially property, plant, and equipment—could contain expenditures that were capitalized when they should have been expensed. A better definition of the population would be all repairs and maintenance work orders authorized during the period.

*Step 2a—Define the sampling unit*

The population is made up of individual sampling units that may be individual transactions, documents, customer or vendor balances, or an individual entry. The auditor must consider the efficiency of the audit when selecting the sampling unit. For example, it may be more efficient to define the sampling unit as the individual sales invoice—rather than as the individual accounts receivable, which may be made up of several invoices.

*Step 2b—Consider the completeness of the population*

The physical representation of the population must be consistent with the definition of the population. For example, the auditor may be concerned with all cash disbursements made during the period and define the population as all cancelled checks during the period. The auditor must determine that the defined population is complete; otherwise, a representative sample cannot be drawn from the population.

*Step 2c—Identify individually significant items*

The population should be reviewed for items that should be individually examined because of the audit exposure related to these items. Items that should be examined individually include large-dollar items, related-party transactions, and accounts with a history of errors. When items are examined individually, they are not part of the sampling results; however, these items must be considered in determining the possible misstatement in the population. There is, therefore, no sampling risk associated with these items.

*Step 3—Choose an audit sampling technique*

Initially, the auditor must determine whether a non-statistical or a statistical sampling approach should be employed. As stated earlier, AU-C 530 indicates no preference of one over the other. Whether a non-statistical or a statistical sampling approach is used, many different types of sampling techniques are used in practice. Irrespective of the sampling approach or specific sampling technique the auditor uses, he or she must observe the following steps in the performance of substantive procedures based on sampling.

*Step 4—Determine the sample size*

The auditor must use professional judgment to determine the sample size. The decision process for determining the sample size is the same for non-statistical sampling as it is for statistical sampling. In statistical sampling the auditor will quantify the relevant factors, whereas in non-statistical sampling the factors will be described in a less structured manner.

The audit decision process for determining the sample size as described in AU-C 530 is summarized in Exhibit AU-C 530-2.

*Step 4a—Consider variations within the population*

A basic concept in sampling is the need to obtain a representative sample from the population. If the population is composed of various items, the auditor must examine a sufficiently large sample to be reasonably assured that a representative sample has been selected.

For accounting populations, the variation within a population may be expressed in dollar amounts. It is not unusual for an accounting population to be composed of a few large balances, several medium balances, and numerous smaller balances. The required sample size increases as the variability in the population increases.

# § 530 • Audit Sampling

## EXHIBIT AU-C 530-2—AUDIT JUDGMENT FACTORS USED TO DETERMINE SAMPLE SIZE FOR SUBSTANTIVE PROCEDURES

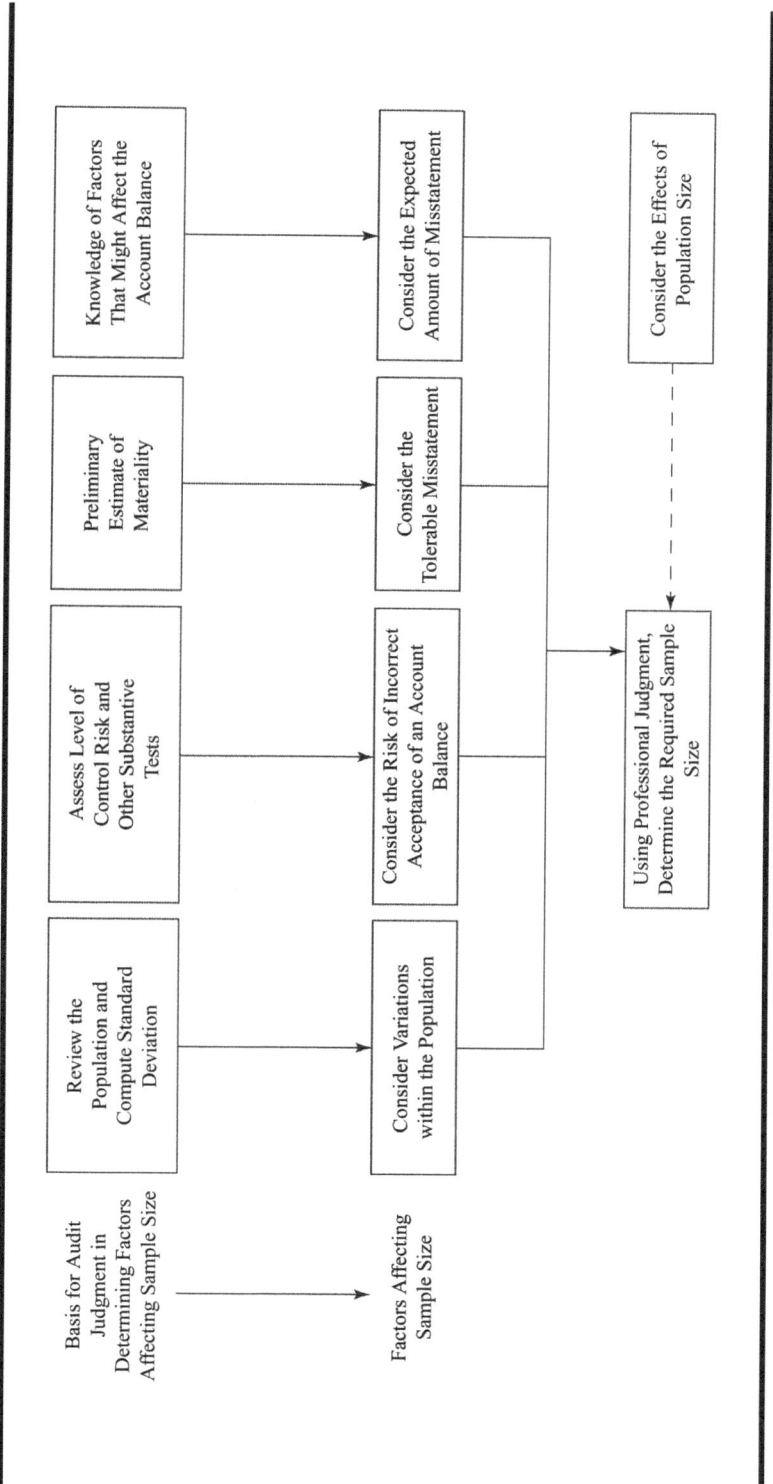

When nonstatistical sampling is employed, the auditor may review the population or the prior years' audit documentation to acquire an understanding of the variation within the population. When a classical variable statistical sampling technique is employed, the auditor measures the variation in the population by computing the estimate of the standard deviation of the sample mean.

It may be efficient to stratify a population with a high degree of variation. "Stratification" simply means that the population is divided into groups (strata) of sampling units that have the same or approximately the same dollar values, and samples are selected from each group. Stratification is necessary to reduce the effect of the variation in the population on the size of the sample. (In both nonstatistical sampling and statistical sampling, as the variation increases, the auditor needs to select a larger sample size.)

**ENGAGEMENT STRATEGY:** When probability proportional to size (PPS) sampling is used, there is no need to consider the variation within the population, because this technique automatically considers that factor since it is a combination of both attribute sampling and variable estimation.

*Step 4b—Consider the acceptable level of risk*

When considering whether to accept or reject the results of a sample, the auditor is faced with the risks of (1) incorrect rejection of a balance and (2) incorrect acceptance of a balance. The risk of incorrect rejection of a balance is the risk that the results of a sample will lead the auditor to conclude that the recorded account balance is materially misstated when, in fact, the recorded account balance is not materially misstated. The risk of incorrect acceptance of a balance is the risk that the results of a sample will lead the auditor to conclude that the recorded account balance is not materially misstated when, in fact, the recorded account balance is materially misstated.

In determining an acceptable level of risk of incorrect acceptance for tests of details, the auditor should consider (1) the assessed risk of material misstatement (inherent risk and control risk) and (2) the risk that other relevant substantive procedures (including substantive analytical procedures) would not detect a material misstatement. These risk factors and interrelationships must be considered in non-statistical sampling plans as well as in statistical sampling plans. These relationships are in the following manner:

$$TD = AR/(IR \times CR \times AP)$$

where:

- $AR$ = the allowable audit risk that monetary misstatements equal to tolerable misstatement might remain undetected for the account balance or class of transactions and related assertions after the auditor has completed all audit procedures deemed necessary.
- $IR$ = the susceptibility of an assertion to a material misstatement assuming there are no related internal controls.

- CR = the risk that a material misstatement that could occur in an assertion will not be prevented or detected on a timely basis by the entity's internal controls. (The auditor assesses control risk on the basis of the sufficiency of audit evidence obtained to support the effectiveness of internal controls.)
- AP = the risk that analytical procedures and other relevant substantive procedures would fail to detect misstatements that could occur in an assertion equal to tolerable misstatement, given that such misstatements occur and are not detected by the internal control.
- TD = the allowable risk of incorrect acceptance for the test of details, given that misstatements equal to tolerable misstatement occur in an assertion and are not detected by internal control or analytical procedures and other relevant substantive procedures.

The above equation emphasizes relationships among the various factors that the auditor must consider when determining the allowable risk of incorrect acceptance. For example, as control risk rises, the allowable risk of incorrect acceptance must decrease to achieve a stated level of audit risk. That relationship is based on the simple logic that as the perceived effectiveness of internal control decreases, the auditor is less willing to establish a high allowable risk of incorrect acceptance of an account balance. Stated in terms of its effect on sample size, it is necessary to increase the size of the sample as control risk increases to reduce the level of risk of incorrect acceptance. Thus, from the perspective of sample size and all other factors remaining constant, there is an inverse relationship between control risk and the allowable risk of incorrect acceptance.

Although the relationships established in the above equation are intuitive, it is unlikely that an auditor would assign an absolute value to audit risk; rather he or she would evaluate the risk in an abstract manner. Even when statistical sampling is employed, most auditors would use the relationships established by the equation as a guide, avoiding a strict and comprehensive quantitative approach arrived at by simply plugging in risk factors. When an auditor insists on a strictly quantitative approach, that does not imply that judgment has been removed from the process. In a strictly quantitative approach, the process may appear to be unbiased but, as discussed in this section, the risk factors are based on a number of decisions that depend heavily on professional judgments. Those judgments are the same for non-statistical sampling and statistical sampling.

*Step 4c—Consider the tolerable misstatement*

The tolerable misstatement is an estimate of the maximum monetary misstatement that may exist in an account balance or group of transactions when combined with misstatement in other accounts, without causing the financial statements to be materially misstated. The tolerable misstatement is based on the auditor's definition of "materiality," or the maximum amount by which the financial statements could be misstated and still be in accordance with generally accepted accounting principles. There is an inverse relationship between the tolerable misstatement and the required sample size. Thus, the sample size must be increased when the tolerable misstatement is decreased.

Tolerable misstatement is related to the auditor's planned level of materiality for the financial statements as a whole such that tolerable misstatement when combined for all planned audit procedures does not exceed materiality for the financial statements. Thus, auditors should set tolerable misstatement for a specific audit procedure at an amount less than the financial statements so that when the results are aggregated, the required level of overall assurance is obtained.

*Step 4d—Consider the expected amount of misstatement*

An estimate of the expected amount of misstatement in a particular account balance or group of transactions is based on the following factors:
- Understanding of the entity's business,
- Prior years' tests of the population,
- Results of a pre-audit sample, and
- Results of tests of controls.

The required sample size increases as the auditor's estimate of the expected amount of misstatement in the population increases.

---

**PLANNING AID REMINDER:** In practice it is often difficult to determine the expected amount of misstatement, but this can be overcome by combining the effects of the tolerable misstatement and the expected amount of misstatement. This can be accomplished by establishing a materiality threshold and then dividing that amount by "about 2" in order to establish the tolerable misstatement. For example, if materiality is established at $100,000, then the tolerable misstatement would be about $50,000 ($100,000/2). Then only the (adjusted) tolerable misstatement would be used to determine the required sample size.

---

*Step 4e—Consider the population size*

The population size generally has an effect on the sample size, depending on which sampling technique the auditor employs.

*Step 5—Determine the method of selecting the sample*

The auditor must select sampling units from the defined population in such a way that each sampling unit has a chance of being selected. The auditor's objective is to select a representative sample of all items from the population. If statistical sampling is used, the sample selection must be random.

*Step 6—Perform the sampling plan*

Once the sample has been selected, the auditor should apply appropriate audit procedures. If the auditor is unable to perform an audit procedure on a sampling unit selected for examination, alternative audit procedures should be considered. If the sampling unit does not have an effect on the conclusion the auditor reaches concerning the acceptability of the population, alternative audit procedures do not have to be applied, and the sampling unit may be treated as a misstatement for evaluation purposes. In addition, the auditor should determine whether the inability to apply an audit procedure has an effect on the assessed level of control risk or the assessment of risk on representations made by the client.

## Step 7—Evaluate the sample results

After testing the sample units, the auditor should evaluate the sample results to determine whether the account balance or group of transactions is correct and in accordance with generally accepted accounting principles.

## Step 7a—Project the misstatement to the population and consider sampling risk

The misstatements discovered in the sampling units should be projected to the total population. In its simplest form, a $2,000 misstatement in a sample that represents 20% of the population would be projected as a total misstatement of $10,000 ($2,000/20%). The method of projecting the misstatement to the total population will depend on the type of sampling technique the auditor uses.

If the projected misstatement is greater than the tolerable misstatement, the account balance cannot be accepted as correct. If the projected misstatement is significantly less than the tolerable misstatement, the auditor may conclude that the account balance is not materially misstated. For example, if the projected misstatement is $10,000 and the tolerable misstatement is $50,000, in most instances the risk of accepting an incorrect balance would be acceptable. As the projected misstatement approaches the tolerable misstatement, the risk of accepting an incorrect balance increases, and the auditor must use professional judgment in deciding whether to accept a balance as correct. For example, if the projected misstatement is $40,000 and the tolerable misstatement is $50,000, in most instances the risk of accepting an incorrect balance would not be acceptable.

## Step 7b—Consider the qualitative aspects of misstatements and reach an overall conclusion

Each misstatement the auditor discovers by testing the sample should be evaluated to determine why the misstatement was made and whether the misstatement has an effect on other phases of the engagement. For example, the discovery of a fraudulent act would have broader implication to the auditor than the discovery of a routine error.

The results of the substantive procedures may suggest that the assessed level of control risk was too low. Such a condition would require the auditor to consider whether substantive procedures should be expanded.

## Step 8—Document the sampling procedures

The auditor should consider the following matters for documentation in the audit files:

- Description of audit procedures and objectives tested;
- Definition of population and sampling unit;
- Definition of a misstatement;
- Basis for establishment of risk of incorrect acceptance, incorrect rejection, tolerable misstatement, and expected misstatement;

- Audit sampling technique used;
- Method of sampling selection;
- Description of sampling procedures performed and list of misstatements discovered [deviations should be classified as unintentional and (suspected) intentional acts]; and
- Evaluation of sample and summary of overall conclusions.

### NON-STATISTICAL SAMPLING FOR TESTS OF DETAIL

This section is based on the discussion in the previous section, but it focuses exclusively on non-statistical sampling for tests of detail. The guidance provided here is based on material in Chapter 5 of the AICPA's Audit Guide *Audit Sampling* (a new edition of this Guide was released by the AICPA as of December 1, 2019).

## Promulgated Procedures Checklist

The auditor may use the following steps to apply non-statistical sampling concepts to tests of details:

- Identify individually significant items,
- Determine the sample size,
- Select the sample, and
- Evaluate the sample results.

## Analysis and Application of Procedures

### *Identify Individually Significant Items*

Initially the auditor should review the items that make up the population to determine whether certain items should be tested 100% rather than sampled. The items selected for 100% testing might be based on the dollar value of the item or unusual characteristics of the item. For example, an auditor may review the trial balance of accounts receivable and decide that all receivables that exceed $1,000 should be selected for confirmation. Generally larger-dollar amounts within a population are selected for 100% testing based on the auditor's judgment.

### *Determine the Sample Size*

The size of the sample in non-statistical sampling is based on professional judgment. The auditor cannot simply decide to use a rule of thumb in all engagements and expect to satisfy professional standards or to perform an effective engagement. For example, if the auditor has a rule of thumb that he or she always confirms 10% of the dollar value of accounts receivable, that approach is a violation of generally accepted auditing standards.

The Audit Guide *Audit Sampling* points out that when an auditor uses non-statistical sampling to perform test of details, the following four factors (discussed in the previous section) must be taken into consideration:

1. Population variation,
2. Risk of incorrect acceptance,
3. Tolerable misstatement and expected misstatement, and
4. Population size.

Although these factors sound like concepts that are found in a statistics course, they are actually based on common sense.

---

**PLANNING AID REMINDER:** Although the auditor must take the four factors listed above into consideration in determining the size of the sample, he or she does not have to quantify these factors. Also, some auditors believe that there is some simple solution to determining sample size that does not have to take into consideration the four factors listed above. There is no simple rule-of-thumb solution. An auditor must take these factors into consideration and use professional judgment to determine the size of a sample, even when non-statistical sampling is used.

---

*Population variation*

In general, the more homogenous the population, the smaller the sample size can be. That is, for example, if the trial balance of accounts receivable is made up of balances that range from $150 to $220, there is little variation in the population. For this reason, an auditor can test relatively few items in order to get a representative sample of the accounts receivable. On the other hand, if the range of balances in accounts receivable is from $5 to $25,000, this population exhibits more variability and it would be necessary to test a larger number of accounts receivable.

---

**ENGAGEMENT STRATEGY:** In practice it is unlikely that an accounting population will have as small degree of variation as suggested in the above paragraph; however, it is possible to divide the population into groupings (population stratification) and thus significantly reduce the degree of variation in each grouping. Also, it should be remembered that a group of the population may be tested 100% and evaluated separately. Stratification and testing some of the items 100% will almost always reduce the overall size of the sample.

---

The auditor can get a feel for the variation within a population by reviewing the items that make up the population. For example, a simple review of the trial balance of accounts receivable should give the auditor a reasonable impression of the variability of the population. A more precise measurement of variability can be determined quickly if the trial balance is digitized and can be subjected to analysis by various file analyzers. For example, if the trial balance of accounts receivable is maintained in a spreadsheet file, such as an Excel spreadsheet, it might be possible to create statistics such as the variance or standard deviation of the population.

*Risk of incorrect acceptance*

As discussed earlier in this section, an interplay exists among audit risk, inherent risk, and control risk. These relationships can be summarized as follows:

- When the combined inherent and control risks are assessed at a lower level, a greater risk of incorrect acceptance for planned substantive procedures can be established. Under this circumstance, the required sample size is decreased.
- When the combined inherent and control risks are assessed at a higher level, a lower risk of incorrect acceptance for planned substantive procedures can be established. Under this circumstance, the required sample size is increased.
- When the auditor relies more heavily on other substantive procedures (including analytical procedures) to achieve the same audit objective, a greater risk of incorrect acceptance for planned substantive procedures can be established. Under this circumstance, the required sample size is decreased.
- When the auditor relies less heavily on other substantive procedures (including analytical procedures) to achieve the same audit objective, a lesser risk of incorrect acceptance for planned substantive procedures can be established. Under this circumstance, the required sample size is increased.

*Tolerable misstatement and expected misstatement*

The establishment of a sample size in non-statistical sampling must take into consideration the tolerable misstatement (the size of the error that the auditor considers to be tolerable) and the expected misstatement. In general, as the size of the tolerable misstatement increases, the required sample size decreases. For example, if the auditor believes that a tolerable misstatement in the accounts receivable balance is $30,000 rather than $10,000, the number of items that must be in the sample is decreased.

In determining the size of a sample, the auditor should also take into consideration the expected misstatement in the population. As the expected misstatement in the population increases, the required sample size must be increased. That is, if an auditor does not have much faith in the balances under investigation, common sense would require an auditor to test more items from the population.

*Population size*

The size of the population has little effect on the size of the sample. Thus, if one trial balance of accounts receivable has 2,000 line items and another trial balance has 4,000 line items, assuming all other factors are equal, both populations would require essentially the same sample size.

---

**ENGAGEMENT STRATEGY:** It is easy for auditors to overemphasize the size of the population in determining the required sample size for a particular balance. For example, if the auditor has a rule of thumb that he or she samples 10% of the items of the population, the result is a misapplication of auditing standards. In the previous example, the auditor would select 200 items from the first population and 400 items from the second, but that doubling of the sample size in the second population is not supported by sampling concepts. It is far more important for the auditor to thoughtfully look at the other three factors discussed above, rather than population size, in determining the required sample size for a population.

***

***Consider the interplay of the four factors*** The auditor uses professional judgment to evaluate the four factors described above and, based on this evaluation, determines the required sample size. There is no single approach that an auditor should use to make this determination; however, for illustrative purpose the AICPA *Audit Sampling* Guide describes the following as an approach that an auditor may consider:

- Consider the level of inherent risk.
- Consider the effectiveness of controls related to the financial statement assertions.
- Establish the risk of incorrect acceptance.
- Establish a tolerable misstatement level.
- Evaluate the effect of other related tests of details.
- Determine the population reported amount.
- Compute the preliminary sample size.
- Adjust the preliminary sample size.

***

**ENGAGEMENT STRATEGY:** The AICPA Audit Guide *Audit Sampling* is careful not to endorse any particular method for determining sample size but describes the usefulness of the approach described above as follows: The model is provided only to illustrate the relative effect of different planning considerations on sample size; it is not intended as a substitute for professional judgment. The auditor can find this approach useful to get a feel for how various assessments of the four factors described earlier can have on the required sample size.

***

***Consider the level of inherent risk*** Initially the auditor assesses the level of inherent risk related to the particular assertions in the financial statements that will be tested once the sample is selected. Inherent risk is the susceptibility of an assertion to a material misstatement, assuming that there are no related controls. AU-C 500 (*Audit Evidence*) attempts to provide the logical framework for the audit process by identifying the following broad assertions that must be tested:

- Assertions for classes of transactions.
- Assertions for account balances.
- Assertions for presentation and disclosure.

***Consider the effectiveness of controls related to the financial statement assertions*** Once the specific financial statement assertions are identified, the auditor should consider the effectiveness of the controls related to the prevention and detection of material misstatements related to the assertions. Control risk is the risk that a material misstatement that could occur in an assertion will not be prevented or detected on a timely basis by the entity's internal control.

*Establish the risk of incorrect acceptance* The judgments made in the first two steps should be combined and the auditor should determine the risk of incorrect acceptance (which was described earlier in this section). That is, inherent risk and control risk related to specific assertions included in the financial statements provide insight into how much risk the auditor is willing to accept for those particular assertions. Although there are innumerable levels that could be identified in practice, some auditors think about the risk of incorrect acceptance using quantitative measures such as 5%, 10%, 15%, and so forth, whereas other auditors qualitatively express the risk of incorrect acceptance using the following categories:

- Maximum,
- Slightly below maximum,
- Moderate, and
- Low.

If the auditor believes that particular assertions have a high inherent risk and that the controls related to the assertions are weak, the maximum level of incorrect acceptance should be established. On the other hand, if there is relatively low inherent risk related to assertions and the related controls are effective, a low level of incorrect acceptance should be established.

*Establish a tolerable misstatement level* The tolerable misstatement is an estimate of the maximum monetary misstatement that may exist in an account balance or group of transactions when combined with misstatement in other accounts, without causing the financial statements to be materially misstated.

*Evaluate the effect of other related tests of details* When a single audit procedure is performed, the results of that procedure often test the validity of more than one assertion that appears in the financial statements. For this reason, the auditor should assess the risk that other audit procedures may have an impact on the assertions that are the focus of the current sample determination using the following framework:

- *Maximum risk* No other substantive procedures are performed to test the same assertions.
- *Moderate risk* Other substantive procedures that are performed to test the same assertions are expected to be moderately effective in detecting material misstatements in those assertions.
- *Low risk* Other substantive procedures that are performed to test the same assertions are expected to be highly effective in detecting material misstatements in those assertions.

*Determine the population reported amount* The dollar value of the population is simply the amount reported in the financial statements less items that make up this value that are to be tested 100%.

*Compute the preliminary sample size* The preliminary sample size is a function of the auditor's determination of the risk of incorrect acceptance, expected rate of misstatement in the population, tolerable misstatement, and the reported population amount. Tolerable misstatement, the reported population amount, and the risk of incorrect acceptance were discussed earlier. The expected rate of misstatement is the expected monetary misstatement that may exist in an account balance or group of transactions. The illustrative sample sizes in Exhibit AU-C 530-3 are based on Table 4.5 from the Audit Guide.

*EXHIBIT AU-C 530-3—ILLUSTRATIVE SAMPLE SIZES*

| Risk of Incorrect Acceptance | Ratio of Expected Misstatement to Tolerable Misstatement | Tolerable Misstatement as % of Population | Sample Size |
|---|---|---|---|
| 5% | 0 | 5% | 60 |
| 5% | .20 | 5% | 93 |
| 5% | .20 | 2% | 232 |
| 10% | 0 | 5% | 47 |
| 10% | .20 | 5% | 69 |
| 10% | .20 | 3% | 114 |
| 15% | 0 | 5% | 38 |
| 15% | .20 | 5% | 55 |
| 15% | 0 | 2% | 95 |

As Exhibit AU-C 530-3 illustrates, holding other factors constant, the sample size increases given (1) a lower risk of incorrect acceptance, (2) a larger ratio of expected misstatement to tolerable misstatement, and (3) a smaller ratio of tolerable misstatement as a percentage of the reported population amount.

***Adjust the preliminary sample size*** The preliminary sample size must be adjusted upward because non-statistical rather than statistical sampling is used. The AICPA Audit Guide *Audit Sampling* notes that "auditors typically adjust the sample size from 10% to 50% if the sample is not selected in a statically efficient manner." For example, if a population that has a great deal of variation has not been stratified, the auditor should increase the preliminary sample size.

To illustrate this approach, assume an auditor is trying to decide the sample size for the confirmation of accounts receivable under the following conditions:

- *Consider the level of inherent risk* This particular audit procedure is concerned with the existence of accounts receivable, and the level of inherent risk is considered to be moderate based on the nature of accounts receivable and other factors related to the client.

- *Consider the effectiveness of controls related to the financial statement assertions* Based on the evaluation of the client's internal control related to the processing of accounts receivable and cash receipts, the auditor has concluded that internal controls are weak and control risk is assessed at the maximum level.

- *Evaluate the effect of other related tests of details* The auditor has identified another audit procedure that will help to determine the existence of accounts receivable (e.g., the review of subsequent cash receipts) and has assessed the risk that other substantive procedures will fail to detect a material misstatement as *moderate*.

- *Establish the risk of incorrect acceptance* The auditor considers the assessed level of inherent risk (moderate), control risk (maximum), and the effect of other related tests of details (moderate) in determining the risk of incorrect acceptance. The auditor decides to assess the risk of incorrect acceptance at 10% (or, qualitatively, at a level *slightly below maximum*).

- *Establish a tolerable misstatement level* Based on the assessment of materiality, the auditor decides to establish a tolerable misstatement level of $11,500.

- *Estimate the expected misstatement level* Based on the auditor's previous experience auditing accounts receivable for this client, expected misstatement is $2,000.

- *Determine the population reported amount* The general ledger balance of accounts receivable is reported at $250,000 but accounts receivable that exceed $4,000 will be tested 100%. The accounts that will be tested 100% are reported at $20,000. Thus, the population subject to sampling has a reported amount of $230,000.

- *Compute the preliminary sample size* The auditor has established the risk of incorrect acceptance at 10%. Expected misstatement, $2,000, is approximately 20% of tolerable misstatement, $11,500. And tolerable misstatement is 5% of the population balance subject to sampling ($11,500 / $230,000). Using the table in Exhibit AU-C 530-3, the preliminary sample size is 69 sample items (i.e., customer accounts receivable balances to be confirmed).

- *Adjust the preliminary sample size* The auditor, based on the review of the trial balance of accounts receivable, decided not to stratify the sample (except for the items that are tested 100%), even though there was a moderate amount of variation in the account balances. For this reason, the auditor decided to increase the size of the sample by 30%. Thus, the required sample size is 90 (69 × 1.3).

## Select the Sample

Once the sample size has been determined, the sample itself should be selected so that each item in the population has a chance of selection (representative sample). One way to select the sample is to divide the population into categories based on dollar values, selecting more items from the category with the greatest dollar value. The allocation in Exhibit AU-C 530-4 illustrates this approach based on the example presented earlier in this section.

## EXHIBIT AU-C 530-4—SELECTING THE SAMPLE

| Category | Reported Amount | Allocation Fraction | Total Required Sample Size | Sample Size for Category |
|---|---|---|---|---|
| $1 to $500 | 100,000 | 100/230 | 90 | 39 |
| $501 to $2,000 | 80,000 | 80/230 | 90 | 31 |
| $2,001 to $4,000 | 50,000 | 50/230 | 90 | 20 |
| Totals | $230,000 | | | 90 |

Thus, 39 receivables will be selected from those receivables that have a balance of $500 or less, and so on. Within each category, the specific items selected for confirmation could be selected on a random basis or an interval basis.

**OBSERVATION:** In this example, the population has been stratified for sample selection purposes but not for sample evaluation purposes.

### Evaluate the Sample Results

In order to evaluate the sample results when a non-statistical sampling approach is used, the auditor must do the following:

- Project the misstatement in the population,
- Consider the sampling risk, and
- Consider qualitative characteristics.

*Project the misstatement in the population*

Once the specific items are selected for testing, the appropriate audit procedures are performed. Based on the performance of the audit procedures, the auditor would determine the amount of the misstatements found in the sample items. This misstatement must then be projected to the total population. To continue with the current illustration, assume the 90 accounts selected for confirmation have a total account balance of $23,000 and assume that the auditor discovered misstatements equal to $600. The projected total misstatement for the sampled population would be $6,000 ($600 / [$23,000 / $230,000]).

When the auditor has tested a segment of the population 100%, the misstatement found for these items must be added to the projected total misstatement for the sampled item in order to determine the projected total misstatement for the total population. For example, in the current illustration all receivables with a balance greater than $4,000 were tested. If the misstatement discovered in this group of receivables was $1,000, the projected total misstatement for the population would be $7,000 ($6,000 + $1,000).

## Consider sampling risk

Once the auditor has determined the projected total misstatement for the population, he or she must be careful not to draw a conclusion about the population based on this single estimate. That is, the auditor cannot say that the best estimate of the misstatement is a specific amount ($7,000 in the current example), but rather he or she must recognize that sampling risk must be considered. Sampling risk arises because not all the items in the population were tested; therefore, the best estimate of the misstatement is not a single amount but a range around that single amount.

Determining, based on the sampling results, whether a population's dollar value is probably not misstated involves a considerable amount of professional judgment. The focus of the judgment is the relationship between the tolerable misstatement and the projected misstatement. The broad generalizations in Exhibit AU-C 530-5 are helpful in making that judgment.

### EXHIBIT AU-C 530-5—MISSTATEMENTS AND PROFESSIONAL JUDGMENT

| Relationship of Projected Misstatement and Tolerable Misstatement for the Sample | Examples | Analysis and Judgment |
|---|---|---|
| The projected misstatement is significantly less than the tolerable misstatement. | Assume the projected misstatement is $1,000 and the tolerable misstatement is $9,000. | The projected misstatement is so much less than the tolerable misstatement, it is probably unlikely that the actual misstatement (if the entire population were sampled) would be greater than the tolerable misstatement. *Conclusion:* The auditor is reasonably assured that the population balance is not misstated. |
| The projected misstatement is equal to or greater than the tolerable misstatement. | Assume the projected misstatement is $10,000 and the tolerable misstatement is $9,000. | The projected misstatement implies that the balance is materially misstated. *Conclusion:* The auditor may request that the client review the population for possible adjustment. Once adjustments are made, the auditor should reevaluate the balance to determine whether it is acceptable. |
| The projected misstatement is neither close to nor far from the tolerable misstatement. | Assume the projected misstatement is $7,500 and the tolerable misstatement is $9,000. | When the projected misstatement is neither close to nor far from the tolerable misstatement, the decision process becomes more difficult because the conclusion that can be drawn is not as obvious as it is in the two situations described above. |
| | | *Conclusion:* Under this circumstance, the auditor might want to (1) increase the sample size (concluding that the original sample might not have been representative) or (2) perform alternative audit procedures in order to obtain additional evidence concerning the possible misstatement of the population. |

*Consider qualitative characteristics*

When a misstatement is discovered, an auditor should not mechanically respond to the misstatement as simply part of the projection of the total misstated amount in the population. Each misstatement should be analyzed to determine whether it arose from an error (an unintentional action) or from possible fraud (an intentional action). If fraud is suspected, the auditor should follow the guidance established in AU-C 240 (*Consideration of Fraud in a Financial Statement Audit*).

## EXHIBIT AU-C 530-6—REQUIRED SAMPLE SIZE FOR NON-STATISTICAL TESTS OF DETAILS

Use the following procedures as a guide for determining the required sample size for the performance of tests of details based on a non-statistical sampling approach. The checklist is only a guide, and professional judgment should be exercised to determine how it should be modified by revising or adding procedures. Initial and date each procedure as it is completed. Each procedure should be cross-referenced to an audit schedule that is the basis for the judgment or factor that is used to determine the required sample size.

Client Name: _____

Account Balance or Transactions Tested: _____

Date of Financial Statements: _____

| | | Initials | Date | Audit Documentation Reference |
|---|---|---|---|---|
| 1. | Establish the level of inherent risk.<br>—Maximum<br>—Slightly below maximum<br>—Moderate<br>—Low | _____ | _____ | _____ |
| 2. | Consider the effectiveness of controls related to the financial statement assertions (control risk).<br>—Maximum<br>—Slightly below maximum<br>—Moderate<br>—Low | _____ | _____ | _____ |
| 3. | Establish the risk of incorrect acceptance.<br>—Maximum<br>—Slightly below maximum<br>—Moderate<br>—Low | _____ | _____ | _____ |

|   |   | Initials | Date | Audit Documentation Reference |
|---|---|---|---|---|
| 4. | Establish a tolerable misstatement level, both as a dollar amount and as a percentage of the population amount subject to sampling procedures. _____ | _____ | _____ | _____ |
| 5. | Estimate the expected misstatement amount, both as a dollar amount and as a percentage of tolerable misstatement. _____ | | | |
| 6. | Evaluate the effect of other related tests of details.<br>—Maximum<br>—Slightly below maximum<br>—Moderate<br>—Low | _____ | _____ | _____ |
| 7. | Determine the population reported amount subject to sampling procedures.<br>$ _____ | _____ | _____ | _____ |
| 8. | Compute the preliminary sample size using the table in Exhibit AU-C 530-3 or using Table 4.5 in the AICPA's *Audit Sampling* Guide.<br>Preliminary sample size: _____ | | | |
| 9. | Adjust the preliminary sample size.<br>Required sample size: _____ | _____ | _____ | _____ |

Reviewed by: _____

Date: _____

# SECTION 540

# AUDITING ACCOUNTING ESTIMATES, INCLUDING FAIR VALUE ACCOUNTING ESTIMATES, AND RELATED DISCLOSURES

## Authoritative Pronouncements

SAS-122—Statements on Auditing Standards: Clarification and Recodification

SAS-134—Auditor Reporting and Amendments, Including Amendments Addressing Disclosures in the Audit of Financial Statements

SAS-136—Forming an Opinion and Reporting on Financial Statements of Employee Benefit Plans Subject to ERISA

SAS-141—Amendment to Effective Dates of SAS Nos. 134-140

SAS-142—Audit Evidence

SAS-143—Auditing Accounting Estimates and Related Disclosures

SAS-144—Amendments to AU-C Sections 501, 540, and 620 Related to the Use of Specialists and the Use of Pricing Information Obtained from External Information Sources

## Overview

AU-C 540 describes the auditor's responsibilities related to accounting estimates, including fair value accounting estimates, and related disclosures. During the audit, the auditor's objective is to obtain sufficient appropriate audit evidence about whether accounting estimates, including fair value accounting estimates, and related disclosures, in the financial statements are adequate and reasonable. Accounting estimates are approximations of financial statement elements, items, or accounts that are made to measure past transactions or events (loss contingency arising from pending lawsuits) or to measure assets (net realizable value of accounts receivable) or liabilities (accrual related to warranty contracts). Many factors, such as the availability of reliable data, the required complexity of the evaluation process, and the extent to which assumptions must be made by management, can increase the likelihood of accounting estimates leading to material misstatement in the financial statements and affect their susceptibility to management bias.

**IMPORTANT NOTICE FOR 2022:** In July 2020, the AICPA Auditing Standards Board (ASB) issued SAS No. 143, *Auditing Accounting Estimates and Related Disclosures*, which supersedes AU-C 540 and amends various other sections in the professional standards. The new SAS begins with an explanation of the nature of accounting estimates and how they can vary widely in nature and are required to be made by management when monetary amounts cannot be directly observed. The measurement of amounts is subject to estimation uncertainty, which reflects inherent limitations in the knowledge or data. These limitations give rise to inherent subjectivity and variation in measurement outcomes. Although the guidance in SAS No. 143 applies to all accounting estimates, the degree to which an accounting estimate is subject to estimation uncertainty will vary substantially. Therefore, SAS No. 143 recognizes that the nature, timing, and extent of the risk assessment and further audit procedures required will vary in relation to the estimation uncertainty and the assessment of the related risks of material misstatement. The ASB is coordinating the effective date of SAS No. 143 with the effective date of a proposed new SAS, *Understanding the Entity and Its Environment and Assessing the Risks of Material Misstatement*, which was under consideration by the ASB at the time this edition of the *GAAS Guide* was being prepared. SAS No. 143 does not become effective until audits of financial statements for periods ending on or after December 15, 2023, which is consistent with the date in the proposed new standard. As a result, this AU-C reflects existing auditing standards requirements. Updates to reflect SAS No. 143 will occur in the next edition of the *GAAS Guide*.

---

**IMPORTANT NOTICE FOR 2022:** In June 2021, the AICPA Auditing Standards Board (ASB) issued SAS No. 144, *Amendments to AU-C Sections 501, 540, and 620 Related to the Use of Specialists and the Use of Pricing Information Obtained from External Information Sources*, that amends AU-C 540 to add a new appendix addressing the use of pricing information obtained from external information sources to be used as audit evidence for estimates related to fair value instruments. It provides guidance for the auditor to consider when using pricing information from a single pricing service, multiple pricing services, or a broker or dealer. SAS No. 144 does not become effective until audits of financial statements for periods ending on or after December 15, 2023, which is consistent with the effective date of SAS No. 143. As a result, this AU-C reflects existing auditing standards requirements. Updates to reflect SAS No. 144 will occur in the next edition of the *GAAS Guide*.

---

**FRAUD POINTER:** As described in AU-C 240 (*Consideration of Fraud in a Financial Statement Audit*), one of the three conditions of fraud is the presence of "opportunities," or circumstances that allow fraud to be perpetrated. The presence of accounting estimates in financial statements can create significant opportunities for management to materially misstate financial statements due to the complexity involved in the estimation process and the need for assumptions to be made by management when developing an estimate. As auditors identify and evaluate factors related to fraud risks, they should consider the extent to which estimates are required in client financial statements and identify whether indicators of potential unintentional or intentional management bias exist.

---

Accounting estimates involve the use of judgment based on information available when the financial statements are prepared and may involve assumptions regarding matters that are uncertain at the time the estimate is made. While uncertainty about matters may exist, the auditor is not responsible for predicting future events that could have impacted the estimates made had they been known at the time of the audit.

> **OBSERVATION:** A difference between an accounting estimate and the amount originally recognized or disclosed in the financial statements does not necessarily indicate a misstatement of the financial statements; the difference could be due to estimation uncertainty.

Auditing estimates that are part of financial statements can often prove to be a significant engagement challenge because they often require a considerable amount of professional judgment. The AICPA has published the Audit Practice Guide *Auditing Estimates and Other Soft Accounting Information,* which is summarized in a Practitioner's Aid at the end of this section (see Exhibit AU-C 540-1).

- The fair value of an asset or liability might have to be estimated depending on the information available regarding that value. Determining the fair value of an asset that is held or a liability that exists is relatively easy if there is an established public market. For example, the fair value of an investment in the equity securities of a public company is generally readily determinable based on prices reflected in public markets. However, the more an item is unique and less like a commodity, the less likely it is that there is an established market with a large number of buyers and sellers to provide reliable information about the item's fair value at a particular point in time.

> **PLANNING AND REMINDER:** AU-C 540 does not identify audit procedures for specific types of assets and liabilities that must be measured or disclosed at their estimated fair values. The auditor must be aware of other standards (e.g., AU-C 501, *Audit Evidence—Specific Considerations for Selected Items*) that provide guidance that is more specific.

> **PUBLIC COMPANY IMPLICATION:** In December 2018, the PCAOB issued AS-2501 (*Auditing Accounting Estimates, Including Fair Value Measurement*).The goal of this new standard is to establish a single auditing standard that sets forth a uniform risk-based approach for auditing accounting estimates. The PCAOB developed this new standard partially in response to findings from the PCAOB inspections process where a number of issues related to the auditing of those estimates and disclosures were identified that the PCAOB believed warranted clarification in auditing standards. Additionally, a number of the financial reporting frameworks have changed in areas involving accounting estimates and the use of fair value accounting. Thus, the PCAOB has embarked on this project to update auditing standards related to the audit of accounting estimates. The PCAOB has also previously issued Staff Audit Practice Alerts that continue to be relevant, which are summarized below. AS-2501 was approved by the SEC in July 2019. The effective date is for audits of fiscal years ending on or after December 15, 2020.

**PUBLIC COMPANY IMPLICATION:** The PCAOB's Staff Audit Practice Alert No. 2 (*Matters Related to Auditing Fair Value Measurements of Financial Instruments and the Use of Specialists*) is designed to provide guidance related to auditing fair values, particularly in light of the FASB's ASC 820 (*Fair Value Measurements*). The auditor needs to understand the company's process for determining fair value measurements and disclosures, including related internal controls. The auditor should also evaluate whether (1) management's assumptions in determining fair value are reasonable and not inconsistent with market information, (2) management reliance on historical financial information continues to be justified (e.g., use of historical default rates may not be appropriate when credit markets are deteriorating), and (3) the company's determination of fair value is applied consistently and whether this is appropriate. For example, a company may apply a model consistently in determining fair value but because of changes in the environment it may be more appropriate for the company to change the relative weights of model inputs. In addition, the auditor should recognize that model inputs based on the company's own data are generally more susceptible to bias and take appropriate audit steps to respond to this increased risk. Finally, U.S. GAAP provides for many required disclosures relating to fair value measurements. The auditor needs to recognize that material disclosures that depart from U.S. GAAP represent a misstatement of the financial statements.

---

**PUBLIC COMPANY IMPLICATION:** The PCAOB's Staff Audit Practice Alert No. 4 (*Auditor Considerations Regarding Fair Value Measurements, Disclosures, and Other-than-Temporary Impairments*) is designed to inform auditors about the potential implications on annual audits and interim reviews of three former FASB Staff Positions (FSPs): (1) FSP FAS 157-4 (*Determining Fair Value When the Volume and Level of Activity for the Asset or Liability Have Significantly Decreased and Identifying Transactions That Are Not Orderly*), (2) FSP FAS 115-2 and FAS 124-2 (*Recognition and Presentation of Other-than-Temporary-Impairments*), and (3) FSP FAS 107-1 and APB 28-1 (*Interim Disclosures about Fair Value of Financial Instruments*). The guidance in these now superseded FSPs is incorporated in ASC 820 (*Fair Value Measurements and Disclosures*), ASC 320 (*Investments—Debt and Equity Securities*), and ASC 825 (*Financial Instruments*), respectively. PCAOB Staff Audit Practice Alert No. 4 states that the auditor should include inquiries about the application of these FSPs in a review of interim financial information. For audits of financial statements, Practice Alert 4 emphasizes the need for auditors to obtain sufficient appropriate evidence to support accounting estimates, including their measurement and disclosure. For example, in certain cases the guidance in ASC 320 (*Investments—Debt and Equity Securities*) requires losses from other-than-temporary impairments to be separated between credit losses and other factors. Such a determination involves significant judgment. Practice Alert 4 also reminds auditors of their responsibility to read other information in documents containing interim and annual financial statements. If this other information is inconsistent with the financial statements, either the audit report, financial statements, or the other information needs to be changed. The application of these FSPs may require communication to the audit committee because their application might involve a change in (1) accounting policy, (2) accounting estimates, (3) the process by which management develops sensitive estimates, and (4) the auditor's judgment about the quality, not just the acceptability, of the client's accounting policies. These required disclosures to the audit committee pertain to both annual audits and interim reviews.

## Definitions

| | |
|---|---|
| Accounting estimate | An approximation of a monetary amount, including an amount measured at fair value, in the absence of a precise means of measurement. |
| Auditor's point estimate or auditor's range | The amount (point estimate) or range of amounts (auditor's range) derived from audit evidence for use in evaluating management's point estimate. |
| Estimation uncertainty | The susceptibility of an accounting estimate and related disclosures to an inherent lack of precision in its measurement. |
| Management bias | A lack of neutrality by management in the preparation and presentation of information. |
| Management's point estimate | The amount selected by management for recognition or disclosure in the financial statements as an accounting estimate. |
| Outcome of an accounting estimate | The actual monetary amount resulting from the resolution of the underlying transactions, events, or conditions addressed by the accounting estimate. |

## Requirements

The auditor is presumptively required to perform the following procedures with respect to accounting estimates in an audit of a client's financial statements:

### Risk Assessment and Related Procedures

1. Obtain an understanding of the following to provide a basis for identifying and assessing risks of material misstatement for accounting estimates:

The applicable financial reporting framework's requirements relevant to accounting estimates and related disclosures.

    a. How management identifies transactions, events, or conditions requiring recognition or disclosure of accounting estimates. To do this, inquire of management about changes in circumstances that may create the need for new or revised accounting estimates.

    b. How management makes accounting estimates and the data estimates are based on, including the method used for estimation, relevant controls, use of a specialist, assumptions underlying the estimates, if a change in the estimation method is needed and why, and any assessment by management of the effect of estimation uncertainty.

This understanding should be obtained when performing risk assessment and related procedures to obtain an understanding of the entity and its environment.

2. Review the outcome of accounting estimates from prior-period financial statements or re-estimates made by management during the current period to identify any relevant information for identifying and assessing risks of material misstatement for accounting estimates made in the current period finan-

cial statements. This review is not intended to question the auditor's prior judgments made based on the information available at that time.

## Identifying, Assessing, and Responding to the Risks of Material Misstatement

3. Evaluate the degree of estimation uncertainty associated with an accounting estimate when identifying and assessing the risks of material misstatement.

4. Using judgment, determine whether any accounting estimates with a high level of estimation uncertainty give rise to significant risks.

5. Determine, based on the assessed risks of material misstatement, whether (1) management has appropriately applied the applicable financial reporting framework's requirements relevant to the accounting estimate and (2) the estimation methods used are appropriate and consistently applied, and whether any changes in estimates or estimation methods are appropriate.

6. To respond to the assessed risks of material misstatement, perform one or more of the following procedures depending on the nature of the accounting estimate:

   a. Determine if events occurring up to the date of the auditor's report provide audit evidence regarding the accounting estimate.

   b. Test how management made the estimate and the data on which the estimate is based by evaluating if the measurement method used is appropriate, management's assumptions are reasonable given the measurement objectives of the applicable financial reporting framework, and the data on which the estimate is based are sufficiently reliable for the auditor's purposes.

   c. Test the operating effectiveness of controls over how management made the estimate and use appropriate substantive procedures.

   d. Develop a point estimate or range to evaluate management's point estimate. If using different assumptions or methods from management, obtain a sufficient understanding of management's assumptions and methods to establish that the auditor's point estimate or range accounts for relevant variables and to evaluate any significant differences from management's point estimate. If using a range, narrow the range based on available audit evidence until all outcomes in the range are considered reasonable.

7. When responding to assessed risks of material misstatement for accounting estimates, consider whether specialized skills or knowledge are needed to obtain sufficient appropriate audit evidence.

## Responding to Significant Risks

8. Evaluate the following matters for accounting estimates that create significant risks:

   a. How management considered and rejected alternative assumptions or outcomes or otherwise addressed estimation uncertainty in making the estimate.

   b. If significant assumptions used by management are reasonable; a significant assumption is one for which a reasonable variation in the assumption would materially affect the measurement of the accounting estimate.

   c. Management's intent and ability to carry out specific courses of action as relevant to the reasonableness of significant assumptions or the appropriate application of the applicable financial reporting framework.

9. If, in the auditor's judgment, management has not adequately addressed the effects of estimation uncertainty for estimates creating significant risks, develop a range to use to evaluate the estimates' reasonableness if necessary.

10. Obtain sufficient appropriate audit evidence for accounting estimates that create significant risks about whether management's decision regarding recognition of the estimates in the financial statements and the measurement basis selected for the estimates are in accordance with the requirements of the applicable financial reporting framework.

## Evaluating Reasonableness of Accounting Estimates

11. Evaluate whether the audit evidence demonstrates that accounting estimates in the financial statements are reasonable or misstated given the applicable financial reporting framework.

## Disclosures

12. Obtain sufficient appropriate audit evidence about whether disclosures related to accounting estimates in the financial statements are in accordance with the requirements of the applicable financial reporting framework.

13. For accounting estimates that create significant risks, evaluate the adequacy of disclosure in the financial statements of their estimation uncertainty given the applicable financial reporting framework.

## Management Bias

14. Review management judgments and decisions in making accounting estimates to identify any indicators of management bias. Indicators of management bias do not in themselves constitute misstatements for purposes of concluding as to the reasonableness of individual accounting estimates.

## Documentation

15. Document:

   a. The basis for conclusions about the reasonableness of accounting estimates that create significant risks and their disclosure.

   b. Any indicators of possible management bias.

---

**IMPORTANT NOTICE FOR 2022:** In July 2020, the AICPA Auditing Standards Board (ASB) issued SAS No. 142, *Audit Evidence*, which supersedes AU-C 500 (*Audit Evidence*) and amends various other sections, including AU-C 540, in the professional standards. This SAS addresses the evolving nature of business and audit services and issues that include the use of emerging technologies by both preparers and auditors, audit data analytics (ADA), the application of professional skepticism, the expanding use of external information sources as audit evidence, and, more broadly, the accuracy, completeness, and reliability of audit evidence. This SAS is effective for audits of financial statements for periods ending on or after December 15, 2022.

## Analysis and Application of Procedures

*Risk Assessment and Related Procedures*

The auditor is required to perform certain procedures to provide a basis for identifying and assessing the risks of material misstatement for accounting estimates. However, these procedures may not need to be performed if events occurring after management's estimate was made, such as settlement of litigation, sale of an impaired asset, or collection of receivables, have significantly reduced the risk of material misstatement related to the accounting estimate.

*Obtain an understanding of the applicable financial reporting framework requirements*

Obtaining an understanding of the applicable financial reporting framework assists the auditor in understanding how the entity develops its accounting estimates. The framework's requirements may detail certain conditions for recognizing accounting estimates, methods for measuring accounting estimates, and conditions requiring or allowing measurement at fair value or disclosure. The framework may also guide management's determination of point estimates when alternatives exist; for example, a framework may require management to select a point estimate that is the most likely outcome or to use a discounted probability-weighted expected value. Some frameworks may not allow entities to recognize accounting estimates in the financial statements if a high degree of estimation uncertainty exists.

*Obtain an understanding of how management identifies the need for accounting estimates*

To obtain an understanding of how management identifies transactions, events, and conditions that require recognition or disclosure of accounting estimates, the auditor may predominantly use management inquiry if management identifies these events using their knowledge and experience. If management has a more structured process for identifying these events, the auditor may perform risk assessment procedures directed at that process. If the auditor identifies a need for an accounting estimate during the audit that management failed to identify, he or she should determine if this constitutes a significant deficiency or material weakness in internal control of the entity's risk assessment process. Exhibit AU-C 540-2 lists common financial statement estimates that require evaluation by an auditor.

The auditor also inquires of management about changes in circumstances that may create the need for new or revised accounting estimates. These inquiries may include questions about whether:

- The entity has engaged in new types of transactions that could require accounting estimates.
- Terms of transactions or accounting policies relating to accounting estimates have changed.
- Regulatory changes or new events or conditions have occurred that may create the need for new or revised accounting estimates.

*Obtain an understanding of how management makes accounting estimates*

The auditor is required to obtain an understanding of how management makes accounting estimates and the data on which the estimates are based. In addition to the required considerations, the auditor may also consider the types of accounts or transactions the estimates relate to, management's use of recognized measurement techniques in making estimates, and how management has taken into account the effect of any changes in circumstances occurring between the date of the estimate and the period end.

The method of measurement management uses to form accounting estimates is often not prescribed by the applicable financial reporting framework. In these situations, the auditor may evaluate management's consideration of the nature of the item being estimated in selecting an estimation method and whether the entity's industry has commonly used estimation methods. If management has internally developed a method of making an accounting estimate or departs from a commonly used industry method, there may be a greater risk of material misstatement.

In obtaining an understanding of relevant controls, the auditor may consider:

- The competence and experience of those making the accounting estimates.
- How the completeness, relevance, and accuracy of data used to develop estimates is determined and how accounting estimates are reviewed and approved, including the assumptions and inputs.
- The segregation of duties between those making the accounting estimates and those committing the entity to the underlying transactions.
- The extent to which the entity uses a service organization to provide accounting estimates or the data supporting those estimates.
- The design and development, or selection, of a particular model for making a particular estimate.
- The use, maintenance, periodic validation of integrity, and security controls over unauthorized changes of a model used to make accounting estimates.

When obtaining an understanding about the assumptions underlying the accounting estimates, the auditor may consider:

- The nature and significance of the assumptions.
- How management assesses if assumptions are relevant, complete, and internally consistent.
- Whether assumptions relate to matters within, or outside of, management's control.
- The nature and extent of documentation supporting the assumptions.

Because management supports assumptions with information from different sources of varying relevance and reliability, the reliability of assumptions will also vary depending on the degree of subjectivity involved. When considering fair value accounting estimates, assumptions rely on what knowledgeable and willing arm's-length parties would use to determine fair value. These assumptions may be based on observable inputs, such as independent market data, or unobservable inputs, such as the entity's own judgments. The auditor's assessment of the risks of material misstatement for an accounting estimate increases as the estimation uncertainty increases, and estimation uncertainty increases as subjectivity related to the estimate increases.

In obtaining an understanding of any changes in management's methods for making accounting estimates, the auditor should evaluate whether these changes are reasonable. When considering management's assessment of the effect of estimation uncertainty, the auditor may examine whether management has considered alternative assumptions or outcomes, how management determines an estimate when there are several outcome scenarios, and whether management monitors and responds to the outcome of prior-period accounting estimates.

*Reviewing prior-period accounting estimates*

The nature and extent of the auditor's review of prior-period accounting estimates is a matter of professional judgment and the outcome of every prior-period accounting estimate is not required to be reviewed. The extent of review may increase for estimates with high estimation uncertainty or those that changed significantly since the prior period audit. This review can provide the auditor with:

- Information about the effectiveness of management's prior-period estimation process, which can help the auditor judge the likely effectiveness of the current process;
- Audit evidence pertinent to the current period re-estimation of prior-period accounting estimates;
- Audit evidence of matters that may require disclosure in the financial statements; and
- Information identifying circumstances that increase the susceptibility of accounting estimates to possible management bias.

A difference between the outcome of an accounting estimate and the amount recognized in prior-period financial statements does not necessarily represent a misstatement. However, it may represent a misstatement if the difference exists due to information that was available to management or that could be reasonably expected to have been obtained and taken into account when the prior period financial statements were finalized.

---

**FRAUD POINTER:** To address the ever-present risk of management override of internal control, AU-C 240 requires the auditor in every audit to review accounting estimates for biases that could result in material misstatements due to fraud. As part of that review, AU-C 240 requires the auditor to perform a retrospective review of significant accounting estimates reflected in the financial statements of the prior year. The purpose of this retrospective review is to determine whether management judgments and assumptions related to the estimates indicate possible management bias. The management judgments and assumptions examined by the auditor should include those estimates that are based on highly sensitive assumptions or are otherwise significantly impacted by management's judgment. In performing this retrospective review, the auditor is able to take advantage of the benefit of hindsight to determine the extent of bias on the part of management in developing the prior-year estimate. When bias is detected, the auditor should evaluate whether it indicates a risk of material misstatement due to fraud.

## Identifying, Assessing, and Responding to the Risks of Material Misstatement

In assessing the risks of material misstatement, the auditor may consider:
- The actual or expected magnitude of an accounting estimate.
- The difference between management's recorded accounting estimate and that expected by the auditor.
- If management used a specialist in making the accounting estimate.
- The outcome of the review of prior-period accounting estimates.

*Estimation uncertainty*

The auditor is also required to evaluate the degree of estimation uncertainty associated with an accounting estimate. The degree of estimation uncertainty may influence the estimate's susceptibility to bias. Estimation uncertainty may be influenced by several factors:
- The extent to which the estimate depends on judgment.
- The sensitivity of the estimate to changes in assumptions.
- The existence of recognized measurement techniques that may mitigate the estimation uncertainty.
- The forecast period's length and the relevance of data from past events in forecasting future events.
- The availability of reliable data from external sources.
- The extent to which the estimate is based on observable or unobservable inputs.

An accounting estimate may be material to the financial statements even if the estimate is for a seemingly small amount if there is a high degree of estimation uncertainty associated with the estimate. Under some circumstances, the estimation uncertainty may be so high that it gives rise to significant risks. When a significant risk related to an accounting estimate is identified, the auditor should obtain an understanding of the entity's controls, including control activities.

In some cases, the estimation uncertainty is so high that a reasonable accounting estimate cannot be made, thereby precluding recognition of the item in the financial statements or the measurement of its fair value. In these situations, the auditor may question whether the applicable financial reporting framework permits recognition of the item in the financial statements.

*Management's adherence to applicable financial reporting framework and basis for changes*

The auditor's consideration of management's application of the requirements of the applicable financial reporting framework as it relates to accounting estimates is focused on those aspects that may result in misapplication or differing interpretations. The auditor may use his or her understanding of the entity and its environment, perform additional audit procedures, or obtain additional evidence in determining whether the framework's requirements were applied appropriately.

The auditor also considers management's reasons for making any changes in accounting estimates or in methods for making accounting estimates to ensure that changes are not arbitrary and are based on a change in circumstances or new information. This is because an arbitrary change can result in inconsistent financial statements, give rise to a financial statement misstatement, or be an indicator of possible management bias. The auditor uses professional judgment to determine whether management's reasons for any changes are sound and adequate.

If the auditor is engaged to communicate key audit matters, the auditor may need to consider an accounting estimate that has been identified as having high estimation uncertainty as a key audit matter.

*Procedures responding to assessed risks of material misstatement*

The auditor may decide which procedures to perform to respond to the assessed risks of material misstatement related to an accounting estimate depending on the nature of the accounting estimate, if the procedure is expected to provide the auditor with sufficient appropriate audit evidence, the assessed risk of material misstatement, and whether the assessed risk is a significant risk. Some accounting estimates may only require the auditor to perform one procedure, while others may necessitate a combination of procedures to obtain sufficient appropriate audit evidence.

*Considering events occurring up to the date of the auditor's report*

The auditor may consider events occurring up to the date of the auditor's report to respond to the assessed risks of material misstatement for an accounting estimate if those events are expected to occur and to provide audit evidence confirming or contradicting the accounting estimate. If events contradict the accounting estimate, this may be an indication that management has ineffective processes for making estimates or that management bias exists in making accounting estimates. For fair value accounting estimates, this procedure may not be an appropriate response, because events occurring after the date of the estimate may not be relevant to the measurement of fair value at the balance sheet date.

**PLANNING AID REMINDER:** The auditor is required under AU-C 560 to perform audit procedures to obtain sufficient appropriate audit evidence that any events occurring between the financial statement date and auditor's report date that require financial statement identification or disclosure have been identified and are appropriately reflected in the financial statements. Therefore, even if the auditor does not use this procedure to consider specific accounting estimates, he or she may still consider many accounting estimates when following AU-C 560 procedures because their measurement depends on events occurring during this time.

*Testing how management made the accounting estimate*

It may be appropriate for the auditor to test how management made an accounting estimate and the data on which the estimate is based if (1) the accounting estimate is a fair value estimate based on observable and unobservable inputs, (2) the accounting estimate is derived from routine data processing of the entity's accounting system, (3) the accounting estimate is based on a large population of similar items that are not significant individually, or (4) the auditor's review of similar prior-period accounting estimates suggests that management's current-period process is likely to be effective. The auditor is required to evaluate whether the data on which the estimate is based are sufficiently reliable and relevant by obtaining evidence about the accuracy and completeness of the data and evaluating whether the data are sufficiently precise and detailed, including evaluation of the source of the data.

Testing of how management made the accounting estimate may involve:

- Testing whether the data on which the estimate is based is accurate, complete, relevant, and sufficiently precise and detailed for the auditor's purposes, and whether the estimate has been properly determined using such data and management assumptions;
- Determining how management accounted for the effect of any events occurring between the date of the estimate and the reporting date;
- Recalculating the accounting estimate and reviewing information about the estimate for internal consistency; and
- Considering management's review and approval process.

In testing how management made an accounting estimate, the auditor evaluates whether the method used to make the estimate was appropriate in the circumstances. Absent any requirements by the applicable financial reporting framework, a method or model's appropriateness depends on the auditor's professional judgment. Factors the auditor may consider in determining the appropriateness of management's methods or models include whether management has a reasonable rationale for selecting the method; management sufficiently evaluated and appropriately applied any criteria provided to support the selected method; the method is appropriate and the data are sufficient given the nature of the estimate and the requirements of the applicable financial reporting framework; and the method is appropriate in relation to the entity's business, industry, and operating environment.

If the entity uses a model to make accounting estimates (which may be particularly likely for fair value accounting estimates), the auditor may consider some of the following factors such as whether:

- The model is commercially available or proprietary.
- The model is validated prior to usage and periodically reviewed, ensuring continued validity for its intended use. Validation may involve evaluating the model's theoretical soundness, the completeness and consistency of its inputs with market practices, and its output compared to actual transactions.

- Appropriate change control policies and procedures exist.
- The model is periodically tested for validity.
- Adjustments are made to the model's output.
- The model is adequately documented.

The auditor does not offer an opinion on the assumptions, valuation models, or the underlying data themselves. Rather, the auditor's tests are performed in the context of auditing the client's financial statements. If the auditor identifies significant assumptions used by management to make accounting estimates, these may indicate a high degree of estimation uncertainty related to the estimate, which may give rise to a significant risk. The auditor may consider many factors in evaluating the reasonableness of management's assumptions, such as if the assumptions:

- Appear reasonable, both individually and in conjunction with other assumptions.
- Are interdependent and internally consistent.
- Appropriately reflect observable market assumptions for fair value estimates.
- Are reasonable in light of other assumptions.
- Are consistent with the entity's plans and the economic environment.
- Are consistent with the entity's prior experience as it may relate to future events, any relevant assumptions made in prior periods, and any other assumptions relating to the financial statements.

The auditor should pay attention to the consistency of management's assumptions and valuation approaches and to any changes in these approaches or assumptions to ensure that changes in circumstances are reflected in the appropriate changes in management approaches and assumptions.

Management's intent and ability to carry out particular courses of action may affect the auditor's judgment of the reasonableness of the assumptions used. However, this information may not be permitted to be taken into account when using certain financial reporting frameworks or for fair value accounting estimates. When the auditor is obtaining audit evidence about management's intents and abilities, his or her procedures may include:

- Review of management's history of carrying out its stated intentions,
- Review of written plans and other documentation,
- Inquiry of management about its reasons for a particular course of action,
- Review of events occurring between the date of the financial statements and the auditor's report date, and
- Evaluation of the entity's ability to carry out a particular course of action given its economic circumstances.

The auditor may consider additional factors when evaluating the reasonableness of management's assumptions related to fair value accounting estimates, including how management incorporated market-specific inputs into developing its assumptions; if assumptions are consistent with observable market conditions and the characteristics of the item being measured; the relevance and reliability of the sources of market-participant assumptions and how management selected the assumptions to use when several assumptions exist; and how management considered assumptions used for comparable transactions, assets, or liabilities.

If the auditor is evaluating the reasonableness of assumptions related to fair value accounting estimates based on unobservable inputs, he or she may consider how management identified characteristics of market participants relevant to the accounting estimate, modified assumptions to reflect its view of assumptions market participants would use, whether the best information available in the circumstances was incorporated, and how the assumptions used account for comparable transactions, assets, or liabilities. If there are unobservable inputs, the auditor will likely need to combine evaluation of management's assumptions with other response procedures to assessed risks in order to obtain sufficient appropriate audit evidence.

*Testing the operating effectiveness of controls*

The auditor may test the operating effectiveness of controls over how management made the accounting estimate when management uses a well-designed, implemented, and maintained process for making estimates. Examples of this include when controls exist for management or those charged with governance to review and approve accounting estimates or when the accounting estimate is derived from routing data processing by the entity's accounting system.

---

**PLANNING AID REMINDER:** AU-C 330 requires the auditor to test the operating effectiveness of controls when the auditor's assessment of risks of material misstatement at the relevant assertion level include an expectation that controls over the process are operating effectively or when substantive procedures alone do not provide sufficient appropriate audit evidence at the relevant assertion level.

---

*Developing a point estimate or range*

Developing a point estimate or range to evaluate management's point estimate may be useful to the auditor when:

- An estimate is not derived from routine data processing by the accounting system.
- The auditor's review of similar prior-period accounting estimates suggests management's current-period process is unlikely to be effective.
- The entity lacks well-designed or properly implemented controls over management's process for making accounting estimates.
- Management's point estimate is contradicted by events occurring between the financial statement date and the auditor's report date.
- Alternative sources of data are available to the auditor to make a point estimate or range.

The auditor's decision as to whether to develop a point estimate or a range may depend on what is most effective in the circumstances, what is prescribed by the applicable financial reporting framework, the availability of data, the estimation uncertainty involved with the accounting estimate, and the model used. Actual development by the auditor of a point estimate or range may occur by using a commercially available or proprietary model; further developing management's consideration of alternative assumptions or outcomes; engaging a specialist; or making reference to other comparable conditions, transactions, events, or markets for comparable assets or liabilities.

When using a range to evaluate the reasonableness of management's point estimate, the auditor should ensure the range is sufficiently narrow to enable a conclusion about whether the accounting estimate is misstated. To ensure that all range outcomes are considered reasonable, the auditor may narrow the range based on available audit evidence until all outcomes in the range are considered reasonable and may eliminate range outliers that are judged by the auditor to be unlikely to occur. For the auditor's range to be adequate for this evaluation, the range generally has to be narrowed to be less than or equal to performance materiality. However, this is not possible in some circumstances, and in those cases, the accounting estimate may still be able to be recognized but the estimation uncertainty associated with the estimate may be so high that is gives rise to a significant risk.

---

**IMPORTANT NOTICE FOR 2022:** In May 2019, the AICPA's Auditing Standards Board (ASB) issued SAS No. 134 titled *Auditor Reporting and Amendments, Including Amendments Addressing Disclosures in the Audit of Financial Statements* that makes significant changes to the auditor's report, including the ability to communicate key audit matters (KAMs) in the auditor's report. SAS No. 134 also includes conforming amendments to other AU-C sections, including amendments to AU-C 540 to acknowledge that when an accounting estimate has been identified as having high estimation uncertainty, the auditor may determine that to be a KAM to be communicated in the auditor's report. Originally, the effective date of SAS No. 134 was for audits of financial statements periods ending on or after December 15, 2020, with early implementation **not** permitted. However, the ASB's issuance of SAS No. 141, *Amendment to the Effective Dates of SAS Nos. 134-140*, extended the effective date to December 15, 2021, in order to provide more time for firms to implement SAS No. 134 in light of the effect of the coronavirus pandemic. While SAS No. 141 allows for early implementation of SAS No. 134, the ASB recommends that SAS Nos. 134-140 be implemented concurrently.

---

*Considering the need for specialized skills or knowledge*

For the majority of accounting estimates, it is unlikely that specialized skills or knowledge will be needed; however, the auditor may decide there is a need for those specialized skills or knowledge in some circumstances. Matters that may affect the auditor's decision include:

- The nature of the underlying asset, liability, or equity component in a particular business or industry;
- The degree of estimation uncertainty;
- The involvement of complex calculations or specialized models;

- The complexity of the requirements of the applicable financial reporting framework relevant to accounting estimates, including whether there are areas subject to differing interpretations or inconsistent or developing practices; and
- The procedures the auditor intends to undertake to respond to assessed risks.

## Responding to Significant Risks

The auditor's substantive procedures in auditing accounting estimates that give rise to significant risks are focused on how management assessed the effect of estimation uncertainty on the estimate, the effect that uncertainty may have on the appropriateness of the estimate's recognition in the financial statements, and the adequacy of related disclosures. Management's method for dealing with alternative outcomes or assumptions of accounting estimates is not as important as whether management has assessed how estimation uncertainty may affect the estimates. If management has not considered alternative outcomes or assumptions, the auditor may need to discuss how the effects of estimation uncertainty on the accounting estimate have been addressed with management.

**PLANNING AID REMINDER:** An assumption may be considered to be significant if a reasonable variation in the assumption would materially affect the measurement of the accounting estimate. The auditor may be able to evaluate the assumptions through inquiries of, and discussions with, management along with the other audit procedures to obtain sufficient appropriate evidence. Information derived from management's strategic analysis and risk management may provide additional input for the auditor.

Circumstances in which the auditor may determine management's consideration of the effects of estimation uncertainty on the accounting estimates giving rise to significant risks is inadequate include:

- Sufficient appropriate audit evidence could not be obtained through the auditor's evaluation of how management addressed the effects of estimation uncertainty and it is unlikely that other audit evidence can be obtained.
- Further exploration of the degree of estimation uncertainty related to an accounting estimate is needed, such as when the auditor is aware of a wide variation of outcomes for similar estimates.
- Indicators of management bias in making accounting estimates may exist.

**OBSERVATION:** When evaluating the appropriateness of recognizing or not recognizing specific accounting estimates in the financial statements, the auditor may determine in the case of an estimate not requiring financial statement recognition that there is a need to draw the reader's attention to a significant uncertainty by adding an emphasis-of-matter paragraph to the auditor's report.

## Evaluating Reasonableness of Accounting Estimates

If the auditor has developed a point estimate, the difference between the auditor's point estimate and management's point estimate is a misstatement. If the auditor has developed a range, the difference between management's point estimate and the nearest point of the auditor's range is a misstatement. A misstatement may also occur if the auditor concludes that management made an arbitrary change in an estimate or the method of making the estimate. Furthermore, evaluation of the reasonableness of accounting estimates and related disclosures included in the notes to the financial statements, whether required by the applicable financial reporting framework or disclosed voluntarily, involves the same considerations as when auditing an accounting estimate recognized in the financial statements.

---

**OBSERVATION:** The purpose of the audit of accounting estimates is to determine whether estimates are reasonable. Thus, an auditor might conclude that an estimate is reasonable even though it is not the best estimate. The difference between the reasonable estimate and the best estimate should not necessarily be treated as a misstatement; however, if most estimates appear to reflect a particular bias, such as the tendency to understate expenses, the auditor should consider whether all misstatements combined could result in a material misstatement.

---

**PLANNING AID REMINDER:** The auditor is required under AU-C 260 (*The Auditor's Communication with Those Charged with Governance*) to communicate with those charged with governance about the qualitative aspects of the entity's significant accounting practices, including accounting estimates and to inform those charged with governance about management's process for forming sensitive accounting estimates and the basis for the auditor's conclusions regarding the reasonableness of those estimates.

---

## Disclosures

Disclosures related to accounting estimates in the financial statements may be required by the applicable financial reporting framework or disclosed voluntarily. Disclosures may include information about the assumptions and estimation method used, the basis for selecting the estimation method, the effect of any changes to the estimation method from the prior period, and the sources and implications of estimation uncertainty.

For accounting estimates giving rise to significant risks, additional disclosure about their estimation uncertainty may be required the greater the range is of possible outcomes of the accounting estimate in relation to materiality. In some cases, the auditor may ask management to describe the circumstances related to estimation uncertainty in the notes to the financial statements. If the auditor believes management's disclosure of estimation uncertainty in the financial statements is inadequate or misleading, modifications to his or her opinion may be appropriate.

*Management Bias*

If the auditor becomes aware of indicators of management bias, the conclusion about the appropriateness of the auditor's risk assessment and related responses may be affected and the auditor may need to consider the implications for the rest of the audit. These indicators may also affect the auditor's evaluation of whether the financial statements as a whole are free from material misstatement.

Indicators of possible management bias with respect to accounting estimates include:

- Changes in an accounting estimate or method for making the estimate based on management's subjective assessment that there has been a change in circumstances,
- Use of an entity's own assumptions for fair value accounting estimates when those assumptions are inconsistent with observable market assumptions,
- Selection or construction of significant assumptions that yield a point estimate favorable for management objectives, and
- Selection of a point estimate that may indicate a pattern of optimism or pessimism.

**FRAUD POINTER:** Fraudulent financial reporting enforcement actions issued by the SEC often highlight cases involving asset overstatements. Assets related to fair value measurement and disclosure might involve heightened fraud risk because of the significant opportunities for management to perpetrate fraud related to those accounts. The significant dependence on management assumptions and the related complexities associated with measuring and disclosing fair value instruments can create significant opportunities for management to engage in fraud.

## Practitioner's Aids

Exhibit AU-C 540-1 discusses nonauthoritative guidance that is helpful in the audit of so-called soft accounting information (estimates). This exhibit summarizes an approach explained in the AICPA's Audit Practice Guide *Auditing Estimates and Other Soft Accounting Information*. The Audit Practice Guide is available for purchase from the AICPA.

**EXHIBIT AU-C 540-1—NONAUTHORITATIVE GUIDANCE FOR AUDITING SOFT ACCOUNTING INFORMATION**

The AICPA's Audit Practice Guide *Auditing Estimates and Other Soft Accounting Information* provides the following broad guidelines for the audit of accounting estimates:

- Auditing soft accounting information and engagement planning.
- Evaluating the persuasiveness of audit evidence related to soft accounting information.
- Communicating the nature of soft accounting information.

## Auditing Soft Accounting Information and Engagement Planning

Financial statements are based on a variety of accounting estimates ranging from the percentage of accounts receivable expected to be uncollectible to actuarial assumptions required by ASC 715 (*Compensation—Retirement Benefits*) in order to recognize pension expense. The client needs to understand and appreciate the role of estimates in the financial reporting process and that the determination of those estimates is the responsibility of the client, not the auditor.

For the planning phase of the engagement, the Audit Practice Guide addresses the following issues:

- Identify estimates with high risk.
- Determine the client's involvement in accounting estimates.
- Advise and support the client in making accounting estimates.

### Identify estimates with high risk

Financial statements incorporate a variety of estimates. During the planning stage of an engagement the auditor should identify areas where there is a high degree of risk for specific estimates. One factor that can help mitigate the risk related to a particular estimate is the client's established procedures. For example, internal reports that are timely reviewed and are the basis of managerial action can help ensure that an estimate is well understood and to some degree controlled. On the other hand, poorly designed procedures increase the likelihood that an estimate that has not received an appropriate amount of attention harbors a relatively high degree of risk. The Audit Practice Guide identifies the following as conditions that can increase the audit risk related to estimates:

- The client might be new and its previous years' financial statements might have been compiled or audited and the client might not have given adequate attention to the role of estimates in financial reporting.

- The client might have switched from another comprehensive basis of accounting to U.S. GAAP-based reporting. For example, many estimates are based on the accrual accounting concept and if a cash or modified accrual basis has been used by the client, procedures related to the development of estimates might be nonexistent.

- There has been an issuance of new accounting standards that contain accounting and reporting requirements that rely on client estimates. For example, ASC 360 (*Property, Plant, and Equipment*) requires under certain conditions the estimate of future net cash flows to determine whether a long-lived asset has a cost-recoverability problem.

- The operations of the client have changed in a manner whereby previous years' experience with estimating account balances is no longer relevant or is less relevant to current estimates. For example, the client has added a line of electronic components that is characterized by rapid technological change compared to previously manufactured components. Previously

employed procedures for identifying inventory that needs to be written down might not be appropriate for the new components.
- The customer base of the client has been modified. For example, the client might have decided to sell its products in foreign markets and has limited experience with collection issues related to accounts receivable.

*Determine the client's involvement in accounting estimates*

The Audit Practice Guide notes that once the estimates that have a higher degree of audit risk are identified, the next step is to determine the extent to which the client has developed an information base to address the estimation issue. This approach should include asking the following questions:
- What are the specific procedures used by the client to develop the data?
- Are the data collected by the client relevant to the account estimate and sufficient to make a reliable estimate?
- What are the procedures (model) used by the client to convert the data into the account estimate?
- Are the procedures used logical and does the process represent a reasonable approximation of the existing conditions?

In the audit of some clients, especially small or newly organized companies, it is possible that the client's procedures do not address many, if any, accounting estimates. This could be especially true of companies dominated by a manager-owner. The Audit Practice Guide points out that under this condition the auditor must determine whether the lack of procedures requires the auditor to withdraw from the engagement or remain in the engagement and help the client develop reasonable estimates for the preparation of the financial statements.

The Audit Practice Guide states that "when the estimates or soft accounting information are vital to the management of the business and are pervasive throughout the financial statements, the client's lack of a process for making these estimates should lead you to consider whether the entity is even auditable." For example, assume that a client manufactures a component for a large computer manufacturer and the controls in the supply chain are so deficient that the client often has fairly large quantities of inventory that become obsolete and of nominal value. If the client has maintained no records from previous years' inventory obsolescence experience, it is possible that the engagement is not auditable if current levels of inventory are material.

**OBSERVATION:** If the client has essentially no procedures related to the development of an estimate fundamental to the financial statements but still believes that the financial statements are auditable, the auditor should consider whether the condition gives rise to a significant deficiency or material weakness in internal control.

*Advise and Support the Client in Making Accounting Estimates*

On the other hand, the client's lack of procedures related to estimating account balances does not always imply that a prudent auditor should withdraw from an engagement. In many small engagements the client lacks the in-house expertise to fully understand the role of estimations in financial reporting or develop appropriate data to make those estimations. Obviously the auditor cannot simply walk away from these engagements (assuming they are auditable) but, rather, must develop a commonsense approach to the situation. The Audit Practice Guide describes the following as an approach that could be useful under this circumstance:

- Explain the role of estimates to the client.
- Assist the client in developing an estimation model.
- Assist the client in developing relevant key assumptions.
- Assist the client in obtaining relevant information about key assumptions.
- Let the client make the final assumptions.
- Assist the client in making the final estimate.

*Explain the role of estimates to the client*

Many individuals with a limited financial background (including businesspeople) see accounting as black and white with no room for estimates; it can be a challenge to explain to such individuals the accrual basis of accounting. The way an auditor conveys the explanation is personal and dependent upon his or her imagination. It is often best to leave out all of the jargon and technical references and find an everyday, close-to-home context to explain the need for estimates. In the final analysis an auditor must take time to educate the client and make sure they are committed to "getting the numbers right."

*Assist the client in developing an estimation model*

All estimates are based on a model (mathematical equation), some of which are simple and some of which are elaborate. For example, the aging of accounts receivable in order to estimate the amount of uncollectible accounts is based on a model with two or more variables (the bad-account percentage increases with the age of the account).

The key to developing a successful model (one that represents more or less the real world) is inquisitiveness in the context of the client's operations. The client brings to this project a thorough understanding of its operations and should be able to rely on in-house expertise to be reasonably certain that all of the relevant factors are considered. An auditor brings to this project a more limited knowledge of the client but a great deal of experience with various other clients and industries. Furthermore, the auditor brings a degree of rigor that might not always be the domain of the client. For example, the auditor can analyze factors raised by the client and determine which are relevant, how they interrelate with one another, and the possible financial outcome of their interplay.

Finally, an auditor should be careful not to restrict the scope of the information that may be gathered to deal with the estimation issue. The Audit Practice Guide notes that "many practitioners make the mistake of building a model based only on the information they know exists." With the explosion of informa-

*Assist the client in developing relevant key assumptions*

The auditor should discuss with the client the key assumptions that are likely to be the basis for developing an acceptable account estimate. The assumptions may include a variety of factors such as management's desire to maintain strong customer relations (the liberal application of a warranty clause), reliable costs estimates (for pending lawsuits), and business strategies that relate to future cash flow assumptions (in applying the cost recoverability test to various assets).

*Assist the client in obtaining relevant information about key assumptions*

Often a client needs help in the collection of information that relates to the key assumptions identified by the client. This is a research task that can include searching databases and other sources of information maintained by industry trade associations, business libraries, and reference sources maintained by the client. As sources of information are identified the auditor must determine whether the information is relevant to the estimate that needs to be made by the client. Like all accounting information, the information must be relevant to the estimation that needs to be made, reliable, and sufficient to support the assertions that will be made in the financial statements.

*Let the client make the final assumptions*

Even though the auditor is involved in developing the procedures used to make an account estimate, professional standards require that the client, not the auditor, make the assumptions related to the estimation. This is often a very difficult phase of the process. Up to this point the auditor has worked with the client to develop the approach and suddenly the auditor must tell the client that the client has the responsibility for developing an estimate that is included in the financial statements. The client knows that the estimates he or she develops must be acceptable to the auditor and often asks "What is the correct number?" The auditor should point out that it is not so much the specific number that an auditor is concerned with but, rather, the client's approach in developing the number. After all, the estimate is just that, an estimate. The Audit Practice Guide notes that it may be helpful to explain to the client the thought process that the auditor goes through in determining whether the process and assumptions used by the client are acceptable. For example, the auditor would raise the following questions as part of the audit process:

- Are the assumptions internally consistent with one another and consistent with other information developed?
- Do the assumptions reflect current changes and trends that are likely to have an effect on the eventual payments or write-downs related to the estimate?
- Are the assumptions consistent with the client's future plans?

*Assist the client in making the final estimate*

The final estimate made by the client must satisfy the client as well as the auditor and is fundamentally a trade-off between the cost of developing a highly precise estimate and the materiality of the estimate to the financial statements. If the estimate is clearly not material to the financial statements, a minimum amount of time should be devoted to the process. As the materiality of the estimate increases the auditor must be prepared to expend more audit effort in order to reduce the audit risk to an acceptable level.

Only a seasoned auditor who is familiar with the client and the client's industry should make the decision on how important an estimate is and how much audit time should be allocated to the process. The Audit Practice Guide points out that the auditor should also realize that becoming familiar with a particular estimation process should not be limited to the context of the client. For example, building expertise in a particular area can (1) benefit other audit engagements who have a similar issue or (2) build "valuable skills that later clients will pay for."

**PLANNING AID REMINDER:** The auditor might not have the expertise to develop an estimation process or evaluate the process used by the client, in which case the guidance established by AU-C 620 (*Using the Work of an Auditor's Specialist*) should be observed.

## Evaluating the Persuasiveness of Audit Evidence Related to Soft Accounting Information

Audit evidence related to estimates is different from that which supports historical cost transactions reflected in the financial statements. Past transactions can be corroborated by inspecting documentation, confirming specifics related to the transactions, or performing other, similar audit procedures that generally created high-quality audit evidence. Estimates are future related because they are based on subsequent decisions, events, or transactions and the quality of audit evidence to corroborate estimates will be somewhat limited. The Audit Practice Guide states that in order to be comfortable with an estimate the following two factors are important to the audit process:

1. The reliability of the estimation process, and
2. The quality of the assumptions used in the estimation process.

*The reliability of the estimation process*

There is an inverse relationship between the time and effort expended by management to develop an estimate and the audit risk related to the estimate. That is, if management has little interest in a particular estimate, the level of audit risk is greater than when management's approach to the estimate is both thoughtful and rigorous. The Audit Practice Guide points out that the following are factors of a reliable estimation process:

- Management's good faith effort,
- The appropriateness of the estimation model, and
- The quality of information used to make the estimate.

**Management's good faith effort** In determining whether the estimation process is reliable, management's attitude toward the process should be considered. The

Audit Practice Guide notes that good faith effort includes (1) being diligent in developing appropriate assumptions, (2) being cautious so as not to include misleading information in the financial statements, and (3) incorporating information that is consistent with management's plans and strategies.

*The appropriateness of the estimation model* An appropriate balance can only be created when the model used is a reasonable representation of the real-world conditions that affect the estimate. Key elements of the model should be investigated to determine whether they are consistent with the existing conditions. For example, if a warranty liability is being estimated and one of the key elements of the estimation model is that only parts and not repair service are covered by the warranty, the auditor should determine whether in practice service costs are also covered depending on the nature of the relationship between the client and its customers.

*The quality of information used to make the estimate* Obviously the auditor must be reasonable in determining the quality of information that is acceptable in developing an estimate. Professional judgment must be exercised based on the costs to the client and the benefits of producing financial statements that are not materially misstated.

*The quality of the assumptions used in the estimation process*

The Audit Practice Guide identifies the following as techniques that can be used to evaluate the appropriateness of estimates made by the client:

- Use of hindsight,
- Identify ranges of estimates, and
- Use alternative approaches.

*Use of hindsight* In limited situations an auditor may be able to review transactions and events that occur during the stub period (after the date of the financial statements but before the financial statements are released). For example, if a client made an estimate for returned goods that were shipped before the end of the year, a review of returned goods during the stub period might provide important insight into whether the estimate was reasonable.

*Identify ranges of estimates* One thing that is almost always certain about a point estimate is that it will be wrong. In most situations the auditor develops an acceptable range for the estimate, and if the client's estimate falls within that range, the auditor might be satisfied with the account balance.

---

**OBSERVATION:** The Audit Practice Guide warns that "the process used to develop a range should be as rigorous" as the process used to develop a point estimate.

---

*Use alternative approaches* Often the auditor can use alternative ways to determine whether an estimation process used by the client is acceptable. For example, an estimate for warranty costs for a new product could have been made by the client using assessments made by its engineering staff. As an alternative approach, the auditor could select a previously introduced product and review the warranty cost pattern for that product to see if it is reasonably consistent with the one developed by the client. The Audit Practice Guide notes that "wide differences in the results obtained from two or more valid models should be a red flag that causes you to investigate further."

---

**OBSERVATION:** The Audit Practice Guide points out that there are three types of estimates that are required by financial accounting standards, namely (1) management's ability and intent, (2) estimates of future cash flows, and (3) fair value estimates. For example, (1) ASC 320 (*Investments—Debt and Equity Securities*) requires that management classify investments into three possible portfolios that are accounted for in three different ways, (2) ASC 360 (*Property, Plant, and Equipment*) requires a client to estimate future cash flows for certain long-lived assets, and (3) ASC 718 (*Compensation—Stock Compensation*) requires that the fair value of compensatory stock option plans be determined. All of these estimation approaches present challenges for the auditor in determining whether the soft accounting information is not misleading as reported in the financial statements.

---

## Communicating the Nature of Soft Accounting Information

The inherent nature of estimates constrains the precision and effectiveness of financial reporting. No matter how sophisticated the client's procedure for constructing estimates or how rigorous the auditor's evaluation of those estimates, the information in the current financial statements that is based on estimates is tentative to some degree. The uncertainty related to estimates needs to be communicated to users in a way that allows them to build that uncertainty into their decision making process. The Audit Practice Guide lists the following two broad techniques that can help users better understand this uncertainty:

1. Required disclosures, and
2. Optional disclosures.

### Required disclosures

Financial reporting mandates a variety of required disclosures that specifically focus on uncertainties related to financial reporting. ASC 275 (*SOP 94-6, Disclosure of Certain Significant Risks and Uncertainties*) provides the "primary guidance on disclosures related to estimates and soft accounting information." ASC 275 requires certain disclosures when the following conditions are present:

- It is at least reasonably possible that the estimate of the effect on the financial statements of a condition, situation, or set of circumstances that existed at the date of the financial statements will change in the near term due to one or more future confirming events.
- The effect of the change would have a material effect on the financial statements.

If the above conditions are present, the following disclosures should be made:

- If an estimate requires disclosure under ASC 450 (*Contingencies*) or another pronouncement, an indication also shall be made that it is at least

reasonably possible that a change in the estimate will occur in the near term.
- An estimate that does not require disclosure under ASC 450 (*Contingencies*) (such as estimates associated with long-term operating assets and amounts reported under profitable long-term contracts) may meet the standards described above and, if so, require the following: (1) disclosure of its nature and (2) an indication that it is reasonably possible that a change in the estimate will occur in the near term.

The scope of ASC 275 (*Risks and Uncertainties*) is general and can apply to a variety of financial reporting issues as indicated by the following examples that are included in the pronouncement:
- Inventory subject to rapid technological obsolescence.
- Specialized equipment subject to technological obsolescence.
- Valuation allowances for deferred tax assets based on future taxable income.
- Capitalized motion picture film product costs.
- Capitalized computer software costs.
- Deferred policy acquisition costs of insurance enterprises.
- Valuation allowances for commercial and real estate loans.
- Environmental remediation-related obligations.
- Litigation-related obligations.
- Contingent liabilities for obligations of other entities.
- Amounts reported for long-term obligations (e.g., pensions and other postretirement benefits).
- Estimated net proceeds recoverable, the provisions for expected loss to be incurred, etc., on disposition of a business or assets.
- Amounts reported for long-term contracts.

*Optional disclosures*

Disclosures are not limited to those required by specific accounting pronouncements. The general disclosure principle requires that financial statements include information that could reasonably make a difference in assessments made by financial statement users. This general disclosure principle provides both management and the auditor with an opportunity to step back from the promulgated standards and ask whether the financial statements convey a reasonable description of the financial position and results of operations of the client. The Audit Practice Guide points out that the following optional disclosures may be helpful in portraying the risks and uncertainties related to soft accounting information:
- Disclose significant estimates.
- Describe limitations of estimates.
- Describe models used to make estimates.
- Describe the basis used to make assumptions.
- Describe recognition criteria.

- Explain why an estimate cannot be made.
- Disclose the time period related to future cash flow estimates.

***Disclose significant estimates*** The listing of estimates used by a client in the preparing of financial statements has become boilerplate and for that reason not very informative. As a supplement, the auditor may encourage the client to disclose and explain significant estimates that are fundamental to presentation of the financial statements.

***Describe limitations of estimates*** One of the misconceptions of financial reporting is the implication that a number presented is correct with no room for imprecision. This impression can be remedied to some extent by the client's describing the uncertainty related to specific significant estimates used to prepare the financial statements. Management should supplement boilerplate language with a succinct description of the risks that management is aware of and planned strategies to address these issues.

***Describe models used to make estimates*** The Audit Practice Guide points out that in some instances, such as one-time events, it is helpful to describe in a note to the financial statements "significant features of the process, the key assumptions made, and the rationale for such assumptions." These disclosures could remind the readers of the financial statements of the uncertainty associated with a particular account balance and the practical difficulties with making a reasonable estimate based on existing conditions.

***Describe the basis used to make assumptions*** Along with describing the elements related to the model used to make an estimate it may be equally insightful to the financial statement reader to be informed of "the rationale, the sources of information, and the thought process" used to construct assumptions that were fundamental to making the estimate.

***Describe recognition criteria*** In some instances, it is not apparent or obvious to a financial statement user the criteria that were used to make an estimate. For example, ASC 450 (Contingencies) uses terms such as "probable," "reasonably possible," and "remote" in determining whether a loss contingency is to be recorded, disclosed in a note, or omitted from the financial statements. Descriptions of these terms in the context of the specific estimates may assist the user in understanding the degree of uncertainty related to certain account balances.

***Explain why an estimate cannot be made*** In some instances, management is unable to make a reasonable estimate because of the lack of relevant information even after an appropriate estimation process has been constructed and executed. Rather than simply state in a note to the financial statements that an estimate cannot be made, the disclosure may "explain why a particular estimate cannot be made and give some indication of when an estimate will be possible."

***Disclose the time period related to future cash flow estimates*** Accounting estimates may be in part based on estimates of future cash flows. Disclosing the period of time used for the estimate and why a particular length of time was used can better convey to the financial statement user the degree of uncertainty surrounding an estimate.

## EXHIBIT AU-C 540-2—COMMON FINANCIAL STATEMENT ESTIMATES REQUIRING AUDITOR EVALUATION

### Assets
- Allowance for doubtful accounts.
- Allowance for sales returns and allowances.
- Evaluation of when a software vendor has established technological feasibility for the purpose of capitalizing computer software development costs.
- Estimates of fair-market value of available-for-sale and trading securities (not traded in an active market).
- Impairment of long-lived assets and intangible assets.
- Inventory obsolescence reserve.
- Recoverability of deferred tax assets (more likely than not).
- Useful lives and salvage values of fixed assets.
- Useful lives of intangible assets (those without an indefinite useful life).

### Liabilities
- Discount rate, assumed return on plan assets, among other assumptions, for defined benefit pension plans.
- Discount rate, health-care-cost trend rate, among other estimates, for retiree health-care-benefit plans.
- Salvage value for leased assets, implicit rate of return in a lease contract, among other estimates, for lease contracts.
- Warranty obligations.

### Revenues
- Percentage-of-completion for long-term construction contracts.
- Sales discounts.
- Sales returns.

### Expenses
- Amortization expense.
- Bad debts expense.
- Cost of goods sold.
- Depreciation expense.
- Income tax expense.
- Pension expense (income).
- Postretirement benefit expense other than pension.
- Warranty expense.

### Gains and Losses
- Loss on asset impairment.
- Unrealized gains and losses on nonpublic or thinly traded securities.

# SECTION 550

# RELATED PARTIES

## Authoritative Pronouncements

SAS-122—Statements on Auditing Standards: Clarification and Recodification

SAS-135—Omnibus Statement on Auditing Standards—2019

SAS-136—Forming an Opinion and Reporting on Financial Statements of Employee Benefit Plans Subject to ERISA

SAS-141—Amendment to Effective Dates of SAS Nos. 134-140

## Overview

An audit of financial statements cannot be expected to provide assurance that all related-party transactions were identified. However, an auditor must be alert for the possible occurrence of related-party transactions and should evaluate them with a higher degree of skepticism than transactions that are executed by parties that are not related. AU-C 550 establishes guidelines for evaluating related-party relationships and transactions that are discovered during an audit engagement.

While related-party transactions may occur in the normal course of business and carry no higher a risk of material misstatement than an arm's length transaction, in some circumstances, related-party transactions may give rise to higher risks of material misstatement of the financial statements. This increased risk of material misstatement associated with related-party transactions may be due to increased complexity, ineffective transaction identification or tracking, transaction terms or conditions different from the market, or management motivations to engage in or conceal fraud.

The auditor is responsible for identifying, assessing, and responding to risks of material misstatement that arise from the entity's failure to account for or disclose related-party relationships or transactions according to the applicable financial reporting framework. These procedures are important because the auditor should be able to conclude, based on the audit evidence obtained, whether related-party relationships and transactions prevent the financial statements from being fairly presented. Professional guidelines for related-party transactions are contained in AU-C 550 and ASC 850 (*Related Party Disclosures*).

**IMPORTANT NOTICE FOR 2022:** In May 2019, the AICPA's Auditing Standards Board (ASB) issued SAS No. 135 titled *Omnibus Statement on Auditing Standards—2019* that includes amendments to various AU-C sections. SAS No. 135 amends AU-C 550 to incorporate some of the guidance in PCAOB Auditing Standards that addresses auditor responsibilities regarding related parties. SAS No. 135 adds requirements to AU-C 550 to heighten the auditor's focus on related parties and relationships and transactions with related parties. More specifically, the new standard (1) enhances requirements to identify related parties, particularly previously unidentified or undisclosed related parties or significant related-party transactions, (2) includes potential inquiries about background information concerning related parties, (3) enhances the auditor's response to the risks of material misstatement associated with related-party relationships and transactions, including procedures to test the accuracy and completeness of the related parties and relationships and transactions with related parties identified by the entity, taking into account the information gathered during the audit, and (4) provides application material regarding these enhanced requirements, including examples. SAS No. 135 adds requirements for the auditor to inquire about any related-party transactions that have not been authorized or approved in accordance with the entity's established policies or procedures regarding the authorization and approval of transactions with related parties. And, the auditor should inquire about the business purpose of entering into a transaction with a related party versus an unrelated party. The auditor will also need to add inquiries about any related-party transactions for which exceptions have been granted. Finally, the auditor is required to inquire of those charged with governance about their understanding of the entity's relationship and transactions with related parties and whether those charged with governance have any concerns related to those relationships and transactions. Originally, the effective date of SAS No. 135 was for audits of financial statements periods ending on or after December 15, 2020, with early application **not** permitted. However, the ASB's issuance of SAS No. 141, *Amendment to the Effective Dates of SAS Nos. 134-140*, extended the effective date to December 15, 2021, in order to provide more time for firms to implement SAS No. 135 in light of the effect of the coronavirus pandemic. While SAS No. 141 allows for early implementation of SAS No. 135, the ASB recommends that SAS Nos. 134-140 be implemented concurrently.

## Definitions

| | |
|---|---|
| Arm's-length transaction | A transaction conducted on such terms and conditions between a willing buyer and seller who are unrelated, acting independently of each other, and pursuing their own best interests. |
| Related party | This term is defined by U.S. GAAP as an entity affiliate; an entity for which the investing entity should account for its investments using the equity method; beneficial employee trusts that are managed by entity management; principal owners and management of the entity and their immediate families; any party that may, or does, deal with the entity and has ownership, control, or significant influence over the management or operating policies of another party to the extent that an arm's-length transaction might not be achieved. |

**PUBLIC COMPANY IMPLICATION:** The PCAOB's Auditing Standard AS-2410 (*Related Parties: Amendments to Certain PCAOB Auditing Standards Regarding Significant Unusual Transactions and Other Amendments to PCAOB Auditing Standards*) contains guidance in the areas of related-party transactions (RPTs), significant unusual transactions, and financial relationships and transactions with executive officers. The PCAOB guidance combines these three areas into a single standard because of their potential relationship with executive officers. In auditing RPTs, the standard requires the auditor to (1) perform procedures to understand the company's relationships and transactions with related parties, including transactions with related parties that were modified during the period under audit; (2) evaluate whether the company has properly identified its related parties and transactions with them; (3) perform additional procedures if undisclosed (by management) related parties or related-party transactions are discovered by the auditor; (4) perform specific procedures for those RPTs required to be disclosed in the financial statements or that are identified as a significant risk; and (5) communicate to the audit committee the auditor's evaluation of the company's identification of, accounting for, and disclosure of RPTs.

AS-2410 also includes requirements for the consideration of fraud in an audit. The PCAOB describes a "significant unusual transaction" as one that is outside the normal course of business for the company or that otherwise appears unusual because of the transaction's timing, size, or nature. In auditing significant unusual transactions, the standard requires the auditor to (1) perform procedures to identify significant unusual transactions; (2) perform procedures to determine whether the significant unusual transaction has a business purpose and, if so, to understand that purpose; and (3) consider whether the transaction may have been entered into to commit financial reporting fraud or conceal a misappropriation of assets. The PCAOB's standard requires the auditor to obtain an understanding of the company's financial relationships and transactions with executive officers, including executive compensation arrangements. Specifically, AS-2410 requires the auditor to consider whether executive compensation arrangements may create an incentive or pressure for the company to achieve certain operating results or financial position.

## Requirements

The auditor is required to perform the following procedures with respect to related-party relationships and transactions:

### Risk Assessment and Related Procedures

1. Obtain information relevant to identifying the risks of material misstatements associated with related-party relationships and transactions.

2. As part of the required engagement team discussion, consider the susceptibility of the financial statements to material misstatement due to fraud or error that could result from the entity's related-party relationships and transactions.

3. Inquire of management and others within the entity about:
   a. The identity of the entity's related parties, including any changes from the prior period;
   b. The nature of the relationships between the entity and related parties;
   c. The business purpose of entering into a transaction with a related party versus an unrelated party; and
   d. Whether any transactions occurred, were modified, or terminated between the entity and related parties during the period and, if so, inquire about the type and purpose of the transactions.

4. Inquire of management and others within the entity and perform other appropriate risk assessment procedures to obtain an understanding of any controls management has established to:

    a. Identify, account for, and disclose related-party relationships and transactions;
    b. Authorize and approve significant transactions and arrangements with related parties outside the normal course of business or with related parties; and
    c. Authorize and approve significant unusual transactions, and arrangements outside the normal course of business.

   Inquiries should include asking about any related-party transactions that have not been authorized or approved in accordance with the entity's policies and procedures or any transactions for which exceptions to those policies or procedures occurred.

5. Inquire of those charged with governance about their understanding of the entity's relationships and transactions with related parties that are significant to the entity and whether any of those charged with governance have concerns regarding relationships or transactions with related parties, and, if so, the substance of those concerns.

6. Remain alert during the audit for information indicating the existence of related-party relationships or transactions not previously identified or disclosed to the auditor when inspecting records or documents, in particular, the following: bank and legal confirmations, minutes of meetings of shareholders and those charged with governance, and other records or documents the auditor considers necessary in the entity's circumstances.

7. If significant unusual transactions outside the entity's normal course of business are identified when performing audit procedures, inquire of management about the nature of the transactions and whether related parties could be involved.

8. Share relevant information about the entity's related parties with engagement team members.

## *Identification and Assessment of the Risks of Material Misstatement*

9. Identify and assess the risks of material misstatement associated with related-party relationships and transactions and determine whether any of those risks are significant risks. Identified significant related-party transactions outside the entity's normal course of business should be considered as giving rise to significant risks.

10. When identifying and assessing risks of material misstatement due to fraud, incorporate consideration of related parties as part of the auditor's consideration of fraud risk factors when performing risk assessment and related procedures.

## *Responses to the Risks of Material Misstatement*

11. Design and perform further audit procedures to obtain sufficient appropriate audit evidence about the assessed risks of material misstatement associated with related-party transactions.

12. Evaluate whether the entity has properly identified its related-party relationships and transactions, including inquiry as to how management tests the accuracy and completeness of the related-party transactions identified by the entity.

13. If arrangements or information are identified suggesting the existence of related-party relationships or transactions that management has not previously identified or disclosed to the auditor, determine whether the underlying circumstances confirm their existence.

14. If previously unidentified or undisclosed related parties or significant related-party transactions are identified:
    a. Promptly communicate the relevant information to other engagement team members.
    b. Request that management identify all transactions with those related parties for the auditor's further evaluation.
    c. Inquire why the entity's controls over related-party relationships and transactions failed to enable their identification or disclosure.
    d. Perform appropriate substantive audit procedures relating to the newly identified related parties or significant related-party transactions.
    e. Reconsider the risk that other related parties or significant related-party transactions may exist that management has not identified or disclosed to the auditor and perform any necessary additional audit procedures.
    f. Evaluate the implications for the audit if management's nondisclosure appears intentional.

15. For identified significant related-party transactions outside the entity's normal course of business:
    a. Inspect any underlying contracts or agreements and evaluate whether the business rationale or lack thereof suggests the transactions may have been entered into to engage in or conceal fraud; the transactions' terms are consistent with management's explanations; and the transactions have been appropriately accounted for and disclosed.
    b. Obtain audit evidence that the transactions have been appropriately authorized and approved.

16. If management asserts in the financial statements that a related-party transaction was conducted on terms equivalent to an arm's length transaction, obtain sufficient appropriate audit evidence about the assertion.

17. To assess the risk of material misstatements associated with entity's accounts with affiliates, the auditor should perform procedures on balances with affiliated entities as of concurrent dates, even if fiscal years of the respective entities differ.

## *Evaluation of Identified Related-Party Relationships and Transactions*

18. In forming an opinion on the financial statements, evaluate whether identified related-party relationships and transactions are appropriately accounted for and disclosed and whether the effects of related-party relationships and transactions prevent fair presentation of the financial statements.

## *Communication with Those Charged with Governance*

19. Unless all of those charged with governance are involved in managing the entity, communicate significant matters arising during the audit in connection with the entity's related parties.

## *Documentation*

20. Include the names of identified related parties and the nature of related-party relationships in the audit documentation.

## Analysis and Application of Procedures

*Nature of Related-Party Relationships and Transactions*

While requirements for the accounting treatment and disclosure of related-party relationships and transactions are prescribed by financial reporting frameworks and accounting pronouncements, related-party transactions are typically not required to be accounted for differently than transactions with unrelated parties. It is important, however, to ensure that the substance rather than the form of related-party transactions is recognized in the financial statements.

In addition to relationships that may lead to the auditor's identification of a related-party transaction, certain transactions suggest that the parties may be related. AU-C 550 lists the following as examples:

- Contracts that carry no interest rate or that carry an unrealistic interest rate.
- Real estate transactions that are made at a price significantly different from appraised values.
- Nonmonetary transactions that involve the exchange of similar assets.
- Loan agreements that contain no repayment schedule.

---

**PUBLIC COMPANY IMPLICATION:** Because related-party transactions are not conducted at arm's length, there is often a lack of independence and objectivity between management and the related party. In light of this, SOX prohibits related-party transactions that involve personal loans to executives of public companies. It is now illegal for any public company to extend or maintain credit, to arrange for the extension of credit, or to renew the extension of credit in the form of a personal loan to any director or executive officer of the company. These restrictions do not apply to any loan, such as a home loan or credit card agreement, made by a bank or other insured financial institution under normal banking operations using market terms. Auditors of public companies should be alert for prohibited loans to executives and deal with them as illegal acts.

---

Finally, certain conditions may increase the possibility that a related-party transaction may occur. These conditions include the following:

- Inadequate working capital or lines of credit,
- Earnings forecast that was too optimistic,
- Too great a dependence on one or a few products or customers,
- A declining industry,
- Excess capacity,
- Significant legal problems, and
- Exposure to technological changes.

> **OBSERVATION:** Although these conditions do not usually result in related-party transactions, they indicate that the auditor must be more alert to the increased possibility.

---

> **FRAUD POINTER:** AU-C 240 notes that the presence of significant related-party transactions not in the ordinary course of business or with related parties who are not audited or who are audited by another firm can create opportunities for management or others to engage in fraudulent financial reporting. When evaluating business transactions involving previously unidentified related parties, auditors should exercise appropriate professional skepticism.

## Risk Assessment and Related Procedures

### Understanding related-party relationships and transactions

As part of the engagement team discussion considering the financial statements' susceptibility to misstatements that could result from the entity's related-party relationships or transactions, matters such as the following may be addressed:

- The nature and extent of the entity's related-party relationships and transactions;
- The importance of maintaining professional skepticism regarding those risks of material misstatement;
- Records, documents, or circumstances that could indicate the existence of unidentified or undisclosed related-party relationships or transactions;
- The importance management and those charged with governance place on proper accounting for and disclosure of such relationships and transactions;
- Circumstances or conditions that may give rise to related parties that might not be identified by management or disclosed to the auditor; and
- Specific considerations of how related parties may be involved in fraud.

---

> **PLANNING AID REMINDER:** The principal auditor and other auditors of related entities should exchange information on the names of known related parties in the early stages of their examinations.

---

Information regarding the identity of the entity's related parties may be readily available to the auditor if the entity has an information system that tracks this information to enable the entity to meet disclosure requirements; however, this is not always the case. The auditor's inquiries regarding the identity of related parties may occur as part of the engagement acceptance or continuance process or as part of the risk assessment procedures and related activities performed to obtain information about the entity and its environment. Information about the identity of related parties is also obtained through management's written representations disclosing the identity of related parties that management is aware of and asserting that such related-party relationships and transactions have been appropriately accounted for and disclosed.

> **ENGAGEMENT STRATEGY:** Management is more likely to be aware of relationships of economic significance to the entity so inquiries may be more effective if the auditor focuses on significant transactions the entity engages in and asks if those parties are related parties.

Management is responsible for designing, implementing, and monitoring controls over related-party relationships and transactions so that they are appropriately accounted for and disclosed and those charged with governance are responsible for overseeing management's performance of this responsibility. To obtain an understanding of controls over related-party relationships and transactions, the auditor makes inquiries of management and others within the entity such as those charged with governance, internal auditors, legal counsel, the chief ethics officer, the chief compliance officer, the human resources director, and personnel who initiate, authorize, process, or record significant transactions outside the entity's normal course of business or those who supervise or monitor such personnel.

> **FRAUD POINTER:** Management override of controls is often involved in fraudulent financial reporting when controls appear to be operating effectively. The risk of management override is increased with related parties because management may be presented with greater incentives and opportunities to perpetrate fraud.

AU-C 550 lists factors the auditor may consider in obtaining his or her understanding of internal control over related-party relationships and transactions:

- Communication and enforcement of internal ethics codes.

- Policies and procedures for the disclosure of management's and those charged with governance's interests in related-party transactions.

- Assignment of responsibilities for initiating, recording, summarizing, and disclosing related-party transactions.

- Disclosure and discussion between management and those charged with governance of significant related-party transactions outside the entity's normal course of business, including whether those charged with governance questioned the business rationale for such transactions.

- Guidelines approval of for related-party transaction when actual or perceived conflicts of interest exist.

- Periodic reviews by internal auditors.

- Proactive action taken by management to resolve related-party disclosure issues.

- The existence of whistle-blowing policies and procedures.

> **ENGAGEMENT STRATEGY:** If controls over related-party transactions and relationships are deficient or nonexistent, sufficient appropriate audit evidence may not be able to be obtained. In these circumstances, the auditor should consider the implications for the audit and the opinion in the auditor's report.

*Reviewing documents or records for related-party information and arrangements*

Entity documents and records that may provide information about related-party relationships and transactions not previously identified or disclosed to the auditor include: income tax returns; information supplied to regulatory authorities; shareholder registers identifying principal shareholders; statements of conflicts of interest from or contracts and agreements with management and those charged with governance; records of investments and benefit plans; significant contracts and agreements not in the ordinary course of business; invoices and correspondence from professional advisors; life insurance policies acquired; significant contracts renegotiated during the period; capital financing arrangements with entities other than financial institutions; economic development arrangements for capital additions; and prior year audit documentation.

Third-party confirmations and prior years' audit documentation are additional documentation that may provide the auditor with relevant information. The auditor may also obtain relevant information by inquiring of a predecessor auditor regarding that auditor's knowledge of existing relationships and the extent of management involvement in material transactions.

An arrangement is a formal or informal agreement between an entity and one or more other parties for reasons such as establishing a business relationship, conducting certain types of transactions, or providing designated services or financial support. Arrangements may indicate the presence of related-party relationships or transactions in certain circumstances, including participation in unincorporated partnerships with other parties, agreements for provision of services to certain parties under terms and conditions outside the entity's normal course of business, or guarantees and guarantor relationships.

When the auditor is identifying significant unusual transactions, such transactions may include the following as listed in AU-C 550:

- Complex equity transactions such as corporate restructurings or acquisitions,
- Transactions with offshore entities in jurisdictions with less rigorous corporate laws or regulations,
- Leases or provision of services to another party with no consideration exchanged,
- Sales transactions with unusually large discounts or returns,
- Transactions with circular arrangements such as a commitment to repurchase, and
- Transactions under contracts when terms are changed before expiration.

*Sharing information with the engagement team*

When sharing relevant information obtained about the entity's related parties with other members of the engagement team, the auditor may share information about the nature of related-party relationships and transactions and about significant or complex related-party relationships or transactions that may require special audit consideration, especially if management or those charged with governance are financially involved. This sharing of information is most useful in the beginning stages of an audit.

*Identification and Assessment of the Risks of Material Misstatement*

If a related party exerts dominant influence over an entity or its management, that is a fraud risk factor which, when combined with other fraud risk factors, may indicate significant risks of material misstatement due to fraud. Factors indicating a related party may be exerting dominant influence include the following:

- The related party has vetoed business decisions of management or those charged with governance.
- Significant transactions are referred to the related party for final approval.
- Business proposals by the related party receive little debate.
- Transactions involving the related party are rarely independently reviewed and approved.
- The related party helped found the entity and still participates in managing the entity.

*Responses to the Risks of Material Misstatement*

The nature, timing, and extent of the auditor's further audit procedures to respond to the risks of material misstatement associated with related-party relationships and transactions will depend on the nature of those risks and the entity's circumstances.

If there is a significant risk that certain related-party transactions have not been properly accounted for or disclosed, the auditor may perform substantive audit procedures such as:

- Confirming transaction details with the related parties,
- Inspecting evidence held by other parties to the transaction,
- Confirming or discussing significant transaction information with intermediaries,
- Referring to public information sources when there is reason to believe that significant transactions with unfamiliar parties may lack substance, and
- Obtaining information about the financial capability of other parties to the transaction.

**ENGAGEMENT STRATEGY:** Since the audit risk associated with management's assertions concerning related-party transactions is generally higher than the audit risk associated with other transactions, the audit procedures that are applied to related-party transactions should be more extensive or effective. For example, to obtain additional evidence or a better understanding of a related-party transaction, the auditor may apply selected audit procedures to, or may actually audit, the financial statements of the related party as part of the engagement strategy.

---

**PLANNING AID REMINDER:** In some circumstances, substantive audit procedures will not provide the auditor with sufficient appropriate audit evidence and testing the entity's controls over related-party relationships and transactions will be required.

---

If there is a significant risk of material misstatement due to fraud because of a related party with dominant influence, the auditor may perform the following procedures to identify any need for further substantive audit procedures: inquire of management, those charged with governance, and the related party; inspect significant contracts with the related party; perform appropriate background research; and review any employee whistle-blowing reports.

*Newly identified related-party relationships or transactions*

Substantive audit procedures that may be appropriate for the auditor to perform related to newly identified related-party relationships and transactions include the following:

- Inquiring about the nature of the entity's relationships with the newly identified related parties and other external parties presumed to have significant knowledge of the entity and its business,
- Analyzing accounting records for transactions with the newly identified related parties, and
- Verifying terms and conditions of transactions with newly identified related parties and evaluating whether those transactions have been appropriately accounted for and disclosed.

---

**FRAUD POINTER:** If management appears to have intentionally failed to disclose related-party relationships or transactions, the auditor should consider whether to reevaluate the reliability of management's representations and responses to the auditor's inquiries.

---

*Significant related-party transactions outside the entity's normal course of business*

The auditor considers the business rationale of significant related-party transactions outside the entity's normal course of business to evaluate whether these transactions indicate the presence of any fraud risk factors. In evaluating the business rationale of these transactions, the auditor may consider whether: the transaction is overly complex, has unusual terms, lacks an apparent logical business reason for its occurrence, involves previously unidentified related parties, or is processed in an unusual manner. The auditor may also consider whether management has discussed the transaction's nature and accounting with those charged with governance and whether management is emphasizing a particular accounting treatment instead of following the underlying economics of the transaction.

> **PLANNING AID REMINDER:** The auditor is required to understand the business rationale for significant related-party transactions. AICPA Practice Alert 03-1 (*Audit Confirmations*) states that confirmation of the terms of related-party transactions can help auditors obtain this understanding. Specifically, the auditor might confirm the transaction amount and terms, including any guarantees, with the other party to the transaction. Because client management may be on both sides of a related-party transaction, the auditor should consider confirming the terms of the transaction with intermediaries (e.g., agents, attorneys, banks, guarantors).

A transaction that appears inconsistent with the nature of the related party's business or that is materially inconsistent with management's explanations may represent a fraud risk. Furthermore, if management's explanations are inconsistent with the transaction, the auditor is required to consider the reliability of management's explanations and representations on other significant matters.

Proper authorization and approval of such significant related-party transactions by management, those charged with governance, or shareholders may provide audit evidence that these transactions have been appropriately considered and reflected in the financial statements. However, authorization and approval may not be sufficient to conclude whether risks of material misstatement due to fraud are absent because they may be ineffective in circumstances when there is collusion between related parties or the entity is subject to the dominant influence of a related party.

*Assertions regarding the terms of related-party transactions*

It is typically difficult for the auditor to substantiate an assertion by management that the terms of a transaction were equivalent to those prevailing in an arm's length transaction. Even if audit evidence is available supporting the price of a transaction, other terms and conditions of the transaction may be impracticable to confirm. Therefore, there may be a risk that management's assertion regarding such a transaction is materially misstated.

Management may support an assertion that the terms of a related-party transaction are equivalent to those of an arm's length transaction by having an external specialist determine and confirm a market value, terms, and conditions for the transaction or by comparing the transaction's terms to those of an identical or similar transaction with an unrelated party or to known market terms from broadly similar transactions on an open market. The auditor may evaluate management's support for such an assertion by considering the appropriateness of management's process for supporting the assertion or by verifying the source of and testing the data supporting the assertion for accuracy, completeness, and relevance.

> **ENGAGEMENT STRATEGY:** If the auditor believes management's assertion that the terms of a related-party transaction are equivalent to an arm's length transaction is unsubstantiated or sufficient appropriate audit evidence to support the assertion cannot be obtained, he or she should consider the implications for the audit and the audit opinion in accordance with AU-C 705.

> **ENGAGEMENT STRATEGY:** If management does not adequately substantiate its representation with respect to the related-party transaction, the auditor should express a qualified or adverse opinion on the financial statements if the matter is considered material.

### Evaluation of Identified Related-Party Relationships and Transactions

Appropriate disclosure of related-party transactions may not be achieved if the disclosures are not understandable, which could occur if the business rationale and effects of the transaction on the financial statements are unclear or misstated or key terms, conditions, or other elements of the transactions necessary to understand them are not appropriately disclosed.

### Communication with Those Charged with Governance

Significant related-party matters the auditor may communicate with those charged with governance include the following listed in AU-C 550:

- Nondisclosure by management of related-party relationships or transactions.
- Significant related-party transactions identified that have not been appropriately authorized and approved.
- Disagreement with management regarding the accounting for and disclosure of significant related-party transactions.
- Noncompliance with applicable laws or regulations prohibiting or restricting specific types of related-party transactions.
- Difficulties in identifying the entity that ultimately controls the entity.

> **PLANNING AID REMINDER:** The auditor should consider obtaining written representations from senior management of an entity and its board of directors regarding whether they or other related parties were involved in transactions with the entity.

*Determine whether the client has made appropriate disclosures for related-party transactions that have been identified*

The Financial Accounting Standards Board (FASB) requires disclosure of related-party transactions that (1) are not eliminated in consolidated or combined financial statements and (2) are necessary to understand the entity's financial statements.

If separate financial statements of an entity that has been consolidated are presented in a financial report that includes the consolidated financial statements, duplicate disclosure of the related-party transactions is not necessary. Thus, disclosure of the related-party transactions in the consolidated statements is all that is required. However, disclosure of related-party transactions is required in separate financial statements of (1) a parent company, (2) a subsidiary, (3) a corporate joint venture, or (4) an investee that is less than 50% owned. The minimum financial statement disclosures required by ASC 850 (*Related Parties*) for related-party transactions that (1) are not eliminated in consolidation or combination and (2) are necessary to the understanding of the financial statements are as follows:

- The nature of the related-party relationship. The name of the related party should also be disclosed if it is essential to the understanding of the relationship.
- A description of the related-party transactions, including amounts and other pertinent information for each period in which an income statement is presented.
- Related-party transactions of no amount, or of nominal amounts, must also be disclosed. In other words, all information that is necessary for an understanding of the effects of the related-party transactions on the financial statements must be disclosed, assuming this information is material.
- The effects of any change in terms between the related parties from terms used in prior periods. In addition, the dollar amount of transactions for each period in which an income statement is presented must be disclosed.
- If not apparent in the financial statements, (1) the terms of related-party transactions, (2) the manner of settlement to related-party transactions, and (3) the amount due to, or due from, related parties must all be disclosed.
- The nature of any control relationship, even if there were no transactions between the related parties, must be disclosed in all circumstances.

The amount of information disclosed for related-party transactions must be sufficient for the user of the financial statements to be able to understand the related-party transaction. Thus, the disclosure of the total amount of a specific type of related-party transaction, or the effects of the relationship between the related parties, may be all that is necessary. The auditor must determine whether the related-party transaction affects the financial statements to such a degree that they are materially misstated and must modify the report accordingly.

---

**OBSERVATION:** One cannot assume that a related-party transaction is consummated in the same manner as an arm's-length transaction. Disclosures or other representations of related-party transactions in financial statements should not, under any circumstances, indicate that the transaction was made on the same basis as an arm's-length transaction.

## SECTION 560

# SUBSEQUENT EVENTS AND SUBSEQUENTLY DISCOVERED FACTS

### Authoritative Pronouncements

SAS-122—Statements on Auditing Standards: Clarification and Recodification

SAS-135—Omnibus Statement on Auditing Standards—2019

SAS-136—Forming an Opinion and Reporting on Financial Statements of Employee Benefit Plans Subject to ERISA

SAS-141—Amendment to Effective Dates of SAS Nos. 134-140

### Overview

AU-C 560 addresses the auditor's responsibilities relating to subsequent events and subsequently discovered facts in a financial statement audit. The responsibilities of a predecessor auditor for subsequent events and subsequently discovered facts when reissuing an auditor's report on prior period financial statements are also addressed.

There are two types of subsequent events generally identified by financial reporting frameworks:

1. Those providing evidence of conditions that existed at the date of the financial statements.

2. Those providing evidence of conditions that arose after the date of the financial statements but before the date of the auditor's report.

The auditor seeks to obtain sufficient appropriate audit evidence about whether subsequent events are appropriately reflected in the financial statements in accordance with the applicable financial reporting framework. Another objective of the auditor is to respond appropriately to subsequently discovered facts. For predecessor auditors, the objective is to determine if reissuing a previously issued auditor's report on prior period financial statements to be presented with audited financial statements of a subsequent period on a comparative basis is still appropriate.

The auditor's report should be dated no earlier than the date on which the auditor has gathered sufficient audit evidence to support the opinion. The auditor has not obtained sufficient audit evidence to support the opinion until (1) the audit documentation has been reviewed, (2) the financial statements, including required disclosures have been prepared, and (3) management and those charged with governance (as appropriate) have accepted responsibility for the financial statements. Accordingly, the date of the auditor's report on amended financial statements cannot be earlier than the date of approval of the amended financial statements.

The term "audited financial statements" refers to the financial statements together with the auditor's report on the financial statements. While AU-C 560 describes the auditor's responsibilities for subsequent events and subsequently discovered facts in a financial statement audit, the auditor may have additional responsibilities related to subsequent events when audited financial statements are included in other documents subsequent to their issuance. These responsibilities are not addressed in AU-C 560, but may relate to legal or regulatory requirements involving private placement offerings, exempt public offerings, or other public offerings in jurisdictions outside the United States.

## Definitions

| | |
|---|---|
| Date of the auditor's report | The date that the auditor dates the report on the financial statements. |
| Date of the financial statements | The date of the end of the latest period covered by the financial statements. |
| Subsequent events | Events occurring between the date of the financial statements and the date of the auditor's report. |
| Subsequently discovered facts | Facts that become known to the auditor after the date of the auditor's report that, had they been known to the auditor at that date, may have caused the auditor to amend the auditor's report. |

## Requirements

The auditor is presumptively required to perform the following procedures related to subsequent events and subsequently discovered facts:

### *Subsequent Events*

1. Perform audit procedures designed to obtain sufficient appropriate audit evidence that all subsequent events have been identified. If previously performed audit procedures provide satisfactory conclusions about a matter, additional audit procedures do not need to be performed.

2. Audit procedures should cover the period from the date of the financial statements to the date of the auditor's report as much as is practicable. The nature and extent of audit procedures should take the auditor's risk assessment into account and include the following:

   a. Obtain an understanding of procedures management established to identify subsequent events;

   b. Inquire of management and those charged with governance (as appropriate) about whether any events occurred after the date of the financial statements that might affect the statements;

   c. Read any minutes of meetings of the entity's owners, management, and those charged with governance held after the date of the financial statements and inquire about matters discussed at any such meeting if minutes are not yet available; and

   d. Read the latest of any subsequent interim financial statements of the entity.

3. Determine if each subsequent event that is identified and requires adjustment of, or disclosure in, the financial statements is appropriately reflected in the financial statements in accordance with the applicable financial reporting framework.

## Subsequently Discovered Facts

4. After the date of the auditor's report, the auditor is not obligated to perform any audit procedures regarding the financial statements. If the auditor becomes aware of a subsequently discovered fact before or after the report release date, (1) discuss the matter with management and those charged with governance (as appropriate) and (2) determine if the financial statements need amendment and, if so, inquire how management intends to address the matter in the financial statements.

5. If management amends the financial statements, perform the necessary audit procedures on the revision and either:

   a. Date the auditor's report as of a later date; extend the audit procedures performed for subsequent events to the date of the new auditor's report; and request written representations from management as of the new date of the auditor's report.

   b. Include an additional date in the auditor's report on the amended financial statements limited to that amendment, indicating the audit procedures on subsequently discovered facts are limited to that amendment, and request written representations from management as of the additional date about whether any information has come to management's attention that would cause management to believe any previous representations should be modified, or any other events have occurred subsequent to the financial statements date that would require adjustment to, or disclosure in, the financial statements.

   c. If a subsequently discovered fact became known to the auditor after the report release date and the audited financial statements had already been made available to third parties, the auditor should assess whether steps taken by management are timely and appropriate to ensure that anyone receiving those financial statements is informed of the situation, including that the audited financial statements are not to be relied on.

   d. If a subsequently discovered fact became known to the auditor after the report release date and the opinion on the amended financial statements is different from the opinion previously expressed, an emphasis-of-matter or other-matter paragraph should be included disclosing (1) the date of the auditor's previous report, (2) the type of opinion previously expressed, (3) the substantive reasons for the different opinion, and (4) that the auditor's opinion on the amended financial statements is different from the auditor's previous opinion.

6. If management does not amend the financial statements and the auditor believes the statements need to be amended:

   a. If a subsequently discovered fact becomes known to the auditor before the report release date, express a modified (qualified or adverse) opinion as required and release the auditor's report.

   b. If a subsequently discovered fact becomes known to the auditor after the report release date and the audited financial statements have not been made available to third parties, notify management and those charged with governance not to make the audited financial statements available until amendments have been made and a new auditor's report has been provided. If the audited financial statements are made available to third parties without the necessary amendments, take appropriate action to seek to prevent reliance on the auditor's report.

c. If a subsequently discovered fact becomes known to the auditor after the report release date and the audited financial statements have been made available to third parties, assess whether steps taken by management are timely and appropriate to ensure that anyone receiving those financial statements is informed of the situation, including that the audited financial statements are not to be relied on. If the necessary steps are not taken by management, inform management and those charged with governance that the auditor will seek to prevent future reliance on the auditor's report. If the necessary steps are still not taken despite such notification, take appropriate action to seek to prevent reliance on the auditor's report.

## *Predecessor Auditor's Reissuance of the Auditor's Report in Comparative Financial Statements*

7. A predecessor auditor may be requested to reissue a previously issued auditor's report on prior period financial statements when those financial statements are to be presented on a comparative basis with audited financial statements of a subsequent period. In this situation, the predecessor auditor should perform the following procedures to determine if the previously issued auditor's report is still appropriate before reissuing the report:

   a. Read the subsequent period financial statements being presented on a comparative basis.

   b. Compare the prior period financial statements reported on with the subsequent period financial statements to be presented on a comparative basis.

   c. Inquire of and obtain a representation letter from management of the former client at or near the date of reissuance stating (1) whether any information has come to management's attention that would cause them to believe any previous representations should be modified and (2) whether any events have occurred after the date of the most recent prior period financial statements reported on by the predecessor auditor that would require adjustment to or disclosure in the financial statements.

   d. Obtain a representation letter from the successor auditor stating whether the successor auditor's audit revealed any matters that in his or her opinion might have a material effect on or require disclosure in the financial statements reported on by the predecessor auditor.

8. If, in performing the above procedures, a subsequently discovered fact becomes known to the predecessor auditor, follow the guidance for auditors becoming aware of subsequently discovered facts after the report release date. However, in circumstances where management amends the financial statements and the predecessor auditor does not plan to issue a new auditor's report or if management does not revise the financial statements when the predecessor auditor believes they need to be revised, the only step the auditor must take is to assess whether the steps taken by management are timely and appropriate to ensure that anyone receiving those financial statements is informed of the situation, including that the audited financial statements are not to be relied on.

## Analysis and Application of Procedures

*Subsequent Events*

The specified audit procedures that the auditor is required to perform relating to subsequent events are not necessarily the only procedures the auditor will perform to obtain sufficient appropriate audit evidence. The auditor may perform audit procedures for other purposes in the audit that also provide evidence about subsequent events. The auditor's risk assessment may be such that he or she includes procedures such as review or testing of accounting records or transactions occurring between the date of the financial statements and the auditor's report date in order to obtain sufficient appropriate audit evidence.

Furthermore, the audit procedures performed to obtain evidence about subsequent events may depend on the availability of information, the manner in which the entity's accounting records have been maintained, and the extent to which information has been prepared since the date of the financial statements. For example, the entity may not have prepared interim financial statements or minutes of meetings of management or those charged with governance. In this instance, the auditor may inspect the entity's books and records. In addition to the required audit procedures, the auditor may consider it necessary to apply additional audit procedures, such as reading the most recent available budgets, cash flow forecasts, and other related management reports for periods after the date of the financial statements.

> **PLANNING AID REMINDER:** The auditor should request written representation from management and those charged with governance (as appropriate) as of the date of the auditor's report that all subsequent events have been adjusted or disclosed in the financial statements.

When inquiring of management or those charged with governance about whether any subsequent events have occurred, the auditor may make specific inquiries on particular matters:

- The current status of items accounted for on the basis of preliminary or inconclusive data.
- Any new commitments, borrowings, or guarantees entered into.
- Any planned or executed sales or acquisitions of assets.
- Any increases in capital, issuance of debt instruments, or plans for or existence of a merger or liquidation agreement.
- Any assets that have been appropriated by the government or destroyed.
- Any developments regarding contingencies.
- Any unusual accounting adjustments that are planned or performed.
- Any events likely to occur or that have occurred bringing the appropriateness of accounting policies used in the financial statements into question.
- Any events that occurred relevant to the measurement of estimates or provisions made in the financial statements.

- Any events that occurred relevant to the recoverability of assets.
- Any changes in the entity's related parties and whether there have been any significant transactions with related parties.
- Any significant unusual transactions.

---

**IMPORTANT NOTICE FOR 2022:** In May 2019, the AICPA's Auditing Standards Board (ASB) issued SAS No. 135 titled *Omnibus Statement on Auditing Standards—2019* that includes amendments to various AU-C sections. SAS No. 135 amends AU-C 560 to add additional inquiries the auditor should make of management. Specifically, SAS No. 135 now requires the auditor to add to the inquiries about subsequent events whether (1) there have been any changes in the entity's related parties, (2) there have been any significant new related-party transactions, and (3) the entity has entered into any significant unusual transactions. Originally, the effective date of SAS No. 135 was for audits of financial statements periods ending on or after December 15, 2020, with early application **not** permitted. However, the ASB's issuance of SAS No. 141, *Amendment to the Effective Dates of SAS Nos. 134-140*, extended the effective date to December 15, 2021, in order to provide more time for firms to implement SAS No. 135 in light of the effect of the coronavirus pandemic. While SAS No. 141 allows for early implementation of SAS No. 135, the ASB recommends that SAS Nos. 134-140 be implemented concurrently.

---

**ENGAGEMENT STRATEGY:** When agreeing to the terms of the audit engagement, the auditor may include that management will inform the auditor of subsequent events and subsequently discovered facts.

---

## Subsequently Discovered Facts that Become Known to the Auditor before the Report Release Date

When an amendment to the financial statements is made and the auditor limits the audit procedures performed to that amendment, the auditor's report will be dual-dated. Under this approach, the report is dated based on the original audit report date and an additional date is noted in the report:

March 3, 20X5, except as to Note X, which is as of March 15, 20X5.

If the auditor dual-dates the report, that informs users of the financial statements that the procedures he or she performed after the original date of the auditor's report are limited to the amendment of the financial statements. The auditor is allowed to dual-date the report in certain circumstances, but is never required to dual-date the report and may always extend audit procedures on subsequent events to the date of the auditor's report on the amended financial statements if desired. If the financial statements are revised, management's written representations are required as of the later auditor's report date. In these situations, the auditor may request management provide a new representation letter or may agree to accept a written representation that addresses whether there are any changes to the previously provided written representations and what those changes are.

> **OBSERVATION:** If the financial statements are revised by disclosing an event that arose after the original audit report date in a separate financial statement note labelled as unaudited, the auditor is not required to perform any procedures on the revision and the auditor's report date stays the same.

## Subsequently Discovered Facts that Become Known to the Auditor after the Report Release Date

The auditor's responsibility to investigate whether subsequently discovered information existed at the date of the auditor's report does not change even when he or she has resigned or been discharged from the engagement. However, the specific procedures the auditor performs may vary depending on factors such as the time elapsed since the report release date and any legal implications such as those regarding confidentiality.

If management amends the financial statements to reflect a subsequently discovered fact, the steps taken to ensure that anyone in receipt of the financial statements is informed of this amendment may depend on the circumstances:

- Issue amended financial statements with appropriate disclosure of the matter as soon as practicable.
- If the issuance of amended financial statements and a new auditor's report is not imminent, notify anyone known or likely to be relying on the financial statements and auditor's report that they are not to be relied upon and that amended financial statements and a new auditor's report will be issued.
- If issuance of the subsequent period's financial statements is imminent, include appropriate disclosure of the matter in those financial statements.

> **PLANNING AID REMINDER:** Additional requirements exist for audits performed under *Government Auditing Standards* in circumstances where management amends the financial statements to reflect a subsequently discovered fact. These requirements include procedures such as reporting directly to appropriate officials when management does not take the necessary steps.

If the auditor notifies management not to make the financial statements available to third parties and management does so or the auditor notifies management or those charged with governance to take necessary steps to prevent reliance by third parties on the auditor's report on the financial statements and these steps are not taken, the auditor's course of action depends on his or her legal rights and obligations. The auditor may consider it appropriate to seek legal advice under these circumstances.

The auditor may take the following steps, depending on the circumstances, to prevent reliance on the auditor's report to the extent applicable:

- Notify management and those charged with governance that the auditor's report is not to be associated with the financial statements or to be relied upon.
- Notify any applicable regulatory agencies that the auditor's report should no longer be relied on and request that the agency take the appropriate steps to accomplish the necessary disclosure.
- Notify persons known or likely to be relying on the financial statements that the auditor's report should no longer be relied on to the extent practicable.

The notifications by the auditor to third parties may contain different information depending on the circumstances. If the auditor is able to determine that the financial statements need amendment, notification may include: (1) a description of the nature of the matter and its effects on the financial statements and (2) a description of the effect on the auditor's report if the matter had been known to the auditor at the date of the report and not reflected in the financial statements. The notification should avoid comments concerning the conduct or motives of any person. If the auditor is unable to determine if the financial statements need amendment, a notification may indicate that information became known to the auditor that, if true, causes the auditor to believe that the auditor's report should not be relied on. The notification does not need to describe the specific matter.

*Predecessor Auditor's Reissuance of the Auditor's Report in Comparative Financial Statements*

A request by an entity's management or those charged with governance that the predecessor auditor provide additional copies of the auditor's report after the report release date does not constitute a reissuance of the report. Therefore, the auditor is not responsible for performing any procedures regarding events that may have occurred between the date of the auditor's report and the date of the release of additional copies.

While a predecessor auditor may agree to reissue an audit report on prior period financial statements to be presented in comparative financial statements with audited financial statements of a subsequent period, the auditor is not required to reissue the auditor's report. The predecessor auditor may decline reissuing the report if circumstances such as the current form or manner of presentation of the prior period financial statements make the predecessor's previous audit report inappropriate.

## Practitioner's Aids

Exhibit AU-C 560-1 illustrates an audit program for subsequent events.

### EXHIBIT AU-C 560-1—SUBSEQUENT EVENTS AUDIT PROGRAM

Use the following procedures as a guide to identify subsequent events that occur after the date of the financial statements but before the date of our audit report. This audit program is only a guide, and professional judgment should be exercised to determine how it should be modified by revising or adding procedures.

Initial and date each procedure as it is completed. If the procedure is not relevant to this particular engagement, place "N/A" (not applicable) in the space provided for an initial.

Client Name: _____

Date of Financial Statements: _____

Audit Report Date: _____

|  |  | Initials | Date | Audit Documentation Reference |
|---|---|---|---|---|
| 1. | Inquire of and discuss with appropriate management personnel whether any material contingent liabilities or commitments existed at the date of the balance sheet or shortly thereafter. | _____ | _____ | _____ |
| 2. | Inquire of and discuss with appropriate management personnel whether any significant change in owners' equity, long-term debt, or working capital has occurred since the date of the balance sheet. | _____ | _____ | _____ |
| 3. | Inquire of and discuss with appropriate management personnel whether any material adjustments have been made during the subsequent period. | _____ | _____ | _____ |
| 4. | Inquire of and discuss with appropriate management personnel the status of items that were accounted for in the financial statements on the basis of tentative or preliminary data. | _____ | _____ | _____ |
| 5. | Read the latest minutes of stockholders', directors', and other committee meetings that occurred during the subsequent period. | _____ | _____ | _____ |
| 6. | Obtain from the client's legal counsel a description and evaluation of any impending litigation, claims, and contingent liabilities. | _____ | _____ | _____ |

|    |    | Initials | Date | Audit Documentation Reference |
|----|----|----------|------|-------------------------------|
| 7. | Obtain a letter of representation from management regarding any events occurring during the subsequent period that require adjustment or disclosure. | _____ | _____ | _____ |
| 8. | Read the latest interim financial statements and compare them to (a) the year-end financial statements and (b) the interim financial information for the previous year. | _____ | _____ | _____ |
| 9. | Review journal entries made after the end of the year for unusual amounts, unusual activity, or other unusual characteristics. | _____ | _____ | _____ |
| 10. | Determine whether the client is considering changing any of its accounting policies or procedures. | _____ | _____ | _____ |
| 11. | Perform any other procedures deemed appropriate depending on the results of the procedures described above. | _____ | _____ | _____ |

Reviewed by: _____

Date: _____

_____

---

# EXHIBIT AU-C 560-2—DISCOVERY OF FACTS AFTER THE DATE OF THE REPORT

Use the following procedures, which are adapted from guidance found in AU-C 560, as a guide for evaluating the discovery of facts after the date of the report. The program is only a guide, and professional judgment should be exercised to determine how the guidance established in the auditing standard should be adapted to a particular engagement.

Initial and date each procedure as it is completed. If the procedure is not relevant to this engagement, place "N/A" (not applicable) in the space provided for an initial.

Client Name: _____

Date of Financial Statements: _____

|  | Initials | Date | Audit Documentation Reference |
|---|---|---|---|

1. Determine whether the discovered facts are relevant to the financial statements by considering the following factors:
   - The report would have been affected if the CPA had known the information at the date of the audit report, _____ _____ _____
   - The matter would have been reflected in the financial statements, and _____ _____ _____
   - The CPA believes that there are third-party users relying on or likely to rely on the financial statements who would attach importance to the subsequently discovered information. _____ _____ _____

2. If the conditions described in 1 above exist, advise the client to inform third-party users currently relying or likely to rely on the financial statements, following the general guidance:
   - When the effects of the subsequently discovered information can be determined quickly, and the issuance of more current financial statements is not imminent, revised financial statements and a revised report should be issued. (Both the financial statements and the report should describe the reason for the revision.) _____ _____ _____

|  | Initials | Date | Audit Documentation Reference |
|---|---|---|---|

- When the issuance of more recent financial statements is imminent, the disclosure of the revision can be made in the more recent financial statements; the earlier financial statements need not be reissued. _____ _____ _____
- When the effects of the subsequently discovered information cannot be determined without a prolonged investigation, third-party users who are currently relying or likely to rely on the financial statements and the associated report should be notified not to rely on them and should be informed that revised financial statements and a revised audit report will be issued when an investigation is completed. _____ _____ _____

3. If the client refuses to make appropriate disclosures to third-party users, inform each member of the board of directors of the refusal. _____ _____ _____

4. If the board of directors is notified but appropriate disclosures to third-party users still are not made, discuss the matter with legal counsel. _____ _____ _____

5. If it appears there are or will be third-party users who will rely on the financial statements, consider the following:

- Notify the client that the CPA's report should no longer be associated with the client's financial statements. _____ _____ _____

|  | Initials | Date | Audit Documentation Reference |
|---|---|---|---|

- Notify regulatory agencies having jurisdiction over the client that the CPA's report should no longer be associated with the client's financial statements. _____ _____ _____
- To the extent practical, the CPA should notify each third-party user known to be relying on the financial statements that the auditor's report should no longer be relied upon. _____ _____ _____

6. If the matters have been satisfactorily investigated and the subsequent information considered reliable, disclosures to regulatory authorities and third-party users should include the following:
    - The nature of the subsequently acquired information and the effects on the financial statements. _____ _____ _____
    - The effects of the subsequently acquired information on the CPA's report, if the information had been known to him or her at the date of the report and it had not been reflected in the financial statements. _____ _____ _____

7. If a satisfactory investigation is not conducted, make the following disclosure to regulatory authorities and third-party users:
    - Describe the general nature of the problem (specific details are not required). _____ _____ _____

|  | Initials | Date | Audit Documentation Reference |
|---|---|---|---|

- State that the effects of the problem cannot be substantiated because the client did not cooperate in the investigation of the matter. _____ _____ _____

- State that if the information is correct, the CPA believes that his or her report should no longer be associated with the client's financial statements. No disclosure should be made unless the CPA believes that the financial statements are likely to be misleading and that his or her audit report should no longer be relied upon. _____ _____ _____

8. Other engagement procedures: _____
_____

Reviewed by: _____

Date: _____

## SECTION 570

# THE AUDITOR'S CONSIDERATION OF AN ENTITY'S ABILITY TO CONTINUE AS A GOING CONCERN

## Authoritative Pronouncements

SAS-132—The Auditor's Consideration of an Entity's Ability to Continue as a Going Concern

SAS-134—Auditor Reporting and Amendments, Including Amendments Addressing Disclosures in the Audit of Financial Statements

SAS-136—Forming an Opinion and Reporting on Financial Statements of Employee Benefit Plans Subject to ERISA

SAS-141—Amendment to Effective Dates of SAS Nos. 134-140

## Overview

Financial statements are usually prepared based on the assumption that an entity will continue as a going concern. SAS No. 132 addresses the auditor's responsibilities in the audit of financial statements relating to an entity's ability to continue as a going concern. It also provides guidance about implications to the auditor's report.

Some financial reporting frameworks include requirements for management to evaluate an entity's ability to continue as a going concern for a reasonable period of time and to provide disclosures related to the entity's ability to continue as a going concern. FASB standards (codified in ASC Subtopic 205-40, *Presentation: Going Concern*) set forth management's responsibility to evaluate whether there is substantial doubt about an entity's ability to continue as a going concern within one year after the date that the financial statements are issued (or are available to be issued) and to provide note disclosures related to those circumstances. Additionally, GASB Statement No. 56, *Codification of Accounting and Financial Reporting Guidance Contained in the AICPA Statements on Auditing Standards*, establishes guidance related to going concern for governmental entities. Other financial reporting frameworks may not include explicit requirements for management to assess an entity's ability to continue as a going concern. However, when the going concern principle is a fundamental principle in the preparation of financial statements, management is still required to make that assessment even if there is no explicit requirement to do so.

**OBSERVATION:** The FASB defines *substantial doubt* as being probable, with *probable* being defined in the same manner as it is used in evaluating contingencies (see ASC 450), and defines a *reasonable period of time* as one year from the date the financial statements are issued (or are available to be issued). Therefore, management would conclude that there is substantial doubt about the entity's ability to continue as a going concern if it is probable that the entity will be unable to meet its obligations as they become due within one year after the date the financial statements are issued.

SAS No. 132 (*The Auditor's Consideration of an Entity's Ability to Continue as a Going Concern*) states that as part of an audit, the auditor should evaluate conditions or events discovered during the engagement that raise questions about the appropriateness of the going-concern assumption. The auditor may identify such conditions or events at various points during the engagement, including during the performance of analytical procedures, when reading responses received from the entity's legal counsel, and when evaluating the entity's compliance with restrictions imposed by loan agreements. SAS No. 132 requires that the auditor reach his or her own conclusion on the appropriateness of management's use of the going concern basis of accounting, when relevant, in the preparation of the financial statements.

SAS No. 132 applies to all audits of financial statements, regardless of whether a general purpose or special purpose framework is used. Financial statements are prepared based on the going concern assumption, unless the liquidation basis of accounting is appropriate. When a company decides or is forced to liquidate, the going-concern concept is not appropriate and assets should be presented at their estimated net realizable values, and legally enforceable liabilities should be classified according to priorities established by law. SAS No. 132 does not apply to an audit of financial statements prepared using the liquidation basis of accounting.

Although the auditor is responsible for including an emphasis-of-matter section in the auditor's report when a substantial-doubt question arises, he or she is not responsible for predicting the outcome of future events. Thus, the liquidation of an entity (even within one year of the date of the financial statements) does not imply that the audit was substandard when a going concern section had not been included in the auditor's report. Similarly, the absence of a going concern section in the auditor's report should not be taken as assurance that the entity will continue as a going concern for a reasonable period of time. The auditor's evaluation is based on his or her knowledge of relevant conditions and events that exist at, or have occurred prior to, the date of the auditor's report.

**PLANNING AID REMINDER:** Information that raises questions about going concern generally relates to the entity's ability to meet its maturing obligations without selling operating assets, restructuring debt, or revising operations based on outside pressures or similar strategies.

**IMPORTANT NOTICE FOR 2022:** In May 2019, the AICPA's Auditing Standards Board (ASB) issued SAS No. 134 titled *Auditor Reporting and Amendments, Including Amendments Addressing Disclosures in the Audit of Financial Statements* that makes significant changes to the auditor's report, including the ability to communicate key audit matters (KAMs) in the auditor's report. SAS No. 134 amends the auditor report illustrations contained in AU-C 570 that are to be used when the auditor concludes that substantial doubt about the entity's ability to continue as a going concern for a reasonable period of time remains. The amendments conform those illustrations to the language in the new auditor's report, including a requirement that the communication about going concern be in a separate section of the auditor's report with the heading "Substantial Doubt About the Entity's Ability to Continue as a Going Concern." Originally, the effective date of SAS No. 134 was for audits of financial statements periods ending on or after December 15, 2020, with early implementation **not** permitted. However, the ASB's issuance of SAS No. 141, *Amendment to the Effective Dates of SAS Nos. 134-140*, extended the effective date to December 15, 2021, in order to provide more time for firms to implement SAS No. 134 in light of the effect of the coronavirus pandemic. While SAS No. 141 allows for early implementation of SAS No. 134, the ASB recommends that SAS Nos. 134-140 be implemented concurrently.

## Definitions

| | |
|---|---|
| Reasonable period of time | A period of time as required by the applicable financial reporting framework; if no such requirement exists, within one year after the date that the financial statements are issued. |

## Requirements

The auditor is presumptively required to perform the following procedures in evaluating the entity's ability to continue as a going concern.

### Performing Risk Assessment Procedures

1. As part of an auditor's performance of risk assessment procedures during planning to assess the risk of material misstatement, the auditor should be alert for conditions or events that might raise substantial doubt about an entity's ability to continue as a going concern for a reasonable period of time. The auditor would also determine if management has performed its own going concern assessment.

### Evaluating Relevant Information Obtained during the Course of the Engagement

2. As the audit is performed, the auditor should continue to consider whether the procedures performed during the audit identify conditions or events that create substantial doubt about the entity's ability to continue as a going concern for a reasonable period of time. If so, the auditor should consider the need to obtain additional information about such conditions or events.

### Considering Management's Evaluation

3. The auditor should consider management's evaluation of whether conditions and events raise substantial doubt about the entity's ability to continue as a going concern for a reasonable period of time, which is defined by the applicable financial reporting framework. The auditor would use the same time period that management uses to make its evaluation to conform to the applicable financial reporting framework. The auditor also should inquire of management about its knowledge of conditions or events beyond the period of management's evaluation that might impact the entity's ability to continue as a going concern.

> **OBSERVATION:** FASB standards (ASC 205-40, *Presentation: Going Concern*) require management to evaluate the entity's going concern status when preparing both annual and interim financial statements.

## *Performing Additional Procedures if Conditions or Events Are Identified*

4. When conditions or events are identified that raise substantial doubt about the entity's ability to continue as a going concern for a reasonable period of time, the auditor should perform additional audit procedures to obtain sufficient appropriate audit evidence to determine whether such doubt exists. These procedures would include:
   a. Asking management to make its going concern evaluation, if it has not been performed.
   b. Considering whether management plans, if effectively implemented, would mitigate the auditor's concerns regarding the entity's ability to continue as a going concern for a reasonable period of time.
   c. Evaluating underlying data and assumptions used by management if they have prepared a cash flow forecast. When management's plans include financial support to be provided by third parties or the entity's owner-manager, the auditor should obtain sufficient appropriate *written* evidence about the *intent* of such supporting parties to provide the necessary financial support. The auditor should also obtain sufficient appropriate evidence about their *ability* to provide such support.

## *Written Representations*

5. Certain written representations are needed if the auditor concludes, before considering management's plans, that there is substantial doubt about the entity's ability to continue as a going concern for a reasonable period of time. These written representations are:
   a. Management's plans designed to address the conditions and events giving rise to the auditor's going-concern doubts, including management's view as to the likelihood that these plans can be effectively implemented.
   b. That the financial statements disclose the principal conditions and events giving rise to the going-concern doubts and management's plans for addressing these conditions and events.

## *Evaluating the Use of the Going Concern Basis of Accounting*

6. Based on the evidence obtained, the auditor should evaluate the appropriateness of management's use of the going concern basis of accounting used when preparing the financial statements and then the auditor should conclude whether there are conditions or events, considered in the aggregate, that raise substantial doubt about an entity's ability to continue as a going concern for a reasonable period of time.

## *Consideration of Financial Statement Effects*

7. When the auditor concludes that substantial doubt exists about the entity's ability to continue as a going concern, the auditor should evaluate the adequacy of the financial statements disclosures that are required by the applicable financial reporting framework.

8. After reviewing management's plans, the auditor may conclude that substantial doubt about the entity's going-concern status has been alleviated. If so, the auditor should consider the need for, and evaluate the adequacy of, disclosure of the principal conditions and events that originally gave rise to his or her going-concern doubts. Both the conditions and events initially giving rise to the auditor's going-concern doubts and the effect of mitigating factors, including management plans, are to be evaluated for disclosure.

9. If the applicable financial reporting framework (e.g., FASB standards codified in sub-topic ASC 205-40) contains disclosure requirements based on management's assessment of the entity's going concern status, the auditor's assessment of the financial statement effects is to be based on the disclosure requirements in the applicable financial reporting framework.

## Consideration of the Effects on the Auditor's Report

10. The auditor should include a separate section in the auditor's report with the heading "Substantial Doubt About the Entity's Ability to Continue as a Going Concern" that draws attention to the note in the financial statements that discloses the conditions and events identified and management's plans that deal with these conditions or events and that these conditions or events indicate that substantial doubt exists about the entity's ability to continue as a going concern for a reasonable period of time.

11. The auditor's going-concern section should include a description about the entity's ability to continue as a going concern for a reasonable period of time that is consistent with those included in the financial reporting framework. For example, for financial statements based on FASB standards, the auditor would include the phrase "substantial doubt about its (the entity's) ability to continue as a going concern" or similar language that includes the words "substantial doubt" and "going concern." When an auditor concludes that there is substantial doubt about an entity's ability to continue as a going concern, the audit report should not use language that suggests that the conclusion is conditional on future events. For example, conditional terminology such as "if the company is unable to obtain refinancing, there may be substantial doubt about the company's ability to continue as a going concern" is precluded.

12. If the entity's disclosures regarding going-concern status are inadequate, the auditor should issue a qualified or adverse opinion due to a U.S. GAAP departure and the auditor should modify the Basis of Opinion section header of the report to say "Basis for Qualified (or Adverse) Opinion" and state in that section that substantial doubt exists and the financial statements do not adequately disclose that matter.

## Communication with Those Charged with Governance

13. If the auditor concludes that substantial doubt about the entity's ability to continue as a going concern exists, he or she should communicate to those charged with governance:

    a. The nature of the conditions or events identified that raise substantial doubt,

    b. The auditor's consideration of management's plans,

    c. Whether management's use of the going concern basis of accounting is appropriate in the preparation of the financial statements,

    d. The possible effects of these conditions or events on the financial statements and related disclosures, and

    e. The effects on the auditor's report.

## Comparative Presentations

14. During the current year, a question of substantial doubt contained in an auditor's report on a prior year's financial statements may no longer be applicable. Under this circumstance, the going concern section should not be repeated in the auditor's report on the comparative financial statements.

## Eliminating a Going-Concern Section from a Reissued Report

15. After the auditor has issued a report that refers to a going-concern issue, the client may request the auditor to reissue the report and remove the going-concern reference because the client believes the circumstances that led to the uncertainty have changed. Because the request by the client constitutes a new engagement, the auditor is not obligated to accept it. If the auditor accepts the engagement, the circumstances related to the going-concern issue should be examined to determine whether it is appropriate to revise the report. If the auditor accepts the new engagement, he or she should perform the following procedures:

   a. Audit the event or transaction that prompted the request to delete the going-concern section.
   b. Perform procedures related to subsequent events at or near the reissuance date of the report.
   c. Consider the factors related to the going-concern concept as described in AU-C 570.

---

**ENGAGEMENT STRATEGY:** In addition to the listed procedures, the auditor should conduct other procedures he or she deems appropriate. Based on the results of applying those procedures, the auditor should reassess the going-concern status of the client.

---

## Documentation

16. The auditor should document the following in the audit files when a going-concern issue has been raised and investigated based on the standards discussed in AU-C 570:

   a. Conditions or events that are the basis for the going-concern substantial doubt.
   b. Elements of management's plans that have a significant effect on overcoming the adverse effects of the conditions or events identified above.
   c. Audit procedures performed and evidence gathered related to the significant elements of management's plans.
   d. The auditor's conclusion about the ability of the client to continue as a going concern for a reasonable period of time.
   e. If the auditor concludes that there is substantial doubt about the client continuing as a going concern, document the possible effects on the financial statements (including disclosures).
   f. If the auditor concludes that the substantial doubt issue has been alleviated, document the conclusion regarding the need for, and adequacy of, disclosure of the conditions or events.
   g. The conclusion regarding whether a going-concern section should be included in the audit report.

h. If disclosures in the financial statements concerning the going-concern issue are inadequate, document the conclusion regarding whether the audit report should be qualified or an adverse opinion should be expressed.

## Analysis and Application of Procedures

*Management's Evaluation an Entity's Ability to Continue*

Most financial reporting frameworks, such as that established by the FASB, include explicit requirements for management to evaluate the entity's ability to continue as a going concern for a reasonable period of time. When financial reporting frameworks require management to make an evaluation of the entity's ability to continue as a going concern, the auditor would consider that evaluation as part of assessing management's use of the going concern basis of accounting and to determine if substantial doubt is present. The auditor's evaluation may include consideration of the process used by management to make its evaluation and any assumptions used by management, including consideration of management's plans and their feasibility in being implemented to alleviate substantial doubt.

When accounting frameworks include a specific requirement for management to evaluate a going concern, most frameworks specify the timeframe to be evaluated. The FASB specifies reasonable period of time to be "within one year after the date the financial statements are issued," while the GASB specifies a reasonable period of time to be "twelve months beyond the date of the financial statements." The International Accounting Standards Board specifies a reasonable period of time to be "at least, but not limited to, one year from the end of the reporting period." SAS No. 132 also requires the auditor to make an inquiry of management about its knowledge of conditions or events beyond the period of management's evaluation that may have an effect on the entity's ability to continue as a going concern.

When evaluating management's evaluation of whether there is substantial doubt the auditor is likely to consider the process used by management to evaluate a going concern, any assumptions included in management's evaluation, and the feasibility of management's plans to remove any substantial doubt. When the financial reporting framework requires an evaluation by management, the auditor's procedures to evaluate management's compliance with that framework generally serve as the basis for the auditor's conclusion about the entity's ability to continue as a going concern for a reasonable period of time.

When financial reporting frameworks do not require management to make an explicit evaluation, the auditor should still obtain from management its assessment of the entity's ability to continue as a going concern when the going concern basis of accounting is a fundamental principle in the preparation of financial statements. The auditor's evaluation of a going concern would focus on the time period that is within one year after the date the financial statements are issued.

The FASB standards actually use the term substantial doubt about an entity's ability to continue as a going concern, while other financial reporting frameworks may use terms that are different, but similar in concept to the terms used by the FASB.

> **PLANNING AID REMINDER:** When a financial reporting framework requires an explicit management evaluation of a going concern, the lack of a detailed analysis performed by management may suggest the presence of a deficiency in internal control over financial reporting.

*Evaluate relevant information obtained during the course of the engagement*

In addition to considering management's evaluation of the entity's ability to continue as a going concern for a reasonable period of time, the auditors also remain sensitive to implications pertaining to a going concern in the audit evidence collected during the audit. Procedures that the auditor otherwise would perform—identifying and assessing risk, gathering audit evidence in response to risks, and audit completion steps—are typically sufficient to identify conditions or events that suggest that there may be substantial doubt as to the entity's ability to continue as a going concern for a reasonable period of time. Examples of these audit procedures include:

- Risk assessment procedures;
- Analytical procedures;
- Subsequent events review;
- Review compliance with financial agreements (e.g., debt, loan);
- Reading relevant minutes (e.g., meetings of stockholders, the board of directors, and important board committees);
- Review of the attorney letter regarding litigation, claims, and assessments; and
- Confirmation with related and third parties of commitments to provide or maintain financial support.

As the auditor performs procedures throughout the remainder of the audit, he or she continues to remain alert for audit evidence about conditions or events that might raise substantial doubt about the entity's ability to continue as a going concern. The auditor may need to revise his or her risk assessment and adjust the planned audit procedures as new information emerges. SAS No. 132 provides the examples in Exhibit AU-C 570-1 as conditions and events that may raise substantial doubt about an entity's ability to continue as a going concern.

## EXHIBIT AU-C 570-1—CONDITIONS AND EVENTS THAT MAY RAISE A SUBSTANTIAL-DOUBT QUESTION

| Condition or Event | Specific Example |
|---|---|
| Negative trends | • Recurring operating losses<br>• Working capital deficiencies<br>• Negative cash flows from operations<br>• Adverse key financial ratios |
| Other indications of possible financial difficulties | • Default on loan or similar financial difficulties<br>• Arrearages in dividends<br>• Denial of usual trade credit from vendors<br>• Restructuring of debt<br>• Noncompliance with statutory capital requirements<br>• Need to seek new sources of financing<br>• Need to sell substantial assets |
| Internal matters | • Labor difficulties, such as work stoppages<br>• Substantial dependence on the success of a particular project<br>• Uneconomic long-term commitments<br>• Need to significantly revise operations |
| External matters or similar matters that might affect the entity's ability to continue operations | • Legal proceedings, legislation<br>• Loss of key franchise, license, or patent<br>• Loss of principal customer or vendor<br>• Occurrence of uninsured catastrophe |

**FRAUD POINTER:** SEC enforcement actions alleging violations of the antifraud provisions of the securities acts often find that companies involved in fraud were financially distressed in periods preceding the fraud. Fraud companies often face net losses or experience downward trends in net income preceding the first year of the fraud. As auditors observe conditions affecting an entity's ability to continue as a going concern, they should consider whether those conditions create significant incentives or pressures that might lead management to perpetrate fraudulent financial reporting.

*Identify and Evaluate Management's Plans Related to a Going Concern*

Some of the conditions noted above may be mitigated by plans of management to address such conditions or events that create substantial doubt about the entity's ability to continue as a going concern. Exhibit AU-C 570-2 lists plans and factors that might represent examples of plans management has to address the substantial doubt about the entity's ability to continue as a going concern for a reasonable period of time.

**EXHIBIT AU-C 570-2—PLANS AND FACTORS RELEVANT TO THE EVALUATION OF MANAGEMENT'S PLANS**

| Planned Action | Factors Relevant to Evaluation of Planned Action |
|---|---|
| Sale of assets | • Restrictions on the sale of assets<br>• Likely marketability of assets<br>• Effects from sale of assets |
| Borrow or restructure debt | • Likelihood of raising funds based on existing or committed debt arrangements<br>• Existing or committed arrangements for restructuring debt or obtaining guarantees for loans<br>• Restrictions on ability to borrow or use assets as collateral |
| Reduce or delay expenditures | • Feasibility of reducing or postponing expenditures<br>• Effects of reducing or postponing expenditures |
| Increase ownership equity | • Feasibility of increasing equity based on existing or committed arrangements<br>• Flexibility of dividend policy<br>• Ability to raise funds from affiliates or other investors |

*Evaluating Management's Plans*

Management's plans to address substantial doubt about the entity's ability to continue as a going concern may include some of the above-planned actions. The auditor may choose to perform audit procedures to evaluate the feasibility of those plans. That might include evaluating any forecasts management has developed about cash flows or profits, analyzing interim financial statements, reviewing debt agreements, minutes of shareholder or board of director meetings, making inquiries of management, and evaluating the feasibility of management's plans to liquidate assets, borrow funds, restructure debt, increase capital, or delay expenditures, among other matters.

Prospective financial information may be an important part of evaluating management's plans for addressing the conditions and events giving rise to the going-concern doubts. If so, the auditor should evaluate the prospective financial information and consider the adequacy of the support for the assumptions underlying the prospective financial information.

In some cases, the substantial doubt may be eliminated by management's plans to obtain financial support from third parties or the entity's owner-manager. In that situation, the auditor will need to obtain written evidence about the intent of such supporting parties. That might be in the form of a written evidence provided by management of a commitment from the supporting parties or it might be in the form of a confirmation obtained directly from the supporting parties. In addition to obtaining written evidence about the intent of supporting parties, the auditor should also obtain sufficient appropriate evidence about the supporting parties' ability to provide support.

### Considering Adequacy of Disclosure

If the auditor concludes that substantial doubt exists about the client's ability to continue in existence, care must be taken to ensure that presentations and related disclosures in the financial statements are properly reflected. For example, under FASB standards, the entity must include a statement in the notes to the financial statements indicating that there is substantial doubt about the entity's ability to continue as a going concern within one year of the date that the financial statements are issued. That disclosure would include information about the conditions or events that raise substantial doubt, management's evaluation of those conditions and events, and its plans to mitigate the conditions or events. Depending on the circumstances, the auditor may decide that additional disclosures are necessary.

Disclosure might include the following:

- Conditions or events that gave rise to the substantial doubt concerning continued existence.
- Possible effects of the conditions or events.
- Management's assessments concerning the significance of the conditions or events.
- Other factors that may aggravate or mitigate the conditions or events.
- Management's strategies that will attempt to deal with the adverse conditions or events.
- Possible discontinuance of operations.

### Consideration of the Effects on the Auditor's Report

Exhibit AU-C 570-3 provides an example of a going-concern section of the auditor's report when the auditor concludes substantial doubt exists, management's plans do not alleviate that doubt, and the entity is required by the financial reporting framework to include a statement in the notes to the financial statements that substantial doubt exists. When the auditor includes a going-concern section, the introductory, scope, and opinion paragraphs make no reference to that section.

**IMPORTANT NOTICE FOR 2022:** As a reminder, in May 2019, the AICPA's Auditing Standards Board (ASB) issued SAS No. 134 titled *Auditor Reporting and Amendments, Including Amendments Addressing Disclosures in the Audit of Financial Statements* that makes significant changes to the auditor's report, including the ability to communicate key audit matters (KAMs) in the auditor's report. SAS No. 134 amends the auditor report illustrations contained in AU-C 570 that are to be used when the auditor concludes that substantial doubt about the entity's ability to continue as a going concern for a reasonable period of time remains. The amendments conform those illustrations to the language in the new auditor's report, including a requirement that the communication about going concern be in a separate section of the auditor's report with the heading "Substantial Doubt About the Entity's Ability to Continue as a Going Concern." Originally, the effective date of SAS No. 134 was for audits of financial statements periods ending on or after December 15, 2020, with early implementation **not** permitted. However, the ASB's issuance of SAS No. 141, *Amendment to the Effective Dates of SAS Nos. 134-140*, extended the effective date to December 15, 2021, in order to provide more time for firms to implement SAS No. 134 in light of the effect of the coronavirus pandemic. While SAS No. 141 allows for early implementation of SAS No. 134, the ASB recommends that SAS Nos. 134-140 be implemented concurrently.

## EXHIBIT AU-C 570-3—GOING-CONCERN SECTION WHEN MANAGEMENT'S STATEMENT IS REQUIRED

The accompanying financial statements have been prepared assuming that the Company will continue as a going concern. As discussed in Note X to the financial statements, the Company is involved in litigation concerning alleged patent infringement that could substantially impede operations if the charges are upheld and the Company has stated that substantial doubt exists about the Company's ability to continue as a going concern. Management's evaluation of the events and conditions and management's plans in regard to the litigation are also described in Note X. The financial statements do not include any adjustments that might result from the outcome of this uncertainty. Our opinion is not modified with respect to this matter.

The going-concern section should be included in subsequent auditor's reports as long as substantial doubt about the entity's existence continues. If the substantial-doubt condition ceases in a future period, there is no need to include the substantial-doubt section for reports that cover previous periods in which the substantial-doubt condition was originally applicable.

**ENGAGEMENT STRATEGY:** To not include the going concern section is not a change in the opinion expressed by the auditor; therefore, not including the section does not require that the auditor observe the report guidelines concerning changes of opinions.

## Comparative Presentations

The modification of the auditor's report because of a substantial-doubt question in the current year does not imply that the auditor's report on a prior year's financial statements (presented on a comparative basis) should also be modified.

## EXHIBIT AU-C 570-4—EVALUATING AN ENTITY'S ABILITY TO CONTINUE AS A GOING CONCERN

Use the following procedures as a guide for evaluating an entity's ability to continue as a going concern. The program is only a guide, and professional judgment should be exercised to determine how the guidance established should be adapted to a particular engagement.

Initial and date each procedure as it is completed. If the procedure is not relevant to this engagement, place "N/A" (not applicable) in the space provided for an initial.

Client Name: _____

Date of Financial Statements: _____

| | | Initials | Date | Audit Documentation Reference |
|---|---|---|---|---|
| 1. | Determine requirements of the financial reporting framework used by management, including whether management must evaluate the entity's ability to continue as a going concern. | _____ | _____ | _____ |
| 2. | When performing risk assessment procedures, consider whether conditions or events raise substantial doubt about the entity's ability to continue as a going concern. | _____ | _____ | _____ |
| 3. | Obtain and consider management's evaluation of whether there are conditions or events that raise substantial doubt about the entity's ability to continue as a going concern. | _____ | _____ | _____ |
| 4. | Identify and evaluate management's plans related to going concern. | _____ | _____ | _____ |
| 5. | Continue to evaluate relevant information obtained during the remainder of the engagement. | _____ | _____ | _____ |
| 6. | Consider the effect of the evidence on disclosures and the audit report. | _____ | _____ | _____ |
| 7. | Consider whether the following disclosures in the financial statements are appropriate: | _____ | _____ | _____ |

|  | Initials | Date | Audit Documentation Reference |
|---|---|---|---|
| • Factors that are the basis for raising the question of going concern | _____ | _____ | _____ |
| • Possible effects on the financial statements of the factors that raised the question of going concern | _____ | _____ | _____ |
| • Management's assessment of the significance of the factors and any mitigating circumstances | _____ | _____ | _____ |
| • Possible discontinuance of operations | _____ | _____ | _____ |
| • Management's plans to deal with the current circumstances (including relevant prospective information) | _____ | _____ | _____ |
| • Information related to asset recoverability and classification and the amount and classification of liabilities | _____ | _____ | _____ |

Other engagement procedures: _____

_____

_____

_____

Reviewed by: _____

Date: _____

**OBSERVATION:** If through performing other audit procedures the auditor identifies conditions and events that may raise questions about the entity's ability to continue as a going concern and management has not developed plans to address the issue, he or she would ordinarily conclude that doubts about the going-concern issue are valid and would consider modifying his or her report in a manner required by SAS No. 132.

# SECTION 580

# WRITTEN REPRESENTATIONS

## Authoritative Pronouncements

SAS-122—Statements on Auditing Standards: Clarification and Recodification

SAS-135—Omnibus Statement on Auditing Standards—2019

SAS-136—Forming an Opinion and Reporting on Financial Statements of Employee Benefit Plans Subject to ERISA

SAS-141—Amendment to Effective Dates of SAS Nos. 134-140

SAS-143—Auditing Accounting Estimates and Related Disclosures

## Overview

During the course of an engagement, the client's personnel make a variety of representations in response to questions raised by the auditor. Generally accepted auditing standards require that in order to reduce the likelihood of misunderstandings between the client and the auditor, written representations be obtained from the client to confirm explicit and implicit representations made by management during the engagement. Providing written rather than oral representations may prompt more rigorous consideration of matters by management and improve the quality of the representation.

Written representations received from management are audit evidence, and they often support other audit evidence the auditor obtains. For example, the auditor may inspect client documentation to determine whether there are liens against certain capital assets; however, the auditor should obtain a written representation from management stating that no liens exist. In other instances, written representations by management may be a source of audit evidence to support an assertion stated or implied in the financial statements. For example, certain current liabilities may be classified as noncurrent based on the guidance established by ASC 470 (*Debt*). Part of that guidance requires that management must intend to refinance the obligation on a long-term basis. Under this circumstance, the auditor's support for management's intent may be management's written representation in addition to other sources of audit evidence. In general, written representations are not a substitute for other auditing procedures necessary to form the basis for the auditor's opinion and do not provide sufficient appropriate audit evidence about matters on their own.

> **PLANNING AID REMINDER:** Because of the importance of written representations as a source of audit evidence, if management modifies or does not provide a requested written representation it may alert the auditor to the existence of a significant issue.

**FRAUD POINTER:** In enforcement actions against auditors, an overreliance on inquiry as a form of evidence often has/been mentioned. Auditors have/often cited for a failure to corroborate management's explanations with other evidence. Instead, auditors relied on only management's representations or failed to challenge inconsistent explanations or explanations that were refuted by other evidence.

AU-C 580 details the auditor's responsibilities to obtain written representations from management and those charged with governance, as appropriate, in a financial statement audit. Other AU-Cs, listed in Exhibit AU-C 580-2, contain subject matter-specific requirements for written representations. The requirements of these other AU-Cs do not limit AU-C 580's application. The auditor's objectives in applying AU-C 580 are to obtain written representations from management and those charged with governance indicating they believe they have fulfilled their responsibility for the preparation and fair presentation of financial statements and for the completeness of information provided to the auditor; to support other audit evidence relevant to the financial statements or financial statement assertions with written representations if required by the auditor or other AU-C sections; and to respond appropriately to written representations that are provided or are not provided as requested.

**PLANNING AID REMINDER:** Sometimes practitioners draft a representation letter for management to develop and sign; however, when doing so, practitioners should make sure that management understands the content that is in the representation letter before signing it and presenting it to the auditor. The auditor should consider discussing the content of the letter with management before management signs the letter and the auditor should consider documenting that discussion in the working papers.

## Definitions

| | |
|---|---|
| Written representation | A written statement by management provided to the auditor to confirm certain matters or to support other audit evidence; this does not include financial statements, the assertions therein, or supporting books and records. |
| Management | In AU-C 580, the term "management" should be read as "management and, when appropriate, those charged with governance." |

## Requirements

The auditor is presumptively required to adhere to the following guidance in obtaining written representations from management in an audit of the financial statements:

*Management from Whom Written Representations Are Requested*

1. Request written representations from management with appropriate responsibilities for the financial statements and knowledge of the matters concerned.

## Written Representations Requested about Management's Responsibilities

2. Management should represent in writing that it has fulfilled its responsibility for preparing and fairly presenting the financial statements in accordance with the applicable financial reporting framework and for the design, implementation, and fair presentation of financial statements that are free from material misstatement, whether due to fraud or error.

3. Management should represent in writing that it has provided the auditor with all relevant information and access as agreed upon in the audit engagement terms and all transactions have been recorded and are reflected in the financial statements.

## Other Written Representations Requested

Written representations should address the following:

4. Management acknowledges its responsibility for the design, implementation, and maintenance of internal control to prevent and detect fraud and has disclosed to the auditor (1) the results of its assessment of the risk that the financial statements may be materially misstated due to fraud; (2) its knowledge of fraud or suspected fraud involving management, employees with significant internal control roles, and others where fraud could have a material effect on the financial statements, and (3) its knowledge of any communicated allegations of fraud or suspected fraud.

5. Management has disclosed to the auditor all known or suspected instances of noncompliance with laws and regulations that have effects that should be considered when preparing the financial statements.

6. Representation about management's belief of whether the effects of uncorrected misstatements are immaterial individually or in the aggregate to the financial statements as a whole, including a summary of those items.

7. Management has disclosed to the auditor and accounted for and disclosed all actual or possible litigation and claims of which it has knowledge that have effects that should be considered when preparing the financial statements in accordance with the applicable financial reporting framework.

8. Representation about management's belief regarding whether significant assumptions it used in making accounting estimates are reasonable.

9. Management has disclosed to the auditor the identity of all of the entity's related parties and all the related-party transactions and relationships it is aware of and has appropriately accounted for and disclosed such relationships and transactions.

10. Management has made the adjustments or disclosures required by the applicable financial reporting framework regarding events occurring subsequent to the date of the financial statements.

11. The auditor should request other written representations determined to be necessary to support other audit evidence relevant to the financial statements or specific financial statement assertions.

---

**IMPORTANT NOTICE FOR 2022:** In May 2019, the AICPA's Auditing Standards Board (ASB) issued SAS No. 135 titled *Omnibus Statement on Auditing Standards—2019* that includes amendments to various AU-C sections. SAS No. 135 amends AU-C 580 to enhance guidance related to obtaining representations about related parties and related-party transactions. Originally, the effective date of SAS No. 135 was for audits of financial statements periods ending on or after December 15, 2020, with early application **not** permitted. However, the ASB's issuance of SAS No. 141, *Amendment to the Effective Dates of SAS Nos. 134-140*, extended the effective date to December 15, 2021, in order to provide more time for firms to implement SAS No. 135 in light of the effect of the coronavirus pandemic. While SAS No. 141 allows for early implementation of SAS No. 135, the ASB recommends that SAS Nos. 134-140 be implemented concurrently.

---

**IMPORTANT NOTICE FOR 2022:** In July 2020, the AICPA Auditing Standards Board (ASB) issued SAS No. 143, *Auditing Accounting Estimates and Related Disclosures*, which supersedes AU-C 540 (*Auditing Accounting Estimates, Including Fair Value Accounting Estimates, and Related Disclosures*) and amends various other sections including AU-C 580 in the professional standards. The SAS begins with an explanation of the nature of accounting estimates and how they can vary widely in nature and are required to be made by management when monetary amounts cannot be directly observed. The measurement of amounts is subject to estimation uncertainty, which reflects inherent limitations in the knowledge or data. These limitations give rise to inherent subjectivity and variation in measurement outcomes. Although the guidance in SAS No. 143 applies to all accounting estimates, the degree to which an accounting estimate is subject to estimation uncertainty will vary substantially. Therefore, SAS No. 143 recognizes that the nature, timing, and extent of the risk assessment and further audit procedures required will vary in relation to the estimation uncertainty and the assessment of the related risks of material misstatement. The ASB is coordinating the effective date of SAS No. 143 with the effective date of a proposed new SAS, *Understanding the Entity and Its Environment and Assessing the Risks of Material Misstatement*, which was under consideration by the ASB at the time this edition of the *GAAS Guide* was being prepared. SAS No. 143 does not become effective until audits of financial statements for periods ending on or after December 15, 2023, which is consistent with the date in the proposed new standard. As a result, this AU-C reflects existing auditing standards requirements. Updates to reflect SAS No. 143 will occur in the next edition of the *GAAS Guide*.

---

## *Date and Form of Written Representations*

12. The date of written representations should be as of the date of the auditor's report on the financial statements and cover all financial statements and periods referred to in the auditor's report.

13. Written representations should be in the form of a representation letter addressed to the auditor.

## *Written Representations with Doubtful Reliability or Not Provided*

14. Determine the effect any concerns about management's competence, integrity, ethical values, diligence, or its commitment to and enforcement of these qualities may have on the reliability of representations and audit evidence in general.

15. If written representations are inconsistent with other audit evidence, perform audit procedures to attempt to resolve the matter. If the matter remains unresolved, reconsider the assessment of management's competence, integrity, ethical values, diligence, and its commitment to and enforcement of

these qualities and the effect this may have on the reliability of representations and audit evidence in general.

16. If the auditor concludes the written representations are not reliable, appropriate action should be taken, including determining the possible effect on the opinion in the auditor's report in accordance with AU-C 705 (*Modifications to the Opinion in the Independent Auditor's Report*).

17. Disclaim an opinion on the financial statements in accordance with AU-C 705 (*Modifications to the Opinion in the Independent Auditor's Report*) or withdraw from the engagement if management does not provide the required written representations about its responsibilities or there is sufficient doubt about management's integrity to make the auditor conclude that those representations provided are unreliable.

18. If one or more requested written representations are not provided by management, (1) discuss the matter with management, (2) reevaluate management's integrity and the effect this may have on the reliability of representations and audit evidence in general, and (3) take appropriate action, including determining the possible effect on the opinion in the auditor's report in accordance with AU-C 705.

## Analysis and Application of Procedures

### Management from Whom Written Representations Are Requested

The auditor requests representations from those within the entity who have sufficient knowledge of and responsibility for the matters covered in the representations. Individuals with this knowledge are typically the management of an entity, but may also include those charged with governance or other individuals within the entity with specialized knowledge regarding representation matters such as actuaries, staff engineers, or internal counsel. The auditor may request that management confirm in its representations that it has inquired of others as appropriate to gain sufficient knowledge about the matters represented.

Management may include qualifying language in its representations indicating that representations are made to the base of its knowledge of belief. This type of qualification is reasonable for the auditor to accept if he or she believes the representations are being made by those with sufficient knowledge of and responsibilities for the matters included.

### Written Representations Requested about Management's Responsibilities

Written representations about management's responsibilities are important to the audit because the auditor is not able to obtain sufficient appropriate audit evidence about management's fulfilment of its responsibilities without obtaining confirmation from management. These written representations act to confirm that management has fulfilled the responsibilities it agreed to and acknowledged in the terms of the audit engagement. In the case of audits of governmental entities with broader mandates than other entities, management may be responsible for additional written representations confirming that transactions and events have been carried out in accordance with law, regulation, or other authority.

When management represents that it has provided the auditor with all relevant information, this includes matters such as:

- The completeness and availability of all minutes of meetings of stockholders, directors, and committees of directors; and
- The completeness of communications from regulatory agencies concerning noncompliance with or deficiencies in financial reporting practices.

The auditor may also request that management reconfirm its acknowledgment and understanding of its responsibilities in its written representations, especially when certain conditions exist: those signing the audit engagement terms no longer have the relevant responsibilities, the audit engagement terms were prepared in a previous year, there is an indication that management misunderstands its responsibilities, or changes in circumstances make reconfirmation appropriate. Any reconfirmation should be unconditional.

*Other Written Representations Requested*

When management makes representations about uncorrected misstatements, they may not believe some of those items are misstatements and may add wording to this effect along with their reasons for this belief in the representations.

**PLANNING AID REMINDER:** Even though the auditor obtains written representations from management about uncorrected misstatements, he or she still needs to form a conclusion on the effect of uncorrected misstatements in accordance with AU-C 450 (*Evaluation of Misstatements Identified during an Audit*).

Management's representations about whether its assumptions used in making accounting estimates are reasonable may include the following matters for accounting estimates recognized or disclosed in the financial statements:

- The appropriateness of the measurement processes used in determining accounting estimates in the context of the applicable financial reporting framework and the consistency in the processes' application.
- That assumptions appropriately reflect management's intent and ability to carry out specific courses of action on the entity's behalf.
- That accounting estimate disclosures are complete and appropriate under the applicable financial reporting framework.
- That no subsequent event requires adjustment to the accounting estimates and disclosures included in the financial statements.

For accounting estimates not recognized or disclosed in the financial statements, representations may include the following regarding the appropriateness of the basis used by management:

- Determination that the recognition or disclosure criteria of the applicable financial reporting framework have not been met.

- Overcoming a presumption regarding the use of fair value set forth under the entity's applicable financial reporting framework for those accounting estimates not measured or disclosed at fair value.

When evaluating management's judgments and intentions, the auditor may consider factors such as the entity's history in carrying out its stated intentions, its reasons for choosing and ability to pursue a particular course of action, and whether other information obtained during the course of the audit exists that may be inconsistent with management's judgment and intent.

The auditor may request written representations from those charged with governance regarding related parties in certain circumstances: when they have approved related-party transactions that materially affect the financial statements or involve management; when they have represented details of certain related-party transactions orally to the auditor; or when they have financial or other interests in the related parties or related-party transaction. The auditor is also required to communicate the written representations requested from management with those charged with governance.

The auditor may request additional written representations from management beyond those required about matters such as:

- Whether the selection and application of accounting policies are appropriate.
- Whether certain matters, such as the following, have been recognized, measured, presented, or disclosed in accordance with the applicable financial reporting framework when they are relevant:
  — The existence of plans or intentions that may affect the carrying value or classification of assets or liabilities.
  — Actual and contingent liabilities.
  — The existence of satisfactory title to assets, liens, or encumbrances on assets, and assets pledged as collateral.
- Compliance with aspects of contractual agreements that may affect the financial statements.
- Whether any side agreements or other arrangements (either written or oral) exist that have not been disclosed to the auditor.
- Whether management has communicated all internal control deficiencies it is aware of.
- Specific assertions in the financial statements to provide support about management's judgment or intent regarding those assertions.

**FRAUD POINTER:** AU-C 240 requires the auditor to make specific inquiries of management related to the risk of material misstatements due to fraud and written representations related to these inquiries are important to obtain regardless of the entity's size because of the nature of fraud and the difficulty for the auditor in detecting material misstatements due to fraud.

Representations made by management may be limited to items that are material to the client's financial statements, if "management and the auditor have reached an understanding on materiality for this purpose." That understanding, expressed either in quantitative or qualitative terms, may be part of the management representation letter. However, some items that are the basis for management representations do not relate to dollar values and therefore are not affected by materiality considerations. For example, the management representation that all financial records and related data have been made available to the auditor is not subject to a materiality threshold.

---

**FRAUD POINTER:** AU-C 580 specifically notes that materiality does not apply to representations related to management's acknowledgment regarding its responsibility for the design, implementation, and maintenance of internal control to prevent and detect fraud.

---

## Date and Form of Written Representations

Written representations are required audit evidence so the auditor's report date cannot be dated before the date of the written representations. If the auditor has obtained a written representation about a specific assertion during the course of the audit, he or she may need to request an updated written representation as of the date of the auditor's report. Although management needs to make written representations about all periods referred to in the auditor's report, the auditor and management may agree to a form of written representation that addresses whether there are any changes to written representations about prior periods and what those changes are. In some situations, management will not have been present during all the periods referred to in the auditor's report; however, this does not diminish their responsibilities for making written representations covering the entire relevant period.

---

**PUBLIC COMPANY IMPLICATION:** SOX requires the auditor of a public company to issue an audit report on the financial statements and, for accelerated filers, a report on the effectiveness of internal control over financial reporting. The audit of financial statements and the audit of internal controls are to be integrated and the report dates should be the same. As a result, auditors may consider combining representations from management related to the audit of financial statements with representations made by management about internal control matters. Management representations required by AS-2201 should be included in the combined representation letter.

---

In some circumstances, management does not provide a signed representation letter to the auditor by the date of the auditor's report. In these situations, the auditor may accept management's oral confirmation that they have reviewed and will sign the representation letter without exception as of the date of the auditor's report as sufficient evidence to date the report. However, the report may not be released before the signed representation letter is obtained.

> **PLANNING AID REMINDER:** AU-C 560 provides guidance for situations in which the auditor's report should be "dual-dated." AU-C 580 points out that the auditor should consider whether it is appropriate to obtain updated written representations when a subsequent event creating a dual-dating situation occurs.

### Written Representations with Doubtful Reliability or Not Provided

When a management representation contradicts evidence the auditor has obtained, the auditor may consider whether the risk assessment remains appropriate or needs revision and the nature, timing, and extent of further audit procedures to respond to the revised risks.

> **FRAUD POINTER:** AU-C 200 provides practical insight into the auditor's reliance on statements made by management. It states, "The auditor neither assumes that management is dishonest nor assumes unquestioned honesty . . . a belief that management and those charged with governance are honest and have integrity does not relieve the auditor of the need to maintain professional skepticism or allow the auditor to be satisfied with less than persuasive audit evidence when obtaining reasonable assurance."

The auditor may be sufficiently concerned about the competence, integrity, ethical values, or diligence of management or about its commitment to or enforcement of these qualities that the risk of management misrepresentation is such that an audit cannot be conducted. In these situations, the auditor may consider withdrawing from the engagement where permitted by law or regulation unless those charged with governance put appropriate corrective measures in place. Even if such measures are put in place, they may not be sufficient for the auditor to issue an unmodified audit opinion.

If the auditor concludes that written representations made by management regarding fulfilment of its responsibilities are not reliable due to doubts about management integrity or if management does not provide those representations, he or she should disclaim an opinion on the financial statements because the possible effects on the financial statements are pervasive. Modification of the written representation that was requested does not necessarily mean that the representation was not provided and the reasons for the modification may affect the opinion in the auditor's report. Furthermore, based on the nature of the representations not obtained or the circumstances of management's refusal to provide written representations, the auditor, rather than disclaiming an opinion or withdrawing from the engagement, may conclude that a qualified opinion is appropriate.

### Practitioner's Aids

Exhibit AU-C 580-1 illustrates a management representation letter similar to the one included in Exhibit 1 of AU-C 580, in which there are no exceptions to the written representations requested.

## EXHIBIT AU-C 580-1—MANAGEMENT REPRESENTATION LETTER

*(Entity letterhead)*

(To Auditor) (Date)

This representation letter is provided in connection with your audit of the financial statements of XYZ Company, which comprise the balance sheet as of December 31, 20X5, and the related statements of income, changes in stockholders' equity and cash flows for the year then ended, and the related notes to the financial statements, for the purpose of expressing an opinion as to whether the financial statements are presented fairly, in all material respects, in accordance with the accounting principles generally accepted in the United States (U.S. GAAP).

Certain representations in this letter are described as being limted to matters that are material. Items are considered material, regardless of size, if they involve an omission or misstatement of accounting information that, in the light of surrounding circumstances, makes it probable that the judgment of a reasonable person relying on the information would be changed or influenced by the omission or misstatement.

Except where otherwise stated below, immaterial matters less than $[*amount*] collectively are not considered to be exceptions that require disclosure for the purpose of the following representations. This amount is not necessarily indicative of amounts that would require adjustment to or disclosure in the financial statements.

We confirm, [*to the best of our knowledge and belief, having made such inquiries as we considered necessary for the purpose of appropriately informing ourselves*] [as of (date of auditor's report)]:

*Financial Statements*

- We have fulfilled our responsibilities, as set out in the terms of the audit engagement dated [*date*] for the preparation of the financial statements in accordance with U.S. GAAP.
- We acknowledge our responsibility for the design, implementation, and maintenance of internal control relevant to the preparation and fair presentation of financial statements that are free from material misstatement, whether due to fraud or error.
- We acknowledge our responsibility for the design, implementation, and maintenance of internal control to prevent and detect fraud.
- Significant assumptions used by us in making accounting estimates, including those measured at fair value, are reasonable.
- Related party relationships and transactions have been appropriately accounted for and disclosed in accordance with the requirements of U.S. GAAP.
- All events subsequent to the date of the financial statements and for which U.S. GAAP requires adjustment or disclosure have been adjusted or disclosed.

- The effects of uncorrected misstatements are immaterial, both individually and in the aggregate, to the financial statements as a whole. A list of the uncorrected misstatements is attached to the representation letter.
- [*Any other matters the auditor may consider appropriate.*]

Information Provided

- We have provided you with:
  - Access to all information, of which we are aware that is relevant to the preparation and fair presentation of the financial statements such as records, documentation and other matters;
  - Additional information that you have requested from us for the purpose of the audit; and
  - Unrestricted access to persons within the entity from whom you determined it necessary to obtain audit evidence.
- All transactions have been recorded in the accounting records and are reflected in the financial statements.
- We have disclosed to you the results of our assessment of the risk that the financial statements may be materially misstated as a result of fraud.
- We have [*no knowledge of any*] [*disclosed to you all information that we are aware in relation to*] fraud or suspected fraud that affects the entity and involves (a) management, (b) employees who have significant roles in internal control, or (c) others where the fraud could have a material effect on the financial statements.
- We have [*no knowledge of any*] [*disclosed to you all information in relation to*] allegations of fraud or suspected fraud affecting the entity's financial statements communicated by employees, former employees, analysts, regulators, or others.
- We have disclosed to you all known instances of non-compliance or suspected non-compliance with laws and regulations whose effects should be considered when preparing financial statements.
- We [*have disclosed to you all known actual or possible*] [*are not aware of any pending or threatened*] litigation and claims whose effects should be considered when preparing the financial statements [*and we have not consulted legal counsel concerning litigation or claims*].
- We have disclosed to you the identity of the entity's related parties and all the related party relationships and transactions of which we are aware.

[*Any other matters that the auditor may consider necessary.*]

[*Name of Chief Executive Officer and Title*]

[*Name of Chief Financial Officer and Title*]

---

Exhibit AU-C 580-2 identifies other AU-C sections that have requirements for specific written representations if relevant to the audit as well as written representations recommended by AICPA Audit Guides for use in certain situations if the auditor decides that a written representation to provide corroborative audit evidence is necessary.

# EXHIBIT AU-C 580-2—ADDITIONAL REQUIREMENTS FOR WRITTEN REPRESENTATIONS

## AU-C Sections with Written Representation Requirements

- AU-C 560, *Subsequent Events and Subsequently Discovered Facts* (paragraph 19)
- AU-C 570, *Going Concern*
- AU-C 700, *Forming an Opinion and Reporting on Financial Statements* (paragraph 52)
- AU-C 935, *Compliance Audits* (paragraph 23)

## Conditions AICPA Audit Guides Recommend May Require Written Representations

*General*

- Unaudited interim financial information accompanies the financial statements
- The effect of a new accounting principle is unknown
- Financial circumstances are strained and management discloses its intentions and the entity's ability to continue as a going concern
- The value of specific significant long lived assets or identifiable intangibles may be impaired
- The entity has a variable interest in another entity
- A specialist's work has been used by the entity

*Assets*

- Disclosure of compensating balances or other arrangements involving restrictions on cash balances, lines of credit, or similar arrangements is required
- Management intends to and has the ability to hold to maturity debt securities classified as held-to-maturity
- Management considers the decline in value of debt or equity securities to be temporary
- Management has determined the fair value of significant financial instruments that do not have readily determinable market values
- There are financial instruments with off-balance-sheet risk and concentrations of credit risk
- There are unusual circumstances in determining the application of equity accounting
- There are loans to executive officers, nonaccrued loans, or zero interest rate loans

*Liabilities*
- Short term debt can be refinanced on a long term basis and management intends to do so
- Tax-exempt bonds have been issued
- Management intends to reinvest undistributed earnings of a foreign subsidiary
- An actuary has been used to measure pension liabilities and cost
- There is involvement with a multiemployer plan
- Postretirement benefits have been eliminated
- Employee layoffs that would otherwise lead to curtailment of a benefit plan are intended to be temporary
- Management intends to continue to make or not make frequent amendments to its pension or other postretirement benefit plans, which may affect the amortization period of prior service cost, or has expressed a substantive commitment to increase benefit obligations

*Equity*
- Capital stock repurchase options or agreements or capital stock reserved for options, warrants, conversions, or other requirements exist

# SECTION 585

# CONSIDERATION OF OMITTED PROCEDURES AFTER THE REPORT RELEASE DATE

## Authoritative Pronouncements

SAS-122—Statements on Auditing Standards: Clarification and Recodification

## Overview

AU-C 585 provides guidance when the auditor concludes, subsequent to the report release date, that one or more procedures necessary given the circumstances existing at the time of the audit were omitted from an engagement. AU-C 585 does not apply when an auditor's work is at issue in a threatened or pending legal proceeding or regulatory investigation. When the auditor becomes aware of a fact after the report release date that may have caused the auditor to amend his or her report had it been known at that date, the guidance in AU-C 560 (*Subsequent Events and Subsequently Discovered Facts*) is applicable.

> **OBSERVATION:** Disclosure that procedures were omitted often comes as a result of a quality review or peer review of the auditor's engagement.

## Definition

Omitted procedure — An auditing procedure considered necessary to be performed in the circumstances existing at the time of the financial statement audit, which was not performed.

## Requirements

The auditor is presumptively required to perform the following procedures when considering the omission of audit procedures after the report release date:

1. When the auditor concludes subsequent to the report release date there is an omitted procedure, he or she should assess any effect of the omitted procedure on the auditor's current ability to support the previously expressed audit opinion.

2. If the auditor concludes an omitted procedure impairs his or her current ability to support the previously expressed audit opinion and the auditor believes there are users relying or likely to rely on the previously released report, the omitted procedure or alternative procedures should be performed to determine whether there is a satisfactory basis for the auditor's previously expressed opinion. The procedures performed should be documented in accordance with AU-C 230 (*Audit Documentation*), including the circumstances encountered; new or additional procedures performed, audit evidence obtained, conclusions reached, and

their effect on the auditor's report; and when and by whom the changes to audit documentation were made and reviewed.

3. When subsequent performance of an omitted procedure or alternative procedure causes the auditor to becomes aware of facts about the financial statements that existed at the report date that would have affected the auditor's opinion had he or she been aware of them, the auditor should follow the requirements in AU-C 560 regarding subsequently discovered facts that become known to the auditor after the report release date.

## Analysis and Application of Procedures

Initially, the auditor should assess the importance of the omitted audit procedure within the context of the engagement to determine any effect it has on his or her current ability to support the previously expressed audit opinion. This assessment may include a review of the audit documentation, discussions with other personnel within the firm, and reevaluation of the audit's overall scope. An omitted procedure may be compensated for by other audit procedures applied or a subsequent audit may provide evidence supporting a previously expressed opinion.

> **OBSERVATION:** After the report release date, even though the auditor has no responsibility to perform a retrospective review of audit work performed, there may be circumstances in which the auditor becomes aware of an omitted procedure.

If the auditor is unable to apply an omitted or alternative audit procedure, he or she may consult an attorney and discuss the appropriateness of the following actions:

- Notification of regulatory authorities (SEC, etc.); and
- Notification of persons relying, or likely to rely, on the financial statements.

## Practitioner's Aid

*EXHIBIT AU-C 585-1—OMISSION OF ENGAGEMENT PROCEDURES DISCOVERED AFTER THE REPORT RELEASE DATE*

Use the following procedures, as a guide for evaluating the omission of engagement procedures discovered after the report release date. The program is only a guide, and professional judgment should be exercised to determine how the guidance established in the auditing standards should be adapted to a particular engagement.

Initial and date each procedure as it is completed. If the procedure is not relevant to this engagement, place "N/A" (not applicable) in the space provided for an initial.

Client Name: _____

Date of Financial Statements: _____

|   |   | Initials | Date | Audit Documentation Reference |
|---|---|---|---|---|
| 1. | Establish the level of inherent risk. | _____ | _____ | _____ |
| 2. | Assess the significance of omitted procedures and consider whether to apply audit procedures. | _____ | _____ | _____ |
| 3. | If doing so is appropriate, apply the omitted procedures and consider the effect that the evidence gathered has on the auditor's conclusions. | _____ | _____ | _____ |
| 4. | Determine the proper course of action if significant procedures or alternative procedures cannot be performed. | _____ | _____ | _____ |

Other engagement procedures: _____

Reviewed by: _____

Date: _____

# AU-C 600
# Using the Work of Others

| Section 600: | Special Considerations—Audits of Group Financial Statements (Including the Work of Component Auditors) | 6002 |
|---|---|---|
| Section 610: | Using the Work of Internal Auditors | 6027 |
| Section 620: | Using the Work of an Auditor's Specialist | 6038 |

## SECTION 600

## SPECIAL CONSIDERATIONS—AUDITS OF GROUP FINANCIAL STATEMENTS (INCLUDING THE WORK OF COMPONENT AUDITORS)

### Authoritative Pronouncements

SAS-122—Statements on Auditing Standards: Clarification and Recodification

SAS-127—Omnibus Statement on Auditing Standards—2013

SAS-134—Auditor Reporting and Amendments, Including Amendments Addressing Disclosures in the Audit of Financial Statements

SAS-135—Omnibus Statement on Auditing Standards—2019

SAS-137—The Auditor's Responsibilities Relating to Other Information Included in Annual Reports

SAS-138—Amendments to the Description of the Concept of Materiality

SAS-No. 141—Amendment to Effective Dates of SAS Nos. 134-140

SAS Interpretation 1—Auditor of Participating Employer in a Governmental Pension Plan (April 2014)

### Overview

As part of an audit of group financial statements, the group engagement partner must abide by the requirements in AU-C 220 (*Quality Control for an Engagement Conducted in Accordance with Generally Accepted Auditing Standards*). The guidance in AU-C 600 helps the group engagement partner to meet these requirements when component auditors are involved in the audit. This guidance can also be useful to the auditor when adapted to situations other than group audits where other auditors are involved in an audit (e.g., observing an inventory count at a remote location).

AU-C 600 helps the auditor decide whether to act as the auditor of the group financial statements. It also provides guidance to the auditor in communicating with component auditors. The auditor is to obtain sufficient appropriate audit evidence regarding the components' financial information and the consolidation process to express a group audit opinion. The evidence needed is affected by audit risk, which in a group audit includes the risk that the component auditor and group engagement team may not detect a misstatement in the component information that could cause a material misstatement of the group financial statements.

AU-C 600 also assists the auditor is determining whether reference should be made to the audit of a component auditor in the auditor's report on the group financial statements. If the group engagement partner assumes responsibility for the work of component auditors, the group auditors should be involved in the work of the component auditors as it relates to expressing a group audit opinion; if the group engagement partner does not assume responsibility for the component auditors' work, reference should be made to the audit of a component auditor in the group auditor's report.

---

**IMPORTANT NOTICE FOR 2022:** In May 2019, the AICPA's Auditing Standards Board (ASB) issued SAS No. 134 titled *Auditor Reporting and Amendments, Including Amendments Addressing Disclosures in the Audit of Financial Statements* that makes significant changes to the auditor's report, including the ability to communicate key audit matters (KAMs) in the auditor's report. SAS No. 134 amends all the auditor report illustrations contained in AU-C 600 to conform those reports to the language in the new auditor's report. Originally, the effective date of SAS No. 134 was for audits of financial statements periods ending on or after December 15, 2020, with early implementation **not** permitted. However, the ASB's issuance of SAS No. 141, *Amendment to the Effective Dates of SAS Nos. 134-140*, extended the effective date to December 15, 2021, in order to provide more time for firms to implement SAS No. 134 in light of the effect of the coronavirus pandemic. While SAS No. 141 allows for early implementation of SAS No. 134, the ASB recommends that SAS Nos. 134-140 be implemented concurrently.

---

**IMPORTANT NOTICE FOR 2022:** In December 2019, the AICPA's Auditing Standards Board (ASB) issued SAS No. 138 titled *Amendments to the Description of the Concept of Materiality* to align the materiality concepts discussed in auditing standards, including AU-C 200, with the definition of materiality used by the U.S. judicial system, the PCAOB auditing standards, and the Financial Accounting Standards Board (FASB). The FASB aligned its definition of materiality in August 2018 to be consistent with the U.S. judicial system and other U.S. standards setters and regulators. The ASB believes it is in the public interest to eliminate existing inconsistencies in definitions of materiality used. The U.S. judicial system defines misstatement as material if there is "**substantial likelihood** that a reasonable shareholder **would** consider it important" whereas existing auditing standards define a misstatement as material if it "**could reasonably be expected to** influence the judgment of a reasonable person." The effective date of the amendment is for audits of financial statements for periods ending on or after December 15, 2021.

---

**OBSERVATION:** AU-C 600 replaces what was previously AU 543 (*Part of an Audit Performed by Other Independent Auditors*). The scope of AU-C 600 is broader than the scope of AU 543. In addition, the term "principal auditor" from AU 543 has been replaced by the terms "group engagement partner," "group engagement team," or "auditor of the group financial statements," depending on the context.

## Definitions

| | |
|---|---|
| Component | An entity or business activity for which group or component management prepares financial information that is required by the applicable financial reporting framework to be included in the group financial statements. |
| Component auditor | An auditor who performs work on the financial information of a component that will be used as evidence for the group audit. A component auditor can be part of the same firm as the group engagement partner; it can be a firm that belongs to the same network as the group engagement partner's firm; or it can be another firm. |
| Component management | Management responsible for preparing the financial information of a component. |
| Component materiality | The materiality for a component determined by the group engagement team for the purposes of a group audit. |
| Consolidation process | Includes the recognition, measurement, presentation, and disclosure of components' financial information in the group financial statements through inclusion, consolidation, proportionate consolidation, the equity or cost methods of accounting, or aggregation in combined financial statements of the financial information of components that have no parent but are under common control. |
| Group | All the components (always more than one) whose financial information is included in the group financial statements. |
| Group audit | The audit of group financial statements. |
| Group audit opinion | The audit opinion of the group financial statements. |
| Group engagement partner | The partner or other person in the firm responsible for the group audit engagement, its performance, and the group audit opinion issued on behalf of the firm; this may include joint engagement partners when joint auditors conduct a group audit. |
| Group engagement team | The group engagement partner, partners, and staff who establish the overall group audit strategy, communicate with component auditors, perform work on the consolidation process, and evaluate the conclusions drawn from the audit evidence in order to form an opinion on the group financial statements. |
| Group financial statements | Financial statements that include the financial information of more than one component, or combined financial statements aggregating the financial information prepared by components that have no parent but are under common control. |
| Group management | Management responsible for preparing and presenting group financial statements. |
| Group-wide controls | Controls over financial reporting designed, implemented, and maintained by group management. |
| Significant component | A component identified by the group engagement team that is of individual financial significance to the group or, due to its nature or circumstances, is likely to include significant risks of material misstatement of the group financial statements. |

**IMPORTANT NOTICE FOR 2022:** In 2016, the PCAOB had issued a proposal that would amend the existing guidance on supervising other auditors, and that would replace the existing guidance when a divided-opinion report is issued. The PCAOB's proposal (*Proposed Amendments Relating to the Supervision of Audits Involving Other Auditors and Proposed Auditing Standard—Dividing Responsibil-

*ity for the Audit with Another Accounting Firm*) is designed to ensure greater participation by the lead auditor in engagements involving other auditors. As of June 2021, this exposure draft was still outstanding. Under the proposal, AS-1205 would be superseded and the lead auditor would no longer be able to take responsibility for the work performed by other auditors (in those cases where a divided-responsibility report is not issued) unless the lead auditor supervised the work performed by the other auditors. The proposal requires the lead auditor to: (1) perform certain procedures to supervise the work performed by other auditors, (2) determine whether the lead auditor's firm has sufficient participation in the audit to issue an opinion, the determination of which would have to be reviewed by the engagement quality reviewer, and (3) document the other auditors' working papers that were reviewed by the lead auditor but not retained by the lead auditor. If the lead auditor desires to issue a divided-responsibility opinion, the portion of the financial statements audited by the referred-to auditor would continue to be disclosed in the audit report. In addition, the proposed new standard requires the lead auditor to: (1) obtain a representation from the referred-to auditor that the firm is duly licensed in the jurisdiction(s) where work is performed, (2) determine whether the referred-to auditor is registered with the PCAOB, and (3) name the referred-to auditor in the audit report. In September 2017, the PCAOB issued a Supplemental Request for Comment related to this proposal to seek input on possible revisions. The PCAOB is currently evaluating the feedback received.

## Requirements

The group engagement team is presumptively required to perform the following procedures in audits of group financial statements:

### *Responsibility*

1. The group engagement partner is responsible for the direction, supervision, and performance of the group audit engagement in compliance with professional standards, legal and regulatory requirements, and the firm's policies and procedures and for determining if the issued audit report is appropriate in the circumstances.

### *Acceptance and Continuance*

2. The group engagement partner should determine whether sufficient appropriate audit evidence will be able to be obtained about the consolidation process and the financial information of components for the group engagement team to serve as the auditor of the group financial statements and formulate a group audit opinion. For this determination, the group engagement team should obtain a sufficient understanding of the group, its components, and their environments to identify components that are likely to be significant.

3. The group engagement partner should determine whether the work of the group engagement team and the work of component auditors will be sufficient for the group engagement team to serve as the group auditor.

4. If the group engagement partner concludes that sufficient appropriate audit evidence will not be able to be obtained through the group engagement team's work or involvement in the work of component auditors due to

restrictions imposed by group management or other reasons, and this may result in a disclaimer of a group audit opinion, the partner should:
- a. Not accept the engagement if it is a new engagement,
- b. Withdraw from the engagement if it is a continuing engagement, and
- c. Disclaim an opinion on the group financial statements if prohibited from declining or withdrawing from the engagement due to law or regulation.

5. The group financial statements auditor is required to agree upon the terms of the group audit engagement. This is a mandatory requirement (rather than a presumptively mandatory requirement).

## Overall Audit Strategy and Audit Plan

6. The group engagement team should establish and the group engagement partner should review and approve an overall group audit strategy and audit plan. In developing the group audit plan, the group engagement partner should assess the extent to which the work of component auditors will be used and whether the group audit report will reference the audit of a component auditor.

## Obtaining an Understanding

7. Identify and assess the risks of material misstatement by obtaining an understanding of the entity and its environment through (1) enhancing the understanding of the group, its components, their environments, and group-wide controls obtained during acceptance and continuance; and (2) an understanding of the consolidation process, including the instructions issued by group management to components. This understanding should be sufficient to confirm or revise the initial identification of components likely to be significant and to assess the risks of material misstatement of the group financial statements whether due to fraud or error.

8. Obtain an understanding of:
- a. A component auditor's independence, professional competence, and understanding and willingness to comply with the ethical requirements relevant to the group audit.
- b. The extent the group engagement team will be able to be involved in the work of the component auditor.
- c. Whether the group engagement team will be able to obtain information affecting the consolidation process from a component auditor.
- d. If a component auditor operates in a regulatory environment that actively oversees auditors.

9. If a component auditor is not independent, or the auditor is seriously concerned that the component auditor does not understand or will not comply with ethical requirements or lacks professional competence, obtain sufficient appropriate audit evidence relating to the financial information of the component without using the work of or making reference to the audit of the component auditor in the group auditor's report.

## Whether to Make Reference to a Component Auditor in the Group Audit Report

10. The group engagement partner should decide whether to make reference to a component auditor in the group audit report.

11. Reference can be made to the audit of a component auditor when (1) the component and group financial statements are prepared using the same

financial reporting framework, and (2) the component auditor has performed a financial statement audit of the component in accordance with GAAS, or Public Company Accounting Oversight Board (PCAOB) auditing standards when required, and issued an unrestricted auditor's report. If certain conditions are met, the standards permit the group auditor to make reference to the audit of a component auditor in the group auditor's report when the component's financial statements are prepared using a different financial reporting framework than that used for the group financial statements. In that situation, the auditor's report on the group financial statements must disclose that the group auditor is taking responsibility for evaluating the appropriateness of the adjustments to convert the component's financial statements to the financial reporting framework used by the group.

**OBSERVATION:** If the component auditor performed the audit using auditing standards other than GAAS or, where applicable, PCAOB standards, the engagement partner may evaluate whether these standards meet the requirements of GAAS. In general, International Auditing Standards (IASs), promulgated by the International Auditing and Assurance Standards Board, are more likely to meet the requirements of GAAS than are other auditing frameworks. When the group auditor is making reference to the audit of a component auditor and has determined that the component auditor performed additional procedures in order to meet the requirements of GAAS, the auditor's report on the group financial statements should indicate the set of auditing standards used by the component auditor and that additional audit procedures were performed by the component auditor to meet the relevant requirements of GAAS.

12. If reference will be made to the audit of a component auditor in the group audit report, obtain sufficient appropriate audit evidence about those components by:

   a. Performing all of the required procedures except those applicable when assuming responsibility for the work of a component auditor.

   b. Identifying significant findings and issues by reading the components' financial information and any component auditor's report and, if necessary, communicating with the component auditor.

13. If reference is made to the audit of a component auditor in the group audit opinion, the group audit report should clearly indicate the division of responsibility between the component auditor and group engagement team. Disclose in the report the magnitude of the portion of the financial statements audited by the component auditor.

14. If the component auditor is named in the group audit report, the express permission of the component auditor should be obtained and the component auditor's report should be presented with the group auditor's report.

15. If the component auditor's opinion is modified or includes an emphasis-of-matter or other-matter paragraph, the group engagement partner should determine the effect this may have on the group auditor's report, and, where appropriate, should modify the opinion or include an emphasis of matter or other matter paragraph in the group auditor's report.

16. If assuming responsibility for the work of a component auditor, do not make reference to the component auditor in the group auditor's report.

*Materiality*

17. Determine:

   a. Materiality, including performance materiality, for the group financial statements as a whole when establishing the overall group audit strategy.

   b. Materiality to be applied to any particular classes of transactions, account balances, or disclosures in the group financial statements for which there is a substantial likelihood that misstatements less than materiality for the statements as a whole would influence the judgments of reasonable users taken on the basis of the group financial statements.

   c. Component materiality for components on which an audit or review will be performed, which should be lower than materiality for the group financial statements as a whole to reduce the risk that aggregate detected and undetected misstatements exceed materiality.

   d. The threshold above which misstatements cannot be regarded as clearly trivial to the group financial statements.

---

**IMPORTANT NOTICE FOR 2022:** In December 2019, the AICPA's Auditing Standards Board (ASB) issued SAS No. 138 titled *Amendments to the Description of the Concept of Materiality* to align the materiality concepts discussed in auditing standards, including AU-C 200, with the definition of materiality used by the U.S. judicial system, the PCAOB auditing standards, and the Financial Accounting Standards Board (FASB). The FASB aligned its definition of materiality in August 2018 to be consistent with the U.S. judicial system and other U.S. standards setters and regulators. The ASB believes it is in the public interest to eliminate existing inconsistencies in definitions of materiality used. The U.S. judicial system defines misstatement as material if there is **"substantial likelihood** that a reasonable shareholder **would** consider it important" whereas existing auditing standards define a misstatement as material if it **"could reasonably be expected to** influence the judgment of a reasonable person." The effective date of the amendment is for audits of financial statements for periods ending on or after December 15, 2021.

---

*Response to Assessed Risks*

18. Design and implement appropriate responses to address the assessed risks of material misstatement of the financial statements. The group or component auditor should test the operating effectiveness of controls if the procedures to be performed on the consolidation process or the components' financial information is based on an expectation that group-wide controls are operating effectively or substantive procedures alone cannot provide sufficient appropriate audit evidence at the assertion level.

*Consolidation Process*

19. Design and perform further audit procedures on the consolidation process to respond to the assessed risks of material misstatement of the group financial statements arising from the consolidation process, including evaluating whether all components have been included in the group financial statements.

20. Evaluate the appropriateness, completeness, and accuracy of consolidation adjustments and reclassifications and the existence of any fraud risk factors or indicators of possible management bias.

21. If a component's financial information has not been prepared in accordance with the same accounting policies as the group financial statements, evaluate whether that financial information has been appropriately adjusted for purposes of preparing and presenting group financial statements.

22. Determine whether the financial information the component auditor identifies as reporting on is the information that is incorporated in the group financial statements.

23. If the group financial statements contain the financial statements of a component with a different financial reporting period-end, evaluate whether appropriate adjustments have been made to those financial statements in accordance with the applicable financial reporting framework.

## Subsequent Events

24. When audits are performed on the financial information of components, procedures should be performed that are designed to identify events at those components that occur between the date of the financial information of the components and the group auditor's report date that may require adjustment or disclosure in the group financial statements.

## Communication with the Component Auditor

25. Communicate requirements to the component auditor on a timely basis and include:
   a. A request that the component auditor confirm their cooperation with the group engagement team knowing the context in which the component auditor's work will be used.
   b. Relevant ethical and independence requirements.
   c. A list of related parties prepared by group management and any other related parties the group engagement team is aware of, including the nature of the entity's relationship and transactions with related parties. Request the component auditor communicate on a timely basis any related parties not previously identified. The group engagement team should identify such additional related parties to other component auditors.
   d. Identified significant risks of material misstatement of the group financial misstatements due to fraud or error that are relevant to the component auditor.

26. Request that component auditors communicate matters relevant to the conclusion for the group audit, including:
   a. Whether the component auditor complied with relevant ethical requirements, including independence and professional competence;
   b. Identification of the financial information of the component the component auditor is reporting on; and
   c. The component auditor's overall findings, conclusions, or opinion.

## Evaluating Audit Evidence

27. Evaluate a component auditor's communication, discuss significant findings and issues arising from that evaluation with the component auditor, component management, or group management as appropriate.

28. Evaluate whether sufficient appropriate audit evidence to base the group audit opinion on has been obtained from the audit procedures performed on the consolidation process and the work performed by the group and component auditors on the financial information of the components.

29. The group engagement partner should evaluate the effect on the group audit opinion of any uncorrected misstatements and any instances in which sufficient appropriate audit evidence has been unable to be obtained.

## Communication with Management and Those Charged with Governance of the Group

30. Communicate material weaknesses and significant deficiencies in internal control identified by the group auditor or component auditors to group management and those charged with governance of the group.

31. Communicate identified fraud or information indicating a fraud may exist on a timely basis to the appropriate level of group management.

32. When a component auditor is engaged to audit a component's financial statements and the group engagement team becomes aware of a matter that may be significant to the component's financial statements but that component management may not be aware of (such as potential litigation, plans for abandonment of material operating assets, subsequent events, or significant legal agreements), request that group management inform component management of the matter. If group management refuses to communicate this information, discuss the matter with those charged with governance of the group. If the matter remains unresolved, consider whether, given legal and professional responsibility considerations, to advise the component auditor not to issue the auditor's report on the component's financial statements until the matter is resolved and whether to withdraw from the engagement.

33. Communicate the following matters with those charged with governance of the group:

    a. An overview of the type of work to be performed on the financial information of the components, including the basis for a decision to make reference to the audit of a component auditor in the group auditor's report.

    b. An overview of the nature of the planned involvement by the group auditor in the work to be performed by component auditors on the financial information of significant components.

    c. Instances in which evaluation of the work of a component auditor gives rise to a concern about the quality of that auditor's work.

    d. Any limitations on the group audit (e.g., restrictions on access to information).

    e. Fraud or suspected fraud involving group or component management, employees with significant roles in group-wide controls, or others in which a material misstatement of the group financial statements has or may have resulted from fraud.

## Documentation

34. Document:

    a. An analysis of components indicating significant components and the type of work performed on the components' financial information.

    b. Components for which the auditor's report on the group financial statements refers to the reports of component auditors.

c. Written communications between the group engagement team and the component auditors about the group engagement team's requirements.

d. For components for which the auditor is making reference to the audit of a component auditor, the financial statements of the component and the auditor's report on the component.

## Additional Requirements Applicable When Assuming Responsibility for the Work of a Component Auditor

35. Evaluate the appropriateness of performance materiality at the component level.

36. Determine the type of work to be performed by the group or component auditors on the financial information of components and the nature, timing, and extent of involvement in the work of component auditors.

37. If a component is significant due to its individual financial significance to the group, the group or component auditor should perform an audit of the financial information of the component to meet the needs of the group engagement team, using component materiality.

38. If a component is significant because it is likely to include significant risks of material misstatement of the group financial statements due to qualitative factors, the group or component auditor should use component materiality and perform one or more of the following:

a. An audit of the component's financial information to meet group engagement team needs.

b. An audit of one or more account balances, classes of transactions, or disclosures, or specified audit procedures relating to the likely significant risks of material misstatement.

39. If a component is not a significant component, perform analytical procedures at the group level.

40. If sufficient appropriate audit evidence cannot be obtained from work performed on the financial information of significant components, group-wide controls and the consolidation process, and from analytical procedures performed at the group level, select additional non-significant components and the group or component auditor should perform one or more of the following on the selected components:

a. A review or audit of the component's financial information to meet the group engagement team's needs, using component materiality.

b. An audit of one or more account balances, classes of transactions, or disclosure.

c. Specified audit procedures.

Vary the selection of individual components over a period of time.

41. If a component auditor audits or performs audit procedures on the financial information of a significant component, the group auditor should be involved in the component auditor's assessment of significant risks of material misstatement to the group financial statements, although the nature, timing, and extent of involvement will vary based on the understanding of the component auditor. Involvement should, at a minimum, include:

a. Discussing the component's business activities of significance to the group with the component auditor or component management,

b. Discussing the susceptibility of the component to material misstatement of the financial information through fraud or error with the component auditor, and

c. Reviewing the component auditor's documentation of identified significant risks of material misstatement of the group financial statements.

42. If significant risks of material misstatement to the group financial statements have been identified in a component, evaluate the appropriateness of further audit procedures to be performed to respond to those identified significant risks and determine if it is necessary to be involved in the further audit procedures depending on the group auditor's understanding of the component auditor.

43. If component auditors perform work other than audits of components' financial information at the request of the group engagement team, request that the component auditors notify the group engagement team if they become aware of subsequent events that may require adjustment or disclosure in the group financial statements.

44. Communication between the group auditor and the component auditor should include:

   a. The nature of the work to be performed by the component auditor, and the nature and content of the component auditor's communication with the group auditor at the conclusion of this work;

   b. When the component auditor performs an audit or review: (1) component materiality; (2) any amounts lower than component materiality for particular account balances, transaction classes, and disclosures; and (3) the threshold above which misstatements cannot be viewed as clearly trivial;

   c. Whether the component auditor has complied with the group engagement team's requirements;

   d. Information on instances of noncompliance with laws or regulations at the component or group level that could lead to a material misstatement of the group financial statements;

   e. Significant risks of material misstatement of the group financial statements due to fraud or error in the component and the component auditor's responses to those risks;

   f. A list of corrected and uncorrected misstatements (does not need to include clearly trivial misstatements) of the financial information of the component;

   g. Indicators of possible management bias regarding accounting estimates and the application of accounting principles;

   h. Description of any identified material weaknesses and significant deficiencies in internal control at the component level;

   i. Other significant findings and issues the component auditor communicated or expects to communicate to those charged with governance of the component, including fraud or suspected fraud involving component management, employees with significant roles in internal control at the component level, or others in which a material misstatement of the financial information of the component has resulted from fraud; and

j. Any other matters that may be relevant to the group audit or that the component auditor wishes to draw to the attention of the group engagement team, including exceptions noted in the written representations the component auditor requested from component management.

45. If the component auditor's work is concluded to be insufficient, determine additional procedures to be performed and whether they will be performed by the component or group auditor.

46. The group auditor should evaluate material weaknesses and significant deficiencies in internal control identified by a component auditor, and determine which of these items to communicate to group management and those charged with governance of the group.

47. Document the nature, timing, and extent of the involvement in the work performed by the component auditors on significant components including any review of relevant parts of the component auditors' audit documentation and conclusions of that review.

## Analysis and Application of Procedures

### Components and Component Auditors

Components are entities or business activities for which management prepares financial information. This is often based on organizational structure, and components may be subsidiaries of a parent, joint ventures, or investees accounted for by the cost or equity method of accounting; however, components may be also identified based on function, process, product or service, or geographical location. Furthermore, there may be different levels of components within a group financial reporting system such that components may be identified at aggregated levels rather than individually. These aggregated components may constitute a component for the purposes of a group audit and may constitute a group for preparation of group financial statements incorporating all of the encompassed individual components. Therefore, there may be multiple group audits that occur within one group financial reporting system.

When identifying significant components, the auditor considers quantitative and qualitative factors. The auditor may, using professional judgment, apply a percentage to a chosen benchmark to identify components of individual financial significance.

Component auditors may include auditors working for a network firm, auditors working in a different office of the group engagement partner's firm, or even group engagement team members working on a component's financial information at the request of the group engagement team. However, an auditor performing work on a component that will not be used to provide evidence for the group audit is not a component auditor.

### Responsibility

Group engagement partners are responsible for the group audit opinion; however, component auditors remain responsible for their overall findings, conclusions, and opinions on the components' financial information.

## Acceptance and Continuance

The group engagement team obtains an understanding of the group, its component, and their environments as part of the decision to accept or continue the engagement. This understanding may be obtained from information provided by or communication with group management or from communication with component management, component auditors, or the previous group engagement team when applicable. The auditor's understanding may incorporate matters such as:

- Group structure,
- Component business activities that are significant to the group,
- Use of service organizations,
- A description of group-wide control,
- Complexity of the consolidation process,
- If there will be any component auditors outside of the group engagement partner's firm or network and group management's rationale for that decision, and
- If the group engagement team will have unrestricted access to the necessary people and information and will be able to perform necessary work on the components' financial information.

If the engagement is a continuing engagement, the ability to obtain sufficient appropriate audit evidence may be affected by significant changes, such as changes in group structure, components' business activities significant to the group, the composition of management or those charged with governance of the group or of significant components, group-wide controls, the applicable financial reporting framework, or concerns of the group engagement team regarding the integrity and competence of group or component management.

Determination of whether to act as the group financial statement auditor may include factors such as the group engagement team's involvement in significant components, and the extent of the group engagement team's knowledge of the overall financial statements. If a group does not contain any significant components, the auditor should be able to act as the group financial statement auditor if the group engagement team will be able to perform the work on the financial information of some of the components and be involved in the work of component auditors on the financial information of other components to the extent necessary to obtain sufficient appropriate audit evidence.

---

**PLANNING AID REMINDER:** In determining whether to act as the auditor for governmental group financial statement audits, the auditor also considers his or her engagement by the primary government as the auditor of the financial reporting entity and his or her responsibility for auditing the primary government's general or other primary operating fund.

---

The group engagement team may have restricted access to information due to group management or other circumstances. If information access is restricted because of circumstances, sufficient appropriate audit evidence may still be able to be obtained if the component is not significant. However, if the component is significant and reference will not be made to the component auditor in the group auditor's report, sufficient appropriate audit evidence about that component will not be able to be obtained. If information is restricted because of group management and the component is significant, the group engagement team will not be able to obtain sufficient appropriate audit evidence. Sufficient appropriate audit evidence may be able to be obtained about a component that is not significant even if information is restricted by group management, but the reason for the restriction may affect the group audit opinion because it may affect the reliability of group management responses and representations.

---

**OBSERVATION:** The group engagement team uses professional judgment to determine the materiality and pervasiveness of an inability to obtain sufficient appropriate audit evidence about a significant component. If the effect of this inability is material but not pervasive, a qualified opinion should be expressed. However, if the effect of this inability is material and pervasive, a disclaimer of opinion should be expressed.

---

The terms of engagement agreed upon by the group engagement partner identify the applicable financial reporting framework and may include matters such as whether reference to the component auditor's audit will be made in the auditor's report on the group financial statements; the group engagement team's need for unrestricted communication between the group engagement team and component auditors; having any important communications between component auditors, management, and those charged with governance, or between regulatory authorities and components related to financial reporting matters communicated; necessary access to components' management, those charged with governance, auditors, and information; and permission to perform work or request a component auditor perform work on components' financial information as necessary.

## Obtaining an Understanding

### Understanding the entities and their environments

When obtaining an understanding of the entity and its environment to identify and assess the risks of material misstatement, specific matters to consider that may be relevant to a group audit engagement include group-wide controls and matters relating to the applicable financial reporting framework, the consolidation process, consolidation adjustments, and the instruction issued by group management to components.

The instructions from group management to components often cover the accounting policies to be applied, a reporting timetable, and statutory and disclosure requirements applicable to the group financial statements such as segment identification and reporting, related-party relationships and transactions, and intragroup account balances, transactions, and unrealized profits. The auditor's understanding of these instructions may include:

- The clarity and practicality of the instructions for completing the reporting package, which consists of a standard format for providing financial information for incorporation into the group financial statements;
- Whether the instructions adequately describe the characteristics of the applicable financial reporting framework; and
- Whether the instructions provide for disclosure sufficient to comply with applicable financial reporting framework requirements, identification of consolidation adjustments, and the approval of the financial information by component management.

---

**IMPORTANT NOTICE FOR 2022:** In May 2019, the AICPA's Auditing Standards Board (ASB) issued SAS No. 135 titled *Omnibus Statement on Auditing Standards—2019* that includes amendments to various AU-C sections. SAS No. 135 amends AU-C 600 to add requirements for the group engagement team to include with its list of related parties prepared by group management information about the nature of the entity's relationships and transactions with those related parties. Originally, the effective date of SAS No. 135 was for audits of financial statements periods ending on or after December 15, 2020, with early application **not** permitted. However, the ASB's issuance of SAS No. 141, *Amendment to the Effective Dates of SAS Nos. 134-140*, extended the effective date to December 15, 2021, in order to provide more time for firms to implement SAS No. 135 in light of the effect of the coronavirus pandemic. While SAS No. 141 allows for early implementation of SAS No. 135, the ASB recommends that SAS Nos. 134-140 be implemented concurrently.

---

The auditor should obtain an understanding sufficient to identify and assess the risks of material misstatement of the group financial statements, whether due to error or fraud. Information used to identify the risks of material misstatement due to fraud may include:

- Group management's assessment of the risks of the group financial statements being materially misstated due to fraud;
- Group management's process for identifying and responding to identified or likely fraud risks, how those charged with governance of the group monitor that process, and controls that group management has established to mitigate those risks;
- Whether particular components are likely to have a fraud risk; and
- Responses of group or component management, those charged with governance of the group, internal audit, or component auditors to inquiries of the group engagement team regarding knowledge of any actual, suspected, or alleged fraud affecting a component or group.

There are many conditions and events that may indicate risks of material misstatement of the group financial statements. Examples of these conditions that are specific to a group audit engagement include: a complex group structure, nonexistent or ineffective group-wide controls, uncertainties regarding which components' financial information to consolidate in the group financial statements, prior occurrences of intragroup account balances not balancing or reconciling on consolidation, complex transactions accounted for in multiple components, use of different accounting policies in component and group financial statements, components with different financial year-ends, and prior occurrences of incomplete consolidation adjustments.

The required discussion among key members of the engagement team about the susceptibility of an entity to material misstatement of the financial statements, emphasizing the risks due to fraud, may include component auditors based on the group engagement partner's determination. This discussion provides auditors with the opportunity to share information and ideas about the group and its components and business risks, the potential for management bias or override and the existence of fraud risk factors, and identified or indicated instances of fraud or noncompliance with laws or regulations.

*Understanding the component auditor*

The group engagement partner's decision about whether to use the component auditor's work to provide audit evidence for the group audit and whether to make reference to the component auditor's audit in the auditor's report on the group financial statements may be influenced by factors such as differences in the financial reporting framework or auditing or other standards applied in preparing the component and group financial statements, whether the component's financial statement audit will be completed in time to meet the group reporting timetable, and whether the group engagement team is able to be involved in the work of the component auditor.

---

**PLANNING AID REMINDER:** It is not necessary to obtain an understanding of auditors of components for which the group engagement team only plans to perform analytical procedures at a group level.

---

The nature, timing, and extent of the group engagement team's procedures to obtain an understanding of a component auditor depend on previous knowledge of or experience with the component auditor and the degree to which the group engagement team and component auditor are subject to the same policies and procedures, laws and regulations, education and training, professional oversight and standards, and language and culture.

In the first year working with a component auditor, this understanding may be obtained by:

- Determining that the component auditor is aware that : the component's financial statements will be included in the group financial statements; the component auditor's report will be relied upon; the group financial statement auditor will make reference to the component auditor's report in the opinion on the group financial statements or the group engagement team will be involved in the work of the component auditor; and matters affecting the elimination of intercompany transactions and accounts and the uniformity of accounting practices among the components in the group financial statements will be reviewed.

- Evaluating results of the quality control monitoring system if the group engagement team and component auditor are under common monitoring policies and procedures at a firm or network.
- Visiting a component auditor or requesting a component auditor to confirm or complete questionnaires about matters that the group engagement team is required to obtain an understanding of.
- Discussing a component auditor with colleagues in the group engagement partner's firm or with a reputable third party with knowledge of the component auditor.

In later years, the group engagement team's previous experience may provide sufficient understanding of the component auditor. Then, the group engagement team may just request that the component auditor confirm any changes in matters they are required to obtain an understanding.

The understanding of a component auditor's professional competence may include whether the component auditor possesses: a sufficient understanding of the standards applicable to the group audit, the special skills necessary to perform the work on a particular component's financial information, and a sufficient understanding of the applicable financial reporting framework. Inquiries about the professional competence of a component auditor may be made of the AICPA, the component auditor's state board of accountancy or state or local CPA society, or the corresponding foreign professional organization.

If the group engagement team has less than serious concerns about a component auditor's professional competence or the component auditor is operating in an environment that does not actively oversee auditors, by being involved in the work of the component auditor or performing additional risk assessment or further audit procedures on the component's financial information, that auditor's work may still be able to be used. However, greater involvement by the group auditor cannot remedy a lack of independence on the part of a component auditor. If the component auditor is not subject to the AICPA Code of Professional Conduct, compliance with the International Federation of Accountants *Code of Ethics for Professional Accountants* will suffice.

---

**OBSERVATION:** In some foreign jurisdictions, the group auditor may be precluded from accessing the workpapers of a component auditor. This issue has been particularly acute in China. This problem can be partially addressed by having the component auditor prepare a memorandum discussing the matters documented in the aforementioned workpapers. However, in the case of the audit of a public company, the PCAOB would not likely view a memorandum as a substitute for the group auditor having access to the workpapers of the component auditor.

---

### *Whether to Make Reference to a Component Auditor in the Group Audit Report*

The decision about whether to refer to the audit of a component auditor in the group audit report is made separately for each component auditor such that none, some, or all of the component auditors may be referred to in the group audit report. If the group engagement partner assumes responsibility for the work of a component auditor, no reference to the component auditor should be made in the group audit report because it could cause a reader to misinterpret the degree of responsibility the group auditor is assuming.

**OBSERVATION:** While the group audit report typically may not refer to the audit of a component auditor if the component's financial statements were prepared using a different financial reporting framework than the group financial statements, this restriction does not apply to group financial statements prepared in accordance with a reporting framework that provides for the inclusion of component financial statements prepared in accordance with a different financial reporting framework. Both the Governmental Accounting Standards Board and Federal Accounting Standards Advisory Board reporting frameworks have such provisions.

**PUBLIC COMPANY IMPLICATION:** PCAOB AS-1215 (*Audit Documentation and Amendment to Interim Auditing Standards*) provides documentation guidelines involving the use of principal and other auditors for public companies. AS-1215 specifies appropriate audit documentation when the principal auditor does not refer to the work of the other auditors. The principal auditor must obtain and review the following prior to issuing his or her audit report: (1) an engagement completion document; (2) a list of significant fraud risk factors, the other auditor's response, and the results from these procedures; (3) information on any matters that are inconsistent with or contradict the auditor's final conclusions; (4) any findings that affect the consolidating or combining of accounts in the consolidated financial statements; (5) the information necessary for the principal auditor to reconcile the amounts audited by the other auditor to the consolidated financial statements; (6) a schedule of audit adjustments, including the nature and cause of each adjustment; (7) a listing of all significant deficiencies and material weaknesses in internal control, with each group listed separately; (8) management representation letters; and (9) any matters to be communicated to the audit committee. In addition to these documentation requirements, the principal auditor should consider discussing the other auditors' audit procedures and related results, and consider reviewing the audit programs used by other auditors.

When reference is made to the audit of a component auditor in the group audit report, the magnitude of the portion of the financial statements audited by the component auditor may be disclosed by stating the dollar amounts or percentages of total assets, total revenues, and other criteria as appropriate. If multiple component auditors participated, the portion of the financial statements covered by their work may be stated as an aggregate amount. Exhibit AU-C 600-1 displays an example of a group audit report that makes reference to a component auditor.

> **OBSERVATION:** Reference to a component auditor in the group audit report reflects that the group financial statement auditor is not assuming responsibility for the component auditor's work and the source of the audit evidence referenced for such components; it does not indicate a qualified opinion.

## Materiality

The component materiality levels determined by the group engagement team to assist in establishing the overall audit strategy for a component may be different for different components and, when added together, component materiality levels may exceed group materiality.

Component materiality is determined by the group engagement team, regardless of whether the group engagement partner is making reference to the audit of the component auditor. For purposes of the group audit, component materiality is required to be lower than group materiality in order to reduce the risk that the aggregate of detected and undetected misstatements in the group financial statements exceeds the materiality for the group financial statements as a whole. Any misstatements identified in components' financial information that exceed the threshold above which they cannot be regarded as clearly trivial should be communicated to the group engagement team.

## Consolidation Process

When evaluating the appropriateness, completeness, and accuracy of consolidation adjustments and reclassifications, the group engagement team may:

- Evaluate if significant adjustments appropriately reflect their underlying events and transactions;
- Determine whether significant adjustments are properly supported, sufficiently documented, and correctly calculated, processed, and authorized by group and component management as appropriate;
- Check the reconciliation and elimination of intragroup account balances, transactions, and unrealized profits; and
- Communicating with the component auditor, regardless of whether the group financial statement audit report references the audit of the component auditor.

## Subsequent Events

When the group audit report on the financial statements references the audit of a component auditor, procedures to identify subsequent events between the date of the component auditor's report and the group auditor's report may include:

- Obtaining an understanding of procedures group management has established to identify such subsequent events;
- Requesting that the component auditor update subsequent event procedures to the date of the group financial statements auditor's report;

- Obtaining written representations from component management regarding subsequent events;
- Reading the component's interim financial information and inquiring of group management;
- Reading board meeting minutes for meeting held since the financial statement date;
- Reading the subsequent year's capital and operating budgets;
- Inquiring of group management about currently known facts, decisions, or conditions expected to have a significant effect on financial position or results of operations for subsequent event items; and
- Considering the implications for the group financial statements auditor's report if the group engagement team is unable to obtain sufficient appropriate audit evidence regarding subsequent events.

## Additional Requirements Applicable When Assuming Responsibility for the Work of a Component Auditor

Performance materiality levels are determined to reduce the risk that the aggregated detected and undetected misstatements in a component's financial information exceed component materiality. The group engagement team may set component materiality at the level of performance materiality for the component. The component auditor uses component materiality to evaluate the individual or aggregate materiality of uncorrected detected misstatements.

An audit of a component's financial information adapted to meet group engagement team needs may refer to an audit performed in accordance with GAAS with the exception of performing audit procedures on tax and other accounts for which procedures will be performed at a group financial statement level. Another adaptation may be that the results of the component audit will be communicated in a form to meet the group engagement team's needs.

The group engagement team's determination of the type of work to be performed on a component's financial information and the nature, timing, and extent of involvement in the work of a component auditor will depend on many factors, such as:

- The component's significance,
- Identified significant risks of material misstatement of the group financial statements,
- Evaluation of design and implementation of group-wide controls, and
- Understanding of the component auditor.

The group engagement team's involvement in the work of a component auditor may include the following procedures:

- Obtaining an understanding of the component and its environment by meeting with component management or auditors,
- Reviewing the overall audit strategy and plan of the component auditors,

- Performing risk assessment procedures to identify and assess the risks of material misstatement at the component level alone or with the component auditors,
- Designing and performing further audit procedures alone or with the component auditors,
- Participating in key meetings between component auditors and component management, and
- Reviewing relevant parts of component auditors' audit documentation.

For a component identified as significant because it is likely to include significant risks of material misstatement due to qualitative factors, the group engagement team may be able to identify and perform or request that a component auditor perform an audit solely of account balances, classes of transactions, or disclosures affected by those risks.

In some circumstances, work is required to be performed on components that are not significant in order to obtain sufficient appropriate audit evidence to base the group audit opinion on. In some group audits, there may be no significant components and it is likely that in these circumstances additional work will be required to be performed at the component level to obtain sufficient appropriate audit evidence. The group engagement team's decision regarding which and how many components to select and what work to perform on these components may be affected by factors such as:

- The extent of audit evidence expected from significant components' financial information;
- If the component is newly formed or acquired;
- If significant changes have occurred in the component;
- If any work has been performed at the component by internal audit and its effect on the group audit;
- If components apply common systems and processes;
- The operating effectiveness of group-wide controls;
- Abnormal fluctuations identified by analytical procedures performed at the group level;
- The individual financial significance of, or risk posed by, the component compared to other non-significant components; and
- Whether the component is otherwise already subject to an audit.

An audit of a non-significant component may have already been performed for component management, in which case the group engagement partner may decide to use that work to provide audit evidence. If this occurs, the decision about whether to make reference to the work of the component auditor in the group audit report must be made.

## Communication with the Component Auditor

Communication of the group engagement team's requirements to the component auditor is often accomplished using a letter of instruction. A letter of instruction may contain guidance on required communications as well as additional matters that may be relevant to the planning or conduct of the work of the component auditor. The component auditor often communicates with the group engagement team using a memorandum or report of work performed. However, required communication between the group engagement team and component auditor may not need to be written; for example, communication may be accomplished through visits to the component auditor or review of the component auditor's audit documentation. Required communication is also often accomplished through means other than writing when a member of the group engagement team is also a component auditor.

---

**OBSERVATION:** A governmental entity may provide pension benefits to its employees by participating in a governmental pension plan. For example, a city, county, or municipality may provide pension benefits to its employees by participating in the pension plan offered by the state where the local governmental unit is located. In accordance with Interpretation 1 of AU 600, a governmental pension plan is not a component of the employer (e.g., not a component of the local governmental unit). As such, the auditor of the employer (local governmental unit) should not refer to the audit report issued by the auditor of the governmental pension plan.

---

**IMPORTANT NOTICE FOR 2022:** As a reminder, in May 2019, the AICPA's Auditing Standards Board (ASB) issued SAS No. 134 titled *Auditor Reporting and Amendments, Including Amendments Addressing Disclosures in the Audit of Financial Statements* that makes significant changes to the auditor's report, including the ability to communicate key audit matters (KAMs) in the auditor's report. SAS No. 134 amends all the auditor report illustrations contained in AU-C 600 to conform those reports to the language in the new auditor's report. Originally, the effective date of SAS No. 134 was for audits of financial statements periods ending on or after December 15, 2020, with early implementation **not** permitted. However, the ASB's issuance of SAS No. 141, *Amendment to the Effective Dates of SAS Nos. 134-140*, extended the effective date to December 15, 2021, in order to provide more time for firms to implement SAS No. 134 in light of the effect of the coronavirus pandemic. While SAS No. 141 allows for early implementation of SAS No. 134, the ASB recommends that SAS Nos. 134-140 be implemented concurrently.

## Practitioner's Aid

Exhibit AU-C 600-1 illustrates an auditor's report in which reference is made to the work of a component auditor.

## EXHIBIT AU-C 600-1—REFERENCE TO THE WORK OF ANOTHER AUDITOR IN THE AUDIT REPORT

### Independent Auditor's Report

[Appropriate Addressee]

*Report on the Audit of the Consolidated Financial Statements*

*Opinion*

We have audited the consolidated financial statements of X Company and its subsidiaries, which comprise the consolidated balance sheets as of December 31, 20X5 and 20X4, and the related consolidated statements of income, changes in stockholders' equity, and cash flows for the years then ended, and the related notes to the financial statements.

In our opinion, based on our audits and the report of the other auditors, the accompanying consolidated financial statements present fairly, in all material respects, the financial position of X Company and its subsidiaries as of December 31, 20X5 and 20X4, and the results of their operations and their cash flows for the years then ended in accordance with accounting principles generally accepted in the United States of America.

We did not audit the financial statements of Z Company, a wholly owned subsidiary, which statements reflect total assets constituting 15 percent and 12 percent, respectively, of consolidated total assets at December 31, 20X1 and 20X0, and total revenues constituting 18 percent and 14 percent, respectively, of consolidated total revenues for the years then ended. Those statements were audited by other auditors, whose report has been furnished to us, and our opinion, insofar as it relates to the amounts included for Z Company, is based solely on the report of the other auditors.

*Basis for Opinion*

We conducted our audits in accordance with auditing standards generally accepted in the United States of America (GAAS). Our responsibilities under those standards are further described in the Auditor's Responsibilities for the Audit of the Financial Statements section of our report. We are required to be independent of X Company and to meet our other ethical responsibilities, in accordance with the relevant ethical requirements relating to our audits. We believe that the audit evidence we have obtained is sufficient and appropriate to provide a basis for our audit opinion.

*Responsibilities of Management for the Financial Statements*

Management is responsible for the preparation and fair presentation of the consolidated financial statements in accordance with accounting principles generally accepted in the United States of America, and for the design, implementation, and maintenance of internal control relevant to the preparation and fair presentation of consolidated financial statements that are free from material misstatement, whether due to fraud or error.

In preparing the consolidated financial statements, management is required to evaluate whether there are conditions or events, considered in the aggregate, that raise substantial doubt about X Company's ability to continue as a going concern for a reasonable period of time as defined by accounting principles generally accepted in the United States of America.

*Auditor's Responsibilities for the Audit of the Financial Statements*

Our objectives are to obtain reasonable assurance about whether the consolidated financial statements as a whole are free from material misstatement, whether due to fraud or error, and to issue an auditor's report that includes our opinion. Reasonable assurance is a high level of assurance but is not absolute assurance and therefore is not a guarantee that an audit conducted in accordance with GAAS will always detect a material misstatement when it exists. The risk of not detecting a material misstatement resulting from fraud is higher than for one resulting from error, as fraud may involve collusion, forgery, intentional omissions, misrepresentations, or the override of internal control. Misstatements are considered material if, individually or in the aggregate, they could reasonably be expected to influence the economic decisions of users made on the basis of these consolidated financial statements.

In performing an audit in accordance with GAAS, we:

- Exercise professional judgment and maintain professional skepticism throughout the audit.
- Identify and assess the risks of material misstatement of the consolidated financial statements, whether due to fraud or error, and design and perform audit procedures responsive to those risks. Such procedures include examining, on a test basis, evidence regarding the amounts and disclosures in the financial statements.
- Obtain an understanding of internal control relevant to the audit in order to design audit procedures that are appropriate in the circumstances, but not for the purpose of expressing an opinion on the effectiveness of X Company's internal control. Accordingly, no such opinion is expressed.
- Evaluate the appropriateness of accounting policies used and the reasonableness of significant accounting estimates made by management, as well as evaluate the overall presentation of the consolidated financial statements.
- Conclude, whether, in our judgment, there are conditions or events, considered in the aggregate, that raise substantial doubt about X Company's ability to continue as a going concern for a reasonable period of time.

We are required to communicate with those charged with governance regarding, among other matters, the planned scope and timing of the audit, significant audit findings, and certain internal control–related matters that we identified during the audit.

*Other Information*

Management is responsible for the other information [*included in the annual report*]. The other information comprises the [*information included in the annual report*] but does not include the financial statements and our auditor's report thereon. Our opinion on the financial statements does not cover the other information, and we do not express an opinion or any form of assurance thereon.

In connection with our audit of the financial statements, our responsibility is to read the other information and consider whether a material inconsistency exists between the other information and the financial statements, or the other information otherwise appears to be materially misstated. If, based on the work performed, we conclude that an uncorrected material misstatement of the other information exists, we are required to describe it in our report.

*Report on Other Legal and Regulatory Requirements*

[*The form and content of this section of the auditor's report would vary depending on the nature of the auditor's other reporting responsibilities.*]

[*Signature of auditor's firm*]

[*City and state where the auditor's report is issued*]

[*Date of the auditor's report*]

# SECTION 610

# USING THE WORK OF INTERNAL AUDITORS

## Authoritative Pronouncements

SAS-128—Using the Work of Internal Auditors

## Overview

An internal audit function, if it exists, is part of the client's internal control. AU-C 315 (*Understanding the Entity and Its Environment and Assessing the Risks of Material Misstatement*) requires the auditor to obtain an understanding of the entity's internal control. In doing do, the auditor may determine that the entity's internal audit function may be relevant to the audit if internal audit's responsibilities and activities are related to financial reporting, especially as part of the monitoring component of internal control. The auditor should obtain an understanding of the internal audit function as part of obtaining an understanding of the entity and its environment, including its internal controls.

Internal audit can often inform the auditor about the entity and its environment and significant matters affecting the work of the auditor, including the assessment of the risk of material misstatements. AU-C 610 contains relevant guidance that addresses the external auditor's responsibilities if using the work of internal auditors. This includes either or both:

- Using the work of the internal audit function in obtaining audit evidence; and
- Using internal auditors to provide direct assistance under the direction, supervision, and review of the external auditor.

SAS No. 128 *does not apply* if the entity does not have an internal audit function. And, an internal audit function may consist of a variety of activities, some or all of which might not be related to the recording, processing, and reporting of financial information.

If the entity has an internal audit function, the requirements in SAS No. 128 relating to using the work of that function *do not apply* if:

- The responsibilities and activities of the function are not relevant to the audit, or
- The external auditor does not expect to use the work of the function in obtaining audit evidence, based on his or her preliminary understanding of the function obtained because of procedures performed under AU-C 315 (*Understanding the Entity and Its Environment and Assessing the Risks of Material Misstatement*).

In addition, nothing requires the external auditor to use the work of the internal audit function to modify the nature or timing, or reduce the extent, of audit procedures to be performed directly by the external auditor. The external auditor maintains responsibility for the establishment of the overall audit strategy. The requirements in AU-C 610 relating to direct assistance do not apply if the external auditor does not plan to use internal auditors to provide direct assistance.

The external auditor has sole responsibility for the audit opinion expressed, and that responsibility is not reduced by the external auditor's use of the work of the internal audit function or the use of internal auditors to provide direct assistance on the engagement. This section provides guidance to assist the auditor in using that work.

> **PUBLIC COMPANY IMPLICATION:** In 2003, the New York Stock Exchange (NYSE) changed its listing requirements to mandate that all NYSE registrants have an internal audit function. NASDAQ has considered a similar requirement, but withdrew its proposal for further consideration.

## Definitions

Direct assistance — The use of internal auditors to perform audit procedures under the direction, supervision, and review of the external auditor.

Internal audit function — A function of an entity that performs assurance and consulting activities designed to evaluate and improve the effectiveness of the entity's governance, risk management, and internal control processes.

## Requirements

To determine if the work of the internal audit function can be used in the audit of the financial statements, the auditor must perform the following procedures:

### Evaluating the Internal Audit Function

1. As part of the determination of whether internal audit's work can be used as part of the auditor's audit evidence-gathering procedures, the external auditor evaluates:

   a. Whether the extent of internal audit's organizational status and relevant policies and procedures support the objectivity of internal auditors,

   b. Internal audit's level of competence, and

   c. Whether internal audit applies a systematic and disciplined approach to its work, including quality control.

2. There may be circumstances that warrant not using the work of internal audit. The external auditor should not use the work of internal audit if:

   a. The organizational status of internal audit and its relevant policies and procedures do not support internal audit's objectivity,

   b. The competence of internal audit is not sufficient, or

   c. Internal audit does not apply a systematic and disciplined approach to its work, including quality control.

## Using the Work of Internal Audit: Determining Nature and Extent of Work of Internal Audit

3. To determine the nature and extent of the work of internal audit that can be used in obtaining audit evidence, the external auditor should consider the nature, timing, and extent of the work internal audit has performed or plans to perform. Part of that consideration is an assessment of the relevance of that work to the external auditor's overall audit strategy and audit plan.

4. Even though the external auditor may use the work of internal audit, the external auditor should make all significant judgments in the audit engagement, even when the work of internal audit may be relevant to those judgments.

5. A number of factors may impact the extent of the external auditor's use of the work of internal audit. The external auditor should perform more work directly and use less of the work by internal auditor when:

    a. More judgment is involved in planning and performing relevant audit procedures or evaluating the audit evidence obtained.

    b. The organizational status of internal audit or its policies and procedures are less likely to support the objectivity of internal auditors.

    c. The assessed risk of material misstatement at the assertion level is higher, especially when those risks involve significant risks.

    d. Internal auditor's competence is less.

6. If the auditor also plans to use internal auditors to provide direct assistance, the external auditor should evaluate in the aggregate the use of the work of internal audit in obtaining audit evidence along with the use of internal audit in direct assistance to ensure the external auditor is sufficiently involved in the audit, given the auditor's responsibility to issue the audit opinion.

## Communicating with Those Charged with Governance

7. The external auditor is required by AU-C 260 (*The Auditor's Communication with Those Charged with Governance*) to communicate to those charged with governance matters related to an overview of the scope and timing of the audit. When making those communications, the auditor should describe how the external auditor has planned to use the work of internal audit in obtaining audit evidence.

## Using the Work of Internal Audit to Obtain Audit Evidence

8. The external auditor should coordinate with the internal audit function when the external auditor plans to use the work of internal audit in obtaining audit evidence.

9. To obtain an understanding of the nature and extent of audit procedures performed by internal audit, the external auditor should read the reports of the internal audit function that relate to the work where the external auditor plans to use the work of internal audit.

10. When the external auditor plans to use the work of internal audit to obtain audit evidence, the external auditor should perform sufficient audit procedures related to the work of internal audit in order to evaluate:

    a. If the work of internal audit was properly planned, performed, supervised, reviewed, and documented.

    b. If sufficient appropriate audit evidence was obtained to enable internal audit to reach reasonable conclusions.

c. If the conclusions reached are appropriate in the circumstances, and whether internal audit's reports are consistent with the results of the work performed.

11. A number of factors will help determine the nature and extent of the external auditor's procedures. For example, the following factors may impact the external auditor's evaluation:

    a. The amount of judgment involved in planning and performing relevant audit procedures and evaluating audit evidence obtained,

    b. The assessed risk of material misstatement,

    c. The level of competency of internal audit, and

    d. The organizational status of internal audit, including its policies and procedures.

12. The external auditor should reperform some of the work of internal audit.

13. Before finalizing the audit, the external auditor should evaluate whether information obtained during the audit affects his or her conclusions about internal audit's competence, organizational status, and its application of a systematic and disciplined approach to its work. The external auditor should also evaluate whether the nature and extent of the use of internal audit's work remains appropriate.

## Using the Work of Internal Audit to Provide Direct Assistance

14. The external auditor may determine that it may be effective and efficient to use internal audit to provide direct assistance on the audit. To do so, the external auditor should evaluate the existence and significance of threats to the objectivity of internal auditors who will be providing the direct assistance, including any safeguards to reduce or eliminate the threats. The external auditor should also evaluate the competency of the internal auditors who will be performing the direct assistance.

15. The use of internal audit to provide direct assistance should not occur if:

    a. Internal audit lacks the competence needed to perform the proposed work.

    b. Internal audit is lacking the objectivity necessary to perform the proposed work.

16. In determining whether to use internal audit to provide direct assistance, the following factors that impact the external auditor's evaluation should be considered:

    a. The amount of judgment involved in planning and performing relevant audit procedures and evaluating audit evidence obtained,

    b. The assessed risk of material misstatement, and

    c. The external auditor's evaluation of the level of competency of internal audit, the existence of threats to the internal auditor's objectivity, including the effectiveness of safeguards to reduce or eliminate the threats.

## Communicating with Those Charged with Governance

17. Similar to when the external auditor plans to use the work of internal audit to obtain audit evidence, the external auditor should communicate to those charged with governance how the external auditor plans to use the work of internal auditors to provide direct assistance. AU-C 260 (*The Auditor's Communication with Those Charged with Governance*) addresses communicating to those

charged with governance matters related to an overview of the scope and timing of the audit.

## Using the Work of Internal Audit to Provide Direct Assistance

18. Because the external auditor has sole responsibility for the audit opinion expressed, he or she should evaluate whether, in the aggregate, using internal auditors to provide direct assistance or to obtain audit evidence would still result in the external auditor still being sufficiently involved in the audit.

19. Before using internal audit to provide direct assistance, the external auditor should obtain written acknowledgment from management or those charged with governance that internal auditors providing direct assistance will be allowed to follow the instructions of the external auditor and that the entity will not intervene in the work of internal audit performed for the external auditor.

20. The work of internal audit should be directed, supervised, and reviewed by the external auditor. That oversight should take into account the following:

   a. The nature, timing, and extent of direction, supervision, and review should be responsive to the outcome of the evaluation factors in paragraph 16, above,

   b. The external auditor should instruct the internal auditors to bring accounting and auditing issues identified during the audit to the attention of the external auditor, and

   c. The external auditor should test some of the work performed by internal audit as part of the external auditor's review.

21. Before finalizing the audit, the external auditor should evaluate whether information obtained during the audit affects his or her conclusions about internal audit's competence, organizational status, and its application of a systematic and disciplined approach to its work. The external auditor should also evaluate whether the nature and extent of the use of internal audit's work remains appropriate.

## Documentation

22. If the external auditor uses the work of internal audit to obtain audit evidence, the external auditor should include the following in the audit documentation:

   a. Results of the evaluation of internal audit's competence, organizational status, and whether it applies a systematic and disciplined approach, including quality control.

   b. The nature and extent of the work used (this would also include the period covered by, and the results of, such work) and the basis for the external auditor's decision to use such work.

   c. Audit procedures performed by the external auditor to evaluate the adequacy of the work used, including the procedures performed by the external auditor to reperform some of the body of work of the internal audit function in obtaining audit evidence.

23. If the external auditor uses the work of internal audit to provide direct assistance, the external auditor should include the following in the audit documentation:

   a. Evaluation of the existence and significance of threats to the objectivity of the internal auditors, as well as any safeguards applied to reduce or eliminate the threats, and the level of competence of the internal auditors to provide the direct assistance.

b. The basis for the decision regarding the nature and extent of the work performed by internal auditors.
c. The external auditor's review of the internal auditor's work (this would include the testing by the external auditor of some of the work performed by internal auditors).
d. Working papers prepared by the internal auditors who provided direct assistance on the audit.

24. Because the external auditor has sole responsibility for the audit opinion expressed, he or she should include in the audit documentation his or her evaluation of whether, in the aggregate, using internal auditors to provide direct assistance or to obtain audit evidence still results in the external auditor still being sufficiently involved in the audit.

## Analysis and Application of Procedures

SAS No. 128 defines

- The conditions necessary to enable the external auditor to be able to use the work of internal auditors, and
- The necessary work effort to obtain sufficient appropriate evidence that the work of the internal audit function or internal auditors providing direct assistance is adequate for the purposes of the audit.

The requirements are designed to provide a framework for the external auditor's judgments regarding the use of the work of internal auditors to prevent inappropriate use of such work.

## Conditions Necessary to Use the Work of Internal Audit

AU-C 315 (*Understanding the Entity and Its Environment and Assessing the Risks of Material Misstatement*) addresses how the knowledge and experience of the internal audit function can inform the external auditor's understanding of the entity and its environment, including identification and assessment of risks of material misstatement. AU-C 315 also explains how effective communication between the internal and external auditors creates an environment in which the external auditor can be informed of significant matters that may affect the external auditor's work.

The external auditor may be able to use the work of the internal audit function in a constructive and complementary manner, dependent on:

- Whether the internal audit function's organizational status and relevant policies and procedures adequately support the objectivity of the internal auditors,
- The level of competency of the internal audit function, and
- Whether the function applies a systematic and disciplined approach.

SAS No. 128 addresses the external auditor's responsibilities when, based on the external auditor's understanding of the internal audit function obtained as a result of procedures performed under AU-C 315, the external auditor expects to use the work of the internal audit function in obtaining audit evidence. Such use of that work modifies the nature or timing, or reduces the extent, of audit procedures to be performed directly by the external auditor. SAS No. 128 also applies if the external auditor is considering using internal auditors to provide direct assistance under the direction, supervision, and review of the external auditor.

## Evaluating Organizational Status

As part of determining whether the work of internal auditors can be used, SAS No. 128 also requires the auditor to evaluate whether the internal audit function's organizational status and relevant policies and procedures support the objectivity of the internal auditors. "Objectivity" refers to the ability to perform tasks without allowing bias, conflict of interest, or undue influence of others to override professional judgments.

> **OBSERVATION:** The standard of objectivity is different from the standard of independence. Although it could be argued that it is simply a matter of semantics, the differentiation is based on the reasonable assumption that an internal auditor cannot achieve independence, because he or she is an employee of the client.

Factors that may affect the external auditor's determination about objectivity of internal audit include the following:

- Does the organizational status of the internal audit function support the ability of the function to be free from bias, conflict of interest, or undue influence of others to override professional judgments. For example, does the internal audit function report to:
    - Management, but with direct access to those charged with governance?
    - An officer with appropriate authority?
    - Those charged with governance?
- Is the internal audit function free of any conflicting responsibilities? For example, does internal audit have any managerial or operational duties or responsibilities that are outside the internal audit function?
- Do those charged with governance oversee employment decisions related to the internal audit function?
- Has management or those charged with governance placed any constraints or restrictions on the internal audit function?
- Are internal auditors members of relevant professional organizations that obligate them to comply with standards related to objectivity?

## Evaluating Competence

As part of determining whether the work of internal auditor can be used, SAS No. 128 requires the auditor to evaluate the competence of the internal audit function. The "competence" of the internal audit function refers to the attainment and maintenance of knowledge and skills of the function as a whole at the level required to enable the assigned tasks to be performed diligently and with the appropriate level of quality.

Factors that may affect the external auditor's determination about competence include the following:
- Is the internal audit function adequately and appropriately resourced relative to the size of the entity and the nature of its operations?
- Do policies for hiring, training, assigning internal auditors to internal audit engagements exist?
- Do internal auditors have adequate training and proficiency in auditing? For example, do they have relevant professional designations and experience?
- Do the internal auditors possess the required knowledge relating to the entity's financial reporting and the applicable financial reporting framework and does the internal audit function possess the necessary skills to perform the work related to the entity's financial statements?
- Are internal auditors members of relevant professional bodies or do they have certifications that oblige them to comply with relevant professional standards, including continuing education requirements?

**OBSERVATION:** A high level of competence cannot compensate for an organizational status and policies and procedures that do not adequately support the objectivity of the internal auditors. Equally, an organizational status and relevant policies and procedures that adequately support the objectivity of the internal auditors cannot compensate for the lack of sufficient competence of the internal audit function.

## Evaluating the Application of a Systematic and Disciplined Approach

Consistent with international auditing standards, SAS No. 128 introduces the concept of "a systematic and disciplined approach." Before being able to use the work of the internal audit function, the auditor must evaluate whether the internal auditor has applied a *systematic and disciplined approach, including quality control* to planning, performing, supervising, reviewing, and documenting its activities that may be performed within the entity.

The following factors may affect the external auditor's determination of whether the internal audit function applies a systematic and disciplined approach:
- Is there any evidence of the existence and use of documented internal audit procedures or guidance covering areas such as risk assessment, work programs, documentation, or reporting?
- Are the procedures adequate and is their nature and extent commensurate with the nature and size of the internal audit function relative to the complexity of the entity?
- Does the internal audit function have appropriate quality control policies and procedures or quality control requirements in standards set by relevant professional bodies for internal auditors? For example, does internal audit have policies and procedures related to leadership, human resources, or engagement performance?

The external auditor's determination of whether the internal audit function applies a systematic and disciplined approach is intended to address the risk that the external auditor inappropriately uses internal audit-like work performed in an informal, unstructured, or ad-hoc manner.

The application of a systematic and disciplined approach to planning, performing, supervising, reviewing, and documenting its activities distinguishes the activities of the internal audit function from other monitoring control activities that may be performed within the entity.

## Determining Nature and Extent of Internal Audit Work to Be Used

To determine the nature and extent of internal audit work that may be used by the external auditor, SAS No. 128 notes that the external auditor should consider the nature, timing, and extent of the work that has been performed, or is planned to be performed, by the internal audit function, and its relevance to the external auditor's overall audit strategy and audit plan.

Because the external auditor has sole responsibility for the audit opinion expressed, the external auditor should make all significant judgments in the audit engagement, including when using the work of the internal audit function in obtaining audit evidence. As the degree of judgment involved in planning and performing the audit procedures or evaluating audit evidence increases, the need for the external auditor to perform more procedures directly increases.

The work of internal audit may be able to help the external auditor modify the nature or timing, or reduce the extent, of further audit procedures performed directly by the external auditor. For example, the internal audit function may have performed or may be planning to perform tests of relevant controls upon which the external auditor intends to rely in determining the nature, timing, and extent of substantive procedures. Or, the internal audit function may have performed or may be planning to perform substantive procedures that the external auditor also plans to perform. Additionally, the external auditor may be able to coordinate work with the internal auditors and reduce the number of the entity's components where the external auditor would otherwise need to perform audit procedures.

If the external auditor plans to use the work of the internal audit function in obtaining such evidence, the external auditor should discuss the planned use of the work with the function as a basis for coordinating their respective activities. The external auditor should read the reports of the internal audit function that relate to the work of the function the external auditor plans to use to obtain an understanding of the nature and extent of audit procedures the internal audit function performed and the related findings.

The external auditor should perform sufficient audit procedures on the body of work the internal audit function as a whole that the external auditor wants to use to determine its adequacy for purposes of the audit. Those procedures should include the evaluation of whether:

- The work of the function was properly planned, performed, supervised, reviewed, and documented.
- Sufficient appropriate evidence was obtained to enable the function to draw reasonable conclusions.
- Conclusions reached are appropriate in the circumstances, and the reports are prepared by the function are consistent with the results of the work performed.

---

**FRAUD POINTER:** AU-C 240 requires auditors to inquire of internal audit personnel, if there is an internal audit function, about internal audit's views related to the risks of fraud. Auditors must also inquire about whether internal audit has performed any procedures to identify or detect fraud during the year and whether management has responded satisfactorily to internal audit's findings regarding fraud risks. Auditors must also ask internal audit whether they have knowledge of any fraud or suspected fraud.

---

## Determining Nature and Extent that Internal Audit Can Provide Direct Assistance

The external auditor may consider using internal auditors to perform direct assistance to carry out audit procedures that otherwise would be performed directly by the external auditor. In this situation, the external auditor is under the direction, supervision, and review of the external auditors.

Before assigning the internal auditors specific tasks, the external auditor should evaluate the existence and significance of threats to the objectivity of the internal auditor who will provide the direct assistance, and they should evaluate the level of competence of the internal auditors who will be providing the direct assistance.

To determine the extent of direct assistance that might be provided, the external auditor should consider the materiality of the financial statement amounts involved and the assessed risk of material misstatement, and the amount of judgment required. As materiality, risk of misstatement, or amount of judgment increases, the need for the external auditor to perform the procedures goes up.

Examples of activities that would not be appropriate for internal auditors to provide direct assistance include the following:

- Making required inquiries of entity personnel or those charged with governance related to the identification of fraud risks and determining the procedures to respond to such risks.
- Determination of unpredictable audit procedures.

## Conditions When the Work of Internal Audit Should Not Be Used

The external auditor should not use the work of the internal audit function in obtaining audit evidence if the external auditor determines that:

- The function's organizational status and relevant policies do not adequately support the objectivity of internal auditors,
- The function lacks sufficient competence, or
- The function does not apply a systematic and disciplined approach, including quality control.

## Communication with Those Charged with Governance

As part of the normal communications with those charged with governance about the overview of the planned scope and timing of the audit, the external auditor should communicate how the external auditor plans to use the work of internal auditors. The planned use of the work of internal audit function in obtaining audit evidence is an integral part of the external auditor's overall audit strategy and, therefore, is relevant to those charged with governance for their understanding of the proposed audit approach.

## Documentation

When auditors use the work of internal audit, the external auditor's documentation should include the following:
- Results of their evaluation of internal audit's competence, organizational status and objectivity, and the application of a systematic and disciplined approach, including quality control.
- The nature and extent of the work used and the basis for that decision.
- The audit procedures performed by the external auditor to evaluate the adequacy of the work used, including the procedures performed by the external auditor to re-perform some of the work.

When the external auditor uses internal auditors to perform direct assistance on the audit, the external auditor should also document the following:
- The evaluation and existence of threats to the objectivity of the internal auditors, as well as any safeguards applied to reduce or eliminate the threats, and the level of competence of the internal auditors used to provide the direct assistance.
- The basis for the decision regarding the nature and extent of the work performed by the internal auditors.
- The nature and extent of the external auditor's review of the internal auditors' work, including testing of some of the work.
- The working papers prepared by the internal auditors who provide the direct assistance on the audit engagement.

# SECTION 620

## USING THE WORK OF AN AUDITOR'S SPECIALIST

### Authoritative Pronouncements

SAS-122—Statements on Auditing Standards: Clarification and Recodification

SAS-144—Amendments to AU-C Sections 501, 540, and 620 Related to the Use of Specialists and the Use of Pricing Information Obtained from External Information Sources

SAS Interpretation 1—The Use of Legal Interpretations as Audit Evidence to Support Management's Assertion That a Transfer of Financial Assets Has Met the Isolation Criterion in Paragraphs 7-14 of Financial Accounting Standards Board *Accounting Standards Codification* 860-10-40

### Overview

In some instances, the dollar amounts reflected in the financial statements are based on audit evidence that an auditor is not capable of evaluating. For example, pension costs depend on an actuarial analysis that is usually beyond the expertise of an auditor. AU-C 620 provides guidance in engagements that require the services of an auditor's specialist. An auditor's specialist is a person or firm that possesses specialized knowledge or skill in a nonaccounting or nonauditing field, whose work is used by the auditor to assist in obtaining sufficient appropriate audit evidence.

The guidance in AU-C 620 does not apply when the auditor consults someone with expertise in a specialized area of accounting or auditing, as these circumstances are addressed in AU-C 220 (*Quality Control for an Engagement Conducted in Accordance with Generally Accepted Auditing Standards*) and AU-C 300 (*Planning an Audit*). AU-C 620 also does not apply when the auditor uses the work of someone with expertise other than accounting or auditing when that specialist's work is used by the entity to assist in preparing its financial statements, a situation covered by the guidance in AU-C 500 (*Audit Evidence*).

---

**ENGAGEMENT STRATEGY:** An entity's use of information technology is likely to have a significant impact on internal control. AU-C 315 notes that the auditor should consider whether specialized IT skills are needed for the auditor to understand the effect of IT on the audit. In some instances, an outside IT specialist is needed to inquire of client IT personnel about IT-based transaction processing and related automated controls, including examination of system documentation and planning and performance of tests of IT controls. An auditor who engages an IT specialist should have sufficient IT-related knowledge to communicate the audit objectives to the specialist, to evaluate whether the specialist's procedures satisfy audit objectives, and to evaluate the results of the specialist's work.

**FRAUD POINTER:** As part of the auditor's mandated responses to address the risk of management override of internal controls, AU-C 240 (*Consideration of Fraud in a Financial Statement Audit*) requires the auditor to examine journal entries and other adjustments for evidence of possible material misstatements due to fraud. AU-C 240 notes that journal entries and other adjustments might only exist in electronic form for entities that use IT in the financial reporting process. In some circumstances, an IT specialist might be needed to extract electronic evidence needed by the auditor to test journal entries and other adjustments.

---

**PUBLIC COMPANY IMPLICATION:** In December 2018, the PCAOB issued AS-1210 (*Auditor's Use of the Work of Specialists*). The goal of this new standard is to amend existing PCAOB Auditing Standards to expand guidance related to the use of the work performed by specialists. AS-1210 provides specific guidance related to the use of company-employed specialists, auditor-employed specialists, and auditor-engaged specialists. In developing this new standard, the PCAOB noted that its inspection process has observed substantial variation in practice as to how auditors use the work of specialists and how they evaluate the work performed by specialists. For example, it has noted that auditors have failed to adequately evaluate the assumptions used by company specialists to develop fair value measurements and auditors have failed to consider contradictory evidence or issues raised by an auditor's specialist. AS-1210 was approved by the SEC in July 2019 and its effective date is for audits of fiscal years ending on or after December 15, 2020.

---

**IMPORTANT NOTICE FOR 2022:** In June 2021, the AICPA Auditing Standards Board (ASB) issued SAS No. 144, *Amendments to AU-C Sections 501, 540, and 620 Related to the Use of Specialists and the Use of Pricing Information Obtained from External Information Sources*, that amends AU-C 540 to expand the application guidance related to obtaining agreement on the respective roles and responsibilities of the auditor and the auditor's specialists, including the specialist's responsibilities for testing source data, evaluating significant assumptions used by the entity or management's specialists, and evaluating the methods used by the entity or management's specialists to develop an accounting estimate. SAS No. 144 also provides examples of when the auditor may conclude that the work of the auditor's specialist is not adequate for the auditor's purposes. SAS No. 144 does not become effective until audits of financial statements for periods ending on or after December 15, 2023, which is consistent with the effective date of SAS No. 143. As a result, this AU-C reflects existing auditing standards requirements. Updates to reflect SAS No. 144 will occur in the next edition of the *GAAS Guide*.

---

While the auditor may use the work of an auditor's specialist as appropriate audit evidence, the audit opinion expressed is the sole responsibility of the auditor. Therefore, the auditor must decide whether to use the work of an auditor's specialist and if that work is adequate for the auditor's purposes.

## Definitions

| | |
|---|---|
| Auditor's specialist | An individual or organization possessing expertise in a field other than accounting or auditing, whose work in that field is used by the auditor to assist in obtaining sufficient appropriate audit evidence. The specialist may be an internal specialist who is a partner, staff, or temporary staff member of the auditor's firm or a network firm or an external specialist. |
| Expertise | Skills, knowledge, and experience in a particular field. |
| Management's specialist | An individual or organization possessing expertise in a field other than accounting or auditing, whose work in that field is used by the entity to assist in preparing its financial statements. |

## Requirements

The auditor is presumptively required to perform the following procedures when using the work of an auditor's specialist in an audit engagement:

1. Determine whether to use the work of an auditor's specialist if expertise in an area other than accounting or auditing is needed to obtain sufficient appropriate audit evidence.
2. Determine the nature, timing, and extent of audit procedures related to the auditor's specialist and his or her work, considering matters such as:
   a. The nature of and risks of material misstatement in the matter of the specialist's work,
   b. The significance of the specialist's work in the context of the audit,
   c. The auditor's knowledge of and experience with prior work of the specialist, and
   d. Whether the specialist is subject to the auditor's firm's quality control policies and procedures.
3. Evaluate whether the auditor's specialist's competence, capability, and objectivity are adequate for the auditor's purposes. If the specialist is external, inquire about interests and relationships that could threaten the specialist's objectivity.
4. Obtain a sufficient understanding of the specialist's field of expertise to determine the nature, scope, and objectives of the specialist's work and to evaluate the adequacy of that work for the auditor's purposes.
5. When appropriate, agree in writing with the auditor's specialist regarding:
   a. The nature, scope, and objectives of the specialist's work;
   b. The respective roles and responsibilities of the auditor and the specialist;
   c. The nature, timing, and extent of communication between the auditor and specialist, including the form of any report to be provided by the specialist; and
   d. The need for the auditor's specialist to observe confidentiality requirements.

6. Evaluate the adequacy of the auditor's specialist's work for the auditor's purposes, including:
    a. The relevance and reasonableness of the specialist's findings or conclusions and their consistency with other audit evidence;
    b. Obtaining an understanding and evaluating the relevance and reasonableness of any significant assumptions and methods used considering the specialist's rationale and support as well as the auditor's other findings and conclusions; and
    c. The relevance, completeness, and accuracy of any significant source data used.
7. If the auditor determines the work of the auditor's specialist is not adequate for the auditor's purposes, he or she should agree with the specialist on the nature and extent of further work to be performed by the specialist or perform additional audit procedures appropriate to the circumstances.
8. An auditor's specialist's work should not be referred to in an auditor's report with an unmodified opinion.
9. The auditor should not refer to the work of the auditor's specialist in a report containing an unmodified opinion. But, if an auditor's external specialist's work is referred to in an auditor's report to help understand a modification to the audit opinion, the auditor's report should indicate that such reference does not reduce the auditor's responsibility for the audit opinion.

## Analysis and Application of Procedures

### Auditor's Specialist

An auditor's specialist has expertise in fields other than accounting or auditing, such as:

- The valuation of complex financial instruments, land and buildings, plants and machinery, jewelry, works of art, antiques, intangible assets, assets and liabilities assumed in business combinations, and assets that may have been impaired.
- The actuarial calculation of liabilities associated with insurance contracts or employee benefit plans.
- The estimation of oil or gas reserves.
- The valuation of environmental liabilities and site cleanup costs.
- The interpretation of contracts, laws, and regulations.
- The analysis of complex or unusual tax compliance issues.
- The determination of physical characteristics relating to quantity on hand or condition.

While it is often clear whether a specialist has expertise in accounting or auditing or in another field, in some cases making this distinction will require the use of professional judgment. In these situations, the auditor may use applicable professional rules and standards regarding education and competency requirements for accountants and auditors to help make these decisions. Sometimes a specialist may possess expertise in accounting or auditing as well as in another field. In these circumstances, the decision about whether that individual is an auditor's specialist depends on the nature of the work performed by the individual that the auditor is using for the audit.

> **OBSERVATION:** An auditor's specialist may be an individual or an organization, so the auditor may consider the personal attributes of the individual and the managerial attributes of the organization, such as its system of quality control, in evaluating the competence, capabilities, and objectivity of the specialist.

## Need for an Auditor's Specialist

The auditor may determine an auditor's specialist is needed to assist in one or more phases of the audit. The decision to use the work of an auditor's specialist may help the auditor fulfill requirements under AU-C 220 that the engagement team and any external auditor's specialists have the appropriate competence and capabilities to perform the audit and under AU-C 300 to determine the nature, timing, and extent of resources necessary to perform the engagement.

Even if an auditor is not a specialist in a relevant field other than accounting or auditing, he or she may be able to obtain a sufficient understanding of the field to perform the audit without an auditor's specialist. Experience auditing entities requiring this type of expertise or education or professional development in the relevant field may contribute to this understanding.

When deciding whether to use an auditor's specialist, the auditor may consider the following: if management used a specialist to prepare the financial statements; the nature, significance, complexity, and risks of material misstatement of the matter; and the expected nature of the procedures to respond to identified risks, including the auditor's knowledge of and experience with specialists' work in such matters and the availability of alternative sources of evidence.

> **PUBLIC COMPANY IMPLICATION:** The PCAOB has issued Staff Audit Practice Alert No. 2 (*Matters Related to Auditing Fair Value Measurements of Financial Instruments and the Use of Specialists*), which includes a discussion of the auditor's use of a specialist in auditing fair values. The auditor should consider using a specialist when he or she lacks the necessary skill and knowledge to plan and perform audit procedures relating to fair value measurements in the financial statements. The auditor should be more likely to use a specialist given a greater client use of unobservable inputs, greater complexity in valuation techniques, and fair value amounts that are large. If the auditor chooses to rely on the work of a specialist, he or she must obtain an understanding of the specialist's methods and evaluate whether they will result in a measurement that is in accordance with U.S. GAAP. In addition, the auditor needs to evaluate the specialist's assumptions. Finally, the auditor should evaluate the

specialist's qualifications, including his or her experience in performing the type of work that the auditor is considering relying upon.

Management's specialists may be used to address the increased risks of material misstatement that can occur when expertise other than accounting is needed for management to prepare the financial statements. If a management's specialist has been used, the auditor's decision about whether to use an auditor's specialist may also include the nature, scope, and objectives of the management's specialist's work; if the specialist is employed by the entity; the extent to which entity management can influence or control their work; the specialist's competence and capabilities; whether the specialist is subject to technical performance standards or other professional or industry requirement; any entity controls over their work; and the auditor's ability to evaluate the work of management's specialists without the use of an auditor's specialist.

*Auditor's Firm's Quality Control Policies and Procedures*

In accordance with SQCS-8, *A Firm's System of Quality Control,* if an auditor's specialist is part of the auditor's firm or part of a network firm, he or she is subject to the quality control policies and procedures of the firm. However, if the auditor's specialist is external to the auditor's firm, he or she is not a member of the engagement team and is not subject to the firm's quality control policies and procedures.

AU-C 220 guidance allows engagement teams to rely on the firm's system of quality control unless the engagement partner determines it is inappropriate to do so. The extent of the auditor's reliance depends on the nature, timing, and extent of the audit procedures with respect to matters such as: competence and capabilities, objectivity, the auditor's evaluation of the adequacy of the auditor's specialist's work, adherence to regulatory and legal requirements through monitoring processes, and agreement with the auditor's specialist.

**PLANNING AID REMINDER:** Reliance on the firm's system of quality control does not reduce the auditor's responsibility to meet AU-C 620's requirements.

*Competence, Capabilities, and Objectivity of the Auditor's Specialist*

Information about the competence, capabilities, and objectivity of an auditor's specialist may come from sources such as: personal experience with prior work of the specialist, discussions with the specialist or with others familiar with the specialist's work, knowledge of the specialist's qualifications and works published by the specialist, or the auditor's firm's quality control policies and procedures. In evaluating the specialist's competence, capabilities, and objectivity, the auditor may consider:

- If the specialist's work is subject to technical performance standards or other professional or industry requirements.
- The relevance of the specialist's competence to the matter his or her work will be used for.

- The specialist's competence related to relevant accounting and auditing requirements.
- Whether unexpected events, changes in conditions, or audit evidence obtained from results of audit procedures indicate the auditor's initial evaluation of the specialist's competence, capabilities, and objectivity needs to be reconsidered.

If the objectivity of an auditor's specialist is threatened, safeguards created by external structures, the specialist's work environment, or the audit engagement may eliminate or reduce those threats. The role of the auditor's specialist and the significance of his or her work to the audit impact the evaluation of the significance of threats to their objectivity. In some situations, such as when the auditor's specialist is also a management's specialist, safeguards may not be sufficient to reduce these threats to an acceptable level.

To evaluate the specialist's objectivity, the auditor may inquire of the entity and specialist about any interests or relationships between the entity and specialist that may affect objectivity such as financial interests, business and personal relationships, the provision of other services, as well as any applicable safeguards that could reduce objectivity threats to an acceptable level. If the auditor believes the relationship between the entity and the specialist may impair the specialist's objectivity, additional procedures may be performed to determine if the specialist's findings are reasonable.

### Obtaining an Understanding of the Auditor's Specialist's Field of Expertise

The auditor may find the following relevant in obtaining an understanding of the auditor's specialist's field of expertise:
- Whether the specialist's field has specialized areas relevant to the audit.
- Whether any professional standards or legal or regulatory requirements apply.
- The assumptions, methods, and applicable models used by the auditor's specialist and whether they are generally accepted in the specialist's field and appropriate for financial reporting purposes.
- The nature of internal and external data or information used by the specialist.

### Agreement with the Auditor's Specialist

Regardless of whether the auditor's specialist is internal or external, the nature, scope and objectives of the specialist's work, the respective roles and responsibilities of the auditor and specialist, and the nature, timing, and extent of communication between the auditor and specialist should be agreed upon.

Agreement on the nature, scope, and objectives of the specialist's work may include discussion of relevant technical performance standards or other professional or industry requirements the specialist will adhere to. Agreement on the roles and responsibilities of the auditor and specialist may include who will perform detailed testing of the source data, consent for the auditor to discuss the specialist's findings or conclusions with the entity and others and to include details of these finding or conclusions in the basis for a modified opinion in the auditor's report if needed.

> **ENGAGEMENT STRATEGY:** The auditor may need to inform the specialist that his or her work will be used to substantiate certain assertions in the financial statements. It generally would be necessary to ensure that the specialist understands the need to provide a "usable link" between the specialist's work and the assertions to be substantiated. Essentially, the prudent auditor must make sure that the technical nature of the specialist's work makes sense in the context of the audit engagement. This should be determined early in the strategy planning for the engagement.

This agreement may also determine access to and retention of each party's working papers, as the working papers of a specialist who is part of the engagement team are part of the audit documentation but the working papers of an external auditor's specialist are not part of the audit documentation absent an agreement otherwise. Agreement on the nature, timing, and extent of communication between the auditor and specialist is also important and, in situations when the specialist's work relates to the auditor's conclusions regarding a significant risk, both a formal written report at the conclusion of the specialist's work and oral reports as the work progresses may be appropriate.

The auditor's specialist should abide by the same confidentiality provisions of relevant ethical requirements as the auditor. Law or regulation may impose additional requirements. Additionally, the entity may request that auditor's external specialists agree to specific confidentiality provisions.

The agreement between the auditor and auditor's specialist may or may not be written. If there is no written agreement, evidence of the agreement may be included in the auditor's planning documentation or the policies and procedures of the auditor's firm. No documentation may be required if, for example, the auditor's firm has protocols detailing the circumstances in which the work of a specialist is used. In establishing an agreement with the auditor's specialist, it is important to consider the implications of any reservation, limitation, or restriction on the specialist's work. A more detailed or written agreement may be preferred if some of the following factors exist:

- The specialist will have access to sensitive or confidential entity information.
- The auditor and specialist have different roles and responsibilities than would normally be expected.
- Multijurisdictional legal or regulatory requirements apply.
- The matter the specialist's work relates to is highly complex.
- The auditor has not previously used work performed by the specialist.
- The specialist's work is extensive and significant in the context of the audit.

A written agreement between the auditor and auditor's external specialist is often in the form of an engagement letter. Exhibit AU-C 620-1 provides a listing of matters the auditor may consider including in an engagement letter or other agreement with an auditor's external specialist.

## Evaluating the Adequacy of an Auditor's Specialist's Work

The nature, timing, and extent of the auditor's procedures to evaluate the adequacy of the auditor's specialist's work are affected by the auditor's: evaluation of the specialist's competence, capabilities, and objectivity; familiarity with the specialist's field of expertise; and the nature of work performed by the specialist. To evaluate the adequacy of the specialist's work, the auditor may:

- Make inquiries of the specialist;
- Review the specialist's working papers and reports;
- Perform corroborative procedures such as observing the specialist's work, examining published data, confirming relevant matters with third parties, performing detailed analytical procedures, and reperforming calculations;
- Discuss with another specialist with relevant expertise when the auditor's specialist's findings or conclusions are not consistent with audit evidence; and
- Discuss the specialist's report with management.

When the auditor considers the relevance and reasonableness of the specialist's findings or conclusions, he or she may include whether the findings and conclusions are: presented in a manner consistent with the specialist's profession or industry; clearly expressed, referring to the agreed objectives, scope of work performed, and standards applied; based on an appropriate period taking into account subsequent events as appropriate; and based on appropriate consideration of any errors or deviations encountered.

If the auditor's specialist is evaluating management's underlying assumptions and methods, the auditor primarily performs procedures to evaluate whether the specialist has adequately reviewed those methods. If the specialist is developing an estimate or range for the auditor to compare with management's estimate, the auditor primarily performs procedures to evaluate the assumptions and methods used by the specialist.

**OBSERVATION:** The guidance in AU-C 540 (*Auditing Accounting Estimates, Including Fair Value Accounting Estimates, and Related Disclosures*) about the auditor obtaining sufficient appropriate audit evidence regarding management's assumptions and methods may also assist the auditor in evaluating a specialist's assumptions and methods.

If a specialist's work uses significant assumptions and methods, the auditor's evaluation of those assumptions and methods may include whether they are:

- Generally accepted in the specialist's field;
- Consistent with the requirements of the applicable financial reporting framework;

- Dependent on the use of specialized models; and
- Consistent with management's assumptions and methods, and the reason for and effect of any inconsistencies.

When the auditor considers the relevance, completeness, and accuracy of source data significant to the specialist's work, he or she may test the data by verifying the origin of the data, obtaining an understanding of and possibly testing the internal controls over the data and its transmission to the specialist, and reviewing the data for completeness and internal consistency. In some situations, such as when the data is highly technical in relation to the specialist's field, the specialist may test the source data. When this occurs, the auditor may inquire of the specialist or supervise or review the specialist's test to evaluate the data's relevance, completeness, and accuracy.

If the auditor's specialist's work is not adequate for the auditor's purposes and additional work performed by the auditor or specialist cannot resolve the matter, a modified opinion may need to be expressed in the auditor's report because the auditor has not obtained sufficient appropriate audit evidence.

## *If Applicable, Consider Using a Specialist's Work to Determine Whether There Has Been a Transfer of Financial Assets as Defined by ASC-860*

ASC 860 (*Accounting for Transfers of Financial Assets*) provides the following guidance for determining when the transfer of financial assets may be treated as a sale:

> The transferred financial assets have been isolated from the transferor—put presumptively beyond the reach of the transferor and its creditors, even in bankruptcy or other receivership.

Determining whether the above condition (the isolation criterion) has been satisfied is "largely a matter of law." The need for the work of a specialist (lawyer) generally depends on the complexity of the transfer. When the transfer is routine and there is no continuing involvement in the assets by the transferor, the use of a lawyer may not be necessary. On the other hand, if the transfer involves complex legal structures, the opinion of a legal specialist may be required.

When it is concluded that the opinion of a legal specialist is needed, the following factors should be considered in assessing the adequacy of the legal opinion:

- The legal experience of the specialist in the area (including exposure to the U.S. Bankruptcy Code and other relevant statutes),
- An understanding by the auditor of the assumptions that are used by the legal specialist, and
- The performance by the auditor of appropriate tests on relevant information that has been provided to the specialist by management.

**OBSERVATION:** The specialist's work is usually expressed "in the form of a reasoned legal opinion that is restricted to particular facts and circumstances relevant to the specific transaction." If the auditor concludes that the legal opinion provided by the specialist is inadequate or inappropriate, the auditor must determine how the audit report should be modified.

**PLANNING AID REMINDER:** Interpretation 1 of AU-C 620 provides guidance for the auditor regarding his or her responsibilities in determining whether to use the work of a legal specialist to obtain pervasive evidence to support management's assertion related to the transfer of assets.

## Practitioner's Aid

**EXHIBIT AU-C 620-1—CONSIDERATIONS FOR INCLUSION IN AN AGREEMENT BETWEEN THE AUDITOR AND AN AUDITOR'S EXTERNAL SPECIALIST**

**Nature, Scope, and Objectives of the Specialist's Work**
- Nature and scope of procedures the specialist will perform
- Specialist's objectives in the context of materiality and risk considerations concerning the matter of the specialist's work and the applicable financial reporting framework when relevant
- Relevant technical performance standards or professional or industry requirements the specialist will follow
- The assumptions, methods, and models the specialist will use and their authority
- The effective date or testing period for the matter of the specialist's work and requirements regarding subsequent events

**Roles and Responsibilities of the Auditor and the Auditor's External Specialist**
- Relevant auditing and accounting standards and regulatory or legal requirements
- The specialist's consent to the auditor's intended use of the specialist's report including any reference to or disclosure of it to others
- The nature and extent of the auditor's review of the specialist's work
- Whether the auditor or specialist will test source data
- The specialist's access to the entity's records, files, personnel, and specialists engaged by the entity
- Procedures for communication between the specialist and the entity
- Access of the auditor and the specialists to each other's working papers
- Ownership and control of working papers during and after the engagement
- The specialist's responsibility to perform work with due skill and care
- The specialist's competence and capability to perform the work
- The expectation that the specialist will use all his or her knowledge that is relevant to the audit
- Any restriction on the specialist's association with the auditor's report
- Any agreements to inform the specialist of the auditor's conclusions regarding the specialist's work

**Communications and Reporting**
- Methods and frequency of communication including how the specialist's findings or conclusions will be reported and identification of engagement team members who will communicate with the specialist
- When the specialist will complete the work and report findings or conclusions to the auditor

- The specialist's responsibility to communicate promptly any potential delay in completing the work, any potential reservation or limitation on his or her findings or conclusions, and any instances of the entity restricting the specialist's access to records, files, personnel, or specialists engaged by the entity
- The specialist's responsibility to communicate to the auditor all information the specialist believes may be relevant to the audit
- The specialist's responsibility to communicate circumstances that may threaten his or her objectivity and any relevant safeguards that may eliminate or reduce such threats to an acceptable level

**Confidentiality**
- The need for the specialist to observe confidentiality requirements, including the confidentiality provisions of relevant ethical requirements that apply to the auditor and any additional requirements that may be imposed by law or regulation

# AU-C 700
# Audit Conclusions and Reporting

| Section 700: | Forming an Opinion and Reporting on Financial Statements | 7002 |
| Section 701: | Communicating Key Audit Matters in the Independent Auditor's Report | 7022 |
| Section 703: | Forming an Opinion and Reporting on Financial Statements of Employee Benefit Plans Subject to ERISA | 7028 |
| Section 705: | Modifications to the Opinion in the Independent Auditor's Report | 7047 |
| Section 706: | Emphasis-of-Matter Paragraphs and Other-Matter Paragraphs in the Independent Auditor's Report | 7067 |
| Section 708: | Consistency of Financial Statements | 7076 |
| Section 720: | Other Information in Documents Containing Audited Financial Statements | 7081 |
| Section 725: | Supplementary Information in Relation to the Financial Statements as a Whole | 7089 |
| Section 730: | Required Supplementary Information | 7097 |

# SECTION 700

# FORMING AN OPINION AND REPORTING ON FINANCIAL STATEMENTS

## Authoritative Pronouncements

SAS-122—Statements on Auditing Standards: Clarification and Recodification

SAS-131—Amendment to Statement on Auditing Standards No. 122 Section 700, *Forming an Opinion and Reporting on Financial Statements*

SAS-134—Auditor Reporting and Amendments, Including Amendments Addressing Disclosures in the Audit of Financial Statements

SAS-136—Forming an Opinion and Reporting on Financial Statements of Employee Benefit Plans Subject to ERISA

SAS-137—The Auditor's Responsibilities Relating to Other Information Included in Annual Reports

SAS-138—Amendments to the Description of the Concept of Materiality

SAS-141—Amendment to Effective Dates of SAS Nos. 134-140

SAS-143—Auditing Accounting Estimates and Related Disclosures

**IMPORTANT NOTICE FOR 2022:** In May 2019, the AICPA's Auditing Standards Board (ASB) issued SAS No. 134 titled *Auditor Reporting and Amendments, Including Amendments Addressing Disclosures in the Audit of Financial Statements* that makes significant changes to the auditor's report, including the ability to communicate key audit matters (KAMs) in the auditor's report. SAS No. 134 changes the wording in the standard auditor's report. The most notable changes include (1) moving the "Opinion" section to be presented first in the auditor's report followed by the "Basis for Opinion," (2) adding to the Basis of Opinion section an affirmative statement that the auditor is required to be independent and to meet other ethical responsibilities, (3) including new descriptions of management's responsibilities for assessing the entity's ability to continue as a going concern, if the applicable financial reporting framework contains such a requirement, (4) expanding the description of responsibilities of management for the preparation and fair presentation of the financial statements, and (5) adding new descriptions of the auditor's responsibilities. The most notable change included in SAS No. 134 is that it allows, but does not require, the auditor to be engaged to communicate KAMs in the auditor's report. Guidance for auditors in those circumstances in which KAMs are communicated in the auditor's report are provided in new AU-C 701. Originally, the effective date of SAS No. 134 was for audits of financial statements periods ending on or after December 15, 2020, with early implementation **not** permitted. However, the ASB's issuance of SAS No. 141, *Amendment to the Effective Dates of SAS Nos. 134-140*, extended the effective date to December 15, 2021, in order to provide more time for firms to implement SAS No. 134 in light of the effect of the coronavirus pandemic. While

SAS No. 141 allows for early implementation of SAS No. 134, the ASB recommends that SAS Nos. 134-140 be implemented concurrently.

**PUBLIC COMPANY IMPLICATIONS:** Similar to the AICPA, the PCAOB adopted in 2017 a new auditing standard AS-3101 (*The Auditor's Report on an Audit of Financial Statements When the Auditor Expresses an Unqualified Opinion*) that changed the standard unqualified opinion audit report for public companies. The most notable change is that AS-3101 requires the auditor (1) to describe critical audit matters in the audit report and (2) to disclose the tenure of the audit firm as auditor. The PCAOB's new standard describes critical audit matters as those audit matters that are communicated, or are required to be communicated, to the audit committee that (1) related to accounts or disclosures that are material to the financial statements, and (2) involved especially challenging, subjective, or complex judgments. The auditor's report on financial statements of SEC registrants should now (1) identify the critical audit matter, (2) describe why the auditor concluded that the item was a critical audit matter, (3) describe how the critical audit matter was addressed in the audit, and (4) refer to the relevant financial statement accounts and disclosures affected by the critical audit matter. Notice that the PCAOB requires the auditor to communicate critical audit matters, whereas the proposed changes to AICPA auditing standards for nonpublic company audits allows, but does not require, the auditor to communicate KAMs.

**IMPORTANT NOTICE FOR 2022:** In July 2019, the AICPA's Auditing Standards Board (ASB) issued SAS No. 136, *Forming an Opinion and Reporting on Financial Statements of Employee Benefit Plans Subject to ERISA*. The new guidance is specific to audits of financial statements of employee benefit plans (EBPs) subject to the Employee Retirement Income Security Act of 1974 (ERISA). The ASB issued SAS No. 136 to address the auditor's responsibility to form an opinion and report on the audit of financial statements of EBPs, including reporting on specific plan provisions related to the ERISA plan financial statements. The most notable aspect of SAS No. 136 is that it changes the form and content of the auditor's report issued as a result of an audit of ERISA plan financial statements. The SAS creates a separate, stand-alone reporting section that is codified as new AU-C 703. For audits of ERISA plan financial statements only, the guidance in AU-C 703 would apply in place of the guidance in AU-C 700. Originally, SAS No. 136 was to become effective for audits of ERISA plan financial statements for period ending on or after December 15, 2020, with early adoption not permitted. However, the ASB's issuance of SAS No. 141, *Amendment to the Effective Dates of SAS Nos. 134-140*, extended the effective date to December 15, 2021, in order to provide more time for firms to implement SAS No. 136 in light of the effect of the coronavirus pandemic. While SAS No. 141 allows for early implementation of SAS No. 136, the ASB recommends that SAS Nos. 134-140 be implemented concurrently.

## Overview

AU-C 700 provides the auditor with guidance regarding forming an opinion on financial statements in addition to the form and content of the auditor's report on the financial statement audit. AU-C 700 guidance covers audits of complete sets of financial statements prepared in accordance with a fair presentation framework. This section does not apply to forming an opinion on financial statements of employee benefit plans subject to the Employment Retirement Income Security Act of 1974 (ERISA).

The auditor's objectives in adhering to AU-C 700 are to form an opinion on the financial statements based on an evaluation of the audit evidence obtained and to express that opinion clearly through a written report that includes a description of the opinion's basis. An additional aim of this standard is to promote consistency in the auditor's report, which increases the credibility of audit reporting and promotes the user's understanding and identification of any unusual circumstances that have occurred. This section allows, but does not require, the communication of key audit matters.

## Definitions

| | |
|---|---|
| Comparative financial statements | A complete set of financial statements for one or more prior periods that is included for comparison with the current period financial statements. |
| Comparative information | Prior period information presented for purposes of comparison with current period amounts or disclosures that is not in the form of a complete set of financial statements (e.g., condensed financial statements or summarized financial information). |
| Condensed financial statements | Historical information presented in less detail than a complete set of financial statements prepared in accordance with an appropriate financial reporting framework (this information may be presented as unaudited financial information or as comparative information). |
| General purpose financial statements | Financial statements prepared in accordance with a general purpose framework. |
| General purpose framework | A financial reporting framework designed to meet the common financial information needs of a wide range of users. |
| Unmodified opinion | An opinion expressed by the auditor when the auditor concludes that the financial statements are presented fairly, in all material respects, in accordance with the applicable financial reporting framework. |

---

**IMPORTANT NOTICE FOR 2022:** The PCAOB's auditing standard AS-3101 (*The Auditor's Report on an Audit of Financial Statements When the Auditor Expresses an Unqualified Opinion*) requires the auditor (1) to describe critical audit matters in the audit report and (2) to disclose the tenure of the audit firm as auditor. The PCAOB's standard describes critical audit matters as those audit matters that are communicated, or are required to be communicated, to the audit committee that (1) related to accounts or disclosures that are material to the financial statements, and (2) involved especially challenging, subjective, or complex judgments. The auditor's report related to an SEC registrants financial statements should (1) identify the critical audit matter, (2) describe why the auditor concluded that the item was a critical audit matter, (3) describe how the critical audit matter was addressed in the audit, and (4) refer to the relevant financial statement accounts and disclosures affected by the critical audit matter.

---

**PUBLIC COMPANY IMPLICATION:** The PCAOB requires disclosure of the engagement partner's name in a Form AP, Auditor Reporting of Certain Audit Participants, filed with the PCAOB within 35 days after a public company's Form 10-K report is filed. In addition, the involvement of other accounting firms in performing the audit is disclosed on Form AP. More specifically, disclosure is required of the names, locations (city, state or city, country), and extent of involvement (as a percentage of the total audit hours) of other accounting firms that participated in the audit, if any firm's work constituted 5% or more of total audit hours. The extent of involvement can either be presented as a single number or as a range (e.g., 5%–10%, 10%–20%, 20%–30%, etc. of the total audit hours). In addition, for accounting firms that perform less than 5% of the total audit hours, the total number of such firms and the aggregate percentage of total audit work performed is disclosed on Form AP. Participation in the audit by nonaccounting firms (e.g., offshored work that is affiliated with, but legally distinct from, the registered accounting firm) does not have to be disclosed. Hours performed by the following parties can be excluded in computing total audit hours: (1) engagement quality reviewer; (2) persons performing an Appendix K review; (3) specialists engaged, but not employed, by the auditor; (4) internal auditors, other company personnel, or third parties who provide assistance in the internal control over financial reporting (ICFR) audit and who are under the direction of management or the audit committee; and (5) internal auditors who provide direct external audit assistance. Accounting firms are permitted, but are not required, to also disclose the name of the engagement partner and the involvement of other accounting firms in the auditor's report.

---

## Requirements

The auditor is presumptively required to perform the following procedures when forming an opinion and reporting on financial statements:

### Forming an Opinion

1. Form an opinion on whether the financial statements are presented fairly, in all material respects, in accordance with the applicable financial reporting framework.

2. Reach a conclusion as to whether reasonable assurance has been obtained that the financial statements as a whole are free from material misstatement, whether due to fraud or error. The conclusion should take into account the auditor's conclusions about whether sufficient appropriate audit evidence has been obtained and whether uncorrected misstatements are material either individually or in the aggregate, as well as the evaluations detailed in requirements 3 through 6 that the auditor makes in forming an opinion on the financial statements.

3. Evaluate whether the financial statements are prepared, in all material respects, in accordance with the applicable financial reporting framework. Consider the qualitative aspects of the entity's accounting practices, including indicators of possible bias in management's judgments.

4. Evaluate whether, given the requirements of the applicable financial reporting framework:
    a. Financial statements adequately disclose the significant accounting policies selected and applied;
    b. Accounting policies selected and applied are appropriate and consistent with the applicable financial reporting framework;
    c. Accounting estimates are reasonable;
    d. Financial statement information presented is relevant, reliable, comparable, and understandable;
    e. Financial statements provide adequate disclosures to enable the intended users to understand the effect of material transactions and events on the information conveyed in the statements; and
    f. Appropriate titles and terminology are used in the financial statements.

**IMPORTANT NOTICE FOR 2022:** In July 2020, the AICPA Auditing Standards Board (ASB) issued SAS No. 143, *Auditing Accounting Estimates and Related Disclosures*, which supersedes AU-C 540 (*Auditing Accounting Estimates, Including Fair Value Accounting Estimates, and Related Disclosures*) and amends various other sections, including AU-C 700, in the professional standards. The SAS begins with an explanation of the nature of accounting estimates and how they can vary widely in nature and are required to be made by management when monetary amounts cannot be directly observed. The measurement of amounts is subject to estimation uncertainty, which reflects inherent limitations in the knowledge or data. These limitations give rise to inherent subjectivity and variation in measurement outcomes. Although the guidance in SAS No. 143 applies to all accounting estimates, the degree to which an accounting estimate is subject to estimation uncertainty will vary substantially. Therefore, SAS No. 143 recognizes that the nature, timing, and extent of the risk assessment and further audit procedures required will vary in relation to the estimation uncertainty and the assessment of the related risks of material misstatement. The ASB is coordinating the effective date of SAS No. 143 with the effective date of a proposed new SAS, *Understanding the Entity and Its Environment and Assessing the Risks of Material Misstatement*, which was under consideration by the ASB at the time this edition of the *GAAS Guide* was being prepared. SAS No. 143 does not become effective until audits of financial statements for periods ending on or after December 15, 2023, which is consistent with the date in the proposed new standard. As a result, this AU-C reflects existing auditing standards requirements. Updates to reflect SAS No. 143 will occur in the next edition of the *GAAS Guide*.

5. Evaluate whether the financial statements achieve fair presentation by considering the overall presentation, structure, and content of the statements and whether the financial statements and related notes represent the underlying transactions and events in a manner that achieves fair presentation.

**IMPORTANT NOTICE FOR 2022:** In May 2019, the AICPA's Auditing Standards Board (ASB) issued SAS No. 134 titled *Auditor Reporting and Amendments, Including Amendments Addressing Disclosures in the Audit of Financial Statements* to revise the auditor's report and to amend various AU-C sections to heighten the auditor's focus on disclosures throughout the process of auditing financial statements. SAS No. 134 adds additional emphasis for the auditor to consider the appropriateness of disclosures in the financial statements, particularly the qualitative aspects of those disclosures, as the auditor forms an opinion on the financial statements.

6. Evaluate whether the financial statements adequately refer to or describe the applicable financial reporting framework.

## Form of Opinion

7. Express an unmodified opinion when the auditor concludes that the financial statements are presented fairly, in all material respects, in accordance with the applicable financial reporting framework.

8. Modify the opinion in the auditor's report if the auditor (1) concludes that the financial statements as a whole are materially misstated based on the audit evidence obtained or (2) is unable to obtain sufficient appropriate audit evidence to conclude that the financial statements as a whole are free from material misstatement.

9. If the auditor concludes that the financial statements do not achieve fair presentation, discuss the matter with management and, depending or how the matter is resolved, determine whether a modification of the auditor's opinion is necessary.

## Auditor's Report

**OBSERVATION:** AU-C 700 requires that the audit report contain section headings to clearly define each section of the report.

10. The report should be in writing.

11. The report should have a title that includes the word independent.

12. The report should be addressed as required by the engagement circumstances.

13. The first section includes the heading "Opinion." In this section, the auditor should identify the entity whose financial statements are audited and the specific financial statements audited, with reference to the footnotes and time periods covered.

14. If an unmodified opinion is expressed, the opinion should state the auditor's conclusion that the financial statements present fairly, in all material respects, the financial position of the entity as of the balance sheet date and results of its operations and its cash flows for the period then ended in accordance with the applicable financial reporting framework, which should be identified along with its origin.

15. The section following the "Opinion" section should be titled "Basis for Opinion" and in that section the auditor should state that the audit was conducted in accordance with generally accepted auditing standards in the United States of America (U.S. GAAS). This section should also include a reference to the section in the auditor's report that describes the auditor's responsibilities under GAAS, a statement that the auditor is independent of the entity, and statement that the auditor believes the audit evidence obtained is sufficient and appropriate to provide a basis for the auditor's opinion.

16. If there are substantial doubts about the entity's ability to continue as a going concern, the auditor should report in accordance with AU-C 570 (*The Auditor's Consideration of an Entity's Ability to Continue as a Going Concern*).

17. When the auditor is engaged to communicate key audit matters, the auditor should comply with AU-C 701.

18. A section with the heading, "Responsibilities of Management for the Financial Statements" should be included. This section should describe management's responsibility for the preparation and fair presentation of the financial statements in accordance with the applicable financial reporting framework, including its responsibility for the design, implementation, and maintenance of internal control relevant to the preparation and fair presentation of financial statements that are free from material misstatement, whether due to fraud or error. The auditor's report should not refer to any separate management statement about management's responsibilities if a description of management's responsibilities is included in a document containing the auditor's report.

19. A section with the heading "Auditor's Responsibilities for the Audit of the Financial Statements" should be included. This section should include the following statements:

   a. The auditor's responsibility is to obtain reasonable assurance about whether the financial statements as a whole are free from material misstatement and to express an opinion on the financial statements based on the audit.

   b. The audit was conducted in accordance with GAAS and the United States is the country of origin of those standards, which require that the auditor plan and perform the audit to obtain reasonable assurance about whether the financial statements are free from material misstatement. The report should also include a statement that reasonable assurance is a high level of assurance but is not absolute assurance and therefore not a guarantee that the audit will always detect a material misstatement when one exists.

   c. An audit involves performing procedures to obtain audit evidence about the amounts and disclosures in the financial statements and the procedures selected depend on the auditor's judgment, including the assessment of the risks of material misstatement of the financial statements, whether due to fraud or error. The report should also state that the risk of not detecting a material misstatement due to fraud is higher than one resulting from an error.

   d. Risk assessments involve consideration of internal control relevant to the entity's preparation and fair presentation of the financial statements in order to design audit procedures that are appropriate in the circumstances, but not for the purpose of expressing an opinion on the effectiveness of the entity's internal control, and accordingly, no such opinion is expressed. If the auditor is responsible for expressing an opinion on the effectiveness of internal control in conjunction with the financial statement audit, omit the phrase in the audit report that the auditor's consideration of internal control is not for the purpose of expressing an opinion on the effectiveness of the entity's internal control, and accordingly, no such opinion is expressed.

   e. Misstatements are considered material if there is substantial likelihood that, individually or in the aggregate, they would influence the judgment made by a reasonable user on the basis of the audited financial statements.

f. The auditor is responsible for exercising professional judgment and maintaining professional scepticism throughout the audit. The auditor also identifies and assesses risks of material misstatement of the financial statements and designs and performs procedures in response to those risks. That is done on a test basis.

g. The auditor obtains an understanding of internal control relevant to the audit to design audit procedures, not to express an opinion on those internal controls. Thus, no such opinion in expressed.

h. An audit includes evaluating the appropriateness of the accounting policies used and the reasonableness of significant accounting estimates made by management, as well as the overall presentation of the financial statements.

i. The auditor arrives at a conclusion about whether there are conditions or events that raise substantial doubt about the entity's ability to continue as a going concern for a reasonable period of time.

j. The auditor concludes an acknowledgment that the auditor is required to communicate certain matters with those charged with governance.

20. If reporting responsibilities in addition to those under GAAS to report on the financial statements are addressed in the auditor's report on the financial statements, address those responsibilities in a separate section in the auditor's report subtitled, "Report on Other Legal and Regulatory Requirements," or another title as appropriate for the section's content.

21. If the audit report includes a separate section on other reporting responsibilities, the report should contain a subtitle, "Report on the Audit of Financial Statements," encompassing the main section of the audit report, which should precede the section on other reporting responsibilities.

22. The manual or printed signature of the auditor's firm should be included.

23. The city and state where the auditor's report is issued.

24. The report should be dated no earlier than the date on which the auditor has obtained sufficient appropriate audit evidence on which to base the opinion on the financial statements, including evidence that the audit documentation has been reviewed, all the statements and related notes comprising the financial statements have been prepared, and management has asserted that they have taken responsibility for the financial statements.

25. If an audit is conducted in accordance with GAAS and another set of auditing standards, the auditor may indicate that the audit was also conducted in accordance with that other set of auditing standards in the report. This reference should not be made unless the audit was conducted in accordance with both sets of standards in their entirety. If the report refers to another set of auditing standards, identify the set of auditing standards and their country of origin.

---

**PLANNING AID REMINDER:** An auditor may be engaged to conduct an audit in accordance with GAAS and the International Standards on Auditing (ISAs) issued by the International Auditing and Assurance Standards Board (IAASB). SAS No. 134 includes an illustrative auditor's report (see Illustration No. 4) when the audit has been conducted in accordance with both auditing standards generally accepted in the United States of America and ISAs. ISA 700 (Revised), *Forming an Opinion and Reporting on Financial Statements*, allows the auditor to use the layout or wording of the national auditing standards (e.g., GAAS), provided (1) there are no conflicts between the requirements in GAAS and the

ISAs that would lead to a different conclusion with respect to the opinion, and (2) the layout or wording addresses, and is not inconsistent with, certain of the required minimum reporting elements in ISA 700 (Revised).

Similarly, there are situations in which an auditor may be required by law or regulation, or voluntarily agrees, to perform an audit engagement in accordance with PCAOB standards for an entity whose audit is not subject to PCAOB oversight. SAS No. 134 includes an illustrative report (see Illustration No. 8) when the audit has been conducted by a firm that is not a PCAOB-registered firm in accordance with GAAS and the Auditing Standards of the PCAOB.

---

26. If an audit is conducted in accordance with PCAOB standards but is not within PCAOB jurisdiction, the auditor must also conduct the audit in accordance with GAAS. Any reference to PCAOB standards in such an auditor's report should use the form required by PCAOB standards, amended to state that the audit was also conducted in accordance with GAAS.

## *Comparative Financial Statements*

27. If comparative financial statements are presented, whether due to requirements of the applicable financial reporting framework or because management elected to provide the information, the auditor's report should refer to each period for which financial statements are presented and on which an audit opinion is expressed.

28. If expressing an opinion on all periods presented, a continuing auditor should update the report on the financial statements of the prior comparative periods with those of the current period. The auditor's report on comparative financial statements should not be dated earlier than the date on which the auditor has obtained sufficient appropriate audit evidence on which to support the opinion for the most recent audit.

29. If comparative information is presented but not covered by the auditor's opinion, the auditor should clearly indicate in the auditor's report the nature of any work performed by the auditor and the degree of responsibility the auditor is taking.

---

**OBSERVATION:** Comparative information, rather than comparative financial statements, typically denotes condensed financial statements or summarized financial information.

---

30. If comparative information for prior periods is presented and the auditor is requested to express an opinion on all periods presented, he or she should consider whether the information included for prior periods is sufficiently detailed to constitute a fair presentation in accordance with the applicable financial reporting framework.

31. Determine whether the comparative financial statements or comparative information has been prepared in accordance with the relevant requirements of the applicable financial reporting framework.

32. Evaluate whether (1) the comparative financial statements or comparative information agrees with the amounts and disclosures presented in the prior period or has been restated for the correction of a material misstatement or adjusted for the retrospective application of an accounting principle when applicable and (2) the accounting policies reflected in the comparative financial statements or comparative information are consistent with those applied

in the current period or, if there have been changes in accounting policies, if those changes have been properly accounted for and adequately presented and disclosed.

33. If the auditor becomes aware of a possible material misstatement in the comparative financial statements or comparative information while performing the current period audit, perform any additional audit procedures necessary in the circumstances to obtain sufficient appropriate audit evidence to determine whether a material misstatement exists. If the auditor audited the prior period's financial statements and becomes aware of a material misstatement in those financial statements, also follow the relevant requirements in AU-C 560. If the prior period financial statements are restated, determine that the comparative financial statements or comparative information agrees with the restated financial statements.

34. Request written representations for all periods referred to in the auditor's opinion. Obtain a specific written representation regarding any restatement made to correct a material misstatement in a prior period that affects the comparative financial statements.

35. If reporting on prior period financial statements in connection with the current period audit and the auditor's opinion on the prior period statements differs from the opinion the auditor previously expressed, disclose the following matters in an emphasis-of-matter or other-matter paragraph:
    a. The date of the auditor's previous report;
    b. The type of opinion previously expressed;
    c. The substantive reasons for the different opinion; and
    d. That the auditor's opinion on the amended financial statements is different from the auditor's previous opinion.

36. If prior period financial statements were audited by a predecessor auditor and the predecessor auditor's report on those statements is not reissued, state in an other-matter paragraph that the prior period financial statements were audited by a predecessor auditor, the type of opinion that was expressed and the reasons for any modification of the opinion, the nature of any emphasis-of-matter or other-matter paragraph included in the predecessor's report, and the date of that report.

37. If prior period financial statements were reported on by a predecessor auditor without modification and the auditor concludes that a material misstatement exists that affects the prior period statements, follow the communication requirements in AU-C 510 (*Opening Balances—Initial Audit Engagements, Including Reaudit Engagements*). If the prior period financial statements are amended and the predecessor auditor agrees to issue a new auditor's report on the amended statements, express an opinion only on the current period.

38. If prior period financial statements were compiled or reviewed and are presented comparatively with current period financial statements without the report on the prior period being reissued, an other-matter paragraph should be included in the current period auditor's report with:
    a. The service performed in the prior period;
    b. The date of the report on that service;
    c. A description of any material modification noted in that report; and
    d. A statement that the service was less in scope than an audit and does not provide the basis for the expression of an opinion on the financial statements.

39. If prior period financial statements were not audited, reviewed, or compiled, state in an other-matter paragraph that the auditor has not audited,

reviewed, or compiled the prior period financial statements and assumes no responsibility for them.

## Other Information Presented in the Financial Statements

40. Information that is presented as part of the basic financial statements even though it is not required by the applicable financial reporting framework should be covered by the auditor's opinion if it cannot be clearly differentiated.

---

**PLANNING AID REMINDER:** Interpretation 2 of AU-C 700 addresses reporting by the federal government. In addition to consolidated financial statements, the Federal Accounting Standards Advisory Board requires three additional statements in the consolidated financial report of the U.S. government: a Statement of Long-Term Fiscal Projections, a Statement of Social Insurance, and a Statement of Changes in Social Insurance. These three statements are referred to as sustainability financial statements. Interpretation 2 indicates that an auditor may report on these sustainability financial statements in accordance with GAAS. Since the sustainability financial statements do not articulate with the consolidated financial statements, the opinions on the two sets of financial statements are independent of each other.

---

## Analysis and Application of Procedures

### Forming an Opinion

The auditor considers qualitative aspects of accounting practices in evaluating whether the financial statements are prepared in all material respects in accordance with the requirements of the applicable financial reporting framework. The auditor may identify indicators of a lack of neutrality that cause the financial statements as a whole to be materially misstated. Possible indicators include the selective correction of misstatements brought to management's attention during the audit and possible management bias in making accounting estimates.

When preparing the financial statements, management makes a number of judgments about the amounts and disclosures in the financial statements. The auditor also evaluates whether the financial statements achieve fair presentation. In making this evaluation, the auditor applies his or her judgment about the fairness of presentation in the context of the applicable financial reporting framework. This also includes evaluation of whether the financial statements appropriately disclose the significant accounting policies.

The auditor's evaluation of whether the financial statements achieve fair presentation, including disclosure, is a matter of professional judgment. The auditor's evaluation includes consideration of the facts and circumstances of the entity that is applied in the context of the financial reporting framework.

The financial statements should adequately refer to or describe the applicable financial reporting framework. It is only appropriate to state that the financial statements are prepared in accordance with an applicable financial reporting framework if the statements comply with all framework requirements that are effective during the period covered by the statements. Describing the applicable financial reporting framework with imprecise qualifying or limiting language, such as "in substantial compliance with," is not adequate because it may mislead financial statement users.

---

**PLANNING AID REMINDER:** When the auditor is engaged to report on financial statements prepared in accordance with a special purpose framework and is required by law or regulation to use a specific layout, form, or wording of the auditor's report, guidance in AU-C 800 (*Special Considerations—Audits of Financial Statements Prepared in Accordance with Special Purpose Frameworks*) applies.

---

The financial statements may be prepared in accordance with one financial reporting framework and contain sufficient description in the notes to the financial statements to also comply with another framework. In this situation, the information is considered an integral part of the financial statements if it cannot be clearly differentiated and is therefore covered by the auditor's opinion.

*Form of Opinion*

If the financial statements do not achieve fair presentation even though they were prepared in accordance with the requirements of a fair presentation framework, fair presentation may be able to be achieved by providing additional disclosures in the financial statements beyond those specifically required or, in rare circumstances, departing from a framework requirement.

Rule 1.320.001 (*Accounting Principles*) of the AICPA Code of Professional Conduct describes the requirements for the auditor in situations where a departure from a framework requirement has a material effect on the financial statements as a whole, but the financial statements would have been misleading without the departure. Under these circumstances, the auditor may still issue an unqualified opinion but should describe the departure, its approximate effects if practicable, and the reasons why compliance with the principle would result in a misleading statement in an emphasis-of-matter paragraph in the auditor's report. The other paragraphs in the audit report are not modified, and no reference is made to the emphasis-of-matter paragraph in the opinion paragraph.

---

**OBSERVATION:** Although Rule 1.320.001 of the Code may be needed to provide flexibility in the application of accounting principles, the rule must be used with a great deal of caution. When the rule is used, the auditor is, in effect, promulgating an accounting rule for a specific client, which is a heavy responsibility to undertake. Not surprisingly, there are very few examples where Rule 1.320.001 has been employed concerning the adaptation of different accounting methods.

---

*Auditor's Report*

Including the word "independent" in the title of the auditor's report indicates that the auditor has met all of the relevant ethical requirements regarding independence. The auditor's report may be addressed to the client, its board of directors, or its stockholders. For an unincorporated client, the report may be addressed to the partners or the sole proprietor. When an audit is performed at the request of a party other than the management or owners of the audited entity, the report may be addressed to the party that requested the audit.

> **OBSERVATION:** A written report includes those issued in hard copy format and those using an electronic medium.

> **PUBLIC COMPANY IMPLICATION:** Under SOX, the audit committee of the client's board of directors is directly responsible for the appointment, compensation, and oversight of the auditor. As such, the client in a public company audit is now the audit committee. Therefore, public company audit reports are not addressed to the company or to the company's management.

The auditor's report must begin with the section titled "Opinion." That is followed by the section titled, "Basis for Opinion," that provides context about the auditor's opinion. Because the "Opinion" section should identify each statement comprising the financial statements, if a statement of changes in stockholders' equity accounts or statement of comprehensive income is included, those statements should be identified in the introductory paragraph. However, these statements do not need to be reported on separately in the opinion paragraph because changes in stockholders' equity accounts and comprehensive income are part of the presentation of financial position, results of operations, and cash flows.

The auditor may include the page numbers containing the financial statements in the audit report to help users identify the statements to which the audit report relates if the statements will be included in a document containing other information.

The auditor should not make additional references beyond those required to be made in the management responsibility section of the audit report because such references may lead users to erroneously believe that the auditor is providing assurances regarding management representations about their responsibilities contained in the management report.

In the auditor's responsibility section of the audit report, the auditor should only state that the audit was conducted in accordance with GAAS if the auditor has complied with the requirements of all AU-C sections relevant to the audit.

> **PUBLIC COMPANY IMPLICATION:** The auditor's opinion relates to whether the financial statements are fairly presented. Auditors have historically assumed that if the financial statements are in accordance with U.S. GAAP, then the financial statements are fairly stated. This assumption might no longer be valid for public company audits. For example, Section 302 of SOX requires management to certify whether the financial statements fairly present in all material respects the financial condition and results of operations of the entity. There is no reference to

compliance with U.S. GAAP in evaluating whether the financial statements are fairly stated. All auditors, but particularly public company auditors, should only issue an unqualified report if the client's financial statements accurately represent the economics of the client's financial position and results of operations, regardless of compliance with U.S. GAAP.

Financial statements are fairly presented in accordance with U.S. GAAP if the statements are in accordance with either U.S. GAAP or International Financial Reporting Standards (IFRS) as issued by the International Accounting Standards Board (IASB). This reflects the fact that AICPA Council has designated the IASB as the body to promulgate international financial reporting standards under Rules 202 and 203 of the AICPA's Code of Professional Conduct. The auditor would state in the management responsibility and opinion paragraphs of the audit report that the financial statements were prepared in accordance with IFRS as issued by the IASB rather than in accordance with U.S. GAAP.

The auditor may have the responsibility to report on matters in addition to his or her responsibility under GAAS to report on the financial statements. Other reporting responsibilities are addressed in a separate section of the auditor's report in order to provide clear differentiation. Relevant laws and regulations will dictate whether the auditor is required or permitted to report on these other responsibilities within the auditor's report on the financial statements or in a separate report. Additional reporting responsibilities may include requirements under *Government Auditing Standards* to report on internal control over financial reporting and on compliance with laws, regulations, and provisions of contracts or grant agreements.

The auditor's signature in some circumstances may be required by law or regulation to include the personal name and signature of the auditor in addition to the auditor's firm. Also, in some situations, the auditor may be required to declare his or her professional accountancy designation or the auditor or firm's recognition by the appropriate licensing agency in the audit report. In some cases, law or regulation may allow for the use of electronic signatures.

In audits involving an engagement quality control review, the audit report may not be released before the review is completed. Some audits require final approval of the financial statements by governmental legislative bodies before the statements are issued; this approval is not necessary for the auditor to reach the conclusion that sufficient appropriate audit evidence has been obtained. The date of financial statement approval for the purposes of GAAS in these situations is the earlier of the date that those with the recognized authority determine that all financial statements and related notes have been prepared and the date that those with recognized authority assert that they have taken responsibility for the statements.

An audit may be performed in accordance with GAAS and another set of auditing standards such as International Standards on Auditing (ISAs), PCAOB auditing standards, or *Government Auditing Standards*. If an audit is conducted in accordance with another set of auditing standards in addition to GAAS, then the auditor's responsibility paragraph of the standard audit report is modified to read as follows (for illustrative purposes it is assumed that the other set of auditing standards satisfied were those established by the International Auditing and Assurance Standards Board):

> We conducted our audit in accordance with auditing standards generally accepted in the United States of America and in accordance with International Standards on Auditing.

---

**PLANNING AID REMINDER:** If an audit is performed in accordance with GAAS and ISAs, the auditor may reference Appendix B, Substantive Differences Between the International Standards on Auditing and Generally Accepted Auditing Standards, of the AICPA's *Codification of Statements on Auditing Standards*. This appendix identifies ISA sections that may require documentation and procedures in addition to GAAS to help the auditor plan and perform the audit in accordance with the ISAs.

---

An audit may be performed in accordance with PCAOB standards as well as GAAS even though the audit is not within PCAOB jurisdiction. This may occur with audits for clearing agencies, futures commission merchants, and other entities registered with the U.S. Commodities Futures Trading Commission; financial statements included in securities offering documents pursuant to Regulation A of the Securities and Exchange Act of 1933; or for nonissuers that are contractually obligated or desire to obtain such an audit. In these circumstances, the scope paragraph of the auditor's report is required to state the audit was conducted in accordance with "the standards of the Public Company Oversight Board (United States)." Referencing "the standards" indicates compliance with PCAOB professional practice and auditing standards, whereas referencing "the auditing standards" limits compliance to PCAOB auditing standards. Engagement circumstances will determine the level of compliance the auditor should report.

---

**PUBLIC COMPANY IMPLICATION:** If an audit is being conducted on the financial statements of an entity within PCAOB jurisdiction, the AICPA Code of Professional Conduct requires AICPA members to conduct the audit in accordance with PCAOB standards; however, the audit is not required to also be conducted in accordance with GAAS.

---

## Comparative Financial Statements

In an audit report on comparative financial statements, the auditor may express differing opinions on the financial statements of different periods. The auditor may issue an updated report on prior period financial statements in conjunction with the auditor's report on the current period financial statements. An updated report is different from a reissued report in that it considers information the auditor has become aware of during the current period financial statement audit.

---

**OBSERVATION:** If comparative information is presented that is not in the form of a complete set of financial statements, it is not considered comparative financial statements and the auditor does not need to issue an opinion on the information.

If only summarized comparative financial information for prior periods is presented, the auditor is not required to report on that summarized information. If the client requests the auditor to express an opinion on summarized comparative financial information for prior periods, additional detail may need to be added to that information or the opinion in the audit report may need to be modified.

The auditor may express a different opinion on the prior period financial statements than the opinion previously expressed due to circumstances or events the auditor becomes aware of during the current period audit that materially affect the prior period financial statements. In these situations, the auditor may have additional reporting responsibilities detailed in AU-C 560 that are designed to prevent future reliance on the auditor's previously issued report on the prior period financial statements.

If the prior year's financial statements have been restated and the predecessor auditor previously reporting on those statements is unable or unwilling to reissue the audit report on those statements, an other-matter paragraph of the successor auditor's report may state that the predecessor auditor reported on the prior year's financial statements before they were restated. When the successor auditor has been engaged to audit the restatement adjustments, and has applied sufficient procedures to determine that the adjustments are appropriate, the following paragraph may be added to the successor auditor's report in the other-matter paragraph section:

> As part of our audit of the 20X5 financial statements, we also audited the adjustments described in Note X that were applied to restate the 20X4 financial statements. In our opinion, such adjustments are appropriate and have been properly applied. We were not engaged to audit, review, or apply any procedures to the 20X4 financial statements of the Company other than with respect to such adjustments and, accordingly, we do not express an opinion or any other form of assurance on the 20X4 financial statements taken as a whole.

**PLANNING AID REMINDER:** In determining the nature, timing, and extent of audit procedures related to the restatement or amendment adjustments, the successor auditor should consider the guidance established by AU-C 560.

**PUBLIC COMPANY IMPLICATION:** The PCAOB staff has issued a series of questions and answers surrounding auditor reporting responsibilities when prior-period financial statements are adjusted. Adjustments to prior-period financial statements can relate to reporting a discontinued operation, restatements to correct errors, and retrospective applications of changes in accounting principles. Either the predecessor or successor auditor may audit the adjustments to the prior-period financial statements, as long as the auditor is independent and registered with the PCAOB. If the predecessor auditor audits the adjustments, the predecessor auditor should dual date his or her report and the successor auditor should obtain an understanding of the adjustments and their effects on the current-period financial statements. In deciding whether the successor auditor can audit the adjustments or has to re-audit the prior-period financial statements, the successor auditor should consider (1) the extent of the adjustments, (2) the reason for the adjustments, and (3) the cooperation of the predecessor auditor. In addition, the successor auditor must have completed the audit of the current-period financial statements to audit adjustments to prior-period financial statements.

---

If the prior period financial statements were not audited, but were reviewed, the other-matter paragraph may read as follows:

> The 20X4 financial statements were reviewed by us (other accountants) and our (their) report thereon, dated March 1, 20X5, stated we (they) were not aware of any material modifications that should be made to those statements for them to be in conformity with accounting principles generally accepted in the United States of America. However, a review is substantially less in scope than an audit and does not provide a basis for the expression of an opinion on the financial statements as a whole.

If the prior period financial statements were compiled, the other matter paragraph may read as follows:

> The 20X4 financial statements were compiled by us (other accountants) and our (their) report thereon, dated March 1, 20X5, stated we (they) did not audit or review those financial statements and, accordingly, express no opinion or other form of assurance on them.

If the prior period financial statements were not audited, reviewed, or compiled, the other matter paragraph may read as follows:

> The accompanying balance sheet of X Company as of December 31, 20X4, and the related statements of income and cash flows for the year then ended were not audited, reviewed, or compiled by us and, accordingly, we do not express an opinion or any other form of assurance on them.

---

**PLANNING AID REMINDER:** A successor auditor can report on restated financial statements previously audited by a predecessor auditor in the manner described above only when reporting on comparative financial statements. Thus, a successor auditor cannot report only on the restatement adjustments.

---

### Other Information Presented in the Financial Statements

Additional information may be presented in the financial statements that is not required by the applicable financial reporting framework, but that is not able to be clearly differentiated from the financial statements because of its nature and manner of presentation. This information should typically be covered by the auditor's opinion; however, if the information is clearly differentiated and is not necessary to fairly present the financial position, operating results, or cash flows on which the auditor is reporting, it may be identified as *unaudited* or *not covered by the auditor's report*.

## Practitioner's Aid

**IMPORTANT NOTICE FOR 2022:** As a reminder, in May 2019, the AICPA's Auditing Standards Board (ASB) issued SAS No. 134 titled *Auditor Reporting and Amendments, Including Amendments Addressing Disclosures in the Audit of Financial Statements* that makes significant changes to the auditor's report, including the ability to communicate key audit matters (KAMs) in the auditor's report. SAS No. 134 changes the wording in the standard auditor's report. Originally, the effective date of SAS No. 134 was for audits of financial statements periods ending on or after December 15, 2020, with early implementation **not** permitted. However, the ASB's issuance of SAS No. 141, *Amendment to the Effective Dates of SAS Nos. 134-140*, extended the effective date to December 15, 2021, in order to provide more time for firms to implement SAS No. 134 in light of the effect of the coronavirus pandemic. While SAS No. 141 allows for early implementation of SAS No. 134, the ASB recommends that SAS Nos. 134-140 be implemented concurrently. The following exhibits reflect the new report language contained in SAS No. 134.

### EXHIBIT AU-C 700-1—STANDARD UNMODIFIED AUDITOR'S REPORT

### INDEPENDENT AUDITOR'S REPORT

[Appropriate Addressee]

**Report on the Financial Statements**

*Opinion*

We have audited the consolidated financial statements of X Company and its subsidiaries, which comprise the consolidated balance sheets as of December 31, 20X5 and 20X4, and the related consolidated statements of income, changes in stockholders' equity, and cash flows for the years then ended, and the related notes to the financial statements.

In our opinion, the accompanying consolidated financial statements referred to above present fairly, in all material respects, the financial position of X Company and its subsidiaries as of December 31, 20X5 and 20X4, and the results of their operations and cash flows for the years then ended in accordance with accounting principles generally accepted in the United States of America.

*Basis for Opinion*

We conducted our audits in accordance with auditing standards generally accepted in the United States of America (GAAS). Our responsibilities under those standards are further described in the Auditor's Responsibilities for the Audit of the Financial Statements section of our report. We are required to be independent of X Company and to meet our other ethical responsibilities, in accordance with the relevant ethical requirements relating to our audits. We believe that the audit evidence we have obtained is sufficient and appropriate to provide a basis for our audit opinion.

*Responsibilities of Management for the Financial Statements*

Management is responsible for the preparation and fair presentation of these consolidated financial statements in accordance with accounting principles generally accepted in the United States of America, and for the design, implementation, and maintenance of internal control relevant to the preparation and fair presentation of consolidated financial statements that are free from material misstatement, whether due to fraud or error.

In preparing the financial statements, management is required to evaluate whether there are conditions or events, considered in the aggregate, that raise substantial doubt about X Company's ability to continue as a going concern for a reasonable period of time as defined by accounting principles generally accepted in the United States of America.

*Auditor's Responsibilities for the Audit of the Financial Statements*

Our objectives are to obtain reasonable assurance about whether the financial statements as a whole are free from material misstatement, whether due to error or fraud, and to issue an auditor's report that includes our opinion. Reasonable assurance is a high level of assurance but is not absolute assurance and therefore is not a guarantee that an audit conducted in accordance with GAAS will always detect a material misstatement when it exists. The risk of not detecting material misstatement resulting from fraud is higher than for one resulting from error, as fraud may involve collusion, forgery, or intentional misrepresentations, or the override of internal control. Misstatements are considered material if, individually or in the aggregate, they could reasonably be expected to influence the economic decisions of users made on the basis of these financial statements.

In performing an audit in accordance with GAAS, we:

- Exercise professional judgment and maintain professional skepticism throughout the audit.
- Identify and assess the risks of material misstatement of the financial statement, whether due to fraud or error, and design and perform audit procedures responsive to those risks. Such procedures include examining, on a test basis, evidence regarding the amounts and disclosures in the financial statements.
- Obtain an understanding of internal control relevant to the audit in order to design audit procedures that are appropriate in the circumstances, but not for the purpose of expressing an opinion on the effectiveness of X Company's internal control. Accordingly, no such opinion is expressed.
- Evaluate the appropriateness of accounting policies used and the reasonableness of significant accounting estimates made by management, as well as evaluate the overall presentation of the financial statements.
- Conclude whether, in our judgment, there are conditions or events, considered in the aggregate, that raise substantial doubt about X Company's ability to continue as a going concern for a reasonable period of time.

We are required to communicate with those charged with governance regarding, among other matters, the planned scope and timing of the audit, significant audit findings, and certain internal control-related matters that we identified during the audit.

*Other Information [Included in the Annual Report]*

Management is responsible for the other information [*included in the annual report*]. The other information comprises the [*information included in the annual report*] but does not include the financial statements and our auditor's report thereon. Our opinion on the financial statements does not cover the other information, and we do not express an opinion or any form of assurance thereon.

In connection with our audit of the financial statements, our responsibility is to read the other information and consider whether a material inconsistency exists between the other information and the financial statements, or the other information otherwise appears to be materially misstated. If, based on the work performed, we conclude that an uncorrected material misstatement of the other information exists, we are required to describe it in our report.

*Report on Other Legal and Regulatory Requirements*

[*Form and content of this section of the auditor's report will vary depending on the nature of the auditor's other reporting responsibilities.*]

[*Auditor's firm signature*]

[*Auditor's city and state*]

[*Date of the auditor's report*]

## SECTION 701

# COMMUNICATING KEY AUDIT MATTERS IN THE INDEPENDENT AUDITOR'S REPORT

### Authoritative Pronouncements

SAS-122—Statements on Auditing Standards: Clarification and Recodification

SAS-134—Auditor Reporting and Amendments, Including Amendments Addressing Disclosures in the Audit of Financial Statements

SAS-141—Amendment to Effective Dates of SAS Nos. 134-140

SAS-143—Auditing Accounting Estimates and Related Disclosures

**IMPORTANT NOTICE FOR 2022:** In May 2019, the AICPA's Auditing Standards Board (ASB) issued SAS No. 134 titled *Auditor Reporting and Amendments, Including Amendments Addressing Disclosures in the Audit of Financial Statements* that makes significant changes to the auditor's report. Most notably, SAS No. 134 allows, but does not require, the auditor to be engaged to communicate key audit matters (KAMs) in the auditor's report. SAS No. 134 creates this new AU-C 701 to contain guidance for auditors in those circumstances in which KAMs are communicated in the auditor's report. SAS No. 134 defines a KAM as "Those matters that, in the auditor's professional judgment, were of most significance in the audit of the financial statements of the current period. Key audit matters are selected from matters to be communicated with those charged with governance." Originally, the effective date of SAS No. 134 was for audits of financial statements periods ending on or after December 15, 2020, with early implementation **not** permitted. However, the ASB's issuance of SAS No. 141, *Amendment to the Effective Dates of SAS Nos. 134-140*, extended the effective date to December 15, 2021, in order to provide more time for firms to implement SAS No. 134 in light of the effect of the coronavirus pandemic. While SAS No. 141 allows for early implementation of SAS No. 134, the ASB recommends that SAS Nos. 134-140 be implemented concurrently.

**PUBLIC COMPANY IMPLICATIONS:** Similar to the AICPA, the PCAOB adopted in 2017 a new auditing standard AS-3101 (*The Auditor's Report on an Audit of Financial Statements When the Auditor Expresses an Unqualified Opinion*) that changed the standard unqualified opinion audit report for public companies. The most notable change is that AS-3101 requires the auditor (1) to describe critical audit matters in the audit report and (2) to disclose the tenure of the audit firm as auditor. The PCAOB's standard describes critical audit matters as those audit matters that are communicated, or are required to be communicated, to the audit committee that (1) related to accounts or disclosures that are material to the financial statements, and (2) involved especially challenging, subjective, or complex judgments. The auditor's report on financial statements of SEC registrants should (1) identify the critical audit matter, (2) describe why the auditor concluded that the item was a critical audit matter, (3) describe how the critical audit matter was addressed in the audit, and (4) refer to the relevant financial statement accounts and disclosures affected by the critical audit matter. Notice that the PCAOB requires the auditor to communicate critical audit matters, whereas AICPA auditing standards for nonpublic company audits allow, but do not require, the auditor to communicate KAMs.

## Overview

AU-C 701 provides the auditor with guidance regarding the auditor's responsibility to communicate key audit matters in the auditor's report when management engages the auditor to do so. This section includes guidance to help the auditor apply judgment in determining what might constitute a key audit matter, and it provides guidance on auditor reporting of key audit matters. While not required in all audits, the communication of key audit matters helps to increase transparency about the audit that has been performed.

The communication of key audit matters is based on work conducted by the auditor in forming an opinion on the financial statements as a whole. Communication of key audit matters is not intended to substitute for required disclosures in the financial statements or to substitute for a modified opinion on the financial statements, or to communicate substantial doubt about the entity's ability to continue as a going concern.

This section applies when the auditor of a complete set of general purpose financial statements is engaged to communicate key audit matters. The auditor is prohibited by AU-C 705 from communicating key audit matters when the auditor expresses an adverse opinion or disclaims an opinion on the financial statements, unless required by law or regulation.

## Definitions

| | |
|---|---|
| Key audit matters | Those matters that, in the auditor's professional judgment, were of most significance in the audit of the financial statements of the current period. Key audit matters are selected from matters communicated with those charged with governance. |

## Requirements

The auditor is presumptively required to perform the following procedures when engaged to communicate key audit matters:

### Determination of Key Audit Matters

1. Using the population of matters communicated with those charged with governance, the auditor should determine those matters that required significant auditor attention, including matters such as areas of higher assessed risk of material misstatement or significant risks, significant auditor judgment, estimates having high estimation uncertainty, or the effect on the audit of significant events or transactions. The auditor should determine those matters to be of most significance and which are key audit matters.

**IMPORTANT NOTICE FOR 2022:** In July 2020, the AICPA Auditing Standards Board (ASB) issued SAS No. 143, *Auditing Accounting Estimates and Related Disclosures*, which supersedes AU-C 540 (*Auditing Accounting Estimates, Including Fair Value Accounting Estimates, and Related Disclosures*) and amends various other sections, including AU-C 701, in the professional standards. The new SAS begins with an explanation of the nature of accounting estimates and how they can vary widely in nature and are required to be made by management when monetary amounts cannot be directly observed. The measurement of amounts is subject to estimation uncertainty, which reflects inherent limitations in the knowledge or data. These limitations give rise to inherent subjectivity and variation in measurement outcomes. Although the guidance in SAS No. 143 applies to all accounting estimates, the degree to which an accounting estimate is subject to estimation uncertainty will vary substantially. Therefore, SAS No. 143 recognizes that the nature, timing, and extent of the risk assessment and further audit procedures required will vary in relation to the estimation uncertainty and the assessment of the related risks of material misstatement. The ASB is coordinating the effective date of SAS No. 143 with the effective date of a proposed new SAS, *Understanding the Entity and Its Environment and Assessing the Risks of Material Misstatement*, which is under consideration by the ASB at the time this edition of the *GAAS Guide* was prepared. SAS No. 143 does not become effective until audits of financial statements for periods ending on or after December 15, 2023, which is consistent with the date in the proposed new standard. As a result, this AU-C reflects existing auditing standards requirements. Updates to reflect SAS No. 143 will occur in the next edition of the *GAAS Guide*.

## *Communicating Key Audit Matters*

2. Key audit matters should each be described in a separate section of the auditor's report that has the title "Key Audit Matters" and that states that key audit matters are those matters that were communicated with those charged with governance and in the auditor's judgment were of most significance. This section should clearly state that the auditor does not provide a separate opinion on those matters.

3. Communication of key audit matters are not to be a substitute for modification of the auditor's opinion.

4. The information provided about the key audit matter should include discussion of why the matter was considered to be one of most significance to the audit and how the matter was addressed. It should also include reference to related disclosures in the financial statements, if any.

5. There may be circumstances when the auditor does not communicate a matter that is a key audit matter. For example, a law or regulation may preclude disclosure or the auditor may determine that there may be adverse consequences of doing so that outweigh the public benefit (this would be rare).

6. If the auditor determines that there are no key audit matters to communicate, the auditor should state so in the "Key Audit Matters" section of the report.

## Relationship of Key Audit Matters and Other Elements of the Auditor's Report

7. While matters that give rise to substantial doubt about an entity's ability to continue as a going concern are by their nature key audit matters, the auditor should not report on those in the "Key Audit Matters" section of the auditor's report. Instead, those matters would be addressed in the section that describes that substantial doubt as discussed in AU-C 570.

## Communication with Those Charged with Governance

8. The auditor should communicate with those charged with governance all matters determined to be key audit matters. When there are no key audit matters, the auditor should communicate that.

## Documentation

9. Audit documentation should include the matters that required significant auditor attention and the auditor's rationale for determining whether the matter was a key audit matter or not. When the auditor determines that there are no key audit matters, the documentation should include the rationale for that determination.

10. If the auditor determines that a key audit matter is not communicated in the auditor's report, the auditor should communicate the rationale for the decision to not include that matter in the report.

# Analysis and Application of Procedures

## Determination of Key Audit Matters

The communication of key audit matters provides additional information for users of the financial statements that helps them understand those matters that are of most significance to the audit. The determination of key audit matters is based on and selected from matters communicated to those charged with governance and includes those that required significant auditor attention in performing the audit. From that, the auditor then determines those that were of most significance to the audit. Those represent the key audit matters. Key audit matters are limited to those of most significance to the current period financial statements audited, even when comparative financial statements are presented.

The concept of significant auditor attention recognizes the reality that more judgment is involved in planning and performing procedures in response to higher assessed risks of material misstatement. Challenges in obtaining sufficient appropriate evidence or challenges in forming an opinion may be indicative of a key audit matter. Other potential key audit matters may relate to areas of complexity, significant management or auditor judgment, or matters that affect the overall audit strategy. AU-C 260 (*The Auditor's Communication With Those Charged With Governance*) and AU-C 220 (*Quality Control for an Engagement Conducted in Accordance With Generally Accepted Auditing Standards*) include specific required communications with those charged with governance that may require significant auditor attention.

During the planning stage of the audit, the auditor may develop a preliminary view about matters that may be key audit matters. Areas that might represent key audit matters include areas of higher risk of material misstatement, including significant risks, areas of significant management or auditor judgment, including accounting estimates, and the effects on the audit of significant events and transactions.

### Most Significant Matters

When determining whether a matter is a key audit matter, the auditor may consider the nature and extent of communications with those charged with governance as a signal of matters that are most significant in the audit. The importance of a matter to financial statement users, including the matter's materiality, may help in the auditor's determination of whether the matter is a key audit matter. Other considerations may include the nature and extent of uncorrected misstatements, subjectivity involved in management's selection of an accounting policy, difficulties in applying audit procedures or evaluating the results of procedures, or the severity of control deficiencies.

### Communication of Key Audit Matters

The order of presentation of key audit matters in the "Key Audit Matters" section of the report is a matter of professional judgment. The information might be presented based on relative importance or it might be in the same order as relevant disclosures appear in the financial statements. Similarly, the description of the key audit matter is a matter of professional judgment. The description needs to be sufficient to provide a succinct and balanced description of the key audit matter. The description might include original information that has not already been disclosed by management, although that should be avoided when possible.

The description of the key audit matter should address why it is considered to be a matter of most significance in the audit and how the matter was addressed. It should not merely be a reiteration of what is disclosed in the financial statements. However, reference can be made to disclosures to help users understand how management has addressed the matter.

The amount of detail provided in the auditor's report to describe how a key audit matter was addressed in the audit is a matter of professional judgment. The description might include a brief overview of procedures performed, the outcome of the procedures, and key observations regarding the matter. The auditor should ensure that the description does not imply that the matter has not been appropriately resolved in the audit.

There may be circumstances where law or regulation prohibits the communication of a key audit matter. It is rare that a key audit matter will not be communicated. That determination should take into account the facts and circumstances related to the matter.

### Communication with Those Charged with Governance

The timing of communications of key audit matters with those charged with governance may vary. Some key audit matters may be communicated to those charged with governance during planning while others may be communicated when discussing audit findings. The auditor may find it helpful to provide those charged with governance a draft of the auditor's report that includes communications of key audit matters. If the auditor determines that there are no key audit matters to communicate, that determination should be discussed with those charged with governance.

## Documentation

The audit documentation should include documentation of professional judgments in determining among items communicated with those charged with governance those matters that require significant auditor attention and whether those matters are key audit matters. That might include documentation of the auditor's communication with those charged with governance.

## SECTION 703

# FORMING AN OPINION AND REPORTING ON FINANCIAL STATEMENTS OF EMPLOYEE BENEFIT PLANS SUBJECT TO ERISA

## Authoritative Pronouncements

SAS-136—Forming an Opinion and Reporting on Financial Statements of Employee Benefit Plans Subject to ERISA

SAS-138—Amendments to the Description of the Concept of Materiality

SAS-140—Amendments to AU-C Sections 725, 730, 930, 935, and 940 to Incorporate Auditor Reporting Changes from SAS Nos. 134 and 137

SAS-141—Amendment to Effective Dates of SAS Nos. 134-140

SAS-143—Auditing Accounting Estimates and Related Disclosures

**IMPORTANT NOTICE FOR 2022:** In July 2019, the AICPA's Auditing Standards Board (ASB) issued SAS No. 136, *Forming an Opinion and Reporting on Financial Statements of Employee Benefit Plans Subject to ERISA*. The new guidance is specific to audits of financial statements of employee benefit plans (EBPs) subject to the Employee Retirement Income Security Act of 1974 (ERISA). The ASB issued SAS No. 136 to address the auditor's responsibility to form an opinion and report on the audit of financial statements of EBPs, including reporting on specific plan provisions related to the ERISA plan financial statements. The most notable aspect of SAS No. 136 is that it changes the form and content of the auditor's report issued as a result of an audit of ERISA plan financial statements. The new SAS creates a separate, stand-alone reporting section that is codified as new AU-C 703. For audits of ERISA plan financial statements only, the guidance in AU-C 703 would apply in place of the guidance in AU-C 700. Originally, SAS No. 136 was to become effective for audits of ERISA plan financial statements for period ending on or after December 15, 2020, with early adoption not permitted. However, the ASB's issuance of SAS No. 141, *Amendment to the Effective Dates of SAS Nos. 134-140*, extended the effective date to December 15, 2021, in order to provide more time for firms to implement SAS No. 136 in light of the effect of the coronavirus pandemic. While SAS No. 141 allows for early implementation of SAS No. 136, the ASB recommends that SAS Nos. 134-140 be implemented concurrently.

## Overview

AU-C 703 provides the auditor with guidance regarding the auditor's responsibility to form an opinion on the financial statements of employee benefit plans (EBPs) subject to the Employee Retirement Income Security Act of 1974 (ERISA). It also provides guidance regarding the form and content of the auditor's report issued as a result of an audit of ERISA plan financial statements. This section applies to an audit of a complete set of general purpose financial statements of EBPs subject to ERISA. AU-C 703 does not apply to plans that are not subject to ERISA.

The Form 5500 series developed by the Department of Labor (DOL), the IRS, and the Pension Benefit Guaranty Corporation (PBGC) can be used by EBPs to satisfy the annual reporting requirements under Title I and Title IV of ERISA. ERISA requires that certain supplemental schedules accompany the ERISA plan financial statements. This section describes the auditor's responsibilities relating to reporting on the ERISA-required supplemental schedules. The requirements in AU-C 703 are specific to ERISA plan audit engagements; however, it does not contain all the requirements necessary to form an opinion and report on ERISA plan financial statements.

SAS No. 136 addresses the auditor's responsibilities for forming an opinion on ERISA plan financial statements when management elects to have an audit performed in accordance with ERISA Section 103(a)(3)(C). In those engagements, the audit need not extend to any statements or information related to assets held for investment of the plan by a bank or similar institution or an insurance carrier that is regulated, supervised and subject to periodic examination by a state or federal agency, provided that the statements or information regarding assets so held are prepared and certified to by the bank or similar institution or insurance carrier in accordance with DOL rules.

## Definitions

There are no defined terms in AU-C 703.

## Requirements

The auditor is presumptively required to perform the following procedures when engaged to form an opinion on the financial statements of employee benefit plans (EBPs) subject to the Employee Retirement Income Security Act of 1974 (ERISA):

*Acceptance of the Engagement*

> 1. In addition to other preconditions required by other auditing standards, the auditor should obtain agreement with management that it acknowledges and understands its responsibilities for maintaining a current plan instrument and for administering the plan and determining that the plan's transactions are presented and disclosed in the ERISA plan financial statements in conformity with the plan's provisions.
>
> 2. When management has elected to have an ERISA Section 103(a)(3)(C) audit, the auditor should also determine that management has assessed whether that kind of audit is permissible for the plan, the investment information is prepared and certified by a qualified institution, the certification meets the requirements, and the certified investment information is appropriately measured, presented, and disclosed.
>
> 3. Management agrees to provide the auditor with a draft of the Form 5500 that is substantially complete.

## Risk Assessment and Response

4. The auditor should assess the risk of material misstatements in the financial statements subject to ERISA. The auditor should obtain and read the most current plan instrument for the audit period to assess the risk of misstatement. The plan instrument is essential to understanding the plan and performing audit procedures in response to the assessed risks.

5. The auditor should also consider whether management has performed the relevant Internal Revenue Code (IRC) compliance tests regarding the plan's tax status.

6. The auditor should evaluate whether prohibited transactions identified by management or as part of the audit have been appropriately reported in the required supplemental schedules. If the auditor identifies any prohibited transactions, those matters should be discussed with management and determination of whether the supplemental schedules require revision should be made.

7. When the auditor identifies items that are not in accordance with the criteria specified, the auditor should determine if the items are reportable findings. Reportable findings include an identified instance of noncompliance or suspected noncompliance with laws or regulations, a finding arising from the audit that is significant and relevant to those charged with governance, and an indication of deficiencies in internal control identified during the audit that have not been communicated to management by other parties that the auditor believes are of sufficient importance.

## Communication with Management or Those Charged with Governance

8. The auditor should communicate in writing with those charged with governance, on a timely basis, reportable findings. The auditor should not issue a written communication stating that no reportable findings were identified in the audit.

## Procedures for ERISA Section 103(a)(3)(C) Audit

9. When management elects to have an ERISA Section 103(a)(3)(C) audit, the auditor assess management's assessment of whether the entity issuing the certification is a DOL qualified institution. Any concerns about that qualification should be discussed with management and those charged with governance.

10. The auditor should identify the investment information that is certified. The auditor should perform procedures related to the certified investment information including reading the certification, comparing the certified investment information with related information presented and disclosed in the ERISA plan financial statements and supplemental schedules, and reading disclosures relating to the certified investment information to assess whether they are in accordance with the presentation and disclosure requirements of the applicable financial reporting framework. If inaccuracies or otherwise incomplete or unsatisfactory information is identified, the auditor should discuss those matters with management and perform additional procedures.

11. The auditor should perform audit procedures on the financial statement information not covered by the certification. Plans may hold investments whereby only a portion is covered by the certification. In that case, the auditor should perform audit procedures on that investment information.

## Written Representations

12. In addition to required representations outlined in AU-C 580 (*Written Representations*), the auditor should request the following written representation:
    a. That management has provided the auditor with the most current plan instrument, including amendments;
    b. Management's acknowledgment of its responsibility for administering the plan and determining that the plan's transactions are presented and disclosed in the ERISA plan financial statements in accordance with the plan's provisions; and
    c. Acknowledgment that even with the election to have an ERISA Section 103(a)(3)(C) audit, management retains responsibility for the financial statements and for determining that the audit is permissible under the circumstances, the investment information is prepared and certified by a qualified institution and that the certification meets the applicable requirements, and the certified investment information is appropriately measured, presented, and disclosed.

## Forming an Opinion

13. The auditor should form an opinion on whether the ERISA plan financial statements are presented fairly, in all material respects. To do so, the auditor should determine if the auditor has obtained reasonable assurance about whether the ERISA plan financial statements as a whole are free of material misstatement, whether due to fraud or error.

14. The auditor should evaluate whether the ERISA plan financial statements are prepared in accordance with the requirements of the applicable financial reporting framework. That should include evaluation of the ERISA plan financial statements' disclosure of significant accounting policies selected and applied, accounting estimates made by management, and whether the information presented is relevant, reliable, comparable and understandable.

15. The auditor's evaluation should also include consideration of the overall presentation, structure, and content of the ERISA plan financial statements and whether they represent the underlying transactions and events in a manner that leads to fair presentation.

## Form of Opinion

16. When the ERISA plan financial statements are presented fairly in all material respects in accordance with the applicable financial reporting framework, the auditors should express an unqualified opinion.

17. The auditor modified the opinion if the auditor concludes that the ERISA plan financial statements are materially misstated or the auditor is unable to obtain sufficient appropriate audit evidence to conclude whether the financial statements are materially misstated.

18. When the financial statements do not present fairly, the auditor should discuss the matter with management and then determine if the opinion should be modified.

## Form 5500 Filing Considerations

19. The auditor should obtain and read the Form 5500 prior to the dating of the auditor's report in order to identify material inconsistencies with the audited ERISA plan financial statements. If material inconsistencies are identi-

fied, the auditor should consider if the financial statements or the Form 5500 should be revised.

20. The auditor should communicate with those charged with governance the auditor's responsibilities with respect to the Form 5500.

21. If the auditor identifies a material misstatement of fact, the auditor should discuss the matter with management. Any material misstatements of fact that remain uncorrected should be communicated by the auditor with those charged with governance.

## Auditor's Report on ERISA Plan Financial Statements Other than for an ERISA Section 103(a)(3)(C) Audit

22. The auditor's report should be in writing.

23. The report should have a title that indicates clearly that the report is from the independent auditor.

24. The report should be addressed to the appropriate recipients.

25. The first section of the report should contain the auditor's opinion, which identifies the plan financial statements audited and that the plan is subject to ERISA, the titles of the financial statements and references to the notes and the dates covered by each financial statement. That section should have the heading "Opinion."

26. The opinion should state that, in the auditor's opinion, the accompanying financial statements present fairly in all material respects in accordance with the applicable financial reporting framework.

27. The report should include a section following the "Opinion" section with the heading "Basis for Opinion." That section should state the audit was conducted in accordance with GAAS and should refer to the section of the report that describes the auditor's responsibilities. It should also include a statement that the auditor is required to be independent of the plan. And, it should state whether the auditor believes the audit evidence obtained is sufficient and appropriate to provide a basis for the auditor's opinion.

28. When applicable, the auditor should report on the entity's ability to continue as a going concern. And, if the auditor is engaged to communicate key audit matters, the auditor should do so in accordance with AU-C 701.

29. The auditor's report should include a section with the heading "Responsibilities of Management for the Financial Statements" which includes description of management's responsibility for the financial statements and responsibility for considering the entity's ability to continue as a going concern, responsibility for maintaining a current plan instrument, and administering the plan and presenting and disclosing transactions in the financial statements in accordance with plan provisions.

30. The auditor's report should also include a section "Auditor's Responsibilities for the Audit of the Financial Statements" that state that the objectives of the auditor and that describe the auditor's responsibilities in performing an audit in accordance with GAAS.

31. When auditing ERISA plan financial statements, the auditor is required to report on whether the ERISA required supplemental schedules are fairly stated in relationship to the financial statements as a whole.

32. The auditor addresses other responsibilities in performing an ERISA plan financial statement audit that are in addition to those required by GAAS.

33. The auditor's report should contain the manual or printed signature of the auditor's firm and it should name the city and state where the auditor's report is issued.

34. The auditor's report should be dated no earlier than the date on which the auditor has obtained sufficient appropriate audit evidence on which to base the auditor's opinion.

35. Information that is not required by the applicable financial reporting framework but is presented as part of the basic financial statements should be covered by the auditor's opinion if it cannot be clearly differentiated.

---

**OBSERVATION:** An auditor may indicate that the audit was also conducted in accordance with another set of auditing standards, such as International Standards on Auditing (ISAs) or Government Auditing Standards. The auditor should not refer to having conducted an audit in accordance with another set of auditing standards in addition to GAAS unless the audit was conducted in accordance with both sets of standards in their entirety.

---

## *Comparative Financial Statements*

36. When comparative financial statements are presented, the auditor's report should refer to each period for which the financial statements are presented and on which an opinion is expressed.

37. When expressing an opinion on all periods presented, a continuing auditor should update the report on the financial statements of one or more prior periods presented on a comparative basis with those of the current year.

38. The auditor should perform procedures to determine if the comparative financial statements have been presented in accordance with the relevant requirements.

39. If the auditor becomes aware of possible misstatements in the comparative financial statements, the auditor should perform additional procedures to determine if a material misstatement exists.

40. The auditor should request written representations for all periods referred to in the auditor's opinion.

41. If the financial statements of a prior period were audited by a predecessor auditor, and the predecessor auditor's opinion is not reissued, the auditor should describe the predecessor auditor's involvement in an other-matters paragraph.

42. When current period financial statements are audited and presented in comparative form with prior period financial statements for which a compilation or review was performed and the report on the prior period is not reissued, the auditor should include an other-matter paragraph in the report that describes the work related to the prior period financial statements.

## Auditor's Report on ERISA Section 103(a)(3)(C) Audit

43. The auditor's report should be in writing.

44. The report should have a title that indicates clearly that the report is from the independent auditor.

45. The report should be addressed to the appropriate recipients.

46. The first section of the auditor's report should include a description of the scope and nature of the ERISA Section 103(a)(3)(C) audit and should have the

heading "Scope and Nature of the ERISA Section 103(a)(3)(C) Audit." This section should include the following:

a. Identification of the plan whose financial statements have been audited.
b. That the auditor performed an audit of the financial statements of a plan subject to the ERISA Section 103(a)(3)(C) audit.
c. Titles of each statement that comprises the financial statement and the dates or periods covered by each statement.
d. Reference to footnotes.
e. Statement that management has elected to have the audit performed in accordance with ERISA Section 103(a)(3)(C) and that the audit need not extend to any statements or information related to assets held for investment of the plan by a bank or similar institution or insurance carrier that is regulated or supervised, and subject to periodic examination by a state or federal agency, provided that the statements or information regarding assets so held are prepared and certified to by the bank or similar institution or insurance carrier in accordance with DOL rules.
f. Statement that management has obtained a certification from a qualified institution stating that the certified investment information is complete and accurate.
g. That management has provided the auditor with the most current plan instrument, including amendments.

47. The next section of the report should contain the auditor's opinion, which identifies the plan financial statements audited and that the plan is subject to ERISA, the titles of the financial statements, and references to the notes and the dates covered by each financial statement. That section should have the heading "Opinion."

48. The opinion should state that, in the auditor's opinion, the accompanying financial statements present fairly in all material respects in accordance with the applicable financial reporting framework and that the information in the accompanying financial statements related to assets held by and certified to by a qualified institution agrees to, or is derived from, in all material respects, the information prepared and certified by an institution that management determined meets the requirements of ERISA Section 103(a)(3)(C).

49. The report should include a section following the "Opinion" section with the heading "Basis for Opinion." That section should state the audit was conducted in accordance with GAAS and should refer to the section of the report that describes the auditor's responsibilities. It should also include a statement that the auditor is required to be independent of the plan. And, it should state whether the auditor believes the audit evidence obtained is sufficient and appropriate to provide a basis for the auditor's opinion.

50. When applicable, the auditor should report on the entity's ability to continue as a going concern. And, if the auditor is engaged to communicate key audit matters, the auditor should do so in accordance with AU-C 701.

51. The auditor's report should include a section with the heading "Responsibilities of Management for the Financial Statements" which includes description of management's responsibility for the financial statements, responsibility for the election of ERISA Section 103(a)(3)(C), responsibility for considering the entity's ability to continue as a going concern, responsibility for maintaining a current plan instrument, and administering the plan and presenting and disclosing transactions in the financial statements in accordance with plan provisions.

52. The auditor's report should also include a section "Auditor's Responsibilities for the Audit of the Financial Statements" that state that the objectives of the auditor and that describe the auditor's responsibilities in performing an audit in accordance with GAAS.

53. The auditor's report should state that the audit did not extend to the certified investment information, except for obtaining and reading the certification, comparing the certified investment information with the related information presented and disclosed in the financial statements, and reading the disclosures relating to the certified investment information to assess whether they are in accordance with the presentation and disclosure requirements of the applicable financial reporting framework.

54. The auditor's report should also state that the objective of the ERISA Section 103(a)(3)(C) audit is not to express an opinion about whether the financial statements are as a whole presented fairly, in accordance with the financial reporting framework.

55. When the auditor concludes that a modification to the auditor's opinion on the ERISA plan financial statements is necessary, the auditor should apply the requirements in AU-C 705.

56. The auditor's report should include a separate section with the heading "Supplemental Schedules Required by ERISA." This section should include the title of the supplemental schedules and periods covered, a statement that the supplemental schedules are presented for purposes of additional analysis and are not a required part of the financial statements but are supplementary information required by DOL, a statement that the schedules are the responsibility of management and derived from the underlying accounting and other records used to prepare the financial statements, and a statement that the information included in the supplemental schedules, other than that agreed to or derived from the certified investment information, has been subjected to auditing procedures. For information included in the supplemental schedules that agreed to or is derived from the certified investment information, a statement should be included that the auditor compared such information to the related certified investment information.

57. The separate section should also include a statement that in forming the auditor's opinion on the supplemental schedules, the auditor evaluated whether the supplemental schedules, other than the information agreed to or derived from the certified investment information, including their form and content, are presented in conformity with DOL requirements. It also should include a statement whether in the auditor's opinion, the form and content of the supplemental schedules are presented in all material respects in conformity with DOL requirements and the information in the supplemental schedules related to assets held by and certified to by a qualified institution agrees to, or is derived from, in all material respects, the information prepared and certified by an institution that management determines meets the requirements of ERISA Section 103(a)(3)(C).

58. If the auditor issues a qualified ERISA Section 103(a)(3)(C) opinion on the ERISA plan financial statements and the qualifications have an effect on the ERISA-required supplemental schedules, the auditor's report should include a statement that, in the auditor's opinion, except for the effects of [the matters described in the report explaining the qualification] on the [identified] supplemental schedules the form and content of the supplemental schedules comply with DOL requirements and the information in the supplemental schedules related to assets held by and certified to by a qualified institution agrees to, or is derived from, in all material respects, the information prepared and certi-

fied by an institution that management determines meets ERICA Section 103(a)(3)(C).

59. If the auditor's report contains an adverse opinion or disclaimer of opinion, the auditor is precluded from expressing an opinion on the supplementary schedules.

60. The auditor addresses other responsibilities in performing an ERISA plan financial statement audit that are in addition to those required by GAAS.

61. The auditor's report should contain the manual or printed signature of the auditor's firm and it should name the city and state where the auditor's report is issued.

62. The auditor's report should be dated no earlier than the date on which the auditor has obtained sufficient appropriate audit evidence on which to base the auditor's opinion.

63. Information that is not required by the applicable financial reporting framework but is presented as part of the basic financial statements should be covered by the auditor's opinion if it cannot be clearly differentiated.

## Reporting on Supplemental Schedules

64. ERISA requires that certain supplemental schedules accompany the ERISA plan financial statements. The financial statements may also be accompanied by information that is not required by ERISA. The auditor should report on whether the ERISA-required supplemental schedules are fairly stated, in all material respects, in relation to the financial statements as a whole. Reporting guidance that applies is contained in AU-C 725.

65. When reporting on ERISA required supplemental schedules, in accordance with AU-C 725, the reporting elements should be appropriately modified to reflect the fact that the supplemental schedules are presented for purposes of additional analysis and are not a required part of the financial statements but are supplementary information required by the DOL, among other matters.

66. When the auditor's report on the audited ERISA plan financial statements contains an adverse opinion or disclaimer of opinion, the auditor is precluded from expressing an opinion on the ERISA-required supplemental schedules.

67. The report should have a title that indicates clearly that the report is from the independent auditor.

## Analysis and Application of Procedures

ERISA oversees management's operating and reporting practices related to EBPs and establishes reporting requirements for covered plans. The DOL and IRS have authority to issue regulations governing the administration of EBPs, including the reporting and disclosure requirements to be included in the annual filing with the DOL. The DOL and the Pension Benefit Guaranty Corporation (PBGC) jointly developed the Form 5500 series of reporting that EBPs use to satisfy annual reporting requirements. The IRS, DOL, and PBGC have consolidated their reporting and disclosure requirements into the Form 5500 to minimize the filing burden for plan management.

Management is responsible for the selection of an acceptable financial reporting framework. The auditor considers accounting estimates. The plan administrator manages the day-to-day administration and decisions for the plan. ERISA contains a requirement for annual audits of EBP financial statements by an independent qualified public accountant. ERISA and DOL regulations require additional information to the disclosed in the financial statements or presented in supplemental schedules. ERISA also contains a requirement for the auditor to report on whether certain supplemental schedules are presented fairly, in all material respects, in relation to the financial statements as a whole.

Management can elect an ERISA Section 103(a)(3)(C) audit when a qualified institution certifies both the accuracy and completeness of investment information submitted to the plan administrator. A qualified institution is an organization that is a bank or similar institution that holds plan assets or an insurance carrier which provides benefits under the plan or holds plan assets, that is regulated, supervised, and subject to periodic examination by a state or federal agency that prepares and certifies the investment information. An ERISA Section 103(a)(3)(C) audit is unique to EBPs and is not considered a scope limitation.

Auditors can find interpretative guidance in the AICPA's Audit and Accounting Guide, *Employee Benefit Plans*, to apply SAS No. 136.

## Engagement Acceptance

Management is responsible for preparing the financial statements reflected in Form 5500. A draft of Form 5500 that is substantially complete includes the forms and schedules that could have a material effect, involving both quantitative and qualitative considerations, on the information in the financial statements and supplemental schedules required by ERISA. If the auditor assists in drafting the Form 5500, the auditor should consider the AICPA Code of Professional Conduct requirements for independence and should establish and document in writing his or her understanding of the services to be performed.

## Risk Assessment and Audit Responses

Auditing standards require the auditor of an EBP to establish an overall audit strategy that guides the development of the audit plan, which includes risk assessment procedures and further audit procedures. The auditor obtains an understanding of the plan and its environment, including its internal controls, and performs risk assessment procedures to identify and assess risks of material misstatement at the financial statement and assertion levels. In response to those risks, the auditor designs and performs further audit procedures.

The EBP is required by ERISA to have a written plan instrument that includes requirements that satisfy the IRC. Management is responsible for determining that the plan's transactions are presented and disclosed in the ERISA plan financial statements in accordance with the plan instrument. Many of the financial statement amounts in ERISA plan financial statements are determined from provisions specified in the plan instrument. For example, the plan outlines who is eligible to participate in the plan and the plan provisions outline the types of contributions and distributions that can be made from the plan.

Some plans are granted special tax status for the contributions and earnings on plan investments are exempt from taxation. To determine if a plan is operating within the specific guidelines established by the plan document, management is required to conduct certain compliance tests.

> **IMPORTANT NOTICE FOR 2022:** In July 2020, the AICPA Auditing Standards Board (ASB) issued SAS No. 143, *Auditing Accounting Estimates and Related Disclosures*, which supersedes AU-C 540 (*Auditing Accounting Estimates, Including Fair Value Accounting Estimates, and Related Disclosures*) and amends various other sections, including AU-C 703, in the professional standards. The new SAS begins with an explanation of the nature of accounting estimates and how they can vary widely in nature and are required to be made by management when monetary amounts cannot be directly observed. The measurement of amounts is subject to estimation uncertainty, which reflects inherent limitations in the knowledge or data. These limitations give rise to inherent subjectivity and variation in measurement outcomes. Although the guidance in SAS No. 143 applies to all accounting estimates, the degree to which an accounting estimate is subject to estimation uncertainty will vary substantially. Therefore, SAS No. 143 recognizes that the nature, timing, and extent of the risk assessment and further audit procedures required will vary in relation to the estimation uncertainty and the assessment of the related risks of material misstatement. The ASB is coordinating the effective date of SAS No. 143 with the effective date of a proposed new SAS, *Understanding the Entity and Its Environment and Assessing the Risks of Material Misstatement*, which is under consideration by the ASB at the time this edition of the *GAAS Guide* was prepared. SAS No. 143 does not become effective until audits of financial statements for periods ending on or after December 15, 2023, which is consistent with the date in the proposed new standard. As a result, this AU-C reflects existing auditing standards requirements. Updates to reflect SAS No. 143 will occur in the next edition of the *GAAS Guide*.

## *Communications with Management or Those Charged with Governance*

Auditing standards contain a number of required communications with those charged with governance, including matters involving noncompliance with laws and regulations and significant findings and issues from the audit. Within the context of an ERISA plan audit, this might include operational errors that have been identified by the auditor as part of the audit when testing the plan provisions. The auditor and the engaging party may need to agree to who are the appropriate persons for purposes of fulfilling the required communications with those charged with governance. Some plans have formal boards of trustees and others may only have a named fiduciary who is often the plan sponsor.

Auditing standards require the auditor to communicate in writing to those charged with governance on a timely basis any significant deficiencies or material weaknesses identified during the audit. When the auditor identifies instances where the plan provisions were not followed, those instances might represent a deficiency in internal control. The communication of reportable findings related to plan provisions may outline the plan provision related to the reportable finding and may provide more explanation about the reportable findings and the related impact on the financial statements. The auditor may want to discuss reporting findings with the plan administrator before providing a written communication to allow the administrator the ability to take corrective action.

### ERISA Section 103(a)(3)(C) Audits

Management has the ability to elect an ERISA Section 103(a)(3)(C) audit. Doing so does not represent a scope limitation. However, that election is only available for certain EBPs that meet ERISA requirements. The auditor evaluates management's assessment of that qualification.

In an ERISA Section 103(a)(3)(C) audit, a qualified institution may certify some or all plan activity. The auditor agrees and reviews reconciliations of the certified investment information with the amounts in the ERISA plan financial statements and related investment disclosures as well as the investment information included in the ERISA-required supplemental schedules. The auditor performs additional procedures when the investment information cannot be agreed to or derived from the certified information. If the auditor determines that the certified investment information has not been appropriately measured, presented, or disclosed, communication of that finding should be made to management who may request that the trustee or custodian recertify or amend the certification.

### Written Representations

The AICPA Audit and Accounting Guide, *Employee Benefit Plans*, provides helpful guidance on representations that may be appropriate when auditing ERISA plan financial statements.

### Forming an Opinion

As the auditor evaluates management judgments about the amounts and disclosures in the ERISA plan financial statements, including qualitative aspects of the plan's accounting practices, the auditor may become aware of bias in those judgments. Indication of possible bias does not automatically constitute a misstatement; however, it does affect the auditor's evaluation of whether the financial statements as a whole are free from material misstatement.

The auditor evaluates whether the plan financial statements appropriately disclose the significant accounting policies used and evaluates the understandability of those financial statements. Fair presentation requires the inclusion of an adequate description of the applicable financial reporting framework in the financial statements. Some financial reporting frameworks acknowledge explicitly or implicitly the concept of fair presentation. The auditor's evaluation of whether the plan financial statements are presented fairly is a matter of professional judgment. This may include discussions with management and those charged with governance about their views of why a certain presentation or disclosure was selected and alternatives they considered.

### Form 5500 Filing Considerations

AU-C 703 requires the auditor to obtain and read the draft Form 5500 prior to dating the auditor's report. That enables the auditor to address possible material inconsistencies and apparent misstatements of facts with management on a timely basis. A misstatement of fact is information contained in the Form 5500 unrelated to matters appearing in the audited ERISA plan financial statements that is incorrectly stated or presented. Form 5500 information may be relevant to the audit. Information contained in the Form 5500 that conflicts with the audited financial statements is an inconsistency, which may raise doubt about the audit conclusions drawn from the audit evidence.

When addressing a material misstatement of fact with management, the auditor may not be able to evaluate the validity of some disclosures included within the draft Form 5500 and management's responses to the auditor's inquiries and may conclude that valid differences of judgment or opinion exist. The auditor may choose to withhold the auditor's report when management refuses to correct a material misstatement of fact.

## Auditor's Reports on ERISA Plan Financial Statements

AU-C 703 contains illustrative reports for auditor reporting on ERISA plan financial statements and it requires specific headings to be used in the report. Illustrations are provided for audit reports on ERISA plan financial statements for situations that are and are not an ERISA Section 103(a)(3)(C) audit.

The following exhibits are related to auditor's report when reporting on financial statements of employee benefit plan subject to ERISA:

- Exhibit AU-C 703-1—Auditor's Report on Financial Statements for a Defined Contribution Retirement Plan Subject to ERISA
- Exhibit AU-C 703-2—Auditor's Report on Financial Statements for a Defined Contribution Retirement Plan Subject to ERISA When Management Elects an ERISA Section 103(a)(3)(C) Audit

## EXHIBIT AU-C 703-1—AUDITOR'S REPORT ON FINANCIAL STATEMENTS FOR A DEFINED CONTRIBUTION RETIREMENT PLAN SUBJECT TO ERISA

### INDEPENDENT AUDITOR'S REPORT

[Appropriate Addressee]

*Opinion*

We have audited the financial statements of XYZ 401(k) Plan, an employee benefit plan subject to the Employee Retirement Income Security Act of 1974 (ERISA), which comprise the statements of net assets available for benefits as of December 31, 20X5 and 20X4, and the related statement of changes in net assets available for benefits for the year ended December 31, 20X5, and the related notes to the financial statements.

In our opinion, the accompanying financial statements present fairly, in all material respects, the net assets available for benefits of XYZ 401(k) Plan as of December 31, 20X5 and 20X4, and the changes in its net assets available for benefits for the year ended December 31, 20X5, in accordance with accounting principles generally accepted in the United States of America.

*Basis for Opinion*

We conducted our audits in accordance with auditing standards generally accepted in the United States of America (GAAS). Our responsibilities under those standards are further described in the Auditor's Responsibilities for the Audit of the Financial Statements section of our report. We are required to be independent of XYZ 401(k) Plan and to meet our other ethical responsibilities, in accordance with the relevant ethical requirements relating to our audits. We believe that the audit evidence we have obtained is sufficient and appropriate to provide a basis for our audit opinion.

*Responsibilities of Management for the Financial Statements*

Management is responsible for the preparation and fair presentation of the financial statements in accordance with accounting principles generally accepted in the United States of America, and for the design, implementation, and maintenance of internal control relevant to the preparation and fair presentation of financial statements that are free from material misstatement, whether due to fraud or error.

In preparing the financial statements, management is required to evaluate whether there are conditions or events, considered in the aggregate, that raise substantial doubt about XYZ 401(k) Plan's ability to continue as a going concern for [*insert the time period set by the applicable financial reporting framework*].

Management is also responsible for maintaining a current plan instrument, including all plan amendments, administering the plan, and determining that the plan's transactions that are presented and disclosed in the financial statements are in conformity with the plan's provisions, including maintaining sufficient records with respect to each of the participants, to determine the benefits due or which may become due to such participants.

*Auditor's Responsibilities for the Audit of the Financial Statements*

Our objectives are to obtain reasonable assurance about whether the financial statements as a whole are free from material misstatement, whether due to fraud or error, and to issue an auditor's report that includes our opinion. Reasonable assurance is a high level of assurance but is not absolute assurance and therefore is not a guarantee that an audit conducted in accordance with GAAS will always detect a material misstatement when it exists. The risk of not detecting a material misstatement resulting from fraud is higher than for one resulting from error, as fraud may involve collusion, forgery, intentional omissions, misrepresentations, or the override of internal control. Misstatements are considered material if, individually or in the aggregate, they could reasonably be expected to influence the economic decisions of users made on the basis of these financial statements.

In performing an audit in accordance with GAAS, we:

- Exercise professional judgment and maintain professional skepticism throughout the audit.
- Identify and assess the risks of material misstatement of the financial statements, whether due to fraud or error, and design and perform audit procedures responsive to those risks. Such procedures include examining, on a test basis, evidence regarding the amounts and disclosures in the financial statements.
- Obtain an understanding of internal control relevant to the audit in order to design audit procedures that are appropriate in the circumstances, but not for the purpose of expressing an opinion on the effectiveness of XYZ 401(k) Plan's internal control. Accordingly, no such opinion is expressed.

- Evaluate the appropriateness of accounting policies used and the reasonableness of significant accounting estimates made by management, as well as evaluate the overall presentation of the financial statements.
- Conclude whether, in our judgment, there are conditions or events, considered in the aggregate, that raise substantial doubt about XYZ 401(k) Plan's ability to continue as a going concern for a [insert the time period set by the applicable financial reporting framework].

We are required to communicate with those charged with governance regarding, among other matters, the planned scope and timing of the audit, significant audit findings, and certain internal control-related matters that we identified during the audit.

*Supplemental Schedules Required by ERISA*

Our audits were conducted for the purpose of forming an opinion on the financial statements as a whole. The supplemental schedules of [*identify title of supplemental schedules and periods covered*] are presented for purposes of additional analysis and are not a required part of the financial statements but are supplementary information required by the Department of Labor's Rules and Regulations for Reporting and Disclosure under ERISA. Such information is the responsibility of management and was derived from and relates directly to the underlying accounting and other records used to prepare the financial statements. The information has been subjected to the auditing procedures applied in the audits of the financial statements and certain additional procedures, including comparing and reconciling such information directly to the underlying accounting and other records used to prepare the financial statements or to the financial statements themselves, and other additional procedures in accordance with GAAS.

In forming our opinion on the supplemental schedules, we evaluated whether the supplemental schedules, including their form and content, are presented in conformity with the Department of Labor's Rules and Regulations for Reporting and Disclosure under ERISA.

In our opinion, the information in the accompanying schedules is fairly stated, in all material respects, in relation to the financial statements as a whole, and the form and content are presented in conformity with the Department of Labor's Rules and Regulations for Reporting and Disclosure under ERISA.

[*Signature of the auditor's firm*]

[*City and state where the auditor's report is issued*]

[*Date of the auditor's report*]

§ 703 • Reporting on Financial Statements   7043

EXHIBIT AU-C 703-2—AUDITOR'S REPORT ON FINANCIAL STATEMENTS FOR A DEFINED CONTRIBUTION RETIREMENT PLAN SUBJECT TO ERISA WHEN MANAGEMENT ELECTS AN ERISA SECTION 103(a)(3)(C) AUDIT

## INDEPENDENT AUDITOR'S REPORT

[Appropriate Addressee]

*Scope and Nature of the ERISA Section 103(a)(3)(C) Audit*

We have performed audits of the financial statements of XYZ 401(k) Plan, an employee benefit plan subject to the Employee Retirement Income Security Act of 1974 (ERISA), as permitted by ERISA Section 103(a)(3)(C) (ERISA Section 103(a)(3)(C) audit). The financial statements comprise the statements of net assets available for benefits as of December 31, 20X2 and 20X1, and the related statement of changes in net assets available for benefits for the year ended December 31, 20X2, and the related notes to the financial statements.

Management, having determined it is permissible in the circumstances, has elected to have the audits of XYZ 401(k) Plan's financial statements performed in accordance with ERISA Section 103(a)(3)(C) pursuant to 29 CFR 2520.103-8 of the Department of Labor's Rules and Regulations for Reporting and Disclosure under ERISA. As permitted by ERISA Section 103(a)(3)(C), our audits need not extend to any statements or information related to assets held for investment of the plan (investment information) by a bank or similar institution or insurance carrier that is regulated, supervised, and subject to periodic examination by a state or federal agency, provided that the statements or information regarding assets so held are prepared and certified to by the bank or similar institution or insurance carrier in accordance with 29 CFR 2520.103-5 of the Department of Labor's Rules and Regulations for Reporting and Disclosure under ERISA (qualified institution).

Management has obtained certifications from a qualified institution as of December 31, 20X5 and 20X4, and for the year ended December 31, 20X5, stating that the certified investment information, as described in Note X to the financial statements, is complete and accurate.

*Opinion*

In our opinion, based on our audits and on the procedures performed as described in the Auditor's Responsibilities for the Audit of the Financial Statements section

- the amounts and disclosures in the accompanying financial statements, other than those agreed to or derived from the certified investment information, are presented fairly, in all material respects, in accordance with accounting principles generally accepted in the United States of America.
- the information in the accompanying financial statements related to assets held by and certified to by a qualified institution agrees to, or is derived from, in all material respects, the information prepared and certified by an institution that management determined meets the requirements of ERISA Section 103(a)(3)(C).

*Basis for Opinion*

We conducted our audits in accordance with auditing standards generally accepted in the United States of America (GAAS). Our responsibilities under those standards are further described in the Auditor's Responsibilities for the Audit of the Financial Statements section of our report. We are required to be independent of XYZ 401(k) Plan and to meet our other ethical responsibilities, in accordance with the relevant ethical requirements relating to our audits. We believe that the audit evidence we have obtained is sufficient and appropriate to provide a basis for our ERISA Section 103(a)(3)(C) audit opinion.

*Responsibilities of Management for the Financial Statements*

Management is responsible for the preparation and fair presentation of the financial statements in accordance with accounting principles generally accepted in the United States of America, and for the design, implementation, and maintenance of internal control relevant to the preparation and fair presentation of financial statements that are free from material misstatement, whether due to fraud or error. Management's election of the ERISA Section 103(a)(3)(C) audit does not affect management's responsibility for the financial statements.

In preparing the financial statements, management is required to evaluate whether there are conditions or events, considered in the aggregate, that raise substantial doubt about XYZ 401(k) Plan's ability to continue as a going concern for [*insert the time period set by the applicable financial reporting framework*].

Management is also responsible for maintaining a current plan instrument, including all plan amendments, administering the plan, and determining that the plan's transactions that are presented and disclosed in the financial statements are in conformity with the plan's provisions, including maintaining sufficient records with respect to each of the participants, to determine the benefits due or which may become due to such participants.

*Auditor's Responsibilities for the Audit of the Financial Statements*

Except as described in the Scope and Nature of the ERISA Section 103(a)(3)(C) Audit section of our report, our objectives are to obtain reasonable assurance about whether the financial statements as a whole are free from material misstatement, whether due to fraud or error, and to issue an auditor's report that includes our opinion. Reasonable assurance is a high level of assurance but is not absolute assurance and therefore is not a guarantee that an audit conducted in accordance with GAAS will always detect a material misstatement when it exists. The risk of not detecting a material misstatement resulting from fraud is higher than for one resulting from error, as fraud may involve collusion, forgery, intentional omissions, misrepresentations, or the override of internal control. Misstatements are considered material if, individually or in the aggregate, they could reasonably be expected to influence the economic decisions of users made on the basis of these financial statements.

In performing an audit in accordance with GAAS, we:

- Exercise professional judgment and maintain professional skepticism throughout the audit.

- Identify and assess the risks of material misstatement of the financial statements, whether due to fraud or error, and design and perform audit procedures responsive to those risks. Such procedures include examining, on a test basis, evidence regarding the amounts and disclosures in the financial statements.

- Obtain an understanding of internal control relevant to the audit in order to design audit procedures that are appropriate in the circumstances, but not for the purpose of expressing an opinion on the effectiveness of the XYZ 401(k) Plan's internal control. Accordingly, no such opinion is expressed.
- Evaluate the appropriateness of accounting policies used and the reasonableness of significant accounting estimates made by management, as well as evaluate the overall presentation of the financial statements.
- Conclude whether, in our judgment, there are conditions or events, considered in the aggregate, that raise substantial doubt about XYZ 401(k) Plan's ability to continue as a going concern for a reasonable period of time.

Our audits did not extend to the certified investment information, except for obtaining and reading the certification, comparing the certified investment information with the related information presented and disclosed in the financial statements, and reading the disclosures relating to the certified investment information to assess whether they are in accordance with the presentation and disclosure requirements of accounting principles generally accepted in the United States of America.

Accordingly, the objective of an ERISA Section 103(a)(3)(C) audit is not to express an opinion about whether the financial statements as a whole are presented fairly, in all material respects, in accordance with accounting principles generally accepted in the United States of America.

We are required to communicate with those charged with governance regarding, among other matters, the planned scope and timing of the audit, significant audit findings, and certain internal control-related matters that we identified during the audit.

*Supplemental Schedules Required by ERISA*

The supplemental schedules of [*identify the title of supplemental schedules and periods covered*] are presented for purposes of additional analysis and are not a required part of the financial statements but are supplementary information required by the Department of Labor's Rules and Regulations for Reporting and Disclosure under ERISA. Such information is the responsibility of management and was derived from and relates directly to the underlying accounting and other records used to prepare the financial statements. The information included in the supplemental schedules, other than that agreed to or derived from the certified investment information, has been subjected to auditing procedures applied in the audits of the financial statements and certain additional procedures, including comparing and reconciling such information directly to the underlying accounting and other records used to prepare the financial statements or to the financial statements themselves, and other additional procedures in accordance with GAAS. For information included in the supplemental schedules that agreed to or is derived from the certified investment information, we compared such information to the related certified investment information.

In forming our opinion on the supplemental schedules, we evaluated whether the supplemental schedules, other than the information agreed to or derived from the certified investment information, including their form and content, are presented in conformity with the Department of Labor's Rules and Regulations for Reporting and Disclosure under ERISA.

In our opinion

- the form and content of the supplemental schedules, other than the information in the supplemental schedules that agreed to or is derived from the certified investment information, are presented, in all material respects, in conformity with the Department of Labor's Rules and Regulations for Reporting and Disclosure under ERISA.
- the information in the supplemental schedules related to assets held by4 and certified to by a qualified institution agrees to, or is derived from, in all material respects, the information prepared and certified by an institution that management determined meets the requirements of ERISA Section 103(a)(3)(C).

[Signature of the auditor's firm]

[City and state where the auditor's report is issued]

[Date of the auditor's report]

# SECTION 705

# MODIFICATIONS TO THE OPINION IN THE INDEPENDENT AUDITOR'S REPORT

## Authoritative Pronouncements

SAS-122—Statements on Auditing Standards: Clarification and Recodification

SAS-123—Omnibus Statement on Auditing Standards—2011

SAS-134—Auditor Reporting and Amendments, Including Amendments Addressing Disclosures in the Audit of Financial Statements

SAS-137—The Auditor's Responsibilities Relating to Other Information Included in Annual Reports

SAS-141—Amendment to Effective Dates of SAS Nos. 134-140

## Overview

AU-C 705 addresses the auditor's responsibilities to issue an appropriate report and clearly express an appropriately modified opinion when he or she concludes that a modification to the auditor's opinion on the financial statements is necessary. A modified opinion is necessary if the auditor concludes that the financial statements as a whole are materially misstated, or if the auditor is unable to obtain sufficient appropriate evidence to form an opinion on the financial statements. The three types of modified opinions that may be issued are a qualified opinion, adverse opinion, and disclaimer of opinion. The type of modification issued depends on the nature of the matter causing the modification and the auditor's judgment about the pervasiveness of the effects or possible effects of the matter on the financial statements.

---

**IMPORTANT NOTICE FOR 2022:** In May 2019, the AICPA's Auditing Standards Board (ASB) issued SAS No. 134 titled *Auditor Reporting and Amendments, Including Amendments Addressing Disclosures in the Audit of Financial Statements* that makes significant changes to the auditor's report, including the ability to communicate key audit matters (KAMs) in the auditor's report. SAS No. 134 amends the guidance in AU-C 705 related to modifications of the opinion in the auditor's report to conform those modifications to the new form and content of the auditor's report. Originally, the effective date of SAS No. 134 was for audits of financial statements periods ending on or after December 15, 2020, with early implementation **not** permitted. However, the ASB's issuance of SAS No. 141, *Amendment to the Effective Dates of SAS Nos. 134-140*, extended the effective date to December 15, 2021, in order to provide more time for firms to implement SAS No. 134 in light of the effect of the coronavirus pandemic. While SAS No. 141 allows for early implementation of SAS No. 134, the ASB recommends that SAS Nos. 134-140 be implemented concurrently.

**OBSERVATION:** The guidance in AU-C 706 should be followed if the auditor considers it necessary or is required to include additional communications in the auditor's report that are not audit opinion modifications.

**PUBLIC COMPANY IMPLICATIONS:** Similar to the AICPA, the PCAOB adopted in 2017 a new auditing standard AS-3101 (*The Auditor's Report on an Audit of Financial Statements When the Auditor Expresses an Unqualified Opinion*) that changed the standard unqualified opinion audit report for public companies. That new standard also made changes to the guidance that addresses explanatory language in the auditor's report and situations where the auditor departs from an unqualified opinion (i.e., qualified opinions, scope limitations, adverse opinions, disclaimers of opinion).

## Definitions

| | |
|---|---|
| Modified opinion | A qualified opinion, adverse opinion, or disclaimer of opinion |
| Pervasive | Effects or possible effects on the financial statements of misstatements that are undetected due to an inability to obtain sufficient appropriate audit evidence and in the auditor's judgment are not confined to specific financial statement elements, accounts, or items, if so confined, represent or could represent a substantial proportion of the financial statements, or are fundamental disclosures to users' understanding of the financial statements |

## Requirements

The auditor is presumptively required to perform the following procedures when deciding whether to issue a modified opinion and, if a modified opinion is to be issued, in issuing the modified opinion in the independent auditor's report:

### Audit Opinion Modifications

1. Modify the audit report opinion when:
    a. The auditor concludes that, based on the audit evidence obtained, the financial statements as a whole are materially misstated; or
    b. The auditor is unable to obtain sufficient appropriate audit evidence to conclude that the financial statements as a whole are free from material misstatement.

2. Express a qualified opinion when (1) sufficient appropriate audit evidence has been obtained to conclude that misstatements, individually or in the aggregate, are material but not pervasive to the financial statements, or (2) sufficient appropriate audit evidence is unable to be obtained on which to base the opinion, but the auditor concludes that the possible effects of undetected misstatements could be material but not pervasive to the financial statements.

3. Express an adverse opinion when sufficient appropriate audit evidence has been obtained to conclude that misstatements, individually or in the aggregate, are material and pervasive to the financial statements.

4. Disclaim an opinion when sufficient appropriate audit evidence is unable to be obtained on which to base the opinion, but the auditor concludes that the possible effects of undetected misstatements could be material and pervasive to the financial statements.

5. If, after accepting an engagement, management limits the scope of the audit such that the auditor considers the need to express a qualified opinion or to disclaim an opinion likely, request that management remove the limitation. If management refuses to remove the limitation, communicate the matter to those charged with governance (unless all of those charged with governance are part of management) and determine if it is possible to obtain sufficient appropriate audit evidence by performing alternative procedures.

6. If a management imposed limitation causes an inability to obtain sufficient appropriate audit evidence and the possible effects of undetected misstatements could be material but not pervasive to the financial statements, the auditor should qualify the opinion. If the undetected misstatements could be material and pervasive to the financial statements, the auditor should disclaim an opinion or withdraw from the audit when practicable. Before withdrawal from the audit, communicate to those charged with governance any matters regarding misstatements identified during the audit that would have caused a modification of the opinion.

7. If expressing an adverse opinion or disclaiming an opinion on the financial statements as a whole, the audit report should not include an unmodified opinion with respect to the same financial reporting framework on a single financial statement or specific financial statement element, account, or item because to do so would be contradictory.

8. If the auditor expects to modify the opinion in the auditor's report, communicate with those charged with governance the circumstances leading to the expected modification and the proposed wording of the modification.

9. If the auditor is not independent but is required by law or regulation to report on the financial statements, the auditor should disclaim an opinion and indicate that he or she is not independent. The auditor has the option as to whether or not to disclose the reason(s) for his or her lack of independence, but if the auditor discloses the reasons for a lack of independence all of the relevant reasons should be disclosed.

## *Reporting on Audit Opinion Modifications*

10. The opinion paragraph should be titled "Qualified Opinion," "Adverse Opinion," or "Disclaimer of Opinion" when the opinion is modified.

11. If the opinion is qualified due to a material misstatement in the financial statements or an inability to obtain sufficient appropriate audit evidence, the opinion paragraph should state that, in the auditor's opinion, except for the effects (possible effects if the qualification is due to lack of sufficient evidence) of the matter(s) described in the "Basis for Qualified Opinion" section of the auditor's report, the financial statements present fairly, in all material respects, in accordance with the applicable financial reporting framework.

12. If an adverse opinion is expressed, the opinion paragraph should state that, in the auditor's opinion, because of the significance of the matter(s) described in the "Basis for Adverse Opinion" section of the auditor's report, the financial statements do not present fairly in accordance with the applicable reporting framework.

13. If an opinion is disclaimed, the opinion paragraph should state that, because of the significance of the matter(s) described in the "Basis for Disclaimer of Opinion" section of the auditor's report, the auditor has not been

able to obtain sufficient appropriate audit evidence to provide a basis for an audit opinion, and, accordingly, an opinion is not expressed on the financial statements.

14. Directly before the opinion paragraph, include a basis for modification section in the audit report describing the matter giving rise to the modification appropriately entitled "Basis for Qualified Opinion," "Basis for Adverse Opinion," or "Basis for Disclaimer of Opinion." The report should also be modified to state that the auditor was engaged to audit the financial statements rather than state the financial statements have been audited.

15. The "Basis for Opinion" heading should be modified applicable to be "Basis for Qualified Opinion," "Basis for Adverse Opinion," or "Basis for Disclaimer of Opinion." This section should also include a description of the matter giving rise to the modification.

16. The basis for modification section should include a description and quantification of the financial effects of material misstatements relating to specific financial statement amounts or quantitative disclosures if practicable; or, if not practicable, that should be stated in the paragraph.

17. The basis for modification section should include an explanation of how material misstatements of financial statements related to narrative disclosures are misstated.

18. If a material financial statement misstatement relates to the omission of information required to be presented or disclosed: discuss the omission with those charged with governance; describe the nature of the omitted information in the "Basis of Opinion" section; and include the omitted information if sufficient appropriate audit evidence about the information has been obtained and it is practicable to do so.

19. If the modification is due to an inability to obtain sufficient appropriate audit evidence, the "Basis for Opinion" section should include the reasons for that inability.

20. If an adverse opinion is expressed or an opinion is disclaimed, the auditor should describe in the "Basis for Opinion" section any other matters the auditor is aware of that would have required a modification of opinion and their effects.

21. If a qualified or adverse opinion is expressed, the description of the auditor's responsibility in the audit report should be amended to state that the auditor believes that the audit evidence obtained is sufficient and appropriate to provide a basis for the auditor's modified opinion.

22. If there is a disclaimer of opinion due to an inability to obtain sufficient appropriate evidence, the auditor should amend the description of the auditor's responsibilities to reflect that while engaged to conduct an audit of the entity's financial statements, the auditor was unable to obtain sufficient appropriate audit evidence to provide a basis for an audit opinion on the financial statements.

23. If an adverse opinion or disclaimer of opinion is expressed, the auditor's report should not include a "Key Audit Matters" section.

## Analysis and Application of Procedures

### Audit Opinion Modifications

One reason for an audit opinion modification is that the auditor concludes, based on the audit evidence obtained, that the financial statements as a whole are materially misstated. This conclusion takes into account the auditor's evaluation of any uncorrected misstatements in the financial statements that were identified when following the guidance in AU-C 450. Material misstatements may be related to the appropriateness or application of the selected accounting policies or the appropriateness of the adequacy of disclosures in the financial statements or the presentation of the financial statements.

The appropriateness of the selected accounting policies is evaluated based on whether the selected policies are in accordance with the applicable financial reporting framework or the financial statements and related notes represent the underlying transactions and events in a manner achieving fair presentation. Material misstatements related to the appropriateness of accounting policies may also occur when the entity has changed accounting policies and not complied with the requirements of the applicable financial reporting framework in accounting for and disclosing this change.

Material misstatements related to the application of the selected accounting policies may occur due to the method of application (e.g., due to an unintentional error in applying the policy), or when management has not applied the selected policies in accordance with the applicable financial reporting framework, or has not applied policies consistently between periods or to similar transactions or events.

Material misstatements related to the appropriateness of financial statement presentation or adequacy of disclosures in the financial statements may occur due to several factors: the financial statements may not provide all the disclosures required by the applicable financial reporting framework or all those necessary to achieve fair presentation; the disclosures may not be presented in accordance with the applicable financial reporting framework; or information required to be presented by the applicable financial reporting framework may be omitted due to lack of a required statement or other lack of disclosure in the financial statements.

Another reason the auditor may modify the audit opinion is due to a scope limitation, or an inability to obtain sufficient appropriate audit evidence to conclude that the financial statements as a whole are free from material misstatement. A scope limitation does not arise from an inability to perform a specific procedure if the auditor is able to obtain sufficient appropriate audit evidence by performing alternative procedures. Scope limitations may arise from the following three sources:

1. *Circumstances beyond the entity's control* The entity's accounting records have been destroyed or seized indefinitely by governmental authorities.
2. *Circumstances relating to the nature or timing of the auditor's work* The timing of the auditor's appointment prevents the observation of the physical inventory count and the auditor is unable to perform other appropriate procedures, substantive procedures alone are determined to be insufficient but the entity's controls are not effective, or the auditor is unable to obtain an investee's audited financial statements when accounting for long-term investments, or the auditor is not able to obtain

sufficient appropriate audit evidence for an investee accounted for by the investor (client) using the equity method of accounting.
3. *Limitations imposed by management* Management prevents the auditor from observing the physical inventory count or from requesting external confirmation of specific account balances.

---

**PLANNING AID REMINDER:** Management limitations may have additional audit implications related to the auditor's assessment of fraud risks and consideration of engagement continuance.

---

When the auditor is unable to obtain sufficient appropriate audit evidence due to a management-imposed limitation and is considering either disclaiming an opinion or withdrawing from the engagement, his or her ability to withdraw may depend on several factors. It may not be practical to withdraw from the audit if the auditor has already substantially completed the audit and the auditor may instead decide to disclaim an opinion. In some circumstances, law or regulation or an audit appointment prohibiting withdrawal before audit completion or the end of a certain period may prevent withdrawal.

---

**OBSERVATION:** There are circumstances in which an auditor may disclaim an opinion or express an adverse opinion on certain portions of the audit and still express an unmodified opinion on other portions of the audit. The auditor may express an unmodified opinion on the financial position and disclaim an opinion on the results of operations and cash flows of an entity because this does not constitute disclaiming an opinion on the financial statements as a whole. In audits of governmental entities, the auditor expresses or disclaims an opinion for each opinion unit, so the audit report may include an unmodified opinion about one or more opinion units and a modified opinion about one or more other opinion units.

---

By communicating with those charged with governance about the circumstances leading to an expected audit opinion modification and the proposed wording of the modification: the auditor gives notice to those charged with governance of any intended modifications and the reasons for those modifications; the auditor seeks agreement of those charged with governance about the facts of the matter causing the expected modification or confirms matters of disagreement with management as such; and, those charged with governance have an opportunity to provide the auditor with further information and explanations about the matter causing the expected modification.

*Reporting on Audit Opinion Modifications*

Including a basis for modification section following the opinion section when the opinion is modified helps to promote consistency in the form and content of the audit report, which increases users' understanding and helps identify unusual circumstances when they occur. When describing the quantification of the financial effects of the material misstatement causing a modified opinion in the basis for modification section, the auditor may reference the notes to the financial statements if they include such a disclosure. As one example, if inventory is overstated, the financial effects of the material misstatements that the auditor describes in the basis for modification section may include the effects on income before taxes, income taxes, net income, and equity.

> **PLANNING AID REMINDER:** Section 1.700.001 (*Confidential Client Information*) of the AICPA Code of Professional Conduct states that the auditor should not disclose any confidential client information without the client's specific consent. The auditor uses confidential client information in the audit, but may not disclose that information unless it is required to be disclosed or presented in order for the financial statements to comply with the applicable financial reporting framework.

If an opinion is being modified because of omitted information, the auditor should include that omitted information in the report as long as it is practicable to do so. Practicable means that the information has been prepared by management or is otherwise reasonably obtainable from management's accounts and records. However, the auditor should not assume the role of a preparer of financial information—for example, the auditor should not prepare a basic financial statement that is otherwise missing.

> **OBSERVATION:** When the audit opinion is modified due to an inability to obtain sufficient appropriate audit evidence, it is not appropriate for the scope of the audit to be explained in a note to the financial statements because the description of audit scope is the auditor's responsibility, not management's.

When an audit opinion is qualified, phrases such as "with the foregoing explanation" or "subject to" are not appropriate for the opinion paragraph because they are not sufficiently clear or forceful. Wording such as "fairly presented, in all material respects, when read in conjunction with Note X" is also not appropriate because it is likely to be misunderstood. If an audit opinion is qualified due to a scope limitation, wording such as "In our opinion, except for the above-mentioned limitation on the scope of our audit" is unacceptable because it bases the qualification on the restriction rather than the possible effects on the financial statements.

## Practitioner's Aids

> **IMPORTANT NOTICE FOR 2022:** As a reminder, in May 2019, the AICPA's Auditing Standards Board (ASB) issued SAS No. 134 titled *Auditor Reporting and Amendments, Including Amendments Addressing Disclosures in the Audit of Financial Statements* that makes significant changes to the auditor's report, including the ability to communicate key audit matters (KAMs) in the auditor's report. SAS No. 134 changes the wording in the standard auditor's report and it amends the guidance in AU-C 705 related to modifications of the opinion in the auditor's report to conform those modifications to the new form and content of the auditor's report. Originally, the effective date of SAS No. 134 was for audits of financial statements periods ending on or after December 15, 2020, with early

implementation **not** permitted. However, the ASB's issuance of SAS No. 141, *Amendment to the Effective Dates of SAS Nos. 134-140*, extended the effective date to December 15, 2021, in order to provide more time for firms to implement SAS No. 134 in light of the effect of the coronavirus pandemic. While SAS No. 141 allows for early implementation of SAS No. 134, the ASB recommends that SAS Nos. 134-140 be implemented concurrently.

The following exhibits related to modified auditor's reports are presented in this section:

- Exhibit AU-C 705-1—Qualified Auditor's Report Due to Material Misstatement
- Exhibit AU-C 705-2—Qualified Auditor's Report Due to Inadequate Disclosure
- Exhibit AU-C 705-3—Adverse Auditor's Report
- Exhibit AU-C 705-4—Qualified Auditor's Report Because of a Scope Limitation
- Exhibit AU-C 705-5—Disclaimer Report
- Exhibit AU-C 705-6—Auditor's Report on Comparative Financial Statements with Unmodified Prior-Year Opinion and Modified Current-Year Opinion

Exhibits AU-C 705-1 and AU-C 705-5 provide examples of complete auditor's reports with modified opinions. Exhibits AU-C 705-2, AU-C 705-3, AU-C 705-4, and AU-C 705-6 provide examples of changes to the auditor's responsibility paragraph, the basis for modification and opinion paragraphs of auditor's reports with modified opinions.

## EXHIBIT AU-C 705-1—QUALIFIED AUDITOR'S REPORT DUE TO MATERIAL MISSTATEMENT

### INDEPENDENT AUDITOR'S REPORT

[*Appropriate Addressee*]

**Report on the Financial Statements**

We have audited the financial statements of X Company, which comprise the balance sheets as of December 31, 20X5 and 20X4, and the related statements of income, changes in stockholders' equity, and cash flows for the years then ended, and the related notes to the financial statements.

In our opinion, except for the effects of the matter described in the Basis for Qualified Opinion section of our report, the accompanying financial statements present fairly, in all material respects, the financial position of X Company as of December 31, 20X5 and 20X4, and the results of its operations and its cash flows for the years then ended in accordance with accounting principles generally accepted in the United States of America.

*Basis for Qualified Opinion*

X Company has stated inventories at cost in the accompanying balance sheets. Accounting principles generally accepted in the United States of America require inventories to be stated at the lower of cost or market. If the Company stated inventories at the lower of cost or market, a write down of $XXX and $XXX would have been required as of December 31, 20X5 and 20X4, respectively. Accordingly, cost of sales would have been increased by $XXX and $XXX, and net income, income taxes, and stockholders' equity would have been reduced by $XXX, $XXX, and $XXX, and $XXX, $XXX, and $XXX, as of and for the years ended December 31, 20X5 and 20X4, respectively.

We conducted our audits in accordance with auditing standards generally accepted in the United States of America (GAAS). Our responsibilities under those standards are further described in the Auditor's Responsibilities for the Audit of the Financial Statements section of our report. We are required to be independent of X Company and to meet our other ethical responsibilities, in accordance with the relevant ethical requirements relating to our audits. We believe that the audit evidence we have obtained is sufficient and appropriate to provide a basis for our qualified audit opinion.

*Responsibilities of Management for the Financial Statements*

Management is responsible for the preparation and fair presentation of the financial statements in accordance with accounting principles generally accepted in the United States of America, and for the design, implementation, and maintenance of internal control relevant to the preparation and fair presentation of financial statements that are free from material misstatement, whether due to fraud or error.

In preparing the financial statements, management is required to evaluate whether there are conditions or events, considered in the aggregate, that raise substantial doubt about X Company's ability to continue as a going concern for a reasonable period of time as defined by accounting principles generally accepted in the United States of America.

*Auditor's Responsibilities for the Audit of the Financial Statements*

Our objectives are to obtain reasonable assurance about whether the financial statements as a whole are free from material misstatement, whether due to fraud or error, and to issue an auditor's report that includes our opinion. Reasonable assurance is a high level of assurance but is not absolute assurance and therefore is not a guarantee that an audit conducted in accordance with GAAS will always detect a material misstatement when it exists. The risk of not detecting a material misstatement resulting from fraud is higher than for one resulting from error, as fraud may involve collusion, forgery, intentional omissions, misrepresentations, or the override of internal control. Misstatements are considered material if, individually or in the aggregate, they could reasonably be expected to influence the economic decisions of users made on the basis of these financial statements.

In performing an audit in accordance with GAAS, we:

- Exercise professional judgment and maintain professional skepticism throughout the audit.
- Identify and assess the risks of material misstatement of the financial statements, whether due to fraud or error, and design and perform audit procedures responsive to those risks. Such procedures include examin-

ing, on a test basis, evidence regarding the amounts and disclosures in the financial statements.

- Obtain an understanding of internal control relevant to the audit in order to design audit procedures that are appropriate in the circumstances, but not for the purpose of expressing an opinion on the effectiveness of X Company's internal control. Accordingly, no such opinion is expressed.
- Evaluate the appropriateness of accounting policies used and the reasonableness of significant accounting estimates made by management, as well as evaluate the overall presentation of the financial statements.
- Conclude whether, in our judgment, there are conditions or events, considered in the aggregate, that raise substantial doubt about X Company's ability to continue as a going concern for a reasonable period of time.

We are required to communicate with those charged with governance regarding, among other matters, the planned scope and timing of the audit, significant audit findings, and certain internal control–related matters that we identified during the audit.

*Other Information [Included in the Annual Report]*

Management is responsible for the other information [*included in the annual report*]. The other information comprises the [*information included in the annual report*] but does not include the financial statements and our auditor's report thereon. Our opinion on the financial statements does not cover the other information, and we do not express an opinion or any form of assurance thereon.

In connection with our audit of the financial statements, our responsibility is to read the other information and consider whether a material inconsistency exists between the other information and the financial statements, or the other information otherwise appears to be materially misstated. If, based on the work performed, we conclude that an uncorrected material misstatement of the other information exists, we are required to describe it in our report.

*Report on Other Legal and Regulatory Requirements*

[*Form and content of this section of the auditor's report will vary depending on the nature of the auditor's other reporting responsibilities.*]

[*Auditor's firm signature*]

[*Auditor's city and state*]

[*Date of the auditor's report*]

## EXHIBIT AU-C 705-2—QUALIFIED AUDITOR'S REPORT DUE TO INADEQUATE DISCLOSURE

### Report on the Audit of the Financial Statements

*Qualified Opinion*

We have audited the financial statements of X Company, which comprise the balance sheets as of December 31, 20X5 and 20X4, and the related statements of income, changes in stockholders' equity, and cash flows for the years then ended, and the related notes to the financial statements.

In our opinion, except for the omission of the information described in the Basis for Qualified Opinion section of our report, the accompanying financial statements present fairly, in all material respects, the financial position of X Company as of December 31, 20X1 and 20X0, and the results of its operations and its cash flows for the years then ended in accordance with accounting principles generally accepted in the United States of America.

*Basis for Qualified Opinion*

X Company's financial statements do not disclose [*describe the nature of the omitted information that is not practicable to present in the auditor's report*]. In our opinion, disclosure of this information is required by accounting principles generally accepted in the United States of America.

We conducted our audits in accordance with auditing standards generally accepted in the United States of America (GAAS). Our responsibilities under those standards are further described in the Auditor's Responsibilities for the Audit of the Financial Statements section of our report. We are required to be independent of X Company and to meet our other ethical responsibilities, in accordance with the relevant ethical requirements relating to our audits. We believe that the audit evidence we have obtained is sufficient and appropriate to provide a basis for our qualified audit opinion.

*Responsibilities of Management for the Financial Statements*

Management is responsible for the preparation and fair presentation of the financial statements in accordance with accounting principles generally accepted in the United States of America, and for the design, implementation, and maintenance of internal control relevant to the preparation and fair presentation of financial statements that are free from material misstatement, whether due to fraud or error.

In preparing the financial statements, management is required to evaluate whether there are conditions or events, considered in the aggregate, that raise substantial doubt about X Company's ability to continue as a going concern for a reasonable period of time as defined by accounting principles generally accepted in the United States of America.

*Auditor's Responsibilities for the Audit of the Financial Statements*

Our objectives are to obtain reasonable assurance about whether the financial statements as a whole are free from material misstatement, whether due to fraud or error, and to issue an auditor's report that includes our opinion. Reasonable assurance is a high level of assurance but is not absolute assurance and therefore is not a guarantee that an audit conducted in accordance with GAAS will always detect a material misstatement when it exists. The risk of not detecting a material misstatement resulting from fraud is higher than for one resulting from error, as fraud may involve collusion, forgery, intentional omissions, misrepresentations, or the override of internal control. Misstatements are considered material if, individually or in the aggregate, they could reasonably be expected to influence the economic decisions of users made on the basis of these financial statements.

In performing an audit in accordance with GAAS, we:

- Exercise professional judgment and maintain professional skepticism throughout the audit.
- Identify and assess the risks of material misstatement of the financial statements, whether due to fraud or error, and design and perform audit

procedures responsive to those risks. Such procedures include examining, on a test basis, evidence regarding the amounts and disclosures in the financial statements.

- Obtain an understanding of internal control relevant to the audit in order to design audit procedures that are appropriate in the circumstances, but not for the purpose of expressing an opinion on the effectiveness of X Company's internal control. Accordingly, no such opinion is expressed.
- Evaluate the appropriateness of accounting policies used and the reasonableness of significant accounting estimates made by management, as well as evaluate the overall presentation of the financial statements.
- Conclude whether, in our judgment, there are conditions or events, considered in the aggregate, that raise substantial doubt about X Company's ability to continue as a going concern for a reasonable period of time.

We are required to communicate with those charged with governance regarding, among other matters, the planned scope and timing of the audit, significant audit findings, and certain internal control–related matters that we identified during the audit.

*Other Information [Included in the Annual Report]*

Management is responsible for the other information [*included in the annual report*]. The other information comprises the [*information included in the annual report*] but does not include the financial statements and our auditor's report thereon. Our opinion on the financial statements does not cover the other information, and we do not express an opinion or any form of assurance thereon.

In connection with our audit of the financial statements, our responsibility is to read the other information and consider whether a material inconsistency exists between the other information and the financial statements, or the other information otherwise appears to be materially misstated. If, based on the work performed, we conclude that an uncorrected material misstatement of the other information exists, we are required to describe it in our report.

*Report on Other Legal and Regulatory Requirements*

[*Form and content of this section of the auditor's report will vary depending on the nature of the auditor's other reporting responsibilities.*]

[*Auditor's firm signature*]

[*Auditor's city and state*]

[*Date of the auditor's report*]

## EXHIBIT AU-C 705-3—ADVERSE AUDITOR'S REPORT

**Report on the Audit of the Consolidated Financial Statements**

*Adverse Opinion*

We have audited the consolidated financial statements of X Company and its subsidiaries, which comprise the consolidated balance sheet as of December 31, 20X5, and the related consolidated statements of income, changes in stockholders' equity, and cash flows for the year then ended, and the related notes to the financial statements.

In our opinion, because of the significance of the matter discussed in the Basis for Adverse Opinion section of our report, the accompanying consolidated financial statements do not present fairly the financial position of X Company and its subsidiaries as of December 31, 20X5, or the results of their operations or their cash flows for the year then ended in accordance with accounting principles generally accepted in the United States of America.

*Basis for Adverse Opinion*

As described in Note #, X Company has not consolidated the financial statements of subsidiary ABC Company that it acquired during 20X5 because it has not yet been able to ascertain the fair values of certain of the subsidiary's material assets and liabilities at the acquisition date. This investment is therefore accounted for on a cost basis by the Company. Under accounting principles generally accepted in the United States of America, the subsidiary should have been consolidated because it is controlled by the Company. Had ABC Company been consolidated, many elements in the accompanying consolidated financial statements would have been materially affected. The effects on the consolidated financial statements of the failure to consolidate have not been determined. We believe that the audit evidence we have obtained is sufficient and appropriate to provide a basis for our qualified audit opinion.

*Responsibilities of Management for the Financial Statements*

Management is responsible for the preparation and fair presentation of the consolidated financial statements in accordance with accounting principles generally accepted in the United States of America, and for the design, implementation, and maintenance of internal control relevant to the preparation and fair presentation of consolidated financial statements that are free from material misstatement, whether due to fraud or error.

In preparing the consolidated financial statements, management is required to evaluate whether there are conditions or events, considered in the aggregate, that raise substantial doubt about X Company's ability to continue as a going concern for a reasonable period of time as defined by accounting principles generally accepted in the United States of America.

*Auditor's Responsibilities for the Audit of the Financial Statements*

Our objectives are to obtain reasonable assurance about whether the consolidated financial statements as a whole are free from material misstatement, whether due to fraud or error, and to issue an auditor's report that includes our opinion. Reasonable assurance is a high level of assurance but is not absolute assurance and therefore is not a guarantee that an audit conducted in accordance with GAAS will always detect a material misstatement when it exists. The risk of not detecting a material misstatement resulting from fraud is higher than for one resulting from error, as fraud may involve collusion, forgery, intentional omissions, misrepresentations, or the override of internal control. Misstatements are considered material if, individually or in the aggregate, they could reasonably be expected to influence the economic decisions of users made on the basis of these consolidated financial statements.

In performing an audit in accordance with GAAS, we:

- Exercise professional judgment and maintain professional skepticism throughout the audit.
- Identify and assess the risks of material misstatement of the consolidated financial statements, whether due to fraud or error, and design and perform audit procedures responsive to those risks. Such procedures include examining, on a test basis, evidence regarding the amounts and disclosures in the financial statements.
- Obtain an understanding of internal control relevant to the audit in order to design audit procedures that are appropriate in the circumstances, but not for the purpose of expressing an opinion on the effectiveness of X Company's internal control. Accordingly, no such opinion is expressed.
- Evaluate the appropriateness of accounting policies used and the reasonableness of significant accounting estimates made by management, as well as evaluate the overall presentation of the consolidated financial statements.
- Conclude whether, in our judgment, there are conditions or events, considered in the aggregate, that raise substantial doubt about X Company's ability to continue as a going concern for a reasonable period of time.

We are required to communicate with those charged with governance regarding, among other matters, the planned scope and timing of the audit, significant audit findings, and certain internal control–related matters that we identified during the audit.

*Other Information [Included in the Annual Report]*

Management is responsible for the other information [*included in the annual report*]. The other information comprises the [*information included in the annual report*] but does not include the financial statements and our auditor's report thereon. Our opinion on the financial statements does not cover the other information, and we do not express an opinion or any form of assurance thereon.

In connection with our audit of the financial statements, our responsibility is to read the other information and consider whether a material inconsistency exists between the other information and the financial statements, or the other information otherwise appears to be materially misstated. If, based on the work performed, we conclude that an uncorrected material misstatement of the other information exists, we are required to describe it in our report.

*Report on Other Legal and Regulatory Requirements*

[*Form and content of this section of the auditor's report will vary depending on the nature of the auditor's other reporting responsibilities.*]

[*Auditor's firm signature*]

[*Auditor's city and state*]

[*Date of the auditor's report*]

EXHIBIT AU-C 705-4—QUALIFIED AUDITOR'S REPORT BECAUSE OF A SCOPE LIMITATION

## Report on the Audit of the Financial Statements

*Qualified Opinion*

We have audited the financial statements of X Company, which comprise the balance sheet as of December 31, 20X5, and the related statements of income, changes in stockholders' equity, and cash flows for the year then ended, and the related notes to the financial statements.

In our opinion, except for the possible effects of the matter described in the Basis for Qualified Opinion section of our report, the accompanying financial statements present fairly, in all material respects, the financial position of X Company as of December 31, 20X5, and the results of its operations and its cash flows for the year then ended in accordance with accounting principles generally accepted in the United States of America.

*Basis for Qualified Opinion*

X Company's investment in ABC Company, a foreign affiliate acquired during the year and accounted for under the equity method, is carried at $XXX on the balance sheet at December 31, 20X5, and X Company's share of ABC Company's net income of $XXX is included in X Company's net income for the year then ended. We were unable to obtain sufficient appropriate audit evidence about the carrying amount of X Company's investment in ABC Company as of December 31, 20X5, and X Company's share of ABC Company's net income for the year then ended because we were denied access to the financial information, management, and the auditors of ABC Company. Consequently, we were unable to determine whether any adjustments to these amounts were necessary.

We conducted our audit in accordance with auditing standards generally accepted in the United States of America (GAAS). Our responsibilities under those standards are further described in the Auditor's Responsibilities for the Audit of the Financial Statements section of our report. We are required to be independent of X Company and to meet our other ethical responsibilities, in accordance with the relevant ethical requirements relating to our audit. We believe that the audit evidence we have obtained is sufficient and appropriate to provide a basis for our qualified audit opinion.

*Responsibilities of Management for the Financial Statements*

Management is responsible for the preparation and fair presentation of the financial statements in accordance with accounting principles generally accepted in the United States of America, and for the design, implementation, and maintenance of internal control relevant to the preparation and fair presentation of financial statements that are free from material misstatement, whether due to fraud or error.

In preparing the financial statements, management is required to evaluate whether there are conditions or events, considered in the aggregate, that raise substantial doubt about X Company's ability to continue as a going concern for a reasonable period of time as defined by accounting principles generally accepted in the United States of America.

*Auditor's Responsibilities for the Audit of the Financial Statements*

Our objectives are to obtain reasonable assurance about whether the financial statements as a whole are free from material misstatement, whether due to fraud or error, and to issue an auditor's report that includes our opinion. Reasonable assurance is a high level of assurance but is not absolute assurance and therefore is not a guarantee that an audit conducted in accordance with GAAS will always detect a material misstatement when it exists. The risk of not detecting a material misstatement resulting from fraud is higher than for one resulting from error, as fraud may involve collusion, forgery, intentional omissions, misrepresentations, or the override of internal control. Misstatements are considered material if, individually or in the aggregate, they could reasonably be expected to influence the economic decisions of users made on the basis of these financial statements.

In performing an audit in accordance with GAAS, we:

- Exercise professional judgment and maintain professional skepticism throughout the audit.
- Identify and assess the risks of material misstatement of the financial statements, whether due to fraud or error, and design and perform audit procedures responsive to those risks. Such procedures include examining, on a test basis, evidence regarding the amounts and disclosures in the financial statements.
- Obtain an understanding of internal control relevant to the audit in order to design audit procedures that are appropriate in the circumstances, but not for the purpose of expressing an opinion on the effectiveness of X Company's internal control. Accordingly, no such opinion is expressed.
- Evaluate the appropriateness of accounting policies used and the reasonableness of significant accounting estimates made by management, as well as evaluate the overall presentation of the financial statements.
- Conclude whether, in our judgment, there are conditions or events, considered in the aggregate, that raise substantial doubt about X Company's ability to continue as a going concern for a reasonable period of time.

We are required to communicate with those charged with governance regarding, among other matters, the planned scope and timing of the audit, significant audit findings, and certain internal control–related matters that we identified during the audit.

*Other Information [Included in the Annual Report]*

Management is responsible for the other information [*included in the annual report*]. The other information comprises the [*information included in the annual report*] but does not include the financial statements and our auditor's report thereon. Our opinion on the financial statements does not cover the other information, and we do not express an opinion or any form of assurance thereon.

In connection with our audit of the financial statements, our responsibility is to read the other information and consider whether a material inconsistency exists between the other information and the financial statements, or the other information otherwise appears to be materially misstated. If, based on the work performed, we conclude that an uncorrected material misstatement of the other information exists, we are required to describe it in our report.

Report on Other Legal and Regulatory Requirements

[Form and content of this section of the auditor's report will vary depending on the nature of the auditor's other reporting responsibilities.]

[Auditor's firm signature]

[Auditor's city and state]

[Date of the auditor's report]

---

EXHIBIT AU-C 705-5—DISCLAIMER REPORT

---

### INDEPENDENT AUDITOR'S REPORT

[Appropriate Addressee]

**Report on the Audit of the Financial Statements**

*Disclaimer of Opinion*

We were engaged to audit the financial statements of X Company, which comprise the balance sheet as of December 31, 20X5, and the related statements of income, changes in stockholders' equity, and cash flows for the year then ended, and the related notes to the financial statements.

We do not express an opinion on the accompanying financial statements of X Company. Because of the significance of the matter described in the Basis for Disclaimer of Opinion section of our report, we have not been able to obtain sufficient appropriate audit evidence to provide a basis for an audit opinion on the financial statements.

*Basis for Disclaimer of Opinion*

X Company's investment in ABC Company, a joint venture, is carried at $XXX on the Company's balance sheet, which represents over 90 percent of the Company's net assets as of December 31, 20X5. We were not allowed access to the management and the auditors of ABC Company. As a result, we were unable to determine whether any adjustments were necessary relating to the Company's proportional share of ABC Company's assets that it controls jointly, its proportional share of ABC Company's liabilities for which it is jointly responsible, its proportional share of ABC Company's income and expenses for the year, and the elements making up the statements of changes in stockholders' equity and cash flows.

*Responsibilities of Management for the Financial Statements*

Management is responsible for the preparation and fair presentation of the financial statements in accordance with accounting principles generally accepted in the United States of America, and for the design, implementation, and maintenance of internal control relevant to the preparation and fair presentation of financial statements that are free from material misstatement, whether due to fraud or error.

In preparing the financial statements, management is required to evaluate whether there are conditions or events, considered in the aggregate, that raise substantial doubt about X Company's ability to continue as a going concern for a reasonable period of time as defined by accounting principles generally accepted in the United States of America.

*Auditor's Responsibilities for the Audit of the Financial Statements*

Our responsibility is to conduct an audit of X Company's financial statements in accordance with auditing standards generally accepted in the United States of America and to issue an auditor's report. However, because of the matter described in the Basis for Disclaimer of Opinion section of our report, we were not able to obtain sufficient appropriate audit evidence to provide a basis for an audit opinion on these financial statements.

We are required to be independent of X Company and to meet our other ethical responsibilities, in accordance with the relevant ethical requirements relating to our audit.

*Report on Other Legal and Regulatory Requirements*

[Form and content of this section of the auditor's report will vary depending on the nature of the auditor's other reporting responsibilities.]

[Auditor's firm signature]

[Auditor's city and state]

[Date of the auditor's report]

---

## EXHIBIT AU-C 705-6—AUDITOR'S REPORT ON COMPARATIVE FINANCIAL STATEMENTS WITH UNMODIFIED PRIOR-YEAR OPINION AND MODIFIED CURRENT-YEAR OPINION

### Report on the Audit of the Financial Statements

*Qualified Opinion*

We have audited the financial statements of X Company, which comprise the balance sheets as of December 31, 20X5 and 20X4, and the related statements of income, changes in stockholders' equity, and cash flows for the years then ended, and the related notes to the financial statements.

In our opinion, except for the effects on the accompanying 20X1 financial statements of not capitalizing certain lease obligations as described in the Basis for Qualified Opinion section of our report, the financial statements present fairly, in all material respects, the financial position of X Company as of December 31, 20X5 and 20X4, and the results of its operations and its cash flows for the years then ended in accordance with accounting principles generally accepted in the United States of America.

*Basis for Qualified Opinion on the 20X5 Financial Statements*

X Company has excluded, from property and debt in the accompanying 20X5 balance sheet, certain lease obligations that were entered into in 20X5 that, in our opinion, should be capitalized in accordance with accounting principles generally accepted in the United States of America. If these lease obligations were capitalized, property would be increased by $XXX, long-term debt by $XXX, and retained earnings by $XXX as of December 31, 20X5, and net income and earnings per share would be increased (decreased) by $XXX and $XXX, respectively, for the year then ended.

We conducted our audits in accordance with auditing standards generally accepted in the United States of America (GAAS). Our responsibilities under those standards are further described in the Auditor's Responsibilities for the Audit of the Financial Statements section of our report. We are required to be independent of X Company and to meet our other ethical responsibilities, in accordance with the relevant ethical requirements relating to our audit. We believe that the audit evidence we have obtained is sufficient and appropriate to provide a basis for our qualified audit opinion on the 20X5 financial statements and for our opinion on the 20X4 financial statements.

*Responsibilities of Management for the Financial Statements*

Management is responsible for the preparation and fair presentation of the financial statements in accordance with accounting principles generally accepted in the United States of America, and for the design, implementation, and maintenance of internal control relevant to the preparation and fair presentation of financial statements that are free from material misstatement, whether due to fraud or error.

In preparing the financial statements, management is required to evaluate whether there are conditions or events, considered in the aggregate, that raise substantial doubt about X Company's ability to continue as a going concern for a reasonable period of time as defined by accounting principles generally accepted in the United States of America.

*Auditor's Responsibilities for the Audit of the Financial Statements*

Our objectives are to obtain reasonable assurance about whether the financial statements as a whole are free from material misstatement, whether due to fraud or error, and to issue an auditor's report that includes our opinion. Reasonable assurance is a high level of assurance but is not absolute assurance and therefore is not a guarantee that an audit conducted in accordance with GAAS will always detect a material misstatement when it exists. The risk of not detecting a material misstatement resulting from fraud is higher than for one resulting from error, as fraud may involve collusion, forgery, intentional omissions, misrepresentations, or the override of internal control. Misstatements are considered material if, individually or in the aggregate, they could reasonably be expected to influence the economic decisions of users made on the basis of these financial statements.

In performing an audit in accordance with GAAS, we:

- Exercise professional judgment and maintain professional skepticism throughout the audit.
- Identify and assess the risks of material misstatement of the financial statements, whether due to fraud or error, and design and perform audit procedures responsive to those risks. Such procedures include examining, on a test basis, evidence regarding the amounts and disclosures in the financial statements.
- Obtain an understanding of internal control relevant to the audit in order to design audit procedures that are appropriate in the circumstances, but not for the purpose of expressing an opinion on the effectiveness of X Company's internal control. Accordingly, no such opinion is expressed.
- Evaluate the appropriateness of accounting policies used and the reasonableness of significant accounting estimates made by management, as well as evaluate the overall presentation of the financial statements.

- Conclude whether, in our judgment, there are conditions or events, considered in the aggregate, that raise substantial doubt about X Company's ability to continue as a going concern for a reasonable period of time.

We are required to communicate with those charged with governance regarding, among other matters, the planned scope and timing of the audit, significant audit findings, and certain internal control–related matters that we identified during the audit.

Report on Other Legal and Regulatory Requirements

[*Form and content of this section of the auditor's report will vary depending on the nature of the auditor's other reporting responsibilities.*]

[*Auditor's firm signature*]

[*Auditor's city and state*]

[*Date of the auditor's report*]

# SECTION 706

## EMPHASIS-OF-MATTER PARAGRAPHS AND OTHER-MATTER PARAGRAPHS IN THE INDEPENDENT AUDITOR'S REPORT

### Authoritative Pronouncements

SAS-122—Statements on Auditing Standards: Clarification and Recodification

SAS-134—Auditor Reporting and Amendments, Including Amendments Addressing Disclosures in the Audit of Financial Statements

SAS-137—The Auditor's Responsibilities Relating to Other Information Included in Annual Reports

SAS-140—Amendments to AU-C Sections 725, 730, 930, 935, and 940 to Incorporate Auditor Reporting Changes from SAS Nos. 134 and 137

SAS-141—Amendment to Effective Dates of SAS Nos. 134-140

### Overview

AU-C 706 provides the auditor with guidance on the use of emphasis-of-matter paragraphs and other-matter paragraphs in the auditor's report. These paragraphs are additional communications included when the auditor judges it is necessary to, in an emphasis-of-matter paragraph, draw users' attention to a matter that is appropriately presented or disclosed in the financial statements but is of such importance that it is fundamental to users' understanding of the financial statements or, in an other-matter paragraph, to draw users' attention to any other-matter relevant to users' understanding of the audit, the auditor's responsibilities, or the auditor's report as appropriate.

Some AU-Cs contain specific requirements for the auditor to include an emphasis-of-matter paragraph or other-matter paragraph in the auditor's report. See Exhibit AU-C 706-1 for a listing of these AU-Cs. The guidance in AU-C 706 applies regarding the form and placement of these required paragraphs.

---

**OBSERVATION:** AU-C 706 addresses emphasis-of-matter paragraphs and other-matter paragraphs included due to the auditor's judgment; however, the other AU-Cs listed in Exhibit AU-C 706-1 require the use of emphasis-of-matter and other-matter paragraphs and do not leave their inclusion up to the auditor's discretion.

---

**IMPORTANT NOTICE FOR 2022:** In May 2019, the AICPA's Auditing Standards Board (ASB) issued SAS No. 134 titled *Auditor Reporting and Amendments, Including Amendments Addressing Disclosures in the Audit of Financial Statements* that makes significant changes to the auditor's report, including the ability to communicate key audit matters (KAMs) in the auditor's report. SAS No. 134

also includes amendments to conform guidance in AU-C 706 to clarify the relationship between emphasis-of-matter paragraphs and the communications of KAMs in the auditor's report. The new standard notes that the use of an emphasis-of-matter paragraph is not a substitute for a description of individual KAMs. It also requires the auditor to use appropriate heading for an emphasis-of-matter paragraph that includes the term "Emphasis of Matter." Originally, the effective date of SAS No. 134 was for audits of financial statements periods ending on or after December 15, 2020, with early implementation **not** permitted. However, the ASB's issuance of SAS No. 141, *Amendment to the Effective Dates of SAS Nos. 134-140*, extended the effective date to December 15, 2021, in order to provide more time for firms to implement SAS No. 134 in light of the effect of the coronavirus pandemic. While SAS No. 141 allows for early implementation of SAS No. 134, the ASB recommends that SAS Nos. 134-140 be implemented concurrently.

---

**PUBLIC COMPANY IMPLICATIONS:** Similar to the AICPA, the PCAOB adopted in 2017 a new auditing standard AS-3101 (*The Auditor's Report on an Audit of Financial Statements When the Auditor Expresses an Unqualified Opinion*) that changed the standard unqualified opinion audit report for public companies. That standard also made changes to the guidance that addresses explanatory language in the auditor's report and situations where the auditor departs from an unqualified opinion (i.e., qualified opinions, scope limitations, adverse opinions, disclaimers of opinion).

---

## Definitions

| | |
|---|---|
| Emphasis-of-matter paragraph | A paragraph included in the auditor's report at the auditor's discretion or as required by GAAS that refers to a matter appropriately presented or disclosed in the financial statements that, in the auditor's judgment, is of such importance that it is fundamental to users' understanding of the financial statements. |
| Other-matter paragraph | A paragraph included in the auditor's report at the auditor's discretion or as required by GAAS that refers to a matter other than those presented or disclosed in the financial statements that, in the auditor's judgment, is relevant to users' understanding of the audit, the auditor's responsibilities, or the auditor's report. |

## Requirements

The auditor is presumptively required to perform the following procedures when including an emphasis-of-matter paragraph or other-matter paragraph in the auditor's report:

1. An emphasis-of-matter paragraph should be included only if sufficient appropriate audit evidence has been obtained that the matter is not materially misstated in the financial statements and should refer only to information presented or disclosed in the financial statements.

2. An emphasis-of-matter paragraph should: (1) be included within a separate section of the auditor's report with an appropriate heading such as "Emphasis

of Matter," (2) clearly reference the matter being emphasized and where relevant disclosures fully describing the matter can be found in the financial statements, and (3) state that the auditor's opinion is not modified regarding the emphasized matter.

3. An other-matter paragraph should be in a separate section with a heading such as "Other Matter," provided that the matter is not deemed to be a key audit matter to be communicated in the auditor's report.

4. If the auditor expects to include an emphasis-of-matter or other-matter paragraph in the report, communicate this expectation and the paragraph's proposed wording with those charged with governance.

## Analysis and Application of Procedures

*Relationship between Key Audit Matters and Emphasis-of-Matter Paragraphs*

Key audit matters are selected from matters communicated with those charged with governance, which include significant findings from the audit of the financial statements. When the auditor is engaged to communicate key audit matters in the auditor's report, the use of emphasis-of-matter paragraphs cannot be a substitute for the description of the key audit matter.

*Emphasis-of-Matter Paragraph*

The following are matters that the auditor may want to emphasize (in addition to those matters in Exhibit AU-C 706-1 that are required to be emphasized):

- There is uncertainty as to the future outcome of exceptional litigation or regulatory action.
- A major catastrophe has had or continues to have a significant effect on the entity's financial position.
- There have been significant transactions with a related party.
- A significant subsequent event has taken place.

---

**PLANNING AID REMINDER:** An emphasis-of-matter paragraph should not contain more information than the related financial statement presentation or disclosure because this may imply that the matter was not appropriately presented or disclosed.

---

Including an emphasis-of-matter paragraph does not affect the auditor's opinion and does not act as a substitute for either (1) the auditor expressing a qualified or adverse opinion or disclaiming an opinion when required or (2) financial statement disclosures that the applicable financial reporting framework requires management to make.

The placement of the emphasis-of-matter paragraph depends on the nature of the information to be communicated and the auditor's judgment about the relative significance of such information to the intended users compared to other elements required to be reported.

### Other-Matter Paragraph

There are several circumstances in which inclusion of an other-matter paragraph may be necessary or desired. When the auditor is unable to withdraw from an engagement even though the possible effect of a management-imposed scope limitation is pervasive, an other-matter paragraph may be needed to explain why withdrawal is not permitted. If the auditor reports on two sets of financial statements prepared by the same entity in accordance with different financial reporting frameworks, an other-matter paragraph may be included referring to the entity's preparation of another set of financial statements in accordance with another general purpose framework and the auditor's issuance of a report on those financial statements. Further explanation of the auditor's responsibilities or of the auditor's report may be included in an other-matter paragraph where required or permitted by law, regulation, or generally accepted practice.

---

**PLANNING AID REMINDER:** An other-matter paragraph is not used to address an auditor's additional reporting responsibilities in addition to the responsibilities under GAAS to report on the financial statements, an auditor's performance of and reporting on additional specified procedures, or the expression of an opinion on specific matters.

---

An other-matter paragraph clearly indicates that the matter discussed is not required to be presented and disclosed in the financial statements. Information that should not be included in an other-matter paragraph includes information the auditor is prohibited by law, regulation, or other professional standards from including or information that is required to be provided by management.

The placement of an other-matter paragraph in the auditor's report depends on the nature of the information being communicated.

---

**PLANNING AID REMINDER:** If an other-matter paragraph on a particular matter continues to recur on successive engagements, the auditor may determine it is unnecessary to repeat the required communications with those charged with governance on each engagement.

---

## Practitioner's Aids

---

**IMPORTANT NOTICE FOR 2022:** As a reminder, in May 2019, the AICPA's Auditing Standards Board (ASB) issued SAS No. 134 titled *Auditor Reporting and Amendments, Including Amendments Addressing Disclosures in the Audit of Financial Statements* that makes significant changes to the auditor's report, including the ability to communicate key audit matters (KAMs) in the auditor's report. SAS No. 134 changes the wording in the standard auditor's report. SAS No. 134 also includes amendments to conform guidance in AU-C 706 to clarify the relationship between emphasis-of-matter paragraphs and the communications of KAMs in the auditor's report and to conform the reporting the language to the new form of auditor's report. Originally, the effective date of SAS No. 134 was for audits of financial statements periods ending on or after December 15,

2020, with early implementation **not** permitted. However, the ASB's issuance of SAS No. 141, *Amendment to the Effective Dates of SAS Nos. 134-140*, extended the effective date to December 15, 2021, in order to provide more time for firms to implement SAS No. 134 in light of the effect of the coronavirus pandemic. While SAS No. 141 allows for early implementation of SAS No. 134, the ASB recommends that SAS Nos. 134-140 be implemented concurrently.

## EXHIBIT AU-C 706-1—AUDITING STANDARDS REQUIRING EMPHASIS-OF-MATTER PARAGRAPHS AND OTHER-MATTER PARAGRAPHS

### AU-Cs with Requirements for Emphasis-of-matter Paragraphs

- AU-C 560, *Subsequent Events and Subsequently Discovered Facts* (paragraph 16c)
- AU-C 703, *Forming an Opinion and Reporting on Financial Statements of Employee Benefit Plans Subject to ERISA* (paragraph 92)
- AU-C 708, *Consistency of Financial Statements* (paragraphs 8–9 and 11–13)
- AU-C 800, *Special Considerations—Audits of Financial Statements Prepared in Accordance with Special Purpose Frameworks* (paragraphs 19 and 21)

### AU-Cs with Requirements for Other-matter Paragraphs

- AU-C 560, *Subsequent Events and Subsequently Discovered Facts* (paragraph 16c)
- AU-C 700, *Forming an Opinion and Reporting on Financial Statements* (paragraphs 55–56 and 58–59)
- AU-C 703, *Forming an Opinion and Reporting on Financial Statements of Employee Benefit Plans Subject to ERISA* (paragraphs 53, 92–93, 95–96, 120, and 132)
- AU-C 800, *Special Considerations—Audits of Financial Statements Prepared in Accordance with Special Purpose Frameworks* (paragraph 20)
- AU-C 806, *Reporting on Compliance with Aspects of Contractual Agreements or Regulatory Requirements in Connection with Audited Financial Statements* (paragraph 13)
- AU-C 905, *Alert that Restricts the Use of the Auditor's Written Communication* (paragraph 1)

## EXHIBIT AU-C 706-2—AUDITOR'S REPORT WITH EMPHASIS-OF-MATTER PARAGRAPH

### INDEPENDENT AUDITOR'S REPORT

[*Appropriate Addressee*]

**Report on the Audit of the Financial Statements**

*Opinion*

We have audited the financial statements of X Company, which comprise the balance sheet as of December 31, 20X5, and the related statements of income, changes in stockholders' equity, and cash flows for the year then ended, and the related notes to the financial statements.

In our opinion, the accompanying financial statements present fairly, in all material respects the financial position of X Company as of December 31, 20X5, and the results of its operations and its cash flows for the year then ended in accordance with accounting principles generally accepted in the United States of America.

*Basis for Opinion*

We conducted our audit in accordance with auditing standards generally accepted in the United States of America (GAAS). Our responsibilities under those standards are further described in the Auditor's Responsibilities for the Audit of the Financial Statements section of our report. We are required to be independent of X Company and to meet our other ethical responsibilities, in accordance with the relevant ethical requirements relating to our audit. We believe that the audit evidence we have obtained is sufficient and appropriate to provide a basis for our audit opinion.

*Emphasis of Matter*

As discussed in Note # to the financial statements, X Company is a defendant in a lawsuit [*briefly describe the nature of the litigation consistent with the Company's description in the note to the financial statements*]. Our opinion is not modified with respect to this matter.

*Responsibilities of Management for the Financial Statements*

Management is responsible for the preparation and fair presentation of the financial statements in accordance with accounting principles generally accepted in the United States of America, and for the design, implementation, and maintenance of internal control relevant to the preparation and fair presentation of financial statements that are free from material misstatement, whether due to fraud or error.

In preparing the financial statements, management is required to evaluate whether there are conditions or events, considered in the aggregate, that raise substantial doubt about X Company's ability to continue as a going concern for a reasonable period of time as defined by accounting principles generally accepted in the United States of America.

*Auditor's Responsibilities for the Audit of the Financial Statements*

Our objectives are to obtain reasonable assurance about whether the financial statements as a whole are free from material misstatement, whether due to fraud or error, and to issue an auditor's report that includes our opinion. Reasonable assurance is a high level of assurance but is not absolute assurance and therefore is not a guarantee that an audit conducted in accordance with GAAS will always detect a material misstatement when it exists. The risk of not detecting a material misstatement resulting from fraud is higher than for one resulting from error, as fraud may involve collusion, forgery, intentional omissions, misrepresentations, or the override of internal control. Misstatements are considered material if, individually or in the aggregate, they could reasonably be expected to influence the economic decisions of users made on the basis of these financial statements.

In performing an audit in accordance with GAAS, we:

- Exercise professional judgment and maintain professional skepticism throughout the audit.
- Identify and assess the risks of material misstatement of the financial statements, whether due to fraud or error, and design and perform audit procedures responsive to those risks. Such procedures include examining, on a test basis, evidence regarding the amounts and disclosures in the financial statements.
- Obtain an understanding of internal control relevant to the audit in order to design audit procedures that are appropriate in the circumstances, but not for the purpose of expressing an opinion on the effectiveness of X Company's internal control. Accordingly, no such opinion is expressed.
- Evaluate the appropriateness of accounting policies used and the reasonableness of significant accounting estimates made by management, as well as evaluate the overall presentation of the financial statements.
- Conclude whether, in our judgment, there are conditions or events, considered in the aggregate, that raise substantial doubt about X Company's ability to continue as a going concern for a reasonable period of time.

We are required to communicate with those charged with governance regarding, among other matters, the planned scope and timing of the audit, significant audit findings, and certain internal control–related matters that we identified during the audit.

*Report on Other Legal and Regulatory Requirements*

[*Form and content of this section of the auditor's report will vary depending on the nature of the auditor's other reporting responsibilities.*]

[*Auditor's firm signature*]

[*Auditor's city and state*]

[*Date of the auditor's report*]

---

## EXHIBIT AU-C 706-3—AUDITOR'S REPORT WITH OTHER-MATTER PARAGRAPH

---

### INDEPENDENT AUDITOR'S REPORT

[*Appropriate Addressee*]

**Report on the Audit of the Financial Statements**

*Opinion*

We have audited the financial statements of X Company, which comprise the balance sheets as of December 31, 20X5 and 20X4, and the related statements of income, changes in stockholders' equity, and cash flows for the years then ended, and the related notes to the financial statements.

In our opinion, the accompanying financial statements present fairly, in all material respects, the financial position of X Company as of December 31, 20X5 and 20X4, and the results of its operations and its cash flows for the years then ended in accordance with accounting principles generally accepted in the United States of America.

*Basis for Opinion*

We conducted our audits in accordance with auditing standards generally accepted in the United States of America (GAAS). Our responsibilities under those standards are further described in the Auditor's Responsibilities for the Audit of the Financial Statements section of our report. We are required to be independent of X Company and to meet our other ethical responsibilities, in accordance with the relevant ethical requirements relating to our audits. We believe that the audit evidence we have obtained is sufficient and appropriate to provide a basis for our audit opinion.

*Other Matter*

In our report dated April 1, 20X5, we expressed an opinion that the 20X4 financial statements did not fairly present the financial position, results of operations, and cash flows of X Company in accordance with accounting principles generally accepted in the United States of America because of two departures from such principles: (1) X Company carried its property, plant, and equipment at appraisal values, and provided for depreciation on the basis of such values, and (2) X Company did not provide for deferred income taxes with respect to differences between income for financial reporting purposes and taxable income. As described in Note #, the Company has changed its method of accounting for these items and restated its 20X4 financial statements to conform with accounting principles generally accepted in the United States of America. Accordingly, our present opinion on the restated 20X4 financial statements, as presented herein, is different from that expressed in our previous report.

*Responsibilities of Management for the Financial Statements*

Management is responsible for the preparation and fair presentation of the financial statements in accordance with accounting principles generally accepted in the United States of America, and for the design, implementation, and maintenance of internal control relevant to the preparation and fair presentation of financial statements that are free from material misstatement, whether due to fraud or error.

In preparing the financial statements, management is required to evaluate whether there are conditions or events, considered in the aggregate, that raise substantial doubt about X Company's ability to continue as a going concern for a reasonable period of time as defined by accounting principles generally accepted in the United States of America.

*Auditor's Responsibilities for the Audit of the Financial Statements*

Our objectives are to obtain reasonable assurance about whether the financial statements as a whole are free from material misstatement, whether due to fraud or error, and to issue an auditor's report that includes our opinion. Reasonable assurance is a high level of assurance but is not absolute assurance and therefore is not a guarantee that an audit conducted in accordance with GAAS will always detect a material misstatement when it exists. The risk of not detecting a material misstatement resulting from fraud is higher than for one resulting from error, as fraud may involve collusion, forgery, intentional omissions, misrepresentations, or the override of internal control. Misstatements are considered material if, individually or in the aggregate, they could reasonably be expected to influence the economic decisions of users made on the basis of these financial statements.

In performing an audit in accordance with GAAS, we:

- Exercise professional judgment and maintain professional skepticism throughout the audit.
- Identify and assess the risks of material misstatement of the financial statements, whether due to fraud or error, and design and perform audit procedures responsive to those risks. Such procedures include examining, on a test basis, evidence regarding the amounts and disclosures in the financial statements.
- Obtain an understanding of internal control relevant to the audit in order to design audit procedures that are appropriate in the circumstances, but not for the purpose of expressing an opinion on the effectiveness of X Company's internal control. Accordingly, no such opinion is expressed.
- Evaluate the appropriateness of accounting policies used and the reasonableness of significant accounting estimates made by management, as well as evaluate the overall presentation of the financial statements.
- Conclude whether, in our judgment, there are conditions or events, considered in the aggregate, that raise substantial doubt about X Company's ability to continue as a going concern for a reasonable period of time.

We are required to communicate with those charged with governance regarding, among other matters, the planned scope and timing of the audit, significant audit findings, and certain internal control–related matters that we identified during the audit.

*Report on Other Legal and Regulatory Requirements*

*[Form and content of this section of the auditor's report will vary depending on the nature of the auditor's other reporting responsibilities.]*

*[Auditor's firm signature]*

*[Auditor's city and state]*

*[Date of the auditor's report]*

# SECTION 708

# CONSISTENCY OF FINANCIAL STATEMENTS

## Authoritative Pronouncements

SAS-122—Statements on Auditing Standards: Clarification and Recodification

SAS-136—Forming an Opinion and Reporting on Financial Statements of Employee Benefit Plans Subject to ERISA

## Overview

AU-C 708 provides guidance to the auditor in evaluating the consistency of financial statements and applying the effect of that evaluation on the auditor's report. The auditor should communicate in the report when the comparability of financial statements is materially affected by a change in accounting principle or by adjustments to correct a material misstatement in previously issued financial statements.

> **PUBLIC COMPANY IMPLICATION:** The PCAOB's AS-2820 (*Evaluating Consistency of Financial Statements and Conforming Amendments*) requires the auditor to evaluate whether financial statements between periods are comparable. Financial statements might not be comparable because of a change in accounting principle or an adjustment to correct a misstatement in previously issued financial statements. If there is a change in accounting principle, the auditor should evaluate whether (1) the new accounting principle is generally accepted, (2) the accounting for the change in accounting principle is in accordance with U.S. GAAP, (3) the disclosures surrounding the change are adequate, and (4) the change in accounting principle is preferable. Assuming these four criteria are met, the auditor should add an explanatory paragraph to the audit report describing the lack of consistency in the financial statements. If the four criteria are not met, the financial statements are not in accordance with U.S. GAAP and the auditor should issue either an adverse opinion or a qualified opinion.
>
> If the financial statements are not comparable because of a change in accounting principle due to the adoption of a new FASB standard, the explanatory paragraph should state that the company has changed its method of accounting due to the adoption of the specific FASB standard and refer the reader to the particular note describing the change. If the financial statements are not comparable because of a voluntary change in accounting principle, the explanatory paragraph should refer to the elective nature of the change and refer the reader to the particular note describing the change.
>
> In addition, if the financial statements are adjusted to correct a material misstatement in previously issued financial statements, the auditor's report should include an explanatory paragraph describing the lack of consistency due to the correction of the previously issued financial statements (i.e., the financial statements for earlier years included for comparative purposes in the current

year's filing will differ from previously filed statements). Finally, a change in how items are classified in the financial statements does not need to be recognized in the auditor's report unless it represents a change in accounting principle or the correction of a material misstatement.

## Definition

Current period   The most recent year upon which the auditor is reporting.

## Requirements

The auditor is presumptively required to perform the following procedures when considering the consistency of financial statements:

### *Evaluating Consistency*

1. Evaluate whether financial statement comparability between periods has been materially affected by a change in accounting principle or adjustments to correct a material misstatement in previously issued financial statements.

   a. If the auditor's opinion is only on the current period's financial statements, the auditor's evaluation should address the consistency between the current period and the preceding period (regardless of whether the financial statements for the preceding period are included).

   b. If the auditor's opinion covers two or more periods, the auditor's evaluation should address the consistency between the periods presented and covered by the auditor's report, as well as the consistency between the earliest period reported on and the prior period if financial statements for the prior period are included with the financial statements that the auditor is reporting on.

2. Evaluate whether the financial statements for the periods reported on are consistent with previously issued financial statements for the respective periods. This evaluation is particularly important when a change in accounting principle is retrospectively applied to earlier periods presented for comparative purposes.

### *Change in Accounting Principle*

3. Evaluate a change in accounting principle to determine whether:

   a. The newly adopted accounting principle and the method of accounting for the effect of the change are in accordance with the applicable financial reporting framework.

   b. Disclosures related to the change are appropriate and adequate.

   c. The entity has justified that the alternative accounting principle is preferable.

4. If the criteria in the preceding paragraph are met and the effect of the change on the financial statements is material, include an emphasis-of-matter paragraph in the auditor's report describing the change in accounting principle and referring to the entity's disclosure. If the criteria in the preceding paragraph are not met, evaluate whether the accounting change results in a material misstatement and if there is a need for the auditor's opinion to be modified.

5. Include an emphasis-of-matter paragraph relating to a change in accounting principle in the auditor's report in the period of change and all subsequent periods until the new accounting principle is applied in all periods presented. An emphasis-of-matter paragraph is only needed in the period of change if the change is accounted for by retrospective application to the financial statements of all prior periods presented.

6. Evaluate and report on a change in accounting estimate inseparable from the effect of a related change in accounting principle in the same manner as a change in accounting principle.

7. If a change in reporting entity results in financial statements that are, in effect, those of a different reporting entity, include an emphasis-of-matter paragraph in the auditor's report describing the change in reporting entity and referring to the entity's disclosure, unless the change in reporting entity is due to a transaction or event. The requirements in paragraph 5 also apply to a change in the reporting entity.

8. If an entity's financial statements contain an investment accounted for by the equity method, evaluate the consistency of the investee's financial statements. If the investee has made a change in accounting principle that is material to the investing entity's financial statements, an emphasis-of-matter paragraph should be included in the auditor's report describing that change. The requirements in paragraph 5 apply in this case as well.

## Correction of a Material Misstatement in Previously Issued Financial Statements

9. Include an emphasis-of-matter paragraph in the auditor's report when financial statements are restated to reflect adjustments to correct a material misstatement in previously issued financial statements. This paragraph does not need to be repeated in subsequent periods.

10. The emphasis-of-matter paragraph should (*a*) state that the previously issued financial statements have been restated for the correction of a material misstatement in the respective period and (*b*) refer to the entity's disclosure of the correction of the material misstatement.

11. If the financial statement disclosures relating to the restatement correcting a material misstatement in previously issued financial statements are not adequate, address this inadequacy as described in AU-C 705 (*Modifications to the Opinion in the Independent Auditor's Report*).

## Change in Classification

12. Evaluate a material change in financial statement classification and the related disclosure to determine whether that change is also a change in accounting principle or an adjustment to correct a material misstatement in previously issued financial statements, in which case the applicable requirements described above should be followed.

**OBSERVATION:** Under current GAAS, changes and material reclassifications in previously issued financial statements to improve comparability with the current year's financial statements do not have to be referred to in the auditor's report. Under AU-C 708, the auditor needs to evaluate whether a material change in financial statement classification is a change in accounting principle or a correction of a material misstatement.

## Analysis and Application of Procedures

*Evaluating Consistency*

The auditor's report implies that the auditor is satisfied as to the comparability of the financial statements presented unless the report explicitly states otherwise. Therefore, if no change in accounting principle has occurred or a change in accounting principle or its method of application has occurred but the effect is immaterial, consistency does not need to be referred to in the auditor's report.

*Change in Accounting Principle*

A change in accounting principle is a change in accounting principle or a change in the method of applying an accounting principle, in accordance with the applicable financial reporting framework, when (*a*) two or more accounting principles apply or (*b*) the accounting principle formerly used is no longer in accordance with the applicable financial reporting framework. The applicable financial reporting framework generally provides the method of accounting for the change in accounting principle and the related disclosures.

An entity's justification for a change in accounting principle is generally adequate if an accounting pronouncement is issued that requires the use of a new principle, interprets an existing principle, expresses a preference for an accounting principle, or rejects a specific principle, so long as the change is made in accordance with the applicable financial reporting framework.

An example of an emphasis-of-matter paragraph for a change in accounting principle due to the adoption of a new accounting pronouncement follows:

> As discussed in Note X to the financial statements, in [*insert year(s) of financial statements that reflect the accounting method change*], the entity adopted new accounting guidance [*description of new accounting guidance*]. Our opinion is not qualified with respect to this matter.

An example of an emphasis-of-matter paragraph for a voluntary change in accounting principle not due to the adoption of a new accounting pronouncement follows:

> As discussed in Note X to the financial statements, the entity has elected to change its method of accounting for [*describe accounting method change*] in [*insert year(s) of financial statements that reflect the accounting method change*]. Our opinion is not qualified with respect to this matter.

---

**ENGAGEMENT STRATEGY:** If a change in accounting principle does not have a material effect on the financial statements in the current year but is expected to have a material effect in later years, the auditor is not required to recognize this change in his or her report. However, the applicable financial reporting framework may include a requirement to disclose this situation in the notes to the financial statements.

---

A change in reporting entity that would not require recognition in the auditor's report is one resulting from a "transaction or event, such as the creation, cessation, or complete or partial purchase or disposition of a subsidiary or other business unit." The auditor should include an emphasis-of-matter paragraph for changes in the reporting entity that are not the result of a transaction or event, including:

- Consolidated or combined financial statements are presented in the current year, but individual financial statements were presented in the previous year.
- Consolidated financial statements for the current year do not include the same subsidiaries that were used to prepare the previous year's consolidated financial statements.
- Combined financial statements for the current year do not include the same companies that were used to prepare the previous year's combined financial statements.

*Correction of a Material Misstatement in Previously Issued Financial Statements*

The correction of a material misstatement includes a change in accounting principle from one that is not in accordance with the applicable financial reporting framework to one that is in accordance with that framework. If adjustments have been made to correct a material misstatement in previously issued financial statements, AU-C 560 (*Subsequent Events and Subsequently Discovered Facts*) provides guidance as to the auditor's responsibilities.

An example of an emphasis-of-matter paragraph when there has been a correction of a material misstatement in previously issued financial statements follows:

> As discussed in Note X to the financial statements, the 20X5 financial statements have been restated to correct a misstatement. Our opinion is not modified with respect to this matter.

*Change in Classification*

Changes in classification that would require recognition in the auditor's report include reclassifications in previously issued financial statements occurring because the items were classified incorrectly in the previously issued statements. In situations where reclassifications in previously issued financial statements are due to changes in the entity's business or operating structure, the auditor may need to obtain further understanding of the underlying business rationale for these changes to determine whether the changes require recognition in the auditor's report.

# SECTION 720

## OTHER INFORMATION IN DOCUMENTS CONTAINING AUDITED FINANCIAL STATEMENTS

### Authoritative Pronouncements

SAS-123—Omnibus Statement on Auditing Standards—2011

SAS-137—The Auditor's Responsibilities Relating to Other Information Included in Annual Reports

SAS-141—Amendment to Effective Dates of SAS Nos. 134-140

### Overview

The auditor's report may be included in an entity's annual report that contains other information, including both financial or nonfinancial information. For example, a company's annual report may include a message from the chief executive officer and descriptions of operations and future plans, as well as a variety of charts and graphs accompanied by explanations.

AU-C 720 establishes the responsibilities of the independent auditor with respect to other information in (*a*) annual reports sent to holders of securities, (*b*) annual reports of government and charitable or philanthropic organizations available to the public, and (*c*) other documents reviewed by the auditor at the client's request.

---

**IMPORTANT NOTICE FOR 2022:** In July 2019, the AICPA's Auditing Standards Board (ASB) issued SAS No. 137, *The Auditor's Responsibilities Relating to Other Information Included in Annual Reports.* That new SAS addresses the auditor's responsibilities related to other information, whether financial or nonfinancial, included in the entity's auditor's report. SAS No. 137 superseded the guidance in AU-C 720. SAS No. 137 retains the existing responsibility in AU-C 720 for the auditor to read and consider the other information included in the annual report to determine whether there is a material inconsistency between the other information and the financial statements. The ASB issued this new guidance because it believed that in practice the guidance in AU-C 720 was being applied more broadly than intended. SAS No. 137 clarifies the scope of the documents that the auditor is required to subject to the procedures, and it includes a new title to reflect the more specific focus on annual report documents. Originally, the effective date of SAS No. 137 was for audits of financial statements periods ending on or after December 15, 2020, with early implementation **not** permitted. However, the ASB's issuance of SAS No. 141, *Amendment to the Effective Dates of SAS Nos. 134-140*, extended the effective date to December 15, 2021, in order to provide more time for firms to implement SAS No. 137 in light of the effect of the coronavirus pandemic. While SAS No. 141

allows for early implementation of SAS No. 137, the ASB recommends that SAS Nos. 134-140 be implemented concurrently.

---

**PLANNING AID REMINDER:** A designated accounting standard setter such as the Financial Accounting Standards Board (FASB) may have issued guidance or standards regarding the form and content of other information. AU-C 720 addresses this other information when it is voluntarily presented in a document containing the audited financial statements and auditor's report, but if the other information is required to be included by a designated accounting standard setter, the auditor should follow the guidance in AU-C 730.

---

Although not required to audit the other information in the annual report, the auditor must read it to determine whether—compared with the information presented in the financial statements—there is (*a*) a material inconsistency or (*b*) a material misstatement of fact. By reading the other information, the auditor can respond appropriately if other information is presented that could undermine the credibility of the audited financial statements and the auditor's report.

## Definitions

| | |
|---|---|
| Annual report | A document, or combination of documents, typically prepared on an annual basis by management or those charged with governance in accordance with law, regulation, or custom, the purpose of which is to provide owners (or similar stakeholders) with information on the entity's operations and the entity's financial results and financial position as set out in the financial statements. An annual report contains, accompanies, or incorporates by reference the financial statements and the auditor's report thereon and usually includes information about the entity's developments, its future outlook and risks and uncertainties, a statement by the entity's governing body, and reports covering governance matters. Annual reports include annual reports of governments and organizations for charitable or philanthropic purposes and are available to the public. |
| Misstatement of the other information | A misstatement of the other information exists when the other information is incorrectly stated or otherwise misleading. |
| Other information | Financial and nonfinancial information (other than the financial statements or the auditor's report thereon) that is included in the entity's annual report. |

---

**IMPORTANT NOTICE FOR 2022:** The PCAOB adopted in 2017 auditing standard AS-3101 (*The Auditor's Report on an Audit of Financial Statements When the Auditor Expresses an Unqualified Opinion*) that requires the auditor (1) to describe critical audit matters in the audit report and (2) to disclose the tenure of the audit firm as auditor. The PCAOB's new standard describes critical audit matters as those audit matters that are communicated, or are required to be communicated, to the audit committee that (1) related to accounts or disclosures that are material to the financial statements, and (2) involved especially challenging, subjective, or complex judgments. The auditor's report on financial statements of SEC registrants will now (1) identify the critical audit matter, (2) describe why the auditor concluded that the item was a critical audit matter, (3) describe how the critical audit matter was addressed in the audit, and (4) refer to the relevant financial statement accounts and disclosures affected by the critical audit matter.

---

**PUBLIC COMPANY IMPLICATION:** In October 2013, the PCAOB issued guidance codified as AS-2701 (*Auditing Supplemental Information Accompanying Audited Financial Statements and Related Amendments to PCAOB Standards*) to provide additional guidance related to the auditor's responsibility to "read and consider" other information in documents containing audited financial statements. This guidance was partially motivated by the increasing attention to and inclusion of non-GAAP financial measures and operational measures included in annual reports, registration statements, earnings releases, and other communications. When non-GAAP measures are included in an annual report, such as in the section on management's discussion and analysis, those measures are considered "other information" and are subject to the requirements of AS-2701. Under that section, the auditor has a "read and consider" responsibility, but the auditor does not have responsibility to perform procedures related to information presented in other communications, such as earnings releases, investor presentations, or analyst calls. The revised standard enhanced the auditor's responsibility under AS-2701.

---

## Requirements

The auditor is presumptively required to perform the following procedures on other information in documents containing audited financial statements:

### Reading Other Information

1. Determine with management and obtain management's written acknowledgment about which document(s) comprise the annual report and the entity's anticipated manner and timing of the issuance of those documents.

2. Arrange with management or those charged with governance to obtain the documents that comprise the annual report prior to the auditor's report date, or, if that is not possible, read other information as soon as practicable.

---

**OBSERVATION:** Sometimes a portion of the documents will not be available until after the date of the auditor's report. In those circumstances, the auditor should request that management provide a written representation that the final version of the documents will be provided when available and prior to the issuance by the entity.

---

3. Communicate with those charged with governance the auditor's responsibilities and procedures performed with respect to the other information and the related results.

4. Read other information in documents containing audited financial statements and the auditor's report to identify any material inconsistencies with the audited financial statements. The auditor should compare selected amounts or other items in the other information with such amounts that are in the financial statements.

5. The auditor should remain alert for a material inconsistency that may exist between the other information and the auditor's knowledge obtained in the audit and for a material misstatement of fact that may exist or be otherwise misleading. The auditor is not responsible for searching for incomplete or omitted other information.

## Material Inconsistencies

6. If a material inconsistency is identified when reading the other information, the auditor should discuss the inconsistency with management, and if necessary, perform other procedures to conclude whether a material misstatement exists in either the audited financial statements or other information.

7. If the auditor concludes that a material misstatement of the other information exists, the auditor should request management to revise the other information. When the information is corrected, the auditors should determine that the correction has been made. If the information is not corrected, the auditor should communicate that to those charged with governance and request correction be made.

8. If revision of the other information is necessary and management refuses to make the revision prior to the date of the auditor's report, the auditor should communicate the matter to those charged with governance and consider how it might impact the auditor's report. The auditor may communicate a decision to withhold the auditor's report or withdraw from the engagement.

9. If the auditor concludes that a material misstatement of the other information exists after the date of the auditor's report, the auditor should request management to revise the other information. If the other information is not revised after communicating with those charged with governance, the auditor should seek to have the uncorrected material misstatement brought to the attention of anyone in receipt of the financial statements and the auditor's report. The auditor should do so with the auditor's legal rights in consideration.

10. When the auditor determines that a material misstatement in the financial statements exists, the auditor should respond according to provisions of AU-C 315, AU-C 450, and AU-C 560.

## Reporting

11. The auditor should include a separate section in the auditor's report on the financial statements with the heading "Other Information" or other appropriate heading.

12. The "Other Information" section should include a statement that management is responsible for the other information and it should identify the other information, with a statement that notes the other information does not include the financial statements and the auditor's report thereon.

13. The "Other Information" section should also include a statement that the auditor's opinion on the financial statements does not cover the other information and that the auditor does not express an opinion or any form of assurance on the other information.

14. The "Other Information" section should state that the auditor is responsible for reading the other information and consider whether a material inconsistency exists between the other information and the financial statements or the other information otherwise appears to be materially misstated. The auditor also includes a statement that if, based on the work performed, the auditor concludes that an uncorrected misstatement of the other information exists, the auditor is required to describe it in the auditor's report.

15. If the auditor determines that an uncorrected material misstatement of the other information exists, the "Other Information" section should also state that the auditor has concluded that an uncorrected material misstatement of the other information exists and include description of the misstatement in the auditor's report.

## *Documentation*

16. The auditor should document the procedures required by AU-C 720.

17. The auditor should also document the final version of the other information on which the auditor has performed the work.

# Analysis and Application of Procedures

## *Annual Report*

An annual report is typically prepared on an annual basis, but it may cover financial statements sometimes prepared for a period that is more or less than a year. It may be made available in printed or electronic form and it may be in a single document or separate documents. Sometimes laws and regulations define the content of an annual report.

## *Other Information*

Items that may comprise other information include the following:

- Chairman's statement or corporate governance statement;
- A report on operations by management or those charged with governance;
- Financial summaries or highlights;
- Employment data;
- Planned capital expenditures;
- Financial ratios;
- Names of officers and directors; and
- Selected quarterly data.

"Other information" does not include information on a company's website, information contained in analyst briefings, or a press release or cover letter accompanying the document containing audited financial statements and the auditor's report.

## *Reading Other Information*

The other information is not required to be referenced in the auditor's report on the financial statements. However, an explanatory paragraph disclaiming an opinion on the other information may be included to prevent users from inferring an unintended level of assurance on the other information. An example of such an explanatory paragraph follows:

> Our audit was conducted for the purpose of forming an opinion on the basic financial statements as a whole. The [*identify the other information*] is presented for purposes of additional analysis and is not a required part of the basic financial statements. Such information has not been subjected to the auditing

procedures applied in the audit of the financial statements, and, accordingly, we do not express an opinion or provide any assurance on it.

The auditor may find an agreement with management helpful in obtaining the other information on a timely basis. The auditor may also consider delaying release of his or her report until the client provides the auditor with the other information.

## Misstatements of Other Information

A misstatement of other information may be an inconsistency, a misstatement of fact, or information that is otherwise misleading because it is obscure or incomplete. An inconsistency is present when the other information conflicts with information in the financial statements. A material misstatement of fact is present when other information that is unrelated to matters appearing in the financial statements is incorrectly stated or presented.

It may be more difficult to identify a material misstatement of fact in an annual report, because the nature of much of the other information will be nonaccounting and beyond the expertise of the auditor. The auditor may conclude valid differences of judgment or opinion exist if he or she is unable to evaluate the validity of some disclosures in the other information or of management's responses to inquiries.

When material inconsistencies are identified in other information obtained prior to the report release date and management refuses to make revisions, the auditor may use legal counsel's advice to decide on further appropriate action. In instances where withdrawal from the engagement is not legally permitted, the auditor may issue a report to those charged with governance and the appropriate statutory body detailing the identified inconsistency.

When material inconsistencies are identified in other information obtained subsequent to the report release date and management agrees to make revisions, the auditor's procedures may include reviewing steps taken by management to inform recipients of the issued financial statements, auditor's report, and other information of the revision. If management refuses to make revisions the auditor deems necessary, the auditor may take further action including obtaining advice from legal counsel.

**FRAUD POINTER:** AU-C 720 is vague in this area of material misstatement, because it relies on the auditor's limited expertise in relation to the other information. In other words, the auditor must proceed with caution. However, if the auditor discovers a material misstatement of other information and the client refuses to change the other information but the auditor still issues a report, it might be wise for the auditor to follow the reporting format prescribed when a material misstatement is encountered in the financial statements or accompanying notes.

If the auditor concludes there is a material misstatement of fact that management refuses to correct, the auditor may take further actions including obtaining advice from legal counsel, withholding his or her report if not already issued, or withdrawing from the engagement.

Exhibits 720-1 and 720-2 contain examples of the "Other Information" section of the auditor's report.

- Exhibit AU-C 720-1—Other Information Section to be Included in the Auditor's Report Related to Other Information Included in the Annual Report and Auditor Has Not Identified an Uncorrected Material Misstatement
- Exhibit AU-C 720-2—Other Information Section to be Included in the Auditor's Report Related to Other Information Included in the Annual Report and Auditor Has Concluded That an Uncorrected Material Misstatement Exists

**EXHIBIT AU-C 720-1—OTHER INFORMATION SECTION TO BE INCLUDED IN THE AUDITOR'S REPORT RELATED TO OTHER INFORMATION INCLUDED IN THE ANNUAL REPORT AND AUDITOR HAS NOT IDENTIFIED AN UNCORRECTED MATERIAL MISSTATEMENT**

*Other Information [Included in the Annual Report]*

Management is responsible for the other information [*included in the annual report*]. The other information comprises the [*information included in the annual report*] but does not include the financial statements and our auditor's report thereon. Our opinion on the financial statements does not cover the other information, and we do not express an opinion or any form of assurance thereon.

In connection with our audit of the financial statements, our responsibility is to read the other information and consider whether a material inconsistency exists between the other information and the financial statements, or the other information otherwise appears to be materially misstated. If, based on the work performed, we conclude that an uncorrected material misstatement of the other information exists, we are required to describe it in our report.

**EXHIBIT AU-C 720-2—OTHER INFORMATION SECTION TO BE INCLUDED IN THE AUDITOR'S REPORT RELATED TO OTHER INFORMATION INCLUDED IN THE ANNUAL REPORT AND AUDITOR HAS CONCLUDED THAT AN UNCORRECTED MATERIAL MISSTATEMENT EXISTS**

*Other Information [Included in the Annual Report]*

Management is responsible for the other information [*included in the annual report*]. The other information comprises the [*information included in the annual report*] but does not include the financial statements and our auditor's report thereon. Our opinion on the financial statements does not cover the other information, and we do not express an opinion or any form of assurance thereon.

In connection with our audit of the financial statements, our responsibility is to read the other information and consider whether a material inconsistency exists between the other information and the financial statements, or the other information otherwise appears to be materially misstated. If, based on the work performed, we conclude that an uncorrected material misstatement of the other information exists, we are required to describe it in our report. As described below, we have concluded that such an uncorrected material misstatement of the other information exists.

[*Description of material misstatement of the other information*]

# SECTION 725

# SUPPLEMENTARY INFORMATION IN RELATION TO THE FINANCIAL STATEMENTS AS A WHOLE

## Authoritative Pronouncements

SAS-119—Supplementary Information in Relation to the Financial Statements as a Whole

SAS-136—Forming an Opinion and Reporting on Financial Statements of Employee Benefit Plans Subject to ERISA

SAS-137—The Auditor's Responsibilities Relating to Other Information Included in Annual Reports

SAS-138—Amendments to the Description of the Concept of Materiality

SAS-140—Amendments to AU-C Sections 725, 730, 930, 935, and 940 to Incorporate Auditor Reporting Changes from SAS Nos. 134 and 137

SAS-141—Amendment to Effective Dates of SAS Nos. 134-140

SAS Interpretation 1—Dating the Auditor's Report on Supplementary Information

## Overview

AU-C 725 applies to engagements where the auditor expresses an opinion on whether supplementary information is fairly stated, in all material respects, in relation to the financial statements as a whole. The supplementary information that this AU-C 725 applies to is not required in order for the financial statements to be fairly presented in accordance with the applicable financial reporting framework. When the auditor is performing an audit of an employee benefit plan subject to ERISA, AU-C 703 (*Forming an Opinion and Reporting on Financial Statements of Employee Benefit Plans Subject to ERISA*) applies. The requirements in paragraph .09 of AU-C 725 are replaced by AU-C 703 for such audits only.

This guidance may also be applied if the auditor is engaged to express an opinion on whether required supplementary information is fairly stated in all material respects in relation to the financial statements as a whole. However, AU-C 720 addresses the auditor's responsibilities for information other than the financial statements, auditor's report and required supplementary information, and AU-C 730 addresses the auditor's responsibilities for information required by a designated accounting standard setter to accompany an entity's basic financial statements. Furthermore, if the auditor is engaged to express an opinion on specified elements, accounts, or items of financial statements for the purpose of a separate presentation, the guidance in AU-C 805 applies. An engagement to examine supplementary information or an assertion related to the supplementary information may also be performed in accordance with the attestation standards.

## Definitions

Supplementary information
: Information other than the financial statements, auditor's report, and required supplementary information that is not considered necessary for the financial statements to be fairly presented in accordance with the applicable financial reporting framework. This information includes details, explanations, or historical summaries of financial statement items, consolidating information, statistical data, and other information which may come from sources outside the accounting system or the entity. This information may be presented with or separate from the audited financial statements. Supplementary information may be prepared in accordance with an applicable financial reporting framework, management's criteria, or by regulatory, contractual, or other requirements.

---

**PUBLIC COMPANY IMPLICATION:** PCAOB AS-2701 (*Auditing Supplemental Information Accompanying Audited Financial Statements and Related Amendments to PCAOB Standards*) provides guidance when the auditor of a company's financial statements is engaged to examine and report on supplemental information accompanying financial statements that have been audited in accordance with PCAOB standards. Supplemental information is often in the form of schedules, and often is presented in response to a regulatory requirement. For example, supplemental information is required by the Securities and Exchange Commission related to the Commission's oversight of brokers and dealers (e.g., SEC Rule 17a-5). As a result, in auditing brokers and dealers, the requirements of AS-2701 should be coordinated with the requirements of the PCAOB's two attestation standards related to compliance or exemption reports required by the SEC. However, AS-2701 also applies when the supplemental information is voluntarily provided, when the auditor is engaged to report on that supplemental information in relation to the financial statements taken as a whole (and the financial statements have been audited in accordance with PCAOB standards).

AS-2701 requires the auditor to (1) determine that the supplement information reconciles to underlying accounting (or other) records or to the financial statements; (2) test the completeness and accuracy of the supplemental information, if not already tested as part of the audit of the financial statements; and (3) evaluate whether the form and content of the supplemental information complies with any applicable regulatory requirement or other applicable criteria. The auditor should accumulate detected misstatements as a result of audit procedures and communicate these misstatements to management on a timely basis so that management can make needed corrections. The auditor should evaluate whether detected misstatements related to the supplemental information are material, both individually and in the aggregate, in determining whether the supplemental information is fairly stated in relation to the financial statements taken as a whole; otherwise, the auditor should disclaim an opinion. Unless precluded by regulatory requirement, the auditor's opinion on the supplemental information can either be in the auditor's report on the financial statements or in a separate report on the supplemental information.

## Requirements

The auditor is presumptively required to apply the following procedures for reporting on supplementary information in relation to the financial statements as a whole:

*Procedures*

1. Determine the following in order to express an opinion on whether supplementary information is fairly stated in all material respects in relation to the financial statements as a whole:
    a. Supplementary information relates to the same period as the financial statements and was derived from and directly relates to the underlying accounting and other records used to prepare those statements.
    b. The financial statements were audited, an adverse opinion or disclaimer or opinion was not issued, and the auditor served as the principal auditor in the engagement.
    c. The supplementary information will accompany the audited financial statements or the entity will make those statements readily available.

2. Obtain management's agreement that it acknowledges and understands its responsibility:
    a. To prepare the supplementary information in accordance with the applicable criteria.
    b. To provide the auditor with the written representations described in requirement 3f.
    c. To include the auditor's report on the supplementary information in any document containing the supplementary information and indicate the auditor has reported on that information.
    d. To present the supplementary information with the audited financial statements or make the audited financial statements readily available to the supplementary information's intended users no later than the date the supplementary information and auditor's report on that information are issued.

3. Perform the following procedures in addition to procedures performed during the financial statement audit, using the same materiality level used in the financial statement audit, in order to express an opinion on whether supplementary information is fairly stated in all material respects in relation to the financial statements as a whole:
    a. Inquire of management about the purpose of supplementary information and the criteria used to prepare that information.
    b. Obtain an understanding about the methods of preparing the information including whether those methods have changed from prior periods and the reasons why as well as whether the form and content of the information complies with established criteria.
    c. Compare and reconcile the information to the financial statements or to the underlying accounting and other records used in preparing the financial statements.
    d. Inquire of management about any significant assumptions or interpretations underlying the information's measurement or presentation.
    e. Evaluate the appropriateness and completeness of the information, considering procedures performed and other knowledge obtained during the financial statement audit.

f. Obtain written representations from management: acknowledging responsibility for the supplementary information; stating that the information's form and content is in accordance with prescribed guidelines; stating that measurement and presentation methods have not changed from the prior period or the reasons for any such changes; about any significant assumptions or interpretations underlying information measurement or presentation; and that when supplementary information is not presented with the audited financial statements those statements will be made readily available to the supplementary information's intended users no later than the date the supplementary information and auditor's report are issued.

4. The auditor has no responsibility for considering subsequent events with respect to the supplementary information. However, if information comes to the auditor's attention before or after the auditor's report on the financial statements is released regarding events that affect the financial statements, he or she should follow the guidance in AU-C 560.

---

**IMPORTANT NOTICE FOR 2022:** In December 2019, the AICPA's Auditing Standards Board (ASB) issued SAS No. 138, *Amendments to the Description of the Concept of Materiality*, to align the materiality concepts discussed in auditing standards, including AU-C 700, with the definition of materiality used by the U.S. judicial system, the PCAOB auditing standards, and the Financial Accounting Standards Board (FASB). The FASB aligned its definition of materiality in August 2018 to be consistent with the U.S. judicial system and other U.S. standards setters and regulators. The ASB believes it is in the public interest to eliminate existing inconsistencies in definitions of materiality used. The U.S. judicial system defines misstatement as material if there is **"substantial likelihood** that a reasonable shareholder **would** consider it important"** whereas existing auditing standards define a misstatement as material if it **"could reasonably be expected to** influence the judgment of a reasonable person." Also, in April 2020, the ASB issued SAS No. 140, *Amendments to AU-C Sections 725, 730, 930, 935, and 940 to Incorporate Auditor Reporting Changes from SAS Nos. 134 and 137*. SAS No. 140 amends the reporting illustrations in AU-C 725. Originally, the effective date of these amendments was for audits of financial statements for periods ending on or after December 15, 2020. However, the ASB's issuance of SAS No. 141, *Amendment to the Effective Dates of SAS Nos. 134-140*, extended the effective date to December 15, 2021, in order to provide more time for firms to implement SAS Nos. 134 and 140 in light of the effect of the coronavirus pandemic. The ASB recommends that SAS Nos. 134-140 be implemented concurrently.

---

## Reporting

5. If the auditor expresses an opinion on the supplementary information in relation to the financial statements as a whole that is presented with the financial statements, include a separate section in the auditor's report on the financial statements with the heading "Supplementary Information" or in a separate report on the supplementary information. The "Supplementary Information" section of the auditor's report on the financial statements should include the following statements:

   a. The audit was conducted for the purpose of forming an opinion on the financial statements as a whole.

b. Supplementary information is presented for additional analysis purposes and is not a required part of the financial statements.

c. Supplementary information is management's responsibility and was derived from and directly relates to the underlying accounting and other records used to prepare the financial statements.

d. Supplementary information has been subjected to the auditing procedures applied in the financial statement audit and certain additional procedures, including comparing and reconciling such information directly to the underlying accounting and other records used to prepare the financial statements and other additional procedures as prescribed by auditing standards generally accepted in the United States of America.

e. If the financial statement opinion is unqualified and the supplementary information is fairly stated, include a statement that, in the auditor's opinion, the other supplementary information is fairly stated in all material respects, in relation to the financial statements as a whole.

f. If the financial statement opinion is qualified and the qualification has an effect on the supplementary information, include a statement that, in the auditor's opinion, except for the effects on the supplementary information of (refer to the paragraph in the auditor's report explaining the qualification), such information is fairly stated in all material respects in relation to the financial statements as whole.

6. If the auditor expresses an opinion on supplementary information and the audited financial statements are not presented with the supplementary information, the report on the supplementary information should include all of the above elements and: a reference to the financial statement report, the date of that report, the opinion expressed on the financial statements, and any report modifications.

7. If an adverse opinion or disclaimer of opinion is issued on the financial statements, the auditor may not express an opinion on the supplementary information and may withdraw from the engagement to report on such information where permitted by law or regulation. If the auditor does not withdraw from the engagement, the report on the supplementary information should state that because of the significance of the matter disclosed in the auditor's report, it is inappropriate to and the auditor does not express an opinion on the supplementary information.

8. The date of the auditor's opinion on the supplementary information should not be earlier that the date on which the auditor completed the required procedures.

9. If the auditor concludes the supplementary information is materially misstated in relation to the financial statements as a whole, he or she should discuss the matter with management and propose appropriate revision of such information. If management does not revise the supplementary information, the auditor should modify the auditor's opinion on such information and describe the misstatement in the auditor's report, or, if a separate report is being issued on the supplementary information, withhold the auditor's report on the supplementary information.

## Analysis and Application of Procedures

*Reporting on Supplementary Information*

While the auditor is not obligated to report on supplementary information presented outside the basic financial statements, he or she may choose to apply auditing procedures to such information in order to express an opinion on that information. Management information not directly related to the basic financial statements is not ordinarily subjected to auditing procedures. However, when that information has been obtained or derived from accounting records the auditor has tested, the auditor may be in a position to express an opinion on such information in relation to the financial statements as a whole.

---

**PLANNING AID REMINDER:** Interpretation 1 of AU-C 725 provides guidance when reporting on supplementary information after the date of the auditor's report on the financial statements so that the auditor can make it clear that no additional procedures were performed on the audited financial statements subsequent to the date of the auditor's report on those financial statements.

---

*Procedures*

To express an opinion on other supplementary information in relation to the financial statements as a whole, the auditor is not required to obtain a separate understanding of internal control or assess fraud risk. The auditor may consider testing accounting or other records through observation or examination of source documents or other procedures ordinarily performed in a financial statement audit to evaluate the appropriateness and completeness of the supplementary information.

---

**PLANNING AID REMINDER:** The materiality level used for the supplementary information is the overall audit materiality used in the financial statement audit, or, for the entire governmental entity in a government audit. Therefore, the procedures required to express an opinion on the supplementary information in relation to the financial statements as a whole do not need to be as extensive as if the auditor was expressing an opinion on the supplementary information by itself.

---

Other guidance the auditor may follow in determining whether supplementary information is fairly stated in relation to the financial statements as a whole includes:

- Obtaining an updating representation letter in accordance with AU-C 580;
- Performing subsequent events procedures in accordance with AU-C 560; and
- Sending the client's lawyer a letter of inquiry regarding supplementary information in accordance with AU-C 501.

Audited financial statements are considered readily available if a third-party user can obtain the statements without any further action by the entity. For example, financial statements available on an entity's website are readily available, but if the statements are only available upon request they are not readily available.

**ENGAGEMENT STRATEGY:** The auditor may consider restricting the use of a separate report on supplementary information to avoid potential misinterpretation or misunderstanding of supplementary information that is not presented with the financial statements (see AU-C 905 for further guidance).

## Practitioner's Aids

Exhibit AU-C 725-1 provides an example of a section that may be used in the auditor's report on the financial statements when the auditor is engaged to report on supplementary information in relation to the financial statements as a whole, an unqualified opinion is being issued on the financial statements, and the auditor has concluded that the supplementary information is fairly stated, in all material respects, in relation to the financial statements as a whole.

### EXHIBIT AU-C 725-1—SUPPLEMENTARY INFORMATION SECTION IN AUDITOR'S REPORT USED WHEN REPORTING ON SUPPLEMENTARY INFORMATION

*Supplementary Information*

Our audit was conducted for the purpose of forming an opinion on the financial statements as a whole. The [*identify accompanying supplementary information*] is presented for purposes of additional analysis and is not a required part of the financial statements. Such information is the responsibility of management and was derived from and relates directly to the underlying accounting and other records used to prepare the financial statements. The information has been subjected to the auditing procedures applied in the audit of the financial statements and certain additional procedures, including comparing and reconciling such information directly to the underlying accounting and other records used to prepare the financial statements or to the financial statements themselves, and other additional procedures in accordance with auditing standards generally accepted in the United States of America. In our opinion, the information is fairly stated in all material respects in relation to the financial statements as a whole.

Exhibit AU-C 725-2 provides a reporting example the auditor may use when reporting separately on supplementary information in relation to the financial statements as a whole, an unqualified opinion has been issued on the financial statements, and an unqualified opinion is being issued on the supplementary information.

## EXHIBIT AU-C 725-2—REPORTING ON SUPPLEMENTARY INFORMATION SEPARATELY FROM THE FINANCIAL STATEMENTS AS A WHOLE

We have audited the financial statements of ABC Entity as of and for the year ended December 31, 20X5, and have issued our report thereon dated [*date of the auditor's report on the financial statements*] which contained an unqualified opinion on those financial statements. Our audit was performed for the purpose of forming an opinion on the financial statements as a whole. The [*identify accompanying supplementary information*] is presented for purposes of additional analysis and is not a required part of the financial statements. Such information is the responsibility of management and was derived from and relates directly to the underlying accounting and other records used to prepare the financial statements. The information has been subjected to the auditing procedures applied in the audit of the financial statements and certain additional procedures, including comparing and reconciling such information directly to the underlying accounting and other records used to prepare the financial statements or to the financial statements themselves, and other additional procedures in accordance with auditing standards generally accepted in the United States of America. In our opinion, the information is fairly stated in all material respects in relation to the financial statements as a whole.

# SECTION 730

# REQUIRED SUPPLEMENTARY INFORMATION

## Authoritative Pronouncements

SAS-120—Required Supplementary Information

SAS-137—The Auditor's Responsibilities Relating to Other Information Included in Annual Reports

SAS-140—Amendments to AU-C Sections 725, 730, 930, 935, and 940 to Incorporate Auditor Reporting Changes from SAS Nos. 134 and 137

## Overview

Although required supplementary information is not part of the basic financial statements, certain designated entities must disclose such information. The required supplementary information is considered to be an essential part of the financial report for these designated entities. Although this information does not have to be audited, certain prescribed procedures established by AU-C 730 must be applied. The auditor's objective in performing these procedures is to communicate through his or her report whether any of the required supplementary information has not been presented and whether any material modifications have been identified that should be made to the required supplementary information for it to conform with guidelines established by a designated accounting standard setter. AU-C 720 specifies the auditor's responsibilities for other information that is not required supplementary information.

## Definitions

| | |
|---|---|
| Required supplementary information | Information a designated accounting standard setter required to accompany an entity's basic financial statements. This differs from other types of information outside the basic financial statements because a designated accounting standards setter considers the information an essential part of the financial reporting of certain entities and because authoritative guidelines for the measurement and presentation of the information have been established. |
| Designated accounting standard setter | A body designated by the AICPA council to establish U.S. GAAP pursuant to Rule 1.310 (*Compliance with Standards*) and Rule 1.320 (*Accounting Principles*). Designated bodies are the Federal Accounting Standards Advisory Board (FASAB), the Financial Accounting Standards Board (FASB), the Governmental Accounting Standards Board (GASB), and the International Accounting Standards Board (IASB). |
| Basic financial statements | Financial statements presented in accordance with an applicable financial reporting framework as established by a designated accounting standard setter, excluding required supplementary information. |

| | |
|---|---|
| Applicable financial reporting framework | The financial reporting framework used by management and those charged with governance in preparing the financial statements that is acceptable given the nature of the entity and the objective of the financial statements, or that is required by law or regulation. |
| Prescribed guidelines | The authoritative guidelines established by the designated accounting standard setter for the methods of measurement and presentation of the required supplementary information. |

## Requirements

The auditor is presumptively required to perform the following procedures in fulfilling responsibilities related to required supplementary information:

*Procedures*

1. Apply the following procedures to required supplementary information:
    a. Inquire of management about methods of preparing the information, including whether it has been prepared according to prescribed guidelines, whether any significant assumptions or interpretations underlie its measurement or presentation, and whether measurement or presentation methods have changed since the prior period and reasons for the changes.
    b. Compare the information for consistency with management's responses to the foregoing inquiries, the audited financial statements, and other knowledge obtained during the financial statement audit.
    c. Obtain written representations from management regarding the topics of management inquiry in item 1a and acknowledging responsibility for the required supplementary information.
2. If unable to complete these procedures, consider whether management contributed to the inability to complete the procedures, and, if so, inform those charged with governance.

*Reporting*

3. Include separate section with the heading "Required Supplementary Information" in the auditor's report referring to the required supplementary information. If some or all of the required supplementary information is presented, the separate section should include the following elements:
    a. A statement that [*identify the applicable financial reporting framework*] require that the [*identify the required supplementary information*] be presented to supplement the basic financial statements.
    b. A statement that such information is the responsibility of management, although not a part of the basic financial statements, is required by [*identify designated accounting standard setter*], who considers it to be an essential part of financial reporting for placing the basic financial statements in an appropriate operational, economic, or historical context.
    c. If the auditor is able to complete the prescribed procedures related to the required supplementary information: (1) a statement that the auditor has applied limited procedures, which consisted of inquiries of management and other limited procedures, as prescribed by auditing standards generally accepted in the United States of America regarding the methods of measurement and presentation of the required supplementary information; and (2) a statement that the lim-

ited procedures do not provide the auditor with evidence sufficient to express an opinion or any other form of assurance on the information.

d. If the auditor is unable to complete the prescribed procedures related to the required supplementary information: (1) a statement that the auditor was unable to apply to the information certain limited procedures prescribed by auditing standards generally accepted in the United States of America because [*state the reasons*]; and (2) a statement that the auditor does not express an opinion or any other form of assurance on the information.

e. If some of the required supplementary information is omitted: (1) a statement that management has omitted [*description of the missing required supplementary information*] that [*identify the applicable financial reporting framework*] require to be presented to supplement the basic financial statements; (2) a statement that such missing information, although not a part of the basic financial statements, is required by [*identify designated accounting standard setter*] who considers it to be an essential part of financial reporting for placing the basic financial statements in an appropriate operational, economic, or historical context; and (3) a statement that the auditor's opinion on the basic financial statements is not affected by the missing information.

f. If the measurement or presentation of the required supplementary information departs materially from prescribed guidelines, a statement that the auditor's opinion on the basic financial statements is not affected but that material departures from prescribed guidelines exist [*describe the material departures from the applicable financial reporting framework*].

g. If the auditor has unresolved doubts about whether the required supplementary information conforms to prescribed guidelines, a statement that although the auditor's opinion on the basic financial statements is not affected, the results of the limited procedures have raised doubts regarding whether material modifications should be made to the information for it to conform with guidelines established by [*identify designated accounting standard setter*].

4. If all of the required supplementary information is omitted, the explanatory paragraph should just include the statements described in requirement 3e.

## Analysis and Application of Procedures

*Reporting*

Required supplementary information is not part of the basic financial statements, so the auditor's opinion on the financial statements is not affected by the entity's presentation or lack of presentation of the required supplementary information. If the entity omits presentation of required supplementary information, the auditor does not have a responsibility to present that information.

## Practitioner's Aid

Exhibit AU-C 730-1 provides an example of separate section that can be used in the auditor's report when the required supplementary information is included, the auditor has applied the specified procedures, and no material departures from the prescribed guidelines have been identified.

## EXHIBIT AU-C 730-1—REQUIRED SUPPLEMENTARY INFORMATION SECTION IN AUDITOR'S REPORT WHEN REPORTING ON SUPPLEMENTARY INFORMATION

*Required Supplementary Information*

[*Identify the applicable financial reporting framework (for example,* accounting principles generally accepted in the United States of America)] require that the [*identify the required supplementary information*] on page XX be presented to supplement the basic financial statements. Such information, although not a part of the basic financial statements, is required by [*identify designated accounting standard setter*], who considers it to be an essential part of financial reporting for placing the basic financial statements in an appropriate operational, economic, or historical context. We have applied certain limited procedures to the required supplementary information in accordance with auditing standards generally accepted in the United States of America, which consisted of inquiries of management about the methods of preparing the information and comparing the information for consistency with management's responses to our inquiries, the basic financial statements, and other knowledge we obtained during our audit of the basic financial statements. We do not express an opinion or provide any assurance on the information, because the limited procedures do not provide us with sufficient evidence to express an opinion or provide any assurance.

# AU-C 800
# Special Considerations

| | | |
|---|---|---|
| Section 800: | Special Considerations—Audits of Financial Statements Prepared in Accordance with Special Purpose Frameworks ................................. | 8002 |
| Section 805: | Special Considerations—Audits of Single Financial Statements and Specific Elements, Accounts or Items of a Financial Statement ............................ | 8014 |
| Section 806: | Reporting on Compliance with Aspects of Contractual Agreements or Regulatory Requirements in Connection with Audited Financial Statements ................ | 8024 |
| Section 810: | Engagements to Report on Summary Financial Statements ................................... | 8029 |

# SECTION 800

# SPECIAL CONSIDERATIONS—AUDITS OF FINANCIAL STATEMENTS PREPARED IN ACCORDANCE WITH SPECIAL PURPOSE FRAMEWORKS

## Authoritative Pronouncements

SAS-122—Statements on Auditing Standards: Clarification and Recodification

SAS-127—Omnibus Statement on Auditing Standards—2013

SAS-139—Amendments to AU-C Sections 800, 805, and 810 to Incorporate Auditor Reporting Changes from SAS No. 134

## Overview

An auditor may be engaged to audit financial statements that are not prepared in accordance with U.S. GAAP, but rather are prepared in accordance with a special purpose framework. Special purpose frameworks as contemplated by AU-C 800 are those involving a cash, tax, regulatory, or contractual basis of accounting. The auditor's objectives in these situations are to appropriately address the special considerations relevant to engagement acceptance, engagement planning and performance, and forming an opinion and reporting on the financial statements.

> **OBSERVATION:** The cash, tax, and regulatory bases of accounting are often referred to as an other comprehensive basis of accounting (OCBOA). The term "OCBOA" has been replaced by the term "special purpose framework" as part of the clarification and recodification project.

## Definitions

| | |
|---|---|
| Special purpose financial statements | Financial statements prepared in accordance with a special purpose framework. |
| Special purpose framework | A financial reporting framework other than U.S. GAAP, which is one of the following bases of accounting: |
| • Cash basis | The cash receipts and disbursements basis of accounting, and modifications of the cash basis having substantial support, such as recording depreciation on fixed assets. |
| • Tax basis | The basis of accounting the entity uses to file its income tax return for the period covered by the financial statements. |
| • Regulatory basis | A basis of accounting the entity uses to comply with the requirements or financial reporting provisions of a regulatory agency with jurisdiction over the entity. |

- Contractual basis   A basis of accounting the entity uses to comply with an agreement between the entity and one or more third parties other than the auditor.
- Other   A basis of accounting that uses a definite set of logical, reasonable criteria that is applied to all material items appearing in financial statements to the bases of accounting defined as special purpose frameworks.

## Requirements

The auditor is presumptively required to perform the following procedures when performing an audit of financial statements prepared in accordance with a special purpose framework:

### Engagement Acceptance

1. Determine the acceptability of the financial reporting framework applied in preparing the financial statements. Obtain an understanding of the purpose for which the financial statements are prepared, the intended users, and the steps management has taken to determine that the applicable financial reporting framework is acceptable in the circumstances.

2. Establish whether the preconditions for an audit are present. Obtain management's agreement that it acknowledges and understands its responsibility to include all informative disclosures that are appropriate for the special purpose framework used to prepare the entity's financial statements including:

   a. A description of the special purpose framework, a summary of significant accounting policies, and how the framework differs from U.S. GAAP (the effects of differences do not need to be quantified);
   
   b. Informative disclosures similar to those required by U.S. GAAP if the financial statements contain items similar or the same as those in financial statements prepared in accordance with U.S. GAAP;
   
   c. If prepared in accordance with a contractual basis of accounting, a description of any significant interpretations of the contract on which the financial statements are based; and
   
   d. Additional disclosures beyond those specifically required by the framework that may be necessary for the financial statements to achieve fair presentation.

### Engagement Planning and Performance

3. Comply with all AU-C sections relevant to the audit, adapting all relevant AU-C sections as necessary in the engagement circumstances.

4. Obtain an understanding of the entity's selection and application of accounting policies. If the financial statements are prepared in accordance with a contractual basis of accounting, understand any significant interpretations of the contract management made in preparing the special purpose financial statements. Interpretations are significant if adoption of another reasonable interpretation would have produced a material difference in the information presented in the financial statements.

### Audit Opinion and Reporting

5. Apply the requirements in AU-C 700 (*Forming an Opinion and Reporting on Financial Statements*) or AU-C 703 (*Forming an Opinion and Reporting on Finan-*

cial Statements of Employee Benefit Plans Subject to ERISA) when forming an opinion and reporting on special purpose financial statements. If the auditor concludes a modification to the opinion is necessary, apply the requirements in AU-C 705 (*Modifications to the Opinion in the Independent Auditor's Report*).

6. Evaluate whether the financial statements adequately refer to or describe the applicable financial reporting framework. This involves an evaluation of whether the financial statements (1) are suitably titled, (2) include a summary of significant accounting policies, (3) adequately describe how the special purpose framework differs from U.S. GAAP although quantification of effects of the differences is not required, and (4) if the financial statements have been prepared in accordance with a contractual basis of accounting, whether any significant interpretations of the contract on which the financial statements are based are adequately described.

7. Evaluate whether the financial statements achieve fair presentation. In audits of special purpose financial statements containing the same or similar items to those in financial statements prepared in accordance with U.S. GAAP, evaluate whether the financial statements include informative disclosures similar to those required by U.S. GAAP. Evaluate whether additional disclosures beyond those specifically required by the framework, related to matters not specifically identified in the financial statements, are necessary to fairly present the financial statements. Regardless of whether the going concern basis of accounting is relevant, the auditors should conclude whether or not conditions and events raise substantial doubt about the entity's ability to continue as a going concern for a reasonable period of time. When such substantial doubt exists, evaluate the adequacy of the financial statement disclosures.

8. The auditor's report on special purpose financial statements should follow the guidance in AU-C 700, but also should include:

   a. If management has a choice of financial reporting frameworks in preparing the financial statements, the explanation of management's responsibility for the financial statements should also reference its responsibility for determining that the applicable financial reporting framework is acceptable in the circumstances.

   b. If the financial statements are prepared in accordance with a regulatory or contractual basis of accounting, the report should describe the purpose for which the financial statements are prepared or refer to a note in the financial statements containing that information.

9. Unless the auditor is reporting on financial statements prepared in accordance with a regulatory basis that are intended for general use, the auditor's report should contain an emphasis-of-matter section under an appropriate heading that (1) alerts users of the auditor's report that the financial statements are prepared in accordance with the [*special purpose framework*], (2) refers to the note to the financial statements that describes that framework, and (3) states that the special purpose framework is a basis of accounting other than U.S. GAAP. When a description of the purpose for which the financial statements are prepared is required, the emphasis-of-matter section should include a statement that, as a result, the financial statements may not be suitable for another purpose.

10. Unless the auditor is reporting on financial statements prepared in accordance with a regulatory basis that are intended for general use, if the financial statements are prepared in accordance with a contractual or regulatory basis of accounting, the auditor's report should include an other-matter paragraph under an appropriate heading restricting use of the report to those within the

entity, parties to the contract or agreements, or regulatory agencies with jurisdiction over the entity.

11. If the special purpose financial statements are prepared in accordance with a regulatory basis of accounting and those statements and the auditor's report are intended for general use, express an opinion on whether the financial statements are prepared in accordance with U.S. GAAP. In a separate paragraph, express an opinion on whether the financial statements are prepared in accordance with the special purpose framework.

12. If required by law or regulation to use a specific layout, form, or wording of the auditor's report, the report should refer to GAAS only if it includes, at a minimum, each of the following elements:

   a. A title that clearly states that it is the report of the independent auditor;
   b. An addressee;
   c. An "Opinion" section that identifies the special purpose financial statements that have been audited and contains an expression of opinion on those statements and a reference to the special purpose framework used to prepare the financial statements and, if applicable, an opinion on whether the special purpose financial statements are presented fairly in all material respects in accordance with GAAP;
   d. A description of the purpose for which the financial statements are prepared when required by regulatory or contractual basis of accounting;
   e. A statement that the auditor is required to be independent of the entity and to meet the auditor's other ethical responsibilities;
   f. When applicable, a section that addresses the reporting requirements related to substantial doubt about an entity's ability to continue as a going concern;
   g. A description of management's responsibilities for the preparation and fair presentation of the special purpose financial statements that address, and is consistent with, the requirements of AU-C 700;
   h. A reference to management's responsibility for determining that the applicable financial reporting framework is acceptable;
   i. If applicable, a reference to the law or regulation and a description of the auditor's responsibilities for an audit of financial statements that addresses and is consistent with AU-C 700;
   j. If applicable, a section that addresses the reporting requirements in AU-C 720 related to the auditor's responsibility for other information contained in the annual report;
   k. An emphasis-of-matter section that indicates the financial statements are prepared in accordance with a special purpose framework, that refers to the note in the financial statements describing that framework, and that states that the special purpose framework is a basis of accounting other than U.S. GAAP;
   l. An other-matter paragraph restricting the use of the auditor's report;
   m. The signature of the auditor's firm;
   n. The city and state where the auditor's report is issued; and
   o. The date of the auditor's report.

> **OBSERVATION:** A contractual or regulatory basis of accounting that is based on U.S. GAAP, but that does not require compliance with all of U.S. GAAP, cannot be described as conforming to U.S. GAAP but rather must be described as a contractual or regulatory basis of accounting.

## Analysis and Application of Procedures

*Engagement Acceptance*

Financial reporting frameworks applied in preparing the financial statements are presumed to be acceptable if the framework is prescribed by law or regulation or it encompasses standards established by an organization authorized to promulgate standards for special purpose financial statements. In other situations, the auditor will need to use professional judgment to evaluate the acceptability of the financial reporting framework.

In evaluating whether the financial statements achieve fair presentation according to the applicable financial reporting framework, consider the overall presentation, structure, and content of the financial statements and whether the financial statements and related notes represent the underlying transactions and events in a manner that achieves fair presentation.

> **OBSERVATION:** The auditor may want to discuss with management and with those charged with governance how an audit of special purpose financial statements differs from an audit of general purpose financial statements.

*Engagement Planning and Performance*

An AU-C section is relevant to the audit and to be complied with when the AU-C section is in effect and the circumstances addressed by the AU-C exist. However, requirements of various AU-C sections may need to be adapted to suit the circumstances of a particular engagement. For example, judgments about materiality are generally considered based on the common financial information needs of users as a group, while for special purpose financial statements considering the financial information needs of the intended users may be sufficient.

> **OBSERVATION:** The requirements of AU-C 260 (*The Auditor's Communication with Those Charged with Governance*) apply when those charged with governance are responsible for overseeing the preparation of the financial statements. However, in the case of special purpose financial statements, those charged with governance may not have this responsibility so the requirements of AU-C 260 may not be relevant to the audit unless the auditor is also auditing the general purpose financial statements or has otherwise agreed to such communications.

## Audit Opinion and Reporting

When financial statements based on a special purpose framework are prepared, the auditor should determine whether the financial statements are properly labeled. Care must be taken in titling financial statements so that a reader of the statements will not infer that the financial statements are prepared in accordance with U.S. GAAP. When U.S. GAAP-based financial statements are presented, the financial statements are referred to as balance sheet (or statement of financial position), statement of income (or statement of operations), and statement of cash flows. When special purpose financial statements are presented, it would be inappropriate to refer to a financial statement as a balance sheet or a statement of financial position. Instead, for example, if the financial statements are prepared on a modified cash basis, the title might be "Statement of Assets and Liabilities—Modified Cash Basis." If the financial statements are prepared on a regulatory accounting basis an appropriate name would be "Balance Sheet—Regulatory Accounting Basis."

> **PLANNING AID REMINDER:** In describing how the special purpose framework differs from U.S. GAAP, only material differences are ordinarily addressed.

> **PUBLIC COMPANY IMPLICATION:** For public companies, an audit report on special purpose financial statements must state that the audit was conducted in accordance with standards of the Public Company Accounting Oversight Board.

In order for special purpose financial statements to achieve fair presentation, all informative disclosures that are appropriate for the applicable financial reporting framework should be included. Disclosures in special purpose financial statements may differ from U.S. GAAP disclosures by providing information that communicates the substance of the requirements or by substituting qualitative information for some of the quantitative information required by U.S. GAAP. For example, disclosing repayment terms of significant long-term borrowings without providing the summary of principal reduction during each of the next five years may be sufficient to communicate information about future principal reduction.

> **PLANNING AID REMINDER:** There is no comprehensive list of minimum disclosures for special purpose financial statements. Professional judgment must be used to determine whether the basic concept of adequate disclosure has been achieved in the special purpose financial statements.

Special purpose financial statements may or may not be prepared in accordance with an applicable financial reporting framework that includes the going concern basis of accounting. The going concern basis of accounting is relevant to a special purpose framework if that framework requires management to use a basis of accounting other than the going concern basis of accounting. For example, the AICPA's *Financial Reporting Framework for Small-and Medium-Sized Entities*

(FRF for SMEs) requires management to assess whether the going concern basis of accounting is appropriate but the cash or tax basis of accounting do not. Depending on the financial reporting framework, the auditor's report may need to be adapted related to going concern.

Special purpose financial statements prepared in accordance with a regulatory framework are intended for general use when the financial statements and auditor's report are intended to be used by parties other than those within the entity and regulatory agencies with jurisdiction over the entity or when the financial statements and auditor's report are distributed by the entity to parties other than the regulatory agencies with jurisdiction over the entity. In this instance, an emphasis-of-matter paragraph indicating that the financial statements are prepared in accordance with a special purpose framework and an other-matter paragraph restricting the use of the auditor's report are not required. However, the auditor is required to opine on whether the special purpose financial statements are prepared in accordance with U.S. GAAP as well as in accordance with the special purpose framework.

If the auditor wishes to preclude general use of the report, he or she may, in agreeing with the terms of the engagement, reach an understanding with and obtain agreement from management that the use of the auditor's report will be restricted to those identified in the report. When issuing a restricted use report, if the auditor decides after the audit report has been released to add parties other than the parties originally specified in the report, the auditor should follow the guidance in AU-C 905.

---

**PLANNING AID REMINDER:** In some circumstances, the auditor may consider it appropriate to restrict the use of the auditor's report for a report on financial statements prepared in accordance with a cash or tax basis of accounting.

---

## Practitioner's Aids

Examples of reporting on special purpose frameworks are included to illustrate of the requirements of AU-C 800.

Exhibit AU-C 800-1 includes the various special purpose frameworks and reporting requirements that apply to each.

# EXHIBIT AU-C 800-1—SPECIAL PURPOSE FRAMEWORKS AND REPORTING REQUIREMENTS

|  | Cash Basis | Tax Basis | Regulatory Basis (Restricted Use) | Regulatory Basis (General Use) | Contractual Basis |
|---|---|---|---|---|---|
| **Opinion(s)** | Single opinion on special purpose framework | Single opinion on special purpose framework | Single opinion on special purpose framework | Dual opinion on special purpose framework and U.S. GAAP | Single opinion on special purpose framework |
| **Description of purpose for which special purpose financial statements are prepared** | No | No | Yes | Yes | Yes |
| **Emphasis-of-matter paragraph required (emphasizing use of the special purpose framework)** | Yes | Yes | Yes | No | Yes |
| **Other-matter paragraph required (restricting the use of the report)** | No | No | Yes | No | Yes |

Exhibit AU-C 800-2 contains an example of an independent auditor's report on cash-based financial statements.

# EXHIBIT AU-C 800-2—INDEPENDENT AUDITOR'S REPORT ON CASH-BASED FINANCIAL STATEMENTS

## INDEPENDENT AUDITOR'S REPORT

[*Appropriate Addressee*]

**Report on the Audit of the Financial Statements**

*Opinion*

We have audited the financial statements of XYZ Partnership, which comprise the statement of assets and liabilities arising from cash transactions as of December 31, 20X5, and the related statement of revenue collected and expenses paid for the year then ended, and the related notes to the financial statements.

In our opinion, the accompanying financial statements present fairly, in all material respects, the assets and liabilities arising from cash transactions of XYZ

Partnership as of December 31, 20X5, and its revenue collected and expenses paid during the year then ended in accordance with the cash basis of accounting described in Note X.

*Basis for Opinion*

We conducted our audit in accordance with auditing standards generally accepted in the United States of America (GAAS). Our responsibilities under those standards are further described in the Auditor's Responsibilities for the Audit of the Financial Statements section of our report. We are required to be independent of XYZ Partnership, and to meet our other ethical responsibilities, in accordance with the relevant ethical requirements relating to our audit. We believe that the audit evidence we have obtained is sufficient and appropriate to provide a basis for our audit opinion.

*Emphasis of Matter — Basis of Accounting*

We draw attention to Note X of the financial statements, which describes the basis of accounting. The financial statements are prepared on the cash basis of accounting, which is a basis of accounting other than accounting principles generally accepted in the United States of America. Our opinion is not modified with respect to this matter.

*Responsibilities of Management for the Financial Statements*

Management is responsible for the preparation and fair presentation of the financial statements in accordance with the cash basis of accounting described in Note X, and for determining that the cash basis of accounting is an acceptable basis for the preparation of the financial statements in the circumstances. Management is also responsible for the design, implementation, and maintenance of internal control relevant to the preparation and fair presentation of financial statements that are free from material misstatement, whether due to fraud or error.

*Auditor's Responsibilities for the Audit of the Financial Statements*

Our objectives are to obtain reasonable assurance about whether the financial statements as a whole are free from material misstatement, whether due to fraud or error, and to issue an auditor's report that includes our opinion. Reasonable assurance is a high level of assurance but is not absolute assurance and therefore is not a guarantee that an audit conducted in accordance with GAAS will always detect a material misstatement when it exists. The risk of not detecting a material misstatement resulting from fraud is higher than for one resulting from error, as fraud may involve collusion, forgery, intentional omissions, misrepresentations, or the override of internal control. Misstatements are considered material if there is a substantial likelihood that, individually or in the aggregate, they would influence the judgment made by a reasonable user based on the financial statements.

In performing an audit in accordance with GAAS, we:

- Exercise professional judgment and maintain professional skepticism throughout the audit.
- Identify and assess the risks of material misstatement of the financial statements, whether due to fraud or error, and design and perform audit procedures responsive to those risks. Such procedures include examining, on a test basis, evidence regarding the amounts and disclosures in the financial statements.

- Obtain an understanding of internal control relevant to the audit in order to design audit procedures that are appropriate in the circumstances, but not for the purpose of expressing an opinion on the effectiveness of XYZ Partnership's internal control. Accordingly, no such opinion is expressed.
- Evaluate the appropriateness of accounting policies used and the reasonableness of significant accounting estimates made by management, as well as evaluate the overall presentation of the financial statements.
- Conclude whether, in our judgment, there are conditions or events, considered in the aggregate, that raise substantial doubt about XYZ Partnership's ability to continue as a going concern for a reasonable period of time.

We are required to communicate with those charged with governance regarding, among other matters, the planned scope and timing of the audit, significant audit findings, and certain internal control–related matters that we identified during the audit.

*Report on Other Legal and Regulatory Requirements*

[*The form and content of this section of the auditor's report would vary depending on the nature of the auditor's other reporting responsibilities.*]

[*Signature of the auditor's firm*]

[*City and state where the auditor's report is issued*]

[*Date of the auditor's report*]

---

Exhibit AU-C 800-3 provides an example of an independent auditor's report on financial statements prepared in accordance with a regulatory basis of accounting and intended for general use.

## EXHIBIT AU-C 800-3—INDEPENDENT AUDITOR'S REPORT ON FINANCIAL STATEMENTS PREPARED IN ACCORDANCE WITH A REGULATORY BASIS OF ACCOUNTING AND INTENDED FOR GENERAL USE

---

### INDEPENDENT AUDITOR'S REPORT

[*Appropriate Addressee*]

**Report on the Audit of the Financial Statements**

***Opinions***

We have audited the financial statements of XYZ Government Authority, which comprise the statement of net position—regulatory basis as of December 31, 20X5, and the related statements of revenues, expenses, and changes in net position—regulatory basis and cash flows—regulatory basis for the year then ended, and the related notes to the financial statements.

*Unmodified Opinion on Regulatory Basis of Accounting*

In our opinion, the accompanying financial statements present fairly, in all material respects, the regulatory basis net position of XYZ Government Authority as of December 31, 20X5, and the regulatory basis revenues, expenses, and changes in net position and regulatory basis cash flows thereof for the year then ended in accordance with the financial reporting provisions of Section Y of Regulation Z of Any State Statutes described in Note X.

*Adverse Opinion on U.S. Generally Accepted Accounting Principles*

In our opinion, because of the significance of the matter discussed in the Basis for Adverse Opinion on U.S. Generally Accepted Accounting Principles section of our report, the financial statements do not present fairly, in accordance with accounting principles generally accepted in the United States of America, the financial position of XYZ Government Authority as of December 31, 20X5, or the changes in net position and cash flows thereof for the year then ended.

*Basis for Opinions*

We conducted our audit in accordance with auditing standards generally accepted in the United States of America (GAAS). Our responsibilities under those standards are further described in the Auditor's Responsibilities for the Audit of the Financial Statements section of our report. We are required to be independent of XYZ Government Authority, and to meet our other ethical responsibilities, in accordance with the relevant ethical requirements relating to our audit. We believe that the audit evidence we have obtained is sufficient and appropriate to provide a basis for our audit opinions.

*Basis for Adverse Opinion on U.S. Generally Accepted Accounting Principles*

As described in Note X of the financial statements, the financial statements are prepared by XYZ Government Authority on the basis of the financial reporting provisions of Section Y of Regulation Z of Any State Statutes, which is a basis of accounting other than accounting principles generally accepted in the United States of America, to meet the requirements of Any State Statutes. The effects on the financial statements of the variances between the regulatory basis of accounting described in Note X and accounting principles generally accepted in the United States of America, although not reasonably determinable, are presumed to be material and pervasive.

*Responsibilities of Management for the Financial Statements*

Management is responsible for the preparation and fair presentation of the financial statements in accordance with the financial reporting provisions of Section Y of Regulation Z of Any State Statutes. Management is also responsible for the design, implementation, and maintenance of internal control relevant to the preparation and fair presentation of financial statements that are free from material misstatement, whether due to fraud or error.

*Auditor's Responsibilities for the Audit of the Financial Statements*

Our objectives are to obtain reasonable assurance about whether the financial statements as a whole are free from material misstatement, whether due to fraud or error, and to issue an auditor's report that includes our opinion. Reasonable assurance is a high level of assurance but is not absolute assurance and therefore is not a guarantee that an audit conducted in accordance with GAAS will always detect a material misstatement when it exists. The risk of not detecting a material misstatement resulting from fraud is higher than for one resulting from error, as fraud may involve collusion, forgery, intentional omissions, misrepresentations, or the override of internal control. Misstatements are considered material if there is a substantial likelihood that, individually or in the aggregate, they would influence the judgment made by a reasonable user based on the financial statements.

In performing an audit in accordance with GAAS, we:

- Exercise professional judgment and maintain professional skepticism throughout the audit.
- Identify and assess the risks of material misstatement of the financial statements, whether due to fraud or error, and design and perform audit procedures responsive to those risks. Such procedures include examining, on a test basis, evidence regarding the amounts and disclosures in the financial statements.
- Obtain an understanding of internal control relevant to the audit in order to design audit procedures that are appropriate in the circumstances, but not for the purpose of expressing an opinion on the effectiveness of XYZ Government Authority's internal control. Accordingly, no such opinion is expressed.
- Evaluate the appropriateness of accounting policies used and the reasonableness of significant accounting estimates made by management, as well as evaluate the overall presentation of the financial statements.
- Conclude whether, in our judgment, there are conditions or events, considered in the aggregate, that raise substantial doubt about XYZ Government Authority's ability to continue as a going concern for a reasonable period of time.

We are required to communicate with those charged with governance regarding, among other matters, the planned scope and timing of the audit, significant audit findings, and certain internal control-related matters that we identified during the audit.

**Report on Other Legal and Regulatory Requirements**

[*Form and content of this section of the auditor's report will vary depending on the nature of the auditor's other reporting responsibilities.*]

[*Signature of the auditor's firm*]

[*City and state where the auditor's report was issued*]

[*Date of the auditor's report*]

# SECTION 805

# SPECIAL CONSIDERATIONS—AUDITS OF SINGLE FINANCIAL STATEMENTS AND SPECIFIC ELEMENTS, ACCOUNTS OR ITEMS OF A FINANCIAL STATEMENT

## Authoritative Pronouncements

SAS-122—Statements on Auditing Standards: Clarification and Recodification

SAS-139—Amendments to AU-C Sections 800, 805, and 810 to Incorporate Auditor Reporting Changes from SAS No. 134

SAS Interpretation 1—Auditor of Governmental Cost-Sharing Multiple-Employer Pension Plan (April 2014)

SAS Interpretation 2—Auditor of Governmental Agent Multiple-Employer Pension Plan

## Overview

An auditor may be engaged to audit a single financial statement or a specific element, account, or item of a financial statement. The financial statement or financial statement element audited may be prepared in accordance with either a general or special purpose framework. The auditor's objective in performing this type of audit is to appropriately address the special considerations relevant to engagement acceptance, engagement planning and performance, and forming an opinion and reporting on the financial statement or financial statement element audited.

> **OBSERVATION:** AU-C 805 does not apply to a component auditor's report that is issued based on work performed on a component's financial information at a group engagement team's request for the purposes of an audit of group financial statements.

## Definitions

| | |
|---|---|
| Element of a financial statement | Element, account, or item of a financial statement, including its related notes. Examples include: accounts receivable, allowance for doubtful accounts receivable, inventory, the liability for accrued benefits of a private pension plan, the recorded value of identified intangible assets, the liability for "incurred but not reported" claims in an insurance portfolio, schedules of externally managed assets and income of a private pension plan, schedules of disbursements in relation to a lease property, and schedules of profit participation or employee bonuses. |

| | |
|---|---|
| Single financial statement | Single financial statements include the related notes. Examples include statements of income, operations, retained earnings, cash flows, assets and liabilities, changes in owner's equity, revenue and expenses, operations by product lines, and balance sheet. |

## Requirements

The auditor is presumptively required to perform the following procedures when auditing a single financial statement or a specific element of a financial statement:

### Engagement Acceptance

1. Comply with all AU-C sections relevant to the audit.

2. If not also engaged to audit the entity's complete set of financial statements, determine whether the audit of a single financial statement or a specific financial statement element in accordance with GAAS is practicable. Also determine whether procedures on interrelated items will be able to be performed as necessary to meet the audit objective.

3. Obtain an understanding of the purpose for which the single financial statement or specific element of a financial statement is prepared, the intended users, and the steps management has taken to determine that the application of the financial reporting framework is acceptable.

4. Determine the acceptability of the financial reporting framework applied in preparing the single financial statement or element, including whether (1) the framework's application will result in a presentation with adequate disclosures to enable intended users to understand the information conveyed in the financial statement or financial statement element and (2) the effect of material transactions and events on the information conveyed in the financial statement or element.

### Engagement Planning and Performance

5. Adapt all AU-C sections relevant to the audit as necessary in the engagement circumstances.

6. Perform procedures on interrelated items as necessary to meet the objective of the audit. Many financial statement items are interrelated—for example, sales and receivables, inventory and payables, fixed assets and depreciation. If auditing a specific financial statement element and the element is, or is based upon, the entity's stockholders' equity or net income or the equivalent, perform procedures necessary to obtain sufficient appropriate audit evidence to enable expressing an opinion about financial position (and results of operations in the case of net income), excluding classification or disclosure matters that are not relevant to the audit of that element.

7. If auditing a single financial statement, determine materiality for the single financial statement as a whole. If auditing one or more specific elements of a financial statement, determine materiality for *each* individual element reported on rather than the aggregate of the elements or the complete financial statements as a whole.

---

**PLANNING AID REMINDER:** The management of a governmental cost-sharing multiple-employer pension plan may prepare a schedule of employer allocations and a schedule of pension amounts using the AICPA's whitepaper *Governmen-*

tal Employer Participation in Cost-Sharing Multiple-Employer Plans: Issues Related to Information for Employer Reporting*. The auditor of the governmental pension plan may be engaged to audit these schedules. In accordance with Interpretation 1 of AU 805 the amounts in these schedules are considered elements or items and therefore should be audited following the guidance in AU 805. Moreover, materiality is to be determined for each individual element reported on rather than the aggregate elements. In addition, materiality is to be determined separately for the schedule of employer allocations, and separately for the net pension liability, total deferred inflows of resources, total deferred outflows of resources, and total pension expense. In a similar fashion, management of a governmental agent multiple-employer pension plan may prepare a schedule of changes in fiduciary net position using the AICPA's whitepaper *Governmental Employer Participation in Agent Multiple-Employer Plans: Issues Related to Information for Employer Reporting*. The auditor of the agent plan may be engaged to audit the schedule of changes in fiduciary net position by employer. In accordance with Interpretation 2 of AU 805 the amounts in this schedule are considered elements or items and therefore should be audited following the guidance in AU 805. Moreover, materiality is to be determined separately for fiduciary net position and changes in fiduciary net position. If the auditor of the agent plan is engaged to report separately on fiduciary net position and change in net position for each employer included in the multiple employer plan, then materiality is to be determined separately for each employer.

8. Regardless of whether the going concern basis of accounting is relevant to the preparation of the special purpose financial statements, the requirements of AU-C 570 (*The Auditor's Consideration of an Entity's Ability to Continue as a Going Concern*) apply and the auditor should conclude whether there are conditions or events that raise substantial doubt about the entity's ability to continue as a going concern for a reasonable period of time. When such substantial doubt exists, the auditor should evaluate the adequacy of the financial statement disclosures.

## Audit Opinion and Reporting

9. Apply the requirements in AU-C 700 (*Forming an Opinion and Reporting on Financial Statements*) or AU-C 703 (*Forming an Opinion and Reporting on Financial Statements of Employee Benefit Plans Subject to ERISA*) when forming an opinion and reporting on a single financial statement or a specific financial statement element.

10. If auditing a single financial statement or a specific financial statement element in conjunction with an audit of the entity's complete set of financial statements, issue a separate auditor's report and express a separate opinion for each engagement. The auditor also should indicate the date of the auditor's report on the complete set of financial statements and the nature of opinion expressed on those statements under an appropriate heading.

11. Unless the auditor issues an adverse opinion or disclaims an opinion on the complete set of financial statements, an audited single financial statement or specific financial statement element may be published together with the entity's audited complete set of financial statements if its presentation is sufficiently differentiated from the complete set of financial statements. If the auditor concludes these presentations are not sufficiently differentiated, he or she should ask management to remedy the situation and not release the auditor's report on the single financial statement or specific financial statement element until the auditor is satisfied with the differentiation. The audi-

tor's report on the single financial statement or specific financial statement element should also be differentiated from the report on the complete set of financial statements.

12. If the opinion in the auditor's report on the complete set of financial statements is modified, determine the effect this may have on the opinion on a single financial statement or specific financial statement element.

13. In the audit of a specific financial statement element, if the modified opinion on the complete set of financial statements is relevant to the audit of the specific element or an interrelated item of the specific element:

   a. Express an adverse opinion on the specific element when the modification on the complete set of financial statements is due to a material misstatement.

   b. Disclaim an opinion on the specific element when the modification on the complete set of financial statements is due to an inability to obtain sufficient appropriate audit evidence.

14. If the auditor expresses an adverse opinion or disclaims an opinion on the complete set of financial statements, an unmodified opinion on an audit of a specific element included in those financial statements should only be expressed if (1) that opinion is expressed in an auditor's report that is not published together with and does not otherwise accompany the auditor's report containing the adverse opinion or disclaimer of opinion and (2) the specific element does not constitute a major portion of the entity's complete set of financial statements and is not, or is not based upon, the entity's stockholders' equity or net income or the equivalent.

15. If the auditor expresses an adverse opinion or disclaims an opinion on the complete set of financial statements, an unmodified opinion should not be expressed on a single financial statement that is part of that complete set of financial statements because a single financial statement is deemed to constitute a major portion of a complete set of financial statements.

16. If the auditor's report on a complete set of financial statements includes an emphasis-of- matter or other-matter paragraph that is relevant to the audit of the single financial statement or specific element, include an emphasis-of-matter or other-matter paragraph in the auditor's report in accordance with AU-C 706 (*Emphasis-of-Matter Paragraphs and Other-Matter Paragraphs in the Independent Auditor's Report*).

17. When reporting on an incomplete presentation that is otherwise in accordance with generally accepted accounting principles, include an emphasis-of-matter paragraph in the auditor's report that (1) states the purpose for which the presentation is prepared and refers to a financial statement note describing the basis for the presentation and (2) indicates that the presentation is not intended to be a complete presentation of the entity's assets, liabilities, revenues, or expenses.

---

**OBSERVATION:** A practitioner could be engaged to review or to perform agreed-upon procedures to a single financial statement or specific element. In these cases, the guidance in AT-C 210 and AT-C 215, respectively, would apply.

## Analysis and Application of Procedures

*Engagement Acceptance*

The auditor is required to comply with all relevant ethical requirements as well as all AU-C sections relevant to the audit. Each requirement in a relevant AU-C section should be complied with unless the requirement is conditional and the condition does not exist. In rare circumstances, the auditor may judge it necessary to depart from a presumptively mandatory requirement in a relevant AU-C section by performing alternative audit procedures to achieve the intent of that requirement.

In determining whether an audit of a single financial statement or a specific financial statement element in accordance with GAAS is practicable, the auditor may find that the relevant AU-C sections require an amount of audit effort disproportionate to the element being audited. For example, considering the going concern status of the entity may be relevant even when retained to audit a specific element. In these circumstances, the auditor may discuss with management whether another type of engagement, such as an agreed-upon procedures or review engagement may be more practicable.

A single financial statement or specific financial statement element may be prepared using a financial reporting framework established by an authorized or recognized standards setting organization for the preparation of a complete set of financial statements. In these circumstances, the auditor needs to determine if that framework is acceptable for presenting the single financial statement or financial statement element with adequate disclosures. In making this determination, the auditor may consider:

- Whether the framework is explicitly or implicitly restricted to preparing complete sets of financial statements.

- Whether the single financial statement or financial statement element will fully comply with each framework requirement relevant to that statement or element and whether the presentation will include the related notes.

- Whether the single financial statement or financial statement element, if necessary to achieve fair presentation, will need disclosures beyond those specifically required by the framework (or, in rare cases, will need to depart from a requirement of the framework).

The auditor may be requested to audit an incomplete presentation that is otherwise in accordance with U.S. GAAP. This incomplete presentation may be requested by an entity or required by a regulatory agency, contract, or agreement and is generally regarded as a single financial statement. If the incomplete presentation is required by a regulatory agency, contract, or agreement, the auditor may determine it is more appropriate for the description of the applicable financial reporting framework to refer to the regulatory or contractual basis of accounting rather than to refer to U.S. GAAP. If the auditor makes this determination, AU-C 800 would also be relevant.

## Engagement Planning and Performance

AU-C sections relevant to the audit include AU-C sections that are in effect that address circumstances existing in the audit. AU-C sections such as AU-C 240, AU-C 550, and AU-C 570 are relevant even in audits of financial statement elements because the element could, in principle, be misstated or impacted due to fraud, related-party transactions, or the incorrect application of the going concern assumption.

---

**ENGAGEMENT STRATEGY:** In audits of single financial statements or financial statement elements when the auditor is also engaged to audit the entity's complete set of financial statements, audit evidence obtained as part of the audit of the entity's complete set of financial statements may be able to be used in the single financial statement or financial statement element audit.

---

Because the auditor determines materiality for the audit of a single financial statement or financial statement element separately from materiality for the complete set of financial statements, the nature, timing, and extent of audit procedures will typically be more extensive for the element audited than if that element was being considered in an audit of the complete financial statements as a whole.

## Audit Opinion and Reporting

If the opinion in an auditor's report on an entity's complete set of financial statements is modified and that modification is relevant to the audit of a single financial statement or financial statement element, the modification is considered material and pervasive with respect to that financial statement or element. Modifications the auditor may consider not relevant to the audit of a single financial statement or financial statement element include those solely related to classification or disclosure.

---

**OBSERVATION:** If the auditor is retained to audit accounts receivable and if the auditor's report on the financial statements as a whole is modified related to revenues, this modification would be relevant to the audit of the specific element, accounts receivable, because of the interrelated nature of revenues and accounts receivable.

---

The auditor may decide it is appropriate to include an other-matter paragraph in the audit report on a financial statement or financial statement element describing the modification to the opinion on the entity's complete set of financial statements even when that modified opinion, emphasis-of-matter paragraph, or other-matter paragraph does not relate to the audited financial statement or financial statement element. This may be done if the auditor judges it to be relevant to the users' understanding of the audited financial statement, financial statement element, or the related auditor's report.

> **OBSERVATION:** In the auditor's report on a complete set of financial statements, the auditor is permitted to express a disclaimer of opinion on the results of operations and cash flows and an unmodified opinion on the financial position since the disclaimer is not being issued on the financial statements as a whole.

If an auditor reports on an incomplete presentation that is otherwise in accordance with U.S. GAAP and is prepared in accordance with a regulatory or contractual basis of accounting, the requirement to include an emphasis-of-matter paragraph in the auditor's report does not apply and the auditor should follow the guidance in AU-C 800.

The applicable financial reporting framework may not address whether management is required to make a going concern assessment for a single financial statement or a specific element, account, or item of a financial statement. Thus, the description in the auditor's report of management's responsibilities related to going concern may not be relevant or may need to be adjusted. Similarly, the statement of auditor's responsibilities may also need to be adjusted.

Determining if a matter included in the auditor's report on the complete set of financial statements is relevant in the context of an engagement to report on a single financial statement or a specific element of a financial statement involves professional judgment.

When applicable, key audit matters communicated in the auditor's report may have implications for an audit of a single financial statement or specific element of a financial statement.

## Practitioner's Aids

Examples of auditor's reports on a single financial statement and on a specific financial statement element are illustrated in the following exhibits.

Exhibit AU-C 805-1 contains an auditor's report on a single financial statement.

### EXHIBIT AU-C 805-1—AUDITOR'S REPORT ON A SINGLE FINANCIAL STATEMENT

**INDEPENDENT AUDITOR'S REPORT**

[*Appropriate Addressee*]

**Report on the Financial Statement**

*Opinion*

We have audited the balance sheet of XYZ Company as of December 31, 20X5, and the related notes (the financial statement).

In our opinion, the accompanying financial statement presents fairly, in all material respects, the financial position of XYZ Company as of December 31, 20X5, in accordance with accounting principles generally accepted in the United States of America.

### Basis for Opinion

We conducted our audit in accordance with auditing standards generally accepted in the United States of America (GAAS). Our responsibilities under those standards are further described in the Auditor's Responsibilities for the Audit of the Financial Statement section of our report. We are required to be independent of XYZ Company and to meet our other ethical responsibilities, in accordance with the relevant ethical requirements relating to our audit. We believe that the audit evidence we have obtained is sufficient and appropriate to provide a basis for our audit opinion.

### Responsibilities of Management for the Financial Statement

Management is responsible for the preparation and fair presentation of the financial statement in accordance with accounting principles generally accepted in the United States of America, and for the design, implementation, and maintenance of internal control relevant to the preparation and fair presentation of the financial statement that is free from material misstatement, whether due to fraud or error.

### Auditor's Responsibilities for the Audit of the Financial Statement

Our objectives are to obtain reasonable assurance about whether the financial statement as a whole is free from material misstatement, whether due to fraud or error, and to issue an auditor's report that includes our opinion. Reasonable assurance is a high level of assurance but is not absolute assurance and therefore is not a guarantee that an audit conducted in accordance with GAAS will always detect a material misstatement when it exists. The risk of not detecting a material misstatement resulting from fraud is higher than for one resulting from error, as fraud may involve collusion, forgery, intentional omissions, misrepresentations, or the override of internal control. Misstatements are considered material if there is a substantial likelihood that, individually or in the aggregate, they would influence the judgment made by a reasonable user based on the financial statement.

In performing an audit in accordance with GAAS, we:

- Exercise professional judgment and maintain professional skepticism throughout the audit.
- Identify and assess the risks of material misstatement of the financial statement, whether due to fraud or error, and design and perform audit procedures responsive to those risks. Such procedures include examining, on a test basis, evidence regarding the amounts and disclosures in the financial statement.
- Obtain an understanding of internal control relevant to the audit in order to design audit procedures that are appropriate in the circumstances, but not for the purpose of expressing an opinion on the effectiveness of XYZ Company's internal control. Accordingly, no such opinion is expressed.
- Evaluate the appropriateness of accounting policies used and the reasonableness of significant accounting estimates made by management, as well as evaluate the overall presentation of the financial statement.
- Conclude whether, in our judgment, there are conditions or events, considered in the aggregate, that raise substantial doubt about XYZ Company's ability to continue as a going concern for a reasonable period of time.

We are required to communicate with those charged with governance regarding, among other matters, the planned scope and timing of the audit, significant audit findings, and certain internal control-related matters that we identified during the audit.

Report on Other Legal and Regulatory Requirements

[*The form and content of this section of the auditor's report would vary depending on the nature of the auditor's other reporting responsibilities.*]

[*Signature of the auditor's firm*]

[*City and state where the auditor's report is issued*]

[*Date of the auditor's report*]

Exhibit AU-C 805-2 contains an auditor's report on a specific element, account, or item of a financial statement when the audit was performed in conjunction with an audit on the entity's complete set of financial statements.

## EXHIBIT AU-C 805-2—AUDITOR'S REPORT ON A SPECIFIC ELEMENT, ACCOUNT, OR ITEM OF A FINANCIAL STATEMENT

### INDEPENDENT AUDITOR'S REPORT

[*Appropriate Addressee*]

**Report on the Audit of the Schedule**

*Opinion*

We have audited the schedule of accounts receivable of XYZ Company as of December 31, 20X5, and the related notes (the schedule).

In our opinion, the accompanying schedule presents fairly, in all material respects, the accounts receivable of XYZ Company as of December 31, 20X5, in accordance with accounting principles generally accepted in the United States of America.

*Basis for Opinion*

We conducted our audit in accordance with auditing standards generally accepted in the United States of America (GAAS). Our responsibilities under those standards are further described in the Auditor's Responsibilities for the Audit of the Schedule section of our report. We are required to be independent of XYZ Company and to meet our other ethical responsibilities, in accordance with the relevant ethical requirements relating to our audit. We believe that the audit evidence we have obtained is sufficient and appropriate to provide a basis for our audit opinion.

*Responsibilities of Management for the Schedule*

Management is responsible for the preparation and fair presentation of the schedule in accordance with accounting principles generally accepted in the United States of America and for the design, implementation, and maintenance of internal control relevant to the preparation and fair presentation of the schedule that is free from material misstatement, whether due to fraud or error.

### Auditor's Responsibilities for the Audit of the Schedule

Our objectives are to obtain reasonable assurance about whether the schedule as a whole is free from material misstatement, whether due to fraud or error, and to issue an auditor's report that includes our opinion. Reasonable assurance is a high level of assurance but is not absolute assurance and therefore is not a guarantee that an audit conducted in accordance with GAAS will always detect a material misstatement when it exists. The risk of not detecting a material misstatement resulting from fraud is higher than for one resulting from error, as fraud may involve collusion, forgery, intentional omissions, misrepresentations, or the override of internal control. Misstatements are considered material if there is a substantial likelihood that, individually or in the aggregate, they would influence the judgment made by a reasonable user based on the schedule.

In performing an audit in accordance with GAAS, we:

- Exercise professional judgment and maintain professional skepticism throughout the audit. • Identify and assess the risks of material misstatement of the schedule, whether due to fraud or error, and design and perform audit procedures responsive to those risks. Such procedures include examining, on a test basis, evidence regarding the amounts and disclosures in the schedule.
- Obtain an understanding of internal control relevant to the audit in order to design audit procedures that are appropriate in the circumstances, but not for the purpose of expressing an opinion on the effectiveness of XYZ Company's internal control. Accordingly, no such opinion is expressed.
- Evaluate the appropriateness of accounting policies used and the reasonableness of significant accounting estimates made by management, as well as evaluating the overall presentation of the schedule.
- Conclude whether, in our judgment, there are conditions or events, considered in the aggregate, that raise substantial doubt about XYZ Company's ability to continue as a going concern for a reasonable period of time.

We are required to communicate with those charged with governance regarding, among other matters, the planned scope and timing of the audit, significant audit findings, and certain internal control-related matters that we identified during the audit.

### Other Matter

We have audited, in accordance with GAAS, the financial statements of XYZ Company as of and for the year ended December 31, 20X5, and our report thereon, dated March 15, 20X6, expressed an unmodified opinion on those financial statements.

### Report on Other Legal and Regulatory Requirements

[*The form and content of this section of the auditor's report would vary depending on the nature of the auditor's other reporting responsibilities.*]

[*Signature of the auditor's firm*]

[*City and state where the auditor's report is issued*]

[*Date of the auditor's report*]

# SECTION 806

## REPORTING ON COMPLIANCE WITH ASPECTS OF CONTRACTUAL AGREEMENTS OR REGULATORY REQUIREMENTS IN CONNECTION WITH AUDITED FINANCIAL STATEMENTS

### Authoritative Pronouncements

SAS-122—Statements on Auditing Standards: Clarification and Recodification

### Overview

An auditor may be asked to provide assurance on an entity's compliance with aspects of contractual agreements or regulatory requirements in connection with a financial statement audit (often referred to as a by-product report). The relevant financial statement audit may be of either general purpose or special purpose financial statements. Financial statement users, such as banks and regulatory agencies, may request that an entity's auditor specifically state whether the entity has observed a particular contract clause, covenant requirement, or administrative regulation. For example, a loan agreement may require that the entity's working capital not be less than a certain dollar amount.

In these situations, the auditor may provide negative assurance about the entity's compliance based on the financial statement audit. Negative assurance consists of a statement that nothing came to the auditor's attention as a result of performing procedures for the financial statement audit that caused the auditor to believe the entity did not comply with specified aspects of contractual agreements or regulatory requirements.

**PLANNING AID REMINDER:** If engaged to perform a compliance audit, the auditor should follow the guidance in AU-C 935 (*Compliance Audits*). If engaged to provide assurance on compliance with specific laws, regulations, rules, contracts, or grants that are not related to the financial statements, or to report on the effectiveness of internal control with respect to compliance, the auditor should follow the guidance in AT-C 315.

### Requirements

The auditor is presumptively required to perform the following procedures when reporting on compliance with aspects of contractual agreements or regulatory requirements in connection with audited financial statements:

1. Only include a statement in the auditor's report on compliance that nothing came to the auditor's attention causing the auditor to believe that the entity failed to comply with specified aspects of the contractual

agreements or regulatory requirements as they relate to accounting matters when:

   a. The auditor has not identified any instances of noncompliance.

   b. The applicable covenants or regulatory matters relate to matters that have been subjected to audit procedures in the financial statement audit.

   c. The auditor expressed an unmodified or qualified opinion on the financial statements related to the applicable covenants or regulatory requirements.

2. If instances of noncompliance are identified, describe those instances in the report on compliance.

3. If the auditor expressed an adverse opinion or disclaimed an opinion on the financial statements, a report on compliance should only be issued when instances of noncompliance are identified and the wording of the report should be appropriately modified.

4. Notwithstanding the requirements in the foregoing items 1 through 3, the auditor is not precluded from issuing a report on compliance if such a report is required by another set of auditing standards and the auditor has been engaged to audit the financial statements in accordance with GAAS and the other set of auditing standards.

5. Provide the report on compliance in writing as either (1) a separate report or (2) one or more paragraphs included in the auditor's report accompanying the financial statements.

6. If reporting on compliance with aspects of contractual agreements or regulatory requirements in a separate report, include:

   a. A title with the word "independent," indicating the report is from an independent auditor;

   b. An appropriate addressee;

   c. A paragraph stating that the financial statements were audited in accordance with GAAS, that the United States is the country of origin of those standards, and the date of the auditor's report on those financial statements;

   d. If the auditor's report on the financial statements is modified, a statement describing the nature of the modification;

   e. A reference to the specific covenants or paragraphs of the contractual agreement or regulatory requirement and (1) if no instances of noncompliance are identified, a statement that nothing came to the auditor's attention causing him or her to believe that the entity failed to comply with specified aspects of the contractual agreements or regulatory requirements related to accounting matters, or, (2) if instances of noncompliance are identified, a description of the contractual agreements or regulatory requirements and the identified areas of noncompliance;

f. A statement that the report is being provided in connection with the financial statement audit;

g. A statement that the audit's primary focus was not obtaining knowledge about compliance and had the auditor performed additional procedures, other matters regarding noncompliance with the specific covenants or paragraphs of the contractual agreement or regulatory requirement may have come to the auditor's attention;

h. A paragraph including a description and the source of any significant interpretations made by the entity's management relating to the provisions of a relevant agreement;

i. A paragraph restricting the report's use to management, those charged with governance, others within the organization, the regulatory agency responsible for the provisions, or other parties to the contract or agreement;

j. The manual or printed signature of the auditor's firm, and the city and state where the auditor practices; and

k. The date of the report, which should be the same date as the auditor's report on the financial statements.

7. If reporting on compliance with aspects of contractual agreements or regulatory requirements within the auditor's report on the financial statements, include:

a. An other-matter paragraph referencing the specific covenants or paragraphs of the contractual agreement or regulatory requirement and (1) if no instances of noncompliance are identified, a statement that nothing came to the auditor's attention causing him or her to believe that the entity failed to comply with specified aspects of the contractual agreements or regulatory requirements related to accounting matters, or, (2) if instances of noncompliance are identified, a description of those identified instances;

b. A statement that the communication is being provided in connection with the financial statement audit;

c. A statement that the audit was not primarily directed toward obtaining knowledge about compliance and, had the auditor performed additional procedures, other matters regarding noncompliance with the specific covenants or paragraphs of the contractual agreement or regulatory requirement may have come to the auditor's attention;

d. A paragraph with a description and source of any significant interpretations of contractual provisions or regulatory requirements made by the entity's management; and

e. A paragraph restricting the report's use to management, those charged with governance, others within the organization, the regulatory agency responsible for the provisions, or other parties to the contract or agreement.

## Analysis and Application of Procedures

A restriction on the use of the report is necessary because the aspects of the contractual agreements or regulatory requirements being reported on are developed for and directed to only those parties to the agreement or contract or the regulatory agency responsible for the requirements.

> **OBSERVATION:** If the auditor's report on compliance with aspects of contractual agreements or regulatory requirements is included in his or her report on the financial statements, the restriction on the report's use to specified parties applies to the entire auditor's report. However, if a separate report on compliance with aspects of contractual agreements or regulatory requirements is issued, then only that report will be restricted as to use by the specified parties.

When there are identified instances of noncompliance and the entity has obtained a waiver for the noncompliance, the auditor may include a statement that a waiver has been obtained in the report on compliance. Regardless of whether a waiver has been obtained, all instances of noncompliance are required to be described in the report on compliance.

If the auditor has included an emphasis-of-matter paragraph in the report on the financial statements as a whole (e.g., a going-concern paragraph), the auditor may include that same paragraph in the report on compliance.

Exhibit AU-C 806-1 is an example of a separate auditor's report on compliance when there are no identified instances of noncompliance.

## Practitioner's Aid

*EXHIBIT AU-C 806-1—SEPARATE AUDITOR'S REPORT ON COMPLIANCE WITH ASPECTS OF CONTRACTUAL AGREEMENTS*

### INDEPENDENT AUDITOR'S REPORT

We have audited, in accordance with auditing standards generally accepted in the United States of America, the financial statements of X Company, which comprise the balance sheet as of December 31, 20X5, and the related statements of income, changes in stockholders' equity, and cash flows for the year then ended, and the related notes to the financial statements, and have issued our report thereon dated February 20, 20X6.

In connection with our audit, nothing came to our attention that caused us to believe that X Company failed to comply with the terms, covenants, provisions, or conditions of the restrictive terms of the loan agreement dated March 4, 20X0, as explained in Section A of the agreement with First State Bank insofar as they relate to accounting matters. However, our audit was not directed primarily toward obtaining knowledge of such noncompliance. Accordingly, had we performed additional procedures, other matters may have come to our attention regarding the Company's noncompliance with the above-referenced terms, covenants, provisions, or conditions of the loan agreement, insofar as they relate to accounting matters.

This report is intended solely for the information and use of the board of directors and management of X Company and First State Bank and is not intended to be and should not be used by anyone other than these specified parties.

[*Auditor's signature*]

[*Auditor's city and state*]

[*Date of the auditor's report*]

# SECTION 810

# ENGAGEMENTS TO REPORT ON SUMMARY FINANCIAL STATEMENTS

## Authoritative Pronouncements

SAS-122—Statements on Auditing Standards: Clarification and Recodification

SAS-137—The Auditor's Responsibilities Relating to Other Information Included in Annual Reports

SAS-139—Amendments to AU-C Sections 800, 805, and 810 to Incorporate Auditor Reporting Changes from SAS No. 134

## Overview

AU-C 810 is applicable to engagements to report separately on summary financial statements that are derived from financial statements audited in accordance with GAAS by the same auditor. The auditor issues an opinion as to whether the summary financial statements are materially consistent with the audited financial statements from which they are drawn. In these situations, the auditor's objectives are: to determine if it is appropriate to accept such an engagement; if the engagement is accepted, to form an opinion on the summary financial statements based on an evaluation of the conclusions drawn from the audit evidence obtained; and to clearly express that opinion through a written report with a description of the basis for that opinion.

In some instances, summary financial statements are required to accompany the basic financial statements by the standard setter responsible for the financial reporting framework being used. In this instance, the requirements of AU-C 730 (*Required Supplementary Information*) are applicable.

---

**OBSERVATION:** When an auditor reports on financial statements that present comparative information with summarized prior period financial information, the applicable reporting guidance is described in AU-C 700 (*Forming an Opinion and Reporting on Financial Statements*).

---

## Definitions

| | |
|---|---|
| Applied criteria | Criteria applied by management in preparation of the summary financial statements. |

| Summary financial statements | Historical financial information derived from, but containing less detail than, the financial statements that provides a structured representation consistent with that provided by the financial statements of the entity's economic resources or obligations at a point in time or the changes therein for a period of time. These statements are separately presented, and are not shown as comparative information. |
|---|---|

## Requirements

The auditor is presumptively required to observe the following guidelines in an engagement to report on summary financial statements:

### Engagement Acceptance

1. An auditor should only accept an engagement to report on summary financial statements in accordance with AU-C 810 if that auditor has been engaged to conduct an audit in accordance with GAAS of the financial statements from which the summary financial statements are derived.

2. Before accepting an engagement to report on summary financial statements:
   a. Determine whether the applied criteria are acceptable, including whether the criteria (1) are unbiased so summary financial statements are not misleading; (2) permit reasonably consistent qualitative or quantitative measurements so information in the summary financial statements agrees with or can be recalculated from the related information in the audited financial statements; (3) are sufficiently complete so the summary financial statements contain the necessary information and are at an appropriate level of aggregation to not be misleading; and (4) are relevant to the summary financial statements in view of their purpose.
   b. Obtain management's agreement that it acknowledges and understands its responsibility (1) for preparing the summary financial statements in accordance with the applied criteria; (2) to provide the auditor with written representations; (3) to make the audited financial statements readily available to the intended users of the summary financial statements; and (4) to include the auditor's report on the summary financial statements in any document containing the summary financial statements and indicates the auditor has reported on them.
   c. Obtain management's written agreement about the expected form and content of the report on summary financial statements, including that circumstances may cause the report to differ from this expectation.

3. Do not accept the engagement to report on the summary financial statements if the applied criteria are not acceptable or management's agreement is unable to be obtained.

### Engagement Procedures

4. Perform the following procedures, and any other procedures considered necessary, on the summary financial statements to provide the basis for the auditor's opinion on those statements:
   a. Evaluate whether the statements' summarized nature is adequately disclosed and the audited financial statements are identified.

b. If not accompanied by the audited financial statements, evaluate whether the summary financial statements clearly describe where the audited financial statements are available and whether the audited financial statements are readily available to the intended users of the summary financial statements.
c. Evaluate whether the applied criteria are adequately disclosed.
d. Compare the summary statements with the audited statements to determine if the summary financial statements agree with or can be recalculated from the related information in the audited financial statements.
e. Evaluate whether the summary statements are prepared in accordance with the applied criteria.
f. Evaluate whether the necessary information in included at the appropriate level of aggregation to not be misleading in view of the purpose of the summary financial statements.

## Written Representations

5. Request management provide written representations in the form of a representation letter addressed to the auditor for all summary financial statements and periods referred to in the auditor's report on the summary financial statements for the following matters:
   a. Management has prepared the summary financial statements in accordance with the applied criteria and believes the applied criteria to be acceptable.
   b. Management will make the audited financial statements readily available to the intended users of the summary financial statements upon issuance of the summary financial statements, if the summary financial statements will not be accompanied by the audited financial statements.
   c. If the date of the auditor's report on the summary financial statements is later than the date of the auditor's report on the audited financial statements: (1) whether any information has come to management's attention causing it to believe any previous representations on the audited financial statements need to be modified and (2) whether any events have occurred subsequent to the date of the audited financial statements that may require adjustment of, or disclosure in, the audited financial statements.

6. The date of the written representations should be as of the date of the auditor's report on the summary financial statements.

## Audit Opinion and Reporting

7. If the auditor concludes an unmodified opinion on the summary financial statements is appropriate, the auditor's opinion should state that the summary financial statements are consistent, in all material respects, with the audited financial statements from which they have been derived, in accordance with the applied criteria.

8. If the summary financial statements are not consistent, in all material respects, with the audited financial statements, in accordance with the applied criteria, and management does not agree to make the necessary changes, express an adverse opinion on the summary financial statements.

9. If the auditor's opinion on the audited financial statements contains an adverse opinion or a disclaimer of opinion, the auditor should withdraw from

the engagement where permissible under applicable law or regulation. If the auditor is not able to withdraw and issues an auditor's report on the summary financial statements, the auditor's report should:

    a. State that the auditor's report on the audited financial statements contains an adverse opinion or disclaimer of opinion;

    b. Describe the basis for that adverse opinion or disclaimer of opinion; and

    c. State that because of that adverse opinion or disclaimer of opinion it is inappropriate to express, and the auditor does not express, an opinion on the summary financial statements.

10. The auditor's report on the summary financial statements should include the following elements:

    a. Title clearly indicating it as the report of an independent auditor;

    b. An addressee;

    c. Identification of: (1) the summary financial statements on which the auditor is reporting, including the title of each statement included and (2) the audited financial statements from which the summary financial statements have been derived;

    d. An expression of an opinion;

    e. A statement that the summary financial statements do not contain all the disclosures required by the financial reporting framework applied in preparing the audited financial statements, and that reading the summary financial statements is not a substitute for reading the audited financial statements;

    f. Reference to the auditor's report on the audited financial statements, the date of that report, and, if it is the case, the fact that an unmodified opinion is expressed on the audited financial statements;

    g. If the date of the auditor's report on the summary financial statements is later than the date of the auditor's report on the audited financial statements, a statement that the summary and audited financial statements do not reflect the effect of any events occurring subsequent to the date of the auditor's report on the audited financial statements;

    h. Description of management's responsibility for the summary financial statements including its responsibility for preparing the summary financial statements in accordance with the applied criteria;

    i. Statement that the auditor is responsible for expressing an opinion on the summary financial statements based on procedures required by GAAS and that the United States is the country of origin of those standards, including that: (1) procedures consist principally of comparing the summary financial statements with the related information in the audited financial statements from which the summary statements have been derived and evaluating whether the summary financial statements are prepared in accordance with the applied criteria and (2) if the date of the auditor's report on the summary financial statements is later than the date of the auditor's report on the audited financial statements, the auditor did not perform any audit procedures regarding the audited financial statements after the date of the report on the audited statements;

    j. Signature of the auditor's firm;

    k. City and state where the auditor's report was issued; and

    l. Date of the auditor's report.

11. Date the auditor's report on the summary financial statements no earlier than:

    a. The date on which sufficient appropriate audit evidence has been obtained on which to base an opinion, including evidence that management and those charged with governance as appropriate have prepared and taken responsibility for the summary financial statements.

    b. The date of the auditor's report on the audited financial statements.

12. If the auditor's report on the summary financial statements is dated later than the date of the auditor's report on the audited financial statements and the auditor becomes aware of subsequently discovered facts, do not release the auditor's report on the summary financial statements until consideration of those facts in relation to the audited financial statements has been completed in accordance with AU-C 560.

13. If the auditor's report on the audited financial statements contains a qualified opinion, an emphasis-of-matter paragraph, an other matter paragraph, a going concern section, or communication of key audit matters, the auditor's report on the summary financial statements should (1) state that the auditor's report on the audited financial statements contains such an opinion, paragraph, or section, (2) describe the basis for that opinion on the financial statements and the effect thereof, or (3) describe the matter referred to in the emphasis-of-matter, other-matters paragraph, or "Going Concern" section in the auditor's report on the audited financial statements.

## Other Matters

14. If the auditor's report on the audited financial statements is for restricted use or alerts readers that the audited financial statements are prepared in accordance with a special purpose framework, a similar restriction or alert should be included in the auditor's report on the summary financial statements.

15. If the audited financial statements contain comparative financial statements but the summary financial statements do not, determine if this omission is reasonable in the circumstances of the engagement. Determine the effect of an unreasonable omission on the auditor's report on the summary financial statements.

16. If the summary financial statements contain comparative financial statements, and if the prior year summary statements were reported on by another auditor and the predecessor auditor's report on the prior period's summary financial statements is not reissued the auditor's report on the summary financial statements should state:

    a. Summary financial statements of the prior period were audited by a predecessor auditor;

    b. The type of opinion expressed by the predecessor auditor and the reasons for any modified opinion; and

    c. The date of that report.

17. If the summary financial statements contain comparative summary financial statements that were not reported on by any auditor, the auditor's report on the summary financial statements should state that the comparative summary financial statements were not reported on by the auditor and therefore the auditor does not express an opinion on the comparative summary financial statements.

18. Evaluate whether any unaudited information presented with the summary financial statements is clearly differentiated from the summary financial statements. If the auditor concludes unaudited information is not clearly differentiated, he or she should ask management to change the presentation of the unaudited information. If management refuses to do so, the auditor should explain in the auditor's report on the summary financial statements that such information is not covered by the report and accordingly, the auditor does not express an opinion on the information.

19. Read other information included in a document containing the summary financial statements and related auditor's report to identify any material inconsistencies with the summary financial statements or the audited financial statements. If a material inconsistency or material misstatement of fact is identified, he or she should discuss the matter with management and consider appropriate further action in the circumstances. And, in the case of a material inconsistency, the auditor should determine if the summary financial statements or the other information needs to be revised.

20. If an entity intends to state that the auditor has reported on summary financial statements in a document containing the statements but not the auditor's report, the auditor should request management include the auditor's report in the document. If management refuses, the auditor should take appropriate action to prevent being inappropriately associated with the summary financial statements in that document.

21. If the auditor reports on an entity's financial statements but not its summary financial statements and the entity plans to refer to the auditor and the fact that summary financial statements are derived from the audited financial statements, the auditor should be satisfied that the reference to the auditor applies to the auditor's report on the audited financial statements, and the statement does not give the impression that the auditor has reported on the summary financial statements. If the auditor is not satisfied that this is the case, he or she should request management to:

   a. Change the statement to satisfy these criteria,
   b. Not refer to the auditor in the document, or
   c. Engage the auditor to report on the summary financial statements and include the related auditor's report in the document.

If management refuses, the auditor should advise the entity that he or she disagrees with the reference to the auditor and carry out appropriate actions to prevent from being inappropriately associated with the summary financial statements in that document.

## Analysis and Application of Procedures

### Engagement Acceptance

If the auditor has not also audited the financial statements from which the summary financial statements are derived, application of the guidance in AU-C 810 will not provide sufficient appropriate evidence on which to base an opinion on the summary financial statements and the auditor should not accept the engagement.

In many cases, the criteria for preparing summary financial statements may be established by an authorized or recognized standards setting organization or by law or regulation, in which case the auditor may presume the criteria used are acceptable. In circumstances when the auditor must determine whether the applied criteria are acceptable, however, he or she may consider the nature of the entity, the purpose of the summary financial statements, the information needs of the intended users of the summary financial statements, and whether the applied criteria will result in summary financial statements that are not misleading in the circumstances. In the absence of established criteria for summary financial statements, management will have to develop the criteria. Reference to industry practice may be appropriate in this instance.

Summary financial statements are aggregated versions of the audited financial statements with limited disclosures so they contain an increased risk that information necessary for the statements to not be misleading is not there, especially when there are no existing criteria established for the preparation of summary financial statements.

Because of these limitations, reading summary financial statements is not a substitute for reading the audited financial statements. Therefore, the auditor must obtain management's agreement acknowledging its responsibility for making the audited financial statements readily available to the intended users of the summary financial statements. Audited financial statements are considered readily available if a third-party user can obtain the statements without any further action by the entity. For example, indicating that the audited financial statements are available upon request is not consistent with these statements being readily available.

## Engagement Procedures

Adequate disclosure of the summarized nature of summary financial statements and the identity of the audited financial statements may be provided by a title such as "Summary Financial Statements Prepared from the Audited Financial Statements as of and for the Year Ended December 21, 20X5."

## Audit Opinion and Reporting

The very nature of summary financial statements is that they are presented in less detail than audited financial statements. For this reason, they do not fairly present the financial position or results of operation of an entity. When an auditor is engaged to report on summary financial statements derived from audited financial statements, the auditor should report in a different manner than when he or she reports on the complete financial statements to prevent users from assuming all the disclosures necessary for complete financial statements are included. In some cases, if the auditor expresses a qualified opinion on financial statements, he or she may decide it is inappropriate to express an opinion on the summary financial statements. If so, the auditor should follow the reporting guidance from paragraph 9.

Summary financial statements, due to their summarized nature, are either consistent or not consistent in all material respects with the audited financial statements in accordance with the applied criteria. If the summary financial statements are consistent with the audited financial statements, an unmodified opinion is appropriate; if the statements are not consistent and management refuses to make the necessary changes then an adverse opinion is appropriate.

> **OBSERVATION:** Because of the summarized nature of summary financial statements, a qualified opinion on the summary statements is not appropriate.

*Other Matters*

When comparative financial statements are included in the audited financial statements, it is presumed that the summary financial statements will also contain comparatives. However, if the summary financial statements do not contain comparatives, the auditor should determine whether that omission is reasonable. This decision may be affected by the nature and objective of the summary financial statements, the applied criteria, or the information needs of the intended users of the summary financial statements.

*Auditor Association*

Management may indicate in a document including summary financial statements that the auditor has reported on these summary statements but not include the auditor's report, or management may refer to the auditor in a document containing the summary financial statements even though the auditor was not engaged to audit the summary statements. The auditor should request management to remedy either of these situations (see paragraphs 20 and 21 for additional details). In situations where management does not take the action the auditor requests, the auditor may inform the intended users and other known third-party users of inappropriate reference to the auditor including that the auditor did not report and does not express an opinion on the summary financial statements. The auditor may also consider it appropriate to seek legal advice.

## Practitioner's Aid

Exhibit AU-C 810-1 is an example of a report on summary financial statements containing an unmodified opinion that is dated after the date of the auditor's report on the audited financial statements.

**EXHIBIT AU-C 810-1—REPORT ON SUMMARY FINANCIAL STATEMENTS WITH AN UNMODIFIED OPINION DATED AFTER THE DATE OF THE AUDITOR'S REPORT ON THE AUDITED FINANCIAL STATEMENTS**

---

**INDEPENDENT AUDITOR'S ON SUMMARY FINANCIAL STATEMENTS**

[*Appropriate Addressee*]

*Opinion*

The summary financial statements, which comprise the summary balance sheet as of December 31, 20X5, the summary income statement, summary statement of changes in stockholders' equity, and summary cash flow statement for the year then ended, and the related notes, are derived from the audited financial statements of XYZ Company as of and for the year ended December 31, 20X5. We expressed an unmodified audit opinion on those audited financial statements in our report dated February 15, 20X6.

In our opinion, the accompanying summary financial statements of XYZ Company as of and for the year ended December 31, 20X5 referred to above are consistent, in all material respects, with the audited financial statements from which they have been derived, on the basis described in Note X.

*Summary Financial Statements*

The summary financial statements do not contain all the disclosures required by [*describe financial reporting framework applied in the preparation of the financial statements of XYZ Company*]. Reading the summary financial statements and the auditor's report hereon, therefore, is not a substitute for reading the audited financial statements and the auditor's report thereon. The summary financial statements and the audited financial statements do not reflect the effects of events that occurred subsequent to the date of our report on the audited financial statements.

*Responsibility of Management for the Summary Financial Statements*

Management is responsible for the preparation of the financial statements in accordance with the criteria described in Note X.

*Auditor's Responsibility*

Our responsibility is to express an opinion on whether the summary financial statements are consistent, in all material respects, with the audited financial statements based on our procedures, which were conducted in accordance with auditing standards generally accepted in the United States of America. The procedures consisted principally of comparing the summary financial statements with the related information in the audited financial statements from which the summary financial statements have been derived and evaluating whether the summary financial statements are prepared in accordance with the basis described in Note X. We did not perform any audit procedures regarding the audited financial statements after the date of our report on those financial statements.

[*Signature of the auditor's firm*]

[*City and state where the auditor's report is issued*]

[*Date of the auditor's report*]

# AU-C 900
# Special Considerations in the United States

| Section 905: | Alert That Restricts the Use of the Auditor's Written Communication | 9002 |
| Section 910: | Financial Statements Prepared in Accordance with a Financial Reporting Framework Generally Accepted in Another Country | 9006 |
| Section 915: | Reports on Application of Requirements of an Applicable Financial Reporting Framework | 9015 |
| Section 920: | Letters for Underwriters and Certain Other Requesting Parties | 9021 |
| Section 925: | Filings with the U.S. Securities and Exchange Commission under the Securities Act of 1933 | 9044 |
| Section 930: | Interim Financial Information | 9051 |
| Section 935: | Compliance Audits | 9075 |
| Section 940: | An Audit of Internal Control over Financial Reporting That Is Integrated with an Audit of Financial Statements | 9087 |
| Section 945: | Auditor Involvement with Exempt Offering Documents | 9120 |

# SECTION 905

## ALERT THAT RESTRICTS THE USE OF THE AUDITOR'S WRITTEN COMMUNICATION

### Authoritative Pronouncements

SAS-125—Alert That Restricts the Use of the Auditor's Written Communication

### Overview

AU-C 905 provides the auditor with guidance on when to include an alert as to the intended use of the auditor's report or other written communication, such as letters communicating internal control related matters or presentations addressing communications with those charged with governance, issued in connection with an engagement conducted in accordance with GAAS. While several AU-Cs contain requirements for the auditor to include such an alert, nothing precludes the auditor from including such an alert in other circumstances as he or she considers it necessary. Such an alert restricts the use of the auditor's written communication, and is included in an other-matter paragraph.

The auditor's written communication is to be restricted when the risk exists that the written communication will be misunderstood when taken out of the context in which the communication was intended to be used.

### Definition

Specified parties    The intended users of the auditor's written communication.

### Requirements

The auditor is presumptively required to perform the following procedures related to an alert as to the intended use of the auditor's written communication:

1. Include an alert as to the intended use of a written communication when that communication's subject matter is based on:

    a. Measurement or disclosure criteria the auditor determines are suitable only for a limited number of users presumed to have an adequate understanding of the criteria,

    b. Measurement or disclosure criteria available only to the specified parties, or

    c. Matters identified by the auditor during the course of the engagement that are not the primary objective of the engagement, known as a by-product report.

2. The alert should, unless otherwise specified by other relevant AU-Cs:

    a. State that the written communication is intended for the information and use of the specified parties only;

b. Identify the specified parties, which, in the case of a by-product report, should include only management, those charged with governance, others within the entity, parties to the contract or agreement, or the regulatory agencies with jurisdiction over the entity as appropriate; and

c. State that the written communication is not intended to be and should not be used by anyone other than the specified parties.

3. If the auditor is requested to add other specified parties to an alert, he or she should determine whether to add these parties. In the case of a by-product report, the auditor should not agree to add any specified parties not described in requirement 2b, above.

4. If the auditor agrees to add other parties as specified parties (i.e., permitting these parties to rely on the auditor's written communication), obtain affirmative written acknowledgment from the other parties of their understanding of the nature of the engagement and the measurement or disclosure criteria in the written communication and of the related auditor's written communication.

5. If other parties are added after the release of the auditor's written communication, in addition to the requirements in item 4, above, take one of the following actions:

   a. Amend the written communication to add the other parties but do not change the date of the written communication, or

   b. Provide a written acknowledgment to management and the other parties that such parties have been added as specified parties, stating that no procedures were performed after the date of the written communication or the date the engagement was completed as appropriate.

6. When an engagement is also performed in accordance with *Government Auditing Standards* and the auditor's written communication is issued under requirements in AU-C 265 (*Communicating Internal Control Related Matters Identified in an Audit*), AU-C 806 (*Reporting on Compliance with Aspects of Contractual Agreements or Regulatory Requirements in Connection with Audited Financial Statements*), AU-C 935 (*Compliance Audits*), or AU-C 940 (*An Audit of Internal Control over Financial Reporting That Is Integrated with an Audit of Financial Statements*), the alert language should not be that stated in requirement 2, above, but should instead describe the purpose of the written communication and state that the written communication is not suitable for any other purpose.

---

**OBSERVATION:** AU-C 905 defines certain audit reports as "intended use" reports. The previous language in GAAS referred to "restricted use" reports; the term "restricted use reports" no longer appears in AU-C 905.

## Analysis and Application of Procedures

An alert as to the intended use of the auditor's written communication may be used due to the purpose of the written communication, the nature of procedures applied or the basis of assumptions used in its preparation, the extent to which the procedures performed are generally known or understood, and the potential for the written communication to be misunderstood when taken out of its intended context.

---

**OBSERVATION:** The auditor is not precluded from including an alert as to the intended use of his or her written communication in situations where such an alert is not required. For example, the auditor may want to indicate that an audit report related to general purpose financial statements for use in an acquisition is intended only for the use of specified parties.

---

The auditor is required to issue an alert as to the intended use of a by-product report because the report may be based on matters that were not his or her primary objective during the engagement, so only limited procedures may have been conducted related to the subject of the by-product report and its intended purpose may be misinterpreted or misunderstood.

The alert as to the intended use of the auditor's written communication may list the specified parties or refer to a listing of the specified parties elsewhere in the written communication. An example of an alert is as follows:

> This [*report, letter, presentation, or communication*] is intended solely for the information and use of [*list or refer to the specified parties*] and is not intended to be and should not be used by anyone other than these specified parties.

Other AU-Cs with requirements for the auditor to include an alert as to intended use in the auditor's written communication, listed in Exhibit AU-C 905-1, may include specific requirements relating to the matters to be included in the alert, including identifying the specified parties (e.g., see AU-C 920, *Letters for Underwriters and Certain Other Requesting Parties*).

The intended use of a general-use communication is not affected if:

- A written communication that includes an alert as to its intended use is included in a document that also contains a written communication for general use, or
- The auditor issues a single combined written communication covering communications that include an alert as to intended-use and general-use communications.

---

**OBSERVATION:** The auditor is not responsible for controlling distribution of the written communication, but he or she may consider informing the entity that the written communication is not intended for distribution to other than the specified parties. The auditor may want to, as part of establishing the engagement terms, obtain an agreement that the entity and specified parties will not distribute the auditor's report to any other parties.

**OBSERVATION:** The combining of written communications intended for general use with communications intended for specified parties does not, as discussed above, restrict the use of the general purpose report. This guidance in AU-C 905 differs from the guidance in the former AU 532, which required the combined report to be restricted to specified parties.

When following *Government Auditing Standards*, the engagement's written communication is generally required by law or regulation to be publicly available. An example of the type of alert to use in these situations follows:

The purpose of this [*report, letter, presentation, or communication*] is to [*describe the purpose of the written communication*]. This [*report, letter, presentation, or communication*] is an integral part of an audit conducted in accordance with Government Auditing Standards in considering [*describe what is being assessed—e.g., internal control over financial reporting*]. Accordingly, this [*report, letter, presentation, or communication*] is not intended to be and should not be used for any other purpose.

## Practitioner's Aid

*EXHIBIT AU-C 905-1—LIST OF STATEMENTS ON AUDITING STANDARDS CONTAINING REQUIREMENTS FOR AN ALERT AS TO THE INTENDED USE OF AN AUDITOR'S WRITTEN COMMUNICATION*

- AU-C 260, *The Auditor's Communication with Those Charged with Governance* (paragraph 17)
- AU-C 265, *Communicating Internal Control Related Matters Identified in an Audit* (paragraphs 14(d), A32, and A38–A39)
- AU-C 725, *Supplementary Information in Relation to the Financial Statements as a Whole* (paragraph A16)
- AU-C 800, *Special Considerations—Audits of Financial Statements Prepared in Accordance with Special Purpose Frameworks* (paragraphs 20, A26–A27, and A33)
- AU-C 806, *Reporting on Compliance with Aspects of Contractual Agreements or Regulatory Requirements in Connection with Audited Financial Statements* (paragraphs 12, 13, and A6–A8)
- AU-C 915, *Reports on Application of Requirements of an Applicable Financial Reporting Framework* (paragraphs 14(f) and A6)
- AU-C 920, *Letters for Underwriters and Certain Other Requesting Parties* (paragraphs 33 and A34)
- AU-C 935, *Compliance Audits* (paragraphs 30, 31(i), and A33)

# SECTION 910

## FINANCIAL STATEMENTS PREPARED IN ACCORDANCE WITH A FINANCIAL REPORTING FRAMEWORK GENERALLY ACCEPTED IN ANOTHER COUNTRY

### Authoritative Pronouncements

SAS-124—Financial Statements Prepared in Accordance with a Financial Reporting Framework Generally Accepted in Another Country

SAS-134—Auditor Reporting and Amendments, Including Amendments Addressing Disclosures in the Audit of Financial Statements

SAS-140—Amendments to AU-C Sections 725, 730, 930, 935, and 940 to Incorporate Auditor Reporting Changes from SAS Nos. 134 and 137

SAS-141—Amendment to Effective Dates of SAS Nos. 134-140

### Overview

AU-C 910 provides guidance to auditors practicing in the United States who are engaged to report on financial statements prepared in accordance with a financial reporting framework that is generally accepted in another country but is not adopted by a body designated by the Council of the AICPA to establish U.S. generally accepted accounting principles (U.S. GAAP) when those audited financial statements are intended for use outside the United States, although this does not preclude the use of these financial statements in the United States. AU-C 910 does not apply to financial statements prepared in accordance with financial reporting frameworks established by any of the bodies designated by the Council of the AICPA to establish U.S. GAAP.

> **OBSERVATION:** AU-C 910 states that the guidance in AU-C 700 (*Forming an Opinion and Reporting on Financial Statements*), rather than in AU-C 910, applies when the auditor is engaged to opine on financial statements prepared in accordance with International Financial Reporting Standards (IFRS) as issued by the IASB. If, however, the financial statements use IFRS as modified by a foreign country (i.e., they deviate from IFRS as originally issued by the IASB), then AU-C 910 applies.

> **OBSERVATION:** AU-C 910 does not apply to engagements to report on financial statements of a U.S. subsidiary of a foreign registrant parent company that are presented in that parent company's filing with the U.S. Securities and Exchange Commission when the subsidiary's financial statements have been prepared in accordance with a financial reporting framework used by the parent company and audited in accordance with GAAS.

**IMPORTANT NOTICE FOR 2022:** In May 2019, the AICPA's Auditing Standards Board (ASB) issued SAS No. 134 titled *Auditor Reporting and Amendments, Including Amendments Addressing Disclosures in the Audit of Financial Statements* that makes significant changes to the auditor's report, including the ability to communicate key audit matters (KAMs) in the auditor's report. SAS No. 134 amends all the auditor report illustrations contained in AU-C 910 to conform those reports to the language in the new auditor's report. Originally, the effective date of SAS No. 134 is for audits of financial statements periods ending on or after December 15, 2020, with early implementation **not** permitted. However, the ASB's issuance of SAS No. 141, *Amendment to the Effective Dates of SAS Nos. 134-140*, extended the effective date to December 15, 2021, in order to provide more time for firms to implement SAS No. 134 in light of the effect of the coronavirus pandemic. While SAS No. 141 allows for early implementation of SAS No. 134, the ASB recommends that SAS Nos. 134-140 be implemented concurrently.

The auditor's objective in an engagement to report on financial statements prepared in accordance with a financial reporting framework generally accepted in another country when the audited financial statements are intended for use outside the United States is to appropriately address the special considerations relevant to engagement acceptance, engagement planning and performance, and forming an opinion and reporting on the financial statements.

## Requirements

The auditor is presumptively required to perform the following procedures when reporting on financial statements prepared in accordance with a financial reporting framework generally accepted in another country:

1. In considering acceptance of an audit engagement, determine the acceptability of the financial reporting framework applied in the preparation of the financial statements. Obtain an understanding of:

    a. The purpose for which the financial statements are prepared and whether the financial reporting framework applied is a fair presentation framework,

    b. The intended users of the financial statements, and

    c. The steps management has taken to determine the financial reporting framework is acceptable in the circumstances.

2. If planning to issue a standard report of another country, obtain an understanding of the legal responsibilities in the other country.

3. Comply with GAAS if financial statements are prepared for use only outside the United States, except for requirements related to report form and content. Determine whether GAAS application requires special consideration in the circumstances of the engagement.

4. Obtain an understanding of the financial reporting framework applied as part of obtaining an understanding of the entity's selection and application of accounting policies.

5. If the agreed-upon terms of an audit engagement require the auditor to apply another country's auditing standards or the International Standards on Auditing (ISAs), obtain an understanding of and apply the relevant auditing standards as well as GAAS (except for requirements related to report form and content if the financial statements are prepared for use only outside the United States).
6. If financial statements are intended for use only outside the United States, report using either:
    a. A U.S. form of report reflecting that the financial statements being reported on have been prepared in accordance with a financial reporting framework generally accepted in another country including the elements required by AU-C 700 (*Forming an Opinion and Reporting on Financial Statements*) and a statement referring to the note to the financial statements describing the basis of presentation of the financial statements on which the auditor is reporting, including identification of the nationality of the accounting principles, or
    b. The standard report form and content of the other country, or that set forth in the ISAs if applicable, provided that such a report would be issued by auditors in the other country in similar circumstances, the auditor understands and has obtained sufficient appropriate audit evidence to support the statements contained in such a report, and he or she has complied with the reporting standards of that country and identifies that country in the report.
7. If financial statements prepared in accordance with a financial reporting framework generally accepted in another country are also intended for use in the United States, report using the U.S. form of the report and include an emphasis-of-matter paragraph in the report (1) identifying the accounting framework used in preparing the financial statements, (2) referring to the note that describes the framework, and (3) indicating that the framework differs from U.S. GAAP.

## Analysis and Application of Procedures

### Audit Planning and Performance

In auditing financial statements prepared in accordance with a financial reporting framework generally accepted in another country that are prepared for use only outside the United States, GAAS should be complied with excepting requirements related to form and content. However, the procedures applied to perform a GAAS audit may need to be modified to reflect differences in the accounting principles used to prepare the financial statements. For example, some financial reporting frameworks used in foreign countries require, or permit, the revaluation of assets. Auditing such revaluations would differ from an audit of U.S. GAAP-based financial statements.

**PLANNING AID REMINDER:** If the financial statements prepared in accordance with a framework generally accepted in another country are likely to be used in the United States, the auditor may consider whether U.S. users are likely to understand the differences between the foreign accounting framework and U.S. GAAP. For example, it may not be appropriate to report on financial statements prepared in accordance with a foreign framework if these statements are going to be included in a private placement memorandum that will be used extensively in the United States.

When the auditor is required to comply with auditing standards of another country, both those standards and GAAS must be observed during the engagement. Thus, some audit procedures will be employed to comply with GAAS, whereas other potentially additional audit procedures will be performed to satisfy auditing standards of the foreign country.

**PLANNING AID REMINDER:** An understanding of a financial reporting framework generally accepted in another country or the auditing standards of another country or the ISAs may be obtained by reading the statutes or professional literature establishing or describing the framework or standards or by consulting with others with appropriate expertise and experience in applying such framework or standards.

## *Preparing an Appropriate Audit Report*

The reporting standards that must be observed in the preparation of the auditor's report on financial statements prepared in accordance with accounting principles of another country are dependent on the purpose of the financial statements. These purposes may be classified as (1) foreign GAAP/foreign use and (2) dual statements (foreign GAAP/U.S. GAAP).

### *Foreign GAAP/Foreign use*

When financial statements of a U.S. entity that are prepared in accordance with accounting principles of another country are to be used exclusively outside the United States, the auditor may use either (1) the U.S.-style auditor's report with a statement referencing the note to the financial statements describing the basis of presentation of the financial statements and identifying the nationality of the accounting principles or (2) the standard auditor's report of the foreign country. An example of a U.S.-style auditor's report on financial statements intended for use only outside the United States is presented in Exhibit AU-C 910-2.

The assertions in the standard auditor's report of another country may be different from those in the U.S.-style standard auditor's report. The fundamental assertion in the U.S.-style standard auditor's report is that the financial statements are prepared in accordance with generally accepted accounting principles. On the other hand, a foreign country's standard auditor's report may imply or state that the financial statements are prepared in compliance with existing statutory regulations. Thus, before issuing a foreign country's standard auditor's report, the U.S. auditor must fully understand the auditing standards, accounting principles, and laws that are applicable in the foreign country. To gain the appropriate understanding, the U.S. auditor might need to consult with persons who are familiar with the auditing standards, accounting principles, and laws of the particular foreign country.

*Dual statements (Foreign GAAP/U.S. GAAP)*

One set of financial statements may be prepared in accordance with U.S. GAAP and a second set in accordance with accounting principles acceptable in a foreign country, to provide relevant information to users in both countries. For the financial statements presented in accordance with U.S. GAAP, the auditor should observe GAAS in preparing the auditor's report. For the financial statements prepared in accordance with accounting principles acceptable in a foreign country and to be used outside of the United States, the auditor may prepare either type of report that is permitted for statements using foreign GAAP for use outside the United States.

Some confusion may arise when the same financial statements of a U.S. entity are prepared on two different accounting bases. AU-C 910 suggests that to reduce the possibility of a misunderstanding, one or both of the audit reports may contain a statement advising the reader of the other audit report, which has been issued on the same financial statements but is based on the accepted accounting principles of another country. The auditor's report also may refer to the note to the financial statements, if presented, that describes the significant differences between the two bases of accounting. An example of the auditor's reference to such a note is as follows:

> We also have reported separately on the financial statements of Company X for the same period presented in accordance with [*specify the financial reporting framework generally accepted*] in [*name of country*]. (The significant differences between the [*specify the financial reporting framework*] and accounting principles generally accepted in the United States of America are summarized in Note 1.)

## Practitioner's Aids

**IMPORTANT NOTICE FOR 2022:** As a reminder, in May 2019, the AICPA's Auditing Standards Board (ASB) issued SAS No. 134 titled *Auditor Reporting and Amendments, Including Amendments Addressing Disclosures in the Audit of Financial Statements* that makes significant changes to the auditor's report, including the ability to communicate key audit matters (KAMs) in the auditor's report. SAS No. 134 amends all the auditor report illustrations contained in AU-C 910 to conform those reports to the language in the new auditor's report. Originally, the effective date of SAS No. 134 is for audits of financial statements periods ending on or after December 15, 2020, with early implementation **not** permitted. However, the ASB's issuance of SAS No. 141, *Amendment to the Effective Dates of SAS Nos. 134-140*, extended the effective date to December 15, 2021, in order to provide more time for firms to implement SAS No. 134 in light of the effect of the coronavirus pandemic. While SAS No. 141 allows for early implementation of SAS No. 134, the ASB recommends that SAS Nos. 134-140 be implemented concurrently.

Exhibit AU-C 910-1 is an example of a U.S. form of auditor's report on financial statements prepared in accordance with a financial reporting framework generally accepted in another country that are also intended for use in the U.S.

## EXHIBIT AU-C 910-1—U.S. FORM OF AUDITOR'S REPORT ON FINANCIAL STATEMENTS THAT ARE ALSO INTENDED FOR USE IN THE U.S.

### INDEPENDENT AUDITOR'S REPORT

[Appropriate Addressee]

**Report on the Financial Statements**

*Opinion on the Financial Statements*

We have audited the financial statements of X Company, which comprise the balance sheet as of December 31, 20X5, and the related statements of income, changes in stockholders' equity, and cash flows for the year then ended, and the related notes to the financial statements, which, as described in note X to the financial statements, have been prepared on the basis of [*specify the financial reporting framework generally accepted*] in [*name of country*].

In our opinion, the accompanying financial statements present fairly, in all material respects, the financial position of X Company as of December 31, 20X5, and the results of its operations and its cash flows for the year then ended in accordance with [*specify the financial reporting framework generally accepted*] in [*name of country*].

*Basis for Opinion*

We conducted our audit in accordance with auditing standards generally accepted in the United States of America (and [*in name of country*]). Our responsibilities under those standards are further described in the Auditor's Responsibilities for the Audit of the Financial Statements section of our report. We are required to be independent of X Company and to meet our other ethical responsibilities, in accordance with the relevant ethical requirements relating to our audit. We believe that the audit evidence we have obtained is sufficient and appropriate to provide a basis for our audit opinion.

*Emphasis of Matter*

As discussed in Note X to the financial statements, the Company prepares its financial statements in accordance with [*specify the financial reporting framework generally accepted*] in [*name of country*], which differ(s) from accounting principles generally accepted in the United States of America. Our opinion is not modified with respect to this matter.

*Responsibilities of Management for the Financial Statements*

Management is responsible for the preparation and fair presentation of the financial statements in accordance with [*specify the financial reporting framework generally accepted*] in [*name of country*], and for the design, implementation, and maintenance of internal control relevant to the preparation and fair presentation of financial statements that are free from material misstatement, whether due to fraud or error.

In preparing the financial statements, management is required to evaluate whether there are conditions or events, considered in the aggregate that raise substantial doubt about the Company's ability to continue as a going concern for [*insert the time period set by the applicable financial reporting framework*].

Auditor's Responsibilities for the Audit of the Financial Statements

Our objectives are to obtain reasonable assurance about whether the financial statements as a whole are free from material misstatement, whether due to fraud or error, and to issue an auditor's report that includes our opinion. Reasonable assurance is a high level of assurance but is not absolute assurance and therefore is not a guarantee that an audit conducted in accordance with generally accepted auditing standards will always detect a material misstatement when it exists. The risk of not detecting a material misstatement resulting from fraud is higher than for one resulting from error, as fraud may involve collusion, forgery, intentional omissions, misrepresentations, or the override of internal control. Misstatements are considered material if, individually or in the aggregate, they could reasonably be expected to influence the economic decisions of users made on the basis of these financial statements.

In performing an audit in accordance with GAAS, we:

- Exercise professional judgment and maintain professional skepticism throughout the audit.
- Identify and assess the risks of material misstatement of the financial statements, whether due to fraud or error, and design and perform audit procedures responsive to those risks. Such procedures include examining, on a test basis, evidence regarding the amounts and disclosures in the financial statements.
- Obtain an understanding of internal control relevant to the audit in order to design audit procedures that are appropriate in the circumstances, but not for the purpose of expressing an opinion on the effectiveness of the Company's internal control. Accordingly, no such opinion is expressed.
- Evaluate the appropriateness of accounting policies used and the reasonableness of significant accounting estimates made by management, as well as evaluate the overall presentation of the financial statements.
- Conclude whether, in our judgment, there are conditions or events, considered in the aggregate, that raise substantial doubt about the Company's ability to continue as a going concern for a reasonable period of time.

We are required to communicate with those charged with governance regarding, among other matters, the planned scope and timing of the audit, significant audit findings, and certain internal control-related matters that we identified during the audit.

[*Signature of the auditor's firm*]

[*City and state where the auditor's report is issued*]

[*Date of the auditor's report*]

---

Exhibit AU-C 910-2 is an example of a U.S. form of auditor's report on financial statements prepared in accordance with a financial reporting framework generally accepted in another country that is intended for use only outside the United States.

*EXHIBIT AU-C 910-2—U.S. FORM OF AUDITOR'S REPORT ON FINANCIAL STATEMENTS INTENDED FOR USE ONLY OUTSIDE THE U.S.*

## INDEPENDENT AUDITOR'S REPORT

[Appropriate Addressee]

**Report on the Financial Statements**

*Opinion*

We have audited the financial statements of X Company, which comprise the balance sheet as of December 31, 20X5, and the related statements of income, changes in stockholders' equity, and cash flows for the year then ended, and the related notes to the financial statements, which, as described in note X to the financial statements, have been prepared on the basis of [*specify the financial reporting framework generally accepted*] in [*name of country*].

In our opinion, the accompanying financial statements present fairly, in all material respects, the financial position of X Company as of December 31, 20X5, and the results of its operations and its cash flows for the year then ended in accordance with [*specify the financial reporting framework generally accepted*] in [*name of country*].

*Basis for Opinion*

We conducted our audit in accordance with auditing standards generally accepted in the United States of America (and [*in name of country*]). Our responsibilities under those standards are further described in the Auditor's Responsibilities for the Audit of the Financial Statements section of our report. We are required to be independent of X Company and to meet our other ethical responsibilities, in accordance with the relevant ethical requirements relating to our audit. We believe that the audit evidence we have obtained is sufficient and appropriate to provide a basis for our audit opinion.

*Responsibilities of Management for the Financial Statements*

Management is responsible for the preparation and fair presentation of the financial statements in accordance with [*specify the financial reporting framework generally accepted*] in [*name of country*], and for the design, implementation, and maintenance of internal control relevant to the preparation and fair presentation of financial statements that are free from material misstatement, whether due to fraud or error.

In preparing the financial statements, management is required to evaluate whether there are conditions or events, considered in the aggregate that raise substantial doubt about the Company's ability to continue as a going concern for [*insert the time period set by the applicable financial reporting framework*].

*Auditor's Responsibilities for the Audit of the Financial Statements*

Our objectives are to obtain reasonable assurance about whether the financial statements as a whole are free from material misstatement, whether due to fraud or error, and to issue an auditor's report that includes our opinion. Reasonable assurance is a high level of assurance but is not absolute assurance and therefore is not a guarantee that an audit conducted in accordance with generally accepted auditing standards will always detect a material misstatement when it exists. The risk of not detecting a material misstatement resulting from fraud is higher than for one resulting from error, as fraud may involve collusion, forgery, intentional omissions, misrepresentations, or the override of internal control. Misstatements are considered material if, individually or in the aggregate, they could reasonably be expected to influence the economic decisions of users made on the basis of these financial statements.

In performing an audit in accordance with GAAS, we:

- Exercise professional judgment and maintain professional skepticism throughout the audit.
- Identify and assess the risks of material misstatement of the financial statements, whether due to fraud or error, and design and perform audit procedures responsive to those risks. Such procedures include examining, on a test basis, evidence regarding the amounts and disclosures in the financial statements.
- Obtain an understanding of internal control relevant to the audit in order to design audit procedures that are appropriate in the circumstances, but not for the purpose of expressing an opinion on the effectiveness of the Company's internal control. Accordingly, no such opinion is expressed.
- Evaluate the appropriateness of accounting policies used and the reasonableness of significant accounting estimates made by management, as well as evaluate the overall presentation of the financial statements.
- Conclude whether, in our judgment, there are conditions or events, considered in the aggregate, that raise substantial doubt about the Company's ability to continue as a going concern for a reasonable period of time.

We are required to communicate with those charged with governance regarding, among other matters, the planned scope and timing of the audit, significant audit findings, and certain internal control–related matters that we identified during the audit.

[*Signature of the auditor's firm*]

[*City and state where the auditor's report is issued*]

[*Date of the auditor's report*]

# SECTION 915

## REPORTS ON APPLICATION OF REQUIREMENTS OF AN APPLICABLE FINANCIAL REPORTING FRAMEWORK

### Authoritative Pronouncements

SAS-122—Statements on Auditing Standards: Clarification and Recodification
SAS-123—Omnibus Statement on Auditing Standards—2011

### Overview

Accountants are often requested to give an informal opinion on how a transaction should or could be accounted for or what type of opinion would be appropriate for a particular set of financial statements. Requests of this nature are frequently associated with prospective clients who are "shopping for an opinion." Unfortunately, such requests have resulted in a significant amount of adverse publicity for the accounting profession. AU-C 915 provides guidance in this sensitive area. AU-C 915 points out that an accountant may be asked by management or other interested parties (1) to explain how an applicable financial reporting framework applies to specific transactions or (2) to increase their knowledge of specific financial reporting issues.

The standards established by AU-C 915 apply to the reporting accountant and help him or her to appropriately address engagement acceptance, planning, performance, and reporting under the following circumstances:

- A written report is prepared on the application of the requirements of an applicable financial reporting framework to specific transactions.
- A written report is prepared on the type of opinion that may be expressed on a specific entity's financial statements.
- Oral advice is offered that the accountant believes is intended to be used by a principal to the transaction as an important factor to be considered in reaching a decision on the application of the requirements of an applicable financial reporting framework to a specific transaction.
- Oral advice is offered by the reporting accountant on the type of opinion that may be expressed on a specific entity's financial statements.

**OBSERVATION:** The scope of AU-C 915 includes oral advice so that the reporting accountant cannot circumvent professional standards simply by not preparing a written report.

**OBSERVATION:** With the increased visibility of accountants in the press and the related close scrutiny of the profession as well as the possibility of litigation, accountants should be particularly careful in accepting engagements covered by AU-C 915.

The standards established by AU-C 915 do not apply to the following circumstances:

- A continuing accountant with respect to the specific entity whose financial statements are being reported upon by the continuing accountant.
- An accountant assisting in litigation or providing expert testimony involving accounting matters.
- An accountant providing professional advice to another accountant in public practice.
- An accountant preparing other communications such as position papers (newsletters, articles, texts, lectures, etc.) on the application of the requirements of an applicable financial reporting framework to an issue unless the guidance is rendered on a specific transaction.

---

**OBSERVATION:** The standards established by AU-C 915 do not provide guidance for a continuing accountant (except as discussed later with respect to the communication between the reporting accountant and the continuing accountant) because the continuing accountant discusses the application of accounting principles to various transactions and the effect of the accounting for such transactions on the auditor's report as part of the normal audit process.

---

## Definitions

| | |
|---|---|
| Continuing accountant | An accountant who has been engaged to report on the financial statements of a specific entity. |
| Hypothetical transaction | A transaction or financial reporting issue that does not involve facts or circumstances of a specific entity. |
| Reporting accountant | An accountant, other than a continuing accountant, in the practice of public accounting who prepares a written report or provides oral advice on the application of the requirements of an applicable financial reporting framework to a specific transaction, or on the type of report that may be issued on a specific entity's financial statements. |
| Specific transaction | A completed or proposed transaction or financial reporting issue involving facts and circumstances of a specific entity. |
| Written report | Any written communication expressing a conclusion on the appropriate application of the requirements of an applicable financial reporting framework to a specific transaction, or on the type of report that may be issued on a specific entity's financial statements. |

## Requirements

The reporting accountant is presumptively required to observe the following performance standards when reporting on the application of requirements of an applicable financial reporting framework:

1. Consider (1) the circumstances under which the written report or oral advice is requested, (2) the purpose of the request, and (3) the intended use of the written report or oral advice in determining whether to accept the engagement. The reporting accountant is not required to be independent.
2. Only accept engagements to issue written reports or provide oral advice on the application of requirements of an applicable financial reporting framework to a specific transaction when the transaction involves facts and circumstances of a specific entity. Engagements to report on hypothetical transactions should not be accepted.
3. Establish an understanding with the entity that management:
    a. Is responsible for the proper accounting treatment and is expected to consult with its continuing accountant;
    b. Acknowledges that the reporting accountant may need to consult with the continuing accountant and that management will authorize the continuing accountant to respond fully to the reporting accountant's inquiries upon request; and
    c. Will notify those charged with governance and the continuing accountant regarding the nature of the engagement.

    If management refuses to authorize the continuing accountant to respond fully to the reporting accountant's inquiries, inquire about the reasons and consider the implications in determining whether to accept the engagement.
4. In planning and performing an engagement:
    a. Obtain an understanding of the form and substance of the specific transactions or the conditions relevant to the type of report that may be issued on a specific entity's financial statements;
    b. Review the relevant requirements of the applicable financial reporting framework as necessary;
    c. Consult with other professionals, specialists, or regulators as necessary;
    d. Perform research or other procedures as appropriate to identify and consider existing creditable precedents or analogies;
    e. Except as noted in item 5, request permission from the entity's management to consult with the continuing accountant and request the entity's management to authorize the continuing accountant to respond fully to the reporting accountant's inquiries; and
    f. Except as noted in item 5, consult with the continuing accountant to determine the available facts relevant to forming a conclusion.
5. Consultation with the continuing accountant as described above is not required when the reporting accountant is engaged to issue a written report or provide oral advice on the application of the requirements of an applicable financial reporting framework to a specific transaction and

is engaged to provide accounting and reporting advice to the entity on a recurring basis and:

a. Does not believe a second opinion is being requested,

b. Has full access to management, and

c. Believes that the relevant information has been obtained in order to provide advice regarding the application of the requirements of an applicable financial reporting framework to that entity's specific transaction.

> **PLANNING AID REMINDER:** The reporting accountant should document its reasons for not consulting with the continuing accountant.

6. The written report should be addressed to the requesting entity such as management or those charged with governance and should include:

    a. A brief description of the nature of the engagement and a statement that the engagement was performed in accordance with AU-C 915;

    b. Identification of the specific entity, a description of the specific transaction, and a statement of the relevant facts, circumstances, and assumptions and the source of such information;

    c. A statement describing the appropriate application of the requirements of an applicable financial reporting framework (including the country of origin) to the specific transaction or type of report that may be issued on the entity's financial statements and a description of the reasons for the accountant's conclusion if appropriate;

    d. A statement that the preparers of the financial statements are responsible for the proper accounting treatment and should consult with their continuing accountant;

    e. A statement that differences in the facts, circumstances, or assumptions presented may change the report;

    f. A separate paragraph at the end of the report including a statement indicating that the report is intended solely for the information and use of the specified parties, identification of the specified parties to whom use is restricted, and a statement that the report is not intended to be and should not be used by anyone other than the specified parties; and

    g. If applicable, an indication that the reporting accountant is not independent. The reporting accountant has the discretion as to whether or not to disclose the reasons for his or her lack of independence. However, if any reason for a lack of independence is disclosed, all such reasons must be disclosed.

## Analysis and Application of Procedures

*Engagement Planning and Performance*

A continuing accountant's responsibilities to respond to the inquiries of a reporting accountant are the same as a predecessor auditor's responsibilities to respond to inquiries of a successor auditor as addressed in AU-C 210 (*Terms of Engagement*). The continuing accountant may be able to provide the reporting accountant with information related to the form and substance of the specific transaction that is otherwise unavailable to the reporting accountant such as the following:

- How management has applied the requirements of an applicable financial reporting framework to similar transactions.
- Whether management disputes the method of accounting recommended by the continuing accountant.
- The continuing accountant's conclusion on the application of the requirements of an applicable financial reporting framework to the specific transaction or the type of opinion that may be rendered on the entity's financial statements.

Engagement of the reporting accountant on a recurring basis may involve financial reporting advisory services or the effective outsourcing of controllership or other financial reporting functions that may allow the accountant to have complete access to management. When the reporting accountant is determining whether consultation with the continuing accountant is necessary, he or she may consider:

- The nature of the engagement,
- Whether full knowledge of the form and substance of the transaction has been obtained,
- How management has applied the requirements of the applicable financial reporting framework to similar transactions in the past, and
- Whether this method of accounting has been discussed with the continuing accountant.

*Reporting*

An example from AU-C 915 of an accountant's report on the application of the requirements of accounting principles to a specific transaction is presented in Exhibit AU-C 915-1. The restriction of use on the written report is not intended to preclude distribution of the report to the continuing accountant.

---

**ENGAGEMENT STRATEGY:** AU-C 915 notes that the reporting standards apply only to written reports but that accountants may find this guidance useful in providing oral advice.

## Practitioner's Aid

Exhibit AU-C 915-1 is an example based on the reporting standards established by AU-C 915 of an accountant's report on the application of accounting principles to a specific transaction.

## EXHIBIT AU-C 915-1—ACCOUNTANT'S REPORT ON THE APPLICATION OF ACCOUNTING PRINCIPLES

[*Introduction*]

We have been engaged to report on the appropriate application of accounting principles generally accepted in the United States of America to the specific transaction described below. This report is being issued to ABC Company for assistance in evaluating accounting principles for the described specific transaction. Our engagement has been conducted in accordance with Statement on Auditing Standards No. 122, section 915 *Reports on Application of Requirements of an Applicable Financial Reporting Framework.*

[*Description of Transaction*]

The facts, circumstances, and assumptions relevant to the specific transaction as provided to us by the management of ABC Company are as follows: [*describe the transaction*]

[*Appropriate Accounting Principles*]

[*Discuss accounting principles generally accepted in the United States of America and how they apply to the described transaction*]

[*Concluding Comments*]

The ultimate responsibility for the decision on the appropriate application of accounting principles generally accepted in the United States of America for an actual transaction rests with the preparers of financial statements, who should consult with their continuing accountants. Our conclusion on the appropriate application of the requirements of accounting principles generally accepted in the United States of America for the described specific transaction is based solely on the facts provided to us as described above; should these facts and circumstances differ, our conclusion may change.

[*Restricted Use*]

This report is intended solely for the information and use of those charged with governance and management of ABC Company and is not intended to be and should not be used by anyone other than these specified parties.

# SECTION 920

# LETTERS FOR UNDERWRITERS AND CERTAIN OTHER REQUESTING PARTIES

## Authoritative Pronouncements

SAS-122—Statements on Auditing Standards: Clarification and Recodification

SAS-129—Amendment to SAS No. 122 Section 920, *Letters for Underwriters and Certain Other Requesting Parties*

SAS-140—Amendments to AU-C Sections 725, 730, 930, 935, and 940 to Incorporate Auditor Reporting Changes from SAS Nos. 134 and 137

SAS-141—Amendment to Effective Dates of SAS Nos. 134-140

## Overview

AU-C 920 provides guidance to auditors in performing engagements to provide (1) letters to requesting parties in conjunction with a nonissuer entity's financial statements included in registration statements filed with the Securities and Exchange Commission (SEC) under the Securities Act of 1933 (the 1933 Act) and (2) letters to a requesting party in conjunction with other securities offerings. AU-C 920 assists the auditor in ensuring a letter with the appropriate form and content is issued to the requesting parties.

> **PLANNING AID REMINDER:** While auditors are often requested to issue comfort letters to requesting parties, generally accepted auditing standards do not require the auditor to accept these engagements.

> **PRACTICE POINTER:** In July 2014, the Auditing Standards Board (ASB) issued SAS No. 129 to address some unintended issues that arose from its efforts to clarify the guidance that previously existed in AU Section 634 (*Letters for Underwriters and Certain Other Requesting Parties*). As part of the ASB's Clarity Project, it redrafted the extant guidance in AU Section 634 as new section AU-C 920 with the intention of merely clarifying that guidance using its clarity drafting conventions and it did not intend to change practice in this area. However, subsequent to the issuance of the redrafted guidance contained in AU-C 920, the ASB became aware of practice issues that were revealed as a result of implementing AU-C 920. SAS No. 129 addresses those concerns and avoids unintended consequences to previous practice. Those revisions are reflected in the guidance in this section.

As part of the registration of securities under the 1933 Act, underwriters of the securities often ask an accountant to provide them with a comfort letter. The comfort letter is not a requirement of the 1933 Act and is not included in the registration statement. However, underwriters request it to assist them in discharging their duty of reasonable investigation and to help establish their affirmative defense under Section 11 of the 1933 Act (often referred to as "Section 11 investigation" or "due diligence"). Therefore, obtaining the accountant's comfort letter is one of many activities that underwriters undertake to respond to the liability imposed on them under Section 11 of the 1933 Act.

A comfort letter may cover subjects such as:

- The auditor's independence;
- Whether the form of the audited financial statements included in the securities offering complies in all material respects with the applicable accounting requirements of the 1933 Act and the related rules and regulations adopted by the SEC;
- Unaudited financial statements, condensed interim financial information, capsule financial information, pro forma financial information, financial forecasts, management's discussion and analysis, and changes in selected financial statement items during a period subsequent to the date and period of the latest financial statements included in the securities offering;
- Tables, statistics, and other financial information included in the securities offering; and
- Negative assurance about whether the form of certain nonfinancial statement information included in the securities offering complies in all material respects with Regulation S-K.

AU-C 920 states that, in addition to underwriters, the auditor may also provide comfort letters to other requesting parties listed below that are conducting a review process substantially consistent with the due diligence process performed if the securities offering were being registered pursuant to the 1933 Act:

- To a selling shareholder, sales agent, or other party with a statutory due diligence defense under Section 11 of the 1933 Act.
- To a broker-dealer or other financial intermediary in connection with the following types of securities offerings:
  — For foreign offerings (e.g., Regulation S, Eurodollar, and other offshore offerings);
  — For transactions that are exempt from the registration requirements of Section 5 of the 1933 Act, including those pursuant to Regulation A, Regulation D, and Rule 144A; and
  — For offerings of securities issued or backed by governmental, municipal, banking, tax-exempt, or other entities that are exempt from registration under the 1933 Act.
- To a buyer or a seller, or both, in connection with acquisition transactions involving an exchange of stock (e.g., Form S-4 or merger proxy situation).

> **OBSERVATION:** AU-C 920 does not cover an auditor's report on a preliminary investigation in connection with a proposed transaction such as a merger or acquisition. The guidance in AT-C 215 may apply to such engagements.

## Definitions

| | |
|---|---|
| Capsule financial information | Unaudited summarized interim information for periods subsequent to the periods covered by the audited financial statements or unaudited condensed interim financial information included in the securities offering. This information is presented in narrative or tabular form and is often provided for the most recent interim period and for the corresponding period of the prior year. |
| Change period | The period for which the auditor gives negative assurance ordinarily beginning immediately after the date and period of the latest financial statements included in the securities offering and ending on the cutoff date. |
| Closing date | The date on which the issuer or selling security holder delivers the securities to the underwriter in exchange for the proceeds of the offering. |
| Comfort letter | A letter issued by an auditor to requesting parties in connection with an entity's financial statements included in securities offerings. |
| Comparison date and comparison period | The dates and periods for which data at the cutoff date and data for the change period are to be compared. |
| Cutoff date | The date through which certain procedures described in the comfort letter are to relate. |
| Effective date | The date on which the securities offering becomes effective. |
| Entity | The party whose financial statements are the subject of the engagement. |
| Negative assurance | A statement that, based on the procedures performed, nothing has come to the auditor's attention causing the auditor to believe that specified matters do not meet specified criteria. For example, there is nothing causing the auditor to believe that material modifications should be made to the unaudited financial statements for them to be in accordance with generally accepted accounting principles. |
| Requesting party | One of the following specified parties requesting a comfort letter, who has negotiated an agreement with the entity: (1) an underwriter or (2) other parties conducting a review process that is or will be substantially consistent with the due diligence process performed when the securities offering is, or if the securities offering were, being registered pursuant to the 1933 Act. |

| | |
|---|---|
| Securities offerings | One of the following types of securities offerings: (1) registration of securities with the SEC under the 1933 Act; (2) foreign offerings, including Regulation S, Eurodollar, and other offshore offerings; (3) transactions that are exempt from the registration requirements of section 5 of the 1933 Act, including those pursuant to Regulation A, Regulation D, and Rule 144A; (4) offerings of securities issued or backed by governmental, municipal, banking, tax-exempt, or other entities that are exempt from registration under the 1933 Act; or (5) acquisition transactions in which there is an exchange of stock. |
| Underwriter | A person who has purchased from or offers or sells for an issuer or a person directly or indirectly controlling, in common control with, or controlled by the issuer in connection with the distribution of any security, or who directly or indirectly participates in any such undertaking or the underwriting of any such undertaking. This does not include a person whose interest is limited to a commission from an underwriter or dealer not in excess of the usual and customary distributors' or sellers' commission. For the purposes of AU-C 920, an underwriter refers to the lead underwriter who negotiates the underwriting or purchase agreement for a group of underwriters whose composition is not determined until shortly before a securities offering becomes effective. |

## Requirements

The auditor is presumptively required to perform the following procedures with respect to letters for underwriters and certain other requesting parties:

### Engagement Acceptance

1. Determine whether to accept the engagement. The auditor is not required to accept an engagement to issue a comfort letter.

2. Only provide a comfort letter in connection with financial statements included in securities offerings to the following requesting parties: (1) underwriters or (2) other parties meeting the definition of a requesting party.

3. Request that the requesting party provide either:

    a. A written opinion from external legal counsel that the requesting party has a statutory due diligence defense under Section 11 of the 1933 Act, or

    b. A representation letter addressed to the auditor and signed by the requesting party that contains the statement "The review process applied to the information relating to the issuer, is, or will be, substantially consistent with the due diligence process that we would perform if this securities offering were being registered pursuant to the Securities Act of 1933. We are knowledgeable with respect to the due diligence process."

4. If a requesting party other than an underwriter requests a comfort letter but does not provide a legal opinion or representation letter, the auditor should not provide negative assurance on the financial statements as a whole, or on any specified elements, accounts, or items of the financial statements and should include the following statements in the comfort letter:

a. It should be understood that we have no responsibility for establishing and did not establish the scope and nature of the procedures enumerated in the preceding paragraphs; rather, the procedures enumerated therein are those that the requesting party asked us to perform. Accordingly, we make no representations regarding questions of legal interpretation or regarding the sufficiency for your purposes of the procedures enumerated in the preceding paragraphs; also, such procedures would not necessarily reveal any material misstatement of the amounts or percentages previously listed as set forth in the offering circular. Further, we have addressed ourselves solely to the foregoing data and make no representations regarding the adequacy of disclosures or whether any material facts have been omitted. This letter relates only to the financial statement items previously specified and does not extend to any financial statement of the company taken as a whole.

b. The foregoing procedures do not constitute an audit conducted in accordance with generally accepted auditing standards. Had we performed additional procedures or had we conducted an audit or a review of the company's [*give dates of any interim financial statements*] consolidated financial statements in accordance with auditing standards generally accepted in the United States of America, other matters might have come to our attention that would have been reported to you.

c. These procedures should not be taken to supplant any additional inquiries or procedures that you would undertake in your consideration of the proposed offering.

d. This letter is solely for your information and to assist you in your inquiries in connection with the offering of the securities covered by the offering circular. It is not to be used, circulated, quoted, or otherwise referred to for any other purpose, including but not limited to the registration, purchase, or sale of securities, nor is it to be filed with or referred to in whole or in part in the offering document or any other document, except that reference may be made to it in any list of closing documents pertaining to the offering of the securities covered by the offering document.

e. We have no responsibility to update this letter for events and circumstances occurring after [*cutoff date*].

5. A comfort letter should not be provided to any party other than a requesting party as defined in AU-C 920.

6. When issuing a letter in accordance with AU-C 920, the auditor should not issue any additional letters or reports to a requesting party in connection with the securities offering he or she is commenting on if commenting on those items is otherwise precluded by AU-C 920.

## Agreeing Upon the Scope of Services

7. Obtain an understanding of the specific matters to be addressed in the comfort letter.

8. Ask to meet with the requesting party and the entity to discuss the procedures to be followed in connection with a comfort letter and clearly state that any assurance regarding the sufficiency of procedures for the requesting party's purposes cannot be provided.

9. The auditor should provide a draft of the form of the letter he or she expects to furnish that covers all matters and uses exactly the same terms that will be

used in the final letter, with the understanding that the comments in the final letter cannot be determined until the procedures underlying it have been performed. Identify the draft letter as a draft to avoid giving the impression that the described procedures have already been performed.

10. In the draft and final comfort letter, clearly describe the procedures the auditor followed. Do not state or imply that the procedures being carried out are those that the auditor considers necessary in order to avoid misunderstandings about the responsibility for the sufficiency of the procedures for the requesting party's purposes.

11. If the auditor is unable to discuss his or her planned procedures with the underwriter, describe in the draft letter those procedures specified in the draft underwriting agreement that the auditor is willing to perform.

12. When the comfort letter relates to group financial statements, the auditor of the group financial statements should read the comfort letters of the component. State in the comfort letter that (*a*) reading the component auditors' letters was one of the procedures followed and (*b*) the other procedures performed by the auditor of the group financial statements relate solely to entities he or she audited and to the group financial statements.

13. AU-C 920 requirements apply to each auditor from whom a comfort letter is requested.

14. In competitive bidding situations where the requesting party's legal counsel acts as the requesting party's representative prior to opening and acceptance of the bid, carry out the discussions and other communications required by AU-C 920 with the legal counsel until the requesting party is selected. In these situations, do not agree to provide a comfort letter addressed to the client, legal counsel, or a nonspecific addressee such as "any or all underwriters to be selected." If the auditor agrees to provide a draft comfort letter, it should include a legend describing the letter's purpose and limitations.

## Comfort Letter Format and Contents

### Date

15. The letter should state that the inquiries and other procedures described in the letter did not cover the period from the cutoff date to the date of the letter.

16. If an additional letter, dated at or shortly before the closing date, is requested, carry out the specified procedures and inquiries as of the cutoff date for each letter. The subsequent letter should only relate to information in the most recently amended securities offering.

### Addressee

17. Address the letter to the requesting party, or the requesting party and the entity, and do not provide the letter to any other parties.

### Introductory paragraph

18. Include an introductory paragraph in the letter identifying the financial statements and the securities offering.

### Auditor's reports

19. The comfort letter should not repeat the report on the audited financial statements included in the securities offering but it should reference this report.

20. If the auditor's report on the audited financial statements included in the securities offering contains an emphasis-of-matter or other-matter paragraph, or a separate section in the auditor's report addressing matters other than

consistency of application of accounting policies, the auditor should refer to that fact and discuss the subject matter of that paragraph in the comfort letter. In situations where the SEC accepts a modified opinion on historical financial statements, refer to the modification and discuss its subject matter in the comfort letter's opening paragraph.

21. Do not provide negative assurance about the auditor's report or audited financial statements reported on in the securities offering by other auditors.

22. If the comfort letter's introductory paragraph refers to reports the auditor previously issued other than the report on the audited financial statements included in the securities offering, do not repeat the reports in the comfort letter or otherwise imply that the auditor is reporting as of the date of the comfort letter or assuming responsibility for the sufficiency of the procedures for the underwriter's purposes.

23. Do not mention in a comfort letter reports issued in accordance with AU-C 265 or any restricted use reports issued to a client in connection with procedures performed on the client's internal control over financial reporting (ICFR) in accordance with AU-C 940.

24. Do not refer to or attach to the comfort letter any restricted use report. An example of a restricted use report is a report on agreed-upon procedures.

*Representations*

25. Refer to the requesting party's representations in the comfort letter when the representation letter has been provided.

*Independence*

26. State in the comfort letter that the auditor is independent with respect to the entity or state the date through which the auditor was independent and identify the applicable independence rules.

*Compliance with SEC requirements*

27. If the auditor is requested to express an opinion on whether the form of the financial statements covered by the auditor's report comply in all material respects with the pertinent accounting requirements adopted by the SEC, state that such compliance is with the applicable accounting requirements of the 1933 Act and the related rules and regulations adopted by the SEC.

28. If financial statements are incorporated in a 1933 Act registration statement by referring to filings under the Securities Exchange Act of 1934 (the 1934 Act), the auditor may refer to whether the form of the audited financial statements included in the registration statement comply in all material respects with the applicable accounting requirements of the 1934 Act and the related rules and regulations adopted by the SEC. However, the auditor should not refer to compliance with the 1934 Act provisions regarding ICFR.

29. If the auditor has been asked to include an opinion in the comfort letter on whether the financial statements covered by the auditor's report comply as to form with the pertinent accounting requirements of the SEC, disclose any existing material departures in the comfort letter.

30. The auditor should only express an opinion about the compliance as to form with requirements under the SEC's adopted rules and regulations for financial statements he or she has audited. If financial statements or financial statement schedules have not been audited, the auditor is limited to providing negative assurance regarding compliance as to form.

31. Do not comment in a comfort letter on compliance as to form of MD&A with the SEC's adopted rules and regulations.

*Comments on information other than audited financial statements*

32. When commenting on information other than audited financial statements in a comfort letter, describe the procedures performed by the auditor, describe the criteria specified by the requesting party, and state that procedures performed with respect to interim periods may not disclose matters of significance regarding matters about which negative assurance is requested.

33. In the comfort letter, do not:

   a. State or imply that the auditor determined that the applied procedures are necessary or sufficient for the requesting party's purposes,

   b. Use terms with uncertain meanings such as general review, limited review, reconcile, check, or test in describing the work unless the procedures encompassed by these terms are described in the comfort letter, and

   c. Make a statement that nothing else has come to the auditor's attention that would be of interest to the requesting party as a result of carrying out the specified procedures.

34. If the report on the audited financial statements in the securities offering is a modified report, consider the effect on providing negative assurance in the comfort letter regarding subsequent interim financial information included in the securities offering or regarding an absence of specified subsequent changes and follow the procedures describe in requirement 20 (above).

35. Obtain an understanding of a client's ICFR for both annual and interim periods when commenting in a comfort letter on (*a*) unaudited interim or condensed interim financial information; (*b*) capsule financial information; (*c*) a financial forecast when historical financial statements provide a basis for one or more significant assumptions for the forecast; or (*d*) changes in selected financial statements items (e.g., capital stock, long-term debt).

36. Provide negative assurance on unaudited interim financial information included in the securities offering only if the auditor has reviewed the interim financial information in accordance with AU-C 930. If the auditor has not conducted a review in accordance with AU-C 930, he or she is limited to reporting procedures performed and findings obtained. Negative assurance provided should be about whether:

   a. Any material modifications should be made to the unaudited interim financial information for it to be in accordance with the applicable financial reporting framework, and

   b. The form of the unaudited interim financial information complies in all material respects with the applicable accounting requirements of the 1933 Act and the related rules and regulations adopted by the SEC, if applicable.

37. If the comfort letter states that the auditor has issued a review report, attach the review report to the letter unless the review report is already included in the securities offering.

38. The letter should specifically identify any unaudited interim financial information and should state that the auditor has not audited the interim financial information in accordance with generally accepted auditing standards and does not express an opinion concerning such information.

39. When the requesting party requests that the auditor provide negative assurance on the unaudited interim financial information or information extracted therefrom, for a monthly period ending after the latest financial statements included in the securities offering, requirements 36–38 (above)

apply and a copy of the unaudited interim financial information should be attached to the comfort letter.

40. Only provide negative assurance about whether selected capsule financial information is in accordance with the applicable financial reporting framework if (*a*) the auditor has reviewed the financial statements underlying the capsule financial information in accordance with AU-C 930, and (*b*) the selected capsule financial information is in accordance with minimal disclosure requirements of the applicable financial reporting framework. If these conditions are not met, the auditor is limited to reporting procedures performed and findings obtained.

41. Only provide negative assurance on selected capsule financial information regarding whether the dollar amounts were determined on a basis substantially consistent with that of the corresponding amounts in the audited financial statements if the auditor has reviewed the financial statements underlying the capsule financial information in accordance with AU-C 930. Otherwise, the auditor is limited to reporting procedures performed and findings obtained.

42. The auditor should not comment in a comfort letter on pro forma financial information unless he or she has an appropriate level of knowledge of the entity's accounting and financial reporting practices.

43. Only provide negative assurance in a comfort letter on pro forma financial information, including negative assurance on the application of pro forma adjustments to historical amounts, the compilation of pro forma financial information, or whether the form of the pro forma financial information complies in all material respects with the applicable accounting requirements of Rule 11-02 of Regulation S-X, if the auditor has obtained the required knowledge of the entity's accounting and financial reporting practices and has performed:

    a. An audit of the annual financial statements, or

    b. A review in accordance with AU-C 930 of the interim financial statements of the entity to which the pro forma adjustments were applied.

If these conditions are not met, the auditor is limited to reporting procedures performed and findings obtained.

44. When performing procedures agreed to with the requesting party on a financial forecast and commenting on them in a comfort letter:

    a. Obtain an understanding of the entity's ICFR for both annual and interim periods,

    b. Perform procedures required by AT-C 305, paragraph 69, for reporting on compilation of a forecast,

    c. Issue a report on the compilation of prospective financial information in accordance with AT-C 305, paragraphs 18–19, and attach that report to the comfort letter, and

    d. Perform additional procedures as requested by the underwriter (or other requesting party) and report on the findings in the comfort letter.

45. Do not provide negative assurance on the results of procedures performed on a financial forecast.

46. The auditor should not provide negative assurance regarding compliance of the forecast with Rule 11-03 of Regulation S-X unless he or she has performed an examination of the forecast in accordance with AT-C 305.

47. A comfort letter should not be issued if the forecast is included in the securities offering unless the forecast is accompanied by an indication that the auditor has not examined the forecast and, therefore, does not express an opinion on it.

48. Base comments regarding subsequent changes in specified financial statement items only on the limited procedures performed with respect to the change period as determined by the requesting party.

49. Provide negative assurance in the comfort letter regarding subsequent changes in specified financial statement items only as of a date less than 135 days from the end of the most recent period for which the auditor has performed an audit or review.

50. If the requesting party requests negative assurance regarding subsequent changes in specified financial statement items as of a later date, then the auditor is limited to reporting procedures performed and findings obtained.

51. Subsequent changes should not be characterized using ambiguous terms (e.g., "adverse"). The auditor should note in the comfort letter if there has been a change in the application of the requirements of the applicable financial reporting framework.

52. The auditor should only comment on the occurrence of changes in specified financial statement items that are not included in the securities offering. If the auditor is aware of a change, increase, or decrease that has occurred during the change period and the amount of the change, increase, or decrease is included in the securities offering, he or she should include the phrase "except for changes, increases, or decreases that the securities offering discloses have occurred or may occur" in the comfort letter. This phrase is not needed when no changes, increases, or decreases in the specified financial statement items are disclosed in the securities offering.

53. Identify in the draft and final form of the comfort letter the dates and periods for which data at the cutoff date and for the change period are to be compared, regardless of specification in the underwriting agreement.

54. If the requesting party requests the use of change periods other than beginning immediately after the date of the latest balance sheet and the latest period presented in the securities offering and ending on the cutoff date, explain the implications of using an earlier date to the requesting party. If the requesting party still desires the use of such change periods, the auditor is permitted to use the periods requested.

*Comments on tables, statistics, and other financial information*

55. Do not comment in a comfort letter on tables, statistics, and other financial information, unless that information is expressed in dollars or percentages and is derived from amounts that have been obtained from accounting records subject to ICFR, or information that has been derived directly from such accounting records by analysis or computation.

56. Do not comment in a comfort letter on quantitative information that has been obtained from an accounting record unless the information is subject to the same controls over financial reporting as the dollar amounts.

57. The auditor should not comment on tables, statistics, and other financial information relating to an unaudited period unless he or she has performed an audit of the client's financial statements for a period including or immediately prior to the unaudited period or completed an audit for a later period, or otherwise obtained knowledge of the client's ICFR.

58. The auditor should not use the term *presents fairly* in comments concerning tables, statistics, and other financial information and should not comment on

information subject to legal interpretation, nonfinancial data presented in MD&A unless the auditor has examined or reviewed the MD&A in accordance with AT-C 395, or on other matters solely because he or she is capable of reading, counting, measuring, or performing other applicable functions.

59. Comments in the comfort letter about tables, statistics, and other financial information included in the securities offering should clearly identify the specific information commented on, include a description of the procedures performed and the findings, expressed in terms of agreement between items compared.

60. The auditor should only comment on the acceptability of allocation methods used in deriving the figures commented on to the extent to which the allocation is made in or can be directly derived by analysis or computation from the client's accounting records. Such comments should clarify that such allocations are arbitrary to a substantial extent, the allocation method used is not the only acceptable one, and other acceptable allocation methods might produce significantly different results.

61. The letter should state that the auditor makes no representations regarding any matter of legal interpretation, the completeness or adequacy of disclosure, and the adequacy of the procedures followed, and that such procedures would not necessarily disclose material misstatements or omissions in the information to which the comments relate.

*Compliance as to form with Regulation S-K*

62. Do not provide negative assurance about whether certain financial information in registration statements that is included because of specific requirements of regulation S-K is in conformity with the Regulation's disclosure requirements unless the information is derived directly or by analysis or computation from the accounting records subject to ICFR and this information is capable of evaluation against reasonable criteria that have been established by the SEC.

63. Do not express an opinion on conformity with Regulation S-K's disclosure requirements.

*Concluding paragraph*

64. The comfort letter should include a concluding paragraph restricting the use of the comfort letter for the information of the addressees and to assist the requesting parties in connection with the securities offering.

*Disclosure of subsequently discovered matters*

65. Inform the entity when matters are discovered that require mention in the final comfort letter that were not mentioned in the draft letter provided to the requesting party. If the entity decides that disclosure will not be made in the securities offering, inform the entity that the matters will be mentioned in the comfort letter and recommend that the requesting party be informed promptly.

## Analysis and Application of Procedures

*Engagement Acceptance*

Exhibit AU-C 920-1 illustrates a representation letter from requesting parties. A letter from an attorney indicating that a party "may" be deemed to be an underwriter or has liability substantially equivalent to that of an underwriter under the securities laws would not meet the AU-C 920 requirement to be considered a "requesting party."

---

**PLANNING AID REMINDER:** Although the auditor is not permitted to provide a comfort letter to any party other than a requesting party, he or she may follow the guidance in AT-C 215 to provide a report on agreed-upon procedures to such parties.

---

*Agreeing Upon the Scope of Services*

While comfort letters are not required under the 1933 Act, receipt of a comfort letter from the auditor is a common condition of the underwriting agreement. In requiring comfort letters from auditors, underwriters are seeking assistance in performing a reasonable investigation of data (unaudited financial information and other data) on the authority of an expert. Unfortunately, what constitutes a reasonable investigation of unaudited data sufficient to satisfy an underwriter's purpose has never been authoritatively established. Therefore, it is only the underwriter who can determine the amount of work sufficient to satisfy his or her due diligence requirement. Accordingly, the auditor carries out procedures that are within his or her professional expertise that will aid underwriters in discharging their responsibility for exercising due diligence, but cannot furnish any assurance on whether those procedures are sufficient for the underwriter's purpose, which paragraph 4 of the sample comfort letter in Exhibit AU-C 920-2 illustrates.

---

**PLANNING AID REMINDER:** If the requesting party refuses to meet together with the entity, the auditor may consider the implications in determining whether to accept the engagement.

---

Acceptance of the draft comfort letter by the requesting party indicates to the auditor that the requesting party considers the procedures described in the letter to be sufficient for its purposes. However, the auditor may wish to further emphasize the point that the requesting party and not the auditor is responsible for the sufficiency of the comfort procedures by including a legend or a concluding paragraph on the draft letter to the underwriter to address its functions and limitations. AU-C 920 contains the following example of such a paragraph:

> This draft is furnished solely for the purpose of indicating the form of letter that we would expect to be able to furnish [*name of requesting party*] in response to their request, the matters expected to be covered in the letter, and the nature of the procedures that we would expect to carry out with respect to such matters. Based on our discussions with [*name of requesting party*], it is our understanding that the procedures outlined in this draft letter are those they wish us to follow. Unless [*name of requesting party*] informs us otherwise, we shall assume that there are no additional procedures they wish us to follow. The text of the letter itself will depend, of course, on the results of the procedures, which we would not expect to complete until shortly before the letter is given and in no event before the cutoff date indicated therein.

In the absence of any discussions with the requesting party, the second sentence of the above paragraph should be revised as follows:

> In the absence of any discussions with [*name of requesting party*], we have set out in this draft letter those procedures referred to in the draft underwriting agreement (of which we have been furnished a copy) that we are willing to follow.

A shelf registration statement enables an entity to register securities under the 1933 Act and then issue these securities over a period of time. At the effective date of the registration statement, an underwriter or lead underwriter may not have been named, although the auditor may have been asked to issue a comfort letter. In these situations, the auditor may issue a draft comfort letter to the entity or the legal counsel representing the underwriter group based on the actual procedures the auditor has performed and include a legend in the draft comfort letter addressing the letter's functions and limitations. The following is an example of such a paragraph as illustrated in AU-C 920:

> This draft describes the procedures that we have performed and represents a letter we would be prepared to sign if the managing underwriter had been chosen and requested such a letter. The text of the final letter will depend, of course, on whether the managing underwriter who is selected requests that these and other procedures be performed to meet his or her needs and whether the managing underwriter requests that any of the procedures be updated to the date of issuance of the signed letter.

A signed comfort letter may be issued to the underwriter selected for the portion of the issue then being offered when the underwriting agreement for an offering is signed and on each closing date.

### Comfort Letter Format and Contents

AU-C 920 provides a variety of sample comfort letters, one of which represents a typical comfort letter and is presented in Exhibit AU-C 920-2.

*Date*

Ordinarily, the comfort letter is dated on or shortly after the underwriting agreement is signed. Usually the underwriting agreement specifies the date to which the procedures described in the letter are to relate. This date, commonly referred to as the cutoff date, is customarily within five business days before the effective date of the registration statement.

---

**PLANNING AID REMINDER:** The auditor should consider whether the period between the cutoff date and the date of the letter provides the auditor with sufficient time to perform the procedures and prepare the letter when deciding whether to accept the engagement.

---

*Auditor's reports*

The requesting party may request that the auditor put the report on the audited financial statements included in the registration statement in the comfort letter, but the auditor is not permitted to do this because of the significance of the date of the auditor's report. The comfort letter's opening paragraph may refer to matters addressed in emphasis-of-matter or other-matter paragraphs or a separate section in the auditor's report that do not affect the opinion on the basic financial statements, such as interim financial information accompanying or included in the notes to the audited financial statements or required supplementary information described in AU-C 730.

A requesting party may request that the auditor comment in the comfort letter on unaudited interim financial information required by item 302(a) of Regulation S-K or required supplementary information. AU-C 930 and AU-C 730 provide guidance for these respective items regarding when the auditor is required to modify the auditor's report on the audited financial statements to refer to such information. If the auditor's report in the registration statement is modified, it is generally referred to in the comfort letter's opening paragraph. If the requesting party requests that the auditor perform procedures with regard to such information in addition to those performed for the review or audit as per AU-C 930 and AU-C 730, the auditor may do so and report the findings.

The auditor may have previously reported on any of the following:

- Summarized financial statements derived from audited financial statements, in accordance with AU-C 810 (*Engagements to Report on Summary Financial Statements*);
- Interim financial information, in accordance with AU-C 930 (*Interim Financial Information*);
- Pro forma financial information, in accordance with AT-C 310 (*Reporting on Pro Forma Financial Information*);
- A financial forecast, in accordance with AT-C 305 (*Prospective Financial Information*); or
- Management's discussion and analysis (MD&A), in accordance with AT-C 395 (*Management's Discussion and Analysis*).

In these situations, in the introductory paragraph of the comfort letter, the accountant may refer to the previously issued reports and, if the reports are not included in the securities offering, they may be attached to the comfort letter.

*Independence*

In conjunction with SEC filings, the underwriting agreement customarily requests that the auditor represent in the comfort letter that he or she is independent. A simple statement, such as the following, suffices:

> We are independent certified public accountants with respect to [*name of client*], within the meaning of the 1933 Act and the applicable rules and regulations thereunder adopted by the SEC.

In a non-SEC filing, a statement such as the following suffices:

> We are independent certified public accountants with respect to [*name of client*], under the "Independence Rule" of the AICPA's Code of Professional Conduct and its interpretations.

Auditors for previously nonaffiliated companies recently acquired by the registrant are not required to have been independent with respect to the company whose shares are being registered. In this situation, the statement regarding independence should be modified, as follows:

> As of [*date of the auditor's most recent report on the financial statements of the client*] and during the period covered by the financial statements on which we reported, we were independent certified public accountants with respect to [*name of client*], under the "Independence Rule" of the AICPA's Code of Professional Conduct and its interpretations.

*Compliance with SEC requirements*

Usually, the underwriting agreement requests that the auditor comment on whether the financial statements comply with SEC requirements. The auditor may do so in the comfort letter by adding a paragraph like the following:

> In our opinion [*include phrase* "except as disclosed in the registration statement," *if applicable*], the [*identify the financial statements and financial statement schedules*] audited by us and included in the registration statement comply as to form in all material respects with the applicable accounting requirements of the 1933 Act and the related rules and regulations adopted by the SEC.

If there is a material departure from the pertinent published SEC requirements, the auditor should disclose such departure in the comfort letter. Normally, representatives of the SEC will have agreed to such a departure. The following is an example of wording to be used in the comfort letter when the SEC has agreed to a departure from its published accounting requirements:

> In our opinion [*include phrase* "except as disclosed in the registration statement," *if applicable*], the consolidated financial statements and financial statement schedules audited by us and included [*incorporated by reference*] in the registration statement comply as to form in all material respects with the applicable accounting requirements of the Act and the related rules and regulations adopted by the SEC; however, as agreed to by representatives of the SEC, separate financial statements and financial statement schedules of ABC Company (an equity investee) as required by Rule 3-09 of Regulation S-X have been omitted.

---

**ENGAGEMENT STRATEGY:** While the auditor should not use the comfort letter to comment on compliance of MD&A's form with rules and regulations adopted by the SEC, he or she may accept an engagement to examine or review MD&A in accordance with AT-C 395.

---

*Comments on information other than audited financial statements*

The auditor's comfort letter often refers to information other than audited financial statements, such as:

- Unaudited interim financial information,
- Capsule financial information,
- Pro forma financial information,
- Financial forecasts, and
- Subsequent changes in specified financial statement items.

The comfort letter should refer to the agreed-upon procedures when commenting on such information with the following exception: when the auditor has been asked to provide negative assurance on interim or capsule financial information, he or she does not need to specify the procedures involved in an AU-C 930 review.

While the auditor is responsible for obtaining a sufficient understanding of internal control over financial reporting (ICFR) for annual and interim periods when commenting in a comfort letter on information described in requirement 35 (above), he or she may have already obtained this understanding through the audit of the entity's financial statements.

The requirements in AU-C 920 related to unaudited condensed interim financial information also apply to complete financial statements and the interim statements may be for a 12-month period ending on a date other than the entity's normal year-end. Exhibit AU-C 920-2 illustrates how the auditor may appropriately comment on unaudited condensed interim financial information when he or she has conducted a review of the information in accordance with AU-C 930. If a review of interim financial information was conducted in accordance with AU-C 930, the auditor may state in the comfort letter that he or she:

- Performed the procedures identified in AU-C 930, or
- Issued a report on the review of the interim financial information.

**PLANNING AID REMINDER:** The auditor may have sufficient knowledge of the entity's accounting and financial reporting practices to comment on pro forma financial information from his or her audit or review of the entity's historical financial statements for the most recent annual or interim period for which the pro forma financial information is presented.

When the auditor performs a compilation on a financial forecast for an entity whose securities are subject to SEC regulation, the SEC's views regarding independence are relevant and independence may be considered impaired when services include preparation or assembly of financial forecasts.

The underwriter often asks the auditor to comment in the comfort letter on subsequent changes in certain financial statement items during the change period. These comments usually relate to (1) changes in capital stock, (2) increases in long-term debt, (3) decreases in net current assets, (4) decreases in stockholders' equity, (5) decreases in net sales, and (6) decreases in total and per-share amounts of income before continuing operations and of net income.

**PLANNING AID REMINDER:** The auditor should base his or her comments on subsequent changes solely on the limited procedures performed, which may include inquiries of company officials and the reading of minutes. (Paragraph 6 of the sample comfort letter in Exhibit AU-C 920-2 illustrates this requirement.)

When the auditor is providing negative assurance regarding the absence of subsequent changes, he or she may express this negative assurance as illustrated in paragraphs 5b and 6 of the sample comfort letter provided in Exhibit AU-C 920-2.

> **PLANNING AID REMINDER:** In the comfort letter, the accountant should use the terms "change," "increase," and "decrease" rather than "adverse change." The term "adverse change" implies that the accountant is making a judgment about the change, which might be misinterpreted by the underwriter.

When the auditor is commenting on subsequent changes, he or she is commenting on the change period as a whole; therefore, changes within the change period that offset each other would not be reported. When more than one auditor is involved in the audit of the financial statements of the entity, the auditor of the group financial statements may comment that there were no changes in consolidated financial statement items even if changes were reported by component auditors. In these situations, the auditor of the group financial statements should make appropriate modifications to the comfort letter commenting on subsequent changes. The modifications consist of an addition to paragraph 4, a substitute for the applicable part of paragraph 5, and an addition to the last sentence of paragraph 6 of the sample comfort letter at the end of this section.

> 4c. We have read the letter dated [*date*] of [*the other auditors*] with regard to [*the related company*].
>
> 5. Nothing came to our attention as a result of the foregoing procedures (which, so far as [*the related company*] is concerned, consisted solely of reading the letter referred to in 4c), however, that caused us to believe that ...
>
> 6. On the basis of these inquiries and our reading of the minutes and the letter dated [*date*] of [*the other auditors*] with regard to [*the related company*], as described in 4, nothing came to our attention that caused us to believe that there was any such change, increase, or decrease, except in all instances for changes, increases, or decreases that the registration statement discloses have occurred or may occur.

*Comments on tables, statistics, and other financial information*

The auditor's comments in the comfort letter regarding the procedures performed and findings obtained concerning tables, statistics, and other financial information may be presented by:

- Individually describing each item of specific information commented on;
- Grouping or summarizing descriptions as long as the procedures and findings are adequately described, the applicability of the descriptions to items in the securities offering is clear, and the descriptions do not imply that the auditor assumes responsibility for the adequacy of the procedures;
- Presenting a matrix that lists the financial information and common procedures used and indicates the procedures applied to the specific items; and
- Identifying procedures performed with specified symbols and identifying items to which those procedures have been applied directly on a copy of the prospectus, which is attached to the comfort letter.

*Compliance as to form with Regulation S-K*

Items that generally meet the requirements for auditors to be able to provide negative assurance about whether that information is in conformity with the disclosure requirements of Regulation S-K include:

- Item 301, "Selected Financial Data";
- Item 302, "Supplementary Financial Information";
- Item 402, "Executive Compensation"; and
- Item 503(d), "Ratio of Earnings to Fixed Charges."

Item 305, "Quantitative and Qualitative Disclosure about Market Risk," does not meet the criteria for the auditor to provide either negative assurance on its conformity with Regulation S-K's disclosure requirements or comments on its qualitative disclosures in the comfort letter because the disclosures are not derived from accounting records subject to ICFR. The quantitative disclosures required by Item 305 may be presented in the form of a tabular presentation, sensitivity analysis, or value-at-risk disclosures and the auditor may perform limited procedures related to tabular presentation to the extent that such information is derived from the accounting records subject to internal control over financial reporting.

> **PLANNING AID REMINDER:** Even though the auditor cannot express an opinion on conformity with the disclosure requirements of Regulation S-K, he or she is permitted to perform procedures and report findings with respect to this information.

*Concluding paragraph*

Paragraph 7 of the sample comfort letter in Exhibit AU-C 920-2 illustrates appropriate wording for a concluding paragraph.

## Practitioner's Aids

Exhibit AU-C 920-1 is an example of a representation letter as illustrated in AU-C 920. Exhibit AU-C 920-2 is an example of a sample comfort letter for a 1933 Act offering as illustrated in AU-C 920.

### EXHIBIT AU-C 920-1—REPRESENTATION LETTER FROM REQUESTING PARTIES

[*Date*]

Dear ABC Accountants:

[*Name of requesting party*], as principal or agent, in the placement of [*identify securities*] to be issued by [*name of issuer*], will be reviewing certain information relating to [*issuer*] that will be included [*incorporated by reference*] in the document [*if appropriate, the document should be identified*], which may be delivered to investors and utilized by them as a basis for their investment decision. This review process, applied to the information relating to the issuer, is [*will be*] substantially consistent with the due diligence review process that an underwriter would perform if this placement of securities [*or issuance of securities in an* acquisition transaction] were being registered pursuant to the Securities Act of 1933 (the Act). We are knowledgeable with respect to the due diligence review process that would be performed if this placement of securities were being registered pursuant to the Act. We hereby request that you deliver to us a "comfort" letter concerning the financial statements of the issuer and certain statistical and other data included in the offering document. We will contact you to identify the procedures we wish you to follow and the form we wish the comfort letter to take.

Very truly yours,

[Name of requesting party]

## EXHIBIT AU-C 920-2—SAMPLE COMFORT LETTER FOR A 1933 ACT OFFERING

June 28, 20X6

[Addressee]

Dear Ladies and Gentlemen:

We have audited the consolidated balance sheets of The Blank Company, Inc. (the company) and subsidiaries, which comprise the consolidated balance sheets as of December 31, 20X5 and 20X4, and the related consclidated statements of income, changes in stockholders' equity, and cash flows for each of the three years in the three-year period ended December 31, 20X5, and the related notes to the consolidated financial statements, all included in the registration statement (no. 33-00000) on Form S-1 filed by the registrant under the Securities Act of 1933 (the Act); our report with respect thereto is also included in that registration statement.[1] The registration statement, as amended on June 28, 20X6, is herein referred to as the registration statement.[2]

In connection with the registration statement:

1. We are independent certified public accountants with respect to the company within the meaning of the 1933 Act and the applicable rules and regulations thereunder adopted by the SEC.

2. In our opinion [included the phrase "except as disclosed in the registration statement," if applicable], the consolidated financial statements audited by us and included in the registration statement comply as to form in all material respects with the applicable accounting require-

---

[1] The example includes financial statements required by SEC regulations to be included in the filing. If additional financial information is covered by the comfort letter, appropriate modifications should be made.

[2] The example assumes that the auditors have not previously reported on the interim financial information. If the accountants have previously reported on the interim financial information, they may refer to that fact in the introductory paragraph of the comfort letter as follows:

Also, we have reviewed the unaudited condensed consolidated financial statements as of March 31, 20X6 and 20X5, and for the three-month periods then ended, as indicated in our report dated May 15, 20X6, which is included (incorporated by reference) in the registration statement. The report may be attached to the comfort letter although restricted use reports should not be attached. The auditors may agree to comment in the comfort letter on whether the interim financial information complies as to form in all material respects with the applicable accounting requirements of the published rules and regulations of the SEC.

ments of the Act and the related rules and regulations adopted by the SEC.

3. We have not audited any financial statements of the company as of any date or for any period subsequent to December 31, 20X5; although we have conducted an audit for the year ended December 31, 20X5, the purpose (and therefore the scope) of the audit was to enable us to express our opinion on the consolidated financial statements as of December 31, 20X5, and for the year then ended, but not on the financial statements for any interim period within that year. Therefore, we are unable to and do not express any opinion on the unaudited condensed consolidated balance sheet as of March 31, 20X6, and the unaudited condensed consolidated statements of income, stockholders' equity, and cash flows for the three-month periods ended March 31, 20X6 and 20X5, included in the registration statement, or on the financial position, results of operations, or cash flows as of any date or for any period subsequent to December 31, 20X5.

4. For purposes of this letter we have read the 20X6 minutes of meetings of the stockholders, the board of directors, and [include other appropriate committees, if any] of the company and its subsidiaries as set forth in the minute books at June 23, 20X6, officials of the company having advised us that the minutes of all such meetings through that date were set forth therein and having discussed with us the unapproved minutes of meetings held on [*dates*], we have carried out other procedures to June 23, 20X6, as follows (our work did not extend to the period from June 24, 20X6, to June 28, 20X6, inclusive):

    a. With respect to the three-month periods ended March 31, 20X6 and 20X5, we have:

        (i) Performed the procedures specified for a review in accordance with auditing standards generally accepted in the United States of America applicable to reviews of interim financial information, on the unaudited condensed consolidated balance sheet as of March 31, 20X6, and unaudited condensed consolidated statements of income, stockholders' equity, and cash flows for the three-month periods ended March 31, 20X6 and 20X5, included in the registration statement.

        (ii) Inquired of certain officials of the company who have responsibility for financial and accounting matters whether the unaudited condensed consolidated financial statements referred to in a(i) comply as to form in all material respects with the applicable accounting requirements of the Act and the related rules and regulations adopted by the SEC.

    b. With respect to the period from April 1, 20X6, to May 31, 20X6, we have:

        (i) Read the unaudited consolidated financial statements of the company and subsidiaries for April and May of both 20X5 and 20X6 furnished us by the company, officials of the company having advised that no such financial statements as of any date or for any period subsequent to May 31, 20X6, were available. [*If applicable:* The financial information for April and May is incomplete in that it omits the statements of cash flows and other disclosures.]

    (ii) Inquired of certain officials of the company who have responsibility for financial and accounting matters whether the unaudited consolidated financial statements referred to in b(i) are stated on a basis substantially consistent with that of the audited consolidated financial statements included in the registration statement.

The foregoing procedures do not constitute an audit conducted in accordance with generally accepted auditing standards. Also, they would not necessarily reveal matters of significance with respect to the comments in the following paragraph. Accordingly, we make no representations regarding the sufficiency of the foregoing procedures for your purposes.

5. Nothing came to our attention as a result of the foregoing procedures, however, that caused us to believe that:[3]

    a. Any material modifications should be made to the unaudited condensed consolidated financial statements described in 4a(i), included in the registration statement, for them to be in conformity with generally accepted accounting principles.[4]

    b. The unaudited condensed consolidated financial statements described in 4a(i) do not comply as to form in all material respects with the applicable accounting requirements of the Act and the related rules and regulations adopted by the SEC.

    c. At May 31, 20X6, there was any change in the capital stock, increase in long-term debt, or decrease in consolidated net current assets or stockholders' equity of the consolidated companies as compared with amounts shown in the March 31, 20X6, unaudited condensed consolidated balance sheet included in the registration statement, or

    d. for the period from April 1, 20X6, to May 31, 20X6, there were any decreases, as compared to the corresponding period in the preceding year, in consolidated net sales or in the total or per-share amounts of income before extraordinary items or of net income, except in all instances for changes, increases, or decreases that the registration statement discloses have occurred or may occur.

---

[3] If there has been a change in accounting principle during the interim period, a reference to that change should be included therein.

[4] AU-C 930 does not require the accountants to modify the report on a review of interim financial information for a lack of consistency in the application of accounting principles provided that the interim financial information appropriately discloses such matters.

6. As mentioned in 4b, company officials have advised us that no consolidated financial statements as of any date or for any period subsequent to May 31, 20X6, are available; accordingly, the procedures carried out by us with respect to changes in financial statement items after May 31, 20X6, have, of necessity, been even more limited than those with respect to the periods referred to in 4. We have inquired of certain officials of the company who have responsibility for financial and accounting matters whether (*a*) at June 23, 20X6, there was any change in the capital stock, increase in long-term debt or any decreases in consolidated net current assets or stockholders' equity of the consolidated companies as compared with amounts shown on the March 31, 20X6, unaudited condensed consolidated balance sheet included in the registration statement or (*b*) for the period from April 1, 20X6, to June 23, 20X6, there were any decreases, as compared with the corresponding period in the preceding year, in consolidated net sales or in the total or per-share amounts of income before extraordinary items or of net income. On the basis of these inquiries and our reading of the minutes as described in 4, nothing came to our attention that caused us to believe that there was any such change, increase, or decrease, except in all instances for changes, increases, or decreases that the registration statement discloses have occurred or may occur.

7. This letter is solely for the information of the addressees and to assist the underwriters in conducting and documenting their investigation of the affairs of the company in connection with the offering of the securities covered by the registration statement, and it is not to be used, circulated, quoted, or otherwise referred to within or without the underwriting group for any purpose, including but not limited to the registration, purchase, or sale of securities, nor is it to be filed with or referred to in whole or in part in the registration statement or any other document, except that reference may be made to it in the underwriting agreement or in any list of closing documents pertaining to the offering of the securities covered by the registration statement.

**Note to Exhibit AU-C 920-2:** This letter assumes the following circumstances: The prospectus includes audited consolidated balance sheets as of December 31, 20X5 and 20X4, and audited consolidated statements of income, stockholders' equity, and cash flows for each of the three years in the period ended December 31, 20X5. The prospectus also includes an unaudited condensed consolidated balance sheet as of March 31, 20X6, and unaudited condensed consolidated statements of income, stockholders' equity, and cash flows for the three-month periods ended March 31, 20X6 and 20X5, reviewed in accordance with AU-C 930 but not previously reported on by the auditor. The cutoff date is June 23, 20X6, and the letter is dated June 28, 20X6. The effective date is June 28, 20X6. Each of the comments in the letter is in response to a requirement of the underwriting agreement. For purposes of this example, the income statement items of the current interim period are to be compared with those of the corresponding period of the preceding year.

**PUBLIC COMPANY IMPLICATION:** Because comfort letters are associated with filings under the federal securities laws, references in Exhibit AU-C 920-2 to "independent certified public accountants" are to be changed to "independent registered public accounting firm" ; references to "generally accepted auditing standards" are to be changed to "standards of the Public Company Accounting Oversight Board (United States)"; and references to "procedures of the American Institute of Certified Public Accountants" are to be changed to "standards of the Public Company Accounting Oversight Board."

## SECTION 925

## FILINGS WITH THE U.S. SECURITIES AND EXCHANGE COMMISSION UNDER THE SECURITIES ACT OF 1933

### Authoritative Pronouncements
SAS-122—Statements on Auditing Standards: Clarification and Recodification

### Overview
AU-C 925 provides the auditor with guidance regarding his or her responsibilities in connection with financial statements of a nonissuer included or incorporated by reference in a registration statement filed with the U.S. Securities and Exchange Commission (SEC) under the Securities Act of 1933, as amended. The auditor's objective is to perform procedures to indicate that the auditor has performed a reasonable investigation as referred to in Section 11(b)(3)(B) of the Securities Act of 1933. These procedures are performed at, or shortly before, the effective date of the registration statement.

### Definitions

| | |
|---|---|
| Auditor's consent | A statement signed by the auditor indicating that the auditor consents to the inclusion of the audit report and other references to the auditor in a registration statement filed under the Securities Act of 1933. |
| Awareness letter | A letter signed and dated by the auditor acknowledging the auditor's awareness that the auditor's review report on unaudited interim financial information is included in a registration statement filed under the Securities Act of 1933. This letter is not part of the registration statements and is often called an acknowledgment letter. |
| Effective date of the registration statement | The date on which the registration statement becomes effective for purposes of evaluating the auditor's liability under Section 11 of the Securities Act of 1933. |

### Requirements
The auditor is presumptively required to perform the following procedures related to filings with the SEC under the Securities Act of 1933.

#### Effective Date of the Registration Statement

1. The effective date of a registration statement is not necessarily the same as the filing date. Therefore, the auditor should request that management advise the auditor of the registration proceedings' progress through the registration statement's effective date.

#### Audited Financial Statements

2. If the auditor's report on audited financial statements is included in a registration statement filed with the SEC under the Securities Act of 1933,

perform the procedures described in AU-C 720 (*Other Information in Documents Containing Audited Financial Statements*) on the prospectus and pertinent portions of the registration statement, including material that is included by reference. Determine that the auditor's name is not being used in a way that indicates a greater responsibility than he or she intends.

3. If the auditor has audited the most recent period for which separate audited financial statements of the entity are included in the registration statement, then he or she should perform the following procedures at or shortly before the registration statement's effective date (these procedures are derived from AU-C 560 (*Subsequent Events and Subsequently Discovered Facts*):

   a. Perform audit procedures to identify subsequent events through a date at or near the effective date of the registration statement that require adjustment or disclosure in the financial statements. The nature and extent of audit procedures should take the auditor's risk assessment into account and should include (1) obtaining an understanding of procedures management established to identify subsequent events, (2) inquiring of management and those charged with governance (as appropriate) about whether any events occurred after the date of the financial statements that might affect the statements, (3) reading any minutes of meetings of the entity's owners, management, and those charged with governance held after the date of the financial statements and inquiring about matters discussed at any such meeting if minutes are not yet available, and (4) reading the latest of any subsequent interim financial statements of the entity.

   b. Obtain an updated written representation letter from management responsible for financial and accounting matters as of a date at or near the effective date of the registration statement and determine that the updated letter addresses whether any information has come to management's attention that would cause them to believe any previous representations should be modified or any events have occurred after the date of the most recent financial statements that would require adjustment to or disclosure in the financial statements.

4. If the auditor has audited the most recent period for which separate audited financial statements of the entity are included in the registration statement and (1) the entity has been acquired by another entity, (2) the acquirer's audited financial statements included in the registration statement reflect a period that includes the date of acquisition, and (3) the auditor is a predecessor auditor because the auditor is not the continuing auditor of the entity, then the auditor may not be able to perform the procedures in requirement 3 (above). Alternatively, the auditor should obtain, through a date at or near the registration statement's effective date:

   a. A representation letter from management of the former client stating whether any information has come to management's attention that would cause them to believe any previous representations should be modified or any events have occurred after the date of the most recent prior-period financial statements reported on by the predecessor auditor that would require adjustment to or disclosure in the financial statements, and

   b. A letter from the successor auditor stating whether his or her audit revealed any matters that might, in the successor auditor's opinion, have a material effect on or require disclosure in the financial statements reported on by the predecessor auditor.

5. If a predecessor auditor audited the entity's separate financial statements for a prior-period included in the registration statement but not for the most

recent period for which the entity's audited financial statements are included in the registration statement, he or she should read the financial statements of the subsequent period to be presented on a comparative basis, compare the prior-period financial statements the predecessor auditor reported on with the subsequent period's financial statements to be presented on a comparative basis, and perform the procedures listed in requirement 4a and 4b (above) through a date at or near the registration statement's effective date.

6. If the auditor becomes aware of subsequently discovered facts, the auditor should not consent to the inclusion of his or her report in the registration statement until all of the procedures specified by AU-C 560 (*Subsequent Events and Subsequently Discovered Facts*) have been performed. If the auditor believes the audited financial statements need to be revised and management does not revise the statements, he or she should determine whether to withhold the auditor's consent.

## *Unaudited Financial Statements or Unaudited Interim Financial Information*

7. If the auditor concludes that unaudited interim financial information or unaudited annual financial statements included in a registration statement filed under the Securities Act of 1933 are not in conformity with the requirements of the applicable financial reporting framework, he or she should request that management revise the information or statements appropriately.

8. If management does not revise the unaudited annual financial statements or unaudited interim financial information appropriately and (1) the auditor has reported on a review of the unaudited annual financial statements or unaudited interim financial information, (2) the auditor's review report is included in the registration statement, and (3) the subsequently discovered facts would have affected the report had they been known to the auditor at the date of the report, then the auditor should follow the guidance in AU-C 560 (*Subsequent Events and Subsequently Discovered Facts*).

9. If management does not revise the unaudited annual financial statements or unaudited interim financial information appropriately and (1) the auditor has not reported on a review of the unaudited annual financial statements or unaudited interim financial information or (2) the auditor's review report is not included in the registration statement, then the auditor should follow the guidance in AU-C 930 to modify the report on the audited financial statements to describe the departure from the requirements of the applicable financial reporting framework contained in the unaudited annual financial statements or unaudited interim financial information.

10. Determine whether to withhold the auditor's consent and, if applicable, the awareness letter.

**PUBLIC COMPANY IMPLICATION:** Certain securities are exempt from registration under the Securities Act of 1933. These securities remain subject to the antifraud provisions of the Act, which prohibit any person from misrepresenting or omitting material facts in an offering or sales of securities. Because the SEC cannot directly regulate such offerings, there is no requirement for auditor involvement with an exempt offering. The AICPA has historically provided guidance in its Audit and Accounting Guides for *State and Local Governments* and *Health Care Entities* regarding an auditor's responsibilities when the auditor's report was included in a municipal security offering document. In 2016, the AICPA Auditing Standards Board (ASB) issued an exposure draft of a proposed new auditing standard that would include performance requirements when the auditor is involved with an exempt offering. The ASB is currently evaluating comments received on the exposure draft of the proposed standard.

## Analysis and Application of Procedures

### Audited Financial Statements

The auditor is responsible for performing a reasonable investigation as described in Section 11(c) of the Securities Act of 1933, and reading the entire prospectus including any documents such as Forms 10-K, 10-Q, and 8-K that are incorporated by reference in the document helps to fulfill this responsibility.

> **PLANNING AID REMINDER:** The auditor may not need to perform the procedures described in AU-C 925 if the filing of a prospectus supplement does not create a new effective date for the auditor even if the filing creates a new effective date for other parties (e.g., the issuing entity).

If the auditor has audited the most recent period for which separate audited financial statements of the entity are included in the registration statement, then in addition to the procedures required, the auditor may consider whether it is appropriate or necessary to inquire of the entity's legal counsel concerning litigation, claims, and assessments.

> **OBSERVATION:** When making the determination as to whether to withhold the auditor's consent, the auditor may consider the need to obtain legal advice.

An entity is only required by the SEC to include an auditor's review report on unaudited interim financial information in the registration statement if the statement states that the unaudited interim financial information has been reviewed by an independent auditor. If an auditor's review report on unaudited interim financial information is included in the registration statement, the auditor should determine that the issuer discloses the fact that an interim review report is not a report on or a part of a registration statement prepared or certified by the auditor within the meaning of Sections 7 and 11 of the Securities Act of 1933 and that the auditor's liability under Section 11 does not extend to the auditor's review report.

### Securities Act of 1933

AU-C 925 states that generally an accountant's responsibility for filings under federal securities statutes is no different from the accountant's responsibility in any other reporting engagement. However, Section 11(a) of the Securities Act of 1933 imposes civil liability on an auditor who has consented to the use of the auditor's report on audited financial statements as part of a registration statement filed under the Securities Act of 1933. Management's disclosure stating that audited financial statements are included in the registration statement in reliance on the auditor's report on the audited financial statements is typically included in the "Experts" section of the registration statement. This disclosure cannot imply that the auditor prepared the financial statements or that the financial statements are not the direct representations of management. An example of this disclosure is provided in Exhibit AU-C 925-1. Section 7 of the Securities Act of 1933 requires an issuer to provide the consent of the auditor whose report on audited financial statements is included in a Securities Act of 1933 registration statement.

An accountant's report on a review of interim financial information is not a report under Section 11. Therefore the auditor does not have the same statutory responsibility for such a report as of the effective date of the registration statement. Management's disclosure that the registration statement includes the auditor's review report on unaudited interim financial information is not included in the "Experts" section of the registration statement. The disclosure may be included in the same section as disclosures on the auditor's report on the audited financial statements under a section titled "Independent Auditors" or something similar or may be included in a separate section. An example of this disclosure is provided in Exhibit AU-C 925-2. The issuer is required to file an awareness letter from an auditor if the auditor's review report on interim financial statements is included in a Securities Act of 1933 registration statement.

Shelf registration occurs when issuers register securities under the Securities Act of 1933 to be offered and sold on a delayed or continuous basis. A base prospectus is included in a shelf registration statement at the time it becomes effective, which generally relies entirely on documents incorporated by reference to make issuer-related disclosures. The base prospectus generally omits information relating to the specific amount of each security to be offered and pricing information, providing that information in a prospectus supplement filed at the time the securities are sold. Information that the issuer does not include in the base prospectus and information provided at a later date may be conveyed to investors by a posteffective amendment to the registration statement, by a prospectus supplement filed pursuant to the Securities Act of 1933 Rule 424(b), or through the incorporation by reference of the information from a report filed under the Securities Exchange Act of 1934 such as Forms 10-K or 8-K.

The effective date for the auditor in connection with a Securities Act of 1933 registration statement is the latest of the below dates:

- The date the original registration statement becomes effective,
- The effective date of any posteffective amendment,
- The filing date of a prospectus supplement if the supplement's filing creates a new effective date for the auditor because it has information the auditor is an expert about requiring a new auditor's consent, or
- The filing date of any report that includes or amends audited financial statements and is incorporated by reference into the already effective registration statement.

The term "expert" is specifically defined in the Securities Act of 1933, so when an issuer refers to the auditor's role in an offering document in connection with a securities offering that is not registered under the Securities Act of 1933, the disclosure is generally in a section labeled "Independent Auditors" rather than "Experts" and there is no reference to the auditor as an expert in the document. This disclosure may be worded as follows:

### INDEPENDENT AUDITORS

The financial statements of Company ABC as of December 31, 20X5 and for the year then ended, included in this offering circular, have been audited by XYZ & Co., independent auditors, as stated in their report appearing herein.

---

**OBSERVATION:** The auditor may agree to be referred to as an expert other than in a Securities Act of 1933 registration statement in situations where the term "expert" is sufficiently defined. For example, the auditor may agree to be named as an expert in an offering document in an intrastate securities offering if applicable state law sufficiently defines the term.

---

If an auditor's report is used in an offering transaction not registered under the Securities Act of 1933, the auditor does not typically have to provide written consent. However, if the auditor does provide written consent, he or she may provide a letter indicating his or her agreement to the inclusion of the auditor's report on the audited financial statements in the offering materials. This letter would typically not be included in the offering materials and may be worded as follows:

> We agree to the inclusion in the offering circular of our report, dated February 5, 20X6, on our audit of the financial statements of Company ABC.

## Practitioner's Aids

Exhibits AU-C 925-1 and AU-C 925-2, reproduced from AU-C 925, illustrate acceptable wording to be included in a registration statement filed under the Securities Act of 1933.

*EXHIBIT AU-C 925-1—DISCLOSURE IN "EXPERTS" SECTION OF A REGISTRATION STATEMENT FILED UNDER THE SECURITIES ACT OF 1933*

---

### EXPERTS

The consolidated balance sheets of ABC Company as of December 31, 20X5, and 20X4, and the related consolidated statements of income and comprehensive income, changes in stockholders' equity, and of cash flows for each of the three years in the period ended December 31, 20X5, included in this prospectus, have been so included in reliance on the report of XYZ & Co., independent auditors, given on the authority of that firm as experts in auditing and accounting.

## EXHIBIT AU-C 925-2—DISCLOSURE THAT INCLUDES THE AUDITOR'S REVIEW REPORT ON UNAUDITED INTERIM FINANCIAL INFORMATION

[*Note: This disclosure may appear in a section labeled as "Experts" or "Independent Auditors."*]

With respect to the unaudited interim financial information of Company ABC for the three-month periods ended March 31, 20X6, and 20X5, included in this prospectus, XYZ & Co. has reported that they have applied limited procedures in accordance with professional standards for a review of such information. However, their separate report dated May 10, 20X6, included herein, states that they did not audit and they do not express an opinion on that interim financial information. Accordingly, the degree of reliance on their report on such information should be restricted in light of the limited nature of the review procedures applied. XYZ & Co. is not subject to the liability provisions of Section 11 of the Securities Act of 1933 for their report on the unaudited interim financial information because that report is not a "report" or a "part" of the registration statement prepared or certified by the accountants within the meaning of Sections 7 and 11 of the Act.

# SECTION 930

## INTERIM FINANCIAL INFORMATION

### Authoritative Pronouncements

SAS-122—Statements on Auditing Standards: Clarification and Recodification

SAS-135—Omnibus Statement on Auditing Standards—2019

SAS-140—Amendments to AU-C Sections 725, 730, 930, 935, and 940 to Incorporate Auditor Reporting Changes from SAS Nos. 134 and 137

SAS-141—Amendment to Effective Dates of SAS Nos. 134-140

### Overview

AU-C 930 provides the auditor of an entity's financial statements guidance when he or she is engaged to review interim financial information of that client. AU-C 930 applies when the auditor is engaged by a nonissuer to review interim financial information if:

- The entity's latest financial statements have been audited by the auditor or a predecessor;

- The auditor has been engaged to audit the current-year financial statements; or, the auditor has audited the entity's latest annual financial statements, the entity's current-year financial statements are expected to be audited, and a new auditor has not been hired as of the beginning of the period being reviewed; and

- The entity prepares its interim financial information in accordance with the same financial reporting framework as that used to prepare the annual financial statements.

AU-C 930 also applies to reviews of condensed interim financial information if all of the following conditions are met:

- The condensed interim financial information purports to conform to an appropriate financial reporting framework, which includes appropriate form and content of interim financial information;

- The condensed interim financial information includes a note that the financial information does not represent complete financial statements and should be read in conjunction with the entity's latest annual audited financial statements; and

- The condensed financial information accompanies the entity's latest audited annual financial statements or such audited annual financial statements are made readily available by the entity, such that a third-party user can obtain the financial statements without any further action by the entity.

**PLANNING AID REMINDER:** AU-C 930 is applicable to interim financial information that is to be reviewed. Interim financial statements may be audited, in which case the auditor follows generally accepted auditing standards. The special accounting practices and modifications established by appropriate financial reporting frameworks such as FASB Accounting Standards Codification (ASC) Topic 270 (*Interim Reporting*) and Article 10 of Securities and Exchange Commission (SEC) Regulation S-X, with respect to accounting principles generally accepted in the United States of America, or International Accounting Standard 34 (*Interim Financial Reporting*) with respect to International Financial Reporting Standards issued by the International Accounting Standards Board, should be followed in the preparation of the interim financial statements.

---

**IMPORTANT NOTICE FOR 2022:** In April 2020, the AICPA's Auditing Standards Board (ASB) issued SAS No. 140, *Amendments to AU-C Sections 725, 730, 930, 935, and 940 to Incorporate Auditor Reporting Changes from SAS Nos. 134 and 137*. SAS No. 140 amends the reporting illustrations in AU-C 930. Originally, the effective date of SAS No. 140 was for audits of financial statements for periods ending on or after December 15, 2020. However, the ASB's issuance of SAS No. 141, *Amendment to the Effective Dates of SAS Nos. 134-140*, extended the effective date to December 15, 2021, in order to provide more time for firms to implement SAS No. 140 in light of the effect of the coronavirus pandemic. The ASB recommends that SAS Nos. 134-140 be implemented concurrently.

---

**OBSERVATION:** The auditor may find the guidance in AU-C 930 useful when he or she is not specifically engaged to perform a review of interim financial information but decides it is appropriate to perform such procedures in connection with the inclusion of the auditor's report on the annual financial statements in an unregistered securities offering document.

---

**PUBLIC COMPANY IMPLICATION:** PCAOB AS-1220 (*Engagement Quality Review*) applies to all firms registered with the PCAOB. In addition to applying to audits performed under PCAOB standards, the standard also applies to reviews. However, the procedures required to be performed by the engagement quality reviewer for a review of interim financial information are more limited. For all such engagements, an engagement review is required to be conducted before the report is issued. The engagement reviewer is required to be a partner of the firm performing the engagement, another person in an equivalent position in the firm, or an individual outside the firm who is associated with a registered public accounting firm. The engagement reviewer is required to have competence, independence, integrity, and objectivity. He or she is required to have the level of competence needed to have an overall responsibility for a comparable engagement. To maintain objectivity, the engagement reviewer is not permitted to make decisions for the engagement team, supervise the team, or assume responsibilities of the team. Review procedures generally involve discussions with engagement personnel and review of documents. Review procedures must be performed with due professional care and professional skepticism. Required engagement quality review procedures are more limited when the service being reviewed is an interim review. In addition, the engagement quality reviewer is required to review documentation in the areas that he or she reviewed. The firm is not permitted to issue its report (or communicate its conclusion to the client if no report is to be issued) until the engagement quality reviewer grants his or her concurring approval.

## Responsibility and Function of the Auditor

The purpose of an audit is to determine whether the financial statements are presented fairly in accordance with generally accepted accounting principles. A review of interim financial information differs significantly from an audit of financial information because a review does not include the collection of corroborative evidence through the performance of typical substantive audit tests. The review of interim financial information primarily consists of performing certain inquiries and analytical procedures. For these reasons, a review provides limited assurance (i.e., negative assurance) as to whether the interim financial information is fairly presented in accordance with an applicable financial reporting framework.

AU-C 930 states that the purpose of a review is to provide the auditor with a basis for reporting whether material modifications are necessary for the interim financial information to be in conformity with the applicable financial reporting framework. The auditor acquires the basis for reporting by applying the standards for a review of interim financial information in accordance with AU 930. The auditor issues a report containing an expression of limited assurance that, on the basis of the review, he or she is not aware of any material modification that should be made to the interim financial information for it to be in conformity with the applicable financial reporting framework.

## Definition

| | |
|---|---|
| Interim financial information | Financial information prepared and presented in accordance with an applicable financial reporting framework that contains either a complete or condensed set of financial statements covering a period or periods less than one full year or a 12-month period ending on a date other than the entity's fiscal year-end. |

## Requirements

The auditor is presumptively required to perform the following procedures when reporting on interim financial information.

### Acceptance

1. Follow the procedures for initial engagements required by paragraphs 11-12 of AU-C 210 (*Terms of Engagement*) before accepting an engagement to perform an initial review of an entity's interim financial information.

2. Before accepting an engagement to review interim financial information:

a. Determine whether the financial reporting framework to be applied in preparing the interim financial information is acceptable.

b. Obtain management's agreement that it acknowledges and understands its responsibilities for (1) preparing interim financial information in accordance with the applicable financial reporting framework; (2) designing, implementing, and maintaining sufficient internal control to provide a reasonable basis for the preparation of that information; (3) providing the auditor with access to all information relevant to preparing the interim financial information that management is aware of, additional information the auditor requests from management for purposes of the review, and unrestricted access to entity personnel for the auditor to make necessary inquiries; and (4) including the auditor's review report in any document containing interim financial information that indicates such information has been reviewed by the entity's auditor.

3. Do not accept the proposed engagement if the financial reporting framework to be applied in preparing the interim financial information is unacceptable or the agreement with management regarding its responsibilities as described in requirement 2b (above) has not been obtained.

4. Agree on engagement terms with management or those charged with governance and record the agreed-upon terms in an engagement letter or other suitable written agreement that includes the engagement objectives and scope, management's responsibilities as described in requirement 2b (above), the auditor's responsibilities, the limitations of a review engagement, and identification of the applicable financial reporting framework for preparing the interim financial information.

## *Interim Financial Information Review Procedures*

5. The auditor should have a sufficient understanding of the entity and its environment including its internal control as it relates to preparing annual and interim financial information to be able to identify the types of potential material misstatements in the interim financial information and consider the likelihood of their occurrence and to select the inquiries and analytical procedures that will provide a basis for reporting on whether the auditor is aware of any material modifications that should be made to the interim financial information for it to be in accordance with the applicable financial reporting framework. In order to obtain or update this understanding, the auditor should perform the following procedures:

a. Read documentation of the preceding year's audit and of reviews of prior interim periods of the current year and corresponding interim periods of the prior year to the extent necessary to enable identification of matters that may affect the current-period interim financial information, considering the nature of any corrected material misstatements, matters identified in any summary of uncorrected misstatements, identified risks of material misstatement due to fraud including the risk of management override of controls, and significant financial accounting and reporting matters that may be of continuing significance such as significant deficiencies and material weaknesses.

b. Read the most recent annual and comparable prior interim period financial information.

c. Consider the results of any audit procedures performed related to the current year's financial statements.

d. Inquire of management about changes in the entity's business activities.

e. Inquire of management about the identity of all related parties and the nature of any transactions with those parties.

f. Inquire of management about whether significant changes in internal control have occurred after the preceding annual audit or prior review of interim financial information related to preparing interim financial information, including changes in the entity's policies, procedures, and personnel and the nature and extent of any changes.

6. Apply the following analytical procedures to the interim financial information to identify and provide a basis for inquiry about the relationships and individual items that appear to be unusual and may indicate a material misstatement.

- a. Compare the interim financial information with comparable information for the immediately preceding interim period, if applicable, and with the corresponding periods in the previous year, considering knowledge about changes in the entity's business and specific transactions.
- b. Consider plausible relationships among financial and relevant nonfinancial information.
- c. Compare recorded amounts or ratios developed from recorded amounts to the expectations developed by identifying and using relationships that are reasonably expected to exist based on the auditor's understanding of the entity and its industry.
- d. Compare disaggregated revenue data.

7. Make the following inquiries and perform the following additional review procedures when reviewing interim financial information:

- a. Read available minutes of meetings of stockholders, directors, and appropriate committees and inquire about matters dealt with at meetings without minutes available to identify matters that may affect the interim financial information.
- b. Obtain reports from any component auditors related to reviews performed on interim financial information of significant components of the reporting entity including its investees or inquire of those auditors if reports have not been issued.
- c. Inquire of management about:
    - i. Whether the interim financial information has been prepared and fairly presented in accordance with the applicable financial reporting framework consistently applied.
    - ii. Unusual or complex situations that may have an effect on the interim financial information.
    - iii. Significant transactions occurring or recognized in the interim period, particularly in the last several days of the interim period.
    - iv. The status of uncorrected misstatements identified during the previous audit and interim review.
    - v. Matters that applying review procedures have raised questions about.
    - vi. Events subsequent to the date of the interim financial information that could have a material effect on the information's presentation.

vii. Management's knowledge of any fraud or suspected fraud affecting the entity involving management, employees with significant internal control roles, or others when the fraud could have a material effect on the financial information.

viii. Whether management is aware of allegations of fraud or suspected fraud affecting the entity.

ix. Significant journal entries and other adjustments.

x. Communications from regulatory agencies.

xi. Significant deficiencies and material weaknesses in the design or operation of internal control as it relates to preparing the annual and interim financial information.

xii. Changes in related parties or significant new related-party transactions.

d. Obtain evidence that the interim financial information agrees or reconciles with the accounting records and inquire of management about the reliability of those records.

e. Read the interim financial information to consider whether, based on the results of the review procedures and other information the auditor is aware of, the information to be reported is in accordance with the applicable financial reporting framework.

f. Read other information in documents containing the interim financial information to consider whether that information or its presentation is materially inconsistent with the interim financial information. If there is a material inconsistency or the auditor becomes aware of information he or she believes to be a material misstatement of fact, use professional judgment to take action.

8. If there is information causing the auditor to question whether the interim financial information is prepared in all material respects in accordance with the applicable financial reporting framework with respect to litigation, claims, and assessments, and the auditor believes the entity's internal or external legal counsel may have information concerning that question, he or she should send an inquiry letter to that legal counsel concerning litigation, claims, and assessments.

9. If (*a*) conditions or events existed at the date of the prior-period financial statements that may indicate substantial doubt about an entity's ability to continue as a going concern, regardless of whether that doubt was alleviated by the auditor's consideration of management's plans, or (*b*) the auditor becomes aware of conditions or events that may indicate the entity's inability to continue as a going concern when performing review procedures on the current-period interim financial information, then inquire of management about its plans for dealing with the adverse effects of the conditions and events and consider the adequacy of the disclosure about such matters in the interim financial information.

**OBSERVATION:** Interpretation 4 of AU 570 (January 2015) states that if the applicable financial reporting framework (e.g., FASB standards under ASU 2014-15) contains disclosure requirements based on management's assessment of the entity's going concern status, the auditor's assessment of the financial statement effects is to be based on the disclosure requirements in the applicable financial reporting framework.

10. Consider the reasonableness and consistency of management's responses given the results of other review procedures and knowledge about the entity's business and internal control.

11. When a matter comes to the auditor's attention causing him or her to question whether the interim financial information has been prepared in accordance with the applicable financial reporting framework in all material respects, he or she should make additional inquiries or perform other procedures to provide a basis for communicating whether the auditor is aware of any material modifications that should be made to the interim financial information.

## Evaluating Interim Review Procedures' Results

12. Accumulate misstatements including inadequate disclosure that are identified in performing review procedures and evaluate these misstatements to determine whether material modification should be made to the interim financial information for it to be in accordance with the applicable financial reporting framework.

## Management's Written Representations

13. Request that management provide written representations for all interim financial information presented and for all periods covered by the review:
    a. That it has fulfilled its responsibility for preparing and fairly presenting the interim financial information in accordance with the applicable financial reporting framework as set out in the engagement terms.
    b. That it acknowledges its responsibility for designing, implementing, and maintaining internal control relevant to the preparation and fair presentation of interim financial statements, including its responsibility to prevent and detect fraud.
    c. That it has disclosed all significant deficiencies and material weaknesses it is aware of in the design or operation of internal control as it relates to preparing the annual and interim financial information.
    d. That is has provided the auditor with all relevant information and access as agreed upon in the engagement terms.
    e. That all transactions have been recorded and are reflected in the interim financial information.
    f. That it has disclosed to the auditor the results of its assessment of the risk that the interim financial information may be materially misstated due to fraud.
    g. That it has disclosed to the auditor its knowledge of fraud or suspected fraud affecting the entity involving management, employees who have significant roles in internal control, or others when the fraud could have a material effect on the interim financial information.
    h. That it has disclosed to the auditor its knowledge of any allegations of fraud or suspected fraud affecting the entity's interim financial information communicated by employees, former employees, regulators, or others.
    i. That it has disclosed to the auditor all known instances of noncompliance or suspected noncompliance with laws and regulations whose effects should be considered when preparing interim financial information.

j. About whether it believes the effects of uncorrected misstatements are immaterial, individually and in the aggregate, to the interim financial information as a whole. A summary of such items should be included in or attached to the written representation.

k. That it has disclosed to the auditor and appropriately accounted for and disclosed in accordance with the applicable financial reporting framework all known actual or possible litigation and claims whose effects should be considered when preparing the interim financial information.

l. About whether it believes significant assumptions it used in making accounting estimates are reasonable.

m. That it has disclosed to the auditor the identity of the entity's related parties and all the related-party relationships and transactions it is aware of and it has appropriately accounted for and disclosed such relationships and transactions.

n. That all events occurring subsequent to the date of the interim financial information have been adjusted or disclosed as required by the applicable financial reporting framework.

14. If the auditor has concerns about the reliability of the representations or if management does not provide the requested representations, the auditor should take appropriate action. If management does not provide the written representations described in requirement 13(a)–(e), the auditor should withdraw from the engagement to review the interim financial information.

## Communications with Management and Those Charged with Governance

15. If the auditor cannot complete the review, he or she should communicate to the appropriate level of management and those charged with governance (a) the reason why the review cannot be completed, (b) that an incomplete review does not provide a basis for issuing a review report so the auditor is precluded from issuing such a report, and (c) any material modifications the auditor is aware of that should be made to the interim financial information for it to be in accordance with the applicable financial reporting framework in accordance with requirements 16-18 (below).

16. Communicate to the appropriate level of management as soon as practicable matters that cause the auditor to believe that (a) material modification should be made to the interim financial information for it to be in accordance with the applicable financial reporting framework or (b) the entity issued interim financial information before completion of a required review.

17. If management does not respond appropriately to the auditor's communication within a reasonable time period, inform those charged with governance of the matters as soon as practicable.

18. If those charged with governance do not respond appropriately to the auditor's communication within a reasonable time period, consider whether to withdraw from the engagement to review the interim financial information and as the entity's auditor.

19. If the auditor becomes aware of fraud, communicate the matter as soon as practicable to the appropriate level of management. If the fraud involves senior management or results in a material misstatement of the interim financial information, communicate the matter directly to those charged with governance. If the auditor becomes aware of matters involving identified or suspected noncompliance with laws and regulations, communicate all matters that are not clearly inconsequential to those charged with governance.

20. Communicate relevant matters of governance interest arising from the interim financial information review to those charged with governance, including (a) significant deficiencies or material weaknesses in internal control as it relates to preparing annual and interim financial information, and (b) any of the matters described in AU-C 260 that have been identified that relate to the interim financial information.

## *Auditor's Review Report on Interim Financial Information*

21. Issue a written report on a review of interim financial information.

22. Include the following information in the written report:

   a. A title that clearly indicates that it is the report of the independent auditor;

   b. An appropriate addressee;

   c. The first section includes the auditor's conclusion and the heading "Results of Review of Interim Financial Information" and the following elements:

   - Name of the entity whose interim financial information has been reviewed;
   - Statement that the interim financial information identified in the report was reviewed;
   - Title of each statement that the interim financial information comprises and reference to the notes;
   - The dates of periods covered by each financial statement comprising the interim financial information; and
   - Statement about whether the auditor is aware of any material modifications that should be made to the accompanying interim financial information for it to be in accordance with the applicable financial reporting framework and that identifies the country of origin of those accounting principles, if applicable.

   d. A section directly following the "Results of Interim Financial Information" section that includes the heading "Basis for the Review Results" and includes the following:

   - Statement that the review was conducted in accordance with generally accepted auditing standards applicable to review of interim financial information and identified the United States as the country of origin of those standards;
   - Statement that a review of interim financial information consists of principally applying analytical procedures and making inquiries of persons responsible for financial and accounting matters;
   - Statement that a review of interim financial information is substantially less in scope than an audit conducted in accordance with GAAS, and accordingly the auditor does not express such an opinion;
   - Statement that the auditor is required to be independent of the entity and to meet other ethical responsibilities; and
   - Statement whether the auditor believes the results of the review procedures provide a reasonable basis for the auditor's conclusion.

e. A section titled "Responsibilities of Management for the Interim Financial Information" explaining that the preparation and fair presentation of the interim financial information is management's responsibility, including the responsibility to design, implement, and maintain internal control sufficient to provide a reasonable basis for the preparation and fair presentation of interim financial information in accordance with the applicable financial reporting framework;

f. The manual or printed signature of the auditor's firm;

g. The city and state where the auditor's report is issued; and

h. The date of the review report, which should be dated no earlier than the date on which the auditor completed procedures sufficient to obtain a basis for reporting whether the auditor is aware of any material modifications that should be made to the interim financial information in order for it to be in accordance with the applicable financial reporting framework, including evidence that (1) all the statements and disclosures that the interim financial information comprises have been prepared and (2) management has asserted that it has taken responsibility for the interim financial information.

23. Determine that management has clearly marked each page of the interim financial information as unaudited.

24. If the auditor is engaged to review the most recent interim period and that financial information will be presented comparatively with prior interim period information that has not been reviewed, the financial information should be accompanied by the auditor's review report stating that the auditor has not reviewed the prior-period interim financial information and that he or she is not responsible for that information.

25. If a condensed balance sheet derived from audited financial statements is presented on a comparative basis with the interim financial information, the auditor should only report on the condensed balance sheet if he or she audited the financial statements the condensed balance sheet was derived from. Make sure that the condensed balance sheet agrees with or can be recalculated from the audited financial statements.

Include a paragraph in the auditor's report on the interim financial information that: identifies the condensed balance sheet on which the auditor is reporting and the audited financial statements the condensed balance sheet was derived from, indicating that the financial statements are not separately presented; refers to the auditor's report on the audited financial statements, including the report date, type or opinion expressed, and the basis for any modified opinion; describes the nature of any emphasis-of-matter paragraph or other-matter paragraph included in the auditor's report; and includes an opinion about whether the condensed balance sheet is consistent in all material respects with the audited financial statements from which it was derived.

26. When interim financial information has not been prepared in accordance with the applicable financial reporting framework in all material respects, consider whether modification of the auditor's review report on the interim financial information is sufficient to disclose the departure.

a. If modification of the standard review report is sufficient to disclose the departure, modify the review report, describing the nature of the departure and the effects on the interim financial information, if practicable. If the departure is due to inadequate disclosure, if practicable, include the information in the review report that the auditor believes is necessary for adequate disclosure in accordance with the applicable financial reporting framework.

b. If modification of the review report is not sufficient to indicate the deficiencies in the financial information as a whole, withdraw from the review engagement and provide no further services regarding that interim financial information.

## Other Considerations

27. If, subsequent to the date of the auditor's review report, the auditor becomes aware that facts existed at the date of the report that might have affected the report had the auditor been aware of those matters, consider the guidance in AU-C 560 (*Subsequent Events and Subsequently Discovered Facts*).

28. If management does not include the auditor's review report in a report, document, or written communication containing the reviewed interim financial information that indicates such information has been reviewed by the entity's auditor, despite having agreed to do so in the terms of the engagement, perform the following procedures:

   a. Request that management amend the report, document, or written communication to include the auditor's review report and reissue the report, document, or written communication;
   
   b. If management does not comply with the request, request that the auditor's name not be associated with the interim financial information or referred to in the report, document, or written communication;
   
   c. If management does not comply with the request, advise management that the auditor will not permit use of the auditor's name or reference to the auditor;
   
   d. Communicate management's noncompliance with the request to those charged with governance;
   
   e. Recommend that the entity consult with its legal counsel about the application of relevant laws and regulations when appropriate; and
   
   f. Consider what other actions might be appropriate.

29. If the auditor issued a modified review report and management issues the interim financial information without including the review report in the document containing the interim financial information, determine the appropriate course of action in the circumstances including whether to withdraw from the engagement to audit the annual financial statements.

30. Include an other-matter paragraph in the auditor's report on the audited financial statements when interim financial information reviewed in accordance with AU-C 930 is included in a document containing audited financial statements, that interim financial information does not appear to be presented in accordance with the applicable financial reporting framework, and the auditor's separate review report referring to that departure is not presented with the information.

31. Disclaim an opinion on the interim financial information in the auditor's report on the audited financial statements when the interim financial information included in a note to the financial statements, including information that has been reviewed in accordance with AU-C 930, is not appropriately marked as unaudited.

## Documentation

32. Prepare documentation in connection with an interim financial information review that will enable an experienced auditor to understand:

   a. The nature, timing, and extent of the review procedures performed;

b. The results of the review procedures and the evidence that was obtained; and

c. Significant findings or issues that arose during the review, the conclusions reached regarding these issues, and significant professional judgments made in reaching those conclusions.

33. Documentation should the written or oral communications required by AU-C 930.

## Analysis and Application of Procedures

*Acceptance*

The written communication documenting the agreed-upon terms of the engagement may encompass the following points:

- The objective of a review of interim financial information is to provide the auditor with a basis for communicating whether he or she is aware of any material modifications that should be made to the interim financial information for it to conform to the applicable financial reporting framework.
- A review includes obtaining sufficient knowledge of the entity's business and its internal control as it relates to the preparation of both annual and interim financial information to:
  — Identify the types of potential misstatements in the interim financial information and consider the likelihood of their occurrence, and
  — Select the inquiries and analytical procedures that will provide the auditor with a basis for communicating whether he or she is aware of any material modifications that should be made to the interim financial information for it to conform to the applicable financial reporting framework.
- Management is responsible for preparing the entity's interim financial information in accordance with the applicable financial reporting framework.
- Management is responsible for designing, implementing, and maintaining internal control over financial reporting (ICFR) sufficient to provide a reasonable basis for preparing and fairly presenting interim financial information in accordance with the applicable financial reporting framework.
- Management is responsible for identifying and ensuring that the entity complies with the laws and regulations applicable to its activities.
- Management is responsible for providing the auditor with access to all information relevant to preparing and fairly presenting the interim financial information that management is aware of, additional information the auditor requests from management for purposes of the review, and unrestricted access to entity personnel for the auditor to make necessary inquiries.

- Management is responsible for including the auditor's review report in any document containing interim financial information that indicates such information has been reviewed by the entity's auditor.

- At the conclusion of the engagement, management will provide the auditor with a letter confirming certain representations made during the review.

- Management is responsible for adjusting the interim financial information to correct material misstatements. Although a review of interim financial information is not designed to obtain reasonable assurance that the interim financial information is free from material misstatement, management also is responsible for affirming in its representation letter to the auditor that the effects of any uncorrected misstatements aggregated by the auditor during the current engagement and pertaining to the current period(s) under review are immaterial, both individually and in the aggregate, to the financial information taken as a whole.

- The auditor is responsible for conducting the review in accordance with auditing standards generally accepted in the United States of America. A review of interim financial information consists principally of performing analytical procedures and making inquiries of persons responsible for financial and accounting matters. It is substantially less in scope than an audit conducted in accordance with generally accepted auditing standards, the objective of which is the expression of an opinion regarding the financial statements taken as a whole. Accordingly, the auditor will not express an opinion on the interim financial information.

- Limitations of a review engagement, including acknowledgment that a review does not provide a basis for expressing an opinion on the interim financial information.

- A review does not provide assurance that the auditor will become aware of all significant matters that would be identified in an audit.

- A review is not designed to provide assurance on internal control or to identify control deficiencies. However, the auditor is responsible for communicating to management and those charged with governance any significant deficiencies or material weaknesses in ICFR that come to his or her attention.

---

**PLANNING AID REMINDER:** AU-C 265 (*Communicating Internal Control Related Matters Identified in an Audit*) requires the auditor of financial statements to communicate in writing to management and those charged with governance significant deficiencies and material weaknesses that were identified. Although an audit of financial statements is not designed to perform procedures to detect control deficiencies, AU-C 265 requires the communications when the auditor identifies significant deficiencies and material weaknesses in ICFR. The ASB adopted the PCAOB definitions of "control deficiency," "significant deficiency," and "material weakness."

**PUBLIC COMPANY REMINDER:** Although a review is not designed to provide assurance on internal control, the auditor's involvement in evaluating internal control on an interim basis is likely to increase because of SEC and PCAOB requirements. First, management must disclose to the auditor (1) all changes during the quarter in ICFR that materially affected, or are likely to materially affect, the entity's internal control, (2) all significant deficiencies and material weaknesses in the design and operation of internal control on a quarterly basis, and (3) any fraud, regardless of materiality, involving management or any other person who plays an important role in the entity's ICFR. Second, because the auditor must issue his or her own opinion on the effectiveness of the entity's ICFR as part of its annual audit report, it seems likely that internal control testing will occur throughout the year.

## Interim Financial Information Review Procedures

*Acquire knowledge of the entity's business and internal control*

In order to successfully execute a review of interim financial information, the auditor must have both an understanding of the client's business and its internal control used to prepare annual as well as interim financial information. This background (1) helps identify financial information that has the greatest potential for misstatement and (2) provides focus in determining which analytical procedures and inquiries should be made. The review is not able to be successfully executed if the entity has significant internal control deficiencies such that the auditor is not able to perform review procedures to obtain a basis for communicating whether the auditor is aware of any material modifications that should be made to the interim financial information for it to be in accordance with the applicable financial reporting framework.

If the auditor has not previously reviewed a client's interim financial information, he or she must nonetheless obtain an adequate understanding of the client's business and its internal control. Specifically, under this circumstance, the auditor may consider obtaining permission from the predecessor auditor to review his or her audit documentation for interim reviews made during the previous year.

**OBSERVATION:** The auditor is responsible for all inquiries made, analytical procedures and other procedures performed, and conclusions reached in an initial interim financial information review.

When the predecessor accountant does not respond to the auditor's inquiries or allow access to audit documentation for previous engagements, the auditor may inquire as to why and can use alternative procedures in order to obtain an adequate understanding of the client's business and internal control.

*Perform analytical procedures, inquiries, and other review procedures*

The specific analytical procedures and related inquiries employed should be based on the accountant's understanding of the client's business and internal control, the results of risk assessments relating to the previous audit, and the auditor's consideration of materiality as it relates to the interim financial information. For example, if there has been a significant change in the entity's control activities, the auditor may consider making additional inquiries and using analytical procedures with more precise expectations.

> **PLANNING AID REMINDER:** In general, expectations for analytical procedures developed in interim financial information reviews are less precise than those developed in an audit and management's responses are not required to be corroborated with other evidence.

Many of the inquiries and review procedures in an interim financial information review can be performed before or at the same time as the entity's preparation of the interim financial information. Performing some review procedures earlier in the interim period allows the auditor to identify and consider significant matters affecting the interim financial information at an earlier date. Some auditing procedures associated with the annual financial statement audit may also be able to be performed at the same time as the interim financial information review.

Generally, apart from the circumstances described in requirement 8 (above), the auditor is not required to make inquiries of the client's lawyer concerning litigation, claims, and assessments in a review of interim financial information. The auditor is also generally not required to collect evidence that might identify conditions or events that raise substantial doubt about the client's ability to continue as a going concern in an interim financial information review apart from the circumstances described in requirement 9 (above). In a review, the auditor is not required to obtain evidence supporting the information that mitigates these conditions and events. If the auditor concludes that the entity's disclosure about its possible inability to continue as a going concern is inadequate, there is a departure from the applicable financial reporting framework and the review report is required to be modified.

### *Evaluating Interim Review Procedures' Results*

The application of review procedures can identify potential misstatements. The auditor may designate an amount below which misstatements are clearly trivial and do not need to be accumulated because their accumulation would not have a material effect on the interim financial information. The auditor may consider factors such as the following in evaluating whether uncorrected misstatements, individually or in the aggregate, are material:

- The amount and the reason for the misstatement,
- The occurrence date of the misstatement (current period or the previous period),
- The basis for determining whether an item is material,
- The possible effect of the misstatement on future interim or annual periods,

- The appropriateness of offsetting a likely misstatement that is based on an estimate with a misstatement that is subject to measurement that is more precise, and
- The possible material effect on future financial information of current balance sheet misstatements that are considered immaterial.

## Management's Written Representations

AU-C 930 requires the auditor to obtain written representations from management for each interim financial information review engagement. An example of a representation letter for the review of interim financial information is presented in Exhibit AU-C 930-1.

> **ENGAGEMENT STRATEGY:** If no uncorrected misstatements are identified, then the requirement for management representation regarding uncorrected misstatements is not relevant and, therefore, is not required.

In addition to the specific representations required by AU-C 930, the auditor should consider the particular characteristics of the client to determine which additional representations should be made by management. For example, a client that operates in an industry addressed by an AICPA Accounting and Auditing Guide should consider whether other representations should be obtained from management. The auditor may request additional representations related to matters specific to the entity's business or industry or support for any assertion that a transaction was conducted on terms equivalent to those prevailing in an arm's-length transaction or whether any side agreements exist that have not been disclosed to the auditor.

> **IMPORTANT NOTICE FOR 2022:** In May 2019, the AICPA's Auditing Standards Board (ASB) issued SAS No. 135 titled *Omnibus Statement on Auditing Standards—2019* that includes amendments to various AU-C sections, including AU-C 930. SAS No. 135 adds to AU-C 930 a suggestion that the auditor may want to request additional representations about support for any assertion that a transaction with a related party was conducted on terms equivalent to those prevailing in an arm's-length transaction and whether any side agreements or other arrangements (either written or oral) exist that may have not been disclosed to the auditor. Originally, the effective date of SAS No. 135 was for audits of financial statements periods ending on or after December 15, 2020, with early application **not** permitted. However, the ASB's issuance of SAS No. 141, *Amendment to the Effective Dates of SAS Nos. 134-140*, extended the effective date to December 15, 2021, in order to provide more time for firms to implement SAS No. 135 in light of the effect of the coronavirus pandemic. While SAS No. 141 allows for early implementation of SAS No. 135, the ASB recommends that SAS Nos. 134-140 be implemented concurrently.

When management does not provide a requested written representation or when the auditor has concerns about the reliability of the representations, the auditor should discuss the matter with management and those charged with governance when appropriate, reevaluate management's integrity and evaluate any effect this has on the reliability of representations and evidence obtained, and consider whether to withdraw from the interim financial information review engagement and as the entity's auditor if applicable.

*Communications with Management and Those Charged with Governance*

The interim financial information review will be incomplete if the auditor is unable to perform appropriate review procedures or the client does not provide the auditor with the necessary written representations. If the auditor is in the situation where he or she is deciding whether to withdraw from the engagement to review the interim financial information and as the entity's auditor, he or she may consult with legal counsel.

---

**OBSERVATION:** If matters concerning possible illegal acts or fraud arise, the auditor should follow the guidance established by AU-C 250 (*Consideration of Laws and Regulations in an Audit of Financial Statements*) and AU-C 240 (*Consideration of Fraud in a Financial Statement Audit*).

---

**OBSERVATION:** If matters concerning internal control deficiencies over financial reporting come to the accountant's attention, the guidance established in AU-C 265 (*Communicating Internal Control Related Matters Identified in an Audit*) should be considered.

---

When the auditor determines that a matter should be communicated to management or those charged with governance, he or she should make such communications, whether in writing or orally, on a sufficiently timely basis to enable those parties to take appropriate action.

*Auditor's Review Report on Interim Financial Information*

If a third party requires a review of the interim financial information but does not require a written review report, the auditor's review report on the interim financial information must still be in writing. Exhibit AU-C 930-2 is an example of a standard review report.

If the auditor has not reviewed the prior-period interim financial information, presented for comparative purposes, and assumes no responsibility for that information, he or she may indicate that in the report by stating:

> The accompanying [*describe the interim financial information or statements*] of X Company and subsidiaries as of September 30, 20X5, and for the three-month period then ended were not reviewed by us, and accordingly, we do not express any form of assurance on it.

Departures from the applicable financial reporting framework may preclude the issuance of a review report or require modification to the standard review report. These departures include inadequate disclosure and changes in accounting policies that are not in accordance with the applicable financial reporting framework.

Exhibit AU-C 930-3 is an example of a review report on interim financial information that has a departure from the applicable financial reporting framework.

When interim financial statements are presented, the information necessary for adequate disclosure will vary depending on the form and content of the interim financial information. For example, condensed financial statements require less extensive disclosures than annual financial statements that present financial position, results of operations, and cash flows in accordance with the applicable financial reporting framework. Exhibit AU-C 930-4 is an example of a review report on interim financial information that includes an inadequate disclosure.

The interim financial information may adequately disclose the existence of substantial doubt about the entity's ability to continue as a going concern or a lack of consistency in the application of accounting principles affecting the interim financial information. Although the foregoing conditions do not require a modification of the review report, an emphasis-of-matter section can be included in the report. Examples of going concern reports are presented in Exhibits AU-C 930-5 and AU-C 930-6.

### Other Considerations

In instances in which a client represents in a filing with a regulatory authority or communications with stockholders or third parties that the included interim information has been reviewed by an auditor, and management refuses to include the review report in the document, then when the auditor is considering other appropriate actions, he or she may wish to contact legal counsel. Interim financial information may be included as supplementary information or as a note to the client's audited financial statements. Under both circumstances, management is responsible for clearly marking the interim information as unaudited. In these situations, the auditor does not need to modify the auditor's report on the audited financial statements to refer to the accompanying interim financial information even if the auditor has reviewed that information.

### Documentation

AU-C 230 (*Audit Documentation*) provides the auditor with additional guidance on determining the form, content, and timing of engagement documentation.

## Practitioner's Aids

The following exhibits are presented in this section:

- Exhibit AU-C 930-1—Management Representation Letter for a Review of Interim Financial Information
- Exhibit AU-C 930-2—Standard Review Report on Interim Financial Information
- Exhibit AU-C 930-3—Modification of Review Report on Interim Financial Information Due to a Departure from the Applicable Financial Reporting Framework

- Exhibit AU-C 930-4—Modification of Review Report on Interim Financial Statements Due to Inadequate Disclosure
- Exhibit AU-C 930-5—Separate Section Related to a Going Concern Issue Referred to in the Previous Audit Report
- Exhibit AU-C 930-6—Separate Section Related to a Going Concern Issue Not Referred to in the Previous Audit Report

## EXHIBIT AU-C 930-1—MANAGEMENT REPRESENTATION LETTER FOR A REVIEW OF INTERIM FINANCIAL INFORMATION

Bluefield Company

1400 Maple Street

Bluefield, NJ 08000

[Date]

Mr. Arthur Oldes

Arthur Oldes & Company

1040 Main Street

Bluefield, NJ 08000

Dear Mr. Oldes:

This representation letter is provided in connection with your review of the [*consolidated*] balance sheet as of June 30, 20X5 and the related [*consolidated*] statements of income, changes in equity and cash flows for the six-month period then ended of Bluefield Company for the purpose of determining whether any material modifications should be made to the [*consolidated*] interim financial information, for it to be in accordance with accounting principles generally accepted in the United States of America (U.S. GAAP) [*including, if appropriate, an indication as to the appropriate form and content of interim financial information (for example, Article 10 of SEC Regulation S-X)*].

We confirm that [, *to the best of our knowledge and belief, having made such inquiries as we considered necessary for the purpose of appropriately informing ourselves*] [*as of (date of auditor's review report)*]:

*Interim Financial Information*

1. We have fulfilled our responsibilities, as set out in the terms of the engagement letter dated [*insert date*] for the preparation and fair presentation of the interim financial information in accordance with U.S. GAAP; in particular the interim financial information is presented in accordance therewith.

2. We acknowledge our responsibility for the design, implementation, and maintenance of internal control relevant to the preparation and fair presentation of interim financial information that is free from material misstatement, whether due to fraud or error.

3. The interim financial information has been adjusted or includes disclosures for all events subsequent to the date of the interim financial information for which U.S. GAAP requires adjustment or disclosure.

4. The effects of uncorrected misstatements are immaterial, both individually and in the aggregate, to the interim financial information as a whole. A list of the uncorrected misstatements is attached to the representation letter.

[*Any other matters the auditor may consider appropriate.*]

Information Provided

5. We have provided you with:
    — Access to all information of which we are aware that is relevant to the preparation and fair presentation of the interim financial information such as records, documentation and other matters;
    — Minutes of the meetings of stockholders, directors, and committees of directors, or summaries of actions of recent meetings for which minutes have not yet been prepared;
    — Additional information that you have requested from use for the purpose of the review; and
    — Unrestricted access to persons within the entity of whom you determined it necessary to make inquiries.

6. We have disclosed to you all significant deficiencies or material weaknesses in the design or operation of internal control of which we are aware, as it relates to the preparation of both annual and interim financial information.

7. We have disclosed to you the results of our assessment of the risk that the interim financial information may be materially misstated as a result of fraud.

8. We have [*no knowledge of any*] [*disclosed to you all information of which we are aware in relation to*] fraud or suspected fraud that affects the entity and involves:
    — Management;
    — Employees who have significant roles in internal control; or
    — Others where the fraud could have a material effect on the interim financial information.

9. We have [*no knowledge of any*] [*disclosed to you all information in relation to*] allegations of fraud or suspected fraud affecting the entity's interim financial information communicated by employees, former employees, analysts, regulators, or others.

10. We have disclosed to you the identity of the entity's related parties and all the related-party relationships and transactions of which we are aware.

[*Any other matters that the auditor may consider necessary.*]

11. We have reviewed our representation letter to you dated [*date of representation letter relating to most recent audit*] with respect to the audited financial statements for the year ended [*prior year-end date*]. We believe that representations A, B, and C within that representation letter do not apply to the interim financial information referred to above. We now confirm those representations D through X, as they apply to the interim financial information referred to above, and incorporate them herein, with the following changes:

   [*Indicate changes*]

12. [*Add any representations related to new accounting or auditing standards that are being implemented for the first time.*]

_____

[Name of chief executive officer and title]

_____

[Name of chief financial officer and title]

_____

[Name of chief accounting officer and title]

---

*EXHIBIT AU-C 930-2—STANDARD REVIEW REPORT ON INTERIM FINANCIAL INFORMATION*

---

### Independent Auditor's Review Report

Board of Directors

Bluefield Company

Bluefield, NJ 08000

*Results of Review of Interim Financial Information*

We have reviewed the accompanying [*describe the interim financial information or statements reviewed*] of Bluefield Company and its subsidiaries as of September 30, 20X1, and for the three-month and nine-month periods then ended, **and the related notes (collectively referred to as the interim financial information***)*.

Based on our review, we are not aware of any material modifications that should be made to the accompanying interim financial information for it to be in accordance with [*identify the applicable financial reporting framework; for example, accounting principles generally accepted in the United States of America*].

*Basis for Review Results*

We conducted our review in accordance with auditing standards generally accepted in the United States of America (GAAS) applicable to reviews of interim financial information. A review of interim financial information consists principally of applying analytical procedures and making inquiries of persons responsible for financial and accounting matters. A review of interim financial information is substantially less in scope than an audit conducted in accordance with GAAS, the objective of which is an expression of an opinion regarding the financial information as a whole, and accordingly, we do not express such an opinion. We are required to be independent of Bluefield Company and to meet our other ethical responsibilities in accordance with the relevant ethical requirements relating to our review. We believe that the results of the review procedures provide a reasonable basis for our conclusion.

*Responsibilities of Management for the Interim Financial Information*

Management is responsible for the preparation and fair presentation of the interim financial information in accordance with [*identify the applicable financial reporting framework; for example, accounting principles generally accepted in the United States of America*] and for the design, implementation, and maintenance of internal control relevant to the preparation and fair presentation of interim financial information that is free from material misstatement, whether due to fraud or error.

[*Signature of the auditor's firm*]

[*City and state where the auditor's report is issued*]

[*Date of the auditor's report*]

---

## EXHIBIT AU-C 930-3—MODIFICATION OF REVIEW REPORT ON INTERIM FINANCIAL INFORMATION DUE TO A DEPARTURE FROM THE APPLICABLE FINANCIAL REPORTING FRAMEWORK

[*Appropriate Addressee*]

**Results of Review of Interim Financial Information**

We have reviewed the accompanying [*describe the interim financial information or statements reviewed*] of Bluefield Company and its subsidiaries as of September 30, 20X5, and for the three-month and nine-month periods then ended, and the related notes (collectively referred to as the interim financial information).

Based on our review, with the exception of the matters described in the following paragraph, we are not aware of any material modifications that should be made to the accompanying interim financial information for it to be in accordance with [*identify the applicable financial reporting framework; for example, accounting principles generally accepted in the United States of America*].

Based on information furnished to us by management, we believe that the Company has excluded from property and debt in the accompanying balance sheet certain lease obligations that we believe should be capitalized to be in accordance with [*identify the applicable financial reporting framework; for example, accounting principles generally accepted in the United States of America*]. This information indicates that if these lease obligations were capitalized at September 30, 20X1, property would be increased by $_____, long-term debt would be increased by $_____, and net income would be increased (decreased) by $_____ and $_____, respectively, for the three-month and nine-month periods then ended.

*Basis for Review Results*

We conducted our review in accordance with auditing standards generally accepted in the United States of America (GAAS) applicable to reviews of interim financial information. A review of interim financial information consists principally of applying analytical procedures and making inquiries of persons responsible for financial and accounting matters. A review of interim financial information is substantially less in scope than an audit conducted in accordance with GAAS, the objective of which is an expression of an opinion regarding the financial information as a whole, and accordingly, we do not express such an opinion. We are required to be independent of Bluefield Company and to meet our other ethical responsibilities in accordance with the relevant ethical requirements relating to our review. We believe that the results of the review procedures provide a reasonable basis for our conclusion.

*Responsibilities of Management for the Interim Financial Information*

Management is responsible for the preparation and fair presentation of the interim financial information in accordance with [identify the applicable financial reporting framework; for example, accounting principles generally accepted in the United States of America] and for the design, implementation, and maintenance of internal control relevant to the preparation and fair presentation of interim financial information that is free from material misstatement, whether due to fraud or error.

[Signature of the auditor's firm]

[City and state where the auditor's report is issued]

[Date of the auditor's report]

## EXHIBIT AU-C 930-4—MODIFICATION OF REVIEW REPORT ON INTERIM FINANCIAL STATEMENTS DUE TO INADEQUATE DISCLOSURE

The following is an example of the second and third paragraphs of a modification of the auditor's review report when such report is modified due to inadequate disclosure:

> Based on our review, with the exception of the matters described in the following paragraph, we are not aware of any material modifications that should be made to the accompanying interim financial information for it to be in accordance with [*identify the applicable financial reporting framework; for example, accounting principles generally accepted in the United States of America*].
>
> Management has informed us that the Company is presently defending a claim regarding [*describe the nature of the loss contingency*] and that the extent of the Company's liability, if any, and the effect on the accompanying interim financial information is not determinable at this time. The interim financial information fails to disclose these matters, which we believe are required to be disclosed in accordance with [*identify the applicable financial reporting framework; for example, accounting principles generally accepted in the United States of America*].

## EXHIBIT AU-C 930-5—SEPARATE SECTION RELATED TO A GOING CONCERN ISSUE REFERRED TO IN THE PREVIOUS AUDIT REPORT

*Substantial Doubt About the Entity's Ability to Continue as a Going Concern*

The accompanying interim financial information has been prepared assuming that the Company will continue as a going concern. Note 4 of the Company's audited financial statements as of December 31, 20X5, and for the year then ended, includes a statement that substantial doubt exists about the Company's ability to continue as a going concern. Note 4 of the Company's audited financial statements also discloses the events and conditions, management's evaluation of the events and conditions, and management's plans regarding these matters, including the fact that the Company was unable to renew its line of credit or obtain alternative financing as of December 31, 20X5. Our auditor's report on those financial statements includes a separate section referring to the matters in Note 4 of those financial statements. As indicated in Note 3 of the accompanying interim financial information as of March 31, 20X6, and for the three months then ended, the Company was still unable to renew its line of credit or obtain alternative financing as of March 31, 20X6, and has stated that substantial doubt exists about the Company's ability to continue as a going concern. The accompanying interim financial information does not include any adjustments that might result from the outcome of this uncertainty.

## EXHIBIT AU-C 930-6—SEPARATE SECTION RELATED TO A GOING CONCERN ISSUE NOT REFERRED TO IN THE PREVIOUS AUDIT REPORT

*Substantial Doubt About the Entity's Ability to Continue as a Going Concern*

The accompanying interim financial information has been prepared assuming that the Company will continue as a going concern. Note 4 of the Company's audited financial statements as of December 31, 20X5, and for the year then ended, discloses that the Company was unable to renew its line of credit or obtain alternative financing as of December 31, 20X5. Our auditor's report on those financial statements includes a separate section referring to the matters in Note 4 of those financial statements, indicating that these matters raised substantial doubt about the Company's ability to continue as a going concern. As indicated in Note 3 of the accompanying interim financial information as of March 31, 20X6, and for the three months then ended, the Company was still unable to renew its line of credit or obtain alternative financing as of March 31, 20X6. Management's evaluation of the conditions and events and management's plans regarding these matters are also disclosed in Note 3. The accompanying interim financial information does not include any adjustments that might result from the outcome of this uncertainty. As indicated in Note X, certain conditions indicate that the Company may be unable to continue as a going concern. The accompanying interim financial information does not include any adjustments that might result from the outcome of this uncertainty.

# SECTION 935

# COMPLIANCE AUDITS

## Authoritative Pronouncements

SAS-117—Compliance Audits

SAS-123—Omnibus Statement on Auditing Standards—2011

SAS-140—Amendments to AU-C Sections 725, 730, 930, 935, and 940 to Incorporate Auditor Reporting Changes from SAS Nos. 134 and 137

SAS-141—Amendment to Effective Dates of SAS Nos. 134-140

## Overview

The guidance in AU-C 935 applies when an auditor is engaged or required by law or regulation to perform a compliance audit in accordance with three sets of requirements—GAAS, the financial auditing standards under *Government Auditing Standards*, and a governmental audit requirement requiring an auditor to express an opinion on compliance. For example, AU-C 935 applies to an audit performed in accordance with the provisions of Office of Management and Budget (OMB) Circular A-133 (*Audits of States, Local Governments and Non-Profit Organizations*).

AU-C 935 does not apply to an engagement that does not require that the audit be performed according to both GAAS and *Government Auditing Standards.* Under these circumstances, the engagement could be performed under AT-C 315 (*Compliance Attestation*), or AT-C 215 (*Agreed-Upon Procedures Engagements*) depending on the government requirements. AT-C 315 is also applicable when the governmental audit requirement requires an examination of an entity's compliance with specified requirements in accordance with the Statements on Standards for Attestation Engagement or an examination of an entity's internal control over compliance. If an entity is required to have a compliance audit and an examination of internal control over compliance, AU-C 935 applies to the compliance audit and AT-C 315 applies to the examination. Law or regulation does not always prescribe which standards the auditor should follow, so he or she will need to use professional judgment in this determination.

AU-C 935 assists the auditor in applying GAAS to a compliance audit, which is often performed in conjunction with a financial statement audit. While AU-C 100-700 and 900 address financial statement audits, only AU-C 100-300 and 500 can generally be adapted to a compliance audit's objectives. When planning and performing a compliance audit, the auditor should obtain sufficient appropriate audit evidence to support the auditor's opinion. However, the auditor is not required to translate each financial statement audit procedure into a compliance audit procedure. AU-C 935 provides the auditor with more specific guidance on how to adapt and apply relevant AU-C sections to a compliance audit.

Management is responsible for the entity's compliance with compliance requirements in a compliance audit. Management's responsibilities include (*a*) identifying the entity's government programs and understanding and complying with compliance requirements, (*b*) establishing and maintaining effective controls that provide reasonable assurance that the entity administers government programs in compliance with compliance requirements, (*c*) evaluating and monitoring the entity's compliance with compliance requirements, and (*d*) taking corrective action when instances of noncompliance are identified, including findings of the compliance audit.

In a compliance audit, the auditor's objective is to obtain sufficient appropriate audit evidence to form an opinion and report at the level specified in the governmental audit requirement on whether the entity complied in all material respects with the applicable compliance requirements. The auditor also has the objective of identifying any audit and reporting requirements specified in the governmental audit requirement that are supplementary to GAAS and *Governmental Auditing Standards* and perform procedures to address those requirements.

---

**IMPORTANT NOTICE FOR 2022:** In April 2020, the AICPA's Auditing Standards Board (ASB) issued SAS No. 140, *Amendments to AU-C Sections 725, 730, 930, 935, and 940 to Incorporate Auditor Reporting Changes from SAS Nos. 134 and 137*. SAS No. 140 amends the reporting illustrations in AU-C 935. Originally, the effective date of SAS No. 140 was for audits of financial statements for periods ending on or after December 15, 2020. However, the ASB's issuance of SAS No. 141, *Amendment to the Effective Dates of SAS Nos. 134-140*, extended the effective date to December 15, 2021, in order to provide more time for firms to implement SAS No. 140 in light of the effect of the coronavirus pandemic. The ASB recommends that SAS Nos. 134-140 be implemented concurrently.

---

## Definitions

| | |
|---|---|
| Applicable compliance requirements | Compliance requirements that are subject to the compliance audit. |
| Audit findings | Matters the auditor is required to report on in accordance with the governmental audit requirement. |
| Audit risk of noncompliance | Risk that the auditor expresses an inappropriate audit opinion on the entity's compliance when material noncompliance exists; function of the risks of material noncompliance and detection risk of noncompliance. |
| Compliance audit | A program-specific or organization-wide audit of an entity's compliance with applicable compliance requirements. |
| Compliance requirements | Laws, statutes, regulations, rules, and provisions of contracts or grant agreements applicable to a government program with which the entity is required to comply. |

§ 935 • *Compliance Audits*

| | |
|---|---|
| Deficiency in internal control over compliance | A deficiency in internal control over compliance exists when the design or operation of a control over compliance does not allow management or employees to prevent, or detect and correct, noncompliance on a timely basis in the course of their normal activities. |
| Detection risk of noncompliance | The risk that the procedures the auditor performs to reduce audit risk of noncompliance to an acceptably low level will not detect existing noncompliance that could be material, either individually or when aggregated with other instances of noncompliance. |
| Governmental audit requirement | Government requirement established by law, regulation, rule, or provision of contracts of grant agreements requiring that an entity undergo an audit of its compliance with applicable compliance requirements related to one or more government programs that the entity administers. |
| *Government Auditing Standards* | Standards and guidance issued by the Comptroller General of the United States, U.S. Government Accountability Office for financial audits, reviews of financial statements, attestation engagements, and performance audits; also known as generally accepted government auditing standards (GAGAS) or the Yellow Book. |
| Government program | The means by which governmental entities achieve their objectives |
| Grantor | A government agency that funds the government program. |
| Known questioned costs | Questioned costs specifically identified by the auditor; a subset of likely questioned costs. |
| Likely questioned costs | The auditor's best estimate of total questioned costs developed by extrapolating from audit evidence obtained, for example, by projecting known questioned costs identified in an audit sample to the entire population from which the sample was drawn. |
| Material noncompliance | If not otherwise defined in the governmental audit requirement, noncompliance with the applicable compliance requirements is considered quantitatively or qualitatively material if there is substantial likelihood that either individually or when aggregated, it would influence the judgment made by a reasonable user of the report on compliance about the entity's compliance with the requirements of the government program as a whole. |
| Material weakness in internal control over compliance | A deficiency or combination of deficiencies in internal control over compliance such that there is a reasonable possibility that material noncompliance with a compliance requirement will not be prevented, or detected and corrected, on a timely basis. A reasonable possibility exists when the event's likelihood is reasonably possible or probable. |
| Organization-wide audit | An audit of an entity's financial statements and of its compliance with the applicable compliance requirements as they relate to one or more government programs that the entity administers. |
| Pass-through entity | An entity that receives an award from a grantor or other entity and distributes all or part of it to another entity to administer a government program. |

| | |
|---|---|
| Program-specific audit | An audit of an entity's compliance with applicable compliance requirements as they relate to one government program that the entity administers performed in conjunction with an audit of the entity's or program's financial statements. |
| Questioned costs | Costs that are questioned by the auditor because 1) of a violation or possible violation of compliance requirements, 2) of lack of support by adequate documentations, or 3) the incurred costs appear unreasonable and do not reflect a prudent person's actions in the circumstances. |
| Risk of material noncompliance | The risks that material noncompliance exists prior to the audit; consists of the inherent risk of noncompliance and the control risk of noncompliance. |
| Significant deficiency in internal control over compliance | A deficiency or combination of deficiencies in internal control over compliance that is less severe than a material weakness in internal control over compliance yet important enough to merit attention by those charged with governance. |

## Requirements

The auditor is presumptively required to perform the following procedures when performing a compliance audit:

### Planning and Performing a Compliance Audit

1. Adapt and apply the relevant AU-C sections to the objectives of a compliance audit.

2. Establish and apply materiality levels for the compliance audit based on the governmental audit requirement.

3. Determine which of the entity's government programs and compliance requirements to test.

4. For each government program and compliance requirement tested, perform risk assessment procedures to understand the applicable compliance requirements and the entity's internal control over compliance with the applicable compliance requirements.

5. In performing risk assessment procedures, ask management if there are findings and recommendations in written communications from previous audit or attestation engagements or monitoring that directly relate to the compliance audit's objectives. Gain an understanding of management's response to any findings and recommendations that could have a material effect on the entity's compliance with applicable compliance requirements and use this information to identify and assess risks of material noncompliance and determine the nature, timing, and extent of the audit procedures for the compliance audit and the extent to which testing the implementation of any corrective actions is applicable to the audit objectives.

6. Assess the risks of material noncompliance due to fraud or error for each applicable compliance requirement and consider whether any of those risks are pervasive, affecting the entity's compliance with many compliance requirements.

7. Develop an overall response to any pervasive risks of material noncompliance identified.

8. Design and perform further audit procedures, including tests of details, in response to the assessed risks of material noncompliance to obtain sufficient appropriate audit evidence about the entity's compliance with each applicable

compliance requirement. Risk assessment procedures, tests of controls, and analytical procedures by themselves are not sufficient to address these risks.

9. Tests of controls and their operating effectiveness over each applicable compliance requirement should be performed in response to the assessed risks of material noncompliance if (1) the auditor's risk assessment includes an expectation of the operating effectiveness of controls over compliance related to the applicable compliance requirements, (2) substantive procedures alone do not provide sufficient appropriate audit evidence, or (3) tests of controls over compliance are required by the governmental audit requirement.

10. Perform procedures to address any additional audit requirements specified in the governmental audit requirement supplementary to GAAS and *Government Auditing Standards*.

11. If a governmental agency provides guidance for performing a compliance audit that conflicts with current GAAS or *Government Auditing Standards*, comply with the most current applicable GAAS and *Government Auditing Standards* rather than the outdated or conflicting guidance.

12. Request written representations from management tailored to the entity and the governmental audit requirement stating management's:

    a. Acknowledgment of responsibility for understanding and complying with the compliance requirements;

    b. Acknowledgment of responsibility for establishing and maintaining controls providing reasonable assurance that the entity administers government programs in accordance with the compliance requirements;

    c. Identification and disclosure to the auditor of all of its government programs and related activities subject to the governmental audit requirement;

    d. Making available to the auditor all contracts, grant agreements, amendments, and any other correspondence relevant to the programs and related activities subject to the governmental audit requirement;

    e. Disclosure to the auditor of all known noncompliance with the applicable compliance requirements or stating that there was no such noncompliance;

    f. Belief as to whether the entity has complied with the applicable compliance requirements excepting any noncompliance disclosed to the auditor;

    g. Making available to the auditor all documentation related to compliance with the applicable compliance requirements;

    h. Interpretation of any applicable compliance requirements subject to varying interpretations;

    i. Disclosure to the auditor of any communications from grantors and pass-through entities about possible noncompliance with applicable compliance requirements, including communications to the date of the auditor's report;

    j. Disclosure to the auditor of findings received and related corrective actions taken up to the date of the auditor's report for previous audits, attestation engagements, and internal or external monitoring that directly relate to the compliance audit's objectives;

    k. Disclosure to the auditor of all known noncompliance with the applicable compliance requirements subsequent to the period covered by the auditor's report or stating that there is no known noncompliance; and

    l. Responsibility for taking corrective action on audit findings of the compliance audit.

13. The auditor should request additional representations from management related to the entity's compliance with the applicable compliance requirements if he or she finds it necessary.

14. Perform audit procedures up to the date of the auditor's report to obtain sufficient appropriate audit evidence that all subsequent events related to the entity's compliance during the period covered by the auditor's compliance report have been identified. Take into account the risk assessment in determining the nature and extent of such audit procedures which should include but are not limited to inquiring of management about and considering any relevant internal auditors' reports, other auditors' reports, and reports from grantors and pass-through entities about the entity's noncompliance that were issued during the subsequent period; and information about the entity's noncompliance obtained through other professional engagements performed for that entity.

15. While the auditor has no obligation to perform procedures related to the entity's compliance subsequent to the period covered by the audit report, if he or she becomes aware of noncompliance after the period covered by the report but before the report release date that needs to be disclosed to avoid misleading users of the report, he or she should discuss the matter with management and those charged with governance as appropriate and include an other-matter paragraph describing the nature of the noncompliance in the report.

16. Evaluate the sufficiency and appropriateness of the audit evidence obtained.

17. Form an opinion at the level specified by the governmental audit requirement on whether the entity complied in all material respects with the applicable compliance requirements and report appropriately. Evaluate likely questioned costs and other material noncompliance that may not result in questioned costs.

## *Reporting on a Compliance Audit*

18. If the auditor's report on compliance is combined with a report on internal control over compliance required by the governmental audit requirement, the following items should be addressed in the reports:

*Report on Compliance*

  a. The report on compliance should precede the report on internal control over compliance and include the title "Report on Compliance."

  b. The first section of the report on compliance should include the auditor's opinion (under a heading "Opinion") and state that the entity's compliance with the applicable compliance requirements have been audited and the time period covered by the audit. When expressing an unmodified opinion, state that in the auditor's opinion the entity complied in all material respects with the compliance requirements that are applicable for the period covered.

  c. The report on compliance should include a section following the Opinion that is titled "Basis for Opinion" that states that the audit of compliance was conducted in accordance with GAAS and Government Auditing Standards and the governmental audit requirement. This section also refers to the section of the audit report that describes the auditor's responsibilities under those standards and includes acknowledgment that the auditor is required to be independent. And, the auditor includes a statement that the audit evidence obtained by the auditor is sufficient and appropriate to provide a basis for the opinion and that states the compliance audit does not provide a legal determination of the entity's compliance with the applicable compliance requirements.

d. A statement that management is responsible for compliance with applicable compliance requirements and for establishing and maintaining effective internal control over compliance;

e. A section titled "Responsibilities for the Audit of Compliance" that (1) states the objectives of the audit are to provide reasonable assurance about whether material noncompliance with the applicable compliance requirements occurred, whether due to fraud or error and (2) expresses an opinion on the entity's compliance with the applicable compliance requirements. That section also includes the following statements:

   i. That the risk of not detecting material noncompliance resulting from fraud is higher than that resulting from error.

   ii. That noncompliance with the applicable compliance requirements is considered material if there is substantial likelihood that, individually or in the aggregate, it would influence the judgment made by a reasonable user of the report on compliance.

   iii. A description of the audit in accordance with GAAS, Government Auditing Standards, and the relevant government audit requirement.

   iv. That the auditor is required to communicate certain matters to those charged with governance, including deficiencies related to internal control over compliance.

*Report on Internal Control Over Compliance*

f. The combined report should include a separate section that is titled, "Report on Internal Control Over Compliance" that includes the following items:

   i. The definitions of *deficiency in internal control over compliance* and *material weakness in internal control over compliance, and significant deficiency in internal control over compliance;*

   ii. The auditor's opinion on whether the entity complied with the applicable compliance requirements in all material respects at the level specified by the governmental audit requirement;

   iii. A statement that the auditor considered the entity's internal control over compliance with the applicable compliance requirements in planning and performing the audit to determine the auditing procedures in order to express an opinion on compliance, but not an opinion on the effectiveness of internal control over compliance.

   iv. A statement that the auditor's consideration of the entity's internal control over compliance was not designed to identify all internal control deficiencies that might be significant deficiencies or material weaknesses in internal control over compliance;

   v. A description of any identified material weaknesses and significant deficiencies in internal control over compliance or reference to that description in an accompanying schedule;

vi. If no material weaknesses in internal control over compliance were identified, a statement to that effect; and

vii. A statement that the auditor is not expressing an opinion on internal control over compliance and accordingly no such opinion is expressed.

g. The main or printed signature of the auditor's firm, the city and state where the auditor's report is issued, and the date of the auditor's report, which should not earlier than the date the auditor obtained sufficient appropriate evidence on which to base the auditor's opinion on compliance.

19. If the auditor chooses to issue a separate reports on compliance and on internal control over compliance required by the governmental audit requirement, the separate report on compliance would omit the elements related to internal control over compliance and the separate report on internal control over compliance would omit the elements related to compliance. It would also include the following additional statements:

a. That the auditor audited the entity's compliance with applicable compliance requirements related to [*identify the government program or programs and period audited*] and a reference to the auditor's report on compliance;

b. That the compliance audit was conducted in accordance with GAAS, Government Auditing Standards, and the governmental audit requirement;

c. That management is responsible for the design, implementation, and maintenance of effective internal control over compliance with the requirements of laws, statutes, regulations, rules, and provisions of contracts or grant agreements applicable to government programs.

d. That in planning and performing the compliance audit, the auditor considered the entity's internal control over compliance with the applicable compliance requirements to determine the audit procedures necessary for expressing an opinion on compliance, but not for expressing an opinion on the effectiveness of internal control over compliance; and

e. That the auditor is not expressing an opinion on internal control over compliance.

20. Noncompliance and other matters required to be reported by the governmental audit requirement should be reported in the manner specified by that requirement.

21. The auditor's opinion on compliance should be modified if (1) the compliance audit identifies noncompliance with the applicable compliance requirements that the auditor believes has a material effect on the entity's compliance or (2) there is a restriction on the scope of the compliance audit.

22. Modify the report on compliance only or the separate report on internal control over compliance when referring to another auditor's report as part of the basis for the report.

23. Communicate in writing to management and those charged with governance any identified significant deficiencies and material weaknesses in internal control over compliance, even if there is no governmental audit requirement to report on internal control over compliance.

24. Communicate to those charged with governance the auditor's responsibilities under GAAS (*Government Auditing Standards*) and the governmental audit requirement, an overview of the planned scope and timing of the compliance audit, and significant findings from the compliance audit.

25. If there is a printed form, schedule, or report containing prescribed wording and the auditor has no basis to make such a statement, he or she should reword the document or attach an appropriately worded separate report.

## Documentation

26. The auditor should document the following:
    a. Risk assessment procedures performed, including those performed to gain an understanding of internal control over compliance;
    b. The auditor's responses to the assessed risks of material noncompliance, procedures performed, including any tests of controls over compliance, to test compliance with the applicable compliance requirements and the results of those procedures;
    c. Materiality levels and the basis on which they were determined; and
    d. How compliance with the specific governmental audit requirements supplementary to GAAS and *Government Auditing Standards* was achieved.

## Report Reissuance

27. If a report is reissued, it should include an explanatory paragraph stating the report is replacing a previously issued report, describing the reasons why the report is being reissued, and any changes from the previously issued report. If additional procedures are performed to obtain sufficient appropriate audit evidence for all of the government programs being reported on, the report date should be updated to the date the auditor obtained sufficient appropriate audit evidence about the events causing the auditor to perform the new procedures. If additional procedures are performed to obtain sufficient appropriate audit evidence for some of the government programs being reported on, the report should be dual dated with an updated report date being the date the auditor obtained sufficient appropriate audit evidence regarding the affected government programs and a reference to the affected government programs.

# Analysis and Application of Procedures

## Planning and Performing a Compliance Audit

### Materiality

In a compliance audit, the auditor establishes materiality levels to:
- Determine the nature and extent of risk assessment procedures;
- Identify and assess the risks of material noncompliance;
- Determine the nature, timing, and extent of further audit procedures;
- Evaluate whether the entity complied with the applicable compliance requirements; and
- Report noncompliance findings and other matters required to be reported by the governmental audit requirement.

Materiality is generally considered in relation to the government program as a whole although a different level of materiality may be specified by the governmental audit requirement for particular purposes. For example, OMB Circular A-133 requires reporting findings of noncompliance that are material in relation to one of fourteen types of compliance requirements identified in the OMB *Compliance Supplement*.

*Identifying government programs and applicable compliance requirements*

Some governmental audit requirements specifically identify the applicable compliance requirements, while others, such as the *Compliance Supplement* for OMB Circular A-133, provide a framework for the auditor to determine the applicable compliance requirements. When identifying and obtaining an understanding of applicable compliance requirements, the auditor may consult the *Compliance Supplement* used in OMB Circular A-133 audits, which contains compliance requirements that are typically applicable to federal government programs and suggested audit procedures for those requirements and also provides guidance for identifying compliance requirements for programs that are not included. The auditor may also consult the applicable program-specific audit guide issued by the grantor agency, which contains the compliance requirements pertaining to the government program and suggested audit procedures for those requirements.

If the *Compliance Supplement* or a program-specific audit guide is not applicable, the auditor may perform the following procedures to identify and obtain an understanding of the applicable compliance requirements:

- Read laws, regulations, rules, and provisions of contracts or grant agreements pertaining to the government program;
- Inquire of management and other knowledgeable entity personnel;
- Inquire of appropriate individuals outside the entity, such as the office of the federal, state, or local program official or auditor about the laws and regulations applicable to entities within their jurisdiction or a third-party specialist such as an attorney;
- Read the minutes of meetings of the governing board of the entity being audited;
- Read audit documentation about the applicable compliance requirements prepared during prior years' audits or other engagements; and
- Discuss the applicable compliance requirements with auditors who performed prior years' audits or other engagements.

*Risk assessment and audit procedures*

The nature and extent of risk assessment procedures the auditor performs vary and are influenced by factors such as:

- The newness, complexity, and nature of the applicable compliance requirements;
- The auditor's knowledge of the entity's internal control over compliance with the applicable compliance requirements obtained in previous audits or other professional engagements;

- The services provided by the entity and how they are affected by external factors;
- The level of oversight by the grantor or pass-through entity; and
- How management addresses findings.

In assessing the risks of material noncompliance with the applicable compliance requirements, the auditor may consider the requirements' complexity and susceptibility to noncompliance, how long the entity has been subject to the requirements, how the entity has previously complied with the requirements, the potential effect on the entity of noncompliance, the degree of judgment involved in adhering to the requirements, and the auditor's assessment of the risks of material misstatement in the financial statement audit. Inherent and control risk of noncompliance may be evaluated individually or in combination.

**OBSERVATION:** The risk of material noncompliance may be pervasive to the entity's noncompliance if an entity is experiencing financial difficulty and there is an increased risk grant funds will be diverted for unauthorized purposes or an entity has a history of poor recordkeeping for its government programs.

Audit procedures are designed in a compliance audit to detect intentional and unintentional material noncompliance in order to obtain reasonable, but not absolute, assurance about the entity's compliance. Analytical procedures may contribute some substantive evidence, but are generally less effective in a compliance audit than in a financial statement audit. Tests of details may be used to test for compliance in areas such as grant disbursements or expenditures, eligibility files, cost allocation plans, or periodic reports filed with grantor agencies.

Some governmental audit requirements such as OMB Circular A-133 require tests of the operating effectiveness of controls identified as likely to be effective even if that testing is inefficient. For compliance audits, audit evidence about the operating effectiveness of controls obtained in prior audits is not applicable.

*Supplementary audit requirements*

An example of supplementary audit requirements the auditor may need to adhere to are the requirements in OMB Circular A-133 to perform specified procedures to identify major programs and to follow up on prior audit findings and perform procedures to assess the reasonableness of the summary schedule of prior audit findings.

*Written representations*

Management may include qualifying language in the written representations indicating that representations are made to the best of management's knowledge and belief. This qualifying language is not appropriate for the representations about management's responsibilities for: understanding and complying with the compliance requirements; establishing and maintaining controls that provide reasonable assurance that the entity administers governments programs in accordance with the compliance requirements; and taking corrective action on audit findings of the compliance audit.

## Evaluating audit evidence and forming an opinion

In determining whether an entity has materially complied with the applicable compliance requirements, the auditor may consider factors such as:

- The frequency and nature of noncompliance with the applicable compliance requirements identified during the compliance audit,
- The adequacy of the entity's system for monitoring compliance with the applicable compliance requirements and the possible effect of any noncompliance on the entity, and
- Whether any identified noncompliance with the applicable compliance requirements resulted in likely questioned costs that are material to the government program.

The auditor should consider all noncompliance he or she identified in making this evaluation, regardless of whether the entity corrected the noncompliance after the auditor brought it to management's attention.

## Reporting on a Compliance Audit

The auditor is not precluded from restricting the use of any report to intended users.

**OBSERVATION:** If a report is a matter of public record or available for public inspection, removing personally identifiable information in the report and findings of noncompliance will reduce the likelihood of sensitive information being disclosed.

*Government Auditing Standards* require that when the auditor communicates significant deficiencies or material weaknesses in internal control over compliance to management and those charged with governance, he or she obtain a response, preferably in writing, concerning their views on the findings, conclusions, and recommendations included in the auditor's report on internal control over compliance and any such written response be included in the auditor's report. If the written response is included in a document with the auditor's written communication to management and those charged with governance regarding identified significant deficiencies or material weaknesses in internal control over compliance, the auditor may add a paragraph to the communication disclaiming an opinion on such information.

## Documentation

Specific documentation of how the auditor adapted and applied each of the applicable AU-C sections to the objectives of a compliance audit is not necessary; documentation of the audit strategy, audit plan, and the work performed is sufficient.

# SECTION 940

# AN AUDIT OF INTERNAL CONTROL OVER FINANCIAL REPORTING THAT IS INTEGRATED WITH AN AUDIT OF FINANCIAL STATEMENTS

## Authoritative Pronouncements

SAS-130—An Audit of Internal Control over Financial Reporting That Is Integrated with an Audit of Financial Statements

SAS-135—Omnibus Statement on Auditing Standards—2019

SAS-140—Amendments to AU-C Sections 725, 730, 930, 935, and 940 to Incorporate Auditor Reporting Changes from SAS Nos. 134 and 137

SAS-141—Amendment to Effective Dates of SAS Nos. 134-140

## Overview

The basic concepts of internal control and the auditor's consideration of internal control in a financial statement audit are discussed in AU-C 315 (*Understanding the Entity and Its Environment and Assessing the Risks of Material Misstatement*). Internal control over financial reporting (ICFR) is a process—designed and overseen by those charged with governance, management, and others—designed to provide reasonable assurance that the financial statements are prepared in accordance with the applicable financial reporting framework. Effective internal control provides reasonable assurance over the reliability of financial reporting.

The guidance in AU-C 940 applies only when an auditor is engaged to perform an audit of ICFR that is integrated with a financial statement audit. While integrated audits may be required to be and are often performed by the same auditor, AU-C 940 requires ICFR and financial statement audits to be integrated even if they are performed by different auditors. GAAS standards should be adapted to apply to an ICFR audit that is integrated with a financial statement audit.

The two main objectives of an auditor in an ICFR audit are to:

1. Obtain reasonable assurance about whether material weaknesses exist as of the date specified in management's assessment about ICFR effectiveness; and
2. To express an opinion on the effectiveness of ICFR in a written report and communicate with management and those charged with governance.

The auditor is not required to plan or perform the integrated audit to identify deficiencies less severe than a material weakness. If one or more material weaknesses are found, the entity's ICFR cannot be considered effective. However, the auditor is required to evaluate the effectiveness of all of an entity's relevant control objectives so identification of a material weakness does not relieve the auditor of his or her responsibility to evaluate all remaining relevant control objectives.

---

**IMPORTANT NOTICE FOR 2022:** In April 2020, the AICPA's Auditing Standards Board (ASB) issued SAS No. 140, *Amendments to AU-C Sections 725, 730, 930, 935, and 940 to Incorporate Auditor Reporting Changes from SAS Nos. 134 and 137*. SAS No. 140 amends the reporting illustrations in AU-C 940. Originally, the effective date of SAS No. 140 was for audits of financial statements for periods ending on or after December 15, 2020. However, the ASB's issuance of SAS No. 141, *Amendment to the Effective Dates of SAS Nos. 134-140*, extended the effective date to December 15, 2021, in order to provide more time for firms to implement SAS No. 140 in light of the effect of the coronavirus pandemic. The ASB recommends that SAS Nos. 134-140 be implemented concurrently.

---

## Definitions

| | |
|---|---|
| Audit of ICFR | An audit of the design and operating effectiveness of an entity's ICFR. |
| Control objective | Control objectives address the risks that specified controls are intended to mitigate. In ICFR, control objectives generally relate to a relevant assertion for a significant class of transactions, account balance, or disclosure and address the risk that the specified controls will not provide reasonable assurance that a misstatement or omission in that assertion is prevented, or detected and corrected, on a timely basis. |
| Criteria | Benchmarks used to measure or evaluate the subject matter. |
| Detective control | A control with the objective of detecting and correcting errors or fraud that have occurred and could result in a misstatement of the financial statements. |
| Internal control over financial reporting (ICFR) | A process effected by those charged with governance, management, and other personnel, designed to provide reasonable assurance as to the preparation of reliable financial statements in accordance with the applicable financial reporting framework. ICFR includes policies and procedures that:<br>• Pertain to maintaining records that accurately and fairly reflect the transactions and dispositions of the entity's assets;<br>• Provide reasonable assurance that transactions are recorded to allow for financial statement preparation in accordance with the applicable financial reporting framework and that receipts and expenditures are made in accordance with authorizations by management and those charged with governance; and<br>• Provide reasonable assurance regarding prevention, or timely detection and correction of unauthorized acquisition, use, or disposition of the entity's assets that could have a material effect on the financial statements. |

| | |
|---|---|
| | ICFR has inherent limitations due to its reliance on human diligence and compliance, which can lead to lapses in judgments, circumvention by collusion, or improper management override. Because of these limitations, there is a risk that material misstatements will not be prevented, or detected and corrected, on a timely basis by ICFR. |
| | The auditor's procedures performed as a part of the integrated audit are not part of an entity's ICFR. |
| Management's assessment about ICFR | Management's conclusion, which is included in management's report on ICFR, about the effectiveness of the entity's ICFR based on suitable and available criteria. |
| Preventive control | A control with the objective of preventing errors or fraud that could result in a misstatement of the financial statements. |

## Requirements

The auditor is presumptively required to perform the following procedures when performing an integrated ICFR audit:

### ICFR Audit Preconditions

1. Obtain management agreement that it acknowledges and understands its responsibility for:
   a. Designing, implementing, and maintaining effective ICFR,
   b. Evaluating the effectiveness of the entity's ICFR using suitable and available criteria,
   c. Providing management's assessment about ICFR in a report accompanying the auditor's report,
   d. Supporting its assessment about the effectiveness of the entity's ICFR with sufficient evaluation and documentation, and
   e. Providing the auditor with access to all information management is aware of that is relevant to management's assessment of ICFR, additional information the auditor may require from management for the ICFR audit, and unrestricted access to the entity's people whom the auditor determines are necessary in obtaining audit evidence.

Determine that the as of date corresponds to the balance sheet or period ending date of the period covered by the financial statements.

2. Evaluate the effectiveness of the entity's ICFR using the same suitable and available criteria used by management in its assessment.

### Requesting a Written Assessment

3. Request a written assessment from management about the effectiveness of the entity's ICFR. Management's refusal to provide a written assessment is a scope limitation.

### Integrating the ICFR Audit with the Financial Statement Audit

4. ICFR and financial statement audits have different objectives; however, the integrated audit should be designed to achieve both objectives simultaneously. Tests of controls should be designed to obtain sufficient appropriate audit evidence to support the auditor's opinion on ICFR as of the date specified in management's assessment about ICFR and the auditor's control risk assessments for the financial statement audit.

5. If the ICFR audit engagement is for a period of time, the requirements and guidance in this AU-C should be modified accordingly and the financial statement audit should cover the same period of time.

6. Financial statement auditing procedure results should be taken into account in the auditor's risk assessments and the testing necessary to conclude on the operating effectiveness of a control.

7. If a deficiency in ICFR is identified during the ICFR audit, any effect it has on the nature, timing, and extent of substantive procedures to be performed to reduce audit risk in the financial statement audit to an acceptably low level should be considered.

8. The auditor's conclusion on the effectiveness of controls for the financial statement audit should incorporate the results of any additional tests of controls performed in achieving the objective related to expressing an opinion on the entity's ICFR.

## Planning the ICFR Audit

9. An overall audit strategy should be established setting the scope, timing, and direction of the ICFR audit and guiding the development of the audit plan in accordance with AU-C 300 (*Planning an Audit*).

10. Areas that have a higher risk of existence of a material weakness should have more attention focused on them. An entity's ICFR is less likely to prevent, or detect and correct, a misstatement caused by fraud than one caused by error. Controls that, even if deficient, would not present a reasonable risk of material misstatement to the financial statements do not need to be tested.

11. Evaluate whether the entity's controls sufficiently address identified risks of material misstatement due to fraud and the risk of management override of other controls.

12. Consider whether other information obtained indicates risks of material misstatement due to fraud as required by AU-C 240 (*Consideration of Fraud in a Financial Statement Audit*). If deficiencies are identified during the ICFR audit in controls designed to prevent, or detect and correct, misstatements caused by fraud, those deficiencies should be taken into account when developing the response to risks of material misstatement during the financial statement audit.

13. Obtain a sufficient understanding of the internal audit function and others to identify activities related to ICFR effectiveness that are relevant to planning and performing the ICFR audit.

14. Evaluate the extent to which the work of internal auditors or others will be used to modify the nature, timing, or extent of audit procedures performed. The requirements of AU-C 610 (*Using the Work of Internal Auditors*) should be applied when the work of internal auditors or others will be used in obtaining audit evidence or in providing direct assistance in the ICFR audit.

15. The same materiality should be used for planning and performing the ICFR and financial statement audit.

## Using a Top-Down Approach

16. Use a top-down approach in selecting the controls to test in an ICFR audit.

17. Identify and test entity-level controls that are important to the auditor's conclusion about whether the entity's ICFR is effective.

18. Evaluate the components of ICFR and determine whether the components are present and functioning in ICFR design, implementation, and operation and whether the components are functioning together in an integrated manner to achieve the entity's financial reporting objectives.

19. Evaluate the period-end financial reporting process including procedures: used to enter transaction totals into the general ledger; related to selection and application of accounting policies; used to initiate, authorize, record, and process journal entries in the general ledger; used to record recurring and nonrecurring adjustments to the financial statements; and used for financial statement preparation.

20. As part of the period-end financial reporting process evaluation, assess:
    a. The inputs, procedures performed, and outputs of the processes used by the entity to produce its financial statements;
    b. The extent of information technology (IT) involvement;
    c. Who participates from management;
    d. The locations involved;
    e. The types of consolidating and adjusting entries; and
    f. The nature and extent of process oversight by management and those charged with governance.

21. Identify significant classes of transactions, account balances, and disclosures, and their relevant assertions, by evaluating the qualitative and quantitative risk factors related to the financial statement line items and disclosures and determining likely sources of potential misstatements that would cause the financial statements to be materially misstated.

22. If an entity has components, significant classes of transactions, account balances, and disclosures, and their relevant assertions, should be identified based on the group financial statements.

23. To understand likely sources of potential misstatements and as part of selecting controls to test, the auditor should:
    a. Understand the flow of transactions related to the relevant assertions, including how those transactions are initiated, authorized, recorded, processed, and reported;
    b. Identify points where a misstatement could arise within the entity's processes that could individually, or in combination with other misstatements, be material;
    c. Identify controls management has implemented to address these potential misstatements; and
    d. Identify controls management has implemented over the prevention, or timely detection and correction, of unauthorized acquisition, use, or disposition of the entity's assets that could have a material effect on the financial statements.

> Due to the great degree of judgment necessary in this, the auditor should directly perform these procedures or supervise the work of internal auditors or others providing direct assistance.

24. The auditor should understand how IT affects the entity's flow of transactions and how the entity has responded to risks arising from IT as required by AU-C 315 (*Understanding the Entity and Its Environment and Assessing the Risks of Material Misstatement*).

25. Identify and test controls important to the auditor's conclusion about whether the entity's controls sufficiently address the assessed risk of material misstatement to each relevant assertion.

## Testing Controls

26. Evaluate the design effectiveness of controls by determining whether the entity's controls, if operated as prescribed by people with the necessary authority and competence to perform them effectively, satisfy the entity's control objectives and can effectively prevent, or detect and correct, misstatements caused by errors or fraud that could result in material misstatements in the financial statements.

27. Test the operating effectiveness of controls by determining whether the control is operating as designed and whether the person performing the control possesses the necessary authority and competence to perform the control effectively.

28. The sufficiency and appropriateness of evidence obtained should increase as the risk associated with the control being tested increases.

29. Obtain evidence about the effectiveness of selected controls for each relevant assertion. Evidence does not need to be obtained about the effectiveness of each individual control to meet this requirement.

30. Test the controls selected in order to obtain evidence about whether they are effective.

31. When control deviations are identified, determine the effect of those deviations on the risk assessment of the control being tested, the evidence to be obtained, and the operating effectiveness of the control.

32. Evidence should be obtained that ICFR has operated effectively over a period of time in order to express an opinion on ICFR as of a point in time. The period of time tested may be less than the financial statement period. Tests of controls closer to the as of date should be performed as well as tests over a sufficient period of time to obtain sufficient appropriate audit evidence of operating effectiveness.

33. When the auditor has obtained evidence about the operating effectiveness of controls at an interim date, he or she should determine what additional evidence concerning operations of the controls is necessary in order to report on the effectiveness of controls as of a specific date.

34. The nature, timing, and extent of testing necessary in subsequent year's audits should take into account knowledge obtained during past audits of the entity's ICFR.

35. The nature, timing, and extent of testing should vary to incorporate unpredictability from period to period and respond to changes in circumstances.

## Identifying Deficiencies in ICFR

36. The auditor should determine whether one or more deficiencies in ICFR have been identified based on the audit work performed.

37. Each deficiency identified should be evaluated for severity to determine whether the deficiency, individually or in combination, is a material weakness as of the date specified in management's assessment about ICFR. The auditor should determine as part of this evaluation whether deficiencies affecting the same ICFR component, relevant assertion, or significant class of transactions, account balance, or disclosure, collectively result in a material weakness.

38. Compensating controls should be considered when determining whether a deficiency, individually or in combination, is a material weakness as of the date specified in management's assessment about ICFR. The operating effectiveness of compensating controls should be tested to determine whether they operate at a level of precision that would prevent, or detect and correct, a material misstatement.

39. If the auditor determines a deficiency, individually or in combination, is not a material weakness in ICFR, he or she should consider whether prudent officials with the same knowledge would likely reach the same conclusion.

40. Each deficiency identified should be evaluated for severity to determine whether the deficiency, individually or in combination, is a significant deficiency. The auditor should determine as part of this evaluation whether deficiencies affecting the same ICFR component, relevant assertion, or significant class of transactions, account balance, or disclosure collectively result in a significant deficiency.

## Subsequent Events

41. Inquire of management and those charged with governance as appropriate about whether there were any changes in ICFR or conditions that might significantly affect ICFR subsequent to the as of date but before the auditor's report date. To obtain this information, the auditor should inquire about and read the following for the subsequent period: relevant internal audit reports issued, reports of other independent auditors regarding deficiencies, regulatory agency reports on the entity's ICFR, and information about the entity's ICFR effectiveness from other engagements the auditor performed for the entity.

42. If knowledge is obtained about a material weakness that existed as of the date specified in management's assessment about ICFR, an adverse opinion should be issued. If management's assessment about ICFR states that ICFR is effective, the auditor's report should be modified to state that one or more material weaknesses have been identified but not included in management's report. A description of each material weakness should be included with specific information about its nature and its actual and potential effect on the presentation of the entity's financial statements issued during its existence. The auditor should communicate in writing to those charged with governance that one or more material weaknesses were not disclosed or identified in management's report.

43. If the effect of a subsequent event on the effectiveness of the entity's ICFR as of the date specified in management's assessment about ICFR is unable to be determined, the auditor should disclaim an opinion and should also disclaim an opinion on management's disclosures about any corrective actions taken by the entity.

44. If knowledge is obtained about conditions that arose subsequent to the as of date and before the auditor's report date that have a material effect on the entity's ICFR, the auditor's report should include an emphasis-of-matter section directing the reader's attention to the subsequently discovered fact and its effects as disclosed in management's report or an other-matter paragraph describing the subsequently discovered fact and its effects.

45. The auditor is not responsible for staying informed of events subsequent to the auditor's report date but if facts become known to the auditor after the report date that may have caused a revision to the report had they been known at that time, he or she should respond appropriately.

## Concluding Procedures

46. An opinion on the effectiveness of ICFR should be formed by evaluating evidence from all sources, including the auditor's control testing for the ICFR audit, any additional control testing performed for the financial statement audit, misstatements detected during the financial statement audit, and any identified deficiencies.

47. Review reports issued by internal auditors and others during the year that address ICFR controls and evaluate any deficiencies identified.

48. Evaluate the effect of the findings of substantive procedures performed in the financial statement audit on ICFR effectiveness, including:

   a. Risk assessments in connection with the selection and application of substantive procedures, especially those related to fraud;
   b. Findings regarding noncompliance with laws and regulations;
   c. Findings about related-party transactions and complex or unusual transactions;
   d. Indications of management bias in making accounting estimates and selecting accounting principles; and
   e. The nature and extent of misstatements detected by substantive procedures.

49. After forming an opinion on the effectiveness of the entity's ICFR, evaluate management's report to determine whether it contains:

   a. A statement regarding management's responsibility for ICFR;
   b. A description of the subject matter of the audit (e.g., controls over the preparation of the entity's financial statements in accordance with accounting principles generally accepted in the United States of America);
   c. An identification of the ICFR measurement criteria;
   d. Management's assessment about ICFR;
   e. A description of any material weaknesses; and
   f. The date as of which management's assessment about ICFR is made.

50. If any required element of management's report is incomplete or improperly presented, the auditor should request management revise its report.

51. Obtain written representations from management:

   a. Acknowledging management's responsibility for establishing and maintaining effective ICFR;
   b. Stating that management performed an assessment of the effectiveness of the entity's ICFR and specifying the criteria;
   c. Stating that management did not use the auditor's procedures performed during the integrated audit as part of the basis for its assessment;
   d. Stating management's assessment about the effectiveness of the entity's ICFR based on the criteria as of a specified date;
   e. Stating that management disclosed all deficiencies in ICFR design and operation to the auditor, including separate disclosure of any such deficiencies it believes to be significant deficiencies or material weaknesses;
   f. Describing any fraud resulting in a material misstatement to the entity's financial statements and any other fraud involving senior

management, management, or other employees with a significant role in the entity's ICFR;

g. Stating whether significant deficiencies and material weaknesses identified and communicated to management and those charged with governance during previous engagements have been resolved and specifically identifying any that have not; and

h. Stating whether, subsequent to the date being reported on, there were any changes in ICFR or conditions that might significantly affect ICFR, including any corrective actions taken by management with regard to significant deficiencies and material weaknesses.

52. If management does not provide the required written representations, the auditor should consider this a scope limitation and withdraw from the engagement or disclaim an opinion on ICFR and consider the implications on the financial statement audit.

53. Communicate in writing to management and those charged with governance significant deficiencies and material weaknesses identified during the integrated audit, including any remediated during the integrated audit and any previously communicated but not yet remediated.

54. If the auditor concludes that oversight of the entity's financial reporting and ICFR by the audit committee or similar committee was ineffective, he or she should communicate that conclusion in writing to the board of directors or similar governing body (see Exhibit AU-C 940-2 for an example of a written communication of significant deficiencies and material weaknesses).

55. The written communications in the previous two requirements should be made by the report release date. In the case of a governmental entity, if these written communications would be publicly available prior to management's report on ICFR, the entity's financial statements, and the auditor's report, the written communications should be made no later than 60 days following the report release date.

56. All deficiencies identified during the integrated audit should be communicated to management on a timely basis not to exceed 60 days after the report release date and those charged with governance should be informed of when such communication is expected to be made. Deficiencies that are not significant deficiencies or material weaknesses that were previously identified in written communication by the auditor or others within the entity are not required to be part of this communication.

57. The auditor's report should not indicate that no material weaknesses or less severe deficiencies were identified during the integrated audit because the auditor's report expresses an opinion on the effectiveness of the entity's ICFR and does not provide reasonable assurance that all deficiencies less severe than a material weakness have been identified.

## *Reporting on ICFR*

58. The auditor's written report on the ICFR audit should include the following elements (an example of a combined report on ICFR and the financial statements is included in Exhibit AU-C 940-1):

a. A title that indicates the auditor is *independent* to clearly indicate it is the report of an independent auditor.

b. An addressee that is appropriate.

c. A section titled "Opinion on Internal Control Over Financial Reporting" stating the auditor's opinion on whether the entity maintained, in all material respects, effective ICFR as of the specified date, based on the criteria. This section should identify the entity with a statement that the entity's internal control over financial reporting has been audited as of a specified date and it should refer to the criteria use to evaluate those controls. It should also include the auditor's opinion on whether the entity has maintained, in all material respects, effective ICFR as of the specified date based on the criteria.

d. A section titled "Basis for Opinion" that states the audit was conducted in accordance with GAAS and refers to the section of the auditor's report that describes the auditor's responsibilities under GAAS. This section should also include a statement acknowledging the auditor's responsibility to be independent of the entity and a statement that the auditor believes the audit evidence obtained is sufficient and appropriate to serve as the basis for the auditor's opinion.

e. A section titled "Responsibilities of Management for Internal Control over Financial Reporting" that includes statements that management is responsible for designing, implementing, and maintaining effective ICFR and for its assessment about the effectiveness of ICFR as well as a reference to management's report on ICFR.

f. A section titled "Responsibilities for the Audit of Internal Control Over Financial Reporting" that includes statements that:

  i. The objectives of the audit are to (1) obtain reasonable assurance about whether the effectiveness of ICFR was maintained in all material respects and (2) issue an auditor's report that includes the auditor's opinion on ICFR;

  ii. Reasonable assurance is a high level of assurance but is not absolute assurance and, therefore, is not a guarantee that an audit of ICFR in accordance with GAAS will always detect a material weakness when it exists; and

  iii. The audit conducted in accordance with auditing standards generally accepted in the United States of America requires the auditor to exercise professional judgment and maintain professional scepticism throughout the audit and requires the auditor to obtain an understanding of ICFR, assess the risks that a material misstatement exists, and test and evaluate the design and operating effectiveness of ICFR based on the assessed risks.

g. A section titled "Definition and Inherent Limitations of Internal Control over Financial Reporting" or other appropriate title that includes the definition of ICFR used by management in its report and a paragraph stating that inherent limitations mean ICFR may not prevent, or detect and correct, misstatements and projections of any assessment of effectiveness to future periods are subject to the risk that controls may become inadequate because of changes in conditions or deterioration of compliance with policies or procedures.

h. The manual or printed signature of the auditor's firm.

i. The city and state where the auditor's report is issued.

j. The date of the auditor's report.

59. If separate reports are issued on ICFR and the financial statements, the report on the audited financial statements report should include the following paragraph following the "Opinion" section of that report:

We also have audited, in accordance with auditing standards generally accepted in the United States of America, [*entity name*]'s internal control over financial reporting as of December 31, 20XX, based on [*identify criteria*] and our report dated [*date of report, which should be the same as the date of the report on the financial statements*] expressed [*include nature of opinion*].

The ICFR report should include the following paragraph within the section "Opinion on Internal Control Over Financial Reporting":

> We also have audited, in accordance with auditing standards generally accepted in the United States of America, the [*identify financial statements*] of [*entity name*] and our report dated [*date of report, which should be the same as the date of the report on ICFR*] expressed [*include nature of opinion*].

60. The ICFR report date should be no earlier than the date on which the auditor has obtained sufficient appropriate audit evidence, including evidence that the audit work performed has been reviewed, to support his or her opinion. Because the ICFR audit is integrated with the financial statement audit, the dates of the reports should be the same even if they are issued separately.

## Report Modifications

61. The ICFR report should be modified if any of the following conditions exist:

   a. One or more material weaknesses exist,
   b. Management's report has incomplete or improperly presented elements,
   c. There is a scope limitation on the engagement,
   d. The report references the report of a component auditor as part of the basis for the auditor's opinion, or
   e. Other information is contained in management's report.

## Adverse Opinions

62. Express an adverse opinion on the entity's ICFR if there are deficiencies that, individually or in combination, cause one or more material weaknesses as of the date specified in management's assessment about ICFR unless there is a scope limitation on the engagement.

63. When ICFR is not effective because material weaknesses exist, the auditor's report should define a material weakness and include a statement that one or more material weaknesses have been identified and reference the identification of material weaknesses described in management's assessment about ICFR.

64. If management's report does not include a known material weakness, the auditor's report should be modified to state that one or more material weaknesses have been identified but not included in management's report. A description of each material weakness should be included with specific information about its nature and its actual and potential effect on the presentation of the entity's financial statements issued during its existence. The auditor should communicate in writing to those charged with governance that one or more material weaknesses were not disclosed or identified in management's report.

If management's report includes all material weaknesses but disclosure is not fairly presented in all material respects, the auditor's report should state this conclusion and the information necessary to fairly describe each material weakness.

65. Determine the effect an adverse opinion on ICFR has on the financial statement opinion and disclose as a separate paragraph within the "Adverse

Opinion on Internal Control Over Financial Reporting" section of the report whether the auditor's opinion on the financial statements was affected by the material weakness.

## Management's Report has Incomplete or Improperly Presented Elements

66. If the auditor determines management's report has incomplete or improperly presented elements and management's report is not revised, the auditor should modify the report on ICFR to include an other-matter paragraph describing the reasons for his or her determination. If the issue is with fair presentation of a material weakness, the auditor's report should state that management's report does not fairly describe the material weakness, and the auditor should provide the information necessary to fairly describe each material weakness.

## Scope Limitations

67. If a scope limitation on the ICFR audit arises after accepting the integrated audit engagement, withdraw from the engagement or disclaim an opinion on ICFR and consider the implications on the financial statement audit.

68. Withdraw from the engagement if management refuses to furnish a written assessment about the effectiveness of ICFR. If withdrawal is not possible due to law or regulation, disclaim an opinion on ICFR and consider the implications on the financial statement audit.

69. In a disclaimer due to a scope limitation, the auditor should state that an opinion is not expressed on the effectiveness of ICFR and include the substantive reasons for the disclaimer. The procedures performed and statements describing the characteristics of an ICFR audit should not be included as their inclusion could overshadow the disclaimer.

70. If the auditor disclaims an opinion but has identified a material weakness, the auditor's report should define a material weakness and include statements that (1) if one or more material weaknesses exist, an entity's internal control over financial reporting cannot be considered effective and (2) one or more material weaknesses have been identified and an identification of the material weaknesses described in management's assessment about ICFR. The auditor should also provide users of the report with specific information about the nature of the material weakness and its actual and potential effect on the presentation of the financial statements issued during its existence, and whether the auditor's opinion on the financial statements was affected by the material weakness.

71. If an opinion cannot be expressed due to the scope limitation, the auditor should communicate in writing to management and those charged with governance that the ICFR audit cannot be completed.

## Referencing and Assuming Responsibility for the Work of a Component Auditor

72. AU-C 600 (*Special Considerations—Audits of Group Financial Statements (Including the Work of Component Auditors)*) requires the group engagement partner to evaluate whether sufficient appropriate audit evidence will be able to be obtained through the group engagement team's work or use of the work of component auditors to act as the auditor of and report on the ICFR of the group financial statements.

73. The group engagement partner should determine whether to refer to a component auditor in the ICFR report over group financial statements. A component auditor's audit should not be referenced unless the engagement partner determines the component auditor audited the component's ICFR in

accordance with the relevant requirements of GAAS (or those of the PCAOB, if applicable) and the component auditor's report on ICFR is not restricted as to use.

## *Additional Information*

74. When management includes additional information in its report or in a document containing its report beyond what the auditor is required to evaluate per paragraph 49, the auditor should:
    a. If the additional information is contained in management's report, read the additional information to identify material inconsistencies with management's report and remain alert for material misstatements of fact while reading the additional information.
    b. If the auditor identifies a material inconsistency or becomes aware of a material misstatement of fact, request management to correct the information and to do the following:
        i. Determine the correction has been made, if management agreed to make the correction.
        ii. Communicate the matter to those charged with governance, if management refuses to make the correction.
        iii. If after communicating with those charged with governance the correction is not made, the auditor should (*a*) consider the implications for the auditor's report and communicate with those charged with governance about how the auditor plans to address the material inconsistency or material misstatement of fact in the auditor's report, (*b*) withhold the auditor's report, or (*c*) withdraw from the engagement.
    c. Disclaim an opinion in an other-matters paragraph when any additional information is included in management's report and no material inconsistencies or material misstatements of fact are identified.

# Special Topics

## *Entities with Multiple Components*

75. The group engagement team should assess the risk of material misstatement to the financial statements of a component and correlate the amount of attention devoted to tests of controls on a component with the degree of risk.

76. Controls over specific risks that present a reasonable possibility of material misstatement to the group financial statements should be tested by the group engagement team or by a component auditor.

77. The nature, timing, and extent of tests of controls at components should vary from year to year.

78. The audit scope for equity method investment components should include controls over the reporting in the entity's financial statements, including investee income or loss, investment balance, adjustments to income or loss, and related disclosures.

79. The audit scope should include entities acquired on or before the date of management's assessment about ICFR and discontinued operations that are reported in accordance with the applicable financial reporting framework in the entity's financial statements.

80. Notwithstanding the immediately preceding discussion, if management excludes certain entities from its assessment, the auditor should evaluate whether that is appropriate using his or her judgment. If the auditor concludes it is appropriate, a statement should be included in the "Opinion on Internal Control Over Financial Reporting" or "Basis of Opinion" section of the report a disclosure similar to management's regarding the exclusion of an entity from management's assessment about ICFR and the auditor's audit of ICFR. The auditor should also evaluate the appropriateness of management's disclosure related to the exclusion.

81. If the auditor believes management's disclosure about the exclusion needs to be modified, he or she should communicate the matter first to the appropriate level of management and then to those charged with governance if management does not respond appropriately within a reasonable time period. If management and those charged with governance do not respond appropriately, the auditor's report on ICFR should be modified to include an other-matter paragraph describing the reasons why the auditor believes management's disclosure requires modification.

## *Use of Service Organizations*

82. The activities of a service organization should be considered if one is used by an entity in determining the evidence required to support the auditor's opinion on the effectiveness of an entity's ICFR.

83. Perform the procedures in AU-C 402 (*Audit Considerations Relating to an Entity Using a Service Organization*) on activities performed by a service organization. Evidence should be obtained that controls at the service organization relevant to the auditor's opinion on ICFR are operating effectively.

84. If the auditor plans to use a Type 2 report as audit evidence that controls are operating effectively, he or she should determine whether that report provides sufficient appropriate audit evidence about the effectiveness of the controls to support the auditor's opinion by evaluating:

   a. The time period covered by the tests of controls and its relation to the as of date;

   b. The scope of the service auditor's work, services and processes covered, controls tested, tests performed, and how tested controls relate to the entity's controls; and

   c. The results of those tests of controls and the service auditor's opinion on their operating effectiveness.

85. Determine whether complementary user entity controls identified in the Type 2 report are relevant in addressing the risks of material misstatement and, if so, evaluate the entity's design and implementation of the relevant controls and test their operating effectiveness.

86. In order for the Type 2 report to provide sufficient appropriate audit evidence to support the auditor's opinion on ICFR, the auditor should be satisfied as to the service auditor's professional competence and independence from the service organization and the adequacy of the standards under which the Type 2 report was issued.

87. Inquire of management whether any changes have been identified in the service organization's controls subsequent to the period covered by the service auditor's report. If changes have been identified, evaluate the effect of those changes on the effectiveness of the entity's ICFR. Also evaluate whether the results of other procedures performed indicate any changes in controls at the service organization.

88. Determine whether additional evidence about the operating effectiveness of controls at the service organization should be obtained based on procedures performed by management or the auditor and their results as well as consideration of the following risk factors:
   a. The time elapsed between the time period covered by the tests of controls in the service auditor's report and the as of date.
   b. The significance of the activities of the service organization.
   c. Whether errors have been identified in the service organization's processing.
   d. The nature and significance of any changes in the service organization's controls identified by management or the auditor.

89. Additional procedures should be performed when a significant period of time has elapsed between the time period covered by the tests of controls in the service auditor's report and the as of date to obtain sufficient appropriate audit evidence about the operating effectiveness of the controls at the service organization relevant to the auditor's opinion on ICFR.

90. The auditor should not refer to the service auditor's report when expressing an opinion on ICFR.

### Benchmarking of Automated Controls

91. To determine whether to use benchmarking for testing an automated application control, assess the following risk factors: the extent to which the application control is stable and can be matched to a defined program within an application; and the availability and reliability of a report of the compilation dates of the programs placed in production.

92. Obtain evidence to determine that the automated application control has not changed when using a benchmarking strategy.

93. The baseline of the operation of an automated application control should be reestablished after a period of time. To determine when to reestablish a baseline, evaluate:
   a. The effectiveness of the IT control environment, including controls over application and system software acquisition and maintenance, access controls, and computer operations;
   b. The auditor's understanding of the nature of any changes on the specific programs containing the controls;
   c. The nature and timing of other related tests;
   d. The consequences of errors associated with the benchmarked application control; and
   e. Whether the control is sensitive to other business factors that may have changed.

## Analysis and Application of Procedures

### ICFR Audit Preconditions

An auditor may accept an engagement to report on an entity's internal control only if the following conditions are satisfied:

- Management accepts responsibility for the effectiveness of ICFR.
- Management evaluates the effectiveness of ICFR using a suitable and available control framework.

- Management supports its assessment of the effectiveness of ICFR with sufficient appropriate evidence.
- Management provides a report on the effectiveness of ICFR that accompanies the auditor's report.

---

**PUBLIC COMPANY IMPLICATION:** As a result of the issuance of AS-2201 by the PCAOB, the guidance in AU-C 940 only applies to reporting on an entity's ICFR for nonpublic companies. AU-C 940 largely converges the standards for reporting on ICFR for nonpublic companies with the guidance on reporting on ICFR for public companies as contained in AS-2201.

---

**PUBLIC COMPANY IMPLICATION:** PCAOB Staff Audit Practice Alert No. 11 (*Considerations for Audits of Internal Control over Financial Reporting*) identifies common deficiencies in audits of ICFR, and highlights factors for auditors to consider when performing audits of ICFR. Common inspection deficiencies related to ICFR audits include the auditor's failure to (1) identify and sufficiently test controls relevant to the risk of material misstatement, (2) sufficiently test the design and operating effectiveness of management review controls, (3) sufficiently update the results from testing controls at an interim date to year-end, (4) sufficiently test controls over system-generated data, (5) adequately test the work of others, and (6) adequately evaluate identified control deficiencies. The Audit Practice Alert provides guidance to auditors in risk assessment, selecting controls to test, testing management review controls, testing information technology controls (including controls over systems-generated data and reports), roll-forward testing of controls, using the work of others, and evaluating identified control deficiencies.

---

Management is responsible for documenting its controls and related control objectives, and the documentation serves as a basis for management's internal control assertion. The extent of the documentation needed depends on the size and complexity of the entity. Examples of documentation include (1) policy and accounting manuals, (2) narrative memoranda, (3) flowcharts, (4) decision tables, (5) procedural write-ups, and (6) questionnaires.

Management's monitoring activities also provide evidence as to the design and operating effectiveness of ICFR. Monitoring includes periodically testing and assessing controls, identifying and reporting deficiencies to appropriate individuals in the entity, and taking necessary corrective action. Monitoring can be performed through ongoing activities or separate evaluations.

---

**ENGAGEMENT STRATEGY:** Although management is responsible for the documentation of its internal control, the auditor may be engaged to help management identify the methods they are using to document the controls.

---

**PUBLIC COMPANY IMPLICATION:** The extent to which the auditor can be used to help management document internal controls for a public company is more limited than for private companies. Documentation assistance must be preapproved by the audit committee only after the audit committee carefully considers whether the auditor's involvement in documenting controls would impair the auditor's independence, either in fact or in appearance.

---

ICFR is typically examined as of the end of the entity's fiscal year; however, management may retain the auditor to examine ICFR as of a date other than year-end. Regardless of the date selected, the ICFR audit is required to be integrated with a financial statement audit as of the date specified in management's assessment.

Appropriate criteria against which the effectiveness of the entity's ICFR can be evaluated must be relevant, objective, measurable, and complete, not omitting any relevant factors. The *Internal Control-Integrated Framework* (2013), issued by the Committee of Sponsoring Organizations of the Treadway Commission (2013 COSO framework), and the U.S. Government Accountability Office's *Standards for Internal Control in the Federal Government* (the Green Book) provide suitable and available criteria. If other criteria selected are available only to specified parties, AU-C 905 (*Alert That Restricts the Use of the Auditor's Written Communication*) requires the auditor's report to include an other-matter paragraph restricting the use of the auditor's report.

### Integrating the ICFR Audit with the Financial Statement Audit

The auditor's conclusions about ICFR should affect the financial statement audit. Specifically, the nature, timing, and extent of audit procedures in the financial statement audit should reflect conclusions about the effectiveness of the client's ICFR. In addition, the auditor's findings during the financial statement audit should affect the audit of ICFR; for example, areas where misstatements are identified may suggest that internal control in that area is not effective.

---

**PLANNING AID REMINDER:** Although the ICFR audit should affect (be integrated with) the financial statement audit and vice versa, the auditor typically needs to test more controls in order to issue an ICFR opinion than would be tested when only expressing an opinion on the financial statements.

---

**PLANNING AID REMINDER:** Regardless of the assessed level of risk, the auditor should perform substantive procedures for all relevant assertions for each material account balance, transaction class, and disclosure. Therefore, even if inherent risk is low and internal control is effective, the auditor must still perform some substantive procedures for material account balances, transaction classes, and disclosures.

---

**OBSERVATION:** AU-C 940 requires that an examination of ICFR be integrated with the audit of financial statements. For insured depository institutions (IDIs) subject to Section 112 of the Federal Deposit Insurance Corporation Improvement Act (FDICIA), ICFR includes controls over the preparation of the IDI's financial statements in accordance with U.S. GAAP and with the instructions to the Consolidated Financial Statements for Bank Holding Companies. ICFR also includes controls over preparation of the IDI's schedules equivalent to the basic financial statements in accordance with the Federal Financial Institutions Examination Council Instructions for Consolidated Reports of Condition and Income (Call Report Instructions).

## Planning the ICFR Audit

Proper planning of the engagement requires that the auditor consider factors that may be relevant to forming an opinion related to the entity's ICFR, such as:

- Knowledge of the entity's ICFR based on previous engagements.
- Matters affecting the entity's industry (e.g., financial reporting practices, economic conditions, laws and regulations, and technological changes).
- Matters affecting the entity's business (e.g., organization, operating characteristics, and capital structure).
- The effect of recent changes to the entity, its operations, or its ICFR.
- The auditor's preliminary judgments about materiality and risk.
- Deficiencies previously communicated to management or those charged with governance.
- Legal or regulatory matters affecting the entity.
- The type and extent of available evidence related to assessing ICFR.
- Preliminary judgments about the effectiveness of ICFR.
- Public information about the entity related to the risk of material financial statement misstatements and about the effectiveness of ICFR.
- Knowledge about entity risks obtained as part of the client acceptance and retention process.
- The relative complexity of the entity.

The nature of an entity's controls varies based on its size and complexity, and the documentation of controls is typically more extensive for a larger, more complex entity than for a smaller, less complex one. The auditor should adjust (scale) the risk-based audit approach accordingly. Factors to consider in assessing the complexity of an entity include (1) the number of business lines, (2) the complexity of business processes and financial reporting systems, (3) the relative degree of centralization of the accounting function, (4) involvement by senior management in the day-to-day activities of the business, and (5) the number of levels of management. One additional factor that the practitioner should consider when planning the engagement is the extent to which the internal control is documented.

**IMPORTANT NOTICE FOR 2022:** In May 2019, the AICPA's Auditing Standards Board (ASB) issued SAS No. 135 titled *Omnibus Statement on Auditing Standards—2019* that includes amendments to various AU-C sections, including AU-C 940. SAS No. 135 adds to AU-C 940 to emphasize consideration of significant unusual transactions, particularly controls over significant unusual transactions. Originally, the effective date of SAS No. 135 was for audits of financial statements periods ending on or after December 15, 2020, with early application **not** permitted. However, the ASB's issuance of SAS No. 141, *Amendment to the Effective Dates of SAS Nos. 134-140*, extended the effective date to December 15, 2021, in order to provide more time for firms to implement SAS No. 135 in light of the effect of the coronavirus pandemic. While SAS No. 141 allows for early implementation of SAS No. 135, the ASB recommends that SAS Nos. 134-140 be implemented concurrently.

---

The auditor is specifically required to analyze fraud risk in an audit of ICFR. The auditor should address whether controls adequately address the risk of material misstatement due to fraud and to management override of controls. Controls that might be responsive to fraud risks include:

- Controls over significant unusual transactions, particularly those that occur late in the period or via unusual journal entries;
- Controls over journal entries and adjustments made as part of the period-end financial reporting process;
- Controls over related-party transactions;
- Controls related to significant management estimates; and
- Controls that reduce managerial incentives or pressures to falsify reported financial results.

In an audit of ICFR, the auditor may use work performed by, or receive direct assistance from, internal auditors, entity personnel other than internal auditors, and outside parties working under the direction of management and those charged with governance. In determining how extensively the auditor can rely on the work of others, he or she is to assess the competence and objectivity of other parties that the auditor is considering relying upon. There is a direct relation between reliance and competence and objectivity. Given a higher assessed level of competence and objectivity, the auditor can place greater reliance on work performed by others. In addition, the more audit risk in an area, the greater the need for the auditor to directly perform work on the control and the less reliance that can be placed on the work of others.

### Using a Top-Down Approach

In planning an audit of ICFR, the auditor is to use a top-down approach in identifying risks and controls to test. A top-down approach:

- Begins with controls at the financial statement level;
- Uses the auditor's understanding of overall risks to ICFR;
- Focuses on entity-level controls;
- Works down to controls related to significant accounts and disclosures and related assertions;
- Focuses attention on classes of transactions, accounts, disclosures, and assertions that present a reasonable possibility of material misstatement of the financial statements;

- Verifies the auditor's understanding of the risks in the entity's processes; and
- Selects controls for testing that sufficiently address the assessed risk of material misstatement to each relevant assertion.

*Entity-level controls*

The auditor's evaluation of entity-level controls can change the amount of audit effort needed in testing controls at the account and transaction level (i.e., referred to as control activities in COSO's internal control framework). Entity-level controls include (1) controls related to the control environment, (2) controls related to management override, (3) the entity's risk assessment process, (4) centralized processing and controls, (5) controls that monitor the results of operations, (6) controls to monitor other controls (e.g., internal audit, those charged with governance), (7) controls over the period-end financial reporting process, and (8) programs and controls that address significant business risks.

---

**PLANNING CONSIDERATION:** Controls over management override may be particularly important at a smaller, less complex entity due to senior management's increased involvement in performing controls and in the period-end financial reporting process.

---

Entity-level controls vary in nature and precision. Some entity-level controls, such as certain control environment controls, have only an indirect effect on prevention, detection, or correction of misstatements but may affect the controls selected by the auditor for testing and the tests performed on those controls. Some entity-level controls monitor the effectiveness of other controls and may, when operating effectively, allow for reduced testing of other controls. Some entity-level controls may operate to adequately prevent, or detect and correct, on a timely basis misstatements to relevant assertions, in which case additional controls would not need to be tested related to that risk.

*Evaluating ICFR components*

ICFR is often considered to have five components necessary to an effective ICFR system: (1) control environment, (2) risk assessment, (3) control activities, (4) information and communication, and (5) monitoring activities. The 2013 COSO framework includes principles related to each component that are suitable to all entities. The framework makes the presumption that all principles are relevant and states that management must support a determination that a principle is not relevant with a description of how the associated component is present and functioning in the principle's absence. The guidance that follows is applicable when management uses the 2013 COSO framework. If management uses the Green Book or another framework, the guidance that follows may be adapted as necessary. The principles described below for each component of the ICFR system are relevant to the auditor's evaluation of whether that component is present and functioning in the design, implementation, and operation of ICFR to achieve the entity's financial reporting objectives.

Relevant control environment principles include:
- The entity demonstrates a commitment to integrity and ethical values;
- Those charged with governance demonstrate independence from management and exercise oversight of the development and performance of ICFR in the context of the entity's governance structure (those charged with governance and management may be the same people in smaller entities, in which case independence may not be a necessary requirement);
- Management establishes, with oversight of those charged with governance, structure, reporting lines, and appropriate authorities and responsibilities to achieve the entity's financial reporting objectives;
- The entity demonstrates commitment to attracting, developing, and retaining competent individuals in alignment with the entity's financial reporting objectives; and
- The entity holds individuals accountable for their ICFR responsibilities in pursuit of the entity's financial reporting objectives.

Relevant risk assessment principles include:
- The entity specifies clear financial reporting objectives enabling the identification and assessment of risks related to those objectives;
- The entity identifies and analyzes risks to the entity's achievement of financial reporting objectives to determine how the risks should be managed;
- The entity considers the potential for fraud in assessing risks to the achievement of financial reporting objectives; and
- The entity identifies and assesses changes that could significantly impact ICFR.

Relevant control activity principles to the audit of ICFR include:
- The entity selects and develops control activities that help mitigate risks to achievement of financial reporting objectives to acceptable levels;
- The entity selects and develops general control activities over technology to support achievement of financial reporting objectives; and
- The entity deploys control activities through policies and procedures.

Relevant control activities include those related to each significant class of transactions, account balance, and disclosure, and its relevant assertions.

Relevant information and communication principles include:
- The entity obtains or generates and uses relevant quality information to support ICFR functioning;
- The entity internally communicates information, including financial reporting objectives and responsibilities, necessary to support ICFR functioning; and
- The entity communicates with external parties regarding matters affecting ICFR functioning.

Relevant monitoring principles include:
- The entity selects, develops, and performs ongoing or separate evaluations to determine whether internal control components are present and functioning; and
- The entity evaluates and communicates ICFR deficiencies in a timely manner to those responsible for taking corrective action, including senior management and those charged with governance.

---

**PRACTICE POINTER:** Since the annual period-end financial reporting process occurs after the as of date, controls related to this process often cannot be tested until after the as of date.

---

*Identify significant classes of transactions, account balances, and disclosures, and their relevant assertions*

To perform an effective audit of ICFR, the auditor should identify the client's significant classes of transactions, accounts balances, and disclosures and their relevant assertions. Relevant risks include:
- Size and composition;
- Susceptibility to misstatement due to error or fraud;
- Nature of the account, transaction class, or disclosure;
- Volume of activity and the complexity of transactions;
- Accounting and reporting complexities;
- Exposure to losses;
- Possibility of significant contingent liabilities;
- Existence of related-party transactions; and
- Changes from the prior period.

The accounts, transaction classes, and disclosures, and their relevant assertions identified in an ICFR audit also pertain to a financial statement audit and are therefore the same in an integrated audit.

---

**PRACTICE POINTER:** The components comprising accounts, transaction classes, and disclosures may be subject to significantly different risks and, if this is the case, different controls, responsive to these different risks, should be in place.

---

*Understanding likely sources of misstatement*

Performing a walk-through is often the best way to understand the likely sources of misstatement. A walk-through involves following a transaction from initiation through the entity's processes until it is reflected in the financial records. In addition, a walk-through includes questioning entity personnel about their understanding of procedures and controls, especially at those points where important processing procedures occur. Walk-throughs also include observing the operation of controls, inspecting relevant documents, and, in some cases, reperforming controls. These procedures allow the auditor to understand the process sufficiently to identify points where a necessary control may be missing or designed ineffectively.

> **PLANNING CONSIDERATION:** Inquiry alone is not sufficient to achieve the objective of understanding likely sources of potential misstatements.

Identifying risks and controls within IT is not a separate process; rather, it is integrated in the top-down approach.

*Selecting controls to test*

Determination of which controls should be tested depends on which controls, individually or in combination, sufficiently address the assessed risk of material misstatement to a relevant assertion. One control may address the assessed risk of material misstatement for multiple assertions or it may take multiple controls to address the assessed risk of material misstatement for a single assertion.

## Testing Controls

*Evaluating design effectiveness*

Design effectiveness can be tested using inquiry, observation, and inspection of relevant documentation. Walk-throughs that incorporate the foregoing procedures are often sufficient for evaluating design effectiveness. Control objectives may be achieved differently in smaller, less complex entities; for example, fewer accounting employees could limit the ability to segregate duties and cause the entity to use different controls to meet its control objectives.

*Testing operating effectiveness*

In testing the operating effectiveness of ICFR, the tests should be designed to determine (1) how the control was applied, (2) whether the control was applied consistently, and (3) who applied the control. The auditor can make these determinations by applying a variety of examination procedures, including inquiry, inspection of documents, observation of activities, and reapplication or reperformance of internal control procedures. Inquiry is not sufficient by itself; the guidance in AU-C 330 (*Performing Audit Procedures in Response to Assessed Risks and Evaluating the Audit Evidence Obtained*) provides guidance on what procedures might be appropriate in combination with inquiry to test the operating effectiveness of controls.

In assessing the competence of those responsible for an entity's financial reporting and associated controls, the auditor can take into consideration the competence of any third parties that assist in financial reporting functions for the entity as well as the competence of entity personnel.

*Match evidence to risk*

The audit evidence needed depends on the risk associated with the control (more risk, more evidence needed; less risk, less evidence). It generally takes less evidence to conclude a control is not effective than it does to conclude a control is operating effectively.

The risk associated with a control includes the risk that the control is not effective and, if the control is not effective, the risk that a material weakness exists. Factors affecting the risk associated with a control include:
- Nature and materiality of the misstatements that the control addresses;
- Inherent risk associated with the account and assertions;
- Changes in the volume or nature of transactions;
- The account's history of errors;
- Effectiveness of entity-level controls;
- Nature of the control;
- Frequency of the control's operation (e.g., daily, weekly, monthly, etc.);
- Extent to which the control relies on the effectiveness of other controls;
- Competence of the personnel performing the control or monitoring performance, and whether there has been turnover in these individuals;
- Whether the control is manual or automated; and
- Complexity of the control, and extent of judgment needed to apply the control.

> **PRACTICE POINTER:** A smaller, less complex entity may have simple information systems that use off-the-shelf packaged software. Assuming no modifications, the auditor's tests of IT controls may simply focus on the application controls built into the packaged software, assuming that the entity's IT general controls are effective.

*Determine nature, timing, and extent of testing*

The auditor should vary the nature, timing, and extent of his or her testing in response to the risk associated with a control.

> **ENGAGEMENT STRATEGY:** The absence of misstatements in an account balance, transaction class, or disclosure related to a control does not necessarily mean that the control is effective. A control should be tested directly in order to conclude that it is effective. However, the absence of misstatements can affect the auditor's risk assessment and determination of what testing is needed to conclude on the control's operating effectiveness.

The nature of testing relates to the type of auditing procedures performed. Not all auditing procedures are equally effective. Generally, the quality of audit evidence obtained follows this descending order: (1) reperformance, including recalculation, (2) inspection of relevant documentation, (3) observation, and (4) inquiry. Exclusive reliance on inquiry, given that inquiry generally provides the weakest form of evidence, is insufficient for testing a control.

> **ENGAGEMENT STRATEGY:** The nature of evidence gathered depends on the extent of the client's documentation of control procedures. Some controls (e.g., tone at the top, management's philosophy and operating style) do not provide

documentary evidence, and the lack of documentary evidence may be more pronounced in smaller entities. In cases where documentary evidence is lacking, the auditor may have to rely on inquiry, observation of activities, and review of less formal documentation. Where inquiry is an important procedure, the auditor may want to consider asking similar questions of multiple individuals, including client personnel in operating positions.

Testing may identify control deviations, instances where controls do not operate as designed. The existence of a control deviation should be evaluated by the auditor to determine whether the entity is still able to effectively achieve its control objectives.

Testing controls over a longer period of time provides more evidence than testing controls over a shorter period of time. Testing controls closer to the as of date provides more evidence than testing controls earlier in the year, although controls have to be tested over a period that is long enough to assess their operating effectiveness. In addition, the more extensively (i.e., sample size) a control is tested, the more evidence the testing provides.

An entity may remediate control deficiencies during the year. If sufficient time remains in the year to test the design and operating effectiveness of the remediated control, the auditor does not have to test the superseded control for the ICFR audit; however, he or she does need to consider the effect of deficiencies in the superseded control in planning the financial statement audit.

An auditor may test the operating effectiveness of a control as of an interim date and desire to roll forward his or her conclusion to the period-end date. The auditor needs more evidence as to the continuing effectiveness of the control if (1) the risks associated with the control are greater, (2) the evidence obtained about the control's operating effectiveness at the interim date was limited, (3) there is a longer period of time between the interim date and the year-end date, and (4) changes have occurred in internal control since the interim date. Inquiry alone may be sufficient as a roll-forward procedure if the factors above suggest there is a low risk that controls are no longer effective.

*Subsequent years' audits*

Factors affecting the risk of a control in subsequent years' audits include the control risk factors previously described as well as the nature, timing, and extent of procedures performed in prior audits; the results from prior years' testing of the control; and whether changes have occurred in the control or its operations since the prior audit. Consideration of these factors could lead the auditor to reduce risk from the prior year and reduce testing or conversely to increase risk and the associated testing required.

*Identifying deficiencies in ICFR*

The severity of an identified deficiency depends on the magnitude of the potential misstatement as a result of the deficiency and the likelihood that a misstatement will occur as a result of the deficiency. Factors that affect the magnitude of a potential misstatement are (1) the financial statement amounts or transaction totals affected by the deficiency and (2) the volume of activity in the account or transaction class affected by the deficiency. In evaluating deficiencies, the auditor should recognize that the likelihood of a small misstatement is greater than the likelihood of a large misstatement. Also, the maximum amount by which an account can be overstated is generally the account's recorded balance; accounts can be understated by more than the recorded amount. Factors that affect the likelihood of a misstatement are:

- Nature of accounts, transactions, disclosures, and assertions;
- Cause and frequency of exceptions detected as a result of ICFR deficiencies;
- Susceptibility of related asset or liability to loss or fraud;
- Subjectivity, complexity, and judgment involved with the account;
- Relation of the control to other controls;
- Interaction among the deficiencies;
- Possible future consequences of the deficiency; and
- The importance of controls to the financial reporting process (e.g., controls related to monitoring, fraud, selection and application of significant accounting policies, related-party transactions, significant nonroutine transactions, period-end financial reporting process).

**PLANNING AID REMINDER:** The severity of a deficiency does not depend on whether a misstatement has already occurred.

Multiple deficiencies that affect the same class of transactions, account, disclosure, assertion, or internal control component increases the likelihood that a material weakness exists. In some cases, clients have a second control that compensates for a deficiency in the tested control. A compensating control can limit the severity of an identified deficiency (in the tested control) and thereby prevent the deficiency from rising to the level of a significant deficiency or material weakness. However, a compensating control does not eliminate the underlying deficiency. In order for a compensating control to mitigate a control deficiency, it must operate at a level of precision sufficient to prevent, or detect and timely correct, a material misstatement in the financial statements.

There are certain indicators that suggest that a material weakness may exist:

- Identification of fraud committed by senior management, regardless of materiality.
- Restatements of previously issued financial statements to correct a material misstatement due to error or fraud.
- Identification of a material misstatement by the auditor in the financial statements being audited that was not detected by management (i.e., the auditor is not part of the client's internal control system).
- Ineffective oversight of financial reporting and internal control by those charged with governance.

> **PLANNING AID REMINDER:** When a material weakness exists, the auditor should report directly on the effectiveness of internal control rather than on the written assertion.

## Concluding Procedures

*Obtaining written representations*

> **PLANNING AID REMINDER:** Sometimes practitioners draft a representation letter for management to develop and sign; however, when doing so, practitioners should make sure that management understands the content that is in the representation letter before signing it and presenting it to the accountant. The accountant should consider discussing the content of the letter with management before management signs the letter and should also consider documenting that discussion in the working papers.

*Communicating ICFR-related matters*

The auditor is to communicate in writing to management and those charged with governance all significant deficiencies and material weaknesses identified during the integrated audit. If any of these significant deficiencies or material weaknesses were previously communicated, the auditor can simply refer to the communication by date.

> **PLANNING AID REMINDER:** AU-C 265 (*Communicating Internal Control Related Matters Identified in an Audit*) does not apply to integrated audits.

The entity may be able to remediate internal control deficiencies during the year if it receives timely communication. Therefore, the auditor can orally communicate to management significant internal control matters. However, oral communication does not eliminate the auditor's responsibility to communicate significant deficiencies and material weaknesses in writing, even if the matters are remediated during the year.

Whereas a financial statement audit requires written communication of only significant deficiencies and material weaknesses, all identified deficiencies must be communicated in writing in an ICFR audit even if they are not significant deficiencies or material weaknesses because the focus of an ICFR audit is on identifying ICFR deficiencies. The auditor's communication only needs to include identified deficiencies as all deficiencies may not have been identified through audit procedures performed.

## Reporting on ICFR

If an audit is also conducted in accordance with *Government Auditing Standards*, the auditor may state that the audit was conducted in accordance with the auditing standards generally accepted in the United States and the standards applicable to financial audits contained in the *Government Auditing Standards* issued by the Comptroller General of the United States. If the audit report refers to *Government Auditing Standards* and significant ICFR deficiencies are identified, the auditor is required to add the following other-matter paragraphs to the report:

> In accordance with *Government Auditing Standards*, we are required to report findings of significant deficiencies. A significant deficiency is a deficiency, or a combination of deficiencies, in internal control that is less severe than a material weakness, yet important enough to merit attention by those charged with governance. We consider the deficiencies in XYZ Company's internal control described below [*or in the accompanying schedule of findings*] to be significant deficiencies.
>
> *Government Auditing Standards* require the auditor to perform limited procedures on XYZ Company's response, described below [*or in the accompanying schedule of findings*] to the findings identified in our audit of internal control over financial reporting. XYZ Company's response was not subjected to the other auditing procedures applied in the audit of internal control over financial reporting and, accordingly, we express no opinion on the response.

## Report Modifications

*Adverse opinions and scope limitations*

AU-C 705 (*Modifications to the Opinion in the Independent Auditor's Report*) provides guidance on adverse opinions and disclaimers of opinion for financial statement audits that can be adapted and applied to ICFR audits as needed.

A scope limitation is due to the auditor being unable to obtain sufficient appropriate audit evidence, which could occur due to circumstances beyond the entity's control, circumstances related to the nature and timing of the auditor's work, or limitations imposed by management. If the auditor determines insufficient appropriate audit evidence will be available and an opinion will not be able to be expressed, no additional work is required to be performed prior to issuing a disclaimer of opinion. If the auditor withdraws from the integrated audit, he or she may still be engaged to audit the financial statements. If this is the case, knowledge obtained in the integrated audit should be considered when deciding whether to accept an engagement or when performing the financial statement audit.

*Referencing and Assuming Responsibility for the Work of a Component Auditor*

It is important to note that the group engagement partner's decision whether to reference or assume responsibility for the work of a component auditor in the ICFR report over the group financial statements may be different from the same decision over the entity's financial statement audit.

*Additional Information*

The auditor is to disclaim an opinion on additional information included in management's report by adding an additional last paragraph to the auditor's standard ICFR report.

> **PLANNING AID REMINDER:** The last paragraph may be worded as follows: "We did not perform auditing procedures on [*describe additional information, such as management's cost-benefit statement*], and accordingly, we do not express an opinion or provide any assurance on it."

## Special Topics

*Entities with multiple components*

There may be some situations where the auditor determines it is appropriate for management to limit its assessment by excluding certain entities, such as recently acquired entities for which management has not had sufficient time to assess controls. However, management should not exclude a recently acquired entity from its assessment for more than one year from the acquisition date or for more than one annual management report on ICFR. Law or regulations may also specify other situations where it may be appropriate for management to exclude entities from its assessment and provide guidance as to any necessary disclosures.

*Use of service organizations*

AU-C 402 provides guidance for auditors when the entity being audited uses a service organization. AU-C 402 identifies situations when the service organization's services and controls are part of a user entity's information system, in which case they are also part of the user entity's ICFR.

Procedures for obtaining evidence of whether relevant service organization controls are operating effectively include one or more of the following: (1) obtaining and reading a Type 2 report, or (2) performing or using another auditor to perform appropriate tests of controls at the service organization. A Type 1 report does not include a description of tests of controls or their results or the service auditor's opinion on the operating effectiveness of controls, and, therefore, does not provide evidence in the ICFR audit of the operating effectiveness of controls.

If the auditor determines additional evidence about operating effectiveness of controls at the service organization is required, he or she may evaluate procedures performed by management and their results, contact the service organization through the user entity to obtain specific information, request a service auditor perform procedures to supply the needed information, or visit the service organization and perform audit procedures.

Changes in a service organization's controls subsequent to the period covered by the service auditor's report that the auditor may need to evaluate include:

- Changes communicated to management from the service organization;
- Changes in personnel with whom management interacts at the service organization;
- Changes in design or implementation controls necessary to achieve control objectives;

- Changes in reports or other data received from the service organization;
- Changes in contracts or service level agreements; and
- Errors identified in the service organization's processing, identified noncompliance with laws and regulations, or fraud.

*Benchmarking of automated controls*

For many clients, automated controls are increasingly important. Automated controls are generally less susceptible to human failure and therefore can allow for a benchmarking strategy to be applied. Benchmarking is the process of testing an automated application control to establish a baseline that, with effective IT general controls, can provide the auditor with sufficient evidence that the control is effective without performing tests of operating effectiveness. Benchmarking can be especially suitable for controls with low risk factors and for entities using purchased software with low risk of program changes.

## Practitioner's Aids

The following exhibits are presented in this section:

- Exhibit AU-C 940-1—Combined Report Expressing an Unmodified Opinion on ICFR and on the Financial Statements
- Exhibit AU-C 940-2—Written Communication of Significant Deficiencies and Material Weaknesses

## EXHIBIT AU-C 940-1—COMBINED REPORT EXPRESSING AN UNMODIFIED OPINION ON ICFR AND ON THE FINANCIAL STATEMENTS

### INDEPENDENT AUDITOR'S REPORT

[*Appropriate Addressee*]

**Report on the Financial Statements and Internal Control Over Financial Reporting**

We have audited the financial statements of W Company, which comprise the balance sheet as of December 31, 20XX, and the related statements of income, changes in stockholders' equity, and cash flows for the year then ended, and the related notes to the financial statements. In our opinion, the accompanying financial statements present fairly, in all material respects, the financial position of W Company as of December 31, 20XX, and the results of its operations and its cash flows for the year then ended in accordance with accounting principles generally accepted in the United States of America.

We have also audited W Company's internal control over financial reporting as of December 31, 20XX, based on [*identify criteria*]. In our opinion, W Company maintained, in all material respects, effective internal control over financial reporting as of December 31, 20XX, based on [*identify criteria*].

**Basis for Opinions**

We conducted our audits in accordance with auditing standards generally accepted in the United States of America (GAAS). Our responsibilities under those standards are further described in the "Auditor's Responsibilities for the Audits of the Financial Statements and Internal Control Over Financial Reporting" section of our report. We are required to be independent of W Company and to meet our other ethical responsibilities, in accordance with the relevant ethical requirements relating to our audits. We believe that the audit evidence we have obtained is sufficient and appropriate to provide a basis for our audit opinions.

**Responsibilities of Management for the Financial Statements and Internal Control over Financial Reporting**

Management is responsible for the preparation and fair presentation of the financial statements in accordance with accounting principles generally accepted in the United States of America, and for the design, implementation, and maintenance of effective internal control over financial reporting relevant to the preparation and fair presentation of financial statements that are free from material misstatement, whether due to fraud or error. Management is also responsible for its assessment about the effectiveness of internal control over financial reporting, included in the accompanying [*title of management's report*].

In preparing the financial statements, management is required to evaluate whether there are conditions or events, considered in the aggregate, that raise substantial doubt about W Company's ability to continue as a going concern [*insert the time period set by the applicable financial reporting framework*].

**Auditor's Responsibilities for the Audits of the Financial Statements and Internal Control Over Financial Reporting**

Our objectives are to obtain reasonable assurance about whether the financial statements as a whole are free from material misstatement whether due to fraud or error, and about whether effective internal control over financial reporting was maintained in all material respects, and to issue an auditor's report that includes our opinions.

Reasonable assurance is a high level of assurance but is not absolute assurance and, therefore, is not a guarantee that an audit of financial statements or an audit of internal control over financial reporting conducted in accordance with GAAS will always detect a material misstatement or a material weakness when it exists. The risk of not detecting a material misstatement resulting from fraud is higher than for one resulting from error, as fraud may involve collusion, forgery, intentional omissions, misrepresentations, or the override of internal control. Misstatements are considered to be material if there is a substantial likelihood that, individually or in the aggregate, they would influence the judgment made by a reasonable user based on the financial statements.

In performing an audit of financial statements and an audit of internal control over financial reporting in accordance with GAAS, we:

- Exercise professional judgment and maintain professional skepticism throughout the audits.

- Identify and assess the risks of material misstatement of the financial statements, whether due to fraud or error, and design and perform audit procedures responsive to those risks. Such procedures include examining, on a test basis, evidence regarding the amounts and disclosures in the financial statements.

- Obtain an understanding of internal control relevant to the financial statement audit in order to design audit procedures that are appropriate in the circumstances.

- Obtain an understanding of internal control over financial reporting relevant to the audit of internal control over financial reporting, assess the risks that a material weakness exists, and test and evaluate the design and operating effectiveness of internal control over financial reporting based on the assessed risk.

- Evaluate the appropriateness of accounting policies used and the reasonableness of significant accounting estimates made by management, as well as evaluate the overall presentation of the financial statements.

- Conclude whether, in our judgment, there are conditions or events, considered in the aggregate, that raise substantial doubt about W Company's ability to continue as a going concern for a reasonable period of time.

We are required to communicate with those charged with governance regarding, among other matters, the planned scope and timing of the audit, significant audit findings, and certain internal control-related matters that we identified during the financial statement audit.

### Definition and Inherent Limitations of Internal Control over Financial Reporting

An entity's internal control over financial reporting is a process effected by those charged with governance, management, and other personnel, designed to provide reasonable assurance regarding the preparation of reliable financial statements in accordance with accounting principles generally accepted in the United States of America. An entity's internal control over financial reporting includes those policies and procedures that (1) pertain to the maintenance of records that, in reasonable detail, accurately and fairly reflect the transactions and dispositions of the assets of the entity; (2) provide reasonable assurance that transactions are recorded as necessary to permit preparation of financial statements in accordance with accounting principles generally accepted in the United States of America, and that receipts and expenditures of the entity are being made only in accordance with authorizations of management and those charged with governance; and (3) provide reasonable assurance regarding prevention, or timely detection and correction of unauthorized acquisition, use, or disposition of the entity's assets that could have a material effect on the financial statements.

Because of its inherent limitations, internal control over financial reporting may not prevent, or detect and correct, misstatements. Also, projections of any assessment of effectiveness to future periods are subject to the risk that controls may become inadequate because of changes in conditions, or that the degree of compliance with the policies or procedures may deteriorate.

### Report on Other Legal and Regulatory Requirements

[*Form and content of this section of the auditor's report will vary depending on the nature of the auditor's other reporting responsibilities.*]

[*Signature of the auditor's firm*]

[*City and state where the auditor's report is issued*]

[*Date of the auditor's report*]

## EXHIBIT AU-C 940-2—WRITTEN COMMUNICATION OF SIGNIFICANT DEFICIENCIES AND MATERIAL WEAKNESSES

To Management and [identify the body of individuals charged with governance, such as the entity's board of directors] of W Company:

In connection with our audit of W Company's (the Company) financial statements as of December 31, 20XX, and for the year then ended, and our audit of the Company's internal control over financial reporting as of December 31, 20XX (integrated audit), auditing standards generally accepted in the United States of America require that we advise you of the following matters relating to internal control over financial reporting (internal control) identified during our integrated audit.

Our responsibility is to plan and perform our integrated audit to obtain reasonable assurance about whether the financial statements are free from material misstatement, whether due to fraud or error, and whether effective internal control was maintained in all material respects (i.e., whether material weaknesses exist as of the date specified in management's assessment). The integrated audit is not designed to detect deficiencies that, individually or in combination, are less severe than a material weakness.

A deficiency in internal control exists when the design or operation of a control does not allow management or employees, in the normal course of performing their assigned functions, to prevent, or detect and correct, misstatements on a timely basis. A material weakness is a deficiency, or a combination of deficiencies, in internal control, such that there is a reasonable possibility that a material misstatement of the entity's financial statements will not be prevented, or detected and corrected, on a timely basis. [We consider the following deficiencies in the Company's internal control to be material weaknesses:]

[Describe the material weaknesses that were identified during the integrated audit and provide an explanation of their potential effects. The auditor may separately identify those material weaknesses that exist as of the date specified in management's assessment about ICFR by referring to the auditor's report.]

A significant deficiency is a deficiency, or a combination of deficiencies, in internal control that is less severe than a material weakness, yet important enough to merit attention by those charged with governance. [We consider the following deficiencies in the Company's internal control over financial reporting to be significant deficiencies:]

[Describe the significant deficiencies that were identified during the integrated audit and provide an explanation of their potential effects.]

This communication is intended solely for the information and use of management, [identify the body or individuals charged with governance], others within the organization, and [identify any governmental authorities to which the auditor is required to report] and is not intended to be and should not be used by anyone other than these specified parties.

[Auditor's signature]

[Auditor's city and state]

[Date]

# SECTION 945

# AUDITOR INVOLVEMENT WITH EXEMPT OFFERING DOCUMENTS

## Authoritative Pronouncements

SAS-133—Auditor Involvement with Exempt Offering Documents

SAS-137—The Auditor's Responsibilities Relating to Other Information Included in Annual Reports

## Overview

AU-C 945 addresses the auditor's responsibilities when the auditor is involved with an exempt offering document. Exempt offerings are defined as securities exempt from registration under the Securities Act of 1933, as amended, or franchise offerings regulated by the Federal Trade Commission (FTC). These securities remain subject to the antifraud provisions of that act and the provisions prohibit any person from misrepresenting or omitting material facts in an offering or sale of securities. The U.S. SEC cannot directly regulate such offerings, so there is no requirement by the SEC for auditor involvement with exempt offerings. Accordingly, an auditor generally is not required to participate in or undertake any procedures with respect to an exempt offering. Franchise offerings regulated by the FTC are similar in that there is no requirement for auditor involvement with such offerings.

An exempt offering document is the disclosure document that provides financial and nonfinancial information related to the entity issuing the exempt offering (or in the case of a franchise offering, the franchisor) and the offering itself. Entities that issue exempt offerings may include an auditor's report in an offering document without obtaining the auditor's permission as no laws or rules prohibit such an inclusion.

AU-C 945 applies when (1) the auditor's report on financial statements or the auditor's review report on interim financial information of an entity is included or incorporated by reference in an offering document related to (*a*) securities, when either the transaction or securities themselves are exempt from registration under the Securities Act of 1933, as amended or (*b*) franchise offerings regulated by the FTC or applicable state franchise laws, and (2) the auditor performs one or more specified activities related to the exempt offering document.

The guidance in AU-C 945 requires the auditor to perform procedures and respond appropriately when the auditor concludes that the information included or incorporated by reference in the document could undermine the credibility of the financial statements and the auditor's report. The guidance also requires the auditor to perform procedures and respond to facts that become known to the auditor after the date of the auditor's report that, had they been known to the auditor at that date, may have caused the auditor to revise the auditor's report.

## Definitions

| | |
|---|---|
| Exempt offering documents | The disclosure document that provides financial and nonfinancial information related to the entity issuing the exempt offering (or in the case of a franchise offering, the franchisor) and the offering itself. |
| Security | Security has the meaning as defined in Section 2(a)(1) of the Securities Act of 1933, as amended. |

## Requirements

*Triggers of Involvement with Exempt Offering Documents*

1. The conditions that trigger involvement of the auditor with an exempt offering document occur when both (1) the auditor's report is included in the exempt document and (2) the auditor performs one or more of the following activities with respect to the exempt offering document:
   a. Helping with the preparation of information included in the exempt offering document.
   b. Reading, at the request of the entity, drafts of the exempt offering document.
   c. Issuing a comfort letter or similar letter or issuing an agreed-upon-procedures report in lieu of a comfort or similar letter on information included in the exempt offering document.
   d. Participating in due diligence discussions with placement agents, broker-dealers, underwriters, and other financial intermediaries involved with the exempt offering.
   e. Issuing a practitioner's attestation report on information relating to the exempt offering.
   f. Providing written agreement for the use of the auditor's report in the exempt offering document.
   g. Updating the auditor's report for inclusion in the exempt offering document.
2. When the auditor is deemed to be involved with an exempt offering document, the auditor is required to perform procedures in AU-C 945 at or shortly before the date of distribution, circulation, or submission of the exempt offering document or any subsequent similar activities related to the exempt offering.

*Procedures Related to Other Information in Exempt Offering Document*

3. The procedures in AU-C 720 (*Other Information in Documents Containing Audited Financial Statements*) apply when the auditor is involved with an exempt offering document. As part of the performance of those procedures, the auditor should determine if the role of the auditor described

in the exempt offering document indicates a greater responsibility than the auditor intends.

4. Auditors involved with exempt offerings should perform procedures to identify events occurring between the date of the auditor's report and the date of distribution, circulation, or submission of the exempt offering document that, had they been known to the auditor as of the date of the auditor's report, may have caused the auditor to revise the auditor's report. These procedures include the following:

   a. Gaining an understanding of what, if any, procedures management has performed to identify such events.

   b. Asking management and those charged with governance whether such events have occurred that might impact the financial statements.

   c. Obtaining and reading the minutes of meetings of the entity's management and those charged with governance that have been held since the date of the auditor's report and inquiring about matters discussed at any such meetings for which minutes are not yet available.

   d. Reading the entity's most recent subsequent interim financial statements, if any.

5. Auditors involved with exempt offerings should obtain updated written representations from management that include the following:

   a. Whether any information has come to management's attention that would cause management to believe that any of the previous representations should be modified.

   b. Whether any events have occurred subsequent to the date of the auditor's report that would require adjustment to, or disclosure in, the financial statements.

   c. Whether management has provided complete sets of minutes of meetings of the entity's management and those charged with governance, or summaries of actions of recent meetings for which minutes have not yet been prepared since previous representations were provided.

   d. Whether management has provided communications received from regulatory agencies concerning noncompliance with, or deficiencies in, financial reporting practices since previous representations were provided.

6. There may be circumstances where a predecessor auditor's report on a prior period is included in the exempt offering document but the predecessor auditor did not audit the entity's most current separate financial statements included in the exempt offering document and the predecessor is involved with the exempt offering. AU-C 945 outlines procedures that the predecessor auditor should perform that include the following:

> a. Reading the financial statement of the subsequent period to be presented on a comparative basis.
>
> b. Comparing the prior-period financial statements that the predecessor auditor reported on with the financial statements of a subsequent period to be presented on a comparative basis.
>
> c. Asking and requesting certain written representations from management of the former client, at or near the date of distribution, circulation, or submission of the exempt document.
>
> d. Obtaining a representation letter from the successor auditor stating whether the successor auditor's audit identified any matters that might have a material effect on, or require disclosure in, the financial statements reported on by the predecessor auditor.
>
> 7. Sometimes a predecessor auditor of an acquired entity is involved with an exempt offering document and the acquirer's audited financial statements included in the exempt document reflect a time period that includes the date of acquisition. In those situations, the predecessor auditor may be unable to perform all the procedures in AU-C 945. When that occurs, the predecessor auditor should obtain written representations from management of the former client, and a representation letter from the successor auditor.
>
> 8. When the auditor identifies subsequent events that may require adjustment of, or disclosure in, the financial statements or reviewed interim financial information, the auditor should not agree to the inclusion of the auditor's report in the exempt offering document until the auditor's consideration of the subsequent events, including the effect on the auditor's report, has been satisfactorily evaluated. If the auditor becomes aware of subsequently discovered facts, the auditor should not agree to the inclusion in the auditor's report in the exempt offering document until the auditor's consideration of the subsequently discovered facts, including the effect on the auditor's report, has been satisfactorily evaluated.
>
> 9. When management does not revise the financial statements to address situations that the auditor believes need to be revised, the auditor should not agree to the inclusion of the auditor's report in the exempt document.

## Analysis and Application of Procedures

Exhibit AU-C 945-1 contains examples of exempt offering documents. Sometimes the exempt offering is referred to as an offering circular, offering memorandum, offering statement, or franchise disclosure document.

As part of an engagement planning process, the auditor may want to include terms in the engagement letter that require the entity to obtain permission from the auditor before using the auditor's report in connection with an exempt offering. Including these provisions in the engagement letter would not trigger "involvement" by the auditor in the exempt offering document. Exhibit AU-C 945-2 includes example language that may be included in an engagement letter.

*Triggers of Involvement*

AU-C 945 requires the auditor to apply the performance procedures when both of the following conditions exist (which means the auditor is involved):

- The auditor's report is included in the exempt offering document.
- The auditor performs, one or more of the following activities with respect to the exempt offering document:
  — Assisting the entity in preparing information included in the offering document;
  — Reading a draft of the offering document at the entity's request;
  — Issuing a comfort or similar letter in accordance with AU-C 920 (*Letters for Underwriters and Certain Other Requesting Parties*) or an attestation engagement report in lieu of a comfort or similar letter on information included in the offering document;
  — Participating in due diligence discussions with underwriters, placement agents, broker-dealers, or other financial intermediaries in connection with an offering document;
  — Issuing an attestation report on information relating to the offering;
  — Providing written agreement (e.g., an inclusion letter) for the use of the auditor's report in the offering document; and
  — Updating an auditor's report for inclusion in the offering document.

Sometimes the auditor may become aware of an offering document through a communication from an entity or through the receipt of a draft exempt document from an underwriter, placement agent, broker-dealer, or the entity. Mere awareness of the auditor about the exempt offering document does not trigger involvement.

---

**OBSERVATION:** One of the triggers of involvement is assisting with the preparation of information included in the offering document. That is predicated on the assumption that the auditor is reasonably aware that the information will be included in a specific exempt offering document. If the auditor is involved in helping the entity prepare information for the entity's internal purposes and the entity later includes that information in an exempt offering document, that event would not trigger involvement of the auditor in the exempt offering document.

If the auditor provides written or oral comments to the entity on the exempt offering document, that would be treated as involvement with the exempt offering, thereby requiring the auditor to consider the provisions of AU-C 945. Reading the document without providing written or oral comments also triggers auditor involvement with the exempt offering document.

---

**OBSERVATION:** Sometimes the entity may wish to make reference to the auditor's role in connection with the exempt offering document as an "expert."

Because the term "expert" is generally undefined, AU-C 945 notes that the reference should be to "Independent Auditors" (or something similar), unless the term "expert" is sufficiently defined.

### Issuance of Comfort Letters or Similar Letters

If the auditor is requested to issue a comfort letter to underwriters for an exempt offering document, the auditor would address the responsibilities in AU-C 920. When a comfort letter is requested by a party other than a requesting party as defined in AU-C 920, the auditor should not provide that party with a comfort letter or similar letter. Instead, the auditor may accept an engagement to perform agreed-upon procedures requested by that party in accordance with the attestation standards and may issue a practitioner's report.

### Due Diligence Discussions

Sometimes underwriters and their counsel may request to meet with the entity's auditors to discuss the specific exempt offering document. Often these meetings are referred to as oral due diligence meetings. Auditors should use their professional judgment as to whether they should participate and, if so, which questions in an oral due diligence meeting can be addressed.

### Practitioner Attestation Report

A practitioner may be engaged to perform an attestation engagement on information related to the exempt offering document. If the practitioner is the auditor whose report accompanies the financial statements included in the exempt offering document, the auditor is deemed to be involved with the exempt offering document. But, if the practitioner is not the auditor, the practitioner engaged to perform the attestation engagement is not deemed to be involved with the exempt offering document.

### Written Agreements for Use of the Auditor's Report

The auditor may be requested to provide a written agreement to include the auditor's report in the exempt offering document. This inclusion letter may also be referred to as an agree-to-include letter, an acknowledgment letter, or an awareness letter. Exhibit AU-C 945-3 includes an example inclusion letter.

> **OBSERVATION:** Exempt offerings may have multiple stages. A single offering could involve multiple applications of AU-C 945. Therefore, it is important for the auditor to request management to keep the auditor advised of the progress of the preparation of the exempt offering document proceedings through the final distribution, circulation, or submission of the final exempt offering document.

### Subsequent Events and Subsequently Discovered Facts

When the auditor is involved with an offering document, the auditor should perform the following procedures described in AU-C 560 (*Subsequent Events and Subsequently Discovered Facts*):

- Procedures designed to identify events occurring between the date of the auditor's report and the date of the distribution, circulation, or submission of the exempt offering document that, had they been known to the auditor as of the date of the auditor's report, may have caused the auditor to revise the auditor's report.
- Obtain updated written representations from management.

If the auditor identifies subsequent events that may require adjustment of, or disclosure in, the audited financial statements or reviewed interim financial information, the auditor should not agree to the inclusion of the auditor's report until the auditor's consideration of the subsequent events has been satisfactorily evaluated in accordance with AU-C 560.

If the auditor becomes aware of subsequently discovered facts, the auditor should not agree to the inclusion of the auditor's report until the auditor's consideration of the subsequently discovered facts, including the effect on the auditor's report, has been satisfactorily evaluated in accordance with AU-C 560.

If management does not revise the financial statements in circumstances in which the auditor believes they need to be revised, in addition to following the requirements in AU-C 560, the auditor should not agree to the inclusion of the auditor's report in the offering document.

## Practitioner's Aids

Exhibit AU-C 945-1 contains examples of exempt offering documents. Sometimes the exempt offering is referred to as an offering circular, offering memorandum, offering statement, or franchise disclosure document.

### EXHIBIT AU-C 945-1—EXAMPLES OF EXEMPT SECURITIES AND EXEMPT TRANSACTIONS

The Securities Act of 1933 provides for two broad types of exemptions to the requirement that securities be registered with the SEC under Section 5 of the 1933 Act: exempt securities (under Section 3 of the 1933 Act) and exempt transactions (generally under Section 4 and 4A of the 1933 Act). With Section 3 exempt securities, the exemption lies with the nature of the security, and thus, each transaction involving that security will itself be exempt. With Section 4 exempt transactions, however, the exemption is applicable only to a single transaction and does not necessarily carry over to subsequent transactions. Each transaction involving that security must be analyzed to determine if it too is exempt from Section 5 registration requirements. The following list is not intended to be comprehensive. The exemptions listed are frequently subject to conditions and definitional limitations that are not summarized here.

**Exempt securities:** Examples of exempt securities include the following:

a. Securities issued or guaranteed by federal, state, and local governments, including most industrial development bonds.

b. Any security issued or guaranteed by banks or employee benefit plans.

c. Short-term commercial paper with maturity of nine months or less.

d. Securities issued by non-profit religious, educational or charitable organizations.

e. Securities issued by savings and loans and farmer's cooperatives.
f. Railroad equipment trusts.
g. Certificates of receivers and trustees issued with court approval.
h. Insurance policies and annuity contracts.
i. Equity securities issued in connection with the acquisition by a bank holding company of a savings association.
j. Securities issued by certain church employee plans.
k. Security futures products and standardized options.

**Exempt transactions:** Examples of exempt transactions include the following:
a. Transactions by any person other than an issuer, underwriter, or dealer.
b. Transactions by an entity not involving any public offering (the "private placement" exemption), including offerings under Regulation D Rule 506 and Rule 144A.
c. Transactions by a dealer, with certain exemptions.
d. Brokers' transactions executed on customer orders.
e. Offers or sales by an entity to accredited investors (under certain conditions).
f. Regulation CF transactions (crowdfunding).
g. Private resales of securities.
h. Small issues of securities, including Regulation A offerings and offerings under Rules 504 and 505 of Regulation D.
i. Voluntary exchanges between an entity and security holders.
j. Judicially or administratively approved exchanges.
k. Intrastate offerings.

**Other common exemptions:** Examples of other common exemptions include these:
a. Rule 701 exemptions for compensatory arrangements.
b. Regulation S (offshore offers and sales).
c. Franchise offerings.

Exhibit AU-C 945-2 includes example language that may be included in an engagement letter.

## EXHIBIT AU-C 945-2—EXAMPLE TERMS FOR INCLUSION IN ENGAGEMENT LETTERS

> The Entity may wish to include our report on these financial statements in an exempt offering document. The Entity agrees that the aforementioned auditor's report, or reference to our Firm, will not be included in any such offering document without our prior permission or consent. Any agreement to perform work in connection with an exempt offering document, including an agreement to provide permission or consent, will be a separate engagement.

Exhibit AU-C 945-3 includes an example inclusion letter.

## EXHIBIT AU-C 945-3—EXAMPLE OF AN INCLUSION LETTER
## INDEPENDENT AUDITOR'S INCLUSION LETTER

We agree to the inclusion [*or incorporation by reference*] in the [*name of Offering Document*] dated [*insert issuance date of Offering Document*] of our report, dated [*insert date of auditor's report on the financial statements*], on our audit of the financial statements of [*name of Entity*] as of December 31, 20X2 [*and 20X1*], and for the year[*s*] then ended.

# AT-C Section
# Statements on Standards for Attestation Engagements

| | | |
|---|---|---|
| Preface: | Codification of Statements on Standards for Attestation Engagements ................................................. | 10,002 |
| Section 100: | Common Concepts ................................................. | 10,005 |
| Section 105: | Concepts Common to All Attestation Engagements ........... | 10,005 |
| Section 200: | Level of Service .................................................... | 10,024 |
| Section 205: | Assertion-Based Examination Engagements .................. | 10,024 |
| Section 206: | Direct Examination Engagements ............................... | 10,057 |
| Section 210: | Review Engagements ............................................. | 10,065 |
| Section 215: | Agreed-Upon Procedures Engagements ....................... | 10,091 |
| Section 300: | Subject Matter ...................................................... | 10,104 |
| Section 305: | Prospective Financial Information ............................... | 10,104 |
| Section 310: | Reporting on Pro Forma Financial Information ............... | 10,122 |
| Section 315: | Compliance Attestation ........................................... | 10,135 |
| Section 320: | Reporting on an Examination of Controls at a Service Organization Relevant to User Entities' Internal Control over Financial Reporting ............................................................ | 10,150 |
| Section 395: | Management's Discussion and Analysis ...................... | 10,172 |

# CODIFICATION OF STATEMENTS ON STANDARDS FOR ATTESTATION ENGAGEMENTS

## Preface

The preface summarizes the overall structure and key components of the Statements on Standards to Attestation Engagements, which are referred to as the attestation standards or SSAEs. These standards outline the requirements and related guidance for examination, review, and agreed-upon procedures attestation engagements.

## Organizational Structure of the Attestation Standards

The attestation standards are codified into sections that are identified by "AT-C," which are summarized following this Preface.

There are three levels of service contained in the attestation standards:

1. Examination Level;
2. Review Level; and
3. Agreed-Upon Procedures Level.

These levels of service can be applied to a variety of types of subject matters.

The first AT-C 105 includes concepts that apply to all attestation engagements. That section is followed by AT-C 205, AT-C 210, and AT-C 215, which contain the requirements and additional guidance for examination level, review level, and agreed-upon procedures level attestation engagements, respectively. Thus, when performing an examination level engagement, the practitioner would comply with both AT-C 105 and AT-C 205.

The remaining AT-C sections include additional requirements for the following specific subject matter attestation engagements:

- AT-C 305—Prospective Financial Information
- AT-C 310—Reporting on Pro Forma Financial Information
- AT-C 315—Compliance Attestation
- AT-C 320—Reporting on an Examination of Controls at a Service Organization Relevant to User Entities' Internal Control over Financial Reporting
- AT-C 395—Management's Discussion and Analysis

When performing an attestation engagement for one of the above specified subject matter engagements, the practitioner would follow the guidance in that the AT-C section for that specified subject matter engagement in addition to the guidance in AT-C 105 and the guidance in the relevant AT-C section for the applicable level of service. For example, if a practitioner is engaged to perform an agreed-upon procedures compliance attestation engagement, the practitioner would follow the guidance in AT-C 105, AT-C 215, and AT-C 315.

## Purpose of an Attestation Engagement

The attestation standards define the purpose of an attestation engagement as providing "users of information, generally third parties, with an opinion, conclusion, or findings regarding the reliability of subject matter or an assertion about the subject matter, as measured against suitable and available criteria." The objective of an attestation engagement report is to increase confidence about the subject matter for users of that information.

## Responsibilities in an Attestation Engagement

When performing an attestation engagement, the practitioner is responsible for complying with the requirements contained in the SSAEs. The subject matter and the related assertion about that subject matter are the responsibility of a responsible party, although the attestation standards do permit the practitioner to assist the responsible party in developing or presenting the subject matter.

## Performance

When performing an attestation engagement, the practitioner must:

- Be capable of performing and possess the competencies required to perform the respective engagement.
- Maintain and apply professional judgment as he or she plans and completes the performance requirements of the engagement.
- Apply professional skepticism throughout the engagement.
- Ensure that he or she is in compliance with relevant ethical requirements.

Depending on the level of service applicable to the attestation engagement, the practitioner has different performance responsibilities:

- Examination Level—In an examination level of service, the practitioner expresses an opinion about the subject matter. Thus, the practitioner must obtain reasonable assurance about the subject matter or an assertion about the subject matter.
- Review Level—In a review level of service, the practitioner expresses a conclusion about whether the subject matter (or an assertion about the subject matter) requires any material modification for it to comply with the criteria. To provide this conclusion, the practitioner obtains limited assurance.
- Agreed-Upon Procedures Level—In an agreed-upon procedures engagement, the practitioner reports on the application of agreed-upon procedures, which are determined by specific parties. In an agreed-upon procedures engagement, the practitioner does not issue an opinion or conclusion.

## Reporting

The practitioner issues a report applicable to the specific level of service performed. For an examination level of service, the practitioner issues an opinion, and for a review level of service the practitioner issues a conclusion. In an agreed-upon procedures engagement, the practitioner issues a report describing the specific procedures performed and the findings identified by the performance of those procedures.

# SECTION 100

# COMMON CONCEPTS

# SECTION 105

# CONCEPTS COMMON TO ALL ATTESTATION ENGAGEMENTS

## Authoritative Pronouncements

SSAE-18—Attestation Standards: Clarification and Recodification

SSAE-19—Agreed-Upon Procedures Engagements

SSAE-21—Direct Examination Engagements

SSAE Interpretation 1—Responding to Requests for Reports on Matters Relating to Solvency

SSAE Interpretation 2—Applicability of Attestation Standards to Litigation Services

SSAE Interpretation 3—Providing Access to or Copies of Engagement Documentation to a Regulator

SSAE Interpretation 4—Performing and Reporting on an Attestation Engagement under Two Sets of Attestation Standards

---

**IMPORTANT NOTICE FOR 2022:** In December 2019, the ASB issued Statement on Standards for Attestation Engagements (SSAE) No. 19 (*Agreed-Upon Procedures Engagements*), which revises performance and reporting requirements and application guidance for all agreed-upon procedures engagements. SSAE No. 19 superseded AT-C 215 (*Agreed-Upon Procedures Engagements*). It more closely harmonizes the attestation standards with the International Standards on Assurance Engagements (ISAEs) and it provides more flexibility for practitioners when performing agreed-upon procedures engagements, including no longer requiring the practitioner to request a written assertion from the responsible party when the practitioner is reporting directly on the subject matter. SSAE No. 19 became effective for agreed-upon procedures reports dated on or after July 15, 2021. Early implementation is permitted.

---

**IMPORTANT NOTICE FOR 2022:** In September 2020, the ASB issued Statement on Standards for Attestation Engagements (SSAE) No. 21 (*Direct Examination Engagements*), that adds a new AT-C 206 (*Direct Examination Engagements*) to the attestation standards that enable practitioners to perform an examination engagement in which the practitioner obtains reasonable assurance by measuring or evaluating underlying subject matter against criteria and expressing an opinion that conveys the results of that measurement or evaluation. SSAE No. 21 allows the entity in an examination engagement to not provide an assertion about whether the underlying subject matter is in accordance with the criteria. SSAE No. 21 amends some of the definitions and terminology contained in AT-C 105. SSAE No. 21 is effective for examination reports dated on or after June 15, 2022.

## Overview

Statements on Standards for Attestation Engagements (SSAEs) establish attestation standards that must be satisfied by a CPA in public accounting when he or she is "engaged to issue or does issue a practitioner's examination, review, or agreed-upon procedures report on subject matter, or an assertion about subject matter (the assertion), that is the responsibility of another party" except in the following circumstances:

- Engagements performed in accordance with Statements on Auditing Standards (SASs).
- Engagements performed in accordance with Statements on Standards for Accounting and Review Services (SSARSs).
- Engagements performed in accordance with Statements on Standards for Tax Services.

This AT-C section applies to all attestation engagements that are subject to the SSAEs. Additional AT-C sections contain guidance that applies specifically to examination, review, and agreed-upon procedures engagements, including certain specific subject matter attestation engagements. Note that as a result of the issuance of SSAE No. 21 and the introduction of direct examination engagements, references in AU-C 105 to the term "examination" is inclusive of both assertion-based and direct examination engagements.

**OBSERVATION:** In accordance with Interpretation 4 of AT-C 105, a practitioner may perform and report on an attestation engagement in accordance with AICPA attestation standards in addition to another set of attestation standards, such as those issued by the International Auditing and Assurance Standards Board (IAASB) or the PCAOB, as long as both sets of attestation standards are followed in their entirety.

**PLANNING AID REMINDER:** This guidance does not apply to performance audits performed according to *Government Auditing Standards* unless the practitioner is also engaged to conduct an AICPA attestation engagement or issues a practitioner's examination, review, or agreed-upon procedures report.

In conducting an attestation engagement, the practitioner's overall objectives are:

- To apply the requirements relevant to the attestation engagement,
- To report on the underlying subject matter or subject matter information (or assertion) and communicate as required by the applicable AT-C section in accordance with the results of the practitioner's procedures, and
- To implement engagement-level quality control procedures that provide reasonable assurance that the attestation engagement complies with professional standards and applicable legal and regulatory requirements.

The subject matter of an attestation engagement can be varied and can provide assurance on data such as the following:

- Historical or prospective performance or condition, such as historical financial information, prospective financial information, performance measurements, and backlog data.
- Physical characteristics, such as the number of square feet in a building.
- Historical events, such as the price of commodities on a specified date.
- Analytical material, such as break-even analysis.
- Systems and processes, such as internal controls.
- Compliance with established procedures, such as laws and regulations.

---

**PLANNING AID REMINDER:** Attestation standards apply only to litigation service engagements in which a practitioner is engaged to issue or does issue an examination, a review, or an agreed-upon procedures report on subject matter, or an assertion about the subject matter that is the responsibility of another party.

---

In attestation engagements, the underlying subject matter is the responsibility of a party other than the practitioner. In an assertion-based examination engagement or a review engagement, a party other than the practitioner makes an assertion about whether the subject matter is measured or evaluated in accordance with suitable criteria. In a direct examination engagement, the responsible party does not provide an assertion about the results of the measurement or evaluation of the underlying subject matter against the criteria.

If the responsible party refuses to provide a written assertion when it is required for the engagement:

- The practitioner is required to withdraw from an examination or review engagement if permitted by law or regulation where the engaging party is also the responsible party;
- The practitioner is required to disclose the refusal in his or her report and restrict the report's use to the engaging party in an examination or review engagement where the engaging party is not the responsible party; and
- The practitioner is required to disclose the refusal in his or her report in an agreed-upon procedures report.

Practitioners who perform an attestation engagement are required by ET Section 1.310.001 (*Compliance with Standards Rule*) of the AICPA's Professional Standards to comply with standards put forth by bodies designated by the Council of the AICPA. Firm quality control standards relate to the firm's attestation practice as a whole and should allow the firm to have reasonable assurance that its personnel comply with professional standards and legal and regulatory requirements and that practitioners' reports issued are appropriate. While attestation standards and quality control standards are related, if a firm has deficiencies in its system of quality control or violates specific policies or controls, it does not mean that a particular attestation engagement was not performed in accordance with SSAEs.

## Definitions

| | |
|---|---|
| Assertion | Any declaration or set of declarations about whether the underlying subject matter is based on or in accordance with the criteria. An assertion is subject matter information. |
| Attestation engagement | An engagement performed under the attestation standards. There are four types of attestation engagements: *Assertion-based examination engagement*—Reasonable assurance is obtained by collecting sufficient appropriate evidence about the responsible party's measurement or evaluation of the underlying subject matter against criteria in order to be able to draw reasonable conclusions about whether the subject matter is in accordance with or based on the criteria or the assertion is fairly stated in all material respects. The same level of assurance is obtained as in a financial statement audit. *Direct examination engagement*—Reasonable assurance by measuring or evaluating the underlying subject matter against the criteria and performing other procedures to obtain sufficient appropriate evidence to express an opinion that conveys the results of that measurement or evaluation. In a direct examination engagement, the responsible party does not provide an assertion. *Review engagement*—Limited assurance is obtained by collecting sufficient appropriate review evidence about the responsible party's measurement or evaluation of underlying subject matter against criteria in order to express a conclusion about whether any material modification should be made to the subject matter information for it to be in accordance with or based on the criteria or to the responsible party's assertion for it to be fairly stated. The same level of assurance is obtained as in a financial statement review. *Agreed-upon procedures engagement*—Specific procedures are performed on underlying subject matter or subject matter information and reports on the findings without providing an opinion or conclusion. |
| Attestation risk | The risk in an examination or review engagement that, when the subject matter information or assertion is materially misstated, the practitioner expresses an inappropriate opinion or conclusion. |

§ 105 • Concepts Common to All Attestation Engagements        10,009

| | |
|---|---|
| Criteria | The benchmarks used to measure or evaluate the subject matter.<br>**PLANNING AID REMINDER:** Suitable criteria are required for measurement and evaluation of subject matter to be reasonably consistent. Suitability is dependent on circumstances and the practitioner should use professional judgment in determining suitability. Suitability is not affected by the assurance level provided. |
| Documentation completion date | The date the practitioner has assembled a complete and final set of documentation in the engagement file for retention. |
| Engagement circumstances | The context of the engagement including the engagement terms; whether it is an examination, review or agreed-upon procedures engagement; the underlying subject matter characteristics; the criteria; the information needs of the intended users; relevant characteristics of the responsible party and engaging party (if different) and their environment; and other matters such as events, transactions, conditions and practices, and relevant laws and regulations that may have a significant effect on the engagement. |
| Engagement documentation | The record of procedures performed, relevant evidence obtained, and conclusions or findings reached by the practitioner (the workpapers). |
| Engagement partner | The partner or other person in the firm responsible for the attestation engagement, its performance, the report issued on the firm's behalf, and who has the appropriate authority from a professional, legal, or regulatory perspective. |
| Engagement team | All partners and staff performing the engagement and any individuals engaged by the firm to perform attestation procedures on the engagement. The engagement team does not include a practitioner's external specialist, engagement quality control reviewer, or those in the client's internal audit function providing direct assistance. |
| Engaging party | The party engaging the practitioner to perform the attestation engagement who may be management or those charged with governance of the responsible party, a governmental body or agency, the intended users, or another third party. |
| Evidence | Information used by the practitioner to arrive at the opinion, conclusion, or findings stated in his or her report. |
| Firm | A form of organization permitted by law or regulation whose characteristics conform to resolutions of the Council of the AICPA that is engaged in the practice of public accounting. |
| Fraud | An intentional act involving deception that results in a misstatement in the subject matter or assertion. |
| General use | Use of a practitioner's report that is not restricted to specific parties. |
| Internal audit function | An entity function that performs assurance and consulting activities designed to evaluate and improve the effectiveness of the entity's governance, risk management, and internal control processes. |

| | |
|---|---|
| Interpretative publications | Interpretations of SSAEs, exhibits to SSAEs, guidance on attestation engagements including in AICPA audit and accounting guides, and AICPA attestation Statements of Position, to the extent that those statements are applicable to such engagements. |
| Misstatement | A difference between the measurement or evaluation of the underlying subject matter and the appropriate measurement or evaluation of the underlying subject matter in accordance with (or based on) the criteria. Misstatements can be intentional or unintentional, qualitative or quantitative, and include omissions. Misstatements may be referred to as deviations, exceptions, or instances of noncompliance in some engagements. |
| Network firm | A firm or other entity that belongs to a network as defined in ET Section 0.400 (*Definitions*) in the AICPA Professional Standards. |
| Noncompliance with laws or regulations | Intentional or unintentional acts of omission or commission by the entity that are contrary to laws or regulations. These acts include transactions entered into by the entity, in the name of the entity, or on its behalf by those charged with governance, management, or employees. Noncompliance does not include personal misconduct unrelated to the underlying subject matter or subject matter information by the entity's employees, management, or those charged with governance. |
| Other attestation publications | Publications other than interpretative publications. These include AICPA attestation publications not defined as interpretative publication; attestation articles in the *Journal of Accountancy* and other professional journals; continuing professional education programs and other instructional materials, textbooks, guidebooks, attestation programs, and checklists; and other publications from state CPA societies, other organizations, and individuals. |
| Other practitioner | An independent practitioner who is not part of the engagement team who performs work on information that the engagement team will use as evidence. Another practitioner may be part of the practitioner's firm, a network firm, or another firm. |
| Practitioner | Those conducting the attestation engagement, typically the engagement partner or other members of the engagement team or the firm. The term engagement partner rather than practitioner is used if a standard intends the engagement partner fulfill the requirement or responsibility. |
| Practitioner's specialist | An individual or organization with expertise other than accounting or attestation, whose work is used by the practitioner to assist in obtaining evidence for the service being provided. A practitioner's specialist may be internal, part of the practitioner's firm or a network firm, or external. |
| Professional judgment | The application of relevant training, knowledge, and experience, within the context provided by attestation and ethical standards, in making informed decisions about actions appropriate to the engagement circumstances. |
| Professional skepticism | An attitude that includes a questioning mind, being alert to conditions that may indicate possible misstatement due to fraud or error, and a critical assessment of evidence. |
| Reasonable assurance | A high but not absolute level of assurance. |

| | |
|---|---|
| Report release date | The date the practitioner gives the engaging party permission to use the practitioner's report. |
| Responsible party | The party responsible for the underlying subject matter, which is a party other than the practitioner. In an assertion-based examination or review engagement, if the nature of the underlying subject matter is such that no such party exists, a party who has a reasonable basis for making a written assertion about the underlying subject matter may be deemed to be the responsible party. |
| Specified party | The intended users to whom use of the practitioner's report is limited. |
| Subject matter information | The outcome of the measurement or evaluation of the underlying subject matter against the criteria. An assertion about whether the underlying subject matter is in accordance with the criteria is a form of subject matter information. |
| Underlying subject matter | In an examination or review engagement, the phenomenon measured or evaluated by applying criteria. In an agreed-upon procedures engagement, the phenomenon upon which the procedures are performed. |

## Requirements

The practitioner is presumptively required to perform the following procedures when conducting an attestation engagement in accordance with the attestation standards:

### Conduct of an Attestation Engagement in Accordance with the Attestation Standards

1. When performing an attestation engagement, the practitioner should comply with this section; AT-C 205 (*Assertion Based Examination Engagements*), AT-C 210 (*Review Engagements*), or AT-C 215 (*Agreed-Upon Procedures Engagements*) as applicable; and any other section where subject matter AT-C section guidance exists that is relevant to the engagement.

2. Only represent compliance with this or any other section of the attestation standards if the practitioner has complied with all requirements of this section and all other relevant sections.

3. If a practitioner issues reports for services performed under other professional standards, those reports should be written to be clearly distinguishable from and not confused with a report issued under the attestation standards.

4. The practitioner should understand the entirety of each section of the attestation standards that is relevant to the engagement in order to understand its objectives and properly apply its requirements.

5. Comply with each requirement of all attestation standards relevant to the engagement, subject to requirement 9, unless the entire section is not relevant to the engagement or it is a conditional requirement that is not relevant because the condition does not exist.

6. If an attestation engagement is performed for the benefit of a government body or agency and the practitioner agrees to follow specified government standards, guides, procedures, statutes, rules, and regulations, all of those requirements should be followed in addition to any applicable attestation standards.

7. If law or regulation requires the practitioner to use a prescribed form of report that is unacceptable or requires a statement to be made that the practitioner has no basis to make, the prescribed report should be reworded or an appropriately worded practitioner's report should be attached separately.

8. Attestation standards use two categories of professional requirements to describe the degree of responsibility imposed on the practitioner:

   a. *Unconditional requirements.* The practitioner must comply in all cases in which the requirement is relevant. Attestation standards use the word "must" to indicate an unconditional requirement.

   b. *Presumptively mandatory requirements.* The practitioner must comply in all cases in which the requirement is relevant except in rare circumstances discussed in requirement 9. Attestation standards use the word "should" to indicate a presumptively mandatory requirement.

9. In rare circumstances, the practitioner may judge it necessary to depart from a relevant presumptively mandatory requirement. In these circumstances, alternative procedures should be performed to achieve the intent of that requirement. The need to depart from a relevant presumptively mandatory requirement is only expected to occur if the requirement is for performance of a specific procedure that, in the engagement circumstances, would be ineffective in achieving the intent of the requirement.

10. Applicable interpretive publications should be considered in planning and performing the attestation engagement.

11. Use professional judgment and assess the relevance and appropriateness of applying attestation guidance included in another attestation publication given the engagement circumstances.

## Acceptance and Continuance

12. The engagement partner should be satisfied that appropriate procedures regarding the acceptance and continuance of client relationships and attestation engagements have been followed and should determine that any conclusions reached are appropriate.

## Preconditions for an Attestation Engagement

13. The practitioner must be independent when performing an attestation engagement in accordance with the attestation standards unless law or regulation requires the practitioner to accept the engagement.

14. To establish that the preconditions for an attestation engagement are present, the practitioner should, on the basis of preliminary knowledge of the engagement circumstances and discussion with the appropriate party, determine whether the responsible party is a party other than the practitioner and takes responsibility for the underlying subject matter and whether the engagement exhibits all of the following characteristics:

   a. The subject matter is appropriate.

   b. In an examination or review engagement, the criteria to be applied in the preparation and evaluation of the subject matter are suitable and will be available to the intended users.

   c. The practitioner expects to be able to obtain the evidence needed to arrive at his or her opinion, conclusion, or findings including:

      i. Access to all information the appropriate party is aware of that is relevant to the engagement;

ii. Access to additional information the practitioner may request from the appropriate party for the purpose of the engagement; and
   iii. Unrestricted access to those in the appropriate parties from whom the practitioner determines it necessary to obtain evidence.
  d. The practitioner's opinion, conclusion, or findings, as appropriate to the engagement, should be contained in a practitioner's report.

15. If the above preconditions are not present, the practitioner should discuss the matter with the engaging party to try to resolve the issue.

16. An attestation engagement should only be accepted when the practitioner:
  a. Has no reason to believe that relevant ethical requirements, including independence, will not be satisfied;
  b. Is satisfied that those performing the engagement have the appropriate competence and capabilities;
  c. Has determined that all preconditions for an attestation engagement have been met; and
  d. Has reached a common understanding as to engagement terms, including the practitioner's reporting responsibilities, with the engaging party.

17. If it is discovered after engagement acceptance that one or more preconditions for an attestation engagement are absent, the practitioner should discuss the matter with the appropriate parties and determine: whether the matter can be resolved; whether it is appropriate to continue with the engagement; and, if the matter cannot be resolved but it is appropriate to continue the engagement, whether to communicate the matter in the practitioner's report, and if the matter is to be communicated in the practitioner's report, how to do so.

## Acceptance of a Change in Engagement Terms

18. A change in engagement terms should not be agreed to if there is no reasonable justification for the change. If a change in engagement terms occurs, the practitioner should not disregard evidence obtained prior to the change.

19. If a practitioner concludes, using his or her professional judgment, there is reasonable justification to change engagement terms to perform a lower level of service than that of the original engagement terms, then the practitioner should comply with the standards and reporting of the lower level of service. The practitioner's report should not reference the original engagement, procedures that may have been performed, or scope limitations that resulted in the changed engagement.

## Using the Work of Other Practitioners

20. When the practitioner expects to use the work of other practitioners, he or she should:
  a. Obtain an understanding of whether the other practitioner is independent and understands and will comply with the ethical requirements relevant to the engagement.
  b. Obtain an understanding of the other practitioner's professional competence.
  c. Communicate clearly with the other practitioner about the scope and timing of the other practitioner's work and findings.

d. If assuming responsibility for the work of the other practitioner, be involved in that work.
e. Evaluate whether the other practitioner's work is adequate for the practitioner's purposes.
f. Determine whether to make reference to the other practitioner in the practitioner's report.

## Quality Control

21. The engagement partner should be satisfied that:
    a. The engagement team and any practitioner's external specialists have the appropriate competence, including underlying subject matter and criteria knowledge, and capabilities to perform the engagement in accordance with professional standards and applicable legal and regulatory requirements and to enable an appropriate practitioner's report to be issued.
    b. The engagement team will be able to be involved sufficiently in the work of an other practitioner and a practitioner's external specialist when their work is to be used in accepting responsibility for the opinion, conclusion, or findings on the underlying subject matter or subject matter information (or assertion).
    c. Those involved in the engagement have been informed of their responsibilities, the objectives of procedures they are to perform, and matters that may affect the nature, timing, and extent of those procedures.
    d. Engagement team members have been directed to bring significant questions raised during the engagement to the engagement partner's attention so their significance may be assessed.

22. The engagement partner should take responsibility for the overall quality of each attestation engagement, including the following:
    a. Appropriate procedures are performed regarding engagement acceptance and continuance;
    b. The engagement is properly planned and performed, including appropriate supervision, to comply with professional standards and applicable legal and regulatory requirements;
    c. Reviews are performed in accordance with the firm's review policies and procedures and engagement documentation is reviewed on or before the date of the practitioner's report;
    d. Appropriate engagement documentation is maintained to provide evidence that the practitioner's objectives are achieved and the engagement is performed in accordance with relevant attestation standards and legal and regulatory requirements; and
    e. The engagement team is appropriately consulting on difficult or contentious matters.
    f. Appropriate attention has been given and action taken to obtain any evidence on noncompliance with relevant ethical requirements of members of the engagement, remaining alert through observation and inquiries as necessary for any evidence of noncompliance.

## Engagement Documentation

23. Engagement documentation should be prepared on a timely basis.

24. Engagement documentation should be assembled in a final engagement file no later than 60 days following the practitioner's report release date.

25. Documentation should not be deleted or discarded after the documentation completion date until the end of the retention period.

26. If it is necessary to amend or add engagement documentation after the documentation completion date, the practitioner should document the specific reasons for making the amendments or additions and when and by whom they were made and reviewed.

27. Engagement documentation is the property of the practitioner and this ownership is recognized by the statutes of some jurisdictions. Reasonable procedures should be followed to retain engagement documentation for a sufficient length of time to meet the practitioner's needs and satisfy any applicable legal or regulatory record retention requirements.

28. Because engagement documentation often contains confidential information, reasonable procedures should be adopted to maintain the confidentiality of that information.

29. Reasonable procedures should be adopted to prevent unauthorized access to engagement documentation.

30. If there has been a departure from a relevant presumptively mandatory requirement, the practitioner should document the justification for the departure and how the alternative procedures performed were sufficient to achieve the intent of that requirement.

## Engagement Quality Control Review

31. For an engagement the firm has determined requires an engagement quality control review:

   a. The engagement partner should take responsibility for discussing with the engagement quality control reviewer significant findings or issues from the engagement, including those identified during the engagement quality control review, and not release the practitioner's report until the engagement quality control review is complete; and

   b. The engagement quality control reviewer should objectively evaluate significant judgments the engagement team made and conclusions reached in formulating the practitioner's report. The evaluation should include:

      i. Discussing significant findings or issues with the engagement partner;

      ii. Reading the written subject matter information (or assertion) and the proposed practitioner's report;

      iii. Reading engagement documentation related to significant judgments the engagement team made and the related conclusions it reached; and

      iv. Evaluating the decisions reached in formulating the practitioner's report and considering whether the proposed practitioner's report is appropriate.

## Professional Skepticism and Professional Judgment

32. Attestation engagements should be planned and performed with professional skepticism, which is maintained throughout the engagement.

33. Records and documents may be accepted as genuine unless there is reason to doubt their authenticity. If conditions are identified during an attestation

engagement that cause the practitioner to believe records or documents may not be authentic or may have portions omitted, he or she should investigate further.

34. Professional judgment should be exercised in planning and performing an attestation engagement.

## Analysis and Application of Procedures

### Attestation Risk

Attestation risk has three components, although all components may not be present or significant in all engagements. The relevance of each component to an engagement depends on factors such as the nature of the underlying subject matter or subject matter information (or assertion) and the type of engagement being performed. Risks the practitioner does not directly influence are inherent risk, the susceptibility of the underlying subject matter to a material misstatement before considering any related controls, and control risk, the risk that a material misstatement could occur and not be prevented or detected and corrected by internal control systems in a timely manner. The practitioner does directly influence detection risk, the risk that procedures performed by the practitioner will not detect a material misstatement.

The overall attestation risk cannot be quantified, but the CPA must exercise professional judgment in order to assess inherent risk and control risk and establish an appropriate level of detection risk. The generalized relationships in Exhibit AT-C 105-1 can be used to establish an acceptable level of detection risk.

### EXHIBIT AT-C 105-1—ACCEPTABLE LEVEL OF DETECTION RISK

| Assessed Risk | Effect on Detection Risk Level |
| --- | --- |
| Inherent risk is assessed to be relatively high. | Detection risk should be established at a relatively low level. |
| Inherent risk is assessed to be relatively low. | Detection risk should be established at a relatively high level. |
| Control risk is assessed to be relatively high. | Detection risk should be established at a relatively low level. |
| Control risk is assessed to be relatively low. | Detection risk should be established at a relatively high level. |

In an examination engagement, the practitioner can achieve an acceptably low level of attestation risk to support his or her opinion by relying on search and verification procedures, such as physical observation, confirmation, and inspection, in addition to inquiry and analytical procedures. Assurance is reasonable rather than absolute due to factors such as the use of selective testing, the inherent limitations of internal control, the fact that a lot of evidence used is persuasive rather than conclusive, the use of professional judgment in evaluating evidence and forming conclusions, and the characteristics of the underlying subject matter when evaluated or measured against the criteria. In a review engagement, attestation risk is greater and the assurance provided is limited, less than that provided by an examination. Therefore, procedures performed are generally less extensive and limited to inquiry and analytical procedures.

> **PLANNING AID REMINDER:** Attestation risk is not applicable to agreed-upon procedures engagements because no opinion or conclusion is provided in the practitioner's report on findings.

## Conduct of an Attestation Engagement in Accordance with the Attestation Standards

To ensure that a practitioner's report in connection with services performed under other professional standards is not confused with a report issued under the attestation standards, the phrase "was conducted in accordance with attestation standards established by the American Institute of Certified Public Accountants" needs to be included.

> **PLANNING AID REMINDER:** Interpretation 1 of AT-C 105 notes that the accountant should not provide any form of assurance, through an examination, review, or agreed-upon procedures engagement, regarding matters related to an entity's solvency. However, as clarified by Interpretation 2 of AT-C 105, an accountant may provide expert testimony before a trier of fact on matters related to solvency, such as legal or regulatory proceedings before a trier of fact in connection with the resolution of a dispute between two or more parties.

> **PLANNING AID REMINDER:** The practitioner is not prohibited from combining reports issued under the attestation standards with reports issued under other professional standards.

Attestation standards contain both professional requirements and related guidance in applying the standard. In fulfilling professional responsibilities, the practitioner has a responsibility to consider the entire text of the relevant AT-C sections of the attestation standards. The related guidance in an attestation standard is also referred to as "application and explanatory material." Application and explanatory material in a SSAE is intended to be descriptive rather than imperative (i.e., it does not impose a performance obligation upon the practitioner). For example, explanatory material may (1) explain the objective of the professional requirements, (2) explain why particular attestation procedures are recommended or required, and (3) provide additional information that the practitioner may find helpful in applying his or her professional judgment. Explanatory material may discuss other procedures or actions that the practitioner might perform. These other procedures or actions are suggestive and do not impose a professional requirement on the practitioner. These suggested procedures and actions are denoted by the words "may," "might," and "could."

> **ENGAGEMENT STRATEGY:** In attestation engagements where the practitioner is required to comply with requirements in addition to attestation standards, the attestation standards do not override laws or regulations governing the engagement. If the attestation engagement is performed only in accordance with laws and regulations that differ from the attestation standards, the engagement may not comply with the attestation standards.

In addition to the attestation standards, there are other sources of guidance on performing attestation engagements. These other sources of guidance are attestation interpretations, interpretative publications, and other attestation publications.

Interpretative publications are not attestation standards, but represent recommendations on the application of the attestation standards in specific circumstances, including engagements for entities in specialized industries. Interpretative publications are issued under the authority of the relevant senior technical committee. Examples include interpretations of SSAEs, SSAE exhibits, attestation guidance in AICPA Audit and Accounting Guides, and AICPA attestation Statements of Position.

Other attestation publications have no authoritative status, but the practitioner may consider and apply this guidance if it is relevant and appropriate to the engagement. In evaluating whether an attestation publication is appropriate, the practitioner should consider (1) the degree to which the publication is recognized as helpful in understanding and applying SSAEs, and (2) the degree to which the issuer or author is recognized as an authority on attestation matters.

> **OBSERVATION:** An attestation publication that has been reviewed by the AICPA Audit and Attest Standards Staff is presumed to be appropriate.

## Preconditions for an Attestation Engagement

When considering independence for an attestation engagement, ET Section 1.297 (*Independence Standards for Engagements Performed in Accordance with Statements on Standards for Attestation Engagements*) from the AICPA Professional Standards provides special independence requirements for services performed under the attestation standards. ET Section 1.210 (*Conceptual Framework*) from the AICPA Professional Standards discusses threats to independence.

> **PUBLIC COMPANY IMPLICATION:** The PCAOB also has jurisdiction over standard setting for attestation engagements performed for public companies. When assessing independence related to an attestation engagement for a public company, registered public accounting firms must ensure that they are in compliance with all of the SEC's rules, PCAOB's rules, and Part 1.200 of the AICPA's Code of Professional Conduct.

All attestation engagements have an engaging party, a responsible party, the practitioner, and the intended users. In some engagements, the engaging party is different from the responsible party. In other engagements, the engaging party, the responsible party, and the intended users may all be the same.

Evidence that the responsible party takes responsibility for the underlying subject matter may be in the form of an engagement letter, representation letter, subject matter presentation, written assertion, or reference to legislation, regulation, or a contract.

For the underlying subject matter of an engagement to be appropriate, it should be identifiable, able to be consistently measured or evaluated against the criteria, and able to undergo procedures for obtaining sufficient appropriate audit evidence to support an opinion, conclusion, or findings. The responsible party should have processes in place that provide a reasonable basis for measuring or evaluating the subject matter or assertion. An underlying subject matter's ability to be precisely measured or evaluated and the persuasiveness of available evidence may depend on its characteristics, such as whether related information is qualitative or quantitative or relates to a point in time or covers a period in time.

> **PLANNING AID REMINDER:** If the underlying subject matter is not appropriate for an examination, it is also not appropriate for a review engagement.

For criteria to be considered suitable, they should have all of the following four characteristics:

1. Objective (free from bias),
2. Measurable (provide a reasonable basis for the consistent measurement of the underlying subject matter),
3. Complete (no relevant factors that would alter a conclusion are omitted), and
4. Relevant (related to the underlying subject matter).

There is no single source of criteria for the various attestation engagements, and the practitioner must use professional judgment to determine whether a specific set of criteria is suitable to a particular underlying subject matter.

> **PLANNING AID REMINDER:** Criteria developed by an appropriate professional group that follows due process procedures are ordinarily considered suitable. For example, the Auditing Standards Board's guidance in SOP 2003-02 (*Attest Engagements on Greenhouse Gas Emissions Information*) is considered suitable in performing attestation engagements relating to the existence and ownership of greenhouse gas emissions credits. Conversely, in other cases, a client (or other parties or groups that do not follow due process procedures and that do not represent a group of experts) may develop criteria to be used for the attest engagement. In such cases, the practitioner must use the four characteristics listed above to determine the suitability of the criteria established for the attest engagement.

> **OBSERVATION:** In some engagements, the appropriateness of criteria may apply only to parties that have participated in the establishment of the criteria or that have a particular level or type of expertise. In these circumstances the practitioner should restrict the use of the engagement report.

If criteria are specifically designed for the underlying subject matter or assertion of the engagement, they are not suitable if the underlying subject matter, assertion, or practitioner's report is misleading to the intended users. In these circumstances, it is helpful for the intended users or engaging party to acknowledge the criteria are suitable; if the acknowledgment is absent, it may affect steps taken to assess the suitability of the criteria and the information provided about the criteria in the practitioner's report.

Criteria need to be available to intended users under at least one of the following circumstances:

1. The criteria are publicly available.
2. The criteria are clearly presented in the presentation of the subject matter information or the assertion.
3. The criteria are clearly presented in the practitioner's report.
4. The criteria are commonly understood and are not unique to the attest engagement.
5. The criteria are available only to the specified parties (and therefore the availability of auditor's report is restricted).

The practitioner's ability to obtain needed evidence may be impacted by the nature of the relationship between the responsible and engaging parties and the practitioner and could be a factor in determining engagement acceptance. The quality and quantity of evidence is affected by the characteristics of the underlying subject matter or subject matter information and other circumstances, such as the unavailability of evidence expected to exist whether due to adequacy of information systems, entity retention policies or restrictions by the responsible party.

*Acceptance of a Change in Engagement Terms*

Reasonable justification for a change in engagement terms may be a change in circumstances that changes the responsible party or engaging party's requirements or a misunderstanding regarding the type of engagement originally requested. However, a change in engagement terms may not be reasonable if it appears to be requested due to incorrect, incomplete, or unsatisfactory information, for example, to avoid a modified opinion or disclaimer of opinion. If the practitioner and engaging party cannot agree to a change in engagement terms and the practitioner cannot continue the original engagement, he or she may withdraw from the engagement where possible by law or regulation.

*Using the Work of Other Practitioners*

The practitioner may use the work of other practitioners to obtain sufficient appropriate evidence for the attestation engagement. Regardless, the practitioner remains responsible for the direction, supervision, and performance of the engagement in compliance with professional standards, applicable laws and regulations, and firm policies and procedures and for determining whether the practitioner's report issued is appropriate in the circumstances.

Whether or not the engagement partner assumes responsibility for or makes reference to the other practitioner, the practitioner is required to communicate clearly with the other practitioner and evaluate the adequacy of his or her work for the engagement. The nature, timing, and extent of this involvement are affected by the practitioner's knowledge of the other practitioner and whether they are subject to common quality control policies and procedures.

## Quality Control

The engagement partner must consider the competence and capabilities of the engagement team and any practitioner's external specialists and in doing so, may consider matters such as their:

- Understanding of and experience with engagements of similar size and complexity;
- Understanding of professional standards and applicable legal and regulatory requirements;
- Technical expertise including any relevant IT and specialized subject-matter areas;
- Knowledge of relevant industries;
- Ability to apply professional judgment; and
- Understanding of the firm's quality control policies and procedures.

## Engagement Documentation

Documentation prepared on a timely basis is more likely to be accurate than if it were prepared at a later time. Completion of the final engagement file must occur by 60 days after the practitioner's report release date. Completing the file should not involve performing new procedures or drawing new conclusions, but administrative changes may be made to documentation during this process, such as discarding superseded documents, documenting previously agreed-upon evidence, and adding information received after the report release date.

Attestation documentation should be retained for the period of time that meets the objectives of the CPA firm (for example, the need for internal reviews) and satisfies the legal or regulatory requirements imposed by the state or regulatory authorities.

---

**PUBLIC COMPANY IMPLICATION:** The PCAOB requires auditors to retain audit documentation for seven years from the audit report release date. The PCAOB will presumably develop retention requirements for documentation in support of attest engagements at some future point.

---

**PLANNING AID REMINDER:** Accountants are sometimes required by law, regulation, or contract to provide a regulator access to engagement documentation and the regulator may request copies of the engagement documentation.

Interpretation 3 of AT-C 105 provides guidance on steps the accountant may take to respond to these types of regulator requests. These steps include (1) advising the client of the request, (2) making arrangements with the regulator for the review, (3) maintaining control over the engagement documentation, and (4) considering submission of a letter to the regulator to clarify expectations between the accountant and the regulator.

## Engagement Quality Control Review

While there are several required elements an engagement quality control reviewer should evaluate in performing their review, additional matters may be considered such as:

- The engagement team's evaluation of firm independence for the engagement;
- Whether appropriate consultation on differences of opinion or other difficult or contentious matters has occurred and the conclusions that were reached; and
- Whether selected engagement documentation being reviewed is representative of the significant judgments made and supports the conclusions reached.

## Professional Skepticism and Professional Judgment

By using professional skepticism, the practitioner does not assume a party is either dishonest or honest. Therefore, the practitioner needs to obtain sufficient appropriate evidence for the engagement. Professional skepticism involves critically assessing the evidence obtained while being alert to contradictory evidence, information that causes the practitioner to question document reliability and inquiry responses, and circumstances that may indicate fraud or that suggest the need for additional procedures to be performed.

The professional judgment of a practitioner is based on competencies needed to achieve reasonable judgments and is developed through relevant training, knowledge, and experience. Professional judgment can be evaluated by considering whether the judgment reached reflects a competent application of the attestation standards and measurement or evaluation principles and is appropriate given the facts and circumstances known to the practitioner at the date of his or her report.

**ENGAGEMENT STRATEGY:** Consulting on difficult or contentious matters during an engagement can assist the practitioner in making informed and reasonable judgments.

Professional judgment is needed in examination and review engagements to make decisions about matter such as:

- Materiality and attestation risk;
- The nature, timing, and extent of procedures used to meet the relevant requirements and obtain evidence;
- Evaluating whether sufficient appropriate audit evidence has been obtained for the engagement type;
- Evaluating the responsible party's judgments in applying the criteria in assertion-based examination engagements or review engagements; and
- Drawing conclusions based on evidence obtained.

# SECTION 200

## LEVEL OF SERVICE

# SECTION 205

## ASSERTION-BASED EXAMINATION ENGAGEMENTS

### Authoritative Pronouncements

SSAE-18—Attestation Standards: Clarification and Recodification

SSAE-20—Amendments to the Description of the Concept of Materiality

SSAE-21—Direct Examination Engagements

SSAE Interpretation 1—Reporting on Attestation Engagements Performed in Accordance with Government Auditing Standards

SSAE Interpretation 2—Reporting on the Design of Internal Control

### Overview

This AT-C section contains performance and reporting requirements and application guidance for assertion-based examination engagements. The objectives of an assertion-based examination are to:

- Obtain reasonable assurance about whether the subject matter is free from material misstatement as measured or evaluated against the criteria (**Note:** The term "subject matter" encompasses terms such as underlying subject matter and subject matter information);
- Express an opinion in a written report about whether, in all material respects, (1) the subject matter is in accordance with or based on the criteria or (2) the responsible party's assertion is fairly stated; and
- Communicate further as required by the attestation standards.

**IMPORTANT NOTICE FOR 2022:** In September 2020, the ASB issued Statement on Standards for Attestation Engagements (SSAE) No. 21 (*Direct Examination Engagements*), that adds a new AT-C 206 (*Direct Examination Engagements*) to the attestation standards that enable practitioners to perform an examination engagement in which the practitioner obtains reasonable assurance by measuring or evaluating underlying subject matter against criteria and expressing an opinion that conveys the results of that measurement or evaluation. SSAE No. 21 allows the entity in an examination engagement to not provide an assertion about whether the underlying subject matter is in accordance with the criteria. SSAE No. 21 retitled AT-C 205 to reflect the fact that this section now specifically applies to assertion-based examination engagements whereby the entity evaluates whether the subject matter is in accordance with the stated criteria. SSAE No. 21 is effective for examination reports dated on or after June 15, 2022.

---

**PUBLIC COMPANY IMPLICATION:** The PCAOB has issued an attestation standard pertaining to examinations of brokers and dealers. The standard (*Examination Engagements Regarding Compliance Reports of Brokers and Dealers*) addresses an auditor's examination of compliance reports. This attestation standard is designed to help protect customer funds held by broker-dealers by improving the quality of compliance information used by the Securities and Exchange Commission (SEC) in overseeing broker-dealers.

The SEC has recently instituted new requirements (under Exchange Act Rule 17a-5) requiring broker-dealers to prepare compliance or exemption reports, and requiring PCAOB-registered auditors to examine or review such reports. Broker-dealers that hold customer securities or funds must maintain a certain capital level, and must maintain a certain reserve of funds or qualified securities. These requirements around capital and liquidity are designed to enhance market confidence and to safeguard investors, both of which are especially important when adverse market events occur. Broker-dealers holding customer funds must prepare and file a compliance report. Broker-dealers not holding customer funds must file an exemption report to claim an exemption from the compliance-reporting requirements. In addition, broker-dealers must file audited financial statements and supporting schedules with the SEC.

The attestation standard requires the auditor to obtain sufficient appropriate evidence to provide reasonable assurance that the broker-dealer (1) maintained effective internal control over compliance during the most recent fiscal year, (2) had effective internal control over compliance at year-end, (3) complied with the net capital rule and reserve requirement rule at year-end, and (4) based its statement as to compliance on its books and records. The standard provides guidance on (1) planning the engagement; (2) testing controls, both design and operating effectiveness; (3) performing compliance tests; (4) evaluating results; and (5) subsequent events, representation letters, and reporting.

---

## Definitions

| | |
|---|---|
| Appropriateness of evidence | The measure of the quality of evidence, or its relevance and reliability in providing support for the practitioner's opinion. |
| Modified opinion | A qualified opinion, adverse opinion, or disclaimer of opinion. |
| Risk of material misstatement | The risk that the subject matter is not, in all material respects, in accordance with or based on the criteria or that the assertion is not fairly stated. |
| Sufficiency of evidence | The measure of the quantity of evidence, affected by the risks of material misstatement and evidence quality. |
| Test of controls | A procedure designed to evaluate the operating effectiveness of controls in preventing, or detecting and correcting, material misstatements in the subject matter. |

## Requirements

The practitioner is presumptively required to perform the following procedures when conducting an examination engagement:

### Conduct of an Examination Engagement

1. When performing an examination engagement, the practitioner should comply with AT-C Sections 105 and any subject-matter AT-C section relevant to the engagement.

### Preconditions for an Examination Engagement

2. If a practitioner is not independent but is required by law or regulation to accept the engagement and report on the subject matter or assertion, the practitioner should disclaim an opinion and state that he or she is not independent. The reasons for the lack of independence do not have to be provided; however, if they are provided, all reasons for the lack of independence should be included.

### Agreeing on Engagement Terms

3. Engagement terms should be agreed upon with the engaging party and should be specified in sufficient detail in an engagement letter or other suitable written agreement.

4. Engagement terms should include:

   a. Engagement scope and objective;

   b. Practitioner responsibilities;

   c. A statement that the engagement will be conducted in accordance with attestation standards established by the American Institute of Certified Public Accountants;

   d. Responsible party and, if different, engaging party responsibilities;

   e. A statement about the inherent limitations of an examination engagement;

   f. Identification of the criteria for the measurement, evaluation, or disclosure of the subject matter; and

   g. An acknowledgment that the engaging party agrees to provide the practitioner with a representation letter at the end of the engagement.

5. In a recurring engagement, the terms do not need to be modified if they are still suitable, but the practitioner should remind the engaging party of the engagement terms and document that reminder.

### Requesting a Written Assertion

6. Request a written assertion from the responsible party about the measurement or evaluation of the underlying subject matter against the criteria. If the responsible party refuses to provide a written assertion and it is also the engaging party, the practitioner is required to withdraw from the engagement where permitted by law and regulations. If the responsible party refuses to provide a written assertion and it is not the engaging party, the practitioner is required to disclose that refusal in the practitioner's report and restrict its use to the engaging party.

§ 205 • Examination Engagements    10,027

## Planning and Performing the Engagement

7. An overall engagement strategy should be established, setting the scope, timing, and direction of the engagement and guiding development of the engagement plan.

8. To establish an overall engagement strategy:

   a. Identify the engagement characteristics that define its scope and determine the engagement's reporting objectives in order to plan engagement timing and the nature of the required communications;

   b. Using professional judgment, consider significant factors in directing the engagement team's efforts;

   c. Consider the results of preliminary engagement activities, such as client acceptance, and whether knowledge gained on other engagements for the entity is relevant; and

   d. Determine the nature, timing, and extent of resources necessary to perform the engagement.

9. Develop a plan that includes a description of:

   a. The nature, timing, and extent of planned risk assessment procedures;

   b. The nature, timing, and extent of planned further procedures; and

   c. Other planned procedures required for the engagement to comply with the attestation standards.

## Risk Assessment Procedures

10. Obtain an understanding of the subject matter and other engagement circumstances sufficient to enable identification and assessment of the risks of material misstatement in the subject matter and to provide a basis for designing and performing procedures to respond to the assessed risks and obtain reasonable assurance to support the practitioner's opinion.

11. As part of obtaining an understanding of the subject matter, the practitioner should obtain an understanding of internal control over the preparation of the subject matter relevant to the engagement, including evaluating the design of relevant controls and determining whether they have been implemented by performing procedures in addition to inquiry of responsible personnel. The practitioner also should make inquiries to determine whether the responsible party has an internal audit function (and, if so, understand the main activities and main findings of that function) or whether they have used any specialists in the preparation of the subject matter.

## Materiality in Engagement Planning and Performance

12. Consider materiality for the subject matter when establishing the overall engagement strategy.

13. Reconsider materiality for the subject matter if the practitioner becomes aware of information during the engagement that would have caused a different determination of materiality initially.

---

**IMPORTANT NOTICE FOR 2022:** In December 2019, the AICPA's Auditing Standards Board (ASB) issued Statement on Attestation Standards (SSAE) No. 20 (*Amendments to the Description of the Concept of Materiality*) to align the materiality concepts discussed in attestation standards, including AT-C 205, with the definition of materiality used by the U.S. judicial system, the PCAOB auditing standards, and the Financial Accounting Standards Board (FASB). The FASB aligned its definition of materiality in August 2018 to be consistent with the U.S. judicial system and other U.S. standards setters and regulators. The ASB believes it is in the public interest to eliminate existing inconsistencies in definitions of materiality used. The U.S. judicial system defines misstatement as material if there is **"substantial likelihood** that a reasonable shareholder **would** consider it important,"whereas existing attestation standards define a misstatement as material if it **"could reasonably be expected to** influence the judgment of a reasonable person." SSAE No. 20 became effective for practitioner examination reports dated on or after December 15, 2020.

## Identifying Risks of Material Misstatement

14. Identify and assess risks of material misstatement to design and perform further procedures whose nature, timing, and extent are responsive to assessed risks of material misstatement and allow the practitioner to obtain reasonable assurance about whether the subject matter is in accordance with or based on the criteria in all material respects.

## Responding to Assessed Risks and Obtaining Evidence

15. Obtain reasonable assurance by obtaining sufficient appropriate evidence to reduce attestation risk to an acceptably low level to allow the practitioner to draw reasonable conclusions on which to base his or her opinion.

16. Design and implement overall responses to address the assessed risks of material misstatement for the subject matter or assertion.

## Further Procedures

17. Design and perform further procedures whose nature, timing, and extent are responsive to the assessed risks of material misstatement:

    a. Considering the reasons for the assessment given to the risk of material misstatement, including the likelihood of material misstatement due to the subject matter characteristics and whether the practitioner intends to rely on the operating effectiveness of controls in determining the nature, timing and extent of other procedures; and

    b. Obtaining more persuasive evidence the higher the assessment of risk.

18. Consider the relevance and reliability of information to be used as evidence when designing and performing procedures. If evidence obtained from multiple sources is inconsistent, the practitioner has doubts about the reliability of information to be used as evidence, or responses to inquiries are inconsistent or otherwise unsatisfactory, determine what procedure modifications or additions are needed to resolve the matter and consider the effect of the matter on any other aspects of the engagement.

19. Design and perform tests of controls to obtain sufficient appropriate evidence about the operating effectiveness of relevant controls if:

    a. The practitioner intends to rely on the operating effectiveness of controls in determining the nature, timing, and extent of other procedures;

    b. Procedures other than tests of controls do not provide sufficient appropriate audit evidence; or

    c. The subject matter is internal control.

20. If tests of controls are designed and performed to test operating effectiveness and deviations are identified, specific inquiries and other necessary procedures should be performed to understand these matters and their potential consequences. Determine whether:
   a. The tests of controls performed provide an appropriate basis for reliance on the controls;
   b. Additional tests of controls are necessary; or
   c. The potential risks of misstatement need to be addressed using other procedures.

21. Tests of details or analytical procedures related to the subject matter should be designed and performed regardless of the assessed risks of material misstatement, except when the subject matter is internal control.

22. In designing and performing analytical procedures in response to assessed risks:
   a. Determine the suitability of specific analytical procedures for the subject matter, with consideration of the assessed risks of material misstatement and any related tests of details;
   b. Evaluate the reliability of data from which the practitioner's expectation is developed, taking into account the source, comparability, nature, and relevance of available information and controls over their preparation; and
   c. Develop a sufficiently precise expectation to identify possible material misstatements, considering whether analytical procedures will be performed alone or in combination with tests of details.

23. Investigate any fluctuations or relationships that are inconsistent or differ significantly from expectations that are identified by analytical procedures by:
   a. Inquiring of the responsible party and obtaining additional evidence relevant to the responses; and
   b. Performing other procedures needed in the circumstances.

24. Based on the assessed risks of material misstatement, evaluate whether:
   a. The responsible party appropriately applied relevant requirements to any estimated amounts; and
   b. The methods for making estimates are appropriate, applied consistently and any changes in reported estimates or the methods used to make estimates are appropriate.

25. To respond to an assessed risk of material misstatement related to an estimate, do one or more of the following, considering the nature of the estimates:
   a. Determine whether events occurring up to the date of the practitioner's report provide evidence regarding the estimate.
   b. Test how the responsible party made the estimate and the data on which it is based, evaluating whether an appropriate measurement method was used, reasonable assumptions were used by the responsible party, and the data on which the estimate is based are sufficiently reliable for the practitioner's purposes.
   c. Test the operating effectiveness of the controls over how the responsible party made the estimate together with other appropriate further procedures.
   d. Develop a point estimate or range to evaluate the responsible party's estimate. If the practitioner uses different assumptions or methods than the responsible party, an understanding of the responsible

party's assumptions and methods should be obtained sufficiently to determine the practitioner is taking into account relevant variables and to evaluate any significant differences from the responsible party's point estimate. If the practitioner concludes use of a range is appropriate, the range should be narrowed by the available evidence until all outcomes within the range are considered reasonable.

26. If sampling is used, consider the purpose of the procedure and population characteristics when designing the sample. Sampling involves:

   a. Determining a sufficient sample size to reduce sampling risk to an acceptably low level;

   b. Selecting items for the sample so there is a reasonable expectation that the sample is representative of the relevant population and likely to provide a reasonable basis for conclusions about the population;

   c. Treating a selected item for which designed procedures or suitable alternative procedures are unable to be performed as a deviation from the prescribed control in a test of controls or a misstatement in a test of details;

   d. Investigating the nature and cause of identified deviations and misstatements and evaluating their possible effect on the purpose of the procedure and other areas of the engagement;

   e. Evaluating the sample results, including sampling risk, and projecting misstatements found in the sample to the population; and

   f. Evaluating whether use of sampling has provided an appropriate basis for conclusions about the population being tested.

## *Fraud, Laws, and Regulations*

27. The practitioner should:

   a. Consider whether risk assessment procedures and other procedures performed to understand the subject matter indicate risk of material misstatement due to fraud or noncompliance with laws or regulations;

   b. Inquire of appropriate parties to determine whether they are aware of any actual, suspected, or alleged fraud or noncompliance with laws or regulations affecting the subject matter;

   c. Evaluate whether there are unusual or unexpected relationships within the subject matter or between the subject matter and other related information that indicate risks of material misstatement due to fraud or noncompliance with laws or regulations; and

   d. Evaluate whether other information obtained indicates risk of material misstatement due to fraud or noncompliance with laws or regulations.

28. Respond appropriately when suspected or actual fraud or noncompliance with laws and regulations affecting the subject matter is identified during the engagement.

## *Revision of Risk Assessment*

29. The assessment of risk of material misstatement may change during an engagement if additional evidence is obtained that is inconsistent with the evidence on which the original assessment was based. In these circumstances, the assessment should be revised and planned procedures modified accordingly.

## Evaluating the Reliability of Information Produced by the Entity

30. Evaluate whether information produced by the entity is sufficiently reliable for the practitioner's purposes. If needed, this evaluation may include obtaining evidence about the accuracy and completeness of the information and evaluating whether the information is sufficiently precise and detailed for the practitioner's purposes.

## Using the Work of a Practitioner's Specialist

31. If the work of a practitioner's specialist is expected to be used, the practitioner should do the following:

    a. Evaluate whether the practitioner's specialist has the necessary competence, capabilities, and objectivity for the practitioner's purposes. When considering objectivity, inquire about interests and relationships that could create a threat to objectivity.

    b. Obtain a sufficient understanding of the field of expertise of a practitioner's specialist to determine the nature, scope, and objectives and evaluate the adequacy of their work for the practitioner's purposes.

    c. Agree with the practitioner's specialist regarding:

        i. The nature, scope, and objectives of their work;

        ii. The roles and responsibilities of the practitioner and the specialist;

        iii. The nature, timing, and extent of communication between the practitioner and specialist, including the form of any report or documentation the specialist will provide; and

        iv. The need for the specialist to observe confidentiality requirements.

    d. Evaluate the adequacy of the specialist's work for the practitioner's purposes including:

        i. The relevance and reasonableness of the specialist's findings and conclusions and their consistency with other evidence;

        ii. Obtaining an understanding of and evaluating the relevance and reasonableness of any significant assumptions and methods used by the specialist in the circumstances, considering the reasoning and support provided by the specialist and its relation to the practitioner's other findings and conclusions; and

        iii. The relevance, completeness, and accuracy of any source data significant to the specialist's work.

32. If the practitioner determines the specialist's work is not adequate for his or her purposes, the practitioner should agree with the specialist as to the nature and extent of further work the specialist will perform or perform additional procedures appropriate to the circumstances.

33. In determining the appropriate nature, timing, and extent of procedures a practitioner will perform when using the work of a practitioner's specialist, consider the following:

    a. The significance of the specialist's work in the context of the engagement.

    b. The nature of the matter to which the specialist's work relates.

    c. The risks of material misstatement in the matter to which the specialist's work relates.

d. The practitioner's knowledge of and experience with previous work performed by that specialist.
  e. Whether the specialist is subject to the practitioner's firm's quality control policies and procedures.

## Using the Work of Internal Auditors

34. When the internal audit function's work is expected to be used to obtain evidence or to provide direct assistance, determine whether the work can be used for the purposes of the examination by evaluating:
   a. The competence level of the internal audit function or individual internal auditors providing direct assistance;
   b. The extent to which the internal audit function's organizational status and relevant policies and procedures support its objectivity, or for internal auditors providing direct assistance, the existence of threats to their objectivity and the related safeguards applied to reduce or eliminate those threats; and
   c. The systematic and disciplined approach, including quality control, used by the internal audit function.

35. When using the work of the internal audit function, perform sufficient procedures on the work that the practitioner is planning to use to determine its adequacy for the engagement, including reperforming some of that work.

36. Before using internal auditors to provide direct assistance, obtain written acknowledgment from the responsible party that internal auditors providing direct assistance will be allowed to follow the practitioner's instructions and that the responsible party will not intervene in the internal auditor's work for the practitioner.

37. Direct, supervise, and review the work of internal auditors when using their work to provide direct assistance to the practitioner.

38. The practitioner has sole responsibility for the opinion expressed and should make all significant judgments in the engagement, including when to use the work of the internal audit function in obtaining evidence. To prevent undue reliance on the internal audit function, the practitioner should plan to perform more of the work directly:
   a. The more judgment is involved in planning and performing relevant procedures or evaluating the evidence obtained;
   b. The higher the assessed risk of material misstatement;
   c. The less the internal audit function's organizational status and relevant policies and procedures adequately support their objectivity; and
   d. The lower the competence level of the internal audit function.

39. Before the engagement's conclusion, evaluate whether the use of the work of the internal audit function or internal auditors to provide direct assistance results in the practitioner being sufficiently involved in the examination given his or her sole responsibility for the opinion expressed.

## Evaluating the Results of the Procedures

40. Accumulate misstatements, other than those that are clearly trivial, identified during the engagement.

41. Evaluate the sufficiency and appropriateness of the evidence obtained in the context of the engagement and attempt to obtain further evidence if necessary. Consider all relevant evidence, regardless of whether it appears to

corroborate or contradict the measurement or evaluation of the subject matter against the criteria.

42. If it is not possible to obtain necessary further evidence, issue a modified opinion (see requirement 63).

## Considering Subsequent Events and Subsequently Discovered Facts

43. Inquire whether the responsible party and engaging party are aware of any events subsequent to the period or point in time covered by the engagement up to the date of the practitioner's report that could have a significant effect on the subject matter or assertion and apply appropriate procedures to obtain evidence about such events. Take appropriate action if the practitioner becomes aware through inquiry or other means that a subsequent event has occurred that is of such a nature and significance that its disclosure is necessary to prevent report users from being misled and it is not adequately disclosed in the responsible party's subject matter or assertion.

44. The practitioner has no responsibility to perform any procedures regarding the subject matter or assertion after the date of the practitioner's report. However, the practitioner should respond appropriately to facts he or she becomes aware of after the date of the report that may have caused the report to be revised had the practitioner been aware of those facts at the date of the practitioner's report.

## Written Representations

45. Request written representations from the responsible party in the form of a letter addressed to the practitioner. The representations should:
   a. Include the responsible party's assertion about the subject matter based on the criteria;
   b. State that all relevant matters are reflected in the measurement or evaluation of the subject matter or assertion;
   c. State that all known matters contradicting the subject matter or assertion and any communication from regulatory agencies or others affecting the subject matter or assertion have been disclosed to the practitioner, including communications received between the end of the period addressed in the written assertion and the date of the practitioner's report;
   d. Acknowledge responsibility for the subject matter and assertion, selecting the criteria when applicable, and determining that those criteria are appropriate for the responsible party's purposes;
   e. State that any known events subsequent to the period or point in time of the subject matter being reported on that would have a material effect on the subject matter or assertion have been disclosed to the practitioner;
   f. State that it has provided the practitioner with all relevant information and access;
   g. State that it believes the effects of any uncorrected misstatements are immaterial, individually and in the aggregate, to the subject matter;
   h. State that any significant assumptions used in making material estimates are reasonable; and
   i. State that the responsible party has disclosed to the practitioner all internal control deficiencies relevant to the engagement of which it is aware, its knowledge of any actual, suspected, or alleged fraud or

noncompliance with laws or regulations affecting the subject matter and other matters the practitioner determines are appropriate.

46. When the engaging party is different from the responsible party and the responsible party refuses to provide the above written representations, inquire of the responsible party about the representations and try to obtain oral responses.

47. When the engaging party is different from the responsible party, request additional written representations from the engaging party in the form of a letter addressed to the practitioner. The representations should:

    a. Acknowledge that the responsible party is responsible for the subject matter and assertion;

    b. Acknowledge the engaging party's responsibility for selecting the criteria when applicable;

    c. Acknowledge the engaging party's responsibility for determining those criteria are appropriate for its purposes;

    d. State that the engaging party is not aware of any material misstatements in the subject matter or assertion;

    e. State that the engaging party has disclosed to the practitioner all known events subsequent to the period or point in time of the subject matter being reported on that would have a material effect on the subject matter or assertion; and

    f. Address other matters the practitioner determines are appropriate.

48. When written representations are directly related to matters that are material to the subject matter, evaluate their reasonableness and consistency with other evidence obtained, including other representations, and consider whether those making the representations can be expected to be well informed on those matters.

49. The date of the written representation should be as of the date of the practitioner's report and should address the subject matter and periods covered by the practitioner's opinion.

## *Requested Written Representations Not Provided or Not Reliable*

50. When the engaging party is the responsible party and one or more written representations are not provided, or the practitioner concludes there is sufficient doubt about the competence, integrity, ethical values, or diligence of those providing the written representations, or the practitioner concludes the written representations are otherwise not reliable:

    a. Discuss the matter with the appropriate parties;

    b. Reevaluate the integrity of those from whom representations were requested or received and evaluate the effect of this on the reliability of representations and other evidence; and

    c. If any matters are not resolved to the practitioner's satisfaction, take appropriate action.

51. When the engaging party is not the responsible party and one or more written representations are not provided by the responsible party:

    a. If the practitioner receives oral responses to his or her inquiries that allow the practitioner to conclude he or she has sufficient appropriate evidence to form an opinion about the subject matter, the practitioner's report should contain a separate paragraph restricting the use of the report to the engaging party; and

b. If the practitioner does not receive oral responses to his or her inquiries, a scope limitation exists and the practitioner should determine the effect on his or her report or withdraw from the engagement.

## Other Information

52. If the practitioner is willing to allow the inclusion of the practitioner's report in a document containing the subject matter or assertion and other information, read the other information to identify any material inconsistencies with the subject matter, assertion, or practitioner's report. If, using professional judgment, the practitioner identifies a material inconsistency or material misstatement of fact, he or she should discuss the matter with the responsible party and take further action as appropriate.

## Description of Criteria

53. Evaluate whether the written description of the subject matter or assertion adequately refers to or describes the criteria.

## Forming the Opinion

54. Form an opinion about whether, in all material respects, the subject matter is in accordance with or based on the criteria or the assertion is fairly stated by evaluating the practitioner's conclusions regarding the sufficiency and appropriateness of evidence obtained and whether uncorrected misstatements are material, individually or in the aggregate.

55. Evaluate, based on the evidence obtained, whether the presentation of the subject matter or assertion is misleading within the context of the engagement.

## Preparing the Practitioner's Report

56. The practitioner's report should be in writing.

57. A practitioner should report directly on the subject matter or on a written assertion, which should either accompany the practitioner's report or be clearly stated in the practitioner's report.

## Content of the Practitioner's Report

58. The examination report should contain the following:
   a. A title that includes the word independent.
   b. An appropriate addressee.
   c. An identification or description of the subject matter or assertion being reported on, including the period or point in time to which its measurement or evaluation relates.
   d. An identification of the criteria against which the subject matter was measured or evaluated.
   e. A statement that identifies the responsible party and its responsibility for its assertion or for the subject matter in accordance with or based on the criteria and the practitioner's responsibility to express an opinion on the subject matter or assertion based on the examination.
   f. Unless the practitioner is disclaiming an opinion, a statement that:
      i. The examination was conducted in accordance with attestation standards established by the American Institute of Certified Public Accountants;

ii. Those standards require the practitioner to plan and perform the examination to obtain reasonable assurance about whether, in all material respects, the subject matter is in accordance with or based on the criteria or the responsible party's assertion is fairly stated; and

iii. The practitioner believes the evidence obtained is sufficient and appropriate to provide a reasonable basis for the practitioner's opinion.

g. Unless the practitioner is disclaiming an opinion, a description of the nature of an examination engagement.

h. A statement that describes any significant inherent limitations associated with the measurement or evaluation of the subject matter against the criteria.

i. The practitioner's opinion about whether, in all material respects, the subject matter is in accordance with or based on the criteria or the responsible party's assertion is fairly stated.

j. The manual or printed signature of the practitioner's firm.

k. The city and state where the practitioner practices.

l. The date of the practitioner's report, which should be no earlier than the date on which the practitioner has obtained sufficient appropriate evidence on which to base the practitioner's opinion, including evidence that:

i. The attestation documentation has been reviewed;

ii. The written presentation of the subject matter has been prepared if applicable; and

iii. The responsible party has provided a written assertion, or when the responsible party is not the engaging party an oral assertion.

*Restricted-use paragraph*

59. The use of the practitioner's report should be restricted and include an alert in a separate paragraph when:

a. The practitioner determines that the criteria used to evaluate the subject matter are only appropriate for a limited number of parties who have participated in establishing the criteria or who can be presumed to have an adequate understanding of the criteria;

b. The criteria used to evaluate the subject matter are only available to specified parties; and

c. The engaging party is not the responsible party, and the responsible party provides oral but not written representations required. In this case, use of the report should be restricted to the engaging party.

60. The alert should state that the practitioner's report is intended solely for the information and use of the specified parties, identify those parties, and state that the practitioner's report is not intended to be and should not be used by anyone other than the specified parties.

61. If the engagement is also performed in accordance with *Government Auditing Standards* the alert restricting use of the practitioner's report should instead include a description of the purpose of the practitioner's report and a statement that the report is not suitable for any other purpose.

## Reference to the Practitioner's Specialist

62. The work of a practitioner's specialist should not be referred to in a practitioner's report containing an unmodified opinion.

## Modified Opinions

63. Modify the opinion by issuing a qualified, adverse, or disclaimer, when, using professional judgment, either of the following circumstances exist and the effect is or may be material:
    a. The practitioner is unable to obtain sufficient appropriate evidence to conclude that the subject matter is in accordance with or based on the criteria in all material respects.
    b. The practitioner concludes based on evidence obtained that the subject matter is not in accordance with or based on the criteria in all material respects.

64. When the practitioner's opinion is modified, include a separate paragraph in the practitioner's report describing the matter causing the modification.

65. Express a qualified opinion when:
    a. Sufficient appropriate evidence is obtained but the practitioner concludes there are material misstatements, individually or in the aggregate, but they are not pervasive to the subject matter, or
    b. Sufficient appropriate evidence is unable to be obtained but the practitioner concludes that possible undetected misstatements could be material but not pervasive to the subject matter.

66. When a qualified opinion is expressed due to a material misstatement of the subject matter, state that in the practitioner's opinion, except for the effects of the matters giving rise to the modification, the subject matter is presented in accordance with or based on the criteria, in all material respects. When the opinion is modified due to an inability to obtain sufficient appropriate evidence, the phrase "except for the possible effects of the matter(s) ..." should be used in the modified opinion.

67. Express an adverse opinion when sufficient appropriate evidence is obtained and the practitioner concludes misstatements, individually or in the aggregate, are both material and pervasive to the subject matter.

68. When expressing an adverse opinion, state that, in the practitioner's opinion, because of the significance of matters causing the modification the subject matter is not presented in accordance with or based on the criteria, in all material respects.

69. Disclaim an opinion when the practitioner is unable to obtain sufficient appropriate evidence on which to base the opinion and the practitioner concludes that possible effects on the subject matter of any undetected misstatements could be both material and pervasive.

70. When an opinion is disclaimed due to an inability to obtain sufficient appropriate evidence, the practitioner's report should state that because of the significance of the matters giving rise to the modification, the practitioner has not been able to obtain sufficient appropriate evidence to provide a basis for an examination opinion and accordingly, the practitioner does not express an opinion on the subject matter.

71. When a qualified or adverse opinion is expressed, the description of the practitioner's responsibility should be amended to state that the practitioner believes the evidence obtained is sufficient and appropriate to provide a basis for the practitioner's modified opinion.

72. When an opinion is disclaimed due to an inability to obtain sufficient appropriate evidence, the practitioner's report should be amended to state that the practitioner was engaged to examine the subject matter or assertion. The description of the practitioner's responsibility and description of an examination should be amended to state only the following:

"Our responsibility is to express an opinion on the subject matter or assertion based on conducting the examination in accordance with attestation standards established by the American Institute of Certified Public Accountants."

"Because of the limitation on the scope of our examination discussed in the preceding paragraph, the scope of our work was not sufficient to enable us to express, and we do not express, an opinion on whether the subject matter referred to above is in accordance with or based on the criteria, in all material respects."

73. If a modified opinion is expressed because of a scope limitation but there is also a matter the practitioner is aware of that caused the subject matter to be materially misstated, the practitioner's report should include a clear description of the scope limitation and the matter causing the subject matter to be materially misstated.

74. If the practitioner concludes conditions exist that, individually or in combination, result in one or more material misstatements based on the criteria, the practitioner's opinion should be modified and a qualified or adverse opinion should be expressed directly on the subject matter, not on the assertion, even if the misstatement is acknowledged in the assertion.

75. The practitioner's opinion on the subject matter or assertion should be clearly separated from any paragraphs emphasizing matters related to the subject matter or any other reporting responsibilities.

76. When the opinion is modified, reference to an external specialist is permitted if the reference is relevant to understanding the modification to the opinion; however, the practitioner's report should indicate that the practitioner's responsibility for the opinion is not reduced.

## *Responsible Party Refuses to Provide a Written Assertion*

77. If the engaging party is the responsible party and refuses to provide the practitioner with a written assertion, withdraw from the engagement where withdrawal is possible under applicable laws and regulations.

78. Disclaim an opinion if law and regulation do not allow the practitioner to withdraw from the engagement.

79. If the engaging party is not the responsible party and the responsible party refuses to provide the practitioner with a written assertion, the practitioner may report on the subject matter but should disclose the refusal in the report and restrict its use to the engaging party.

## *Communication Responsibilities*

80. Communicate to the responsible party and engaging party (if different) known and suspected fraud and noncompliance with laws and regulations, uncorrected misstatements, and relevant internal control deficiencies identified during the engagement.

81. If noncompliance with laws or regulations that are not relevant to the subject matter are identified or suspected, determine whether the practitioner has a responsibility to report such noncompliance to parties other than the responsible and engaging parties.

## Documentation

82. Prepare engagement documentation that is sufficient to determine:
    a. The nature, timing, and extent of the procedures performed to comply with relevant attestation standards and applicable legal and regulatory requirements, including:
        i. The identifying characteristics of the specific items or matters tested;
        ii. Who performed the engagement work and the date such work was completed;
        iii. Discussions with the responsible party or others about significant findings or issues, including the nature of those findings or issues and when and with whom the discussions occurred;
        iv. When the engaging party is the responsible party and will not provide one or more requested written representations or the practitioner concludes there is sufficient doubt about the competence, integrity, ethical values, or diligence of those providing the written representations or written representations are otherwise not reliable;
        v. When the engaging party is not the responsible party and the responsible party will not provide required written representations, the oral responses to the practitioner's inquiries regarding the representations; and
        vi. Who reviewed the engagement work performed and the date and extent of that review.
    b. The results of the procedures performed and evidence obtained.

83. If information is identified that is inconsistent with the practitioner's final conclusion regarding a significant finding or issue, document how the inconsistency was addressed.

84. If new or additional procedures are performed or new conclusions are drawn after the date of the practitioner's report, document the circumstances encountered; the new or additional procedures performed, evidence obtained, conclusions reached, and their effect on the practitioner's report; and when and by whom the documentation changes were made and reviewed.

## Analysis and Application of Procedures

### Agreeing on Engagement Terms

The engagement letter or written agreement can further describe the practitioner's responsibilities by including statements that:

- An examination is designed to obtain reasonable assurance that the subject matter as measured or evaluated against the criteria is free from material misstatement; and
- The objective of an examination engagement is to provide a written opinion in a practitioner's report about whether, in all material respects, the subject matter is in accordance with or based on the criteria or the assertion is fairly stated.

> **PLANNING AID REMINDER:** It is in the interest of both the practitioner and the engaging party to document the engagement terms in writing before the engagement begins. Many lawsuits against accountants grow out of misunderstandings, both real and fabricated, about the nature of the engagement and the party's responsibilities. Management may claim that they did not read the engagement letter, or did not understand it, and simply signed what the accountant gave them to sign. Although not required by attestation standards, the accountant may want to discuss the engagement letter with the client to ensure understanding of its terms and conditions, and document the discussion via memo.

A statement about the inherent limitations of an examination engagement in the engagement letter or written agreement could indicate "because of the inherent limitations of an examination engagement together with the inherent limitations of internal control, an unavoidable risk exists that some material misstatements may not be detected, even though the examination is properly planned and performed in accordance with the attestation standards."

### Requesting a Written Assertion

The responsible party's written assertion could vary according to engagement circumstances. Examples of assertions that meet the requirements of the attestation standard include the following:

- The entity maintained effective internal control over the subject matter based on the criteria.
- The subject matter is presented in accordance with (or based on) the criteria.
- The subject matter achieved the objectives, for example, when the objectives are the criteria.
- The subject matter is presented fairly, based on the criteria.

> **PLANNING AID REMINDER:** In situations where the current responsible party was not in place for the entire period covered by the practitioner's report, they are still responsible for the subject matter as a whole and a written assertion for the entire relevant period should be obtained.

The responsible party should accept responsibility for its assertion and the subject matter even in circumstances where the practitioner is engaged to assist in measuring or evaluating the subject matter against the criteria.

### Planning and Performing the Engagement

It is important to adequately plan the engagement as it can assist in ensuring important areas are focused on, potential problems are identified on a timely basis, the engagement is performed effectively and efficiently, work is properly assigned to engagement team members and properly reviewed, and coordination of work with other practitioners and practitioner's specialists is facilitated.

The nature and extent of planning will vary with the engagement, influenced by factors such as engagement complexity, prior experience, and size of the engagement team. Matters that may influence the nature and extent of planning include:

- Engagement characteristics defining its scope, including engagement terms, characteristics of the subject matter, and the criteria;
- The expected timing and the nature of the required communications;
- The results of preliminary engagement activities such as client acceptance and whether knowledge gained on other engagements for the entity is relevant;
- The engagement process and choices among alternative measurement or evaluation methods;
- The practitioner's understanding of the appropriate parties and their environment, including the risks that the subject matter may be materially misstated;
- Identification of intended users and their information needs and consideration of materiality and the components of attestation risk;
- The risk of fraud relevant to the engagement; and
- The effect on the engagement of using the internal audit function.

**PLANNING AID REMINDER:** Planning is ongoing throughout the engagement, and the nature, timing, and extent of planned procedures can be changed during the engagement if there are unexpected events, changes in conditions, or evidence obtained.

The engagement strategy or plan is solely the responsibility of the practitioner and any discussion regarding planning with the appropriate parties does not diminish that responsibility. Furthermore, care should be taken when discussing planning to ensure the effectiveness of the engagement is not compromised, for example, by discussing the nature and timing of detailed procedures and making the procedures too predictable.

**ENGAGEMENT STRATEGY:** Interpretation 2 of AT-C 205 (*Reporting on the Design of Internal Control*) clarifies that an accountant is prohibited from reporting on the suitability of the design of an entity's internal control based solely on the risk assessment procedures an auditor performs to obtain an understanding of the entity and its environment, including internal controls, in an audit of the entity's financial statements. However, Interpretation 2 of AT-C 205 does note that an accountant may perform an examination of the suitability of the design of an entity's internal control under AT-C 205 or agreed-upon-procedures to that subject matter under AT-C 215.

## Risk Assessment Procedures

Obtaining an understanding of the subject matter and engagement circumstances provides the practitioner with a frame of reference for exercising professional judgment throughout the engagement in matters such as:

- Considering the characteristics of the subject matter;
- Assessing suitable criteria;
- Considering significant factors in directing engagement team efforts;
- Establishing and evaluating quantitative materiality levels and considering qualitative materiality levels;
- Developing expectations for analytical procedures;
- Designing and performing procedures; and
- Evaluating evidence and the reasonableness of written representations provided.

The inherent risk assessed by the practitioner related to the subject matter or assertion may be influenced by its complexity, the length of the entity's experience with the subject matter or assertion, and the practitioner's experience with the entity's assessment.

## Materiality in Engagement Planning and Performance

Materiality determinations are made using professional judgment. Both quantitative and qualitative factors may be used, and their relative importance may be specific to the engagement. Quantitative factors relate to the magnitude of misstatements relative to amounts reported for aspects of the subject matter that are expressed numerically or are related to numerical values, such as the number of observed deviations in the operation of a control. Qualitative factors may include:

- The interactions and relative importance of different aspects of the subject matter;
- The clarity and completeness of the wording chosen to express the subject matter;
- The presentation method selected when multiple options are available;
- The nature of a misstatement;
- Whether a misstatement affects compliance with laws or regulations;
- Whether an adjustment affects past, current, or future information about the subject matter;
- Whether a misstatement is intentional or unintentional;
- Whether a misstatement is significant to the practitioner's understanding of known prior communications to users; and
- Whether a misstatement relates to the relationship between the responsible and engaging parties or other parties.

The criteria may discuss materiality in the context of the subject matter, which can be useful to the practitioner in considering materiality. Determinations regarding materiality can be affected by the understanding of the subject matter and the responsible party, which may change during the engagement, and the nature and extent of misstatements identified in prior attestation engagements.

> **PLANNING AID REMINDER:** Materiality is based on the information needs of intended users; therefore, determinations regarding materiality are impacted by engagement circumstances but not by the level of assurance provided.

Misstatements, including omissions, are generally considered to be material if there is a substantial likelihood that, individually or in the aggregate, they would influence the judgment made by intended users based on the subject matter. Practitioners typically do not consider the needs of specific users, but assume that intended users:

- Have reasonable knowledge of and are willing to study the subject matter;
- Understand that the subject matter is measured or evaluated and examined to appropriate materiality levels and understand materiality concepts included in the criteria;
- Understand any inherent limitations in measuring or evaluating the subject matter; and
- Make reasonable judgments based on the subject matter.

*Identifying Risks of Material Misstatement*

The types of procedures performed to obtain evidence typically include inquiry in addition to some combination of inspection, observation, confirmation, recalculation, reperformance, and analytical procedures. Subject-matter specific AT-C sections may have requirements for specific procedures to be performed in a particular type of engagement; however, the exact nature, timing and extent of these procedures is still typically subject to professional judgment and will vary according to engagement circumstances.

*Responding to Assessed Risks and Obtaining Evidence*

An overall response to address the assessed risks of material misstatement for the subject matter or assertion may include: emphasizing maintenance of professional skepticism to the engagement team; assigning more experienced or specialized staff; providing more supervision; incorporating additional unpredictability to procedures; and changing the nature, timing, and extent of procedures. The effectiveness of an entity's control environment can impact the assessment of risks of material misstatement. In an ineffective control environment, for example, the practitioner may choose to perform more procedures at period end rather than at an interim date, obtain more evidence from procedures other than tests of controls, and increase the number of locations to be included in the examination scope.

> **PRACTICE POINTER:** A practitioner may use analytical procedures to gather evidence. An analytical procedure involves comparing actual amounts, or ratios developed from actual amounts, to expectations developed by the practitioner. Practitioner expectations are based on knowledge of the entity and industry, and should reflect plausible relationships that are reasonably expected to exist in light of the practitioner's understanding of the subject matter.

### *Fraud, Laws, and Regulations*

Appropriate responses to suspected or actual fraud may include:
- Discussing the matter with the appropriate parties;
- Requesting the responsible party consult with an appropriately qualified third party, such as the entity's legal counsel or a regulator;
- Considering the implications of the matter to the engagement, including the risk assessment and the reliability of written representations provided;
- Obtaining legal advice about different courses of action;
- Communicating with third parties, such as regulators; and
- Withdrawing from the engagement.

The above procedures are also appropriate in the case of suspected or actual noncompliance with laws and regulations. In addition, it may be appropriate to describe the matter in a separate paragraph in the practitioner's report. However, if the practitioner concludes the noncompliance results in a material misstatement, the opinion should be modified, and if the responsible party prevents the practitioner from obtaining sufficient appropriate evidence to evaluate whether material noncompliance has or is likely to have occurred, the opinion should be modified.

### *Revision of Risk Assessment*

As procedures are performed during the engagement, the practitioner may obtain evidence that prompts performing additional procedures or asking the responsible party to determine if adjustments to the subject matter are appropriate. Additionally, the practitioner may become aware of a matter that causes the practitioner to believe the subject matter may be materially misstated. In both cases, the practitioner's original risk assessment should be revised.

### *Evaluating the Reliability of Information Produced by the Entity*

Evaluating the accuracy and completeness of the entity's information may occur while testing controls over the preparation and maintenance of the information, during performance of the actual procedure applied to the information, or it may require performance of additional procedures.

### *Using the Work of a Practitioner's Specialist*

Integration of the work of a practitioner's specialist with other attestation personnel is facilitated by two-way communication, which increases in importance as the integration level of the specialist's work with the nature, timing, and extent of the overall work effort increases. Practitioners may rely on their firm's system of quality control unless information suggests such reliance is inappropriate; such reliance does not reduce the practitioner's responsibility to meet the requirements of this standard. Furthermore, the extent of reliance on the firm's quality control system varies with engagement circumstances and may impact the nature, timing and extent of procedures regarding matters such as evaluating the adequacy of the work of the practitioner's specialist or agreement with the practitioner's specialist.

Information about the competence, capabilities, and objectivity of a practitioner's specialist may come from sources such as:

- Personal experience with the specialist's work;
- Discussions with the specialist;
- Discussions with others familiar with the specialist's work;
- Knowledge of the specialist's qualifications, licenses, and memberships;
- Published works authored by the specialist; and
- The firm's quality control policies and procedures.

**PLANNING AID REMINDER:** While the practitioner's specialist does not need to have the same proficiency as the practitioner in understanding the attestation standards, the specialist's understanding of relevant attestation standards should be sufficient to allow the specialist to relate his or her work to the engagement objective.

The objectivity of a practitioner's specialist may also be evaluated by inquiring of the responsible and engaging parties about any relationships with the specialist that could affect objectivity and by discussing with the specialist any threats to objectivity such as financial interests, business and personal relationships, or provision of other services by the specialist as well as any applicable safeguards and their adequacy. The practitioner may wish to obtain written representation from the specialist about any such interests or relationships. There may be some situations where safeguards cannot reduce threats to an acceptable level, for example, if a practitioner's specialist is also significantly involved in measuring, evaluating or disclosing the subject matter.

When obtaining an understanding of the field of expertise of the practitioner's specialist, the practitioner may consider if the field has specialty areas relevant to the engagement; whether any professional or other standards and regulatory or legal requirements apply; what assumptions, methods, and models the specialist uses and their general acceptance and relevance to the engagement; and the nature of the information and data used by the specialist.

**ENGAGEMENT STRATEGY:** While the agreement between the practitioner and practitioner's specialist is not required to be in writing, it is often documented in writing in the form of an engagement letter.

## Using the Work of Internal Auditors

The work of an internal audit function may be performed by those with other titles in the entity or may be performed by a third-party service provider. It is the nature of the work performed and the characteristics such as competence, objectivity, and use of a systematic and disciplined approach that determine whether the work can be used, not the title or employer of those performing the work.

While competence and objectivity are both important factors, a high level of competence cannot compensate for a low degree of objectivity and a high degree of objectivity cannot compensate for a low level of competence. Likewise, a high degree of competence and objectivity of the internal auditors cannot compensate for the lack of a systematic and disciplined approach to using the work of the internal audit function.

## Evaluating the Results of the Procedures

The practitioner accumulates uncorrected misstatements during the engagement to evaluate whether, individually or in the aggregate, they are material when forming the practitioner's opinion. "Clearly trivial" is not another expression for "not material." Clearly trivial misstatements are not accumulated because they are of such small magnitude that aggregating would not cause a material misstatement. If there is uncertainty about whether an item is clearly trivial, then it is not considered clearly trivial.

Sufficient appropriate evidence is needed to support the practitioner's opinion and report and is a matter of professional judgment. Sufficiency is a measure of the quantity of evidence, and the quantity needed will be affected by the risks of material misstatement and the quality of evidence obtained. Appropriateness of evidence is a measure of the quality of evidence and is related to its relevance and reliability. The reliability of evidence is dependent on its source, nature, and engagement circumstances. The following are some generalizations as to when evidence is more reliable:

- When obtained from independent sources outside the responsible and engaging parties.
- For internally generated evidence, when related controls are effective.
- When obtained directly from the practitioner rather than indirectly or by inference.
- When evidence is documented.
- When provided by original documents rather than by copy or after converting to electronic form.
- When obtained from different sources if the sources are consistent. (However, evidence from different sources that is contradictory may require performance of additional procedures to resolve the inconsistency.)

## Considering Subsequent Events and Subsequently Discovered Facts

To identify subsequent events, the practitioner may make inquiries and consider information contained in relevant reports issued during the subsequent period by internal auditors, other practitioners, or regulatory agencies or obtained through other professional engagements for the entity. If the responsible party refuses to disclose a subsequent event that should be disclosed, the practitioner may disclose the event in the practitioner's report and modify the opinion or withdraw from the engagement.

> **PLANNING AID REMINDER:** Some subject-matter AT-C sections of the attestation standards have specific subsequent event requirements and related application guidance.

If the practitioner becomes aware of facts subsequent to the date of the practitioner's report that may have caused revision of the report had the practitioner been aware of those facts at the date of the report, he or she should attempt to discover whether those facts existed at the date of the practitioner's report and, if so, whether users of the practitioner's report would likely find these facts important. Discussion between the responsible and engaging parties and the practitioner may be appropriate and consideration may be given to factors such as whether a subsequent practitioner's report will be issued soon, as well as the time elapsed since the original report was issued.

The practitioner may determine that it is necessary for the responsible and engaging parties to notify the users of the practitioner's report if, for example, the subject matter or assertion needs revision or the practitioner is unable to determine if revision is necessary and a subsequent practitioner's report will not be issued imminently. If the responsible and engaging parties do not take steps to prevent users from relying on the practitioner's report, the practitioner may wish to seek legal advice prior to disclosing the situation. A disclosure by the practitioner may describe the nature of the matter and its effect on the subject matter or assertion and the practitioner's report, while avoiding comment on people's conduct or motives.

*Written Representations*

The practitioner generally requests written representations from a member of senior management or those charged with governance. A summary of uncorrected misstatements is often attached to the written representation. Obtaining reliable written representations does not provide sufficient appropriate evidence on its own about any matter and does not affect the nature or extent of other evidence obtained by the practitioner.

> **PLANNING AID REMINDER:** If the responsible party is not the engaging party and written representations are refused, the practitioner should generally seek oral representations from the responsible party and restrict use of the practitioner's report. However, this is not permitted in certain subject-matter specific AT-C sections of the attestation standards.

## Requested Written Representations Not Provided or Not Reliable

When oral representations are obtained in place of written representations (which is only permitted when the responsible party is not the engaging party), the practitioner may consider if any concerns exist about the competence, integrity, ethical values, or diligence of those providing the oral responses that could affect their reliability and impact the practitioner's report.

## Other Information

If the practitioner has permitted the practitioner's report to be included in a document containing the subject matter or assertion as well as other information and the practitioner identifies a material inconsistency or material misstatement of fact, further appropriate action could include:

- Requesting the responsible and engaging parties consult with a qualified third party, such as their legal counsel;
- Obtaining legal advice about different courses of action;
- Communicating with third parties, such as regulators, if required or permissible;
- Describing the material inconsistency in the practitioner's report; and
- Withdrawing from the engagement, where withdrawal is possible.

**OBSERVATION:** Other information is not considered to be information contained on the responsible and engaging parties' websites, as websites are considered to be a means of distribution and not documents for these purposes.

## Description of Criteria

The description of criteria should only state that the subject matter or assertion is prepared in accordance with or based on specific criteria if the subject matter complies with all relevant requirements of those criteria. A description of criteria becomes more important when significant differences exist in various criteria regarding how the subject matter may be treated.

## Forming the Opinion

When considering if sufficient appropriate evidence was obtained on which to form an opinion, the practitioner may consider factors such as:

- The significance of a potential misstatement and its likelihood of having a material effect;
- The effectiveness of the responsible party's responses to address known risks;
- Experience gained during prior engagements with similar potential misstatements;
- The results of procedures performed, including whether specific misstatements were identified;
- The source and reliability of the available information;

- The persuasiveness of the evidence; and
- The practitioner's understanding of the responsible party and its environment.

Information obtained during the engagement may affect the practitioner's assessment of whether uncorrected misstatements are material, individually or in the aggregate. The practitioner may find more misstatements than expected, become aware of discrepancies or conflicting information, or identify previously unrecognized risks of material misstatement through procedures performed.

To evaluate whether the subject matter or assertion presentation is misleading, the practitioner may consider whether additional disclosures are needed to describe, for example, the measurement or evaluation methods used, significant interpretations made, subsequent events, or any changes in measurement or evaluation methods used.

---

**PLANNING AID REMINDER:** The presentation of the subject matter or assertion is not required to disclose all related matters users may consider in making decisions, but the practitioner should ensure the presentation is not misleading.

---

## Preparing the Practitioner's Report

The practitioner's report is required to be in writing, but the format of the report is not standardized. There are basic required elements, and the report may then be tailored to the engagement circumstances. Unless the practitioner has concluded one or more material misstatements exist based on the criteria, the practitioner's report may state that:

- The practitioner examined the subject matter and expresses an opinion on the subject matter;
- The practitioner examined the responsible party's assertion and expresses an opinion on the responsible party's assertion; and
- The practitioner examined the responsible party's assertion and expresses an opinion on the subject matter.

## Content of the Practitioner's Report

The practitioner's report is required to include several elements, including that the practitioner is independent, but the practitioner has some discretion in the manner in which they are included. When identifying the criteria, the practitioner's report may include the criteria or refer to a location where they are readily available.

---

**PLANNING AID REMINDER:** An accountant may be engaged to perform an attestation engagement in accordance with *Generally Accepted Government Auditing Standards* (GAGAS). Those standards set forth additional reporting standards that go beyond the reporting standards in AT-C 205. According to Interpretation 1 of AT-C 205 (*Reporting on Attestation Engagements Performed in Accordance with Government Auditing Standards*), the accountant should modify the scope paragraph of the attestation report to indicate that the examination was "conducted in accordance with attestation standards established by the American Institute of Certified Public Accountants and the standards applicable to attestation engagements contained in GAGAS issued by the Comptroller General of the United States." Additionally, the accountant's attestation report should also disclose any "findings" as described by those standards.

---

Identifying the responsibilities of the responsible party and the practitioner helps to clarify each party's role. When discussing the responsible party's responsibility, the practitioner may want to expand the description to indicate that the responsible party is responsible for the subject matter and the practitioner's role is to independently express an opinion about it. The practitioner may also want to include discussion that the responsible party is responsible for preparing and presenting the subject matter in accordance with or based on the criteria, including designing, implementing, and maintaining internal control to prevent or detect and correct misstatement of the subject matter, due to fraud or error.

The language to satisfy the requirement for a statement that the practitioner has planned and performed the examination to obtain reasonable assurance may be tailored to the engagement circumstances, such as "to obtain reasonable assurance about whether:

- The entity maintained effective internal control over the subject matter, based on the criteria, in all material respects."
- The subject matter is presented in accordance with [*or based on*] the criteria, in all material respects."
- The subject matter achieves the objectives, in all material respects."
- The subject matter is presented fairly, in all material respects, based on the criteria."

To describe the nature of an examination engagement, the practitioner may state that:

- An examination involves performing procedures to obtain evidence about the subject matter and that the nature, timing, and extent of the procedures selected depend on the practitioner's judgment, including an assessment of the risks of material misstatement of the subject matter, whether due to fraud or error.
- An examination also involves examining evidence about the subject matter or assertion.
- In assessing the risks of material misstatement, internal control relevant to the subject matter was considered to design appropriate procedures but not to express an opinion on the effectiveness of internal control and no such opinion is expressed.

The practitioner may be requested to provide a description of the procedures performed and their results in a separate section of the practitioner's report. Addition of this information may increase the risk that the report could be misunderstood if taken out of context; this increased risk may lead the practitioner to add a restricted-use paragraph to the report. When considering whether to include this type of description, the practitioner may consider whether:

- The description will likely overshadow or cause users to misunderstand the opinion;
- The parties making the request have a reasonable and appropriate basis for the request;
- The parties have an understanding of the nature and subject matter of the engagement and experience in using the information in such reports; and
- The practitioner's procedures performed directly relate to the subject matter of the engagement.

---

**PLANNING AID REMINDER:** When describing significant inherent limitations, note that some AT-C sections of the attestation standards require identification of specific inherent limitations (e.g., reporting on prospective financial information).

---

The practitioner considers the relevant ethical requirements, including those in the AICPA Code of Professional Conduct and in other sources that may be applicable due to rules and requirements of laws and regulations that affect the engagement.

The practitioner's opinion can be stated in terms of the subject matter and the criteria:

> In our opinion, the schedule of investment returns of Alpha Company for the year ended December 31, 20XX, is in accordance with [or based on] the XYZ criteria set forth in Note 1, in all material respects.

The opinion can also be stated in terms of an assertion made by the responsible party:

> In our opinion, management's assertion that the accompanying schedule of investment returns of Alpha Company for the year ended December 31, 20XX, is in accordance with [or based on] the XYZ criteria set forth in Note 1, is fairly stated, in all material respects.

One practitioner's report can cover more than one aspect of a subject matter or assertion. Separate opinions or conclusions can be contained in the same report; for example, some aspects or assertions can be examined and some can be reviewed or some can have unmodified opinions and some can have modified opinions. A practitioner can also report on a subject matter or assertion at multiple dates or covering multiple periods of time; when this occurs, for criteria to be clearly described, they should identify the criteria for each period and any changes in criteria between periods.

*Restricted-use paragraph*

A restricted-use practitioner's report can be included in a document that also contains a general use practitioner's report and use of the general use report is not affected. A single combined practitioner's report can be issued that includes a restricted-use report and a general use report. As long that the two types of reports are clearly differentiated, use of the general use report is not affected.

> **PLANNING AID REMINDER:** A practitioner is permitted to include an alert restricting the use of the practitioner's report in situations other than those requiring the alert.

A restricted-use alert may identify specified parties by name, by referring to a list, or by identifying the class of parties. The restricted-use alert is intended to avoid misunderstandings related to use of the report. The practitioner may inform the responsible and engaging parties that the practitioner's report is not intended for distribution to those other than the specified parties and reach an agreement that the report will not be distributed to those other than the specified parties. However, the practitioner is not responsible for and cannot control distribution of the practitioner's report after its release.

Restricted-use practitioner reports filed with regulatory agencies may be made available to the public if required by law or regulation. Regulatory agencies may also require access to restricted-use practitioner reports in which they are not a specified party as part of their oversight responsibilities.

### Reference to the Practitioner's Specialist

The practitioner has sole responsibility for the opinion expressed, which is not reduced by using the work of a practitioner's specialist.

### Modified Opinions

There are three types of modified opinions: a qualified opinion, an adverse opinion, and a disclaimer of opinion. The nature of the matter and the pervasiveness of its potential effects are considered when determining which type of opinion is appropriate. Pervasive effects are those that are not confined to specific aspects of the subject matter, are confined to specific aspects but represent a significant portion of the subject matter, or are disclosures that are fundamental to the intended users' understanding of the subject matter. Exhibit AT-C 205-1 illustrates when to use each type of modified opinion:

### EXHIBIT AT-C 205-1—TYPES OF MODIFIED OPINIONS

| Nature of Matter Causing Modification | Practitioner's Professional Judgment About the Pervasiveness of Potential Effects | |
|---|---|---|
| | *Material but Not Pervasive* | *Material and Pervasive* |
| Scope limitation (inability to obtain sufficient appropriate evidence) | Qualified opinion | Disclaimer of opinion |
| Subject matter is materially misstated | Qualified opinion | Adverse opinion |

Scope limitations occur for various reasons. Circumstances beyond the control of the responsible and engaging parties, such as loss of needed documentation, may exist. The nature or timing of the practitioner's work may cause a scope limitation, for example, if the practitioner cannot observe a process because it already occurred. Scope limitations may also occur if the responsible or engaging party imposes limitations on the practitioner, preventing performance of necessary procedures, which may impact the practitioner's consideration of risks of material misstatement and engagement acceptance and continuance. When there is a scope limitation, the practitioner's decision to express a qualified opinion, disclaim an opinion, or withdraw from the engagement depends on the effect of the omitted procedure on the practitioner's ability to express an opinion.

An unmodified opinion may only be issued when the engagement has been conducted in accordance with the attestation standards. All standards are not complied with if the practitioner is unable to perform all necessary procedures. An inability to perform a specific procedure does not constitute a scope limitation if alternative procedures are able to be performed to obtain sufficient appropriate evidence.

### Responsible Party Refuses to Provide a Written Assertion

When the engaging party is not the responsible party and the responsible party refuses to provide a written assertion, the practitioner may report on the subject matter in a report restricted to the use of the engaging party and should disclose the refusal to provide a written assertion in a statement such as:

> Attestation standards established by the American Institute of Certified Public Accountants require that we request a written statement from [*identify the responsible party*] stating that [*identify the subject matter*] that we examined has been accurately measured or evaluated. We requested that [*identify the responsible party*] provide such a written statement but [*identify the responsible party*] refused to do so.

In this situation, the practitioner is only permitted to report on the subject matter and not on an assertion, as a written assertion from the responsible party is required to report on an assertion. If the responsible party's refusal to provide a written assertion leads the practitioner to decide there is a scope limitation and a qualified opinion or disclaimer of opinion is needed, the report does not need to be restricted, but the matter giving rise to the modified opinion should be described.

### Communication Responsibilities

In addition to actual or suspected fraud and noncompliance with laws and regulations, the practitioner may also wish to discuss any bias in the measurement, evaluation, or disclosure of the subject matter with the responsible and engaging parties.

When noncompliance with laws or regulations not relevant to the subject matter is suspected or identified, the practitioner's professional duty to maintain confidentiality of client information may conflict with the practitioner's legal responsibilities, such as in response to a court order or an examination engagement for entities that receive financial assistance from a government entity. In these situations, the practitioner may wish to consult with legal counsel before discussing noncompliance with parties external to the entity. If the examination engagement is being performed in accordance with *Government Auditing Stan-*

*dards,* the practitioner may be required to report on compliance with laws, regulations, and provisions of contracts or grant agreements and to communicate instances of noncompliance to appropriate oversight bodies and funding agencies.

## Documentation

Documentation should not include every matter considered during an engagement but should include a record of the significant findings requiring professional judgment and the related conclusions. The amount of documentation prepared and retained is a matter of professional judgment and may be what the practitioner thinks another experienced practitioner with no history with the engagement would need to understand the work performed and the decisions made.

In addition, documentation typically contains a record of:

- Issues identified regarding compliance with relevant ethical requirements and their resolution;
- Conclusions on compliance with applicable independence requirements and any relevant discussions with the firm supporting those conclusions;
- Conclusions reached regarding the acceptance and continuance of client relationships and attestation engagements; and
- The nature, scope, and conclusions from consultations occurring during the engagement.

## Practitioner's Aids

Exhibit AT-C 205-2 is an illustrative practitioner's report for an examination engagement where the practitioner examined and is reporting on the subject matter.

EXHIBIT AT-C 205-2—ASSERTION-BASED EXAMINATION REPORT—SUBJECT MATTER

### Independent Accountant's Report

[*Appropriate Addressee*]

We have examined the [*identify the subject matter, for example, the accompanying schedule of investment returns of Alpha Company for the year ended December 31, 20XX*]. ABC Company's management is responsible for [*identify the subject matter, for example, presenting the schedule of investment returns*] in accordance with [or based on] [*identify the criteria, for example, the XYZ criteria set forth in Note 1*]. Our responsibility is to express an opinion on [*identify the subject matter, for example, the schedule of investment returns*] based on our examination.

Our examination was conducted in accordance with attestation standards established by the American Institute of Certified Public Accountants. Those standards require that we plan and perform the examination to obtain reasonable assurance about whether [*identify the subject matter, for example, the schedule of investment returns*] is in accordance with [or based on] the criteria, in all material respects. An examination involves performing procedures to obtain evidence about [*identify the subject matter, for example, the schedule of investment returns*]. The nature, timing, and extent of the procedures selected depend on our judgment, including an assessment of the risks of material misstatement of [*identify the subject matter, for example, the schedule of investment returns*], whether due to fraud or error. We believe that the evidence we obtained is sufficient and appropriate to provide a reasonable basis for our opinion.

We are required to be independent and to meet our other ethical responsibilities in accordance with relevant ethical requirements relating to the engagement.

[*Include a description of significant inherent limitations, if any, associated with the measurement or evaluation of the subject matter against the criteria.*]

[*Additional paragraph(s) may be added to emphasize certain matters relating to the attestation engagement or the subject matter.*]

In our opinion, [*identify the subject matter, for example, the schedule of investment returns of Alpha Company for the year ended December 31, 20XX or the schedule of investment returns referred to above*], is presented in accordance with [or based on] [*identify the criteria, for example, the XYZ criteria set forth in Note 1*], in all material respects.

[*Practitioner's signature*]

[*Practitioner's city and state*]

[*Date of practitioner's report*]

---

Exhibit AT-C 205-3 is an illustrative practitioner's report for an examination engagement where the practitioner examined and is reporting on the responsible party's assertion.

## EXHIBIT AT-C 205-3—ASSERTION-BASED EXAMINATION REPORT—ASSERTION

---

### Independent Accountant's Report

[*Appropriate Addressee*]

We have examined management of Alpha Company's assertion that [*identify the assertion, including the subject matter and the criteria, for example, the accompanying schedule of investment returns of Alpha Company for the year ended December 31, 20XX is presented in accordance with [or based on] the XYZ criteria set forth in Note 1*]. Alpha Company's management is responsible for its assertion. Our responsibility is to express an opinion on management's assertion based on our examination.

Our examination was conducted in accordance with attestation standards established by the American Institute of Certified Public Accountants. Those standards require that we plan and perform the examination to obtain reasonable assurance about whether management's assertion is fairly stated, in all material respects. An examination involves performing procedures to obtain evidence about management's assertion. The nature, timing, and extent of the procedures selected depend on our judgment, including an assessment of the risks of material misstatement of management's assertion, whether due to fraud or error.

We believe that the evidence we obtained is sufficient and appropriate to provide a reasonable basis for our opinion.

We are required to be independent and to meet our other ethical responsibilities in accordance with relevant ethical requirements relating to the engagement.

[*Include a description of significant inherent limitations, if any, associated with the measurement or evaluation of the subject matter against the criteria.*]

[*Additional paragraph(s) may be added to emphasize certain matters relating to the attestation engagement or the subject matter.*]

In our opinion, management's assertion that [*identify the assertion, including the subject matter and the criteria, for example, the schedule of investment returns of Alpha Company for the year ended December 31, 20XX is presented in accordance with [or based on] the XYZ criteria set forth in Note 1*] is fairly stated, in all material respects.

[*Practitioner's signature*]

[*Practitioner's city and state*]

[*Date of practitioner's report*]

# SECTION 206

# DIRECT EXAMINATION ENGAGEMENTS

## Authoritative Pronouncements

SSAE-21—Direct Examination Engagements

## Overview

This AT-C section contains performance and reporting requirements and application guidance for direct examination engagements. The objectives of a direct examination are to:

- Obtain reasonable assurance by measuring or evaluating the underlying subject matter against the criteria (**Note:** The term "subject matter" encompasses terms such as underlying subject matter and subject matter information);
- Express an opinion in a written report that conveys the practitioner's results related to that measurement or evaluation; and
- Communicate further as required by the attestation standards.

---

**IMPORTANT NOTICE FOR 2022:** In September 2020, the ASB issued Statement on Standards for Attestation Engagements (SSAE) No. 21 (*Direct Examination Engagements*), that adds a new AT-C 206 (*Direct Examination Engagements*) to the attestation standards that enable practitioners to perform an examination engagement in which the practitioner obtains reasonable assurance by measuring or evaluating underlying subject matter against criteria and expressing an opinion that conveys the results of that measurement or evaluation. SSAE No. 21 allows the entity in an examination engagement to not provide an assertion about whether the underlying subject matter is in accordance with the criteria. SSAE No. 21 retitled AT-C 205 to be *Assertion-Based Examination Engagements*, and it introduced the new AT-C 206, *Direct Examination Engagement*. AT-C 205 specifically applies to assertion-based examination engagements whereby the entity evaluates whether the subject matter is in accordance with the stated criteria, reflecting what has been a traditional examination engagement. AT-C 206 enables entities that do not provide an assertion about whether the underlying subject matter is in accordance with the criteria to undergo an examination engagement. SSAE No. 21 is effective for examination reports dated on or after June 15, 2022.

---

While in a direct examination engagement, the practitioner is not required to request a written assertion from the responsible party, the practitioner is required to apply the other requirements in AT-C 205 to a direct examination engagement. There are no additional defined terms in AT-C 206 beyond those defined in AT-C 105 and 205 for these engagements.

## Definitions

See definitions in AT-C 105 and 205.

## Requirements

The practitioner in a direct examination engagement is required to comply with requirements in AT-C 205 except for those related to obtaining a written assertion from a responsible party. The only exceptions are when (1) the requirement cannot be applied as written due to the nature of the direct examination engagement or (2) the requirements differ from and have been replaced by requirements in AT-C 206, which are summarized next.

*Different Requirements for Direct Examination Engagements*

1. Prior to accepting or continuing a direct examination engagement, the practitioner should make inquiries to understand the intended purpose of the engagement, why this type of engagement is requested, and how the practitioner's report will be used. Inquiries should also include why the responsible party has not measured or evaluated the subject matter against the criteria or, if they have done so, why they are not providing an assertion.

2. In addition to considering the responses to those inquiries, the auditor should evaluate whether to perform a direct examination engagement, while also considering previous engagements performed for the engaging party and initial discussions with the engaging party.

3. The practitioner's engagement letter or other suitable written agreement should include the objectives and scope of the engagement and responsibilities of the practitioner and of the responsible party and the engaging party. That includes acknowledgment that the responsible party is responsible for the underlying subject matter and that either the responsible party or the engaging party are responsible for the selection of the criteria to be used and that the criteria will be suitable and appropriate and available to intended users. The terms of agreement should also include:

    a. A statement about inherent limitations of an examination engagement;

    b. Identification of the criteria to be used for measurement, evaluation, or disclosure of the underlying subject matter; and

    c. Acknowledgment that the engaging party agrees to provide a written representation letter to the practitioner at the end of the engagement.

4. The practitioner should ask the responsible party to provide written representations in a letter to the practitioner at the conclusion of the engagement that include the following:

    a. A statement that all known contradictions of the measurement or evaluation of the underlying subject matter information has been disclosed to the practitioner. That includes communications from regulatory agencies or others affecting the subject matter information.

    b. Acknowledgment that the responsible party is responsible for the underlying subject matter, selection of the criteria (when applicable) and the determination of whether the criteria is suitable and appropriate, and whether it will be available to intended users.

    c. A statement that the responsible party has disclosed any known actual or alleged fraud or noncompliance with laws or regulations affecting the underlying subject matter, all deficiencies known by them in internal control relevant to the subject matter, and other matters the practitioner determines as appropriate.

    d. A statement that the responsible party has disclosed to the practitioner any known events occurring subsequent to the period (or point in time) that would have a material effect on the underlying subject matter or subject matter information.

    e. An acknowledgment that the responsible party has provided the practitioner with all relevant information and access in accordance with the engagement letter or other written terms of agreement.

5. In those situations where the engaging party is not the responsible party, the practitioner should also obtain representations from the engaging party. These include:

    a. Acknowledgments about each of the responsibilities of the engagement party and the responsible party, including that the responsible party is responsible for the underlying subject matter and the engaging party is responsible for selecting the criteria, including determination of its suitability and appropriateness and availability to intended users.

    b. Statement that the engaging party is not aware of any material misstatements in underlying subject matter or subject matter information and that the engaging party has disclosed to the practitioner all known events subsequent to the period (or point in time) of the subject matter information being reporting on that would materially affect the subject matter information.

    c. Other information that the practitioner believes is appropriate.

6. The practitioner's direct examination report should contain the following:

    a. A title that includes the word independent.

    b. An appropriate addressee.

    c. An identification or description of the subject matter or assertion being reported on, including the period or point in time to which its measurement or evaluation relates.

    d. An identification of the criteria against which the subject matter was measured or evaluated.

e. A statement that identifies the responsible party and its responsibility for its the subject matter.

f. A statement that describes the practitioner's responsibility for (1) measuring and evaluating the underlying subject matter against the criteria and performing other procedures, (2) expressing an opinion that describes the practitioner's results from performing the examination, and (3) presenting any subject matter information as part of the practitioner's measurement or evaluation, if applicable.

g. A statement that:
   i. The examination was conducted in accordance with attestation standards established by the American Institute of Certified Public Accountants;
   ii. Those standards require the practitioner to plan and perform the examination to obtain reasonable assurance by measuring and evaluating the underlying subject matter against the criteria and performing additional procedures to obtain sufficient appropriate evidence to express an opinion; and
   iii. The practitioner believes the evidence obtained is sufficient and appropriate to provide a reasonable basis for the practitioner's opinion.

h. A description of the nature of a direct examination engagement.

i. A statement that acknowledges that the practitioner is required to be independent and comply with other ethical responsibilities related to the examination engagement.

j. A statement that describes any significant inherent limitations associated with the measurement or evaluation of the subject matter against the criteria.

k. The manual or printed signature of the practitioner's firm.

l. The city and state where the practitioner practices.

m. The date of the practitioner's report, which should be no earlier than the date on which the practitioner has obtained sufficient appropriate evidence on which to base the practitioner's opinion, including evidence that:
   i. The attestation documentation has been reviewed; and
   ii. The written presentation of the subject matter has been prepared if applicable.

## Analysis and Application of Procedures

*Agreeing on Engagement Terms*

In a direct examination engagement, the responsible party does not provide an assertion. Sometimes, the responsible party may not be able to provide a written assertion because the entity does not have the personnel or processes necessary to have a foundation for an assertion. In other situations, the responsible party may just prefer to have the practitioner measure and evaluate the underlying subject matter against the criteria without requiring the responsible party to provide its own assertion. The practitioner may inquire of the responsible party about the reasons for the direct examination engagement, including whether the responsibility is required by law, regulation, or contract to actually measure and evaluate the underlying subject matter, including a need to provide a written assertion.

While in an assertion-based examination engagement, the practitioner tests subject matter information prepared by the responsible party, the practitioner may increase the extent or change the type of the work to be performed in a direct examination engagement given in a direct examination engagement the practitioner measures or evaluates the underlying subject matter against the criteria and performs risk assessment and further audit procedures to obtain reasonable assurance.

The engagement letter may further describe the objective of a direct examination engagement, including information that acknowledges the engagement is designed to obtain reasonable assurance about whether the subject matter information is free of material misstatement. And, it may describe the nature of the opinion that will be expressed in the practitioner's report. AT-C 206 acknowledges that the practitioner may help the engaging party by recommending, developing, or assisting in the development of the criteria. That may be described in the engagement letter.

## Written Representations

The practitioner often requests written confirmation of oral representations to lower the possibility that there are misunderstandings between the responsible party and the practitioner. Typically, the practitioner requests written confirmation from a member of senior management or those charged with governance. Note, however, that the written representations do not provide sufficient appropriate evidence on their own about any of the matters with which they deal. The practitioner may also include in the request for written representation discussion of what is considered material to the underlying subject matter or subject matter information.

## Content of the Report

The practitioner's report may include the criteria used or refer to them if they are included in the subject matter information or easily available. The report also include information to distinguish the responsibilities of the responsible party and the practitioner. The report may include statements in the description of the nature and direct examination engagement about what is involved in this type of engagement, the practitioner's consideration of internal control, and that the practitioner's judgment informs the nature, timing, and extent of procedures performed.

The practitioner in a direct examination engagement may be asked to provide a description of the procedures performed in a separate section of the report, along with the results that support the opinion. In determining the appropriateness of that disclosure, the practitioner considers the business need, basis for that request, and whether the parties have a sufficient understanding of the nature and underlying subject matter of the engagement and experience using that kind of information.

## Practitioner's Aids

Exhibit AT-C 206-1 includes an illustrative practitioner's report for a direct examination engagement where the practitioner was engaged to measure the rates of return on Beta Company's investment transactions during the year ended December 31, 20XX based on specified criteria and present the rates of return on the investment transactions in a schedule of investment returns.

### EXHIBIT AT-C 206-1—DIRECT EXAMINATION REPORT—MEASUREMENT

**Independent Accountant's Report**

[*Appropriate Addressee*]

We have examined the investment transactions of Beta Company during the year ended December 31, 20XX. Beta Company's management is responsible for its investment transactions during the year ended December 31, 20XX and maintaining a record of those transactions. Our responsibility is to obtain reasonable assurance by measuring the investment transactions of Beta Company during the year ended December 31, 20XX against the XYZ criteria set forth in Note 1 of the accompanying schedule of investment returns to determine the rates of return on those investment transactions and performing other procedures to obtain sufficient appropriate evidence to express an opinion that conveys the results of our measurement based on our examination. We have presented the results of our measurement in the accompanying schedule of investment returns.

Our examination was conducted in accordance with the attestation standards for a direct examination engagement established by the AICPA. Those standards require that we obtain reasonable assurance by measuring the investment transactions of Beta Company during the year ended December 31, 20XX against the XYZ criteria set forth in Note 1 of the accompanying schedule of investment returns and performing other procedures to obtain sufficient appropriate evidence to express an opinion that conveys the results of our measurement or evaluation of the investment transactions of Beta Company during the year ended December 31, 20XX. The nature, timing, and extent of the procedures selected depend on our judgment, including an assessment of the risks of material misstatement of the rates of return on those investment transactions for the year ended December 31, 20XX, as presented in the schedule of investment returns, whether due to fraud or error. We believe that the evidence we obtained is sufficient and appropriate to provide a reasonable basis for our opinion.

We are required to be independent of Beta Company and to meet our other ethical responsibilities, in accordance with relevant ethical requirements relating to our examination engagement.

[*Include a description of significant inherent limitations, if any, associated with the measurement or evaluation of the underlying subject matter against the criteria.*]

§ 206 • Direct Examination Engagements   10,063

*[Additional paragraphs may be added to emphasize certain matters relating to the attestation engagement, the underlying subject matter, or the subject matter information.]*

In our opinion, the rates of return on the investment transactions of Beta Company during the year ended December 31, 20XX included in the accompanying schedule of investment returns of Beta Company for the year ended December 31, 20XX, are fairly presented in accordance with the XYZ criteria set forth in Note 1, in all material respects.

*[Signature of the practitioner's firm]*

*[City and State where the practitioner's report is issued]*

*[Date of the practitioner's report]*

---

Exhibit AT-C 206-2 includes an illustrative practitioner's report for a direct examination engagement where the practitioner was engaged to evaluate a restaurant's food safety practices during the year ended December 31, 20XX based on criteria provided by an outside insurance company and provides an opinion about whether the restaurant's food safety practices and implementation of those practices were in accordance with the criteria.

## EXHIBIT AT-C 206-2—DIRECT EXAMINATION REPORT—EVALUATION

### Independent Accountant's Report

*[Appropriate Addressee]*

We have examined Tasty Restaurant's food safety practices and its implementation of those practices during the year ended December 31, 20XX. Tasty Restaurant's management is responsible for its food safety practices and its implementation of those practices. Our responsibility is to obtain reasonable assurance by measuring Tasty Restaurant's safety practices and its implementation of those practices during the year ended December 31, 20XX against Delta Insurance Company's Best Food Safety Practices for Restaurants and performing other procedures to obtain sufficient appropriate evidence to express an opinion that conveys the results of our evaluation based on our examination.

Our examination was conducted in accordance with the attestation standards for a direct examination engagement established by the AICPA. Those standards require that we obtain reasonable assurance by measuring Tasty Restaurant's food safety practices and its implementation of those practices during the year ended December 31, 20XX against Delta Insurance Company's Best Food Safety Practices for Restaurants and performing other procedures to obtain sufficient appropriate evidence to express an opinion that conveys the results of our evaluation of Tasty Restaurant's food safety practices and its implementation of those practices during the year ended December 31, 20XX. The nature, timing, and extent of the procedures selected depend on our judgment, including an assessment of the risks that Tasty Restaurant's safety practices and its implementation of those practices were not in accordance with Delta Insurance Company's Best Food Safety Practices for Restaurants in all material respects, whether due to fraud or error. We believe that the evidence we obtained is sufficient and appropriate to provide a reasonable basis for our opinion.

We are required to be independent of Tasty Restaurant and to meet our other ethical responsibilities, in accordance with relevant ethical requirements relating to our examination engagement.

[*Include a description of significant inherent limitations, if any, associated with the measurement or evaluation of the underlying subject matter against the criteria.*]

[*Additional paragraphs may be added to emphasize certain matters relating to the attestation engagement, the underlying subject matter, or the subject matter information.*]

In our opinion, Tasty Restaurant's food safety practices and its implementation of those practices during the year ended December 31, 20XX, were in accordance with Delta Insurance Company's Best Food Safety Practices for Restaurants, in all material respects.

[*Signature of the practitioner's firm*]

[*City and State where the practitioner's report is issued*]

[*Date of the practitioner's report*]

# SECTION 210

# REVIEW ENGAGEMENTS

## Authoritative Pronouncements

SSAE-18—Attestation Standards: Clarification and Recodification

SSAE-20—Amendments to the Description of the Concept of Materiality

SSAE-22—Review Engagements

## Overview

This AT-C section contains performance and reporting requirements and application guidance for review engagements. The objectives of a review are to:

- Obtain limited assurance about whether any material modifications should be made to the subject matter in order for it to be in accordance with or based on the criteria;

- Express a conclusion in a written report about whether the practitioner is aware of any material modifications that should be made to the subject matter for it to be in accordance with or based on the criteria or for the assertion to be fairly stated; and

- Communicate further as required by the attestation standards.

**IMPORTANT NOTICE FOR 2022:** In December 2020, the ASB issued Statement on Standards for Attestation Engagements (SSAE) No. 22 (*Review Engagements*), that revises AT-C 210 to make it consistent with the new AT-C 205 (*Assertion-Based Examination Engagements*), that resulted from the issuance of SSAE No. 21 (*Direct Examination Engagements*). SSAE No. 22 also clarifies the types of procedures a practitioner may perform in a review engagement and it revises the reporting requirements for a review engagement, including the ability to issue an adverse opinion. SSAE No. 22 is effective for practitioner's review reports dated on or after June 15, 2022. Early implementation is permitted only if the practitioner also implements early the amendments to AT-C 105 included in SSAE No. 21. The guidance in this section incorporates the provisions in SSAE No. 22.

**PUBLIC COMPANY IMPLICATION:** The PCAOB has issued an attestation standard pertaining to brokers and dealers. The standard, *Review Engagements Regarding Exemption Reports of Brokers and Dealers*, addresses an auditor's review of exemption reports. This attestation standard is designed to help protect customer funds held by broker-dealers by improving the quality of compliance information used by the Securities and Exchange Commission (SEC) in overseeing broker-dealers.

The SEC has recently instituted new requirements (under Exchange Act Rule 17a-5) requiring broker-dealers to prepare compliance or exemption reports, and requiring PCAOB-registered auditors to examine or review such reports. Broker-dealers that hold customer securities or funds must maintain a certain capital level, and must maintain a certain reserve of funds or qualified securities. These requirements around capital and liquidity are designed to enhance market confidence and to safeguard investors, both of which are especially important when adverse market events occur. Broker-dealers holding customer funds must prepare and file a compliance report. Broker-dealers not holding customer funds must file an exemption report to claim an exemption from the compliance-reporting requirements. In addition, broker-dealers must file audited financial statements and supporting schedules with the SEC.

The attestation standard requires the auditor to obtain moderate assurance to support the broker-dealer's assertion that it (1) identified and met the SEC exemption provisions enabling the broker-dealer to not have to file a compliance report, and, if applicable, (2) the broker-dealer identified and described any exception to the applicable exemption requirements. The standard requires the auditor to (1) read the exemption report to understand the broker-dealer's claimed basis for the exemption, (2) perform inquiries and other procedures, (3) evaluate whether evidence suggests that modifications are needed to the broker-dealer's assertions, and (4) obtain representation letters and comply with certain reporting obligations.

## Definitions

| | |
|---|---|
| Appropriateness of review evidence | The measure of the quality of review evidence, or its relevance and reliability in providing support for the practitioner's conclusion. |
| Modified conclusion | A qualified or adverse conclusion. |
| Review evidence | Information used by the practitioner in obtaining limited assurance on which the practitioner's review conclusion is based. |
| Sufficiency of review evidence | The measure of the quantity of evidence, affected by the risks of material misstatement and evidence quality. |

## Requirements

The practitioner is presumptively required to perform the following procedures when conducting a review engagement:

### Conduct of a Review Engagement

1. When performing a review engagement, the practitioner should comply with AT-C 105, this section, and any subject-matter specific AT-C sections relevant to the engagement.

2. Consider whether the nature of review procedures will allow for obtaining sufficient appropriate evidence to obtain limited assurance.

3. A review should not be performed on prospective financial information, internal control, or compliance with requirements of specified laws, regulations, rules, contracts, or grants.

## Agreeing on Engagement Terms

4. Engagement terms should be agreed upon with the engaging party and should be specified in sufficient detail in an engagement letter or other suitable written agreement.

5. Engagement terms should include:
   a. Engagement scope and objective;
   b. Practitioner responsibilities;
   c. A statement that the engagement will be conducted in accordance with attestation standards established by the American Institute of Certified Public Accountants;
   d. Responsible party and, if different, engaging party responsibilities;
   e. A statement that a review is substantially less in scope than an examination and therefore the practitioner does not express an opinion about whether, in all material respects, the subject matter is in accordance with or based on the criteria or the assertion is fairly stated;
   f. Identification of the criteria for the measurement, evaluation, or disclosure of the subject matter; and
   g. An acknowledgment that the engaging party agrees to provide the practitioner with a representation letter at the end of the engagement.

6. In a recurring engagement, the terms do not need to be modified if they are still suitable, but the practitioner should remind the engaging party of the engagement terms and document that reminder.

## Requesting a Written Assertion

7. Request a written assertion from the responsible party about the measurement or evaluation of the underlying subject matter against the criteria. If the responsible party refuses to provide a written assertion and it is also the engaging party, the practitioner is required to withdraw from the engagement where permitted by law and regulations. If the responsible party refuses to provide a written assertion and it is not the engaging party, the practitioner is required to disclose that refusal in the practitioner's report and restrict its use to the engaging party.

## Planning and Performing the Engagement

8. Establish the scope, timing, and direction of the overall engagement and determine the nature, timing and extent of procedures to be carried out to achieve the engagement objectives, with the practitioner exercising professional skepticism in selecting and applying procedures.

9. Obtain a sufficient understanding of the engagement circumstances and subject matter, including the methods used to measure, recognize, and record the subject matter, to provide a basis for identifying areas where material misstatement may arise and for designing and performing procedures in order to achieve the engagement objectives.

10. The practitioner should also make inquiries about whether the responsible party has an internal audit function or whether any specialists have been used in the preparation of the subject matter.

## Materiality in Engagement Planning and Performance

11. Consider materiality when planning and performing the engagement, including determining the nature, timing, and extent of procedures and when

evaluating whether the practitioner is aware of any material modifications that should be made to the subject matter for it to be fairly stated in accordance with or based on the criteria, or for the assertion to be fairly stated.

---

**IMPORTANT NOTICE FOR 2022:** In December 2019, the AICPA's Auditing Standards Board (ASB) issued Statement on Attestation Standards (SSAE) No. 20 (*Amendments to the Description of the Concept of Materiality*) to align the materiality concepts discussed in attestation standards, including AT-C 210, with the definition of materiality used by the U.S. judicial system, the PCAOB auditing standards, and the Financial Accounting Standards Board (FASB). The FASB aligned its definition of materiality in August 2018 to be consistent with the U.S. judicial system and other U.S. standards setters and regulators. The ASB believes it is in the public interest to eliminate existing inconsistencies in definitions of materiality used. The U.S. judicial system defines misstatement as material if there is "**substantial likelihood** that a reasonable shareholder **would** consider it important," whereas existing attestation standards define a misstatement as material if it "**could reasonably be expected to** influence the judgment of a reasonable person." SSAE No. 20 became effective for practitioner examination reports dated on or after December 15, 2020.

---

## Procedures to Be Performed

12. Obtain sufficient appropriate evidence to obtain limited assurance and express a conclusion about whether any material modifications should be made to the subject matter for it to be fairly stated in accordance with or based on the criteria, or for the assertion to be fairly stated.

13. Determine the specific nature, timing, and extent of review procedures using professional judgment and the practitioner's understanding of the subject matter, including the methods the responsible party uses to measure, recognize, and record the subject matter, the engagement circumstances, and the risk that the practitioner's report may fail to be modified when the subject matter is materially misstated. Design and perform analytical procedures, inquiries, and other procedures to obtain sufficient appropriate evidence to obtain limited assurance about whether any material modifications should be made to the subject matter in order for it to be in accordance with or based on the criteria, or the assertion, in order for it to be fairly stated. Inquiry procedures alone are not sufficient to obtain limited assurance.

14. The practitioner's focus should be on areas in which there are increased risks that the subject matter may be materially misstated.

## Analytical Procedures

15. In designing and performing analytical procedures:
    a. Determine how suitable specific analytical procedures are for the subject matter and existing risks;
    b. Evaluate how reliable the data used for the expectation is, based on its source, comparability, nature, and relevance; and
    c. Develop an expectation of recorded amounts or ratios.

16. Investigate any fluctuations or relationships that are inconsistent with or differ significantly from the practitioner's expectations by:
    a. Inquiring of the responsible party about such differences; and
    b. Considering the inquiry responses to determine whether other procedures are needed in the circumstances.

## Inquiries and Other Review Procedures

17. Inquire of the responsible party about:
    a. Whether the subject matter was prepared in accordance with or based on the criteria;
    b. The practices used by the responsible party to measure, recognize, and record the subject matter;
    c. Questions arising as review procedures have been performed; and
    d. Any relevant communications from regulatory agencies or others.

18. Consider the reasonableness and consistency of the responsible party's responses in the context of the results of review procedures and the practitioner's knowledge of the subject matter, criteria, and responsible party.

## Fraud, Laws, and Regulations

19. Inquire of appropriate parties to determine whether they know of any actual, suspected, or alleged fraud or noncompliance with laws or regulations affecting the subject matter.

20. Respond appropriately when suspected or actual fraud or noncompliance with laws and regulations affecting the subject matter is identified during the engagement.

## Incorrect, Incomplete, or Otherwise Unsatisfactory Information

21. If the practitioner becomes aware that information is incorrect, incomplete, or otherwise unsatisfactory while performing review procedures, request that the responsible party consider the effect on the subject matter and communicate its conclusions to the practitioner. Consider the results communicated by the responsible party and any potential effect on the practitioner's report.

22. If the practitioner believes the subject matter may be materially misstated, perform additional procedures sufficient to obtain limited assurance about whether any material modifications should be made to the subject matter in order for it to be in accordance with or based on the criteria, or the assertion, in order for it to be fairly stated.

## Using the Work of a Practitioner's Specialist or Internal Auditors

23. When the work of a practitioner's specialist or internal auditors is expected to be used, apply the requirements in AT-C 205 (*Assertion-Based Examination Engagements*) and the application guidance relevant to a review engagement.

## Evaluating the Results of the Procedures

24. Accumulate misstatements, other than those that are clearly trivial, identified during the engagement.

25. Evaluate the sufficiency and appropriateness of the evidence obtained in the context of the engagement and attempt to obtain further evidence if necessary. Consider all relevant evidence, regardless of whether it appears to corroborate or contradict the measurement or evaluation of the subject matter against the criteria.

26. If the practitioner concludes the subject matter is materially misstated, the practitioner should express a qualified conclusion; if the practitioner is unable

to obtain sufficient review evidence for limited assurance, the practitioner should withdraw from the engagement if possible under applicable law or regulation.

## Considering Subsequent Events and Subsequently Discovered Facts

27. Inquire whether the responsible party and engaging party are aware of any events subsequent to the period or point in time covered by the engagement up to the date of the practitioner's report that could have a significant effect on the subject matter or assertion. Take appropriate action if the practitioner becomes aware through inquiry or other means that a subsequent event has occurred that is of such a nature and significance that its disclosure is necessary to prevent report users from being misled and it is not adequately disclosed in the responsible party's subject matter or assertion.

28. The practitioner has no responsibility to perform any procedures regarding the subject matter or assertion after the date of the practitioner's report. However, the practitioner should respond appropriately to facts the practitioner becomes aware of after the date of the report that may have caused the report to be revised had the practitioner been aware of those facts at the date of the practitioner's report.

## Written Representations

29. Request written representations from the responsible party in the form of a letter addressed to the practitioner. The representations should:

   a. Include the responsible party's assertion about the subject matter based on the criteria.

   b. State that all relevant matters are reflected in the measurement or evaluation of the subject matter or assertion.

   c. State that all known matters contradicting the subject matter or assertion and any communication from regulatory agencies or others affecting the subject matter or assertion have been disclosed to the practitioner, including communications received between the end of the period addressed in the written assertion and the date of the practitioner's report.

   d. Acknowledge responsibility for the subject matter and assertion, selecting the criteria when applicable, and determining that those criteria are appropriate for the responsible party's purposes.

   e. State that the responsible party has disclosed to the practitioner (1) all deficiencies in internal control relevant to the engagement that the responsible is aware, (2) its knowledge of any actual, suspected, or alleged fraud or noncompliance with laws or regulations, and (3) any other matters that the practitioner believes is appropriate.

   f. State that any known events subsequent to the period or point in time of the subject matter being reported on that would have a material effect on the subject matter or assertion have been disclosed to the practitioner.

   g. State that it has provided the practitioner with all relevant information and access.

   h. State that it believes the effects of any uncorrected misstatements are immaterial, individually and in the aggregate, to the subject matter.

   i. State that any significant assumptions used in making material estimates are reasonable.

30. When the engaging party is different from the responsible party and the responsible party refuses to provide the above written representations, inquire of the responsible party about the representations and try to obtain oral responses.

31. When the engaging party is different from the responsible party, request additional written representations from the engaging party in the form of a letter addressed to the practitioner. The representations should:
   a. Acknowledge that the responsible party is responsible for the subject matter and assertion.
   b. Acknowledge the engaging party's responsibility for selecting the criteria when applicable.
   c. Acknowledge the engaging party's responsibility for determining those criteria are appropriate for its purposes.
   d. State that the engaging party is not aware of any material misstatements in the subject matter or assertion.
   e. State that the engaging party has disclosed to the practitioner all known events subsequent to the period or point in time of the subject matter being reported on that would have a material effect on the subject matter or assertion.
   f. Address other matters the practitioner determines are appropriate.

32. When written representations are directly related to matters that are material to the subject matter, evaluate their reasonableness and consistency with other evidence obtained, including other representations, and consider whether those making the representations can be expected to be well informed on those matters.

33. The date of the written representation should be as of the date of the practitioner's report and should address the subject matter and periods covered by the practitioner's conclusion.

## *Requested Written Representations Not Provided or Not Reliable*

34. When the engaging party is the responsible party and one or more written representations are not provided, or the practitioner concludes there is sufficient doubt about the competence, integrity, ethical values, or diligence of those providing the written representations, or the practitioner concludes the written representations are otherwise not reliable:
   a. Discuss the matter with the appropriate parties;
   b. Reevaluate the integrity of those from whom representations were requested or received and evaluate the effect of this on the reliability of representations and other evidence; and
   c. If any matters are not resolved to the practitioner's satisfaction, take appropriate action.

35. When the engaging party is not the responsible party and one or more written representations are not provided by the responsible party:
   a. If the practitioner receives oral responses to his or her inquiries that allow the practitioner to conclude he or she has sufficient appropriate evidence to form a conclusion about the subject matter, the practitioner's report should contain a separate paragraph restricting the use of the report to the engaging party.
   b. If the practitioner does not receive oral responses to his or her inquiries, a scope limitation exists and the practitioner should withdraw from the engagement.

## Other Information

36. If the practitioner is willing to allow the inclusion of the practitioner's report in a document containing the subject matter or assertion and other information, read the other information to identify any material inconsistencies with the subject matter, assertion, or practitioner's report. If, using professional judgment, the practitioner identifies a material inconsistency or material misstatement of fact, he or she should discuss the matter with the responsible party and take further action as appropriate.

## Description of Criteria

37. Evaluate whether the written description of the subject matter or assertion adequately refers to or describes the criteria.

## Forming the Conclusion

38. Form a conclusion about whether the practitioner is aware of any material modifications that should be made to the subject matter in order for it to be in accordance with or based on the criteria or to the responsible party's assertion in order for it to be fairly stated by evaluating the practitioner's conclusions regarding the sufficiency and appropriateness of evidence obtained and whether uncorrected misstatements are material, individually or in the aggregate.

39. Evaluate, based on the evidence obtained, whether the presentation of the subject matter or assertion is misleading within the context of the engagement.

## Preparing the Practitioner's Report

40. The practitioner's report should be in writing.

41. A practitioner should report directly on the subject matter or on a written assertion, which should either accompany the practitioner's report or be clearly stated in the practitioner's report.

## Content of the Practitioner's Report

42. The review report should contain the following:
    a. A title that includes the word independent.
    b. An appropriate addressee.
    c. An identification or description of the subject matter or assertion being reported on, including the period or point in time to which its measurement or evaluation relates.
    d. An identification of the criteria against which the subject matter was measured or evaluated.
    e. A statement that identifies the responsible party and its responsibility for its assertion or for the subject matter in accordance with or based on the criteria and the practitioner's responsibility to express a conclusion on the subject matter or assertion.
    f. A statement that:
        i. The review was conducted in accordance with attestation standards established by the American Institute of Certified Public Accountants;
        ii. Those standards require the practitioner to plan and perform the review to obtain limited assurance about whether any material modifications should be made to the

subject matter in order for it to be in accordance with or based on the criteria or to the responsible party's assertion in order for it to be fairly stated;

    iii. A review is substantially less in scope than an examination and therefore the practitioner does not express an opinion about whether, in all material respects, the subject matter is in accordance with or based on the criteria or the assertion is fairly stated; and

    iv. The practitioner believes the review provides a reasonable basis for the practitioner's conclusion.

g. A statement acknowledging the practitioner is required to be independent and to meet other ethical responsibilities relating to the review engagement.

h. A statement that describes any significant inherent limitations associated with the measurement or evaluation of the subject matter against the criteria.

i. The practitioner's conclusion about whether any material modifications should be made to the subject matter in order for it to be in accordance with or based on the criteria or to the responsible party's assertion in order for it to be fairly stated.

j. The manual or printed signature of the practitioner's firm.

k. The city and state where the practitioner practices.

l. The date of the practitioner's report, which should be no earlier than the date on which the practitioner has obtained sufficient appropriate evidence on which to base the practitioner's conclusion, including evidence that:

    i. The attestation documentation has been reviewed;

    ii. The written presentation of the subject matter has been prepared if applicable; and

    iii. The responsible party has provided a written or oral assertion.

*Restricted-use paragraph*

43. The use of the practitioner's report should be restricted and include an alert in a separate paragraph when:

a. The practitioner determines that the criteria used to evaluate the subject matter are only appropriate for a limited number of parties who have participated in establishing the criteria or who can be presumed to have an adequate understanding of the criteria.

b. The criteria used to evaluate the subject matter are only available to specified parties.

c. The engaging party is not the responsible party, and the responsible party provides oral but not written representations required. In this case, use of the report should be restricted to the engaging party.

44. The alert should state that the practitioner's report is intended solely for the information and use of the specified parties, identify those parties, and state that the practitioner's report is not intended to be and should not be used by anyone other than the specified parties.

45. If the engagement is also performed in accordance with *Government Auditing Standards,* the alert restricting use of the practitioner's report should instead include a description of the purpose of the practitioner's report and a statement that the report is not suitable for any other purpose.

## Reporting on Subject Matter or Written Assertion

46. The practitioner should report on the written assertion or directly on the subject matters. When reporting on the assertion, the assertion be bound with the practitioner's report or the assertion should be clearly stated in the report.

## Reference to the Practitioner's Specialist

47. The work of a practitioner's specialist should not be referred to in a practitioner's report containing an unmodified conclusion.

## Modified Conclusions

48. If the practitioner becomes aware that the subject matter is misstated and the misstatement is not corrected, consider whether modification of the conclusion is adequate to disclose the misstatement. That may include a qualified conclusion or an adverse conclusion.

49. When the practitioner's conclusion is modified, the practitioner should include a separate paragraph in the practitioner's report that describes the nature of the matter giving rise to the modification, including the effects on the subject matter.

50. When the practitioner's conclusion is qualified, include a separate paragraph in the practitioner's report describing the matter causing the qualification. When a qualified conclusion is expressed due to the effects of a matter being material but not pervasive, it should be expressed as being "except for the effects" of the matters giving rise to the qualification.

51. When the effects of a matter are material and pervasive, the practitioner should express an adverse conclusion.

52. If the practitioner concludes that conditions exist that result in one or more material misstatements based on the criteria, the practitioner should modify the conclusion and express a qualified or adverse conclusion directly on the subject matter, not on the assertion, even if the misstatement is acknowledged in the assertion.

53. If the practitioner believes qualifying the conclusion is not adequate to indicate the misstatements in the subject matter, he or she should withdraw from the engagement.

54. The practitioner's conclusion on the subject matter or assertion should be clearly separated from any paragraphs emphasizing matters related to the subject matter or any other reporting responsibilities.

55. When the conclusion is modified, reference to an external specialist is permitted if the reference is relevant to understanding the modification to the conclusion; however, the practitioner's report should indicate that the practitioner's responsibility for the conclusion is not reduced.

56. A scope limitation exists if sufficient appropriate evidence is unable to be obtained and the practitioner should withdraw from the engagement where possible under law or regulation.

## Responsible Party Refuses to Provide a Written Assertion

57. If the engaging party is the responsible party and refuses to provide the practitioner with a written assertion, withdraw from the engagement where withdrawal is possible under applicable laws and regulations.

58. If the engaging party is not the responsible party and the responsible party refuses to provide the practitioner with a written assertion, the practitioner

may report on the subject matter but should disclose the refusal in the report and restrict its use to the engaging party.

## Communication Responsibilities

59. Communicate to the responsible party and engaging party (if different) known and suspected fraud and noncompliance with laws and regulations and uncorrected misstatements. The practitioner should consider responsibilities under the AICPA Code of Professional Conduct and applicable law, if the practitioner encounters known or suspected fraud.

## Documentation

60. Prepare engagement documentation that is sufficient to determine:
   a. The nature, timing, and extent of the procedures performed to comply with relevant attestation standards and applicable legal and regulatory requirements, including:
      i. The identifying characteristics of the specific items or matters tested;
      ii. Who performed the engagement work and the date such work was completed;
      iii. Discussions with the responsible party or others about significant findings or issues, including the nature of those findings or issues and when and with whom the discussions occurred;
      iv. When the engaging party is the responsible party and will not provide one or more requested written representations or the practitioner concludes there is sufficient doubt about the competence, integrity, ethical values, or diligence of those providing the written representations or written representations are otherwise not reliable;
      v. When the engaging party is not the responsible party and the responsible party will not provide required written representations, document the oral responses to the practitioner's inquiries regarding the representations; and
      vi. Who reviewed the engagement work performed and the date and extent of that review; and
   b. The results of the procedures performed and evidence obtained.

61. If information is identified that is inconsistent with the practitioner's final conclusion regarding a significant finding or issue, document how the inconsistency was addressed.

62. If new or additional procedures are performed or new conclusions are drawn after the date of the practitioner's report, document the circumstances encountered; the new or additional procedures performed, evidence obtained, conclusions reached, and their effect on the practitioner's report; and when and by whom the documentation changes were made and reviewed.

# Analysis and Application of Procedures

## Conduct of a Review Engagement

Review procedures are generally limited to inquiries and analytical procedures, but other procedures can be performed if needed to obtain sufficient appropriate evidence to give the practitioner the required level of assurance. A review engagement may not be appropriate however if other procedures cannot be designed to provide sufficient appropriate review evidence.

## Agreeing on Engagement Terms

The engagement letter or written agreement can further describe the practitioner's responsibilities by including statements that:

- A review is designed to obtain limited assurance about whether any material modifications should be made to the subject matter in order for it to be in accordance with or based on the criteria; and
- The objective of a review engagement is to provide a written conclusion in a practitioner's report about whether the practitioner is aware of any material modifications that should be made to the subject matter in order for it to be in accordance with or based on the criteria or the assertion for it to be fairly stated.

> **PLANNING AID REMINDER:** It is in the interest of both the practitioner and engaging party to document the engagement terms in writing before the engagement begins.

## Requesting a Written Assertion

The responsible party's written assertion could vary according to engagement circumstances. Examples of assertions that meet the requirements of the attestation standard include:

- The subject matter is presented in accordance with (or based on) the criteria.
- The subject matter achieved the objectives, for example, when the objectives are the criteria.

> **PLANNING AID REMINDER:** In situations where the current responsible party was not in place for the entire period covered by the practitioner's report, they are still responsible for the subject matter as a whole, and a written assertion for the entire relevant period should be obtained.

The responsible party should accept responsibility for its assertion and the subject matter even in circumstances where the practitioner is engaged to assist in measuring or evaluating the subject matter against the criteria.

## Planning and Performing the Engagement

It is important to adequately plan the engagement as it can assist in ensuring important areas are focused on, potential problems are identified on a timely basis, the engagement is performed effectively and efficiently, work is properly assigned to engagement team members and properly reviewed, and coordination of work with other practitioners and practitioner's specialists is facilitated.

The nature and extent of planning will vary with the engagement, influenced by factors such as engagement complexity, prior experience, and size of the engagement team. Matters that may influence the nature and extent of planning include:

- Engagement characteristics including its scope, engagement terms, characteristics of the subject matter, and the criteria;
- The expected timing and the nature of the required communications;
- The results of preliminary engagement activities such as client acceptance and whether knowledge gained on other engagements for the entity is relevant;
- The engagement process and choices among alternative measurement or evaluation methods;
- The practitioner's understanding of the appropriate parties and their environment, including the risks that the subject matter may be materially misstated;
- Identification of intended users and their information needs and consideration of materiality and the components of attestation risk;
- The risk of fraud relevant to the engagement; and
- The effect on the engagement of using the internal audit function.

**PLANNING AID REMINDER:** Planning is ongoing throughout the engagement and the nature, timing, and extent of planned procedures can be changed during the engagement if there are unexpected events, changes in conditions, or evidence obtained.

The engagement strategy or plan is solely the responsibility of the practitioner, and any discussion regarding planning with the appropriate parties does not diminish that responsibility. Furthermore, care should be taken when discussing planning to ensure the effectiveness of the engagement is not compromised, for example, by discussing the nature and timing of detailed procedures and making the procedures too predictable.

Obtaining an understanding of the subject matter and engagement circumstances provides the practitioner with a frame of reference for exercising professional judgment throughout the engagement in matters such as:

- Considering the characteristics of the subject matter;
- Assessing criteria suitability;
- Considering significant factors in directing engagement team efforts;
- Establishing and evaluating quantitative materiality levels and considering qualitative materiality levels;
- Developing expectations for analytical procedures;
- Designing and performing procedures; and
- Evaluating evidence and the reasonableness of written representations provided.

In some review engagements, an understanding of internal control over the measurement, evaluation, or disclosure of the subject matter may be obtained.

## Materiality in Engagement Planning and Performance

Materiality determinations are made using professional judgment. Both quantitative and qualitative factors may be used and their relative importance may be specific to the engagement. Quantitative factors relate to the magnitude of misstatements relative to amounts reported for aspects of the subject matter that are expressed numerically or are related to numerical values. Qualitative factors may include:

- The interactions and relative importance of different aspects of the subject matter;
- The clarity and completeness of the wording chosen to express the subject matter;
- The presentation method selected when multiple options are available;
- The nature of a misstatement;
- Whether a misstatement affects compliance with laws or regulations;
- Whether an adjustment affects past, current, or future information about the subject matter;
- Whether a misstatement is intentional or unintentional;
- Whether a misstatement is significant to the practitioner's understanding of known prior communications to users; and
- Whether a misstatement relates to the relationship between the responsible and engaging parties or other parties.

The criteria may discuss materiality in the context of the subject matter, which can be useful to the practitioner in considering materiality. Determinations regarding materiality can be affected by the understanding of the subject matter and the responsible party, which may change during the engagement.

---

**PLANNING AID REMINDER:** Materiality is based on the information needs of intended users; therefore, determinations regarding materiality are impacted by engagement circumstances but not by the level of assurance provided.

---

Misstatements, including omissions, are generally considered to be material if there is a substantial likelihood that, individually or in the aggregate, they would influence the judgment made by intended users based on the subject matter. Practitioners typically do not consider the needs of specific users, but assume that intended users:

- Have reasonable knowledge of and are willing to study the subject matter;
- Understand that the subject matter is measured or evaluated and reviewed to appropriate materiality levels and understand materiality concepts included in the criteria;

- Understand any inherent uncertainties in measuring or evaluating the subject matter; and
- Make reasonable judgments based on the subject matter.

## Procedures to Be Performed

Inquiry and analytical procedures generally provide a reasonable basis for obtaining limited assurance. However, the practitioner may determine additional procedures are needed in order to obtain limited assurance and the other procedures performed may be dependent on engagement circumstances. Other procedures, such as inspection, observation, confirmation, recalculation, and reperformance may be needed in order to obtain sufficient appropriate evidence or because evidence obtained during the engagement brings new information to light that requires further investigation. The practitioner may ask the responsible party to examine the matter identified and make appropriate adjustments to the subject matter. If other procedures cannot be designed to provide sufficient appropriate review evidence, a review engagement may not be appropriate.

Subject-matter specific AT-C sections may have requirements for specific procedures to be performed in a particular type of engagement; however, the exact nature, timing and extent of these procedures is still typically subject to professional judgment and will vary according to engagement circumstances.

## Analytical Procedures

The practitioner uses professional judgment in determining the suitability of certain analytical procedures and their limitations, identifying the relationships and data used, and reaching conclusions about the results. The practitioner develops expectations about recorded amounts or ratios by using relationships reasonably expected to exist based on the subject matter, how the responsible party measures, recognizes, and records the subject matter, and the entity's industry.

In a review engagement, analytical procedures are not designed to identify misstatements with the same level of precision as an examination engagement. Furthermore, when significant fluctuations, relationships, or differences are identified, the practitioner can often obtain appropriate review evidence solely by inquiring of the responsible party and considering the responses given without obtaining additional evidence that would be needed in an examination engagement.

## Inquiries and Other Review Procedures

The practitioner is generally not required to corroborate the responsible party's responses with other review evidence.

## Fraud, Laws, and Regulations

Appropriate responses to suspected or actual fraud and noncompliance may include:
- Discussing the matter with the appropriate parties;

- Requesting the responsible party consult with an appropriately qualified third party, such as the entity's legal counsel or a regulator;
- Considering the implications of the matter to the engagement, including the practitioner's planning and the reliability of written representations provided;
- Obtaining legal advice about different courses of action;
- Communicating with third parties, such as regulators; and
- Withdrawing from the engagement.

In the case of suspected or actual noncompliance with laws or regulations, it may be appropriate to describe the matter in a separate paragraph in the practitioner's report. If the practitioner concludes the noncompliance results in a material misstatement, the conclusion should be modified (or, if the effects of the noncompliance are pervasive, the practitioner should withdraw from the engagement if allowable). If the responsible party prevents the practitioner from obtaining sufficient appropriate evidence to evaluate whether material noncompliance has or is likely to have occurred, there is a scope limitation and the practitioner should withdraw from the engagement where possible under law or regulation.

## Evaluating the Results of the Procedures

The practitioner accumulates uncorrected misstatements during the engagement to evaluate whether, individually or in the aggregate, they are material when forming the practitioner's conclusion. "Clearly trivial" is not another expression for "not material." Clearly trivial misstatements are not accumulated because they are of such small magnitude that aggregating would not cause a material misstatement. If there is uncertainty about whether an item is clearly trivial, then it is not considered clearly trivial.

Sufficient appropriate evidence is needed to support the practitioner's conclusion and report and is a matter of professional judgment. Sufficiency is a measure of the quantity of evidence and the quantity needed will be affected by the risks of material misstatement and the quality of evidence obtained. Appropriateness of evidence is a measure of the quality of evidence and is related to its relevance and reliability.

## Considering Subsequent Events and Subsequently Discovered Facts

To identify subsequent events, the practitioner may make inquiries and consider information contained in relevant reports issued during the subsequent period by internal auditors, other practitioners, or regulatory agencies or obtained through other professional engagements for the entity. If the responsible party refuses to disclose a subsequent event that should be disclosed, the practitioner may disclose the event in the practitioner's report and modify the conclusion or withdraw from the engagement.

> **PLANNING AID REMINDER:** Some subject-matter attestation sections have specific subsequent event requirements and related application guidance.

If the practitioner becomes aware of facts subsequent to the date of the practitioner's report that may have caused revision of the report had the practitioner been aware of those facts at the date of the report, he or she should attempt to discover whether those facts existed at the date of the practitioner's report and, if so, whether users of the practitioner's report would likely find these facts important. Discussion between the responsible and engaging parties and the practitioner may be appropriate and consideration may be given to factors such as whether a subsequent practitioner's report will be issued soon, as well as the time elapsed since the original report was issued.

The practitioner may determine that it is necessary for the responsible and engaging parties to notify the users of the practitioner's report if, for example, the subject matter or assertion needs revision or the practitioner is unable to determine if revision is necessary and a subsequent practitioner's report will not be issued imminently. If the responsible and engaging parties do not take steps to prevent users from relying on the practitioner's report, the practitioner may wish to seek legal advice prior to disclosing the situation. A disclosure by the practitioner may describe the nature of the matter and its effect on the subject matter or assertion and the practitioner's report, while avoiding comment on people's conduct or motives.

## Written Representations

The practitioner generally requests written representations from a member of senior management or those charged with governance. A summary of uncorrected misstatements is often attached to the written representations. Obtaining reliable written representations does not provide sufficient appropriate evidence on its own about any matter and does not affect the nature or extent of other evidence obtained by the practitioner.

> **PLANNING AID REMINDER:** If the responsible party is not the engaging party and written representations are refused, the practitioner should generally seek oral representations from the responsible party and restrict use of the practitioner's report. However, this is not permitted in certain subject-matter specific AT-C sections of the attestation standards.

## Requested Written Representations Not Provided or Not Reliable

When oral representations are obtained in place of written representations, the practitioner may consider if any concerns exist about the competence, integrity, ethical values, or diligence of those providing the oral responses could affect their reliability and impact the practitioner's report.

*Other Information*

If the practitioner has permitted the practitioner's report to be included in a document containing the subject matter or assertion and other information, and the practitioner identifies a material inconsistency or material misstatement of fact, further appropriate action could include:

- Requesting the responsible and engaging parties consult with a qualified third party, such as their legal counsel;
- Obtaining legal advice about different courses of action;
- Communicating with third parties, such as regulators, if required or permissible;
- Describing the material inconsistency in the practitioner's report; and
- Withdrawing from the engagement, where withdrawal is possible.

---

**OBSERVATION:** Other information is not considered to be information contained on the responsible and engaging parties' website, as websites are considered to be a means of distribution and not documents for these purposes.

---

*Description of Criteria*

The description of criteria should only state that the subject matter is prepared in accordance with or based on specific criteria if the subject matter complies with all relevant requirements of those criteria. A description of criteria becomes more important when significant differences exist in various criteria regarding how the subject matter may be treated.

*Forming the Conclusion*

When considering if sufficient appropriate evidence was obtained on which to form a conclusion, the practitioner may consider factors such as:

- The significance of a potential misstatement and its likelihood of having a material effect;
- The effectiveness of the responsible party's responses to address known risks;
- Experience gained during prior engagements with similar potential misstatements;
- The results of procedures performed, including whether specific misstatements were identified;
- The source and reliability of the available information;
- The persuasiveness of the evidence; and
- The practitioner's understanding of the responsible party and its environment.

Information obtained during the engagement may affect the practitioner's assessment of whether uncorrected misstatements are material, individually or in the aggregate. The practitioner may find more misstatements than expected, become aware of discrepancies or conflicting information, or identify previously unrecognized risks of material misstatement through procedures performed.

To evaluate whether the subject matter or assertion presentation is misleading, the practitioner may consider whether additional disclosures are needed to describe, for example, the measurement or evaluation methods used, significant interpretations made, subsequent events, or any changes in measurement or evaluation methods used.

> **PLANNING AID REMINDER:** The presentation of the subject matter or assertion is not required to disclose all related matters users may consider in making decisions, but the practitioner should ensure the presentation is not misleading.

*Preparing the Practitioner's Report*

The practitioner's report is required to be in writing, but the format of the report is not standardized. There are basic required elements, and the report may then be tailored to the engagement circumstances. Unless the practitioner has concluded that material misstatements exist and a qualified conclusion is needed, the practitioner's report may state that:

- The practitioner reviewed the subject matter and expresses a conclusion on the subject matter;
- The practitioner reviewed the responsible party's assertion and expresses a conclusion on the responsible party's assertion; and
- The practitioner reviewed the responsible party's assertion and expresses a conclusion on the subject matter.

*Content of the Practitioner's Report*

The practitioner's report is required to include several elements, including that the practitioner is independent, but the practitioner has some discretion in the manner in which they are included. When identifying the criteria, the practitioner's report may include the criteria or refer to a location where they are readily available. Disclosure of the criteria source, measurement or evaluation methods used, significant interpretations made, or whether there have been any changes to measurement or evaluation methods used may be included when relevant.

Identifying the responsibilities of the responsible party and the practitioner helps to clarify each party's role. When discussing the responsible party's responsibility, the practitioner may want to expand the description to indicate that the responsible party is responsible for preparing and presenting the subject matter in accordance with or based on the criteria, including designing, implementing, and maintaining internal control to prevent or detect and correct misstatement of the subject matter, due to fraud or error.

> **PLANNING AID REMINDER:** When describing significant inherent limitations, note that some AT-C sections of the attestation standards require identification of specific inherent limitations.

The practitioner's conclusion can be stated in terms of the subject matter and the criteria:

> Based on our review, we are not aware of any material modifications that should be made to the ABC schedule in order for it to be in accordance with [or based on] the XYZ criteria.

The conclusion can also be stated in terms of an assertion made by the responsible party:

> Based on our review, we are not aware of any material modifications that should be made to management of ABC Company's assertion in order for it to be fairly stated.

One practitioner's report can cover more than one aspect of a subject matter or assertion. Separate opinions or conclusions can be contained in the same report; for example, some aspects or assertions can be examined and some can be reviewed or some can have unmodified conclusions and some can have modified conclusions. A practitioner can also report on a subject matter or assertion at multiple dates or covering multiple periods of time; when this occurs, for criteria to be clearly described, they should identify the criteria for each period and any changes in criteria between periods.

*Restricted-use paragraph*

A restricted-use practitioner's report can be included in a document that also contains a general use practitioner's report and use of the general use report is not affected. A single combined practitioner's report can be issued that includes a restricted-use report and a general use report. As long that the two types of reports are clearly differentiated, use of the general use report is not affected.

> **PLANNING AID REMINDER:** A practitioner is permitted to include an alert restricting the use of the practitioner's report in situations other than those requiring the alert.

A restricted-use alert may identify specified parties by name, by referring to a list, or by identifying the class of parties. The restricted-use alert is intended to avoid misunderstandings related to use of the report. The practitioner may inform the responsible and engaging parties that the practitioner's report is not intended for distribution to those other than the specified parties and reach an agreement that the report will not be distributed to those other than the specified parties. However, the practitioner is not responsible for and cannot control distribution of the practitioner's report after its release.

Restricted-use practitioner reports filed with regulatory agencies may be made available to the public if required by law or regulation. Regulatory agencies may also require access to restricted-use practitioner reports in which they are not a specified party as part of their oversight responsibilities.

### Reference to the Practitioner's Specialist

The practitioner has sole responsibility for the conclusion expressed, which is not reduced by using the work of a practitioner's specialist.

### Modified Conclusions

In a review, when an unmodified conclusion cannot be obtained the practitioner can express a qualified conclusion or an adverse conclusion. The nature of the matter and the pervasiveness of its potential effects are considered when determining which action is appropriate. Pervasive effects are those that are not confined to specific aspects of the subject matter, but represent a significant portion of the subject matter, or are disclosures that are fundamental to the intended users' understanding of the subject matter.

Scope limitations may be known prior to accepting a review engagement, and the practitioner should consider whether he or she expects to be able to obtain the evidence needed to form a conclusion. Other scope limitations may be imposed by the responsible or engaging parties after acceptance of a review engagement; in these circumstances, the practitioner may determine it is appropriate to withdraw from the engagement where possible.

An unmodified conclusion may only be issued when the engagement has been conducted in accordance with the attestation standards. All standards are not complied with if the practitioner is unable to perform all necessary procedures. An inability to perform a specific procedure does not constitute a scope limitation if alternative procedures can be performed to obtain sufficient appropriate evidence.

### Responsible Party Refuses to Provide a Written Assertion

Not being able to obtain written representations from the responsible party generally results in a scope limitation. There may be some exceptions when the engaging party is not the responsible party and the practitioner is able to make inquiries of the responsible party.

When the engaging party is not the responsible party and the responsible party refuses to provide a written assertion, the practitioner may report on the subject matter in a report restricted to the use of the engaging party and should disclose the refusal to provide a written assertion in a statement such as:

> Attestation standards established by the American Institute of Certified Public Accountants require that we request a written statement from [*identify the responsible party*] stating that [*identify the subject matter*] that we examined has been accurately measured or evaluated. We requested that [*identify the responsible party*] provide such a written statement but [*identify the responsible party*] refused to do so.

In this situation, the practitioner is only permitted to report on the subject matter and not on an assertion, as a written assertion from the responsible party is required to report on an assertion.

## Communication Responsibilities

In addition to actual or suspected fraud and noncompliance with laws and regulations, the practitioner may also wish to discuss any internal control deficiencies identified or bias in the measurement, evaluation, or disclosure of the subject matter with the responsible and engaging parties.

## Documentation

Documentation should not include every matter considered during an engagement but should include a record of the significant findings requiring professional judgment and the related conclusions. The amount of documentation prepared and retained is a matter of professional judgment and may be what the practitioner thinks another experienced practitioner with no history with the engagement would need to understand the work performed and the decisions made.

Documentation typically contains a record of:

- Issues identified regarding compliance with relevant ethical requirements and their resolutions;
- Conclusions on compliance with applicable independence requirements and any relevant discussions with the firm supporting those conclusions;
- Conclusions reached regarding the acceptance and continuance of client relationships and attestation engagements; and
- The nature, scope, and conclusions from consultations occurring during the engagement.

## Practitioner's Aids

Exhibit AT-C 210-1 is an illustrative practitioner's report for a review engagement where the practitioner reviewed and is reporting on the subject matter.

### EXHIBIT AT-C 210-1—REVIEW REPORT—SUBJECT MATTER

**Independent Accountant's Review Report**

[*Appropriate Addressee*]

We have reviewed the accompanying schedule of investment returns of Alpha Company for the year ended December 31, 20XX. Alpha Company's management is responsible for presenting the schedule of investment returns in accordance with the XYZ criteria set forth in Note 1. Our responsibility is to express a conclusion on the schedule of investment returns based on our review.

Our review was conducted in accordance with attestation standards established by the American Institute of Certified Public Accountants. Those standards require that we plan and perform the review to obtain limited assurance about whether any material modifications should be made to the schedule of investment returns in order for it to be in accordance with the criteria above. The procedures performed in a review vary in nature and timing from are substantially less in extent than an examination, the objective of which is to obtain reasonable assurance about whether the schedule of investment returns is in accordance with the criteria, in all material respects, in order to express an opinion. Accordingly, we do not express such an opinion. Because of the limited nature of the engagement, the level of assurance obtained in a review is substantially lower than the assurance that would have been obtained had an examination been performed. We believe that the review evidence obtained is sufficient and appropriate to provide a reasonable basis for our conclusion

We are required to be independent and to meet our other ethical responsibilities in accordance with relevant ethical requirements related to the engagement.

[Include a description of the work performed as a basis for the practitioner's conclusion.]

[Include a description of significant inherent limitations, if any, associated with the measurement or evaluation of the subject matter against the criteria.]

[Additional paragraph(s) may be added to emphasize certain matters relating to the attestation engagement or the subject matter.]

Based on our review, we are not aware of any material modifications that should be made to the schedule of investment returns of Alpha Company for the year ended December 31, 20XX, in order for it to be in accordance with the XYZ criteria set forth in Note 1.

[Practitioner's signature]

[Practitioner's city and state]

[Date of practitioner's report]

---

Exhibit AT-C 210-2 is an illustrative practitioner's report for a review engagement where the practitioner reviewed and is reporting on the responsible party's assertion.

## EXHIBIT AT-C 210-2—REVIEW REPORT—ASSERTION

### Independent Accountant's Review Report

[Appropriate Addressee]

We have reviewed management of Alpha Company's assertion that the accompanying schedule of investment returns of Alpha Company for the year ended December 31, 20XX, is presented in accordance with the XYZ criteria set forth in Note 1. Alpha Company's management is responsible for its assertion. Our responsibility is to express a conclusion on management's assertion based on our review.

Our review was conducted in accordance with attestation standards established by the American Institute of Certified Public Accountants. Those standards require that we plan and perform the review to obtain limited assurance about whether any material modifications should be made to management's assertion in order for it to be fairly stated. The procedures performed in a review vary in nature and timing from and are substantially less in extent than an examination, the objective of which is to obtain reasonable assurance about whether management's assertion is fairly stated, in all material respects, in order to express an opinion. Accordingly, we do not express such an opinion. Because of the limited nature of the engagement, the level of assurance obtained in a review is substantially lower than the assurance that would have been obtained had an examination been performed. We believe that the review evidence obtained is sufficient and appropriate to provide a reasonable basis for our conclusion.

We are required to be independent and to meet our other ethical responsibilities in accordance with relevant ethical requirements related to the engagement.

[*Include a description of the work performed as a basis for the practitioner's conclusion.*]

[*Include a description of significant inherent limitations, if any, associated with the measurement or evaluation of the subject matter against the criteria.*]

[*Additional paragraph(s) may be added to emphasize certain matters relating to the attestation engagement or the subject matter.*]

Based on our review, we are not aware of any material modifications that should be made to management of Alpha Company's assertion in order for it to be fairly stated.

This report is intended solely for the information and use of Alpha Company, and is not intended to be, and should not be, used by anyone other than the specified parties.

[*Practitioner's signature*]

[*Practitioner's city and state*]

[*Date of practitioner's report*]

---

Exhibit AT-C 210-3 is an illustrative practitioner's report for a review engagement where the practitioner reviewed and is reporting on subject matter, but the practitioner expresses a qualified conclusion because the review identified conditions that, individually, or in combination, result in one or more material, but not pervasive misstatements of the subject matter.

## EXHIBIT AT-C 210-3—REVIEW REPORT—QUALIFIED CONCLUSION

### Independent Accountant's Review Report

[*Appropriate Addressee*]

We have reviewed the accompanying schedule of investment returns of Alpha Company for the year ended December 31, 20XX. Alpha Company's management is responsible for presenting the schedule of investment returns based on the XYZ criteria set forth in Note 1. Our responsibility is to express a conclusion on the schedule of investment returns based on our review.

Our review was conducted in accordance with attestation standards established by the American Institute of Certified Public Accountants. Those standards require that we plan and perform the review to obtain limited assurance about whether any material modifications should be made to the schedule of investment returns in order for it to be in accordance with the criteria. The procedures performed in a review vary in nature and timing from and are substantially less in extent than an examination, the objective of which is to obtain reasonable assurance about whether the schedule of investment returns is in accordance with the criteria, in all material respects, in order to express an opinion. Accordingly, we do not express such an opinion. Because of the limited nature of the engagement, the level of assurance obtained in a review is substantially lower than the assurance that would have been obtained had an examination been performed. We believe that the review evidence obtained is sufficient and appropriate to provide a reasonable basis for our conclusion.

We are required to be independent and to meet our other ethical responsibilities in accordance with relevant ethical requirements related to the engagement.

[Include a description of the work performed as a basis for the practitioner's conclusion.]

[Include a description of significant inherent limitations, if any, associated with the measurement or evaluation of the subject matter against the criteria.]

[Additional paragraph(s) may be added to emphasize certain matters relating to the attestation engagement or the subject matter.]

Our review identified [describe conditions that resulted in material misstatement or deviation from the criteria].

Based on our review, except for matters described in the preceding paragraph, we are not aware of any material modifications that should be made to the accompanying schedule of investment returns of Alpha Company for the year ended December 31, 20XX in order for it to be in accordance with the criteria of XYZ criteria set forth in Note 1.

[Practitioner's signature]

[Practitioner's city and state]

[Date of practitioner's report]

---

Exhibit AT-C 210-4 is an illustrative practitioner's report for a review engagement where the practitioner reviewed and is reporting on subject matter, but the practitioner expresses an adverse conclusion because the review identified conditions that, individually, or in combination, result in one or more material and pervasive misstatements of the subject matter based on the criteria.

*EXHIBIT AT-C 210-4—REVIEW REPORT—ADVERSE CONCLUSION*

---

### Independent Accountant's Review Report

[Appropriate Addressee]

We have undertaken a review of management of the accompanying schedule of investment returns of Alpha Company for the year ended December 31, 20XX. Alpha Company's management is responsible for presenting the schedule of investment returns based on the XYZ criteria set forth in Note 1. Our responsibility is to express a conclusion on the schedule of investment returns based on our review.

Our review was conducted in accordance with attestation standards established by the American Institute of Certified Public Accountants. Those standards require that we plan and perform the review to obtain limited assurance about whether any material modifications should be made to the schedule of investment returns in order for it to be in accordance with the criteria. The procedures performed in a review vary in nature and timing from and are substantially less in extent than an examination, the objective of which is to obtain reasonable assurance about whether the schedule of investment returns is in accordance with the criteria, in all material respects, in order to express an opinion. Accordingly, we do not express such an opinion. Because of the limited nature of the engagement, the level of assurance obtained in a review is substantially lower than the assurance that would have been obtained had an examination been performed. We believe that the review evidence obtained is sufficient and appropriate to provide a reasonable basis for our conclusion.

We are required to be independent and to meet our other ethical responsibilities in accordance with relevant ethical requirements related to the engagement.

Alpha Company has not [*describe conditions that resulted in the material and pervasive misstatement of the subject matter*]. Had Alpha Company properly accounted for [*describe the material and pervasive misstatement of the subject matter*] many elements in the schedule of investment returns would have been materially affected. The effects on the schedule of investment returns have not been determined.

Based on our review, because of the significance of the matter described in the preceding paragraph, the schedule of investment returns is not in accordance with the XYZ criteria set forth in Note 1. Had we been engaged to perform an examination, other matters might have come to our attention.

[*Practitioner's signature*]

[*Practitioner's city and state*]

[*Date of practitioner's report*]

# SECTION 215

# AGREED-UPON PROCEDURES ENGAGEMENTS

## Authoritative Pronouncements

SSAE-18—Attestation Standards: Clarification and Recodification

SSAE-19—Agreed-Upon Procedures Engagements

SSAE Interpretation 1—Third Party Due Diligence Services Related to Asset-Backed Securitizations: SEC Release No. 34-72936

> **IMPORTANT NOTICE FOR 2022:** In December 2019, the ASB issued Statement on Standards for Attestation Engagements (SSAE) No. 19 (*Agreed-Upon Procedures Engagements*), which revises performance and reporting requirements and application guidance for all agreed-upon procedures engagements. SSAE No. 19 superseded AT-C 215 (*Agreed-Upon Procedures Engagements*). It more closely harmonizes the attestation standards with the International Standards on Assurance Engagements (ISAEs) and it provides more flexibility for practitioners when performing agreed-upon procedures engagements, including no longer requiring the practitioner to request a written assertion from the responsible party when the practitioner is reporting directly on the subject matter. SSAE No. 19 became effective for agreed-upon procedures reports dated on or after July 15, 2021.

## Overview

This section contains performance and reporting requirements and application guidance for agreed-upon procedures (AUP) engagements. The objectives of an AUP engagement are to:

- Apply specific procedures on subject matter;
- Issue a report on the practitioner's findings without stating a conclusion or opinion; and
- Communicate further as required by the attestation standards.

In an AUP engagement, the practitioner issues a report on his or her findings after performing specific procedures on the subject matter, the procedures having been agreed to by the practitioner and the engaging party. In this engagement, the specified procedures can vary greatly, but the engaging party is responsible for determining the appropriateness of the procedures. Because the practitioner's report on agreed-upon procedures contains the procedures performed and the practitioner's findings, the practitioner does not perform an examination or review in an agreed-upon procedures engagement. Thus, an opinion or conclusion is not provided by the practitioner.

The requirements and guidance in AT-C 105 of the attestation standards are also applicable to an AUP engagement and should be followed. The guidance in

AT-C 215 does not apply to other services performed by the practitioner, such as a financial statement audit, review or compilation, other attestation service, or nonattestation service; other relevant professional standards should be used for those services. This section also does not apply to engagements to issue comfort letters to underwriters and other requesting parties; the guidance in AU-C 920 (*Letters for Underwriters and Certain Other Requesting Parties*) should be used for those engagements.

A practitioner's report can contain an AUP report and a report on other services so long as the services provided are clearly distinguishable and applicable professional standards were followed for each service performed (e.g., the practitioner might perform a review of the entity's financial statements and then also perform an agreed-upon procedures engagement for that entity). A restricted-use practitioner's report can be included in a document that also contains a general use practitioner's report and use of the general use report is not affected. A single combined practitioner's report can be issued that includes a restricted-use report and a general use report. As long that the two types of reports are clearly differentiated, use of the general use report is not affected.

## Definition

There are no defined terms in AT-C 215.

## Requirements

The practitioner is presumptively required to perform the following procedures when conducting an AUP engagement:

### Conduct of an AUP Engagement

1. Comply with this section, AT-C 105, and any relevant subject-matter specific sections of the engagement.

### Preconditions for an AUP Engagement

2. The practitioner must be independent when performing an attestation engagement in accordance with the attestation standards unless law or regulation requires the practitioner to accept the engagement and report on the subject matter or assertion. If the practitioner is required by law or regulation to accept the AUP engagement, the practitioner's report should state that the practitioner is not independent and can either omit or include the reasons for the lack of independence. If reasons are included, all such reasons should be included.

3. To establish that the preconditions for an AUP engagement are present, the preconditions in AT-C 105 as well as the following should be present:
    a. The engaging party agrees on the procedures to be performed and acknowledges they are appropriate.
    b. The practitioner determines the procedures can be designed, performed, and reported on.
    c. The procedures are expected to provide reasonably consistent findings using the criteria.
    d. When applicable, the practitioner agrees to apply any applicable threshold for reporting exceptions.

4. If the specified parties do not agree on the procedures to be performed or do not take responsibility for the sufficiency of those procedures, the AUP engagement should not be accepted.

5. The practitioner should establish an understanding with the engaging party on the intended purpose of the engagement, intended users of the agreed-upon procedures report and whether the report is to be restricted, whether this engagement is performed to comply with certain laws or regulations, and whether other parties will be requested to agree to the procedures and their appropriateness.

## *Agreeing on Engagement Terms*

6. Engagement terms should be agreed upon with the engaging party and should be specified in sufficient detail in an engagement letter or other suitable written agreement.

7. The agreement on engagement terms should be addressed to the engaging party.

8. The agreed-upon terms of the engagement should include:
    a. The nature of the engagement;
    b. Identification of the subject matter and the responsible party;
    c. Acknowledgment by the responsible party of their responsibilities for the appropriateness of the procedures and a statement that the engaging party agrees to provide the practitioner a written agreement and acknowledgment that the procedures performed are appropriate;
    d. The responsibilities of the practitioner;
    e. A statement that the engagement will be conducted in accordance with attestation standards established by the American Institute of Certified Public Accountants;
    f. Agreement on procedures by providing a list or reference;
    g. Acknowledgment that the engaging party agrees to provide a representation letter at the conclusion of the engagement;
    h. Identification of any other parties, if known before the engagement begins, that will be requested to agree to the procedures and acknowledge their appropriateness;
    i. If the engaging party is not the responsible party, a statement of written representations may be requested from the responsible party;
    j. Expectations related to the form and content of the practitioner's agreed-upon procedures report, including any restrictions on the report's use;
    k. Disclaimers expected to be in the practitioner's report;
    l. Assistance to be provided to the practitioner;
    m. Any involvement of an external specialist; and
    n. Any agreed-upon thresholds to be applied for reporting exceptions.

## *Procedures to Be Performed*

9. The practitioner should perform the procedures agreed to and acknowledged by the engaging party.

10. The practitioner should not agree to perform procedures that are uncertain in meaning or subject to various interpretations. Unclear language such as "general" or "limited review" or "test" should not be used to describe procedures unless those terms are defined within the agreed-upon procedures.

11. The agreed-upon procedures should be performed and used to provide a reasonable basis for the findings in the practitioner's report but the performance of additional procedures outside the scope of the engagement to obtain additional evidence is not required.

## Using the Work of a Practitioner's External Specialist

12. The practitioner and specified parties should explicitly agree if the practitioner is to be assisted by a practitioner's external specialist in performing an AUP engagement.

13. The nature of the assistance provided by the practitioner's external specialist should be described in the practitioner's report.

## Using the Work of Internal Auditors or Other Practitioners

14. The engagement team or other practitioners, not internal auditors, should perform all of the agreed-upon procedures referred to or listed in the practitioner's report.

## Appropriateness of Procedures

15. The engaging party should provide the practitioner a written agreement of the procedures to be performed, including acknowledgment of their appropriateness, before the practitioner's report is issued. If the engaging party refuses to provide the written agreement and acknowledgment, the practitioner should withdraw from the engagement.

## Findings

16. The results of applying agreed-upon procedures to the specific subject matter should be presented in the form of findings.

17. Because the practitioner of an agreed-upon procedures engagement does not involve an examination or review, the practitioner's report should not express an opinion or conclusion about the subject matter. For example, the report should not state, "Nothing came to our attention that caused us to believe that the subject matter is not in accordance with or based on the criteria, in all material respects, or that the assertion is not fairly stated, in all material respects."

18. The practitioner should report all findings from the performance of the procedures. Any threshold used by the practitioner for determining what is reported should be described in the report.

19. The practitioner should avoid using vague or ambiguous language in reporting findings.

## Written Representations

20. Request written representations from the engaging party in the form of a letter addressed to the practitioner that:

   a. Include the responsible party's statement that they are responsible for the subject matter.

   b. State that the engaging party has obtained from all necessary parties, if applicable, agreement to the procedures and acknowledgment of the appropriateness of those procedures.

   c. State that all known matters contradicting the subject matter and any communication from regulatory agencies or others affecting the subject matter, including those occurring after the end of the period

addressed by the subject matter and before the date of the practitioner's report, have been disclosed to the practitioner.
d. State that it has provided access to all records and other information relevant to the subject matter and agreed-upon procedures to the practitioner.
e. Consider, when the engaging party is not the responsible party, requesting relevant written representations from the responsible party.
f. Acknowledge that it is not aware of a material misstatement in the subject matter.
g. State that it has disclosed other matters the practitioner deems appropriate, including all known subsequent events after the period or point in time of the subject matter being reported on that would have a material effect on the subject matter.
h. Include other representations that the practitioner believes are appropriate.

21. The written representations should address the subject matter and periods covered by the practitioner's findings and should be dated as of the date of the practitioner's AUP report.

## Requested Written Representations Not Provided or Not Reliable

22. When the engaging party is the responsible party and one or more written representations are not provided, or the practitioner concludes there is sufficient doubt about the competence, integrity, ethical values, or diligence of those providing the written representations, or the practitioner concludes the written representations are otherwise not reliable:
    a. Discuss the matter with the appropriate parties;
    b. Reconsider the integrity of those from whom representations were requested or received and evaluate the effect of this on the reliability of representations and other evidence; and
    c. If any matters are not resolved to the practitioner's satisfaction, take appropriate action.

23. When the engaging party is not the responsible party and one or more written representations are not provided by the responsible party:
    a. The practitioner should inquire of the responsible party about and seek oral responses to the requested representations.
    b. If the practitioner does not receive oral responses to his or her inquiries, he or she should take appropriate action.

## Preparing the Report

24. The report should be in writing.

25. The practitioner's AUP report should be in the form of procedures and findings (and should not contain an opinion or a conclusion that the subject matter is in accordance with the criteria).

## Content of the Practitioner's AUP Report

26. The AUP report should be in writing and include:
    a. A title that includes the word independent;
    b. An appropriate addressee;
    c. An identification of the engaging party;

d. An identification of the subject matter and the nature of an AUP engagement;
e. An identification of the responsible party, including a statement that the responsible party is responsible for the subject matter;
f. A statement that the procedures performed were agreed to by the engaging party identified in the practitioner's report and are appropriate to meet the intended purpose of the engagement;
g. An identification in sufficient detail of the intended purpose of the engagement to enable the user to understand the nature of the work performed;
h. A statement that the practitioner's report may not be suitable for any other purpose;
i. A statement that users are responsible for determining whether the procedures performed are appropriate, given the procedures performed may not address all the items of interest and may not meet the needs of all users of the report;
j. A statement that an agreed-upon procedures engagement involves the practitioner performing specific procedures that the engaging party has agreed to and acknowledged as being appropriate for the intended purpose of the engagement and reporting on findings based on the performance of those procedures;
k. Details describing the nature and extent of procedures performed and, if appropriate, the timing of the procedures;
l. A description of the findings from each procedure performed and details of any exceptions found;
m. A description of a threshold, if applicable, established by the engaging party for reporting exceptions;
n. A statement that:
   i. The AUP engagement was conducted in accordance with attestation standards established by the American Institute of Certified Public Accountants,
   ii. The practitioner was not engaged to and did not conduct an examination or review of the subject matter, the objective of which would be the expression of an opinion or conclusion, respectively, on the subject matter,
   iii. The practitioner does not express such an opinion or conclusion, and
   iv. Had other procedures been performed by the practitioner, other matters might have come to his or her attention that would have been reported;
o. A statement that the practitioner is required to be independent of the responsible party and to meet the practitioner's other ethical responsibilities related to the agreed-upon procedures engagement;
p. A description of the nature of assistance provided, if any, by a practitioner's external specialist;
q. Any reservations or restrictions concerning procedures or findings;
r. The manual or printed signature of the practitioner's firm;
s. The city and state where the practitioner's report is issued; and
t. The date of the practitioner's report, which should be no earlier than the date on which the practitioner completed the procedures and determined the findings, including that:

i. The attestation documentation has been reviewed and
   ii. The written presentation of the subject matter has been prepared if applicable.

27. The practitioner should consider if the report should include an alert, in a separate paragraph, that restricts the use of the practitioner's agreed-upon procedures report. The alert should state that the practitioner's report if intended solely for the information and use of the specified parties, identify the specified parties for whom it is intended, and state that the report is not intended to be, and should not be, used by anyone other than the specified parties.

## *Adding Specified Parties*

28. If the practitioner issues a report that includes an alert restricting the use of the report to certain specified parties and the engaging party subsequently requests the practitioner to add a nonparticipant party, the practitioner should determine whether to add the additional specified party. In doing so, the practitioner should consider whether the additional specified party has acknowledged or will be requested to acknowledge that the procedures performed are appropriate for their purposes. If the practitioner determines acknowledgment is necessary, the practitioner should obtain that acknowledgment directly either from the nonparticipant party agreeing or from the engaging party as to the procedures performed and taking responsibility for the appropriateness of the procedures.

29. The practitioner should consider if the report will be reissued to acknowledge the nonparticipant party.

30. If the practitioner acknowledges in writing that the nonparticipant party has been added as a specified party, that acknowledgment should state that no procedures have been performed subsequent to the date of the practitioner's report.

## *Restrictions on the Performance of Procedures*

31. If there are restrictions on performing the agreed-upon procedures, the practitioner should attempt to obtain agreement from the engaging party as to whether those restrictions are appropriate, and if so, the practitioner should describe any restrictions on the performance of procedures.

## *Knowledge of Matters Outside Agreed-Upon Procedures*

32. If matters come to the practitioner's attention during performance of the AUP engagement that significantly contradict the subject matter referred to in the practitioner's report, those matters should be included in the practitioner's report.

## *Communication Responsibilities*

33. Communicate to the responsible party and engaging party (if different) known and suspected fraud and noncompliance with laws and regulations.

## *Documentation*

34. Prepare engagement documentation that is sufficient to determine:
    a. The specified parties' written agreement and acknowledgment of the appropriateness of the procedures performed.
    b. The nature, timing and extent of the procedures performed to comply with relevant attestation standards and applicable legal and regulatory requirements, including:

i. The identifying characteristics of the specific items or matters tested;

ii. Who performed the engagement work and the date such work was completed;

iii. When the appropriate party will not provide one or more requested written representations or the practitioner concludes there is sufficient doubt about the competence, integrity, ethical values, or diligence of those providing the written representations or written representations are otherwise not reliable; and

iv. Who reviewed the engagement work performed and the date and extent of that review.

c. The results of the procedures performed and evidence obtained.

## Analysis and Application of Procedures

*Conduct of an AUP Engagement*

---

**PLANNING AID REMINDER:** Refer to ET Section 1.297.020 (*Agreed-Upon Procedures Engagements Performed in Accordance With Statement on Standards for Attestation Engagements*) of the AICPA *Professional Standards* for the independence requirements unique to an AUP engagement.

---

**PLANNING AID REMINDER:** In October 2017, the AICPA Auditing Standards Board issued a new Statement of Position (SOP) 17-1 titled *Performing Agreed-Upon Procedures Related to Rated Exchange Act Asset-Backed Securities Third Party Due Diligence Services as Defined by SEC Release No. 34-72936*. This SOP provides guidance to practitioners regarding the application of SSAEs to agreed-upon procedures (AUP) attestation engagements related to third-party due diligence services performed in connection with rated asset-backed securities (ABS) issued in accordance with the Securities Exchange Act of 1934, as amended, as those services are defined in the SEC rules as amended or adopted by SEC Release No. 34-72936, *Nationally Recognized Statistical Rating Organizations,* and the accompanying text (the release). This SOP supersedes Attestation Interpretation 1, "Third-Party Due Diligence Services Related to Asset-Backed Securitizations: SEC Release No. 34-72936," of AT-C 9215.

---

*Preconditions for an AUP Engagement*

Generally, the practitioner should communicate directly with the engaging party to determine which procedures are to be performed and to make it clear that the engaging party is responsible for the appropriateness of the procedures. SSAE standards note that when the practitioner is unable to communicate directly with the engaging party, procedures such as the following should be employed:

- Compare the procedures to be applied to written requirements established by the engaging party.
- Discuss with a representative of the engaging party the procedures to be employed.
- Review relevant contracts or correspondence from the specified party.

By taking responsibility for the appropriateness of the procedures to be performed, the specified parties are assuming the risk that procedures performed may be insufficient for their purposes and that they might misunderstand or inappropriately use findings reported by the practitioner.

## Agreeing on Engagement Terms

The practitioner's responsibilities in an AUP engagement are to perform the procedures and report findings. Thus, it is important that the practitioner and the engaging party document the agreed-upon terms of the engagement in an engagement letter or other form of written agreement before the engagement begins. The practitioner does not have the responsibility of determining what procedures would have been necessary had the engagement been another form of attestation engagement.

---

**OBSERVATION:** In an AUP engagement, the practitioner assumes the risk that (1) misapplication of the procedures might result in inappropriate findings being reported, and (2) appropriate findings might not be reported or might be reported inaccurately.

---

## Procedures to Be Performed

While procedures performed may be very limited or very extensive, in order to report on the results of applying agreed-upon procedures, the practitioner needs to do more than read an assertion or specified information about the subject matter. SSAE standards identify the following as appropriate procedures in an AUP engagement:

- Executing a sampling application after agreeing on relevant parameters.
- Inspecting specified documents evidencing certain types of transactions or detailed attributes thereof.
- Confirming specific information with third parties.
- Comparing documents, schedules, or analyses with certain specified attributes.
- Performing specific procedures on work performed by others (including the work of internal auditors).
- Performing mathematical computations.

On the other hand, the following would be inappropriate procedures in an AUP engagement:

- Merely reading the work performed by others solely to describe their findings.
- Evaluating the competency or objectivity of another party.
- Obtaining an understanding about a particular subject.
- Interpreting documents outside the scope of the practitioner's professional expertise.

The practitioner should be specific in the description of procedures performed, for example, by stating the sample size, how the selection was made, the date the procedure was performed, and the information sources used. In describing the nature and extent of procedures performed, vague or ambiguous language such as note, review, evaluate, analyze, check, test, interpret, verify, and examine are generally not acceptable. Acceptable descriptions of procedures performed would include inspect, confirm, compare, agree, trace, inquire, recalculate, observe, and mathematically check.

## Using the Work of a Practitioner's External Specialist

In some AUP engagements, the practitioner and engaging party may agree that it is appropriate for a practitioner to use the work of an external specialist and that agreement may be documented in the agreement on engagement terms.

> **PLANNING AID REMINDER:** As one of the agreed-upon procedures, the practitioner may agree to apply procedures to the work product created by a specialist. This approach is not considered the "use of a specialist" in the context of an AUP engagement. SSAE standards note that the practitioner should not agree to simply read a specialist's report "solely to describe or repeat the findings, or take responsibility for all or a portion of any procedures performed by a specialist or the specialist's work product."

## Using the Work of Internal Auditors or Other Practitioners

The practitioner is responsible for performing the agreed-upon procedures, but he or she may use internal auditors or other personnel to accumulate data and perform other similar procedures. In addition, the practitioner may agree to perform procedures on information included in an internal practitioner's audit documentation; however, SSAE standards point out that the following would be inappropriate:

- Agree to simply read an internal auditor's report for the sole purpose of describing the findings in the engagement report.
- Report any of the findings of procedures performed by internal auditors as the practitioner's findings.
- Prepare an engagement report in a manner that suggests that the practitioner and the internal auditor share responsibility for the performance of the agreed-upon procedures.

## Findings

Findings should not be reported with vague or ambiguous language. The following provides some example agreed-upon procedures along with appropriate and inappropriate descriptions of findings:

| AUP | Appropriate Finding Description | Inappropriate Finding Description |
|---|---|---|
| Recalculate the rate of return on a commercial real-estate investment according to [*an agreed-upon formula*] and determine whether the resulting percentage agreed to the percentage in an identified schedule. | No exceptions were found as a result of applying the procedure. | The resulting percentage approximated the percentage in the identified schedule. |
| Inspect the receiving report dates for an agreed-upon sample of specified receiving report documents and determine whether any of these dates were subsequent to [*date*]. | No receiving dates shown on the sample of receiving report documents were subsequent to [*date*]. | Nothing came to my attention as a result of applying that procedure. |

---

**PLANNING AID REMINDER:** Materiality does not apply to AUP findings unless a definition of materiality has been agreed to by the specified parties.

---

### Requested Written Representations Not Provided or Not Reliable

When the practitioner is unable to obtain requested written or oral representations from the responsible or engaging party or the practitioner questions its reliability, he or she should take appropriate action. Appropriate actions the practitioner may consider are withdrawing from the engagement or determining the effect on the practitioner's report.

### Preparing the Report

The practitioner's report is required to be in writing, but the format of the report is not standardized. There are basic required elements and the report may then be tailored to the engagement circumstances. An example of a practitioner's report is shown in Exhibit AT-C 215-1.

### Content of the Practitioner's AUP Report

The practitioner may be asked to apply agreed-upon procedures to more than one subject matter; in these situations, one practitioner's report may still be produced that refers to all subject matter covered. If the subject matter of an AUP engagement consists of financial statement accounts or elements, the practitioner's report may state that the agreed-upon procedures do not constitute an audit or review of financial statements or any part thereof, the objective of which is the expression of any opinion or conclusion.

AUP reports are restricted to ensure that only those who have agreed on the procedures performed and taken responsibility for the sufficiency of those procedures use the report. Restricted-use practitioner reports filed with regulatory agencies may be made available to the public if required by law or regulation. Regulatory agencies may also require access to restricted-use practitioner reports in which they are not a specified party as part of their oversight responsibilities.

---

**PLANNING AID REMINDER:** An accountant may be engaged to perform an agreed-upon-procedures engagement related to asset-backed securitizations (ABS). SEC Release No. 34-72936 (*Nationally Recognized Statistical Rating Organizations*) describes these as third-party due diligence services. Such services may involve the accountant checking the accuracy of the information or data about the assets provided by the securitizer or originator of the assets. The SEC's Rule requires the issuer or underwriter of any ABS to make publicly available the findings and conclusions of any third-party due diligence report obtained by the issuer or underwriter, and that disclosure include information about the criteria used to make the accountant's evaluations. Additionally, the third-party due diligence service provider must also complete a specific prescribed ABS Form, which includes information about the services performed. Interpretation 1 of AT-C 215 (*Third-Party Due Diligence Services Related to Asset-Backed Securitizations: SEC Release No. 34-72936*) clarifies that the distribution of the procedures or findings in the prescribed ABS Form is not prohibited by AT-C 215. Interpretation 1 of AT-C 215 notes, however, that the accountant may need to reword the prescribed form if the form contains language that may be inconsistent with the accountant's function or that may be misinterpreted.

---

When describing any reservations or restrictions concerning procedures or findings, the practitioner may include explanatory paragraphs about matters such as:

- Stipulated facts, assumptions, or interpretations used in the application of agreed-upon procedures;
- The condition of records, controls, or data to which the procedures were applied;
- Explanation that the practitioner has no responsibility to update the practitioner's report; and
- Explanation that the sample may not be representative of the population.

### Knowledge of Matters Outside Agreed-Upon Procedures

The practitioner is to include in the practitioner's report matters that significantly contradict the subject matter or assertion referred to in the practitioner's report that come to his or her attention other than through the agreed-upon procedures. Examples of such matters that would be included in the practitioner's report are a material weakness that is discovered or a departure from a standard audit report on the entity's financial statements if the AUP engagement relates to an element, account, or item of a financial statement.

## Practitioner's Aid

Exhibit AT-C 215-1 is an illustrative practitioner's report for an AUP engagement where the practitioner applied agreed-upon procedures to and is reporting on a Statement of Commercial Real Estate Investment Performance Statistics.

## EXHIBIT AT-C 215-1—AUP ENGAGEMENT REPORT

### Independent Accountant's Report

[*Appropriate Addressee*]

We have performed the procedures enumerated below, which were agreed to by the audit committees and managements of Alpha Inc. and REAL Fund on the accompanying Statement of Commercial Real Estate Investment Performance Statistics of REAL Fund for the year ended December 31, 20XX. REAL Fund's management is responsible for the Statement of Commercial Real Estate Investment Performance Statistics for the year ended December 31, 20XX.

Alpha Inc. and REAL Fund have agreed to and acknowledged that the procedures performed are appropriate to meet the intended purpose of assisting them in understanding the Statement of Commercial Real Estate Investment Performance Statistics of REAL Fund for the year ended December 31, 20XX. This report may not be suitable for any other purpose. The procedures performed may not address all the items of interest to a user of this report and many not meet the needs of all users of this report and, as such, users are responsible for determining whether the procedures performed are appropriate for their purposes.

The procedures and the associated findings are as follows:

[*Include paragraphs to enumerate procedures and findings, including exceptions identified.*]

We were engaged by Alpha Inc. and REAL Fund to perform this agreed-upon procedures engagement and conducted our engagement in accordance with attestation standards established by the American Institute of Certified Public Accountants. We were not engaged to and did not conduct an examination or review engagement, the objective of which would be the expression of an opinion or conclusion, respectively, on the accompanying Statement of Commercial Real Estate Investment Performance Statistics of REAL Fund for the year ended December 31, 20XX. Accordingly, we do not express such an opinion or conclusion. Had we performed additional procedures, other matters might have come to our attention that would have been reported to you.

We are required to be independent of Alpha Inc. and REAL Fund and to meet our other ethical responsibilities, in accordance with the relevant ethical requirements related to our agreed-upon procedures engagement.

[*Additional paragraphs may be added to describe other matters.*]

[*Signature of the practitioner's firm*]

[*City and State where the practitioner's report is issued*]

[*Date of practitioner's report*]

# SECTION 300

## SUBJECT MATTER

# SECTION 305

## PROSPECTIVE FINANCIAL INFORMATION

### Authoritative Pronouncements

SSAE-18—Attestation Standards: Clarification and Recodification

### Overview

This section contains performance and reporting requirements and application guidance for examination or agreed-upon procedures (AUP) engagements on prospective financial information.

The objectives of an examination of prospective financial information are to:
- Obtain reasonable assurance about whether, in all material respects, the prospective financial information is presented in accordance with the guidelines established by the AICPA and the assumptions underlying the forecast or projection are suitably supported and provide a reasonable basis for the responsible party's forecast or projection, given the hypothetical assumptions.
- Express an opinion in a written report about the above matters.

In an examination of prospective financial information, the practitioner attempts to obtain sufficient appropriate evidence using his or her professional judgment to reduce attestation risk to an acceptably low level to express the above opinion. This opinion does not address whether the prospective results can be achieved because the results are dependent on the actions, plans and assumptions of the responsible party and unexpected events may occur.

The objectives of an AUP engagement of prospective financial information are to:
- Apply the procedures established and agreed-upon by the specified parties who are responsible for the sufficiency of the procedures for their purposes; and
- Issue a written report describing the procedures and findings.

The requirements and guidance in Section 1, *Concepts Common to All Attestation Engagements,* and either Section 2, *Examination Engagements,* or Section 4, *Agreed-Upon Procedures Engagements,* of the attestation standards that pertain to prospective financial information engagements are also applicable and should be followed.

> **PLANNING AID REMINDER:** AT-C 210 (*Review Engagements*) prohibits a practitioner from performing a review of prospective financial information.

The AICPA guide, *Prospective Financial Information*, provides comprehensive guidance on prospective financial information and on application of the guidance in this section.

## Definitions

| | |
|---|---|
| Entity | Any existing or potential unit for which the financial statements could be prepared in accordance with generally accepted accounting principles or special purpose frameworks, such as an individual, partnership, corporation, trust, estate association, or governmental unit. |
| Financial forecast | Prospective financial statements that present, to the best of the responsible party's knowledge and belief, an entity's expected financial position, results of operations, and cash flows. The forecast is based on the responsible party's assumptions about expected future conditions and actions. A forecast may be expressed as a single-point estimate or as a range, which may not be selected in a biased or misleading manner. |
| Financial projection | Prospective financial statements that present, to the best of the responsible party's knowledge and belief, given one or more hypothetical assumptions, an entity's expected financial position, results of operations, and cash flows. The forecast is based on the responsible party's assumptions about expected future conditions and actions, given the hypothetical assumptions. A projection may be expressed as a point estimate or range. |
| Guide | The AICPA guide, *Prospective Financial Information*. |
| Hypothetical assumption | An assumption used in a financial projection or partial presentation of projected information to present a condition or course of action that may or may not occur but is consistent with the projection's purpose. |
| Key factors | Significant matters on which an entity's future results are expected to depend that serve as a foundation for prospective financial information and are the bases for assumptions. Key factors are basic to the entity's operations, encompassing matters affecting sales, production, service, and financing activities. |
| Partial presentation | A presentation of prospective financial information that excludes one or more of the applicable items required for prospective financial statements as described in Section 8 of the Guide. |
| Presentation guidelines | The criteria for presentation and disclosure of prospective financial information. |

| | |
|---|---|
| Prospective financial information | Any financial information about the future that may be presented as complete financial statements or limited to one or more elements, items, or accounts. |
| Prospective financial statements | Financial forecasts or projections including the summaries of significant assumptions and accounting policies. Prospective financial statements may cover a period that has partially expired. Prospective financial statements are not for periods that have completely expired, for pro forma financial statements, or for partial presentations. |

## Requirements

The practitioner is presumptively required to perform the following procedures when conducting an examination or applying agreed-upon procedures to prospective financial information:

## Examination Engagements

### Preconditions for an Examination Engagement

1. The practitioner should not agree to his or her name being used in conjunction with a financial projection that the practitioner believes will be distributed to those who will not be negotiating directly with the responsible party because financial projections are not appropriate for general use.

2. An engagement to examine the following should not be accepted unless required by law or regulation:

   a. A forecast or projection unless the responsible party has agreed to disclose the significant assumptions.

   b. A financial projection unless the responsible party has agreed to identify which assumptions are hypothetical in the presentation and to describe the limitations on the projections' usefulness.

   c. A partial presentation that does not describe the limitations on the usefulness of the presentation.

3. The practitioner should not examine a forecast or projection that does not disclose any of the significant assumptions. If after engagement acceptance the practitioner becomes aware that no significant assumptions are disclosed, he or she should withdraw from the engagement unless required by law to report on the financial forecast or projection, in which case an adverse opinion should be expressed in the practitioner's report.

4. If after engagement acceptance the practitioner becomes aware that one or more significant assumptions are not disclosed, the practitioner's report should describe those assumptions and express an adverse opinion.

5. If after engagement acceptance the practitioner determines a projection fails to identify which assumptions are hypothetical or to describe the limitations on the usefulness of the projection, he or she should withdraw from the engagement unless required by law or regulation to report on the projection, in which case an adverse opinion should be expressed in the practitioner's report.

### Training and Proficiency

6. The practitioner should:

   a. Understand the guidelines for preparation and presentation of prospective financial statements contained in the Guide.

b. Possess or obtain knowledge of the entity's industry and accounting principles and practices of that industry sufficient to allow the practitioner to examine prospective financial information appropriate for an entity in that industry.

c. Obtain knowledge of the key factors on which the entity's prospective financial information is based.

## Requesting a Written Assertion

7. Request a written assertion from the responsible party, whether or not the responsible party is the engaging party. If the responsible party refuses to provide a written assertion, withdraw from the engagement if permitted by applicable laws and regulations.

## Planning

8. Establish an overall engagement strategy that sets the scope, timing, and direction of the engagement and guides development of the engagement plan in accordance with AT-C 205.

## Examination Procedures

9. Examination procedures should be based on consideration of:

    a. The nature and materiality of the information to the prospective financial information as a whole;

    b. The likelihood of material misstatements;

    c. Knowledge obtained during current and previous engagements;

    d. The responsible party's competence with respect to prospective financial information;

    e. The extent to which the responsible party's judgment affects the prospective financial information, for example in selecting significant assumptions used to prepare prospective financial information; and

    f. The support for the responsible party's assumptions.

10. Evaluate whether the responsible party has a reasonably objective basis for the forecast and consider whether sufficiently objective assumptions can be developed for each key factor.

11. Perform the procedures the practitioner considers necessary in the circumstances to report on whether the assumptions underlying the forecast or projection are suitably supported and provide a reasonable basis for the forecast or projection, given the hypothetical assumptions.

12. Evaluate the support for the significant assumptions individually and in the aggregate. An assumption is suitably supported if the preponderance of information supports that assumption. Support does not need to be obtained for hypothetical assumptions but the practitioner should evaluate whether they are consistent with the purpose of the presentation.

13. In evaluating whether the assumptions provide a reasonable basis for the forecast, consider the assumptions in the aggregate. Assumptions that do not have a material effect on the presentation may not need to be individually evaluated but should be included when evaluating the aggregate effect of the assumptions.

14. Evaluate the assumptions related to an expired portion of the prospective period.

15. In evaluating the preparation and presentation of prospective financial information, perform procedures to obtain reasonable assurance about whether the:
   a. Presentation reflects the identified assumptions;
   b. Computations translating the assumptions into prospective amounts are mathematically accurate;
   c. Assumptions are internally consistent;
   d. Appropriate accounting principles are used;
   e. Prospective financial information is presented in accordance with the AICPA presentation guidelines; and
   f. Assumptions have been adequately disclosed in accordance with the AICPA presentation guidelines.

16. Conclude whether the prospective financial information or related disclosures should be revised due to mathematical errors, unreasonable or internally inconsistent assumptions, inappropriate or incomplete presentation, or inadequate disclosure.

## *Written Representations*

17. In an examination of a forecast, in addition to the written representations from the responsible party required by AT-C 205, request written representations from the responsible party that:
   a. The forecast presents the expected financial position, results of operations and cash flows for the forecast period, and reflects the responsible party's judgment of expected conditions and its expected course of action given present circumstances;
   b. The assumptions on which the forecast is based are reasonable and suitably supported; and
   c. If the forecast contains a range, the items subject to the assumptions are reasonably expected to fall within the range and the range was not selected in a biased or misleading manner.

18. In an examination of a projection, in addition to the written representations from the responsible party required by AT-C 205, request written representations from the responsible party that:
   a. Identify the hypothetical assumptions;
   b. Identify any hypothetical assumptions that are improbable;
   c. Describe the limitations on the usefulness of the presentation;
   d. The projection presents the expected financial position, results of operations and cash flows for the projection period, and reflects the responsible party's judgment of expected conditions and its expected course of action given present circumstances and the occurrence of the hypothetical events;
   e. The assumptions on which the projection is based other than the hypothetical assumptions are reasonable and suitably supported; and
   f. If the projection contains a range, given the hypothetical assumptions, the items subject to the assumptions are reasonably expected to fall within the range and the range was not selected in a biased or misleading manner.

19. In an examination of prospective financial information, the written representation required by AT-C 205 regarding whether the subject matter is in accordance with or based on the criteria should indicate that the forecast or

projection is presented in accordance with or based on the guidelines for the presentation of a financial forecast or projection established by the AICPA.

20. The practitioner should request from the responsible party the written representations in AT-C 205 and those applicable above, even if the engaging party is not the responsible party. There is no alternative to obtaining written representations in an examination of prospective financial information. If the responsible party refuses to provide written representations, there is a scope limitation on the engagement sufficient to preclude an unmodified opinion that may be sufficient to cause withdrawal from the engagement where possible under applicable law or regulation.

## Content of the Practitioner's Examination Report

21. The practitioner's examination report on prospective financial information should include the following:
    a. A title that includes the word independent;
    b. An appropriate addressee;
    c. An identification of the prospective financial information being reported on and the period of time to which it relates;
    d. An indication that the criteria against which the prospective financial information was measured or evaluated are the guidelines for the presentation of a forecast or projection established by the AICPA;
    e. A statement that identifies the following:
        i. The responsible party and its responsibility for preparing and presenting the prospective financial information in accordance with the guidelines for the presentation of a forecast or projection established by the AICPA, and
        ii. The practitioner's responsibility is to express an opinion on the prospective financial information based on the practitioner's examination;
    f. Unless the practitioner is disclaiming an opinion, a statement that:
        i. The examination was conducted in accordance with attestation standards established by the AICPA,
        ii. Those standards require that the practitioner plan and perform the examination to obtain reasonable assurance about whether the forecast or projection is presented in accordance with the guidelines for the presentation of a forecast or projection established by the AICPA in all material respects, and
        iii. The practitioner believes sufficient appropriate evidence was obtained to provide a reasonable basis for the practitioner's opinion;
    g. Unless the practitioner is disclaiming an opinion, a description of the nature of an examination engagement;
    h. The practitioner's opinion about whether the forecast or projection is presented in all material respects in accordance with the guidelines for the presentation of a forecast or projection established by the AICPA and whether the underlying assumptions are suitably supported and provide a reasonable basis for the forecast or projection, given the hypothetical assumptions;
    i. A statement indicating that prospective results may not be achieved and describing any other significant inherent limitations;

j. A statement that the practitioner has no responsibility to update the report for events and circumstances occurring after the date of the report;
k. The manual or printed signature of the practitioner's firm;
l. The city and state where the practitioner practices; and
m. The date of the practitioner's report, which should be no earlier than the date on which the practitioner has obtained sufficient appropriate evidence on which to base his or her opinion, including evidence that:
    i. The attestation documentation has been reviewed,
    ii. The prospective financial information has been prepared, and
    iii. The responsible party has provided a written assertion.

22. The practitioner's opinion in an examination of a projection should be conditioned on the hypothetical assumptions; therefore, the opinion should be expressed on whether the assumptions provide a reasonable basis for the projection given the hypothetical assumptions. A practitioner's report on an examination of a projection should also include:
    a. An identification of the hypothetical assumptions;
    b. A statement describing the special purpose for which the projection was prepared;
    c. A separate paragraph containing a restricted-use alert that:
        i. States that the practitioner's report is intended solely for the information and use of the specified parties,
        ii. Identifies the specified parties for whom use is intended, and
        iii. States that the practitioner's report is not intended to be and should not be used by anyone other than the specified parties; and
    d. If the engagement is also performed in accordance with *Government Auditing Standards*, the alert restricting use of the practitioner's report should instead include a description of the purpose of the practitioner's report and a statement that the report is not suitable for any other purpose.

23. When the prospective financial information contains a range, the practitioner's report should include a separate paragraph stating that the responsible party elected to portray the expected results of one or more assumptions as a range.

## Modified Opinions

24. The following are circumstances requiring the practitioner to modify the opinion and the type of modified opinion that should be expressed in each instance:
    a. If the prospective financial information materially departs from the AICPA presentation guidelines in the practitioner's judgment, express a qualified or adverse opinion.
    b. If the prospective financial information fails to disclose assumptions that are significant in the practitioner's judgment or misapplies accounting principles, express an adverse opinion.

c. If one or more significant assumptions are not suitably supported or do not provide a reasonable basis for the forecast or projection, given the hypothetical assumptions, express an adverse opinion.

d. If the practitioner is unable to obtain sufficient appropriate evidence, disclaim an opinion and describe the scope limitation in the practitioner's report.

## Partial Presentations

25. When examining partial presentations, consider whether all significant assumptions have been disclosed and whether key factors affecting elements, accounts, or items interrelated with those in the partial presentation have been considered, including key factors that may not necessarily be obvious to the user of a partial presentation.

26. Partial presentations are generally only appropriate for limited use so practitioners' reports on partial presentations of forecasted and projected financial information should include a description of any limitations on the usefulness of the presentation.

# Agreed-Upon Procedures Engagements

## Preconditions for an AUP Engagement

27. In addition to applying the preconditions for accepting or continuing an AUP engagement in AT-C 105 and AT-C 215, the practitioner should not perform an AUP engagement on a forecast or projection unless the prospective financial information includes a summary of significant assumptions.

## Content of the Practitioner's AUP Report

28. The practitioner's report on the application of agreed-upon procedures to a forecast or projection should include the following:

   a. A title that includes the word "independent."
   b. An appropriate addressee.
   c. An identification of the prospective financial information and the nature of an AUP engagement.
   d. An identification of the specified parties.
   e. A statement that the procedures performed were those agreed to by the specified parties identified in the practitioner's report.
   f. A statement identifying the responsible party and its responsibility for preparing and presenting the forecast or projection in accordance with the guidelines for the presentation of a forecast or projection established by the AICPA.
   g. A statement that:
      i. The sufficiency of the procedures is solely the responsibility of the specified parties; and
      ii. The practitioner makes no representation regarding the sufficiency of the procedures for the purpose for which the practitioner's report has been requested or for any other purpose.
   h. A list of procedures performed or reference to those procedures and related findings.
   i. A description of any agreed-upon materiality limits.

j. A statement that:
   i. The AUP engagement was conducted in accordance with attestation standards established by the American Institute of Certified Public Accountants.
   ii. The practitioner was not engaged to and did not conduct an examination or review of the forecast or projection, the objective of which would be the expression of an opinion or conclusion, respectively, on the forecast of projection.
   iii. The practitioner does not express an opinion or conclusion on:
      1. Whether the presentation of the forecast or projection is in accordance with guidelines for the presentation of a forecast or projection established by the AICPA;
      2. Whether the underlying assumptions are suitably supported; and
      3. Whether the underlying assumptions provide a reasonable basis for the forecast or projection, given the hypothetical assumptions.
   iv. Had other procedures been performed by the practitioner, other matters might have come to his or her attention that would have been reported.
k. A separate paragraph containing an alert restricting use of the practitioner's report that:
   i. States the practitioner's report is intended solely for the information and use of the specified parties,
   ii. Identifies the specified parties for whom use is intended, and
   iii. States that the practitioner's report is not intended to be and should not be used by anyone other than the specified parties.
l. If the engagement is also performed in accordance with *Government Auditing Standards,* the alert restricting use of the practitioner's report should instead include a description of the purpose of the practitioner's report and a statement that the report is not suitable for any other purpose.
m. Any reservations or restrictions concerning procedures or findings.
n. A description of the nature of any assistance provided by a practitioner's external specialist.
o. A caveat that the prospective results may not be achieved.
p. A statement that the practitioner has no responsibility to update the report for events and circumstances occurring after the date of the report.
q. The manual or printed signature of the practitioner's firm.
r. The city and state where the practitioner practices.
s. The date of the practitioner's report, which should be no earlier than the date on which the practitioner completed the procedures and determined the findings, including that:
   i. The attestation documentation has been reviewed,

ii. The prospective financial information has been prepared, and

iii. The responsible party has provided a written assertion, unless the responsible party is unwilling to provide an assertion.

## Analysis and Application of Procedures

Under the attestation standards, a practitioner who is engaged to report on complete or summarized or condensed prospective financial statements must determine whether such statements are intended for general use or for limited use. Prospective financial statements that are issued for general use are those that are intended to be used by parties that are not negotiating directly with the responsible party. Since the parties not negotiating directly are generally unable to make direct inquiries about the prospective financial statements, the most useful presentation for them is one that reflects the responsible party's best knowledge and belief of the expected results. Thus, only a financial forecast is appropriate for general use.

Prospective financial statements that are issued for limited use are those that are intended to be used only by the responsible party and those parties negotiating directly with the responsible party. Since the parties are negotiating directly and are able to make direct inquiries of the responsible party, either a financial forecast or a financial projection is appropriate for limited use.

**ENGAGEMENT STRATEGY:** Pro forma financial statements attempt to reflect the effects of a possible transaction or event on historical financial statements. Pro forma financial statements are not considered to be prospective financial statements. Pro forma financial information is discussed in AT-C 310 (*Reporting on Pro Forma Financial Information*).

## Examination Engagements

### Training and Proficiency

To obtain an understanding of factors that appear key to the entity's future financial results, the practitioner may focus on areas such as costs of production, competitiveness of markets, pace of technology within the industry, and past patterns of revenues, costs, and management policies.

### Planning

SSAE standards identify the following as some of the factors that are important in the proper planning of an examination engagement on prospective financial information:

- Financial reporting framework to be used and the type of presentation.
- Initial assessment of materiality.
- Elements of the prospective financial statements that are likely to require revision.

- Conditions that could change the nature, timing, or extent of examination procedures.
- Understanding of the entity's business environment.
- The responsible party's experience in preparing prospective financial statements.
- The period of time covered by the prospective financial statements.
- The process used to develop the prospective financial statements.

*Examination Procedures*

Evidence must be collected to determine if assumptions used in the preparation of the prospective financial statements are reasonable.

*Financial Forecasts*

The SSAE standards state that in a financial forecast engagement the practitioner can be satisfied with respect to the reasonableness of assumptions made by the responsible party if the examination procedures lead to the following conclusions:

- The responsible party has explicitly identified all key factors expected to materially affect the operations of the entity during the prospective period and has developed appropriate assumptions with respect to such factors.
- The assumptions are suitably supported.

*Financial Projections*

The SSAE standards state that in a financial projection engagement (given the hypothetical assumptions) the practitioner can be satisfied with respect to the reasonableness of assumptions made by the responsible party if the examination procedures lead to the following conclusions:

- The responsible party has explicitly identified all key factors that would materially affect the operations of the entity during the prospective period if the hypothetical assumptions were to materialize and developed appropriate assumptions with respect to such factors.
- The other assumptions are suitably supported given the hypothetical assumptions.

In determining whether there is a preponderance of information to support significant assumptions, judgment is involved and different people may arrive at different reasonable conclusions based on the same information. When evaluating support for significant assumptions in a financial projection, the assumptions can be considered suitably supported if the preponderance of information supports each significant assumption given the hypothetical assumption. The following should be considered when determining whether there is suitable support for assumptions:

- Have sufficient pertinent sources of information about the assumptions been considered? Examples of external sources the practitioner might consider are government publications, industry publications, economic forecasts, existing or proposed legislation, and reports of changing technology. Examples of internal sources are budgets, labor agreements, patents, royalty agreements and records, sales backlog records, debt agreements, and actions of the board of directors involving entity plans.

- Are the assumptions consistent with the sources from which they are derived?

- Are the assumptions consistent with each other?

- Are the historical financial information and other data used in developing the assumptions sufficiently reliable for that purpose? Reliability can be assessed by inquiry and analytical and other procedures, some of which may have been completed in past examinations or reviews of the historical financial statements. If historical financial statements have been prepared for an expired part of the prospective period, the practitioner should consider the historical data in relation to the prospective results for the same period, where applicable. If the prospective financial statements incorporate such historical financial results and that period is significant to the presentation, the practitioner should make a review of the historical information in conformity with the applicable standards.

- Are the historical financial information and other data used in developing the assumptions comparable over the periods specified? Were the effects of any lack of comparability considered in developing the assumptions?

- Are the logical arguments or theory, considered with the data supporting the assumptions, reasonable?

**ENGAGEMENT STRATEGY:** When preparing and presenting prospective financial information, different accounting principles may be used in the prospective period than were used in the historical period if those different principles are consistent with the purpose of the presentation.

Materiality is a highly subjective factor that the practitioner must consider in the examination of prospective financial statements in the same manner as he or she would in the evaluation of historical financial statements. Because of the higher degree of uncertainty associated with prospective financial statements, prospective financial information cannot be expected to be as precise as historical financial information. Thus, the range or reasonableness for evaluating prospective financial information is broader than the range an auditor would use to evaluate historical financial information.

## Content of the Practitioner's Examination Report

The requirements in this section describing the content of a practitioner's examination report constitute all required elements for a report on the examination of prospective financial statements. AT-C 205 of the attestation standards contains the application guidance relating to these required elements.

> **ENGAGEMENT STRATEGY:** When an examination of prospective financial information is part of a larger engagement, such as a business acquisition study, the practitioner's report may be expanded to describe the entire engagement. Section 17 of the Guide, "The Practitioner's Examination Report," provides reporting guidance in this situation.

When a range is included in prospective financial information, the practitioner's report should include a separate paragraph stating that the responsible party elected to portray the expected results of one or more assumptions as a range. A sample of such a paragraph for a forecast containing a range follows:

> "As described in the summary of significant assumptions, management of Alpha Company has elected to portray forecasted [*describe the financial statement element or elements for which the expected results of one or more assumptions fall within a range, and identify assumptions expected to fall within a range, for example, revenue in the amounts of $X,XXX and $Y,YYY, which is predicated upon occupancy rates of XX percent and YY percent of available commercial retail locations*] rather than as a single point estimate. Accordingly, the accompanying forecast presents forecasted financial position, results of operations, and cash flows [*describe one or more assumptions expected to fall within a range, for example, 'at such occupancy rates'*]. However, there is no assurance that the actual results will fall within the range of [*describe one or more assumptions expected to fall within a range, for example, occupancy rates*] presented."

## *Modified Opinions*

SSAEs require the practitioner to issue a qualified opinion when the prospective financial information fails to disclose matters (excluding failure to disclose significant assumptions). For example, the practitioner would issue a qualified opinion when there is a failure to disclose significant accounting policies. A qualified opinion includes "except for" language. When there is a failure to disclose significant assumptions, the SSAEs require the practitioner to issue an adverse opinion.

When expressing a qualified opinion, the opinion should be separated from the paragraph describing the matter giving rise to the qualification. An illustrative paragraph describing the matter giving rise to the qualification and the opinion paragraph when a financial forecast departs from AICPA presentation guidelines follows:

> The forecast does not disclose significant accounting policies. Disclosure of such policies is required by guidelines for the presentation of a forecast established by the American Institute of Certified Public Accountants.
>
> In our opinion, except for the omission of the disclosures related to significant accounting policies as discussed in the preceding paragraph, the accompanying forecast is presented in accordance with the guidelines for the presentation of a forecast established by the American Institute of Certified Public Accountants, and the underlying assumptions are suitably supported and provide a reasonable basis for management's forecast.

In an adverse opinion, the practitioner states that the presentation is not in accordance with AICPA presentation guidelines and, if applicable, that the assumptions are not suitably supported and do not provide a reasonable basis for the prospective financial statements. The paragraphs below illustrate an adverse opinion when the financial forecast contains an unreasonable significant assumption:

> As discussed under the caption "Sales" in the summary of significant forecast assumptions, the forecasted sales include, among other things, revenue from the Company's contracts with government agencies continuing at the current level. The Company's present contracts with government agencies will expire in March 20XX. No new contracts have been signed and no negotiations are under way for new government contracts. Furthermore, the government has entered into contracts with another company to supply the items being manufactured under the Company's present contracts.
>
> In our opinion, the accompanying forecast is not presented in accordance with the guidelines for the presentation of a forecast established by the American Institute of Certified Public Accountants because management's assumptions, as discussed in the preceding paragraph, are not suitably supported and do not provide a reasonable basis for management's forecast.

When disclaiming an opinion, the practitioner describes the matters giving rise to the modified opinion by describing how the examination did not comply with applicable attestation standards. The practitioner states that the examination scope was not sufficient for the expression of an opinion due to the ways in which the examination did not comply with applicable attestation standards. An illustrative practitioner's report on an examination of a financial forecast for which a significant assumption could not be evaluated follows:

> We were engaged to examine the accompanying forecast of Alpha Company, which comprises the forecasted balance sheet as of December 31, 20XX and the related forecasted statements of income, stockholders' equity, and cash flows for the year then ending. Alpha Company's management is responsible for preparing and presenting the forecast in accordance with the guidelines for the presentation of a forecast established by the American Institute of Certified Public Accountants.
>
> As discussed under the caption, "Income From Investee" in the summary of significant forecast assumptions, the forecast includes income from an equity investee constituting 19 percent of forecasted net income, which is management's estimate of the Company's share of the investee's income to be accrued for 20XX. The investee has not prepared a forecast for the year ending December 31, 20XX, and we were therefore unable to obtain suitable support for this assumption.
>
> Because, as described in the preceding paragraph, we are unable to evaluate management's assumption regarding income from an equity investee and other assumptions that depend thereon, the scope of our work was not sufficient to express, and we do not express, an opinion with respect to the presentation of or the assumptions underlying the accompanying forecast.
>
> We have no responsibility to update this report for events and circumstances occurring after the date of this report.

## Partial Presentations

SSAE standards do not establish specific engagement procedures that should be used in a partial presentation engagement, because of the limited content of the presentation. However, the standards do point out that the nature of the information presented in a partial presentation may affect the procedures performed by the practitioner. The nature and extent of procedures performed in a partial presentation examination may be similar to that performed in an examination of prospective financial statements due to the interrelationships of many accounts. Chapter 23 of the Guide addresses partial presentations.

## Agreed-Upon Procedures Engagements

### Content of the Practitioner's AUP Report

The requirements in this section describing the content of a practitioner's AUP report constitute all required elements for a report on the application of agreed-upon procedures to a forecast or projection. AT-C 215 of the attestation standards contains the application guidance relating to these required elements.

## Practitioner's Aids

Exhibit AT-C 305-1 is an illustrative practitioner's report for an examination of a financial forecast.

**EXHIBIT AT-C 305-1—REPORT ON AN EXAMINATION OF A FORECAST**

### Independent Accountant's Report

[Appropriate Addressee]

We have examined the accompanying forecast of Alpha Company, which comprises the forecasted balance sheet as of December 31, 20XX and the related forecasted statements of income, stockholders' equity, and cash flows for the year then ending, based on the guidelines for the presentation of a financial forecast established by the American Institute of Certified Public Accountants. Alpha Company's management is responsible for preparing and presenting the forecast in accordance with the guidelines for the presentation of a forecast established by the American Institute of Certified Public Accountants. Our responsibility is to express an opinion on the forecast based on our examination.

Our examination was conducted in accordance with attestation standards established by the American Institute of Certified Public Accountants. Those standards require that we plan and perform the examination to obtain reasonable assurance about whether the forecast is presented in accordance with the guidelines for the presentation of a forecast established by the American Institute of Certified Public Accountants, in all material respects. An examination involves performing procedures to obtain evidence about the forecast. The nature, timing, and extent of the procedures selected depend on our judgment, including an assessment of the risks of material misstatement of the forecast, whether due to fraud or error. We believe that the evidence we obtained is sufficient and appropriate to provide a reasonable basis for our opinion.

In our opinion, the forecast referred to above is presented, in all material respects, in accordance with the guidelines for the presentation of a forecast established by the American Institute of Certified Public Accountants, and the underlying assumptions are suitably supported and provide a reasonable basis for management's forecast.

There will usually be differences between the forecasted and actual results, because events and circumstances frequently do not occur as expected, and those differences may be material. We have no responsibility to update this report for events and circumstance occurring after the date of this report.

[*Practitioner's signature*]

[*Practitioner's city and state*]

[*Date of practitioner's report*]

Exhibit AT-C 305-2 is an illustrative practitioner's report for an examination of a financial projection.

## EXHIBIT AT-C 305-2—REPORT ON AN EXAMINATION OF A PROJECTION

### Independent Accountant's Report

[*Appropriate Addressee*]

We have examined the accompanying projection of Alpha Company, which comprises the projected balance sheet as of December 31, 20XX and the related projected statements of income, stockholders' equity, and cash flows for the year then ending, based on the guidelines for the presentation of a projection established by the American Institute of Certified Public Accountants. Alpha Company's management is responsible for preparing and presenting the projection based on [*identify the hypothetical assumption, for example,* "the granting of the requested loan as described in the summary of significant assumptions"] in accordance with the guidelines for the presentation of a projection established by the American Institute of Certified Public Accountants. The projection was prepared for [*identify the special purpose, for example,* "the purpose of negotiating a loan to expand Alpha Company's retail outlets"]. Our responsibility is to express an opinion on the projection based on our examination.

Our examination was conducted in accordance with attestation standards established by the American Institute of Certified Public Accountants. Those standards require that we plan and perform the examination to obtain reasonable assurance about whether the projection is presented in accordance with the guidelines for the presentation of a projection established by the American Institute of Certified Public Accountants, in all material respects. An examination involves performing procedures to obtain evidence about the projection. The nature, timing, and extent of the procedures selected depend on our judgment, including an assessment of the risks of material misstatement of the projection, whether due to fraud or error. We believe that the evidence we obtained is sufficient and appropriate to provide a reasonable basis for our opinion.

In our opinion, [*describe the hypothetical assumption, for example,* "assuming the granting of the requested loan for the purpose of expanding Alpha Company's retail outlets as described in the summary of significant assumptions."] the projection referred to above is presented, in all material respects, in accordance with the guidelines for the presentation of a projection established by the American Institute of Certified Public Accountants, and the underlying assumptions are suitably supported and provide a reasonable basis for management's projection given the hypothetical assumption(s).

Even if [*describe hypothetical assumption, for example,* "the loan is granted and the company adds new retail outlets"], there will usually be differences between the projected and actual results because events and circumstances frequently do not occur as expected, and those differences may be material. We have no responsibility to update this report for events and circumstance occurring after the date of this report.

The accompanying projection and this report are intended solely for the information and use of [*identify specified parties, for example,* "Alpha Company and Beta National Bank"] and are not intended to be and should not be used by anyone other than these specified parties.

[*Practitioner's signature*]

[*Practitioner's city and state*]

[*Date of practitioner's report*]

Exhibit AT-C 305-3 is an illustrative practitioner's report on an AUP engagement for a financial forecast.

## EXHIBIT AT-C 305-3—AUP ENGAGEMENT REPORT FOR A FINANCIAL FORECAST

[*Appropriate Addressee*]

We have performed the procedures enumerated below, which were agreed to by the Boards of Directors of Alpha Company and Zeta Company, on the forecasted balance sheet as of December 31, 20XX and the related forecasted statements of income, stockholders' equity, and cash flows of Gamma Company, a subsidiary of Zeta Company, for the year then ending. Gamma Company's management is responsible for preparing and presenting the forecast in accordance with the guidelines for the presentation of a forecast established by the American Institute of Certified Public Accountants. The sufficiency of these procedures is solely the responsibility of those parties specified in this report. Consequently, we make no representation regarding the sufficiency of the procedures enumerated below either for the purpose for which this report has been requested or for any other purpose.

[*Include paragraphs to enumerate procedures and findings.*]

This agreed-upon procedures engagement was conducted in accordance with attestation standards established by the American Institute of Certified Public Accountants. We were not engaged to and did not conduct an examination or review, the objective of which would be the expression of an opinion or conclusion, respectively, about the accompanying forecast. Accordingly, we do not express an opinion or conclusion about whether the forecast is presented in accordance with the guidelines for the presentation of a forecast established by the American Institute of Certified Public Accountants or whether the underlying assumptions are suitably supported or provide a reasonable basis for management's forecast. Had we performed additional procedures, other matters might have come to our attention that would have been reported to you.

There will usually be differences between the forecasted and actual results because events and circumstances frequently do not occur as expected, and those differences may be material. We have no responsibility to update this report for events and circumstances occurring after the date of this report.

This report is intended solely for the information and use of the Boards of Directors of Zeta Company and Alpha Company and is not intended to be and should not be used by anyone other than these specified parties.

[*Practitioner's signature*]

[*Practitioner's city and state*]

[*Date of practitioner's report*]

# SECTION 310

# REPORTING ON PRO FORMA FINANCIAL INFORMATION

## Authoritative Pronouncements

SSAE-18—Attestation Standards: Clarification and Recodification

## Overview

This section contains performance and reporting requirements and application guidance for examination or review engagements on pro forma financial information.

The objectives of an examination of pro forma financial information are to:

- Obtain reasonable assurance about whether, in accordance with or based on the criteria, management's assumptions (management is the responsible party for the purposes of this section) provide a reasonable basis for presenting the significant effects directly attributable to the underlying transaction or event, the related pro forma adjustments give appropriate effect to those assumptions, in all material respects, and the pro forma information properly applies those adjustments to the historical financial statements.
- Express an opinion in a written report about the above matters.

The objectives of a review of pro forma financial information are to:

- Obtain limited assurance about whether, in accordance with or based on the criteria, any material modifications should be made to management's assumptions so that they provide a reasonable basis for presenting the significant effects directly attributable to the underlying transaction or event, the related pro forma adjustments in order for them to give appropriate effect to those assumptions, and the pro forma information in order for it to properly apply those adjustments to the historical financial statements.
- Express a conclusion in a written report about the above matters.

The requirements and guidance in AT-C 105 (*Concepts Common to All Attestation Engagements*) and either AT-C 205 (*Assertion-Based Examination Engagements*) or AT-C 210 (*Review Engagements*) of the attestation standards that pertain to pro forma financial information engagements are also applicable and should be followed.

This section does not apply under several circumstances:

- When performing agreed-upon procedures related to pro forma financial information—in those instances AT-C 105 (*Concepts Common to All Attestation Engagements*) and AT-C 215 (*Agreed-Upon Procedures Engagements*) apply.

- When providing a comfort letter or performing procedures on pro forma financial information in connection with an offering, AU-C 920 (*Letters for Underwriters and Certain Other Requesting Parties*) applies.
- When pro forma financial information is presented in the same document as the basic financial statements and the practitioner is not engaged to report on the pro forma financial information—in those situations AU-C 720 (*Other Information in Documents Containing Audited Financial Statements*) applies and AU-C 925 (*Filings with the U.S. Securities and Exchange Commission under the Securities Act of 1933*) may apply.
- When a transaction that occurred after the balance-sheet date is included in the historical financial statements, such as revision of earnings per share calculations for a stock split.
- When the applicable financial reporting framework requires pro forma financial information in the financial statements or accompanying notes; examples include generally accepted accounting principles requirements in Financial Accounting Standards Board Accounting Standards Codification (ASC) 805 (*Business Combinations*) and ASC 250 (*Accounting Changes and Error Corrections*).

## Definitions

| | |
|---|---|
| Criteria for the preparation of pro forma financial information | The basis and assumptions management used to develop the pro forma financial information that is disclosed in the pro forma financial information. |
| Pro forma financial information | A presentation showing what the significant effects on the historical financial information might have been had a proposed or consummated transaction or event occurred at an earlier date. |

## Requirements

The practitioner is presumptively required to perform the following procedures when conducting an examination or review engagement on pro forma financial information:

*Preconditions for an Examination or Review Engagement*

1. In order to accept an examination or review engagement on pro forma financial information, in addition to the preconditions described in AT-C 105 and AT-C 205:

   a. Determine that the most recent historical financial statements available are included in the document with the pro forma financial information or are readily available and, if interim pro forma financial information is presented, that interim historical financial information for that period is included or available. In a business combination, ensure the historical information for the significant constituent parts of the combined entity is available.

   b. Determine that the historical financial statements described above have been audited if an examination is being performed or have been audited or reviewed if a review is being performed. The audit or review report (if issued) should be included in the document with the pro forma financial information or should be readily available.

c. An appropriate level of knowledge of the accounting and financial reporting practices of the entity will be obtained to perform the procedures necessary to report on the pro forma financial information.

2. The service level provided on the pro forma financial information should not exceed that provided on the related historical financial statements. An examination of pro forma financial information should only be performed if historical financial statements were audited; a review of pro forma financial information should only be performed if historical financial statements were audited or reviewed. In a business combination, the service level provided on the pro forma financial information should not exceed the lowest level of service provided on the historical financial statements of any significant constituent party of the combined entity.

## Requesting a Written Assertion

3. Request a written assertion from management, whether or not the responsible party (management) is the engaging party. If management refuses to provide a written assertion, withdraw from the engagement when possible under applicable laws or regulations.

## Assessing the Suitability of the Applicable Criteria

4. Determine whether management used suitable criteria in preparing and presenting the pro forma financial information, and determine whether the criteria include, at a minimum, that:

  a. The financial information be extracted from audited or reviewed historical financial statements;

  b. The pro forma adjustments be directly attributable to the event or transaction, factually supportable, and consistent with the entity's applicable financial reporting framework and the related accounting policies; and

  c. The pro forma financial information be appropriately presented and include disclosures that enable intended users to understand the information conveyed.

## Understanding the Entity's Accounting and Financial Reporting Policies

5. Obtain an appropriate level of knowledge of the accounting and financial reporting practices of the entity (or of each significant constituent part of the combined entity in a business combination).

## Examination and Review Procedures

6. The following procedures should be applied to the assumptions and pro forma adjustments in an examination or review engagement:

  a. Obtain an understanding of the underlying transaction or event.

  b. In a business combination, obtain an understanding of the accounting and financial reporting practices of each significant constituent part of the combined entity that will enable the practitioner to perform the required procedures. The need to obtain this understanding is not diminished if another practitioner performed the audit or review on the most recent annual or interim historical financial information. In these circumstances, the practitioner should consider whether sufficient knowledge of the accounting and financial reporting practices

§ 310 • *Reporting on Pro Forma Financial Information*  10,125

      can be acquired to perform the procedures necessary to report on the pro forma financial information.

    c. Discuss with management their assumptions regarding the effects of the transaction or event.

    d. Evaluate whether pro forma adjustments are included for all significant effects directly attributable to the transaction or event.

    e. Obtain sufficient evidence in support of such adjustments.

    f. Evaluate whether the presentation of management's assumptions underlying the pro forma adjustments is sufficiently clear and comprehensive.

    g. Evaluate whether the pro forma adjustments are consistent with each other and with the data used to develop them.

    h. Evaluate whether pro forma adjustment computations are mathematically correct and whether the pro forma column reflects proper application of those adjustments to the historical financial statements.

    i. Read the pro forma financial information and evaluate whether the underlying transaction or event, pro forma adjustments, significant assumptions, and any significant uncertainties about these assumptions have been appropriately disclosed and whether the source of the historical financial information on which the pro forma financial information is based has been appropriately identified.

## *Written Representations in an Examination and Review Engagement*

7. In addition to the written representations from management required by AT-C 205 for an examination engagement or by AT-C 210 for a review engagement, request written representations from management that:

    a. It is responsible for the assumptions used in determining the pro forma adjustments;

    b. The assumptions are factually supportable;

    c. The assumptions provide a reasonable basis for presenting the significant effects directly attributable to the underlying transaction or event, the related pro forma adjustments give appropriate effect to those assumptions, and the pro forma column reflects the proper application of those adjustments to the historical financial statements;

    d. The pro forma adjustments are consistent with the entity's applicable financial reporting framework and its accounting policies under that framework; and

    e. The pro forma financial information is appropriately presented and discloses the significant effects directly attributable to the transaction or event.

8. The practitioner should request from management the written representations in AT-C 205 or AT-C 210 as applicable in addition to those above, even if the engaging party is not management. There is no alternative to obtaining written representations in an examination or review of pro forma financial information. If management refuses to provide written representations, there is a scope limitation on the engagement, which in an examination is sufficient to preclude an unmodified opinion and possibly to cause withdrawal from the engagement where possible under applicable law or regulation and in a review is sufficient to cause withdrawal from the engagement.

## Reporting

9. The practitioner's report on pro forma financial information may be combined with the report on historical financial information or it may appear separately. In a combined report, if the date procedures were completed for the examination or review of pro forma financial information is after the date the practitioner obtained the evidence necessary to issue a report on the audit or review of the historical financial information, the report should be dual-dated.

## Content of the Practitioner's Examination Report

10. The practitioner's examination report on pro forma financial information should include the following:

   a. A title that includes the word "independent."
   b. An appropriate addressee.
   c. A reference to the pro forma adjustments included in the pro forma financial information.
   d. A reference to management's description in the pro forma financial information of the transaction or event to which the pro forma adjustments give effect.
   e. An identification or description of the pro forma financial information being reported on, including the point or period of time to which the measurement or evaluation of the pro forma financial information relates.
   f. An identification of the criteria against which the pro forma financial information was measured or evaluated.
   g. A reference to the financial statements from which the historical financial information is derived, a statement that such financial statements were audited, if those statements were audited by another auditor, and a reference to any modification in the auditor's report on the historical financial statements.
   h. A statement that the pro forma adjustments are based on management's assumptions.
   i. A statement that identifies:
      i. Management and its responsibility for the pro forma financial information; and
      ii. The practitioner's responsibility to express an opinion on the pro forma financial information based on the practitioner's examination.
   j. Unless the practitioner is disclaiming an opinion, a statement that:
      i. The examination was conducted in accordance with attestation standards established by the AICPA;
      ii. Those standards require that the practitioner plan and perform the examination by performing procedures to obtain sufficient evidence to provide reasonable assurance about (1) whether, based on the criteria, management's assumptions provide a reasonable basis for presenting the significant effects directly attributable to the underlying transaction or event, and (2) whether the related pro forma adjustments give appropriate effect to those assumptions in all material respects, and the pro forma amounts reflect the proper application of those adjustments to the historical financial statements;

### § 310 • Reporting on Pro Forma Financial Information 10,127

      iii. The practitioner performed procedures to obtain evidence about management's assumptions, the related pro forma adjustments, and the pro forma amounts; and

      iv. The practitioner believes sufficient appropriate evidence was obtained to provide a reasonable basis for the practitioner's opinion.

  k. Unless the practitioner is disclaiming an opinion, a description of the objectives and limitations of pro forma financial information.

  l. The practitioner's opinion about whether, based on the criteria and in all material respects, management's assumptions provide a reasonable basis for presenting the significant effects directly attributable to the underlying transaction or event, the related pro forma adjustments give appropriate effect to those assumptions in all material respects, and the pro forma amounts reflect the proper application of those adjustments to the historical financial statements.

  m. When the circumstances identified in AT-C 205 are applicable, an alert in a separate paragraph restricting use of the report or describing the purpose of the report as applicable.

  n. The manual or printed signature of the practitioner's firm.

  o. The city and state where the practitioner practices.

  p. The date of the practitioner's report, which should be no earlier than the date on which the practitioner has obtained sufficient appropriate evidence on which to base his or her opinion, including evidence that:

      i. The attestation documentation has been reviewed,

      ii. The pro forma financial information has been prepared, and

      iii. Management has provided a written assertion.

## Content of the Practitioner's Review Report

11. The practitioner's review report on pro forma financial information should include the following:

  a. A title that includes the word "independent."

  b. An appropriate addressee.

  c. A reference to the pro forma adjustments included in the pro forma financial information.

  d. A reference to management's description in the pro forma financial information of the transaction or event to which the pro forma adjustments give effect.

  e. An identification or description of the pro forma financial information being reported on, including the point or period of time to which the measurement or evaluation of the pro forma financial information relates.

  f. An identification of the criteria against which the pro forma financial information was measured or evaluated.

  g. A reference to the financial statements from which the historical financial information is derived, and, as applicable, a statement that such financial statements were audited or reviewed. If the practitioner issued a review report on the historical financial statements, reference should be included in regard to a statement that a review report was issued on the historical financial statements (including a statement that those statements were reviewed by another accountant, if so) and a reference to any modification in the accountant's report on the historical financial statements.

h. A statement that the pro forma adjustments are based on management's assumptions.

i. A statement that identifies:
    i. Management and its responsibility for the pro forma financial information; and
    ii. The practitioner's responsibility to express a conclusion on the pro forma financial information based on the practitioner's review.

j. A statement that:
    i. The review was conducted in accordance with attestation standards established by the AICPA;
    ii. Those standards require that the practitioner plan and perform the review to obtain limited assurance about whether, based on the criteria, any material modifications should be made to management's assumptions in order for them to provide a reasonable basis for presenting the significant effects directly attributable to the underlying transaction or event, the related pro forma adjustments in order for them to give appropriate effect to those assumptions, or the pro forma amounts in order for them to reflect the proper application of those adjustments to the historical financial statements;
    iii. A review is substantially less in scope than an examination, the objective of which is to obtain reasonable assurance about whether, based on the criteria, management's assumptions provide a reasonable basis for presenting the significant effects directly attributable to the underlying transaction or event and the related pro forma adjustments give appropriate effect to those assumptions in all material respects and the pro forma amounts reflect the proper application of those adjustments to the historical financial statements in order to express an opinion. Accordingly, the practitioner does not express such an opinion; and
    iv. The practitioner believes the review provides a reasonable basis for the practitioner's conclusion.

k. A description of the objectives and limitations of pro forma financial information.

l. The practitioner's conclusion about whether, based on the review and the criteria, the practitioner is aware of any material modifications that should be made to management's assumptions in order for them to provide a reasonable basis for presenting the significant effects directly attributable to the underlying transaction or event, the related pro forma adjustments in order for them to give appropriate effect to those assumptions, and the pro forma amounts in order for them to reflect the proper application of those adjustments to the historical financial statements.

m. When the circumstances identified in AT-C 210 are applicable, an alert in a separate paragraph restricting use of the report or describing the purpose of the report as applicable.

n. The manual or printed signature of the practitioner's firm.

o. The city and state where the practitioner practices.

p. The date of the practitioner's report, which should be no earlier than the date on which the practitioner has obtained sufficient appropriate evidence on which to base his or her conclusion, including evidence that:

   i. The attestation documentation has been reviewed,

   ii. The pro forma financial information has been prepared, and

   iii. Management has provided a written assertion.

## Analysis and Application of Procedures

Pro forma financial information reflects the effects of applying significant assumptions, such as a proposed transaction, to an enterprise's historical financial statements or information. The more common uses of pro forma financial information include showing the effects of transactions such as a business combination, change in capitalization, change in form of business organization, proposed sale of securities and application of the proceeds, or the disposition of a significant segment of a business. When pro forma financial information is presented, the following should be observed:

- Pro forma financial information should be labeled to distinguish it from historical financial information.

- The transactions or events that are being integrated into the historical financial information and the assumed timing of those transactions or events should be clearly described.

- The historical financial information that is the basis for the pro forma financial information should be clearly identified along with description of the financial accounting framework used to prepare those financial statements.

- The assumptions used by management in constructing the pro forma financial information should be clearly identified.

- Any significant uncertainties related to management's assumptions should be clearly identified.

- A clear indication that the pro forma financial information should be read in conjunction with the related historical financial information.

- It must be clearly stated that the pro forma financial information is not necessarily indicative of what would have occurred had the transaction or event had taken place at an earlier date.

---

**PLANNING AID REMINDER:** Regulation S-X (17 CFR 210.11) provides further guidance on the presentation of pro forma financial information included in Securities and Exchange Commission filings.

*Preconditions for an Examination or Review Engagement*

Historical financial statements, historical interim financial information, and audit reports are readily available if they can be obtained by a third party without any further action by the entity; this would encompass information available on the entity's website, but does not include being available upon request.

> **PUBLIC COMPANY IMPLICATION:** For purposes of pro forma financial information included in in an SEC 8-K, including the historical information included in a prior SEC filing fills the requirement of including the most recent historical financial information.

> **PUBLIC COMPANY IMPLICATION:** For issuers, the PCAOB's AS 4105 (*Reviews of Interim Financial Information*) requires that, if any filing mentions that the interim financial information has been reviewed by an independent public accountant, that the review report be filed if a written report was prepared.

> **PLANNING AID REMINDER:** Some situations may involve entities whose historical financial statements have been audited at year-end while interim financial statements are reviewed. In that case, the practitioner may perform an examination or review of pro forma financial information at year-end; however, the practitioner may only perform a review of pro forma financial information at the interim date.

*Assessing the Suitability of the Applicable Criteria*

Pro forma adjustments are considered factually supportable if the preponderance of information supports each significant assumption underlying the adjustments. It is management's responsibility to factually support significant assumptions.

*Understanding the Entity's Accounting and Financial Reporting Policies*

In obtaining sufficient knowledge of the significant constituent parts of a combined entity in a business combination, the practitioner may wish to communicate with other practitioners who audited or reviewed the relevant historical financial information. Communication may be about topics such as the accounting principles and financial reporting practices used, transactions between the entities, material contingencies, and relevant industry, legal and regulatory, and other external factors for the entity.

*Examination and Review Procedures*

The practitioner must understand the nature of the transaction that is the basis for converting the historical financial statements into pro forma financial information. Obtaining this understanding could include the reading of contracts and agreements between the parties involved in the transaction and by making inquiries of appropriate management personnel.

Professional judgment must be used to determine what constitutes sufficient evidential matter for each pro forma adjustment. For example, the practitioner may obtain appraisal reports to support the assignment of fair values in a purchase transaction or review debt agreements.

---

**ENGAGEMENT STRATEGY:** Generally, a greater level of evidential matter is required in an examination than in a review engagement. Practitioners performing an examination should consider the examination procedures outlined in AT-C 205, while practitioners performing a review should consider the review procedures outlined in AT-C 210.

---

## Reporting

An illustrative example of a statement dual-dating the practitioner's combined report follows:

> March 1, 20X7, except for the paragraphs regarding pro forma financial information for which the date is March 27, 20X7.

## Content of the Practitioner's Examination and Review Reports

The requirements in this section describing the content of a practitioner's examination and review report constitute all required elements for a report on the examination or review of pro forma financial information. AT-C 205 of the attestation standards contains the application guidance relating to these required elements for an examination. AT-C 210 of the attestation standards contains the application guidance relating to these required elements for a review.

When the practitioner considers whether management's assumptions provide a reasonable basis for presenting the significant effects directly attributable to the transaction or event, uncertainty about the consummation of a transaction or event generally does not require modification of the practitioner's report.

# Practitioner's Aids

Exhibit AT-C 310-1 is an illustrative practitioner's examination report on pro forma financial information.

EXHIBIT AT-C 310-1—EXAMINATION REPORT ON PRO FORMA FINANCIAL INFORMATION

---

### Independent Accountant's Report

[*Appropriate Addressee*]

We have examined the pro forma adjustments giving effect to the transaction (or event) described in Note 1 and the application of those adjustments to the historical amounts in the accompanying pro forma condensed balance sheet of Delta Company as of December 31, 20XX, and the related pro forma condensed statement of income for the year then ended (pro forma financial information), based on the criteria in Note 1. The historical condensed financial statements are derived from the historical financial statements of Delta Company, which were audited by us, and of Epsilon Company, which were audited by other accountants, appearing elsewhere herein [*or and are readily available*]. The pro forma adjustments are based on management's assumptions described in Note 1. Delta Company's management is responsible for the pro forma financial information. Our responsibility is to express an opinion on the pro forma financial information based on our examination.

Our examination was conducted in accordance with attestation standards established by the American Institute of Certified Public Accountants. Those standards require that we plan and perform the examination to obtain reasonable assurance about whether, based on the criteria in Note 1, management's assumptions provide a reasonable basis for presenting the significant effects directly attributable to the underlying transaction (or event), and, in all material respects, the related pro forma adjustments give appropriate effect to those assumptions and the pro forma amounts reflect the proper application of those adjustments to the historical financial statements. An examination involves performing procedures to obtain evidence about management's assumptions, the related pro forma adjustments, and the pro forma amounts in the pro forma condensed balance sheet of Delta Company as of December 31, 20XX, and the related pro forma condensed statement of income for the year then ended. The nature, timing, and extent of the procedures selected depend on our judgment, including an assessment of the risks of material misstatement of the pro forma financial information, whether due to fraud or error. We believe that the evidence we obtained is sufficient and appropriate to provide a reasonable basis for our opinion.

The objective of this pro forma financial information is to show what the significant effects on the historical financial information might have been had the underlying transaction (or event) occurred at an earlier date. However, the pro forma condensed financial statements are not necessarily indicative of the results of operations or related effects on financial position that would have been attained had the above-mentioned transaction (or event) actually occurred at such earlier date.

In our opinion, based on the criteria in Note 1, management's assumptions provide a reasonable basis for presenting the significant effects directly attributable to the above-mentioned transaction (or event) described in Note 1, and, in all material respects, the related pro forma adjustments give appropriate effect to those assumptions and the pro forma amounts reflect the proper application of those adjustments to the historical financial statement amounts in the pro forma condensed balance sheet of Delta Company as of December 31, 20XX, and the related pro forma condensed statement of income for the year then ended.

[*Practitioner's signature*]
[*Practitioner's city and state*]
[*Date of practitioner's report*]

---

Exhibit AT-C 310-2 is an illustrative practitioner's review report on pro forma financial information.

## EXHIBIT AT-C 310-2—REVIEW REPORT ON PRO FORMA FINANCIAL INFORMATION

**Independent Accountant's Report**

[*Appropriate Addressee*]

We have reviewed the pro forma adjustments giving effect to the transaction (or event) described in Note 1 and the application of those adjustments to the historical amounts in the accompanying pro forma condensed balance sheet of Delta Company as of June 30, 20XX, and the related pro forma condensed statement of income for the three months then ended (pro forma financial information), based on the criteria in Note 1. These historical condensed financial statements are derived from the historical unaudited financial statements of Delta Company, which were reviewed by us, and of Epsilon Company, which were reviewed by other accountants, appearing elsewhere herein [*or and are readily available*]. The pro forma adjustments are based on management's assumptions as described in Note 1. Delta Company's management is responsible for the pro forma financial information. Our responsibility is to express a conclusion based on our review.

Our review was conducted in accordance with attestation standards established by the American Institute of Certified Public Accountants. Those standards require that we plan and perform our review to obtain limited assurance about whether, based on the criteria in Note 1, any material modifications should be made to management's assumptions in order for them to provide a reasonable basis for presenting the significant effects directly attributable to the underlying transaction (or event), the related pro forma adjustments in order for them to give appropriate effect to those assumptions, or the pro forma amounts in order for them to reflect the proper application of those adjustments to the historical financial statements. A review is substantially less in scope than an examination, the objective of which is to obtain reasonable assurance about whether based on the criteria, management's assumptions provide a reasonable basis for presenting the significant effects directly attributable to the underlying transaction (or event), and, in all material respects, the related pro forma adjustments give appropriate effect to those assumptions and the pro forma amounts reflect the proper application of those adjustments to the historical financial statements, in order to express an opinion. Accordingly, we do not express such an opinion. We believe that our review provides a reasonable basis for our conclusion.

The objective of this pro forma financial information is to show what the significant effects on the historical financial information might have been had the underlying transaction (or event) occurred at an earlier date. However, the pro forma condensed financial statements are not necessarily indicative of the results of operations or related effects on financial position that would have been attained had the above-mentioned transaction (or event) actually occurred at such earlier date.

Based on our review, we are not aware of any material modifications that should be made to management's assumptions in order for them to provide a reasonable basis for presenting the significant effects directly attributable to the above-mentioned transaction (or event) described in Note 1, the related pro forma adjustments in order for them to give appropriate effect to those assumptions, or the pro forma amounts in order for them to reflect the proper application of those adjustments to the historical financial statement amounts in the pro forma condensed balance sheet of Delta Company as of June 30, 20XX, and the related pro forma condensed statement of income for the three months then ended, based on the criteria in Note 1.

[*Practitioner's signature*]

[*Practitioner's city and state*]

[*Date of practitioner's report*]

# SECTION 315

# COMPLIANCE ATTESTATION

## Authoritative Pronouncements

SSAE-18—Attestation Standards: Clarification and Recodification

## Overview

This section contains performance and reporting requirements and application guidance for an engagement in which the practitioner either (1) performs an examination or agreed-upon procedures on an entity's compliance with financial or nonfinancial requirements of specified laws, regulations, rules, contracts, or grants (referred to as compliance with specified requirements) or an assertion about compliance with specified requirements, or (2) performs agreed-upon procedures on the effectiveness of an entity's internal control over compliance with specified requirements.

The requirements and guidance in AT-C 105 (*Concepts Common to All Attestation Engagements*) and either AT-C 205 (*Assertion-Based Examination Engagements*) or AT-C 215 (*Agreed-Upon Procedures Engagements*) of the attestation standards that pertain to compliance are also applicable and should be followed.

The objectives of an examination of an entity's compliance with specified requirements are to:

- Obtain reasonable assurance about whether, in all material respects, an entity complied with the specified requirements; and
- Express an opinion in a written report about whether an entity complied with the specified requirements in all material respects or express an opinion about management's assertion (management is the responsible party for the purposes of this section) about its compliance with the specified requirements is fairly stated in all material respects.

The objectives of an agreed-upon procedures engagement about an entity's compliance or about the entity's internal control over compliance with specified requirements are to:

- Apply agreed-upon procedures established by specified parties who are responsible for the sufficiency of the procedures for their purposes to an entity's compliance or internal control over compliance with specified requirements; and
- Issue a practitioner's written report describing the procedures applied and the practitioner's findings.

**OBSERVATION:** The practitioner's report issued on compliance or internal control over compliance with specified requirements does not serve as a legal determination of the entity's compliance but may be used by legal counsel or others to make such a determination.

**PUBLIC COMPANY IMPLICATION:** The PCAOB has issued two attestation standards, both pertaining to brokers and dealers (these are the first two attestation standards issued by the PCAOB). The first (examination) standard (*Examination Engagements Regarding Compliance Reports of Brokers and Dealers*) addresses an auditor's examination of compliance reports. The second (review) standard (*Review Engagements Regarding Exemption Reports of Brokers and Dealers*) addresses an auditor's review of exemption reports. These attestation standards are designed to help protect customer funds held by broker-dealers by improving the quality of compliance information used by the Securities and Exchange Commission (SEC) in overseeing broker-dealers.

The SEC has recently instituted new requirements (under Exchange Act Rule 17a-5) requiring broker-dealers to prepare compliance or exemption reports, and requiring PCAOB-registered auditors to examine or review such reports. Broker-dealers that hold customer securities or funds must maintain a certain capital level, and must maintain a certain reserve of funds or qualified securities. These requirements around capital and liquidity are designed to enhance market confidence and to safeguard investors, both of which are especially important when adverse market events occur. Broker-dealers holding customer funds must prepare and file a compliance report. Broker-dealers not holding customer funds must file an exemption report to claim an exemption from the compliance-reporting requirements. In addition, broker-dealers must file audited financial statements and supporting schedules with the SEC.

The examination standard requires the auditor to obtain sufficient appropriate evidence to provide reasonable assurance that the broker-dealer (1) maintained effective internal control over compliance during the most recent fiscal year, (2) had effective internal control over compliance at year-end, (3) complied with the net capital rule and reserve requirement rule at year-end, and (4) based its statement as to compliance on its books and records. The examination standard provides guidance on (1) planning the engagement; (2) testing controls, both design and operating effectiveness; (3) performing compliance tests; (4) evaluating results; and (5) subsequent events, representation letters, and reporting.

The review standard requires the auditor to obtain moderate assurance to support the broker-dealer's assertion that it (1) identified and met the SEC exemption provisions enabling the broker-dealer to not have to file a compliance report, and, if applicable, (2) the broker-dealer identified and described any exception to the applicable exemption requirements. The review standard requires the auditor to (1) read the exemption report to understand the broker-dealer's claimed basis for the exemption, (2) perform inquires and other procedures, (3) evaluate whether evidence suggests that modifications are needed to the broker-dealer's assertions, and (4) obtain representation letters and comply with certain reporting obligations.

These attestation standards became effective for examination or review engagements for fiscal years ending on or after June 1, 2014.

Although the standards discussed in this section are concerned with engagements related to compliance with specified requirements, the guidance does not apply to the following engagements:

- Reviews of compliance with specified requirements or an entity's internal control over compliance or an assertion because reviews of this type are prohibited by AT-C 210 (*Review Engagements*).
- Examination engagements to report on an entity's internal control over compliance with specified requirements. (This type of engagement is governed by AT-C 105 and AT-C 205 and additional guidance can be found in AU-C 940 (*An Audit of Internal Control over Financial Reporting That Is Integrated with an Audit of Financial Statements*)).
- Certain audit reports on specified compliance requirements based solely on the audit of financial statements as addressed in AU-C 806 (*Reporting on Compliance with Aspects of Contractual Agreements or Regulatory Requirements in Connection with Audited Financial Statements*).
- Reports on engagements that are subject to the standards established by AU-C 935 (*Compliance Audits*).

## Definitions

| | |
|---|---|
| Compliance with specified requirements | An entity's compliance with specified laws, regulations, rules, contracts, or grants. |
| Internal control over compliance | An entity's internal control over compliance with specified requirements. This is different from, but may include part of, internal control over financial reporting. |
| Material noncompliance | Failure to follow compliance requirements or violation or prohibitions in the specified requirements resulting in quantitatively or qualitatively material noncompliance, either individually or when aggregated with other noncompliance. Defined for the purpose of the engagement by government or other requirements. |

## Requirements

The practitioner is presumptively required to perform the following procedures when conducting a compliance attestation engagement:

## Examination Engagements

### Preconditions for Examination Engagements

1. To be in a position to accept an engagement to examine compliance with specified requirements, in addition to the preconditions described in AT-C 105 and AT-C 205, determine that:

    a. Responsibility for the entity's compliance with specified requirements and the entity's internal control over compliance is acknowledged and accepted by management; and

    b. Management evaluates the entity's compliance with specified requirements.

2. Request a written assertion from management, whether or not the responsible party (management) is the engaging party. If management refuses to

provide a written assertion, withdraw from the engagement where possible under applicable laws and regulations.

## *Reasonable Assurance*

3. Seek to obtain reasonable assurance that the entity complied with the specified requirements in all material respects. Design the examination to detect both intentional and unintentional material noncompliance.

## *Materiality*

4. Consider materiality when establishing the overall engagement strategy.

## *Examination Procedures*

5. Obtain an understanding of the specified requirements by:

   a. Considering the laws, regulations, rules, contracts, and grants pertaining to the specified requirements, including published requirements;

   b. Considering knowledge of the specified requirements obtained from prior engagements and regulatory reports; and

   c. Discussing with appropriate individuals within the entity, for example, the chief financial officer, internal auditors, legal counsel, compliance officer, or grant or contract administrators.

6. If the entity being examined has operations in several components (e.g., locations, branches, subsidiaries, or programs), determine the nature, timing, and extent of testing to be performed at individual components by evaluating factors such as:

   a. The degree to which the specified requirements apply at the component level;

   b. Judgments about materiality;

   c. The degree of records centralization;

   d. The effectiveness of the control environment and management's direct control over the authority delegated and its ability to effectively supervise activities at various locations;

   e. The nature and extent of operations conducted at the various components; and

   f. The similarity of operations over compliance for different components.

7. Obtain a sufficient understanding of relevant portions of internal control over compliance to plan the engagement and assess control risk for compliance with specified requirements. Use this knowledge to identify potential types of noncompliance, consider factors that affect the risk of material noncompliance, and design appropriate tests of compliance when planning the examination.

8. If the engagement involves compliance with regulatory requirements, review reports of relevant examinations and related communications between regulatory agencies and the entity and make appropriate inquiries of the regulatory agencies, including inquiries about examinations in progress.

## Written Representations in an Examination Engagement

9. In addition to the written representations from management required by AT-C 205 for an examination engagement, request written representations from management that:
   a. Acknowledge management's responsibility for establishing and maintaining effective internal control over compliance,
   b. State that management has performed an evaluation of the entity's compliance with specified requirements, and
   c. State management's interpretation of any compliance requirements that have varying interpretations.

10. The practitioner should request from management the written representations in AT-C 205 in addition to those above, even if the engaging party is not management. There is no alternative to obtaining written representations in an engagement to examine compliance. If management refuses to provide written representations, there is a scope limitation on the engagement, which in an examination is sufficient to preclude an unmodified opinion and possibly to cause withdrawal from the engagement where possible under applicable law or regulation.

## Reporting on an Examination

11. Evaluate whether an entity has complied with the specified requirements in all material respects or evaluate management's assertion about its compliance with the specified requirements is fairly stated in all material respects. To do this, evaluate the nature and frequency of identified noncompliance and whether that noncompliance is material given the nature of the compliance requirements.

## Content of the Practitioner's Examination Report

12. The practitioner's examination report on compliance should include the following:
   a. A title that includes the word "independent."
   b. An appropriate addressee.
   c. Identification of the compliance matters being reported on or the assertion about such matters, including the point or period of time to which the measurement or evaluation of compliance relates.
   d. Identification of the specified requirements against which compliance was measured or evaluated.
   e. A statement that identifies:
      i. Management and its responsibility for complying with the specified requirements or for its assertion as applicable; and
      ii. The practitioner's responsibility to express an opinion on the entity's compliance with the specified requirements or on management's assertion about the entity's compliance with the specified requirements based on the practitioner's examination.
   f. Unless the practitioner is disclaiming an opinion, a statement that:
      i. The examination was conducted in accordance with attestation standards established by the AICPA;
      ii. Those standards require that the practitioner plan and perform the examination to obtain reasonable assurance

about whether the entity complied with the specified requirements in all material respects or management's assertion about compliance is fairly stated in all material respects; and

    iii. The practitioner believes sufficient appropriate evidence was obtained to provide a reasonable basis for the practitioner's opinion.

g. Unless the practitioner is disclaiming an opinion, a description of the nature of an examination engagement.

h. A statement describing any significant inherent limitations associated with the measurement or evaluation of the entity's compliance with specified requirements or its assertion thereon.

i. A statement that the examination does not provide a legal determination on the entity's compliance with specified requirements.

j. The practitioner's opinion about whether, in all material respects, (1) the entity complied with the specified requirements, or (2) management's assertion about the entity's compliance with specified requirements is fairly stated.

k. When the circumstances identified in AT-C 205 are applicable, a separate paragraph should be included that contains an alert that restricts use of the report or describes the purpose of the report as applicable.

l. The manual or printed signature of the practitioner's firm.

m. The city and state where the practitioner practices.

n. The date of the practitioner's report, which should be no earlier than the date on which the practitioner has obtained sufficient appropriate evidence on which to base his or her opinion, including evidence that:

    i. The attestation documentation has been reviewed, and

    ii. Management has provided a written assertion.

13. Criteria need to be identified; if they are not contained in the compliance requirements, the practitioner's report should identify the criteria.

## *Modified Opinions*

14. If the practitioner determines there is material noncompliance, the practitioner's report should describe the material noncompliance and the opinion should be modified using the guidance in AT-C 205.

# Agreed-Upon Procedures Engagements

## *Preconditions for an AUP Engagement*

15. In addition to applying the preconditions for accepting or continuing an AUP engagement in AT-C 105 and AT-C 215, in order to accept an AUP engagement on compliance or internal control over compliance with specified requirements, the practitioner should determine that management accepts responsibility for and evaluates the entity's compliance with specified requirements and the entity's internal control over compliance.

16. Obtain an understanding of the specified requirements by:

a. Considering the laws, regulations, rules, contracts, and grants pertaining to the specified requirements, including published requirements;

b. Considering knowledge of the specified requirements obtained from prior engagements and regulatory reports; and

c. Discussing with appropriate individuals within the entity, for example, the chief financial officer, internal auditors, legal counsel, compliance officer, or grant or contract administrators.

## Written Representations in an AUP Engagement

17. In addition to the written representations from management required by AT-C 215 for an AUP engagement, request written representations from management that:

   a. Acknowledge management's responsibility for establishing and maintaining effective internal control over compliance;

   b. State that management has performed an evaluation of the entity's compliance with specified requirements or the entity's controls for establishing and maintaining internal control over compliance and detecting noncompliance with requirements as applicable;

   c. State management's interpretation of any compliance requirements that have varying interpretations; and

   d. State that management has disclosed any known noncompliance occurring subsequent to the period covered by the practitioner's report.

## Content of Practitioner's AUP Report

18. The practitioner's AUP report on compliance should include:

   a. A title that includes the word "independent."
   b. An appropriate addressee.
   c. An indication that the subject matter of the engagement is the entity's compliance at a point or period of time.
   d. An identification of the specified requirements against which the entity's compliance was measured or evaluated.
   e. An indication that management is responsible for the entity's compliance with the specified requirements.
   f. An identification of the specified parties.
   g. A statement that:
      i. The sufficiency of the procedures is solely the responsibility of the specified parties; and
      ii. The practitioner makes no representation regarding the sufficiency of the procedures for the purpose for which the practitioner's report has been requested or for any other purpose.
   h. A list of procedures performed or reference to those procedures and related findings.
   i. A description of any agreed-upon materiality limits.
   j. A statement that:
      i. The AUP engagement was conducted in accordance with attestation standards established by the American Institute of Certified Public Accountants;
      ii. The practitioner was not engaged to and did not conduct an examination or review of the entity's compliance or internal control over compliance, the objective of which

would be the expression of an opinion or conclusion, respectively, on compliance or internal control over compliance;

iii. The practitioner does not express such an opinion or conclusion; and

iv. Had other procedures been performed by the practitioner, other matters might have come to his or her attention that would have been reported.

k. A separate paragraph containing an alert restricting use of the practitioner's report that:

i. States the practitioner's report is intended solely for the information and use of the specified parties,

ii. Identifies the specified parties for whom use is intended, and

iii. States that the practitioner's report is not intended to be and should not be used by anyone other than the specified parties.

l. If the engagement is also performed in accordance with *Government Auditing Standards,* the alert restricting use of the practitioner's report should instead include a description of the purpose of the practitioner's report and a statement that the report is not suitable for any other purpose.

m. Any reservations or restrictions concerning procedures or findings.

n. A description of the nature of any assistance provided by a practitioner's external specialist.

o. The manual or printed signature of the practitioner's firm.

p. The city and state where the practitioner practices.

q. The date of the practitioner's report, which should be no earlier than the date on which the practitioner completed the procedures and determined the findings, including that:

i. The attestation documentation has been reviewed, and

ii. Management has provided a written assertion, unless management is unwilling to provide an assertion.

## Analysis and Application of Procedures

Compliance attestation engagements can be for compliance with specified requirements or the effectiveness of an entity's internal control over compliance with specified requirements. Internal control over compliance only involves the portion of management's internal control relevant to an entity's compliance with specified requirements. This can vary widely and may or may not include accounting procedures depending on whether the compliance with financial or nonfinancial requirements is being evaluated.

**PLANNING AID REMINDER:** The consideration of internal control in a compliance attestation engagement is very similar to the consideration of the internal control in an audit of financial statements. In an audit of financial statements, the auditor (1) obtains an understanding of the entity and its environment, including internal control, (2) determines the planned assessed level of the risk of material misstatement, (3) generally performs tests of controls, and (4) designs substantive procedures based on the assessed level of the risk of material misstatement. In a compliance attestation engagement, the practitioner (1) obtains an understanding of internal control, (2) determines the planned assessed level of control risk, (3) generally performs tests of controls, and (4) designs compliance tests based on the assessed level of control risk. Thus, the only difference is that in a compliance attestation engagement the auditor performs tests of compliance rather than substantive procedures as the final step.

## Examination Engagements

### Preconditions for Examination Engagements

Management's responsibility for the entity's compliance with specified requirements includes identifying the specified requirements; designing, implementing, and maintaining internal control to provide reasonable assurance that the entity complies with those requirements; evaluating and monitoring the entity's compliance; and specifying reports that satisfy legal, regulatory, or contractual requirements.

In evaluating the entity's compliance with specified requirements, the form and extent of management's documentation may vary and may include accounting or statistical data, entity policy manuals, accounting manuals, narrative memoranda, procedural write-ups, flowcharts, completed questionnaires, or internal auditors' reports.

Management's written assertion about compliance with specified requirements may take a number of different forms, such as "management's assertion that ABC Company complied with [*specify compliance requirement*] as of [*date*]." However, an assertion is inappropriate if it is so subjective that people competent in using similar criteria would not ordinarily be able to arrive at similar conclusions.

### Materiality

From a broad perspective, the concept of materiality in a compliance attestation engagement is similar to its role in an audit of financial statements. Immaterial deviations (from U.S. generally accepted accounting principles (U.S. GAAP) or from established or agreed-upon criteria) will generally exist in both types of engagements, but it is unreasonable to direct the focus of the engagements to immaterial items.

Although the concept of materiality applies to both types of engagements, it is probably more difficult to apply the concept in a compliance attestation engagement. First, because the engagement can be directed to a variety of specified requirements, it is very difficult to generalize about the examination approach. Second, the specified requirements may or may not be quantifiable in monetary terms. Third, there has been little research, if any, into what the focal point should be for determining materiality in a compliance attestation engagement. SSAE standards provide little guidance for determining materiality, except to state that the following may affect the determination of materiality:

- The nature of the compliance requirements, which may or may not be quantifiable in monetary terms.
- The nature and frequency of noncompliance identified with appropriate consideration of sampling risk.
- Qualitative considerations, including the needs and expectations of the report's users.

**PLANNING AID REMINDER:** Some compliance attestation engagements require the practitioner to prepare a supplemental report identifying all or certain deviations discovered. Any threshold guidance established for reporting items in the supplemental report should not have an effect on the auditor's determination of a materiality threshold for the primary examination report.

## Examination Procedures

When the practitioner is obtaining an understanding of the design of specific controls over compliance to plan the engagement and assess control risk, he or she may make inquiries of appropriate management and other personal, inspect entity documents, and observe the entity's activities and operations. The procedures used by the practitioner vary by engagement and their nature and extent is affected by:

- The specified requirements' nature, newness, and complexity;
- The practitioner's knowledge of internal control over compliance obtained in prior engagements;
- An understanding of the entity's industry; and
- Judgments about materiality.

**PLANNING AID REMINDER:** To minimize the likelihood of confusion near the completion of the engagement, practitioners may want to discuss with management during the early part of the engagement the fact that management will need to provide a written representation letter at the end of the engagement.

## Content of the Practitioner's Examination Report

The requirements in this section describing the content of a practitioner's examination report constitute all required elements for a report on an examination of compliance with specified requirements. AT-C 205 of the attestation standards contains the application guidance relating to these required elements for an examination.

Criteria should be identified in the compliance requirements or in the practitioner's report. The criteria are generally included in the specified requirements and may be identified as follows: "We have examined management of ABC Company's compliance with [*identify the specified requirements* . . . ]." In the case of a subjectively worded compliance requirement, the criteria used to define the requirement should be included in the practitioner's report.

When the practitioner is required to make significant interpretations of the laws, regulations, rules, contracts, or grants establishing requirements in evaluating compliance with those requirements, he or she may include a paragraph in the practitioner's report describing the interpretations and identifying the source of the interpretations made by the entity's management, such as:

> We have been informed that, under [*name of entity*]'s interpretation of [*identify the compliance requirement*], [*explain the source and nature of the relevant interpretation*].

## *Modified Opinions*

If a qualified opinion is being expressed, the following paragraphs illustrate a paragraph describing the matter causing the qualified opinion and the modified opinion paragraph:

> Our examination disclosed the following material noncompliance with [*type of compliance requirement*] applicable to [*name of entity*] during the [*period*] ended [*date*]. [*Describe noncompliance.*]
>
> In our opinion, except for the material noncompliance described in the preceding paragraph, [*name of entity*] complied, in all material respects, with the aforementioned requirements for the [*period*] ended [*date*].

If an adverse opinion is being expressed, the following paragraphs illustrate a paragraph describing the matter causing the adverse opinion and the modified opinion paragraph:

> Our examination disclosed the following material noncompliance with [*type of compliance requirement*] applicable to [*name of entity*] during the [*period*] ended [*date*]. [*Describe noncompliance.*]
>
> In our opinion, because of the effect of the noncompliance described in the preceding paragraph, [*name of entity*] has not complied with the aforementioned requirements for the [*period*] ended [*date*].

If the practitioner's compliance report includes a qualified or adverse opinion and the practitioner also issued an audit report on the entity's financial statements, the practitioner's compliance report may indicate that the noncompliance was considered during the audit, whether or not the two practitioner's reports are included in the same document. An example of a sentence that could be added to the opinion paragraph of the practitioner's compliance examination report is:

> We considered the effect of these conditions on our audit of the 20XX financial statements. This report on ABC Company's compliance with [*identify the specified requirements*] does not affect our audit report dated [*date of report*] on those financial statements.

---

**PLANNING AID REMINDER:** During the engagement, the practitioner may discover noncompliance that is considered "significant" but not material. Under this circumstance, guidance established by AU-C 265 (*Communication of Internal Control Related Matters Identified in an Audit*) should be considered.

## Agreed-Upon Procedures Engagements

*Preconditions for an AUP Engagement*

Management's responsibility for the entity's compliance with specified requirements includes identifying the specified requirements; establishing and maintaining internal control to provide reasonable assurance that the entity complies with those requirements; evaluating and monitoring the entity's compliance; and specifying reports that satisfy legal, regulatory, or contractual requirements.

In evaluating the entity's compliance with specified requirements, the form and extent of management's documentation may vary and may include accounting or statistical data, entity policy manuals, accounting manuals, narrative memoranda, procedural write-ups, flowcharts, completed questionnaires, or internal auditors' reports.

*Content of Practitioner's AUP Report*

The requirements in this section describing the content of a practitioner's AUP report constitute all required elements for a report on the application of agreed-upon procedures related to an entity's compliance with specified requirements. AT-C 215 of the attestation standards contains the application guidance relating to these required elements for an AUP engagement.

An AUP engagement may relate to compliance with specified requirements in addition to the entity's internal control over compliance. One practitioner's report may be issued to address both and the first sentence of the introductory paragraph could state:

> We have performed the procedures enumerated below, related to [*name of entity*]'s compliance with [*identify the specified requirements*] during the [*period*] ended [*date*] and [*name of entity*]'s internal control over compliance with the aforementioned compliance requirements as of [*date*].

When the practitioner is required to make significant interpretations of the laws, regulations, rules, contracts, or grants establishing requirements in evaluating compliance with those requirements, he or she may include a paragraph in the practitioner's report describing the interpretations and identifying the source of the interpretations made by the entity's management, such as:

> We have been informed that, under [*name of entity*]'s interpretation of [*identify the compliance requirement*], [*explain the source and nature of the relevant interpretation*].

## Practitioner's Aids

Exhibit AT-C 315-1 is an illustrative practitioner's examination report on an entity's compliance with specified requirements.

*EXHIBIT AT-C 315-1—EXAMINATION ON COMPLIANCE WITH SPECIFIED REQUIREMENTS*

**Independent Accountant's Report**

[*Appropriate addressee*]

We have examined ABC Company's compliance with [*identify the specified requirements, for example, the requirements listed in Attachment 1*] during the period January 1, 20X7 to December 31, 20X7. Management of ABC Company is responsible for ABC Company's compliance with those specified requirements. Our responsibility is to express an opinion on ABC Company's compliance with the specified requirements based on our examination.

Our examination was conducted in accordance with attestation standards established by the American Institute of Certified Public Accountants. Those standards require that we plan and perform the examination to obtain reasonable assurance about whether ABC Company complied, in all material respects, with the specified requirements referenced above. An examination involves performing procedures to obtain evidence about whether ABC Company complied with the specified requirements. The nature, timing and extent of the procedures selected depend on our judgment, including an assessment of the risks of material noncompliance, whether due to fraud or error. We believe that the evidence we obtained is sufficient and appropriate to provide a reasonable basis for our opinion.

Our examination does not provide a legal determination of ABC Company's compliance with specified requirements.

In our opinion, ABC Company complied, in all material respects, with [*identify the specified requirements, for example, the requirements listed in Attachment 1*] during the period January 1, 20X7 to December 31, 20X7.

[*Practitioner's signature*]

[*Practitioner's city and state*]

[*Date of practitioner's report*]

Exhibit AT-C 315-2 is an illustrative practitioner's examination report on management's assertion about compliance with specified requirements.

*EXHIBIT AT-C 315-2—EXAMINATION ON MANAGEMENT'S ASSERTION CONCERNING COMPLIANCE WITH SPECIFIED REQUIREMENTS*

**Independent Accountant's Report**

[*Appropriate addressee*]

We have examined ABC Company's assertion that ABC Company complied with [*identify the specified requirements, for example, the requirements listed in*

Attachment 1] during the period January 1, 20X7 to December 31, 20X7. ABC Company's management is responsible for its assertion. Our responsibility is to express an opinion on management's assertion about ABC Company's compliance with the specified requirements based on our examination.

Our examination was conducted in accordance with attestation standards established by the American Institute of Certified Public Accountants. Those standards require that we plan and perform the examination to obtain reasonable assurance about whether management's assertion about compliance is fairly stated, in all material respects. An examination involves performing procedures to obtain evidence about whether management's assertion is fairly stated, in all material respects. The nature, timing, and extent of the procedures selected depend on our judgment, including an assessment of the risks of material misstatement of management's assertion, whether due to fraud or error. We believe that the evidence we obtained is sufficient and appropriate to provide a reasonable basis for our opinion.

Our examination does not provide a legal determination of ABC Company's compliance with specified requirements.

In our opinion, management's assertion that ABC Company complied [identify the specified requirements, for example, the requirements listed in Attachment 1] is fairly stated, in all material respects.

[Practitioner's signature]

[Practitioner's city and state]

[Date of practitioner's report]

---

Exhibit AT-C 315-3 is an illustrative practitioner's AUP report on an entity's compliance with specified requirements.

## EXHIBIT AT-C 315-3—AUP REPORT ON COMPLIANCE WITH SPECIFIED REQUIREMENTS

---

### Independent Accountant's Report on Applying Agreed-Upon Procedures

[Appropriate addressee]

We have performed the procedures enumerated below, which were agreed to by the management of ABC Company, related to ABC Company's compliance with [identify the specified requirements, for example, the requirements listed in Attachment 1] during the period January 1, 20X7 to December 31, 20X7. ABC Company's management is responsible for its compliance with those requirements. The sufficiency of these procedures is solely the responsibility of those parties specified in this report. Consequently, we make no representations regarding the sufficiency of the procedures enumerated below either for the purpose for which this report has been requested or for any other purpose.

[Include paragraphs to enumerate procedures and findings]

This agreed-upon procedures engagement was conducted in accordance with attestation standards established by the American Institute of Certified Public Accountants. We were not engaged to and did not conduct an examination or review, the objective of which would be the expression of an opinion or conclusion, respectively, on compliance with specified requirements. Accordingly, we do not express such an opinion or conclusion. Had we performed additional procedures, other matters might have come to our attention that would have been reported to you.

This report is intended solely for the information and use of the management of ABC Company, and is not intended to be and should not be used by anyone other than these specified parties.

[Practitioner's signature]

[Practitioner's city and state]

[Date of practitioner's report]

---

Exhibit AT-C 315-4 is an illustrative practitioner's AUP report related to an entity's internal control over compliance with specified requirements.

## EXHIBIT AT-C 315-4—AUP REPORT ON INTERNAL CONTROL OVER COMPLIANCE WITH SPECIFIED REQUIREMENTS

---

**Independent Accountant's Report on Applying Agreed-Upon Procedures**

[Appropriate addressee]

We have performed the procedures enumerated below, which were agreed to by the management of ABC Company, related to ABC Company's internal control over compliance with [identify the specified requirements, for example, the requirements listed in Attachment 1] as of December 31, 20X7. ABC Company's management is responsible for its internal control over compliance with those requirements. The sufficiency of these procedures is solely the responsibility of those parties specified in this report. Consequently, we make no representations regarding the sufficiency of the procedures enumerated below either for the purpose for which this report has been requested or for any other purpose.

[Include paragraphs to enumerate procedures and findings]

This agreed-upon procedures engagement was conducted in accordance with attestation standards established by the American Institute of Certified Public Accountants. We were not engaged to and did not conduct an examination or review, the objective of which would be the expression of an opinion or conclusion, respectively, on compliance with specified requirements. Accordingly, we do not express such an opinion or conclusion. Had we performed additional procedures, other matters might have come to our attention that would have been reported to you.

This report is intended solely for the information and use of the management of ABC Company, and is not intended to be and should not be used by anyone other than these specified parties.

[Practitioner's signature]

[Practitioner's city and state]

[Date of practitioner's report]

# SECTION 320

## REPORTING ON AN EXAMINATION OF CONTROLS AT A SERVICE ORGANIZATION RELEVANT TO USER ENTITIES' INTERNAL CONTROL OVER FINANCIAL REPORTING

### Authoritative Pronouncements

SSAE-18—Attestation Standards: Clarification and Recodification

### Overview

AT-C 320 addresses examination engagements performed by a service auditor to report on controls at service organizations that provide services to user entities when those controls are likely to be relevant to the user entities' internal control over financial reporting (ICFR). Relevant controls may pertain to assertions about presentation and disclosure related to account balances, classes of transactions or disclosures, or to evidence the user auditor evaluates or uses in applying audit procedures.

> **PLANNING AID REMINDER:** The guidance in this AT-C section is applicable to service auditors and it is designed as a complement to the guidance for user auditors that is located in the Statements on Auditing Standards (SASs) contained in AU-C 402 (*Audit Considerations Relating to an Entity Using a Service Organization*). Thus, the service auditor reports prepared under the guidance in this chapter may provide appropriate evidence for user auditors as described in AU-C 402.

AT-C 320 may also be helpful when performing an examination engagement under AT-C 205 (*Assertion-Based Examination Engagements*) to report on controls at a service organization that are not likely relevant to financial reporting, such as those affecting user entities' compliance with specified requirements, production, or quality control or those when management at the service organization is not responsible for the system design. While this chapter may be helpful when performing these engagements, reports issued under this chapter should not include any controls not likely to be relevant to user entities' ICFR and should not combine reporting on those controls that are likely to be relevant with those that are not likely to be relevant to ICFR.

> **PLANNING AID REMINDER:** If a practitioner is engaged to perform an agreed-upon procedures engagement related to an entity's internal control over compliance with specified requirements, he or she should comply with the guidance in AT-C 315 (*Compliance Attestation*).

This chapter does not provide guidance related to some other engagements a practitioner may perform, including an examination and report on a user entity's transactions or balances maintained by a service organization or an agreed-upon procedures engagement related to the controls of a service organization or to transactions or balances of a user entity maintained by a service organization performed under AT-C 215 (*Agreed Upon Procedures Engagements*).

When a service auditor is engaged to examine internal control at organizations that are relevant to user entities' ICFR, the practitioner should follow the guidance in this AT-C section in addition to the requirements in AT-C 105 (*Concepts Common to All Attestation Engagements*) and AT-C 205. AT-C 105 requires applicable interpretive guidance to be considered; in this type of engagement, the AICPA guide *Service Organizations: Reporting on Controls at a Service Organization Relevant to User Entities' Internal Control Over Financial Reporting* is relevant and should be considered. AT-C 205 allows for a practitioner to report directly on the subject matter or on management's assertion; however, for engagements conducted under this chapter, the service auditor should only report directly on the subject matter.

---

**PLANNING AID REMINDER:** If management is not responsible for and is unable to make an assertion on the design of controls, the service auditor will not be able to give an opinion on the operating effectiveness of controls due to the link between suitability of design of controls and their operating effectiveness. Instead, the practitioner may perform agreed-upon procedures under AT-C 215 or an examination of whether the controls were operating as described under AT-C 205.

---

The objectives of the service auditor in an engagement under AT-C 320 are (1) to obtain reasonable assurance about whether in all material respects and based on suitable criteria management's description of the service organization's system is presented fairly as the system that was designed and implemented and that the controls are suitably designed (and operated effectively when included in the scope of the engagement) to achieve the control objectives stated in management's description, and (2) to express an opinion in a written report in accordance with the findings.

## Definitions

| | |
|---|---|
| Carve-out method | Method of dealing with services provided by a subservice organization in which management's description identifies the nature of the services provided by the subservice organization. Management's description and the scope of the service auditor's engagement exclude the subservice organization's relevant control objectives and related controls. |
| Complementary subservice organization controls | Controls that management of the service organization assumes, in the design of the service organization's system, will be implemented by subservice organizations that are necessary to achieve the control objectives stated in management's description of the service organization's system. |

| | |
|---|---|
| Complementary user entity controls | Controls the management of the service organization assumes, in the design of the service organization's system, will be implemented by user entities that are necessary to achieve the control objectives stated in the management's description of the service organization's system. |
| Control objectives | The aim or purpose of specified controls at the service organization that ordinarily address the risks the controls are intended to mitigate. |
| Controls at a service organization | Policies and procedures at a service organization that are likely relevant to user entities' ICFR. These policies and procedures are designed, implemented, and documented to provide reasonable assurance about achievement of control objectives relevant to the services covered by the service auditor's report. |
| Inclusive method | Method of addressing the services provided by a subservice organization in which the service organization's system description identifies the nature of the services provided by the subservice organization as well as the subservice organization's relevant control objectives and related controls. |
| Management's description of a service organization's system and a service auditor's report on that description and on the suitability of the design of controls (type 1 report) | service auditor's report comprising (1) management's description of the service organization's system; (2) a written assertion by the service organization's management about whether, based on the criteria and as of a specified date, management's description of the service organization's system fairly presents such system's design and implementation, and the controls related to the description's control objectives were suitably designed to achieve those objectives; and (3) a service auditor's report expressing an opinion on these written assertions. |
| Management's description of a service organization's system and a service auditor's report on that description and on the suitability of the design and operating effectiveness of controls (type 2 report) | A service auditor's report comprising (1) management's description of the service organization's system; (2) a written assertion by the service organization's management about whether, based on the criteria and throughout the specified period, management's description of the service organization's system fairly presents such system's design and implementation, the controls related to the description's control objectives were suitably designed and operated effectively to achieve those objectives; and (3) a service auditor's report that expresses an opinion on these written assertions and includes a description of the service auditor's tests of controls and their results. |
| Service auditor | A practitioner who reports on controls at a service organization. |
| Service organization | An organization or segment of an organization providing services to user entities that are likely to be relevant to those user entities' ICFR. |
| Service organization's assertion | The written assertion by management of the service organization included in the type 1 and type 2 reports. |
| Service organization's system | The policies and procedures designed, implemented, and documented by the service organization's management to provide user entities with the services covered by the service auditor's report. Management's description of the service organization's system identifies the services covered, the period related to the description, control objectives specified by management or an outside party, any outside party specifying the control objectives, and the related controls. |

| | |
|---|---|
| Subservice organization | A service organization used by another service organization to provide some of the services to user entities that are relevant to those user entities' ICFR. |
| Test of controls | A procedure designed to evaluate the operating effectiveness of controls in achieving the control objectives stated in management's service organization's system description. |
| User auditor | An auditor who audits and reports on user entity financial statements. |
| User entity | An entity that uses a service organization for which controls at the service organization are likely to be relevant to that entity's ICFR. |

## Requirements

The service auditor is presumptively required to perform the following procedures related to reporting on an examination of controls at a service organization relevant to user entities' ICFR.

### *Management and Those Charged with Governance*

1. When required to inquire of, request representations from, communicate with, or otherwise interact with the responsible party (service organization's management), the auditor should determine the appropriate people within management or governance structure with whom to interact, considering who has appropriate responsibilities for and knowledge of the matters concerned.

### *Preconditions*

2. Only continue or accept a service auditor's engagement if the preconditions described in Chapter 1 and the following are met:
    a. Preliminary knowledge of engagement circumstances indicates that management's description of the service organization's system description and scope of the engagement will not be limited to the extent they are not useful to user entities and their auditors.
    b. Management acknowledges and accepts responsibility for:
        i. Preparing the service organization's system description, including the completeness, accuracy, and presentation method of the description and assertion;
        ii. Having a reasonable basis for its assertion;
        iii. Selecting and stating the criteria used in the assertion;
        iv. Specifying and stating the control objectives in the description and identifying any other party specifying control objectives;
        v. Identifying the risks that threaten achievement of the control objectives stated in the description and designing, implementing, and documenting controls that are suitably designed and operating effectively to provide reasonable assurance that the stated control objectives will be achieved; and
        vi. Providing a written assertion accompanying management's description of the service organization's system, both of which will be provided to user entities.

3. If the inclusive method is used, apply the applicable requirements of this chapter along with AT-C 105 and AT-C 205 to the services provided by the subservice organization, including the requirement to obtain management's acknowledgment and acceptance of responsibility as described in the requirement above.

4. If management requests a change in the engagement scope before engagement completion, the service auditor should be satisfied there is reasonable justification for the change before agreeing.

## *Requesting a Written Assertion*

5. Request a written assertion from management of the service organization, whether management is the responsible party or the engaging party. If management refuses to provide a written assertion, withdraw from the engagement when possible under applicable laws and regulations.

## *Assess Criteria Suitability*

6. Assess whether management used suitable criteria in preparing the service organization's system description and evaluating whether controls were suitably designed (and operating effectively if a type 2 report) to achieve the description's stated control objectives.

7. Minimum suitable criteria for evaluating fair presentation of management's description of the service organization's system include:

    a. Whether the description presents how the system was designed and implemented, including, if applicable:

        i. The types of services provided and classes of transactions processed;

        ii. The procedures within automated and manual systems by which services are provided, including procedures by which transactions are initiated, authorized, recorded, processed, corrected, and transferred to the reports and other information prepared for user entities;

        iii. The information used in performing the procedures, including related accounting records, and supporting information for initiation, authorization, recording, processing, correcting, and reporting transactions to user entities;

        iv. How significant events and conditions other than transactions are captured;

        v. The process used to prepare reports and other information for user entities;

        vi. Any services performed by a subservice organization, including whether the inclusive or carve-out method was used;

        vii. Specified control objectives and controls designed to achieve those objectives, including complementary user entity controls and complementary subservice organization controls; and

        viii. Other aspects of the service organization's internal control system relevant to the services provided.

    b. In the case of a type 2 report, whether management's description of the service organization's system includes relevant detail of changes to the system during the period covered by the description.

c. Whether the description does not omit or distort information relevant to the system and acknowledges the description may not include all system aspects important to every user entity and auditor.

8. Minimum suitable criteria for evaluating if controls are suitably designed include whether risks threatening achievement of the description's stated control objectives have been identified by management and if identified controls would, if operating effectively, provide reasonable assurance that those risks would not prevent achievement of the control objectives.

9. Minimum suitable criteria for evaluating whether controls operated effectively to provide reasonable assurance that the stated control objectives were achieved include whether the controls were consistently applied as designed throughout the specified period and whether manual controls were applied by individuals with appropriate competence and authority.

10. Request a written assertion from the responsible party about the measurement or evaluation of the subject matter against the criteria. Determine that management's assertion addresses all of the criteria management used to evaluate that the description was fairly presented and controls were suitably designed (and operating effectively in a type 2 engagement).

## Materiality

11. Evaluate materiality when planning and performing the engagement regarding fair presentation of management's description of the service organization's system and suitability of the design (and operating effectiveness if a type 2 report) of controls to achieve the description's stated control objectives.

## Obtain an Understanding of the Service Organization's System and Assess the Risk of Material Misstatement

12. Obtain an understanding of the service organization's system and controls included in the scope of the engagement, including the processes the service organization uses to prepare the description of the service organization's system, including the determination of control objectives, identify controls designed to achieve the control objectives, and assess the suitability of the design of the controls (and operating effectiveness if a type 2 report).

13. If the service organization has an internal audit function, obtain an understanding of the nature of the internal audit function's responsibilities, how it fits in the organizational structure, and the activities the function will perform or has performed as it relates to the service organization.

14. Identify the risks of material misstatement.

15. Any reports of the internal audit function and regulatory examinations relating to the services provided to user entities and the scope of the engagement should be read to understand the nature and extent of procedures performed and the related findings. The findings should be considered as part of the risk assessment and in determining the nature, timing, and extent of the tests.

## Responding to Assessed Risks and Further Procedures

16. Design and implement overall responses to address the assessed risks of material misstatement for the subject matter and design and perform further procedures whose nature, timing, and extent are based on and responsive to the assessed risks of material misstatement.

## Obtain Evidence

17. Obtain and read management's description of the service organization's system and evaluate whether aspects of the description included in the scope of the engagement are presented fairly, in all material respects, including whether the description's stated control objectives are reasonable, controls identified in the description were implemented, and any complementary user controls, complementary subservice organization controls, and services provided by a subservice organization are adequately described (including whether the inclusive or carve-out method is used).

18. Determine, through inquiries in combination with other procedures, whether the service organization's system has been implemented.

19. Determine whether the controls identified by management in its service organization system description as achieving the control objectives were suitably designed to achieve those objectives by:

    a. Obtaining an understanding of management's process for identifying and evaluating risks threatening achievement of the objectives and assessing the completeness and accuracy of management's identification of those risks,

    b. Evaluating the linkage of controls identified in the description with those risks, and

    c. Determining that the controls have been implemented.

20. For a type 2 engagement, test controls management identified in its description as those that achieve the control objectives and assess their operating effectiveness throughout the period. Evidence obtained in prior engagements does not provide a basis for a reduction in testing even if supplemented with evidence obtained during the current period.

21. Obtain an understanding about changes in the service organization's controls implemented during the period covered by the service auditor's report. Changes significant to user entities and their auditors should be in the service organization's system description or, if not in the description, should be described in the service auditor's report and the effect of such changes on the report should be determined. If superseded controls are relevant to achievement of the description's stated control objectives, determine if it is possible to test the controls before and after the change and, if not, determine the effect on the service auditor's report.

22. When using information produced by the service organization, evaluate whether such information is sufficiently reliable for the service auditor's purposes by obtaining evidence about its accuracy and completeness and evaluating whether the information is sufficiently precise and detailed.

23. When designing and performing tests of controls, perform other procedures such as inspection, observation, or reperformance in combination with inquiry to obtain evidence about how, by whom or what means, and with what consistency the control was applied; determine if any controls to be tested depend on other controls and if it is necessary to obtain evidence about those controls' operating effectiveness; and determine an effective method for selecting the items to be tested to meet the procedure's objectives.

24. Investigate the nature and cause of any deviations identified and determine whether:

    a. Identified deviations are within the expected deviation rate and the control operated effectively,

    b. Additional testing of the control or other controls is necessary to reach a conclusion about operating effectiveness, and

    c. The testing performed provides an appropriate basis for concluding the control did not operate effectively.

25. If the service auditor becomes aware based on the above procedures that any identified deviations are due to fraud by service organization personnel, assess the risk that management's service organization system description is not fairly presented and the controls are not suitably designed or, in a type 2 report, operating effectively.

26. If the service auditor becomes aware that management or other service organization personnel have caused incidents of noncompliance with laws and regulations, fraud or uncorrected misstatements that are not clearly trivial and may affect user entities, determine the effect of such incidents on management's assertion, management's description of the service organization's system, the achievement of control objectives, and the service auditor's report.

## Subsequent Events

27. If the service auditor becomes aware of a subsequent event when performing the subsequent event procedures required by AT-C 205, its nature and significance is such that disclosure is necessary to prevent misleading users of a type 1 or type 2 report, and management has not disclosed information about the event in its description, then disclose the event in the service auditor's report.

## Written Representations

28. Ask management to provide written representations that it has disclosed to the service auditor any of the following about which it is aware: instances of noncompliance with laws and regulations or uncorrected misstatements that may affect user entities; knowledge of any actual, suspected, or alleged fraud by the service organization's management or employees that could adversely affect the fair presentation of management's description of the service organization's system or the completeness or achievement of the description's stated control objectives.

29. If the service organization's system description uses the inclusive method and a subservice organization is used, obtain the written representations described in AT-C 205 and in the requirement above from management of the subservice organization.

30. Request written representations from the responsible party (management of the service organization) in a type 1 or type 2 engagement, even if the responsible party is not the engaging party. If management does not provide one or more of the requested written representations, there is a scope limitation on the engagement sufficient to preclude an unmodified opinion that may be sufficient to cause withdrawal from the engagement where possible under applicable laws and regulations.

## Other Information

31. For situations in which the practitioner is willing to allow a document containing other information to include the practitioner's report on the subject matter or assertion, follow the guidance provided in AT-C 205.

## Preparing the Service Auditor's Report

32. Include the following elements in a service auditor's type 1 or type 2 report:
    a. A title that includes the word "independent."
    b. An appropriate addressee.

c. Identification of:
   i. Management's description of the service organization's system, the function performed by the system and the specified date (or period in a type 2 report) to which the description relates;
   ii. The criteria used to evaluate if the description was fairly presented and the controls were suitably designed (and operating effectively in a type 2 report);
   iii. Any information included in a document containing the service auditor's report that is not covered by the service auditor's report;
   iv. Any services performed by a subservice organization and whether the inclusive or carve-out method was used;
   v. If the inclusive method was used, include a statement that management's description of the service organization's system includes the control objectives and related controls at the subservice organization and the service auditor's procedures included procedures related to the subservice organization; and
   vi. If the carve-out method was used, include a statement that management's description of the service organization's system excludes the control objectives and related controls at the subservice organization, certain specified control objectives can only be achieved if complementary subservice organization controls are suitably designed and operating effectively and the service auditor's procedures do not include complementary subservice organization controls.
d. A statement that the description only includes controls and control objectives management believes are likely to be relevant to user entities' ICFR and does not include those aspects that are not likely relevant.
e. If management's service organization system description refers to the need for complementary user entity controls, a statement that the description's stated control objectives can only be achieved if complementary user entity controls are suitably designed and operating effectively and that the service auditor has not evaluated such suitability.
f. A reference to management's assertion and a statement that management is responsible for:
   i. Preparing the service organization's system description and the assertion, including the completeness, accuracy, and presentation method of the description and assertion;
   ii. Providing the services covered by the service organization's system description;
   iii. Specifying and stating the control objectives in the service organization's system description;
   iv. Identifying the risks that threaten achieving the control objectives;
   v. Selecting the criteria; and

§ 320 • *Reporting on an Examination of Controls* **10,159**

vi. Designing, implementing, and documenting controls to achieve the related control objectives stated in the description.

g. A statement that the service auditor is responsible for expressing an opinion on the fairness of the presentation of management's description of the service organization's system and on the suitability of the design (and operating effectiveness in a type 2 report) of the controls to achieve the related control objectives stated in the description, based on the service auditor's examination.

h. A statement that:

i. The examination was performed in accordance with attestation standards established by the American Institute of Certified Public Accountants;

ii. Those standards require the service auditor to plan and perform the examination to obtain reasonable assurance about whether, in all material respects, based on the criteria in management's assertion, management's description of the service organization's system is fairly presented and the controls are suitably designed as of the specified date (or designed and operating effectively throughout the specified period in a type 2 report) to achieve the related control objectives; and

iii. The service auditor believes the evidence obtained is sufficient and appropriate to provide a reasonable basis for the service auditor's opinion.

i. A statement that an examination of management's service organization system description and the suitability of the design (and operating effectiveness in a type 2 report) of the service organization's controls to achieve the related control objectives stated in the description involves:

i. Performing procedures to obtain evidence about the fairness of the description's presentation and the suitability of the design (and operating effectiveness in a type 2 report) of controls to achieve the control objectives in the description, based on the criteria in management's assertion;

ii. Assessing the risks that management's service organization system description is not fairly presented and that the controls were not suitably designed (or operating effectively in a type 2 report) to achieve the related control objectives;

iii. In a type 2 report, testing the operating effectiveness of the controls management considers necessary to provide reasonable assurance that the related control objectives stated in management's service organization system description were achieved; and

iv. Evaluating the overall presentation of management's service organization system description, the suitability of the control objectives stated in the description, and the suitability of the criteria specified by the service organization in its assertion.

j. A description of the inherent limitations of controls, including that there is a risk that service organization controls may become ineffective in the future when considering any projection of the evaluation of whether management's description is fairly presented or the conclusions about whether the controls are designed (and operating effectively in a type 2 report) to achieve the related control objectives.

k. In a type 1 report, a statement that the service auditor has not performed any procedures regarding the operating effectiveness of controls and therefore does not express an opinion on their effectiveness.

l. In a type 2 report, a reference to a description of the service auditor's test of controls and their results that includes:

    i. Identification of the controls tested;

    ii. Whether all or part of the population was tested;

    iii. The nature of the tests in sufficient detail for user auditors to determine the effects of these tests on their risk assessments;

    iv. Any identified deviations in the operation of controls included in the description, the extent of testing performed and number of items tested that led to identifying the deviations, and the number and nature of the deviations noted regardless of whether the related control objectives were achieved; and

    v. A description of any work of internal auditors that was used in tests of controls and of the service auditor's procedures with respect to that work.

m. The service auditor's opinion on whether, in all material respects, based on the criteria described in management's assertion:

    i. Management's description of the service organization's system fairly presents the system that was designed and implemented as of the specified date (throughout the specified period for type reports);

    ii. The controls related to the control objectives stated in management's description of the service organization's system were suitably designed to provide reasonable assurance that those control objectives would be achieved if the controls operated effectively as of the specified date (throughout the specified period for type reports);

    iii. In a type 2 report, the controls operated effectively to provide reasonable assurance that the control objectives stated in management's description of the service organization's system were achieved throughout the specified period;

    iv. If applicable, a reference to the need for complementary user entity controls to be applied to achieve the related control objectives stated in management's description of the service organization's system; and

    v. If applicable, a reference to the need for complementary subservice organization controls to be applied to achieve the related control objectives stated in management's description of the service organization's system.

n. A restricted-use alert in a separate paragraph that states that the service auditor's report is intended solely for the information and use of management of the service organization, user entities of the service organization's system during some or all of the period covered by the service auditor's report, and the auditors of such user entities' financial statements or ICFR and that the report is not intended to be and should not be used by anyone other than the specified parties.

o. The manual or printed signature of the service auditor's firm.

p. The city and state where the service auditor practices.

q. The date of the service auditor's report, which should be no earlier than the date on which sufficient appropriate audit evidence has been obtained to support the service auditor's opinion, including evidence that:

  i. Management's description of the service organization's system has been prepared,
  
  ii. Management has provided a written assertion, and
  
  iii. The attestation documentation has been reviewed.

33. Modify the opinion and include a clear description of all reasons for the modification if the service auditor concludes that management's service organization system description is not fairly presented in all material respects; controls are not suitably designed to provide reasonable assurance that the description's stated control objectives would be achieved if the controls operated as described; that, in the case of a type 2 report, those controls did not operate effectively; or the service auditor is unable to obtain sufficient, appropriate audit evidence.

34. If the service auditor is disclaiming an opinion due to an inability to obtain sufficient appropriate audit evidence, and has concluded that management's service organization system description is not fairly presented in all material respects; controls are not suitably designed to provide reasonable assurance that the description's stated control objectives would be achieved if the controls operated as described; or that, in the case of a type 2 report, those controls did not operate effectively, he or she should identify these findings in the report.

35. If planning to disclaim an opinion, do not identify the procedures performed or include statements describing the characteristics of a service auditor's engagement in the report so that the disclaimer is not overshadowed.

## Other Communication Responsibilities

36. If the service auditor becomes aware of incidents of noncompliance with laws and regulations, fraud, or uncorrected misstatements attributable to the service organization that may affect user entities, determine whether this information has been communicated appropriately to affected user entities and, if it has not been communicated and management is unwilling to do so, take appropriate action.

# Analysis and Application of Procedures

## Preconditions

Management's documentation of the service organization's system may vary widely depending on the size and complexity of the organization and its monitoring activities. Management's monitoring activities include assessing the effectiveness of internal controls on a timely basis, identifying and reporting deficiencies to appropriate individuals within the service organization, and taking necessary corrective actions. Monitoring takes place through a combination of ongoing activities, which include regular management and supervisory activities and the work of internal auditors, and separate evaluations to ensure controls remain effective over time. The service auditor's report on controls is not a substitute for the service organization's processes to provide a reasonable basis for its assertion.

> **PLANNING AID REMINDER:** If a required precondition is not met and the service auditor is required by regulation or law to accept or continue an engagement, the service auditor needs to determine the effect of the precondition not being met on the service auditor's report.

> **PLANNING AID REMINDER:** The service auditor does not need to be independent of each user entity to perform a service auditor's engagement.

If the inclusive method is being used, the service and subservice organizations should agree on the following:

- The examination scope and the period to be covered by the service auditor's report;
- Acknowledgment from subservice organization management that it will provide the service auditor with a written assertion and representation letter (along with those provided by the service organization);
- The planned content and format of the inclusive description;
- The representatives from each organization who will be responsible for providing each entity's description and integrating the descriptions; and
- For a type 2 report, the timing of the tests of controls.

When evaluating a request from management to change engagement scope, the service auditor may not consider the request reasonably justified if its purpose is to exclude certain control objectives from the engagement or to prevent disclosure of deviations identified at a subservice organization by changing from the inclusive to the carve-out method. A request may be reasonably justified if management wants to remove a control objective that the service auditor concludes is not relevant to a broad range of user entities during the examination period.

*Assess Criteria Suitability*

AT-C 105 provides guidance that can help the service auditor when assessing whether management used suitable criteria. Management or the engaging party is responsible for selecting the criteria and determining they are appropriate for its purposes. The subject matter being measured or evaluated by applying criteria should be capable of evaluation against criteria that are suitable and available to users. Criteria need to be available to user entities and their auditors to understand the basis for the service organization's assertion about management's description of the service organization's system being fairly presented and the suitability of the design (and operating effectiveness in a type 2 report) of controls that address control objectives stated in the system description.

Management's description of the service organization's system and the service auditor's engagement scope include service organization monitoring activities of subservice organization controls. These monitoring activities of the subservice organization may include reviewing and reconciling output reports, holding periodic discussions, making regular site visits, testing controls, reviewing type 1 or type 2 reports on the organization, and monitoring external communications.

*Materiality*

In a service auditor's engagement, materiality in concept relates to the information being reported on, not the user entity's financial statements. Materiality related to the fair presentation of the service organization's system description and design of controls primarily considers qualitative factors such as whether the description includes significant aspects of processing significant transactions or omits or distorts relevant information, or whether the controls, as designed, have the ability to provide reasonable assurance that the description's stated control objectives would be achieved. Materiality related to the operating effectiveness of controls considers quantitative and qualitative factors, such as tolerable and observed deviation rates and the nature and cause of any observed deviations.

> **OBSERVATION:** Materiality is not applied when disclosing identified deviations in the results of the tests of controls, because a deviation may have significance beyond whether it prevents a control from operating effectively.

*Obtain an Understanding of the Service Organization's System and Assess the Risk of Material Misstatement*

Obtaining an understanding of the service organization's system and related controls assists the service auditor in:

- Identifying system boundaries and how the system interfaces with other systems;
- Assessing the fair presentation of the service organization's system description;
- Understanding which controls are necessary to achieve the description's stated control objectives, and whether controls were suitably designed (and operating effectively in the case of a type 2 report) to achieve those objectives; and
- When there is a separate type 1 or type 2 report for a subservice organization, whether management has identified any necessary controls at the service organization or user entities to address relevant complementary user entity controls identified in the carved-out subservice organization's description of its system.

There are many procedures the service auditor may perform to obtain this understanding, including inquiring of management and other service organization personnel, observing operations, inspecting documents and records of transaction processing, inspecting agreements between the service organization and user entities to identify common terms, and reperforming application of controls.

The risk of material misstatement is the risk that, based on the criteria in management's assertion, management's description of the service organization's system is not fairly presented or the controls are not suitably designed (or operating effectively in a type 2 report) to provide reasonable assurance that the control objectives stated in management's description would be achieved. Risks identified may be related to new or significantly changed controls, system changes, processing volumes, personnel or key management, transaction types, products or technologies, or modifications to the service auditor's opinion in the prior-year report.

*Obtain Evidence*

The service auditor plans and performs the engagement to obtain reasonable, not absolute, assurance of detecting errors and omissions in management's service organization system description. Therefore, subsequently discovering that material omissions or errors exist in the description or that there were instances in which control objectives were not achieved does not necessarily mean that there was inadequate planning, performance, or judgment by the service auditor.

In evaluating the fair presentation of the service organization's system description, the auditor may perform procedures such as:

- Considering the user entities' nature and how they are affected by the service organization's services;
- Reading contracts with user entities to understand the service organization's contractual obligations;
- Observing procedures performed by service organization personnel;
- Reviewing the service organization's policy and procedure manuals and other system documentation; and
- Performing walk-throughs of transactions through the service organization's system.

Procedures the auditor may perform to determine whether the system described has been implemented include inquiry of management and other service organization personnel, observation, inspection of records and other documentation, and reperformance of transaction processing and control application.

**PLANNING AID REMINDER:** The service auditor may perform procedures to determine whether the service organization's system has been implemented in conjunction with procedures to obtain an understanding of the system.

When obtaining evidence regarding the design of controls, the auditor should take compensating controls into account. If the auditor evaluates certain activities as ineffective in achieving a particular control objective, compensating controls may exist that still allow the auditor to conclude that controls related to the description's stated control objective are suitably designed to achieve that objective.

In obtaining evidence about the operating effectiveness of controls, evidence about the suitability of control design and implementation may provide evidence of operating effectiveness if there is some automation that provides for consistent operation of the control as it was designed and implemented. Some control procedures do not leave evidence of their operation, so the auditor may need to test operating effectiveness of such procedures throughout the reporting period to obtain sufficient evidence. Evidence about the operating effectiveness of controls cannot be provided by knowledge of satisfactory operation of controls in prior periods. However, the service auditor may consider knowledge of modifications to the prior service auditor's report or observed deviations in a prior engagement when determining the extent of testing needed during the current period.

To determine the effect of changes in service organization controls that were implemented during the period covered by the service auditor's report, the auditor should gather information about the nature and extent of the changes, how they affect processing at the service organization, and how they might affect assertions in financial statements of user entities.

> **OBSERVATION:** Type 2 reports are generally most useful to user entities and their auditors when they cover a substantial portion of the period covered by the user entity's financial statements being audited.

When obtaining evidence about the reliability of information produced by the service organization, the service auditor often uses items such as the following: population lists to select items for testing; lists of data with specific characteristics; exception reports; transaction reconciliations; documentation providing evidence of operating effectiveness of controls, such as user access lists; and system generated reports and other data.

*Written Representations*

Written representations described in the requirements section are separate from management's written assertion that accompanies the service organization's system description provided to user entities. In some circumstances, these written representations may be obtained from parties in addition to service organization management, such as those charged with governance. The service auditor may also consider it necessary to obtain additional representations beyond what is required.

> **PLANNING AID REMINDER:** Sometimes practitioners draft a representation letter for management to develop and sign; however, when doing so, practitioners should make sure that management understands the content in the representation letter before signing it and presenting it to the accountant. The accountant should consider discussing the content of the letter with management

before management signs the letter and documenting that discussion in the working papers.

## Preparing the Service Auditor's Report

The requirements in this chapter describing the content of a service auditor's report constitute all required elements for such a report. AT-C 205 of the attestation standards contains the application guidance relating to these required elements for a service auditor's type 1 or type 2 engagement.

**PUBLIC COMPANY IMPLICATION:** Under the PCAOB's AS-2201, only a type 2 report is acceptable, because the auditor must be comfortable that internal controls at the service organization are properly designed and operating effectively.

In a type 2 report's description of tests of controls, the inclusion of information about causative factors for identified deviations can be useful to readers of the report. If the internal audit function's work has been used in the tests of controls other than as a part of direct assistance, the description of that work and procedures used may be presented at the beginning of the description of tests of controls or by attributing individual tests to internal auditors. This description is the only reference that should be made to the work of the internal audit function in the service auditor's report.

There are many modifications that can be made to service auditor's reports. The AICPA guide, *Service Organizations: Reporting on Controls at a Service Organization Relevant to User Entities' Internal Control over Financial Reporting*, contains examples of elements of modified service auditor's reports.

## Other Communication Responsibilities

When a service auditor becomes aware of noncompliance with laws and regulations, fraud, or uncorrected misstatements at the service organization, there are several actions that may be taken. For example, the service auditor might:

- Obtain legal advice about the consequences of different courses of action;
- Communicate with those charged with governance at the service organization;
- Disclaim an opinion, modify the service auditor's opinion, or add an explanatory paragraph;
- Communicate with third parties such as a regulator when required; and
- Withdraw from the engagement.

## Practitioner's Aids

Exhibit AT-C 320-1 is an example of a type 1 report and Exhibit AT-C 320-2 is an example of a type 2 report.

# EXHIBIT AT-C 320-1—TYPE 1 REPORT

## Independent Service Auditor's Report on Epsilon Service Organization's Description of its [*type or name of*] System and the Suitability of the Design of Controls

To: Epsilon Service Organization

We have examined Epsilon Service Organization's description of its [*type or name of*] system entitled "Epsilon Service Organization's Description of its [*type or name of*] System" for processing user entities' transactions [or *identification of the function performed by the system*], as of [*date*] (description), and the suitability of the design of controls included in the description to achieve the related control objectives, also included in the description, based on the criteria identified in "Epsilon's Service Organization's Assertion" (assertion). The controls and control objectives included in the description are those that management of Epsilon Service Organization believes are likely to be relevant to user entities' internal control over financial reporting and the description does not include those aspects of the [*type or name of*] system that are not likely to be relevant to user entities' internal control over financial reporting.

*Service Organization's Responsibilities*

In [*section number where assertion is presented*], Epsilon Service Organization has provided an assertion about the fairness of the presentation of the description and suitability of the design of the controls to achieve the related controls objectives stated in the description. Epsilon Service Organization is responsible for preparing the description and its assertion, including the completeness, accuracy, and method of presentation of the description and the assertion, providing the services covered by the description, specifying the control objectives and stating them in the description, identifying the risks that threaten the achievement of the control objectives, selecting the criteria stated in the assertion, and designing, implementing, and documenting controls that are suitably designed and operating effectively to achieve the related control objectives stated in the description.

*Service Auditor's Responsibilities*

Our responsibility is to express an opinion on the fairness of the presentation of the description and on the suitability of the design of controls to achieve the related control objectives stated in the description, based on our examination.

Our examination was conducted in accordance with attestation standards established by the American Institute of Certified Public Accountants. Those standards require that we plan and perform our examination to obtain reasonable assurance about whether in all material respects, based on the criteria in management's assertion, the description is fairly presented and the controls were suitably designed to achieve the related control objectives stated in the description as of [*date*]. We believe that the evidence we obtained is sufficient and appropriate to provide a reasonable basis for our opinion.

An examination of a description of a service organization's system and the suitability of the design of controls involves:

- Performing procedures to obtain evidence about the fairness of the presentation of the description of the system and the suitability of the design of the controls to achieve the related control objectives stated in the description, based on the criteria referenced above;

- Assessing the risks that the description is not fairly presented and that the controls were not suitably designed to achieve the related control objectives stated in the description; and
- Evaluating the overall presentation of the description, suitability of the control objectives stated therein, and suitability of the criteria specified by the service organization in its assertion.

*Inherent Limitations*

The description is prepared to meet the common needs of a broad range of user entities and their auditors who audit and report on user entities' financial statements and may not, therefore, include every aspect of the system that each individual user entity may consider important in its own particular environment. Because of their nature, controls at a service organization may not prevent or detect and correct all misstatements in processing or reporting transactions [*or identification of the function performed by the system*]. Also, the projection to the future of any evaluation of the fairness of the presentation of the description, or conclusions about the suitability of the design of the controls to achieve the related control objectives is subject to the risk that controls at a service organization may become ineffective.

*Other Matter*

We did not perform any procedures regarding the operating effectiveness of the controls stated in the description and, accordingly do not express an opinion thereon.

*Opinion*

In our opinion, in all material respects, based on the criteria described in Epsilon Service Organization's assertion:

a. The description fairly presents the [*type or name of*] system that was designed and implemented as of [*date*].

b. The controls related to the control objectives stated in the description were suitably designed to provide reasonable assurance that the control objectives would be achieved if the controls operated effectively as of [*date*].

*Restricted Use*

This report is intended solely for the information and use of Epsilon Service Organization, user entities of Epsilon Service Organization's [*type or name of*] system as of [*date*], and their auditors who audit and report on such user entities' financial statements or internal control over financial reporting and have a sufficient understanding to consider it, along with other information including information about controls implemented by user entities themselves, when assessing the risks of material misstatements of user entities' financial statements. This report is not intended to be and should not be used by anyone other than these specified parties.

[*Service auditor's signature*]

[*Service auditor's city and state*]

[*Date of the service auditor's report*]

EXHIBIT AT-C 320-2—TYPE 2 REPORT

### Independent Service Auditor's Report on Epsilon Service Organization's Description of its [*type or name of*] System and the Suitability of the Design and Operating Effectiveness of Controls

To: Epsilon Service Organization

*Scope*

We have examined Epsilon Service Organization's description of its [*type or name of*] system entitled "Epsilon Service Organization's Description of its [*type or name of*] System" for processing user entities' transaction [*or identification of the function performed by the system*] throughout the period [*date*] to [*date*] (description) and the suitability of the design and operating effectiveness of controls included in the description to achieve the related control objectives also included in the description, based on the criteria identified in "Epsilon Service Organization's Assertion" (assertion). The controls and control objectives included in the description are those that management of Epsilon Service Organization believes are likely to be relevant to user entities' internal control over financial reporting and the description does not include those aspects of the [*type of name of*] system that are not likely to be relevant to user entities' internal control over financial reporting.

*Service Organization's Responsibilities*

In [*section number where the assertion is presented*], Epsilon Service Organization has provided an assertion about the fairness of the presentation of the description and suitability of the design and operating effectiveness of the controls to achieve the related control objectives stated in the description. Epsilon Service Organization is responsible for preparing the description and its assertion, including the completeness, accuracy, and method of presentation of the description and the assertion, providing the services covered by the description, specifying the control objectives and stating them in the description, identifying the risks that threaten the achievement of the control objectives, selecting the criteria stated in the assertion, and designing, implementing, and documenting controls that are suitably designed and operating effectively to achieve the related control objectives stated in the description.

*Service Auditor's Responsibilities*

Our responsibility is to express an opinion on the fairness of the presentation of the description and on the suitability of the design and operating effectiveness of the controls to achieve the related control objectives stated in the description, based on our examination.

Our examination was conducted in accordance with attestation standards established by the American Institute of Certified Public Accountants. Those standards require that we plan and perform the examination to obtain reasonable assurance about whether, in all material respects, based on the criteria in management's assertion, the description is fairly presented and the controls were suitably designed and operating effectively to achieve the related control objectives stated in the description throughout the period [*date*] to [*date*]. We believe that the evidence we obtained is sufficient and appropriate to provide a reasonable basis for our opinion.

An examination of a description of a service organization's system and the suitability of the design and operating effectiveness of the service organization's controls involves:

- Performing procedures to obtain evidence about the fairness of the presentation of the description and the suitability of the design and operating effectiveness of the controls to achieve the related control objectives stated in the description, based on the criteria referenced above.
- Assessing the risks that the description is not fairly presented and that the controls were not suitably designed or operating effectively to achieve the related control objectives stated in the description.
- Testing the operating effectiveness of those controls that management considers necessary to provide reasonable assurance that the related control objectives stated in the description were achieved.
- Evaluating the overall presentation of the description, suitability of the control objectives stated therein, and suitability of the criteria specified by the service organization in its assertion.

*Inherent Limitations*

The description is prepared to meet the common needs of a broad range of user entities and their auditors who audit and report on user entities' financial statements and may not, therefore, include every aspect of the system that each individual user entity may consider important in its own particular environment. Because of their nature, controls at a service organization may not prevent or detect and correct all misstatements in processing or reporting transactions [*or identification of the function performed by the system*]. Also, the projection to the future of any evaluation of the fairness of the presentation of the description, or conclusions about the suitability of the design or operating effectiveness of the controls to achieve the related control objectives is subject to the risk that controls at a service organization may become ineffective.

*Description of Tests of Controls*

The specific controls tested and the nature, timing, and results of those tests are listed in [*section number where the description of tests of controls is presented*].

*Opinion*

In our opinion, in all material respects, based on the criteria described in Epsilon Service Organization's assertion:

   a. The description fairly presents the [*type or name of*] system that was designed and implemented throughout the period [*date*] to [*date*].
   b. The controls related to the control objectives stated in the description were suitably designed to provide reasonable assurance that the control objectives would be achieved if the controls operated effectively throughout the period [*date*] to [*date*].
   c. The controls operated effectively to provide reasonable assurance that the control objectives stated in the description were achieved throughout the period [*date*] to [*date*].

*Restricted Use*

This report, including the description of tests of controls and results thereof in [*section number where the description of tests of controls is presented*], is intended solely for the information and use of Epsilon Service Organization, user entities of Epsilon Service Organization's [*type or name of*] system during some or all of the period [*date*] to [*date*], and their auditors who audit and report on such user entities' financial statements or internal control over financial reporting and have a sufficient understanding to consider it, along with other information including information about controls implemented by user entities themselves, when assessing the risks of material misstatement of user entities' financial statements. This report is not intended to be and should not be used by anyone other than these specified parties.

[*Service auditor's signature*]

[*Service auditor's city and state*]

[*Date of the service auditor's report*]

## SECTION 395

## MANAGEMENT'S DISCUSSION AND ANALYSIS

### Authoritative Pronouncements

SSAE-10—Attestation Standards: Revision and Recodification

> **IMPORTANT NOTICE FOR 2022:** The Auditing Standards Board (ASB) has now completed a project to clarify the Statements on Standards for Attestation Engagements (SSAEs) similar to its clarity project related to Statements on Auditing Standards (SASs) and the Accounting and Review Services Committee's (ARSC's) clarity project related to Statements on Standards for Accounting and Review Services (SSARS). In April 2016, the Auditing Standards Board issued SSAE No. 18 (*Attestation Standards: Clarification and Recodification*), which restructured the attestation standards so that the applicability of any section of the attestation standards to a particular engagement depends on the type of service provided and the subject matter of the engagement. All of the existing attestation standards were superseded by SSAE No. 18 except for extant AT 701 (*Management's Discussion and Analysis*). The ASB does not currently plan to revise AT-C 395 because practitioners report that they rarely perform these engagements. The former AT 701 is being retained in the attestation standards in its current form as AT-C 395. SSAE No. 18 became effective for practitioners' reports dated on or after May 1, 2017.

### Overview

A practitioner may be engaged to examine or review management's discussion and analysis (MD&A) (a written assertion) that is presented to conform to the rules and regulations adopted by the Securities and Exchange Commission (SEC). This service is considered an attestation engagement subject to the standards established in the Statements on Standards for Attestation Engagements (SSAE) standards. Under these standards, the practitioner may perform either an examination or review of MD&A. Examinations and reviews should satisfy the general, fieldwork, and reporting standard discussed in the chapter titled *Concepts Common to All Attestation Engagements* (AT-C 105), as well as the guidance discussed in this chapter.

> **OBSERVATION:** A practitioner may perform an agreed-upon procedures engagement on MD&A if the standards established in the chapter titled *Agreed-Upon Procedures Engagements* (AT-C 215) are observed.

> **OBSERVATION:** Because only public companies are required to prepare an MD&A, presumably most attestation engagements on MD&A have been performed for public companies. The PCAOB has the statutory authority to set

auditing and attestation standards for public companies. It is reasonable to assume that the standards for issuing an attestation report on MD&A for a public company might be modified by the PCAOB in the future.

## EXAMINATION ENGAGEMENT

SSAE standards state that the objective of an examination of MD&A information is for the practitioner to express an opinion on the information taken as a whole by reporting on the following:

- Whether the presentation includes, in all material respects, the required elements of the rules and regulations adopted by the SEC;
- Whether the historical financial amounts have been accurately derived, in all material respects, from the entity's financial statements; and
- Whether the underlying information, determinations, estimates, and assumptions of the entity provide a reasonable basis for the disclosures contained therein.

A practitioner may examine an MD&A presentation in order to express an opinion on the presentation if (1) the practitioner has audited at least the latest financial statements to which the MD&A information pertains, and (2) either the practitioner or a predecessor practitioner has audited the prior years' financial statements to which the MD&A information pertains.

When a predecessor practitioner has audited one or more of the financial statements for the period covered by the MD&A information, the successor practitioner must determine whether it is possible to "acquire sufficient knowledge of the business and of the entity's accounting and financial reporting practices for such period" so that the following can be satisfied:

- The types of potential material misstatements in MD&A can be identified and the likelihood of their occurrence can be determined.
- Procedures can be performed that will provide the practitioner with a basis for expressing an opinion on whether the MD&A presentation includes, in all material respects, the required elements of the rules and regulations adopted by the SEC.
- Procedures can be performed that will provide the practitioner with a basis for expressing an opinion on the MD&A presentation with respect to whether the historical financial amounts have been accurately derived, in all material respects, from the entity's financial statements for such a period.
- Procedures can be performed that will provide the practitioner with a basis for expressing an opinion on whether the underlying information, determinations, estimates, and assumptions of the entity provide a reasonable basis for the disclosures contained therein.

The practitioner examining the MD&A information may decide to review the workpapers (for the financial statement audit and the examination or review of MD&A information) of the predecessor practitioner; however, the review of the predecessor practitioner's workpapers alone does not provide a basis sufficient to express an opinion on the MD&A information that applies to the periods for which the predecessor practitioner was involved. The results of the review of the predecessor practitioner's workpapers should be used to determine the nature, extent, and timing of the examination engagement procedures (which are discussed below) with respect to the MD&A information covered by the work of the predecessor practitioner. In addition, the practitioner should "make inquiries of the predecessor practitioner and management as to audit adjustments proposed by the predecessor practitioner that were not recorded in the financial statements."

> **PLANNING AID REMINDER:** The practitioner should follow the standards established by AU-C 510 (*Opening Balances—Initial Audit Engagements, Including Reaudit Engagements*) to determine whether to accept an audit engagement with respect to the financial statements. When the requested engagement also encompasses the examination of MD&A information, the successor auditor should expand the inquiries directed to the predecessor auditor so that they include questions concerning the previous MD&A engagement. If the successor auditor is requested to examine the MD&A information after being engaged to audit the client's financial statements, the successor auditor should review the predecessor auditor's workpapers related to the previous MD&A engagement.

## Promulgated Procedures Checklist

The practitioner should plan and execute the MD&A engagement in order to determine, with reasonable assurance, whether any material misstatements in the MD&A information exist. SSAE standards require that, in order to achieve this objective, the practitioner perform the following procedures during the engagement:

- Plan the engagement.
- Obtain an understanding of MD&A requirements.
- Obtain an understanding of the client's methods used to prepare MD&A information.
- Consider relevant portions of the entity's internal control applicable to the preparation of MD&A.
- Obtain sufficient evidence, including testing for completeness.
- Consider the effect of events subsequent to the balance-sheet date.
- Obtain written representations from management.
- Prepare an appropriate examination report.

> **PLANNING AID REMINDER:** General guidance for documenting an attest engagement is discussed in AT-C 105 (*Concepts Common to All Attestation Engagements*).

## Analysis and Application of Procedures

*Plan the Engagement*

In an examination engagement, the practitioner must collect evidence sufficient to limit attestation risk to an "appropriate low level." The components of attestation risk in an examination are similar to those that are related to an audit of financial statements, and they are described by the SSAE standards as follows:

- *Inherent risk*—The susceptibility of an assertion within MD&A to a material misstatement, assuming that there are no related controls (inherent risk varies depending on the nature of each assertion included in the MD&A information).

- *Control risk*—The risk that a material misstatement that could occur in an assertion within MD&A and not be prevented or detected on a timely basis by the entity's controls (some control risk will always exist because of the inherent limitations of any internal control).

- *Detection risk*—The risk that the practitioner will not detect a material misstatement that exists in an assertion within MD&A (the establishment of an acceptable level of detection risk is related to the auditor's assessment of inherent risk and control risk).

The foregoing risk factors should be integrated into the planning phase of the engagement by taking into consideration the following factors:

- The anticipated level of attestation risk related to assertions embodied in the MD&A presentation.
- Preliminary judgments about materiality levels for attest purposes.
- The items within the MD&A presentation that are likely to require revision or adjustment.
- Conditions that may require extension or modification of attest procedures.

The focus of the examination of MD&A information is the assertions (explicit or implicit) that are included in the client's MD&A presentation. There are four broad assertions:

1. *Occurrence assertion:* The occurrence assertion is concerned with whether transactions included in the MD&A information actually occurred during the period covered by the presentation.

2. *Consistency assertion:* The consistency assertion focuses on whether the information in the MD&A presentation is consistent with information included in the financial statements and related financial records. The assertion is also concerned with whether nonfinancial data have been "accurately derived from related records."

3. *Completeness assertion:* The completeness assertion is concerned with whether descriptions of transactions and events included in MD&A information are sufficient to adequately reflect the entity's financial condition, changes in financial condition, results of operations, and material commitments for capital resources. This assertion also requires

that relevant "known events, transactions, conditions, trends, demands, commitments, or uncertainties" that will or may affect these transactions and events be properly presented in the MD&A information.

4. *Presentation and disclosure assertion:* The presentation and disclosure assertion focuses on the proper classification, description, and disclosure of information included in the MD&A presentation.

> **ENGAGEMENT STRATEGY:** The assertions listed above are similar to the assertions that the auditor is concerned with when the client's financial statements are audited, and they are discussed in AU-C 500 (*Audit Evidence*) in this guide. However, the examination of assertions related to an MD&A engagement is limited to the assertions described in the SSAE standards (not the assertions described in AU-C 500). For example, if a client asserts that revenues increased due to a strengthening of the dollar relative to other foreign currencies, the auditor should determine the completeness of that assertion, but he or she would not be concerned with the completeness of the assertion related to total revenues, which would have been evaluated as part of the audit of the entity's financial statements.

The practitioner must use professional judgment to determine the specific planning strategy to be used in a particular MD&A engagement; however, SSAE standards note that planning should consider factors such as the following:

- Industry characteristics (such as economic conditions, accounting principles, and legal considerations);
- An understanding of the client's internal control (and recent changes thereto) with respect to the preparation of MD&A information that may have been obtained during the audit of the entity's financial statements;
- Specific characteristics of the entity (such as business form, capital structure, and distribution systems);
- The type of relevant information provided to external parties (such as press releases and presentations to financial analysts);
- The approach the client used to analyze operating activities (such as budgeted versus actual result comparisons) and the types of reports presented to its board of directors to keep the board members informed of day-to-day operations as well as long-range planning strategies;
- Management's familiarity with MD&A rules and regulations;
- The purpose of the MD&A information, if the entity is nonpublic;
- Initial judgments about materiality, inherent risk, and factors related to MD&A internal controls;
- Fraud risk factors and other relevant conditions identified as part of the audit of the entity's latest financial statements;
- The client's documentation to support MD&A information;
- The possible need for a specialist due to the complexity of the material included in the MD&A information (when a specialist is required, the

guidance established by AU-C 620 (*Using the Work of an Auditor's Specialist*) may be followed);

- The existence of an internal audit function (when an internal audit function exists, the guidance established by AU-C 610 (*Using the Work of Internal Auditors*) may be followed); and
- The intended use of the MD&A (if issued by a nonpublic entity).

In addition, the practitioner should take into consideration the results of auditing the client's financial statements. For example, the planning of the MD&A engagement may be affected by such matters as the type of audit adjustments proposed and the types of misstatements identified. If the practitioner's report on the client's financial statements is other than unqualified, that fact may have an impact on the planning of the MD&A engagement.

**ENGAGEMENT STRATEGY:** When the auditor has not previously examined MD&A information for the client, the auditor should obtain an understanding of the internal controls relative to the preparation of the MD&A information for the previous year(s).

Public companies often consist of various subsidiaries, branches, and other operating entities. SSAE standards note that the practitioner should consider factors such as the following in order to determine the procedures to be applied to a particular operating component:

- The significance of each component to the MD&A information taken as a whole,
- The degree to which centralized records are maintained,
- The effectiveness of controls over the various operating components,
- The activities conducted at an operating component location, and
- The similarity of activities and related internal controls at each operating component.

*Obtain an Understanding of MD&A Requirements*

The auditor must develop an understanding of the MD&A rules and regulations adopted by the SEC. These rules and regulations are established in the following SEC publications and related Interpretations:

- Item 303 of Regulation S-K and related Financial Reporting Releases
- Item 303 of Regulation S-B (for small-business issues)
- Item 9 of Form 20-F (for foreign companies)

**PLANNING AID REMINDER:** The SEC rules and regulations listed above establish "reasonable criteria" as required by General Standard No. 3.

## Obtain an Understanding of the Client's Methods Used to Prepare MD&A Information

For developing the MD&A information, the client should have established procedures (similar in concept to its established procedures for the preparation of its financial statements) that conform to the rules and regulations established by the SEC. The practitioner should obtain from the client a description (oral or written) of the procedures the client used to prepare the MD&A information. The description should include such matters as the following:

- The sources of the information,
- The manner in which the information is obtained,
- The factors that management considered relevant in determining the materiality of information, and
- The identification of any changes in procedures from the prior year.

## Consider the Relevant Portions of the Entity's Internal Control Applicable to the Preparation of MD&A

The practitioner must consider the client's internal controls that relate to its preparation of MD&A information in much the same manner as the auditor evaluates internal controls in the audit of an entity's financial statements. In order to satisfy the SSAE standards, the practitioner should follow the steps listed below when considering internal controls in an examination of MD&A information:

**Step 1:** Obtain an understanding of the client's internal controls.

**Step 2:** Assess the control risk.

**Step 3:** Perform tests of controls (when control risk is assessed at a level less than the maximum level).

**Step 4:** Determine the nature, timing, and extent of substantive procedures.

**Step 5:** Document the assessment of control risk.

### Step 1

In all examination engagements, the practitioner must adequately understand those controls relevant to the client's preparation of MD&A information. Relevant controls are concerned with the recording, processing, summarizing, and reporting of financial and nonfinancial data consistent with the assertions embodied in the MD&A presentation. Thus, the practitioner needs to understand internal controls that increase the likelihood that the MD&A information will be prepared in accordance with rules and regulations established by the SEC.

The practitioner generally obtains an understanding of the entity's internal controls that relate to the MD&A presentation by employing the following procedures:

- Making appropriate inquiries of client personnel,
- Inspecting relevant entity documents, and
- Observing relevant control activities.

*Step 2*

Once the practitioner has obtained an understanding of the client's internal control, it is possible to assess the level of control risk for a particular engagement. The practitioner should have documented the system and, based on that documentation, identified potential misstatements (including material omissions of MD&A information). The assessment of the level of control risk provides the practitioner with a general strategy for planning the remaining internal control evaluation. If the practitioner believes the internal control is well designed, the level of control risk will be assessed at a relatively low level for a given assertion.

On the other hand, if the internal control appears to be poorly designed, the level of control risk will be assessed at a maximum level.

*Step 3*

In order to assess control risk at a relatively low level, the practitioner must perform tests of controls. Tests of controls are used to determine the effectiveness of (1) the design of internal controls, and (2) operations of internal controls that relate to the preparation of the MD&A information in accordance with the rules and regulations established by the SEC. For example, if the MD&A information includes statistics, such as the average net sales per square foot of retail space, the auditor must test the internal controls related to how this information is accumulated and reported.

*Step 4*

Based on his or her assessment of inherent risk and assessment of control risk resulting from the understanding of the entity's internal control and perhaps tests of control (if control risk is assessed at a level less than the maximum), the practitioner determines an acceptable level of detection risk. Detection risk is the risk that the practitioner will not detect a material misstatement in an assertion that is included or that should be included in the MD&A presentation. The establishment of a level of acceptable detection risk is used as a basis for determining the nature, timing, and extent of substantive procedures.

*Step 5*

The assessment of control risk for a particular assertion (or group of assertions related to a component of the MD&A presentation) must be documented. The assessment must be related to the results of obtaining an understanding of the client's relevant internal controls and, perhaps, to the performance of tests of controls. SSAE standards note that "the form and extent of this documentation is influenced by the size and complexity of the entity, as well as the nature of the entity's control applicable to the preparation of MD&A."

*Obtain Sufficient Evidence (Including Testing Completeness)*

In order to obtain sufficient evidence to allow the practitioner to offer a reasonable assurance on the client's presentation of MD&A information, SSAE standards require the practitioner to perform the following procedures:

- Read the MD&A and compare the content with the audited financial statements for consistency; compare financial amounts to the audited financial statements and related accounting records and analyses; and recompute the increases, decreases, and percentages disclosed.
- Compare nonfinancial amounts to the audited financial statements, if applicable, or to other records (see the discussion below for nonfinancial data).
- Consider whether the explanations in MD&A are consistent with the information obtained during the audit; through inquiry (including inquiry of officers and other executives having responsibility for operational areas) and inspection of client records, investigate further those explanations that cannot be substantiated by information in the audit workpapers.
- Examine internally generated documents (e.g., variance analyses and business plans or programs) and externally generated documents (e.g., correspondence, contracts, or loan agreements) in support of the existence, occurrence, or expected occurrence of events, transactions, conditions, trends, demands, commitments, or uncertainties disclosed in the MD&A.
- Obtain available prospective financial information (e.g., budgets; sales forecasts; forecasts of labor, overhead, and materials cost; capital expenditure requests; and financial forecasts and projections) and compare such information to forward-looking MD&A disclosures. Ask management about the procedures used to prepare the prospective financial information. Evaluate whether the underlying information, determinations, estimates, and assumptions of the entity provide a reasonable basis for the MD&A disclosures of events, transactions, conditions, trends, demands, commitments, or uncertainties.
- Consider obtaining available prospective financial information relating to prior periods and comparing actual results with forecasted and projected amounts.
- Ask officers and other executives who have responsibility for operational areas (such as sales, marketing, and production) and financial and accounting matters about their plans and expectations for the future that could affect the entity's liquidity and capital resources.
- Consider obtaining external information concerning industry trends, inflation, and changing prices and comparing the related MD&A disclosures with such information.
- Compare the information in MD&A with the rules and regulations adopted by the SEC, and consider whether the presentation includes the required elements of such rules and regulations.
- Read the minutes of meetings to date of the board of directors and other significant committees to identify matters that may affect MD&A; consider whether such matters are appropriately addressed in MD&A.

- Ask officers about the entity's prior experience with the SEC and the extent of comments received upon review of documents by the SEC; read correspondence between the entity and the SEC with respect to such review, if any.
- Obtain public communications (e.g., press releases and quarterly reports) and the related supporting documentation dealing with historical and future results; consider whether MD&A is consistent with such communications.
- Consider obtaining other types of publicly available information (e.g., analyst reports and news articles); compare the MD&A presentation with such information.

*Nonfinancial Data*

MD&A information may include a variety of nonfinancial data, such as number of customers, backorders, and capacity utilization rates. SSAE standards note that the practitioner must determine whether the definitions used by management for such nonfinancial data are reasonable for the particular disclosure in the MD&A and whether there are reasonable criteria for the measurement. If nonfinancial data have such characteristics, the practitioner should apply appropriate examination procedures, taking into consideration the materiality of the data in relationship to the MD&A information taken as a whole and the assessed level of control risk.

*Testing Completeness*

The information (especially explanations) included in MD&A does not arise simply from the client's observance of SEC rules and regulations. As part of the test of completeness, the auditor should consider whether the MD&A discloses matters that could significantly impact future financial condition and results of operations of the entity by considering information that he or she obtained through the following:

- As the result of the audit of the entity's financial statements.
- Through inquiries of the client's personnel with respect to current events, conditions, economic changes, commitments, and uncertainties that are unique to the client or to the industry in which it operates.
- By the application of other engagement procedures.

---

**PLANNING AID REMINDER:** SSAE standards note that if the MD&A engagement is characterized by a high level of inherent risk, it may be appropriate for the practitioner to expand the engagement by performing extended procedures, including additional inquiries of client personnel and examining additional documentation.

---

*Consider the Effect of Events Subsequent to the Balance-Sheet Date*

The practitioner should consider events that may have an effect on the MD&A presentation but occur after the period covered by the MD&A information and prior to the issuance of the examination report. Relevant events would be those that have a material impact on the client's financial condition (including liquidity and capital resources), changes in financial condition, results of operations, and material commitments for capital resources. Attestation standards require that the MD&A presentation disclose subsequent events or matters such as the following:

- Items that are expected to have a material effect on (1) net sales or revenues, and (2) income from continuing operations;
- Items that are expected to have a material effect on the entity's liquidity;
- Items that are expected to have a material effect on the entity's capital resources; and
- Items that are expected to have an impact on the entity in a manner that would make reported financial results a poor predictor of future operating results or financial condition.

The identification of subsequent events may require that the MD&A presentation be adjusted or that additional disclosures be included in the material.

**PLANNING AID REMINDER:** SSAE standards note that when MD&A information is included in a 1933 Securities Act document (or incorporated through reference), examination procedures must be extended to the filing date or "as close to it as is reasonable and practicable in the circumstances." This time extension also applies when the examination report is included in a 1933 Securities Act document.

Generally, the practitioner's fieldwork extends beyond the date of the auditor's report on the client's financial statements. For this reason, SSAE standards (as part of the consideration of the possible occurrence of subsequent events) require that the auditor perform the following procedures:

- Read available minutes of meetings of stockholders, the board of directors, and other appropriate committees; for meetings whose minutes are not available, inquire about matters dealt with at the meetings.
- Read the latest available interim financial statements for periods subsequent to the date of the auditor's report and compare them with the financial statements for the periods covered by the MD&A. Discuss with officers and other executives who have responsibility for operational, financial, and accounting matters (limited where appropriate to major locations) such matters as the following:
  — Whether the interim financial statements have been prepared on the same basis as the audited financial statements;
  — Whether any significant changes took place in the entity's operations, liquidity, or capital resource in the subsequent period;
  — The current status of items in the financial statements for which the MD&A has been prepared that were accounted for on the basis of tentative, preliminary, or inconclusive data; and
  — Whether any unusual adjustments were made during the period from the balance sheet date to the date of inquiry.

- Make inquiries of members of senior management about the current status of matters concerning litigation, claims, and assessments identified during the audit of the financial statements and about any new matters or unfavorable developments. Consider obtaining updated legal letters from legal counsel.

- Consider whether any changes have occurred in economic conditions or in the industry that could have a significant effect on the entity.

- Obtain written representations from appropriate officials about whether any events occurred subsequent to the latest balance sheet date that would require disclosure in the MD&A.

- Make additional inquiries or perform other procedures considered necessary and appropriate to address questions that arise in carrying out the foregoing procedures, inquiries, and discussions.

## Obtain Written Representations from Management

Attest standards require that an auditor obtain written representations from the client in an MD&A examination (and a review) engagement. The purpose of written representations is to confirm oral representations made by management during the engagement and to reduce the likelihood of misunderstandings between the client and the auditor. The written representations may be documented in a client representation letter. Although no comprehensive list of items exists that must be included in a client representation letter (or other form of written communication), SSAE standards identify the following as items that management should include:

- Acknowledgment that management is responsible for the preparation of the MD&A information and that it has prepared the information in accordance with the rules and regulations established by the SEC.

- A statement that the historical financial amounts have been accurately derived from the client's financial statements and are reflected in the MD&A presentation.

- An affirmation of the belief that the underlying information, determinations, estimates, and assumptions provide a reasonable basis for the MD&A presentation.

- A statement that all significant documentation that relates to the compliance with the SEC rules and regulations has been made available.

- Confirmation that complete minutes of all meetings of stockholders, the board of directors, and committees of directors have been made available.

- A statement about whether the client (if it is a public entity) has received relevant communications from the SEC.

- A statement about whether events subsequent to the latest balance sheet date that would require disclosure in the MD&A have occurred.

- A statement about whether forward-looking information is included in MD&A information and, if it is included, whether the following is also true:
  — The forward-looking information is based on the client's best estimate of expected events and operations and is consistent with budgets, forecasts, or operating plans prepared for such periods.
  — The same accounting principles used in the preparation of the financial statements were used to prepare the MD&A presentation.
  — The latest versions of budgets, forecasts, or operating plans have been provided, and the practitioner has been informed of any anticipated changes or modifications to such information that could affect the disclosures contained in the MD&A presentation.
- A statement that, if voluntary information is included and subject to SEC rules and regulations, such voluntary information has been prepared in accordance with SEC rules and regulations.
- A statement that, if pro forma information is included in the MD&A information, the following is also true:
  — The client is responsible for establishing the assumptions upon which the pro forma adjustments are based.
  — The client believes that the assumptions used provide a reasonable basis for the pro forma adjustments, and the pro forma column accurately reflects the application of the adjustments to the historical financial statements.
  — The pro forma information appropriately discloses the significant effects directly attributable to the transaction or event that is the basis for the pro forma adjustments.

**PLANNING AID REMINDER:** Sometimes practitioners draft a representation letter for management to develop and sign; however, when doing so, practitioners should make sure that management understands the content that is in the representation letter before signing it and presenting it to the accountant. The accountant should consider discussing the content of the letter with management before management signs the letter, and the accountant should consider documenting that discussion in the working papers.

**PLANNING AID REMINDER:** The guidance established in AU-C 580 (*Written Representations*) should be followed to determine the date of the representations and who should sign them. When a client refuses to provide the practitioner with appropriate written representations, the practitioner should not issue an unqualified opinion on the MD&A information but, rather, should decide whether a qualified opinion, a disclaimer of opinion, or withdrawal from the engagement is appropriate. (If the engagement is a review, the practitioner should generally withdraw from the engagement.) The fact that a client will not provide an appropriate written representation suggests that the practitioner should not rely on other representations the client has made.

**PLANNING AID REMINDER:** When a client provides written representation concerning a matter but does not allow the practitioner to apply appropriate examination procedures to the matter, the auditor should express a qualified opinion or a disclaimer of an opinion in an examination engagement, and in a review engagement he or she should withdraw.

*Prepare an Appropriate Examination Report*

Based on the results of applying examination procedures, the practitioner should form an opinion on the MD&A presentation. The report must be accompanied by the financial statements covered by the MD&A information, the auditor's report(s) on those financial statements, and the MD&A presentation itself.

**PLANNING AID REMINDER:** When the client is a nonpublic company, one of the following conditions should be met: (1) a written statement should be included in the MD&A information stating that the information has been prepared in accordance with the rules and regulations established by the SEC, (2) a separate written assertion from management should accompany the MD&A presentation, or (3) a separate written assertion from management should be included in the representation letter.

The examination report should include the following items:
- A title that includes the word "independent."
- An identification of the MD&A presentation, including the period that is covered.
- A statement that management is responsible for the preparation of the MD&A pursuant to the rules and regulations adopted by the SEC and a statement that the practitioner's responsibility is to express an opinion on the presentation based on his or her examination.
- A reference to the auditor's report on the related financial statements and, if the report was other than a standard report, the substantive reasons why.
- A statement that the examination was made in accordance with attestation standards established by the American Institute of Certified Public Accountants (AICPA), and a description of the scope of an examination of MD&A.
- A statement that the practitioner believes the examination provides a reasonable basis for the opinion given.
- A paragraph stating the following:
    — That the preparation of MD&A requires management to interpret the criteria, make determinations as to the relevancy of information to be

included, and make estimates and assumptions that affect reported information; and
- That actual results in the future may differ materially from management's present assessment of information regarding the estimated future impact of transactions and events that have occurred or are expected to occur, expected sources of liquidity and capital resources, operating trends, commitments, and uncertainties.
- If the entity is a nonpublic entity, a statement that, although the entity is not subject to the rules and regulations of the SEC, the MD&A presentation is intended to be a presentation in accordance with the rules and regulations adopted by the SEC.
- The practitioner's opinion on the following:
  - Whether the presentation includes, in all material respects, the required elements of the rules and regulations adopted by the SEC;
  - Whether the historical financial amounts have been accurately derived, in all material respects, from the entity's financial statements; and
  - Whether the underlying information, determinations, estimates, and assumptions of the entity provide a reasonable basis for the disclosures contained therein.
- The manual or printed signature of the practitioner's firm.
- The date of the examination report.

Exhibit AT-C 395-1 is an example taken from SSAE-10 of an examination report on an entity's MD&A presentation.

## EXHIBIT AT-C 395-1—EXAMINATION REPORT ON AN ENTITY'S MD&A PRESENTATION

We have examined XYZ Company's Management's Discussion and Analysis taken as a whole, included [*incorporated by reference*] in the Company's [*insert description of registration statement or document*]. Management is responsible for the preparation of the Company's Management's Discussion and Analysis, pursuant to the rules and regulations adopted by the Securities and Exchange Commission. Our responsibility is to express an opinion on the presentation based on our examination. We have audited, in accordance with standards of the Public Company Accounting Oversight Board (United States), the financial statements of XYZ Company as of December 31, 20X5 and 20X4, and for each of the years in the three-year period ending December 31, 20X5. In our report dated [*month*] XX, 20X6, we expressed an unqualified opinion on those financial statements.

Our examination of Management's Discussion and Analysis was made in accordance with attestation standards established by the American Institute of Certified Public Accountants and, accordingly, included examining, on a test basis, evidence supporting the historical amounts and disclosures in the presentation. An examination also includes assessing the significant determinations made by management as to the relevancy of information to be included and the estimates and assumptions that affect reported information. We believe that our examination provides a reasonable basis for our opinion.

The preparation of Management's Discussion and Analysis requires management to interpret the criteria, make determinations as to the relevancy of information to be included, and make estimates and assumptions that affect reported information. Management's Discussion and Analysis includes information regarding the estimated future impact of transactions and events that have occurred or are expected to occur, expected sources of liquidity and capital resources, operating trends, commitments, and uncertainties. Actual results in the future may differ materially from management's present assessment of this information because events and circumstances frequently do not occur as expected.

In our opinion, the Company's presentation of Management's Discussion and Analysis includes, in all material respects, the required elements of the rules and regulations adopted by the Securities and Exchange Commission; the historical financial amounts included therein have been accurately derived, in all material respects, from the Company's financial statements; and the underlying information, determinations, estimates, and assumptions of the Company provide a reasonable basis for the disclosures contained therein.

[Signature]

[Date]

---

**OBSERVATION:** Only public companies are required to file an MD&A with the Securities and Exchange Commission. Such audits are performed in accordance with standards of the Public Company Accounting Oversight Board (United States). If a nonpublic company voluntarily includes an MD&A and retains an accounting firm to issue an attestation report, the audit must be performed in accordance with generally accepted auditing standards.

---

The standard examination report on MD&A presentations may be modified for the following reasons:

- A material element as required by SEC rules and regulations is omitted from the presentation (a qualified or adverse opinion should be expressed).
- Historical financial amounts have not been accurately derived (in all material respects) from the client financial statements (a qualified or adverse opinion should be expressed).
- Underlying information, determinations, estimates, and assumptions used by the client do not provide the practitioner a reasonable basis on which to prepare the MD&A presentation (a qualified or adverse opinion should be expressed).
- The practitioner is unable to perform procedures deemed appropriate for the MD&A engagement (a qualified opinion or a disclaimer of opinion should be expressed, or the practitioner should withdraw from the engagement).

- The practitioner decided to refer to the work of another practitioner.
- The practitioner has been engaged to examine the client MD&A presentation after it has been filed with the SEC.
- The practitioner has decided to emphasize a matter.

### REVIEW ENGAGEMENT

SSAE standards state that the objective of a review of MD&A information is for the practitioner to report on whether any information came to his or her attention to cause him or her to believe that:

- The MD&A presentation does not include, in all material respects, the required elements of the rules and regulations adopted by the SEC;
- The historical financial amounts included therein have not been accurately derived, in all material respects, from the entity's financial statements; and
- The underlying information, determinations, estimates, and assumptions of the entity do not provide a reasonable basis for the disclosures contained therein.

A practitioner may review a MD&A presentation if (1) the practitioner has audited at least the latest financial statements to which the MD&A information pertains, and (2) either the practitioner or a predecessor practitioner has audited the prior years' financial statements to which the MD&A information pertains.

When a predecessor practitioner has audited one or more of the financial statements for the period covered by the MD&A information, the successor practitioner must determine whether it is possible to "acquire sufficient knowledge of the business and of the entity's accounting and financial reporting practices for such period" so that the following can be satisfied:

- The types of potential material misstatements in MD&A can be identified and the likelihood of their occurrence can be determined.
- Procedures can be performed that will provide the practitioner with a basis for determining whether any information obtained in the engagement suggests that:
  — The MD&A information excludes material information required by SEC rules and regulations;
  — The historical financial amounts included in the MD&A information have not been accurately derived from the historical financial statements; and
  — The underlying information, determinations, estimates, and assumptions of the entity do not provide a reasonable basis for the disclosures included in the MD&A presentation.

## Promulgated Procedures Checklist

The practitioner should plan and execute the MD&A engagement in order to provide limited assurance that the material misstatements in the MD&A information will be identified. According to SSAE standards, to achieve this objective, the practitioner should perform the following:

- Plan the engagement.
- Obtain an understanding of MD&A requirements.
- Obtain an understanding of the client's methods used to prepare MD&A information.
- Consider relevant portions of the entity's internal control applicable to the preparation of MD&A.
- Apply analytical procedures and make inquires of management and other appropriate personnel.
- Consider the effect of events subsequent to the balance sheet date.
- Obtain written representations from management.
- Prepare an appropriate review report.

> **PLANNING AID REMINDER:** General guidance for documenting an attest engagement is discussed in AT-C 105 (*Concepts Common to All Attestation Engagements*).

## Analysis and Application of Procedures

*Plan the Engagement*

The practitioner must use professional judgment in determining the specific planning strategy to be used in a particular MD&A engagement; however, SSAE standards note that in planning the review engagement, the practitioner should consider factors such as the following:

- Industry characteristics (such as economic conditions, accounting principles, and legal considerations);
- Specific characteristics of the entity (such as business form, capital structure, and distribution systems);
- Relevant information provided to external parties (such as press releases and presentations to financial analysts);
- Management's familiarity with MD&A rules and regulations;
- The purpose of the MD&A information, if the entity is nonpublic;
- Matters identified during the audit or review of the client's financial statements that may provide insight into the preparation and reporting of MD&A information;
- Matters identified during the examination or review concerning the prior years' MD&A presentations;
- Initial judgments about materiality levels;
- Items that are either relatively complex or subjective that provide a basis for assertions in the MD&A information; and
- The existence of an internal audit function and the degree to which the function was involved in the verification of MD&A information.

### Consider Relevant Portions of the Entity's Internal Control Applicable to the Preparation of MD&A

SSAE standards state that as a basis for performing appropriate analytical procedures and inquiries of client personnel, the practitioner must develop an adequate understanding of the client's internal controls related to its preparation and presentation of MD&A information. Although the standards do not provide specific guidance on how this is to be accomplished, the practitioner's knowledge of internal controls must be sufficient to accomplish the following:

- Identification of types of potential misstatements in MD&A, including types of material omissions, and consideration of the likelihood of their occurrence.
- Selection of the inquiries and analytical procedures that will provide a basis for reporting whether any information causes the practitioner to believe the following:
  — That the MD&A presentation does not include, in all material respects, the required elements of the rules and regulations adopted by the SEC, or that the historical financial amounts included therein have not been accurately derived, in all material respects, from the entity's financial statements; and
  — That the underlying information, determinations, estimates, and assumptions of the entity do not provide a reasonable basis for the disclosures contained therein.

### Apply Analytical Procedures and Make Inquiries of Management and Other Appropriate Personnel

The practitioner should apply a variety of analytical procedures and make specific inquiries of client personnel. The results of these procedures should be evaluated in the context of the practitioner's understanding of other relevant information that he or she knows. Although there is no specific list of analytical procedures and inquiries that should be performed in a review engagement, SSAE standards point out that the auditor should generally employ the following procedures:

- Compare information in the MD&A presentation with the audited financial statement and related accounting records and analyses.
- Recompute increases, decreases, and percentage changes relative to financial amounts included in or derived from the financial statements.
- Compare nonfinancial amounts in the MD&A presentation with audited amounts in the financial statements, if appropriate, or in other records.
- Inquire about the types of records that support the nonfinancial amounts, and determine the existence of the records.

- Determine whether the nonfinancial information is relevant to users and is clearly defined in the MD&A information, and inquire about whether the definition of nonfinancial information was consistently applied.

- Consider whether explanations included in the MD&A presentation are consistent with information obtained as part of the audit of the client's financial statements, and direct any related inquiries to appropriate personnel.

- Compare prospective financial information (such as budgets) to forward-looking information included in the MD&A presentation.

- Make inquiries of relevant personnel concerning procedures used to develop prospective financial information and forward-looking information.

- Consider whether information obtained suggests that underlying information, determinations, estimates, and assumptions of the entity do not provide a reasonable basis for the disclosures of trends, demands, commitments, events, or uncertainties.

- Make inquiries of appropriate operational personnel (such as production and marketing) and financial personnel as to plans that could have an effect on the client's liquidity and capital resources.

- Determine whether the MD&A presentation includes disclosures required by the SEC.

- Consider whether the MD&A presentation properly reflects any relevant matters discussed in the minutes of meetings of the board of directors and other significant committees.

- Make inquiries about the experience the client has had with the SEC relative to MD&A presentations made in previous years, and read any correspondence between the client and the SEC relative to these matters.

- Make inquiries concerning the nature of public communications that include historical and future results. Determine whether those communications are consistent with the MD&A presentation.

Although a review engagement is characterized by the use of analytical procedures and inquiries of management personnel, the practitioner should use whatever procedures he or she deems appropriate (including corroborative procedures) if it appears that the MD&A presentation is "incomplete or contains inaccuracies or is otherwise unsatisfactory."

---

**ENGAGEMENT STRATEGY:** The practitioner might find the general guidance for the application of analytical procedures in AU-C 520 (*Analytical Procedures*) helpful in applying the procedures to a review of MD&A information.

*Obtain an Understanding of MD&A Requirements*

In order to develop an understanding of MD&A requirements established by the SEC for a review engagement, the practitioner should follow the guidance discussed earlier for an examination engagement.

*Obtain an Understanding of the Client's Methods Used to Prepare MD&A Information*

In a review engagement, in order to develop an understanding of the client's methods used to create MD&A information, the auditor should follow the guidance discussed earlier for an examination engagement.

*Consider the Effect of Events Subsequent to the Balance-Sheet Date*

In order to consider the effect of an event occurring subsequent to the balance sheet date in a review engagement, the practitioner should follow the guidance discussed earlier for the occurrence of this situation in an examination engagement.

*Obtain Written Representations from Management*

In a review engagement, the practitioner should obtain written representations similar to those obtained in an examination engagement, as discussed earlier. However, when the client refuses to provide the practitioner with appropriate written representations in a review engagement, the practitioner should withdraw from the engagement.

*Prepare an Appropriate Review Report*

Based on the results of applying review procedures, the practitioner should consider which report would be appropriate to issue on the MD&A presentation. However, the report must be accompanied by the financial statements covered by the MD&A information, the auditor's report(s) on those financial statements, and the MD&A presentation.

---

**PLANNING AID REMINDER:** When the client is a public company and the MD&A presentation covers an interim period, the presentation should be accompanied by (1) the related interim financial statements and the review report applicable to the MD&A presentation, and (2) the most recent comparative financial statements and the related MD&A presentation. (The information may be included by reference to filings with the SEC.)

---

**PLANNING AID REMINDER:** When the client is a nonpublic company, there should be a statement that the MD&A information has been prepared in accordance with rules and regulations established by the SEC. The statement may be included in the MD&A presentation itself or presented as a separate statement that accompanies the MD&A presentation. If the presentation for a nonpublic company relates to an interim period, the MD&A presentation should be accompanied by (1) the entity's most recent annual MD&A presentation and the related examination or review report, and (2) the related interim financial statements and the most recent annual financial statements.

---

The review report should include the following items:

- A title that includes the word "independent."
- An identification of the MD&A presentation, including the period covered.
- A statement that management is responsible for preparing the MD&A pursuant to the rules and regulations adopted by the SEC.
- A reference to the auditor's report on the related financial statements and, if the report was other than a standard report, the substantive reasons for it.
- A statement that the review was made in accordance with attestation standards established by the AICPA.
- A description of the procedures for a review of MD&A.
- A statement that a review of MD&A is substantially less in scope than an examination, the objective of which is an expression of opinion regarding the MD&A presentation and that, accordingly, no such opinion is expressed.
- A paragraph stating the following:
  — That the preparation of MD&A requires management to interpret the criteria, make determinations as to the relevancy of information to be included, and make estimates and assumptions that affect reported information; and
  — That future results may differ materially from management's present assessment of information regarding the estimated future impact of transactions and events that have occurred or are expected to occur, expected sources of liquidity and capital resources, operating trends, commitments, and uncertainties.
- If the entity is a nonpublic entity, a statement that, although the entity is not subject to the rules and regulations of the SEC, the MD&A presentation is intended to be a presentation in accordance with the rules and regulations adopted by the SEC.
- A statement about whether any information came to the practitioner's attention that caused him or her to believe any of the following:
  — That the presentation does not include, in all material respects, the required elements of the rules and regulations adopted by the SEC;
  — That the historical financial amounts have not been accurately derived, in all material respects, from the entity's financial statements; or
  — That the underlying information, determinations, estimates, and assumptions of the entity do not provide a reasonable basis for the disclosures contained therein.

- If the entity is a public entity or nonpublic entity that is making an offering of securities to the public, a statement restricting the use of the report to specified parties.
- The manual or printed signature of the practitioner's firm.
- The date of the review report.

Exhibit AT-C 395-2 is an example taken from SSAE-10 of a report for a review engagement on an entity's MD&A presentation.

## EXHIBIT AT-C 395-2—REVIEW REPORT ON AN ENTITY'S MD&A PRESENTATION

We have reviewed XYZ Company's Management's Discussion and Analysis taken as a whole, included [*incorporated by reference*] in the Company's [*insert description of registration statement or document*]. Management is responsible for the preparation of the Company's Management's Discussion and Analysis pursuant to the rules and regulations adopted by the Securities and Exchange Commission. We have audited, in accordance with the standards of the Public Company Accounting Oversight Board (United States), the financial Statements of XYZ Company as of December 31, 20X5 and 20X4, and for each year in the three-year period ended December 31, 20X5, and in our report date [*month*] XX, 20X6, we expressed an unqualified opinion on those financial statements.

We conducted our review of Management's Discussion and Analysis in accordance with attestation standards established by the American Institute of Certified Public Accounts. A review of Management's Discussion and Analysis consists principally of applying analytical procedures and making inquiries of persons responsible for financial, accounting, and operating matters. It is substantially less in scope than an examination, the objective of which is the expression of an opinion on the presentation. Accordingly, we do not express such an opinion.

The preparation of Management's Discussion and Analysis requires management to interpret the criteria, make determinations as to the relevancy of information to be included, and make estimates and assumptions that affect reported information. Management's Discussion and Analysis includes information regarding the estimated future impact of transactions and events that have occurred or are expected to occur, expected sources of liquidity and capital resources, operating trends, commitments, and uncertainties. Actual results in the future may differ materially from management's present assessment of this information because events and circumstances frequently do not occur as expected.

Based on our review, nothing came to our attention that caused us to believe that the Company's presentation of Management's Discussion and Analysis does not include, in all material respects, the required elements of the rules and regulations adopted by the Securities and Exchange Commission, that the historical financial amounts included therein have not been accurately derived, in all material respects, from the Company's financial statements, or that the underlying information, determinations, estimates, and assumptions of the Company do not provide a reasonable basis for the disclosures contained therein.

The report is intended solely for the information and use of [*list or refer to specified parties*] and is not intended to be and should not be used by anyone other than the specified parties.

[*Signature*]

[*Date*]

---

**OBSERVATION:** Only public companies are required to file an MD&A with the Securities and Exchange Commission. Such audits are performed "in accordance with standards of the Public Company Accounting Oversight Board (United States)." If a nonpublic company voluntarily includes an MD&A and retains an accounting firm to issue an attestation report, the audit must be performed in accordance with generally accepted auditing standards.

---

The standard review report on MD&A presentations may be modified for the following reasons:

- A material element as required by SEC rules and regulations is omitted from the presentation (modify the review report by describing the omission).
- Historical financial amounts have not been accurately derived (modify the review report by describing the misstated information).
- Underlying information, determinations, estimates, and assumptions used by the client do not provide a reasonable basis upon which to prepare the MD&A presentation (modify the review report by describing the deficiency).
- The practitioner decides to emphasize a matter with respect to the MD&A presentation (a standard review report is issued with an explanatory paragraph describing the nature of the matter emphasized).

The practitioner's review report may also be modified when another practitioner has examined or reviewed (and issued a separate report on) MD&A information for a component that represents a significant part of the overall financial statements. Under this circumstance, the principal practitioner's report should refer to the work of the other practitioner as a basis for offering the limited assurance on the MD&A presentation. When the other practitioner has not issued a separate report on the (component) MD&A presentation, there should be no reference to the work of the other practitioner in the review report on the MD&A presentation. (This does not mean that the principal practitioner cannot refer in the review report to the fact that a component's financial statements were audited by another auditor.)

---

**PLANNING AID REMINDER:** When the practitioner is unable to perform appropriate review procedures or the client is unwilling to provide appropriate written representations, the practitioner should not issue a review report on the MD&A presentation.

## OTHER ISSUES

### Combined Reporting

A practitioner may be engaged to report on the results of (1) an examination on an MD&A presentation related to the latest annual financial statements, and (2) a review of an MD&A presentation on interim financial information for a period that is subsequent to the date of the annual financial statements. When the two engagements are "completed at the same time," the practitioner can issue a single report that incorporates both a separate examination format and a separate review format (except that the explanatory paragraph in the review report is omitted).

> **ENGAGEMENT STRATEGY:** In some instances, the client may prepare a combined MD&A presentation for an annual period and an interim period. SSAE standards note that if the discussion of liquidity and capital resources applies only as of the most recent interim period (not as of the date of the annual financial statements), the auditor is "limited to performing the highest level of service that is provided with respect to the historical financial statements of any of the periods covered by the MD&A presentation." Thus, if annual financial statements are audited and the interim financial statements are reviewed, the combined MD&A presentation can be reviewed but cannot be examined.

### Engagement of the Auditor Subsequent to Filing of MD&A Presentation

Public companies are required to report significant subsequent events on Form 8-K, on Form 10-Q, or in a registration statement. They are not required to modify previously filed MD&A presentations for the occurrence of subsequent events. If the practitioner is engaged to examine or review an MD&A presentation after the document has been filed, the auditor should consider whether subsequent events have been reported on Form 8-K or Form 10-Q or in a registration statement, rather than whether the MD&A presentation has been modified to reflect the subsequent event. However, under this circumstance, the following sentence should be added to the opinion paragraph in an examination engagement and to the concluding paragraph in a review engagement:

> The accompanying Management's Discussion and Analysis does not consider events that have occurred subsequent to [*month*] XX, 20X6, the date as of which it was filed with the Securities and Exchange Commission.

> **PLANNING AID REMINDER:** If the client has not notified the SEC of a material subsequent event, the practitioner should express a qualified or adverse opinion on the MD&A presentation in an examination engagement (or in a review engagement appropriately modifying the review report), assuming that the auditor concludes that it is appropriate to issue a report on the MD&A information. This circumstance may occur when the SEC filing has not yet been completed but management intends to make the appropriate filing on a timely basis. However, if the subsequent event is not disclosed in a proper manner, the practitioner must decide whether to withdraw from both the MD&A engagement and the audit engagement.

## Communicating with the Client's Audit Committee

Under the following circumstances (assuming the client refuses to correct the deficiency), the practitioner should communicate the deficiency to the entity's audit committee (or others with equivalent authority):

- Material inconsistencies exist between the MD&A presentation and other information included in the document containing the MD&A material.
- Material inconsistencies exist between the MD&A presentation and the historical financial statements.
- Material omissions are made in the MD&A presentation.
- Material misstatements of facts are made in the MD&A presentation.

**FRAUD POINTER:** If the practitioner has evidence as a result of performing the attestation or review engagement that fraud might have occurred—even if the fraud is inconsequential—it should be communicated to an appropriate level of management.

# AR-C Section
# Statements on Standards for Accounting and Review Services

| | | |
|---|---|---|
| Section 60: | General Principles for Engagements Performed in Accordance with Statements on Standards for Accounting and Review Services | 11,002 |
| Section 70: | Preparation of Financial Statements | 11,016 |
| Section 80: | Compilation Engagements | 11,025 |
| Section 90: | Review of Financial Statements | 11,041 |
| Section 100: | Special Considerations—International Reporting Issues | 11,109 |
| Section 120: | Compilation of Pro Forma Financial Information | 11,116 |

## SECTION 60

# GENERAL PRINCIPLES FOR ENGAGEMENTS PERFORMED IN ACCORDANCE WITH STATEMENTS ON STANDARDS FOR ACCOUNTING AND REVIEW SERVICES

### Authoritative Pronouncements

SSARS-21—Statements on Standards for Accounting and Review Services: Clarification and Recodification

SSARS-23—Omnibus Statement on Standards for Accounting and Review Services—2016

SSARS-24—Omnibus Statement on Standards for Accounting and Review Services—2018

SSARS-25—Materiality in a Review of Financial Statements and Adverse Conclusions

**IMPORTANT NOTICE FOR 2022:** In May 2018, the Accounting and Review Services Committee (ARSC) issued SSARS-24 (*Omnibus Statement on Standards for Accounting and Review Services—2018*) to provide requirements and guidance when an accountant is engaged to perform a compilation or review of financial statements that have been prepared in accordance with a financial reporting framework generally accepted in another country or the accountant is engaged to perform a compilation or review in accordance with SSARS and another set of compilation or review standards. SSARS-24 created a new AR-C 100 section titled "Special Considerations—International Reporting Issues." The issuance of SSARS-24 included conforming changes to AR-C 60 (*General Principles for Engagements Performed in Accordance With Statements on Standards for Accounting and Review Services*) to add a definition for the term *fair presentation framework* and to modify the definition of *financial reporting framework*. The effective date of SSARS-24 was for compilations and reviews of financial statements for periods ending on or after June 15, 2019. The *GAAS Guide* reflects these conforming changes.

### Overview

The Accounting and Review Services Committee (ARSC) issued this guidance to provide general principles that will help accountants better understand their professional responsibilities when performing an engagement in accordance with SSARSs. SSARSs address reviews, compilations and engagements to prepare financial statements by an accountant. However, there may be additional legal, regulatory, or professional obligations applicable to specific engagements that differ from SSARS guidance and it is the responsibility of the accountant to ensure compliance with these obligations.

*§ 60 • General Principles for Engagements*  **11,003**

In February 2020, the Accounting and Review Services Committee (ARSC) issued SSARS-25 (*Materiality in a Review of Financial Statements and Adverse Conclusions*).

**PLANNING AID REMINDER:** SSARS-23 revised AR-C 60 so that it applies to SSARS engagements performed on subject matter other than financial statements, such as preparation or compilation of prospective financial information or the compilation of pro forma information. References in AR-C 60 to financial statements also refer to such other financial information.

**IMPORTANT NOTICE FOR 2022:** In February 2020, the Accounting and Review Services Committee (ARSC) issued SSARS-25 (*Materiality in a Review of Financial Statements and Adverse Conclusions*) to further converge SSARS with International Standards on Review Engagements (ISREs) and to further align it with AICPA Auditing Standards. The ARSC determined that further convergence with International Standard on Review Engagements (ISRE) 2400 (Revised) (*Engagements to Review Historical Financial Statements*) was appropriate and in the public interest and that it is important for the SSARS literature to be closely converged with ISRE 2400 (Revised) to facilitate the accountant's ability to perform and report on engagements in accordance with both sets of standards. Additionally, although there are significant differences between an audit engagement and an engagement performed in accordance with SSARSs, there are certain concepts related to the financial statements that are consistent regardless of the level of service performed on those financial statements. SSARS-25 further aligns the SSARS standards with auditing standards. SSARS-25 revises the definition of *financial statements* in AR-C 60 to be consistent with the definition now in auditing standards and it adds a number of new defined terms. SSARS-25 is effective for engagements performed in accordance with SSARS for periods ending on or after December 15, 2021. Early implementation is permitted.

## Definitions

| | |
|---|---|
| Applicable financial reporting framework | The financial reporting framework adopted by management and, when appropriate, those charged with governance in the preparation and fair presentation of the financial statements that is acceptable in the view of the nature of the entity and the objective of the financial statements or that is required by law or regulation. |
| Designated accounting standard setter | A body designated by the Council of the AICPA to promulgate accounting principles generally accepted in the United States of America pursuant to the "Compliance With Standards Rule" (ET section 1.310.001) and the "Accounting Principles Rule" (ET section 1.320.001) of the AICPA Code of Professional Conduct. |
| Engagement partner | The partner or person in the firm responsible for the engagement, its performance, and the report issued on behalf of the firm, and who has the appropriate authority from a professional, legal, or regulatory body when required. |

| | |
|---|---|
| Engagement team | All partners and staff performing the engagement and any individuals engaged by the firm or a network firm who perform procedures on the engagement. |
| Fair presentation framework | See financial reporting framework. |
| Financial reporting framework | A set of criteria used to determine measurement, recognition, presentation, and disclosure of all material items appearing in the financial statements (e.g., accounting principles generally accepted in the United States of America [U.S. GAAP], International Financial Reporting Standards promulgated by the International Accounting Standards Board, or a special purpose framework). <br> The term fair presentation framework refers to a financial reporting framework that requires compliance with the requirements of the framework and does one of the following: <br> a. Acknowledges explicitly or implicitly that, to achieve fair presentation of the financial statements, it may be necessary for management to provide disclosures beyond those specifically required by the framework. <br> b. Acknowledges explicitly that it may be necessary for management to depart from a requirement of the framework to achieve fair presentation of the financial statements. Such departures are expected to be necessary only in rare circumstances. <br> A financial reporting framework that requires compliance with the requirements of the framework but does not contain the acknowledgment in (a) or (b) is not a fair presentation framework. |
| Financial statements | A structured representation of historical financial information, including disclosures, intended to communicate an entity's economic resources and obligations at a point in time or the changes therein for a period of time in accordance with a financial reporting framework. The term financial statements ordinarily refers to a complete set of financial statements as determined by the requirements of the applicable financial reporting framework but can also refer to a single financial statement. Disclosures comprise explanatory or descriptive information, set out as required, expressly permitted or otherwise allowed by the applicable financial reporting framework, on the face of the financial statement or in the notes, or incorporated therein by reference. <br> The requirements of the applicable financial reporting framework determine the presentation, structure, and content of the financial statements and what constitutes a complete set of financial statements. |
| Firm | An organization practicing public accounting that is permitted by law or regulation and whose characteristics conform to AICPA Council resolutions. |
| General purpose financial statements | Financial statements prepared in accordance with a general purpose framework. |

| | |
|---|---|
| General purpose framework | A financial reporting framework designed to meet the common financial information needs of a wide range of users. |
| Interpretive publications | SSARSs interpretations, exhibits, the AICPA Guide *Preparation, Compilation, and Review Engagements*, applicable guidance in AICPA Audit and Accounting Guides, and applicable AICPA Statements of Position. |
| Other preparation, compilation and review publications | Publications other than interpretive publications. |
| Professional judgment | The application of relevant training, knowledge, and experience within the context provided by SSARSs, accounting and ethical standards in making informed decisions about appropriate courses of action given the circumstances of the engagement. |
| Prospective financial information | Any financial information about the future. The information may be presented as complete financial statements or limited to one or more elements, items, or accounts. |
| Special purpose financial statements | Financial statements prepared in accordance with a special purpose framework. |
| Special purpose framework | A financial reporting framework other than GAAP that is one of the following bases of accounting:<br>a. *Cash basis.* A basis of accounting that the entity uses to record cash receipts and disbursements and modifications of the cash basis having substantial support (e.g., recording depreciation of fixed assets).<br>b. *Tax basis.* A basis of accounting that the entity uses to file its tax return for the period covered by the financial statements.<br>c. *Regulatory basis.* A basis of accounting that the entity uses to comply with the requirements or financial reporting provisions of a regulatory agency to whose jurisdiction the entity is subject (e.g., a basis of accounting that insurance companies use pursuant to the accounting practices prescribed or permitted by a state insurance department).<br>d. *Contractual basis.* A basis of accounting that the entity uses to comply with an agreement between the entity and one or more third parties other than the accountant.<br>e. *Other basis.* A basis of accounting that uses a definite set of logical, reasonable criteria that is applied to all material items appearing in the financial statements (e.g., the AICPA's *Financial Reporting Framework for Small- and Medium-Sized Entities*).<br>The cash basis, tax basis, regulatory basis, and other basis of accounting are commonly referred to as *other comprehensive bases of accounting*. |

## Objective

The objective of this standard is for the accountant to obtain an understanding of the general principles for engagements performed in accordance with SSARSs.

## Requirements

*Ethical Requirements and Professional Judgment*

1. The accountant should comply with relevant ethical requirements.
2. Professional judgment should be exercised when performing an engagement in accordance with SSARSs.

## Engagement Conduct in Accordance with SSARSs

3. Reviews, compilations, and engagements to prepare financial statements must be performed in accordance with SSARSs. An exception is for certain reviews of interim financial statements as discussed in AR-C 90 (*Review of Financial Statements*).

4. The accountant should comply with all AR-C sections relevant to the engagement. An AR-C section is relevant when it is in effect and the circumstances it addresses exist.

5. To understand the objectives and apply the requirements of an AR-C section properly, the accountant should have an understanding of its entire text, including the application and other explanatory material.

6. A compilation or review report should only represent compliance with SSARSs if compliance with the requirements of this and all other relevant AR-C sections has been met.

7. Subject to requirement 9, each requirement of a relevant AR-C section should be complied with unless the requirement is not relevant to the engagement because it is conditional and the condition does not exist.

8. SSARSs use two categories of professional requirements to describe the degree of responsibility imposed on accountants:

    a. *Unconditional requirements*. SSARSs use the word "must" to describe those requirements, which must be complied with in all cases where the requirement is relevant.

    b. *Presumptively mandatory requirements*. SSARSs use the word "should" to describe those requirements, which must be complied with in all cases where the requirement is relevant, except in rare circumstances discussed in requirement 9.

9. In rare circumstances, the accountant may judge it necessary to depart from a relevant presumptively mandatory requirement. This is expected to occur only when the requirement is for a specific procedure to be performed that would be ineffective in achieving the intent of the requirement due to specific engagement circumstances. In these circumstances, alternative procedures should be performed to achieve the intent of the requirement.

10. In the rare instance where the accountant judges it necessary to depart from a relevant presumptively mandatory requirement, the accountant must document the justification for the departure and how the alternative procedures performed in the circumstances were sufficient to achieve the intent of that requirement.

11. Applicable interpretive publications should be considered when performing an engagement in accordance with SSARSs.

12. The relevance and appropriateness of guidance in other preparation, compilation, and review publications should be assessed using professional judgment and considering the circumstances of the engagement.

## Engagement Level Quality Control

13. The engagement partner should possess the appropriate competence and capabilities to perform the engagement and competence in financial reporting for the engagement.
14. The engagement partner should take responsibility for:
    a. Overall engagement quality.
    b. The direction, supervision, planning, and performance of the engagement in compliance with professional standards and applicable legal and regulatory requirements.
    c. The accountant's report being appropriate in the circumstances.
    d. The engagement being performed in accordance with the firm's quality control policies and procedures, including:
        (i) Being satisfied that client acceptance and continuance procedures have been followed and appropriate conclusions reached, including those on management integrity;
        (ii) Being satisfied that the engagement team has the appropriate competence and capabilities to perform the engagement in accordance with professional standards and applicable legal and regulatory requirements and expertise in financial reporting to issue any applicable report; and
        (iii) Taking responsibility for appropriate engagement documentation being maintained.
15. The engagement partner should promptly communicate to the firm any information obtained that would have caused the firm to decline the engagement so that necessary action can be taken.
16. The engagement partner should remain alert through observation and inquiry as necessary for evidence of noncompliance with relevant ethical requirements by members of the engagement team. If there is indication of such noncompliance, the engagement partner and others in the firm should determine the appropriate action.
17. The engagement partner should consider the results of the firm's most recent quality control monitoring process and whether any deficiencies noted may affect the engagement.

## Client Relationship and Engagement Acceptance and Continuance

18. The accountant should not accept an engagement to be performed in accordance with SSARSs if he or she believes relevant ethical requirements will not be satisfied, a preliminary understanding indicates that information needed to perform the engagement is likely to be unavailable or unreliable, or there is cause to doubt management's integrity that is likely to affect performance of the engagement.

19. As a precondition for engagement acceptance the accountant should:
   a. Determine whether the financial reporting framework management selected to apply to financial statement preparation is acceptable.
   b. Obtain management agreement that it acknowledges and understands its responsibility:
      (i) For the selection of the financial reporting framework to be applied in financial statement preparation;
      (ii) For the design, implementation, and maintenance of internal control relevant to the preparation and fair presentation of financial statements that are free from material misstatement whether due to fraud or error, unless the accountant decides to accept responsibility for such internal control;
      (iii) For preventing and detecting fraud;
      (iv) For ensuring that the entity complies with applicable laws and regulations;
      (v) For the accuracy and completeness of records, documents, explanations, and other information, including significant judgments provided for financial statement preparation; and
      (vi) To provide the accountant with access to all information management is aware of that is relevant to the preparation and fair presentation of the financial statements, additional information that may be requested for the purposes of the engagement, and unrestricted access to make inquiry of people within the entity as determined necessary by the accountant.

## Analysis and Application of Procedures

### Financial Statements

Preparation and fair presentation of financial statements require the applicable financial reporting framework to be identified in the context of relevant laws and regulations, the financial statements to be prepared and fairly presented in accordance with that framework, and an adequate description of the framework to be included in the financial statements. Management is required to exercise judgment when making accounting estimates and in selecting and applying accounting policies to ensure they are reasonable given the applicable financial reporting framework. Financial statements may be prepared in accordance with a general purpose or special purpose framework.

Financial reporting frameworks often encompass financial accounting standards issued by an authorized standards-setting organization, legislative or regulatory requirements, or both. There may be other sources that are encompassed in a financial reporting framework or that provide direction on applying financial reporting frameworks, such as the legal and ethical environment, published accounting interpretations and views on emerging accounting issues of varying authority, widely recognized general and industry practices, and accounting literature. Whenever conflicting guidance arises, the source of higher authority should be followed.

Some regulators and other governmental agencies require the entity to prepare financial statements in accordance with a financial reporting framework developed by an authorized or recognized framework, such as the FASB or GASB, but not all requirements of the framework are required by the regulator or agency. In that situation, the frameworks are regulatory bases of accounting. In other situations, the regulator may allow the use of a cash basis or tax basis of accounting; however, for purposes of SSARSs, those are not considered to be regulatory bases of accounting.

The following standards have been put forth by organizations that are authorized or recognized to put forth standards to be used by entities for preparing financial statements in accordance with a general purpose framework:

- The FASB *Accounting Standards Codification,*
- International Financial Reporting Standards issued by the International Accounting Standards Board,
- Statements of Federal Financial Accounting Standards issued by the Federal Accounting Standards Advisory Board for U.S. federal government entities, and
- Statements of Governmental Accounting Standards Board issued by the Governmental Accounting Standards Board for U.S. state and local government entities.

The applicable financial reporting framework used determines the form and content of the financial statements and provides principles that can serve as a basis for developing and applying accounting policies consistent with the framework. The framework used also determines what constitutes a complete set of financial statements. Many frameworks intend for the financial statements to provide information about financial position, financial performance, and entity cash flows. However, for some frameworks a single financial statement and its related notes may be sufficient. Example financial statements, each of which would be accompanied by related notes, include the balance sheet, statement of income or statement of operations, statement of retained earnings, statement of cash flows, statement of assets and liabilities, statement of changes in owners' equity, statement of revenue and expenses, and statement of operations by product lines.

An accountant may be engaged to prepare or perform a compilation or review engagement on a complete set of financial statements or an individual financial statement. These financial statements could be for an annual period or a shorter or longer period; however, if there is a comparative presentation with financial statements for an annual period, the duration should likely be for an annual period.

## Ethical Requirements and Professional Judgment

Relevant ethical requirements the accountant is subject to when performing an engagement in accordance with SSARSs include those in the AICPA Code of

Professional Conduct as well as more restrictive rules of state boards of accountancy and applicable regulatory agencies. The fundamental principles of professional ethics established by the AICPA Code of Professional Conduct include the following:

- Responsibilities,
- The public interest,
- Integrity,
- Objectivity and independence,
- Due care, and
- Scope and nature of services.

Due care requires the accountant to have the competence and capabilities to perform the engagement and issue any applicable reports. QC Section 10 (*A Firm's System of Quality Control*), in the AICPA *Professional Standards*, outlines the firm's responsibilities to establish and maintain its quality control system for engagements performed in accordance with SSARSs and establish policies and procedures to provide reasonable assurance that the firm and its personnel comply with relevant ethical requirements, including those pertaining to independence.

Professional judgment is needed to interpret relevant ethical requirements and SSARSs and make informed decisions throughout the engagement. Professional judgment is expected to be exercised by an accountant who has the training, knowledge, and experience sufficient to achieve reasonable judgments and make informed decisions when performing an engagement in accordance with SSARSs. Consultation within and outside the engagement team and firm when needed can assist the accountant on difficult or contentious matters. Professional judgment is exercised based on known facts and circumstances, including knowledge from prior period engagements with the entity, an understanding of the entity, its environment, its accounting system, and the industry's application of the applicable financial reporting framework, and the extent to which financial statement preparation and presentation requires judgment of management or the accountant.

Professional judgment can be evaluated by determining if the judgment reached demonstrates a competent application of SSARSs and accounting principles that is appropriate and consistent with known facts and circumstances at the time of the financial statement issuance or date of the report. Professional judgment should be documented in accordance with the relevant guidance: AR-C 70 (*Preparation of Financial Statements*), AR-C 80 (*Compilation Engagements*), or AR-C 90 (*Review of Financial Statements*). Decisions not otherwise supported by the facts and circumstances of the engagement or the evidence obtained in a review should not be justified by professional judgment.

*Engagement Conduct in Accordance with SSARSs*

SSARSs are developed and issued by the ARSC and are codified in AR-C sections in AICPA *Professional Standards*. SSARSs provide the standards for unaudited financial statements and other unaudited financial information of non-public companies. These standards describe the general responsibilities of the accountant as well as considerations relevant to specific topics.

---

**PLANNING AID REMINDER:** AR-C sections are permitted to be applied prior to their effective date unless otherwise noted.

---

The accountant may be required to comply with requirements in addition to SSARSs. In these circumstances, following a law or regulation may result in the engagement not complying with SSARSs. The accountant may also conduct a compilation or review in accordance with SSARSs and the International Standard on Related Services 4410 (Revised) (*Compilation Engagements*), International Standard on Review Engagements 2400 (Revised) (*Engagements to Review Historical Financial Statements*), or compilation or review standards of another country that could require additional procedures to be performed in addition to those required by SSARSs.

An AR-C section contains several parts that contribute to an understanding of the requirements of that section. Application and other explanatory material is provided to give more precise explanations of requirements and their intended coverage and to include appropriate examples. Introductory material may provide context by explaining the purpose, scope, and subject matter of the AR-C section and the responsibilities of accountants and others as it relates to the AR-C section. Definitions are also included in many AR-C sections to assist with consistent application and interpretations of SSARSs.

While the accountant should consider relevant interpretative publications when performing an engagement in accordance with SSARSs, it is important to note that interpretive publications are not SSARSs. They are recommendations on the application of SSARSs for particular circumstances and industries. Other preparation, compilation, and review publications may also help the accountant understand and apply SSARSs but are not authoritative. The accountant may presume that other preparation, compilation, and review publications published by the AICPA that have been reviewed by the AICPA Audit and Attest Standards staff are appropriate. These publications are listed in Exhibit AR-C 60-1. Other preparation, review, and compilation publications not reviewed by the AICPA Audit and Attest Standards staff may be useful if they are relevant, helpful in understanding and applying SSARSs, and published by a recognized authority. However, those publications do not have authoritative status and the use of any publication that contradicts a publication reviewed by the AICPA Audit and Attest Standards staff is inappropriate.

*Engagement Level Quality Control*

Engagement teams are responsible for implementing applicable quality control procedures on an engagement and for providing the firm with information on independence. Factors important to engagement quality include performing work that complies with professional standards and legal and regulatory requirements; complying with the firm's applicable quality control policies and procedures; issuing an appropriate report as applicable; and the ability of the engagement team to raise concerns without fear of reprisal.

The engagement team can rely on the firm's quality control system unless there is information that suggests it should not be relied upon. If there are deficiencies in the firm's quality control system, the engagement partner may consider measures taken by the firm to address those deficiencies.

> **OBSERVATION:** A deficiency in the firm's quality control system does not necessarily indicate that an engagement was not performed in accordance with the applicable standards and requirements or that any report issued was not appropriate.

When the engagement partner considers the competence and capabilities of the engagement team, he or she may consider matters such as understanding and practical experience with similar engagements, understanding of professional standards and applicable legal and regulatory requirements, relevant technical expertise, specific industry knowledge, ability to apply professional judgment, and understanding of the firm's quality control policies and procedures.

The engagement partner is responsible for determining whether the conclusions reached regarding engagement acceptance with a new or existing client or engagement continuance are appropriate. Factors such as the integrity of owners, management, and those charged with governance of the entity; the competence and capabilities of the engagement team; the ability of the firm and engagement team to comply with relevant ethical requirements; and any significant findings or issues with implications on client continuance may be considered in this determination. It is not appropriate to accept an engagement if management's integrity is in question to a degree that it would likely affect proper performance of the engagement, unless required by law or regulation.

*Client Relationship and Engagement Acceptance and Continuance*

Engagement continuance and relevant ethical requirements are considered at the beginning of an engagement as well as throughout when circumstances and conditions change.

> **PLANNING AID REMINDER:** When performing a review, ethical requirements concerning independence are relevant. The accountant's independence is impaired if the accountant accepts responsibility for the design and implementation of internal control. In that situation, the accountant would not be able to perform a review of the financial statements.

When determining whether information needed to perform an engagement is likely to be available or reliable, the recommendation of adjusting entries to assist management in finalizing financial statements would not be a cause for doubt. When considering if the financial reporting framework management selected is acceptable, it is relevant to consider the purpose of the financial statements and any law or regulation prescribing a particular financial reporting framework. It may be necessary to discuss management's responsibilities in relation to the financial statements with management in a smaller entity in order to obtain informed agreement as to those responsibilities.

*Acceptability of the Financial Reporting Framework*

The accountant evaluates the acceptability of the financial reporting framework by considering a number of factors, including the nature of the entity, the purpose and nature of the financial statements, and whether regulations or laws mandate a certain framework. Without an acceptable framework, management does not have an appropriate basis for the preparation of the financial statements and the accountant does not have suitable criteria for an engagement in accordance with SSARS.

Some financial reporting frameworks are intended to be used to prepare financial information in a format that can be used by a wide variety of users. These are referred to as general purpose financial statements. The sources of established accounting principles that are generally accepted are accounting principles promulgated by a body designated by the AICPA Council to establish such principles. At other times, financial statements are prepared in accordance with special purpose frameworks, such as law or regulation that prescribe the framework to be used by certain entities.

SSARSs require the accountant to obtain management's agreement that it understands its responsibilities before accepting an SSARS engagement. That may be obtained orally or in writing; however, management's agreement should be subsequently recorded within the written terms of the engagement.

## Practitioner's Aid

*EXHIBIT AR-C 60-1—OTHER PREPARATION, COMPILATION, AND REVIEW PUBLICATIONS*

---

The following is a list of other preparation, compilation, and review publications published by the AICPA that have been reviewed by the AICPA Audit and Attest Standards staff and are presumed to be appropriate.

**Current AICPA Alerts**

*Developments in Review, Compilation, and Financial Statement Preparation Engagements*

*Understanding the Financial Reporting Framework for Small- and Medium-Sized Entities*

*Independence and Ethics Developments*

**AICPA *Technical Practice Aids* Accounting and Compilation and Review Technical Questions and Answers (TIS) Sections**

*Special Purpose Frameworks*

| | |
|---|---|
| TIS Section 1500.07 | Disclosure Concerning Subsequent Events in Special Purpose Financial Statements |
| TIS Section 1800.06 | Applicability of Fair Value Disclosure Requirements in FASB ASC 820 to Financial Statements Prepared in Accordance with a Special Purpose Framework |

### Compilation and Review Engagements

| | |
|---|---|
| TIS Section 9150.04 | Financial Statements Marked As "Unaudited" |
| TIS Section 9150.08 | Supplementary Information |
| TIS Section 9150.09 | Applicability of AR Section 300 to Certain Companies Required to File with Regulatory Bodies |
| TIS Section 9150.10 | Review of Financial Statements Included in a Prescribed Form |
| TIS Section 9150.16 | Reference to Accountant's Report in Notes to Financial Statements |
| TIS Section 9150.18 | Bank Engaged an Accountant to Compile a Financial Statement of Another Entity |
| TIS Section 9150.20 | Reissuance When Not Independent |
| TIS Section 9150.24 | Issuing a Compilation Report on Financial Statements That Omit Substantially All Disclosures After Issuing a Report on the Same Financial Statements That Include Substantially All Disclosures |
| TIS Section 9150.25 | Determining Whether Financial Statements Have Been Prepared by the Accountant |
| TIS Section 9150.26 | The Accountant's Responsibilities for Subsequent Events in Compilation and Review Engagements |
| TIS Section 9150.27 | The Accountant's Reporting Responsibility with Respect to Subsequent Discovery of Facts Existing at the Date of the Report |
| TIS Section 9150.28 | Compilation Engagement When the Accountant Is Performing Management Functions |
| TIS Section 9150.29 | Effects on Compilation and Review Engagements When Management Does Not Assess Whether the Reporting Entity Is the Primary Beneficiary of a Variable Interest Entity and Instructs the Accountant to Not Perform the Assessment |
| TIS Section 9150.30 | Disclosure of Independence Impairment in the Accountant's Compilation Report on Comparative Financial Statements When the Accountant's Independence Is Impaired in Only One Period |
| TIS Section 9150.31 | Break-Even Financial Statements |

### Compilation of Financial Statements

| | |
|---|---|
| TIS Section 1300.17 | Omission of Reconciliation of Net Income to Cash Flow from Operations |
| TIS Section 9160.26 | Compilation and Review—Comparative Financial Statements |
| TIS Section 8900.10 | Successor Accountant Becomes Aware of Information During the Performance of a Compilation or Review That Leads the Successor Accountant to Believe That Financial Statements Reported On by a Predecessor Accountant Who Has Ceased Operations May Require Revision |

### Compilation Reports

| | |
|---|---|
| TIS Section 1300.17 | Omission of Reconciliation of Net Income to Cash Flow from Operations |
| TIS Section 9110.07 | Statement of Cash Receipts and Disbursements |

### Review of Financial Statements

TIS Section 8900.10 — Successor Accountant Becomes Aware of Information During the Performance of a Compilation or Review That Leads the Successor Accountant to Believe That Financial Statements Reported On by a Predecessor Accountant Who Has Ceased Operations May Require Revision

### Review Reports

TIS Section 8800.30 — Making Reference to Review Report
TIS Section 9110.07 — Statement of Cash Receipts and Disbursements

### Other Publications

*Corporations: Checklists and Illustrative Financial Statements*
*The Engagement Letter: Best Practices and Examples*

# SECTION 70

# PREPARATION OF FINANCIAL STATEMENTS

## Authoritative Pronouncements

SSARS-21—Statements on Standards for Accounting and Review Services: Clarification and Recodification

SSARS-23—Omnibus Statement on Standards for Accounting and Review Services—2016

SSARS-25—Materiality in a Review of Financial Statements and Adverse Conclusions

## Overview

This SSARS provides guidance to an accountant engaged to prepare financial statements or prospective financial information. This guidance does not apply when an accountant prepares financial statements only for taxing authorities, for personal financial plans prepared by the accountant, in conjunction with litigation services involving pending or potential legal or regulatory proceedings, in conjunction with business valuation services or when engaged to perform an audit, review, or compilation of the financial statements.

> **PLANNING AID REMINDER:** SSARS-23 revised AR-C 70 so that it applies to SSARS engagements performed to prepare prospective financial information. References in AR-C 70 to financial statements also refer to prospective financial information.

> **IMPORTANT NOTICE FOR 2022:** In February 2020, the Accounting and Review Services Committee (ARSC) issued SSARS-25 (*Materiality in a Review of Financial Statements and Adverse Conclusions*) to further converge SSARS with International Standards on Review Engagements (ISREs) and to further align it with AICPA Auditing Standards. The ARSC determined that further convergence with International Standard on Review Engagements (ISRE) 2400 (Revised) (*Engagements to Review Historical Financial Statements*) was appropriate and in the public interest and that it is important for the SSARS literature to be closely converged with ISRE 2400 (Revised) to facilitate the accountant's ability to perform and report on engagements in accordance with both sets of standards. Additionally, although there are significant differences between an audit engagement and an engagement performed in accordance with SSARSs, there are certain concepts related to the financial statements that are consistent regardless of the level of service performed on those financial statements. SSARS-25 further aligns the SSARS standards with auditing standards. SSARS-25 moves definitions for *applicable financial reporting framework* and *special purpose framework* from AR-C 70 to AR-C 60. SSARS-25 is effective for engagements

performed in accordance with SSARS for periods ending on or after December 15, 2021. Early implementation is permitted.

The services the accountant is performing for the client determine whether he or she is engaged to prepare financial statements and therefore subject to this SSARS or is merely assisting in financial statement preparation and therefore performing a bookkeeping service not subject to this guidance. This determination may require professional judgment and Exhibit AR-C 70-1 provides some examples of services the accountant may perform and whether the guidance in AR-C 70 is applicable.

A preparation engagement is a nonattest service that does not require the accountant to determine independence. In addition, no opinion, conclusion, or report is expressed on the financial statements, so there is no requirement for the accountant to gather evidence or verify the accuracy or completeness of information provided by management.

> **PLANNING AID REMINDER:** The "Nonattest Services" subtopic of the "Independence Rule" of the AICPA *Professional Standards*, ET Section 1.295, addresses considerations when the accountant is performing nonattest services for attest clients. The accountant should use the safeguards described in the subtopic to ensure independence is not impaired in this situation.

## Definitions

| | |
|---|---|
| Financial reporting framework | A set of criteria used to determine measurement, recognition, presentation, and disclosure of all material items appearing in the financial statements. Examples include accounting principles generally accepted in the United States of America (U.S. GAAP), International Financial Reporting Standards promulgated by the International Accounting Standards Board, or a special purpose framework. |
| Management | Those with executive responsibility for an entity's operations, which may include some or all of those charged with governance such as executive members of a governance board or owner-managers. |
| Those charged with governance | The people or organizations responsible for overseeing an entity's strategic direction and its obligations related to accountability, which includes the financial reporting process. |

## Objective

The objective of the accountant is to prepare financial statements according to a specified financial reporting framework.

## Requirements

*Engagement Acceptance and General Principles*

1. In addition to AR-C 70, the accountant is required to comply with AR-C 60 (*General Principles for Engagements Performed in Accordance with Statements on Standards for Accounting and Review Services*).
2. If the accountant is not satisfied with any of the preconditions for accepting an engagement to prepare financial statements, he or she should discuss the matter with management or those charged with governance. The engagement should not be accepted if changes are not made to satisfy the accountant about these matters.

*Agreement on Engagement Terms and Accountant Understanding of Financial Reporting Framework*

3. The accountant should agree on engagement terms with management or those charged with governance, as appropriate. An engagement letter or other suitable written agreement between the parties should document the agreed-upon terms of the engagement and should include the following:
    a. Engagement objectives;
    b. Management responsibilities;
    c. Management agreement that each page of the financial statements will include a statement indicating that no assurance is provided on the financial statements or the accountant will be required to issue a disclaimer to clarify this;
    d. Accountant responsibilities;
    e. Limitations of the engagement to prepare financial statements;
    f. Identification of the applicable financial reporting framework for financial statement preparation; and
    g. Whether the financial statements contain any known departures from the applicable financial reporting framework, including inadequate disclosure or omitting substantially all required disclosures.
4. The engagement letter or other suitable written agreement should be signed by the accountant or the accountant's firm and management or those charged with governance as appropriate.
5. The accountant should obtain an understanding of the applicable financial reporting framework and the significant accounting policies intended to be used in financial statement preparation.

*Preparing the Financial Statements*

6. The accountant should prepare the financial statements using the records, documents, explanations, and other information provided by management.

7. The accountant should ensure a statement is included on each page of the financial statements stating that "no assurance is provided." If such a statement is not included, the accountant should do one of the following:
    a. Issue a disclaimer clarifying that no assurance is provided on the financial statements,
    b. Perform a compilation engagement in accordance with AR-C 80 (*Compilation Engagements*), or
    c. Withdraw from the engagement and inform management of the reasons for withdrawing.
8. If financial statements are prepared in accordance with a special purpose framework, the accountant should include a description of the framework either on the face of or in the notes to the financial statements.
9. If the accountant assists management with significant judgments regarding amounts or disclosures reflected in the financial statements, he or she should ensure management understands and accepts responsibility for those judgments.
10. The accountant should bring to management's attention any incomplete, inaccurate, or otherwise unsatisfactory records, documents, explanations, or other information provided during the engagement and request additional or corrected information. If management fails to provide such additional or corrected information, the accountant should disclose a material misstatement in the financial statements or withdraw from the engagement.
11. If the accountant prepares financial statements, after discussion with management, containing any known departures from the applicable financial reporting framework, including inadequate disclosure, he or she should disclose the material misstatements in the financial statements.
12. If the accountant, after discussion with management, prepares financial statements that omit substantially all disclosures required by the applicable financial reporting framework, he or she should disclose the omission in the financial statements.
13. The accountant should not prepare financial statements that omit substantially all disclosures required by the financial reporting framework if he or she believes such financial statements would be misleading to users of the financial statements.

## *Preparing Prospective Financial Information*

14. Significant assumptions are used to prepare prospective financial information. Because significant assumptions are important to a user's understanding of prospective financial information, the prospective financial information prepared by the accountant should not exclude disclosure of the summary of significant assumptions. Similarly, the accountant should not prepare a financial projection that excludes an identification

of hypothetical assumptions or a description of the limitations on the usefulness of the presentation.

*Documentation*

15. Documentation should be prepared in sufficient detail to provide a clear understanding of the work performed, which minimally includes the engagement letter or other suitable written agreement with management and a copy of the financial statements prepared by the accountant.
16. If, in rare circumstances, the accountant judges it necessary to depart from a presumptively mandatory requirement, he or she must document justification for the departure as well as how alternative procedures performed were sufficient to achieve the intent of the requirement.

## Analysis and Application of Procedures

*Agreement on Engagement Terms and Accountant Understanding of Financial Reporting Framework*

An engagement letter or other suitable written agreement should document the agreed-upon terms of the engagement. Documenting engagement terms helps both the accountant and management by reducing misunderstandings and decreasing the risk that management will expect the accountant to protect against certain risks or perform functions that are the responsibility of management. When a third party has contracted for an engagement, agreeing on engagement terms also helps ensure the conditions for an engagement to prepare financial statements are present.

---

**PLANNING AID REMINDER:** If the agreement on engagement terms is only with those charged with governance that does not relieve the accountant of the requirement in AR-C 60 to obtain management's agreement that it acknowledges and understands its responsibilities.

---

Exhibit AR-C 70-2 provides an example engagement letter for financial statement preparation.

The accountant is required to obtain an understanding of the applicable financial reporting framework and the significant accounting policies intended to be used in financial statement preparation. This requirement does not prevent the accountant from accepting an engagement for an industry in which he or she has no previous experience, but it does mean that he or she is responsible for obtaining the required level of knowledge.

In addition to preparing financial statements in accordance with an applicable financial reporting framework, AR-C 70 also applies to the following other historical or prospective financial information:

- Specified elements, accounts, or items of a financial statement, such as schedules of rentals, royalties, profit participation, or provision for income taxes;

- Supplementary information;
- Required supplementary information;
- Pro forma financial information; and
- Prospective financial information, including budgets, forecasts, or projections.

*Preparing the Financial Statements*

The accountant should ensure a statement of the accountant's involvement with the financial statements appears on each page of the financial statements, including related notes, in order to prevent misunderstandings by financial statement users. This statement is made at management's discretion and may or may not include the accountant or the accountant's firm name. The following are examples of an appropriate statement, but other statements conveying that no assurance is provided would also be acceptable:

- No assurance is provided on these financial statements, and
- These financial statements have not been subjected to an audit or review or compilation engagement, and no assurance is provided on them.

> **PRACTICE POINTER:** SSARS-21 clearly permits the accountant's name to be included in the statement, appearing on each page of the financial statements, indicating that no assurance is being provided on the financial statements, and that a compilation, review, or audit has not been performed. Based on insights from insurers and defense counsel, we believe the accountant's risk is minimized if the accountant's name is not included in the statement.

If such a statement is not made, the accountant should either issue a disclaimer clarifying that no assurance is provided (an example of which can be found in the sample engagement letter in Exhibit AR-C 70-2) or perform a compilation engagement.

If financial statements are prepared in accordance with a special purpose framework, a description of the framework may be included in financial statement titles, notes to the financial statements, or otherwise on the face of the financial statements. Examples of suitable financial statements titles include "Income Statement—Modified Cash Basis" if statements are prepared on a modified cash basis of accounting or "Balance Sheet—Tax Basis" if statements are prepared in accordance with the tax basis of accounting.

If the accountant prepares financial statements that include only selected disclosures in the notes to the financial statements, such disclosures may be labeled "Selected Information—Substantially All Disclosures Required by [*the applicable financial reporting framework*] Are Not Included."

In a preparation engagement, documentation may include significant consultations or significant professional judgments made during the engagement.

## Practitioner's Aids

### EXHIBIT AR-C 70-1—PREPARATION OF FINANCIAL STATEMENTS VERSUS ASSISTANCE IN PREPARING FINANCIAL STATEMENTS

The following table provides examples of services the accountant may be engaged to perform and whether AR-C 70 would apply.

| Examples of Services for Which AR-C 70 Applies | Examples of Services for Which AR-C 70 Does Not Apply |
|---|---|
| Financial statement preparation prior to audit or review by another accountant | Financial statement preparation when the accountant is engaged to perform an audit, review, or compilation of the financial statements |
| Financial statement preparation to be presented alongside the entity's tax return | Financial statement preparation solely for submission to taxing authorities |
| Financial statement preparation to be presented alongside a financial plan | Financial statement preparation for inclusion in personal financial plans prepared by the accountant |
| | Financial statement preparation in conjunction with litigation services involving pending or potential legal or regulatory proceedings |
| | Financial statement preparation in conjunction with business valuation services |
| | Maintaining depreciation schedules |
| | Preparing or proposing certain adjustments, such as those pertaining to deferred income taxes, depreciation, or leases |
| Preparation of single financial statements, such as a balance sheet or income statement or financial statements with substantially all disclosures omitted | Draft footnotes to include in the financial statements |
| Financial statement preparation outside of an accounting software system using the information in the general ledger | General bookkeeping such as entering general ledger transactions or processing payments in an accounting software system |

Exhibit AR-C 70-2 is an example of a standard engagement letter for an engagement to prepare financial statements.

### EXHIBIT AR-C 70-2—PREPARATION OF FINANCIAL STATEMENTS ENGAGEMENT LETTER

To the appropriate representative of ABC Company:

You have requested that we prepare the financial statements of ABC Company, which comprise the balance sheet as of December 31, 20XX, and the related

§ 70 • *Preparation of Financial Statements*  **11,023**

statements of income, changes in stockholders' equity, and cash flows for the year then ended, and the related notes to the financial statements. [*If the financial statements omit the statement of cash flows and the related notes, the previous sentence may be revised to read:* You have requested that we prepare the financial statements of ABC Company, which comprise the balance sheet as of December 31, 20XX, and the related statements of income and changes in stockholders' equity. *The following sentence may then be added:* These financial statements will not include a statement of cash flows and related notes to the financial statements.] We are pleased to confirm our acceptance and our understanding of this engagement to prepare the financial statements of ABC Company by means of this letter.

**Our Responsibilities**

The objective of our engagement is to prepare financial statements in accordance with accounting principles generally accepted in the United States of America based on information provided by you. We will conduct our engagement in accordance with Statements on Standards for Accounting and Review Services (SSARSs) promulgated by the Accounting and Review Services Committee of the AICPA and comply with the AICPA's Code of Professional Conduct, including the ethical principles of integrity, objectivity, professional competence, and due care.

We are not required to, and will not, verify the accuracy or completeness of the information you will provide to us for the engagement or otherwise gather evidence for the purpose of expressing an opinion or a conclusion. Accordingly, we will not express an opinion or a conclusion nor provide any assurance on the financial statements.

Our engagement cannot be relied upon to identify or disclose any financial statements misstatements, including those caused by fraud or error, or to identify or disclose any wrongdoing within the entity or noncompliance with laws or regulations.

**Management Responsibilities**

The engagement to be performed is conducted on the basis that management acknowledges and understands that our role is to prepare financial statements in accordance with accounting principles generally accepted in the United States of America. Management has the following overall responsibilities that are fundamental to our undertaking the engagement to prepare your financial statements in accordance with SSARSs:

    a. The prevention and detection of fraud

    b. To ensure that the entity complies with the laws and regulations applicable to its activities

    c. The accuracy and completeness of the records, documents, explanations, and other information, including significant judgments, you provide to us for the engagement to prepare financial statements

    d. To provide us with:

        (i) Documentation, and other related information that is relevant to the preparation and presentation of the financial statements,

(ii) Additional information that may be requested for the purpose of the preparation of the financial statements, and

(iii) Unrestricted access to persons within ABC Company of whom we determine necessary to communicate.

The financial statements will not be accompanied by a report. However, you agree that the financial statements will clearly indicate that no assurance is provided on them.

[*If the accountant expects to issue a disclaimer, instead of the preceding paragraph, the following may be added:*]

As part of our engagement, we will issue a disclaimer that will state that the financial statements were not subjected to an audit, review, or compilation engagement by us and, accordingly, we do not express an opinion, a conclusion, nor provide any assurance on them.]

**Other Relevant Information**

Our fees for these services . . .

[*The accountant may include language, such as the following, regarding limitation of or other arrangements regarding the liability of the accountant or the entity, such as indemnification to the accountant for liability arising from knowing misrepresentations to the accountant by management (regulators may restrict or prohibit such liability limitation arrangements):*]

You agree to hold us harmless and to release, indemnify, and defend us from any liability or costs, including attorney's fees, resulting from management's knowing misrepresentations to us.]

Please sign and return the attached copy of this letter to indicate your acknowledgement of, and agreement with, the arrangements for our engagement to prepare the financial statements described herein, and our respective responsibilities.

Sincerely yours,

[*Signature of accountant or accountant's firm*]

Acknowledged and agreed on behalf of ABC Company by:

[*Signed*]

[*Name and Title*]

[*Date*]

---

**PRACTICE POINTER:** Indemnification clauses for knowingly making false representations to the accountant are generally acceptable to regulators. However, a blanket indemnification clause, serving to provide limitations on damages, is often not acceptable to regulators. The accountant should consult with counsel before crafting indemnification clauses for inclusion in engagement letters.

# SECTION 80

# COMPILATION ENGAGEMENTS

## Authoritative Pronouncements

SSARS-21—Statements on Standards for Accounting and Review Services: Clarification and Recodification

SSARS-23—Omnibus Statement on Standards for Accounting and Review Services—2016

SSARS-25—Materiality in a Review of Financial Statements and Adverse Conclusions

## Overview

This SSARS provides guidance to an accountant engaged to perform a compilation engagement. In a compilation engagement, no opinion or other assurance is expressed on the financial statements so there is no requirement for the accountant to gather evidence or verify the accuracy or completeness of information provided by management. AR-C 80 may also be applied as needed to other historical or prospective financial information.

---

**PLANNING AID REMINDER:** The issuance of SSARS-22 (*Compilation of Pro Forma Financial Information*) in September 2016 revised the guidance related to the compilation of pro forma information. That revised guidance is included in AR-C 120. When an accountant is engaged to compile pro forma information, the accountant is required to adhere to the guidance in both AR-C 80 and AR-C 120.

---

**PLANNING AID REMINDER:** SSARS-23 revised AR-C 80 so that it applies to SSARS engagements performed on subject matter other than financial statements, such as compilation of prospective financial information, pro forma information, or other historical financial information. References in AR-C 80 to financial statements also refer to such other financial information.

---

**IMPORTANT NOTICE FOR 2022:** In February 2020, the Accounting and Review Services Committee (ARSC) issued SSARS-25 (*Materiality in a Review of Financial Statements and Adverse Conclusions*) to further converge SSARS with International Standards on Review Engagements (ISREs) and to further align it with AICPA Auditing Standards. The ARSC determined that further convergence with International Standard on Review Engagements (ISRE) 2400 (Revised) (*Engagements to Review Historical Financial Statements*) was appropriate and in the public interest and that it is important for the SSARS literature to be closely converged with ISRE 2400 (Revised) to facilitate the accountant's ability to perform and report on engagements in accordance with both sets of standards.

Additionally, although there are significant differences between an audit engagement and an engagement performed in accordance with SSARSs, there are certain concepts related to the financial statements that are consistent regardless of the level of service performed on those financial statements. SSARS-25 further aligns the SSARS standards with auditing standards. SSARS-25 moves definitions for *applicable financial reporting framework* and *special purpose framework* from AR-C 80 to AR-C 60. SSARS-25 is effective for engagements performed in accordance with SSARS for periods ending on or after December 15, 2021. Early implementation is permitted.

## Definitions

| | |
|---|---|
| Basic financial statements | Financial statements excluding supplementary and required supplementary information. |
| Financial reporting framework | A set of criteria used to determine measurement, recognition, presentation, and disclosure of all material items appearing in the financial statements. Examples include accounting principles generally accepted in the United States of America (U.S. GAAP), International Financial Reporting Standards promulgated by the International Accounting Standards Board, or a special purpose framework. |
| Generally accepted accounting principles (GAAP) | In SSARSs, GAAP means generally accepted accounting principles promulgated by bodies designated by the Council of the AICPA pursuant to the "Compliance with Standards Rule" and the "Accounting Principles Rule" of the AICPA Code of Professional Conduct. |
| Management | Those with executive responsibility for an entity's operations, which may include some or all of those charged with governance such as executive members of a governance board or owner-managers. |
| Misstatement | A difference between the amount, classification, presentation, or disclosure of a reported financial item and that required for fair presentation in accordance with the applicable financial reporting framework. Misstatements can occur due to fraud or error. |
| Required supplementary information | Information required by a designated accounting standards-setter to accompany an entity's basic financial statements and considered an essential part of financial reporting for placing the financial statements in an appropriate context. Authoritative guidelines for methods of measuring and presenting the information have been established. Examples include management's discussion and analysis and budgetary comparison statements as required by GASB Statement No. 34, *Basic Financial Statements—and Management's Discussion and Analysis—for State and Local Governments*. |

| | |
|---|---|
| Supplementary information | Information presented outside of the basic financial statements and required supplementary information that is not considered necessary for the fair presentation of the financial statements in accordance with the applicable financial reporting framework. Such information may be presented in a document containing the financial statements subjected to the compilation engagement or separate from the financial statements subjected to the compilation engagement. |
| Those charged with governance | The people or organizations responsible for overseeing the entity's strategic direction and its obligations related to accountability, including the financial reporting process. |

## Objectives

The objective of the accountant in a compilation engagement is to use accounting and financial reporting expertise to assist management in financial statement presentation and to report in accordance with AR-C 80. The accountant is not responsible for obtaining or providing assurance that the financial statements are free from needing material modifications in order to for them to be in accordance with the applicable financial reporting framework.

## Requirements

*Engagement Acceptance and General Principles*

1. In addition to AR-C 80, the accountant is required to comply with AR-C 60 (*General Principles for Engagements Performed in Accordance with Statements on Standards for Accounting and Review Services*).

2. The accountant must determine whether he or she is independent of the entity.

3. As a condition of engagement acceptance, the accountant should obtain management's agreement that it acknowledges and understands its responsibility to include the accountant's compilation report in any document containing financial statements indicating a compilation was performed unless a different understanding is reached and for the preparation and fair presentation of financial statements including all relevant disclosures in accordance with the applicable financial reporting framework. If financial statements are prepared in accordance with a special purpose framework, this includes:

    a. For financial statements containing similar items to financial statements prepared in accordance with U.S. GAAP, a description of the special purpose framework, a summary of significant accounting policies, how the framework differs from U.S. GAAP, and informative disclosures where appropriate;

    b. For financial statements prepared in accordance with a contractual-basis of accounting, a description of any significant interpretations of the contract on which the financial statements are prepared; and

c. Additional disclosures beyond those specifically required by the framework that may be necessary for the special purpose framework to achieve fair presentation.

4. If the accountant is not satisfied with any of the preconditions for accepting a compilation engagement, he or she should discuss the matter with management or those charged with governance. The engagement should not be accepted if changes are not made to satisfy the accountant about these matters.

## Agreement on Engagement Terms and Accountant Understanding of Financial Reporting Framework

5. The accountant should agree on engagement terms with management or those charged with governance as appropriate. An engagement letter or other suitable written agreement between the parties should document the agreed-upon terms of the engagement and should include:

   a. Engagement objectives,
   b. Management responsibilities,
   c. Accountant responsibilities,
   d. Limitations of the compilation engagement,
   e. Identification of the applicable financial reporting framework for financial statement preparation, and
   f. The expected form and content of the accountant's compilation report and a statement that circumstances could cause this form and content to differ.

6. The engagement letter or other suitable written agreement should be signed by the accountant or the accountant's firm and management or those charged with governance as appropriate.

7. The accountant should obtain an understanding of the applicable financial reporting framework and the significant accounting policies intended to be used in financial statement preparation.

## Compilation Procedures

8. The accountant should consider whether the financial statements appear appropriate in form and free from material misstatement given his or her understanding of the applicable financial reporting framework and significant accounting policies.

9. The accountant should bring to management's attention any incomplete, inaccurate, or otherwise unsatisfactory records, documents, explanations, or other information provided during the engagement and request additional or corrected information.

10. The accountant should propose appropriate revisions to management if during the engagement he or she becomes aware that the financial statements do not adequately refer to or describe the applicable financial reporting framework, revisions are required for the financial statements

to be in accordance with the applicable financial reporting framework, or the financial statements are otherwise misleading.

11. The accountant should withdraw from the engagement and inform management of his or her reasons if:

    a. Management fails to provide records, documents, explanations, significant judgments, or other information needed to complete the engagement; or

    b. Management does not make appropriate revisions proposed by the accountant or does not disclose such departures in the financial statements and the accountant determines not to disclose such departures in the compilation report.

> **PRACTICE POINTER:** Before withdrawing from the engagement the accountant should consult with legal counsel.

## Compilation Report

12. The accountant's compilation report should be in writing and

    a. State that management or the owners are responsible for the financial statements;

    b. Identify the financial statements subject to the compilation engagement;

    c. Identify the entity whose financial statements underwent the compilation engagement;

    d. Specify the date or period covered by the financial statements;

    e. State that the accountant performed the compilation engagement in accordance with SSARSs put forth by the ARSC of the AICPA;

    f. State that the accountant did not audit or review the financial statements and was not required to verify the accuracy or completeness of information provided by management so no opinion, conclusion, or assurance is provided on the financial statements;

    g. Include the signature of the accountant or the accountant's firm;

    h. Include the city and state where the accountant practices, which may be indicated on letterhead; and

    i. Include the date of the report, which should be the date the accountant completed the required procedures.

13. If financial statements are prepared in accordance with a special purpose framework, unless the entity omits substantially all disclosures, the compilation report should be modified if the accountant becomes aware that the financial statements do not include:

    a. A description of the special purpose framework;

    b. A summary of significant accounting policies;

c. A description about how the special purpose framework differs from U.S. GAAP, which does not require quantification of these differences; and

d. Informative disclosures similar to those required by U.S. GAAP when the financial statements contain similar items to financial statements prepared in accordance with U.S. GAAP.

14. If financial statements are prepared in accordance with a contractual-basis of accounting, the compilation report should be modified if the financial statements do not adequately describe any significant interpretations of the contract on which the financial statements are based. The accountant should consider whether the financial statements adequately describe any significant interpretations of the contract used as the basis to prepare the financial statements.

15. The compilation report on financial statements prepared in accordance with a special purpose framework should include reference to management's responsibility for determining that the financial reporting framework chosen is acceptable in those circumstances where management has a choice of frameworks to use.

16. The compilation report on financial statements prepared in accordance with a special purpose framework should include a separate paragraph indicating that the financial statements are prepared in accordance with the applicable special purpose framework, referring to the note to the financial statements describing the framework if applicable and stating that the special purpose framework is a basis of accounting other than U.S. GAAP. For special purpose frameworks prepared in accordance with a contractual basis of accounting, the separate paragraph should also state, as a result, that the financial statements may not be suitable for another purpose.

17. If the accountant is not independent with respect to the entity, the accountant's lack of independence should be indicated in a final paragraph of the compilation report.

18. If the accountant elects to describe the reasons his or her independence is impaired, then all such reasons should be included in the description.

19. A compilation report should not be issued on financial statements that omit substantially all disclosures required by the applicable financial reporting framework if the accountant believes those financial statements would be misleading to users.

20. A compilation report on financial statements that omit substantially all disclosures required by the applicable financial reporting framework should include a separate paragraph that includes:

　　a. A statement that management has elected to omit substantially all the disclosures and the statement of cash flows, if applicable, required or ordinarily included by the applicable financial reporting framework;

b. A statement that if omitted disclosures and the statement of cash flows, if applicable, were included in the financial statements, they might influence the user's conclusions about the entity's financial position, results of operations, and cash flows; and

c. A statement that, accordingly, the financial statements are not designed for those who are not informed about such matters.

21. When substantially all disclosures are presented, the compilation report should treat the omission of one or more notes as a departure from the applicable financial reporting framework and disclose the nature of the departure and its known effects in accordance with requirements 22 through 26.

22. The accountant should modify the compilation report to disclosure a departure if he or she becomes aware of a departure from the applicable financial reporting framework that will not be revised and is material to the financial statements.

23. Effects of a departure on the financial statements that have been determined by management or are known to the accountant from his or her procedures should be disclosed.

24. When the effects of a departure on the financial statements have not been determined by management or are not known to the accountant from his or her procedures, the accountant is not required to determine the effects but should state in the report that such determination has not been made by management.

25. If the accountant believes modifying the compilation report does not sufficiently address the deficiencies in the financial statements from a departure, he or she should withdraw from the engagement and provide no further services on those financial statements.

26. The compilation report should not be modified to include a statement that the financial statements are not in conformity with the applicable financial reporting framework.

## Reporting on Prospective Financial Information

27. The accountant's compilation report on prospective financial information should not exclude a summary of significant assumptions, given they are essential to a user's understanding of prospective financial information. The accountant's compilation report should not exclude an identification of the hypothetical assumptions or description of the limitations on the usefulness of the presentation.

28. An accountant's compilation report on prospective financial information should include statements that the forecasted or projected results may not be achieved and the accountant assumes no responsibility to update the report for events and circumstances occurring after the date of the report.

## Supplementary and Required Supplementary Information

29. If a compilation report is provided on financial statements that are accompanied by supplementary information, the accountant should indicate the degree of responsibility he or she is taking with respect to the supplementary information in a separate paragraph in the accountant's compilation report on the financial statements or a separate report on the supplementary information. This separate paragraph or separate report should state:
    a. The supplementary information is presented for purposes of additional analysis and is not a part of the basic financial statements,
    b. The supplementary information is the responsibility of management,
    c. The supplementary information was subjected to the compilation engagement, and
    d. The accountant has not audited or reviewed the supplementary information and does not express an opinion, conclusion, nor provide any form of assurance on such information.
30. If the accountant performed a compilation engagement on the financial statements and the supplementary information, the other-matter paragraph or separate report should state that the information was subject to the compilation engagement, however, the accountant has not audited or reviewed the supplementary information and does not express an opinion, a conclusion, nor provide any assurance on such information.
31. If the accountant performed a compilation engagement on the financial statements but not on the supplementary information, the accountant should include a separate paragraph in the compilation report or issue a separate report stating that the supplementary information, which is the responsibility of management, is presented for purposes of additional analysis but was not subject to the compilation engagement and the accountant does not express an opinion, conclusion, nor provide any assurance on such information.
32. If the accountant performed a compilation engagement on the financial statements and the required supplementary information, an other-matter paragraph should be included in the compilation report to explain that the required supplementary information is included and the accountant performed a compilation engagement on that information.
33. If the accountant performed a compilation engagement on the financial statements but not on the required supplementary information, an other-matter paragraph should be included in the compilation report that contains:
    a. A statement that [identify the applicable financial reporting framework] requires that the [identify the required supplementary information] be presented to supplement the basic financial statements;
    b. A statement that such information, although not a part of the basic financial statement, is required by [identify designated accounting standards-setter], who considers it to be an essential part of financial

reporting for placing the basic financial statements in an appropriate operational, economic or historical context;

c. A statement that the accountant did not perform a compilation, review, or audit on the required supplementary information and, accordingly, does not express an opinion, a conclusion, nor provide any assurance on the information;

d. If some or all of the information is omitted:

   (i) A statement that management has omitted [*description of the missing information*] that [*identify the applicable financial reporting framework*] require to be presented to supplement the basic financial statements, and

   (ii) A statement that such missing information, although not a part of the basic financial statements, is required by [*identify designated accounting standards-setter*], who considers it to be an essential part of financial reporting for placing the basic financial statements in an appropriate operations, economic, or historical context;

e. If the information's measurement or presentation departs materially from prescribed guidelines, a statement that material departures from prescribed guidelines exist [*describe the material departures from the applicable financial reporting framework*]; and

f. If the accountant has unresolved doubts about whether the information is measured or presented in accordance with prescribed guidelines, a statement that the accountant has doubts about whether material modifications should be made to the required supplementary information for it to be presented in accordance with guidelines established by [*identify designated accounting standards-setter*].

## Documentation

34. Documentation should be prepared in sufficient detail to provide a clear understanding of the work performed, which minimally includes the engagement letter or other suitable written agreement with management, a copy of the financial statements, and a copy of the accountant's report.

## Analysis and Application of Procedures

### Engagement Acceptance and General Principles

When the accountant is considering independence, he or she considers independence of mind and independence in appearance. Independence is important because it enhances the accountant's objectivity and ability to act with integrity and it demonstrates an obligation to be fair to both management of the entity as well as users of the financial statements. Authoritative guidance on independence is provided by the "Independence Rule" (ET Section 1.200.001) of the ACIPA Code of Professional Conduct or, in the absence of other guidance, by the "Conceptual Framework for Independence" interpretation (ET Section 1.210.010).

If the accountant determines he or she is not independent, the compilation report must be modified.

## Agreement on Engagement Terms and Accountant Understanding of Financial Reporting Framework

The accountant should agree on engagement terms with management or those charged with governance as appropriate. An engagement letter or other suitable written agreement should document the agreed-upon terms of the engagement. Documenting engagement terms helps both the accountant and management by reducing misunderstandings and decreasing the risk that management will expect the accountant to protect against certain risks or perform functions that are the responsibility of management. For example, even though the accountant may prepare all or part of the financial statements, it is management's responsibility to ensure the financial statements are fairly presented in accordance with the applicable financial reporting framework.

> **PLANNING AID REMINDER:** If the agreement on engagement terms is only with those charged with governance that does not relieve the accountant of the requirement in AR-C 60 to obtain management's agreement that it acknowledges and understands its responsibilities.

> **PLANNING AID REMINDER:** The AICPA Guide, Prospective Financial Information, provides guidance about prospective financial information, including preparation and presentation guidelines for financial forecasts and projections and it also provides suitable criteria for the preparation and presentation of prospective financial information.

Exhibit AR-C 80-1 provides an example engagement letter for financial statement compilations.

The accountant is required to obtain an understanding of the applicable financial reporting framework and the significant accounting policies intended to be used in financial statement preparation. This requirement does not prevent the accountant from accepting an engagement for an industry in which he or she has no previous experience, but it does mean that he or she is responsible for obtaining the required level of knowledge.

## Compilation Procedures

The accountant is not required to make inquiries or perform other procedures to verity, corroborate, or review information supplied by the entity. However, the accountant may become aware that information provided by management is incorrect, incomplete, or otherwise unsatisfactory through voluntary inquiries or procedures performed on information supplied by management, knowledge from prior engagements, or the financial statements themselves. The accountant should bring any such information to management's attention and request additional or corrected information.

The accountant should try to avoid the financial statements' being misleading. If the accountant becomes aware that the entity's ability to continue as a going concern is uncertain during a compilation engagement performed according to a financial reporting framework that presumes financial statements are prepared on a going concern basis, he or she may suggest additional disclosures be made to avoid the financial statements' being misleading. However, if substantially all disclosures required by the applicable financial reporting framework are omitted, disclosure of items such as uncertainty is not required.

If the accountant encounters circumstances that cause consideration of withdrawal from an engagement, he or she may wish to consult legal counsel.

## Compilation Report

Exhibit AR-C 80-2 provides an example of a standard compilation report. The accountant may request management include a reference on each page of the financial statements to the compilation report, such as "See Accountant's Report" or "See Accountant's Compilation Report," to reduce the possibility that users of the financial statements place an unintended level of reliance on the financial statements.

> **PLANNING AID REMINDER:** If the entity only includes disclosures about a few matters, those disclosures may be labeled "Selected Information—Substantially All Disclosures Required by [*identify the applicable financial reporting framework (for example*, Accounting Principles Generally Accepted in the United States of America)] Are Not Included."

If financial statements are prepared in accordance with a special purpose framework, a description of the framework may be included in financial statement titles, notes to the financial statements, or otherwise on the face of the financial statements. Examples of suitable financial statements titles include "Income Statement—Modified Cash Basis" if statements are prepared on a modified cash basis of accounting or "Balance Sheet—Tax Basis" if statements are prepared in accordance with the tax basis of accounting.

In describing how the special purpose framework differs from U.S. GAAP, the accountant is only required to include material differences between the two frameworks and does not need to describe or quantify any immaterial differences. The accountant is not required to include a summary of significant accounting policies and a description about how the special purpose framework differs from U.S. GAAP if the financial statements omit substantially all disclosures and the omission is not intended to mislead users of the financial statements.

The accountant is required to describe the purpose for which the financial statements are prepared when they are prepared in accordance with a regulatory or contractual basis of accounting in order to avoid misunderstandings if the financial statements are used for unintended purposes.

If the accountant is not independent, he or she may disclose a description about the reasons for his or her lack of independence, but if these reasons are disclosed, then all reasons should be included in the description. AR-C 80-3 provides an example of such a report. The following are examples of disclosures for a lack of independence:

- A member of the engagement team had a direct financial interest in the company.
- An immediate family member of a member of the engagement team was employed by the company.
- Certain accounting services performed impaired independence.

**PLANNING AID REMINDER:** AR-C 80 states that the accountant's report should be modified when the accountant is not independent and issues a compilation report for an entity's financial statements. AICPA Technical Practice Aid TIS 9150.30 addresses the situation where the accountant was not independent for the prior year but the issue that impaired independence in the prior year has been subsequently cured. In that situation, the accountant is not required to disclose that his or her independence impairment was subsequently cured. However, the accountant may elect to make such a disclosure as follows: "As of and for the year ended December 31, 20XX, I was not independent with respect to ABC Company. I am currently independent with respect to ABC Company."

If financial statements contain known departures from the applicable financial reporting framework, the accountant should not state that the financial statements are not in conformity with the applicable financial reporting framework in the compilation report, because that would imply an adverse opinion was being expressed on the financial statements and an opinion can only be expressed in an audit engagement. An example compilation report when financial statements contain known departures from the applicable financial reporting framework is presented in Exhibit AR-C 80-4.

## Practitioner's Aids

Exhibit AR-C 80-1 is an example of a standard engagement letter for a compilation.

*EXHIBIT AR-C 80-1—COMPILATION ENGAGEMENT LETTER*

To the appropriate representative of management of ABC Company:

You have requested that we prepare the financial statements of ABC Company, which comprise the balance sheet as of December 31, 20XX, and the related statements of income, changes in stockholders' equity, and cash flows for the year then ended, and the related notes to the financial statements, and perform a compilation engagement with respect to those financial statements. [*If the financial statements omit the statement of cash flows and the related notes, the previous sentence may be revised to read:* You have requested that we prepare the financial statements of ABC Company, which comprise the balance sheet as of December 31, 20XX, and the related statements of income and changes in stockholders' equity, and perform a compilation engagement with respect to those financial statements. *The following sentence may then be added:* These financial statements will not include a statement of cash flows and related notes to the financial statements.] We are pleased to confirm our acceptance and our understanding of this engagement by means of this letter.

**Our Responsibilities**

The objective of our engagement is to

   a. Prepare financial statements in accordance with accounting principles generally accepted in the United States of America based on information provided by you and

   b. Apply accounting and financial reporting expertise to assist you in the presentation of financial statements without undertaking to obtain or provide any assurance that there are no material modifications that should be made to the financial statements in order for them to be in accordance with accounting principles generally accepted in the United States of America.

We will conduct our compilation engagement in accordance with Statements on Standards for Accounting and Review Services (SSARSs) promulgated by the Accounting and Review Services Committee of the AICPA and comply with the AICPA's Code of Professional Conduct, including the ethical principles of integrity, objectivity, professional competence, and due care.

We are not required to, and will not, verify the accuracy or completeness of the information you will provide to us for the engagement or otherwise gather evidence for the purpose of expressing an opinion or a conclusion. Accordingly, we will not express an opinion or a conclusion nor provide any assurance on the financial statements.

Our engagement cannot be relied upon to identify or disclose any financial statements misstatements, including those caused by fraud or error, or to identify or disclose any wrongdoing within the entity or noncompliance with laws or regulations.

**Your Responsibilities**

The engagement to be performed is conducted on the basis that you acknowledge and understand that our role is to prepare financial statements in accordance with accounting principles generally accepted in the United States of America and assist you in the presentation of the financial statements in accordance with accounting principles generally accepted in the United States of America. You have the following overall responsibilities that are fundamental to our undertaking the engagement in accordance with SSARSs:

   a. The preparation and fair presentation of financial statements in accordance with accounting principles generally accepted in the United States of America

   b. The design, implementation, and maintenance of internal control relevant to the preparation and fair presentation of the financial statements

   c. The prevention and detection of fraud

   d. To ensure that the entity complies with the laws and regulations applicable to its activities

   e. To make all financial records and related information available to us

   f. The accuracy and completeness of the records, documents, explanations, and other information, including significant judgments, you provide to us for the engagement

You are also responsible for all management decisions and responsibilities and for designating an individual with suitable skills, knowledge, and experience to oversee our preparation of your financial statements. You are responsible for evaluating the adequacy and results of the services performed and accepting responsibility for such services.

**Our Report**

As part of our engagement, we will issue a report that will state that we did not audit or review the financial statements and that, accordingly, we do not express an opinion, a conclusion, nor provide any assurance on them. [*If the accountant's independence is impaired, the following sentence may be added:* We will disclose that we are not independent in our report.]

**Other Relevant Information**

Our fees for these services . . .

[*The accountant may include language, such as the following, regarding limitation of or other arrangements regarding the liability of the accountant or the entity, such as indemnification to the accountant for liability arising from knowing misrepresentations to the accountant by management (regulators may restrict or prohibit such liability limitation arrangements):*

> You agree to hold us harmless and to release, indemnify, and defend us from any liability or costs, including attorney's fees, resulting from management's knowing misrepresentations to us.]

Please sign and return the attached copy of this letter to indicate your acknowledgement of, and agreement with, the arrangements for our engagement to prepare the financial statements described herein and to perform a compilation engagement with respect to those same financial statements, and our respective responsibilities.

Sincerely yours,

[*Signature of accountant or accountant's firm*]

Acknowledged and agreed on behalf of ABC Company by:

[*Signed*]

[*Name and Title*]

[*Date*]

---

Exhibit AR-C 80-2 is an example of a compilation report on financial statements prepared in accordance with accounting principles generally accepted in the United States of America.

*EXHIBIT AR-C 80-2—STANDARD ACCOUNTANT'S COMPILATION REPORT*

**Accountant's Compilation Report**

[*Appropriate Salutation*]

Management is responsible for the accompanying financial statements of ABC Company, which comprise the balance sheets as of December 31, 20X5 and 20X4 and the related statements of income, changes in stockholders' equity, and cash flows for the years then ended, and the related notes to the financial statements in accordance with accounting principles generally accepted in the United States of America. I (We) have performed compilation engagements in accordance with Statements on Standards for Accounting and Review Services promulgated by the Accounting and Review Services Committee of the AICPA. I (We) did not audit or review the financial statements nor was (were) I (we) required to perform any procedures to verify the accuracy or completeness of the information provided by management. Accordingly, I (we) do not express an opinion, a conclusion, nor provide any form of assurance on these financial statements.

[*Signature of accounting firm or accountant, as appropriate*]

[*Accountant's city and state*]

[*Date*]

---

Exhibit AR-C 80-3 is an example of a compilation report on financial statements prepared in accordance with accounting principles generally accepted in the United States of America when the accountant's independence has been impaired and the accountant decides not to disclose the reason for the independence impairment.

*EXHIBIT AR-C 80-3—COMPILATION REPORT WHEN INDEPENDENCE IS IMPAIRED*

**Accountant's Compilation Report**

[*Appropriate Salutation*]

Management is responsible for the accompanying financial statements of ABC Company, which comprise the balance sheets as of December 31, 20X5 and 20X4 and the related statements of income, changes in stockholders' equity, and cash flows for the years then ended, and the related notes to the financial statements in accordance with accounting principles generally accepted in the United States of America. I (We) have performed compilation engagements in accordance with Statements on Standards for Accounting and Review Services promulgated by the Accounting and Review Services Committee of the AICPA. I (We) did not audit or review the financial statements nor was (were) I (we) required to perform any procedures to verify the accuracy or completeness of the information provided by management. Accordingly, I (we) do not express an opinion, a conclusion, nor provide any form of assurance on these financial statements.

I am (we are) not independent with respect to ABC Company.

[*Signature of accounting firm or accountant, as appropriate*]

[*Accountant's city and state*]

[*Date*]

Exhibit AR-C 80-4 is an example of a compilation report on financial statements disclosing a departure from accounting principles generally accepted in the United States of America.

## EXHIBIT AR-C 80-4—COMPILATION REPORT DISCLOSING A GAAP DEPARTURE

### Accountant's Compilation Report

[*Appropriate Salutation*]

Management is responsible for the accompanying financial statements of ABC Company, which comprise the balance sheets as of December 31, 20X5 and 20X4 and the related statements of income, changes in stockholders' equity, and cash flows for the years then ended, and the related notes to the financial statements in accordance with accounting principles generally accepted in the United States of America. I (We) have performed compilation engagements in accordance with Statements on Standards for Accounting and Review Services promulgated by the Accounting and Review Services Committee of the AICPA. I (We) did not audit or review the financial statements nor was (were) I (we) required to perform any procedures to verify the accuracy or completeness of the information provided by management. Accordingly, I (we) do not express an opinion, a conclusion, nor provide any form of assurance on these financial statements.

Accounting principles generally accepted in the United States of America require that land be stated at cost. Management has informed me (us) that ABC Company has stated its land at appraised value and that if accounting principles generally accepted in the United States of America had been followed, the land account and stockholders' equity would have been decreased by $500,000.

[*Signature of accounting firm or accountant, as appropriate*]

[*Accountant's city and state*]

[*Date*]

# SECTION 90

# REVIEW OF FINANCIAL STATEMENTS

## Authoritative Pronouncements

SSARS-21—Statements on Standards for Accounting and Review Services: Clarification and Recodification

SSARS-23—Omnibus Statement on Standards for Accounting and Review Services—2016

SSARS-24—Omnibus Statement on Standards for Accounting and Review Services—2018

SSARS-25—Materiality in a Review of Financial Statements and Adverse Conclusions

---

**IMPORTANT NOTICE FOR 2022:** In May 2018, the Accounting and Review Services Committee (ARSC) issued SSARS-24 (*Omnibus Statement on Standards for Accounting and Review Services—2018*) to provide requirements and guidance when an accountant is engaged to perform a compilation or review of financial statements that have been prepared in accordance with a financial reporting framework generally accepted in another country or the accountant is engaged to perform a compilation or review in accordance with SSARS and another set of compilation or review standards. SSARS-24 created a new AR-C 100 section titled "Special Considerations—International Reporting Issues." The issuance of SSARS-24 includes changes to AR-C 90 to primarily clarify responsibilities related to the evaluation of the going concern assumption, including specific written representation from management regarding disclosures relevant to that assumption, among other matters. The effective date of SSARS-24 was for compilations and reviews of financial statements for periods ending on or after June 15, 2019. These conforming changes have been incorporated in this *GAAS Guide*.

---

**IMPORTANT NOTICE FOR 2022:** In February 2020, the Accounting and Review Services Committee (ARSC) issued SSARS-25 (*Materiality in a Review of Financial Statements and Adverse Conclusions*) to further converge SSARS with International Standards on Review Engagements (ISREs) and to further align it with AICPA Auditing Standards. The ARSC determined that further convergence with International Standard on Review Engagements (ISRE) 2400 (Revised) (*Engagements to Review Historical Financial Statements*) was appropriate and in the public interest and that it is important for the SSARSs literature to be closely converged with ISRE 2400 (Revised) to facilitate the accountant's ability to perform and report on engagements in accordance with both sets of standards. Additionally, although there are significant differences between an audit engagement and an engagement performed in accordance with SSARSs, there are certain concepts related to the financial statements that are consistent regardless of the level of service performed on those financial statements. SSARS-25 further aligns the SSARS standards with auditing standards. SSARS-25 moves definitions for *applicable financial reporting framework, designated accounting standard setter* and *special purpose framework* from AR-C 90 to AR-C 60 and it adds a number of new defined terms to AR-C 90. Furthermore, SAS No. 25 includes other revisions to AR-C 90 to more closely converge with ISRE 2400 (Revised). SSARS-25 is effective for engagements performed in accordance with SSARS for periods ending on or after December 15, 2021. Early implementation is permitted.

## Overview

Accountants are required to comply with the provisions of AR-C 90 when engaged to review financial statements. A review of financial statements involves the accountant expressing a conclusion regarding the entity's financial statements in accordance with a financial reporting framework, with that conclusion based on limited assurance. The accountant's basis for that conclusion is based on the performance of primarily analytical procedures and inquiries to obtain sufficient appropriate review evidence. If the accountant becomes aware of a matter that leads the accountant to believe the financial statements are materially misstated, the accountant designs and performs additional procedures to reach a conclusion.

The accountant may review the basic financial statements or only one financial statement as long as there is no restriction on the accountant's scope of inquiry and analytical procedures. The guidance in AR-C 90 may also be applied as necessary to engagements to review other historical financial information, such as selected elements or schedules of financial statements, supplementary information, required supplementary information, or financial information included in a tax return.

**PLANNING AID REMINDER:** SSARS-23 clarifies that AR-C 90 does not apply to engagements to review pro forma financial information. Reviews of pro forma financial information are to be performed in accordance with Statements on Standards for Attestation Engagements (SSAEs).

If the accountant is engaged to review interim financial information and the following three conditions exist, the applicable guidance is AU-C 930 (*Interim Financial Information*), not AR-C 90:

1. The entity's latest annual financial statements have been audited by the accountant or a predecessor.
2. The accountant has been engaged to audit the entity's current year financial statements or audited the prior financial statements and, in situations when it is expected that the current year financial statements will be audited, the appointment of another accountant to the audit the current year financial statements is not effective prior to the beginning of the period covered by the review.

3. The entity prepares its interim financial information in accordance with the same financial reporting framework used to prepare its annual financial statements.

## Definitions

| | |
|---|---|
| Analytical procedures | Analysis of plausible relationships among financial and nonfinancial data to evaluate financial information. May encompass investigation of identified fluctuations or relationships that are inconsistent or differ significantly from expected values. |
| Comparative financial statements | A complete set of financial statements for one or more prior periods included for comparison with current-period financial statements. |
| Emphasis-of-matter paragraph | A paragraph in the accountant's review report that is either required by SSARSs or is included to refer to a matter appropriately presented or disclosed in the financial statements that in the accountant's professional judgment is fundamental to users' understanding of the financial statements. |
| Error | Mistakes in the financial statements, including arithmetic or clerical mistakes, or mistakes in the application of accounting principles, including inadequate disclosure. |
| Experienced accountant | An individual with practical review experience and an understanding of review processes, SSARSs and applicable legal and regulatory requirements, the entity's business environment, and review and financial reporting issues relevant to the industry. |
| Financial reporting framework | A set of criteria used to determine measurement, recognition, presentation, and disclosure of all material items appearing in the financial statements. Examples include accounting principles generally accepted in the United States of America (U.S. GAAP), International Financial Reporting Standards promulgated by the International Accounting Standards Board, or a special purpose framework. |
| Financial statements | A structured representation of historical financial information, including related notes. Financial statements typically refer to a complete set of financial statements as determined by the applicable financial reporting framework but may also refer to a single financial statement. |
| Fraud | An intentional act resulting in a misstatement in the financial statements. |
| Generally accepted accounting principles (GAAP) | GAAP means generally accepted accounting principles promulgated by bodies designated by the Council of the AICPA pursuant to the "Compliance with Standards Rule" and the "Accounting Principles Rule" of the AICPA Code of Professional Conduct. |
| Historical financial information | Financial information about an entity that is primarily derived from the entity's accounting system about economic events occurring in past time periods or about economic conditions or circumstances at past points of time. |
| Inquiry | Inquiry consists of seeking information of knowledgeable persons within or outside the entity. |

| | |
|---|---|
| Limited assurance | A level of assurance that is less than the reasonable assurance obtained in an audit engagement but is at an acceptable level as the basis for the conclusion expressed in the accountant's review report. |
| Management | Those with executive responsibility for the entity's operations. |
| Misstatement | A difference between the amount, classification, presentation, or disclosure of a reported financial item and that required for fair presentation in accordance with the applicable financial reporting framework. |
| Modified conclusion | A qualified conclusion or an adverse conclusion. |
| Noncompliance | Acts of intentional or unintentional omission or commission by the entity that are contrary to prevailing laws or regulations. |
| Other-matter paragraph | A paragraph in the accountant's review report that is either required by SSARSs or is included to refer to a matter other than those presented or disclosed in the financial statements that in the accountant's professional judgment is relevant to the users' understanding of the review, the accountant's responsibilities, or the review report. |
| Pervasive | A term used, in the context of misstatements, to describe the effects on the financial statements of misstatements. Pervasive effects on the financial statements are those that, in the accountant's judgment are not confined to specific elements, accounts, or items of the financial statements; represent or could represent a substantial portion of the financial statements; or, in regard to disclosures, are fundamental to users' understanding of the financial statements. |
| Professional skepticism | An attitude that includes a questioning mind, being alert to conditions that may indicate a possible misstatement due to fraud or error, and a critical assessment of review evidence. |
| Reasonable period of time | The period of time required by the applicable financial reporting framework or, if no such requirement exists, within one year after the date that the financial statements are issued (or within one year after the date that the financial statements are available to be issued, when applicable). |
| Report release date | The date the accountant grants the entity permission to use the accountant's review report. |
| Required supplementary information | Information required by a designated accounting standards-setter to accompany an entity's basic financial statements Authoritative guidelines for methods of measuring and presenting the information have been established. |
| Review documentation | The record of review procedures performed, relevant review evidence obtained, and conclusions reached by the accountant. Also called working papers or workpapers. |
| Review evidence | Information used by the accountant to provide a reasonable basis for obtaining limited assurance. Review evidence includes both information contained in the accounting records underlying the financial statements and other information, which primarily consists of the results of analytical procedures and inquiries. Sufficiency of review evidence is the measure of the quality of review evidence, that is, relevance and reliability in providing support for the conclusions on which the accountant's review report is based. |
| Specified parties | The intended users of the accountant's review report. |

| | |
|---|---|
| Subsequent events | Events occurring between the date of the financial statements and the date of the accountant's review report. |
| Subsequently discovered facts | Facts that may have caused the accountant to revise the accountant's review report had they been known prior to the date of the report. |
| Supplementary information | Information presented outside the basic financial statements and required supplementary information, and that is not considered necessary for the fair presentation of the financial statements in accordance with the applicable financial reporting framework. Such information may be presented in a document containing the reviewed financial statements or separate from the reviewed financial statements. |
| Those charged with governance | The people or organizations responsible for overseeing the entity's strategic direction and its obligations related to accountability, including the financial reporting process. |
| Updated report | A report issued by a continuing accountant that considers information the accountant becomes aware of during a current engagement and re-expresses the accountant's previous conclusions or expresses different conclusions on prior period financial statements reviewed as of the date of the current review report. |
| Written representations | A written statement by management provided to the accountant to confirm certain matters or support other review evidence. |

## Objective

The objective of a review engagement is to obtain limited assurance, primarily through inquiry and analytical procedures, that there are no material modifications that should be made to the financial statements in order for them to be in accordance with the applicable financial reporting framework.

When the accountant considers materiality, he or she considers many factors:

- Any discussion of materiality in the applicable financial reporting framework.
- Misstatements, including omissions, are generally considered material if they could, either individually or in the aggregate, reasonably be expected to influence the economic decisions of users.
- Judgments about materiality are affected by the circumstances as well as the size and nature of a misstatement.
- Judgments about materiality are based on the common financial information needs of users, not on the possible effects of misstatements on individual users.

It is reasonable for the accountant to assume that financial statement users have a reasonable knowledge of business and accounting and are willing to study financial statements diligently; understand that financial statements are prepared, presented, and reviewed to levels of materiality; recognize the uncertainties inherent in measuring amounts based on estimates, judgments, and the consideration of future events; and make reasonable economic decisions on the basis of financial statements.

The accountant uses professional judgment in determining materiality and his or her judgment about what is material to the financial statements as a whole is the same regardless of the level of assurance being provided. There may be situations when the accountant's determination of materiality needs to be revised during the engagement. This may occur due to a change in circumstances that occurred during the engagement, the receipt of new information, or a change in the accountant's understanding of the entity and its environment as a result of performing review procedures.

A review provides less assurance than an audit of financial statements because it does not require many of the significant procedures required in an audit. A review does not contemplate obtaining an understanding of the entity's internal control, assessing fraud risks, tests of accounting records by obtaining sufficient appropriate evidence, or other procedures ordinarily performed in an audit.

## Requirements

*Engagement Acceptance and General Principles*

1. In addition to AR-C 90, the accountant is required to comply with AR-C 60 (*General Principles for Engagements Performed in Accordance with Statements on Standards for Accounting and Review Services*).

2. The accountant must be independent of the entity when performing a review engagement. If the accountant determines independence is impaired during the course of the engagement, he or she should withdraw from the engagement.

3. A review engagement should not be accepted if management or those charged with governance limit the accountant's scope of work to the extent that the accountant believes he or she will be unable to perform review procedures to provide an adequate basis for issuing a report.

4. As a condition of engagement acceptance, the accountant should obtain management's agreement that it acknowledges and understands its responsibilities to provide the accountant with a letter at the end of the engagement confirming certain representations made; include the accountant's review report in any document containing financial statements indicating a review was performed unless a different understanding is reached; and for the preparation and fair presentation of financial statements, including all relevant disclosures in accordance with the applicable financial reporting framework. If financial statements are prepared in accordance with a special purpose framework, this includes:

    a. Describing the special purpose framework, including providing a summary of significant accounting policies, how the framework differs from U.S. GAAP, and providing informative disclosures when the special purpose financial statements contain similar items to those prepared in accordance with U.S. GAAP;

b. For financial statements prepared in accordance with a contractual-basis of accounting, a description of any significant interpretations of the contract on which the financial statements are prepared; and

c. Additional disclosures beyond those specifically required by the framework that may be necessary for the special purpose framework to achieve fair presentation.

5. If the accountant is not satisfied with any of the preconditions for accepting a review engagement, he or she should discuss the matter with management or those charged with governance. The engagement should not be accepted if changes are not made to satisfy the accountant about these matters.

6. The planning and performance of the review by the accountant should be done with professional skepticism.

7. If after the engagement is accepted, the accountant discovers that some of the preconditions to the engagement are not done satisfactorily, the accountant should discuss the matter with management or those charged with governance to determine whether the matter can be resolved and whether it is appropriate to continue with the engagement.

*Agreement on Engagement Terms*

8. The accountant should agree on engagement terms with management or those charged with governance as appropriate prior to beginning the engagement. An engagement letter or other suitable written agreement between the parties should document the agreed-upon terms of the engagement and should include:

    a. Engagement objectives,

    b. Management responsibilities,

    c. Accountant responsibilities,

    d. Limitations of a review engagement, including a statement about a review engagement being substantially less in scope than an audit and, therefore, the accountant will not be expressing an opinion on the financial statements,

    e. Identification of the applicable financial reporting framework for financial statement preparation, and

    f. The expected form and content of the accountant's review report and a statement that circumstances could cause this form and content to differ.

9. The engagement letter or other suitable written agreement should be signed by the accountant or the accountant's firm and management or those charged with governance as appropriate.

10. The accountant should determine what constitutes materiality for the financial statements as a whole in order to design the review procedures

and evaluate the results obtained from those procedures. The accountant should revise the materiality when the accountant becomes aware of information that would have led the accountant to initially determine a different materiality amount.

## Communication with Management and Those Charged with Governance

11. The accountant should timely communicate to management and those charged with governance all matters during a review engagement that are, in the accountant's professional judgment, significant.

## Understanding of the Industry and Knowledge of the Entity

12. The accountant should possess or obtain an understanding of the entity's industry and accounting principles and practices generally used in the industry.

13. The accountant should obtain knowledge about the entity's business and the accounting principles and practices it uses sufficient to identify policies and procedures that are unusual given the entity's industry, and identify areas in the financial statements with increased risk for material misstatement and to design procedures to address those areas.

## Review Procedures

14. The accountant should design and perform inquiries, analytical procedures, and other procedures as appropriate to obtain sufficient appropriate review evidence as a basis for reporting whether he or she is aware of any material modifications that should be made to the financial statements in order for them to be in accordance with the applicable financial reporting framework based on the accountant's:

    a. Understanding of the industry;

    b. Knowledge of the entity; and

    c. Awareness of the risk that the accountant may unknowingly issue an inappropriate review report.

15. Inquiries and analytical procedures should be designed and performed to address all material items in the financial statements, including disclosures, and to address areas the accountant believes are at increased risk for material misstatements.

16. The accountant should apply analytical procedures to the financial statements to identify and provide a basis for inquiry about unusual items and relationships that may indicate a material misstatement. Analytical procedures performed should include:

    a. Comparing financial statements with prior period comparable information, considering any known changes in the entity's business and specific transactions;

    b. Considering plausible relationships among financial and relevant nonfinancial information;

§90 • Review Engagements   11,049

  c. Comparing expectations developed by the accountant using his or her understanding of the entity and its industry to recorded amounts or ratios developed from recorded amounts; and

  d. Comparing applicable disaggregated revenue data.

17. To design and perform analytical procedures, the accountant should:

  a. Determine the suitability of particular analytical procedures;

  b. Consider the reliability of data the accountant is using to develop expectations of recorded amounts or ratios, including their source, comparability, nature, and relevance;

  c. Develop an expectation of recorded amounts or ratios and evaluate whether that expectation is sufficiently precise to provide limited assurance that a misstatement will be identified that could individually or in the aggregate cause material misstatement of the financial statements; and

  d. Determine the difference between recorded amounts and expected values that is acceptable without further investigation and compare the recorded amounts or ratios developed from recorded amounts with the expected values.

18. If analytical procedures identify inconsistent relationships or fluctuations that differ from expected values by a significant amount, the accountant should investigate such differences by making inquiries of management and performing other review procedures as necessary.

19. The accountant should make inquiries of management with responsibility for financial and accounting matters concerning the financial statements about:

  a. Whether the financial statements are prepared and presented fairly in accordance with the applicable financial reporting framework, including how management determined that significant accounting estimates are reasonable in the circumstances;

  b. Related parties and related-party transactions, including their purpose;

  c. Unusual or complex transactions, events, or matters that may affect the financial statements, such as significant changes in the entity's business, significant changes to terms of contracts, and implications of transactions with related parties;

  d. Significant transactions occurring or recognized during the period, especially those in the last few days of the period;

  e. Whether uncorrected misstatements identified during the previous review have been corrected and if so, in what period and for what amount adjusting entries were made;

  f. Matters about which questions arose during the course of applying review procedures;

g. Events subsequent to the date of the financial statements that could have a material effect on the fair presentation of the financial statements;

h. Existence of any actual, suspected, or alleged fraud or noncompliance with provisions of laws and regulations that may have a direct effect on material amounts and disclosures in the financial statements;

i. Basis for management's assessment of the entity's ability to continue as a going concern, and whether there are events or conditions that raise substantial doubt about the entity's ability to continue as a going concern;

j. Material commitments, contractual obligations, or contingencies that have affected or may affect the financial statements;

k. Applicable communications from regulatory agencies;

l. Any litigation, claims, and assessments existing at the date of the balance sheet being reported on, and through the date of management's response to the accountant's inquiry;

m. Actions taken at meetings of stockholders, the board of directors and its committees, or other meetings that may affect the financial statements; and

n. Any other matters the accountant may consider necessary.

20. The accountant should remain alert for indications of related-party relationships or transactions that management has not previously identified or disclosed and make inquiries about those to understand their nature and impact on the financial statements.

21. Communicate any identified or suspected fraud to members of senior management at a level above those involved and communicate any noncompliance with laws or regulations to management. When noncompliance involves senior management, the accountant should communicate that to those charged with governance. The accountant should obtain legal advice if those charged with governance do not provide sufficient information to help the accountant determine the financial statement impact.

22. When the applicable financial reporting framework requires management to evaluate the entity's ability to continue as a going concern for a reasonable period of time, the accountant should perform review procedures about management's evaluation and their plans to mitigate any concerns that raise substantial doubt about the entity's ability to continue as a going concern and the adequacy of related financial statement disclosures.

23. The accountant should consider the reasonableness and consistency of management's responses to inquiries in the context of other review procedures performed and knowledge of the entity. However, there is no requirement to corroborate management's responses with other evidence.

24. The accountant may use the work of another accountant or expert in the course of performing the review. In those circumstances, the accountant should take the steps to be satisfied that the work performed is adequate for the accountant's purposes.

25. The accountant should read the financial statements and consider whether he or she is aware of any information that would indicate the financial statements do not conform to the applicable financial reporting framework.

26. The accountant should obtain and read any reports issued by other accountants on financial statements of significant components, such as subsidiaries and investees.

27. Evidence should be obtained that the financial statements agree or reconcile with the accounting records.

28. If the accountant becomes aware that the financial statements may be materially misstated, the accountant should design and perform additional procedures to conclude whether or not the matter is likely to cause a material misstatement.

29. If the accountant becomes aware while performing review procedures that information is incorrect, incomplete, or otherwise unsatisfactory, he or she should request that management consider and communicate to the accountant the effect of those matters on the financial statements; and consider management's communication and whether such effects indicate the financial statements may be materially misstated.

30. The accountant should evaluate whether sufficient appropriate review evidence has been obtained from the procedures performed. If not, he or she should perform other procedures sufficient to be able to form a conclusion on the financial statements. If the accountant is not able to obtain sufficient appropriate review evidence to form a conclusion, the accountant should withdraw from the engagement.

31. When the accountant becomes aware of subsequent events that require adjustment of, or disclosure in the financial statements, the accountant should request management to consider whether such event is appropriately reflected in the financial statements.

32. The accountant is not required to perform any review procedures after the date of the review report. However, the accountant may become aware of subsequently discovered facts.

    a. If the accountant becomes aware of those facts before the report release date, the accountant should discuss the matter with management and, when appropriate, those charged with governance, and determine if the financial statements require revision, and perform review procedures if the financial statements are revised. If management does not revise the financial statements when the accountant believes they should be revised, the accountant should modify the review report or withdraw from the engagement.

b. If the accountant becomes aware of those facts after the report release date, the accountant should discuss the matter with management and, when appropriate, those charged with governance, and determine how management intends to address the revision and inform anyone in receipt of those financial statements that they are not to be used, if the financial statements require revision, and perform review procedures if the financial statements are revised. If management does not revise the financial statements when the accountant believes they should be revised, the accountant should notify management that the financial statements should not be made available to third parties. If the financial statements have been released, the accountant should determine whether management has taken the necessary steps to inform those in receipt of the financial statements that they should not be used.

*Written Representations*

33. Written representations are review evidence, as they are necessary information required by the accountant in a review of financial statements.
34. Written representations should be requested from members of management with appropriate responsibilities for and knowledge of matters concerning the financial statements.
35. The accountant should request that management provide written representations for all financial statements presented and all periods covered by the review, and that they be dated as of the date of the review report, stating that:
    a. Management has fulfilled its responsibility for preparing and fairly presenting the financial statements in accordance with the applicable financial reporting framework.
    b. Management acknowledges its responsibility for designing, implementing, and maintaining internal control relevant to the preparation and fair presentation of the financial statements, including its responsibility to prevent and detect fraud.
    c. All transactions have been recorded and are reflected in the financial statements.
    d. Management has provided all relevant information and access.
    e. Management has responded fully and truthfully to all of the accountant's inquiries.
    f. Management has disclosed to the accountant their identification of the entity's related parties and all related-party relationships and transactions of which management is aware and that they have appropriately accounted for and disclosed those relationships and transactions.
    g. Management has disclosed to the accountant any significant facts related to their knowledge of fraud or suspected fraud affecting the entity involving management, employees with significant roles in internal control, or others when fraud could have a material effect on the financial statements.

h. Management has disclosed to the accountant knowledge of any allegations of fraud or suspected fraud affecting the entity's financial statements communicated by employees, former employees, regulators, or others.

i. Management has disclosed to the accountant all known instances of noncompliance or suspected noncompliance with laws and regulations whose effects should be considered when preparing financial statements.

j. Management has disclosed all information about the use of the going concern assumption.

k. Management has properly accounted for all events occurring subsequent to the date of the financial statements.

l. Management had disclosed to the accountant whether it believes uncorrected misstatements are immaterial, individually and in the aggregate, to the financial statements as a whole. A summary of such items should be included in or attached to the written representation.

m. Management has disclosed to the accountant all known actual or possible litigation and claims whose effects should be considered when preparing the financial statements and any such items have been appropriately accounted for and disclosed in accordance with the applicable financial reporting framework.

n. Management has disclosed to the accountant whether it believes the significant assumptions it used to make accounting estimates are reasonable.

36. If the accountant determines additional written representations are necessary to support other review evidence relevant to the financial statements, he or she should request such written representations.

37. Written representations should be in the form of a representation letter addressed to the accountant.

38. If management does not provide the required written representations or the accountant doubts management integrity to the extent that the written representations cannot be deemed reliable, the accountant should discuss the matter with management and those charged with governance as appropriate. If the required representations are not provided or the accountant continues to doubt management's integrity, the accountant should withdraw from the engagement.

39. The accountant should evaluate whether the financial statements adequately refer to the applicable financial reporting framework and consider whether the terminology used in the financial statements and related disclosures is appropriate.

40. The accountant should consider the impact on the financial statements of uncorrected misstatements during the review and in the prior year's review and the accountant should consider the overall presentation, structure, and content of the financial statements.

## Arriving at a Conclusion on the Financial Statements

41. When the accountant has obtained limited assurance to conclude that nothing came to the accountant's attention that the financial statements are materially misstated, the accountant should express an unmodified conclusion in the accountant's review report.

42. When the accountant determines that, based on the procedures performed and review evidence obtained, the financial statements are materially misstated, the accountant should express a modified conclusion. In those situations, the accountant's report should include the heading "Qualified Conclusion" or "Adverse Conclusion" for the conclusion paragraph and provide a description of the matter giving rise to the modification.

43. A qualified conclusion is expressed when the accountant concludes that the effects of the matter are material but not pervasive to the financial statements.

44. An adverse conclusion is provided when the accountant concludes the effects of the matter are material and pervasive to the financial statements.

## Reporting on the Financial Statements

45. The accountant's review report should be in writing.

46. The written report should include:

    a. A title that includes the word *independent* (i.e., independent accountant).

    b. An appropriate addressee.

    c. An introductory paragraph:

        (i) Identifying the entity whose financial statements have been reviewed,

        (ii) Stating that the financial statements identified were reviewed,

        (iii) Identifying the financial statements,

        (iv) Specifying the date or period covered by each financial statement,

        (v) Stating that a review primarily involves applying analytical procedures to management's financial data and making inquiries of management, and

        (vi) Stating that a review is substantially less in scope than an audit, and that the accountant does not express an opinion regarding the financial statements as a whole.

    d. A section with the heading "Management's Responsibility for the Financial Statements" that explains management is responsible for the preparation and fair presentation of the financial statements, including responsibility for the design, implementation, and maintenance of internal control to present financial statements free of material misstatement whether due to error or fraud.

e. A section with the heading "Accountant's Responsibility" that states:

   (i) The accountant's responsibility is to conduct the review engagement in accordance with SSARSs promulgated by the Accounting and Review Services Committee of the AICPA. The report should state that those standards require that the accountant perform procedures to obtain limited assurance as to whether the accountant is aware of any material modifications that should be made to the financial statements for them to be in accordance with the applicable financial reporting framework.

   (ii) The accountant believes that results of the review procedures performed by the accountant provide a basis for the accountant's conclusion.

   (iii) The accountant is required to be independent of the entity and to meet other ethical responsibilities.

f. A concluding section with an appropriate heading that states the accountant's conclusion on the financial statements and that identifies the country of origin for the financial reporting framework.

g. When the conclusion is modified, the modified conclusion is provided in a paragraph under the appropriate heading along with a paragraph describing the matters giving rise to the modification.

h. The signature of the accountant or the accountant's firm.

i. The city and state where the accountant practices, which may be indicated on company letterhead.

j. The date of the review report, which should be no earlier than the date the accountant has obtained sufficient appropriate review evidence to serve as the basis for the accountant's conclusion.

---

**PLANNING AID REMINDER:** Interpretation 1 of AR-C 90 indicates that a practitioner may review financial statements in accordance with both the SSARSs and with another set of review standards (e.g., International Standard on Review Engagements (ISRE 2400 Revised), *Engagements to Review Historical Financial Statements*). If the report states that both sets of standards were followed, they must be complied with in their entirety.

---

*Review Report on Financial Statements Prepared in Accordance with a Special Purpose Framework*

47. The review report on financial statements prepared in accordance with a special purpose framework should:

a. Refer to management's responsibility for determining the acceptability of the applicable financial reporting framework when management has a choice of frameworks;

b. Describe the purpose for which the financial statements are prepared or refer to a note in the financial statements containing that information when financial statements are prepared in accordance with a regulatory or contractual basis of accounting;

c. Include an emphasis-of-matter paragraph under an appropriate heading indicating the financial statements are prepared in accordance with the applicable special purpose framework, referring to the note to the financial statements that describes the framework and stating that the special purpose framework is a basis of accounting other than U.S. GAAP; and

d. Include an other-matter paragraph under an appropriate heading restricting the use of the review report when the special purpose financial statements are prepared in accordance with a contractual basis of accounting, regulatory basis of accounting, or other basis of accounting where measurement or disclosure criteria are suitable only for a limited number of users or only available to specified parties.

48. The review report should be modified when the accountant becomes aware that the financial statements do not include:

a. A description of the special purpose framework;

b. A summary of significant accounting policies;

c. An adequate description about how the special purpose framework differs from U.S. GAAP, the effects of which do not need to be quantified;

d. Informative disclosures similar to those required by U.S. GAAP when financial statements contain similar items to financial statements prepared in accordance with U.S. GAAP; or

e. An adequate description of significant contract interpretations if the financial statements are prepared in accordance with a contractual basis of accounting.

## Comparative Financial Statements

49. If comparative financial statements are presented, whether their presentation is required or elected, the accountant's report should refer to each period for which financial statements are presented.

50. A continuing accountant should update the report on one or more prior periods presented on a comparative basis with those of the current period when reporting on all periods presented. The accountant's report on comparative financial statements should not be dated earlier than the date the accountant completed procedures sufficient to obtain limited assurance as a basis for the review report with respect to the current period.

51. A continuing accountant should consider information he or she has become aware of during the current period review when issuing an updated report.
52. The accountant should consider the effects on the review report of any circumstances or events that come to his or her attention during the current engagement that may affect prior-period financial statements.
53. When the accountant's report on prior-period financial statements contains a changed reference to a departure from the applicable financial reporting framework, the review report should include an other-matter paragraph indicating the date of the accountant's previous review report, the circumstances or events causing the change in the reference, and, if applicable, that the prior-period financial statements have been changed.
54. When prior-period financial statements were audited and the auditor's report is not reissued, the review report on the current period financial statements should include an other-matter paragraph indicating:
    a. The prior-period financial statements were previously audited;
    b. The date of the prior-period auditor's report;
    c. The type of opinion issued on the prior-period financial statements;
    d. The substantive reasons for any modified opinion; and
    e. That no auditing procedures were performed after the date of the previous report.

## Emphasis-of-Matter and Other-Matter Paragraphs in the Review Report

55. The accountant should include an emphasis-of-matter paragraph in the review report if he or she considers it necessary to draw users' attention to an appropriately presented or disclosed matter in the financial statements. An emphasis-of-matter paragraph should not be used if the accountant believes the financial statements may be materially misstated.
56. An emphasis-of-matter paragraph in the review report should:
    a. Include the paragraph within a separate section of the report with an appropriate heading, such as "Emphasis of a Matter";
    b. Include a clear reference to the matter being emphasized and where in the financial statements relevant disclosures describing the matter can be found; and
    c. Indicate that the accountant's conclusion is not modified with respect to the matter emphasized.
57. The accountant should include an other-matter paragraph in the review report if he or she considers it necessary to communicate a matter not presented or disclosed in the financial statements that is relevant to the users' understanding of the review, the accountant's responsibilities, or the accountant's review report. An other-matter paragraph should be

included in a separate section with an appropriate heading, such as "Other Matter."

58. When there are adjustments to correct a material misstatement in the previously issued financial statements, the accountant should include an emphasis-of-matter paragraph in the report. The paragraph should include a statement that the previously issued financial statements have been restated for the correction of a material misstatement and a reference to the disclosure of the correction.

59. If the accountant expects to include an emphasis-of-matter or other-matter paragraph in the review report, he or she should communicate this expectation and the proposed wording of this paragraph to management.

*Restrict the Use of the Accountant's Review Report*

60. The review report should include a separate paragraph with an alert restricting its use when the subject matter of the report is based on measurement or disclosure criteria the accountant determines are suitable only for a limited number of users presumed to have an adequate understanding of the criteria or that are available only to specified parties.

61. An alert restricting use of the accountant's review report should:

    a. State that the accountant's review report is intended solely for the information and use of specified parties,

    b. Identify the specified parties for whom use is intended, and

    c. State that the review report is not intended to be and should not be used by anyone other than the specified parties.

62. If the accountant is requested to add parties to a restricted use report, he or she should determine whether to agree to add those parties as specified parties.

63. If other parties are added after the review report is released, the accountant should either:

    a. Amend the review report to add the other parties and not change the date of the review report; or

    b. Provide a written acknowledgment to management and the other parties that those parties have been added as specified parties and that no procedures were performed after the original date of the review report.

*Accountant's Consideration of an Entity's Ability to Continue as a Going Concern*

64. During performance of review procedures, the accountant should consider whether there is any indication of uncertainty about the entity's ability to continue as a going concern for a reasonable period of time. A reasonable period of time is that specified by the applicable financial reporting framework or, if not specified by the framework, one year

after the date that the financial statement being reviewed is available to be issued.

65. When the financial reporting framework requires management to evaluate the entity's ability to continue as a going concern for a reasonable period of time, the accountant should perform review procedures to evaluate whether the going concern basis of accounting is appropriate and to review management's evaluation of whether there are conditions or events that raise substantial doubt about the entity's ability to continue as a going concern. If there are conditions or events that raise such substantial doubt, the accountant evaluates management's plans to mitigate those matters. The review procedures performed by the accountant should also consider the adequacy of the related financial statement disclosures.

---

**OBSERVATION:** If the applicable financial reporting framework is U.S. GAAP, the FASB has defined a "reasonable period of time" for assessing an entity's going concern status as one year from the date the financial statements are issued or are available to be issued (i.e., not as one year from the financial statement date).

---

66. When the accountant concludes that substantial doubt about the entity's ability to continue as a going concern for a reasonable period of time remains, the accountant should include a separate section in the review report with the heading "Substantial Doubt About the Entity's Ability to Continue as a Going Concern" that draws attention to the related note in the financial statements and the conditions or events identified and management's plans to address them. It should also state that the substantial doubt about the entity's ability to continue as a going concern does not impact the accountant's conclusion about the financial statement.

67. If the accountant determines the entity's disclosures regarding its ability to continue as a going concern are inadequate, he or she should express a qualified or adverse conclusion and describe in the "Basis for Qualified (Adverse) Conclusion" section of the report the conditions or events triggering the substantial doubt.

---

**PRACTICE POINTER:** When there is a material departure from the applicable financial reporting framework, the accountant's reporting options are to (1) modify the review report and include in the review report a discussion of known departures from the applicable financial reporting framework (in this instance, the departure would be inadequate going concern disclosure) or (2) withdraw from the review engagement.

---

## Reference to the Work of Other Accountants in an Accountant's Review Report

68. If other accountants reviewed or audited the financial statements of significant components and the accountant of the reporting entity does

not assume responsibility for those reviews or audits, he or she should reference those reviews or audits in the review report, indicating that the work of other accountants was used and including the magnitude of the portion of the financial statements audited or reviewed by the other accountants.

69. The accountant should communicate with the other accountants and determine:

   a. That the other accountants are aware that the financial statements they audited or reviewed are being included in the financial statements the accountant is reporting on and that he or she is relying upon the other accountants' report;

   b. That the other accountants are familiar with and conducted their audit or review in accordance with the applicable financial reporting framework and with SSARSs or auditing standards generally accepted in the United States of America as applicable; and

   c. That matters affecting elimination of intercompany transactions and accounts and the uniformity of accounting practices among components included in the financial statements will be reviewed.

**PRACTICE POINTER:** When the component's financial statements are prepared using a different financial reporting framework from that used for the financial statements of the reporting entity, the accountant should generally not make reference in the review report to the other auditor's review or audit report, although some exceptions may apply if certain conditions are met.

*Supplementary Information and Required Supplementary Information*

70. If a review report is provided on financial statements that are accompanied by supplementary information, the accountant should indicate the degree of responsibility he or she is taking with respect to the supplementary information in an other-matter paragraph in the accountant's review report on the financial statements or a separate report on the supplementary information. This other-matter paragraph or separate report should state:

   a. The supplementary information is presented for purposes of additional analysis and is not a part of the basic financial statements, and

   b. The supplementary information is the responsibility of management and was derived from, and relates directly to, the underlying accounting and other records used to prepare the financial statements.

71. If the accountant reviewed the financial statements and the supplementary information, the other-matter paragraph or separate report should state that the information was subject to the review procedures performed in the review engagement and whether the accountant is aware of any material modifications that should be made to the supplementary information and that the accountant has not audited the supplementary

information and, accordingly, does not express an opinion on such information.

72. If the accountant subjected the supplementary information to the procedures performed in the review of the basic financial statements, the other-matter paragraph or separate report should state that the information was not audited or reviewed and, accordingly, the accountant does not express an opinion, conclusion, nor provide any assurance on such information.

73. The accountant should include an other-matter paragraph in the review report addressing required supplementary information, explaining the following circumstances as applicable:
    a. Required supplementary information is included and the accountant performed a compilation engagement on the information.
    b. Required supplementary information is included and the accountant reviewed the information.
    c. Required supplementary information is included and the accountant did not perform a compilation, review, or audit on the information.
    d. Required supplementary information is omitted.
    e. Some required supplementary information is presented in accordance with prescribed guidelines and some is missing.
    f. Departures from prescribed guidelines have been identified.
    g. The accountant has unresolved doubts about whether required supplementary information is presented in accordance with prescribed guidelines.

74. If the accountant did not perform a compilation or review on the required supplementary information, the other-matter paragraph should include the following statements:
    a. [Identify the applicable financial reporting framework] require that the [identify the required supplementary information] be presented to supplement the basic financial statements.
    b. Such information, although not a part of the basic financial statements, is required by [identify designated accounting standards-setter], who considers it an essential part of financial reporting for placing the basic financial statements in an appropriate operational, economic, or historical context.
    c. The accountant did not perform a compilation, review, or audit on the required supplementary information and, accordingly, does not express an opinion or provide any assurance on the information.
    d. If all or some of the required supplementary information is omitted, statements that:
        (i) Management has omitted [description of the missing required supplementary information] that [identify the applicable financial reporting framework] require to be presented to supplement the basic financial statements.

(ii) Such missing information, although not a part of the basic financial statements, is required by [*identify designated accounting standards-setter*], who considers it an essential part of financial reporting for placing the basic financial statements in an appropriate operational, economic, or historical context.

e. If the information's measurement or presentation departs materially from the prescribed guidelines, a statement that material departures from prescribed guidelines exist [*describe the material departures from the applicable financial reporting framework*].

f. If the accountant has unresolved doubts about whether required supplementary information is presented in accordance with prescribed guidelines, a statement that that accountant has doubts about whether material modifications should be made to the required supplementary information for it to be presented in accordance with guidelines established by [*identify designated accounting standards-setter*].

## *Change in Engagement from Audit to Review*

75. The accountant should consider the following when deciding whether to agree to a request for a change from an audit to a review engagement:
    a. The reason for the request and whether it is caused by a restriction on the scope of the audit engagement, whether caused by management or circumstances;
    b. The additional effort required to complete the audit engagement; and
    c. The estimated additional cost to complete the audit engagement.
76. If audit procedures are substantially complete or the cost to complete the audit is relatively insignificant, the accountant should consider the appropriateness of accepting a change in the engagement.
77. If the accountant decides that the change in engagement is justified, the accountant should comply with applicable review engagement standards and issue an appropriate review report.
78. The review report should not refer to the original engagement, any audit procedures performed, or scope limitations resulting in the change in engagement.
79. If the accountant was engaged to audit an entity's financial statements and management refuses to allow correspondence with the entity's legal counsel, the accountant may not accept an engagement to review those financial statements except in rare circumstances.

## *Documentation*

80. The accountant's review documentation should be sufficient to enable an experienced accountant with no prior connection to the review to understand:
    a. The nature, timing, and extent of review procedures performed;

    b. The results of review procedures performed and review evidence obtained; and

    c. Significant matters arising during the review, conclusions reached on these findings and issues, and significant professional judgments made in reaching these conclusions.

81. Review documentation should include:

    a. The engagement letter or other suitable written agreement with management,

    b. Communications with management regarding the accountant's expectation to include an emphasis-of-matter or other-matter paragraph in the review report,

    c. Communications with management, those charged with governance, and others as relevant to the performance of the review of significant matters arising during the engagement, including the nature of those matters.

    d. Communications with other accountants that have audited or reviewed financial statements of significant components,

    e. How any inconsistencies between information obtained and the accountant's findings regarding significant matters were addressed,

    f. The representation letter, and

    g. A copy of the reviewed financial statements and the accountant's review report.

## Analysis and Application of Procedures

### Engagement Acceptance and General Principles

When determining independence, the accountant can use the guidance provided by the AICPA Code of Professional Conduct.

---

**PLANNING AID REMINDER:** If an accountant's independence is impaired, he or she cannot perform a review engagement. However, this does not prevent the accountant from performing a compilation engagement on the financial statements.

---

### Agreement on Engagement Terms

Documenting engagement terms helps both the accountant and management by reducing misunderstandings and decreasing the risk that management will expect the accountant to protect against certain risks or perform functions that are the responsibility of management. For example, even though the accountant may prepare all or part of the financial statements, it is management's responsibility to ensure the financial statements are fairly presented in accordance with the applicable financial reporting framework.

> **PLANNING AID REMINDER:** If the agreement on engagement terms is only with those charged with governance that does not relieve the accountant of the requirement in AR-C 60 to obtain management's agreement that it acknowledges and understands its responsibilities.

Exhibit AR-C 90-1 provides an example engagement letter for financial statement reviews.

## Communication with Management and Those Charged with Governance

Communication with management and those charged with governance occurs through inquiries performed as part of the review engagement and other communications to improve understanding of matters that arise and foster a constructive working relationship. The timing of these communications will vary and may depend on the significance and nature of the matter as well as any action expected to be taken by management or those charged with governance. Communication may be restricted by law or regulation in some instances. There may be potential conflicts between the accountant's obligations of confidentiality and obligations to communicate, in which case the accountant may consider obtaining legal counsel.

> **PLANNING AID REMINDER:** If the accountant is responsible for communicating matters to those charged with governance, communication of those matters by management to those charged with governance may affect the form or timing of communication but does not relieve the accountant of his or her responsibility.

Matters that may be communicated to management or those charged with governance as appropriate include significant review findings, such as:

- The accountant's views about significant qualitative accounting practices of the entity;
- Significant findings from review procedures, including when the accountant considered it necessary to perform additional procedures;
- Matters that may lead to a modified review report; and
- Any significant difficulties encountered during the review, which in some cases may lead to the accountant's withdrawal from the engagement.

Law or regulation may require the accountant to provide notification of certain matters communicated with those charged with governance or submit copies of certain reports prepared for those charged with governance to regulatory or enforcement bodies. Unless provision of the accountant's written communications with those charged with governance to a third party is required by law or regulation, the accountant may need the consent of management or those charged with governance before sharing these communications.

## Understanding of the Industry and Knowledge of the Entity

The accountant is required to possess or obtain an understanding of the industry in which the entity operates. This requirement does not prevent the accountant from accepting an engagement for an industry in which he or she has no previous experience, but it does mean that he or she is responsible for obtaining the required level of knowledge. To obtain knowledge of the industry, the accountant can refer to AICPA industry guides, industry publications, financial statements of other companies in the industry, textbooks and periodicals, CPE courses, or individuals with knowledge of the industry. To obtain knowledge of the entity, the accountant may perform inquiries of entity personnel, review documents prepared by the entity, or use his or her experience with the entity or its industry.

## Review Procedures

Inquiry and analytical procedures generally provide the accountant with a reasonable basis for obtaining limited assurance. The results of these review procedures may modify the accountant's understanding of areas of increased risk. Exhibit AR-C 90-4 provides an example of a review program and Exhibit AR-C 90-5 provides a checklist that can serve as a guide in performing review procedures.

> **PLANNING AID REMINDER:** In some instances, while performing a review engagement, the accountant may also perform procedures typically performed in an audit. Performance of these procedures does not change the type of engagement; the engagement remains a review.

Analytical procedures may be performed using many different methods, ranging from simple comparisons to complex analyses either at the financial statement level or at the detailed account level. The accountant is to maintain professional skepticism throughout the review engagement, remaining alert for review evidence that contradicts other review evidence or information that brings into question the reliability of responses to inquiries. Professional judgment is used to determine the nature, timing and extent of analytical procedures. While the accountant is not required to corroborate management's responses with other evidence in a review, he or she may wish to perform other review procedures if management is unable to provide an adequate explanation of the results of analytical procedures. Exhibit AR-C 90-7 lists potential analytical procedures that may be used in a review engagement.

> **PLANNING AID REMINDER:** SSARS-21 requires the accountant to independently develop expectations of ratios and account balances before analyzing the entity's information in a review engagement. Exhibit AR-C 90-8 illustrates how an accountant might document expectations in a review engagement.

When making inquiries of management, the accountant may also make inquiries of those charged with governance and others within the entity as appropriate. Exhibit AR-C 90-6 provides a checklist of possible inquiries. The accountant may read minutes from stockholder, board, or committee meetings to meet the requirement to inquire about actions taken at a meeting that could have an effect on the financial statements.

Apart from the required inquiries, the accountant may also make inquiries of management about unusual or complex situations specific to the engagement, such as:

- Business combinations;
- New or complex revenue recognition methods;
- Asset impairment;
- Disposal of a segment of a business;
- Use of derivative instruments and hedging activities;
- Sales and transfers that might lead to a question of management's classification of investments in securities, including management's intent and ability with regards to held-to-maturity securities;
- New stock compensation plans or modifications to existing plans;
- Restructuring charges taken in current and prior periods;
- Significant, unusual, or infrequently occurring transactions;
- Changes in litigation or contingencies;
- Changes in contracts with major customers or suppliers;
- Application of new accounting principles;
- Changes in accounting principles or methods of application;
- Trends and developments affecting accounting estimates;
- Compliance with debt covenants;
- Changes in related parties or significant new related-party transactions;
- Material off-balance sheet transactions, special purpose entities, and other equity investments; and
- Unique terms for debt or capital stock that could affect classification.

When performing a review, the accountant evaluates whether uncorrected misstatements are material, individually or in the aggregate. The accountant's consideration of materiality is made in the context of the applicable financial reporting framework, some of which discuss the concept of materiality. The accountant's determination of materiality is a matter of professional judgment and is affected by the accountant's perception of the financial information needs of the users of financial statements. Some factors that may impact this evaluation are as follows:

- The nature, cause, and amount of the misstatements.
- Whether the misstatements originated in the prior year.
- The potential effect of misstatements on future periods.
- The appropriateness of offsetting a misstatement of an estimate with a misstatement of a precisely measured item.
- Recognition that immaterial balance sheet misstatements could contribute to material misstatements in future periods.

If the accountant concludes the financial statements are materially misstated, the guidance regarding departures from the applicable financial reporting framework should be followed.

If the accountant does not obtain sufficient, appropriate evidence on which to form a conclusion on the financial statements during a review, he or she may extend the work performed or perform other procedures as needed. If neither of these options is practicable, the accountant is required to determine whether the engagement can be completed. These circumstances may occur even if there is no knowledge of a matter causing the accountant to believe the financial statements may be materially misstated.

*Written Representations*

Written representations are an important source of review evidence as the written form may prompt management to thoroughly consider the representations. Furthermore, modification of or refusal to provide representations may make the accountant aware of potential issues.

These representations are typically from members of management such as the entity's CEO and CFO, although in some entities those charged with governance or other parties may also be responsible for the preparation and fair presentation of the financial statements. Management is expected to have sufficient knowledge of the entity's financial statement preparation process on which to base its representations. Management may, in some cases, use qualifying language in its representations indicating that they are made to the best of its knowledge and belief. This type of qualification may be acceptable if the accountant concludes that those making the representations have appropriate responsibilities and knowledge of the matters being represented.

---

**PLANNING AID REMINDER:** Management must not only acknowledge in the representation letter its responsibilities for preparing the financial statements in accordance with the applicable financial reporting framework (including the design, implementation, and maintenance of internal control), but it must also represent that it believes it has effectively fulfilled these responsibilities.

---

Management is required to provide a representation about uncorrected misstatements. However, management might not agree that these items are misstated; in these circumstances, management may want to add to their written representation a statement such as "We do not agree that items X and Y constitute misstatements because of [*description of reasons*]."

In some cases, the accountant may wish to obtain written representations about related parties from those charged with governance as well as management. If those charged with governance have approved related-party transactions materially affecting the financial statements or involving management, have orally represented to the accountant details of certain related-party transactions, or have financial or other interests in the related parties or their transactions, these representations may be warranted.

> **PLANNING AID REMINDER:** Written representations cover all periods referred to in the accountant's review report. Representations may be written to update prior period written representations by addressing any changes to those representations. If current management was not present during all periods referred to in the review report, this does not change their responsibilities for the financial statements as a whole and the accountant should still obtain written representations covering all relevant periods from them.

Management's representations should be made as of the date of the accountant's review report. The accountant does not need to possess the management representation letter as of the date of the accountant's review report as long as management has acknowledged they will sign the letter without exception as of the date of the accountant's review report and it is received before release of the report.

Exhibit AR-C 90-2 is an example management representation letter for financial statement reviews. The accountant may decide based on engagement circumstances or the client's industry that other matters should be specifically included in the letter or that some of the representations included in the illustrative letter are not necessary.

> **PLANNING AID REMINDER:** Sometimes practitioners draft a representation letter for management to develop and sign; however, when doing so, practitioners should make sure that management understands the content that is in the representation letter before signing it and presenting it to the accountant. The accountant should consider discussing the content of the letter with management before management signs the letter and the accountant should consider documenting that discussion in the working papers.

*Reporting on the Financial Statements*

An appropriate title for the report would be "Independent Accountant's Review Report." A review that is incomplete because the accountant was unable to perform the necessary inquiry, analytical procedures and other procedures or because management did not provide a representation letter does not provide the accountant with an adequate basis to issue a review report.

> **PRACTICE POINTER:** The written review report encompasses either a paper or an electronic document.

The review report is typically addressed to those for whom the report is prepared. In most circumstances this would be the entity whose financial statements are being reviewed or those charged with governance. However, in some instances the accountant may be retained to review the financial statements of another entity, in which case the report may be addressed to the client retaining the accountant.

To minimize the possibility that a user could place an unintended level of reliance on the financial statements if they became unattached from the review report, the accountant may wish to include a reference to the review report on each page of the reviewed financial statements, such as "See independent accountant's review report."

Exhibit AR-C 90-3 is an example of a standard accountant's review report.

### Review Report on Financial Statements Prepared in Accordance with a Special Purpose Framework

If financial statements are prepared in accordance with a special purpose framework, a description of the framework may be included in financial statement titles, notes to the financial statements, or otherwise on the face of the financial statements. Examples of suitable financial statements titles include "Income Statement—Modified Cash Basis" if statements are prepared on a modified cash basis of accounting and "Balance Sheet—Tax Basis" if statements are prepared in accordance with the tax basis of accounting.

In describing how the special purpose framework differs from U.S. GAAP, the accountant is only required to include material differences between the two frameworks, and those differences do not need to be quantified. Immaterial differences do not need to be described.

The accountant is required to describe the purpose for which the financial statements are prepared when they are prepared in accordance with a regulatory or contractual basis of accounting in order to avoid misunderstandings if the financial statements are used for unintended purposes.

### Comparative Financial Statements

When comparative financial statements are presented, the level of information included should be comparable for all periods presented. A continuing accountant updates the report on the prior period financial statements when reporting on comparative financial statements. This updated report should be issued in conjunction with the accountant's report on the current period financial statements.

The accountant is required to include an other-matter paragraph in his or her report if the prior period financial statements contain a changed reference to a departure from the applicable financial reporting framework (e.g., the prior report included a reference to a U.S. GAAP departure whereas the current report does not). Changed references include removal of prior references as well as inclusion of new references.

> **PLANNING AID REMINDER:** If a new accounting firm is formed from the merger of two firms, the new firm may accept responsibility for and issue a review report on the financial statements for prior and current periods of a client of one of the two former firms. In the review report or signature, the accountant may state that a merger occurred and name the firms that merged.

## Communicating to Management and Others Regarding Fraud or Noncompliance with Laws and Regulations

The accountant may wish to establish (in advance) with management and those charged with governance as applicable the nature and amount of matters that would not be considered material and thus not require communication.

> **PRACTICE POINTER:** In describing fraud or noncompliance with laws and regulations, often the accountant will describe the potential fraud or noncompliance, how it occurred, and possible effects on the financial statements.

If the accountant becomes aware that fraud or noncompliance with laws or regulations has occurred, he or she is typically not responsible for nor permitted to disclose this information to parties other than the entity's senior management and those charged with governance as applicable. Certain situations may cause the accountant to have a duty to disclose this information: complying with legal and regulatory requirements; communicating to a successor accountant when management has given permission for predecessor and successor accountants to communicate; or responding to a subpoena.

The accountant may need to consider whether withdrawal from an engagement is necessary if management or those charged with governance do not take the necessary remedial action, or when matters regarding fraud or noncompliance with laws and regulations involve the business owner.

## Emphasis-of-Matter and Other-Matter Paragraphs in the Review Report

Emphasis-of-matter paragraphs or other-matter paragraphs are required to be included in the review report when any of the following conditions exist:

- Management revises the financial statements for a subsequently discovered fact that became known to the accountant after the report release date and the accountant's review report on the revised financial statements differs from the accountant's initial review,
- Financial statements are prepared in accordance with a special purpose framework,
- There is a changed reference to a departure from the applicable financial reporting framework when reporting on comparative financial statements,
- The accountant is reporting on comparative financial statements when the prior period was audited,

- The accountant concludes that substantial doubt about the entity's ability to continue as a going concern for a reasonable period of time remains,
- Non-required supplementary information accompanies reviewed financial statements and the accountant's review report, or
- Required supplementary information is included.

Other circumstances that the accountant may consider sufficient to warrant inclusion of an emphasis-of-matter paragraph include:

- Uncertainty regarding the entity's ability to continue as a going concern for a reasonable time period,
- Uncertainty regarding the future outcome of unusually important litigation or regulatory action,
- A major catastrophe with a significant effect on the entity's financial position,
- Significant transactions with related parties, and
- Unusually important subsequent events.

Other-matter paragraphs clearly state that such information is not required to be presented and disclosed in the financial statements. However, other-matter paragraphs do not include information the accountant is prohibited from providing by law, regulation, or professional standards or information that management is required to provide.

**PLANNING AID REMINDER:** An other-matter paragraph on a particular matter may recur in successive review reports; in these cases, the accountant may determine it is unnecessary to repeat the communication to management on each engagement.

## *Alert That Restricts the Use of the Accountant's Review Report*

A general use report is not restricted to specified parties and is normally used in financial statement reports prepared in accordance with an applicable financial reporting framework. However, the accountant is not precluded from restricting the use of any report. A restricted use report is intended only for one or more specified third parties. Alerts restricting use of the review report help prevent misunderstandings that could occur if the report was taken out of its intended context.

The accountant is not responsible for controlling the distribution of the review report. However, he or she may consider informing the client that restricted use reports are not intended for distribution to nonspecified parties. The accountant may wish to obtain the entity's agreement that the entity and specified parties will not distribute the review report to nonspecified parties when establishing engagement terms.

An example of an alert restricting the use of the review report is as follows:

> This report is intended solely for the information and use of [*list or refer to the specified parties*] and is not intended to be, and should not be, used by anyone other than these specified parties.

## Accountant's Consideration of an Entity's Ability to Continue as a Going Concern

Most accounting frameworks, including those issued by the FASB, GASB, and International Accounting Standards Board (IASB), that require that management make an explicit evaluation of the entity's ability to continue as a going concern specify the time period to be examined. For example, the FASB specifies the time period as within one year after the date that the financial statements are issued (or within one year after the date the financial statements are available to be issued). The GASB specifies the time period as 12 months beyond the date of the financial statements while the IASB specifies the time period as at least, but not limited to, one year from the end of the reporting period.

A review is not designed to identify conditions or events that raise substantial doubt about that entity's ability to continue as a going concern. However, the accountant may identify conditions or events that raise substantial doubt. Sometimes that doubt can be mitigated by management's plans, such as plans to dispose of an asset or business, plans to borrow money or restructure debt, plans to reduce or delay expenditures, or plans to increase owner's equity.

Exhibit AR-C 90-9 contains guidance that might be helpful when evaluating an entity's ability to continue as a going concern. If the accountant concludes that management's disclosure of the going concern uncertainty is adequate, he or she would include a separate section in the review report. The following is an example of an appropriate section referring to a going concern uncertainty:

> **Substantial Doubt About the Company's Ability to Continue as a Going Concern**
>
> The accompanying financial statements have been prepared assuming that the Company will continue as a going concern. As discussed in Note X to the financial statements, the Company has suffered recurring losses from operations, and has a net capital deficiency, and has stated that substantial doubt exists about the Company's ability to continue as a going concern. Management's evaluations of the events and conditions and management's plans regarding these matters are also described in Note X. The financial statements do not include any adjustments that might result from the outcome of this uncertainty. Our conclusion is not modified with respect to this matter.

It is not appropriate for the separate section in this situation to include the following:

- If the company continues to suffer recurring losses from operations and continues to have a net capital deficiency, there may be an uncertainty about its ability to continue as a going concern.

- The company has been unable to renegotiate its expiring credit agreements. Unless the company is able to obtain financial support, there is an uncertainty about its ability to continue as a going concern.

## Subsequent Events and Subsequently Discovered Facts

Whether during performance of review procedures or subsequent to the date of the review report but prior to the report's release, the accountant may become aware that a subsequent event requiring adjustment of or disclosure in the reviewed financial statements has occurred.

If the accountant becomes aware of new information after the report release date, he or she should follow the guidance in this SSARS even if the accountant has since withdrawn or been discharged. When determining whether a subsequently discovered fact requires financial statement revision, the requirements of the applicable financial reporting framework should be considered as well as whether the accountant believes users of the financial statements would consider the fact important, the amount of time elapsed since the report was issued, whether subsequent reviewed or audited financial statements have been issued, and any legal implications.

When the accountant concludes that the reviewed financial statements are not to be used, given that the original reviewed financial statements have been released, appropriate notification may include the following depending on the circumstances:

- If the issuance of revised financial statements and review report are not imminent, notify known and potential users of the financial statements and review report that they are not to be used and that revised financial statements and a new review report will be issued;
- Issue revised financial statements with appropriate disclosure of the matter as soon as practicable; and
- If issuance of the subsequent period's reviewed or audited financial statements is imminent, issue the subsequent period's financial statements with appropriate disclosure of the matter.

If management does not take the necessary steps to prevent third parties from using previously issued reviewed financial statements, the accountant may take steps to prevent use of the review report. The accountant's knowledge that people exist who are using the financial statements and accountant's report and would attach importance to the information as well as the accountant's ability to communicate with these people will affect the steps he or she is able to take. Unless otherwise recommended by the accountant's attorney, the accountant may take the following steps in these circumstances as applicable:

- Notify management and those charged with governance that the review report is not to be used,
- Notify regulatory agencies with jurisdiction over the entity that the review report is not to be used, and
- Notify known users of the financial statements that the review report is not to be used; this type of notification may take the form of notifying a regulatory agency with jurisdiction over the entity.

If the accountant is able to determine that the financial statements need revision, the accountant's notification to recipients of the reviewed financial statements may, as permitted by law, regulation, and relevant ethical requirements include a description of the nature of the subsequently discovered information, its effect on the financial statements, and the effect the matter would have had on the review report if the matter was not reflected in the financial statements and the accountant was aware of the matter at the date of the report. The information disclosed should be as precise and factual as possible without going beyond what is reasonably necessary to describe the nature and effects of the information and without commenting on anyone's conduct or motives.

If the accountant is unable to determine that the financial statements need revisions, the accountant's notification to recipients of the reviewed financial statements may indicate that if the information that the accountant became aware of is true, he or she believes the review report is not to be used.

## Reference to the Work of Other Accountants in an Accountant's Review Report

If the accountant refers to the work of other accountants in the review report, an example of appropriate accountant's responsibility and concluding paragraphs of the report is as follows:

### Accountant's Responsibility

My (Our) responsibility is to conduct the review engagements in accordance with Statements on Standards for Accounting and Review Services (SSARSs) promulgated by the Accounting and Review Services Committee of the AICPA. We have not reviewed the financial statements of ZYX Company, a wholly owned subsidiary, whose financial statements reflect total assets constituting 22 percent and 25 percent, respectively, of consolidated total assets at December 31, 20X7 and 20X6, and total revenues constituting 21 percent and 23 percent, respectively, of consolidated total revenues for the years then ended. These statements were reviewed by other accountants, whose report has been furnished to me (us), and our conclusion, insofar as it relates to the amounts included for ZYX Company, is based solely on the report of the other accountants.

SSARSs require me (us) to perform procedures to obtain limited assurance as a basis for reporting whether I am (we are) aware of any material modifications that should be made to the financial statements for them to be in accordance with accounting principles generally accepted in the United States of America. I (We) believe that the results of my (our) procedures provide a reasonable basis for our conclusion.

### Accountant's Conclusion

Based on my (our) reviews, and the report of other accountants, I am (we are) not aware of any material modifications that should be made to the accompanying financial statements in order for them to be in accordance with accounting principles generally accepted in the United States of America.

## Supplementary Information and Required Supplementary Information

If the accountant has reviewed the financial statements and the supplementary information, an appropriate other-matter paragraph may read:

### Other Matter

The accompanying [*identify the supplementary information*] is presented for purposes of additional analysis and is not a required part of the basic financial statements. Such information is the responsibility of management and was derived from, and relates directly to, the underlying accounting and other records used to prepare the financial statements. The supplementary information has been subjected to the review procedures applied in my (our) review of the basic financial statements. I (We) have reviewed the information and, based on my (our) review, I am (we are) not aware of any material modifications that should be made to the supplementary information. I (We) have not audited the supplementary information and do not express an opinion on such information.

The accountant may also wish to include a reference to the review report on each page of the supplementary information, such as "See independent accountant's review report," to minimize the potential for a user to place an unintended level of reliance on the information.

If the accountant has reviewed the financial statements but not the supplementary information, an appropriate other-matter paragraph may read:

*Other Matter*

The accompanying [*identify the supplementary information*] is presented for purposes of additional analysis and is not a required part of the basic financial statements. Such information is the responsibility of management. I (We) have not audited or reviewed such information and I (we) do not express an opinion, a conclusion, nor provide any assurance on it.

## *Change in Engagement from Audit to Review*

An accountant may be requested to change from an audit to a review engagement before completion of the audit. This request may be due to a change in the entity's circumstances affecting its requirements for an audit or a misunderstanding about the nature of services to be provided. Either of these reasons is typically considered a reasonable basis for requesting a change in the engagement.

The request to change the engagement may be due to a restriction on the scope of the audit engagement, whether caused by management or circumstances. When this occurs, the accountant should consider whether this scope restriction potentially impacts information such that it may be incorrect, incomplete, or otherwise unsatisfactory.

## *Documentation*

The accountant may provide additional support for the review documentation through written documentation in other engagement or quality control files or through oral explanations. However, oral explanations alone do not provide sufficient support for the accountant's work or conclusions.

**PLANNING AID REMINDER:** If an engagement partner performs all the review work in an engagement, he or she must still comply with the requirement to prepare review documentation that can be understood by an experienced accountant because external parties may review the documentation.

When considering significant findings or issues arising during the review to document, the accountant may include results of review procedures indicating the financial statements could be materially misstated, actions taken to address those findings, and the basis used for the accountant's conclusions.

## Practitioner's Aids

Exhibit AR-C 90-1 is an example of a standard engagement letter for a review.

### EXHIBIT AR-C 90-1—REVIEW ENGAGEMENT LETTER

To the appropriate representative of management of ABC Company:

You have requested that we prepare the financial statements of ABC Company, which comprise the balance sheet as of December 31, 20XX, and the related statements of income, changes in stockholders' equity, and cash flows for the year then ended, and the related notes to the financial statements, and perform a review engagement with respect to those financial statements. [*If the accountant is performing other nonattest services as part of the engagement, these services may be included as well.*] We are pleased to confirm our acceptance and our understanding of this engagement by means of this letter.

**Our Responsibilities**

The objective of our engagement is to

a. Prepare financial statements in accordance with accounting principles generally accepted in the United States of America based on information provided by you and

b. Obtain limited assurance as a basis for reporting whether we are aware of any material modifications that should be made to the financial statements in order for the statements to be in accordance with accounting principles generally accepted in the United States of America.

We will conduct our engagement in accordance with Statements on Standards for Accounting and Review Services (SSARSs) promulgated by the Accounting and Review Services Committee of the AICPA and comply with the AICPA's Code of Professional Conduct, including the ethical principles of integrity, objectivity, professional competence, and due care.

A review engagement includes primarily applying analytical procedures to your financial data and making inquiries of company management. A review engagement is substantially less in scope than an audit engagement, the objective of which is the expression of an opinion regarding the financial statements as a whole. A review engagement does not contemplate obtaining an understanding of the entity's internal control; assessing fraud risk; testing accounting records by obtaining sufficient appropriate audit evidence through inspection, observation, confirmation, or the examination of source documents; or other procedures ordinarily performed in an audit engagement. Accordingly, we will not express an opinion on the financial statements.

Our engagement cannot be relied upon to identify or disclose any financial statements misstatements, including those caused by fraud or error, or to identify or disclose any wrongdoing within the entity or noncompliance with laws or regulations. However, we will inform the appropriate level of management of any material errors and any evidence or information that comes to our attention during the performance of our review procedures that indicates fraud may have occurred. In addition, we will report to you any evidence or information that comes to our attention during the performance of our review procedures regarding noncompliance with laws and regulations that may have occurred, unless they are clearly inconsequential.

**Your Responsibilities**

The engagement to be performed is conducted on the basis that you acknowledge and understand that our role is to prepare financial statements in accordance with accounting principles generally accepted in the United States of America and to obtain limited assurance as a basis for reporting whether we are aware of any material modifications that should be made to the financial statements in order for the statements to be in accordance with accounting principles generally accepted in the United States of America. You have the following overall responsibilities that are fundamental to our undertaking the engagement in accordance with SSARSs:

   a. The selection of accounting principles generally accepted in the United States of America as the financial reporting framework to be applied in the preparation of the financial statements

   b. The preparation and fair presentation of financial statements in accordance with accounting principles generally accepted in the United States of America and the inclusion of all informative disclosures that are appropriate for accounting principles generally accepted in the United States of America

   c. The design, implementation, and maintenance of internal control relevant to the preparation and fair presentation of the financial statements

   d. Recording and reflecting all transactions in the financial statements

   e. The prevention and detection of fraud

   f. To ensure that the entity complies with the laws and regulations applicable to its activities

   g. To make all financial records and related information available to us

   h. The accuracy and completeness of the records, documents, explanations, and other information, including significant judgments, you provide to us for the engagement

   i. To provide an identification of the entity's related parties and related-party relationships and transactions and to ensure all are appropriately accounted for and properly disclosed

   j. To provide us with unrestricted access to persons within the entity of whom we determine it necessary to make inquiries

   k. To disclose to us all information relevant to the use of the going concern assumption in the financial statements

   l. To properly account for all events occurring subsequent to the date of the financial statements

   m. To provide us, at the conclusion of the engagement, with a letter that confirms certain representations made during the review

You are also responsible for all management decisions and responsibilities and for designating an individual with suitable skills, knowledge, and experience to oversee our preparation of your financial statements. You are responsible for evaluating the adequacy and results of the services performed and accepting responsibility for such services.

**Our Report**

[Insert appropriate reference to the expected form and content of the accountant's review report. Example follows.]

We will issue a written report upon completion of our review of ABC Company's financial statements. Our report will be addressed to the board of directors of ABC Company. We cannot provide assurance that an unmodified accountant's review report will be issued. Circumstances may arise in which it is necessary for us to report known departures from accounting principles generally accepted in the United States of America, add an emphasis-of-matter or other-matter paragraph(s), or withdraw from the engagement. If, for any reason, we are unable to complete the review of your financial statements, we will not issue a report on such statements as a result of this engagement.

**Other Relevant Information**

Our fees for these services . . .

[The accountant may include language, such as the following, regarding limitation of or other arrangements regarding the liability of the accountant or the entity, such as indemnification to the accountant for liability arising from knowing misrepresentations to the accountant by management (regulators may restrict or prohibit such liability limitation arrangements):

> You agree to hold us harmless and to release, indemnify, and defend us from any liability or costs, including attorney's fees, resulting from management's knowing misrepresentations to us.]

Please sign and return the attached copy of this letter to indicate your acknowledgement of, and agreement with, the arrangements for our engagement to prepare the financial statements described herein and to perform a review of those same financial statements, and our respective responsibilities.

Sincerely yours,

[Signature of accountant or accountant's firm]

Acknowledged and agreed on behalf of ABC Company by:

[Signed]

[Name and Title]

[Date]

---

Exhibit AR-C 90-2 is an example of a standard management representation letter for financial statement reviews.

## EXHIBIT AR-C 90-2—MANAGEMENT REPRESENTATION LETTER

[Entity Letterhead]

[To Accountant]

[Date]

This representation letter is provided in connection with your review of the financial statements of ABC Company, which comprise the balance sheets as of December 31, 20X7 and 20X6, and the related statements of income, changes in stockholders' equity and cash flows for the years then ended, and the related notes to the financial statements, for the purpose of obtaining limited assurance as a basis for reporting whether you are aware of any material modifications that should be made to the financial statements in order for the statements to be in accordance with accounting principles generally accepted in the United States of America.

Certain representations in this letter are described as being limited to matters that are material. Items are considered material, regardless of size, if they involve an omission or misstatement of accounting information that, in the light of surrounding circumstances, makes it probable that the judgment of a reasonable person using the information would be changed or influenced by the omission or misstatement.

We represent that [to the best of our knowledge and belief, having made such inquiries as we considered necessary for the purpose of appropriately informing ourselves] [as of (*date of the accountant's review report*)]:

**Financial Statements**

- We acknowledge our responsibility and have fulfilled our responsibilities for the preparation and fair presentation of the financial statements in accordance with accounting principles generally accepted in the United States of America.
- We acknowledge our responsibility and have fulfilled our responsibilities for the design, implementation, and maintenance of internal control relevant to the preparation and fair presentation of financial statements that are free from material misstatement, whether due to fraud or error.
- We have responded truthfully and fully to all of your inquiries.
- Significant assumptions used by us in making accounting estimates, including those measured at fair value, are reasonable.
- Management has properly accounted for all events occurring subsequent to the date of the financial statements and for which the applicable financial reporting framework requires adjustment or disclosure, and it has made the necessary adjustments or disclosures.
- We have disclosed to you whether the assumptions used by us in making accounting estimates are reasonable.
- All events subsequent to the date of the financial statements and for which accounting principles generally accepted in the United States of America requires adjustment or disclosure have been properly accounted for.
- We acknowledge that the effects of uncorrected misstatements are immaterial, both individually and in the aggregate, to the financial statements as a whole.
- The effects of all known actual or possible litigation and claims have been accounted for and disclosed in accordance with accounting principles generally accepted in the United States of America.

[*Any other matters that the accountant may consider appropriate.*]

**Information Provided**

- We have responded fully and truthfully to all inquiries made to us by you during your review.
- We have provided you with

- Access to all information, of which we are aware, that is relevant to the preparation and fair presentation of the financial statements, such as records, documentation, and other matters;
- Minutes of meetings of stockholders, directors, and committees of directors or summaries of actions for recent meetings for which minutes have not yet been prepared;
- Additional information that you have requested from us for the purpose of the review; and
- Unrestricted access to persons within the entity from whom you determined it necessary to obtain review evidence.

* All transactions have been recorded in the accounting records and are reflected in the financial statements.
* We have [no knowledge of any] [disclosed to you all information that we are aware of regarding] fraud or suspected fraud that affects the entity and involves
  - Management,
  - Employees who have significant roles in internal control, or
  - Others when the fraud could have a material effect on the financial statements.
* We have [no knowledge of any] [disclosed to you all information that we are aware of regarding] allegations of fraud, or suspected fraud, affecting the entity's financial statements as a whole communicated by employees, former employees, analysts, regulators, or others.
* We have no plans or intentions that may materially affect the carrying amounts or classification of assets and liabilities.
* We have disclosed to you all known instances of noncompliance or suspected noncompliance with laws or regulations whose effects should be considered when preparing financial statements.
* We [have disclosed to you all known actual or possible] [are not aware of any pending or threatened] litigation and claims whose effects should be considered when preparing the financial statements [and we have not consulted legal counsel concerning litigation or claims].
* We have disclosed to you any other material liabilities or gain or loss contingencies that are required to be accrued or disclosed by FASB ASC 450, *Contingencies*.
* We have disclosed to you the identity of the entity's related parties and all the related-party relationships and transactions of which we are aware.
* No material losses exist (such as from obsolete inventory or purchase or sale commitments) that have not been properly accrued or disclosed in the financial statements.
* The company has satisfactory title to all owned assets, and no liens or encumbrances on such assets exist, nor has any asset been pledged as collateral, except as disclosed to you and reported in the financial statements.
* We have complied with all aspects of contractual agreements that would have a material effect on the financial statements in the event of noncompliance.

- We are in agreement with the adjusting journal entries that you have recommended, and they have been posted to the company's accounts (if applicable).
- All information relevant to the use of the going concern assumption in the financial statements has been disclosed to you.

[*Any other matters that the accountant may consider necessary.*]

———————————————————

[*Name of Chief Executive Officer and Title*]

———————————————————

[*Name of Chief Financial Officer and Title*]

---

Exhibit AR-C 90-3 is an example of a standard review report on comparative financial statements prepared in accordance with accounting principles generally accepted in the United States of America.

## EXHIBIT AR-C 90-3—STANDARD ACCOUNTANT'S REVIEW REPORT

**Independent Accountant's Review Report**

[*Appropriate Addressee*]

I (we) have reviewed the accompanying financial statements of ABC Company, which comprise the balance sheets as of December 31, 20X7 and 20X6, and the related statements of income, comprehensive income, changes in stockholders' equity, and cash flows for the year then ended, and the related notes to the financial statements. A review includes primarily applying analytical procedures to management's (owners') financial data and making inquiries of company management (owners). A review is substantially less in scope than an audit, the objective of which is the expression of an opinion regarding the financial statements as a whole. Accordingly, I (we) do not express such an opinion.

**Management's Responsibility for the Financial Statements**

Management (Owners) is (are) responsible for the preparation and fair presentation of these financial statements in accordance with accounting principles generally accepted in the United States of America; this includes the design, implementation, and maintenance of internal control relevant to the preparation and fair presentation of financial statements that are free from material misstatement whether due to fraud or error.

**Accountant's Responsibility**

My (Our) responsibility is to conduct the review engagements in accordance with Statements on Standards for Accounting and Review Services promulgated by the Accounting and Review Services Committee of the AICPA. Those standards require me (us) to perform procedures to obtain limited assurance as a basis for reporting whether I am (we are) aware of any material modifications that should be made to the financial statements for them to be in accordance with accounting principles generally accepted in the United States of America. I (We) believe that the results of my (our) procedures provide a reasonable basis for our conclusion.

We are required to be independent of ABC Company and to meet our other ethical responsibilities, in accordance with the relevant ethical requirements related to our reviews.

**Accountant's Conclusion**

Based on my (our) reviews, I am (we are) not aware of any material modifications that should be made to the accompanying financial statements in order for them to be in accordance with accounting principles generally accepted in the United States of America.

[*Signature of accounting firm or accountant, as appropriate*]

[*Accountant's city and state*]

[*Date*]

## EXHIBIT AR-C 90-4—REVIEW PROGRAM

Use the following procedures as a guide for performing a continuing review engagement. This review program is only a guide and professional judgment should be exercised to determine how the procedures should be modified by revising procedures listed or adding procedures to the review program. Before beginning review procedures, the accountant should have applied client acceptance procedures and carefully evaluated whether this is a client the accountant wants to serve.

Initial and date each procedure as it is completed. If the procedure is not relevant to a review engagement, place "N/A" (not applicable) in the space provided for an initial.

Client Name: _____

Date of Financial Statements: _____

Date of Review Report: _____

| | | Initials | Date | Workpaper Reference |
|---|---|---|---|---|
| 1. | Acquire an adequate understanding of accounting principles and practices of the client's industry and methods of applying them. | ___ | ___ | ___ |
| 2. | Develop an understanding of the client's organization. | ___ | ___ | ___ |
| 3. | Develop an understanding of the client's operating characteristics. | ___ | ___ | ___ |
| 4. | Develop an understanding of the nature of the client's assets, liabilities, revenues, and expenses. | ___ | ___ | ___ |
| 5. | Make inquiries concerning the client's accounting principles, practices, and methods. | ___ | ___ | ___ |

|  | | Initials | Date | Workpaper Reference |
|---|---|---|---|---|
| 6. | Make inquiries concerning the client's procedures for recording, classifying, and summarizing transactions and accumulating information for disclosure in the financial statements. | _____ | _____ | _____ |
| 7. | Make inquiries concerning actions taken at meetings of stockholders, board of directors, or other meetings that may affect the financial statements. | _____ | _____ | _____ |
| 8. | Make inquiries concerning the consistent application of U.S. GAAP. | _____ | _____ | _____ |
| 9. | Make inquiries concerning changes in the client's business activities or accounting principles and the implication for financial statements. | _____ | _____ | _____ |
| 10. | Make inquiries concerning occurrence of subsequent events that may have a material effect on the financial statements. | _____ | _____ | _____ |
| 11. | Make inquiries regarding the extent of unusual or complex situations that might exist and have a material effect on the financial statements. | _____ | _____ | _____ |
| 12. | Make inquiries about whether significant transactions occurred or were recognized in the last several days of the reporting period. | _____ | _____ | _____ |
| 13. | Inquire about the status of uncorrected misstatements identified in prior engagements. | _____ | _____ | _____ |
| 14. | Inquire about whether management has knowledge of fraud or suspected fraud affecting the entity that might involve management or others that could materially misstate the financial statements. | _____ | _____ | _____ |
| 15. | Make inquiries concerning the types of significant journal entries or other adjustments that exist. | _____ | _____ | _____ |
| 16. | Inquire regarding whether the client has received communications from regulatory agencies. | _____ | _____ | _____ |
| 17. | Apply analytical procedures to identify relationships and items that appear unusual. | _____ | _____ | _____ |
| 18. | Consider whether other professional services are needed before starting the review engagement. | _____ | _____ | _____ |

|  | Initials | Date | Workpaper Reference |
|---|---|---|---|
| 19. If appropriate, obtain reports from other accountants. | _____ | _____ | _____ |
| 20. Consider whether other review procedures should be performed on the basis of the results of performing the minimum review procedures. | _____ | _____ | _____ |
| 21. Read the financial statements to consider if they conform with U.S. GAAP. | _____ | _____ | _____ |
| 22. Obtain a client representation letter. | _____ | _____ | _____ |
| 23. Other review procedures: _____ |  |  |  |

Reviewed By: _____

Date: _____

## EXHIBIT AR-C 90-5—REVIEW QUESTIONNAIRE CHECKLIST

Use the following checklist as an initial start for performing review procedures, of course customizing them to the unique aspects of the engagement. The checklist is only a guide, and professional judgment should be exercised to determine how the checklist should be modified by revising questions listed or adding questions to the checklist where appropriate.

Initial and date each question as it is considered. If the question is not relevant to a review engagement, place "N/A" (not applicable) in the space provided for an initial. If the answer to the question is "No" or if additional explanation is needed, provide a cross-reference to another workpaper.

Client Name: _____

Date of Financial Statements: _____

|  | Initials | Date | Workpaper Reference |
|---|---|---|---|
| 1. Have we acquired an adequate understanding of specialized accounting principles and practices of the client's industry by: |  |  |  |
| • Reviewing relevant AICPA Accounting/Audit Guides? | _____ | _____ | _____ |
| • Reviewing financial statements of other entities in the same industry? | _____ | _____ | _____ |
| • Consulting with other individuals familiar with accounting practices in the specialized industry? | _____ | _____ | _____ |
| • Reading periodicals, textbooks, and other publications? | _____ | _____ | _____ |
| • Performing other procedures? | _____ | _____ | _____ |
| 2. Have we developed an understanding of the client's organization, including: |  |  |  |

|  | Initials | Date | Workpaper Reference |
|---|---|---|---|

- The form of business organization? ___ ___ ___
- The history of the client? ___ ___ ___
- The principals involved in the organizational chart or similar analysis? ___ ___ ___
- Other relevant matters, such as significant changes in the business activities and organization? ___ ___ ___

3. Have we developed an understanding of the client's operating characteristics, including:
   - An understanding of the client's products and services? ___ ___ ___
   - Identification of operating locations? ___ ___ ___
   - An understanding of production methods? ___ ___ ___
   - Other operating characteristics or significant changes made to those operations? ___ ___ ___

4. Have we developed an understanding of the nature of the client's assets, liabilities, revenues, and expenses by:
   - Reviewing the client's chart of accounts? ___ ___ ___
   - Reviewing the previous year's financial statements? ___ ___ ___
   - Considering the relationships between specific accounts and the nature of the client's business? ___ ___ ___
   - Considering how management determines significant accounting estimates and considers their reasonableness? ___ ___ ___
   - Performing other procedures? ___ ___ ___

5. Have we made inquiries concerning accounting principles, practices, and methods? ___ ___ ___

6. Have we made inquiries concerning the accounting procedures used by the client, including:
   - Recording transactions? ___ ___ ___
   - Classifying transactions? ___ ___ ___
   - Summarizing transactions? ___ ___ ___
   - Accumulating information for making disclosures in the financial statements? ___ ___ ___
   - Other accounting procedures? ___ ___ ___

|  | Initials | Date | Workpaper Reference |
|---|---|---|---|

7. Have we made inquiries concerning the effect on the financial statements due to actions taken at meetings of:
   - Stockholders? _____ _____ _____
   - The board of directors? _____ _____ _____
   - Other committees? _____ _____ _____
8. If there were changes in the application of accounting principles:
   - Did the change in accounting principle include the adoption of another acceptable accounting principle? _____ _____ _____
   - Was the change properly justified? _____ _____ _____
   - Were the effects of the change presented in the financial statements, including adequate disclosure, in a manner consistent with ASC 250, *Accounting Changes and Error Corrections*? _____ _____ _____
   - Were there other matters that we took into consideration? _____ _____ _____
9. Have we made inquiries concerning changes in the client's business activities that may require the adoption of different accounting principles, and have we considered the implication of this change for the financial statements? _____ _____ _____
10. Have we made inquiries concerning the occurrence of events subsequent to the date of the financial statements that may require:
    - Adjustments to the financial statements? _____ _____ _____
    - Disclosures in the financial statements? _____ _____ _____
11. Have we made inquiries regarding the extent of unusual or complex situations that might exist and that have a material effect on the financial statements? _____ _____ _____
12. Have we made inquiries about whether significant transactions occurred or were recognized in the last several days of the reporting period? _____ _____ _____
13. Have we inquired about the status of uncorrected misstatements identified in prior engagements? _____ _____ _____

§ 90 • Review Engagements 11,087

|  | Initials | Date | Workpaper Reference |
|---|---|---|---|

14. Have we inquired regarding whether management has any knowledge of fraud or suspected fraud affecting the entity that might involve management or others that could materially misstate the financial statements? _____ _____ _____

15. Have we made inquiries concerning the types of significant journal entries or other adjustments that exist? _____ _____ _____

16. Have we inquired regarding whether the client has received communications from regulatory agencies? _____ _____ _____

17. Have we performed analytical procedures, including:
    - Comparing current financial statements with comparable prior period(s)? _____ _____ _____
    - Comparing current financial statements with anticipated results? _____ _____ _____
    - Studying financial statement elements and expected relationships? _____ _____ _____
    - Other analytical procedures? _____ _____ _____
    - Documenting our expectations? _____ _____ _____

18. Have we considered whether other professional services are needed in order to complete the review engagement, including:
    - Preparing a working trial balance? _____ _____ _____
    - Preparing adjusting journal entries? _____ _____ _____
    - Consulting matters fundamental to the preparation of acceptable financial statements? _____ _____ _____
    - Preparing tax returns? _____ _____ _____
    - Providing bookkeeping or data processing services that do not include the generation of financial statements? _____ _____ _____
    - Considering other services that may be necessary before a review can be performed? _____ _____ _____

19. Have we obtained reports from other CPA(s) who reported on the financial statements of components of the client-reporting entity? _____ _____ _____

|  | Initials | Date | Workpaper Reference |
|---|---|---|---|

20. Have we read the financial statements to determine whether they appear to be in accordance with U.S. GAAP based on the information that has come to our attention? _____ _____ _____

21. Have we obtained a client representation letter? _____ _____ _____

22. Have we used other procedures to resolve questions during the review arrangement? _____ _____ _____

Reviewed By: _____

## EXHIBIT AR-C 90-6—INQUIRY CHECKLIST FOR A REVIEW ENGAGEMENT

Use this checklist to prompt thinking about example inquiries that might be made concerning accounting procedures used by the client. The checklist is only a guide, and professional judgment should be exercised to determine how the checklist should be modified by revising questions listed or adding questions where appropriate.

If a question is not relevant to a review engagement, place "N/A" (not applicable) in the space provided for a comment. If an additional explanation is needed in response to the question, provide a cross-reference to another workpaper. Note the source of the information in the space provided after each question.

Client Name: _____

Date of Financial Statements: _____

Sources of Information: _____

_____

_____

_____

Date: _____

|  | Yes | No | Date of Inquiry | Comment |
|---|---|---|---|---|

**GENERAL**

1. What are the procedures for recording, classifying, and summarizing transactions in the financial statements, including relevant disclosures? _____ _____ _____ _____

2. Do general ledger control accounts agree with subsidiary ledger accounts? _____ _____ _____ _____

|   | Yes | No | Date of Inquiry | Comment |
|---|---|---|---|---|

3. Have the financial statements been prepared in accordance with generally accepted accounting principles consistently applied? _____ _____ _____ _____

## CASH

1. Have bank balances been reconciled with book balances? _____ _____ _____ _____
   Source:

2. Have old or unusual reconciling items between bank balances and book balances been reviewed and adjustments made where necessary? _____ _____ _____ _____
   Source:

3. Has a proper cutoff of cash transactions been made? _____ _____ _____ _____
   Source:

4. Are there any restrictions on the availability of cash balances? _____ _____ _____ _____
   Source:

5. Have cash funds been counted and reconciled with control accounts? _____ _____ _____ _____
   Source:

6. Have cash overdrafts been classified as current liabilities? _____ _____ _____ _____
   Source:

7. Have amounts that represent temporary investments been identified and reclassified? _____ _____ _____ _____
   Source:

## INVESTMENTS IN MARKETABLE EQUITY SECURITIES

1. Have investments in marketable equity securities been classified into trading securities and available-for-sale securities? _____ _____ _____ _____
   Source:

2. Have trading securities and available-for-sale securities been carried at market value on the balance sheet? _____ _____ _____ _____
   Source:

3. Has management determined market value based on prices in active markets and, if not, how has market value been obtained? _____ _____ _____ _____
   Source:

4. Have available-for-sale securities been classified into a current and noncurrent portfolio? _____ _____ _____ _____
   Source:

|   | Yes | No | Date of Inquiry | Comment |
|---|---|---|---|---|

5. Have unrealized changes in the market value of trading securities since the prior year's financial statements been recorded in the income statement? ____ ____ ____ ____

    Source:

6. Has the cumulative difference between the market value of available-for-sale securities and their book value been recorded as a component of stockholders' equity? Have changes in this account been recognized as a component of Other Comprehensive Income during the year? ____ ____ ____ ____

    Source:

7. Have marketable equity securities been evaluated to determine reductions that are other than temporary? ____ ____ ____ ____

    Source:

8. Have gains or losses from the sale of marketable equity securities been reported on the income statement? ____ ____ ____ ____

    Source:

9. Have dividends received on marketable equity securities been reported on the income statement? ____ ____ ____ ____

    Source:

10. Has an analysis been made to accrue dividends declared but not paid at the end of the period? ____ ____ ____ ____

    Source:

11. Have reclassifications between trading securities and available-for-sale securities been accounted for in accordance with ASC 320, *Investments—Debt and Equity Securities,* and related FASB Staff Guidance? ____ ____ ____ ____

    Source:

INVESTMENTS IN DEBT SECURITIES

1. Have investments in marketable debt securities been classified into trading securities, available-for-sale securities, and hold-to-maturity securities? ____ ____ ____ ____

    Source:

|     |     | Yes | No | Date of Inquiry | Comment |
| --- | --- | --- | --- | --- | --- |
| 2. | Have trading securities and available-for-sale securities been carried at market value on the balance sheet? <br> Source: | \_\_\_\_ | \_\_\_\_ | \_\_\_\_ | \_\_\_\_ |
| 3. | Has management determined market value based on prices in active markets and, if not, how has market value been determined? <br> Source: | \_\_\_\_ | \_\_\_\_ | \_\_\_\_ | \_\_\_\_ |
| 4. | Have hold-to-maturity securities been carried at amortized cost, where amortized cost is determined using the effective interest method (unless the results from using the straight-line method of amortizing premium or discount are immaterially different)? <br> Source: | \_\_\_\_ | \_\_\_\_ | \_\_\_\_ | \_\_\_\_ |
| 5. | Have available-for-sale securities and hold-to-maturity securities been classified into a current and noncurrent portfolio? <br> Source: | \_\_\_\_ | \_\_\_\_ | \_\_\_\_ | \_\_\_\_ |
| 6. | Have unrealized changes in the market value of trading securities since the prior year's financial statements been recorded in the income statement? <br> Source: | \_\_\_\_ | \_\_\_\_ | \_\_\_\_ | \_\_\_\_ |
| 7. | Has the cumulative difference between the market value of available-for-sale securities and their book value been recorded as a component of stockholders' equity? Have changes in this account been recognized as a component of Other Comprehensive Income during the year? <br> Source: | \_\_\_\_ | \_\_\_\_ | \_\_\_\_ | \_\_\_\_ |
| 8. | Have marketable debt securities been evaluated to determine reductions that are other than temporary? <br> Source: | \_\_\_\_ | \_\_\_\_ | \_\_\_\_ | \_\_\_\_ |
| 9. | Have gains or losses from the sale of marketable debt securities been reported on the income statement? <br> Source: | \_\_\_\_ | \_\_\_\_ | \_\_\_\_ | \_\_\_\_ |
| 10. | Has interest income been recognized on the income statement, including an analysis of accrued interest income at the end of the period? <br> Source: | \_\_\_\_ | \_\_\_\_ | \_\_\_\_ | \_\_\_\_ |

|  | Yes | No | Date of Inquiry | Comment |
|---|---|---|---|---|

**RECEIVABLES**

1. Has a reasonable allowance been made for doubtful accounts?
   Source:
2. Have receivables considered uncollectible been written off?
   Source:
3. If appropriate, has interest been reflected?
   Source:
4. Has a proper cutoff of sales transactions been made?
   Source:
5. Are there any receivables from employees or related parties?
   Source:
6. Are any receivables pledged, discounted, or factored?
   Source:
7. Have receivables been properly classified between current and noncurrent?
   Source:
8. Have noncurrent receivables been evaluated to determine whether they carry a reasonable interest rate?
   Source:

**INVENTORIES**

1. Have inventories been physically counted? (If not, how have inventory quantities been determined?)
   Source:
2. Have general ledger control accounts been adjusted to agree with physical inventories?
   Source:
3. If physical inventories are taken at a date other than the balance sheet date, have appropriate procedures been used to record changes in inventory between the date of the count and the balance sheet date?
   Source:
4. Were consignments in or out considered in taking physical inventories?
   Source:

§ 90 • Review Engagements  **11,093**

|   | Yes | No | Date of Inquiry | Comment |
|---|---|---|---|---|

5. Has inventory been valued using an inventory method consistent with that of the previous period?
   Source:
6. Does inventory cost include material, labor, and overhead where applicable?
   Source:
7. Have write-downs for obsolescence or cost in excess of net realizable value been made?
   Source:
8. Have proper cutoffs of purchases, goods in transit, and returned goods been made?
   Source:
9. Are there any inventory encumbrances?
   Source:
10. Have there been any exchanges during the period that involve similar items?
    Source:

PROPERTY, PLANT, AND EQUIPMENT

1. Have gains or losses on disposal of property or equipment been properly reflected?
   Source:
2. Have the criteria for capitalizing property, plant, and equipment been established, and have they been applied during the fiscal period?
   Source:
3. Does the repairs and maintenance account only include expenses?
   Source:
4. Are property, plant, and equipment stated at cost?
   Source:
5. Have depreciation methods been applied in a consistent manner?
   Source:
6. Are there any unrecorded additions, retirements, abandonments, sales, or trade-ins?
   Source:

|   |   | Yes | No | Date of Inquiry | Comment |
|---|---|---|---|---|---|

7. Does the client have material lease agreements, and have they been properly reflected in the financial statements? \_\_\_\_ \_\_\_\_ _____ _____
   Source:
8. Is any property, plant, or equipment mortgaged or otherwise encumbered? \_\_\_\_ \_\_\_\_ _____ _____
   Source:
9. Have there been any exchanges during the period that involved similar items? \_\_\_\_ \_\_\_\_ _____ _____
   Source:
10. Has the client evaluated its fixed assets for possible evidence of impairment and, if impaired, has the appropriate write-off been recognized on the income statement? \_\_\_\_ \_\_\_\_ _____ _____
    Source:

PREPAID EXPENSES

1. Have the items included in prepaid expenses been evaluated to determine whether they are appropriately classified as prepayments? \_\_\_\_ \_\_\_\_ _____ _____
   Source:
2. Has a rational and systematic method been used to amortize prepaid expenses, and has the method been used in a manner consistent with the previous period? \_\_\_\_ \_\_\_\_ _____ _____
   Source:

INTANGIBLE ASSETS

1. Have the items included in intangible assets been evaluated to determine whether they are appropriately classified as intangible assets? \_\_\_\_ \_\_\_\_ _____ _____
   Source:
2. Have intangible assets with indefinite useful lives been evaluated for possible impairment and, if impaired, has the appropriate write-off been recognized on the income statement? \_\_\_\_ \_\_\_\_ _____ _____
   Source:
3. Has the straight-line method been used to amortize the cost of intangible assets with determinative useful lives and has the amortization method been used in a manner consistent with the previous period? \_\_\_\_ \_\_\_\_ _____ _____
   Source:

|  | Yes | No | Date of Inquiry | Comment |
|---|---|---|---|---|

**OTHER ASSETS**

1. Have the items included in other assets been evaluated to determine whether they are appropriately classified?
   Source:
2. Has each item classified as other assets been accounted for in accordance with U.S. GAAP?
   Source:
3. Have any of the other assets been mortgaged or otherwise encumbered?
   Source:

**ACCOUNTS AND NOTES PAYABLE AND ACCRUED LIABILITIES**

1. Have all significant payables been reflected in the financial statements?
   Source:
2. Have all short-term liabilities been properly classified?
   Source:
3. Have all significant accruals, such as payroll, interest, and provisions for pension and profit-sharing plans, been properly reflected in the financial statements?
   Source:
4. Have any of the liabilities been collateralized?
   Source:
5. Are there any payables to employees or related parties?
   Source:

**LONG-TERM LIABILITIES**

1. Have the terms and other provisions of long-term liability agreements been properly reflected in the financial statements?
   Source:
2. Have liabilities been evaluated to determine whether they are properly classified as noncurrent?
   Source:
3. Has interest expense been properly reflected in the financial statements?
   Source:

|  | Yes | No | Date of Inquiry | Comment |
|---|---|---|---|---|

4. Has there been compliance with restrictive covenants of loan agreements? \_\_\_\_ \_\_\_\_ \_\_\_\_ \_\_\_\_
   Source:
5. Have any of the long-term liabilities been collateralized or subordinated? \_\_\_\_ \_\_\_\_ \_\_\_\_ \_\_\_\_
   Source:
6. Has pension liability been determined in accordance with ASC 715, *Compensation—Retirement Benefits* (including, if applicable, the computation of a minimum liability)? \_\_\_\_ \_\_\_\_ \_\_\_\_ \_\_\_\_
   Source:

INCOME AND OTHER TAXES

1. Has provision been made for current- and prior-year federal income taxes payable? \_\_\_\_ \_\_\_\_ \_\_\_\_ \_\_\_\_
   Source:
2. Have any assessments or reassessments been received and are tax examinations in process? \_\_\_\_ \_\_\_\_ \_\_\_\_ \_\_\_\_
   Source:
3. Have differences between accounting methods used in the financial statements and those used in the tax return been properly reflected in the financial statements? \_\_\_\_ \_\_\_\_ \_\_\_\_ \_\_\_\_
   Source:
4. Has the income statement been prepared to reflect intraperiod income tax allocation? \_\_\_\_ \_\_\_\_ \_\_\_\_ \_\_\_\_
   Source:
5. Has provision been made for state and local income, franchise, sales, and other taxes payable? \_\_\_\_ \_\_\_\_ \_\_\_\_ \_\_\_\_
   Source:
6. If a deferred tax asset exists, is its realization more likely than not and, if not, is a valuation allowance account recorded? \_\_\_\_ \_\_\_\_ \_\_\_\_ \_\_\_\_
7. Do uncertain tax positions exist and, if so, are the provisions of ASC 740, *Accounting for Uncertainty in Income Taxes*, appropriately applied?

OTHER LIABILITIES, CONTINGENCIES, AND COMMITMENTS

1. Have the items included in other liabilities been evaluated to determine whether they are properly classified? \_\_\_\_ \_\_\_\_ \_\_\_\_ \_\_\_\_

|  | Yes | No | Date of Inquiry | Comment |
|---|---|---|---|---|

Source:

2. Have the items included in other liabilities been evaluated to determine whether they are current or noncurrent? \_\_\_\_\_ \_\_\_\_\_ _____ _____

   Source:

3. Are there any contingent liabilities such as discounted notes, drafts, endorsements, warranties, litigation, unsettled asserted claims, and unasserted potential claims? \_\_\_\_\_ \_\_\_\_\_ _____ _____

   Source:

4. Are there any material contractual obligations for construction or purchase of real property and equipment and any commitments or options to purchase or sell company securities? \_\_\_\_\_ \_\_\_\_\_ _____ _____

   Source:

EQUITY

1. Have changes in equity accounts for the period been properly accounted for and presented in the financial statements? \_\_\_\_\_ \_\_\_\_\_ _____ _____

   Source:

2. Have all classes of authorized capital stock been identified and properly reflected in the financial statements? \_\_\_\_\_ \_\_\_\_\_ _____ _____

   Source:

3. Has the par or stated value of the various classes of stock been identified and properly reflected in the financial statements? \_\_\_\_\_ \_\_\_\_\_ _____ _____

   Source:

4. Has there been a reconciliation between the number of outstanding shares of capital stock and subsidiary records? \_\_\_\_\_ \_\_\_\_\_ _____ _____

   Source:

5. Have capital stock preferences, if any, been properly disclosed? \_\_\_\_\_ \_\_\_\_\_ _____ _____

   Source:

6. Have stock options been granted? \_\_\_\_\_ \_\_\_\_\_ _____ _____

   Source:

7. Has the client made any acquisitions of its own capital stock? \_\_\_\_\_ \_\_\_\_\_ _____ _____

   Source:

|  | Yes | No | Date of Inquiry | Comment |
|---|---|---|---|---|

8. Has a determination been made as to whether there are any restrictions on retained earnings or other capital accounts? \_\_\_\_ \_\_\_\_ _____ _____

   Source:

### REVENUES AND EXPENSES

1. Has the propriety and reasonableness of revenue recognition methods been considered? \_\_\_\_ \_\_\_\_ _____ _____

2. Has there been a proper cutoff for the recognition of revenues from the sale of major products and services? \_\_\_\_ \_\_\_\_ _____ _____

   Source:

3. Has there been a proper cutoff for the measurement of expenses and purchases of inventory made during the period? \_\_\_\_ \_\_\_\_ _____ _____

   Source:

4. Are revenues and expenses properly classified in the financial statements? \_\_\_\_ \_\_\_\_ _____ _____

   Source:

5. Has an evaluation been made to determine whether the financial statements properly include discontinued operations or unusual or infrequently occurring items? \_\_\_\_ \_\_\_\_ _____ _____

   Source:

### OTHER

1. Have there been any material transactions between the client and related parties? \_\_\_\_ \_\_\_\_ _____ _____

   Source:

2. Have there been evaluations to determine whether there are any material uncertainties? \_\_\_\_ \_\_\_\_ _____ _____

   Source:

3. Has the status of material uncertainties previously disclosed been evaluated? \_\_\_\_ \_\_\_\_ _____ _____

   Source:

4. Are there any subsequent events that have a material effect on the financial statements? \_\_\_\_ \_\_\_\_ _____ _____

   Source:

§ 90 • Review Engagements  11,099

|  | Yes | No | Date of Inquiry | Comment |
|---|---|---|---|---|

**CONSOLIDATION**

1. Have all subsidiaries been evaluated to determine whether they should be included in the consolidated financial statements?
   Source:

2. Have all divisions and branches been included in the client's financial statements?
   Source:

3. Have all intercompany and intracompany accounts and transactions been eliminated?
   Source:

4. For intercorporate investments not consolidated, has the appropriateness of the investment's carrying amount been made (i.e., cost, equity method, or fair value based on the fair value option)?
   Source:

5. Has there been any change in the accounting for an intercorporate investment?
   Source:

**STATEMENT OF CASH FLOWS**

1. Has a statement of cash flows been prepared?
   Source:

2. Has there been an evaluation to determine whether the focus of the statement should be cash, or cash and cash equivalents?
   Source:

3. If the direct method of determining cash flows from operations is not used, has a supplemental reconciliation been included in the financial statement disclosures?
   Source:

## EXHIBIT AR-C 90-7—ANALYTICAL PROCEDURES FOR A REVIEW ENGAGEMENT

Use this form to document the performance of analytical procedures for a review engagement. The form is only a guide, and professional judgment should be exercised to determine how the form should be modified by omitting or adding analytical procedures.

Client Name: _____

Date of Financial Statements: _____

*COMPARISON OF CURRENT FINANCIAL STATEMENTS WITH COMPARABLE PRIOR-PERIOD FINANCIAL STATEMENTS*

The following ratios were computed:
- Using financial data that reflect review adjustments proposed to date.
- Using financial data that do not reflect review adjustments.

*Formula*

**LIQUIDITY RATIOS**

1. Current ratio — $\dfrac{\text{Current assets}}{\text{Current liabilities}}$

2. Acid-test ratio — $\dfrac{\text{Quick assets}}{\text{Current liabilities}}$

3. Days' sales in accounts receivable — $\dfrac{\text{Average accounts receivable} \times 365 \text{ Days}}{\text{Net Credit Sales}}$

4. Current liabilities to total assets — $\dfrac{\text{Current liabilities}}{\text{Total assets}}$

**ACTIVITY RATIOS**

1. Inventory turnover — $\dfrac{\text{Cost of goods sold}}{\text{Average inventory}}$

2. Receivable turnover — $\dfrac{\text{Net credit sales}}{\text{Average accounts receivable}}$

3. Asset turnover — $\dfrac{\text{net sales}}{\text{Average total assets}}$

4. Gross profit percentage — $\dfrac{\text{Gross profit}}{\text{Net sales}}$

**PROFITABILITY RATIOS**

1. Bad debt to sales — $\dfrac{\text{Bad debt expense}}{\text{Net sales}}$

2. Rate of return on total assets used — $\dfrac{\text{Net income}}{\text{Total assets}}$

3. Rate of return on equity (investment) — $\dfrac{\text{Net income}}{\text{Total equity}}$

4. Net margin — $\dfrac{\text{Net income}}{\text{Net sales}}$

**COVERAGE RATIOS**

1. Debt to total assets — $\dfrac{\text{Total debt}}{\text{Total assets}}$

2. Interest expense to sales — $\dfrac{\text{Interest expense}}{\text{Net sales}}$

§ 90 • Review Engagements   11,101

|   |   | Formula |
|---|---|---|
| 3. | Number of times interest earned | $\dfrac{\text{Income before interest and taxes}}{\text{Interest expense}}$ |

OTHER RATIOS

|   |   | |
|---|---|---|
| 1. | Effective tax rate | $\dfrac{\text{Income taxes}}{\text{Income before Taxes}}$ |
| 2. | Bad debt rate | $\dfrac{\text{Allowance for bad debts}}{\text{Accounts receivable}}$ |
| 3. | Depreciation rate | $\dfrac{\text{Depreciation expense}}{\text{Depreciable property}}$ |
| 4. | Accounts payable to purchases | $\dfrac{\text{Accounts payable}}{\text{Purchases}}$ |
| 5. | Dividend rate | $\dfrac{\text{Dividends}}{\text{Common stock (market value)}}$ |
| 6. | Interest rate | $\dfrac{\text{Interest expense}}{\text{Average interest-bearing Debt}}$ |
| 7. | Payroll rate | $\dfrac{\text{Payroll expense}}{\text{Net sales}}$ |
| 8. | Dividend return | $\dfrac{\text{Dividend income}}{\text{Average equity investments}}$ |
| 9. | Interest income return | $\dfrac{\text{Interest income}}{\text{Average debt investments}}$ |

COMPARISON OF CURRENT FINANCIAL STATEMENTS WITH ANTICIPATED RESULTS

|   |   | | 20XX | |
|---|---|---|---|---|
| Acct # | Account Name | Actual | Budgeted | Difference |
|  | Cash in bank—name |  |  |  |
|  | Petty cash |  |  |  |
|  | Cash in bank—payroll |  |  |  |
|  | Investment marketable equity securities (current) |  |  |  |
|  | Accounts receivable |  |  |  |
|  | Allowance for doubtful accounts |  |  |  |
|  | Other receivables (current) |  |  |  |
|  | Accrued interest receivable |  |  |  |
|  | Notes receivable (current) |  |  |  |
|  | Discount on notes receivable |  |  |  |

|        |              |        | 20XX     |            |
|--------|--------------|--------|----------|------------|
| Acct # | Account Name | Actual | Budgeted | Difference |
| | Dividends receivable | | | |
| | Inventory (year-end balance) | | | |
| | Prepaid insurance | | | |
| | Prepaid rent | | | |
| | Prepaid advertising | | | |
| | Land | | | |
| | Buildings | | | |
| | Accumulated depreciation—buildings | | | |
| | Delivery equipment | | | |
| | Accumulated depreciation—delivery equipment | | | |
| | Fixtures | | | |
| | Accumulated depreciation—fixtures | | | |
| | Office equipment | | | |
| | Accumulated depreciation—office equipment | | | |
| | Property—capital leases | | | |
| | Investment—marketable equity securities (noncurrent) | | | |
| | Other receivables (noncurrent) | | | |
| | Land held for investment | | | |
| | Accounts payable | | | |
| | Accrued liabilities | | | |
| | Payroll taxes and other withholdings | | | |
| | Interest payable | | | |
| | Notes payable | | | |
| | Discounts/premiums—notes payable | | | |
| | Obligations—capital leases (current) | | | |
| | Dividends payable | | | |
| | Income taxes payable | | | |
| | Notes payable (noncurrent) | | | |
| | Bonds payable | | | |
| | Discounts/premiums—bonds payable | | | |
| | Obligation—capital leases (noncurrent) | | | |
| | Common stock | | | |
| | Paid-in capital in excess of par | | | |
| | Treasury stock | | | |
| | Accumulated other comprehensive income | | | |

| Acct # | Account Name | Actual | 20XX Budgeted | Difference |
|---|---|---|---|---|
| | Unappropriated retained earnings | | | |
| | Appropriated retained earnings | | | |
| | Sales | | | |
| | Sales returns and allowances | | | |
| | Sales discounts | | | |
| | Cost of goods sold | | | |
| | Purchases | | | |
| | Freight-in | | | |
| | Bad debt expense | | | |
| | Utilities expense | | | |
| | Travel expense | | | |
| | Advertising expense | | | |
| | Delivery expense | | | |
| | Miscellaneous expense | | | |
| | Insurance expense | | | |
| | Rent expense | | | |
| | Professional fees expense | | | |
| | Salaries and wages expense | | | |
| | Payroll taxes expense | | | |
| | Depreciation expense— buildings | | | |
| | Depreciation expense—delivery equipment | | | |
| | Depreciation expense—fixtures | | | |
| | Depreciation expense—office equipment | | | |
| | Depreciation expense—capital leases | | | |
| | Repairs and maintenance expense | | | |
| | Miscellaneous income | | | |
| | Dividend income | | | |
| | Interest income | | | |
| | Interest expense | | | |
| | Loss/gain on sale of assets | | | |
| | Loss on exchange of assets | | | |
| | Loss due to permanent decline in value of security investments | | | |
| | Loss/gain on sale of investments | | | |
| | Income tax expense | | | |
| | Totals | | | |

STUDY OF FINANCIAL STATEMENT ELEMENTS AND UNEXPECTED RELATIONSHIPS

| Unexpected Relationships | Summary of Analysis |
|---|---|
| | |

OTHER ANALYTICAL PROCEDURES

Summary of findings: _____

_____

Prepared By: _____

Date: _____

Reviewed By: _____

Date: _____

# EXHIBIT AR-C 90-8—DOCUMENTING EXPECTATIONS WHEN PERFORMING ANALYTICAL PROCEDURES IN A REVIEW ENGAGEMENT

In review engagements, the accountant must perform inquiry and analytical procedures to provide the basis for the review report. When performing analytical procedures, the accountant first forms an expectation of the recorded amounts or ratios in such a way that a material difference between the expectation and the recorded amount or ratio is indicative of a possible material misstatement requiring further explanation. An accountant cannot perform effective analytical procedures without first developing expectations as to the results of those analytical procedures.

Based on his or her understanding of the client and its industry, the accountant develops expectations by identifying plausible relationships that are reasonably expected to exist. Several data sources might be used by the accountant to form the expectation. The following is an example of how an accountant might document his or her expectations.

## Documenting an Expectation Related to an Increase in Revenue

An accountant is engaged to conduct a review of financial statements of a company that manufactures medical products for use in cancer treatments. Because of increased cancer detection rates due to advanced medical technologies, the accountant reasonably expects product sales to have increased during the fiscal period due to greater demand for cancer treatment products. Using his or her knowledge of the client, the accountant expects a 10% to 15% increase in sales. Additionally, the accountant concludes that receivables should increase, and that loans payable and interest expense would also increase due to additional borrowing of funds to handle production demands.

### Example Documentation

Lifeway Medical Supply Corporation
Analytical Procedures
For the Year Ended December 31, 20X9

*Expectations*

The following are factors that should affect the relationship between current and prior-year revenue account amounts:

- Increase in cancer treatment spending due to earlier cancer detection and treatment improvements in the medical field, resulting in increased product sales. Expected increase is between 10% and 15%. A similar expectation exists for an increase in accounts receivable.
- To fund expenses related to additional production demands, the client borrowed additional funds from its lenders. Thus, loans payable and interest expense is expected to increase between 10% and 15%.
- No significant increases are expected in either days sales in inventory or inventory turnover. Although there will be some inventory buildup, it is not expected to correspond with an increase in sales because the cancer treatment products are expected to be sold near the date of completion. Increases in days sales in inventory or inventory turnover are not expected to change by more than 5%.

Balance sheets are available for the current year and the prior two years and income statements accounts are available for the current and prior year.

*Trend Analysis*

|  | December 31, 20X9 | December 31, 20X8 | Change | Percentage Change |
|---|---|---|---|---|
| Sales | $5,000,000 | $4,350,000 | $650,000 | 14.94% |
| Cost of Sales | $3,560,000 | $3,132,000 | $428,000 | 13.67% |
| Gross margin | $1,440,000 | $1,218,000 |  |  |
| Gross margin as a percentage of sales | 28.80% | 28.00% |  |  |
| Selling expenses | $460,000 | $368,000 | $92,000 | 25.00% |
| Interest expense | $96,000 | $84,000 | $12,000 | 14.29% |

*Balance Sheet Ratio Analysis*

|  | December 31, 20X9 | December 31, 20X8 | December 31, 20X7 |
|---|---|---|---|
| Accounts Rec., net | $2,200,000 | $1,686,000 | $1,406,000 |
| Inventory | $2,000,000 | $1,664,000 | $1,388,000 |
| Notes Payable | $996,000 | $874,000 | $836,000 |

*Change in Receivables*

Accounts receivable increased 30.5% from the prior year, which is in excess of the expected increase of between 10% and 15%. As a result, additional inquiries about the increase in accounts receivable will be made of the client and the associated reasons will be documented.

*Days in Receivables*

Days sales in receivables = Accounts receivables, net at end of period / (Net sales/365)

Days in Receivables for 20X9:

$2,200,000 / ($5,000,000 / 365) = 160.6 days

Days in Receivables for 20X8:

$1,686,000 / ($4,350,000 / 365) = 141.5 days

The increase in 19 days sales in receivables (160.6 - 141.5 days) represents a 13.5% increase. Inquiries about the increase in days sales in receivables will be made as part of the additional inquiries about the increase in accounts receivable.

*Change in Inventory*

Inventory increased 20.2% from the prior year, which is in excess of the expected increase of between 10 and 15% that would be associated with the increase in sales by the same percentage amounts. As a result, additional inquiries about the increase in inventory will be made of the client and the associated reasons will be documented.

*Days sales in inventory*

Days sales in inventory = Inventory at end of period / (Total cost of goods sold / 365)

Days sales in inventory for 2009:

$2,000,000 / ($3,560,000 / 365) = 205.1 days

Days sales in inventory for 2008:

$1,664,000 / ($3,132,000 / 365) = 193.9 days

The increase of 11.2 days sales in inventory (205.1 - 193.9 days) represents a 5.8% increase. Because this increase is greater than expected, further inquiries will be made of the client and reasons for the difference will be documented.

*Inventory Turnover*

Inventory turnover = Cost of goods sold / Average inventory

Inventory turnover for 20X9:

$3,560,000 / (($2,000,000 + $1,664,000) / 2) = 1.94 times

Inventory turnover for 20X8:

$3,132,000 / (($1,664,000 + $1,388,000) / 2) = 2.05 times

The inventory turnover decrease of 5.4% is beyond the expected change of no more than 5%. Because this change is greater than expected, further inquiries will be made of the client and reasons for the difference will be documented.

The increase of 13.9% in notes payable is also reasonable when considered in light of the corresponding increase in interest expense and the expectation associated with the notes payable account. However, because the increase in selling expenses is 25%, additional inquiries about that increase will be made of the client and the associated reasons will be documented.

## EXHIBIT AR-C 90-9—CONSIDERING GOING CONCERN

An entity's continuation as a going concern is assumed in financial reporting in the absence of significant information to the contrary. Often information that indicates uncertainty about an entity's ability to continue as a going concern relates to its ability to continue to meet its obligations as they become due without substantial disposition of assets outside the ordinary course of business, restructuring debt, externally forced revisions of its operations, or similar actions.

*Conditions Often Leading to Substantial Doubt*

Certain conditions, when considered together and depending on their significance, may lead to there being substantial doubt about an entity's ability to continue as a going concern for a reasonable period of time. These conditions or events include the following:

- Negative trends such as recurring operating losses, working capital deficiencies, negative cash flows from operating activities, adverse key financial ratios
- Other indications of possible financial difficulties such as default on loan or similar agreements, arrearages in dividends, denial of usual trade credit from suppliers, debt restructuring, noncompliance with statutory capital requirements, need to seek new sources or methods of financing or to dispose of substantial assets
- Internal matters such as work stoppages or other labor difficulties, substantial dependence on the success of a particular project, uneconomic long-term commitments, need to significantly revise operations

- External matters that have occurred such as legal proceedings, legislation, or similar matters that might jeopardize an entity's ability to operate; loss of a key franchise, license, or patent; loss of a principal customer or supplier; uninsured or underinsured catastrophe such as a drought, earthquake, or flood.

*Management's Plans to Address Conditions*

Management should have plans to address these identified adverse conditions and events. Examples of management's plans might include the following:

- Plans to dispose of assets: Considerations should be made about
    — Whether there are any restrictions on the disposal of assets
    — The marketability of assets to be sold
    — Potential direct or indirect effects of the disposal of assets
- Plans to borrow money or restructure debt: Considerations should be made about
    — Availability of debt financing
    — Existing or committed arrangements to restructure debt
    — Possible effects of management's borrowing plans on existing restrictions on additional borrowing
- Plans to reduce or delay expenditures: Considerations should be made about
    — Feasibility of plans to reduce overhead or administrative expenditures
    — Impact of reduced or delayed expenditures
- Plans to increase ownership equity: Considerations should be made about
    — Feasibility of plans to increase ownership equity, including existing or committed arrangements to raise additional capital
    — Existing or committed arrangements to reduce current dividend requirements

*Financial Statement Disclosure*

When management concludes that there is substantial doubt about the entity's ability to continue as a going concern, management should consider disclosing the following:

- Conditions and events giving rise to the assessment of an uncertainty about the entity's ability to continue as a going concern for a reasonable period of time
- The possible effects of such conditions and events and management's evaluation of their significance as well as any mitigating factors
- Possible discontinuation of operations
- Management's plans, including relevant prospective information
- Information about the recoverability or classification of recorded asset amounts or the amounts or classification of liabilities.

# SECTION 100

# SPECIAL CONSIDERATIONS—INTERNATIONAL REPORTING ISSUES

## Authoritative Pronouncements

SSARS-24—Omnibus Statement on Standards for Accounting and Review Services—2018

> **IMPORTANT NOTICE FOR 2022:** In May 2018, the Accounting and Review Services Committee (ARSC) issued SSARS-24 (*Omnibus Statement on Standards for Accounting and Review Services—2018*) to provide requirements and guidance when an accountant is engaged to perform a compilation or review of financial statements that have been prepared in accordance with a financial reporting framework generally accepted in another country or the accountant is engaged to perform a compilation or review in accordance with SSARS and another set of compilation or review standards. SSARS-24 created this new AR-C 100 section titled "Special Considerations—International Reporting Issues." The effective date of SSARS-24 was for compilations and reviews of financial statements for periods ending on or after June 15, 2019. The guidance in SSARS-24 has been incorporated in this *GAAS Guide*.

## Overview

An accountant may be engaged to perform a compilation or review of financial statements prepared using a financial reporting framework not adopted by a body designated by the Council of the AICPA to establish U.S. GAAP, but that is generally accepted in another country. And the accountant may be engaged to perform that compilation or review in accordance with SSARS and another set of compilation or review standards. This section contains guidance for those situations.

## Objective

The objective of this standard is for the accountant to appropriately consider the unique considerations of this type of engagement when accepting, performing, and planning the engagement and reporting on the financial statements.

## Requirements

*Engagement Acceptance Consideration*

1. As part of the accountant's considerations when accepting an engagement to compile or review financial statements prepared in accordance with a financial reporting framework generally accepted in another country, the accountant should seek to understand the purpose for

which the financial statements are prepared and whether the financial reporting framework is a fair presentation framework and the steps management has taken to determine that the framework is acceptable in the circumstances. The accountant should also understand who comprise the intended users of the financial statements.

2. When the financial statements are to be used outside the United States, the accountant should obtain an understanding of the legal responsibilities involved.

## Consideration of Framework Generally Accepted in Another Country

3. The accountant should obtain an understanding of the framework that is generally accepted in another country. The accountant should comply with the provisions in AR-C 80 for compilations and AR-C 90 for reviews.

4. The accountant should determine if he or she is independent of the entity for which he or she is engaged to compile pro forma financial information.

## Use of Another Set of Compilation and Review Standards

5. The accountant may be engaged to perform the compilation or review using another set of compilation or review standards in addition to SSARS. In that circumstance, the accountant should obtain an understanding of and apply those relevant standards, in addition to SSARS.

## Reporting

6. When the financial statements that are compiled or reviewed are intended to be used only outside the United States, the accountant should use either the report format in SSARS or the report form and content in accordance with another set of compilation and review standards. If the report is prepared in accordance with SSARS, the report would include a statement that refers to the note in the financial statements that describes the basis of the presentation of the financial statements, including identification of the country of origin, if the financial reporting framework is generally accepted in another country.

7. When the financial statements that are compiled or reviewed will be used in the United States, the accountant should report in accordance with SSARS.

8. The accountant can only refer to having conducted the compilation or review in accordance with both SSARS and another set of compilation and review standards if the accountant used both sets of those standards in his or her engagement. In that situation, the accountant's compilation or review report should identify the other set of compilation or review standards, as well as its origin.

## Analysis and Application of Procedures

Sometimes an accountant may be engaged to compile or review financial statements prepared in accordance with another financial reporting framework issued by a body that is not one designated by the AICPA Council. AR-C 80 and 90 apply to compilations and reviews, respectively, of financial statements prepared in accordance with financial reporting frameworks established by bodies designated by the Council, including International Financial Reporting Standards (IFRS) issued by the IASB. AR-C 100 provides guidance when the financial reporting framework is not issued by a body designated by the Council.

### Engagement Acceptance

As part of accepting the engagement, the accountant should obtain an understanding of the purpose for which the financial statements are prepared based on the financial reporting framework generally accepted in another country and the intended users of those financial statements. Based on that consideration, the accountant may conclude that the financial statements are not appropriate for wide distribution in the United States, particularly in light of the different legal requirements that may exist.

### Understanding the Financial Reporting Framework

SSARS requires the accountant to obtain an understanding of the applicable financial reporting framework and significant accounting policies used to prepare the financial statements. That understanding may be obtained by reading the statutes or professional literature that describe that framework.

### Different Set of Compilation and Review Standards Applied

The accountant may be engaged to comply with another set of compilation and review standards other than SSARS, in addition to complying with SSARS. Those standards may require the accountant to perform procedures in addition to those required by SSARS. The accountant may read the statutes, professional literature, and codification of those standards to obtain an understanding of those standards. The accountant may also consult with persons having expertise in applying that set of standards.

### Reporting

AR-C 100 includes different illustrations of the accountant's compilation and review reports on financial statements prepared in accordance with a financial reporting framework generally accepted in another country performed in accordance with SSARS and another set of compilation and review standards.

## Practitioner's Aids

Exhibits AR-C 100-1 and AR-C 100-2 include examples of compilation reports on financial statements prepared in accordance with a financial reporting framework generally accepted in another country.

*EXHIBIT AR-C 100-1—ACCOUNTANT'S COMPILATION REPORT ON FINANCIAL STATEMENTS PREPARED IN ACCORDANCE WITH A FINANCIAL REPORTING FRAMEWORK GENERALLY ACCEPTED IN ANOTHER COUNTRY PERFORMED IN ACCORDANCE WITH SSARS AND ANOTHER SET OF COMPILATION STANDARDS AND THE FINANCIAL STATEMENTS ARE INTENDED FOR USE ONLY OUTSIDE THE UNITED STATES*

Management is responsible for the accompanying financial statements of ABC Company, which comprise the balance sheets as of December 31, 20X2 and 20X1, and the related statements of income, changes in stockholders' equity, and cash flows for the years then ended, and the related notes to the financial statements, which, as described in Note 1 to the financial statements, have been prepared in accordance with [*specify the financial reporting framework generally accepted*] in [*name of country*]. I (We) have performed compilation engagements in accordance with Statements on Standards for Accounting and Review Services promulgated by the Accounting and Review Services Committee of the AICPA and in accordance with [*identify the other set of compilation standards*]. I (We) did not audit or review the financial statements nor was (were) I (we) required to perform any procedures to verify the accuracy or completeness of the information provided by management. I (We) do not express an opinion, a conclusion, nor provide any assurance on these financial statements.

[*Signature of accounting firm or accountant, as appropriate*]

[*Accountant's city and state*]

[*Date of the accountant's report*]

*EXHIBIT AR-C 100-2—ACCOUNTANT'S COMPILATION REPORT ON FINANCIAL STATEMENTS PREPARED IN ACCORDANCE WITH A FINANCIAL REPORTING FRAMEWORK GENERALLY ACCEPTED IN ANOTHER COUNTRY PERFORMED IN ACCORDANCE WITH SSARS AND ANOTHER SET OF COMPILATION STANDARDS AND THE FINANCIAL STATEMENTS ARE ALSO INTENDED FOR USE IN THE UNITED STATES*

Management is responsible for the accompanying financial statements of ABC Company, which comprise the balance sheets as of December 31, 20X2 and 20X1, and the related statements of income, changes in stockholders' equity, and cash flows for the years then ended, and the related notes to the financial statements, which, as described in note 1 to the financial statements, have been prepared in accordance with [*specify the financial reporting framework generally accepted*] in [*name of country*]. I (We) have performed compilation engagements in accordance with Statements on Standards for Accounting and Review Services promulgated by the Accounting and Review Services Committee of the AICPA and in accordance with [*identify the other compilation standards*]. I (We) did not audit or review the financial statements nor was (were) I (we) required to perform any procedures to verify the accuracy or completeness of the information provided by management. I (We) do not express an opinion, a conclusion, nor provide any assurance on these financial statements.

I (We) draw attention to Note 1 of the financial statements, which describes the basis of accounting. The financial statements are prepared in accordance with [*specify the financial reporting framework generally accepted*] in [*name of country*], which is a basis of accounting other than accounting principles generally accepted in the United States of America.

[*Signature of accounting firm or accountant, as appropriate*]

[*Accountant's city and state*]

[*Date of the accountant's report*]

Exhibits AR-C 100-3 and AR-C 100-4 include examples of review reports on financial statements prepared in accordance with a financial reporting framework generally accepted in another country.

## EXHIBIT AR-C 100-3—ACCOUNTANT'S REVIEW REPORT ON FINANCIAL STATEMENTS PREPARED IN ACCORDANCE WITH A FINANCIAL REPORTING FRAMEWORK GENERALLY ACCEPTED IN ANOTHER COUNTRY PERFORMED IN ACCORDANCE WITH SSARS AND ANOTHER SET OF COMPILATION STANDARDS AND THE FINANCIAL STATEMENTS ARE INTENDED FOR USE ONLY OUTSIDE THE UNITED STATES

### Independent Accountant's Review Report

[*Appropriate Addressee*]

I (We) have reviewed the accompanying financial statements of ABC Company, which comprise the balance sheets as of December 31, 20X2 and 20X1, and the related statements of income, changes in stockholders' equity, and cash flows for the years then ended, and the related notes to the financial statements. A review includes primarily applying analytical procedures to management's (owners') financial data and making inquiries of company management (owners). A review is substantially less in scope than an audit, the objective of which is the expression of an opinion regarding the financial statements as a whole. Accordingly, I (we) do not express such an opinion.

**Management's Responsibility for the Financial Statements**

Management (Owners) is (are) responsible for the preparation and fair presentation of these financial statements, which, as described in Note 1 to the financial statements, have been prepared in accordance with [*specify the financial reporting framework generally accepted*] in [*name of country*] this includes the design, implementation, and maintenance of internal control relevant to the preparation and fair presentation of financial statements that are free from material misstatement whether due to fraud or error.

**Accountant's Responsibility**

My (Our) responsibility is to conduct the review engagements in accordance with Statements on Standards for Accounting and Review Services promulgated by the Accounting and Review Services Committee of the AICPA and in accordance with [*identify the other review standards*]. Those standards require me (us) to perform procedures to obtain limited assurance as a basis for reporting whether I am (we are) aware of any material modifications that should be made to the financial statements for them to be in accordance with [*specify the financial* reporting framework generally accepted] in [name of country]. I (We) believe that the results of my (our) procedures provide a reasonable basis for my (our) conclusion.

**Accountant's Conclusion**

Based on my (our) reviews, I am (we are) not aware of any material modifications that should be made to the accompanying financial statements in order for them to be in accordance with [specify the financial reporting framework generally accepted] in [name of country].

[Signature of accounting firm or accountant, as appropriate]

[Accountant's city and state]

[Date of the accountant's review report]

---

## EXHIBIT AR-C 100-4—ACCOUNTANT'S REVIEW REPORT ON FINANCIAL STATEMENTS PREPARED IN ACCORDANCE WITH A FINANCIAL REPORTING FRAMEWORK GENERALLY ACCEPTED IN ANOTHER COUNTRY PERFORMED IN ACCORDANCE WITH SSARS AND ANOTHER SET OF REVIEW STANDARDS AND THE FINANCIAL STATEMENTS ARE ALSO INTENDED FOR USE IN THE UNITED STATES

### Independent Accountant's Review Report

[Appropriate Addressee]

I (We) have reviewed the accompanying financial statements of ABC Company, which comprise the balance sheets as of December 31, 20X2 and 20X1, and the related statements of income, changes in stockholders' equity, and cash flows for the years then ended, and the related notes to the financial statements. A review includes primarily applying analytical procedures to management's (owners') financial data and making inquiries of company management (owners). A review is substantially less in scope than an audit, the objective of which is the expression of an opinion regarding the financial statements as a whole. Accordingly, I (we) do not express such an opinion.

**Management's Responsibility for the Financial Statements**

Management (Owners) is (are) responsible for the preparation and fair presentation of these financial statements, which, as described in Note 1 to the financial statements, have been prepared in accordance with [specify the financial reporting framework generally accepted] in [name of country]; this includes the design, implementation, and maintenance of internal control relevant to the preparation and fair presentation of financial statements that are free from material misstatement whether due to fraud or error.

**Accountant's Responsibility**

My (Our) responsibility is to conduct the review engagements in accordance with Statements on Standards for Accounting and Review Services promulgated by the Accounting and Review Services Committee of the AICPA and in accordance with [identify the other review standards]. Those standards require me (us) to perform procedures to obtain limited assurance as a basis for reporting whether I am (we are) aware of any material modifications that should be made to the financial statements for them to be in accordance with [specify the financial reporting framework generally accepted] in [name of country]. I (We) believe that the results of my (our) procedures provide a reasonable basis for my (our) conclusion.

**Accountant's Conclusion**

Based on my (our) reviews, I am (we are) not aware of any material modifications that should be made to the accompanying financial statements in order for them to be in accordance with [specify the financial reporting framework generally accepted] in [name of country].

**Basis of Accounting**

I (We) draw attention to Note X of the financial statements, which describes the basis of accounting. The financial statements are prepared in accordance with [specify the financial reporting framework generally accepted] in [name of country], which is a basis of accounting other than accounting principles generally accepted in the United States of America. My (Our) conclusion is not modified with respect to this matter.

[Signature of accounting firm or accountant, as appropriate]

[Accountant's city and state]

[Date of the accountant's review report]

# SECTION 120

# COMPILATION OF PRO FORMA FINANCIAL INFORMATION

## Authoritative Pronouncements

SSARS-22—Compilation of Pro Forma Financial Information

## Overview

The Accounting and Review Services Committee completed its project on clarifying SSARS with the issuance of SSARS-22 that provides performance and reporting requirements and application guidance for accountants engaged to perform a compilation engagement on pro forma financial information.

## Definitions

| | |
|---|---|
| Pro forma financial information | A presentation that shows what the significant effects on historical financial information might have been had a consummated or proposed transaction (or event) occurred at an earlier date. |

## Objective

The objective of this standard is for the accountant to apply accounting and financial reporting expertise to assist management in the presentation of pro forma financial information and report in accordance with this section.

## Requirements

*Compliance with General Principles*

1. When engaged to perform a compilation engagement on pro forma financial information, the accountant should not only comply with AR-C 120, but should also comply with the general principles in AR-C 60.

*Independence*

2. The accountant should determine if he or she is independent of the entity for which he or she is engaged to compile pro forma financial information.

*Obtaining Agreement with Management of Responsibilities*

3. As part of the acceptance and continuance of the engagement to compile pro forma financial information, the accountant should obtain an agreement with management that:

    a. Management is responsible for preparing the pro forma financial information and its fair presentation in accordance with the applicable financial reporting framework.

b. Management will include the following in any document that contains the pro forma financial information:
   (i) The entity's most recent year's complete financial statements.
   (ii) Historical interim financial information for the applicable period if pro forma financial information is presented for an interim period.
   (iii) The relevant historical financial information for the significant constituent parts of the combined entity when the pro forma financial information involves a business combination.
c. Management will ensure that the financial statements of the entity on which the pro forma financial information is based have been subjected to a compilation, review, or audit engagement. (In the case of a business combination, this would include financial statements for each significant constituent part of the combined entity.)
d. Management will include the accountant's compilation or review report or the auditor's report on the financial statements in a document that contains the pro forma financial information.
e. Management will present with the pro form financial information a summary of significant assumptions.
f. Prior to including the accountant's compilation report in any document containing the pro form financial information that indicates the entity's accountant has performed a compilation on such pro forma financial information, management will obtain the accountant's permission.

4. The accountant should discuss with management if the accountant is not satisfied with any of the matters noted above (or in AR-60).

5. The accountant should agree upon the terms of the engagement with management or those charged with governance and that agreement should be documented in an engagement letter or other suitable form of written agreement. That agreement should be signed by the accountant (or the accountant's firm) and management or those charged with governance. It should document the following:
   a. Engagement objectives.
   b. Management responsibilities.
   c. Responsibilities of the accountant.
   d. Limitations of the engagement to compile pro forma financial information.
   e. Acknowledgment of the applicable financial reporting framework for the preparation of the pro forma financial information.
   f. The anticipated form and content of the accountant's compilation report, including statements if there may be circumstances where the report may not be in its expected form.

*Knowledge and Understanding of the Entity's Financial Reporting Framework*
   6. The accountant should obtain an understanding of the applicable financial reporting framework used in the preparation of the pro forma financial information.

---

**PLANNING AID REMINDER:** If the entity is a combined entity, the accountant should obtain an understanding of the significant accounting policies adopted by management of each constituent part of the combined entity. The level of understanding would be equivalent to that which would have been required to have been obtained by the accountant performing a compilation engagement with respect to the financial statements of each entity for the most recent annual or interim period for which the pro forma financial information is presented.

---

*Compilation Procedures*
   7. The accountant should perform the following procedures when compiling pro forma financial information:
      a. Ensure compliance with AR-C 80.
      b. Obtain an understanding of the underlying transaction or event that provides the basis for the pro forma financial information.
      c. Ensure management fulfills its agreement to include the following items in the document containing the pro forma financial information:
         (i) The entity's most recent year's complete financial statements.
         (ii) Historical interim financial information for the applicable period if pro forma financial information is presented for an interim period.
         (iii) The relevant historical financial information for the significant constituent parts of the combined entity when the pro forma financial information involves a business combination.
      d. Ensure that management has fulfilled its responsibility to have the financial statements of the entity on which the pro forma financial information is based compiled, reviewed, or audited.
      e. Ensure that management fulfills its agreement to include the accountant's compilation or review report, or the auditor's report on the financial statements in any document that contains the pro forma financial information.

*Accountant's Compilation Report*
   8. The accountant's compilation report on the pro forma financial information should be written and comply with provisions in AR-C 80. The report should also include the following:
      a. Reference to the financial statements from which the historical financial information is derived to compile the pro forma financial information. That reference should also state whether such financial statements were subject to a compilation, review, or audit engagement.

b. Reference to any modification of the audit, review, or compilation report on the historical financial information.

c. Description of the nature and limitations of pro forma financial information.

## *Documentation*

9. The accountant should prepare documentation that is sufficient to provide a clear understanding of the work performed. That would include:

   a. Engagement letter or other suitable form of written documentation with management.

   b. Results of the compilation procedures performed to compile the pro forma financial information.

   c. Copy of the pro forma financial information.

   d. Copy of the accountant's compilation report.

## Analysis and Application of Procedures

The objective of pro forma financial information is to show what the significant effects on historical financial information might have been had a consummated or proposed transaction (or event) occurred at an earlier date. Pro forma financial information is commonly used to show the effects of transactions such as the following:

- Business combination.
- Change in capitalization.
- Disposition of a significant portion of the business.
- Change in the form of business organization or status as an autonomous entity.
- Proposed sale of securities and the application of the proceeds.

Pro forma financial information is generally achieved by applying pro forma adjustments to historical financial statements. Pro forma adjustments should be based on management's assumptions and give effect to all significant effects directly attributable to the transaction (or event). And, those pro forma adjustments should be stated on a basis consistent with the financial reporting framework of the reporting entity.

### *Accountant's Responsibility for Pro Forma Financial Information*

An engagement to compile pro forma financial information may be undertaken as a separate engagement or in conjunction with a compilation, review, or an audit of financial statements. When an accountant is engaged to compile pro forma financial information, he or she should establish an understanding with the entity, in writing, regarding the services to be performed. The understanding should include a description of the nature and limitations of the services to be performed and a description of the report.

When an accountant is engaged to compile pro forma financial information, he or she must adhere to the performance requirements contained in AR-C 60 and AR-C 80 for compilations. Before issuing the compilation report, the accountant should read the compiled pro forma financial information, including the summary of significant assumptions, and consider whether it appears to be appropriate in form and free of obvious material errors. When reading the pro forma financial information, the accountant should consider whether that information adequately describes the underlying transaction (or event), the pro forma adjustments, the significant assumptions, and significant uncertainties, if any, about those assumptions. The accountant should also ensure that the historical information on which the pro forma financial information is derived has been appropriately identified.

The pro forma financial information should be labeled to distinguish it from other historical financial information. And, the pro forma financial information should also include adequately disclosed financial information that describes the transaction or event that is reflected by the pro forma financial information and the date it is assumed to occur on. In addition, the pro forma financial information should describe the financial reporting framework of the financial statements, the source of the historical financial information that the pro forma financial information is based on, the significant assumptions used to compile the pro forma adjustments, and any significant uncertainties regarding those assumptions.

SSARS-22 specifies the basic elements of a compilation report on pro forma financial information. Each page of the compiled pro forma financial information should include a reference, such as "See Accountant's Compilation Report."

> **PLANNING AID REMINDER:** If the accountant is not independent of the entity whose pro forma financial information is the subject of the compilation, the accountant should modify the accountant's compilation report to reflect the lack of independence.

Exhibit AR-C 120-1 is an example of a compilation report on pro forma financial information.

## *EXHIBIT AR-C 120-1—ACCOUNTANT'S COMPILATION REPORT ON PRO FORMA FINANCIAL INFORMATION*

> Management is responsible for the accompanying pro forma condensed balance sheet of ABC Company as of December 31, 20X1, and the related pro forma condensed statement of income for the year then ended (pro forma financial information), based on the criteria in Note 1. The historical condensed financial statements are derived from the financial statements of ABC Company, on which I (we) performed a compilation engagement, and of DEF Company, on which other accountants performed a compilation engagement. The pro forma adjustments are based on management's assumptions described in Note 1. I (We) have performed a compilation engagement in accordance with Statements on Standards for Accounting and Review Services promulgated by the Accounting

and Review Services Committee of the AICPA. I (we) did not examine or review the pro forma financial information nor was (were) I (we) required to perform any procedures to verify the accuracy or completeness of the information provided by management. Accordingly, I (we) do not express an opinion, a conclus on, nor provide any form of assurance on the pro forma financial information.

The objective of this pro forma financial information is to show what the significant effects on the historical financial information might have been had the underlying transaction (or event) occurred at an earlier date. However, the pro forma condensed financial statements are not necessarily indicative of the results of operations or related effects on financial position that would have been attained had the above mentioned transaction (or event) actually occurred at such earlier date.

[*Additional paragraph(s) may be added to emphasize certain matters relating to the compilation engagement or the subject matter.*]

[*Signature of accounting firm or accountant, as appropriate*]

[*Accountant's city and state*]

[*Date of the accountant's report*]

# Accounting Resources on the Web

**Accounting Research Manager®** http://www.AccountingResearchManager.com
*Accounting Today* **magazine** http://www.accountingtoday.com
**AICPA** http://www.aicpa.org
**AICPA Guidance Related to OMB Circular A-133** https://www.aicpa.org/interestareas/governmentalauditquality/resources/singleaudit/uniformguidanceforfederalrewards.html
**AICPA Member Insurance Programs Information - Professional Liability** http://www.cpai.com/business-insurance/professional-liability/index
**American Accounting Association** http://aaahq.org
**American Legal Publishing Corp.** https://codelibrary.amlegal.com/
**American Public Power Association (APPA)** https://www.publicpower.org/
**American Water Works Association** http://www.awwa.org
**Association for Budgeting and Financial Management (ABFM)** http://www.abfm.org
**Association of Certified Fraud Examiners (ACFE)** http://www.acfe.com
**Association of College and University Auditors (ACUA)** http://www.acua.org
**Association of Financial Guaranty Insurers (AFGI)** http://www.afgi.org
**Association of Government Accountants (AGA)** http://www.agacgfm.org
**Association of Latino Professionals in Finance and Accounting (ALPFA)** http://www.alpfa.org
**Association of Local Government Auditors** http://www.GovernmentAuditors.org
**Association of School Business Officials International** http://www.asbointl.org
**Automated Clearing House** https://fiscal.treasury.gov/ach/
**Bloomberg Markets** https://www.bloomberg.com/markets/rates-bonds/government-bonds/us
**BoardSource** http://www.boardsource.org
**Bond Buyer** http://www.bondbuyer.com
**Bureau of Labor Statistics** http://www.bls.gov
**Bureau of the Fiscal Service (Treasury Dept.)** http://www.fiscal.treasury.gov
**CCH Publications** www.cchcpelink.com/books
**Check Payment Systems Association** http://www.cpsa-checks.org
**Code of Federal Regulations** http://www.gpo.gov/fdsys/browse/collectionCfr.action
**Compliance Supplement** https://www.whitehouse.gov/omb/office-federal-financial-management/
**Congress.gov** https://congress.gov

Council of State Governments (CSG) http://www.csg.org
Council of the Inspectors General on Integrity & Efficiency (CIGIE) http://www.ignet.gov
Council on Foundations http://www.cof.org
CPE www.cchcpelink.com
Department of Education OIG's Non-Federal Audit Team http://www2.ed.gov/about/offices/list/oig/nonfed/index.html
Electronic Municipal Market Access (EMMA) http://emma.msrb.org
Electronic Privacy Information Center http://epic.org
FASB http://www.fasb.org
FASB Accounting Standards Codification (ASC) http://asc.fasb.org/home
Federal Accounting Standards Advisory Board (FASAB) http://www.fasab.gov
Federal Agencies Web Locator http://www.usa.gov
Federal Audit Clearinghouse http://harvester.census.gov/facweb
Federal Digital System (FDsys) http://www.gpo.gov/fdsys
Federal Inspectors General (IGnet) http://www.ignet.gov
Federal Register http://www.gpo.gov/fdsys/browse/collection.action?collectionCode=FR
GASB http://www.gasb.org
GASB Governmental Accounting Research System (GARS) online https://gars.gasb.org
General Code Publishers http://www.generalcode.com
General Services Administration http://www.gsa.gov
*Governing* magazine http://www.governing.com
Government Accountability Office http://www.gao.gov
Government Auditing Standards https://www.gao.gov/yellowbook
Government Finance Officers Association (GFOA) http://www.gfoa.org
Government Publishing Office http://www.gpo.gov
GuideStar http://www.guidestar.org
Health and Human Services (HHS) http://www.hhs.gov
Health and Human Services (HHS) Grants/Contracts http://www.hhs.gov/grants/
HUD Office of Public and Indian Housing (PIH) https://www.hud.gov/program_offices/public_indian_housing
HUD Real Estate Assessment Center (REAC) https://www.hud.gov/program_offices/public_indian_housing/reac
IFRS Foundation and the IASB http://www.ifrs.org
Information for Tax-Exempt Organizations https://www.irs.gov/charities-non-profits/exempt-organizations-help-from-the-irs#:~:text=You%20may%20direct%20technical%20and,(toll%2Dfree%20number).

**Institute of Internal Auditors, The (IIA)** http://www.theiia.org
**Institute of Management Accountants (IMA)** http://www.imanet.org
**IntelliConnect®** http://IntelliConnect.cch.com
**Intergovernmental Audit Forums** http://www.auditforum.org
**Internal Revenue Service (IRS)** http://www.irs.gov
**International City/County Management Association** http://www.icma.org
**International Institute of Municipal Clerks (IIMC)** http://www.iimc.com
**Investment Company Institute (ICI)** http://www.ici.org
**Legal Information Institute (Cornell Law School)** https://www.law.cornell.edu/
**LSU Libraries Government Documents** http://www.lib.lsu.edu/collections/govdocs
**Minority Business Development Agency** http://www.mbda.gov
**Municipal Code Corporation (MCC)** http://www.municode.com
**Municipal Securities Rulemaking Board (MSRB)** http://www.msrb.org
**NACHA—The Electronic Payments Association** http://www.nacha.org
**National Association of Asian American Professionals (NAAAP)** http://www.naaap.org
**National Association of Black Accountants, Inc.** http://www.nabainc.org
**National Association of Bond Lawyers** http://www.nabl.org
**National Association of College and University Business Officers (NACUBO)** http://www.nacubo.org
**National Association of Counties (NACO)** http://www.naco.org
**National Association of Housing and Redevelopment Officials (NAHRO)** http://www.nahro.org
**National Association of Regional Councils** http://www.narc.org
**National Association of State Agencies for Surplus Property** http://www.nasasp.org
**National Association of State Auditors, Comptrollers, and Treasurers (NASACT)** http://www.nasact.org
**National Association of State Boards of Accountancy (NASBA)** http://www.nasba.org
**National Association of State Budget Officers** http://www.nasbo.org
**National Association of State Retirement Administrators** http://www.nasra.org
**National Center for Charitable Statistics** http://nccs.urban.org
**National Conference of State Legislatures (NCSL)** http://www.ncsl.org
**National Council of Nonprofits** http://www.CouncilOfNonprofits.org
**National Federation of Municipal Analysts (NFMA)** http://www.nfma.org
**National Governors Association (NGA)** http://www.nga.org

National Labor Relations Board https://www.nlrb.gov
National League of Cities (NLC) http://www.nlc.org
National Rural Development Partnership http://www.rd.usda.gov
Native American Finance Officers Association (NAFOA) http://www.nafoa.org
North American Industry Classification System (NAICS) https://www.census.gov/naics/
Occupational Employment Statistics http://stats.bls.gov/oes/home.htm
Office of Federal Contract Compliance Programs (OFCCP) http://www.dol.gov/ofccp
Office of Management and Budget http://www.whitehouse.gov/omb
Office of Women's Business Ownership (SBA) https://www.sba.gov/offices/headquarters/wbo
OMB Grants Management http://www.omb.ri.gov/grants/
OMB Grants Management Forms https://obamawhitehouse.archives.gov/omb/grants_forms
OMB Submissions to the Federal Register https://www.federalregister.gov/agencies/management-and-budget-office
Privacy Foundation http://www.privacyfoundation.org
Prompt Payment Act Interest Rate http://www.fms.treas.gov/prompt/rates.html
Securities and Exchange Commission http://www.sec.gov
Securities Industry and Financial Markets Association (SIFMA) http://www.sifma.org/
Software and Information Industry Association (SIIA) http://www.siia.net
Sterling Codifiers, Inc. http://www.sterlingcodifiers.com
The Library of Congress http://www.loc.gov
The White House http://www.whitehouse.gov
USA.gov http://www.usa.gov
USA.gov for Nonprofits http://www.usa.gov/Business/Nonprofit.shtml
U.S. Census Bureau: Federal, State, and Local Government Page http://www.census.gov/govs/
U.S. Code Search http://uscode.house.gov
U.S. Conference of Mayors http://www.usmayors.org
U.S. Department of Agriculture http://www.usda.gov
U.S. Department of Commerce http://www.commerce.gov
U.S. Department of Defense http://www.defense.gov
U.S. Department of Education http://www.ed.gov
U.S. Department of Energy http://www.energy.gov
U.S. Department of Health and Human Services http://www.hhs.gov

**U.S. Department of Housing and Urban Development** http://www.hud.gov
**U.S. Department of Labor** http://www.dol.gov
**U.S. Department of State** http://www.state.gov
**U.S. Department of the Interior** http://www.doi.gov
**U.S. Department of the Treasury's Listing of Approved Sureties** http://www.fiscal.treasury.gov/fsreports/ref/suretyBnd/c570.htm
**U.S. Department of Transportation** http://www.dot.gov
**U.S. Dept. of Treasury Bureau of the Fiscal Service** http://www.fiscal.treasury.gov
**U.S. Environmental Protection Agency** http://www.epa.gov
**U.S. GAO Bid Protest Decisions** http://www.gao.gov/legal/
**U.S. Government Forms** http://www.gsa.gov/forms
**U.S. House of Representatives** http://www.house.gov
**U.S. House of Representatives Current Floor Proceedings** http://clerk.house.gov/floorsummary/floor.aspx
**U.S. HUD Client Information and Policy System** http://portal.hud.gov/hudportal/HUD?src=/program_offices/administration/hudclips
**U.S. HUD Office of Inspector General** http://www.hudoig.gov
**U.S. HUD Office of Labor Relations** https://www.hud.gov/program_offices/davis_bacon_and_labor_standards
**U.S. Postal Service** http://www.usps.com
**U.S. Senate** http://www.senate.gov
**U.S. Small Business Administration** http://www.sba.gov
**U.S. Transportation and Safety Administration** http://www.tsa.gov
**U.S. Treasury** http://www.treasury.gov
**Veterans Affairs** http://www.va.gov
**Wolters Kluwer** www.taxna.wolterskluwer.com
**Yellow Book** http://www.gao.gov/yellowbook/overview
**ZIP+4 Code lookup** http://www.usps.com/zip4

# Cross-Reference

13,001

## STATEMENTS ON AUDITING STANDARDS (SASs) AND SAS INTERPRETATIONS

| ORIGINAL PRONOUNCEMENT | GAAS GUIDE REFERENCE |
|---|---|
| Note: *SAS-122 through SAS-128 recodified and superseded all outstanding SASs through SAS-121 except SAS-117, SAS-118, SAS-119, and SAS-120. SAS-118 was later superseded by SAS-137.* | |
| **SAS-117—Compliance Audits** | AU-C 935 |
| **SAS-118—Other Information in Documents Containing Audited Financial Statements** | Superseded by SAS-137 |
| **SAS-119—Supplementary Information in Relation to the Financial Statements as a Whole** | AU-C 725 |
| • Auditing Interpretation 1 of AU 725 (October 2011)—Dating the Auditor's Report on Supplementary Information | |
| **SAS-120—Required Supplementary Information** | AU-C 730 |
| **SAS-122—Statements on Auditing Standards: Clarification and Recodification** | |
| Principles Underlying an Audit Conducted in Accordance with Generally Accepted Auditing Standard | Preface to Codification of Statement on Auditing Standards |
| Overall Objectives of the Independent Auditor and the Conduct of an Audit in Accordance with Generally Accepted Auditing Standards | AU-C 200 |

| ORIGINAL PRONOUNCEMENT | GAAS GUIDE REFERENCE |
|---|---|
| Terms of Engagement | AU-C 210 |
| Quality Control for an Engagement Conducted in Accordance with Generally Accepted Auditing Standards | AU-C 220 |
| Audit Documentation | AU-C 230 |
| • Auditing Interpretation 1 of AU 230 (October 2011)—Providing Access to or Copies of Audit Documentation to a Regulator | |
| Consideration of Fraud in a Financial Statement Audit | AU-C 240 |
| Consideration of Laws and Regulations in an Audit of Financial Statements | AU-C 250 |
| The Auditor's Communication with Those Charged with Governance | AU-C 260 |
| Communicating Internal Control Related Matters Identified in an Audit | AU-C 265 |
| • Auditing Interpretation 1 of AU 265 (January 2012)—Communication of Significant Deficiencies and Material Weaknesses Prior to Completion of the Compliance Audit for Participants in Office of Management and Budget Single Audit Act Pilot Project | |
| • Auditing Interpretation 2 of AU 265 (January 2012)—Communication of Significant Deficiencies and Material Weaknesses Prior to Completion of the Compliance Audit for Auditors That Are Not Participants in Office of Management and Budget Single Audit Act Pilot Project | |
| • Auditing Interpretation 3 of AU 265 (January 2012)—Appropriateness of Identifying No Significant Deficiencies or No Material Weaknesses in an Interim Communication | |
| Planning an Audit | AU-C 300 |

| ORIGINAL PRONOUNCEMENT | GAAS GUIDE REFERENCE |
|---|---|
| Understanding the Entity and Its Environment and Assessing the Risks of Material Misstatement | AU-C 315 |
| Materiality in Planning and Performing an Audit | AU-C 320 |
| Performing Audit Procedures in Response to Assessed Risks and Evaluating the Audit Evidence Obtained | AU-C 330 |
| Audit Considerations Relating to an Entity Using a Service Organization | AU-C 402 |
| Evaluation of Misstatements Identified During the Audit | AU-C 450 |
| Audit Evidence | AU-C 500 |
| • Auditing Interpretation 1 of AU 500 (October 2011)—The Effect of an Inability to Obtain Audit Evidence Relating to Income Tax Accruals | |
| • Auditing Interpretation 2 of AU 500 (April 2014)—Auditor of Participating Employer in a Governmental Cost-Sharing Multiple-Employer Pension Plan | |
| • Auditing Interpretation 3 of AU 500 (June 2014)—Auditor of Participating Employer in a Governmental Agent Multiple-Employer Pension Plan | |
| Audit Evidence—Specific Considerations for Selected Items | AU-C 501 |
| External Confirmations | AU-C 505 |
| Opening Balances—Initial Audit Engagements, Including Reaudit Engagements | AU-C 510 |
| Analytical Procedures | AU-C 520 |
| Audit Sampling | AU-C 530 |
| Auditing Accounting Estimates, Including Fair Value Accounting Estimates and Related Disclosures | AU-C 540 |
| Related Parties | AU-C 550 |
| Subsequent Events and Subsequently Discovered Facts | AU-C 560 |

| ORIGINAL PRONOUNCEMENT | GAAS GUIDE REFERENCE |
|---|---|
| Written Representations | AU-C 580 |
| Consideration of Omitted Procedures after the Report Release Date | AU-C 585 |
| Special Considerations—Audits of Group Financial Statements (Including the Work of Component Auditors) | AU-C 600 |
| • Auditing Interpretation 1 of AU 600 (April 2014)—Auditor of Participating Employer in a Governmental Pension Plan | |
| Using the Work of an Auditor's Specialist | AU-C 620 |
| • Auditing Interpretation 1 of AU 620 (October 2011)—The Use of Legal Interpretations as Audit Evidence to Support Management's Assertion That a Transfer of Financial Assets Has Met the Isolation Criterion in Paragraphs 7-14 of Financial Accounting Standards Board *Accounting Standards Codification* 860-10-40 | |
| Forming an Opinion and Reporting on Financial Statements | AU-C 700 |
| Communicating Key Audit Matters in the Independent Auditor's Report | AU-C 701 |
| Modifications to the Opinion in the Independent Auditor's Report | AU-C 705 |
| Emphasis-of-Matter Paragraphs and Other-Matter Paragraphs in the Independent Auditor's Report | AU-C 706 |
| Consistency of Financial Statements | AU-C 708 |
| Special Considerations—Audits of Financial Statements Prepared in Accordance with Special Purpose Frameworks | AU-C 800 |
| Special Considerations—Audits of Single Financial Statements and Specific Elements, Accounts or Items of a Financial Statement | AU-C 805 |

| ORIGINAL PRONOUNCEMENT | GAAS GUIDE REFERENCE |
|---|---|
| • Auditing Interpretation 1 of AU 805 (April 2014)—Auditor of Governmental Cost-Sharing Multiple-Employer Pension Plan | |
| • Auditing Interpretation 2 of AU 805 (June 2014)—Auditor of Governmental Agent Multiple-Employer Pension Plan | |
| Reporting on Compliance with Aspects of Contractual Agreements or Regulatory Requirements in Connection with Audited Financial Statements | AU-C 806 |
| Engagements to Report on Summary Financial Statements | AU-C 810 |
| Reports on Application of Requirements of an Applicable Financial Reporting Framework | AU-C 915 |
| Letters for Underwriters and Certain Other Requesting Parties | AU-C 920 |
| Filings with the U.S. Securities and Exchange Commission under the Securities Act of 1933 | AU-C 925 |
| Interim Financial Information | AU-C 930 |
| **SAS-123—Omnibus Statement on Auditing Standards—2011** | AU-C 200, AU-C 230, AU-C 260, AU-C 705, AU-C 720, AU-C 915, AU-C 935 |
| **SAS-124—Financial Statements Prepared in Accordance with a Financial Reporting Framework Generally Accepted in Another Country** | AU-C 910 |
| **SAS-125—Alert That Restricts the Use of the Auditor's Written Communication** | AU-C 905 |
| **SAS-126—The Auditor's Consideration of an Entity's Ability to Continue as a Going Concern** | Superseded by SAS-132 |

**13,006** *Cross-Reference*

| ORIGINAL PRONOUNCEMENT | GAAS GUIDE REFERENCE |
|---|---|
| SAS-127—Omnibus Statement on Auditing Standards—2013 | AU-C 600, AU-C 800 |
| SAS-128—Using the Work of Internal Auditors | AU-C 610 |
| SAS-129—Amendment to SAS No. 122 Section 920, Letters for Underwriters and Certain Other Requesting Parties | AU-C 920 |
| SAS-130—An Audit of Internal Control over Financial Reporting That Is Integrated with an Audit of Financial Statements | AU-C 265, AU-C 940 |
| SAS-131—Amendment to Statement on Auditing Standards No. 122 Section 700, Forming an Opinion and Reporting on Financial Statements | AU-C 700 |
| SAS-132—The Auditor's Consideration of an Entity's Ability to Continue as a Going Concern | AU-C 570 |
| SAS-133—Auditor Involvement with Exempt Offering Documents | AU-C 945 |
| SAS-134—Auditor Reporting and Amendments, Including Amendments Addressing Disclosures in the Audit of Financial Statements | AU-C 200, AU-C 210, AU-C 220, AU-C 230, AU-C 240, AU-C 260, AU-C 300, AU-C 315, AU-C 320, AU-C 330, AU-C 450, AU-C 510, AU-C 540, AU-C 570, AU-C 600, AU-C 700, AU-C 701, AU-C 705, AU-C 706, AU-C 910 |
| SAS-135—Omnibus Statement on Auditing Standards—2019 | AU-C 210, AU-C 240, AU-C 260, AU-C 265, AU-C 315, AU-C 330, AU-C 500, AU-C 510, AU-C 550, AU-C 560, AU-C 580, AU-C 600, AU-C 930, AU-C 940 |

Cross-Reference **13,007**

| ORIGINAL PRONOUNCEMENT | GAAS GUIDE REFERENCE |
|---|---|
| SAS-136—Forming an Opinion and Reporting on Financial Statements of Employee Benefit Plans Subject to ERISA | AU-C 200, AU-C 220, AU-C 240, AU-C 330, AU-C 450, AU-C 501, AU-C 510, AU-C 540, AU-C 550, AU-C 560, AU-C 580, AU-C 570, AU-C 700, AU-C 703, AU-C 725, AU-C 708 |
| SAS-137—The Auditor's Responsibilities Relating to Other Information Included in Annual Reports | AU-C 210, AU-C 230, AU-C 260, AU-C 450, AU-C 600, AU-C 700, AU-C 705, AU-C 706, AU-C 720, AU-C 725, AU-C 730, AU-C 810, AU-C 945 |
| SAS-138—Amendments to the Description of the Concept of Materiality | AU-C 200, AU-C 320, AU-C 450, AU-C 600, AU-C 700, AU-C 703, AU-C 725 |
| SAS-139—Amendments to AU-C Sections 800, 805, and 810 to Incorporate Auditor Reporting Changes from SAS No. 134 | AU-C 800, AU-C 805, AU-C 810 |
| SAS-140—Amendments to AU-C Sections 725, 730, 930, 935, and 940 to Incorporate Auditor Reporting Changes from SAS Nos. 134 and 137 | AU-C 703, AU-C 705, AU-C 725, AU-C 730, AU-C 910, AU-C 920, AU-C 930, AU-C 935, AU-C 940 |
| SAS-141—Amendment to the Effective Dates of SAS Nos. 134-140 | AU-C 200, AU-C 210, AU-C 220, AU-C 230, AU-C 240, AU-C 260, AU-C 300, AU-C 315, AU-C 320, AU-C 450, AU-C 510, AU-C 540, AU-C 550, AU-C 560, AU-C 570, AU-C 580, AU-C 600, AU-C 700, AU-C 701, AU-C 703, AU-C 705, AU-C 706, AU-C 720, AU-C 725, AU-C 910, AU-C 920, AU-C 930, AU-C 935, AU-C 940 |
| SAS-142—Audit Evidence | AU-C 200, AU-C 230, AU-C 315, AU-C 330, AU-C 500, AU-C 501, AU-C 530, AU-C 540 |
| SAS-143—Auditing Accounting Estimates and Related Disclosures | AU-C 200, AU-C 230, AU-C 240, AU-C 260, AU-C 501, AU-C 540, AU-C 580, AU-C 700, AU-C 701, AU-C 703 |

| ORIGINAL PRONOUNCEMENT | GAAS GUIDE REFERENCE |
|---|---|
| SAS-144—Amendments to AU-C Sections 501, 540, and 620 Related to the Use of Specialists and the Use of Pricing Information Obtained from External Information Sources | AU-C 501, AU-C 540, AU-C 620 |

## STATEMENTS ON QUALITY CONTROL STANDARDS (SQCSs)

| ORIGINAL PRONOUNCEMENT | GAAS GUIDE REFERENCE |
|---|---|
| SQCS-8—A Firm's System of Quality Control | AU-C 220 |

- No Interpretations

## STATEMENTS ON STANDARDS FOR ACCOUNTING AND REVIEW SERVICES (SSARSs) AND SSARS INTERPRETATIONS

**Note:** *SSARS-21 recodified and superseded all outstanding SSARSs through SSARS-20 except for SSARS-14, which is codified as AR 120. SSARS-14 was later superseded by SSARS-22. All compilation and review interpretations of the SSARS have been considered in the development of SSARS-21 and either incorporated accordingly or considered for inclusion in the AICPA Guide* Review, Compilation, and Financial Statement Preparation Engagements: Engagements Performed in Accordance with SSARSs.

| ORIGINAL PRONOUNCEMENT | GAAS GUIDE REFERENCE |
|---|---|
| SSARS-14—Compilation of Pro Forma Financial Information | Superseded by SSARS-22 |
| SSARS-21—Statements on Standards for Accounting and Review Services: Clarification and Recodification | AR-C 60, AR-C 70, AR-C 80, AR-C 90 |

| ORIGINAL PRONOUNCEMENT | GAAS GUIDE REFERENCE |
|---|---|
| SSARS-22—Compilation of Pro Forma Financial Information | AR-C 120 |
| SSARS-23—Omnibus Statement on Standards for Accounting and Review Services—2016 | AR-C 60, AR-C 70, AR-C 80, AR-C 90 |
| SSARS-24—Omnibus Statement on Standards for Accounting and Review Services—2018 | AR-C 60, AR-C 90, AR-C 100 |
| SSARS-25—Materiality in a Review of Financial Statements and Adverse Conclusions | AR-C 60, AR-C 70, AR-C 80, AR-C 90 |

## STATEMENTS ON STANDARDS FOR ATTESTATION ENGAGEMENTS (SSAEs) AND SSAE INTERPRETATIONS

| ORIGINAL PRONOUNCEMENT | GAAS GUIDE REFERENCE |
|---|---|
| Note: *SSAE-18 recodified and superseded all outstanding SSAEs through SSAE-17 except extant AT section 701,* Management's Discussion and Analysis, *which is now codified as AT-C section 395.* | |
| SSAE-18—Attestation Standards: Clarification and Recodification | |
| Preface | AT-C Preface |
| Concepts Common to All Attestation Engagements | AT-C 105 |
| • SSAE Interpretation 1 of AT-C 105 (April 2016)—Responding to Requests for Reports on Matters Relating to Solvency | |
| • SSAE Interpretation 2 of AT-C 105 (April 2016)—Applicability of Attestation Standards to Litigation Services | |
| • SSAE Interpretation 3 of AT-C 105 (April 2016)—Providing Access to or Copies of Engagement Documentation to a Regulator | |

## 13,010  Cross-Reference

| ORIGINAL PRONOUNCEMENT | GAAS GUIDE REFERENCE |
|---|---|
| • SSAE Interpretation 4 of AT-C 105 (May 2017)—Performing and Reporting on an Attestation Engagement Under Two Sets of Attestation Standards | |
| Assertion-Based Examination Engagements | AT-C 205 |
| • SSAE Interpretation 1 of AT-C 205 (April 2016)—Reporting on Attestation Engagements Performed in Accordance with Government Auditing Standards | |
| • SSAE Interpretation 2 of AT-C 205 (April 2016)—Reporting on the Design of Internal Control | |
| Review Engagements | AT-C 210 |
| Agreed-Upon Procedures Engagements | AT-C 215 |
| • SSAE Interpretation 1 of AT-C 215 (April 2016)—Third Party Due Diligence Services Related to Asset-Backed Securitizations: SEC Release No. 34-72936 | |
| Prospective Financial Information | AT-C 305 |
| Reporting on Pro Forma Financial Information | AT-C 310 |
| Compliance Attestation | AT-C 315 |
| Reporting on an Examination of Controls at a Service Organization Relevant to User Entities' Internal Control over Financial Reporting | AT-C 320 |
| Management's Discussion and Analysis | AT-C 395 |
| **SSAE-19—Agreed-Upon Procedures Engagements** | AT-C 105, AT-C 215 |
| **SSAE-20—Amendments to the Description of the Concept of Materiality** | AT-C 205, AT-C 210 |
| **SSAE-21—Direct Examination Engagements** | AT-C 105, AT-C 205, AT-C 206 |
| **SSAE-22—Review Engagements** | AT-C 210 |

# Index

## A

ABA (American Bar Association), *Statement of Policy Regarding Lawyers' Responses to Auditor's Requests for Information* . . . 5028

Absolute assurance . . . 1002-1003

Accountants
. communication between predecessor and successor accountants. *See* Predecessor and successor accountant communication
. compilation of financial statements
. accountant's compilation reports . . . 11,038-11,039
. financial reporting frameworks, accountant's report . . . 9020
. pro forma financial information—compilation, accountant responsibility . . . 11,120-11,121

Accounting and Review Services Committee (ARSC). *See specific* SSARS

Accounting estimates . . . 5117-5145
. analysis and application of procedures . . . 5124-5135
. . disclosures . . . 5134
. . evaluation of reasonableness . . . 5134
. . identifying, assessing and responding to risks of material misstatement . . . 5127-5133
. . management bias . . . 5135
. . response to significant risks . . . 5133
. . risk assessment . . . 5124-5127
. authoritative pronouncements . . . 5117
. common estimates requiring auditor evaluation . . . 5145
. definitions . . . 5121
. overview . . . 5117-5121
. practitioner's aids . . . 5135-5145
. requirements . . . 5121-5123
. . disclosures . . . 5123
. . documentation . . . 5123
. . evaluation of reasonableness . . . 5123

Accounting estimates—continued
. requirements—continued
. . identifying, assessing and responding to risks of material misstatement . . . 5122
. . management bias . . . 5123
. . response to significant risks . . . 5122-5123
. . risk assessment . . . 5121-5122
. soft accounting information
. . auditing . . . 5135-5140
. . evaluation of persuasiveness of evidence . . . 5140-5142
. . nonauthoritative guidance . . . 5135-5140

Accounting Principles Board. *See specific APB*

Accounting Standards Codification (ASC). *See specific ASC*

Agreed-upon procedures engagements . . . 10,091-10,103
. analysis and application of procedures . . . 10,098-10,102
. . agreeing on engagement terms . . . 10,099
. . conduct of . . . 10,098
. . findings . . . 10,101
. . internal auditors or other practitioners, using work of . . . 10,100
. . matters outside agreed-upon procedures, knowledge of . . . 10,102
. . practitioner's AUP report, content of . . . 10,101-10,102
. . practitioner's external specialist, using work of . . . 10,100
. . preconditions for . . . 10,098-10,099
. . preparation of report . . . 10,101
. . procedures to performed . . . 10,099-10,100
. . requested written representations not provided or not reliable . . . 10,101
. authoritative pronouncements . . . 10,091
. definition . . . 10,092
. overview . . . 10,091-10,092
. practitioner's aid . . . 10,103
. report . . . 10,103
. requirements . . . 10,092-10,098
. . adding specified parties . . . 10,097

**AGR**

**Index**

Agreed-upon procedures engagements—continued
. requirements—continued
. . agreeing on engagement terms . . . 10,093
. . appropriateness of procedures . . . 10,094
. . communication responsibilities . . . 10,097
. . conduct of . . . 10,092
. . documentation . . . 10,097-10,098
. . findings . . . 10,094
. . internal auditors or other practitioners, using work of . . . 10,094
. . matters outside agreed-upon procedures, knowledge of . . . 10,097
. . practitioner's AUP report, content of . . . 10,095-10,097
. . practitioner's external specialist, using work of . . . 10,094
. . preconditions for . . . 10,092-10,093
. . preparation of report . . . 10,095
. . procedures to performed . . . 10,093-10,094
. . requested written representations not provided or not reliable . . . 10,095
. . written representations . . . 10,094-10,095

AICPA. *See* American Institute of Certified Public Accountants (AICPA)

American Bar Association (ABA), *Statement of Policy Regarding Lawyers' Responses to* . . . 5028

American Institute of Certified Public Accountants (AICPA). *See also specific Standard*
. *Analytical Procedures* . . . 5064
. *Auditing Derivative Instruments, Hedging Activities, and Investments in Securities* . . . 5019
. *Auditing Estimates and Other Soft Accounting Information* . . . 5119, 5135
. *Auditing Revenue in Certain Industries* . . . 2084
. *Audit Sampling* . . . 5081, 5096, 5106, 5109, 5111, 5116
. Code of Professional Conduct. *See* Code of Professional Conduct
. *CPA Letter* . . . 2005

American Institute of Certified Public Accountants (AICPA).—continued
. *Forming an Opinion and Reporting on Financial Statements of Employee Benefit Plans Subject to ERISA* . . . 7003, 7028-7046
. "Management Override of Internal Controls: The Achilles' Heel of Fraud Prevention" . . . 2076, 3033

Practice Alerts. *See specific Practice Alert*
. State and Local Governments and Health Care Entities . . . 9046
. Technical Practice Aids. *See* Technical Practice Aids

Analytical procedures . . . 5062-5079
. analysis and application of procedures . . . 5063-5071
. . analytical procedures . . . 5063-5069
. . assisting in forming overall conclusion . . . 5071
. . evaluation of results . . . 5068-5069
. . formation of auditor expectations . . . 5064
. . identification of differences . . . 5067
. . inherent precision . . . 5065-5067
. . investigation of differences . . . 5067-5068
. . investigation of results . . . 5071
. . nature of account or assertion . . . 5064-5065
. . reliability . . . 5065
. . substantive analytical procedures . . . 5069-5071
. authoritative pronouncements . . . 5062
. definitions . . . 5062
. documentation of effect of . . . 5071-5072
. final analytical review . . . 5077-5079
. overview . . . 5062
. performance of . . . 5072-5077
. practitioner's aids . . . 5071-5079
. requirements . . . 5062-5063

*Analytical Procedures* (AICPA) . . . 5064

APB 28-1 (*Interim Disclosures about Fair Value of Financial Instruments*)
. accounting estimates . . . 5120
. audit evidence—specific considerations . . . 5022

AR-C 60 (*Framework for Preparing and Reporting on Compilation and Review Engagements*) . . . 11,002-11,015

AR-C 70 (*Preparation of Financial Statements*) . . . 11,016-11,024

AR-C 80 (*Compilation of Financial Statements*) 11,025-11,040. *See also* Compilation of financial statements

AR-C 90 (*Review of Financial Statements*) 11,041-11,108. *See also* Review of financial statements

AR-C 100 (*Special Considerations — International Reporting Issues*) . . . 11,041, 11,109-11,115 *See also* International reporting issues, special considerations

AR-C 120 (*Compilation of Pro Forma Financial Information*) 11,116-11,121. *See also* Pro forma financial information—compilation

ARSC (Accounting and Review Services Committee). *See specific* SSARS

AS-1101
. fraud . . . 2066

AS-1105 (*Audit Evidence*)
. analytical procedures . . . 5064
. audit evidence . . . 5005

AS-1201 (*Supervision of the Audit Engagement*)
. audit planning . . . 3003
. materiality . . . 3062

AS-1210 (*Using the Work of an Auditor-Engaged Specialist*) . . . 3083-3084, 50105011

AS-1215 (*Audit Documentation*) . . . 2057

AS-1215 (*Audit Documentation and Amendment to Interim Auditing Standards*) . . . 6019

AS-1220 (*Engagement Quality Review*) . . . 9052-9053

AS-2101 (*Audit Planning*)
. audit planning . . . 3003
. fraud . . . 2066
. materiality . . . 3062

AS-2110 (*Identifying and Assessing Risks of Material Misstatement*)
. analytical procedures . . . 5064
. fraud . . . 2066

AS-2201
. internal control—audit . . . 9102
. written representations . . . 5195

AS-2301 (*The Auditor's Responses to the Risks of Material Misstatement*)
. analytical procedures . . . 5064
. fraud . . . 2066
. response to assessed risks . . . 3068

AS-2410 (*Related Parties: Amendments to Certain PCAOB Auditing Standards Regarding Significant Unusual Transactions and Other Amendments to PCAOB Auditing Standards*) . . . 5147-5148
. fraud . . . 2067-2068

AS-2701 (*Auditing Supplemental Information Accompanying Audited Financial Statements and Related Amendments to PCAOB Standards*) . . . 7083, 7090

AS-2810 (*Evaluating Audit Results*)
. analytical procedures . . . 5064
. fraud . . . 2066
. response to assessed risks . . . 3068

AS-2820 (*Evaluating Consistency of Financial Statements and Conforming Amendments*) . . . 7076

AS-3101 (*The Auditor's Report on an Audit of Financial Statements When the Auditor Expresses an Unqualified Opinion*) . . . 7003, 7022-7023, 7082-7083

ASC 270 (*Interim Reporting*) . . . 9052

ASC 275 (*Disclosure of Certain Significant Risks and Uncertainties*) . . . 5142

ASC 320 (*Investments—Debt and Equity Securities*)
. accounting estimates . . . 5120, 5142
. audit evidence—specific considerations . . . 5022

ASC 350 (*Intangibles—Goodwill and Other*) . . . 5019

**ASC**

# 14,004 Index

ASC 360 (*Property, Plant, and Equipment*) . . . 5136, 5142

ASC 360-20 (*Real Estate Sales*) . . . 2084

ASC 450 (*Contingencies*) . . . 2099
. accounting estimates . . . 5142-5143
. audit evidence—specific considerations . . . 5036

ASC 470 (*Debt*) . . . 5188

ASC 470-40 (*Product Financing Arrangements*) . . . 2084

ASC 605 (*Revenue Recognition*) . . . 2084

ASC 715 (*Compensation—Retirement Benefits*) . . . 5136

ASC 718 (*Compensation—Stock Compensation*) . . . 5142

ASC 815 (*Derivatives and Hedging*) . . . 5019

ASC 820 (*Fair Value Measurements and Disclosures*)
. accounting estimates . . . 5120
. audit evidence—specific considerations . . . 5021-5022

ASC 825 (*Financial Instruments*)
. accounting estimates . . . 5120
. audit evidence—specific considerations . . . 5022

ASC 850 (*Related Party Disclosures*) . . . 5146, 5159

ASC 860 (*Accounting for Transfers of Financial Assets*) . . . 6047-6048

ASC 952 (*Franchisors*) . . . 2084

ASC 958 (*Not-for-Profit Entities*) . . . 5021

ASC 985 (*Software*) . . . 2084

Assertion level . . . 2015

Assertion-Based Examination Engagements . . . 10,024
. authoritative pronouncements . . . 10,024
. analysis and application of procedures . . . 10,039-10,054
. . agreeing on engagement terms . . . 10,039-10,040

Assertion-Based Examination Engagements—continued
. analysis and application of procedures—continued
. . communication responsibilities . . . 10,053-10,054
. . criteria, description of . . . 10,048
. . documentation . . . 10,054
. . evaluating results of procedures . . . 10,046
. . fraud, laws, and regulations . . . 10,044
. . identifying risks of material misstatement . . . 10,043
. . internal auditors, using work of . . . 10,046
. . materiality in engagement planning and performance . . . 10,042-10,043
. . modified opinions . . . 10,052-10,053
. . opinion formation . . . 10,048-10,049
. . other information . . . 10,048
. . planning and performing . . . 10,040-10,041
. . practitioner's report . . . 10,049-10,052
. . practitioner's specialist . . . 10,044-10,045, 10,052
. . reliability of information produced by entity, evaluation of . . . 10,044
. . responding to assessed risks and obtaining evidence . . . 10,043-10,044
. . responsible party refuses to provide written assertion . . . 10,053
. . restricted-use paragraph . . . 10,051-10,052
. . risk assessment . . . 10,042, 10,044
. . subsequent events and subsequently discovered facts . . . 10,046-10,047
. . written assertion, request for . . . 10,040
. . written representations . . . 10,047-10,048
. definitions . . . 10,025
. examination report—assertion . . . 10,055-10,056
. examination report—subject matter . . . 10,054-10,055
. MD&A . . . 10,173-10,174
. overview . . . 10,024-10,025
. practitioner's aids . . . 10,054-10,056
. requirements . . . 10,026-10,039
. . agreeing on engagement terms . . . 10,026
. . communication responsibilities . . . 10,038

**ASC**

# Index

**Assertion-Based Examination Engagements—**continued
. requirements—continued
. . conduct of . . . 10,026
. . criteria, description of . . . 10,035
. . documentation . . . 10,039
. . evaluating results of procedures . . . 10,032-10,033
. . fraud, laws, and regulations . . . 10,030
. . identifying risks of material misstatement . . . 10,028
. . internal auditors, using work of . . . 10,032
. . materiality in engagement planning and performance . . . 10,027
. . modified opinions . . . 10,037-10,038
. . opinion formation . . . 10,035
. . other information . . . 10,035
. . planning and performing . . . 10,027
. . practitioner's report . . . 10,035-10,036
. . practitioner's specialist . . . 10,031-10,032, 10,037
. . preconditions for . . . 10,026
. . procedures . . . 10,028-10,030
. . reliability of information produced by entity, evaluation of . . . 10,031
. . responding to assessed risks and obtaining evidence . . . 10,028
. . responsible party refuses to provide written assertion . . . 10,038
. . restricted-use paragraph . . . 10,036
. . risk assessment . . . 10,027, 10,030
. . subsequent events and subsequently discovered facts . . . 10,033
. . written assertion, request for . . . 10,026
. . written representations . . . 10,033-10,035

**Assertions**
. analytical procedures, nature of account or assertion . . . 5064-5065
. response to assessed risks, assertion level responses
. . analysis and application of procedures . . . 3072-3075
. . requirements . . . 3068-3069
. understanding entity and its environment . . . 3037-3038

**Assessment of risk.** *See* Risk assessment

**AT-C 105** (*Concepts Common to all Attestation Engagements*) 10,005-10,023. *See also* Attestation engagements
. compliance attestation . . . 10,135
. MD&A . . . 10,172
. service organizations—reporting . . . 10,151

**AT-C 205** (*Assertion-Based Examination Engagements*) 10,024-10,056, 10,057. *See also* Assertion-Based Examination Engagements
. compliance attestation . . . 10,135
. service organizations—reporting . . . 10,151

**AT-C 206** (*Direct Examination Engagements*) 10,057-10,064. *See also* Direct Examination Engagements
. compliance attestation . . . 10,122
. service organizations—reporting . . . 10,138

**AT-C 210** (*Review Engagements*) 10,065-10,090. *See also* Review Engagements
. compliance attestation . . . 10,137

**AT-C 215** (*Agreed-Upon Procedures Engagements*) 10,005-10,006, 10,091-10,103. *See also* Agreed-Upon Procedures Engagements
. compliance attestation . . . 10,135
. compliance audits . . . 9075
. MD&A . . . 10,172
. service organizations—reporting . . . 10,151
. underwriters' letters . . . 9023, 9032

**AT-C 305** (*Prospective Financial Information*) 10,002, 10,104. *See also* Prospective Financial Information
. underwriters' letters . . . 9029, 9034

**AT-C 310** (*Reporting on Pro Forma Financial Information*) 10,002, 10,122-10,134. *See also* Pro forma financial information—reporting
. underwriters' letters . . . 9034

**AT-C 315** (*Compliance Attestation*) 10,002. *See also* Compliance Attestation
. compliance audits . . . 9075

**AT-C 320** (*Reporting on an Examination of on Controls at a Service Organization Relevant to User Entities' Internal Control over Financial Reporting*) 4007, 10,002. *See also* Service organizations—reporting

**AT-**

# Index

AT-C 395 (*Management's Discussion and Analysis*) 10,002. *See also* Management's discussion and analysis
. underwriters' letters . . . 9034-9035

Attestation, compliance. *See* Compliance attestation

Attest engagements
. analysis and application of procedures . . . 10,016-10,023
. . acceptance of change in engagement terms . . . 10,020
. . attestation risk . . . 10,016-10,017
. . conduct of . . . 10,017-10,018
. . engagement documentation . . . 10,021-10,022
. . engagement quality control review . . . 10,022
. . other practitioners, using work of . . . 10,020-10,021
. . preconditions for . . . 10,018-10,020
. . professional skepticism and professional judgment . . . 10,022-10,023
. . quality control . . . 10,021
. authoritative pronouncements . . . 10,005
. common concepts . . . 10,005-10,023
. definitions . . . 10,008-10,011
. organizational structure of . . . 10,002-10,003
. overview . . . 10,006-10,008
. performance . . . 10,003
. purpose of . . . 10,003
. requirements . . . 10,011-10,016
. . acceptance and continuance . . . 10,012
. . acceptance of change in engagement terms . . . 10,013
. . conduct of . . . 10,011-10,012
. . engagement documentation . . . 10,014-10,015
. . engagement quality control review . . . 10,015
. . other practitioners, using work of . . . 10,013-10,014
. . preconditions for . . . 10,012-10,013
. . professional skepticism and professional judgment . . . 10,015-10,016
. . quality control . . . 10,014
. responsibilities . . . 10,003

AU-C 200 (*Overall Objectives of the Independent Auditor and the Conduct of an Audit in Accordance with Generally Accepted Auditing Standards*) 2002-2023. *See also* Objectives of auditors
. Rule 3101 compared . . . 2018, 2019
. terms of engagement . . . 2029

AU-C 210 (*Terms of Engagement*) 2024-2038. *See also* Terms of engagement
. audit documentation . . . 2058
. audit planning . . . 3004
. financial reporting frameworks . . . 9019
. interim financial information . . . 9053
. opening balances . . . 5054

AU-C 220 (*Quality Control for an Engagement Conducted in Accordance with Generally Accepted Auditing Standards*) 2039-2048. *See also* Quality control for engagements
. audit documentation . . . 2058-2059
. audit planning . . . 3004
. group financial statements . . . 6002
. quality control . . . 2010
. specialists . . . 6038, 6042, 6043
. terms of engagement . . . 2024

AU-C 230 (*Audit Documentation*) 2049-2064. *See also* Audit documentation
. audit evidence . . . 5011
. interim financial information . . . 9068-9069
. omitted procedures . . . 5201

AU-C 240 (*Consideration of Fraud in a Financial Statement Audit*) 2065-2092, 9090. *See also* Fraud
. accounting estimates . . . 5118, 5126-5127
. audit documentation . . . 2059
. audit evidence—specific considerations . . . 5019, 5024, 5026, 5028
. audit sampling . . . 5083-5084, 5088, 5115
. communication—those charged with governance . . . 2115
. evaluation of misstatements identified during audit . . . 4016, 4022
. interim financial information . . . 9067
. internal auditors . . . 6036
. internal control—communication . . . 2124
. objectives of auditors . . . 2014, 2017
. related parties . . . 5152

**AT-**

**AU-C 240** (*Consideration of Fraud in a Financial Statement Audit*) 2065-2092, 9090.—continued
. single financial statements . . . 8019
. specialists . . . 6038-6039
. terms of engagement . . . 2032-2033
. understanding entity and its environment . . . 3024-3025, 3027, 3040, 3043, 3045
. written representations . . . 5194

**AU-C 250** (*Consideration of Laws and Regulations in an Audit of Financial Statements*) 2093-2101. *See also* Consideration of laws and regulations
. audit documentation . . . 2059
. audit evidence—specific considerations . . . 5027
. communication—those charged with governance . . . 2115
. evaluation of misstatements identified during audit . . . 4022
. interim financial information . . . 9067
. internal control—communication . . . 2124
. objectives of auditors . . . 2017

**AU-C 260** (*The Auditor's Communication with Those Charged with Governance*) 2102-2117. *See also* Communication—those charged with governance
. accounting estimates . . . 5134
. audit documentation . . . 2059
. audit planning . . . 3008
. fraud . . . 2083
. interim financial information . . . 9059
. restrictions on use of written communication . . . 9005
. special purpose frameworks . . . 8006

**AU-C 265** (*Communicating Internal Control Related Matters Identified in an Audit*) 2118-2129, 9113. *See also* Internal control—communication
. audit documentation . . . 2059
. communication—those charged with governance . . . 2115
. interim financial information . . . 9063, 9067
. restrictions on use of written communication . . . 9003, 9005
. terms of engagement . . . 2030

**AU-C 265** (*Communicating Internal Control Related Matters Identified in an Audit*) 2118-2129, 9113.—continued
. underwriters' letters . . . 9027

**AU-C 300** (*Planning an Audit*) 3002-3016, 9090. *See also* Audit planning
. audit documentation . . . 2059
. specialists . . . 6038, 6042

**AU-C 315** (*Understanding the Entity and its Environment and Assessing the Risks of Material Misstatements*) 3017-3059, 9087, 9091. *See also* Understanding entity and its environment
. analytical procedures . . . 5062
. audit documentation . . . 2059-2060
. audit planning . . . 3004
. communication—those charged with governance . . . 2108
. fraud . . . 2089, 3026
. internal audits . . . 6032-6033
. internal control—reporting . . . 6028
. opening balances . . . 5059
. specialists . . . 6038

**AU-C 320** (*Materiality in Planning and Performing an Audit*) 3060-3066. *See also* Materiality
. audit documentation . . . 2060
. evaluation of misstatements identified during audit . . . 4012

**AU-C 330** (*Performing Audit Procedures in Response to Assessed Risks and Evaluating the Audit Evidence Obtained*) 3067-3089, 5012, 9109. *See also* Response to assessed risks
. accounting estimates . . . 5131
. analytical procedures . . . 5062
. audit documentation . . . 2060
. audit planning . . . 3004
. external confirmations . . . 5039, 5042
. response to assessed risks . . . 3069
. understanding entity and its environment . . . 3042

**AU-C 402** (*Audit Considerations Relating to an Entity Using a Service Organization*) 4001-4011. *See also* Service organizations—audit considerations
. service organizations—reporting . . . 10,150

**AU-**

AU-C 450 (*Evaluation of Misstatement Identified During the Audit*) 4012-4023. *See also* Evaluation of misstatements identified during audit
. audit documentation . . . 2060
. materiality . . . 3060, 3062
. modification of opinions . . . 7051
. written representations . . . 5193

AU-C 500 (*Audit Evidence*) 5002-5012. *See also* Audit evidence
. audit evidence—specific considerations . . . 5015
. audit sampling . . . 5109
. external confirmations . . . 5039
. MD&A . . . 10,176
. response to assessed risks . . . 3069
. SAS Interpretation 1 (*The Effect of an Inability to Obtain Audit Evidence Relating to Income Tax Accruals*) . . . 5002
. SAS Interpretation 2 (*Auditor of Participating Employer in a Governmental Cost-Sharing Multiple-Employer Pension Plan*) . . . 5002
. SAS Interpretation 3 (*Auditor of Participating Employer in a Governmental Agent Multiple-Employer Pension Plan*) . . . 5002
. specialists . . . 6038

AU-C 501 (*Audit Evidence—Specific Considerations for Selected Items*) 5013-5038. *See also* Audit evidence
. accounting estimates . . . 5119
. audit documentation . . . 2060
. supplementary information . . . 7094

AU-C 505 (*External Confirmations*) 5039-5053. *See also* External confirmations
. fraud . . . 2090

AU-C 510 (*Opening Balances—Initial Audit Engagements, Including Reaudit Engagements*) 5054-5061. *See also* Opening balances
. audit planning . . . 3010
. MD&A . . . 10,174
. terms of engagement . . . 2033

AU-C 520 (*Analytical Procedures*) 5062-5079. *See also* Analytical procedures
. fraud . . . 2081, 2089-2090

AU-C 520 (*Analytical Procedures*) 5062-5079.—continued
. MD&A . . . 10,191
. understanding entity and its environment . . . 3026

AU-C 530 (*Audit Sampling*) 5080-5116. *See also* Audit sampling

AU-C 540 (*Auditing Accounting Estimates, Including Fair Value Accounting Estimates, and Related Disclosures*) 5117-5145. *See also* Accounting estimates
. audit documentation . . . 2061
. audit evidence—specific considerations . . . 5019
. communication—those charged with governance . . . 2115
. fraud . . . 2080, 2091
. specialists . . . 6046

AU-C 543 (*Part of an Audit Performed by Other Independent Auditors*) . . . 6003

AU-C 550 (*Related Parties*) 5146-5159. *See also* Related parties
. audit documentation . . . 2061
. fraud . . . 2089
. single financial statements . . . 8019

AU-C 560 (*Subsequent Events and Subsequently Discovered Facts*) 5160-5173. *See also* Subsequent events and subsequently discovered facts
. accounting estimates . . . 5128
. consistency of financial statements . . . 7080
. emphasis-of-matter paragraphs and other-matter paragraphs . . . 7071
. filings with SEC under 1933 Act . . . 9045-9046
. forming opinions . . . 7011, 7017
. interim financial information . . . 9061
. omitted procedures . . . 5201-5202
. other information . . . 7084
. summary financial statements . . . 8033
. supplementary information . . . 7092, 7094
. written representations . . . 5196, 5198

AU-C 570 (*The Auditor's Consideration of an Entity's Ability to Continue as a Going Concern*) 5174-5187. *See also* Going concerns
. audit documentation . . . 2061

AU-

**Index** **14,009**

AU-C 570 (*The Auditor's Consideration of an Entity's Ability to Continue as a Going Concern*) 5174-5187.—continued
. objectives of auditors . . . 2017
. single financial statements . . . 8019
. understanding entity and its environment . . . 3028
. written representations . . . 5198

AU-C 580 (*Written Representations*) 5188-5200. *See also* Written representations
. fraud . . . 2075-2076, 2091-2092
. MD&A . . . 10,184-10,185
. supplementary information . . . 7094
. terms of engagement . . . 2028

AU-C 585 (*Consideration of Omitted Procedures After the Report Release Date*) 5201-5203. *See also* Omitted procedures

AU-C 600 (*Special Considerations—Audits of Group Financial Statements (Including the Work of Component Auditors)*) 6002-6026, 9098. *See also* Group financial statements
. audit documentation . . . 2061
. audit evidence—specific considerations . . . 5020
. audit planning . . . 3002
. SAS Interpretation 1 (*Auditor of Participating Employer in a Governmental Pension Plan*) . . . 6002
. service organizations . . . 4007

AU-C 610 (*Using the Work of Internal Auditors*) 6027-6037, 9090. *See also* Internal auditors
. audit documentation . . . 2061
. MD&A . . . 10,177
. understanding entity and its environment . . . 3036

AU-C 620 (*Using the Work of an Auditor's Specialist*) 6038-6049. *See also* Specialists
. accounting estimates . . . 5140
. MD&A . . . 10,177
. understanding entity and its environment . . . 3041

AU-C 700 (*Forming an Opinion and Reporting on Financial Statements*) 7002-7021. *See also* Forming opinions
. emphasis-of-matter paragraphs and other-matter paragraphs . . . 7071

AU-C 700 (*Forming an Opinion and Reporting on Financial Statements*) 7002-7021.—continued
. financial reporting frameworks—generally accepted in other countries . . . 9008
. single financial statements . . . 8016
. special purpose frameworks . . . 8003-8004
. summary financial statements . . . 8029
. written representations . . . 5198

AU-C 701 . . . 7022-7027
. audit documentation . . . 2062

AU-C 703 (*Forming an Opinion and Reporting on Financial Statements of Employee Benefit Plans Subject to ERISA*) . . . 7003, 7028-7046, 7089

AU-C 705 (*Modifications to the Opinion in the Independent Auditor's Report*) 7047-7066, 9114. *See also* Modification of opinions
. audit evidence—specific considerations . . . 5015, 5018, 5025, 5029
. consideration of laws and regulations . . . 2094
. consistency of financial statements . . . 7078
. related parties . . . 5158
. service organizations—audit considerations . . . 4005
. special purpose frameworks . . . 8004
. written representations . . . 5192

AU-C 706 (*Emphasis-of-Matter Paragraphs and Other-Matter Paragraphs in the Independent Auditor's Report*) 7067-7075. *See also* Emphasis-of-matter paragraphs and other-matter paragraphs
. modification of opinions . . . 7047
. single financial statements . . . 8017

AU-C 708 (*Consistency of Financial Statements*) 7076-7080. *See also* Consistency of financial statements
. emphasis-of-matter paragraphs and other-matter paragraphs . . . 7071

AU-C 720 (*Other Information in Documents Containing Audited Financial Statements*) 7081-7088. *See also* Other information
. audit documentation . . . 2062
. communication—those charged with governance . . . 2115

**AU-**

AU-C 720 (*Other Information in Documents Containing Audited Financial Statements*) 7081-7088.—continued
. filings with SEC under 1933 Act . . . 9045
. required supplementary information . . . 7097
. supplementary information . . . 7089

AU-C 725 (*Supplementary Information in Relation to the Financial Statements as a Whole*) 7089-7096. *See also* Supplementary information
. restrictions on use of written communication . . . 9005

AU-C 730 (*Required Supplementary Information*) 7097-7100. *See also* Required supplementary information
. other information . . . 7082
. summary financial statements . . . 8029
. supplementary information . . . 7089
. underwriters' letters . . . 9034

AU-C 800 (*Special Considerations—Audits of Financial Statements Prepared in Accordance with Special Purpose Frameworks*) 8002-8013. *See also* Special purpose frameworks
. emphasis-of-matter paragraphs and other-matter paragraphs . . . 7071
. restrictions on use of written communication . . . 9005
. single financial statements . . . 8018, 8020
. terms of engagement . . . 2028

AU-C 805 (*Special Considerations—Audits of Single Financial Statements and Specific Elements, Accounts or Items of a Financial Statement*) 8014-8023. *See also* Single financial statements
. SAS Interpretation 1 (*Auditor of Governmental Cost-Sharing Multiple-Employer Pension Plan*) . . . 8014
. SAS Interpretation 2 (*Auditor of Governmental Agent Multiple-Employer Pension Plan*) . . . 8014

AU-C 806 (*Reporting on Compliance with Aspects of Contractual Agreements or Regulatory Requirements in Connection with Audited Financial Statements*) 8024-8028. *See*

AU-C 806 (*Reporting on Compliance with Aspects of Contractual Agreements or Regulatory Requirements in Connection with Audited Financial Statements*) 8024-8028.—continued
*also* Contractual or regulatory compliance reporting
. compliance attestation . . . 10,137
. emphasis-of-matter paragraphs and other-matter paragraphs . . . 7071
. restrictions on use of written communication . . . 9003, 9005

AU-C 810 (*Engagements to Report on Summary Financial Statements*) 8029-8037. *See also* Summary financial statements
. underwriters' letters . . . 9034

AU-C 905 (*Alert that Restricts the Use of the Auditor's Written Communication*) 9002-9005, 9103. *See also* Restrictions on use of written communication
. emphasis-of-matter paragraphs and other-matter paragraphs . . . 7071
. special purpose frameworks . . . 8008

AU-C 910 (*Financial Statements Prepared in Accordance with a Financial Reporting Framework Generally Accepted in Another Country*) 9006-9014. *See also* Financial reporting frameworks—generally accepted in other countries

AU-C 915 (*Reports on Application of Requirements of an Applicable Financial Reporting Framework*) 9015-9020. *See also* Financial reporting frameworks
. audit documentation . . . 2062
. restrictions on use of written communication . . . 9005

AU-C 920 (*Letters for Underwriters and Certain Other Requesting Parties*) 9021-9043. *See also* Underwriters' letters
. restrictions on use of written communication . . . 9004, 9005
. underwriters' letters . . . 9021

AU-C 925 (*Filings with the U.S. Securities and Exchange Commission Under the Securities Act of 1933*) 9044-9050. *See also* Filings with SEC under 1933 Act

**AU-**

# Index

AU-C 930 (*Interim Financial Information*) 9051-9074. *See also* Interim financial information
. audit documentation . . . 2062
. filings with SEC under 1933 Act . . . 9046
. review of financial statements . . . 11,042
. underwriters' letters . . . 9028-9029, 9034, 9036

AU-C 935 (*Compliance Audits*) 9075-9087. *See also* Compliance audits
. audit documentation . . . 2062
. communication—those charged with governance . . . 2115
. compliance attestation . . . 10,137
. contractual or regulatory compliance reporting . . . 8024
. restrictions on use of written communication . . . 9003, 9005
. written representations . . . 5198

AU-C 940 (*An Audit of Internal Control over Financial Reporting That Is Integrated with an Audit of Financial Statements*) 9003, 9087-9119. *See also* Internal control of financial statement audit
. compliance attestation . . . 10,137

AU-C 945 (*Auditor Involvement with Exempt Offering Documents*) 9120-9128. *See also* Exempt offering documents

Audit documentation . . . 2049-2064
. analysis and application of procedures . . . 2051-2058
. . assembly and retention of final audit file . . . 2056-2058
. . procedures performed and evidence obtained . . . 2052-2056
. . timely preparation . . . 2052
. analytical procedures, documentation of effect of . . . 5071-5072
. applicable AU-Cs . . . 2058-2062
. audit planning . . . 3009-3010
. audit sampling . . . 5097, 5105-5106
. authoritative pronouncements . . . 2049
. communication—those charged with governance . . . 2107
. compilation of financial statements . . . 11,033

Audit documentation—continued
. compliance audits
. . analysis and application of procedures . . . 9087
. . requirements . . . 9083
. consideration of laws and regulations . . . 2096
. definitions . . . 2050
. evaluation of misstatements identified during audit . . . 4016
. fraud . . . 2072
. going concerns . . . 5179-5180
. group financial statements . . . 6010-6011
. interim financial information
. . analysis and application of procedures . . . 9068
. . requirements . . . 9061-9062
. internal auditors . . . 6031-6032, 6037
. letter to regulatory agency . . . 2062-2064
. overview . . . 2049
. practitioner's aids . . . 2058-2064
. quality control for engagements . . . 2044
. related parties . . . 5150
. requirements
. . assembly and retention of final audit file . . . 2051
. . procedures performed and evidence obtained . . . 2050-2051
. . timely preparation . . . 2050
. response to assessed risks
. . analysis and application of procedures . . . 3084
. . requirements . . . 3072
. SOX and . . . 2056-2057
. understanding entity and its environment
. . analysis and application of procedures . . . 3049-3050
. . requirements . . . 3024

Audit evidence . . . 5002-5038
. analysis and application of procedures . . . 5004-5012, 5019-5031
. . analytical procedures . . . 5007-5008
. . audit procedures . . . 5005-5008
. . entity-produced information . . . 5010-5011
. . external confirmations . . . 5007
. . impairment losses . . . 5023-5024

**AUD**

**14,012**         *Index*

Audit evidence—continued
 . analysis and application of procedures—continued
 . . inconsistent or doubtful evidence . . . 5011-5012
 . . inquiries . . . 5008
 . . inspection . . . 5006
 . . inventory . . . 5024-5026
 . . investments in derivative instruments or securities . . . 5019-5020
 . . investments in derivative instruments or securities based on fair value measurement . . . 5021-5023
 . . investments in securities based on financial results . . . 5020-5021
 . . litigation, claims and assessments . . . 5027-5030
 . . management's specialists, use of . . . 5030-5031
 . . observation . . . 5006
 . . recalculation . . . 5006
 . . relevance . . . 5008-5009
 . . reliability . . . 5009
 . . reperformance . . . 5006
 . . segment information . . . 5030
 . . sufficient appropriate evidence . . . 5004-5005
 . audit inquiry letter to legal counsel . . . 5035-5035
 . . management requesting list of litigation, claims and assessments . . . 5037-5038
 . authoritative pronouncements . . . 5002, 5013
 . confirmation request for inventory held by third party . . . 5034-5035
 . definitions . . . 5003, 5014
 . inventory observation procedures . . . 5031-5033
 . overview . . . 5002-5003, 5013-5014
 . practitioner's aids . . . 5031-5038
 . requirements . . . 5003-5004, 5014-5019
 . . impairment losses . . . 5015-5016
 . . inventory . . . 5016
 . . investments in derivative instruments or securities based on fair value measurement . . . 5015
 . . investments in securities based on financial results . . . 5015

Audit evidence—continued
 . requirements—continued
 . . litigation, claims and assessments . . . 5017-5018
 . . management specialists . . . 5019
 . . segment information . . . 5018

*Auditing Derivative Instruments, Hedging Activities, and Investments in Securities* (AICPA) . . . 5019

*Auditing Estimates and Other Soft Accounting Information* (AICPA) . . . 5119, 5135

*Auditing Revenue in Certain Industries* (AICPA) . . . 2084-2086

Auditing Standards (AS). *See specific AS*

Auditing Standards Board. *See specific Standard*

Audit opinions
 . forming. *See* Forming opinions
 . modification of. *See* Modification of opinions

Auditors. *See specific topic*

*The Auditor's Report on an Audit of Financial Statements When the Auditor Expresses an Unqualified Opinion* . . . 2104, 7004-7005, 7082-7083

Audit planning . . . 3002-3016
 . analysis and application of procedures . . . 3005-3010
 . . communication—those charged with governance . . . 3008
 . . development of plan . . . 3008-3009
 . . discussion among key engagement team members . . . 3005
 . . documentation . . . 3009-3010
 . . initial audit engagements . . . 3010
 . . overall strategy . . . 3005-3008
 . . preliminary engagement activities . . . 3005
 . . specialized skills . . . 3009
 . authoritative pronouncements . . . 3002
 . checklist . . . 3010-3016
 . overview . . . 3002-3003
 . practitioner's aids . . . 3010-3016
 . requirements . . . 3003-3005
 . SOX and . . . 3007

**AUD**

Audit sampling . . . 5080-5116
. analysis and application of procedures . . . 5083-5086
. . acceptable level of risk . . . 5102-5103
. . allowable risk of assessing control risk too low . . . 5093
. . choice of technique . . . 5099
. . completeness of population . . . 5089, 5099
. . deviation conditions . . . 5088
. . deviation rate . . . 5095
. . documentation . . . 5097, 5105-5106
. . effect of population size . . . 5094
. . evaluation of results . . . 5085-5086, 5095, 5105, 5113-5115
. . expected amount of misstatement . . . 5104, 5108
. . expected population deviation rate . . . 5093-5094
. . individually significant items . . . 5099, 5106
. . method of selection of sample . . . 5089, 5104
. . nature and cause of deviations and misstatements . . . 5085
. . objectives of test . . . 5087-5088, 5098
. . other sampling . . . 5090-5091
. . overall conclusion . . . 5097
. . performance of audit procedures . . . 5085
. . performance of sampling plan . . . 5095, 5104-5105
. . period covered by test . . . 5089
. . population . . . 5088-5089, 5098-5099
. . population size . . . 5104, 5108
. . projection of misstatements . . . 5085, 5105, 5113
. . qualitative aspects of deviations . . . 5096-5097
. . qualitative aspects of misstatements . . . 5105
. . random-number sampling . . . 5090
. . risk of incorrect acceptance . . . 5107-5108
. . sample design . . . 5083
. . sample size . . . 5083-5084, 5091, 5099, 5106-5107
. . sampling risk . . . 5095-5096
. . sampling unit . . . 5089, 5099
. . selection of items . . . 5084

Audit sampling—continued
. analysis and application of procedures—continued
. . selection of sample . . . 5112-5113
. . statistical versus non-statistical sampling methods . . . 5094-5095
. . systematic sampling . . . 5090
. . tolerable misstatement . . . 5103-5104, 5108
. . tolerable rate . . . 5093
. . variations within population . . . 5100
. audit judgment factors . . . 5092, 5101
. authoritative pronouncements . . . 5080
. definitions . . . 5081-5082
. misstatements and professional judgment . . . 5114
. non-statistical sampling in tests of details . . . 5106-5116
. overview . . . 5080-5081
. practitioner's aids . . . 5115-5116
. promulgated procedures checklist . . . 5086-5087, 5098, 5106
. requirements . . . 5082
. sample size
. . illustration . . . 5111
. . non-statistical tests . . . 5115-5116
. selection of sample . . . 5112-5113
. SOX and . . . 5088
. tests of controls . . . 5086
. tests of details . . . 5097
. . non-statistical sampling . . . 5106-5116

*Audit Sampling* (AICPA) . . . 5080, 5096, 5106, 5109, 5111, 5116

AUP engagements. *See* Agreed-upon procedures engagements

**B**

Balances. *See* Opening balances

**C**

Checklists. *See specific topic*

Circular A-133 (*Audits of States, Local Governments and Non-Profit Organizations*) . . . 9075, 9084, 9085

Clients
. MD&A, obtaining understanding of client's methods . . . 10,178, 10,192
. opening balances, client consent and acknowledgment letter . . . 5061
. terms of engagement, prospective client evaluation form . . . 2036-2038

Code of Ethics for Professional Accountants (International Federation of Accountants) . . . 6018

Code of Professional Conduct (AICPA)
. conceptual framework approach . . . 2010
. Rule 101, *Independence*
. . objectives of auditors . . . 2011
. Rule 102, *Interim Ethics Standards* . . . 2011
. Rule 202, *Compliance with Standards*
. . forming opinions . . . 7015
. Rule 203, *Accounting Principles*
. . forming opinions . . . 7015
. threats and safeguard approach . . . 2010

Committee of Sponsoring Organizations of the Treadway Commission (COSO)
. *Enterprise Risk Management for Cloud Computing* . . . 3035
. *Enterprise Risk Management—Integrated Framework* . . . 3034
. "Fraudulent Financial Reporting 1998-2007: An Analysis of U.S. Public Companies" . . . 2073
. *Internal Control—Integrated Framework*. *See* Internal Control—Integrated Framework
. *Risk Assessment in Practice* . . . 3044
. understanding entity and its environment and . . . 3032, 3034

Communication
. fraud
. . to regulatory and enforcement authorities . . . 2083-2084
. . to those charged with governance . . . 2071-2072, 2083
. group financial statements
. . with component auditor . . . 6009, 6022-6023
. . with those charged with governance . . . 6010

Communication—continued
. internal control. *See* Internal control—communication
. MD&A, communication with audit committee . . . 10,197
. predecessor and successor accountants. *See* Predecessor and successor accountant communication
. restrictions on. *See* Restrictions on use of written communication
. SOX and
. . internal control . . . 2118-2119, 2123-2125
. . with those charged with governance . . . 2109
. terms of engagement, communication with predecessor auditor . . . 2031-2033
. with those charged with governance. *See* Communication—those charged with governance
. understanding entity and its environment, information and communication systems . . . 3034-3035

Communication—those charged with governance . . . 2102-2117
. analysis and application of procedures . . . 2108-2115
. . communication process . . . 2112-2115
. . matters to be communicated . . . 2110-2112
. . those charged with governance . . . 2108-2109
. audit planning . . . 3008
. authoritative pronouncements . . . 2102
. definitions . . . 2104
. fraud
. . analysis and application of procedures . . . 2083
. . requirements . . . 2071-2072
. group financial statements . . . 6010
. interim financial information
. . analysis and application of procedures . . . 9067
. . requirements . . . 9058-9059
. overview . . . 2102-2104
. practitioner's aids . . . 2115-2117
. requirements . . . 2105-2108
. . communication process . . . 2107
. . documentation . . . 2107

Communication—those charged with governance—continued
. requirements—continued
. . matters to be communicated . . . 2105-2106
. . those charged with governance . . . 2105
. SOX and . . . 2109
. topic and nature of . . . 2116-2117

Compilation of financial statements . . . 11,025-11,040
. accountant's compilation reports . . . 11,029-11,031, 11,035-11,036, 11,038-11,039
. analysis and application of procedures . . . 11,033-11,036
. . accountant's compilation reports . . . 11,035-11,036
. . accountant understanding of financial reporting framework . . . 11,034
. . agreement on engagement terms . . . 11,034
. . compilation procedures . . . 11,034-11,035
. . engagement acceptance . . . 11,033-11,034
. authoritative pronouncements . . . 11,025
. compilation procedures . . . 11,028-11,031, 11,034-11,035
. definitions . . . 11,026-11,027
. engagement letters . . . 11,036-11,038
. GAAP, departure from . . . 11,040
. impairment of independence . . . 11,039
. objectives . . . 11,027
. overview . . . 11,025-11,026
. practitioner's aids . . . 11,036-11,040
. reporting requirements . . . 11,027-11,033
. . accountant's compilation reports . . . 11,029-11,031
. . accountant understanding of financial reporting framework . . . 11,028
. . agreement on engagement terms . . . 11,028
. . compilation procedures . . . 11,028-11,029
. . documentation . . . 11,033
. . engagement acceptance . . . 11,027-11,028
. . reporting on prospective financial information . . . 11,031
. . supplementary information . . . 11,032-11,033

Compliance attestation . . . 10,135-10,149
. agreed-upon procedures engagements and . . . 10,140-10,142, 10,146
. . on compliance with specified requirements . . . 10,148-10,149
. . on internal control over compliance with specified requirements . . . 10,149
. analysis and application of procedures . . . 10,142-10,143
. authoritative pronouncements . . . 10,135
. examination engagements . . . 10,137-10,140, 10,143-10,145
. examinations
. . on compliance with specified requirements . . . 10,147
. . on management's assertion concerning compliance with specified requirements . . . 10,147-10,148
. overview . . . 10,135-10,137
. practitioner's aids . . . 10,147-10,149
. requirements . . . 10,137

Compliance audits . . . 9075-9086
. analysis and application of procedures . . . 9083-9086
. . documentation . . . 9086
. . planning and performance . . . 9083-9086
. . reporting . . . 9086
. authoritative pronouncements . . . 9075
. definitions . . . 9076-9078
. overview . . . 9075-9076
. requirements . . . 9078-9083
. . documentation . . . 9083
. . planning and performance . . 9078-9080
. . reissuance of reports . . . 9083
. . reporting . . . 9080-9083

CON-2 (*Qualitative Characteristics of Accounting Information*)
. evaluation of misstatements identified during audit . . . 4019-4021
. materiality . . . 3060

Confidentiality
. Code of Professional Conduct. *See* Code of Professional Conduct

Confirmations
. external confirmations. *See* External confirmations

**CON**

Confirmations—continued
. fraud . . . 2090

Consideration of laws and regulations . . . 2093-2101
. analysis and application of procedures . . . 2096-2101
. . compliance with laws and regulations . . . 2097-2098
. . management responsibilities . . . 2096
. . procedures when noncompliance identified or suspected . . . 2098-2100
. . reporting identified or suspected noncompliance . . . 2100-2101
. authoritative pronouncements . . . 2093
. definitions . . . 2094
. overview . . . 2093-2094
. requirements . . . 2094-2096
. . compliance with laws and regulations . . . 2094-2095
. . documentation . . . 2096
. . procedures when noncompliance identified or suspected . . . 2095
. . reporting identified or suspected noncompliance . . . 2095-2096

Consistency of financial statements . . . 7076-7080
. analysis and application of procedures
. . change in accounting principle . . . 7079-7080
. . change in classification . . . 7080
. . correction of material misstatements . . . 7080
. . evaluation . . . 7079
. authoritative pronouncements . . . 7076
. definitions . . . 7077
. overview . . . 7076-7077
. requirements . . . 7077-7078
. . change in accounting principle . . . 7077-7078
. . change in classification . . . 7078
. . correction of material misstatements . . . 7078
. . evaluation . . . 7077

Contractual or regulatory compliance reporting . . . 8024-8028
. analysis and application of procedures . . . 8027

Contractual or regulatory compliance reporting—continued
. auditor's reports . . . 8027-8028
. authoritative pronouncements . . . 8024
. overview . . . 8024
. practitioner's aids . . . 8027-8028
. requirements . . . 8024-8026

Control risk . . . 2016

COSO. *See* Committee of Sponsoring Organizations of the Treadway Commission

*CPA Letter* (AICPA) . . . 2005

**D**

Deficiencies
. internal control—communication . . . 2125-2126
. . communicating deficiencies . . . 2124
. . identifying deficiencies and evaluating severity . . . 2121-2123
. . written communication about significant deficiencies and material weaknesses . . . 2126-2127

Derivative instruments, audit evidence
. analysis and application of procedures . . . 5019-5020
. . investments in derivative instruments or securities based on fair value measurement . . . 5021-5023
. requirements . . . 5015

Detection risk . . . 2016

Direct Examination Engagements . . . 10,057-10,064
. analysis and application of procedures . . . 10,060-10,062
. . agreeing on engagement terms . . . 10,060-10,061
. . content of report . . . 10,061-10,062
. . written representations . . . 10,061
. authoritative pronouncements . . . 10,057
. definitions . . . 10,058
. evaluation . . . 10,063-10,064
. measurement . . . 10,062-10,063
. overview . . . 10,057
. practitioner's aids . . . 10,062-10,064
. requirements . . . 10,058-10,060

# Index

Disclosures
. accounting estimates
.. analysis and application of procedures . . . 5134
.. requirements . . . 5123
. fraud, adequacy of financial statement disclosures . . . 2092
. interim financial information, inadequate disclosure . . . 9073
. modification of opinions, inadequate disclosure . . . 7056-7058
. response to assessed risks, presentation and disclosure . . . 3071

Documentation. *See* Audit documentation

## E

Employee benefit plans subject to ERISA, forming an opinion and reporting on financial statements of . . . 7028-7046
. analysis and application of procedures . . . 7036-7046
.. auditor's reports on ERISA plan financial statements . . . 7040
.. communications with management or those charged with governance . . . 7038
.. engagement acceptance . . . 7037
.. ERISA section 103(a)(3)(C) audits . . . 7039
.. forming an opinion . . . 7039
.. Form 5500 filing considerations . . . 7039-7040
.. risk assessment and audit responses . . . 7037-7038
.. written representations . . . 7039
. authoritative pronouncements . . . 7028
. defined contribution retirement plan . . . 7040-7046
. definitions . . . 7029
. overview . . . 7029
. requirements . . . 7029-7036
.. acceptance of engagement . . . 7029
.. communication with management or those charged with governance . . . 7030
.. comparative financial statements . . . 7033-7036
.. forming an opinion . . . 7031
.. form of opinion . . . 7031

Employee benefit plans subject to ERISA, forming an opinion and reporting on financial statements of—continued
. requirements—continued
.. Form 5500 filing considerations . . . 7031-7033
.. procedures for ERISA Section 103(a)(3)(C) audit . . . 7030
.. risk assessment and response . . . 7030
.. written representations . . . 7031
. supplemental schedules, reporting on . . . 7036

Emphasis-of-matter paragraphs and other-matter paragraphs . . . 7067-7075
. analysis and application of procedures . . . 7069-7070
.. emphasis-of-matter paragraphs . . . 7069
.. other-matter paragraphs . . . 7070
. auditing standards . . . 7071
. auditor's reports
.. emphasis-of-matter paragraphs . . . 7071-7073
.. other-matter paragraphs . . . 7073-7075
. authoritative pronouncements . . . 7067
. definitions . . . 7068
. overview . . . 7067-7068
. practitioner's aids . . . 7070-7075
. requirements . . . 7068-7069

Engagement letters
. compilation of financial statements . . . 11,036-11,038
. preparation of financial statements . . . 11,022-11,024
. review of financial statements . . . 11,076-11,078
. terms of engagement . . . 2034-2036

Engagements
. agreed-upon procedures engagements. *See* Agreed-upon procedures engagements
. attest engagements. *See* Attest engagements
. examination engagements. *See* Examination engagements
. quality control. *See* Quality control for engagements
. review engagements. *See* Review engagements

Engagements—continued
. terms of. See Terms of engagement

*Enterprise Risk Management for Cloud Computing* (COSO) . . . 3035

*Enterprise Risk Management—Integrated Framework* (COSO) . . . 3034

Entity, understanding. See Understanding entity and its environment

Environment, understanding. See Understanding entity and its environment

Estimates. See Accounting estimates

Evaluation of misstatements identified during audit . . . 4012-4023
. aggregating and netting misstatements . . . 4021-4023
. . GAAP and . . . 4023
. . intentional misstatements . . . 4022
. analysis and application of procedures . . . 4015-4018
. . accumulating identified misstatements . . . 4015
. . communicating and correcting misstatements . . . 4016-4017
. . consideration of identified misstatements . . . 4016
. . documentation . . . 4018
. . effect of uncorrected misstatements . . . 4017-4018
. authoritative pronouncements . . . 4012
. checklist . . . 4018-4019
. definitions . . . 4013
. materiality, assessing . . . 4019-4021
. overview . . . 4012-4013
. practitioner's aids . . . 4018-4023
. requirements . . . 4013-4014
. SAB-99 and . . . 4019-4023

Evidence. See Audit evidence

Examination reports
. MD&A . . . 10,185-10,186
. pro forma financial information—reporting . . . 10,130-10,131

Exempt offering documents . . . 9120-9128

Exempt offering documents—continued
. analysis and application of procedures . . . 9123-9126
. . comfort or similar letters, issuance of . . . 9125
. . due diligence discussions . . . 9125
. . practitioner attestation report . . . 9125
. . subsequent events and subsequently discovered facts . . . 9125-9126
. . triggers of involvement . . . 9124-9125
. . written agreements for use of auditor's report . . . 9125
. authoritative pronouncements . . . 9120
. definitions . . . 9121
. overview . . . 9120-9121
. practitioner's aids . . . 9126-9128
. . engagement letters, example terms for inclusion in . . . 9127
. . exempt securities and exempt transactions, examples of . . . 9126-9127
. . inclusion letter independent auditor's inclusion letter, example of . . . 9128
. requirements . . . 9121-9126
. . procedures related to other information . . . 9121-9123
. . triggers of involvement with . . . 9121

External confirmations . . . 5039-5053
. accounts receivable
. . confirmation . . . 5051-5052
. . summary of statistics . . . 5053
. analysis and application of procedures . . . 5041-5048
. . evaluation of evidence . . . 5048
. . exceptions . . . 5047
. . external confirmation procedures . . . 5041-5044
. . management refusal to allow auditor to send confirmation request . . . 5044
. . negative confirmations . . . 5047-5048
. . nonresponses . . . 5046-5047
. . oral responses . . . 5045-5046
. . positive response necessary to obtain sufficient appropriate evidence . . . 5047
. . reliability of responses . . . 5044-5045
. authoritative pronouncements . . . 5039
. definitions . . . 5040
. long-term lease obligation . . . 5049-5050
. mortgage lease obligation . . . 5050-5051

**ENT**

External confirmations—continued
- negative confirmation . . . 5049
- overview . . . 5039
- positive confirmation . . . 5048-5049
- practitioner's aids . . . 5048-5053
- requirements . . . 5040-5041

## F

Fair value, investments in derivative instruments or securities based on
- analysis and application of procedures . . . 5021-5023
- requirements . . . 5015

FAS 124-2 (*Recognition and Presentation of Other-than-Temporary-Impairment*)
- accounting estimates . . . 5120
- audit evidence—specific considerations . . . 5022

FASB (Financial Accounting Standards Board). *See specific Standard*

FASB Staff Positions (FSP). *See specific FSP*

Filings with SEC under 1933 Act . . . 9044-9050
- analysis and application of procedures . . . 9047-9049
- . audited financial statements . . . 9047
- . Securities Act of 1933 . . . 9047-9049
- auditor's review report on unaudited financial information . . . 9049-9050
- authoritative pronouncements . . . 9044
- definitions . . . 9044
- "experts" section . . . 9049
- overview . . . 9044
- practitioner's aids . . . 9049-9050
- requirements . . . 9044-9047
- . audited financial statements . . . 9044-9046
- . effective date of registration statement . . . 9044
- . unaudited financial statements . . . 9046-9047

Financial Accounting Standards (FAS). *See specific FAS*

Financial Accounting Standards Board (FASB). *See specific Standard*

Financial reporting frameworks . . . 9015-9020
- accountant's report . . . 9020
- analysis and application of procedures . . . 9019
- . engagement planning and performance . . . 9019
- . reporting . . . 9019
- authoritative pronouncements . . . 9015
- definitions . . . 9016
- overview . . . 9015-9016
- practitioner's aids . . . 9020
- requirements . . . 9016-9018

Financial reporting frameworks—generally accepted in other countries . . . 9006-9014
- analysis and application of procedures . . . 9008-9010
- . audit planning and performance . . . 9008-9009
- . preparation of audit report . . . 9009-9010
- authoritative pronouncements . . . 9006
- overview . . . 9006-9007
- practitioner's aids . . . 9010-9014
- requirements . . . 9007-9008
- U.S. form of auditor's report
- . intended for use in U.S. . . . 9011-9012
- . intended for use only outside U.S. . . . 9013-9014

Financial statements. *See specific topic*
- comparative financial statements. *See* Comparative financial statements
- compilation of. *See* Compilation of financial statements
- consistency of. *See* Consistency of financial statements
- group financial statements. *See* Group financial statements
- personal financial statements. *See* Personal financial statements
- review of. *See* Review of financial statements
- single financial statements. *See* Single financial statements
- specified elements, accounts or items. *See* Specified elements, accounts or items of financial statements
- summary financial statements. *See* Summary financial statements

Forecasts. *See* Financial forecasts and projections

Form 8-K
. filings with SEC under 1933 Act . . . 9047, 9048
. MD&A and . . . 10,196

Form 10-K
. filings with SEC under 1933 Act . . . 9047, 9048

Form 10-Q
. filings with SEC under 1933 Act . . . 9047
. MD&A and . . . 10,196

Form 20-F . . . 10,177

Forming opinions . . . 7002-7021
. analysis and application of procedures . . . 7012-7018
. . auditor's report . . . 7014-7016
. . comparative financial statements . . . 7016-7018
. . forming opinion . . . 7012-7013
. . form of opinion . . . 7013
. . other information . . . 7018-7019
. authoritative pronouncements . . . 7002
. definitions . . . 7004
. overview . . . 7004
. practitioner's aids . . . 7019-7021
. requirements . . . 7005-7012
. . auditor's report . . . 7007-7010
. . comparative financial statements . . . 7010-7011
. . forming opinion . . . 7005-7007
. . form of opinion . . . 7007
. . other information . . . 7012
. SOX and . . . 7014
. standard unmodified auditor's report . . . 7019-7021

Frameworks
. financial reporting frameworks. *See* Financial reporting frameworks
. special purpose frameworks. *See* Special purpose frameworks

Fraud . . . 2065-2092

Fraud—continued
. analysis and application of procedures . . . 2072-2084
. . auditor unable to continue engagement . . . 2082-2083
. . characteristics of fraud . . . 2072-2073
. . communication—those charged with governance . . . 2083
. . communication with regulatory and enforcement authorities . . . 2083-2084
. . discussion among engagement team . . . 2074-2075
. . evaluation of audit evidence . . . 2081-2082
. . professional skepticism . . . 2073-2074
. . response to assessed risks . . . 2078-2081
. . risk assessment procedures . . . 2075-2078
. audit procedures . . . 2087-2092
. . accounting estimates . . . 2091
. . adequacy of financial statement disclosures . . . 2092
. . analytical procedures . . . 2089-2090
. . appropriate audit risk level . . . 2087-2088
. . appropriate confirmations . . . 2090-2091
. . appropriate management representations . . . 2091-2092
. . cutoff tests and vouch transactions . . . 2090
. . evaluation of evidence . . . 2092
. . fraud in financial statements . . . 2089
. . internal control over revenue recognition . . . 2089
. . inventory . . . 2091
. . knowledge of business . . . 2088
. . related-party transactions . . . 2089
. authoritative pronouncements . . . 2065
. definitions . . . 2067
. guidance for auditing revenue in certain industries . . . 2084-2086
. indicators of improper revenue recognition . . . 2086-2087
. . absence of agreement . . . 2086
. . incomplete earnings process . . . 2087
. . lack of delivery . . . 2087
. overview . . . 2065-2067
. practitioner's aids . . . 2084-2092

# Index

Fraud—continued
- requirements . . . 2068-2072
- - auditor unable to continue engagement . . . 2071
- - communication—those charged with governance . . . 2071-2072
- - discussion among engagement team . . . 2068-2069
- - documentation . . . 2072
- - evaluation of audit evidence . . . 2071
- - identification and assessment of risks of material misstatement . . . 2069
- - professional skepticism . . . 2068
- - response to assessed risks . . . 2070
- - risk assessment procedures . . . 2069
- service organizations—audit considerations, noncompliance and uncorrected misstatements . . . 4005, 4010

"Fraudulent Financial Reporting 1998-2007: An Analysis of U.S. Public Companies" (COSO) . . . 2073

FSP FAS 107-1 (*Interim Disclosures about Fair Value of Financial Instruments*) . . . 5120

FSP FAS 115-2 (*Recognition and Presentation of Other-than-Temporary-Impairment*)
- accounting estimates . . . 5120
- audit evidence—specific considerations . . . 5022

FSP FAS 157-4 (*Determining Fair Value When the Volume and Level of Activity for the Asset or Liability Have Significantly Decreased and Identifying Transactions That Are Not Orderly*)
- accounting estimates . . . 5120
- audit evidence—specific considerations . . . 5022

## G

Generally accepted accounting principles (GAAP)
- accounting estimates . . . 5136
- audit evidence . . . 5008
- - specific considerations . . . 5020
- compilation of financial statements, departure from GAAP . . . 11,040
- establishment of . . . 9006

Generally accepted accounting principles (GAAP)—continued
- evaluation of misstatements identified during audit, aggregating and netting misstatements . . . 4023
- written representations . . . 5197

Generally accepted auditing standards (GAAS). *See specific topic*

Going concerns . . . 5174-5187
- analysis and application of procedures . . . 5180-5185
- - comparative presentations . . . 5186
- - consideration of effects on auditor's report . . . 5184
- - consideration of adequacy of disclosure . . . 5184
- - evaluation of relevant information . . . 5181
- - evaluation of management's plans . . . 5183-5184
- - identification and evaluation of management's plans . . . 5183
- - management's evaluationentity's ability to continue . . . 5180-5183
- authoritative pronouncements . . . 5174
- conditions and events raising substantial doubt question . . . 5182-5183
- definitions . . . 5176
- evaluation of entity s ability to continue as . . . 5186-5187
- overview . . . 5174-5176
- plans and factors relevant to evaluation of management's plans . . . 5183
- practitioner's aids . . . 5186-5187
- requirements . . . 5176-5180
- - communication with those charged with governance . . . 5178
- - comparative presentations . . . 5179
- - consideration of effects on auditor's report . . . 5178
- - consideration of financial statement effects . . . 5177-5178
- - course of engagement, evaluating relevant information obtained during . . . 5176
- - documentation . . . 5179-5180

# 14,022 Index

Going concerns—continued
. requirements—continued
.. elimination of going-concern paragraph from reissued report . . . 5179
.. going concern basis of accounting, evaluating use of . . . 5177
.. management's evaluation . . . 5176-5177
.. performing additional procedures . . . 5177
.. performing risk assessment procedures . . . 5176
.. written representations . . . 5177
. substantial doubt, existence of . . . 5182-5183

Governance, communication with those charged with. *See* Communication—those charged with governance

*Government Auditing Standards*
. compliance audits . . . 9076, 9078-9080, 9083, 9086
. forming opinions . . . 7015
. objectives of auditors . . . 2010, 2017
. restrictions on use of written communication . . . 9003, 9005
. subsequent events and subsequently discovered facts . . . 5166

Group financial statements . . . 6002-6026
. analysis and application of procedures . . . 6013-6023
.. acceptance and continuance . . . 6014-6015
.. assuming responsibility for work of component auditor . . . 6021-6022
.. communication with component auditor . . . 6022-6023
.. components and component auditors . . . 6013
.. consolidation process . . . 6020
.. materiality . . . 6020
.. obtaining understanding . . . 6015-6020
.. reference to component auditor . . . 6018-6020
.. responsibility . . . 6013
.. subsequent events . . . 6020-6021
. authoritative pronouncements . . . 6002
. definitions . . . 6004
. overview . . . 6002-6003
. practitioner's aids . . . 6023-6026

Group financial statements—continued
. reference to work of another auditor . . . 6023-6026
. requirements . . . 6005-6013
.. acceptance and continuance . . . 6005-6006
.. assuming responsibility for work of component auditor . . . 6011-6013
.. audit strategy and audit plan . . . 6006
.. communication—those charged with governance . . . 6010
.. communication with component auditor . . . 6009
.. consolidation process . . . 6008-6009
.. documentation . . . 6010-6011
.. evaluation of audit evidence . . . 6009-6010
.. materiality . . . 6008
.. obtaining understanding . . . 6006
.. reference to component auditor . . . 6006-6007
.. response to assessed risks . . . 6008
.. responsibility . . . 6005
.. subsequent events . . . 6009

# I

ICFR. *See* Internal control—reporting

Independence
. Code of Professional Conduct. *See* Code of Professional Conduct
. compilation of financial statements
.. impairment of independence . . . 11,039

Independent auditor's report . . . 7022-7027
. analysis and application of procedures . . . 7025-7027
.. communication of key audit matters . . . 7026
.. communication with those charged with governance . . . 7026-7027
.. documentation . . . 7027
.. key audit matters, determination of . . . 7025-7026
.. most significant matters . . . 7026
. authoritative pronouncements . . . 7022
. communicating key audit matters in . . . 7022-7027
. definitions . . . 7023

**GOV**

Independent auditor's report—continued
. overview ... 7023
. requirements ... 7023-7025
.. communicating key audit matters ... 7024
.. communication with those charged with governance ... 7025
.. documentation ... 7025
.. key audit matters, determination of ... 7023-7024
.. relationship of key audit matters and other elements of auditor's report ... 7025

Inherent limitations of audits ... 2016-2017

Inherent risk ... 2016

Inquiries
. audit evidence ... 5008
. analysis and application of procedures ... 9062-9068
.. acceptance ... 9062-9064
.. auditor's review report ... 9067-9068
.. communication—those charged with governance ... 9067
.. documentation ... 9068
.. evaluation ... 9065-9066
.. management's written representations ... 9066-9067
.. other considerations ... 9068
.. review procedures ... 9064-9065
. authoritative pronouncements ... 9051
. definitions ... 9053
. emphasis-of-matter paragraphs
.. not referred to in previous audit report ... 9074
.. referred to in previous audit report ... 9073-9074
. interim financial information ... 9051-9074
. MD&A, inquiries of management and other personnel ... 10,190-10,191
. management representation letter ... 9069-9071
. modification of review report
.. departure from applicable financial reporting framework ... 9072-9073
.. inadequate disclosure ... 9073

Inquiries—continued
. overview ... 9051-9053
.. responsibility and function of auditor ... 9053
. practitioner's aids ... 9068-9074
. requirements ... 9053-9062
.. acceptance ... 9053-9054
.. auditor's review report ... 9059-9061
.. communication—those charged with governance ... 9058-9059
.. documentation ... 9061-9062
.. evaluation ... 9057
.. management's written representations ... 9057-9058
.. other considerations ... 9061
.. review procedures ... 9054-9057
. standard review report ... 9071-9072

Internal auditors ... 6027-6037
. analysis and application of procedures ... 6032
. authoritative pronouncements ... 6027
. communication with those charged with governance ... 6037
. competence, evaluation of ... 6033-6034
. conditions necessary to use work of ... 6032-6033
. conditions when work should not be used ... 6036-6037
. documentation ... 6037
. nature and extent and direct assistance ... 6036
. nature and extent of work to be used, determination of ... 6035-6036
. organizational status, evaluation of ... 6033
. overview ... 6027-6028
. requirements ... 6028-6032
.. communicating with those charged with governance ... 6029, 6030-6031
.. direct assistance, provision of ... 6030, 6031
.. documentation ... 6031-6032
.. evaluating function ... 6027
.. evidence ... 6029-6030
.. nature and extent of work, determination of ... 6029
. systematic and disciplined approach, evaluation of ... 6034-6035

INT

Internal control—communication . . . 2118-2129
. analysis and application of procedures . . . 2121-2125
. . communicating deficiencies . . . 2123-2125
. . identifying deficiencies and evaluating severity . . . 2121-2123
. authoritative pronouncements . . . 2118
. deficiencies . . . 2125-2126
. definitions . . . 2119
. material weaknesses in small business enterprises . . . 2127-2129
. overview . . . 2118-2119
. practitioner's aids . . . 2125-2129
. requirements . . . 2120-2121
. SOX and . . . 2118-2119, 2123-2124
. written communication about significant deficiencies and material weaknesses . . . 2126-2127

Internal control of financial statement audit . . . 9087-9119
. analysis and application of procedures . . . 9101-9109
. . entity-level controls . . . 9106
. . ICFR audit preconditions . . . 9101-9103
. . ICFR audit with financial statement audit, integration of . . . 9103-9104
. . ICFR audit, planning of . . . 9104-9105
. . ICFR components, evaluation of . . . 9106-9108
. . misstatement, sources of . . . 9108-9109
. . selecting controls to test . . . 9109
. . significant classes of transactions, account balances, and disclosures and relevant assertions . . . 9108
. . top-down approach, use of . . . 9105-9106
. authoritative pronouncements . . . 9087
. automated controls . . . 9101, 9116
. combined report expressing unmodified opinion on ICFR and on financial statements . . . 9116-9118
. communicating ICFR-related matters . . . 9113
. definitions . . . 9088-9089
. entities with multiple components . . . 9115
. multiple components, entities with . . . 9099-9100

Internal control of financial statement audit—continued
. practitioner's aids . . . 9116-9119
. overview . . . 9087-9088
. report modifications . . . 9114-9115
. reporting on ICFR . . . 9113-9114
. requirements . . . 9059-9099
. . additional information . . . 9099
. . adverse opinions . . . 9097-9098
. . component auditor, referencing and assuming responsibility for work of . . . 9098-9099
. . concluding procedures . . . 9094-9095
. . ICFR audit preconditions . . . 9089
. . ICFR audit with financial statement audit, integration of . . . 9089-9090
. . ICFR audit, planning of . . . 9090
. . identifying deficiencies in ICFR . . . 9092-9093
. . limitations . . . 9098
. . management's report incomplete or improperly presented elements . . . 9098
. . report modifications . . . 9097
. . subsequent events . . . 9093
. . testing controls . . . 9092
. . top-down approach, use of . . . 9090-9092
. . written assessment, request for . . . 9089
. . written report on ICFR . . . 9095-9097
. service organizations, use of . . . 9100-9101, 9115-9116
. testing controls . . . 9109-9113
. . design effectiveness, evaluation of . . . 9109
. . determine nature, timing, and extent of testing . . . 9110-9111
. . identifying deficiencies . . . 9111-9113
. . match evidence to risk . . . 9109-9110
. . subsequent years' audits . . . 9111
. . testing operating effectiveness . . . 9109
. written communication of significant deficiencies and material weaknesses . . . 9119
. written representations . . . 9113

*Internal Control—Integrated Framework* (COSO)
. understanding entity and its environment . . . 3032

Internal control—reporting
. service organizations—reporting. *See* Service organizations—reporting

International Federation of Accountants . . . 6018

International reporting issues, special considerations . . . 11,109-11,115
. accountant's compilation report on financial statements . . . 11,112-11,115
. analysis and application of procedures
. . different set of compilation and review standards applied . . . 11,111
. . engagement acceptance . . . 11,111
. . financial reporting framework, understanding . . . 11,111
. . reporting . . . 11,111
. authoritative pronouncements . . . 11,109
. objective . . . 11,109
. overview . . . 11,109
. practitioner's aids . . . 11,111-11,115
. requirements
. . compilation and review standards, use of another set of . . . 11,110
. . consideration of framework generally accepted in another country . . . 11,110
. . engagement acceptance consideration . . . 11,109-11,110
. . reporting . . . 11,110

Inventory
. audit evidence
. . analysis and application of procedures . . . 5024-5026
. . confirmation request for inventory held by third party . . . 5034-5035
. . inventory observation procedures . . . 5031-5033
. . requirements . . . 5016
. fraud . . . 2091
. response to assessed risks . . . 3087-3088

**L**

Laws, consideration of. *See* Consideration of laws and regulations

Letters
. audit inquiry letter to legal counsel . . . 5035-5037
. . management requesting list of litigation, claims and assessments . . . 5037-5038
. engagement letters
. . compilation of financial statements . . . 11,036-11,038
. . preparation of financial statements . . . 11,022-11,024
. . review of financial statements . . . 11,076-11,078
. . terms of engagement . . . 2034-2036
. management representation letters
. . review of financial statements . . . 9069-9071
. . written representations . . . 5197-5198
. opening balances, letter of understanding from predecessor auditor to successor auditor . . . 5059-5060
. underwriters. *See* Underwriters' letters

**M**

"Management Override of Internal Controls: The Achilles' Heel of Fraud Prevention" (AICPA) . . . 2076, 3033

Management representation letters
. review of financial statements . . . 9069-9071
. written representations . . . 5197-5198

Management's discussion and analysis (MD&A) . . . 10,172-10,197
. analysis and application of procedures . . . 10,175-10,188, 10,189-10,197
. . analytical procedures . . . 10,190-10,191
. . effect of events subsequent to balance-sheet date . . . 10,181-10,183
. . nonfinancial data . . . 10,181
. . obtaining understanding of client's methods . . . 10,178, 10,192
. . obtaining understanding of requirements . . . 10,177, 10,192
. . obtaining written representations . . . 10,183-10,185, 10,192
. . planning engagement . . . 10,175-10,177, 10,189

**MAN**

Management's discussion and analysis (MD&A)—continued
. analysis and application of procedures—continued
.. preparation of examination report... 10,185-10,186
.. preparation of review report... 10,192-10,195
.. relevant portions of internal control... 10,178-10,179, 10,190
.. subsequent events... 10,192
.. sufficient evidence... 10,179-10,181
.. testing completeness... 10,181
. authoritative pronouncements... 10,172
. combined reporting... 10,196
. communication with audit committee... 10,197
. engagement of auditor subsequent to filing of presentation... 10,196
. examination engagements... 10,173-10,174
. examination report... 10,186-10,187
. overview... 10,172
. promulgated procedures checklist... 10,174, 10,188-10,189
. review engagement... 10,188
. review report... 10,194-10,195

Materiality... 3060-3066
. analysis and application of procedures... 3063-3066
.. performance materiality considerations... 3065-3066
.. during planning phase of engagement... 3063-3065
.. revision of materiality levels... 3066
. authoritative pronouncements... 3060
. definitions... 3062
. evaluation of misstatements identified during audit... 4019-4021
. group financial statements
.. analysis and application of procedures... 6020
.. requirements... 6008
. overview... 3060-3062
. requirements... 3062-3063

Material misstatements. *See* Misstatements

Material weaknesses
. internal control—communication
.. material weaknesses in small business enterprises... 2127-2129
.. written communication about significant deficiencies and material weaknesses... 2126-2127

MD&A. *See* Management's discussion and analysis

Misstatements
. accounting estimates
.. analysis and application of procedures... 5127-5133
.. requirements... 5122
. correction of
.. analysis and application of procedures... 7080
.. requirements... 7078
. evaluation of. *See* Evaluation of misstatements identified during audit
. fraud
.. identification and assessment of risks of material misstatement... 2069
.. noncompliance and uncorrected misstatements... 4005, 4010
. modification of opinions, qualified auditor's report... 7054-7056
. opening balances, possible misstatements reported on by predecessor auditor... 5056
. other information
.. analysis and application of procedures... 7086-7088
. related parties
.. analysis and application of procedures... 5155-5158
.. requirements... 5149
. risks of... 2016
. service organizations—audit considerations
.. analysis and application of procedures... 4010
.. requirements... s4007
. understanding entity and its environment
.. analysis and application of procedures... 3046-3049

**MAT**

Misstatements—continued
- understanding entity and its environment—continued
  - heightened risk of material misstatement . . . 3058-3059
  - relationship of assessed risks of material misstatement and auditor's responses . . . 3085
  - requirements . . . 3022-3024

Modification of opinions . . . 7047-7066
- adverse auditor's report . . . 7058-7060
- analysis and application of procedures . . . 7050-7053
  - modification of opinions . . . 7050-7052
  - reporting on modification of opinions . . . 7052-7053
- authoritative pronouncements . . . 7047
- definitions . . . 7048
- disclaimer report . . . 7063-7064
- overview . . . 7047
- practitioner's aids . . . 7053-7066
- qualified auditor's report
  - inadequate disclosure . . . 7056-7058
  - material misstatement . . . 7054-7056
  - scope limitations . . . 7060-7063
- requirements . . . 7048-7050
  - modification of opinions . . . 7048-7049
  - reporting on modification of opinions . . . 7049-7050
- unmodified prior-year opinion and modified current-year opinion . . . 7064-7066

Monitoring
- quality control for engagements
  - analysis and application of procedures . . . 2048
  - requirements . . . 2044
- understanding entity and its environment . . . 3036

## O

Objectives of auditors . . . 2002-2023
- authoritative pronouncements . . . 2002
- definitions . . . 2004-2006
- overview . . . 2002-2004
- practitioner's aids . . . 2021-2023

Objectives of auditors—continued
- professional skepticism . . . 2022-2023
- requirements . . . 2007-2021
  - in AU-C sections . . . 2018-2019
  - audit risk . . . 2015-2017
  - compliance with . . . 2019-2020
  - ethical requirements . . . 2010-2013
  - failure to achieve objective . . . 2021
  - interpretive publications . . . 2020
  - nature and content of GAAS . . . 2017-2018
  - other auditing publications . . . 2021
  - preparation of financial statement . . . 2009-2010
  - professional judgment . . . 2014-2015
  - professional skepticism . . . 2013-2014
  - sufficient appropriate evidence . . . 2015
- SOX and . . . 2009, 2011

Omitted procedures . . . 5201-5203
- analysis and application of procedures . . . 5202
- authoritative pronouncements . . . 5201
- definitions . . . 5201
- engagement procedures discovered after report release date . . . 5202-5203
- overview . . . 5201
- practitioner's aids . . . 5202-5203
- requirements . . . 5201-5202

Opening balances . . . 5054-5061
- analysis and application of procedures . . . 5056-5059
  - audit conclusions and reporting . . . 5059
  - audit procedures . . . 5056-5059
- authoritative pronouncements . . . 5054
- client consent and acknowledgment letter . . . 5061
- definitions . . . 5055
- letter of understanding from predecessor auditor to successor auditor . . . 5059-5060
- overview . . . 5054
- practitioner's aids . . . 5059-5061
- requirements . . . 5055-5056
  - audit conclusions and reporting . . . 5056
  - audit procedures . . . 5055-5056
  - possible misstatements reported on by predecessor auditor . . . 5056

Opinions
. forming. *See* Forming opinions
. modification of. *See* Modification of opinions

Other information . . . 7081-7088
. analysis and application of procedures . . . 7085-7088
. . misstatements of . . . 7086-7088
. . other information . . . 7085
. . reading other information . . . 7085-7086
. authoritative pronouncements . . . 7081
. definitions . . . 7082
. overview . . . 7081-7082
. requirements . . . 7083-7085
. . documentation . . . 7085
. . material inconsistencies . . . 7084
. . reporting . . . 7084-7085
. . reading other information . . . 7083-7084

Other-matter paragraphs. *See* Emphasis-of-matter paragraphs and other-matter paragraphs

Overall financial statement level . . . 2015

**P**

PCAOB. *See* Public Company Accounting Oversight Board

Planning. *See* Audit planning

Practice Alert No. 01-1 (*Common Peer Review Recommendations*) . . . 2040

Practice Alert No. 03-1 (*Audit Confirmations*)
. external confirmations . . . 5042-5043, 5046
. fraud . . . 2090-2091
. related parties . . . 5157

Practice Alert No. 10 (*Maintaining and Applying Professional Skepticism in Audits*) . . . 2013

Practice Alert No. 98-2 (*Professional Skepticism and Related Topics*) . . . 2021

Preparation of financial statements . . . 11,016-11,024

Preparation of financial statements—continued
. analysis and application of procedures . . . 11,020-11,021
. . accountant understanding of financial reporting framework . . . 11,020-11,021
. . agreement on engagement terms . . . 11,020-11,021
. . financial statements, preparation of . . . 11,021
. assistance in preparing financial statements versus . . . 11,022
. authoritative pronouncements . . . 11,016
. definitions . . . 11,017
. engagement letter . . . 11,022-11,024
. objectives . . . 11,017
. overview . . . 11,016-11,017
. practitioner's aids . . . 11,022-11,024
. requirements . . . 11,018-11,020
. . accountant understanding of financial reporting framework . . . 11,018
. . agreement on engagement terms . . . 11,018
. . documentation . . . 11,020
. . engagement acceptance . . . 11,018
. . financial statements, preparation of . . . 11,018-11,019
. . preparing prospective financial information . . . 11,019-11,020

Principles of audits . . . 1002-1003

Professional skepticism
. fraud
. . analysis and application of procedures . . . 2073-2074
. . requirements . . . 2068
. objectives of auditors . . . 2022-2023
. . requirements . . . 2013-2014

Pro forma financial information
. compilation of. *See* Pro forma financial information—compilation
. reporting. *See* Pro forma financial information—reporting

Pro forma financial information—compilation . . . 11,116-11,121
. accountant responsibility . . . 11,119-11,120
. analysis and application of procedures . . . 11,119-11,121

Pro forma financial information—
compilation—continued
. authoritative pronouncements . . . 11,116
. defined . . . 11,116
. overview . . . 11,116
. requirements . . . 11,116-11,117
. . accountant's compilation report . . . 11,118-11,119
. . compliance with general principles . . . 11,116
. . compilation procedures . . . 11,116
. . documentation . . . 11,119
. . entity's financial reporting framework, knowledge and understanding of . . . 11,118
. . independence . . . 11,116
. . management of responsibilities, obtaining agreement with . . . 11,116-11,117

Pro forma financial information—reporting . . . 10,122-10,134
. analysis and application of procedures . . . 10,129-10,131
. . applicable criteria, assessing suitability of . . . 10,130
. . entity's accounting and financial reporting policies . . . 10,130
. . examination and review procedures . . . 10,130-10,131
. . practitioner's examination and review reports, content of . . . 10,131
. . preconditions for examination or review engagement . . . 10,130
. . reporting . . . 10,131
. authoritative pronouncements . . . 10,122
. definitions . . . 10,123
. examination reports . . . 10,131-10,132
. overview . . . 10,122-10,123
. practitioner's aids . . . 10,131-10,134
. requirements . . . 10,123-10,129
. . applicable criteria, assessing suitability of . . . 10,124
. . entity's accounting and financial reporting policies . . . 10,124
. . examination and review procedures . . . 10,124-10,125
. . reporting . . . 10,126

Pro forma financial information—reporting—continued
. requirements—continued
. . practitioner's examination report, content of . . . 10,126-10,127
. . practitioner's review report, content of . . . 10,127-10,129
. . preconditions for examination or review engagement . . . 10,123-10,124
. . written assertion, request for . . . 10,124
. . written representations in examination and review engagement . . . 10,125
. review reports . . . 10,133-10,134

Projections. *See* Financial forecasts and projections

Prospective Financial Information . . . 10,104-10,121
. agreed-upon procedures engagements
. . practitioner's AUP report, content of . . . 10,111-10,113, 10,118
. . preconditions for . . . 10,111
. . report for financial forecast . . . 10,120-10,121
. analysis and application of procedures . . . 10,113
. authoritative pronouncements . . . 10,104
. definitions . . . 10,105-10,106
. examination engagements
. . financial forecasts . . . 10,114
. . financial projections . . . 10,114-10,115
. . planning . . . 10,107, 10,113-10,114
. . modified opinions . . . 10,110-10,111, 10,116-10,117
. . practitioner's examination report, content of . . . 10,109-10,110, 10,115-10,116
. . partial presentations . . . 10,111, 10,117-10,118
. . preconditions for . . . 10,106
. . procedures . . . 10,107-10,108, 10,114
. . training and proficiency . . . 10,106-10,107, 10,113
. . written assertion, request for . . . 10,107
. . written representations . . . 10,108-10,109
. overview . . . 10,104-10,105
. practitioner's aids . . . 10,118-10,121
. report on examination of forecast . . . 10,118-10,119

**PRO**

# 14,030 Index

Prospective Financial Information—continued
. report on examination of projection . . . 10,119-10,120
. requirements . . . 10,106

Public Company Accounting Oversight Board (PCAOB). *See also specific Standards*
. AS-1210 (*Using the Work of an Auditor-Engaged Specialist*) . . . 3083-3084, 5010-5011
. AS-2501 (*Auditing Accounting Estimates, Including Fair Value Measurement and Related Disclosures*) . . . 5119
. AS-3101 (*The Auditor's Report on an Audit of Financial Statements When the Auditor Expresses an Unqualified Opinion*) . . . 2104, 7004-7005, 7082-7083
. AS-2410 (*Related Parties: Proposed Amendments to Certain PCAOB Standards Regarding Significant Unusual Transactions and Other Proposed Amendments to PCAOB Auditing Standards*) . . . 2067-2068, 2104-2105, 3018-3019, 5147-5148
. Rule 3101 . . . 2018, 2019
. Rule 3502 . . . 2012
. Rule 3520 . . . 2012
. Rule 3521 . . . 2012
. Rule 3522 . . . 2012
. Rule 3523 . . . 2012
. Rule 3524 . . . 2012
. Rule 3525 . . . 2012
. Rule 3526 . . . 2011
. Staff Audit Practice Alerts. *See specific Staff Audit Practice Alert*
. *Supervision of Audits Involving Other Auditors and Proposed Auditing Standard—Dividing Responsibility for the Audit with Another Accounting Firm* (proposed amendments) . . . 6004-6005

Purpose of audits . . . 1002

## Q

Quality control for engagements . . . 2039-2048

Quality control for engagements—continued
. analysis and application of procedures . . . 2045-2048
. . consultations . . . 2047
. . engagement partner responsibilities . . . 2045-2047
. . engagement quality control review . . . 2047-2048
. . monitoring . . . 2048
. authoritative pronouncements . . . 2039
. client and audit engagement acceptance and continuance . . . 2045
. definitions . . . 2041-2042
. engagement performance . . . 2046-2047
. engagement team assignment . . . 2045-2046
. overview . . . 2039-2040
. requirements . . . 2042-2044
. . differences of opinion . . . 2043-2044
. . documentation . . . 2044
. . engagement partner responsibilities . . . 2042-2043
. . engagement quality control reviewer responsibilities . . . 2043
. . monitoring . . . 2044

## R

Reasonable assurance . . . 1002

Reasonableness
. accounting estimates
. . analysis and application of procedures . . . 5134
. . requirements . . . 5123

Regulation D . . . 9024

Regulations, consideration of. *See* Consideration of laws and regulations

Regulation S-B . . . 10,177

Regulation S-K
. MD&A and . . . 10,177
. underwriters' letters . . . 9031, 9038

Regulation S-X
. interim financial information . . . 9052
. underwriters' letters . . . 9029, 9035

**PUB**

Regulatory compliance reporting. *See* Contractual or regulatory compliance reporting

Related parties . . . 5146-5159
. analysis and application of procedures . . . 5151-5159
. . communication—those charged with governance . . . 5158-5159
. . evaluation of identified relationships and transactions . . . 5158
. . identification and assessment of risk of material misstatement . . . 5155
. . nature of relationships and transactions . . . 5151-5152
. . response to risks of material misstatement . . . 5155-5158
. . risk assessment and related procedures . . . 5152-5155
. authoritative pronouncements . . . 5146
. definitions . . . 5147
. overview . . . 5146-5147
. requirements . . . 5148-5150
. . communication—those charged with governance . . . 5150
. . documentation . . . 5150
. . evaluation of identified relationships and transactions . . . 5150
. . identification and assessment of risk of material misstatement . . . 5149
. . responses to risks of material misstatement . . . 5149-518
. . risk assessment and related procedures . . . 5148-5149
. SOX and . . . 5151

AS-2410 (*Related Parties: Proposed Amendments to Certain PCAOB Standards Regarding Significant Unusual Transactions and Other Proposed Amendments to PCAOB Auditing Standards*) . . . 2067-2068, 2104-2105, 3018-3019, 5147-5148

Reliability
. analytical procedures . . . 5065
. audit evidence . . . 5009
. external confirmations, reliability of responses . . . 5044-5045

Reliability—continued
. written representations, of doubtful reliability or not provided . . . 5191-5192, 5196

Reporting requirements
. compilation of financial statements. *See* Compilation of financial statements
. compilation reports. *See* Compilation reports
. compliance audits
. . analysis and application of procedures . . . 9086
. . requirements . . . 9080-9083
. contractual or regulatory compliance reporting. *See* Contractual or regulatory compliance reporting
. examination reports. *See* Examination reports
. internal control. *See* Internal control—reporting
. modification of opinions
. . analysis and application of procedures . . . 7052-7053
. . requirements . . . 7049-7050
. opening balances
. . analysis and application of procedures . . . 5059
. . requirements . . . 5056
. overview . . . 1003
. pro forma financial information. *See* Pro forma financial information—reporting
. required supplementary information . . . 7098-7099
. review reports. *See* Review reports
. service organizations. *See* Service organizations—reportings
. single financial statements
. . analysis and application of procedures . . . 8018-8020
. . requirements . . . 8015-8017
. special purpose frameworks
. . analysis and application of procedures . . . 8007-8008
. . requirements . . . 8003-8006
. summary financial statements
. . analysis and application of procedures . . . 8035
. . requirements . . . 8031-8034

**REP**

Reporting requirements—continued
. supplementary information
.. analysis and application of procedures . . . 7094-7095
.. requirements . . . 7091-7093

Representations, written. *See* Written representations

Required supplementary information . . . 7097-7100
. analysis and application of procedures . . . 7099
. authoritative pronouncements . . . 7097
. definitions . . . 7097-7098
. explanatory paragraph . . . 7100
. overview . . . 7097
. practitioner's aids . . . 7099-7100
. requirements . . . 7098-7099
.. procedures . . . 7098
.. reporting . . . 7098-7099

Response to assessed risks . . . 3067-3089
. analysis and application of procedures . . . 3072-3084
.. assertion level responses . . . 3073-3075
.. documentation . . . 3084
.. operating effectiveness of controls . . . 3078
.. overall responses . . . 3072
.. selecting items for testing . . . 3082
.. substantive procedures . . . 3078-3082
.. sufficiency and appropriateness of evidence . . . 3082-3084
.. tests of controls . . . 3075-3078
. authoritative pronouncements . . . 3067
. decision tree . . . 3086
. definitions . . . 3068
. fraud
.. analysis and application of procedures . . . 2078-2081
.. requirements . . . 2070
. group financial statements . . . 6008
. overview . . . 3067-3068
. practitioner's aids . . . 3084-3089
. requirements . . . 3068-3072
.. assertion level responses . . . 3068-3069
.. documentation . . . 3072
.. overall responses . . . 3068
.. presentation and disclosure . . . 3071

Response to assessed risks—continued
. requirements—continued
.. selecting items for testing . . . 3071
.. substantive procedures . . . 3070-3071
.. sufficiency and appropriateness of evidence . . . 3071-3072
.. tests of controls . . . 3069-3070
. service organizations—audit considerations
.. analysis and application of procedures . . . 4010
.. requirements . . . 4006-4007
. substantive procedures
.. inventory assertions, relevant to . . . 3087-3088
.. roll forward from interim to period end . . . 3088-3089

Responsibilities of auditors . . . 1002

Restrictions on use of written communication . . . 9002-9005
. analysis and application of procedures . . . 9004-9005
. authoritative pronouncements . . . 9002
. definitions . . . 9002
. list of statements . . . 9005
. overview . . . 9002
. practitioner's aids . . . 9005
. requirements . . . 9002-9003

Revenue recognition
. indicators of improper revenue recognition . . . 2086-2087
.. absence of agreement . . . 2086
.. incomplete earnings process . . . 2087
.. lack of delivery . . . 2087
. internal control over . . . 2089

Review Engagements . . . 10,065-10,090
. analysis and application of procedures . . . 10,075-10,086
.. analytical procedures . . . 10,079
.. communication responsibilities . . . 10,086
.. conduct of . . . 10,075-10,076
.. criteria, description of . . . 10,082
.. documentation . . . 10,086
.. engagement terms, agreeing on . . . 10,075
.. evaluating results of procedures . . . 10,080
.. forming conclusion . . . 10,082-10,083

Review Engagements—continued
- analysis and application of procedures—continued
  - fraud, laws, and regulations . . . 10,079-10,080
  - inquiries and other review procedures . . . 10,079
  - materiality in engagement planning and performance . . . 10,078-10,079
  - modified conclusions . . . 10,085
  - other information . . . 10,082
  - planning and performing engagement . . . 10,076-10,078
  - practitioner's report . . . 10,083-10,085
  - practitioner's specialist, reference to . . . 10,085
  - procedures to performed . . . 10,079
  - responsible party refuses to provide written assertion . . . 10,085
  - restricted-use paragraph . . . 10,084-10,085
  - subsequent events and subsequently discovered facts . . . 10,080-10,081
  - written assertion, request for . . . 10,076
  - written representations . . . 10,081
- authoritative pronouncements . . . 10,065
- definitions . . . 10,066
- overview . . . 10,065-10,066
- practitioner's aids . . . 10,086-10,090
- requirements . . . 10,066-10,075
  - analytical procedures . . . 10,068
  - communication responsibilities . . . 10,075
  - conduct of . . . 10,066
  - criteria, description of . . . 10,072
  - documentation . . . 10,075
  - engagement terms, agreeing on . . . 10,067
  - evaluating results of procedures . . . 10,069-10,070
  - fraud, laws, and regulations . . . 10,069
  - forming conclusion . . . 10,072
  - incorrect, incomplete, or otherwise unsatisfactory information . . . 10,069
  - inquiries and other review procedures . . . 10,069
  - materiality in engagement planning and performance . . . 10,067-10,068
  - modified conclusions . . . 10,074
  - other information . . . 10,072

Review Engagements—continued
- requirements—continued
  - planning and performing engagement . . . 10,067
  - practitioner's report . . . 10,072-10,073
  - practitioner's specialist or internal auditors, using work of . . . 10,069, 10,074
  - procedures to performed . . . 10,068
  - responsible party refuses to provide written assertion . . . 10,074-10,075
  - requested written representations not provided or not reliable . . . 10,071
  - restricted-use paragraph . . . 10,073
  - subsequent events and subsequently discovered facts . . . 10,070
  - written assertion, request for . . . 10,067
  - written representations . . . 10,070-10,071
- review report—adverse conclusion . . . 10,089-10,090
- review report—assertion . . . 10,087-10,088
- review report—qualified conclusion . . . 10,088-10,089
- review report—subject matter . . . 10,086-10,087

Review of financial statements . . . 11,041-11,108
- accountant's review report . . . 11,081-11,082
- analytical procedures . . . 11,099-11,104
  - documentation of expectations . . . 11,105-11,107
- analysis and application of procedures . . . 11,063-11,076
  - agreement on engagement terms . . . 11,063
  - change in engagement from audit to review . . . 11,075
  - communication—those charged with governance . . . 11,064
  - communicating to management regarding fraud or noncompliance with laws and regulations . . . 11,070
  - comparative financial statements . . . 11,069-11,070
  - documentation . . . 11,075-11,076
  - emphasis of matter . . . 11,070-11,071
  - engagement acceptance . . . 11,063-11,064

**REV**

Review of financial statements—continued
. analysis and application of procedures—continued
.. financial statements prepared in accordance with special purpose framework . . . 11,069
.. going concern, ability to continue as . . . 11,072
.. independent accountant's review report . . . 11,068-11,069
.. knowledge of the entity . . . 11,065
.. reference to work of another auditor . . . 11,074
.. restricted use of accountant's review report . . . 11,071-11,072
.. review procedures . . . 11,065-11,067
.. subsequent events . . . 11,073-11,074
.. supplementary information . . . 11,074-11,075
.. written representations . . . 11,067-11,068
. authoritative pronouncements . . . 11,041
. definitions . . . 11,043-11,045
. engagement letters . . . 11,076-11,078
. going concern
.. ability to continue as . . . 11,058-11,059, 11,072
.. consideration of . . . 11,107-11,108
. inquiry checklist . . . 11,088-11,099
. management representation letter . . . 11,078-11,081
. objective . . . 11,045-11,046
. overview . . . 11,042-11,043
. practitioner's aids . . . 11,076-11,108
. questionnaire checklist . . . 11,084-11,088
. requirements . . . 11,046-11,063
.. accountant's review report . . . 11,054-11,055
.. agreement on engagement terms . . . 11,047-11,048
.. change in engagement from audit to review . . . 11,062
.. communication—those charged with governance . . . 11,048
.. comparative financial statements . . . 11,056-11,057
.. documentation . . . 11,062-11,063
.. emphasis of matter . . . 11,057-11,058

Review of financial statements—continued
. requirements—continued
.. engagement acceptance . . . 11,046-11,047
.. financial statements, arriving at conclusion on . . . 11,054
.. financial statements prepared in accordance with a special purpose framework . . . 11,055-11,056
.. going concern, ability to continue as . . . 11,058-11,059
.. knowledge of entity . . . 11,048
.. reference to work of another auditor . . . 11,059-11,060
.. restricted use of accountant's review report . . . 11,058
.. review procedures . . . 11,048-11,052
.. supplementary information . . . 11,060-11,062
.. written representations . . . 11,052-11,054
. review program . . . 11,082-11,084

Review reports
. filings with SEC under 1933 Act . . . 9049-9050
. interim financial information
.. analysis and application of procedures . . . 9067-9068
.. requirements . . . 9059-9061
.. standard review report . . . 9071-9072
. MD&A . . . 10,192-10,195
. modification of
.. departure from applicable financial reporting framework . . . 9072-9073
.. inadequate disclosure . . . 9073

Risk assessment
. accounting estimates
.. analysis and application of procedures . . . 5124-5127
.. requirements . . . 5121-5122
. fraud
.. analysis and application of procedures . . . 2075-2078
.. requirements . . . 2069
. related parties
.. analysis and application of procedures . . . 5152-5155
.. requirements . . . 5148-5149
. response. *See* Response to assessed risks

# Index 14,035

Risk assessment—continued
. understanding entity and its environment
. . analysis and application of procedures . . . 3024-3027
. . requirements . . . 3019-3020

*Risk Assessment in Practice* (COSO) . . . 3044

Rule 144 . . . 9024

Rule 424(b) . . . 9048

## S

SAB-99 (*Materiality*)
. evaluation of misstatements identified during audit . . . 4019-4023
. materiality . . . 3065

Sampling. *See* Audit sampling

Sarbanes-Oxley Act of 2002
. audit documentation . . . 2056-2057
. audit planning . . . 3007
. audit sampling . . . 5088
. forming opinions . . . 7014
. internal control
. . communication . . . 2118-2119, 2123-2124
. objectives of auditors . . . 2009, 2011
. related parties . . . 5151
. service organizations—audit considerations . . . 4009
. terms of engagement . . . 2030-2031
. understanding entity and its environment . . . 3032, 3039
. written representations . . . 5195

SAS-117 (*Compliance Audits*) . . . 9075

SAS-119 (*Supplementary Information in Relation to the Financial Statements as a Whole*) . . . 7089

SAS-120 (*Required Supplementary Information*) . . . 7097

SAS-122 (*Statements on Auditing Standards: Clarification and Recodification*)
. accounting estimates . . . 5117
. analytical procedures . . . 5062
. audit documentation . . . 2049
. audit evidence
. . specific considerations . . . 5013
. audit planning . . . 3002

SAS-122 (*Statements on Auditing Standards: Clarification and Recodification*)—continued
. audit sampling . . . 5080
. communication—those charged with governance . . . 2102
. consideration of laws and regulations . . . 2093
. consistency of financial statements . . . 7076
. contractual or regulatory compliance reporting . . . 8024
. emphasis-of-matter paragraphs and other-matter paragraphs . . . 7067
. evaluation of misstatements identified during audit . . . 4012
. external confirmations . . . 5039
. filings with SEC under 1933 Act . . . 9044
. financial reporting frameworks . . . 9015
. forming opinions . . . 7002
. fraud . . . 2065
. independent auditor's report . . . 7022
. interim financial information . . . 9051
. internal control—communication . . . 2118
. materiality . . . 3060
. modification of opinions . . . 7047
. objectives of auditors . . . 2002
. omitted procedures . . . 5201
. opening balances . . . 5053
. quality control for engagements . . . 2039
. related parties . . . 5146
. response to assessed risks . . . 3067
. service organizations . . . 4003
. single financial statements . . . 8014
. specialists . . . 6038
. special purpose frameworks . . . 8002
. subsequent events and subsequently discovered facts . . . 5160
. summary financial statements . . . 8029
. terms of engagement . . . 2024
. understanding entity and its environment . . . 3017
. underwriters' letters . . . 9021
. written representations . . . 5188

SAS-123 (*Omnibus Statement on Auditing Standards—2011*)
. communication—those charged with governance . . . 2102
. compliance audits . . . 9075
. financial reporting frameworks . . . 9015

**SAS**

**14,036**                               *Index*

SAS-123 (*Omnibus Statement on Auditing Standards—2011*)—continued
. modification of opinions . . . 7047
. objectives of auditors . . . 2002
. other information . . . 7081

SAS-124 (*Financial Statements Prepared in Accordance with a Financial Reporting Framework Generally Accepted in Another Country*) . . . 9006

SAS-125 (*Alert that restricts the Use of the Auditor's Written Communication*) . . . 9002

SAS-127 (*Omnibus Statement on Auditing Standards-2013*) . . . 6002, 8002

SAS-128 (*Using the Work of Internal Auditors*) . . . 6027, 6032

SAS-129 (*Letters for Underwriters and Certain Other Requesting Parties*) . . . 9021

SAS-130 (*An Audit of Internal Control over Financial Reporting That Is Integrated with an Audit of Financial Statements*) . . . 9087
. internal control—communication . . . 2118

SAS-131 (*Forming an Opinion and Reporting on Financial Statements*) . . . 7002

SAS-132 (*The Auditor's Consideration of an Entity's Ability to Continue as a Going Concern*) . . . 5174-5175

SAS-133 (*Auditor Involvement with Exempt Offering Documents*) . . . 9120

SAS-134 (*Auditor Reporting and Amendments, Including Amendments Addressing Disclosures in the Audit of Financial Statements*) . . . 2002, 2004, 2024, 2030, 2039, 2048, 2049, 2055, 2065, 2066, 2102, 2103, 3002-3003, 3017, 3035, 3037-3038, 3047, 3061, 3067, 3071, 4012, 4013, 5054, 5059, 5117, 5132, 5174, 5175-5176, 5185, 6002, 6003, 6023, 7002, 7006-7007, 7019, 7022, 7047, 7053-7054, 7067-7068, 7070-7071, 9006, 9007, 9010

SAS-135 (*Omnibus Statement on Auditing Standards—2019*) . . . 2024, 2032, 2065, 2102, 2103, 2113-2114, 2118, 3017, 3067, 3078-3079, 5002, 5054, 5058, 5146-5147, 5160, 5165, 5188, 5190-5191, 6002, 6016, 9051, 9066, 9087, 9104

SAS-136 (*Forming an Opinion and Reporting on Financial Statements of Employee Benefit Plans Subject to ERISA*) . . . 5174, 7003, 7028-7046, 7089
. accounting estimates . . . 5117
. audit evidence . . . 5013
. consistency of financial statements . . . 7076
. evaluation of misstatements identified during audit . . . 4012
. fraud . . . 2065
. forming opinions . . . 7002
. objectives of auditors . . . 2002
. opening balances . . . 5054
. quality control for engagements . . . 2039
. related parties . . . 5146
. response to assessed risks . . . 3067
. subsequent events and subsequently discovered facts . . . 5160
. written representations . . . 5188

SAS-137 (*The Auditor's Responsibilities Relating to Other Information Included in Annual Reports*) . . . 2024, 7047, 7067, 7089, 7097
. audit documentation . . . 2049
. communication—those charged with governance . . . 2102
. evaluation of misstatements identified during audit . . . 4012
. exempt offering documents . . . 9120
. forming opinions . . . 7002
. group financial statements . . . 6002
. modification of opinions . . . 7047
. other information . . . 7081-7082
. summary financial statements . . . 8029

SAS-138 (*Amendments to the Description of the Concept of Materiality*) . . . 2002, 7028, 7089
. evaluation of misstatements identified during audit . . . 4012
. forming opinions . . . 7002
. group financial statements . . . 6002, 6003
. materiality . . . 3060

SAS-139 (*Amendments to AU-C Sections 800, 805, and 810 to Incorporate Auditor Reporting Changes from SAS No. 134*)
. single financial statements . . . 8014
. special purpose frameworks . . . 8002
. summary financial statements . . . 8029

**SAS**

# Index 14,037

SAS-140 (*Amendments to AU-C Sections 725, 730, 930, 935, and 940 to Incorporate Auditor Reporting Changes from SAS Nos. 134 and 137*) . . . 7028, 7089, 7097, 9006
. compliance audits . . . 9075
. interim financial information . . . 9051, 9052, 9066
. internal control of financial statement audit . . . 9087, 9088, 9105
. underwriters' letters . . . 9021

SAS-141 (*Amendment to the Effective Dates of SAS Nos. 134-140*) . . . 2002, 2024, 3079, 5174, 5185, 7028, 7089, 9006, 9010
. accounting estimates . . . 5132
. audit documentation . . . 2049
. audit planning . . . 3002, 3003
. communication—those charged with governance . . . 2102, 2103-2104
. compliance audits . . . 9075
. evaluation of misstatements identified during audit . . . 4012, 4013
. fraud . . . 2065-2067
. forming opinions . . . 7002
. group financial statements . . . 6002, 6003, 6016
. independent auditor's report . . . 7022
. interim financial information . . . 9051
. internal control of financial statement audit . . . 9087, 9088
. materiality . . . 3060
. modification of opinions . . . 7047
. opening balances . . . 5054, 5059
. other information . . . 7081
. quality control for engagements . . . 2039
. related parties . . . 5146
. response to assessed risks . . . 3071
. specialists . . . 6038
. subsequent events and subsequently discovered facts . . . 5160, 5165
. understanding entity and its environment . . . 3017, 3030, 3035, 3037
. underwriters' letters . . . 9021
. written representations . . . 5188, 5191

SAS-142 (*Audit Evidence*) . . . 2002, 2007, 3067
. accounting estimates . . . 5123
. audit documentation . . . 2049

SAS-142 (*Audit Evidence*)—continued
. audit evidence
. . specific considerations . . . 5013
. audit sampling . . . 5080, 5081
. response to assessed risks . . . 3069
. understanding entity and its environment . . . 3017, 3020

SAS-143 (*Auditing Accounting Estimates and Related Disclosures*) . . . 2002, 2004, 2008-2009, 7028, 7038
. accounting estimates . . . 5117-5118
. audit documentation . . . 2049, 2051
. audit evidence . . . 5013-5014
. communication—those charged with governance . . . 2102
. fraud . . . 2065
. forming opinions . . . 7002, 7006
. independent auditor's report . . . 7022, 7024
. written representations . . . 5188, 5191

SAS-144 (*Amendments to AU-C Sections 501, 540, and 620 Related to the Use of Specialists and the Use of Pricing Information Obtained from External Information Sources*)
. accounting estimates . . . 5117, 5118
. audit evidence
. . specific considerations . . . 5012, 5014
. specialists . . . 6039

Scope limitations
. modification of opinions . . . 7060-7063

SEC. *See* Securities and Exchange Commission

Securities, audit evidence
. analysis and application of procedures . . . 5019-5020
. . investments in derivative instruments or securities based on fair value measurement . . . 5021-5023
. . investments in securities based on financial results . . . 5020-5021
. requirements
. . investments in derivative instruments or securities based on fair value measurement . . . 5015
. . investments in securities based on financial results . . . 5015

**SEC**

Securities Act of 1933. *See also* Filings with SEC under 1933 Act
. exempt offering documents . . . 9120
. MD&A and . . . 10,182
. underwriters' letters . . . 9021-9024, 9027-9028, 9032, 9034-9035, 9038

Securities and Exchange Commission (SEC). *See also specific Rule, Regulation or Form*
. filings with. *See* Filings with SEC under 1933 Act
. MD&A and. *See* Management's discussion and analysis
. public entity clients and regulations . . . 2011-2012
. public interest entities . . . 2110
. Staff Accounting Bulletins (SAB). *See specific SAB*

Securities Exchange Act of 1934
. underwriters' letters . . . 9027

Service organizations—audit considerations . . . 4003-4011
. analysis and application of procedures
. . fraud, noncompliance and uncorrected misstatements . . . 4010
. . response to assessed risks . . . 4010
. . service auditor's report . . . 4009-4010
. . understanding of services provided . . . 4007-4009
. . user auditor, reporting by . . . 4011
. authoritative pronouncements . . . 4003
. definitions . . . 4005-4006
. overview . . . 4003-4004
. requirements . . . 4006-4007
. . fraud, noncompliance and uncorrected misstatements . . . 4007
. . response to assessed risks . . . 4006-4007
. . service auditor's report . . . 4006
. . understanding of services provided . . . 4006
. . user auditor, reporting by . . . 4007
. SOX and . . . 4009
. user auditors
. . reporting by . . . 4007, 4011
. . role of . . . 4004

Service organizations—reporting . . . 10,150-10,171

Service organizations—reporting—continued
. analysis and application of procedures . . . 10,161-10,166
. . communication . . . 10,166
. . criteria suitability . . . 10,162-10,163
. . materiality . . . 10,163
. . obtaining evidence . . . 10,164-10,165
. . obtaining understanding of system and assess risk of material misstatement . . . 10,163-10,164
. . preconditions . . . 10,161-10,162
. . preparation of service auditor's report . . . 10,166
. . written representations . . . 10,165-10,166
. authoritative pronouncements . . . 10,150
. definitions . . . 10,151-10,153
. overview . . . 10,150-10,151
. practitioner's aids . . . 10,166-10,171
. requirements . . . 10,153-10,161
. . communication . . . 10,161
. . criteria suitability . . . 10,154-10,155
. . management and those charged with governance . . . 10,153
. . materiality . . . 10,155
. . obtaining evidence regarding description . . . 10,156-10,157
. . obtaining understanding of system and assess risk of material misstatement . . . 10,155
. . other information . . . 10,157
. . preconditions . . . 10,153-10,154
. . preparation of service auditor's report . . . 10,157-10,161
. . responding to assessed risks and further procedures . . . 10,155
. . subsequent events . . . 10,157
. . written assertion, request for . . . 10,154
. . written representations . . . 10,157
. type 1 report . . . 10,167-10,168
. type 2 report . . . 10,169-10,171

Single financial statements . . . 8014-8023
. analysis and application of procedures . . . 8018-8020
. . audit opinion and reporting . . . 8019-8020
. . engagement acceptance . . . 8018
. . engagement planning and performance . . . 8019

**SEC**

Single financial statements—continued
. auditor's reports . . . 8020-8022
. . specific element, account or item . . . 8022-8023
. authoritative pronouncements . . . 8014
. definitions . . . 8014-8015
. overview . . . 8014
. practitioner's aids . . . 8020-8023
. requirements . . . 8015-8017
. . audit opinion and reporting . . . 8016-8017
. . engagement acceptance . . . 8015
. . engagement planning and performance . . . 8015-8016

Skepticism, professional
. fraud
. . analysis and application of procedures . . . 2073-2074
. . requirements . . . 2068
. objectives of auditors . . . 2022-2023
. . requirements . . . 2013-2014

SOP 17-1 (*Performing Agreed-Upon Procedures Related to Rated Exchange Act Asset-Backed Securities Third Party Due Diligence Services as Defined by SEC Release No. 34-72936*) . . . 10,098

SOP 94-6 (*Disclosure of Certain Significant Risks and Uncertainties*) . . . 5142

SOX. *See* Sarbanes-Oxley Act of 2002

Specialists . . . 6038-6049
. analysis and application of procedures . . . 6041-6048
. . agreement with auditor's specialist . . . 6044-6046
. . auditor's specialist . . . 6041-6042
. . competence, capabilities and objectivity . . . 6043-6044
. . evaluation of adequacy of work . . . 6046-6047
. . need for auditor's specialist . . . 6042-6043
. . quality control policies and procedures . . . 6042-6043
. . transfers of financial assets . . . 6047-6048
. . understanding of field of expertise . . . 6044
. authoritative pronouncements . . . 6038

Specialists—continued
. considerations for inclusion in agreements . . . 6049-6050
. definitions . . . 6040
. overview . . . 6038-6039
. practitioner's aids . . . 6049-6050
. requirements . . . 6040-6041

Special purpose frameworks . . . 8002-8013
. analysis and application of procedures . . . 8006-8008
. . audit opinion and reporting . . . 8007-8008
. . engagement acceptance . . . 8006
. . engagement planning and performance . . . 8006
. authoritative pronouncements . . . 8002
. cash-based financial statements . . . 8009-8011
. definitions . . . 8002-8003
. financial statements prepared in accordance with regulatory basis of accounting and intended for general use . . . 8011-8013
. overview . . . 8002
. practitioner's aids . . . 8008-8012
. requirements . . . 8003-8006
. . audit opinion and reporting . . . 8003-8006
. . engagement acceptance . . . 8003
. . engagement planning and performance . . . 8003
. . reporting . . . 8009

SQCS-8 (*A Firm's System of Quality Control*)
. quality control for engagements . . . 2039, 2046
. specialists . . . 6043

SSAE-10 (*Attestation Standards: Revision and Recodification*)
. MD&A . . . 10,172

SSAE-18 (*Attestation Standards: Clarification and Recodification*) . . . 10,005, 10,024, 10,091

SSAE-19 (*Agreed-Upon Procedures Engagements*) . . . 10,005, 10,091

SSAE-20 (*Amendments to the Description of the Concept of Materiality*) . . . 10,005, 10,024, 10,027-10,028

**SSA**

SSAE-21 (*Direct Examination Engagements*) . . . 10,005, 10,024-10,025, 10,057

SSAE-22 (*Review Engagements*) . . . 10,065

SSARS-21 (*Statements on Standards for Accounting and Review Services: Clarification and Recodification*)
. compilation of financial statements . . . 11,025
. general principles for engagements . . . 11,002
. preparation of financial statements . . . 11,016
. review of financial statements . . . 11,041

SSARS-22 (*Compilation of Pro Form Financial Information*)
. pro forma financial information . . . 11,116

SSARS-23 (*Omnibus Statement on Standards for Accounting and Review Services—2016*)
. compilation of financial statements . . . 11,025
. general principles for engagements . . . 11,002
. preparation of financial statements . . . 11,016
. prospective financial information . . . 11,002
. review of financial statements . . . 11,041

SSARS-24 (*Omnibus Statement on Standards for Accounting and Review Services—2016*)
. general principles for engagements . . . 11,002
. review of financial statements . . . 11,040
. special considerations — international reporting issues . . . 11,109

SSARS-25 (*Materiality in a Review of Financial Statements and Adverse Conclusions*)
. compilation of financial statements . . . 11,025-11,026
. general principles for engagements . . . 11,002, 11,003
. preparation of financial statements . . . 11,016-11,017
. review of financial statements . . . 11,041-11,042

Staff Accounting Bulletins (SAB). *See specific SAB*

Staff Audit Practice Alert No. 2 (*Matters Related to Auditing Fair Value Measurements of Financial Instruments and the Use of Specialists*)
. accounting estimates . . . 5120
. audit evidence . . . 5021-5022
. specialists . . . 6042-6043
. understanding entity and its environment . . . 3028

Staff Audit Practice Alert No. 3 (*Audit Considerations in the Current Economic Environment*) . . . 3027-3028

Staff Audit Practice Alert No. 4 (*Auditor Considerations Regarding Fair Value Measurements, Disclosures, and Other-than-Temporary Impairments*) . . . 5022, 5120-5121

Staff Audit Practice Alert No. 11 (*Considerations for Audits of Internal Control over Financial Reporting*) . . . 3019, 9102

Staff Audit Practice Alert No. 12 (*Matters Related to Auditing Revenue in an Audit of Financial Statements*) . . . 5004

Staff Audit Practice Alert No. 14 (*Improper Alteration of Audit Documentation*) . . . 2051-2052, 2057

*Statement of Policy Regarding Lawyers' Responses to Auditor's Requests for Information* (ABA) . . . 5028

Statements of Financial Accounting Concepts (CON). *See specific CON*

Statements of Position (SOP). *See specific SOP*

Statements on Auditing Standards (SAS). *See specific SAS*

Statements on Quality Control Standards (SQCS). *See specific SQCS*

Statements on Standards for Accounting and Review Services (SSARS) 11,002-11,015. *See also* specific SSARS
. analysis and application of procedures . . . 11,008-11,013
. . acceptance and continuance . . . 11,012-11,013
. . client relationship . . . 11,012-11,013
. . engagement conduct . . . 11,010-11,011

Statements on Standards for Accounting and Review Services (SSARS) 11,002-11,015.—continued
- analysis and application of procedures—continued
  - ethical requirements . . . 11,009-11,010
  - financial statements . . . 11,008-11,009
  - financial reporting framework, acceptability of . . . 11,013
  - professional judgment . . . 11,009-11,010
  - quality control . . . 11,011-11,012
- authoritative pronouncements . . . 11,002
- definitions . . . 11,003-11,005
- objectives . . . 11,005
- other preparation, compilation and review publications . . . 11,013-11,015
- overview . . . 11,002-11,003
- practitioner's aids . . . 11,013-11,015
- requirements . . . 11,005-11,008
  - acceptance and continuance . . . 11,008
  - client relationship . . . 11,007-11,008
  - engagement conduct . . . 11,006-11,007
  - ethical requirements . . . 11,005-11,006
  - professional judgment . . . 11,005-11,006
  - quality control . . . 11,007

Statements on Standards for Attestation Engagements (SSAE). 10,002-10,004. *See also specific SSAE*
- organizational structure of . . . 10,002-10,003
- performance . . . 10,003
- purpose of . . . 10,003
- reporting . . . 10,004
- responsibilities in . . . 10,003

Subsequent events and subsequently discovered facts . . . 5160-5173
- analysis and application of procedures . . . 5164-5167
  - predecessor auditor's reissuance of report . . . 5167
  - subsequent events . . . 5164-5165
  - subsequently discovered facts known after report release date . . . 5166-5167
  - subsequently discovered facts known before report release date . . . 5165-5166
- authoritative pronouncements . . . 5160
- definitions . . . 5161

Subsequent events and subsequently discovered facts—continued
- discovery of facts after date of report . . . 5169-5173
- overview . . . 5160-5161
- practitioner's aids . . . 5167-5173
- requirements . . . 5161-5163
  - predecessor auditor's reissuance of report . . . 5163
  - subsequent events . . . 5161
  - subsequently discovered facts . . . 5162-5163
- subsequent events audit program . . . 5167-5169

Successor and predecessor accountant communication. *See* Predecessor and successor accountant communication

Summary financial statements . . . 8029-8037
- analysis and application of procedures . . . 8034-8036
  - audit opinion and reporting . . . 8035-8036
  - auditor association . . . 8036
  - engagement acceptance . . . 8034-8035
  - engagement procedures . . . 8035
  - other matters . . . 8036
- authoritative pronouncements . . . 8029
- definitions . . . 8029-8030
- overview . . . 8029
- practitioner's aids . . . 8036-8037
- requirements . . . 8030-8034
  - audit opinion and reporting . . . 8031-8033
  - engagement acceptance . . . 8030
  - engagement procedures . . . 8030-8031
  - other matters . . . 8033-8034
  - written representations . . . 8031
- unmodified opinions, reports with . . . 8036-8037

Supplementary information . . . 7089-7096
- analysis and application of procedures . . . 7094-7095
  - procedures . . . 7094-7095
  - reporting . . . 7094
- authoritative pronouncements . . . 7089
- definitions . . . 7090
- explanatory paragraph . . . 7095
- overview . . . 7089
- practitioner's aids . . . 7095-7096

**SUP**

# 14,042 Index

Supplementary information—continued
. required supplementary information. *See* Required supplementary information
. requirements . . . 7091-7093
. . procedures . . . 7091-7092
. . reporting . . . 7092-7093
. separate reporting . . . 7096

## T

Technical Practice Aids
. internal control—communication . . . 2122
. response to assessed risks . . . 3075
. understanding entity and its environment . . . 3036, 3039

Terms of engagement . . . 2024-2038
. analysis and application of procedures . . . 2027-2034
. . agreement on audit engagement terms . . . 2029-2031
. . change in audit engagement terms . . . 2033-2034
. . communication with predecessor auditor . . . 2031-2033
. . preconditions for audit . . . 2027-2029
. . recurring audits . . . 2033
. authoritative pronouncements . . . 2024
. definitions . . . 2025
. engagement letters . . . 2034-2036
. overview . . . 2024
. practitioner's aids . . . 2034-2038
. prospective client evaluation form . . . 2036-2038
. requirements . . . 2025-2027
. SOX and . . . 2030-2031

Tests. *See* Audit sampling

Those charged with governance, communication with. *See* Communication—those charged with governance

Treadway Commission. *See* Committee of Sponsoring Organizations of the Treadway Commission

## U

Underlying principles of audits . . . 1002-1003

Understanding entity and its environment . . . 3017-3059
. analysis and application of procedures
. . auditor objectives . . . 3036-3037
. . control activities . . . 3035-3036
. . documentation . . . 3049-3050
. . entity and its environment . . . 3027-3031
. . information and communication systems . . . 3034-3035
. . internal control components . . . 3031-3037
. . monitoring . . . 3036
. . relevant assertions . . . 3037-3038
. . risk assessment procedures . . . 3024-3027
. . risks of material misstatement . . . 3046-3049
. . understanding internal control . . . 3039-3046
. authoritative pronouncements . . . 3017
. control activities germane to internal control . . . 3056
. control environment elements . . . 3053
. definitions . . . 3018
. external factors . . . 3051
. heightened risk of material misstatement . . . 3058-3058
. objectives of information systems . . . 3055
. overview . . . 3017
. practitioner's aids . . . 3050-3059
. relationship of assessed risks of material misstatement and auditor's responses . . . 3085
. relevant standards of financial reporting . . . 3052
. requirements . . . 3019-3024
. . documentation . . . 3024
. . entity and its environment . . . 3020
. . risk assessment procedures . . . 3019-3020
. . risks of material misstatement . . . 3022-3024
. . understanding internal control . . . 3020-3022
. risk assessment by entity . . . 3054
. small and midsized entities . . . 3057-3058
. SOX and . . . 3032, 3039

Underwriters' letters . . . 9021-9043

Underwriters' letters—continued
. analysis and application of procedures . . . 9031-9038
. . agreement upon scope of services . . . 9032-9033
. . comfort letters . . . 9033-9038
. . engagement acceptance . . . 9031-9032
. authoritative pronouncements . . . 9021
. definitions . . . 9023-9024
. overview . . . 9021-9023
. practitioner's aids . . . 9038-9043
. representation letter . . . 9038-9039
. requirements . . . 9024-9031
. . agreement upon scope of services . . . 9025-9026
. . comfort letters . . . 9026-9031
. . engagement acceptance . . . 9024-9025
. sample comfort letter . . . 9039-9043

Using work of others
. internal auditors. *See* Internal auditors
. specialists. *See* Specialists

# W

Work of others
. internal auditors. *See* Internal auditors
. specialists. *See* Specialists

Written representations . . . 5188-5200
. additional requirements . . . 5199-5200

Written representations—continued
. analysis and application of procedures . . . 5192-5196
. . date and form . . . 5195-5196
. . management from whom representations requested . . . 5192
. . other representations requested . . . 5193-5195
. . representations of doubtful reliability or not provided . . . 5196
. . representations requested about management's responsibilities . . . 5192-5193
. authoritative pronouncements . . . 5188
. definitions . . . 5189
. going concerns . . . 5177
. management representation letter . . . 5197-5198
. overview . . . 5188-5189
. practitioner's aids . . . 5196-5200
. requirements . . . 5189-5192
. . date and form . . . 5191
. . management from whom representations requested . . . 5189
. . other representations requested . . . 5190
. . representations of doubtful reliability or not provided . . . 5191-5192
. . representations requested about management's responsibilities . . . 5190
. SOX and . . . 5195